A NEW SYSTEMATIC THEOLOGY OF THE CHRISTIAN FAITH

A NEW SYSTEMATIC THEOLOGY OF THE CHRISTIAN FAITH

ROBERT L. REYMOND

THOMAS NELSON PUBLISHERS
Nashville

Copyright © 1998, Thomas Nelson, Inc.
Published in Nashville, Tennessee, by Thomas Nelson, Inc.
All rights reserved. No portion of this publication may be reproduced,
stored in a retrieval system or transmitted in any form by any means—electronic,
mechanical, photocopying, recording, or any other—except for brief quotations in
printed reviews, without the prior written permission of the publisher.

Scripture quotations as noted are from the following sources:
The *New International Version* of the Bible (NIV), copyright © 1983 by the International
Bible Society. Used by permission of Zondervan Bible Publishers.
The *King James Version* of the Bible (KJV).

Library of Congress Cataloging-in-Publication Data

Reymond, Robert L.
A new systematic theology of the Christian faith / Robert Reymond.
p. cm.
Lectures delivered at Covenant Theological Seminary, St. Louis, Mo.
and Knox Theological Seminary, Fort Lauderdale, Fla.
Includes bibliographical references and index.
ISBN 0-8499-1317-9 (hardcover)
1. Theology, Doctrinal.   2. Reformed Church—Doctrines.   I. Title.
BT75.2.R49   1997
230'.51—dc21
97-12939
CIP

Printed in the United States of America
3 4 5 6   03 02 01 00

A Special Dedication

To
Shirley, my life's companion,
who daily brings the joy and order of music
to my life

Contents

Preface	xix
Introduction	xxv
The Justification of Theology as an Intellectual Discipline	xxvi
Christ's Own Theological Method	xxvii
The Church's Mandate to Disciple the Nations	xxviii
The Apostolic Model	xxviii
The Activity of the New Testament Church	xxx
The Divine Inspiration and Authority of Holy Scripture	xxxi
The Theological Task	xxxii
General Aspects of the Theological Task	xxxii
Specific Aspects of the Reformed Theological Task	xxxiv

PART ONE—A WORD FROM ANOTHER WORLD

1	**The Fact of Divine Revelation**	3
	The Revelational Process	4
	Old Testament Evidence	5
	New Testament Evidence	10
	The Neoorthodox Objection	12
	Language Philosophy's Objection	17
2	**The Inspired Nature of Holy Scripture**	25
	The Bible Message's "Revealedness"	25
	Old Testament Evidence	25
	New Testament Evidence	30
	The Bible's "Inspiredness"	37
	Christ's Authentication of Scripture	44

	The New Testament Writers' Identification of Scripture with God's Word	47
	Hermeneutical Implications	49
3	**The Attributes of Holy Scripture**	55
	The Bible's Necessity	56
	The Bible's Inspiration	59
	The Formation and Close of the Church's Canon	60
	Biblical Infallibility	70
	The Bible's Authority	73
	The Bible's Self-Authentication	79
	The Bible's Sufficiency	83
	The Bible's Perspicuity	87
	The Bible's Finality	88
4	**The Nature of Biblical Truth**	95
	The Nature of the Bible's Assertions about God and our Resultant Knowledge of God	96
	Paradox as a Hermeneutical Category	103
5	**The Bible as the Ποῦ Στῶ for Knowledge and Personal Significance**	111
	The Justification of Knowledge	111
	The Justification of Man's Personal Significance	116

PART TWO—GOD AND MAN

6	**Introduction to the Doctrine of God**	129
	The One True God	130
	Why I Believe in the God of the Bible	131
	The Ontological Argument	132
	The Empirical Arguments	135
7	**The Names and Nature of God**	153
	The Significant Titles and Names of God	153
	The Nature of God	160
	The Relation Between God's Nature and God Himself	161
	Classifications of the Attributes	163
	Analysis of the Shorter Catechism Definition	164
	Excursus on God's Glory	165
	God Is Spirit	166
	Infinite, Eternal, and Unchangeable in His Being	168
	Infinite in His Being	168
	Eternal in His Being	172
	Unchangeable in His Being	177

	Infinite, Eternal, and Unchangeable in His Wisdom	184
	Infinite, Eternal, and Unchangeable in His Power	191
	Infinite, Eternal, and Unchangeable in His Holiness	193
	Infinite, Eternal, and Unchangeable in His Justice	196
	Infinite, Eternal, and Unchangeable in His Goodness	199
	Infinite, Eternal, and Unchangeable in His Truth	201
8	**God as Trinity**	**205**
	The Doctrine's Revelational Ground	206
	The Historical Nature of Its Revelation	207
	The Deity of the Son	211
	Old Testament Predictions of a Divine Messiah	212
	Jesus' Self-Testimony to His Deity	214
	The Title "Son of Man"	214
	The Title "Son (of God)"	218
	The Unity of the Son and the Father	229
	The Son's Eternal Preexistence	230
	Jesus' Acts	232
	Jesus' Divine Attributes	234
	Jesus' Teaching	235
	Paul's Christology	237
	The Non-Pauline New Testament Witness	270
	James's Christology	270
	The Christology of Hebrews	272
	Peter's Christology	278
	The Synoptists' Christology	292
	Jude's Christology	295
	John's Christology	296
	Old Testament Yahweh Passages Applied to Jesus	311
	A Summary of θεός, *Theos*, as a Christological Title	312
	The Deity and Personal Subsistence of the Holy Spirit	312
9	**The Trinity in the Creeds**	**317**
	Analysis of the Nicene Creed and Its Christology	317
	Its Major Affirmations	318
	Three Issues	319
	The Meaning of "Person"	319
	The Relation of the Three to the One	320
	The Father's Eternal Generation of the Son	324
	Analysis of the Niceno-Constantinopolitan Creed's Pneumatology	331
	Westminster's Trinitarianism: Nicene or Reformed?	338

10   The Eternal Decree of God   343
    The Debate over Divine Sovereignty and Human Freedom   346
      Pinnock's Thesis   347
      Pinnock's Proposal   348
      Pinnock's Proposal Analyzed   350
        Failure to Solve the Problem   350
        A Faulty Norm for Theological Construction   355
      The Biblical Perspective   356
        Old Testament Illustrations   358
        New Testament Illustrations   364
      Why God is Not the Author or Chargeable Cause of Sin   372
      A Biblical Theodicy   376
      A Critique of Pinnock's Specific Errors   378
        Adam's Creation and Fall   378
        Man's Cumulative Degeneration   379
        God's Counteractive Grace   380

11   God's Works of Creation and Providence   383
    God's Work of Creation   383
      The Historical Integrity of Genesis 1–11   383
      Creatio Ex Nihilo?   384
        The New Jewish Version (NJV)   385
        The Anchor Bible (AB) Genesis   387
      The Days of Creation   392
      The Age of the Universe   394
      The Purpose of the Created Universe   396
    God's Works of Providence   398
      His Ordinary Works of Providence   399
      His Special Works of Providence   404
        The Covenant of Works   404
        The Covenant of Grace and *Heilsgeschichte*   405
        The Revelatory Process and Miracles   407

12   The Biblical View of Man   415
    Man as Covenant Creature of God   416
      The Constituent Elements of Human Nature   418
      The Origin of the Soul   424
      Man as the *Imago Dei*   425
        The Biblical Data and Their Syntactical Significance   425
        The Nature of the Image   427
      The Covenant of Works   430

The Exegetical Basis for the Presence of a Covenant in Genesis 2	430
The Nature of the Genesis 2 Covenant	431
The Representative Feature of the Covenant of Works	434
The Covenant's Continuing Normativeness	439
Man as Covenant Breaker	440
The Nature of the Fall	440
Seven Effects of the Fall	446
The Natural State of Fallen Man	450
Total Depravity	450
Total Inability	453
Real Guilt	456

Part Three — Our "So Great Salvation"

13 God's Eternal Plan of Salvation — 461

The Fact and Central Elements of God's Eternal Plan	462
God's Eternal Purpose	463
Christ's Cross Work in the Plan	465
God's Foreknowledge and Predestination of the Elect in the Plan	465
The Election of Men in the Plan	466
The Nature of God's Eternal Plan	467
Who Saves Men?	468
How Does God Save Men?	470
In Whom Does God Do His Saving Work?	471
For Whom Did Christ Do His Cross Work?	473
The Amyraldian Scheme	475
The Principle Governing the Order of the Decrees	479
Infralapsarianism: the Historical Principle	479
Supralapsarianism: the Teleological Principle	488
The Primacy of the Particularizing Principle	489
Two Exegetical Objections Considered	490
The Purposing Principle Governing the Rational Mind	492
Four Theological Objections Considered	496

14 The Unity of the Covenant of Grace — 503

Five Arguments for the Unity of the Covenant of Grace	512
The Salvific Definitiveness of the Abrahamic Covenant	512
The Salvific Principles Exhibited in the Exodus	518
The Prophecies of Moses and the Prophets Concerning the New Testament Age	521

SYSTEMATIC THEOLOGY

The Church of Jesus Christ as the Present-Day Expression of the One People of God	525
Identical Requisite Conditions of Salvation in Both Testaments	528
A Disclaimer and a Response	535
Critique of the Dispensationalists' Scriptural Rationale	537
Matthew 13:11, 17, 34–35	537
Ephesians 3:2–6, 9; Colossians 1:25–27	540
Two Tragic Implications	542

15 The Supernatural Christ of History — 545

The Historicity of Jesus' Virginal Conception	547
The Biblical Data	547
Church Testimony	548
The Purpose of the Virginal Conception	550
The Historicity of Jesus' Miracles	553
The Biblical Data	553
Critical Responses	554
Evangelical Responses	556
Their Significance	557
The Historicity of Jesus' Transfiguration	559
Its Background	559
Its Historicity	561
The "Metamorphosis" Itself	563
The Voice From the Cloud	564
The Disciples' Question	564
The Historicity of Jesus' Resurrection	565
The First Strand of Evidence: The Empty Tomb	566
The Stolen Body Theory	566
The Swoon Theory	567
The Second Strand of Evidence: Jesus' Postcrucifixion Appearances	569
Critical Views Considered	571
The Historicity of Jesus' Ascension	575
The Biblical Data	575
Its Significance	578

16 The Christ of the Early Councils — 583

The Apostolic Fathers	584
The Apologists	586
The Antignostic Fathers	589
Origen of Alexandria	593
Monarchianism	596

	The Arian Controversy and the Council of Nicaea	597
	Appollinariansim and the Council of Constantinople	601
	Nestorianism and the Council of Ephesus	603
	Eutychianism and the Council of Chalcedon	606
	Analysis of the Definition of Chalcedon and Its Christology	608
	Departures from the Definition	615
17	**The Character of the Cross Work of Christ**	623
	The Body of Christ	625
	The Blood of Christ	625
	The Cross of Christ	627
	The Death of Christ	627
	Christ's Entire Life Work "One Righteous Act" of Obedience	629
	The Biblical Data	629
	The Character of His Obedience	630
	The Purpose of His Obedience	631
	Christ's Cross Work an Obedient Work of Sacrifice	631
	His Work as High Priest	632
	His Work as the Lamb of God	632
	His Work as a Sacrifice	632
	His Work as an Offering	632
	The Significance of His Death as a Sacrifice	633
	Christ's Obedient Cross Work of Propitiation	635
	Expiation or Propitiation?	636
	The Godward Reference in Propitiation	639
	Christ's Obedient Cross Work of Reconciliation	643
	God's Alienation or Man's?	644
	Pagan or Christian?	651
	Christ's Obedient Cross Work of Redemption	651
	Deliverance by Power or Redemption by Price?	651
	Jesus' Testimony	653
	Peter's Testimony	654
	John's Testimony	654
	The Author of Hebrews' Testimony	654
	Paul's Testimony	655
	Redemption's Godward Reference	656
	Redemption's Manward References	656
	Christ's Obedient Cross Work of Destruction	658
	Satan's Names and Titles	659
	Satan's Actions	659
	Power-Aspects of the Kingdom of Darkness	660

	Christ's Triumphant Kingdom Activity over Satan	660
	A Summary of the Scriptural Categories of Christ's Cross Work	663
	The Absolute Necessity of Christ's Cross Work	664
	The Perfection of Christ's Cross Work	667
18	**The Divine Design Behind the Cross Work of Christ**	**671**
	Ten Lines of Evidence for the Doctrine of Particular Redemption	673
	The Particularistic Vocabulary of Scripture	673
	God's Redemptive Love Not Inclusive of Fallen Angels	675
	The Irreversible Condition of Lost Men Already in Hell When Christ Died	675
	The Limited Number of People, by Divine Arrangement, Who Actually Hear the Gospel	676
	Christ's High-Priestly Work Restricted to the Elect	677
	The Father's Particularistic Salvific Will and Work	677
	The Death to Sin and Resurrection to Newness of Life of All Those for Whom Christ Died	678
	The Implication in the Particularity of the Gift of Faith	679
	The Intrinsic Efficacy of Christ's Cross Work Necessarily Exclusivistic	679
	An Atonement of High Value Necessarily Exclusive of an Atonement of Universal Extension	681
	Exposition of the Allegedly Universalistic Passages	683
	The "All" Passages	685
	The "World" Passages	696
	The "Christians Can Perish" Passages	698
19	**The Application of the Benefits of the Cross Work of Christ**	**703**
	Scriptural Warrant For the Aspects and the Order of Application	704
	The Skeletal Framework of the *Ordo* in Romans 8:29–30: Effectual Calling, Justification and Glorification	704
	The Position of Repentance Unto Life in the Skeletal Framework	706
	The Position of Faith in Jesus Christ in the Skeletal Framework	707
	The Positions of Adoption and Regeneration in the Skeletal Framework	707
	Adoption	707
	Regeneration	708
	The Position of Definitive Sanctification in the Skeletal Framework	710

CONTENTS

The Positions of Progressive Sanctification and Perseverance in Holiness in the Skeletal Framework	710
The Completed Order of Application	711
The Specific Acts and Processes in the Order of Application	711
Two Divine Acts	712
Effectual Calling	712
Regeneration (New Birth)	718
Two Divine-Human Activities (Conversion)	721
Repentance Unto Life	721
Faith in Jesus Christ	725
Union with Christ	736
Three Divine Acts	739
Justification	739
Definitive Sanctification	756
Adoption and the Sealing of the Spirit	759
Two Divine-Human Activities	767
Progressive Sanctification	767
Perseverance of the Saints	781
A Final Divine Act - Glorification	795

PART FOUR—THE CHURCH

20	**The Nature and Foundation of the Church**	805
	The "Assembly" in the Old Testament	805
	The "Assembly" in the New Testament	810
	Jesus' Use of *Ekklēsia*	811
	Matthew 16:18	811
	Matthew 18:17	824
	The *Ekklēsia* in Acts 1–12	825
	The *Ekklēsia* in James	827
	The *Ekklēsia* in Acts 13–28	828
	The *Ekklēsia* in Paul's Letters	830
	The *Ekklēsia* in Hebrews	831
	The *Ekklēsia* in Peter's Letters	833
	The *Ekklēsia* in Jude	834
	The *Ekklēsia* in John's Letters	834
	The *Ekklēsia* in John's Apocalypse	835
21	**The Attributes and Marks of the Church**	837
	The Attributes of the True Church	838
	The Church's Oneness	839

	The Church's Holiness	842
	The Church's Catholicity	843
	The Church's Apostolicity	844
	The Papal Interpretation of the Attributes	846
	The Protestant "Marks" of the True Church	849
	The True Proclamation of the Word of God	851
	The Right Administration of the Sacraments	852
	The Faithful Exercise of Church Discipline	853
	Confessional Witness to the Marks of the True Church	855
22	**The Authority and Duties of the Church**	861
	The Authority of the Church	861
	Its Source	861
	Its Nature	865
	The Duties of the Church	868
	The Duty to Worship and to Serve God	868
	The Duty to Bear Witness to Divine Truth	878
	The Duty to Evangelize and to Grow the Church	880
	The Duty to Administer the Sacraments	885
	The Duty to Minister to the Saints	885
	The Nature of Ministry	886
	The Scope of Ministry	886
	The Goal of Ministry	888
	The Duty to Govern Its Affairs	888
	Authority to Enforce the Laws of Christ	888
	Authority to Draw Up Constitutions and Manuals of Church Order	889
	Authority to Discipline the Unruly and Reprobate	890
	Authority to Separate Itself from Error and Unbelief	890
	The Duty to Perform Deeds of Benevolence and Mercy	892
23	**The Government of the Church**	895
	Presbyterianism	896
	Its History	897
	The Duties of the Eldership	897
	Qualifications of the Eldership	899
	The Diaconate	899
	Presbyterian Connectionalism	900
	Episcopacy	904
	Congregationalism	906
	Erastianism	907
	The Significance of Presbyterian Church Government	908

CONTENTS

24	**The Church's Means of Grace**	911
	The Word of God as a Means of Grace	913
	The Efficacy of the Word	915
	The Ministry of the Word	916
	The Sacraments as Means of Grace	917
	Baptism	923
	Old Testament Background	923
	Institution	924
	Import	925
	Apostolic Baptisms in the New Testament	926
	Exposition of the Pauline References to Baptism	927
	Mode	930
	Paedobaptism	935
	Efficacy	950
	The Lord's Supper	955
	Terminology	956
	Institution	956
	Observance	957
	The Relation of Christ's Presence to the Elements	959
	Import	964
	Prayer as a Means of Grace	967
	Biblical Vocabulary	968
	Prayer in the Bible	969
	Significant Discourses on Prayer in Church History	971
	Efficacy of Prayer	973

PART FIVE—LAST THINGS

25	**Biblical Eschatology**	979
	The Debate Over Eschatology	981
	Classic Liberal Eschatology	981
	Consistent Eschatology	982
	Realized Eschatology	983
	Existential Eschatology	984
	Dispensational Eschatology	985
	Old Testament Eschatology	986
	New Testament Eschatology	988
	John the Baptist's Eschatology	990
	Jesus' Eschatology	991
	His Kingdom of Heaven Parables	994

[*xvii*]

	His Olivet Discourse	999
	Did Jesus Miscalculate the Time of His Parousia?	1006
	Summary of Jesus' Eschatology	1008
	James's Eschatology	1009
	Paul's Eschatology	1009
	The Present State	1016
	The Intermediate State	1017
	The Future State	1019
	The Eschatology of Hebrews	1040
	Peter's Eschatology	1043
	Jude's Eschatology	1046
	John's Eschatology	1046
	John's Gospel Eschatology	1046
	John's Epistolary Eschatology	1047
	The Eschatology of John's Apocalypse	1047
26	**Downgrade Trends in Contemporary Evangelical Eschatology**	1067
	The Denial of a Literal Return of Christ	1067
	Eternal Punishment Construed as Annihilation	1068
	The Non-Necessity of Conscious Faith in Jesus Christ for Final Salvation	1085

Appendices

A	Two Modern Christologies	1095
B	The New Testament *Antilegomena*	1105
C	The Historicity of Paul's Conversion	1113
D	Anselm's Satisfaction View of the Atonement	1121
E	The Five Points of Calvinism	1125
F	Whom Does the Man in Romans 7:14–25 Represent?	1127
G	Selected General Theological Bibliography	1133

Indexes

Biblical References	1143
Old Testament	1143
New Testament	1156
Persons	1191
Subjects	1201

Preface

The publication of a systematic theology of the Christian religion is always a momentous event, particularly for the author, inasmuch as such a work intends to display a professional lifetime of reflection upon all of the major themes (*loci communes* or "standard places") of Holy Scripture and their implications for historical and contemporary points of view. This is true even though over sixty systematic theologies (Gabriel Fackre calls them "theologies-in-the-round")—some evangelical, some ecumenical, some experiential—have been published in the English-speaking world alone since the late 1970s.[1]

This present volume attempts to set forth a systematic theology of the Christian faith that will pass biblical muster. My years of study and teaching have persuaded me that such a construction must take on the contours of what the theological world characterizes as a *Reformed* theology. It must be ultimately God-centered in all its pronouncements and resist every human effort to intrude an unbiblical "analogy of being" (*analogia entis*) into the biblical thought-forms, that is to say, to put an "and" or "plus" where the Bible puts "only" or "alone." For example, in theological methodology it must not say, "I understand *and* I believe," but, "I believe in order that I may understand"; in soteriology it must not urge "God *and* man," but rather "God only" as Savior; it must not teach "faith *and* good works" as the instruments for justification, but rather "faith alone."

The contents of this work are essentially the classroom lectures that I delivered while teaching systematic theology over a period of twenty-two years at Covenant Theological Seminary in St. Louis, Missouri, and seven years at Knox Theological Seminary in Fort Lauderdale, Florida. These lectures were written for required courses in the Master of Divinity programs in these two seminaries. Over the last

---

1. Gabriel Fackre, "The Revival of Systematic Theology," *Interpretation* 49, no. 3 (1995): 230.

fifteen years or so I have provided my lectures to my students in written syllabus form, and by taking this approach I found that I could cover far more material in class, and the students possessed my basic lectures in their entirety without having to concentrate on taking copious notes. My first reason for offering them now to a larger reading public is that my students have encouraged me hundreds of times over the years to do so. So in a very real sense you, my current reader, as you move through these chapters are sitting in my seminary classroom and witnessing my attempt to unveil the Big Picture within the divine Mind which, I am convinced, the one living and true God has revealed to men in Holy Scripture for their eternal salvation and spiritual benefit.[2]

A second reason I offer this volume to a wider audience is that those of us who teach in the Reformed tradition at the seminary level have had to look to Louis Berkhof's revered (and trustworthy) but somewhat dated *Systematic Theology* for our basic one-volume English textbook in the field of systematics, and then we have had to supplement Berkhof with readings from such theological giants as Charles and A. A. Hodge, Benjamin B. Warfield, John Murray, and G. C. Berkouwer. While I am fully aware that no systematic theology will ever be written that will make all supplementation no longer necessary, I have attempted to draw upon the best insights of both biblical and historical theologians and to engage their disciplines as I have gone about fulfilling my fundamental responsibility of setting forth a systematic theology that will pass biblical muster. I hope, of course, that my "systematics" will commend itself, in its attempt to be both biblical and interesting, to other teachers of the Reformed faith. I would be sufficiently rewarded for my labors if any should find it to be "what they are looking for" for their own students.

My third and primary reason for desiring to see these lectures in published form is because I love the gospel of our Lord Jesus Christ and I love the church for which he died. But the church—*his* church—for many years now has been regaled, both in its seminary classrooms and from multitudes of its pulpits, with subbiblical portrayals of what the true gospel of God is. I refer to the Pelagian, semi-Pelagian, semi-semi-Pelagian, Arminian, apostate, and name-it-and-claim-it "gospels" which

---

2. The so-called postmodern theologians for some time now have been urging that the church should respect ambiguity and shun all attempts to formulate a synoptic or "systematic" vision of things, in other words, acknowledge that there is no *predetermined* Big Picture of anything to be discovered. Therefore, they say: "Just draw your own Picture for there is no Big Picture to be discovered." Of course, these theologians refuse to recognize that their declamation, "There is no Big Picture," is itself a Big Picture, complete with its own theology, cosmology, anthropology, Christology, soteriology, and eschatology. The problem with their Big Picture, however, is its fragmentation, incoherence, and failure to come to grips even with how the world really works.

For a brief but informative discussion of postmodernist theology, see Alister McGrath, *Christian Theology: An Introduction* (Oxford: Blackwell, 1994), 102–5.

abound on every hand. To all these false "gospels" the Reformed faith is the only antidote. For me the Reformed faith is not simply a creed the church may relegate now or at some future time to the dustbin of history; for me, its propagation is both a *passion* and a *mission*. Because I believe that the Reformed expression of the gospel is the eternal truth of the one living and true God, I believe that my representation of the gospel of Christ can serve as a corrective to these other "gospels," which are really not the everlasting gospel at all. I hope, of course, that my effort here will contribute to the education of the church at a time when evidence exists all about us that the church has literally "lost her evangelical mind" and is floundering in anti-intellectualism and unbiblical thought. If I can to any degree provide a corrective to this current state of affairs, I will be amply rewarded for all my efforts.

While I have written from a Reformed perspective, I have not slavishly followed the established pattern of "orthodox" or "Reformed" thought when it did not commend itself to me because of its failure to conform in some way to what I perceive to be the teaching of Holy Scripture. For example, in my treatment of the doctrine of Scripture in part one, I have presented it from what is known in apologetic circles as the presuppositional perspective, which I think is more God-honoring than any other alternative. In chapter six I argue that Reformed Christians should not employ, as many of them do, the traditional arguments for the existence of God. In chapter seven I have declined to classify the divine attributes, and I remain unconvinced by any exegesis (or philosophical argument) that I have seen to date that God's eternality necessarily entails the quality of supratemporality or timelessness. Throughout this chapter my main concern is that my reader will be confronted by the God of the Bible rather than the God of the Schoolmen, the latter of which often appears to be more "Greek" than biblical. In chapter nine, I urge upon my reader the Reformation view of the Trinity, which is distinctly different in some respects from the "Niceno-Constantinopolitan" representation of that doctrine which held sway within Christendom for over thirteen hundred years before it was challenged by John Calvin and which, regrettably, is still espoused unwittingly by too many of his followers. In chapter ten, while showing the inherent weaknesses and unbiblical character of Arminianism, I affirm—over against some Reformed thinkers who prefer to represent such things as simply mysteries for which the Bible provides no answers—that God is the decretal Cause of evil in the sense that he is the sole ultimate decretal Cause of all things. I also argue there for the equal ultimacy of, though not an exact identity of divine causality behind, election and reprobation in the divine decree. In chapter eleven I argue, over against a good many Reformed thinkers, that the creation itself has never ultimately had any other than a redemptive *raison d'être,* and that to insist otherwise provides a ground which "lends aid and comfort" to a non-Reformed methodological natural theology. In chapter twelve I urge, over against what I view as a downgrade trend among some Reformed thinkers, that Reformed theology must retain its classic insistence upon an original covenant of works between God and Adam. And in chapter thirteen I espouse a supralapsarian order of the divine decrees, but I offer my own order there inasmuch as the order customarily offered by supralapsarians is inconsistent with their own best insights. I trust the ideas presented throughout the book will advance the on-going discussions in their respective areas among theologians and laypersons alike.

Certain people have been of great personal help to me in my professional development; without them this book would never have been written. First, I want to express my lasting appreciation for Robert G. Rayburn, the first (and late) president of Covenant Theological Seminary, St. Louis, who recommended me when I was only a fledgling theologian to the board of the seminary for a teaching position in the department of systematic theology. I owe a great debt of gratitude to the Covenant Board itself, which hired me and always encouraged all of us on the faculty to write, giving us sabbaticals to do so. I also want to acknowledge my indebtedness to R. Laird Harris, the first dean of faculty under whom I served at Covenant Seminary, and the late J. Oliver Buswell Jr., professor of systematic theology in the systematics department there, both of whom assumed the role of "senior scholar" for me through my earlier years of working under their direction and tutelage. A very special word of appreciation has to go to my dear friend, David C. Jones, who was my colleague in the systematic theology department at Covenant Seminary longer than any other person and who by his scholarly example taught me more than he will ever know about proper theological method and the eternal significance of the theological task.

To the board of Knox Theological Seminary I stand indebted for granting me a sabbatical in order to put the finishing touches on this work. I am indeed grateful for this thoughtful provision.

To Roger R. Nicole, visiting professor of theology at Reformed Theological Seminary, Orlando, whose friendship has graced my life for several years now and whose encyclopedic knowledge of theology I can only dream of acquiring, I must express profound gratitude for reading my systematic theology in its entirety in manuscript form and making many valuable suggestions (most of which I took). To John M. Frame, professor of apologetics and systematic theology at Westminster Theological Seminary in California, and William Edgar, professor of apologetics at Westminster Theological Seminary in Philadelphia, both of whom sharpened my argument in chapter six, I am also very grateful. Finally, I want to thank all my numerous students, who through the years have offered scores of suggestions which have greatly improved the accuracy and presentation of the material.

To all these people—humble, gentle servants of Christ, who in more ways than I can possibly express taught me by both words and example what Christian servanthood is—I, with great delight and deep appreciation, humbly dedicate this book. Any commendation a discerning readership accords it is theirs also; any and all errors and deficiencies which remain are to be traced to me alone.

Fort Lauderdale, Florida
March 1997

Introduction

[handwritten annotation: The doctrine of God]

As the word itself suggests, "theology"[1] (from the Latin *theologia*, in turn from the Greek θεολογία, *theologia*) in its broad sense speaks of intellectual or rational ("reasoned") discourse about God or things divine.[2] As the intelligent effort to understand and explicate the whole Bible viewed as revealed truth, "theology" in the broad encyclopedic sense encompasses the disciplines of the classical divinity curriculum with its four departments of exegetical (or biblical), historical, systematic, and practical theology.[3]

By "systematic theology"—the department of theology with which this book is primarily concerned—I refer to the discipline that answers the question, "What does the whole Bible teach us about a given topic?" Stated more technically, systematic theology is that methodological study of the Bible that views the Holy Scriptures as a *completed* revelation, in distinction from the disciplines of Old Testament theology, New Testament theology, and biblical theology, which approach the Scriptures as an *unfolding* revelation. Accordingly, the systematic theologian, viewing the Scriptures as a completed revelation, seeks to understand holistically the plan, purpose, and didactic intention of the divine mind revealed in Holy Scripture,

---

1. Before "theology" became the common term, the church spoke of it as *sacra doctrina* ("sacred teaching").
2. In its narrow sense—"theology proper"—we employ it to refer to the doctrine of God and take up such topics as his nature, his trinity in unity and unity in trinity, but in the present context we are construing theology in its broad sense as simply rational discourse about God.
3. For a solid contemporary discussion and defense (as long as their essential unity is maintained) of the four departmental disciplines of the classical curriculum, see Richard A. Muller, *The Study of Theology: From Biblical Interpretation to Contemporary Formulation* (Grand Rapids, Mich.: Zondervan, 1991).

and to arrange that plan, purpose, and didactic intention in orderly and coherent fashion as articles of the Christian faith.[4]

Systematic theology covers, as integral parts of Holy Scripture's total body of sacred truth, the theological topics of Holy Scripture itself, God, man, Christ, salvation, the church, and last things. Also falling within this discipline's province are articulation of a believer's pattern of life (personal and social ethics) and the Christian presentation of truth to those outside the church (apologetics).[5]

THE JUSTIFICATION OF THEOLOGY AS AN INTELLECTUAL DISCIPLINE

Theology, as defined above, however, has fallen upon hard times. One may recall here Søren Kierkegaard's lampooning definition of a theologian as "a professor of the fact that Another has suffered,"[6] while Jaroslav J. Pelikan's reminder that the nearest equivalents to the term "theologian" in the New Testament are "scribes and Pharisees"[7] does not help to make the work of the theologian any more appealing either to the church or to the world at large. Indeed, as the Western world has become increasingly a "secular city," more and more men and women within as well as without the church argue that it is impossible even to say anything

---

4. J. Gresham Machen in his address, "Westminster Theological Seminary: Its Purpose and Plan," delivered at the opening of Westminster Seminary in Philadelphia, September 25, 1929, states that systematic theology "seeks to set forth, no longer in the order of the time when it was revealed [biblical theology] but in the order of logical relationships, the grand sum of what God has told us in his Word."

   Klaus Bockmuehl in "The Task of Systematic Theology," in *Perspectives on Evangelical Theology*, ed. Kenneth S. Kantzer and Stanley N. Gundry (Grand Rapids, Mich.: Baker, 1979), states that systematic theology, "a service for the church, in the church," denotes the intellectual effort to produce "a summary of Christian doctrine, an ordered summary or synopsis of the themes of teaching in Holy Scripture." He goes on to say that the systematic theologian should "collect the different, dispersed propositions on essential themes or topics of the OT and the NT and put them together in an order that fits the subject-matter in hand . . . [and he is] to do this in the light of the history of theology which very much is a history of the interpretation of important biblical passages" (4).

5. "Old Princeton" (before 1929) and the Warfield school make apologetics a separate department of theology and place it at the head of the other four departments of theological encyclopedia because, as a discipline, it alone presumably "presupposes nothing." See Robert L. Reymond, *The Justification of Knowledge* (Phillipsburg, N.J.: Presbyterian and Reformed, 1984), 4, 47–70, for my reasons for rejecting this reconstruction.

6. Søren Kierkegaard, *Journals*, ed. and trans. Alexander Dru (Oxford: Oxford University Press, 1938), no. 1362.

7. Jaroslav J. Pelikan, "The Functions of Theology," in *Theology in the Life of the Church*, ed. Robert W. Bertram (Philadelphia: Fortress, 1963), 3.

INTRODUCTION

meaningful about God. Accordingly, Gordon H. Clark begins his book *In Defense of Theology* with the following assessment: "Theology, once acclaimed 'the Queen of the Sciences,' today hardly rises to the rank of a scullery maid; it is often held in contempt, regarded with suspicion, or just ignored."[8] If Clark's judgment is correct, the Christian might well conclude that he should be done with theology as an intellectual discipline altogether and devote his time to some mental pursuit holding out promise of higher esteem. The issue can be pointedly framed: How is theology—construed as an intellectual discipline that *deserves* the church's highest interest and the lifelong occupation of human minds—to be justified today? Still more pointedly: Why should *I*, as a Christian, engage myself for a lifetime in scholarly reflection on the message and content of Holy Scripture? And why should I continue to do it in the particular way that the church (in her best moments) has done it in the past? I would offer the following five reasons why we should engage ourselves in the theological enterprise:

1. Christ's own theological method;
2. Christ's mandate to his church to disciple and to teach;
3. the apostolic model;
4. the apostolically approved example and activity of the New Testament church;
5. the very nature of Holy Scripture.

Christ's Own Theological Method

All four Evangelists depict Jesus of Nazareth as entering deeply into the engagement of mind with Scripture and drawing from it fascinating deductions about himself. For example, on numerous occasions, illustrated by the following New Testament passages, he applied the Old Testament to himself:

Luke 4:16–21: "He went to Nazareth, where he had been brought up, and on the Sabbath day he went into the synagogue, as was his custom. And he stood up to read. The scroll of the prophet Isaiah was handed to him. Unrolling it, he found the place where it is written:

> The Spirit of the Lord is on me, because he has anointed me to preach good news to the poor. He has sent me to proclaim freedom for the prisoners and recovery of sight for the blind, to release the oppressed, to proclaim the year of the Lord's favor.

---

8. Gordon H. Clark, *In Defense of Theology* (Milford, Mich.: Mott, 1984), 3.

Then he rolled up the scroll, gave it back to the attendant and sat down. The eyes of everyone in the synagogue were fastened on him, and he began by saying to them: 'Today this scripture is fulfilled in your hearing.' "

John 5:46: "If you believed Moses, you would believe me, for he wrote about me."

Luke expressly informs us that later, "beginning with Moses and all the Prophets, [the glorified Christ] *explained* [διερμήνευσεν, *diermēneusen*] to them what was said in all the Scriptures concerning himself" (Luke 24:27; see also 24:44–47). *Such an extensive engagement of his mind in Scripture exposition involved our Lord in theological activity in the highest conceivable sense.* It is Christ himself then who established for his church the pattern and end of all theologizing—the *pattern:* we must make the exposition of Scripture the basis of our theology; the *end:* we must arrive finally at him in all our theological labors.

The Church's Mandate to Disciple the Nations

After determining for his church the pattern and end of all theology, the glorified Christ commissioned his church to disciple the nations, baptizing and teaching his followers to obey everything that he had commanded them (Matt. 28:18–20). The Great Commission then places upon the church specific *intellectual* demands. There is the *evangelistic* demand to contextualize without compromise the gospel proclamation in order to meet the needs of every generation and culture. There is the *didactic* demand to correlate the manifold data of Scripture in our minds and to apply this knowledge to all phases of our thinking and conduct.[9] And there is the *apologetic* demand to justify the existence of Christianity as the revealed religion of God and to protect its message from adulteration and distortion (see Tit. 1:9). Theology has risen in the life of the church in response to these concrete demands of the Great Commission. The theological enterprise serves then the Great Commission as it seeks to explicate in a logical and coherent manner for men everywhere the truth God has revealed in Holy Scripture about himself and the world he has created.

The Apostolic Model

Such activity as eventually led to the church's engagement in theology is found not only in the example and teaching of Jesus Christ but also in the rest of the New

---

9. See John Murray, "Systematic Theology," *Westminster Theological Journal* 25 (May 1963), 138. This article is reprinted in *Collected Writings of John Murray* (Edinburgh: Banner of Truth, 1982) 4:1–21.

INTRODUCTION

Testament. Paul wasted no time after his baptism in his effort to "prove" (συμβιβάζων, *symbibazōn*) to his fellow Jews that Jesus is the Son of God and the Christ (Acts 9:20–22). Later, as a seasoned missionary he entered the synagogue in Thessalonica "and on three Sabbath days *he reasoned* [διελέξατο, *dielexato*] with them from the Scriptures, *explaining* [διανοίγων, *dianoigōn*] and *proving* [παρατιθέμενος, *paratithemenos*] that the Christ had to suffer and rise from the dead" (Acts 17:2–3). The learned Apollos "vigorously refuted the Jews in public debate, *proving* [ἐπιδεικνὺς, *epideiknys*] from the Scriptures that Jesus was the Christ" (Acts 18:28).

Nor is Paul's evangelistic "theologizing" limited to the synagogue. While waiting for Silas and Timothy in Athens, Paul "reasoned" (διελέγετο, *dielegeto*) not only in the synagogue with the Jews and the God-fearing Greeks but also in the marketplace day by day with those who happened to be there (Acts 17:17). This got him an invitation to address the Areopagus, which he did in terms that could be understood by the Epicurean and Stoic philosophers gathered there but without any accommodation of his message to what they were prepared to believe. Then, in addition to that three-month period at Ephesus during which he spoke boldly in the synagogue "arguing persuasively" about the kingdom of God (Acts 19:8), Paul "dialogued" daily in the lecture hall of Tyrannus (hardly the name his parents gave him; more likely, the name his students gave him), not hesitating, as he would say later to the Ephesian elders, to preach anything that would be helpful to them and to teach them publicly and from house to house, declaring to both Jews and Greeks that they must turn to God in repentance and have faith in Jesus Christ (Acts 20:20–21).

We also see in Paul's letter to the Romans his theological exposition of the message entrusted to him—both in the broad outline and essential content of the gospel he preached and in the theologizing method which he employed. Note should be taken of the brilliant "theological flow" of the letter: how he moves logically and systematically from the plight of the human condition to God's provision of salvation in Christ, then, in turn, on to the results of justification, the two great objections to the doctrine (justification by faith alone grants license to sin and nullifies the promises God made to Israel as a nation), and finally on to the Christian ethic that God's mercies require of us.

It detracts in no way from Paul's "inspiredness" (see 1 Thess. 2:13; 2 Pet. 3:15–16; 2 Tim. 3:16) to acknowledge that he reflected upon and bolstered his theological conclusions by appeals to earlier conclusions, biblical history, and even his own personal relationship to Jesus Christ as he unfolded his doctrinal perception of the gospel of God under the Spirit's superintendence. One finds these theological reflections and deductions embedded in Romans in the very heart of some of the apostle's most radical assertions. For example, at least ten times, after stating a specific proposition, Paul asks: "What shall we say then?" and proceeds to "deduce by good and necessary consequence" the conclusion he desired his readers to reach

(Rom. 3:5, 9; 4:1; 6:1, 15; 7:7; 8:31; 9:14, 30; 11:7). In the fourth chapter the apostle draws the theological conclusions that circumcision is unnecessary to the blessing of justification and that Abraham is the spiritual father of the uncircumcised Gentile believer from the simple observation based on Old Testament history that "Abram believed the Lord, and he credited it to him as righteousness" (Gen. 15:6) some fourteen years *before* he was circumcised (Gen. 17:24)—striking *theological* deductions to draw in his particular religious and cultural milieu simply from the "before and after" relationship between two *historical* events! Then, to prove that "at the present time there is a remnant chosen by grace" (Rom. 11:5), Paul simply appeals to his own status as a Christian Jew (Rom. 11:1), again a striking theological assertion to derive from the simple fact of his own faith in Jesus.

The apostolic model of exposition of, reflection upon, and deduction from Scripture supports our engagement in the theological enterprise. If we are to help our generation understand the Scriptures, we too must deduce and arrange conclusions from what we have gained from our exegetical labors in Scripture and be ready to "dialogue" with men. Engagement in and the result of this task is theology.

The Activity of the New Testament Church

Engagement of our minds in theology as an intellectual discipline based upon the Holy Scriptures gains additional support from the activity of the New Testament church. The New Testament calls our attention again and again to a body of saving truth, as in 2 Thessalonians 2:15—"the traditions," Romans 6:17—"the pattern of doctrine," Jude 3—"the faith once for all delivered to the saints," 1 Timothy 6:20—"the deposit," and "the faithful sayings" of Paul's pastoral letters (1 Tim. 1:15; 3:1; 4:7–9; 2 Tim. 2:11–13; Tit. 3:4–8). These descriptive terms and phrases indicate that already in the days of the apostles the theologizing process of reflecting upon and comparing Scripture with Scripture, collating, deducing, and framing doctrinal statements into creedal formulae approaching the character of church confessions had begun (examples of these creedal formulae may be seen in Rom. 1:3–4; 10:9; 1 Cor. 12:3; 15:3–4; 1 Tim. 3:16 as well as in the "faithful sayings" of the Pastorals).[10] Furthermore, all of this was done with the full knowledge and approval of the apostles themselves. Indeed, the apostles themselves were personally involved in this theologizing process. In Acts 15:1–16:5, for example, the apostles labored

---

10. An excellent survey of this material may be found in J. N. D. Kelly, "Creedal Elements in the New Testament," in *Early Christian Creeds* (London: Longmans, Green, 1950).

INTRODUCTION

as elders in the deliberative activity of preparing a conciliar theological response to the issue being considered then for the church's guidance.

Hence, when we today, under the guidance of the Spirit of God and in faith, come to Holy Scripture and with our best intellectual tools make an effort to explicate its propositions and precepts, trace its workings in the world, systematize its teachings and formulate them into creeds, and propagate its message to the world, we are standing squarely in the theologizing process already present in and conducted by the church of the apostolic period.

The Divine Inspiration and Authority of Holy Scripture

As we will argue in part one, the Bible is the revealed Word of God. Christ, the Lord of the church, regarded the Old Testament as such, and he gave the church ample reason to regard the New Testament in the same way. This means that the God and Father of our Lord Jesus Christ—indeed, the Triune God—"is really there and he has spoken." If he is there, then he must be someone people should know. And if he has spoken to us in and by the Scriptures of the Old and New Testaments, then that fact alone is sufficient warrant to study the Scriptures. Stated another way, if God has revealed truth about himself, about us, and about the relationship between himself and us in Holy Scripture, then we should study Holy Scripture. It is as simple as that. Indeed, if we take seriously the biblical truth that only in the light of God's Word will we understand anything as we should (Ps. 36:9), we *must* study Holy Scripture, or what amounts to the same thing, we must engage our minds in the pursuit of *theological* truth. Not to be interested in the study of Holy Scripture, *if the one living and true God has revealed himself therein,* is the height of spiritual folly.

For these five reasons the church must remain committed to the theological task. And it can do so with the full assurance that its labors will not be a waste of time and energy. For no intellectual pursuit will prove to be more rewarding ultimately than the acquisition of a knowledge of God and of his ways and works. Indeed, so clear is the scriptural mandate for the theological enterprise that the church's primary question should not be whether it should engage itself in theology or not—the Lord of the church and his apostles leave it no option here. The church *must* be engaged in theology if it is to be faithful to him. Rather, what should be of greater concern to the church is whether, in its engagement in theology, it is listening as intently and submissively as it should to its Lord's voice speaking to his church in Holy Scripture. In sum, the church's primary concern should be, not whether to engage in theology, but is its theology correct? Is it orthodox? Or perhaps better: Is it *biblical*?

THE THEOLOGICAL TASK

Precisely how the theological task is described will be determined by the *Sitz im Leben* of the individual theologian, governed as he is by his own intellectual qualifications, socio/historical situation, learning, and theological station.

General Aspects of the Theological Task

With Louis Berkhof, I believe that the theological task in general is both a constructive and a demonstrative one, both a critical and a defensive one—

1. *Constructive* in that the theologian, dealing primarily with the dogmas embodied in the confession of his church, seeks to combine them into a systematic whole—not always an easy task since the connecting links between many truths that are merely stated in a general way must be discovered, supplied, and formulated in such a way that the organic connection of the several dogmas becomes clear, with new lines of development being suggested which are in harmony with the theological structure of the past;

2. *Demonstrative* in that the theologian must not by his systematizing of dogmas merely describe what his church urges others to believe but also must demonstrate the truth of it by *showing exegetically that every part of it is rooted deeply in the subsoil of Scripture*, offering biblical proof for the separate dogmas, for their connecting links, and for any new elements which he may suggest;

3. *Critical* in that the theologian must allow for the possibility of a departure from the truth at some point or other in his church's dogmas and in the systematic system which he himself proposes, meaning, first, that if he detects errors anywhere, he must seek to remedy them in the proper way, and second, if he discovers lacunae, he must endeavor to supply what is lacking (for Reformed theologians this aspect of the theological task is captured in the motto *ecclesia reformata semper reformanda*—"a Reformed church is always reforming"); and

4. *Defensive* in that the theologian, concerned as he is with the search for absolute truth, must not only take account of previous historical departures from the truth in order to avoid them himself, but he must also

ward off all current heretical attacks on the true dogmas embodied in his church's system.[11]

With regard to the task of *systematic* theology in particular, I concur with Gabriel Fackre that it should be (1) *comprehensive,* that is, cover all of the standard teachings of the Scriptures, (2) *coherent,* that is, demonstrate the interrelationships of the several topics, (3) *contextual,* that is, interpret, whenever and wherever possible, the sweep of doctrine in terms of current issues and idioms, and (4) *conversational,* that is, engage historical and contemporary points of view.[12]

And with Klaus Bockmuehl, I believe that the systematic theologian himself (1) "must encourage . . . and exercise the ministry of teaching in the church" and "reactivate [the] catechetical function in order to confirm both churches and individual believers so that they are not being driven around by alien doctrines and finally destroyed"; (2) must alter his form of expression, whenever and wherever possible, away from that of Greek metaphysical concepts of thought and language to that of the biblical dynamism that was concerned with the *history* of God's deeds of mercy; and (3) against the philosophy of the lordship of man, "must call for the reversal of [modern society's] decision of secularism [i.e., godlessness]" and again "publicly assert and encourage to assert the lordship of God . . . [and] announce God truly as God to a generation forgetful of this fundamental fact."[13]

---

11. Louis Berkhof, *Introductory Volume to Systematic Theology* (Grand Rapids, Mich.: Eerdmans, 1932), 58–59. For a similar opinion, see Pelikan ("The Functions of Theology," *passim*) who urges that theology as a discipline must still fulfill the following five functions in the modern church if the church is to be faithful to the greatest of all the commandments: "You shall love the Lord your God with all your heart, with all your soul, and with all your mind":
    1. The *confessional* function, that is, to assist the concrete church or denomination it serves to respond more deeply to its tradition;
    2. The *conserving* function, that is, to preserve the rich tradition of Christian history;
    3. The *catholic* function, that is, to carry on the "great conversation" with the church fathers and to remind the church of her transdenominational obligations;
    4. The *critical* function, that is, to speak out against any and every theological enterprise that is neither relevant nor responsible by allowing Scripture continually to sit in judgment on the church; and
    5. The *correlating* function, that is, really to hear what the secularist is saying about his world, evil, death, and so on, and to seek to correlate the secularist's questions with Christian answers.
12. Gabriel Fackre, "The Revival of Systematic Theology," *Interpretation* 49, no. 3 (1995): 230.
13. Klaus Bockmuehl, "The Task of Systematic Theology," *Perspectives on Evangelical Theology,* 10–14. See appendix A, "Two Modern Christologies," for my illustration of what the theological task entails today.

Specific Aspects of the Reformed Theological Task

With these general aspects of the theological task guiding him, the Reformed systematic theologian is specifically responsible to provide his readers with (1) organized cognitive information that is radically biblical (this is simply what it means to be "Reformed") and (2) to do so in such a way that such information will encourage growth both in ministerial skills and in specific heart attitudes toward the things of the Spirit.

The Reformed systematician should provide his readers with *cognitive information* concerning

1. the major *loci* and cardinal doctrines of Christian theology as set forth in Holy Scripture (what he gives his readers should be, with no change in basic content, *preachable* and *teachable* material);

2. the historic faith of the early church and the manner in which the church articulated and expressed its faith in such creeds and symbols as the Apostles' Creed, the Nicene Creed, the Niceno-Constantinopolitan Creed, the Definition of Chalcedon, and the so-called Athanasian Creed;

3. the distinctive nature, richness, and beauty of the Reformed faith as the teaching of Holy Scripture, and as interpreted, expounded, and exhibited in John Calvin's *Institutes of the Christian Religion* and the great national Reformed confessions, particularly the Westminster Confession of Faith and the Westminster Assembly's Catechisms, Larger and Shorter;

4. Reformed orthodoxy and its validity as the most viable contemporary expression of scriptural orthodoxy;

5. dominant motifs of contemporary theology from the posture of Reformed biblicism and confessionalism;

6. philosophical, ideological, and religious themes of contemporary thought where they affect the content of the Christian gospel construed as including both Christian proclamation and Christian teaching.

The Reformed systematician is also responsible to impart this cognitive information in a way that will encourage his readers to grow in certain specific religious affections, specifically in their

1. reverence for the Holy Scriptures as God's Word to us and as the final instructional source and norm for faith and life;

INTRODUCTION

2. constant readiness to see God's kingdom and the unity of the biblical covenants as the hermeneutical key to the understanding of Holy Scripture;

3. appreciation for the Reformed theological heritage;

4. perseverance in their effort to grow as systematic theologians;

5. respect for the work of others who have addressed themselves to the systematic task, e.g., Origen, Augustine, Thomas Aquinas, John Calvin, William Ames, Francis Turretin, Jonathan Edwards, Heinrich Heppe, Charles and A. A. Hodge, William G. T. Shedd, James Henley Thornwell, Robert Lewis Dabney, Abraham Kuyper, Herman Bavinck, Augustus Hopkins Strong, Benjamin B. Warfield, Francis Pieper, Louis Berkhof, J. Oliver Buswell Jr., Gerrit C. Berkouwer, John Murray, John H. Gerstner, and Wayne Grudem;[14]

6. awe as those who have been granted the great privilege to study the "mind of Christ" as revealed in Holy Scripture;

7. soberness as those who have been called to spread God's word of judgment to the peoples of the world;

8. joy as those who have been called to proclaim God's word of grace to the same people;

9. meekness as those who recognize that they too must live by and under that same Word which they study and apply to the lives of others;

10. boldness to apply the doctrinal insights they gain winsomely and practically to Christian living and to a world in great need;

11. sincere concern for a biblically faithful evangelization of a lost world and for the juridical subjugation of the nations under the "general equity" of Christ's current messianic rule (Westminster Confession of Faith, XIX/iv); and

12. humble, prayerful reliance upon God for all of these things, with the perpetual prayer that the "favor of the Lord will rest upon them and establish the work of their hands" (Ps. 90:17).

With this perception of the task of theology—and of a Reformed systematic theology in particular—governing our thinking, we will now begin our journey

---

14. See appendix G, "Selected General Theological Bibliography," for further information about these and other theologians.

into the fascinating and dazzlingly rich world of theology as an intellectual discipline. Since all true theology must have an appropriate ground, we will begin with a propaedeutic treatment of Holy Scripture as the only legitimate ground for authoritative theological predications. Then we will address in turn the classical theological *loci,* namely, the doctrines of God (or theology proper), man as covenant creature and covenant breaker, the nature of Christ's incarnation, his salvation in both its accomplished and applied aspects, the church and its attributes and marks, its authority and duties, its government, and its sacraments, and finally, the marvelous but perplexing intricacies of "last things."

PART ONE

A Word from Another World

CHAPTER ONE

The Fact of Divine Revelation

HUNDREDS of the world's space scientists are spending vast sums from their nations' treasuries trying to make meaningful contact with imagined rational beings living in deep space. It is an extremely questionable undertaking for many reasons, but the insatiable thirst for a word to us from another world drives them on in a pursuit that has to date yielded nothing.

The Christian church believes that it already possesses such a word from "outer space," or, more accurately, a word from *beyond* space, even from the Triune God of heaven himself. My aim in part one of this work is to set forth a major portion of the evidence for the teaching that the Bible is indeed God's revealed and inspired Word from another world to the inhabitants of this world. We will show that though written entirely by men, it is also entirely the Word of the living God, because the Spirit of God inspired men to write it in the whole and in the part. The relation between the human authors and the Spirit of God, however, was not one of simple cooperation or coauthorship. Men could not (and would not) have written the Bible apart from the Spirit's superintending activity. The Holy Spirit, then, is the author of Scripture in a more profound and original sense than the human writers ever could (or would) have been. God is the primary author of Holy Scripture, with the human writers being the authors of Scripture only insofar as the Spirit mandated, initiated, and provided their impulse to write. Never did the Bible, either in the whole or in the part, exist for a moment apart from its Spirit-mandated and inspired character. Consequently, to regard the Bible as only a generally reliable library of ancient documents composed by human authors, as even some evangelicals are willing for the unbeliever to do (at least at first) as part of their apologetic strategy,[1] is to overlook the most fundamental fact about the Bible and the Bible's major claim about itself.

This conviction that the Holy Spirit is the primary author of Scripture entails yet another conviction, namely, that the Spirit's superintending influence upon the minds of the Bible writers insured that they would write precisely what God wanted them to. So, since the God of truth by the Spirit of truth inspired the Bible writers to write what he wanted them to write, the final effect was an *inerrant* autograph or original. And if we fail to recognize within the Scriptures our Master's voice speaking his infallible truth to us from his world to our world, we destroy ourselves not only epistemically but also personally, for we abandon the only foundation for the certainty of knowledge and the only "meaning base" by which we may truly know the One infinite, personal God and thereby ourselves as persons of dignity and worth.[2]

THE REVELATIONAL PROCESS

The Bible teaches that God revealed himself to people "at many times and in various ways" (Heb. 1:1–2).[3] The most common nominal expressions in the Old Testament for this revelatory idea are the phrases "the word of Yahweh [or God]" ([אֱלֹהִים] יְהוָה דְּבַר, *dᵉbar yhwh* [*ʾᵉlōhîm*]), which occurs scores of times, and "the law [of Yahweh]" ([יהוה] תּוֹרַת, *tōraṯ* [yhwh]), the proper meaning of which is "instruction," which in turn strongly suggests "authoritative divine communication."[4] The primary Old Testament verb expressing the revelatory idea is גָּלָה, *gālâh*, occurring some twenty-two times, the root meaning of which appears to be "nakedness," and

---

1. See Benjamin B. Warfield, *The Inspiration and Authority of the Bible* (Philadelphia: Presbyterian and Reformed, 1948), 210; John Warwick Montgomery, *History and Christianity* (Downers Grove, Ill.: InterVarsity Press, 1972), 25–26; R. C. Sproul, John Gerstner, and Arthur Lindsley, *Classical Apologetics* (Grand Rapids, Mich.: Zondervan, 1984), 137–55. But Christians should not tell unbelievers that they may presuppose less than the whole truth about the Bible.
2. See Robert L. Reymond, *The Justification of Knowledge* (Phillipsburg, N.J.: Presbyterian and Reformed, 1976), where I have argued that the Bible is our only foundation for the certainty of knowledge. Essential to my argument there is the concept that the Bible as divine revelation is necessarily *self-validating* or *self-authenticating,* carrying as it does within itself its own divine *indicia* (see 15–16; see also Westminster Confession of Faith, I/v). I would also insist that the Bible provides us with our only foundation for justifying our personal meaning and value.
3. By "revelation" I refer first of all to the divine act whereby God deliberately discloses an unknown and unknowable (unknowable, that is, to the *unaided* mind of human beings) portion of his knowledge of himself and/or of his purpose for his creation. In this sense only a part of the Bible is revelation, the rest being the reporting of events or axiomatic judgments and so on. But the term may also refer to the Bible as a whole when the Bible as a message from God is viewed as the product of the Holy Spirit's "inspiring" activity.
4. Warfield, *Inspiration and Authority of the Bible,* 99–100.

which, when applied to revelation, seems to suggest the removal of obstacles to "perception," for the prophet is often spoken of as a "seer" (רֹאֶה, rō'eh, or חֹזֶה, hōzeh) who "sees" visions (מַרְאֶה, mar'eh, חָזוֹן, h°zôn, חָזוּת, hāzût, חִזָּיוֹן, hizzayôn) (see Isa. 1:1; 2:1; 13:1; 29:10–11; Jer. 38:21; Lam. 2:14; Ezek. 1:3, 4; 13:3; Amos 1:1; Mic. 1:1; Hab. 1:1; 2:1).[5] Occasionally the verb יָדַע, yāda', in its causative stem ("to make known") is also employed in the sense of "revealing" (Pss. 25:4; 98:2). In the New Testament the primary word groups for the revelatory idea are formed from the verbs ἀποκαλύπτω (apokalyptō, "to reveal"; see ἀποκάλυψις, apokalypsis, "revelation") and φανερόω (phaneroō, "to manifest"; see ἐπιφάνεια, epiphaneia, "manifestation").[6]

What was it that God revealed? He revealed (1) both his existence and something of his nature, as well as his moral precepts, through man's nature as *imago Dei* (Prov. 20:27; Rom. 2:15), (2) his glory, in creation and nature, in a nonpropositional manner (Ps. 19:1, 3 [NIV mg]; Rom. 1:20), and (3) his wisdom and power, both through his acts of ordinary providence[7] and his mighty acts in the "history of salvation" or *Heilsgeschichte* (e.g., see the sparing of Noah's family at the flood, the exodus, the Incarnation, Christ's cross and resurrection). These "mighty acts of God in history," of course, required the *propositional* explanations that always accompanied them (Amos 3:7) and without which the acts would have been left to their observers to interpret the best they could. Indeed, more than thirty-eight hundred times the writers of the Old Testament introduce their messages with such statements as "the mouth of the Lord has spoken," "the Lord says," "the Lord spoke," "hear the word of the Lord," "thus has the Lord shown to me," or "the word of the Lord came unto me, saying."[8] Consider the following data.[9]

Old Testament Evidence

In the *Prepatriarchal Age* (Gen. 1–11) God spoke directly and propositionally to Adam, having apparently assumed a manlike form for that purpose (Gen. 2:16–17;

---

5. Ibid., 97.
6. Ibid., 97–98; see also George W. Knight III, *Prophecy in the New Testament* (Dallas: Presbyterian Heritage, 1988), 13, fn. 8, for a helpful discussion of the several nuances present in the New Testament occurrences of the words formed from ἀποκαλύπτω, *apokalyptō*.
7. General revelation—that is, God's revelation in humanity, in creation generally, and in his ordinary acts of providence—makes possible all the knowledge that humans as *humans* have (see Acts 17:26–29a). Common grace makes possible all the knowledge that humans as *sinners* have by inhibiting the sinner's *total* suppression of truth and by providing for life amidst the destructiveness of sin (Ps. 145:9; Matt. 5:44; Luke 6:35-36; Acts 14:16).
8. H. C. Thiessen, *Introduction to the New Testament* (Grand Rapids, Mich.: Eerdmans, 1943), 86.
9. I am indebted to David C. Jones's classroom lecture on the revelatory process given at Covenant Theological Seminary, St. Louis, Missouri, for the outline followed on pp. 5–11.

[5]

3:8), and entered into covenant with him, promising Adam great blessedness for obedience and imposing the sanction of death for disobedience. He also spoke to Cain (4:6–12), to Noah (6:13–21), and to Noah and his sons (9:1, 8).

In *Patriarchal Times* (Gen. 12–50) God again revealed his covenant promises and preceptive will through theophanies ("the angel of the Lord,"[10] Gen. 16:7–13; 28:13 [see 31:11–13]; 32:22–32 [see 48:15–16; Hos. 12:3–4]), and he also spoke through visions (Gen. 12:7; 15:1, 12; 26:24; Job 4:13; 20:8; 33:15) and two types of dreams—dreams in which direct revelations were communicated (Gen. 15:12; 20:3, 6; 28:12; 31:10, 11; 46:2), and symbolic dreams requiring divine interpretations (Gen. 37:5, 6, 10; 40:5–16; 41:1, 5).[11]

In the *Mosaic Period* (Exodus through Deuteronomy) God continued to reveal himself through theophanic media (his "angel," the burning bush, the pillar of cloud and fire) and through visions (Num. 22:20). But the chief organ of revelation was Moses himself, whom God commissioned at the burning bush to be his authorized spokesman and thus a unique prophet in Israel's history (Num. 12:6–8; Deut. 18:18, Hos. 12:13). At the sea God revealed himself as the God of the covenant, saving his people and judging their enemies. Several times we read of Moses recording things that God told him (Exod. 17:14; 24:4, 7; 34:27; Num. 33:2; Deut. 31:9, 24; see John 5:46–47). At the mountain, Moses received "the book of the covenant" (Exod. 24:7—סֵפֶר הַבְּרִית, *sēper habbᵉrîth*; see also "the book of the law," Deut. 31:26), which was regarded as of equal authority with Moses himself. The high priest's Urim and Thummim also became a medium for discerning the Lord's will (Exod. 28:30; Num. 27:21; 1 Sam. 14:41, NIV *mg;* 28:6; Ezra 2:63; Neh. 7:65), while the Levites were commissioned to preserve and to teach the Law (Deut. 17:18; 31:9–13; see Mal. 2:5–7). In this period Moses authored Psalm 90. Also in this period we see spiritism and sorcery expressly forbidden as means for determining the divine will (Lev. 19:26; 20:27; Deut. 18:14).

In the *Age of Conquest* (Joshua through Ruth) the Law of Moses continued to abide as Israel's authority (Josh. 1:7–8; 8:30–35; also called "the book of the law of God," Josh. 24:26), with God continuing to speak to Joshua (Josh. 1:1, 5, passim) and by his angel to such judges as Gideon (Judg. 6:12). He also spoke through a dream to a Midianite soldier (Judg. 7:13–15).

In the great *Age of the Prophets* (Samuel to Malachi; see Acts 3:24) God spoke audibly to Samuel (1 Sam. 3; see also 1 Sam. 10:25: "the regulations of the kingship [which Samuel] wrote down on a scroll [סֵפֶר, *sēper*] and deposited before the Lord," which

---

10. See Robert L. Reymond, *Jesus, Divine Messiah: The Old Testament Witness* (Fearn, Ross-shire, Scotland: Christian Focus Publications, 1990), chap. 1, for discussion of the Old Testament "angel of the Lord."
11. See Benjamin B. Warfield, "Dream," in *Selected Shorter Writings of Benjamin B. Warfield*, ed. John E. Meeter (Nutley, N.J.: Presbyterian and Reformed, 1973), 2:152–66.

underscores Samuel's role in the *inscripturation* of revelation). Samuel in turn organized schools or guilds of prophets (1 Sam. 10:5–11) who were to supplement the Word of God given by Moses, to instruct Israel in the ways of God, and to act as guardians of the theocracy. Also in these "cloisterlike establishments dedicated to religion and learning,"[12] the prophets studied God's revealed law, kept a record of Israel's history,[13] and arranged to preserve their own prophetic writings.

During the time of the united kingdom God spoke to David (1 Sam. 23:2–4) and to Solomon (1 Kings 3:5; 9:2; 2 Chron. 7:12) through prophets such as Nathan (2 Sam. 7:4–17; 12:1–14; 1 Chron. 17:3), through the (at least) seventy-three psalms of David[14] and the two psalms of Solomon, and finally through the wisdom literature of godly, wise men.[15] It was also in this period that a clear distinction was drawn between general and special revelation (see Ps. 19).

During the divided kingdom period, prior to the time of the great writing prophets, God spoke through such prophets as Ahijah (1 Kings 11:29–39; 14:6–16), Shemaiah (1 Kings 12:22–24), Elijah (but see 2 Chron. 21:12–19 for a *written* prophecy by Elijah), Micaiah (1 Kings 22:17–28), and Elisha (2 Kings 2–13), who made both short-term (e.g., 1 Kings 17:1, these to authenticate the prophetic institution in Israel quickly as truly from God) and long-term predictions (e.g., 1 Kings 13:2).

Then from the ninth century down to the fifth century God spoke in visions to the so-called writing prophets—Obadiah and Joel (ninth-century prophets), Jonah, Amos, Hosea, Micah, and Isaiah (eighth-century prophets), Nahum, Zephaniah, Habakkuk, and Jeremiah (seventh-century prophets), Daniel, Ezekiel, Haggai, and Zechariah (sixth-century prophets), and to Malachi (a

---

12. Edwin R. Thiele, *A Chronology of the Hebrew Kings* (Grand Rapids, Mich.: Zondervan, 1977), 55.
13. For example, Samuel, Nathan, and Gad recorded David's history (1 Chron. 29:29); Nathan, Ahijah, and Iddo recorded Solomon's history (2 Chron. 9:29); Shemaiah and Iddo kept a record of Rehoboam's reign (2 Chron. 12:15); Iddo recorded Abijah's history (2 Chron. 13:22); Jehu recorded Jehoshaphat's reign (2 Chron. 20:34); Isaiah recorded the histories of Uzziah and Hezekiah (2 Chron. 26:22; 32:32); and unnamed "seers" recorded Manasseh's history (2 Chron. 33:19). Since the Books of Samuel, Kings, and Chronicles were based upon such records (and surely others like them), the history these biblical books record is true and accurate, drawn from literary sources written by inspired prophets and preserved by their prophetic schools.
14. See 2 Samuel 23:2, where David declares, "The Spirit of the LORD spoke through me; his word was on my tongue." See also Acts 1:16 and 4:24–26 for two interesting New Testament affirmations of this same fact: "the Scripture had to be fulfilled which the Holy Spirit spoke long ago through the mouth of David," and "When [the church] heard this, they raised their voices together in prayer to God. 'Sovereign Lord,' they said, . . . 'You spoke by the Holy Spirit through the mouth of your servant, our father David [in the inscripturated Psalm 2].'"
15. See Bruce K. Waltke, "The Authority of Proverbs: An Exposition of Proverbs 1:2–6," *Presbuterion: Covenant Seminary Review* 12, no. 1 (1987): 65–78.

fifth-century prophet). He also spoke by dreams to Nebuchadnezzar and Daniel (Dan. 2:1, 3, 19, 26; 4:5; 7:1; see also Jer. 23:25, 28, 32; 27:9; 29:8; Zech. 10:2).

As these prophets conveyed God's message to the people, while everything they said was ultimately from God (see 2 Tim. 3:16; 2 Pet. 1:20–21), many times the divine factor so overpowered the human factor that the latter virtually dropped out of sight. As Louis Berkhof notes:

> The prophetic word [often] begins by speaking of God in the third person, and then, without any indication of a transition, continues in the first person. The opening words are words of the prophet, and then all at once, without any preparation of the reader for a change, the human author simply disappears from view, and the divine author speaks apparently without any intermediary, Isa. 19:1, 2; Hos. 4:1–6; 6:1–4; Mic. 1:3–6; Zech. 9:4–6; 12:8, 9. Thus the word of the prophet passes right into that of the Lord without any formal transition. The two are simply fused, and thus prove to be one.[16]

The Old Testament also gives evidence that God clearly instructed several prophets to preserve in writing the revelations he was giving them (see 1 Chron. 29:12, 19; Isa. 8:1; 30:8; Jer. 25:13; 30:1–2; 36:2, 27–28; Ezek. 24:1, 2; 43:11; Dan. 9:2; 12:4; Hab. 2:2; see also here 2 Tim. 3:16; 2 Pet. 1:20–21), justifying the inference that he did so with all of the writing prophets.

The prophets also speak of the Lord's hand being upon them in such a manner that they were constrained—sometimes contrary to their natural desire (Exod. 3:11; 4:10, 13; Jer. 1:6)—to proclaim the divine message (Isa. 8:11; Ezek. 1:3; 3:22; 37:1). Jeremiah expressed the holy compulsion he felt to speak God's message in these words: "His word is in my heart like a fire, a fire shut up in my bones. I am weary of holding it in; indeed, I cannot [וְלֹא אוּכָל, $w^e l\bar{o}$' '$\hat{u}c\bar{a}l$]" (Jer. 20:9).

Throughout this period of kingdom disruption a very evident process of *inscripturation* of the divine Word was also taking place, each biblical book of this period, so inscripturated, becoming a covenant or kingdom document given to the people of God in the history of redemption, with later prophets often recognizing earlier prophetic writings as speaking with absolute authority and citing them as the word of God (see Joel 2:32 and Obad. 17; Amos 1:2 and Joel 3:16; Jer. 26:18 and Mic. 3:12; Jer. 49:14–22 and Obad., passim; Ezek. 14:14, 20; Dan. 9:2 and Jer. 29:10; Zech. 7:12; Mal. 4:4).

It was doubtless also in this period of the great prophets that the twelve psalms of Asaph, the ten psalms of the sons of Korah, the psalm of Heman the Ezrahite, and the psalm of Ethan the Ezrahite were composed and added to Israel's Psalter.

---

16. Louis Berkhof, *Introductory Volume to Systematic Theology* (Grand Rapids, Mich.: Eerdmans, 1932), 149.

THE FACT OF DIVINE REVELATION

We may now summarize the concept of revelation in the Old Testament period:

1. God revealed himself in the context of the "history of redemption" (in which history he acted in mercy and judgment to redeem his people).

2. This "history of redemption" was structured by several covenants that God made with Adam, Noah, Abraham, Israel (both at Sinai and on the Plains of Moab), and David, and by the promised new covenant of Jeremiah 31, each covenant building upon those preceding it as God carried out his salvific purpose.

3. This covenantally structured history, in turn, necessarily entailed and was served by verbal communication of propositional truth, assertions sometimes immediately by and from God himself, sometimes immediately by persons authorized, authenticated, and inspired by him.[17]

4. This revelatory activity that accompanied and served God's redemptive activity was necessarily progressive, its progressiveness possessing an organic character, that is, a perfection at every stage (herein resides one reason why later prophets did not hesitate to cite earlier prophets).[18]

5. These revelations came by means of theophanies, dreams, and visions that accompanied and explained God's redemptive activity, but they culminated in the Mosaic Age and each age afterward in the ongoing "inscripturation" of the Word of God. Certain New Testament descriptions of the Old Testament are noteworthy in this regard in that they suggest that the New Testament writers viewed the Old Testament as a fixed and authoritative literary corpus: "the Law and the Prophets" (ὁ νόμος καὶ οἱ προφῆται, *ho nomos kai hoi prophētai*) Luke 16:16; "Moses and the Prophets" (Μωϋσέα καὶ τοὺς προφῆτας, *Mōusea kai tous prophētas*) Luke 16:29; "the Law of Moses, the Prophets, and Psalms" (τῷ νόμῳ Μωϋσέως καὶ τοῖς προφήταις καὶ ψαλμοῖς, *tō nomō Mōuseōs kai tois prophētais kai psalmois*) Luke 24:44; the "Law" (τῷ νόμῳ, *tō nomō* [a citation from Psalms]) John 10:34; "the Scripture" or "the Scriptures" (ἡ γραφή, *hē graphē*, αἱ

---

17. See part two, chapter eleven, "God's Works of Creation and Providence," for further scriptural proof of this relationship.

18. Geerhardus Vos (*Biblical Theology* [Grand Rapids, Mich.: Eerdmans, 1948], 15–16) expresses this point by drawing an analogy between the revelatory process and the growth of a tree: "It is sometimes contended that the assumption of progress in revelation excludes its perfection at all stages. This would actually be so if the progress were nonorganic. The organic progress is from seed-form to the attainment of full growth; yet we do not say that in the qualitative sense the seed is less perfect than the tree."

γραφαί, *hai graphai*) John 10:35; Rom. 9:17; Luke 24:27; "holy Scriptures" (γραφαῖς ἁγίαις, *graphais hagiais*) Rom. 1:2; the "oracles of God" (τὰ λόγια τοῦ θεοῦ, *ta logia tou theou*) Rom. 3:2; "living oracles" (λόγια ζῶντα, *logia zōnta*) Acts 7:38; "prophetic Scriptures" (γραφῶν προφητικῶν, *graphōn prophētikōn*) Rom. 16:26; and "[the] sacred Scriptures" [τὰ] ἱερὰ γράμματα, ([*ta*] *hiera grammata*) 2 Tim. 3:15.

6. Public reading and teaching of the Word of God followed its inscripturation, in order that the Word of God might be kept before the people as his perpetual revelation to them (Josh. 8:30–35; Neh. 8:1–18; Mal. 4:4–6).

New Testament Evidence

1. In the New Testament age (a much shorter period of time than that of the Old Testament, only covering approximately a hundred years), God reinaugurated the revelatory process that had ceased with Malachi. The first messages were Gabriel's words to Zechariah and to Mary (Luke 1:13–20, 28–37) and five supernatural dreams to Joseph and the Magi (Matt. 1:20; 2:12, 13, 19, 22).

2. God later spoke through John the Baptist, with Luke 3:2 reporting the emergence of revelation with John in words paralleling the Old Testament formula: "The word of God came to John" (ἐγένετο ῥῆμα θεοῦ ἐπὶ Ἰωάννην, *egeneto rhēma theou epi Iōannēn*).

3. Then he revealed his glory, grace, and truth most personally and directly in his incarnate Son who *is* the Word of God (John 1:1, 14, 17; 17:3–8; Heb. 1:1–2)—whose *person* manifested God's name and nature (John 17:6), whose *work* revealed God's work (John 17:4), and whose *words* revealed God's words (John 12:44–50; 17:8).

4. Finally, in the apostolic age God provided the explication of this "Son revelation" by his "Word revelation" through Christ's apostles and prophets (John 16:12–15; 1 Thess. 2:13; 1 Cor. 2:13; 12–14; Eph. 3:5; 2 Pet. 3:15–16).[19]

We may summarize the concept of revelation in the New Testament age with six more points:

1. In the Gospels, Christ the incarnate Word, whom John announced as the Messiah of the Old Testament, claims to have supreme, ultimate, and

---

19. See C. H. Dodd, "The Primitive Preaching," *The Apostolic Preaching and Its Developments* (New York: Harper & Row, 1964), and Leon Morris, *The Apostolic Preaching of the Cross* (London: Tyndale, 1955), for excellent analyses respectively of the gospel that the apostles proclaimed to the pagan world and the theological significance of the cross that the apostles taught to the Christian believer.

THE FACT OF DIVINE REVELATION

absolute authority, the authority of the Lord God himself (see Matt. 9:2; 11:27; 28:18; Luke 21:33).

2. In the Gospels, Christ calls, equips, and sends out apostles to speak and act with his authority, and provides for their continuing authoritative witness (Luke 6:13; 9:1–6 [here they are assigned an "internship" in exercising this authority], John 14:25–26; 16:12–15; 17:20 [here they are assured that they need not rely on their memories for knowledge and accuracy; the Holy Spirit will aid them; here also, as church missionaries, they are to go forth as Christ's "plenipotentiaries," having his authority]).[20]

3. In the New Testament age, following the resurrection and ascension of Christ, the apostles are authenticated as Christ's authoritative representatives by the "marks of the apostle" (Acts 5:12; 2 Cor. 12:12; Heb. 2:4).

4. The apostolic witness, which was in the first instance and for the most part *oral*, progressively culminated in the *written* apostolic tradition, which in turn became authoritative and normative in the church for faith and practice (1 Thess. 2:13; 5:27; 2 Thess. 2:15; 3:6, 14; 2 Cor. 10:8; 13:10; Eph. 3:1–4; Col. 4:16; 1 John 1:1–4; 4:6; John 20:30–31).

5. The church received these apostolic writings as being on a par with the Old Testament Scriptures (explicitly stated in 1 Tim. 5:18 [see Luke 10:7]; 2 Pet. 3:16; implicitly stated in 1 Thess. 5:27; Col. 4:16; 1 Tim. 4:13; Rev. 1:3).[21]

6. The postapostolic church did not "canonize" the New Testament Scriptures but only declared that it had received them as authoritative and thus normative from the beginning as an inspired body of literature. The earliest list containing only the twenty-seven New Testament books occurs in a letter of Athanasius, A.D. 367; the first council to affirm the twenty-seven New Testament books was the Third Council of Carthage, A.D. 397.

In anticipation of an issue that will be addressed more fully in chapter three, namely the cessation of special revelation, it is important to note here that the

---

20. In no sense does the word-revelation through the apostolic organs of revelation detract from the character of Jesus as *the* Word of God or dilute the finality of God's revelation to men in and by Christ inasmuch as it is *his* word which, as Christ's inspired appointees, they declare.
21. In 1 Timothy 5:18 Paul treats the statement of Luke 10:7 under the rubric of "Scripture"; in 2 Peter 3:16 Peter suggests that Paul's writings are Scripture by referring to them in a context where he refers to the "other Scriptures." Then when Paul and John demand that their writings be read in the gathered assemblies of the worshiping churches, along with the reading of the Old Testament, the implication is that their writings were to be treated as normative guides for faith and practice, as the Word of God.

[11]

revelatory process that produced our Old and New Testaments did not flow uninterruptedly. Between Genesis 49:27 and Exodus 2:1 slightly over four hundred years transpired when there was a "blackout" of divine communication to Jacob's family in Egypt. Then with the passing of Malachi, the last of the Old Testament prophets, another four-hundred-year "blackout" ensued before the angel Gabriel appeared to Zechariah the priest, thus commencing the New Testament period of revelation. Such previous revelational "blackouts" should prepare us for the naturalness of the revelational "blackout" that has been in place since the close of the New Testament canon.

THE NEOORTHODOX OBJECTION

In our century a certain sophisticated objection has been registered against the whole idea of a verbal revelation. This objection contends that religious truth by its very nature will always be existential truth—that is, subjective "truth for me," the human existent. It is said that because written or spoken language is always caught in the web of historical relativity, it is inadequate as a conveyor of religious truth to meet the soul's subjective demand for religious certainty; it serves at best as a *Hinweis*—a pointer—to the "existential truth encounter" lying behind and signified by the actual words of Scripture and experienced *nonverbally* by the human existent. In other words, revelation is never propositional but always only personal in terms of the "Christ event," for Christ alone is the Word of God. The Bible becomes then the fallible human witness to the Word of God, and the Holy Spirit inspires, not the Bible, but "faith," recreating the "Christ event" *in us* existentially. It is the believer who is actually "inspired."[22]

Such is the dogmatic pronouncement of classic neoorthodoxy. As one facet of that impressive enterprise of the 1920s, 1930s, and 1940s, it takes its place in the broader vision of that theological novelty which, under the influence of the Kantian distinction between the "phenomenal" and "noumenal" realms,[23] maintained the "qualitative distinction between God and man, between eternity and time." Immanuel Kant (1724–1804) had argued that the *phenomenal* realm, the world of appearances, was controlled by pure reason, while the *noumenal* realm was the realm of God, freedom, and

---

22. It is often said, incorrectly, that the neoorthodox theologian teaches that the Bible "contains" the Word of God. Not so! Nor does he teach that the Bible "becomes" the Word of God in any objective way. Rather, the Bible becomes the instrument that reproduces the "Christ event" *in* one subjectively.

23. For an insightful discussion of the influence of Kantian thought on neoorthodoxy, see John M. Frame, *Cornelius Van Til: An Analysis of His Thought* (Phillipsburg, N.J.: Presbyterian and Reformed, 1995), 353–69.

THE FACT OF DIVINE REVELATION

faith, and was governed by "practical" reason. Accordingly, neoorthodox theologians contended that, while eternity might "touch" time as a tangent touches a circle, it never enters into time. While God, true enough, existentially "speaks" to men, this "revelation" always lurks outside of and behind history in what the proponents of this view referred to as "primal" history *(Urgeschichte),* and it is never to be identified with the words of the Bible or any other book in the A = A sense of the word. This objection, in a word, views the Bible as a (flawed) *record* of God's revelation to human beings but not the revelation itself. Revelation is always a nonverbal *direct theophany* outside ordinary history, and religious truth is always personal or existential truth—the effect of an existential crisis encounter (the "Christ event") between God and the individual human existent.

I would say at least three things in response to this objection to the historic Protestant doctrine of Scripture as the very Word of God.[24] First, whatever one may personally think about the verbal or propositional character of special revelation, he should at least be willing to admit that *Scripture itself affirms that one form—indeed a significant form—of divine disclosure assumed precisely this character.* James Barr, himself certainly no friend of the evangelical doctrine of Scripture, concedes as much in his book *Old and New in Interpretation.* In an appendix to this book entitled "A Note on Fundamentalism," Barr observes: "In modern revelational theologies [by this term he refers to the neoorthodox theologies], it is a stock argument against fundamentalism [by this term he refers to evangelical theology] to say that it depends on a propositional view of revelation, while the right view of revelation is one of encounter, events, history or the like."[25] But Barr believes that one's position must be based upon "an exegesis of the texts as they are"[26] and is thus compelled to acknowledge that the evangelical has read his Bible correctly:

> In so far as it is good to use the term "revelation" at all, it is entirely as true to say that in the Old Testament revelation is by verbal communication as to say that it is by acts in history. We have verbal communication both in that God speaks directly with men and in that men learn from other and earlier men through the verbal form of tradition. When we speak of the highly "personal" nature of the Old Testament God, it is very largely upon this verbal character of his communication with man that we are relying. The acts of God are meaningful because they are set within this frame of verbal communication. God tells what he is

---

24. See I. Howard Marshall, *Biblical Inspiration* (Grand Rapids, Mich.: Eerdmans, 1983), 13–15, for his four telling criticisms of the neoorthodox representation of revelation as always and only personal encounter.
25. James Barr, *Old and New in Interpretation* (London: SCM, 1966), 201.
26. Ibid., 77.

[13]

doing, or tells what he is going to do. He does nothing, unless he tells his servants the prophets (Amos 3:7). A God who acted in history would be a mysterious and supra-personal fate if the action was not linked with this verbal conversation. . . .[27]

There is some reluctance to face the fact of this verbal communication because it is supposed that an apologetic problem is involved. We think that we cannot imagine verbal communication between God and man, and we worry about terrible consequences which would ensue in the Church, and of serious damage to the rationality of our presentation of Christianity, if it were admitted that such verbal communication is important.

But, in the first place, these apologetic considerations should not prevent us from speaking historically about the character of the ancient literature. When we speak of the importance of verbal communication, we are talking as historical-literary scholars about the character of the literature and the forms of expression which it displays. It may well be that as historical scholars we cannot give an adequate account of these phenomena; but we *can* seek to give an adequate account of how they were understood to be, and of the way in which they dominate the form-patterns of the literature.[28]

. . . [W]e may express the matter in this way: that whatever acts and encounters formed the experience of man with God in the Old Testament, the tangible form which they take is that of verbal, linguistic, literary statement. It is this that provides the *content* of all the acts and encounters, and provides the discrimination between one and another and the elements of purpose and personal will. Thus the experience of Israel and its prophets and others crystallizes in the form of sentences and literary complexes which are the articulate form (and thus the knowable form) of the way in which God has related himself to them.[29]

In his article "Revelation Through History in the Old Testament and in Modern Theology,"[30] Barr states this conviction even more strongly:

[W]e come to those texts which have supplied the basic examples for the idea of revelation through history, such as the Exodus story. If you treat this record as revelation through history, you commonly speak as if the basis were the doing of certain divine acts (what, exactly, they were is often difficult to determine), while the present form of tradition in its detail and circumstantiality is "interpretation" of these acts, or "meditation" upon them, or theological reflection prompted by them. Thus one may hear the great revelatory passage of Exodus 3 described as

---

27. Ibid., 77–78.
28. Ibid., 79.
29. Ibid., 80.
30. James Barr, "Revelation Through History in the Old Testament and in Modern Theology," *Interpretation* (April 1963): 193–205.

"interpretation" of this divine act of salvation, or as an inference from the fact that God had led Israel out of Egypt.

But I cannot make this scheme fit the texts, for this is not how the texts represent the Exodus events. Far from representing the divine acts as the basis of all knowledge of God and all communication with him, they represent God as communicating freely with men, and particularly with Moses, before, during, and after these events. Far from the incident at the burning bush being an "interpretation" of the divine acts, it is a direct communication from God to Moses of his purposes and intentions. This conversation, instead of being represented as an interpretation of the divine act, is a precondition of it. If God had not told Moses what he did, the Israelites would not have demanded their escape from Egypt, and the deliverance at the Sea of Reeds would not have taken place.

We may argue, of course, from a critical viewpoint that the stories of such dialogues arose in fact as inference from a divine act already known and believed, and for this there may be good reasons. All I want to say is that if we do this we do it on critical grounds and not on biblical grounds, for this is not how the biblical narrative represents the events. . . .[31]

[D]irect communication [between God and men] is, I believe, an inescapable fact of the Bible and of the Old Testament in particular. God can speak specific verbal messages when he wills, to the men of his choice. But for this, if we follow the way in which the Old Testament represents the incidents, there would have been no call of Abraham, no Exodus, no prophecy. Direct communication from God to man has fully as much claim to be called the core of the tradition as has revelation through events in history. If we persist in saying that this direct, specific communication must be subsumed under revelation through events in history and taken as subsidiary interpretation of the latter, I shall say that we are abandoning the Bible's own representation of the matter for another which is apologetically more comfortable.

And here I want, if I may use an inelegant phrase, to call a particular bluff. It has been frequently represented to us in modern times that there is a "scandal" in the idea of revelation through history [the reader should realize that, from the neoorthodox perspective, it is this "scandal" which is the "scandal" of the gospel which challenges the modern mind and thus is a desirable thing—author], and that the acceptance of it is something seriously difficult for the modern mind, including that even of theologians. The contrary seems to me to be obviously the case. . . . The reason why we use it so much is the very reverse: far from being a central stumbling block to our minds, it is something we use because it is a readily acceptable idea within our theological situation; thus it is one which, in our use of the Bible, enables us to mitigate the difficulty of elements which are

---

31. Ibid., 197.

in fact infinitely more scandalous, elements such as the direct verbal communication of which I have been speaking, or prophetic prediction, or miracles.[32]

What Barr is basically saying is that the neoorthodox scholar should admit that the view of revelation espoused by the evangelical is the view of the Bible itself and that his rejection of the "evangelical view" is based upon extrabiblical philosophico-critical grounds with which he is comfortable, rather than on biblical grounds.

Second, the epistemological basis that neoorthodoxy offers to justify its claim to religious knowledge has all of the apologetic weaknesses of every "leap of faith" theology, specifically, the radical subjectivism and irrationality inherent within every nonverbal religious experience. The human religious existent who would espouse the epistemological views of neoorthodoxy can never be sure that the nonverbal subjective religious encounter concerning which he boasts was with God and not with his own subjective consciousness, if not with Satan himself. How does he know it is a true and not a false religious experience? What reason can he offer to justify his *verbal* explication of his nonverbal religious experience? And why should anyone believe him?

Finally, note the judgment that more recent theological history has rendered respecting these conclusions. What has happened to classic neoorthodoxy? After the radical Bultmannianism of the 1940s and 1950s had carried neoorthodoxy's epistemological implications to their logical conclusions by denying, through its program of "demythologizing" the Jesus of the New Testament, the very possibility of discovering any significant historical facts about him, and by virtually transforming theology into a Heideggerian existential anthropology, it has itself been displaced by the post-Bultmannian "new quest" of the 1960s, 1970s, and 1980s for

---

32. Ibid., 201–2. Barr's contention that it is the "fundamentalist" who has read the Scriptures correctly reminds me of Kirsopp Lake's oft-quoted acknowledgment in his *The Religion of Yesterday and Tomorrow* (Boston: Houghton, 1926), 61:

> It is a mistake often made by educated persons who happen to have but little knowledge of historical theology to suppose that fundamentalism is a new and strange form of thought. It is nothing of the kind; it is the partial and uneducated survival of a theology which was once universally held by all Christians. How many were there, for instance, in Christian churches in the eighteenth century who doubted the infallible inspiration of all Scripture? A few, perhaps, but very few. No, the fundamentalist may be wrong; I think that he is. But it is we who have departed from the tradition, not he; and I am sorry for the fate of anyone who tries to argue with a fundamentalist on the basis of authority. The Bible and the *corpus theologicum* of the Church are on the fundamentalist side.

the *historical* Jesus.³³ A theological vision that talked much about the mighty acts of God in history but refused to identify any historical event as an act of God, that talked much about the Christ of faith but refused to identify Jesus of Nazareth directly with this Christ at any point, and that talked much about the Word of God to man but refused to identify the Bible or any other book directly with this Word of God could not for long fire the imagination or answer the hard questions of thinking people. And a gospel whose Christ is a "phantom," whose cross is merely a symbol, and whose resurrection occurs only in "primal history" and not in the actual history where people experience pain and death and long for deliverance simply has no staying power. Increasing uneasiness with precisely this absence of the historical element in neoorthodoxy has provoked the impetus behind the "new quest for the historical Jesus" presently being conducted by much post-Bultmannian critical New Testament scholarship. And it is a striking commentary on how badly classic neoorthodoxy with its concept of revelation as nonhistorical and existential has fared to note that, whereas Bultmann entitled his existential "life of Jesus" in 1926 simply *Jesus,* Günther Bornkamm, one of his students, entitled his own 1956 "life of Jesus," *Jesus of Nazareth,* which, though its content is anything but a return to orthodoxy, reflects the remarkable shift away from the existential theologies that dominated the academic scene some decades ago.

It is still biblical to insist that Jesus Christ is the incarnate Word of God, the supreme revelation of God, and not a vague "event" that occurs in a nonverbal personal encounter.³⁴ And it is still appropriate to teach that the Bible is the written (propositional) Word of God, divinely inspired and therefore infallible. And the Holy Spirit both inspired the Bible and creates saving faith in the redeemed, illuminating them with respect both to the nature of Scripture itself and to Scripture's message to them.

LANGUAGE PHILOSOPHY'S OBJECTION

A second modern objection to the notion of a verbal or propositional revelation from God to human beings contends that language is simply inadequate as a vehicle of personal communication and surely incapable of expressing literal truth

---

33. This "new quest" for the historical Jesus, being conducted by such men as E. Käsemann, H. Conzelmann, N. Perrin, and R. H. Fuller, is doomed to failure because its search for the authentic sayings of Jesus is governed by the application to the dominical sayings of the faulty criteria of dissimilarity, coherence, and frequency.
34. See Robert L. Reymond, *Jesus, Divine Messiah: The New Testament Witness* (Phillipsburg, N.J.: Presbyterian and Reformed, 1990), for a defense of the doctrine that Jesus was the Son of God incarnate.

about transcendent realities. This objection—rooted in present-day positivistic skepticism—finds expression in poets like Gertrude Stein, novelists like Franz Kafka, playwrights like Samuel Beckett, and philosophers such as Ludwig Wittgenstein and A. J. Ayers. It also finds expression in the widespread Eastern religious ideas (such as Taoism) that stress the inexpressibility of God.

This objection, of course, has its problems, the first being what Vern S. Poythress calls the problem of value. He asks:

> On what basis are we to make judgments about adequacy and inadequacy . . . ? What could we mean by saying that human language is inadequate to talk about God . . . ? In what way is it "inadequate"? And what do we expect talk about God . . . to be like? Our expectations and definitions of "adequacy" . . . are themselves shot through with values, with preferences, desires, standards, and perhaps disappointments at goals that we set but are not reached. Where do these values come from? If God is Lord, we ought to conform our values to *his* standards. Hence there is something intrinsically rebellious about negatively evaluating biblical language [for its adequacy as "God talk"].[35]

Poythress highlights a second epistemological problem:

> How does the objector obtain the necessary knowledge about God, truth, and cultures in order to make a judgment about the adequacy of language for expressing theology and truth, and for achieving cross-cultural communications? How does he do this when he himself is largely limited by the capabilities of his own language and culture?[36]

A radical variant of this objection contends that human language is incapable of expressing literal truth about *anything*.[37] One advocate of this theory, Wilbur Marshall Urban, writes that "strictly speaking, there is no such thing as literal truth in any absolute sense. . . . There are no strictly literal sentences . . . there is no such thing as literal truth . . . and any expression in language contains some symbolic element."[38] Urban insists that to have wholly nonsymbolic truth "is really impos-

---

35. Vern S. Poythress, "Adequacy of Language and Accommodation," in *Hermeneutics, Inerrancy, and the Bible*, ed. Earl D. Radmacher and Robert D. Preus (Grand Rapids, Mich.: Zondervan, 1984), 353.
36. Ibid., 354.
37. See Poythress's article and James I. Packer, "The Adequacy of Human Language," in *Inerrancy*, ed. Norman L. Geisler (Grand Rapids, Mich.: Zondervan, 1980), 197–226, for fuller treatments of this objection.
38. Wilbur Marshall Urban, *Language and Reality* (London: George Allen & Unwin, 1961), 382, 383, 433.

sible in view of the very nature of language and expression. If there were such a thing as wholly non-symbolic truth, it could not be expressed."[39]

This theory of language is based on the premise that human language originated in the squeals and grunts of animals. The first words ever spoken were supposedly nouns or names produced by imitating the sound that an animal or a waterfall made; or if the object made no noise, some more arbitrary method was used to attach a noun to it. But in all events, language had a totally sensory origin; all terms, having their immediate origin in sensory impressions, derive their meaning from the sensory world. Consequently, all language is symbolic. Literal meanings, particularly for metaphysics, are impossible because words can never be completely detached from their sensory origin.

What is one to say concerning such a radical theory? First, such a theory of language is self-defeating. To demonstrate this, one has only to ask the proponent of the theory, which theory he has expressed in language, "Is your theory of language, as you have stated it, literally true?" If he affirms that it is, one only needs to note that, if his statement of the theory is literally true, the theory itself is false, for as a proposition set forth in language it contradicts and thus falsifies the very assertion which it makes—namely, that language cannot express literal truth. If he should rejoin that his statement of the theory is the one exception to the thesis it proposes, one can urge again that this self-serving claim still nullifies the theory. But if he affirms that his stated theory is not literally true, one may simply reject it, and that is the end of the matter. If he should reply that, while the statement of his theory is not literally true, it is (in keeping with the theory itself) *symbolically* true, one only needs to ask, "Symbolically true of what?" Since anything he says in response, according to his own view, could only be symbolically true of something else, and so on *ad infinitum*, his infinite symbolic explanatory regress renders impossible the theorist's effort to justify his first assertion ("The theory is symbolically true").

Second, on a practical level, no one could really live comfortably with the notion that language cannot communicate literal truth. Men and women discourse every day around the world in political, economic, and social situations. They intend, apart from the use of obvious figures of speech such as metaphors (which when interpreted intend literal truth), that their language be understood and received as literally true by their listeners. They, in turn, assume that the words spoken to them will normally be literally true. If people do not understand one another's meanings, they ask for clarification, and if they have reason to suspect the truthfulness of the words spoken to them, there are means at their disposal (cross-examination) to verify or to falsify them. In other words, most people simply do not assume that

---

39. Ibid., 446.

language is freighted with so many inherent theoretical difficulties respecting "that which is to be expressed" that its value as a vehicle for literal truth is reduced to zero, that is, that their verbalizing efforts are so burdened with ambiguous symbols that their words cannot state what they literally mean. John M. Frame elaborates upon this concern and applies his conclusions to the issue of scriptural authority:

> (a) Some sentences are, in one sense, perfectly precise and comprehensive. Take "Washington is the capital of the United States": could that fact be stated more precisely? more comprehensively? (b) Of course, even the aforementioned sentence is not comprehensive in the sense of "saying everything there is to say" about Washington and the U.S. But no human being ever *tries* to say all that, at least if he has any sense at all! Nor does the Bible claim to say "everything" about God. The claim to infallibility does not entail a claim to comprehensiveness in this sense. And where no claim to comprehensiveness is made, lack of comprehensiveness does not refute infallibility. (c) Nor is imprecision necessarily a fault. "Pittsburgh is about 300 miles from Philadelphia" is imprecise in a sense, but it is a perfectly good sentence and is in no usual sense untrue. An "infallible" book might contain many imprecise-but-true statements of this sort. Granted, then, that there is a sense in which language never conveys the "whole truth," we need not renounce on that account any element of the orthodox view of biblical authority.[40]

Now if people normally take the validity of the communication process for granted in regard to daily human discourse, how much more plausible is the notion that the infinite, personal God can communicate literal truth verbally or propositionally. If God is omnipotent, surely he can speak literal nonsymbolic truth to human beings without his intention being warped or freighted with distorting and nullifying ambiguities. In fact, according to Scripture this is precisely what he has done. Our God is a language-using God; he has spoken literal truth to humankind.[41]

---

40. John M. Frame, "God and Biblical Language: Transcendence and Immanence," in *God's Inerrant Word*, ed. John W. Montgomery (Minneapolis: Bethany, 1974), 160.
41. In support of God's "language-using" ability, James I. Packer ("The Adequacy of Human Language," 206–7) has a remarkably interesting paragraph:

> We may take the very explicit witness of the letter to the Hebrews as proof. The writer opens with the great "In time past God *spoke* to our forefathers at many times and in various ways, but in these last days he has *spoken* to us by his Son" (Heb. 1:1–2). The phrase "various ways" recalls the visions, dreams, theophanies, angelic messages, and other forms of direct locution whereby God revealed His mind to His Old Testament messengers. It also indicates the occasional and fragmentary nature of the revelations themselves, at least when seen in the light of the final and definitive self-disclosure that God gave through His incarnate Son,

And if God created people for the purpose of fellowship with him, it is fair to assume that he would have created them with the capacity both to comprehend God's literal truth coming to them *ab extra* and in turn to respond verbally with no loss or distortion of the truth in the verbal interchange (this capacity surely being an aspect of humanity's image-bearing character). This is simply to place language as to its origin and significance within the framework of the teaching of Scripture itself. The Scriptures teach that the human being is the crowning creation of God and all human abilities are of divine origination. Specifically, the Scriptures assert in no uncertain terms that human language, far from having its origin in so-called primitive man's first empirically motivated grunts, is a gift from God. To Moses, who urged his lack of eloquence as an excuse for refusing God's call, God responded: "Who has made man's mouth? . . . Is it not I, the LORD?" (Exod. 4:11). God is the Source and Originator of language, and he created men and women in his own image in order that he and his image bearers might be able to speak literal truth to each other. And the Christian has good and ample reasons for believing that the Scriptures are a trustworthy record of a portion of that divine-human dialogue.

Some have objected to the very idea of God speaking to people. Even if he could so speak, they ask, is it not possible that those who first heard him misunderstood or misconstrued his message to them, and if that is a real possibility, how can one ever be sure that they did not in fact misunderstand his word to them?

Yes, theoretically they could have misunderstood his truth to them and thus have unintentionally misrepresented it to others. But that is precisely the reason, evangelicals contend, in agreement with Scripture itself, that God the Holy Spirit "carried [the prophets] along" as they heard God's message and reported it to others, and superintended them as they permanently recorded his word—precisely in order that they would record it without error (see 1 Cor. 2:13; 2 Pet. 1:20–21).

But what about us? Does not the fact that we can misunderstand the Scriptures nullify any value that they might otherwise have as a vehicle for literal truth? After all, people interpreting the same biblical passage have come to opposite conclusions respecting its meaning. William Temple, archbishop of Canterbury (1942–44),

---

Jesus Christ. But when the writer says that God *spoke* by His Son, what he has in mind is precisely verbal communication, just as when he says that God *spoke* through the prophets. His argument continues with the inference that, because of the Son's supreme dignity, we must pay all the greater attention to the message of the great salvation that He declared and that His first hearers, the apostles, relayed in their spoken testimony (Heb. 2:1–3). The author proceeds to make, or at least to buttress, every positive theological point in his whole exposition, up to the final chapter of the letter, by exposition and application of Old Testament passages—which he cites as what the Father or the Son or the Holy Spirit says to Christian believers (see 1:5–13; 5:5ff.; 8:3–12; 10:30, 37ff.; 12:26; 13:5 for the Father as speaker; 2:11–13; 10:5–9 for Christ as speaker; and 3:7–11; 9:8; 10:15–17 for the Holy Spirit as speaker).

declared that even if God had revealed himself in a verbal way (he personally believed that God had not), the value of this revelation as a verbal communication would be destroyed because of the possibility of human misunderstanding of its intent.[42] But if Temple is correct, the worth of his own book is vitiated on this same principle: because it may be misunderstood, it too is valueless as a statement of literal truth. But apparently Temple did not believe that the possibility that people might misunderstand *his* book destroyed its value. Otherwise, he would not have written it.

While it is true that people can and have misunderstood the Scriptures, sometimes even to their own destruction (see 2 Pet. 3:16), it simply is not true that the Bible is a "wax nose" that can be "punched and shaped" to mean anything that the interpreter wants it to mean. For example, the statement, "God so loved the world that he gave his one and only Son, that whoever believes in him shall not perish but have eternal life," is clear and plain. It means only one thing: The Son of God, the Father's gift of love to undeserving people, will save from eternal perdition and give eternal life to everyone who puts his trust in him. This verse does not and cannot be made to mean that Esarhaddon, king of Assyria, so loved the world that he gave his son for it, or that the world so loved God that it did something for him, or that trust in Jesus Christ will bring one to eternal perdition. The rules of grammar are too inflexible to allow such nonsense! And I feel quite sure that anyone who would maintain that John 3:16 could indeed mean any or all of these things would not want the same hermeneutical rule applied to his own words; otherwise, his words could be construed as supporting the idea of a literally true verbal revelation from God to man![43]

Now, of course, it is true that people can and do interpret the Scriptures differently—indeed, at times so differently that they have come to opposite conclu-

---

42. William Temple, *Nature, Man and God* (London: Macmillan, 1934), 310–11.
43. Walter C. Kaiser Jr., "A Response to 'Author's Intention and Biblical Interpretation,'" in *Hermeneutics, Inerrancy, and the Bible*, ed. Earl D. Radmacher and Robert D. Preus (Grand Rapids, Mich.: Zondervan, 1984), 409, observes:

> A literary work like the Bible can have one and only one correct interpretation and that meaning must be determined by the human author's truth-intention; otherwise, all alleged meanings would be accorded the same degree of seriousness, plausibility, and correctness with no one meaning being more valid or true than the others. . . . This is so fundamental to the process of interpretation that one must temporarily assume this hermeneutical principle is true in order to successfully deny its legitimacy. It is humorous to see how many defenders of some form of multiple sense hermeneutic will demand that they be understood according to the single truth-intention of their use of their own words while arguing that Scriptural words have a plethora of meanings.

sions regarding the meaning of a given Scripture statement. How do we explain this? And does this not destroy the value of the Holy Scriptures as God's written revelation? Well, we must be rational enough and courageous enough to declare that both interpretations cannot be right. They may both be wrong, but they cannot both be right. One interpretation, if not both, needs to be corrected by a rigid application of the canons of grammatico-historical hermeneutics, bearing always in mind the great "analogy of faith" principle that Scripture must interpret Scripture. We must *not* say that language cannot convey precise literal meaning from one mind to another and that therefore even contradictory interpretations may both be right! Far from being incapable of expressing literal truth, language is not only the most capable vehicle by which literal truth may be communicated from one mind to another—it is the *only* such vehicle! For truth can only be expressed propositionally, but propositions cannot be framed apart from language. It is as simple as this: deny to language the capacity to communicate literal truth and one rejects the only means of communicating literal truth from one mind to another. Any denial of this must assume linguistic form, as we have already noted, and in the end only self-destructs if it claims to be literally true.

One final comment: every theory that would endorse the idea that literal truth cannot be revealed or communicated propositionally from God to man because language *per se* is incapable of such is ultimately an attack against Jesus Christ. For in the "days of his flesh" Jesus Christ taught the multitudes using the known languages of Aramaic and Greek, claiming as he did so that he was imparting eternal truth (see, e.g., John 8:26, 40). Thus every denial of the possibility of a literally true verbal revelation from God to mankind strikes directly at Jesus Christ in his role as Prophet and Teacher, for he claimed to be the deliverer of just such a revelation. And those who would be loyal to him must be willing to affirm not only that God can and has revealed himself but also that he has done so in propositional fashion—and in inscripturated fashion at the point of the Christian Scriptures.

Christians must make this propositional or informational revelation the *bedrock* of their faith, for it is only as they believe truth originating from God himself that they can have certainty respecting the validity of their religious convictions.

CHAPTER TWO

The Inspired Nature of Holy Scripture

THE PREVIOUS CHAPTER discussed the biblical data for the fact of a verbal or propositional revelatory process in history. This chapter presents arguments for the Bible's truthfulness when it reports on this revelatory process and its own divinely inspired character. After exegetically grounding the fact of the revelatory process and the Bible message's "revealed" character, I will seek to demonstrate the relationship of this revelatory process to the accompanying process of inspiration.

THE BIBLE MESSAGE'S "REVEALEDNESS"

By the Bible message's "revealedness" I mean that the Bible, with regard to the origin of its subject matter or "message," is a revelation from God. That is to say, it "tells a story" that people simply could not and would not have known without divine aid. God was its Author and Source. He had to tell it to them.

Old Testament Evidence

Evidence abounds within the Old Testament that the prophets were God's messengers and that their message was of divine origin. Consider the following key passages:

EXODUS 4:10–16; 7:1–4

Warfield refers to the Exodus material detailing God's commissioning of Moses and Aaron as "the fundamental passage" for determining what it meant for one to be a true prophet (נָבִיא, *nābî'*).[1] The passages read:

> Moses said to the LORD, "O Lord, I have never been eloquent, neither in the past nor since you have spoken to your servant. I am slow of speech and tongue."
>
> The LORD said to him, "Who gave man his mouth? Who makes him deaf or dumb? Who gives him sight or makes him blind? Is it not I, the LORD? Now go; I will help you speak and will teach you what to say."
>
> But Moses said, "O Lord, please send someone else to do it."
>
> Then the LORD's anger burned against Moses and he said, "What about your brother, Aaron the Levite? I know he can speak well. He is already on his way to meet you, and his heart will be glad when he sees you. You shall speak to him and put words in his mouth; I will help both of you speak and will teach you what to do. He will speak to the people for you, and it will be as if he were your mouth and as if you were God to him. (Exod. 4:10–16)
>
> Then the LORD said to Moses, "See, I have made you like God to Pharaoh, and your brother Aaron will be your prophet [נָבִיא, *nābî'*]. You are to say everything I command you, and your brother Aaron is to tell Pharaoh to let the Israelites go out of his country. But . . . he will not listen to you. (Exod. 7:1–4)

God declares that he who made man's mouth would be with Moses to teach him what to say to the people of Israel and to Pharaoh (Exod. 4:12). When Moses continued to object that he was not eloquent, God declared that Moses would become "like God to Pharaoh" (7:1), and would utilize Aaron as his "prophet" (נָבִיא, *nābî'*) (7:1), and that Aaron would speak to the people and to Pharaoh for Moses "as if he were your mouth and as if you were God to him" (4:16). Accordingly, when Pharaoh refused to hear Aaron, he was actually refusing to listen to Moses (7:4). From this material we see that for Aaron to be Moses' "prophet," two conditions were essential: (1) he could not speak for himself, and (2) the one for whom he spoke had to be for him as "God." According to these passages, then, a true prophet was one who did not put forth his own words or "speak out of his own heart," but rather was "an appointed regular speaker for a divine superior, whose speech carries the authority of the latter."[2] In short, the prophet was God's spokesman.

---

1. Benjamin B. Warfield, "The Biblical Idea of Revelation," in *The Inspiration and Authority of the Bible* (Phillipsburg, N.J.: Presbyterian and Reformed, 1948), 87.
2. Geerhardus Vos, *Biblical Theology* (Grand Rapids, Mich.: Eerdmans, 1948), 210.

NUMBERS 12:6–8

To Aaron and Miriam, who had questioned Moses' authority, God declared:

> When a prophet of the Lord is among you,
> I *reveal myself* [אֶתְוַדָּע, *'etwaddāʻ*] to him *in visions*, [בַּמַּרְאָה, *bammarʼâh*],
> I *speak* [אֲדַבֶּר, *ʼadabēr*] to him *in dreams* [בַּחֲלוֹם, *baḥᵃlôm*].
> But this is not true of my servant Moses;
> he is faithful in all my house.
> With him I *speak face to face* [פֶּה אֶל פֶּה אֲדַבֶּר *peh ʼel peh ʼᵃdaber*],
> clearly *and not in riddles* [וְלֹא בְחִידֹת, *wᵉlōʼ bᵉḥîdōt*];
> he sees the form of the Lord.
> Why then were you not afraid
> to speak against my servant Moses? (Num. 12:6–8)

While the fundamental thrust of this passage is the advocacy of the peculiar favor and superior dignity that Moses enjoyed over all of the other Old Testament prophets,[3] the passage also in a unique way underscores the revelatory character of the Old Testament message as a whole. Whether it be Moses or the other prophets, their message is alike from God (see "I reveal," "I speak"). No distinction is drawn between Moses and the other prophets as to the divine origination and authority of their respective messages. "No suggestion whatever is made of any inferiority, in either the directness or the purity of their supernaturalness, attaching to other organs of revelation."[4] In these regards they are equals.

DEUTERONOMY 18:14–21

This passage provides a guarantee that the prophetic institution and the prophetic message in Israel were of divine origination:

> The nations you will dispossess listen to those who practice sorcery or divination [in order to discern the will of their gods]. But as for you, the Lord your God has not permitted you to do so. The Lord your God will raise up for you a

---

3. I would suggest that the New Testament prophets were to the apostles what the Old Testament prophets were to Moses—"like unto" a prior "superior." In the Old Testament the prophets were to be "like unto" Moses (Deut. 18:15,18) and their message had to agree with Moses' teaching. In the New Testament the prophets were under the authority of apostolic direction (1 Cor. 14:29–31).
4. Warfield, "The Biblical Idea of Revelation," 86.

[27]

prophet [נָבִיא, *nābî'*] like me from among your own brothers. You must listen to him. For this is what you asked of the LORD your God at Horeb on the day of the assembly when you said, "Let us not hear the voice of the LORD our God nor see this great fire anymore, or we will die."

The LORD said to me: "What they say is good. I will raise up for them a prophet like you from among their brothers; I will put my words in his mouth, and he will tell them everything I command him. If anyone does not listen to my words that the prophet speaks in my name, I myself will call him to account. But a prophet who presumes to speak in my name anything I have not commanded him to say, or a prophet who speaks in the name of other gods, must be put to death."

You may say to yourselves, "How can we know when a message has not been spoken by the LORD?" If what a prophet proclaims in the name of the Lord does not take place or come true, that is a message the LORD has not spoken. That prophet has spoken presumptuously. Do not be afraid of him. (Deut. 18:14–21)

Against the background of the pagan practices of sorcery and divination, in which Israel was forbidden to engage (Deut. 18:14), Moses declared that as the alternative God would "raise up for you a prophet like me from among your own brothers," and into his mouth God would put his words. Moses further stated that it is *God's* words that the prophet would speak. There is also the implication in 18:22 that the content of the prophet's message, while not to be restricted to the foretelling of future events, could and would include that element (see "If what a prophet proclaims in the name of the LORD does not take place or come true;" see also Deut. 13:1–3 for the "analogy of faith" test of the Old Testament prophet, that is, his theology must agree with previously revealed teaching).

HABAKKUK 2:2–3

This passage is highly significant for what it teaches us about the nature of biblical prophecy:

> Then the LORD replied:
> "Write down the *revelation* [חָזוֹן, *ḥāzôn*]
>   and make it plain on tablets
>   so that a herald may run with it.
> For the *revelation* [חָזוֹן, *ḥāzôn*] awaits an appointed time;
>   it speaks of the end
>   and will not prove false.
> Though it linger, wait for it;
>   it will certainly come and will not delay. (Hab. 2:2–3)

The first thing to note is that *true prophecy is revelation,* for twice the content of Habakkuk 2 is referred to here by the word חָזוֹן, *ḥāzôn* (literally, "vision"). This means that true prophets were not simply men of political genius or wise thinkers with unusual insight into civic and world affairs. Rather, they were men who spoke as the Holy Spirit "bore them along." Second, we are assured that prophecy can include the *foretelling of future events,* for we are told that "the revelation awaits an appointed time," that "it speaks of the end," and that what it foretells *"will come."* Third, the divine Oracle declares that the vision is *certain of fulfillment:* the prophecy "will not prove false" and "will certainly come [בֹּא יָבֹא, *bō' yābo'*]." In sum, what God was promising, he was certainly going to perform. Fourth, we should note that the prophet is instructed to "write [כְּתֹב, *kᵉtôb*] the vision down and make it plain upon tablets [הַלֻּחוֹת, *halluhôt*]." Clearly, biblical prophecy could and did assume *the concrete form of Scripture.* (In this immediate context the "vision" refers to the revelation that God gives the prophet in Habakkuk 2.) Fifth and finally, its inscripturated character insures its preservation, thereby enabling the "herald" (קוֹרֵא, *qôrē',* lit., "the one who reads" the tablet) to run with its message to others.

JEREMIAH 1:4–10

Explaining the origin of his prophetic mission, Jeremiah declared:

The word of the LORD came to me, saying,
  "Before I formed you in the womb I knew you,
    before you were born I set you apart;
   I appointed you as a prophet to the nations."
  "Ah, Sovereign LORD," I said, "I do not know how to speak; I am only a child."
But the LORD said to me, "Do not say, 'I am only a child.' You must go to everyone I send you to and say whatever I command you. . . ."
Then the LORD reached out his hand and touched my mouth and said to me, "Now I have put my words in your mouth. See, I appoint you over nations and kingdoms to uproot and tear down, to destroy and overthrow, to build and to plant." (Jer. 1:4–10)

Here Jeremiah makes it clear that God had set him apart before he was born—indeed, even before he was conceived—to the prophetic office. Once again, from this passage it is made plain that to be a prophet one had to be commissioned by God and the one so commissioned was under obligation to speak God's words. The prophet's message, in sum, had to originate with God.

In keeping with this conception, hundreds of times we find the expressions, "Thus the LORD says" (כֹּה אָמַר יהוה, *kōh 'āmar yhwh*) or "The word of the LORD came unto me saying" (וַיְהִי דְבַר יהוה אֵלַי לֵאמֹר, *wayᵉhî dᵉbar yhwh 'ēlay lē'mōr*), prefacing the prophets' words.

JEREMIAH 36

Finally, we often find God commanding the prophets to write down their oracles in order to preserve them (Exod. 17:14; 24:4, 7; 34:27; Num. 33:2; Deut. 31:9, 24; 1 Chron. 29:12, 19; Hab. 2:2; Jer. 30:1–2; 36:2, 4, 6, 27–28). Jeremiah 36 is particularly instructive in that it gives a graphic picture of the divine word in the actual process of assuming inscripturated form, highlighting the identification of the divine word with the finished product of Scripture. This chapter shows that, first, the Lord is able to, and does in fact, speak verbally to men; second, what he says is capable of being inscripturated; third, the words which were read from the scroll were the Lord's words and Jeremiah's words—the Lord spoke them, Jeremiah also spoke them—underscoring what Warfield calls the *confluent* relation between divine and human authors;[5] and fourth, the process of inscripturating the Lord's words does not need to impinge harmfully on the purity and integrity of his word, for the words Baruch read at the end of the dictation process, while still the dictated words of Jeremiah, were said to be also the dictated words of the Lord, which words, when destroyed, God required to be replaced by the same words, plus even more.

Taken together, these passages demonstrate that the prophets of Israel knew that they were called of the Lord, sometimes contrary to their own natural desire (see Exod. 3:11; 4:10, 13; Jer. 1:6), to speak his word. So conscious were they of this fact that they often designate the time when and the place where the Lord spoke to them (see Isa. 1:1; 6:1; Jer. 6:3; 26:1; 27:1; 33:1; Ezek. 3:16; 8:1; 12:8). As further evidence that the message they brought to the people came to them *ab extra*, the prophets at times indicated that they did not fully understand something they were saying (see Dan. 12:8, 9; Zech. 1:9; 4:4–5; 1 Pet. 1:10–11).

New Testament Evidence

Several key passages in the New Testament also clearly teach the fact of the Bible message's "revealedness."[6]

---

5. Ibid., 160; see also Clark Pinnock, *Biblical Revelation—The Foundation of Christian Theology* (Chicago: Moody, 1971), 92–95.
6. See Edwin A. Blum, "The Apostles' View of Scripture," in *Inerrancy*, ed. Norman L. Geisler (Grand Rapids, Mich.: Zondervan, 1980), 39–53.

GALATIANS 1:11–2:21

To the Galatians Paul declared that the gospel he preached was *"not according to man* [οὐκ . . . κατὰ ἄνθρωπον, *ouk . . . kata anthrōpon*], for I neither received it from man, nor was I taught it, but [I received it] *through a revelation from Jesus Christ* [δι' ἀποκαλύψεως Ἰησοῦ Χριστοῦ, *di' apokalypseōs Iēsou Christou*]" (Gal. 1:11–12). Paul clearly believed that the gospel he proclaimed, including not only its factual content but also his interpretation of this factual content, originated with the glorified Christ. He argued that he had received his gospel neither from his life situation prior to his conversion (Gal. 1:13–14) nor from his life situation after his conversion (Gal. 1:16–2:10) but precisely *in connection with* his conversion experience (Gal. 1:12, 15). Christ had spoken to him from heaven and had given to him his apostolic office. To question his gospel was by extension to question his Christ-endowed apostolic office; to question his Christ-endowed apostolic office was by extension to question his gospel. And to do this, he thundered, would result in his antagonist's damnation (Gal. 1:8–9). Given then Paul's apostolic authority and the specific gospel he proclaimed as Christ's apostle, one must conclude that if Paul simply wrote down the gospel he was proclaiming (see Rom. 1:1–4, 9, 16–17), what he wrote would be equally divine with respect to its revealed character.

1 THESSALONIANS 2:13

To the Thessalonian Christians Paul wrote: "We . . . constantly thank God, that when you received from us the word of God's message, you accepted it not as the word of men, but for what it really is, the word of God, which also performs its work in you who believe" (1 Thess. 2:13, author's translation). Paul's assertion here describes the message he had proclaimed to the Thessalonians (λόγον ἀκοῆς, *logon akoēs*, lit., "a word of hearing") rather than a letter he had written to them, but even so it is still quite significant that Paul characterizes the message he had proclaimed, not as the word of a man, but as "what it really is, the word of God." Here he underscores the truth that while some might prefer to regard his message as a human message in light of the fact that Paul, a human, was proclaiming it, Paul himself regarded it more basically and fundamentally (ἀληθῶς, *alēthōs*; lit., "truly") as a divine word (see his τοῦ θεοῦ, *tou theou*, and θεοῦ, *theou*; lit., "of God") since God himself was the Source of it. If one had no other statement from the apostle than this one, it could be inferred, with ample justification, that the same ascriptions would hold true with respect to the message he wrote as an apostle. Though he was writing it, it would be, if it was the same message he had proclaimed, in fact the word of God (ἀληθῶς λόγον θεοῦ, *alēthōs logon theou*) insofar as its "revealedness" is concerned, since God himself was still its source.

1 CORINTHIANS 2:6–13

In this passage to the Corinthians, which Charles Hodge describes as "the most formal didactic passage in the whole Bible" on the doctrines of revelation and inspiration,[7] Paul affirmed about himself as an apostle of Christ: "we also are speaking [the thoughts freely given to us by God (from 2:12)], not in words taught by human wisdom, but in [words] taught by the Spirit, *with the Spirit's [words] explicating the Spirit's thoughts* [πνευματικοῖς πνευματικὰ συγκρίνοντες, *pneumatikois pneumatika synkrinontes*]" (1 Cor. 2:13).[8]

The passage is somewhat involved, but Paul's intention is clear. First, he asserts that, proclaiming Christ crucified (that is, the gospel) as he was, he was speaking God's "secret wisdom" (σοφίαν ἐν μυστηρίῳ, *sophian en mystēriō*), a wisdom that none of the "rulers" of his age (which classification includes wise men, scholars, and philosophers; see 1 Cor. 1:20) understood. He describes this message as "secret" wisdom (2:7), for what he was proclaiming, he says, "no [human] eye has seen, no [human] ear has heard, no [human] mind has conceived" (2:9).

Second, in response to the anticipated question as to how he came into possession of this wisdom if it is inaccessible to mortals, Paul states, "God *revealed* [ἀπεκάλυψεν, *apekalypsen*] it to us by his Spirit" (2:10a).

Third, Paul says that the reason that the Spirit can reveal the mind of God is because (being God himself) the Spirit of God knows the thoughts of God (2:11b).

Fourth, Paul states that the reason he as an apostle could speak what the Spirit of God knows is because he had received the Spirit of God (2:12), who *taught* him not only the thoughts of God but also the very words with which to frame them: "['The things which God has freely given us,' by the Spirit (from 2:12b)]." Paul says, "we speak, not in 'taught by human wisdom words,' but in 'taught by the Spirit [words],' with the Spirit's [words] explicating the Spirit's 'things'" (2:13, author's translation).

Finally, Paul asserts that it has to be this way, that is, that one has to receive the Spirit of God in order to comprehend "the things taught by the Spirit," because "the man without the Spirit does not accept the things that come from the Spirit of God, for they are foolishness to him, and he cannot understand them, because they are spiritually discerned [that is, they are discerned through the Spirit]" (2:14).

In sum, Paul asserts here that, in his capacity as an apostle, both the *thoughts* he proclaimed (see his λαλοῦμεν, *laloumen;* lit., "we are speaking") and the *very words* with which they were framed, were not ultimately his but originally were the Spirit's

---

7. Charles Hodge, *Systematic Theology* (Grand Rapids, Mich.: Eerdmans, n.d.), 1:165.
8. Hodge, *Systematic Theology,* 1:162, translates the last phrase as "clothing the truths of the Spirit in the words of the Spirit."

thoughts and words. Paul's statement here shows that it is appropriate to speak of "*verbal* inspiration." And again, one might justly infer from this that if Paul recorded these thoughts in written form, framing them by these Spirit-taught words, what he wrote would equally be the Spirit's thoughts and words in inscripturated form.

2 PETER 3:15–16

Do we find a statement anywhere to the effect that what Paul *wrote* as an apostle was the Word of God? Yes, we do—in the passage that George E. Ladd refers to as the "earliest reference to the fact that the apostolic church regarded the Pauline letters—or at least some of them—as Scripture."[9] In 2 Peter 3:15–16 Peter declares: "Our beloved brother Paul, according to the wisdom given him, wrote to you, as also in all his letters, speaking in them of . . . things . . . which the untaught and unstable distort, as they do *also the rest of the Scriptures* [καὶ τὰς λοιπὰς γραφὰς, *kai tas loipas graphas*], to their own destruction." It is important that we observe four things about this statement. First, Peter declares that what Paul wrote, not just to his (Peter's) readers, but in all his letters, he wrote according to the wisdom *given* him: that is, Paul's letters contain divine wisdom. Second, Peter places Paul's letters within the category of divinely inspired Scripture by his particular turn of phrase, "also the rest of the Scriptures." Third, their divine authority is seen in Peter's statement that when the untaught and unstable distort the meaning of Paul's letters, they do so to their own destruction. Finally, Peter says these things about Paul's letters even though he himself receives a sharp rebuke in one of them for his inconsistent practice at Antioch (see Gal. 2:11), showing thereby that he was willing to place himself under the authority of the apostolic word that was given to Paul.

Peter vouches, then, for both the intrinsically divine origin and the authority of Paul's letters, which is precisely what one might expect in light of the statements that Paul himself makes about the origin of his message.

2 TIMOTHY 3:16

In our discussion of the preceding verse we assumed the divine origin and "revealedness" of the "rest of the Scriptures"; Paul speaks of these in 2 Timothy 3:16 when he declares that "all Scripture is Godbreathed [πᾶσα γραφὴ θεόπνευστος, *pasa graphē theopneustos*]."[10] To grasp his meaning, we must first understand what he

---

9. George E. Ladd, *A Theology of the New Testament* (Grand Rapids, Mich.: Eerdmans, 1974), 605.

intended by the phrase "all Scripture" and then what he meant by "Godbreathed."

At the very least Paul meant by "all Scripture" the Scriptures of the Old Testament. This is apparent from his statement to Timothy in the immediately preceding verse: "From childhood you have known the sacred writings [(τὰ) ἱερὰ γράμματα, (ta) hiera grammata]," meaning by this term the Old Testament that we have in our possession today. But there is sound reason to believe that Paul would have been willing to include, and almost certainly did include, within the technical category of "all Scripture" the New Testament documents, including his own, as well. For when Paul wrote what he did in 1 Corinthians 7, he affirmed sarcastically to those who were claiming to have the Spirit's approval to do otherwise than he had directed: "And I think I also have the Spirit of God [δοκῶ δὲ κἀγὼ πνεῦμα θεοῦ ἔχειν, dokō de kagō pneuma theou echein]" (1 Cor. 7:40). Paul expresses here his awareness that what he wrote as an apostle, he wrote under the Spirit's superinten-

---

10. The RV rendering of Paul's statement by "Every scripture inspired of God is also profitable" necessitates two comments: First, it makes little difference whether πᾶσα γραφή, *pasa graphē*, is translated "every Scripture [passage]" or "all Scripture" in the sense of "the whole [or entirety] of Scripture." The end result is essentially the same. Nigel Turner (*A Grammar of New Testament Greek*, ed. James H. Moulton [Edinburgh: T. & T. Clark, 1963], 3:199) states that πᾶς, *pas*, before an anarthrous noun means "every" in the sense of "any": "not every individual . . . but any you please." Accordingly, he translates πᾶσα γραφή, *pasa graphē*, "whatever is Scripture." But he goes on to say that the "anarthrous πᾶς, [*pas*] also means *all, the whole of,* just as it does when it has the article." Therefore, Turner could just as readily have translated πᾶσα γραφή, *pasa graphē*, "all Scripture" in the sense of "the whole of Scripture." Indeed, in light of the context which favors the notion that Paul is thinking of the Old Testament in its entirety, this is more likely his intended meaning. Paul virtually says this in Romans 15:4 when he states that "everything that was written in the past [ὅσα προεγράφη, *hosa proegraphē*] was written to teach us, so that through endurance and the encouragement of the Scriptures [γραφῶν, *graphōn*] we might have hope" (ὅσος, *hosos*, according to BAGD, sec. 2, 586, when used absolutely as it is here, means "everything that"). C. F. D. Moule (*An Idiom Book of New Testament Greek* [Cambridge: Cambridge University Press, 1953], 95) concurs. He urges that it is "most unlikely" that πᾶσα γραφή, *pasa graphē*, means "every inspired Scripture," and that it "much more probably means *the whole of Scripture.*"

Second, with respect to the RV rendering as a whole, Merrill F. Unger, in his *Introductory Guide to the Old Testament* (Grand Rapids, Mich.: Zondervan, 1956), 25–26, has correctly urged that it is (1) *exegetically weak* since one does not have to be told the obvious, namely, that every Scripture inspired of God is also profitable, (2) *syntactically objectionable* since the RV renders the same construction (a subject followed by two predicate adjectives joined by the conjunction καί, *kai*) in 1 Corinthians 11:30, 2 Corinthians 10:10, 1 Timothy 4:4, and Hebrews 4:12–13 straightforwardly as two coordinate predicate adjectives, (3) *critically precarious* since very few scholars have approved such a rendering, and (4) *doctrinally dangerous* since it suggests that some sacred Scripture may not be the product of the divine breath. See also J. N. D. Kelly's similar comments in his *A Commentary on the Pastoral Letters* (New York: Harper & Row, 1964), 203.

dence. Again, Paul expresses an awareness of the Spirit's superintending influence upon him when he writes in 1 Corinthians 14:37: "If anybody thinks he is a prophet or spiritually gifted, let him acknowledge that what I am writing to you is the Lord's command." In 1 Timothy 5:18 Paul writes, "The Scripture [ἡ γραφή, *hē graphē*] says," and then he proceeds to cite both Deuteronomy 25:4 and Luke 10:7. This can only mean that Paul regarded Luke's Gospel as inspired "Scripture" on a par with Deuteronomy. Thus Paul would have included within his expression "all Scripture" any and every written document that was from God and thus of the nature of "sacred writings," including not only the Old Testament and those portions of the New Testament that were already written but also those portions of the New Testament that were yet to be written. For Paul, whatever was "Scripture" was "Godbreathed"; indeed, precisely because it was "Godbreathed" it was "sacred Scripture."

What specifically does Paul mean when he asserts that all Scripture is "Godbreathed" (θεόπνευστος, *theopneustos*)? The Greek word occurs only here, but A. T. Robertson identifies it as a verbal adjective based upon an old passive participle form.[11] Its closest New Testament analogue (with the θεο-, *theo-* prefix and the -ος, *-os* ending) is θεοδίδακτος, *theodidaktos*, which means "God-taught" (note the passive voice idea), in 1 Thessalonians 4:9. This meaning supports the idea of passive voice action in θεόπνευστος, *theopneustos*, hence our translation "Godbreathed." But what does this mean? Does it mean that God breathed something into the Scriptures, or does it mean that God "breathed out" the Scriptures? After extensive research Warfield concluded that it means the latter—that God "breathed the Scriptures out" from himself, and his conclusion has generally carried the field of scholarly opinion. Stating that "inspired" is "a distinct and even misleading mistranslation," he offers as his reason for this conclusion the following:

> The Greek word in this passage—θεόπνευστος, *theopneustos*—very distinctly does not mean "inspired of God." This phrase is rather the rendering of the Latin, *divinitus inspirata*, restored from the Wyclif ("Al Scripture of God ynspyrid is . . .") and Rhemish ("All Scripture inspired of God is . . .") versions of the Vulgate. The Greek word does not even mean, as the Authorized Version translates it, "given by inspiration of God," although that rendering (inherited from Tindale: "All Scripture given by inspiration of God is . . ." and its successors; see Geneva: "The

---

11. A. T. Robertson, *A Grammar of the Greek New Testament in the Light of Historical Research* (Nashville, Tenn.: Broadman, 1934), 1095–97. See also Warfield's lengthy examination of the voice of θεόπνευστος, *theopneustos*, in his article "God-Inspired Scripture," in *The Inspiration and Authority of the Bible*, 245–96. He also concludes that its voice is passive.

whole Scripture is given by inspiration of God and is . . .") has at least to say for itself that it is a somewhat clumsy, perhaps, but not misleading, paraphrase of the Greek term in the theological language of the day. The Greek term has, however, nothing to say of *inspiring* or of *inspiration*: it speaks only of a "spiring" or "spiration." What it says of Scripture is, not that it is "breathed into by God" or is the product of the Divine "inbreathing" into its human authors, but that it is breathed out by God, "Godbreathed," the product of the creative breath of God. In a word, what is declared by this fundamental passage is simply that the Scriptures are a Divine product without any indication of how God has operated in producing them.[12]

When Paul declared, then, that God "breathed [out]" the Scriptures, he was asserting "with as much energy as he could employ that Scripture is the product of a specifically Divine operation."[13] Said another way, he was asserting the divine origin of the entirety of Scripture, in the whole and in the part, as surely as if he had written πᾶσα γραφὴ ἐκ θεοῦ (*pasa graphē ek theou*, "all Scripture is from God"). Stated differently, he was asserting that the Bible is divine revelation. James S. Stewart correctly asserts that Paul as a Pharisee and later as a Christian believed that "every word" of the Old Testament was "the authentic voice of God."[14]

Moreover, when he characterized the Scriptures as "theopneustic," that is, as being of the character of the very "breath of God breathed out," Paul was asserting something about its nature. Just as God's "breath" (his word) created all the host of heaven (Ps. 33:6), just as his "breath" gave physical life to Adam and to all mankind (Gen. 2:7; Job 33:4), just as his "breath" gave spiritual life to Israel, the "valley of dry bones" (Ezek. 37:1–14), so also his powerful, creative "breath," in its word form, is living and active (Heb. 4:12), imperishable and abiding (1 Pet. 1:23), and through it God's Spirit imparts new life to the soul. As Peter writes in 1 Peter 1:23–25:

> For you have been born again, not of perishable seed, but of imperishable, *through the living and enduring word of God* [διὰ λόγου ζῶντος θεοῦ καὶ μένοντος, *dia logou zōntos theou kai menontos*]. For,
> "All men are like grass,
> and all their glory is like the flowers of the field;
> the grass withers and the flowers fall,
> but the word of the LORD stands forever."

---

12. Warfield, "The Biblical Idea of Inspiration," 132–33; see also 154.
13. Ibid., 133.
14. James S. Stewart, *A Man in Christ* (London: Hodder and Stoughton, 1935), 39.

THE INSPIRED NATURE OF HOLY SCRIPTURE

and this is the word that was preached to you [τοῦτο δέ ἐστιν τὸ ῥῆμα τὸ εὐαγγελισθὲν εἰς ὑμᾶς, *touto de estin to rhēma to euangelisthen eis humas*].

Paul concludes his description of "all Scripture" by saying that it is "useful for teaching, rebuking, correcting and training in righteousness, so that the man of God may be thoroughly equipped for every good work" (2 Tim. 3:16–17).[15] Here Paul asserts the sufficiency of Scripture insofar as the godly man's need for a word-revelation from heaven is concerned.

1 PETER 1:10–12

The prophets, who spoke [lit., prophesied] of the grace that was to come to you, searched intently and with the greatest care, trying to find out the time and circumstances to which the Spirit of Christ in them was pointing when he predicted [προμαρτυρόμενον, *promartyromenon*] the sufferings of Christ and the glories that would follow. It was revealed [ἀπεκαλύφθη, *apekalyphthē*] to them that they were not serving themselves but you when they spoke of the things that have now been told you by those who preach the gospel to you by the Holy Spirit sent from heaven.

Here is an unmistakable affirmation that when the prophets, said here to have been the recipients of divine revelation, prophesied concerning future things, it was the Spirit of Christ in them who was predicting these things.

We must conclude that the Bible speaks of a God who reveals himself propositionally through chosen vessels, and that the Bible represents itself as God's word-revelation or message to needy human beings.

THE BIBLE'S "INSPIREDNESS"

How did God give his word-revelation to men? In a general way the Bible gives an answer to this question. Peter writes: "No prophecy of Scripture arose from one's own interpretation. For prophecy was never brought by the will of man but, by the Holy Spirit being borne along, men spoke from God" (2 Pet. 1:20–21, author's translation).

---

15. I would submit that "every good work" includes the work of apologetics, and would urge that apologetics, when rightly done, will presuppose the revealed truth of Holy Scripture and will base its argumentation on the teachings of the Bible alone as incontrovertible *evidence* for the truthfulness of the Christian position.

The first thing we must do is to consider the context in which these statements occur. False teachers, probably (pre-?) Gnostic enthusiasts, in propagating their γνῶσις, *gnōsis*, theology throughout the Roman Empire, were claiming to have a new word from God that superseded the authoritative word of the Old Testament prophets and the New Testament apostles, and so Peter felt it necessary to respond to their claim before they could infect his flock. He first described their "knowledge" as "sophisticated myths" (σεσοφισμένοις μύθοις, *sesophismenois mythois*, 2 Pet. 1:16) and "made-up stories" (πλαστοῖς λόγοις, *plastois logois*, 2:3). Then he argued that his eye- and ear-witness experience of Jesus' majestic transfiguration—itself the fulfillment of Old Testament Scripture="confirmed [βεβαιότερον, *bebaioteron*] the prophetic word" (1:19a),[16] concerning which word he counseled his readers: "you will do well to pay attention to it, as to a light shining in a dark place, until the Day dawns and the morning star rises in your hearts" (1:19b). Then Peter concluded his response with his classic statement on inspiration: "knowing this first [note his use of the word in which the Gnostic prided himself], that no prophecy of Scripture arose from one's own interpretation. For prophecy was never brought by the will of man, but, by the Holy Spirit being borne along, men spoke from God" (2 Pet. 1:20–21, author's translation).

In this remarkable statement Peter first asserts two negatives about the production of prophecy: first, that no prophecy of Scripture originated in ("arose, came from," γίνεται, *ginetai*) the prophet's estimate of the current state of affairs or in his prognosis about the future, that is, no prophecy of Scripture emerged from his own understanding, and second, that no prophecy of Scripture was motivated by man's will, that is, no prophecy of Scripture came from mere human impulse. By these negatives Peter totally excludes the human element as the ultimate originating cause of Scripture.

Peter then asserts two affirmatives about Scripture prophecy, setting them off over against his previous negatives by the strong adversative ἀλλά (*alla*, "but" or "to the contrary"). Now these affirmatives are as intriguing as the negatives. He declares, first,

---

16. The AV translated βεβαιότερον, *bebaioteron*, by the phrase "more sure"—"We have also a *more sure* word of prophecy"—leaving the impression that the written Word is more certain than the "voice from the Majestic Glory" or the eye- and ear-witness testimony of Peter to that voice. This is unfortunate, for it is the same voice that speaks and the same authority that obtains in both cases. It is true that βεβαιότερον, *bebaioteron*, is a comparative adjective, but here is an instance when the comparative adjective stands in for its superlative counterpart—an occasional occurrence in Greek (see Luke 9:48; 1 Tim. 4:1; 1 Cor. 13:13)—and is to be translated accordingly—"most sure." The thought intended is that the prophetic written Word which spoke of Messiah's glory was rendered "*most* sure," that is, "was covenantally confirmed," by the Transfiguration. See G. Adolf Deissmann, *Bible Studies*, trans. Alexander Grieve (Edinburgh: T. and T. Clark, 1903), 104–9, who argues that βεβαίωσις (*bebaiōsis*) is a technical expression for a legal guarantee, a covenantal certainty or confirmation.

THE INSPIRED NATURE OF HOLY SCRIPTURE

that the prophets spoke from God. This means at the very least that what they spoke did not originate in them but was given to them by God. This affirmation also means, since for Peter what the prophets "spoke" included what they "wrote" (for recall that Peter is describing "prophecy of *Scripture*"), that the prophetic Scriptures themselves came to them from God. As further evidence that Peter included within the category of "speaking" what a prophet "spoke" in and by his writing, one may note what he writes in 2 Peter 3:15–16: "Our beloved brother Paul *wrote* [ἔγραψεν, *egrapsen*] to you, as also in all his letters, *speaking* [λαλῶν, *lalōn*] in them concerning these things."

He tells us, second, that the reason or means whereby the prophets were able to speak from God as they did was that they were being continually borne along (φερόμενοι, *pheromenoi*, present passive participle) by the Holy Spirit as they spoke or wrote. That is, they were under the Spirit's direct superintending influence the entire time they spoke or wrote as prophets. Peter's thought here can be illustrated from Acts 27:15: "when the ship was caught [in the violent wind], and could not face the wind, we gave way to it, and *we were driven along* [ἐφερόμεθα, *epherometha*]" (author's translation). Just as the ship, knowing no will of its own, was "driven" along by the "will" of the wind, so also the prophets, knowing no will of their own in any ultimate sense in the production of the prophetic Scriptures, were "driven" along (same verb root) by the will of the Holy Spirit. Warfield comments:

> What this language of Peter emphasizes—and what is emphasized in the whole account which the prophets give of their own consciousness—is, to speak plainly, the passivity of the prophets with respect to the revelation given through them. This is the significance of the phrase: "it was as borne by the Holy Spirit that men spoke from God." To be "borne" (φέρειν, *pherein*) is not the same as to be led (ἄγειν, *agein*), much less to be guided or directed (ὁδηγεῖν, *hodēgein*): he that is "borne" contributes nothing to the movement induced, but is the object to be moved. The term "passivity" is, perhaps, however, liable to some misapprehension, and should not be overstrained. It is not intended to deny that the intelligence of the prophets was active in the reception of their message; it was by means of their active intelligence that their message was received: their intelligence was the instrument of revelation. It is intended to deny only that their intelligence was active in the production of their message: that it was creatively as distinguished from receptively active. For reception itself is a kind of activity. What the prophets are solicitous that their readers shall understand is that they are in no sense co-authors with God of their messages. Their messages are given them, given them entire, and given them precisely as they are given out by them. God speaks through them: they are not merely His messengers, but "His mouth."[17]

---

17. Warfield, "The Biblical Idea of Revelation," 91.

Does this mean that the prophets were simply secretarial robots through whom the divine Oracle spoke? Against the objection that "in the interest of [the prophets'] personalities, we are asked not to represent God as dealing mechanically with them, pouring His revelations into their souls to be simply received as in so many buckets, or violently wresting their minds from their own proper actions that He may do His own thinking with them"[18]—the objection that would insist that all revelations must be "psychologically mediated" and first made their recipients' "own spiritual possession" in such a sense that the prophets in a real sense are the true and final authors—Warfield reminds his reader of two things.

First, the mode of the communication of the prophetic messages which the objection prefers is directly contradicted by the prophets' own representations of their relations to the revealing Spirit: "In the prophets' own view they were just instruments through whom God gave revelations which came from them, not as their own product, but as the pure word of Jehovah."[19] Warfield continues:

> The plausibility of such questionings [should not] blind us to their speciousness. They exploit subordinate considerations, which are not without their validity in their own place and under their own limiting conditions, as if they were the determining or even the sole considerations in the case, and in neglect of the really determining considerations. God is Himself the author of the instruments He employs for the communication of His messages to men and has framed them into precisely the instruments He desired for the exact communication of His message. There is just ground for the expectation that He will use all the instruments He employs according to their natures; intelligent beings therefore as intelligent beings, moral agents as moral agents. But there is no just ground for asserting that God is incapable of employing the intelligent beings He has Himself created and formed to His will, to proclaim His messages purely as He gives them to them; or of making truly the possession of rational minds conceptions which they have themselves had no part in creating. And there is no ground for imagining that God is unable to frame His own message in the language of the organs of His revelation without its thereby ceasing to be, because expressed in a fashion natural to these organs, therefore purely His message. One would suppose it to lie in the very nature of the case that if the Lord makes any revelation to men, He would do it in the language of men; or, to individualize more explicitly, in the language of the man He employs as the organ of His revelation; and that naturally means, not the language of his nation or circle merely, but his own particular language, inclusive of all that gives individuality to his self-expression. We may speak of this, if we will, as "the accommodation of the revealing God to

---

18. Ibid., 92.
19. Ibid.

the several prophetic individualities." But we should avoid thinking of [this "accommodation"] externally and therefore mechanically, as if the revealing Spirit artificially phrased the message which He gives through each prophet in the particular forms of speech proper to the individuality of each, so as to create the illusion that the message comes out of the heart of the prophet himself. Precisely what the prophets affirm is that their messages do not come out of their own hearts and do not represent the workings of their own spirits. . . . It is vain to say that the message delivered through the instrumentality of [the human] tongue is conditioned at least in its form by the tongue by which it is spoken, if not, indeed, limited, curtailed, in some degree determined even in its matter, by it. Not only was it God the Lord who made the tongue, and who made this particular tongue with all its peculiarities, not without regard to the message He would deliver through it; but His control of it is perfect and complete, and it is as absurd to say that He cannot speak His message by it purely without that message suffering change from the peculiarities of its tone and modes of enunciation, as it would be to say that no new truth can be announced in any language because the elements of speech by the combination of which the truth in question is announced are already in existence with their fixed range of connotation. The marks of the several individualities imprinted on the messages of the prophets, in other words, are only a part of the general fact that these messages are couched in human language, and in no way beyond that general fact affect their purity as direct communications from God.[20]

Second, and as an elaboration upon the conception of the revelatory organs' preparation for the prophetic task which he alludes to in the above comments, Warfield writes:

> Representations are sometimes made as if, when God wished to produce sacred books which would incorporate His will—a series of letters like those of Paul, for example—He was reduced to the necessity of going down to earth and painfully scrutinizing the men He found there, seeking anxiously for the one who, on the whole, promised best for His purpose; and then violently forcing the material He wished expressed through him, against his natural bent, and with as little loss from his recalcitrant characteristics as possible. Of course, nothing of the sort took place. If God wished to give His people a series of letters like Paul's, He prepared a Paul to write them, and the Paul He brought to the task was a Paul who spontaneously would write just such letters.
>
> If we bear this in mind, we shall know what estimate to place upon the common representation to the effect that the human characteristics of the writers must, and in point of fact do, condition and qualify the writings produced by

---

20. Ibid., 92–94.

them, the implication being that, therefore, we cannot get from a man a pure word of God. As light that passes through the colored glass of a cathedral window, we are told, is light from heaven, but is stained by the tints of the glass through which it passes; so any word of God which is passed through the mind and soul of a man must come out discolored by the personality through which it is given, and just to that degree ceases to be the pure word of God. But what if this personality has itself been formed by God into precisely the personality it is, for the express purpose of communicating to the word given through it just the coloring which it gives? What if the colors of the stained-glass window have been designed by the architect for the express purpose of giving to the light that floods the cathedral precisely the tone and quality it receives from them? What if the word of God that comes to His people is framed by God into the word of God it is, precisely by means of the qualities of the men formed by Him for the purpose, through which it is given? When [the long providential process of preparing the men who produced Scripture is taken into account], we can no longer wonder that the resultant Scriptures are constantly spoken of as the pure word of God. We wonder, rather, that an additional operation of God—what we call specifically "inspiration," in its technical sense—was thought necessary.... When we give due place in our thoughts to the universality of the providence of God, to the minuteness and completeness of its sway, and to its invariable efficacy, we may be inclined to ask what is needed beyond this mere providential government to secure the production of sacred books which should be in every detail absolutely accordant with the Divine will.

The answer is, Nothing is needed beyond mere providence to secure such books—provided only that it does not lie in the Divine purpose that these books should possess qualities which rise above the powers of men to produce [such as knowledge of the divine purpose], even under the most complete Divine guidance. For providence is guidance; and guidance can bring one only so far as his own power can carry him. If heights are to be scaled above man's native power to achieve, then something more than guidance, however effective, is necessary. This is the reason for the superinduction, at the end of the long process of the production of Scripture, of the additional Divine operation which we call technically "inspiration." By it, the Spirit of God, flowing confluently in with the providentially and graciously determined work of men, spontaneously producing under the Divine directions the writings appointed to them, gives the product a Divine quality unattainable by human powers alone. Thus these books become not merely the word of godly men, but the immediate word of God Himself, speaking directly as such to the mind and heart of every reader....

It lies equally on the face of the New Testament allusions to the subject that its writers understood that the preparation of men to become vehicles of God's message to man was not of yesterday, but had its beginnings in the very origin of their being. The call by which Paul, for example, was made an apostle of Jesus Christ was sudden and apparently without antecedents; but it is precisely this

Paul who reckons this call as only one step in a long process, the beginnings of which antedated his own existence: "But when it was the good pleasure of God, who separated me, even from my mother's womb, and called me through his grace, to reveal his Son in me" (Gal. i. 15.16; see Jer. i. 5; Isa. xlix. 1.5).[21]

Herein lies the answer to the question, Why did the Spirit of God "bear" the prophets along as they wrote? He superintended them in their writing not only in order to guarantee the books their *revelatory* character (see "spoke *from* God, as they were being borne along") but also to insure their entire *divine* quality and thus their infallible trustworthiness.

Peter's perception of the matter was that the prophets of God spoke and wrote, *as prophets,* solely by and under the superintending influence of the Holy Spirit. The prophets, in sum, were organs of revelation. What they wrote was pure Spirit-inspired revelation. As such, it was inerrant.

Many theologians (e.g., Emil Brunner, Karl Barth, Ernst Käsemann), claim not only that the Bible is anything but noncontradictory in its teachings—it is filled, they say, with errors and contradictions—but also that God, who "delights in surprising us" and who can "draw a straight line with a crooked stick," even speaks to us through its contradictions. So the question naturally arises: Has the evangelical Christian foisted upon Scripture a demand for a doctrinal consistency that Scripture itself does not require? Henri Blocher has quite properly observed:

> At all stages of biblical history, coherence is highly valued, and ascribed to whatever teaching is believed to have come from God. Truth . . . rhymes with eternity, immutable permanence (Ps. 119:160). The law of the Lord is pure, that is, perfectly homogeneous, more thoroughly purged of dross than refined silver and gold; all his ordinances go together as one in their rightness (Ps. 19:9). No miracle may authorize unorthodox prophecies (Dt. 13:1ff). In spite of God's freedom to display new things in history, failure to harmonize with the dominant tone of earlier revelations raises doubts on the authenticity of a message (Je. 28:7ff). Paul exhorts his readers to be of one mind (Phil. 2:2, etc.); they are to grow into the unity of faith (Eph. 3:13), since there is only, under one Lord, one faith and one baptism (v. 5). His preaching is not "Yes" and "No" (2 Cor. 1:18), an echo of Jesus' famous words. . . . Paul insists that his message is identical with that of the other apostles (1 Cor. 15:11). . . . In the face of misinterpretations, 2 Peter 3:16 reaffirms this accord. John highlights the three witnesses' agreement (1 Jn. 5:8), and the Fourth Gospel puts forward a theme of "repetition," not parrot-like indeed, but meeting a concern for identity of substance (Jn. 8:26, 28; 16:13). Discord is a symptom of untruth, as it was in the case of the false witnesses

---

21. Ibid., 155–58, 159.

of Jesus' trial (Mk. 14:56, 59). Contradictors are to be refuted (Rom. 16:17; Tit. 1:9): it could never be done if the standard itself embraced several conflicting theologies. As a matter of fact, the whole logic of our Lord's appeal to Scripture in argument (and similarly of his apostles') would instantly collapse if the presupposition of scriptural coherence were taken away. Even against the Tempter, Jesus relies on the internal consistency of his Father's Word, quoting Scripture to rebuff a twisted use of Scripture. "It is written" would no longer settle an issue if it were conceded that several contradictory views compete with each other on the pages of the Book. The authority of the Word of God would no longer function as it does in Scripture in that case. . . . The men of God who had a part in writing the Bible prized consistency; they ascribed it axiomatically to divine revelation; it belonged to the collection of sacred texts which had been handed down to them and was enlarged through their own ministry.[22]

CHRIST'S AUTHENTICATION OF SCRIPTURE

Because the Holy Scriptures, although written by men, are more fundamentally God's Spirit-inspired, imperishable, coherent Word, they are intrinsically authoritative and man's only infallible rule for faith and life. Jesus Christ, the incarnate Son of God, whom his Father raised from the dead on the third day after death,[23] regarded the Scriptures precisely this way and declared them to be such.[24] Among other things he said about the Old Testament, he declared: "The Scripture cannot be broken [οὐ δύναται λυθῆναι ἡ γραφή, *ou dynatai luthēnai hē graphē*]" (John 10:35). Concerning this statement Warfield declares:

> The word "broken" here is the common one for breaking the law, or the Sabbath, or the like (Jn. v. 18; vii. 23; Mt. v. 19), and the meaning of the declaration is that it is impossible for the Scripture to be annulled, its authority to be withstood, or denied.[25]

---

22. Henri Blocher, "The 'Analogy of Faith' in the Study of Scripture," in *The Challenge of Evangelical Theology* (Edinburgh: Rutherford House, 1987), 29–31.
23. See Robert L. Reymond, *Jesus, Divine Messiah: The Old Testament Witness* (Ross-shire, Scotland: Christian Focus, 1990), and *Jesus, Divine Messiah: The New Testament Witness* (Phillipsburg, N.J.: Presbyterian and Reformed, 1990), for the Old and New Testament witness both to Jesus' deity as the Second Person of the Holy Trinity and to his messianic investiture.
24. Christ's authentication of Scripture as the Word of God is not the only reason the Christian believes the Bible is God's Word but it is certainly a major one. See John W. Wenham, "Christ's View of Scripture," in *Inerrancy*, ed. Norman L. Geisler (Grand Rapids, Mich.: Zondervan, 1980), 3–36; see also his suggestions for further reading, 35–36.
25. Warfield, "The Biblical Idea of Inspiration," 139. Leon Morris comments on this passage: "The term 'broken' is not defined, and it is a word which is not often used of Scripture and the like. . . . But it is perfectly intelligible. It means that Scripture cannot be emptied of its force by being shown to be erroneous" (*The Gospel According to John* [Grand Rapids, Mich.: Eerdmans, 1971], 527).

Likewise, Jesus said: "Do not think that I have come to abolish the Law or the Prophets; I have not come to abolish them but to fulfill them. I tell you the truth, until heaven and earth disappear, not the smallest letter, not the least stroke of a pen, will by any means disappear from the Law until everything is accomplished" (Matt. 5:17–18). He also stated: "It is easier for heaven and earth to pass away than for *one stroke of a letter of the Law to fail* [τοῦ νόμου μίαν κεραίαν πεσεῖν, *tou nomou mian keraian pesein*]" (Luke 16:17).[26]

Again and again Jesus referred to "the Law and the Prophets" (Matt. 5:17; 7:12; 11:13; 22:40), often citing them to settle an issue (Matt. 12:5; 15:3–6; 21:13, 42), and implying as he did so that the Old Testament was for him a fixed canon of authority. He regarded its history as unimpeachable, often choosing for his illustrations the very Old Testament events that prove least acceptable as factual history to the contemporary critical scholar, such as the creation of man in the beginning by a direct act of God (Matt. 19:4–5), the murder of Abel (Matt. 23:35), Noah's flood (Matt. 24:37), the destruction of Sodom and Gomorrah (Matt. 10:15; 11:23–24), the tragic end of Lot's wife (Luke 17:32), and the fish's swallowing of Jonah (Matt. 12:40).

Jesus repulsed the Tempter simply by citing Deuteronomy 8:3, 6:16, and 6:13 (see Matt. 4:4, 7, 10), each time demonstrating his belief in the final authority of the Old Testament by prefixing his citation with "It has been written [and stands so]" (γέγραπται, *gegraptai*, or its Aramaic equivalent), meaning by the expression, "God says" or "It is certainly true" (see also Matt. 11:10; 21:13; 26:24, 31).

Repeatedly Christ asked: "Have you not read [the Scriptures]?" (Matt. 12:3; 19:4; 21:16; 22:31). He ordered the cleansed leper to obey the Mosaic legislation pertaining to cases of cleansing (Matt. 8:4). He taught that John the Baptist fulfilled the prediction of Malachi 3:1 (Matt. 11:10). He regarded words spoken either by Adam or Moses (probably the latter, Gen. 2:24) as ultimately from God (Matt. 19:4). He declared that if someone would not believe Moses and the Prophets, he would not believe God on the basis of a miraculous resurrection (Luke 16:31).[27] He charged that the Sadducees erred concerning the resurrection because they did not know the Scriptures (Matt. 22:29), implying thereby that the Scriptures did not err. He warned that Daniel's prophecy of the abomination of desolation (Dan. 9:27; 11:31; 12:11) was soon to be fulfilled (Matt. 24:15; Luke 21:20).

---

26. According to some critics Jesus often criticized and repudiated parts of the Old Testament. Seven examples have been advanced (his teaching on the sabbath, sacrifice, "clean" foods, the Old Testament ethic, divorce, the *lex talionis*, and one's attitude toward one's enemy). But see Wenham's response to these charges ("Christ's View of Scripture," 23–29).
27. Christian apologists should heed Christ's statement here: evidences, no matter how compelling, will not convince those who have not submitted in faith to God's Word of the truth of the claims of Christianity.

He taught that the Old Testament Scriptures "testified" about him (John 5:39), and that Moses wrote about him (John 5:46–47). After reading Isaiah 61:1–2 aloud in the synagogue at Nazareth, he stated: "Today this scripture is fulfilled in your hearing." He also declared to his disciples: "We are going up to Jerusalem, and everything that is written by the prophets about the Son of Man will be fulfilled" (Luke 18:31). At the Last Supper he declared: "The Son of Man is going just as it has been written about him" (Matt. 26:24), and then he stated: "This Scripture [Isa. 53:12] must be fulfilled in me. Yes, what is written about me is reaching its fulfillment" (Luke 22:37). Then on the Mount of Olives he declared: "This very night you will all fall away on account of me, for it is written, 'I will strike the Shepherd, and the sheep of the flock will be scattered'" (Matt. 26:31). Clearly Jesus believed that the Old Testament spoke explicitly and authoritatively about him. Indeed, so authoritative for Jesus were the prophetic Scriptures that it was more important to him that they be fulfilled than that he escape arrest and the horrible death of crucifixion: "Do you think," he asked Peter, "that I cannot appeal to my Father, and he will at once put at my disposal more than twelve legions of angels? How then shall the Scriptures be fulfilled that it must happen this way? . . . But all this has happened that the Scriptures of the prophets may be fulfilled" (Matt. 26:53–56; Mark 14:49).[28] At his death his thoughts were centered upon Scripture, for he cited Psalm 22:1 just moments before dying (Matt. 27:46). Then after his resurrection the glorified Christ taught his disciples: "This is what I told you while I was still with you: Everything must be fulfilled that is written about me in the Law of Moses, the Prophets and the Psalms" (Luke 24:44; see 24:45–47). Whoever searches the Gospel narratives for himself will be driven to the conclusion of Reinhold Seeberg: "Jesus himself describes and employs the Old Testament as an infallible authority (e.g., Matt. 5:17; Luke 24:44)."[29]

Many critical scholars acknowledge that this is the New Testament's portrayal of Jesus' view of the Old Testament, but they immediately abort the significance of their concession by suggesting (1) that Jesus was simply ignorant of the real origins of the Old Testament, or (2) that, knowing the truth, he accommodated his teaching about the Old Testament to his hearers' views in order to gain a hearing for his own, or (3) that the New Testament representation of Jesus' attitude toward the Old Testament is really a later "church version" that has been

---

28. John puts Jesus' words on a par with the prophecies of the Old Testament when he employs the same "that it might be fulfilled" formula for Jesus' words (John 18:9, 32) that is employed with reference to the fulfillment of Old Testament prophecies.

29. Reinhold Seeberg, *Text-Book of the History of Doctrine* (Grand Rapids, Mich.: Baker, 1952), 1:82.

THE INSPIRED NATURE OF HOLY SCRIPTURE

antedated to the teachings of Jesus. Such assertions, however, have been addressed time and time again by evangelical scholars and shown to be lacking.[30]

Not only did Jesus endorse the Old Testament's divine origin, inspiration, and authority, but he also "preauthenticated" the New. To his disciples he declared: "The Counselor, the Holy Spirit, . . . will teach you all things and will remind you of everything I have said to you" (John 14:26), and "I have much more to say to you, more than you can now bear. But when he, the Spirit of truth, comes, he will guide you into all truth. He will not speak on his own; he will speak only what he hears, and he will tell you what is yet to come. He will bring glory to me by taking from what is mine and making it known to you" (John 16:12–14). Accordingly, the apostles not only shared Christ's view of the Old Testament but also, with his authentication of them as his authoritative messengers and of their message as his word to both church and world, they presented themselves to their auditors as his ambassadors and their message as God's word (see 1 Thess. 2:13), proclaimed "not in words taught . . . by human wisdom but in words taught by the Spirit" (1 Cor. 2:13). They declared that the churches must acknowledge that what they wrote were the commands of Christ (1 Cor. 14:37–38), that the churches should bow before apostolic rulings (1 Cor. 11:2; 2 Thess. 2:5), and that church members who did not do so must be put out of the fellowship (2 Thess. 3:6, 14).

THE NEW TESTAMENT WRITERS' IDENTIFICATION OF SCRIPTURE WITH GOD'S WORD

The New Testament writers, at least four of whom (James, Peter, Matthew, and John) actually knew Christ personally and became witnesses of his resurrection, regarded Scripture as the written yet living Word of God. No clearer proof of this can be given than that provided by Warfield in his analysis of two classes of New Testament passages, each of which,

> when taken separately, throws into the clearest light [the New Testament writers'] habitual appeal to the Old Testament text as to God Himself speaking, while, together, they make an irresistible impression of the absolute identification by their writers of the Scriptures in their hands with the living voice of God. *In one of these classes of passages the Scriptures are spoken of as if they were God; in the other, God is spoken of as if He were the Scriptures;* in the two

---

30. See, e.g., James I. Packer, *"Fundamentalism" and the Word of God* (Grand Rapids, Mich.: Eerdmans, 1959), 59–61; and Wenham, "Christ's View of Scripture," 7–10, 14–16. See also Reymond, *Jesus, Divine Messiah: The New Testament Witness,* chapter two, on Jesus' self-witness.

together, God and the Scriptures are brought into such conjunction as to show that in point of directness of authority *no distinction was made between them....*[31]

Examples of the first class of passages are such as these: Gal. iii. 8, "The Scripture, foreseeing that God would justify the heathen through faith, preached before the gospel unto Abraham, saying, In thee shall all the nations be blessed" (Gen. xii. 1–3); Rom. ix. 17, "The Scripture saith unto Pharaoh, Even for this purpose have I raised thee up" (Ex. ix. 16). It was not, however, the Scripture (which did not exist at the time) that, foreseeing God's purposes of grace in the future, spoke these precious words to Abraham, but God Himself in His own person: it was not the not yet existent Scripture that made this announcement to Pharaoh, but God Himself through the mouth of His prophet Moses. These acts could be attributed to "Scripture" only as the result of such a habitual identification, in the mind of the writer, of the text of Scripture with God as speaking, that it became natural to use the term "Scripture says," when what was really intended was "God, as recorded in Scripture, said."

Examples of the other class of passages are such as these: Matt. xix. 4, 5, "And he answered and said, Have ye not read that he which made them from the beginning made them male and female, and said, For this cause shall a man leave his father and mother, and shall cleave to his wife, and the twain shall become one flesh?" (Gen. ii. 24); Heb. iii. 7, "Wherefore, even as the Holy Ghost saith, Today if ye shall hear his voice," etc. (Ps. xcv. 7); Acts iv. 24, 25, "Thou art God, who by the mouth of thy servant David hast said, Why do the heathen rage and the people imagine vain things" (Ps. ii. 1); Acts xiii. 34, 35, "He that raised him up from the dead, now no more to return to corruption, . . . hath spoken in this wise, I will give you the holy and sure blessings of David" (Isa. lv. 3); "because he saith also in another [Psalm], Thou wilt not give thy holy one to see corruption" (Ps. xvi. 10); Heb. i. 6, "And when he again bringeth in the first born into the world, he saith, And let all the angels of God worship him" (Deut. xxxii. 43); "and of the angels he saith, Who maketh his angels wings, and his ministers a flame of fire" (Ps. civ. 4); "but of the Son, *He saith,* Thy Throne, O God, is for ever and ever," etc. (Ps. xlv. 7); and, "Thou, Lord, in the beginning," etc. (Ps. cii. 26). It is not God, however, in whose mouth these sayings are placed in the text of the Old Testament: they are the words of others, recorded in the text of Scripture as spoken to or of God. They could be attributed to God only through such habitual identification, in the minds of the writers, of the text of Scripture with the utterances of God that it had become natural to use the term "God says" when what was really intended was "Scripture, the Word of God, says."

The two sets of passages, together, thus show an absolute identification, in the minds of these writers, of "Scripture" with the speaking God.[32]

---

31. Benjamin B. Warfield, " 'It Says:' 'Scripture Says:' 'God Says,'" in *The Inspiration and Authority of the Bible* (Philadelphia: Presbyterian and Reformed, 1948), 299, emphasis supplied.
32. Ibid., 299–300.

The entire Bible is revealed, inspired, and authenticated by Christ as God's Word, and identified by the New Testament writers with the living voice of God. We can conclude that the infinite, personal God has spoken to men propositionally in Scripture. The one who makes the Word of the living God the foundation of his or her life stands on solid ground indeed, having both an authoritative basis for knowing what to believe concerning God and what duty God requires of mankind (Westminster Shorter Catechism, Question 3) and a normative ground for the theological task.

HERMENEUTICAL IMPLICATIONS

The Scripture's own doctrine of Scripture has three implications for biblical hermeneutics:

First, the Scripture's doctrine of Scripture, espousing its own revelatory and inspired character, binds us to the grammatical/historical method of exegesis. Packer reminds us:

> The doctrine of inspiration . . . tells us that God has put his words into the mouths, and caused them to be written in the writings, of men whose individuality, as men of their time, was in no way lessened by the fact of their inspiration, and who spoke and wrote to be understood by their contemporaries. Since God has effected an identity between their words and his, the way for us to get into his mind, if we may thus phrase it, is via theirs. Their thoughts and speech about God constitute God's own self-testimony.[33]

But then this means that the exegete, if he is to apprehend God's self-testimony, must seek to put himself in the writer's linguistic, cultural, historical, and religious shoes to discover the writer's intended meaning. And this exegetical effort is what we mean by the *grammatical/historical method* of exegesis, that each biblical document and each part of any given biblical document must be studied in its immediate literary context and the wider situation in which it was written. This will require an understanding of (1) the structure and idioms of the biblical languages, (2) a document's literary genre (is it prose or poetry, history or allegory, parable or apocalypse?), (3) the document's historical background, (4) its geographical conditions, and (5) its *Sitz im Leben* ("life-setting"), that is, what occasioned it? What problem or question did it intend to address?

Second, the Scripture's doctrine of Scripture commits us to the harmonization of Scripture. This is so because the doctrine of inspiration means that the entirety of Scripture,

---

33. James I. Packer, "Biblical Authority, Hermeneutics, and Inerrancy," in *Jerusalem and Athens*, ed. E. R. Geehan (Nutley, N.J.: Presbyterian and Reformed, 1971), 147.

though written over a period of fifteen centuries, is ultimately the product of a single divine mind who is truth itself and who accordingly cannot lie or contradict himself. This means in turn that there is an ultimate organic unity between the Old and New Testaments,[34] and that Scripture can and should be interpreted by Scripture (*Scriptura Scripturae interpres*). Indeed, Scripture is the only *infallible* interpreter of Scripture (Westminster Confession of Faith, I/ix). It also means that Scripture must never be set against itself, and that

> what appears to be secondary and obscure in the Scripture should be studied in the light of what appears primary and plain. This principle obliges us to echo the main emphases of the New Testament and to develop a Christocentric, covenantal, and kerygmatic exegesis of both Testaments; also, it obliges us to preserve a studied sense of proportion regarding what are confessedly minutiae, and not to let them overshadow what God has indicated to be the weightier matters.[35]

This principle of harmony, implying these several things, is what we intend when we refer to the Reformation principle of the *analogia totius Scripturae* ("analogy of the whole of Scripture"). Based upon Paul's expression, "the analogy of the faith" (ἡ ἀναλογία τῆς πίστεως, *hē analogia tēs pisteōs*) in Romans 12:6,[36] the main point of this hermeneutical principle is the studied comparison of all relevant biblical passages on any one topic under the methodological duty

---

34. When the evangelical church affirms the unity of the Old and New Testaments, it should make all due allowance for the progressiveness of revelation and the periodicity in particular of Old Testament revelation determined by the several covenantal arrangements found therein. See John Murray, "The Unity of the Old and New Testaments," *Collected Writings of John Murray* (Edinburgh: Banner of Truth, 1976), 1:23–26.
35. Packer, "Biblical Authority, Hermeneutics, and Inerrancy," 149.
36. Some significant commentators on Romans (e. g., F. F. Bruce, John Murray, C. E. B. Cranfield) urge that Paul means by "faith" here faith in the subjective sense. That is to say, Paul is urging would-be prophets to speak only in conformity with their subjective faith, that is, in dependence upon Christ. Ernst Käsemann, followed by Alphonse Maillot, Heinrich Schlier, and Henri Blocher, on the other hand, argue that it would make no sense at all to suggest that the prophet should judge himself by his own faith, a procedure which would open the door to every kind of false teaching. Accordingly, they urge that Paul intends "faith" here in the objective sense, meaning by it the "pattern of teaching" which had been received (see Rom 6:17). In support of the objective meaning for "faith" here, note (1) the several occurrences in Paul's writings where he employs "faith" in this way (Gal. 1:23; 3:23, 25; 6:10; Eph. 4:5, 13; 1 Tim. 2:7; 3:9; 4:1, 6; 5:8; 6:10, 12, 21; 2 Tim. 3:8; 4:7; Tit. 1:1), and (2) the expression, "measure of faith" (μέτρον πίστεως, *metron pisteōs*), which occurs only three verses earlier. The primary meaning of "measure" is "standard of measurement," which would suggest in this context that God has assigned to every person the function he or she is to fulfill in the church of Christ in accordance with the standard of the "faith" (construing "faith" here as an accusative of reference).

to avoid contradictions. It presupposes biblical coherence, canonical closure, and the organic character of biblical discourse.[37]

Walter C. Kaiser Jr. calls into question an unmodified application of this principle, contending that to permit a piece of subsequent revelation to determine for us an earlier author's intention is to fail to give the progressiveness of revelation its just due and to "level off" the process of revelation in a way overly favorable to the interests of systematic theology.[38] He insists on what he calls the "analogy of (antecedent) Scripture," by which phrase he means that in determining an author's intended meaning in a given passage, in no case is the interpreter to employ teaching from a later passage to "unpack the meaning or to enhance the usability" of the earlier passage. The interpreter must restrict himself to a study of the passage itself and to "affirmations found in passages that *preceded* in time the passage under study."[39]

Aside from the vexing fact, however, that we just do not know for sure the chronological relationship that exists between some portions of Scripture (was Obadiah written before Joel, Psalm "x" before Psalm "y," Mark before Matthew, Colossians before Ephesians, 2 Peter before Jude?) and hence could fail to use an antecedent bit of revelation or misappropriate a subsequent piece of revelation, it is just a fact that there are passages where there is no way the exegete can discern what the author or speaker intended without the benefit of subsequent revelational insight. As one example, apart from the apostles' later authoritative insights found in Acts 2:24–31 and 13:34–37, there is no way that the modern exegete could discern, on the grounds allowed him by Kaiser, that David was not speaking of his own resurrection when he wrote Psalm 16 but was rather speaking *specifically and exclusively* of Messiah's resurrection.

Furthermore, while we would not dispute with Kaiser for a moment that the way into the mind of God is through the biblical writer's mind, it is also true, since the meaning of the writer and that of the divine Author coincide, that to better understand the meaning of the divine Author is to better understand the mind of the writer. Therefore, we should not hesitate to employ later expressions of the divine Author's mind spoken through inspired men to clarify the meaning of earlier expressions of his mind to inspired men. Certainly there are pitfalls in this procedure. We may misinterpret a later piece of revelation and in applying it to an earlier piece misunderstand it too. (This same error can occur, of course, when considering an antecedent piece of revelation!) But as Blocher declares, just because an accurate evaluation of the bearing of later statements on a given

---

37. Blocher, "The 'Analogy of Faith' in the Study of Scripture," 29–34.
38. Walter C. Kaiser Jr., *Toward an Exegetical Theology: Biblical Exegesis for Preaching and Teaching* (Grand Rapids, Mich.: Baker, 1981), 137, 161.
39. Ibid., 140, 136. The emphasis in the latter citation is Kaiser's.

debate of interpretation demands much skill, caution, and tactfulness, "let us not renounce the *analogia fidei;* let us make a better use of it!"[40]

Third, and finally, despite the "occasional" or ad hoc *character of its many literary parts,*[41] *the Scripture's doctrine of Scripture binds us to view its teachings as timeless truths intended "for our instruction, reproof, correction, and training in righteousness."* Not only is this a fair inference from such passages as 2 Timothy 3:16–17, but Paul states this quite plainly in several places:

> Romans 4:23–24: "The words 'it was credited to him' were written not for [Abraham] alone, but also for us, to whom God will credit righteousness—for us who believe in him who raised Jesus our Lord from the dead."
>
> Romans 15:4: "For everything that was written in the past was written to teach us, so that through endurance and the encouragement of the Scriptures we might have hope."
>
> 1 Corinthians 9:9–10: "For it is written in the Law of Moses: 'Do not muzzle an ox while it is treading out the grain.' Is it about oxen that God is concerned? Surely he says this for us, doesn't he? Yes, this was written for us."
>
> 1 Corinthians 10:6, 11: "Now these things occurred as examples to keep us from setting our hearts on evil things as they did. . . . These things happened to them as examples and were written down as warnings for us, on whom the fulfillment of the ages has come."

What is so striking and instructive about Paul's assertions that the Old Testament scriptures were written for *our* instruction is that in his own use of these very Scriptures he

> writes almost as if there were no gap at all between the Scriptures written years before and the "us" for whom they are written as instruction, or as if the analogy and similarities are so great that the gap is thus thereby not only easily bridged but also intended by God to be bridged for he had us also in mind when they were written. This is particularly relevant in that most of the passages are used to urge the appropriate conduct which the Scriptures have indicated. [Paul recognizes that the types and shadows of the ceremonial law and the Jewish theocratic entity have

---

40. Blocher, "The 'Analogy of Faith' in the Study of Scripture," 35.
41. When I speak of the Scripture's *"ad hoc* character" I refer to the fact that every book of the canonical Scriptures was written to a specific individual, church, or people living in a specific time and situation. See Gordon D. Fee, "Reflections on Church Order in the Pastoral Epistles, with Further Reflection on the Hermeneutics of *Ad Hoc* Documents," *Journal of the Evangelical Theological Society* 28, no. 2 (1985): 141–51, for a discussion of this issue in connection with church polity.

respectively been fulfilled and removed with the first advent of Christ.] But in no case does he write about conduct in the realm of morality and say or imply that the Scriptures were not in that case written for our instruction. . . .

Since this principle is true of the OT Scriptures written before the end of the ages has come, how much more is it true of the NT Scriptures written in the period of the end of the ages in which we today and they who originally received it both live. Since the ethical instruction has bridged that most significant gap between OT and NT and applies to us, certainly where there is no real gap of religious moment between us and the NT church we should expect an even more direct correlation between the NT teachings and ourselves. We will not need to argue, as Paul did in 1 Corinthians 10, the analogies between the OT ceremonies and situations and ours, for they will not be ones of analogy but of identity in the religious realm.[42]

Paul's explicit assertion that the Scriptures were written for our instruction means that, while we must distinguish admonitions that are culturally conditioned, such as "Greet one another with a holy kiss" (Rom. 16:16), from those that are not so conditioned in their application, we must resist permitting the "occasional" cultural differences that exist between the New Testament world and our own to nullify all direct application of the Scripture's instruction to us.

---

42. George W. Knight III, "The Scriptures Were Written for Our Instruction," *Journal of the Evangelical Theological Society* 39, no. 1 (1996): 12.

CHAPTER THREE

The Attributes of Holy Scripture

EVERYTHING THAT EXISTS has attributes that define it, make it what it is, and distinguish it from everything else, and so the Holy Scripture has attributes that define it, make it what it is, and distinguish it from all other writings. This chapter deals with seven of the Bible's attributes—its necessity, inspiration, authority, self-authentication, sufficiency, perspicuity, and finality. The first chapter of the great seventeenth-century Protestant creed, the Westminster Confession of Faith, entitled "Of the Holy Scripture," will be used as the framework for my comments.[1]

---

1. The framers of the Confession, by treating the topic of Holy Scripture in chapter one, show their theological astuteness. They were acutely aware that the primary issue in religion is an epistemological one, that of authority. No matter what they later confessed, they knew that they could always be challenged with the questions: "How do you know that what you confess is so? What is your authority for saying what you do?" Accordingly, they address this epistemological issue at the outset, even prior to their treatment of the doctrine of God.

    Benjamin B. Warfield ("The Westminster Doctrine of Holy Scripture," *Selected Shorter Writings of Benjamin B. Warfield*, ed. John E. Meeter [Nutley, N.J.: Presbyterian and Reformed, 1973], 2:561) observes in this connection: "It is in accordance with the fundamental idea and the ordinary practice of the Reformed theology, that the Confession begins its exposition of doctrine with the doctrine of Holy Scripture, as the root out of which all doctrine grows, just because the Scriptures are the fountain from which all knowledge of God's saving purpose and plan flows."

    James Denney, in his *Studies in Theology* (Grand Rapids, Mich.: Baker, 1976 [reprinted from the 1895 edition]), 202–4, errs when he treats Scripture only under the rubric of means of grace by failing to distinguish between the *religious* and the *theological* uses of Scripture. Scripture is intended for uses besides those pertaining to spiritual growth; it is fundamental to all Christian doctrine (see 2 Tim. 3:16–17).

THE BIBLE'S NECESSITY

Although the light of nature, and the works of creation and providence, do so far manifest the goodness, wisdom, and power of God, as to leave men inexcusable; yet are they not sufficient to give that knowledge of God, and of His will, which is *necessary to salvation;* therefore it pleased the Lord, at sundry times, and in divers manners, to reveal Himself, and to declare that [revelation] His will unto His church; and afterwards for the better preserving and propagating of the truth, and for the more sure establishment and comfort of the church against the corruption of the flesh, and the malice of Satan and of the world, to commit the same [revelation which He had declared to be His will unto His church] wholly unto writing; *which maketh the Holy Scripture to be most necessary;* those former ways of God's revealing His will unto His people being now ceased. (Westminster Confession of Faith, I/i, emphasis supplied)

The Confession begins by asserting that although all men and women know God at some level of consciousness or unconsciousness (see Rom. 1:21—γνόντες τὸν θεόν, *gnontes ton theon;* Rom. 1:32—τὸ δικαίωμα τοῦ θεοῦ ἐπιγνόντες, *to dikaioma tou theou epignontes*) because of God's revealing work both within them —that is, "the light of nature" within men and women[2] (John 1:9; Rom. 2:14-15)— and all around them in both his creation and providential care (Ps. 19:1; Acts 14:17; Rom. 1:20),[3] yet this general revelation is not sufficient to give to them the knowledge

---

2. John Calvin spoke of this "light of nature" (*Institutes of the Christian Religion,* trans. Ford Lewis Battles [Philadelphia: Westminster Press, 1960] I.iii.1,3; I.iv.1,4) within men as the *sensus divinitatis, sensus deitatis,* and *semen religionis.* He writes:

   There is within the human mind, and indeed by natural instinct, an awareness of divinity. . . . They who in other aspects of life seem least to differ from brutes still continue to retain some seed of religion. . . . [There is] a sense of deity inscribed in the hearts of all. (*Institutes,* I.iii.1)

   . . . Though the stupid hardness in their minds, which the impious eagerly conjure up to reject God, wastes away, yet the sense of divinity, which they greatly wished to have extinguished, thrives and presently burgeons. From this we conclude that it is not a doctrine that must first be learned in school, but one of which each of us is master from his mother's womb and which nature itself permits no one to forget, although many strive with every nerve to this end. (*Institutes,* I.iii.3)

   . . . God has sown a seed of religion in all men. But scarcely one man in a hundred is met with who fosters it, once received, in his heart, and none in whom it ripens—much less shows fruit in season. (*Institutes,* I.iv.1)

   [Men] entangle themselves in such a huge mass of errors that blind wickedness stifles and finally extinguishes those sparks which once flashed forth to show them God's glory. Yet that seed remains which can in no wise be uprooted: that there is some sort of divinity; but this seed is so corrupted that by itself it produces only the worst fruits. (*Institutes,* I.iv.4)

of God that is necessary for salvation. All it does is leave them in their idolatry without excuse (Rom. 1:20).[4] Therefore, the Confession continues, God revealed himself (propositionally) at many different times and in different ways and declared the content of that special revelatory activity to be his will for his church. This makes the Holy Scripture to be "most necessary," the Confession contends (over against Rome and the Anabaptist mystics), "those former ways of God's revealing His will unto His people being now ceased."[5]

---

3. These verses imply that it is unnecessary for the Christian to try to prove the existence of God to people. They would suggest rather that every human being already knows at some level of consciousness or unconsciousness that God "is really there." The unregenerate, of course, do all they can to suppress this knowledge (Rom. 1:18), although they are never completely successful. It is for this reason that the Bible speaks of the unregenerate person as both knowing God (Rom. 1:21, 32; 2:14–15) and not knowing Him (1 Cor. 1:21; 2:14; 1 Thes. 4:5; 2 Thes. 1:8) at the same time, that is, he knows God is really there but he does not know Him savingly.

    Obviously, there is some psychological complexity here: "The unbeliever knows things at one level of his consciousness that he seeks to banish from other levels . . . he knows God, he knows what God requires, but he does not want that knowledge to influence his decision, except negatively: knowledge of God's will tells him how to disobey God" (John M. Frame, *Apologetics to the Glory of God* [Phillipsburg, N. J., Presbyterian and Reformed, 1994], p. 8). Consequently, to argue as the classical apologist does that proving the existence of God is necessary, at least for some if not for everyone, is to imply that some people do not know God exists, that they are not "religious people," and therefore that they are not guilty before God for refusing to worship Him—facts belied by Romans 1:18–2:16 as a whole.

4. Much more could be said about methodological natural theology, but suffice it here to say that nowhere does the Bible endorse the notion that general revelation was given to provide people the data by which they might, beginning from themselves, reason their way to God. The Bible introduces general revelation alongside special revelation to emphasize man's guilt. The entire effort of Thomistic natural theology to discover God by natural reason apart from Jesus Christ must be judged not only a failure (see 1 Cor. 1:20–21) but also as an unwitting handmaid of the entire revolt of human philosophy against the necessity of special revelation. See Robert L. Reymond, *The Justification of Knowledge* (Phillipsburg, N.J.: Presbyterian and Reformed, 1984), 118–30, and chapter six of this book.

5. Wayne A. Grudem (*The Gift of Prophecy in 1 Corinthians* [Lanham, Md.: University Press of America, 1982]) argues that the New Testament gift of prophecy is still a legitimate gift for the church today, but, basing his view primarily on Acts 21:4, 10–11 and 1 Corinthians 14:29, he declares that the one so engifted, while Spirit-inspired or Spirit-induced, speaks with no "absolute divine authority" and may in fact teach error in detail (78–79). For refutations of this influential but erroneous view, see Richard B. Gaffin Jr., *Perspectives on Pentecost* (Phillipsburg, N.J.: Presbyterian and Reformed, 1979), 65–67; R. Fowler White, "Richard Gaffin and Wayne Grudem on 1 Cor 13:10: A Comparison of Cessationist and Noncessationist Argumentation," *Journal of the Evangelical Theological Society* 35, no. 2 (1992): 173–81, and "Gaffin and Grudem on Ephesians 2:20: In Defense of Gaffin's Cessationist Exegesis," *Westminster Theological Journal* 54 (Fall 1993): 303–20; O. Palmer Robertson, *The Final Word* (Carlisle, Pa.: Banner of Truth, 1993), 85–126; and Edmund P. Clowney, *The Church* (Downers Grove, Ill.: InterVarsity Press, 1995), 257–68.

Here is an affirmation of the *necessity* of Holy Scripture—necessary certainly for salvation and a knowledge of God's will for his church, its most immediate areas of application within the context of the confessional statement itself—but necessary also for the justification of all knowledge and of personal meaning itself.[6]

It is important that we clearly see that the Confession grounds its doctrine of the necessity of Scripture in two antecedent conditions that obtain at the present time, namely, (1) the insufficiency of general revelation, and (2) the cessation of special revelation.[7] If general revelation is insufficient to provide that knowledge of God and of his will that is essential to salvation, and if special revelation has ceased, then *one must go to Scripture if he would learn those things which are "necessary to be known,*

---

6. See Reymond, *The Justification of Knowledge,* and "The Theological Significance of the Biblical Doctrine of Creationism," *Presbyterion* 15 (Fall 1989): 2, 16–26, and chapter five of this book. See also the writings of Francis A. Schaeffer in this connection.

7. The notion of the cessation of special revelation with the passing of the apostles, or more specifically of that divine activity that produced the Holy Scriptures, should not be thought strange. The revelatory process never came in unbroken continuance but rather, in nontechnical language, in "spurts."

    Consider the following facts: Between Genesis 49:1-27, the last time God spoke to or through a Genesis patriarch, which prophecy was spoken by Jacob the year he died in 1858 B.C., and Exodus 3:4, when God spoke to Moses around 1446 B.C., there was a "blackout" of divine communication to Jacob's family in Egypt for over four hundred years. Moses was then raised up to lead God's people out of Egypt and to write the Pentateuch. With reference to the Law of God, Moses warned that nothing was to be added to or taken from the commandments, statutes, and judgments he gave to Israel (Deut. 4:2). No one—neither wives, brothers, children, friends, not even the prophets who would follow him—could add to or take from his Law (see Deut. 12:32–13:8). In short, with respect to the Law *per se,* it was a "closed canon." The Old Testament prophets, of course, did give further revelation as the redemptive process moved toward its consummating goal in Jesus Christ. But in doing so, they did not add to or take away from the Mosaic Law insofar as legislation is concerned but rather continuously called Israel back to obedience to the Mosaic Law (Mal. 4:4). And even their revelational activity ceased after Malachi for a space of another four hundred years. So clearly the Old Testament as a whole became a "closed canon." Consequently, if one avers (see Robert L. Reymond, *What About Continuing Revelations and Miracles in the Presbyterian Church Today?* [Phillipsburg, N.J.: Presbyterian and Reformed, 1977], and George W. Knight III, *Prophecy in the New Testament* [Dallas: Presbyterian Heritage, 1988], 17–23) that the New Testament data supports the position that the New Testament itself has become a "closed canon," the conclusion should not be viewed as foreign to the biblical paradigm.

    One final note: most, if not all, of the biblical scholars and theologians who insist upon the reality of continuing revelation today are apparently also willing to affirm that the Bible is a "closed canon." For this affirmation I am genuinely glad. On the other hand, they seem not to appreciate that the argument for a closed canon, which they affirm, is also the argument for the cessation of revelation, that the two stand or fall together, and that if the revelatory process has in fact continued to this day, then there is no such thing as a truly closed canon.

believed, and observed, for salvation" (I/vii). Moreover, it must be noted that to the degree that one believes that God still speaks directly to men and women today through prophets and glossolalists, just to that same degree he is saying that he does not absolutely need the Bible for a word from God, and accordingly he has abandoned the great Reformation principle of *sola Scriptura*.

THE BIBLE'S INSPIRATION

Under the name of Holy Scripture, or the Word of God written, are now contained all the books of the Old and New Testaments, which are these,
  [The sixty-six books of the Old Testament and New Testaments are then listed by name.]
  All which are given by inspiration of God to be the rule of faith and life.
  The books commonly called Apocrypha, not being of divine inspiration, are no part of the canon of the Scripture, and therefore are of no authority in the Church of God, nor to be any otherwise approved, or made use of, than other human writings. (WCF, I/ii, iii)

First defining the Word of God *extensively* as to its constituent parts, that is, after listing the thirty-nine books of the Old Testament and the twenty-seven books of the New Testament "under the name of Holy Scripture, or the Word of God written," the second article of the Confession of Faith, chapter one, defines the Word of God *intensively* as to its essential character, stating: "All which are *given by inspiration of God, to be the rule of faith and life*" (Larger Catechism, Question 3, adds the word "only" here—"the *only* rule of faith and obedience").

Then, precisely because "the books commonly called Apocrypha" are "not . . . of divine inspiration," the third article goes on to assert, they "are no part of the canon of the Scripture, and therefore are of no authority in the Church of God, nor to be any otherwise approved, or made use of, than other human writings."[8] The reader should take careful note of the four negative things asserted by the Confession about the Apocryphal books: They are *not* inspired; therefore, they are

---

8. The Palestinian Jews never accepted the Apocryphal books, their canon being the same as the Protestant Old Testament (see Josephus, *Against Apion,* 1.41; *Babylonian Talmud,* Yomah 9b, Sota 48b, Sanhedrin 11a). Nor did Jesus or the New Testament writers ever cite from these books. When Paul declared then that the Jews possessed "the oracles of God" (Rom. 3:2), he was implicitly excluding the Apocrypha from those "oracles."
  According to Gleason L. Archer Jr. (*A Survey of Old Testament Introduction* [Chicago: Moody, 1985], 75), the Septuagint, the pre-Christian Alexandrian Jewish translation into Greek of the Hebrew Old Testament, was the only ancient version that included the books of the Apocrypha. This has led some scholars to speak of an "Alexandrian Canon" that had authority among Jews

not canonical, *not* authoritative, and *not* to be approved or made use of by the church in any way different from ordinary human writings.

This article of the Confession raises the related issues of canonics and of inspiration's concomitant effect, namely, biblical infallibility.

The Formation and Close of the Church's Canon

From the beginning of the process of the inscripturation of the Word of God to the present time, the biblical faith has always been a "book religion." That is to say, during this period the people of God have always had a divinely inspired, authoritative canon ("rule" or "standard") comprised of documents which served them as their guide in matters of faith and life. But they did not have to roam the world to find these divinely inspired documents.

In Old Testament times God, as his people's ultimate "canon," announced that prophets were to be his authoritative spokesmen (Deut. 18:14–19), and he himself gave the criteria for discerning the true from the false prophet: (1) He declared in Deuteronomy 18:21–22 that the true prophet's predictions will come to pass (in other words, the true prophet's prophetic word will always be true), and (2) he stated in Deuteronomy 13:1–3 that the true prophet's prophetic message will always be in doctrinal agreement with antecedent redemptive/historical revelation. Here we see God himself establishing what has come to be known as the *analogia fidei* or *analogia doctrinae* principle—subsequent revelation will always accord in content with antecedent revelation. Then he himself authenticated the true prophets by empowering them to work miracles. As we have already noted, Moses, the prophets "like him," and Israel's schools of the prophets carefully collected and preserved the inspired historical and prophetic writings of the nation as they were composed.

---

equal to that of the "Palestinian Canon." But while Philo of Alexandria "quotes frequently from the canonical books of the 'Palestinian Canon,' he never once quotes from any of the apocryphal books" (Archer, 75). Furthermore, Aquila's Greek version, even though it did not contain the Apocrypha, was accepted by Alexandrian Jews in the second century A.D. (Archer, 75). Jerome explained the presence of the Apocrypha in the Alexandrian version by saying that it included both the canonical books and the books that were "ecclesiastical," that is, considered valuable though not inspired (Archer, 76). While it is true that the Septuagint served as the Greek "Bible" of the early church and of the apostles in their mission to the Gentiles, there is no evidence that a New Testament writer cites from any of the Apocryphal books.

Merrill F. Unger, *Introductory Guide to the Old Testament* (Grand Rapids, Mich.: Zondervan, 1956), 81–114, treats the phenomena of the Apocrypha which make it evident that these books are not products of the Spirit's inspiration. See also R. Laird Harris, *Inspiration and Canonicity of the Bible* (Grand Rapids, Mich.: Zondervan, 1957), chapters 6, 8, and Roger Beckwith, *The Old Testament Canon of the New Testament Church and Its Background in Early Judaism* (Grand Rapids, Mich.: Eerdmans, 1986), 338–437.

In New Testament times Jesus Christ—the second Person of the Godhead present with his church as its ultimate "canon"—personally validated for his church the particular Old Testament canon of first-century Palestinian Judaism, namely, the twenty-four books of the Hebrew canon (see his allusion to the tripartite canon of Palestinian Judaism in Luke 24:44), which corresponds to the thirty-nine books of the Protestant Old Testament but not to the forty-six books of the Roman Catholic Old Testament (Rome adds to the undisputed thirty-nine books the books of Tobit, Judith, 1 and 2 Maccabees, the Wisdom of Solomon, Sirach [or Ecclesiasticus], and Baruch). So the first-century church inherited the thirty-nine books of the Old Testament and the oral teaching of Jesus Christ, some of which is recorded in the Gospels (John 21:25; see also Jesus' words in Acts 20:35: "It is more blessed to give than to receive"; not found in any of the Gospels, Paul cites here a dominical saying from oral tradition), as the canonical base for the New Testament canon which appeared in due course.

Christ himself established for his church the "formal authority structure" which would be "the source and standard for all future preaching of the gospel," namely, the apostolate (Mark 3:14; Acts 10:41; Eph 2:20),[9] and he preauthenticated their spoken and written word:

> John 14:26: "the Counselor, the Holy Spirit, whom the Father will send in my name, will teach you all things and *will remind you of everything I have said to you.*" Here Christ promises by implication that the Holy Spirit will oversee the production of the Gospels.
>
> John 16:12–15: "I have much more to say to you, more than you can now bear. But when he, the Spirit of truth, comes, *he will guide you into all truth* [concerning what you cannot bear now]. He will not speak on his own; he will speak only what he hears, and he will tell you what is yet to come." Because the apostles were not able to comprehend the significance of Christ's death at that time, here Christ promises by implication that the Holy Spirit will oversee the production of the New Testament epistles which explicate Christ's cross work. And in his declaration that the Holy Spirit "will tell you what is yet to come," Christ promises by implication that the Holy Spirit will oversee the writing of John's Revelation.

In due course God himself authenticated these New Testament organs of redemptive/historical revelation as his spokesmen by granting them the power to

---

9. Herman N. Ridderbos, *Redemptive History and the New Testament Scriptures* (second revised edition; Phillipsburg, N. J.: Presbyterian and Reformed, 1988), 13.

perform miracles (Acts 14:3; 2 Cor 12:12). These apostles first exercised their authority orally, by preaching rather than by writing, but when they began to write they regarded their own and the other apostles' writings, as we have seen, as of equal authority with their spoken words (2 Thes 2:15; 2 Pet 3:15–16). *Their* authoritative words comprised the apostolic "deposit" or "tradition" which the church was to guard and to which it was to (and to which it did in fact immediately) adhere in matters of faith and life. Thus the apostles—clearly endorsing with their Lord the Old Testament canon of first-century Palestinian Judaism and treating that ancient canon in its entirety as the oracles of God (Rom. 3:2), added to that canon their own writings which both they and the apostolic church also immediately regarded as the Word of God. This much is borne out by Scripture itself and is indisputable.

But the church's coming to an understanding of which books were to comprise the New Testament canon and to the realization that that canon was complete was a slow, almost imperceptible, process. Martin H. Franzmann notes that before 170 A.D. none of the Apostolic Fathers

> explicitly asks or answers the question, "Which books are to be included in the list of those which are normative for the church?" What we do find in the writings of the so-called Apostolic Fathers (Clement of Rome, the Epistle of Barnabas, Ignatius, Polycarp, Hermas, the Teaching of the Twelve Apostles) is, first, a witness to the fact that the books destined to become the New Testament canon are *there*, at work in the church from the first. The books are quoted and alluded to, more often without mention of author or title than by way of formal quotation. Secondly, we find a witness to the fact that the thought and life of the church were being shaped by the content of the New Testament writings from the first, and moreover by the content of all types of New Testament writings. The influence of [all these types] (Synoptic Gospels, Johannine works, Pauline Letters, the Catholic Letters) is clearly discernible. To judge by the evidence of this period, the four Gospels and the letters of Paul were everywhere the basic units in the emerging canon of the New Testament.
>
> And, thirdly, there is some specific witness in these writings to the fact that the New Testament writings assumed a position of authority in the church which they share with no other writings. "The Lord" and "the apostles" appear as authoritative voices besides the Old Testament Scriptures. . . .
>
> Further evidence for the authority exercised by the New Testament writings is found in the fact, recorded by Justin Martyr, that the New Testament writings . . . were read in the worship services of the church, interchangeably with the Old Testament. This is perhaps the most significant bit of evidence for this period.[10]

---

10. Martin H. Franzmann, *The Word of the Lord Grows* (St. Louis: Concordia, 1961), 287–88.

Herman N. Ridderbos concurs with Franzmann's opinion:

> There was never any discussion of the "canonicity" of the majority [and at first of none] of the New Testament writings. The church never regarded those writings as being anything but the authoritative witness to the great time of redemption.... Uncertainty about *some* of [its] writings ... only arose later, as a result of certain actions that occurred within or against the church.[11]

By his last comment Ridderbos is alluding to the time around 160 A.D. when Marcion, the Gnostic heretic, repudiated the entire Old Testament and accepted only a mutilated Luke/Acts and ten "corrected" epistles of Paul as his canon. Thus the question of the New Testament canon became a matter of concern in some regions of the church. And it seems that this later regional uncertainty "damaged the authority a document had from the beginning and destroyed the original certainty of the church" about some New Testament books.[12] Even so, according to the Muratorian Canon or Muratorian Fragment, so named from the librarian of the Ambrosian Library in Milan, Lodovico Muratori, who discovered the document and published it in 1740, which was written by an unknown author (Muratori ascribed it to Caius, an elder in Rome) around 175 A.D.,[13] there seems never to have been any doubt on the part of the church at large concerning the canonical status of twenty New Testament books, namely, the four Gospels, Acts, the thirteen letters of Paul, 1 Peter, and 1 John.[14] The canonical status of the remaining seven New Testament books, namely, James, Hebrews, 2 Peter, 2 John, 3 John, Jude, and Revelation (as well as the canonical status of some other books, such as the Acts of Paul,

---

11. Ridderbos, *Redemptive History*, p. 40. F. F. Bruce, *The Canon of Scripture* (Downers Grove, Ill.,: InterVarsity, 1988), 255, agrees with Franzmann and Ridderbos, writing:
    > The earliest Christians did not trouble themselves about criteria of canonicity; they would not have readily understood the expression. They accepted the Old Testament scriptures as they had received them: the authority of those scriptures was sufficiently ratified by the teaching and example of the Lord and his apostles. The teaching and example of the Lord and his apostles, whether conveyed by word of mouth or in writing, had axiomatic authority for them.
12. Ridderbos, ibid., 44.
13. G. M. Hahneman, *The Muratorian Fragment and the Development of the Canon* (Oxford, Oxford University Press, 1992), has recently challenged the second-century date of the *Fragment*, regarding it as a fourth-century document of eastern origin.
14. Interestingly, the Muratorian author states that the New Testament offices of apostle and prophet were things of the past, as do also Hippolytus (c. 170–c. 236 A.D.) in his "Treatise on Christ and Antichrist," *Anti-Nicene Fathers* (Grand Rapids, Mich.: Eerdmans, 1990 reprint): 5, 204–19, and Chrysostom (c. 347–407 A.D.) later in his *Homilies in First Corinthians* in *Nicene and Post-Nicene Fathers* (Grand Rapids, Mich: Eerdmans, 1989 reprint): Homilies 29, 36.

the Shepherd of Hermas, the Revelation of Peter, and the Epistle of Barnabas, which were finally rejected), continued to be a matter of concern in some regions for about two centuries before they eventually found a fixed place in the church's New Testament canon. But as the several regions of the church grew in their ecumenical ties with one another it became increasingly evident that the doubts concerning these writings were only regional and that these regional doubts contradicted what the larger church had for a long time believed about these matters.

Therefore, during the third century, along with the ever-widening rejection of all the other literary claimants to canonical status, the seven disputed books continued slowly to gain ground in the churches. Yet no commission of theologians or church council met to define or impose a canon on the church. In the fourth century (A.D. 325), since Eusebius of Caesarea could appeal then to nothing "official"— no conciliar decree, no definitive pronouncement that had church authority behind it—he surveyed in his *Ecclesiastical History*, book 3, chapter 25, the status of the various books in the church. And this is what he reports: twenty-seven books then occupied a place of authority in the life of the church. But because there was still some controversy, Eusebius, desiring to be scrupulously accurate, divided the twenty-seven books into the *homologoumena* (the "agreed upon" books) and the *antilegomena* (the "spoken against" books). Among the former he listed twenty-two books: the four Gospels, Acts, fourteen letters of Paul (including Hebrews among the Pauline letters), 1 Peter, 1 John, and the Revelation of John (with the notation, "if it really seem proper"). Among the *antilegomena* ("which are nevertheless recognized by many") he listed five books: James, Jude, 2 Peter, 2 John, and 3 John. Somewhat curiously, if his second placement of John's Revelation is not simply an unwitting error on his part, he lists John's Revelation again, not among the *antilegomena* but among a third group, the *nothoi* (the "rejected" books), with the notation, "if it seem proper, which some, as I said, reject, but which others class among the accepted books." A little over forty years later, in A.D. 367, Athanasius, in his Thirty-Ninth Paschal Letter (often referred to as his "Easter" letter because it announced the official date of Easter to the churches), drawing no distinction as Eusebius had done between *homologoumena* and *antilegomena*, felt the liberty to list the twenty-seven books of Eusebius's canon as "the wellsprings of salvation, from which he who thirsts may take his fill of sacred words." From this date onward the canon of the church was practically determined, and before the end of the fourth century, under the influence of Jerome and Augustine, the church had resolved all the canonical questions to its satisfaction. Accordingly, in A.D. 397 the Third Council of Carthage demanded that nothing be read in the church under the title of divine Scripture except the "canonical" books, and then it affirmed precisely the current collection of twenty-seven New Testament books as the New Testament canon. And because of the near-universal Christian conviction which has prevailed ever

THE ATTRIBUTES OF HOLY SCRIPTURE

since then[15] that the Lord of the church had given these specific books and only these books to his people as the New Testament canon, the church for the last sixteen hundred years has restricted the New Testament canon to the twenty-seven commonly received New Testament books. In sum, from that point on the New Testament canon has been "a literary, historical and theological datum."[16]

Long have Christian scholars, after the fact, debated about what criteria the church employed during the third and fourth centuries to determine a given book's canonicity. It has been urged that the early church applied such criteria as (1) apostolicity (Was a given book written by an apostle or by one so closely associated with an apostle that it received his apostolic endorsement?), (2) antiquity (Since only documents from the apostolic age should be considered as candidates for canonicity, was a given document written in that age?), (3) orthodoxy (Was a given book doctrinally correct, that is, in accord with the "apostolic faith," particularly concerning the person and work of Christ?), (4) catholicity (Was a given book universally or virtually universally accepted throughout the church?), (5) lection (Was a given book being widely read and used in the churches?), and (6) inspiration (Was a given book inspired?), to judge whether any given book was to be viewed as "canonical" or not.[17]

Richard B. Gaffin, Jr., has convincingly argued, however, and I think correctly, given the peculiar mix of books that make up the New Testament, that scholarship has not been able to establish a set of criteria for canonicity which does not at the same time threaten to undermine the New Testament canon as it has come down to us. According to Gaffin, the problems with the several suggested criteria are as follows: (1) The criterion of *apostolicity* does not account for Mark, Luke-Acts, Hebrews,[18] Jude, and most likely James being included. To say that Mark and Luke/Acts are apostolic because the former is "Peter's Gospel" (so Papias) and the latter is "Paul's Gospel" is not sufficient, since we are given no reason to think that apostles could impart their apostolicity to others. Nor does this criterion explain

---

15. The Ethiopian church is the "holdout" here, having both the twenty-seven-book New Testament canon and a longer New Testament canon with seven extra books. This latter canonical tradition must be regarded as aberrant in this respect.
16. Bruce, *The Canon of Scripture*, 250.
17. Ibid., 255–269. Benjamin B. Warfield, "The Westminster Doctrine of Holy Scripture," *Selected Shorter Writings of Benjamin B. Warfield*, edited by John E. Meeter (Nutley, N. J.: Presbyterian and Reformed, 1973), II, 565, declares: "the order of procedure in ascertaining Scripture is to settle first the canon, then its inspiration, and then, as a corollary, its authority." For a contrary view, see R. Laird Harris, *Inspiration and Canonicity of the Bible* (Grand Rapids, Mich.: Zondervan, 1957), 219–80, particularly 280: "the principle of canonicity was inspiration and . . . the test of inspiration was authorship by . . . apostles.
18. I disagree with Gaffin here. See Appendix B.

[65]

why some of Paul's other letters (see 1 Cor. 5:9; 2 Cor. 2:4, 9; Col. 4:16) were not included. (2) The criterion of *antiquity* is really a variation on apostolicity and fails to explain why Paul's "previous" letter (1 Cor. 5:9) which was earlier than Hebrews was not included while Hebrews was included. (3) The criterion of *inspiration*, while certainly necessary to canonicity, cannot explain why Paul's letter to the Laodiceans (Col 4:16), also apostolic and also inspired, was not included. This criterion also faces the insuperable difficulty of demonstrating the inspiration of such books as Mark and Jude. And (4) the criterion of *lection* cannot explain why documents such as the Shepherd of Hermas and the Didache, which were used and occasionally read in public worship, were finally rejected, while there is little to no evidence that such works as 2 Peter, 2 John, 3 John, and Jude were so used. While not denying that criteria such as apostolic authorship and conformity to apostolic orthodoxy were made use of in the early church as it moved toward a consensus on the New Testament canon, Gaffin contends that even the early church's employment of its criteria, whatever they were, were at times defectively applied in reaching what eventually turned out to be right decisions. He has in mind here the book of Hebrews whose authorship the early church (he thinks incorrectly) ascribed to Paul. Furthermore, Gaffin contends, all attempts to demonstrate these criteria subject the absolute authority of the canon to the relativity of historical study and fallible human insight.[19] Regarding this last point Ridderbos also observes:

> no matter how strong the evidence for apostolicity (and therefore for canonicity) may be in many instances and no matter how forceful the arguments in favor of the apostolicity of certain other writings may be, historical judgments cannot be the final and sole ground for the church's accepting the New Testament as canonical. To accept the New Testament on that ground would mean that the church would ultimately be basing its faith on the results of historical investigation.[20]

Of course, if this be the case, one may then ask, how can the church be certain, without a direct statement from God on the matter, that it was only these particular books that he intended should be canonical? How can one be certain that the New Testament does not include a book that should not have been included or that it fails to include a book that should have been included? How can one be certain that the New Testament canon is even closed? And would not the position espoused

---

19. Richard B. Gaffin, Jr., "The New Testament as Canon," *Inerrancy and Hermeneutics*, edited by Harvey M. Conn (Grand Rapids, Mich.: Baker, 1988), 168–70.
20. Ridderbos, ibid., 32–33.

by Gaffin and Ridderbos, if endorsed, involve the church at the very foundation of its faith in a sort of "fideism"?

To such questions no answers can be given that will fully satisfy the mind that desires to think autonomously, that is, independently from Scripture. For regardless of whether or not the Christian scholar thinks he possesses the one right criterion or the one right list of criteria for a given book's canonicity, at some point—and if at no other point, at least at the point of the established number, namely, twenty-seven New Testament books, not twenty-six or twenty-eight—the Christian must accept by faith that the church, under the providential guidance of God's Spirit, got the number and the "list" right since God did not provide the church with a specific list of New Testament books. All that we know for certain about the history of the first four centuries of the church would suggest that God's Spirit providentially led his church—imperceptibly yet inexorably—when it asked its questions, whatever they were, to adopt the twenty-seven documents that the Godhead had determined would serve as the foundation of the church's doctrinal teaching and thus bear infallible witness throughout the Christian era to the great objective central events of redemptive history, and that *this* "apostolic tradition" *authenticated and established itself* over time in the mind of the church as just this infallible foundation and witness.

As for the question concerning canon closure, the sixteen hundred years that have passed since the church resolved all questions regarding the issue of canonicity to its satisfaction, during which period of time no serious attempt has been made anywhere to add an additional document to or to take one away from the New Testament canon, is a strong circumstantial argument for its closure. Even as significant a figure in Reformation times as Martin Luther got nowhere when he raised the question of the canonicity of James, which he termed "an epistle full of straw" because it seemed to focus more on the law than on Christ and the gospel.[21] Moreover, the possibility that a document ever will be presented for inclusion in the canon that, given the fragmented state of the church for the last thousand years, could or would receive the full church's acceptance, is so infinitesimally small that, for all practical purposes, it is non-existent.

---

21. See Luther's *Preface to the New Testament* ("In comparison with [the gospel and first epistle of St. John, St. Paul's epistles, especially those to the Romans, Galatians, and Ephesians, and St. Peter's first epistle], the epistle of St. James is an epistle full of straw, because it contains nothing evangelical.") and his *Preface to the Epistle of St. James* in which he rejects its apostolic authorship and provenance and refuses it "a place among the writers of the true canon" (1) "because, in direct opposition to St. Paul and all the rest of the Bible, it ascribes justification to works," (2) "because, in the whole length of its teaching, not once does it give Christians any instruction or reminder of the passion, resurrection, or spirit of Christ," and (3) because it appeared to him to be written "far later than St. Peter or St. Paul."

In sum, the formation of the twenty-seven-book New Testament canon, after all is said and done, appears ultimately to have been the work, not of men, not even of the church, but of God's Spirit alone. F. F. Bruce notes in this regard:

> Certainly, as one looks back on the process of canonization in early Christian centuries, and remembers some of the ideas of which certain church writers of that period were capable, it is easy to conclude that in reaching a conclusion on the limits of the canon they were directed by a wisdom higher than their own. It may be that those whose minds have been largely formed by scripture as canonized find it natural to make a judgment of this kind. But it is not mere hindsight to say, with William Barclay, that "the New Testament books became canonical because no one could stop them doing so" or even, in the exaggerated language of Oscar Cullmann, that "the books which were to form the future canon *forced themselves on the Church by their intrinsic apostolic authority*, as they do still, because the *Kyrios* Christ speaks in them."[22]

Concluding his own review of the history of canon formation, Franzmann appears to agree with this judgment:

> the New Testament as a collection has a curiously informal and almost casual sort of history. The book that was destined to remain the sacred book for millions of Christians for century upon century came into the church without fanfare, in a quiet, shuffling sort of way. Its history is not at all what *we* should expect the history of a sacred book to be. The story of the Book of Mormon is a good example of how man thinks a sacred book should come to man—miraculously, guaranteed by its miraculousness. The canon is a miracle indeed, but a miracle of another sort, a miracle like the incarnation of our Lord, a miracle in servant's form. Only a God who is really Lord of all history could risk bringing His written word into history in the way the New Testament was actually brought in. Only the God who by His Spirit rules sovereignly over His people could lead His weak, embattled, and persecuted churches to ask the right questions concerning the books that made their claim upon God's people and to find the right answers; to fix with Spirit-guided instinct on that which was genuinely apostolic (whether written directly by an apostle or not) and therefore genuinely authoritative. Only God Himself could make men see that public reading in the churches was a sure clue to canonicity; only the Spirit of God could make men see that a word which commands the obedience of God's people thereby established itself as God's word and must inevitably remove all other claimants from the scene.
>
> This the 27-book canon did. It established itself in the early centuries of the church and maintained itself in the continued life of the church . . . And it will

---

22. Bruce, *The Canon of Scripture*, 282. I do not think that Cullmann's language is "exaggerated" at all.

THE ATTRIBUTES OF HOLY SCRIPTURE

maintain itself henceforth. The question of the limits of the canon may be theoretically open; but the history of the church indicates that it is for practical purposes closed. The 27 books are *there* in the church, at work in the church. They are what Athanasius called them, "the wellsprings of salvation" for all Christendom. And in the last analysis, the church of God can become convinced and remain assured that they are indeed the wellsprings of salvation only by drinking of them.[23]

In response then to the "bottom-line" question, why, of all the literary claimants to canonicity and of all the inspired apostolic writings, did the current twenty-seven books of the New Testament, and only these twenty-seven, finally become the self-authenticating New Testament canon, we must be content simply to say, with Gaffin:

> just these twenty-seven books are what God has chosen to preserve, and he has not told us why. . . .
> In the matter of the New Testament as canon, too, until Jesus comes "we walk by faith, not by sight" (2 Cor. 5:7 RSV). But that faith, grounded in the apostolic tradition of the New Testament, is neither arbitrary nor blind. It has its reasons, its good reasons; it is in conflict only with the autonomy of reason.[24]

Meredith G. Kline has also argued, I believe successfully, that biblical revelation is structurally "covenantal," and as such, because its authoritative words from God are authoritative "treaty words," is intrinsically "canonical" and in a class by itself.[25] As treaty documents of the New Covenant, the Gospels and Acts provide the "historical prologue" of the New Covenant, with the former bearing witness to the ratification of God's covenant with his people in the sacrificial death of Christ, and Acts focusing on the founding of the New Covenant community through apostolic proclamation and providing at the same time the historical framework for the epistles. The New Testament epistles in turn provide the stipulations and sanctions of the New Covenant, that is, they serve as the means of forming and instructing God's covenant community and prosecuting God's covenant lawsuit against his church when the need arises. As such, the New Testament books, along with the Old, functioned *from the beginning* in their character as "treaty documents" to form and structure the New Covenant community and to order its faith and life. Thus the New Testament as treaty-canon—there in the church from the beginning—formed the church and not vice versa, confirming the Reformation's perception of

---

23. Franzmann, *The Word of the Lord Grows*, 294–95.
24. Gaffin, "The New Testament as Canon," 181.
25. Meredith G. Kline, *The Structure of Biblical Authority* (Revised edition; Grand Rapids, Mich.: Eerdmans, 1975], 27–75).

the matter over against Rome's contention that the church determined and formed the canon.

Biblical Infallibility

Warfield defines inspiration as follows: "Inspiration is that extraordinary, supernatural influence (or, passively, the result of it,) exerted by the Holy Ghost on the writers of our Sacred Books, by which their words were rendered also the words of God, *and therefore, perfectly infallible.*"[26] His definition highlights the truth that it is because the Bible is God's Word that the church has always insisted not only upon its revelatory and divine character but also upon inspiration's concomitant effect, infallibility.

What does the word "infallibility" mean? The Westminster Confession uses the word "infallible" in I/v and I/ix ("the *infallible* truth and divine authority thereof"; "The *infallible* rule of interpretation of Scripture, is the Scripture itself"). By it we assert that the Bible is true, that is to say, devoid of, and incapable of teaching, falsehood or error of any kind in all that it intends to affirm.[27] It is internally noncontradictory and doctrinally consistent. Its assertions correspond to what God himself understands is the true and real nature of things.

By "inerrancy" we intend essentially the same thing as "infallibility," namely, that the Bible does not err in any of its affirmations, whether those affirmations be in the spheres of spiritual realities or morals, history or science, and is therefore incapable of teaching error.[28] Because the Bible is God's Word, its assertions are as true as if God spoke to man today directly from heaven.

It is important that we mean by these two words no more and no less than what the Bible itself would permit by its own claims to truthfulness and by its textual phenomena.[29] That is to say, we must not evaluate Scripture according to standards

---

26. Benjamin B. Warfield, "Inspiration and Criticism," *The Inspiration and Authority of the Bible*, 420, emphasis supplied; see also Edward J. Young, *Thy Word Is Truth* (Grand Rapids, Mich: Eerdmans, 1957), 54.
27. The exposition section of the Chicago Statement on Biblical Inerrancy defines "infallible" as follows: "*Infallible* signifies the quality of neither misleading nor being misled and so safeguards in categorical terms the truth that Holy Scripture is a sure, safe, and reliable rule and guide in all matters."
28. The exposition section of the Chicago Statement on Biblical Inerrancy defines "inerrant" as follows: "*Inerrant* signifies the quality of being free from all falsehood or mistake and so safeguards the truth that Holy Scripture is entirely true and trustworthy in all its assertions."
29. For help here, see the Chicago Statement on Biblical Inerrancy, produced by the first International Conference on Biblical Inerrancy, meeting in Chicago, 1978.

of truth and error that are alien to its *Sitz im Leben,* usage or purpose. Such phenomena as a lack of modern technical precision, perceived irregularities of grammar or spelling, observational descriptions of nature, the use of hyperbole and round numbers, the topical arrangement of material, variant selections of material in parallel accounts and the use of free citations should not be used as arguments against tne Scripture's inerrancy.

Many are the objections that have been brought against the doctrine of the Bible's infallibility or inerrancy,[30] including:

1. The Bible contains errors in history and science. *Answer:* Inerrantists do not claim to be able to resolve every historical difficulty that occurs in the Bible. While, admittedly, we will occasionally have difficulty in understanding a historical reference or allusion in Scripture, no historical error has ever been proven to exist in Scripture. This same integrity is true respecting the so-called scientific statements of Scripture.[31] Besides, we must not ground the case for the Bible's inerrancy or lack thereof simply in an inductive study of the Bible's phenomena alone. We must take seriously what it says didactically about itself and study its historical and scientific phenomena in the light of its didactic statements about itself, that is to say, we must approach the Scripture's phenomena not inductively but presuppositionally.[32]

2. The Bible writers never claim inerrancy for themselves. *Answer:* It is true that the Bible writers recognize their own personal finitude and sinfulness and thus their liability to error. Indeed, they insist that everyone is (or may be) a liar (Pss. 58:3; 116:11; Rom. 3:4). But they nevertheless claim inerrancy for the written Word of God which he gave to humankind through them by inspiration (Pss. 19:7–9; 119:86, 138, 142, 144, 151, 160; John 17:17; 2 Tim. 3:16; 2 Pet. 1:20–21). In fact, it is precisely because they could err, that the Spirit's inspiring influence was necessary to keep them from error.

3. The doctrine of inerrancy leads to bondage to a book and thus to spiritual bondage. *Answer:* To the contrary, the doctrine of inerrancy guarantees the truthfulness of Scripture, and truth never binds one unwholesomely. It is truth that sets

---

30. I am indebted to David C. Jones who suggests and responds to the following six objections in his distributed (but unpublished) classroom lecture on inerrancy given at Covenant Theological Seminary.
31. An excellent book treating Bible difficulties is Gleason Archer's *Encyclopedia of Bible Difficulties* (Grand Rapids, Mich.: Zondervan, 1982).
32. See John Murray, "The Infallibility of Scripture," *Collected Writings of John Murray* (Edinburgh: Banner of Truth, 1976): 9–15, for further elucidation of the point that the warrant for holding the doctrine of biblical infallibility is the didactic witness of Scripture to itself and not our ability to prove it at every point to be infallible.

one free from bondage to sin, thus granting true liberty (John 8:32) which is bondage to God and his Christ.

4. Inerrancy obscures or denies the human element that was integrally present in the production of Scripture: "Scripture was written by humans; all humans err; therefore, Scripture must necessarily err," is the argument. *Answer:* This is a fallacious argument. It may be true that to err is human but it is not true that it is intrinsic to humanity necessarily always to err. A human being can and often does utter sentences that contain no errors (e.g., "David killed Goliath"). Accordingly, it is no more essential to the Bible that it *must* err because of its human side than it is essential that Christ must err because of his human nature. His human nature was sinless. Similarly, the Bible's human side is "errorless" because of the Spirit's superintendence of the Bible writers. While this view is often said to be "docetic" ("docetism" was an ancient heresy that denied the true humanity of Christ) in that it "denies the true humanity of Scripture" (it does not do this, of course; rather, it properly recognizes that to be human does not necessarily entail error, and that the Spirit kept the biblical writers from making errors they might otherwise have made), one could argue that the liberal view that denies the Bible's "inspiredness," its concomitant inerrancy, and thus its divine character is in fact "Arian" (Arianism was an ancient heresy that denied the true deity of Christ).

5. Inerrancy shifts the emphasis away from Christ as the proper object of the Christian's worship to Scripture which becomes then the inerrantist's object of worship. *Answer:* This is a groundless charge. No evangelical has ever worshiped the Bible! The evangelical has always recognized that in worship he must move in faith beyond the words of Scripture to the Christ the Scriptures tell him about. But he is also convinced that he must never separate the word of the Christ of Scripture from the word of Scripture itself, since he believes that the latter is the word of the former. Accordingly, to listen to Scripture and to ascribe inerrancy to it is to listen to him and to inscribe inerrancy to him who is the Truth and the source of Scripture's inerrancy.

We must not forget that *the only reliable source of knowledge that we have of Christ is the Holy Scripture.* If the Scripture is erroneous anywhere, then we have no assurance that it is inerrantly truthful in what it teaches about him. And if we have no reliable information about him, then it is precarious indeed to worship the Christ of Scripture, since we may be entertaining an erroneous representation of Christ and thus may be committing idolatry. The only way to avoid this conclusion is to keep the Christ of Scripture and the Scripture itself in vital union with each other—the former the Giver of the latter—and to affirm that the latter is true because it was inspired by the former who is Truth itself (John 14:6).

6. Inerrancy is an apologetic "ploy" on the part of evangelicals to justify their narrow theological stance. *Answer:* This is not so. The evangelical's insistence upon

biblical inerrancy ultimately flows out of his submission to the Scripture's teaching about the nature of God. By nature, God is trustworthy (inerrant); his word is true; he cannot lie. What he declares to human beings must be true, that is, without error. If then the Bible is God's Word (and we have given ample reason to insist that it is), then the Bible must be true, that is, without scientific or historical error or logical contradiction. This is not Cartesian rationalism. It is simply biblical/Christian rationalism.

THE BIBLE'S AUTHORITY

The authority of the Holy Scripture, for which it ought to be believed and obeyed, dependeth not upon the testimony of any man or church, but *wholly upon God* (who is truth itself), the author thereof; and therefore *it is to be believed, because it is the word of God*. (WCF, I/iv, emphasis supplied)

This article, explicating the ground of the Bible's authority, first states the ground wherein the Bible's authority does *not* reside: it does not reside in the testimony of any person or church respecting the Bible. For any person or church to insist that people should believe and obey the Bible because of their testimony to ground its authority in the opinion of fallible men.

Then the article states the sole reason why the Bible ought to be believed and obeyed: because God, who is truth itself,[33] is in a unique sense its author, and therefore because it is the very Word of the one living and true God. In sum, it receives its authority from heaven; it requires no earthly advocacy in regard to the issue of its authority. Its authority is intrinsic and inherent; that is, it is self-validating. In no sense is its authority derived from human testimony.

This article was originally intended to inveigh against the Roman Catholic dogma that the authority of the Bible depends upon the authority of the church. Roman Catholic teaching is that, since it was the church that determined the Scripture canon in the first place,[34] the Scriptures are reliant upon the church for their authority. An unfortunate comment by Augustine is often cited to prove the point: "I would not believe in the Gospel, had not the authority of the Catholic Church

---

33. We must not forget that the authority of Scripture is inevitably bound up with the issue of its inerrant truthfulness. As J. I. Packer observes: "Statements that are not absolutely true and reliable could not be absolutely authoritative" (*"Fundamentalism" and the Word of God*, [Grand Rapids, Mich.: Eerdmans, 1959], 96).
34. The *Baltimore Catechism* declares that "it is only from Tradition (preserved in the Catholic Church) that we can know which of the writings of ancient times are inspired and which are not inspired."

already moved me."[35] Rome's position is based upon the notion that the church canonized the Scriptures, when in fact the church merely received and preserved the already authoritative Scriptures as they were written, and eventually declared to be "canonical" the twenty-seven books that God's Spirit desired should be in the New Testament canon because it could do nothing else.

This position also raises a question about much contemporary apologetic strategy. Classical apologetics, represented by Ligonier apologist R. C. Sproul, argues for the infallible authority of the Bible as the Word of God on the basis of a progression from the premise of the Bible's basic or general reliability or trustworthiness[36] to the conclusion of its infallibility and hence of its divine authoritativeness. This reasoning proceeds as follows:

Premise A: The Bible is a basically or generally reliable and trustworthy document.

Premise B: On the basis of this (generally) reliable document we have sufficient evidence to believe confidently that Jesus Christ is the Son of God.

Premise C: Jesus Christ, being the Son of God, is an infallible authority.

Premise D: Jesus Christ teaches that the Bible is more than generally trustworthy: it is the very Word of God.

Premise E: The Word, in that it comes from God, is utterly trustworthy because God is utterly trustworthy.

Conclusion: On the basis of the infallible authority of Jesus Christ, the church believes the Bible to be utterly trustworthy, i.e., infallible (and therefore authoritative).

Sproul notes that "this progression does not involve *circular* reasoning."[37]

These five premises are stated in a manner, however, which is biased toward the Christian apologist who already believes in the infallibility of Scripture. I do not believe the progression is a valid argument in that the conclusion declares more

---

35. Augustine, *Contra epistolam Manichaei*, 5, 6. See *Catechism of the Catholic Church* (1994), paragraph 119 on page 34. See John Calvin's explanation of Augustine's comment in his *Institutes*, I. vii. 3.
36. Christians should not presuppose less than the truth about the Bible nor should they suggest that unbelievers may presuppose less than the truth about the Bible.
37. R. C. Sproul, *Reason to Believe* (Grand Rapids, Mich.: Zondervan, 1982), 30–31. If this line of reasoning is sound, why should anyone ever use any other line of argument for the Christian faith? Why not just make the case with the unbeliever for the infallible authority of Scripture and argue everything else from this "presupposition"?

than the original premise will allow. If one approaches these issues without Christian presuppositions, one can only conclude at best that the Bible is probably, or even only possibly, God's Word.

With regard to Premise A, can Sproul simply assert that the Bible is generally trustworthy or must he demonstrate it? Surely the latter. But how does one do this? The Bible is a big book, claiming to record accurately the occurrence of hundreds, indeed, thousands of events, most of them purporting to be divinely planned and induced, any one of which, if untrue, would nullify the indefectibility of Scripture. Often there is no archaeological evidence to support the historicity of these events, or even no evidence at all beyond the word of the writers, many of whose identities are doubted by critical scholarship.

Consider for a moment one of the more intriguing biblical events, namely, Jesus' transfiguration. How is one to go about proving it happened and happened the way the Evangelists report it? By citing archaeological evidence? I think we would all admit that we can cite no archaeological evidence for its occurrence. By citing then perhaps what purports to be eyewitness testimony? Just so, surely. But Peter's is the only testimony we have that purports to be such. We have nothing from the other two reported eyewitnesses—James and John. And Matthew, Mark, and Luke who report the event in their respective Gospels were not eyewitnesses but rather second-hand (or even further removed) reporters. So let us say that one cites Peter's purported eyewitness testimony in 2 Peter 1:16–18 as his primary proof for the event's occurrence. Will such an appeal satisfy the skepticism of the secular historian? I do not think so. So now the apologist must begin to amass the requisite evidence showing, first, that it was Peter who in fact wrote these words (the reader should recall here that critical New Testament scholarship, I think wrongly, denies the Petrine authorship of 2 Peter), and second, that when he wrote them he wrote the truth.

Note in the first case that the evidence would have to establish both a first-century date for 2 Peter and an apostolic, indeed Petrine, authorship of the letter. Note too in the second case, since secular assumptions forbid taking the veracity of apostles on faith and because Peter's testimony includes a reference to a voice from heaven, that one would have to establish beyond reasonable doubt the possibility, indeed, the probability of the existence of such a voice and the probability that the voice said what Peter reports that it said. This would take one presumably into the matter of justifying the validity of and then the utilizing of at least one of the so-called arguments for the existence of God—no mean task! And it would require one to demonstrate that a favorable relationship existed between Christ and that voice on the basis of which the voice said what it did. This in turn would necessitate that one enter deeply into the extremely difficult *theological* areas of Christology and Trinitarianism where much that is concluded flows out of an even larger theological vision, namely theism *per se*. This theological vision in turn would need to be justified.

One might also be challenged to demonstrate that the voice from heaven was God's voice and not the voice of a demon who was seeking to mislead Peter. Note as well that the demonstration would not only have to vindicate the veracity of what these particular verses say but also would have to mount independent proofs for at least the general trustworthiness of the teaching of every other verse of the letter. Then one would have to do the same with the secondary sources in the New Testament who report its occurrence—no small task, to say the least.

But let us presume that one accomplished this work to his satisfaction. Now the general trustworthiness of the rest of the Bible writers would have to be demonstrated in the same way with regard to everything else that they report in the Bible, and they report thousands of supernatural events. Of course there simply is no investigatable evidence beyond the report itself for the occurrence of the supernatural events recorded in the Bible, such as the Spirit of God hovering over the waters in Genesis 1:2 or God's hardening of Pharaoh's heart during the Exodus deliverance. Such *theological* statements would have to be accepted on the basis of the "generally reliable" *historical* record corroborated elsewhere. If so, we would be asking the secularist to accept the reliability of the Bible's explicit and replete *supernaturalism* on the basis of the Bible's "generally reliable" *naturalism*. But a great number of natural events would still remain to be investigated and generally corroborated. Some would turn out to be maddeningly resistant to corroboration, I suspect. In fact, very few biblical events, comparatively speaking, can be verified extra-biblically in a way that will satisfy the secularist that they really happened the way the Bible reports them. But for the sake of argument, let us say that one completes this task in due course and is now satisfied that the Bible is a basically or generally trustworthy book, at least in those areas where it can be corroborated. Now he proceeds to draw the stated inferences.

But Premise B, based as it is on Premise A ("The Bible is a basically or generally reliable and trustworthy document"), should really state: "On the basis of this generally reliable and trustworthy document, shown to be so at least in those relatively few areas where we could conduct an investigation, we *possibly* have evidence that Jesus Christ is the Son of God."

But then this means in turn that Premise C should read: "Jesus Christ, *possibly* being the Son of God, is *possibly* therefore an infallible authority." (But this means that his testimony, being only possibly infallible, does not really finally settle this or any other issue. His testimony is just one more part of the total evidence in a possibility construct for some desired conclusion.)

Premise D should then read: "Jesus Christ, *possibly* being accurately portrayed by the Scriptures as the Son of God (Premise B) and therefore *possibly* infallible (Premise C), *possibly* taught infallibly (Premise C) that the Bible is more than generally trustworthy, that is, that it is the very Word of God." (We can say no more than this about Jesus' testimony about the Bible on the basis of a report about him that is represented as only generally reliable.)

Premise E should then read: "The Bible, *possibly* the very Word of God (Premise D), is therefore *possibly* utterly trustworthy, in that the God about whom it speaks is represented as utterly trustworthy in his utterances."

The conclusion should then read: "On the basis of the *possibly* infallible authority of Jesus Christ, the church believes the Bible to be *possibly* utterly trustworthy, i.e., infallible and therefore authoritative."

It seems to me that this is the only way the progression could be rewritten to win the approval of an intelligent nonbeliever schooled in logic. But God is not honored when we draw such conclusions about his Son and his Word from data all of which are really revelational in nature and, as we shall see in our discussion of the Bible's next attribute, are self-authenticating.

The Ligonier apologists, R. C. Sproul, John H. Gerstner, and Arthur Lindsley, offer a variation of this argument in their *Classical Apologetics*:

> Premise A: It is virtually granted that the Bible (not assumed to be inspired) contains generally reliable history.
>
> Premise B: The Bible records miracles as part of its generally reliable history.
>
> Premise C: These miracles authenticate the Bible's messengers and their message.
>
> Conclusion 1: Therefore, the Bible message ought to be received as divine.
>
> Premise D: The Bible message includes the doctrine of its own inspiration.
>
> Conclusion 2: Therefore, the Bible is more than a generally reliable record. It is a divinely inspired record.[38]

The major aspects of my assessment given above register equally against this line of reasoning. Once again the skeptic is being asked by Premise B to accept the supernaturalism of the Bible on the basis of the Bible's "generally reliable history." But as John Frame also declares:

---

38. R. C. Sproul, John Gerstner, Arthur Lindsley, *Classical Apologetics* (Grand Rapids, Mich.: Zondervan, 1984), 141. One could ask again, if this line of reasoning is sound, why should they not argue everything else with the unbeliever on the basis of this "established" fact of the Bible's divine authority?

The authors overestimate, I think, the current scholarly consensus on the reliability of the Gospels. They assume that almost every NT scholar will concede that the Gospels are "generally reliable." I doubt it.[39]

As for their premise that the Gospel miracles authenticate Jesus' message as from God, Frame remarks:

> Even if we grant that some very unusual events took place in the ministry of Jesus [in a footnote at this point Frame writes: "And of course the question must be raised as to *how unusual* an event must be before we call it a miracle"], how can we be sure that these can be explained *only* as a divine attestation to Jesus' authority? It is extremely difficult to prove (apart from Christian presuppositions) the negative proposition that no other cause could have produced these events. The authors need to prove this proposition in order to make their case, but nothing in the book amounts to such a proof.[40]

What Frame is highlighting by his second comment is the problem that always arises when one attempts to prove a universal negative proposition. Such propositions are always extremely difficult, if not impossible, to prove.

Another equally unsalutary argument for the Bible's truthfulness is that which Edward John Carnell advances in *An Introduction to Christian Apologetics* and which Francis A. Schaeffer urges in *The God Who Is There*. Their test for the Bible's truthfulness and thus its authority, to use Carnell's phrase, is "systematic consistency."[41] That is to say, the Bible's claim to truthfulness (1) must pass a rigid application of the law of noncontradiction, that is, its teachings must be internally self-consistent (the "horizontal" test), and (2) must be consistent with or fit all the data of history, archaeology, sociology, scientific cosmogony, and human antiquity, as well as the nature of humankind (the "vertical" test). In response to the question, "How do we know the Bible is true?" Schaeffer writes that

> scientific proof, philosophical proof and religious proof *follow the same rules*. We may have any problem before us which we wish to solve; it may concern a chemical reaction or the meaning of man. After the question has been defined, in each case proof consists of two steps:
>
> > A. The theory must be non-contradictory and must give an answer to the phenomenon in question.

---

39. John M. Frame, "Van Til and the Ligonier Apologetic," *Westminster Theological Journal* 47 (1985): 297.
40. Ibid., 297.
41. Edward John Carnell, *An Introduction to Christian Apologetics* (Grand Rapids, Mich.: Eerdmans, 1948), 106–13.

B. We must be able to live consistently with our theory. For example, the answer given to the chemical reaction must conform to what we observe in the test tube. With regard to man and his "mannishness," the answer given *must conform to what we observe* in a wide consideration of man and how he behaves.[42]

Systematic consistency as a verifiability test, however, is the very test devised by the apostate autonomous man to determine what can and cannot be, and what is and is not true, the very test which has for its theory of fact pure contingency and which has for its goal, at best, only probability! Moreover, how people in general apply the law of noncontradiction to Scripture and how they judge whether or not the Bible "fits all the facts" depend upon their prior *religious* commitment. Unbelievers, using the test for truth which Carnell and Schaeffer grant them, may declare that they find many contradictions in the Bible, and the Bible's view of humankind is the last interpretation the unbeliever will adopt. Using this method no one will be able finally to conclude that the Bible is true in the whole and in the part. I do believe that the Bible is internally self-consistent and that it does "fit the facts" of history and archaeology and so on. But this is because I am a Christian, having been persuaded as a result of the Holy Spirit's regenerating work that the Bible is in fact the authoritative Word of God, that it is intrinsically authoritative and *is to be believed because it is the Word of God*.[43]

THE BIBLE'S SELF-AUTHENTICATION

We may be moved and induced by the testimony of the church to an high and reverent esteem for the Holy Scripture. And the heavenliness of the matter, the efficacy of the doctrine, the majesty of the style, the consent of all the parts, the scope [purpose] of the whole (which is to give all glory to God), the full discovery [disclosure] it makes of the only way of man's salvation, the many other incomparable excellencies, and the entire perfection thereof, *are arguments whereby it doth abundantly evidence itself to be the word of God;* yet, notwithstanding, our full persuasion and assurance of the infallible truth and divine authority thereof, is from the inward work of the Holy Spirit, bearing witness by and with the word in our hearts. (WCF, I/v, emphasis supplied)

---

42. Francis A. Schaeffer, *The God Who Is There* (Downers Grove, Ill.: InterVarsity Press, 1968), 109, emphasis supplied.
43. See Reymond, *The Justification of Knowledge*, 130–48, for a more extensive rebuttal of systematic consistency as man's test of religious truth.

This article asserts both the Bible's *self-authenticating, self-evidencing, self-attesting, self-validating* character as the Word of God and yet also the necessity of the Holy Spirit's saving work if one is to believe it savingly. It recognizes that the Word of God would, of necessity, have to be self-authenticating, self-attesting and self-validating, for if it needed anyone or anything else to authenticate and validate its divine character—based on the principle that the validating source is always the higher and final authority (see Heb. 6:13)—it would not be the Word of God.[44] For while this article recognizes that the testimony of the church to the Bible's divine character, as a motivating appeal for the Bible's claims (a *motivum credibilitatis*), may move Christians (see the "we" and the "our" in the article) to a "high and reverent esteem for the Holy Scripture," it also recognizes that the Bible's ultimate attestation as God's Word does not derive from human or church testimony. Rather, the Bible carries within its own bosom, so to speak, its own divine *indicia*.[45] The article generalizes eight such self-evidencing features: (1) the heavenliness of its subject matter, (2) the efficacy of its doctrine, (3) the majesty of its style, (4) the consent of all its parts, (5) the purpose of the whole, namely, to give all glory to God, (6) the full disclosure it makes of the only way of salvation, (7) its many other incomparable excellencies, and (8) its entire perfection. These, the article states, "are arguments whereby it *doth abundantly evidence itself* to be the word of God."[46]

But if the Bible, as the Confession declares, is self-evidencingly the Word of God, why do not all acknowledge it to be such? The answer is, because something

---

44. When Christ as the incarnate Son of God authenticated the Scriptures, it must be recalled that he was authenticating his own Word, and he was doing it according to his own declared authority in keeping with the principle he enunciated in John 8:14: "Even if I testify on my own behalf, my testimony is valid, for I know where I came from and where I am going." The point to note here is that Jesus validated his claims by appealing to his knowledge of himself, unintimidated by the possible charge of *petitio principii* (Jesus' appeal to self-knowledge here accords with the divine procedure stipulated in Hebrews 6:13: "When God made his promise to Abraham, since there is no one greater for him to swear by, he swore by himself"). Since then the Scriptures are the Word of Christ, one must never separate the words of Scriptures from the words of the Christ of Scripture. It is the same self-attesting Christ speaking in and through both. To doubt the truthfulness of Scripture is to doubt the Christ of Scripture, and to doubt the Christ of Scripture is both immoral and to operate with a false ideal and test of truth.

45. John Calvin in the Latin version of his *Institutes* states (using Greek) that Scripture is αὐτόπιστον, *autopiston*, that is, "self-authenticating" (I.7.5). In the French version of the same work he affirms that the Scripture "carries with[in] itself its [own] credentials" *(porte avec soi sa créance).*

46. Larger Catechism, Question 4, says the same in somewhat different words: "The Scriptures *manifest themselves* to be the word of God, by their majesty and purity, by the consent of all the parts, and the scope of the whole, which is to give all glory to God; by their light and power to convince and convert sinners, to comfort and build up believers unto salvation."

more is needed. What is this lack? The Confession would not for a moment place this inadequacy in the Bible. Rather, taking seriously what the Bible teaches about the darkness of the human heart (see VI/4; Larger Catechism, Question 25), it presupposes here the spiritual blindness of men and women. If we may employ the analogy of a radio station and the home radio, the Confession would say that there is nothing wrong with the radio station's, that is, the Bible's transmission. It is "transmitting" precisely as it should. If its transmission is not received, the problem lies at the reception end, with the "home radio," the human heart. To cite Warfield, man needs "in ordinary language, a new heart, or in the Confession's language, 'the inward work of the Holy Spirit, bearing witness [to these things] by and with the word in our hearts.' "[47]

The reference here in the Confession to "the inward work of the Holy Spirit" is often called the "internal testimony of the Holy Spirit."[48] What precisely is this work? Louis Berkhof replies:

> What is the ground on which our faith in the Word of God rests? Or, perhaps better still, By what means is the conviction respecting the truth of the special revelation of God wrought in our hearts? In answer to these questions Reformed theologians point to the testimony of the Holy Spirit. . . . The Reformers . . . derived their certainty respecting the truth of the divine revelation from the work of the Spirit of God in the hearts of believers. . . .
>
> We should bear in mind that the particular work of the Holy Spirit described by [this] name does not stand by itself, but is connected with the whole work of the Holy Spirit in the application of the redemption wrought in Christ. The Spirit renews the spiritual darkness of the understanding and illumines the heart, so that the glory of God in Christ is clearly seen. . . .
>
> The work of the Holy Spirit enables [men] to accept the revelation of God in Christ, to appropriate the blessings of salvation, and to attain to the assurance of faith. And the testimony of the Holy Spirit is merely a special aspect of His more general work in the sphere of redemption.

After underscoring the two facts that this special testimony of the Spirit neither brings a new revelation, for then this new revelation would call for further attestation ad infinitum, nor is it identical with the faith experience inasmuch as the Spirit's testimony is the efficient cause of faith, Berkhof continues:

---

47. Warfield, "The Westminster Doctrine of Holy Scripture," *Selected Shorter Writings*, 2:567.
48. Paul teaches in 1 Corinthians 2:14–15 that only those who receive the Spirit's enlightenment can savingly accept and understand the truths that come from the Spirit of God. Such truths must be "spiritually discerned" (πνευματικῶς ἀνακρίνεται, *pneumatikōs anakrinetai*).

> The testimony of the Holy Spirit is simply the work of the Holy Spirit in the heart of the sinner by which he removes the blindness of sin, so that the erstwhile blind man, who had no eyes for the sublime character of the Word of God, now clearly sees and appreciates the marks of its divine nature, and receives immediate certainty respecting the divine origin of Scripture. . . .
>
> The Christian believes the Bible to be the Word of God in the last analysis on the testimony which God Himself gives respecting this matter in His Word, and recognizes that Word as divine by means of the testimony of God in his heart. The testimony of the Holy Spirit is therefore, strictly speaking, not so much the final ground of faith, but rather the means of faith. The final ground of faith is Scripture only, or better still, the authority of God which is impressed upon the believer in the testimony of Scripture. The ground of faith is identical with its contents, and cannot be separated from it. But the testimony of the Holy Spirit is the moving cause of faith. We believe Scripture, not because of, but through the testimony of the Holy Spirit.[49]

Edward J. Young likewise responds:

> Of one point we may be sure. [The testimony of the Holy Spirit] is not the communication to us of information beyond what is contained in the Bible. It is not the impartation of new knowledge. It is not a new revelation from God to man. It is rather that aspect of the supernatural work of the new birth in which the eyes of our understanding have been opened so that we, who once were in darkness and bondage of sin, now see that to which formerly we had been blind. . . . Now, at last, the sinner is convinced that this Book is different from all other books. He beholds that it is from God in a sense that is true of no other writing. The divinity of the Scriptures is for the first time clearly perceived, and the voice of the heavenly Father distinctly heard.
>
> It is then from God Himself that we learn the true character of the Scriptures. In the very nature of the case, it must be so. Only God can identify what He Himself has spoken. . . . We Christians need not be ashamed to proclaim boldly that our final persuasion of the Divinity of the Bible is from God Himself. God, in His gentle grace, has identified His Word for us; He has told us that the Bible is from Himself. Those who know Him may not depreciate this doctrine of the internal testimony of the Spirit; those who are His know that God has truly brought them out of darkness into light.[50]

---

49. Louis Berkhof, *Introductory Volume to Systematic Theology* (Grand Rapids, Mich.: Eerdmans, 1932), 182–85.
50. Edward J. Young, *Thy Word Is Truth* (reprint, Edinburgh: Banner of Truth, 1963), 34–35; see also Packer, *"Fundamentalism" and the Word of God*, 119:
    > This part of the Spirit's ministry as His witness to divine truth . . . is a healing of spiritual faculties, a restoring to man of a permanent receptiveness towards divine things, a giving and

THE BIBLE'S SUFFICIENCY

The whole counsel of God, concerning all things necessary for His own glory, man's salvation, faith, and life, is either expressly set down in Scripture, or by good and necessary consequence may be deduced from Scripture: unto which nothing at any time is to be added, whether by new revelations of the Spirit, or traditions of men. Nevertheless, we acknowledge the inward illumination of the Spirit of God to be necessary for the saving understanding of such things as are revealed in the word [already implied in I/v]; and that there are some circumstances concerning the worship of God, and government of the church, common to human actions and societies, which are to be ordered by the light of nature and Christian prudence, according to the general rules of the word, which are always to be observed. (WCF, I/vi, emphasis supplied)

This article, which pits the Reformers' doctrine of *sola Scriptura* off over against both Rome's claims for its tradition and Anabaptist mysticism, affirms the sufficiency of Holy Scripture, properly understood, to inform humankind regarding "the whole counsel of God, concerning all things necessary for His own glory,

---

sustaining of power to recognize and receive divine utterances for what they are. It is given in conjunction with the hearing or reading of such utterances, and the immediate fruit of it is an inescapable awareness of their divine origin and authority.

And when this starts to happen, faith is being born. Faith begins with the according of credence to revealed truths, not as popular, or probable, human opinions, but as words uttered by the Creator, and uttered, not only to mankind in general, but to the individual soul in particular.

See Packer again, *Jerusalem and Athens*, ed. E. R. Geehan (Phillipsburg, N.J.: Presbyterian and Reformed, 1971), 143:

The Scriptures *authenticate themselves* to Christian believers through the convincing work of the Holy Spirit, who enables us to recognize, and bow before, divine realities. It is he who enlightens us to receive the man Jesus as God's incarnate Son, and our Saviour; similarly, it is he who enlightens us to receive sixty-six pieces of human writing as God's inscripturated Word, given to make us "wise unto salvation through faith which is in Christ Jesus" (2 Tim. 3:15). In both cases, this enlightening is not a private revelation of something that has not been made public, but the opening of minds sinfully closed so that they receive evidence to which they were previously impervious. The evidence of divinity is there before us, in the words and works of Jesus in the one case and the words and qualities of Scripture in the other. It consists not of clues offered as a basis for discursive inference to those who are clever enough, as in a detective story, but in the unique force which, through the Spirit, the story of Jesus, and the knowledge of Scripture, always carry with them to strike everyone to whom they come. In neither case, however, do our sinful minds receive this evidence apart from the illumination of the Spirit. The church bears witness, but the Spirit produces conviction, and so, as against Rome, evangelicals insist that it is the witness of the Spirit, not that of the church, which authenticates the canon to us.

man's salvation, faith, and life." Assuming its earlier affirmation that special revelation has ceased, this article then declares that "nothing at any time is to be added [to the Holy Scriptures], whether by [alleged] new revelations of the Spirit, or traditions of men." In short, as Larger Catechism, Question 3, states: "The holy Scriptures of the Old and New Testaments are the word of God, the *only* rule of faith and obedience."

This position assumes, of course, that the revelatory gifts embodied in the living organs of revelation (the apostle, the prophet, and the glossolalist and his translator)—so prominent in the life of the first-century church—passed out of the life of the church with the completion of the inscripturated canon. Ephesians 2:20 places the apostle and the New Testament prophet in the *foundation* of the church, and 2 Timothy 3:16–17 declares that it is Scripture that "thoroughly equip[s] the man of God for every good work."[51] There is also the biblical-theological suggestion, drawn from the historical order of the several New Testament pieces, that a shift took place even within the life of the first-century church away from earlier admonitions to listen to the living voices of prophecies (see 1 Thess. 5:20) to admonitions to read and study the inscripturated Word (see 1 Tim. 4:13). David C. Jones suggests that prophetic and teaching gifts appear to have merged as the canon was completed, with the distinct experience of the Spirit's immediate *inspiration* giving way to the Spirit's *illumination,* working by and with the written word. Joel's prophecy (2:28–32), he suggests, is still programmatic for the entire interadventual period, but to the extent that the New Testament prophets' inspiration ceased, so the prophetic office ceased, and to the extent that their teaching function continues, the prophetic office has merged into the teaching office which continues to the present time.[52] We see this illustrated also by the lists of qualifications given in 1 Timothy 3 and Titus 1, where church officers were to be selected by the church's prudent discernment of their qualifications and not by such direct inspiration as was exhibited earlier in Acts 13:1–2.

It should be carefully observed that the Westminster Assembly is not here inveighing against tradition playing any role in the life of the church; it only opposes tradition being placed on a par with Scripture with respect to authority. Historic Protestantism, and in particular the Reformed church within Protestantism, has always had its traditions, these traditions coming to expression primarily in the great national creeds of Reformed Protestantism. But the framers of these

---

51. According to many scholars, Daniel 9:24, which places the "sealing up of visions and prophecy" within the time frame of the seventy sevens decreed for Daniel's people, also supports the view that verbal revelation ceased with the termination of the apostolic age.
52. David Clyde Jones, "The Gift of Prophecy Today," *The Presbyterian Guardian* (December 1974), 163–64.

creeds never regarded them as possessing intrinsic authority so as to bind men's consciences in matters of faith and morals, expressly stating that "all synods or councils, since the Apostles' times, whether general or particular, may err; and many have erred. Therefore they are not to be made the rule of faith, or practice; but to be used as a help in both" (Westminster Confession, XXXI/iii). In sum, only to the degree that their creedal pronouncements are consonant with the teaching of Scripture are they to be regarded as authoritative, and even so their entire authority is only derived from Scripture itself.

On the other hand, the Roman Catholic Church insists, first, that church tradition possesses an authority equal to that of Scripture itself and, second, that the church should receive and venerate its tradition with the same piety and reverence that it gives the Old and New Testaments.[53] Very cleverly, the *Catechism of the Catholic Church* (1994) blurs the distinction between canonical revelation (which is indisputably authoritative) and Rome's own later tradition (which is noncanonical and therefore not authoritative) when it declares:

> The Tradition here in question comes from the apostles and hands on what they received from Jesus' teaching and example and what they learned from the Holy Spirit. The first generation of Christians did not yet have a written New Testament, and the New Testament itself demonstrates the process of living Tradition. (para. 83)

It is true that the first Christians did not have a written New Testament, but they did have the inspired apostles living among them to give them the authoritative revelational instruction that is referred to as "the traditions," (τὰς παραδόσεις, *tas paradoseis*, lit., "the things passed on") in 2 Thessalonians 2:15. But it is a giant leap in logic simply to assert, because there was such a thing as "apostolic tradition" in the New Testament age, that *that* tradition justifies the positing of an ongoing "process of living Tradition" after the close of the New Testament canon.

The problem with the dual authority of Scripture and later tradition, of course, is that the Scriptures cannot (and in fact do not) really govern the content of tradition, not to mention the fact that with this view of tradition, given Rome's view of itself as a *living* organism in its capacity as the "depository of tradition," there can

---

53. Vatican II's *Dei Verbum*, 9 (November 1965), declares that the church "does not derive her certainty about all revealed truths from the holy Scriptures alone. Both Scripture and Tradition must be *accepted and honored with equal sentiments of devotion and reverence*" (emphasis supplied). It is theological overreaching of the worst kind when some over-zealous Roman Catholic apologists find in the statements of John 20:30 and 21:25 grounds for that communion's many later traditions that contradict New Testament teaching.

never be a codification of or limitation placed upon the content of this tradition. As Charles Elliot states: "So far as we are aware, there is no publication which contains a summary of what the Church believes under the head of tradition."[54] As a result, because tradition is free to aver doctrines which are the very antithesis of Scripture teaching while yet claiming divine authority, becoming thereby bad tradition as recent history will verify (see the papal dogmas of the immaculate conception in 1854, papal infallibility in 1870, and the assumption of Mary in 1950), the church is left vulnerable to every kind of innovation. Moreover, Rome's teaching on tradition impiously implies, since Protestantism self-consciously rejects one of the two "indispensable media of divine revelation," that Protestantism cannot possibly be the church of Christ, when in fact it is Rome with its dogmatic deliverances from the Council of Trent to the present day that is perverting Christian truth by its traditions of men.

A word must be said about the willingness of the Confession to include within the "whole counsel of God" truths that "by good and necessary consequence may be deduced from Scripture." Some Christians have urged that logical deduction adds to Scripture and therefore must be resisted. This is wrong. Validly deduced truths add nothing to the overall truth of Scripture. John Frame has rightly declared:

> Implication does not add anything new [in syllogistic argument]; it merely rearranges information contained in the premises. It takes what is implicit in the premises and states it explicitly. Thus when we learn logical implications of sentences, we are learning more and more of what those sentences *mean*. The conclusion represents part of the meaning of the premises.
> So in theology, logical deductions set forth the meaning of Scripture. . . .
> When it is used rightly, logical deduction adds nothing to Scripture. It merely sets forth what is there. Thus we need not fear any violation of *sola scriptura* as long as we use logic *responsibly*. Logic sets forth the *meaning* of Scripture.[55]

A case in point is the doctrine of the Trinity. In no single passage of Scripture is the full doctrine of the Trinity set forth. But the church has deduced "by good and necessary consequence," as the implicate of all the Scripture data, the doctrine of the Trinity—to be believed as surely as the explicit declaration of Scripture that God is loving!

One final comment. While the framers of the Confession were absolutely convinced of the Scripture's sufficiency and stated as much, they affirm once again here

---

54. Charles Elliot, *Delineation of Roman Catholicism* (London: J. Mason, 1851), 40.
55. John M. Frame, *The Doctrine of the Knowledge of God* (Phillipsburg, N.J.: Presbyterian and Reformed, 1987), 247.

THE BIBLE'S PERSPICUITY

that "the inward illumination of the Spirit of God [is] necessary for the saving understanding of such things as are revealed in the word." In so doing, they indicated their zeal to keep the source of spiritual life where it must always be kept—directly in God alone. It is the Spirit of God, working immediately and directly by and with the Word of God in the hearts of men, who imparts spiritual life!

THE BIBLE'S PERSPICUITY

> All things in Scripture are not alike plain in themselves, nor alike clear unto all; yet those things which are necessary to be known, believed, and observed, for salvation, are so clearly propounded and opened in some place of Scripture or other, that not only the learned, but the unlearned, in a due use of the ordinary means, may attain unto a sufficient understanding of them. (WCF, I/vii)

As a logical corollary to the Bible's representation of its revelatory and inspired nature, the purpose of this entire activity on God's part was to reveal his ways and works in a comprehensible manner to those to whom his revelation originally came. He "spoke and wrote" in order to be understood. And the prophets, apostles, and indeed Jesus himself, addressed their messages to all the people, and never treated them as intellectual pygmies who were incapable of understanding anything of what they said.

While the Confession acknowledges that "all things in Scripture are not alike plain in themselves, nor clear unto all" (it is this fact, among others, that requires diligent application of both the grammatical-historical method of exegesis and the *analogia Scripturae* principle), the Confession affirms, again against Rome, that "those things which are necessary to be known, believed, and observed, for salvation, are so clearly propounded and opened in some place of Scripture or other, that not only the learned, but the unlearned [even the unlearned unbeliever!—author] in a due use of the ordinary means, may attain unto a sufficient understanding of them."[56] As the Psalmist states, God's Word is a lamp to our feet and a light for our pathway (119:105). Note that the Confession declares that "unlearned"

---

56. A. A. Hodge, *A Commentary on the Confession of Faith* (Philadelphia: Presbyterian Board of Publication and Sabbath-School Work, 1869), 63, writes: "Protestants affirm and Romanists deny (a) that every essential article of faith and rule of practice may be clearly learned from the Scripture; and (b) that private and unlearned Christians may be safely allowed to interpret Scripture for themselves." To illustrate Rome's current attitude in this regard one can cite the *Catechism of the Catholic Church* (1994): "the task of interpretation [of the Word of God, whether in its written form or in the form of Tradition] has been entrusted to the bishops in communion with the successor of Peter, the Bishop of Rome" (para. 85).

men through the utilization of "ordinary means" may come to a knowledge of the truth of Scripture. What are these "ordinary means"? Simply the reading, hearing, and study of the Word. For example, one does not need to be "learned," when reading the Gospels or hearing them read or proclaimed, to discover that they intend to teach that Jesus was born of a virgin, lived a sinless life, performed mighty miracles, died on the cross "as a ransom for many," and rose from the dead on the third day after death. These things are plain, lying on the very face of the Gospels. One does not need to be instructed by a preacher to learn that he must believe on Jesus in order to be saved from the penalty his sins deserve. (This includes the unbeliever, who is certainly capable of following an argument.) All one needs to do in order to discover these things, to put it plainly, is to sit down in a fairly comfortable chair, open the Gospels, and with a good reading lamp, read the Gospels like he would read any other book. Of course, if one *believes* these things to be true, leading to the saving of his soul (that is, believes that the Gospels' affirmations correspond to what God himself believes), another factor has intruded itself into the situation—what the Confession has already described both as the "inward work of the Holy Spirit, bearing witness by and with the word in our hearts" and as the "inward illumination of the Spirit of God."

THE BIBLE'S FINALITY

The Old Testament in Hebrew (which was the native language of the people of God of old) and the New Testament in Greek (which at the time of the writing of it was most generally known to the nations), being immediately inspired by God, and by His singular care and providence kept pure in all ages, are therefore authentical [i. e., reliable, trustworthy]; so as in all controversies of religion *the church is finally to appeal unto them*. But because these original tongues are not known to all the people of God who have right unto, and interest in, the Scriptures, and are commanded, in the fear of God, to read and search them, therefore they are to be translated into the language of every people unto which they come, that the word of God dwelling plentifully in all, they may worship him in an acceptable manner, and through patience and comfort of the Scriptures, may have hope. (WCF, I/viii, emphasis supplied)

The Supreme Judge, by which all controversies of religion are to be determined, and all decrees of councils, opinions of ancient writers, doctrines of men, and private spirits, are to be examined, and in whose sentence we are to rest, can be no other but *the Holy Spirit speaking in the Scripture*. (WCF, I/x, emphasis supplied)

No attribute of Scripture is more significant than its attribute of finality, for this attribute is the Bible's response to the burning question of our day: "What should be our *final* authority in all religious controversy?" The Confession declares that "in all controversies of religion, the church is *finally* to appeal unto [the Old and New Testaments in their original languages of Hebrew and Greek respectively]." John Murray quite properly notes that the confessional expression of scriptural finality here is oriented admittedly to the refutation of Rome's appeal to church tradition and the "living voice" of God in the person of the Roman pontiff on the one hand, and to the claim to special revelation by means of mystical inner light on the other,[57] but its teaching militates equally against the claims of Islam respecting the Koran and the Mormon claims respecting the Book of Mormon.[58] By its appeal to the Bible's original languages of Hebrew and Greek, it also opposes the authoritative position which Rome has granted the Latin Vulgate.[59] Murray further writes:

> Since we no longer have prophets, since we do not have our Lord with us as he was with the disciples, and since we do not have new organs of revelation as in apostolic times, Scripture in its total extent, according to the conception entertained by our Lord and his apostles, is the only revelation of the mind and will of God available to us. This is what the finality of Scripture means for us; it is the only extant revelatory Word of God.
>
> ... It is only in and through Scripture that we have any knowledge of or contact with him who is the image of the invisible God ... Without Scripture we are excluded completely from the knowledge, faith, and fellowship of him who is the effulgence of the Father's glory and the transcript of his being, as destitute of the Word of life as the disciples would have been if Jesus had not disclosed himself through his spoken word. ...
>
> Our dependence upon Scripture is total. Without it we are bereft of revelatory Word from God, from the counsel of God "respecting all things necessary for his own glory, man's salvation, faith and life."
>
> ... It is because we have not esteemed and prized the perfection of Scripture and its finality, that we have resorted to other techniques, expedients, and methods of dealing with the dilemma that confronts us all if we are alive to the needs of this hour ... let us also know that it is not the tradition of the past, not a precious heritage, and

---

57. See John Murray, "The Finality and Sufficiency of Scripture," in *Collected Writings of John Murray* (Edinburgh: Banner of Truth, 1976), 1:16–22.
58. By his parable of the wicked farmers (Matt. 21:33–40 and the Synoptic parallels), Jesus taught the finality of his messianic investiture, representing himself as the *last*, the *final* ambassador, after whose sending none higher can come. The New Testament writers, and they alone, became his chosen vessels to give to his church the concluding revelation he wanted it to have (see John 14:25–26; 16:12–15).
59. Because this article says what it says about the original languages, any seminary under the governance of a church court committed to the Westminster Standards is under obligation to teach the original languages to those men who are studying for the ministry.

not the labours of the fathers, that are to serve this generation and this hour, but the Word of the living and abiding God deposited for us in Holy Scripture.[60]

The second half of I/viii declares the right of all to whom the gospel comes to have and use vernacular versions. This is so self-evidently proper that nothing needs to be said about the propriety of the nations possessing the Word of God in their native tongues.

But something should be said about the nature of these translations or versions. Are they to be regarded as the Word of God? Are they authoritative? Are they inspired? We should not hesitate to affirm that to the degree translations and versions capture the authorial intention of the autographs, to that same degree these translations are the Word of God and are therefore authoritative. Theirs, of course, is a *derived* authority, while the authority of the autographs is an intrinsic, immediate and inherent authority. While one may refer to translations and versions as "inspired Scripture" in the sense that they are copies of the inspired autographs, *only the autographs were directly inspired and thus inerrant.* Copies and versions of the autographs are not directly inspired and may contain errors of various kinds.[61] The discipline of textual criticism has demonstrated that variant readings—mostly of an inconsequential nature[62]—have occurred in textual transmission from one level of copying to another through copyists' unintentional mistakes and intentional efforts to provide aids to the reader's comprehension.

---

60. Murray, *Collected Writings*, 1:19–22.
61. For examples of the various kinds of errors that have found their way into extant texts of the New Testament, see Kurt Aland and Barbara Aland, *The Text of the New Testament* (Grand Rapids, Mich.: Eerdmans, 1987), 275–311.
62. Douglas Stuart, "Inerrancy and Textual Criticism," in *Inerrancy and Common Sense*, ed. Roger R. Nicole and J. Ramsey Michaels (Grand Rapids, Mich.: Baker, 1980), 98, writes in this connection:

    The vast majority of textual divergencies involve an inability to choose between equally plausible and usually synonymous wordings, simple haplographies (losses of words) that do not affect the overall meaning of a passage, or conflations (adding words from elsewhere in the same book) which are often quite helpful to the sense of the passage.

    Thus it would not be correct to suggest that the various ancient versions of the Bible are in hopeless disagreement with one another, or that the percentage of textual corruptions is so high as to render questionable large blocks of Scripture. Rather, it is fair to say that the verses, chapters, and books of the Bible would read largely the same, and would leave the same impression with the reader, even if one adopted virtually every possible *alternative* reading to those now serving as the basis for current English translations. In fact, absolutely nothing essential to the major doctrines of the Bible would be affected by any responsible decision in the area of textual criticism. . . .

    A comparison of sample verses from several popular modern English versions of the Bible will give any reader a general idea of what the range of differences between texts might be—the modern English translations are themselves texts, and they roughly parallel the ancient versions in the kinds and varieties of divergencies that are possible under normal circumstances.

It has often been argued that the distinction that evangelicals draw between inerrant autographs and errant apographs (copies) is highly tendentious inasmuch as we are not in possession of the autographs. All we have are errant copies of the autographs, and there is no way to find out whether the errors in the copies were not also present first in the autographs. But it is imperative for *theological* reasons that we insist that any and all textual errors occurred at the apographic levels and *not* in the original autographs. For if God did in fact inspire the original writers to inscripturate his word, we reflect negatively, if not blasphemously, upon his nature as the God of truth, the ultimate Author of Scripture, if we allow for errors in the originals. It would mean, plainly and simply, that the God of truth inspired the production of a rule of faith and practice for his church which contains errors![63]

The significance of the distinction between inerrant autograph and errant apograph may be seen from another angle. What difference would it make, some have asked, if the autographs did contain some of the errors that are present in the copies? Is not the end result of textual criticism and hermeneutics by both nonevangelical and evangelical essentially the same? As far as the results of textual criticism and hermeneutics as such are concerned, the answer to this last query is yes. By sound application of the canons of textual criticism, most by far of the errors in the text may be detected and corrected. And both nonevangelical and evangelical can properly exegete the critically established text. But the nonevangelical who fails to make a distinction between the inerrancy of the autographs and the errancy of the copies, after he has done his textual criticism and grammatical-historical exegesis, is still left with the question, Is the statement which I have now reached by my text-critical work and my hermeneutics true? He can only attempt to determine this on other (extrabiblical) grounds, but he will never know for sure if his determination is correct. The evangelical, however, who

---

63. See Greg L. Bahnsen, "The Inerrancy of the Autographs," in *Inerrancy*, ed. Norman B. Geisler (Grand Rapids, Mich.: Zondervan, 1980), 151–93, for a fuller treatment of this *extremely* important subject. With regard to our immediate concern, Bahnsen employs the following happy illustration:

> My Old Cambridge edition of a Shakespearean play may contain mistaken or disputed words in comparison with the original text of Shakespeare, but that does not lead me to the extreme conclusion that the volume on my desk is not a work of Shakespeare. It *is* Shakespearean—to the degree that it reflects the author's own work, which (because of the generally accepted high degree of correlation) is a qualification that need not be explicitly and often stated. So also my American Standard Version of the Bible contains mistaken or disputed words with respect to the autographic text of Scripture, but it is still the very Word of God . . . to the degree that it reflects the original work of God, which (because of the objective, universally accepted, and outstanding degree of correlation in the light of textual criticism) is a qualification that is very seldom in need of being stated.

draws the distinction between inerrant autograph and errant apograph, once he has done proper text-critical analysis which assures him that he is working with the original text and properly applied the canons of exegesis to that text, rests in the confidence that his labor has resulted in the attainment of truth.

Some critical scholars have suggested that the distinction between inerrant autographs and errant apographs is of fairly recent vintage, indeed, an evangelical ploy to minimize the impact of the "assured results of textual criticism" upon their position. This is erroneous. Augustine's statement, which represents the opinion generally of the Patristic Age, is a sufficient answer to demonstrate that the distinction is not a recent novelty:

> I have learned to defer this respect and honor to the canonical books of Scripture alone, that I most firmly believe that no one of their authors has committed any error in writing. And if in their writings I am perplexed by anything which seems to me contrary to truth, I do not doubt that it is nothing else than either that the manuscript is corrupt, or that the translator has not followed what was said, or that I have myself failed to understand it. But when I read other authors, however eminent they may be in sanctity and learning, I do not necessarily believe a thing is true because they think so, but because they have been able to convince me, either on the authority of the canonical writers or by a probable reason which is not inconsistent with truth. And I think that you, my brother, feel the same way; moreover, I say, I do not believe that you want your books to be read as if they were those of Prophets and Apostles, about whose writings, free of all error, it is unlawful to doubt.[64]

Finally, when the Confession states that *"the Supreme [i.e., Final] Judge, by which all controversies of religion are to be determined, and all decrees of councils, opinions of ancient writers, doctrines of men, and private spirits, are to be examined, and in whose sentence we are to rest, can be no other but the Holy Spirit speaking in the Scripture"* (I/x), we must be clear that this is not a third reference to the *testimonium Spiritus Sancti* (see Arts. v and vi). Murray explains:

> In section x the Confession is dealing with the Scripture as canon, and uses the expression "the Holy Spirit speaking in the Scripture" to remind us that Scripture is not a dead word but the living and abiding speech of the Holy Spirit [see Heb 3:7; 10:15, 17]. The Reformers needed to emphasize this quality of Scripture in order to offset the plea of Rome that a living voice is necessary for the faith and guidance of the Church and also to meet the same argument of enthusiasts for the inner voice of the Spirit in the believer.[65]

---

64. Augustine's *Epist.* 82, to Jerome.
65. Murray, *Collected Writings*, 1:16–17.

In other words, according to I/x, the Scriptures are the Word of God in such a sense that to appeal to them is really to appeal directly to the Holy Spirit himself who speaks in all the Scriptures.

These then are the attributes of Scripture which the Westminster Assembly of divines believed could be legitimately affirmed on the basis of the Scriptures' self-testimony. Liberal and neoorthodox theologians alike have often charged that to ascribe these properties to Scripture is to ascribe to the finite creature perfections properly belonging only to the Creator, and this is to commit blasphemy. Moreover, such reverence as this ascription entails is an act of worship, and this is to commit idolatry, more specifically, bibliolatry.

How shall we respond to these charges? Beside pointing out to these critics that an *infallible* Bible is the only basis upon which they could know for sure what perfections properly belong to the Creator, I would say two further things: First, because the Bible is God's Word, it would necessarily partake of the indefectibility of God. Far from this being blasphemy, I would urge that not to ascribe to *God's* Word the perfection of God's truth is to commit blasphemy. Second, no evangelical has ever worshiped the Bible; rather, he reverences it because it is God's Word and hence the only true light on the path that leads to the one Triune God. Such reverence is not bibliolatry; it is simply the honor properly due the Word of the living God whose word it is. So while it is true that evangelicals seek the Lord who lives "beyond the sacred page," it is equally true that they seek the Lord *through* a study of the sacred pages of his Word which came to them from the world which they have not yet seen except with eyes of faith.

CHAPTER FOUR

The Nature of Biblical Truth

TWO ADDITIONAL MATTERS pertaining to the nature of biblical truth have to be addressed before any treatment of the Bible as God's inspired Word is complete. The first has to do with the nature of the assertions that Holy Scripture makes about God and reality in general: Are they univocally or analogically true? And is the knowledge which we derive from these assertions of Holy Scripture univocally or only analogically true? Some theologians today insist that God's knowledge of himself and of things in general, and human knowledge of these same things, even though the latter accords with God's intended meanings in revealed Scripture, never coincide at any single point. The relationship between these "two knowledge contents" is said to be "analogical" and not "univocal."

The second issue has to do with the matter of paradox. Is paradox a legitimate hermeneutical category in the interpretation of Scripture? Again, in our day some of our finest evangelical scholars insist that, even when correctly interpreted, the Scriptures will often represent their truths to even the *believing* human existent—not least because of its analogical character—in paradoxical terms, that is, in terms "taught unmistakably in the infallible Word of God," which, while "not actually contradictory," nevertheless "cannot possibly be reconciled before the bar of human reason."[1]

---

1. R. B. Kuiper, cited approvingly by George W. Marston, *The Voice of Authority* (Philadelphia: Presbyterian and Reformed, 1960), 16. Kuiper's entire statement is as follows:

    A paradox is not, as Barth thinks, two truths which are actually contradictory. Truth is not irrational. Nor is a paradox two truths which are difficult to reconcile but can be reconciled before the bar of human reason. That is a seeming paradox. But when two truths, both taught unmistakably in the infallible Word of God, cannot possibly be reconciled before the bar of human reason, then you have a paradox.

THE NATURE OF THE BIBLE'S ASSERTIONS ABOUT GOD AND OUR RESULTANT KNOWLEDGE OF GOD

Is biblical revelation about God univocal or analogical? Can we know God as he is in himself, or is an analogical comprehension the most we can hope for?[2] The difference is this: A given predicate applied to separate subjects *univocally* would intend that the subjects possess the predicate in a precisely identical sense. The opposite of univocality is equivocality, which attaches a given predicate to separate subjects in a completely different or unrelated sense. Now lying between univocality and equivocality is analogy. A predicate employed *analogically* intends a relationship between separate subjects based upon comparison or proportion. Can the content of God's knowledge of himself and the content of man's knowledge that is gained from God's verbal revelation be univocal (the same), or must it inevitably be either equivocal (different) or analogical (partly alike, partly not alike, that is, proportional to the specific subject's nature)?

Thomas Aquinas (1224–1274) was one of the first Christian theologians to deal formally with this issue.[3] He was not the first, of course, to address the issue of the nature of knowledge and the functions and limits of language. Augustine (354–430), for example, had grappled with these issues in his treatise *De magistro* and, incidentally, had come to radically different conclusions. Aquinas declared that nothing can properly be predicated of God and man in a univocal sense. To do so and to say, for example, that God and man are both "good" and to intend by "good" the same meaning, is to ignore the difference between the essences of God the Creator (his existence is identical with his essence) and of man the creature (his existence and his essence are two different matters). But Aquinas saw too that to intend an equivocal meaning for "good" would lead to complete ambiguity and epistemological skepticism. Therefore he urged the way of proportionality or analogy as the via media between univocality and equivocality. In other words, the assertion, "God and man are both good," means analogically that man's goodness is proportional to man as God's goodness is proportional to God, but it also means that the goodness intended cannot be the same goodness in both cases. In sum, of this Aquinas was certain: nothing can be predicated of God and man in the univocal sense. Rather, only analogical predication is properly possible when speaking of the relationship between them.

But now a problem arises, for what is it about any analogy that saves it from becoming a complete equivocality? Is it not the univocal element implicit within it?

---

2. I have adapted pages 96–102 from Robert L. Reymond, *Preach the Word!* (Edinburgh: Rutherford House Books, 1990), 17–26.
3. See his *Summa Contra Gentiles* XXXII–XXXIV.

For example, if I assert that an analogy may be drawn between an apple and an orange, do I not intend to suggest that the apple and the orange, obviously different in some respects, are the same in at least one respect? Why, otherwise, would I be drawing attention to the relationship between them? While it is true that the one respect in which I perceive that they are similar will not be immediately apparent to anyone else without further explanation on my part, it should be clear nonetheless to everyone, if I assert that they are analogous one to the other, that I believe that in some sense a univocal feature exists between them—in this case, it may be that I have in mind that they are both fruit, or that they are both spherical, or that they both have extension in space or have mass. I intend to suggest that, for all their differences, they have something in common. The predicate indicates something that is equally true of both. What I am urging here is that the success of any analogy turns on the strength of the univocal element in it. Or as Edward John Carnell has stated, the basis for any analogy is nonanalogical, that is, univocal.[4] Aquinas's dilemma is that he wanted to have his cake and eat it too. He wanted to affirm the analogous relationship between God and man on the one hand, but he denied all univocal coincidence in predication respecting them on the other. But if he affirms the relationship between God and man to be truly analogous, he cannot consistently deny that in some sense a univocal element exists between them. Or if he denies all univocal coincidence in predication between God and man, he cannot continue to speak of the predicative relationship between them as one of analogy. As a matter of fact, Gordon H. Clark has argued that Aquinas's doctrine of the *analogia entis* (analogy of being) between God and man is actually not analogical at all but really an equivocality.[5]

How are we to respond to this issue? Let us consider the pronouncements of the widely respected Reformed theologian Cornelius Van Til. In his theology and in his apologetics Van Til always made it his goal to be true to a single and initial ontological vision—the distinction between the Creator and the creature. Throughout his writings Van Til insisted again and again that human knowledge is and can only be analogical to divine knowledge.[6] What this means for Van Til

---

4. Edward John Carnell, *An Introduction to Christian Apologetics* (Grand Rapids, Mich.: Eerdmans, 1948), 147.
5. If Clark is correct, and I am persuaded that he is, Aquinas's natural theology, which was grounded in his understanding of the *analogia entis,* is also defective, for he was, of necessity, working with two different meanings for the word "existence" as that single predicate applies to God and to sensory data; thus his argument from the existence of sensory data to the existence of God commits the error of equivocating, that is, using a single word with two different meanings in the same argument.
6. See, for example, Cornelius Van Til, *The Defense of the Faith* (Philadelphia: Presbyterian and Reformed, 1955), 56, 65, and *Common Grace* (Philadelphia: Presbyterian and Reformed, 1954), 28.

is the express rejection of any and all qualitative coincidence between the content of God's mind and the content of man's mind. That is to say, according to Van Til, not only is God's knowledge prior to and necessary to man's knowledge, which is always secondary and derivative (with this I am in total agreement), not only is God's knowledge self-validating, whereas man's knowledge is dependent upon God's prior self-validating knowledge for its justification (with this I am also in agreement), but also for Van Til this means that man qualitatively knows nothing as God knows a thing.

In his *An Introduction to Systematic Theology*, Van Til writes: "All human predication is analogical re-interpretation of God's pre-interpretation. Thus the incomprehensibility of God must be taught with respect to *any* revelational proposition."[7] In his introduction to Warfield's *The Inspiration and Authority of the Bible*, Van Til declares:

> When the Christian restates the content of Scriptural revelation in the form of a "system," such a system is based upon and therefore analogous to the "existential system" that God himself possesses. Being based upon God's revelation it is on the one hand, fully true and, on the other hand, *at no point identical* with the content of the divine mind."[8]

In a Complaint filed against the presbytery that voted to sustain Gordon H. Clark's ordination examination, to which Van Til affixed his name as a signatory, it was declared a "tragic fact" that Clark's epistemology "has led him to obliterate the qualitative distinction between the contents of the divine mind and the knowledge which is possible to the creature."[9] The Complaint also affirmed: "We dare not maintain that [God's] knowledge and our knowledge coincide *at any single point.*"[10] It is important to note here that it is not the way that God and human beings know a thing that the Complaint declares is different. Both the complainants and Clark agreed that God knows everything by eternal intuition whereas people learn what they know (excluding certain innate ideas) discursively. Rather, insists Van Til and certain of his students, it is the content of man's knowledge that is qualitatively distinct from God's knowledge.

Because of his particular ontological vision Van Til insists that all verbal revelation coming from God to humans will of necessity be "anthropomorphic," that is,

---

7. Cornelius Van Til, *In Defense of the Faith*, vol. 5, *An Introduction to Systematic Theology* (Nutley, N.J.: Presbyterian and Reformed, 1976), 171, emphasis his.
8. Cornelius Van Til, introduction to *The Inspiration and Authority of the Bible*, by Benjamin B. Warfield (Philadelphia: Presbyterian and Reformed, 1948), 33, emphasis supplied; see also his *An Introduction to Systematic Theology*, 165, for the same contention.
9. Minutes of the Twelfth General Assembly of the Orthodox Presbyterian Church, 1945, 15.
10. Ibid., 14, emphasis original.

it must assume "human form" in order to be understood at the level of creaturely finite comprehension. But Van Til is equally insistent that this divine self-revelation, by the Spirit's enabling illumination, can produce in men a "true" knowledge of God, although their knowledge will be only "analogical" to God's knowledge of himself— it will never correspond to God's knowledge at any single point! How Van Til can regard this "never corresponds" knowledge as "true" knowledge is, to say the least, a serious problem. Perhaps he means that the Creator is willing to regard as "true" the knowledge that men derive from his self-revelation to them even though it is not univocal knowledge at any single point, because due to human finiteness he had to adapt his revelation to creaturely finite comprehension. God's verbal revelation to human beings, in other words, since it is "creature-oriented" (that is, "analogical"), is not a univocal statement of his understanding of himself or of anything else and thus can never produce anything higher than a creaturely ("analogical") comprehension of God or of anything else. If this is what Van Til means, it is difficult to see how, with his explicit rejection of the univocal element (see his "corresponds at no single point") in man's so-called "analogical" knowledge of God, Van Til can rescue such knowledge from being in actuality a total equivocality and no true knowledge at all. It is also difficult to see how he can rescue God from the irrationality in accepting as true what in fact (if Van Til is correct) he knows all the while coincides at no single point with his own knowledge, which is both true and the standard of truth.

Against all this, Clark contended that Van Til's position leads to total human ignorance:

> If God knows all truths and knows the correct meaning of every proposition, and if no proposition means to man what it means to God, so that God's knowledge and man's knowledge do not coincide at any single point, it follows by rigorous necessity that man can have no truth at all.[11]

He further argues:

> If God and man know, there must with the differences be at least one point of similarity; for if there were no point of similarity it would be inappropriate to use the one term knowledge in both cases. . . . If God has the truth and if man has only an analogy [this "analogy" containing no univocal element], it follows that he (man) does not have the truth.[12]

---

11. Gordon H. Clark, "Apologetics," in *Contemporary Evangelical Thought*, ed. Carl F. H. Henry (New York: Harper Channel, 1957), 159.
12. Gordon H. Clark, "The Bible as Truth," *Bibliotheca Sacra* (April 1957): 163.

Clark illustrates his point this way:

> If . . . we think that David was King of Israel, and God's thoughts are not ours, then it follows that God does not think David was King of Israel. David in God's mind was perchance prime minister of Babylon.
>
> To avoid this irrationality, . . . we must insist that truth is the same for God and man. Naturally, we may not know the truth about some matters. But if we know anything at all, what we know must be identical with what God knows. God knows the truth, and unless we know something God knows, our ideas are untrue. It is absolutely essential therefore to insist that there is an area of coincidence between God's mind and our mind. One example, as good as any, is the one already used, viz., David was King of Israel.[13]

Clark concludes:

> If God is omnipotent, he can tell men the plain, unvarnished, literal truth. He can tell them David was King of Israel, he can tell them he is omnipotent, he can tell them he created the world, and . . . he can tell them all this in positive, literal, non-analogical, non-symbolic terms.[14]

Of course, as far as the extent or quantity of their respective knowledge data is concerned, Clark readily acknowledged that God knows more and always will know more than men and women—this hardly even needs saying. But if we are to allow to human beings any knowledge at all, Clark urged, we must insist that if God and man both truly know anything, then what they know must have some point of correspondence as far as the content of their knowledge is concerned. I wholeheartedly concur, and I believe that Francis Schaeffer's dictum is right on target: human beings may indeed have "true though not exhaustive knowledge."

Certain biblical references seem to support Van Til's contention that God's knowledge and man's knowledge are always and at every point qualitatively distinct. Van Til himself pointed to Deuteronomy 29:29, Job 11:7–8, Psalm 145:3, Isaiah 40:28, 55:8–9, Matthew 11:27, Luke 10:22, John 1:18, 6:46, Romans 11:33, and 1 Timothy 6:16 as supporting his contention that with respect to any revelational proposition God still remains, even after the revelatory act, the incomprehensible God.[15] However, a close examination of these verses will show that, while they do not deny the immeasurable wisdom and knowledge of God, they are primarily concerned with

---

13. Gordon H. Clark, "The Axiom of Revelation," in *The Philosophy of Gordon H. Clark*, ed. Ronald H. Nash (Philadelphia: Presbyterian and Reformed, 1968), 76-77.
14. Ibid., 78.
15. Minutes, 12.

underscoring the human need of propositional revelation to know God savingly. Job 11:7–8, Psalm 145:3, Isaiah 40:28, Romans 11:33, and 1 Timothy 6:16, while certainly affirming the infinity of God, need simply mean that men and women, beginning with themselves and refusing the benefit of divine revelation, cannot, as Paul so forcefully declares in 1 Corinthians 1:21, come to God through their own wisdom, or, said somewhat differently, that men and women will always be dependent upon divine informational revelation for a true and saving knowledge of God. Franz Delitzsch captures the essence of the intention of these verses when he comments on Psalm 145:3:

> Of Yahweh's "greatness" . . . there is no searching out, i.e. it is so abysmally deep that no searching can reach its bottom (as in Isa. xl. 28, Job xi. 7 sq.). It has, however, been revealed, and is being revealed continually, and is for this very reason thus celebrated in ver. 4.[16]

As for Deuteronomy 29:29, Matthew 11:27, Luke 10:22, and John 1:18, 6:46 (see v. 45), these verses actually teach that human beings can know God and his thoughts truly to the degree that he reveals himself in his spoken word. Finally, Isaiah 55:8–9 far from depicting "the gulf which separates the divine knowledge from human knowledge,"[17] actually holds out the real possibility that people may know God's thoughts and urges them to turn away from their own thoughts and to learn God's thoughts from him. In 55:7 God calls upon the wicked man to forsake his way and thoughts. Where is he to turn? To the Lord, of course (55:6–7). Why should he forsake his way and thoughts? "Because," says the Lord, "my thoughts are not your thoughts, neither are your ways my ways" (55:8). The entire context, far from affirming that God's ways and thoughts are beyond the capacity of humans to know, on the contrary, expressly calls upon the wicked man to turn away from his ways and thoughts and to seek God's ways and thoughts. In doing so, the wicked man gains ways and thoughts which, just as the heavens transcend the earth, transcend his own. Far from teaching that an unbridgeable gulf exists between God's thoughts and our thoughts, these verses actually call upon the wicked man, in repentance and humility, to seek and to think God's thoughts after him. Again, Franz Delitzsch rightly interprets these verses:

> The appeal, to leave their own way and their own thoughts, and yield themselves to God the Redeemer, and to His word, is urged on the ground of the heaven-wide difference between the ways and thoughts of this God and the despairing

---

16. Franz Delitzsch, *Biblical Commentary on the Psalms* (Grand Rapids, Mich.: Eerdmans, n.d.), 3:389.
17. Minutes, 12.

thoughts of men (Ch. xl. 27, xlix. 24), and their aimless labyrinthine ways.... On what side the heaven-wide elevation is to be seen, is shown by what follows. [God's thoughts] are not so fickle, so unreliable, or so powerless.[18]

None of these verses teaches that man's knowledge of God can be only at best "analogical," in the Van Tilian sense, to God's knowledge. On the contrary, some of them expressly declare that in dependence upon God's propositional self-revelation in Scripture, human beings can know some of God's thoughts truly, that is, univocally (though of course not exhaustively), that is, that they can know a revealed proposition in the same sense that God knows it and has revealed it.

None of this is intended to suggest that the Scriptures contain no figures of speech. Of course they do. For example, the Bible is filled with metaphors (Ps. 18:2—"The LORD is my rock, my fortress") and similes (Isa. 1:30—"You will be like an oak with fading leaves, like a garden without water."). But metaphors and similes intend univocal meanings, and once the appropriate canons of grammatical-historical hermeneutics have determined the precise literal meaning of a metaphor, its meaning must be precisely the same for God as for man.

Christians should be overwhelmed by the magnitude of this simple truth that they take so much for granted—that *the eternal God has deigned to share with us some of the truths that are on his mind. He condescends to elevate us poor undeserving sinners by actually sharing with us a portion of what he knows.* Accordingly, since the Scriptures require that saving faith be grounded in true knowledge (see Rom. 10:13–14), the church must vigorously oppose any linguistic or revelational theory, however well-intended, that would take from men and women the only ground of their knowledge of God and, accordingly, their only hope of salvation. Against the theory of human knowledge that would deny to it the possibility of univocal correspondence at any point with God's mind as to content, it is vitally important that we come down on the side of Christian reason and work with a Christian theory of knowledge that insists upon the possibility of at least some identity between the content of God's knowledge and the content of man's knowledge.[19]

---

18. Franz Delitzsch, *Commentary on Isaiah* (Grand Rapids, Mich.: Eerdmans, n.d.), 2:358.
19. Some of Van Til's students have attempted to extricate their revered mentor from the serious difficulty in which he has ensnared himself. John M. Frame, in his monograph *Van Til: The Theologian* (Phillipsburg, N.J.: Pilgrim, 1976), argues that Van Til means nothing more by his denial of identity of content between the divine and human minds than that God's knowledge, unlike human knowledge, is original and self-validating (21). It is true that Van Til does teach this, and with such teaching I have no quarrel. But I have to agree with Jim Halsey who argues in his review article, "A Preliminary Critique of *Van Til: The Theologian*" (*Westminster Theological Journal* xxxix [Fall 1976]: 120-36), that Van Til indeed intends, because of "ontological considerations," to deny *qualitative* identity of knowledge content in the divine and human minds, and

PARADOX AS A HERMENEUTICAL CATEGORY

Bible students should be solicitous to interpret the Scriptures in a noncontradictory way; they should strive to harmonize Scripture with Scripture because the Scriptures reflect the thought of a single divine mind.[20]

But many of our finest modern evangelical scholars are insisting that even after the human interpreter has understood the Bible correctly, it will often represent its truths to the human existent—even the *believing* human existent—in *paradoxical* terms, that is, in terms "taught unmistakably in the infallible Word of God," which, while not actually contradictory, nevertheless "cannot possibly be reconciled before

---

that Frame has missed Van Til's point (128-31) and accordingly has not accurately represented his theory of knowledge (133). I suggest that the quotations from Van Til which I have already offered support Halsey rather than Frame. Gilbert Weaver, both in *Jerusalem and Athens*, ed. E. R. Geehan (Phillipsburg, N.J.: Presbyterian and Reformed, 1971), 323-27, and in *The Philosophy of Gordon H. Clark* (303-5), also contends that by "human analogical thought" Van Til only intends to refer to the "process of reasoning" in man and not to his knowledge content as such. If this is all that Van Til intends, one wonders what all the fuss was about back in 1945 between Van Til and Clark over the doctrine of the incomprehensibility of God, since both agreed that the divine and human "reasoning processes" were different, God's being eternally "intuitive," man's being in the main discursive. Consequently, I do not agree with Frame or Weaver (neither does Ronald H. Nash), since Van Til himself says, as we have noted, that a proper doctrine of human analogical knowledge will deny all qualitative coincidence between the content of God's knowledge and the content of man's knowledge. But this is no longer analogy at all but a form of equivocality, which God, according to Van Til, chooses to call true although it coincides at no point with truth. This contention ultimately ascribes irrationality to God and ignorance to man, and hence has no legitimate place in a Christian epistemology.

In both his *The Doctrine of the Knowledge of God* (Phillipsburg, N.J.: Presbyterian and Reformed, 1987) and his more recent *Cornelius Van Til: An Analysis of His Thought* (Phillipsburg, N.J.: Presbyterian and Reformed, 1995), 92-93, in connection with his discussion of the Van Til/Clark controversy, Frame has continued to defend (not uncritically by any means, to be sure) Van Til's basic view regarding the analogical character of man's knowledge by insisting that both men, because each emphasized his particular "perspective," simply failed to understood the real concern of the other. He urges that his proposed "multiperspectivalism in theology helps restore the proper balance, because it helps us to see that some doctrines that are apparently opposed are actually equivalent, presenting the same truth from various vantage points" (*Knowledge*, 235; *Analysis*, 170-75). Frame's refusal to dismiss Van Til's faulty "perspective" on human analogical knowledge is, in my opinion, part of the explanation for what I perceive as weaknesses in Frame's own "multiperspectival" approach to theology. For the interested reader who desires a brief but fuller analysis of Frame's approach, I would refer him to Mark W. Karlberg, "On the Theological Correlation of Divine and Human Language: A Review Article," *Journal of the Evangelical Theological Society* 32, no. 1 (1989): 99-105.

20. I have adapted pages 103-10 from Reymond, *Preach the Word!*, 27-34.

the bar of human reason."[21] It is commonly declared, for example, that the doctrines of the Trinity, the hypostatic union of the divine and human natures in the person of Christ, God's sovereignty and human responsibility, unconditional election and the sincere offer of the gospel, and particular redemption and the universal offer of the gospel are all biblical paradoxes, each respectively advancing *antithetical* truths unmistakably taught in the Word of God that cannot possibly be reconciled by human reason.[22] James I. Packer likewise affirms the presence of such paradoxes in Scripture in his *Evangelism and the Sovereignty of God*, although he prefers the term "antinomy" to "paradox." He writes:

> An antinomy—in theology, at any rate—is . . . not a real contradiction, though it looks like one. It is an apparent incompatibility between two apparent truths. An antinomy exists when a pair of principles stand side by side, seemingly irreconcilable, yet both undeniable. . . . [An antinomy] is insoluble. . . . What should one do, then, with an antinomy? Accept it for what it is, and learn to live with it. Refuse to regard the apparent contradiction as real.[23]

Cornelius Van Til even declares that, because human knowledge is "only analogical" to God's knowledge, *all* Christian truth will finally be paradoxical, that is, all Christian truth will ultimately appear to be contradictory to the human existent:

> [Antinomies] are involved in the fact that human knowledge can never be completely comprehensive knowledge. Every knowledge transaction has in it somewhere a reference point to God. Now since God is not fully comprehensible to us we are bound to come into what seems to be contradictions in all our knowledge. Our knowledge is analogical and therefore must be paradoxical.[24]
>
> While we shun as poison the idea of the really contradictory we embrace with passion the idea of the *apparently* contradictory.[25]
>
> *All teaching of Scripture is apparently contradictory.*[26]
>
> All the truths of the Christian religion have of necessity the appearance of being contradictory. . . . We do not fear to accept that which has the appearance of being contradictory. . . . In the case of common grace, as in the case of every other biblical doctrine, we should seek to take all the factors of Scripture teach-

---

21. R. B. Kuiper, cited approvingly by George W. Marston, *The Voice of Authority*, 16.
22. Marston, *The Voice of Authority*, 17, 21, 70, 78, 87.
23. James I. Packer, *Evangelism and the Sovereignty of God* (Chicago: InterVarsity Press, 1961), 18-25.
24. Van Til, *The Defense of the Faith*, 61, emphasis supplied.
25. Cornelius Van Til, *Common Grace and the Gospel* (Philadelphia: Presbyterian and Reformed, 1973), 9.
26. Ibid., 142, emphasis original.

ing and bind them together into systematic relations with one another as far as we can. But we do not expect to have a logically deducible relationship between one doctrine and another. We expect to have only an analogical system.²⁷

What should one say respecting this oft-repeated notion that the Bible will often (always, according to Van Til) set forth its truths in irreconcilable terms? To say the least, one must conclude, if such is the case, that it condemns at the outset as futile even the attempt at the systematic (orderly) theology that Van Til calls for in the last source cited, since it is impossible to reduce to a system irreconcilable paradoxes that steadfastly resist all attempts at harmonious systematization. One must be content simply to live theologically with a series of "discontinuities."²⁸

Now if nothing more could or were to be said, this is already problematical enough because of the implications such a construction carries regarding the nature of biblical truth. But more can and must be said. First, the proffered definition of "paradox" (or antinomy) as two truths which are both unmistakably taught in the Word of God but which also cannot possibly be reconciled before the bar of human reason is itself inherently problematical, for the one who so defines the term is suggesting by implication that either he knows by means of an omniscience that is not normally in human possession that no one is capable of reconciling the truths in question or he has somehow universally polled everyone who has ever lived, is living now, and will live in the future and has discovered that not one has been able, is able, or will be able to reconcile the truths. But it goes without saying that neither of these conditions is or can be true. Therefore, the very assertion that there are paradoxes, so defined, in Scripture is seriously flawed by the terms of the definition itself. There is no way to know if such a phenomenon is present in Scripture. Merely because any number of scholars have failed to reconcile to their satisfaction two given truths of Scripture is no proof that the truths cannot be harmonized. And if just one scholar claims to have reconciled the truths to his or her own satisfaction, this *ipso facto* renders the definition both gratuitous and suspect.

Second, while those who espouse the presence in Scripture of paradoxes are solicitous to point out that these paradoxes are *only* apparent and not actual contradictions, they seem to be oblivious to the fact that, if actually noncontradictory truths can appear as contradictories and if no amount of study or reflection can remove the contradiction, there is no available means to distinguish between this

---

27. Ibid., 165-66.
28. Happily, and not unexpectedly, Van Til's practice here is much better than his theory. In fact, John M. Frame in his *Cornelius Van Til: An Analysis of His Thought*, 161-65, demonstrates that Van Til is "one of the most systematic of thinkers," stressing logical relationships among doctrines "more than almost any other recent theologian" (162).

"apparent" contradiction and a real contradiction. Since both would appear to the human existent in precisely the same form and since neither will yield up its contradiction to study and reflection, how does the human existent know for certain that he is "embracing with passion" only a seeming contradiction and not a real contradiction?

Third (and related to the second point), there is the intrinsic problem of *meaning* in any paradox so defined. What can two truths construed as an unresolvable contradiction mean? What meaning would a four-cornered triangle convey to us? What meaning would a square circle have for us? David Basinger explains:

> If concepts such as human freedom and divine sovereignty are really contradictory at the human level, then . . . they are at the human level comparable to the relationship between a square and a circle. Now let us assume that God has told us in Scripture that he had created square circles. . . . *The fundamental problem would be one of meaning.* We can say the phrase "square circle," and we can conceive of squares and we can conceive of circles. But since a circle is a nonsquare by definition and a square is noncircular by definition, it is not at all clear that we can conceive of a square circle—that is, conceive of something that is both totally a square and totally a circle at the same time. This is because on the human level, language (and thought about linguistic referents) presupposes the law of noncontradiction. "Square" is a useful term because to say something is square distinguishes it from other objects that are not squares. But if something can be a square and also not a square at the same time, then our ability to conceive of, and thus identify and discuss, squares is destroyed. In short, *"square" no longer remains from the human level a meaningful term. And the same is true of the term "circle" in this context.*
>
> But what if we were to add that the concept of a square circle is not contradictory from God's perspective and thus that to him it is meaningful. Would this clarify anything? This certainly tells us something about God: that he is able to think in other than human categories. But it would not make the concept any more meaningful to us. Given the categories of meaning with which we seem to have been created, the concept would remain just as meaningless from our perspective as before.[29]

Fourth—and if the former three difficulties were not enough, this last point, only rarely recognized, should deliver the coup de grace to the entire notion that irreconcilable (only "apparent," of course) contradictions exist in Scripture—once one asserts that a truth may legitimately assume the form of an irreconcilable contradiction, he has given up all possibility of ever detecting a real falsehood. Every

---

29. David Basinger, "Biblical Paradox: Does Revelation Challenge Logic?" *Journal of the Evangelical Theological Society* 30, no. 2 (1987): 208, emphasis supplied.

THE NATURE OF BIBLICAL TRUTH

time he rejects a proposition as false because it "contradicts" the teaching of Scripture or because it is in some other way illogical, the proposition's sponsor only needs to contend that it only appears to contradict Scripture or to be illogical, and that his proposition is simply one of the terms (the Scripture may provide the other) of one more of those paradoxes which we have acknowledged have a legitimate place in our "little systems," to borrow a phrase from Alfred, Lord Tennyson.[30] But this means both the end of Christianity's uniqueness as the revealed religion of God since it is then liable to—nay, more than this, it must be open to—the assimilation of any and every truth claim of whatever kind, and the death of all rational faith.

Now if one has already conceded that the Bible itself can and does teach that truths may come to the human existent in paradoxical terms, it begs the question to respond to this by insisting that one must simply believe what the Bible says about these other claims to truth and reject those that contradict the Bible. Why should either proposition of the "declared" contradiction be preferred to the other when applying Scripture to a contradicting truth claim? Why not simply live with one more unresolved antithesis? The only solution is to deny to paradox, if understood as irreconcilable contradictories, a legitimate place in a Christian theory of truth, recognizing it for what it is—the offspring of an irrational age. If there is to be an offense in Christianity's truth claims, it should be the ethical implications of the cross of Christ and not the irrationality of contradictories proclaimed to men as being both true.

Certainly there are biblical concepts that we cannot fully understand. We may never be able to explain, for example, how God created something from nothing, how he can raise someone from the dead, or how the Spirit of God quickens the unregenerate soul (see John 3:8).[31] Such concepts are *mysteries* to us, but they are not contradictions in terms. Again, it is true that the living God, upon occasion, employed paradoxes (understood as apparent but *reconcilable* contradictories) in his spoken word. But he did so for the same reason that we employ them—as rhetorical or literary devices to invigorate the thought being expressed, to awaken human interest, to intrigue, to challenge the intellect, and to shock and frustrate the lazy mind. But the notion that any of God's truth will always appear to the human

---

30. Tennyson writes:
    Our little systems have their day,
    They have their day and cease to be.
    They are but broken lights of Thee,
    And Thou, O Lord, art more than they.
              —*In Memoriam.*
31. If someday he tells us how he did these things, then of course we will be able to understand them.

existent as contradictory must be rejected. Specifically, the notion that the cardinal doctrines of the faith—the Trinity, the person of Christ, the doctrines of grace—when proclaimed aright must be proclaimed as contradictory constructs is a travesty.

Certainly it is possible for an erring exegete so to interpret two statements of Scripture that he thinks that they teach contradictory propositions. But either he has misinterpreted one statement (maybe both), or he has attempted to relate two statements that were never intended to be related to one another. To affirm otherwise, that is, to affirm that Scripture statements, when properly interpreted, can teach that which for the human existent is both irreconcilably contradictory and yet still true, is to make Christianity and the propositional revelation upon which it is based for its teachings irrational, and this strikes at the rational nature of the God who speaks throughout its pages. God is Truth itself, Christ is the Logos of God, neither can lie, what they say is self-consistent and noncontradictory, and none of this is altered in the revelatory process.

But does not the classical doctrine of the Trinity present, if not a real contradiction, at least an apparent one? The widely acclaimed "paradox" of the Trinity—namely, that three equals one and one equals three—is in fact not one at all. If the numerical adjectives "one" and "three" are intended to describe in both cases the same noun so that the theologian intends to say that one God equals three Gods and three Gods equal one God in the same way that one might say that one apple numerically equals three apples and three apples numerically equal one apple, this is not an apparent contradiction or paradox. This is a real contradiction which not even God can resolve! Nor would he even try to do so! But this is not what the church teaches by its doctrine of the Trinity, although this representation is advanced all too often not only by lay people but also by good theologians. For example, rejecting the traditional distinction that God is one in one sense (essence) and three in another sense (persons), Van Til writes:

> God is a *one-conscious being*, and yet he is a three-conscious being ... the work ascribed to any of the persons is the work of *one absolute person*. ... It is sometimes asserted that we can prove to men that we are not asserting anything that they ought to consider irrational, inasmuch as we say that God is one in essence and three in person. We therefore claim that we have not asserted unity and trinity of exactly the same thing.
>
> Yet this is not the whole truth of the matter. *We do assert that God, that is, the whole Godhead, is one person* ... within the ontological Trinity we must maintain that God is numerically one. He is *one person*. ... Yet, within *the being of the one person* we are permitted and compelled by Scripture to make the distinction between a specific or generic type of being, and *three personal subsistences*.[32]

---

32. Van Til, *An Introduction to Systematic Theology*, 220, 228, 229-30, emphasis supplied.

But no orthodox creed has ever so represented the doctrine. In fact, it is apparent that all of the historic creeds of the church have been exceedingly jealous to avoid the very appearance of contradiction here by employing one noun—"God" or "Godhead"—with the numeral "one" and another noun—"persons"—with the numeral "three." The church has never taught that three Gods are one God or that one person is three persons but rather that "in the unity of the Godhead there are three persons" (Westminster Confession of Faith, II/iii), the Father, the Son, and the Holy Spirit, and that while each is wholly and essentially divine, no one person totally comprehends all that the Godhead is hypostatically. Certainly some of the divine attributes which insure the unity of the Godhead may be unknown to us. But when the Bible refers to the Father and the Son and the Holy Spirit, it intends that we think of three persons, that is, three hypostatically distinct centers of self-consciousness within the Godhead, whereas when it employs the imprecise and flexible title "God," it refers either to the Godhead construed in their unitary wholeness (for example, Gen. 1:26) or to one of the persons of the Godhead, specifically which one to be determined by the context (for example, "God" in Rom. 8:28 refers to the Father while "God" in Rom. 9:5 refers to the Son). Thus construed, the doctrine of the Trinity does not confront us with even an apparent contradiction, much less a real one. *The Triune God is a complex Being but not a contradiction!*

Similarly, the Christian church has never creedally declared that Christ is one person and also two persons or one nature and also two natures. Rather, the church has declared that the Lord Jesus Christ, "being the eternal Son of God, became man, and so was and continues to be God and man, in two distinct natures and one person forever" (Westminster Shorter Catechism, Question 21). Note again: Christ is one person possessing the full complex of divine attributes and the full complex of human attributes. Christ is complex, surely, but he is not a contradiction!

Let no one conclude from this rejection of paradox (as Marston has defined it) as a legitimate hermeneutical category that I am urging a Cartesian rationalism that presupposes the autonomy of human reason and freedom from divine revelation, a rationalism which asserts that it must begin with itself in the build-up of knowledge. But make no mistake: I am calling for a *Christian rationalism* that forthrightly affirms that the divine revelation which it gladly owns and makes the bedrock of all its intellectual efforts is internally self-consistent, that is, noncontradictory. Christians believe that their God is rational, that is, that he is logical. This means that he thinks and speaks in a way that indicates that the laws of logic—the law of identity (A is A), the law of noncontradiction (A is not non-A), and the law of excluded middle (A is either A or non-A)—are laws of thought *original with and intrinsic to himself.* This means that his knowledge is self-consistent. And because he is a God of truth he will not, indeed, he cannot lie (see Tit. 1:2; Heb. 6:18). Accordingly, just because God is rational, self-consistent, and always and necessarily truthful, we should assume that his inscripturated propositional revelation to us—the Holy Scripture—is of necessity also rational, self-consistent, and true. That this view of Holy Scripture is a common Christian conviction is borne out, I would suggest, in the consentient willingness by Christians everywhere to affirm that there are no contradictions in Scripture. The church worldwide has properly seen that the rational character of the one living and true God would of necessity have to be reflected in any propositional self-revelation which he determined to give to human beings, and accordingly has confessed the entire truthfulness (inerrancy) and noncontradictory character of the Word of God. Not to set the goal of quarrying from Scripture a *harmonious* theology devoid of paradoxes is to sound the death knell not only to *systematic* theology but also to *all* theology that would commend itself to men as the truth of the one living and rational God.

CHAPTER FIVE

The Bible as the Ποῦ Στῶ for Knowledge and Personal Significance

WHEN GOD gave his Word to us, he gave us much more than simply basic information about himself. He gave us the ποῦ στῶ, *pou stō*,[1] or base that justifies both our knowledge claims and our claims to personal significance.[2]

THE JUSTIFICATION OF KNOWLEDGE

It is an epistemological axiom that unless there is comprehensive knowledge of all things somewhere there can be no knowledge anywhere. This is because all knowledge data is inextricably interrelated. For the finite knower to begin from himself alone with any datum, whether that datum be subjective or objective, ideal or material, mental or nonmental, and to seek to understand it comprehensively and exhaustively must inevitably lead him to other data, but being finite he cannot examine any datum or all possible relationships of that one datum comprehensively or exhaustively, not to mention examine all the other data in the universe. Furthermore, there is no way he can be assured that the next datum he might have examined at the point at which he concluded his research in his finiteness would

---

1. When Archimedes, the Greek mathematician, working with the simple machine of the lever, said, "Give me *[a place] where I may stand* [ποῦ στῶ] and I will move the world," he was asking for a base for his lever's fulcrum necessarily outside the cosmos. So the Bible is the Christian's extracosmic base for knowledge and meaning.
2. See also Robert L. Reymond, *The Justification of Knowledge* (Phillipsburg, N.J.: Presbyterian and Reformed, 1984) and Reymond, "The Theological Significance of the Biblical Doctrine of Creationism," *Presbyterion* 15, no. 2 (1989): 16–26.

have accorded with all that he had concluded to that point or would have required him to reevaluate his entire enterprise to that point.[3] The only way to escape the force of this fact is to avoid the entire question of epistemology.

The entire history of philosophy up to more recent times may be summarized as precisely man's rational effort,[4] beginning with himself and accepting no outside help, to "examine" enough of certain chosen particularities of the universe—particularities both subjective and objective, ideal and material, mental and nonmental—to find the universals which give to these particularities their meaning. To be somewhat more specific, men have attempted to come to knowledge and then to the justification of their claims to knowledge via the epistemological methods of rationalism or empiricism.

Rationalists, believing that all knowledge begins with innate criterial a priori truths from which further truths are derived by the deductive process, urge that by this method one will arrive at knowledge that is certain. But even if these criterial a priori ideas were to include the laws of logic, our own mental states, and the existence of objective truth, we can, as Frame has urged,

> deduce very little from such a priori ideas. Certainly, we cannot deduce the whole fabric of human knowledge from them or even enough knowledge to constitute a meaningful philosophy. Nothing follows from the laws of logic, taken alone, except possibly more laws of logic. From propositions about our own mental states, nothing follows except further propositions about our own mental states. From the statement "there are objective truths," nothing specific follows, and a statement that tells us nothing specific . . . is not a meaningful statement. . . . Thus if knowledge is limited to the sorts of propositions we have just examined, we will know only about our own minds and not about the real world because our mental states often deceive us. Thus rationalism leaves us not with the body of certainties that Plato and Descartes dreamed of but with no knowledge at all of the real world.[5]

Empiricists, believing that a world of "real facts" is "out there" to be studied and comprehended, urge that knowledge is to be gained through the inductive method

---

3. This is the mistake the Ligonier apologists make when they contend that "the self is the only possible starting place" for the buildup of knowledge (*Classical Apologetics* [Grand Rapids, Mich.: Zondervan, 1984], p. 212).
4. From Hegel's time to the present, many philosophers have given up trying to find purpose and meaning in the world by thinking *rationally*. They have rejected the notion of any real antithesis in logic and have opted for epistemological irrationalism or relativism.
5. John Frame, *The Doctrine of the Knowledge of God* (Phillipsburg, N.J.: Presbyterian and Reformed, 1987), 113.

THE BIBLE AS THE Ποῦ Στῶ

of the scientist—observing, forming hypotheses, experimenting, and inferring conclusions from that experimentation. They are satisfied that such a procedure provides humanity with a program for the achieving of knowledge. But aside from the fact of myriad a priori assumptions that are implicit in the inductive method,[6] one who would consistently follow the empirical approach to knowledge must surrender many claims to knowledge that would otherwise be made without hesitation. For example, to cite Frame:

> (i) Empiricism cannot justify a general proposition, such as "all men are mortal. . . . Similarly, the propositions of logic and mathematics, propositions that claim to be universally true, cannot be established on an empirical basis. (ii) Empiricism cannot justify any statement about the future. . . . (iii) Empiricism cannot justify any statements about ethical values. Statements about sensible facts do not imply anything about ethical goodness or badness, right or wrong, or obligation or prohibition. . . . (iv) [But if empiricism cannot justify the language about ethical values, then it cannot justify any claim to knowledge, for] empiricism cannot justify empiricism. For empiricism is a view of how one *ought* (an ethical "ought") to justify his beliefs, and on an empiricist basis, we cannot justify from sense-experience the proposition that we *ought* to justify our beliefs in that way.
>
> [And, of course,] empiricism rules out claims to know God, if God is thought to be invisible or otherwise resistant to empirical "checking procedures."[7]

Immanuel Kant attempted to avoid the pitfalls of pure rationalism and pure empiricism, neither of which, he averred, can justify its knowledge claims in isolation

---

6. Uncharacteristically, even Warfield, whose entire academic life was dedicated to an evidentialist apologetic that prizes the "facts" and seeks to authenticate the Christian faith as a reasonable faith based on good and sufficient evidence, argues in one place that "if doctrines which stand out of relation to facts are myths, lies, [then] facts which have no connection with what we call doctrine could have no meaning for us whatsoever. It is what we call doctrine which gives all their significance to facts. A fact without doctrine is simply a fact not understood. That intellectual element brought by the mind to the contemplation of facts, which we call 'doctrine' . . . is the condition of any proper comprehension of facts. . . . So closely welded are those intellectual elements—those elements of previous knowledge, or of knowledge derived from other sources—to facts as taken up into our minds in the complex act of apperception, that possibly we have ordinarily failed to separate them, and consequently, in our worship of what we call so fluently "the naked facts," have very little considered what a bare fact is and what little meaning it could have for us." ("The Right of Systematic Theology," *Shorter Selected Writings* [(Nutley, N.J.: Presbyterian and Reformed, 1973], 2:235–36).

   No Van Tilian presuppositionalist could have made a better case for the meaninglessness of "brute facts" and for Van Til's insistence that all apologetic argumentation assumes some basic a priori heart commitment and is thus circular reasoning.

7. Frame, *The Doctrine of the Knowledge of God*, 117–18.

from the other, by formally arguing in his monumental *Critique of Pure Reason* that the knowing subject, although he possesses the innate ideas of space and time as well as twelve specific categories of thought (unity, plurality, totality, reality, negation, limitation, substantiality, causality, reciprocity, possibility and impossibility, existence and nonexistence, and necessity and contingency), also needs the objective facts of the "noumenal world"—the world as it really is apart from our experience—which are brought to him by sensory experience. Otherwise, these "thoughts without percepts" would be "blank" or "empty." On the other hand, if the knowing subject has only the data of the noumenal world streaming via the senses into a mind that is a blank tablet, these "percepts without concepts" would be "blind" or "chaotic." So he argued for the necessary combining of some elements of both rationalism (which provides the form) and empiricism (which provides the "matter") in the acquisition and build-up of knowledge.[8]

However, because the mind's innate ideas and categories of thought impose a structure on the sensory data brought to it, one can never know the objective facts of the world as they really are but only as the mind itself has "created" them.[9] Standing always between the knowing subject and the thing to be known is just the knower's *creative* knowing process itself. But if one can never know "the thing in itself" *(das Ding-an-sich)* but only "the thing as it has been created by the mind," we are left again with skepticism if not total ignorance. Also, Kant's epistemology, as later thinkers noted, raises the prospect of the nonexistence of even his objective noumenal world, for since it is unknowable it cannot be shown to be objective. Furthermore, although he posited a "pre-established harmony" as the basis of his categories in human minds (having rejecting the Christian view of man as a

---

8. Kant's epistemological theory that all knowledge is a combination of the a priori forms and categories of the mind and the flux of sensory experience has grave implications for theology. According to Kant, knowledge of God could only be claimed if either God himself were immediately accessible to our awareness or if "God" were one of the mental categories demonstrably necessary to the ordering and shaping of our understanding. But since God is supposedly pure spirit and thus not directly accessible to us via the senses and since the a priori categories which make thinking possible are inapplicable beyond the sphere of sensation, the human mind cannot legitimately think of God as one, as a cause, as necessary, etc. Nor can his existence be proved, for all assertions of existence depend upon sensory verification. Kant urged, therefore, that the noumenal realm of God, freedom, and immortality—concepts he needed to ground the "categorical imperative" of his ethic—was knowable by "practical reason," that is, by faith. But this faith of course is devoid of concrete data knowable by pure reason.
9. John M. Frame rightly states in his *Cornelius Van Til: An Analysis of His Thought* (Phillipsburg, N.J.: Presbyterian and Reformed, 1995): "Thus, the mind of man not only is its own ultimate authority, but also replaces God as the intelligent planner and creator of the experienced universe" (45). Accordingly, in his *Religion Within the Limits of Reason Alone*, Kant argued that "the human mind can never and must never subject itself to any authority beyond itself" (Frame, 45).

knower created in the divine image for the purpose of cognitive relations with God, the external world, and other selves as the ground for knowledge), Kant can provide no valid reasons why such a pre-established harmony exists. For if, as he contends, knowledge is exclusively a joint product of forms and perceptions, he cannot explain how it is possible to acquire valid information about the categories which for him are purely mental.[10]

It should be apparent that all of these philosophical efforts have ended with dismal results. In more recent times, from Hegel and Kierkegaard to the present, many philosophers, recognizing the failure of this human effort to arrive at the certain knowledge of anything, have concluded that this failure was due to these earlier thinkers thinking rationally (or antithetically). Of course, when Hegel abandoned the biblical concept of rational antithesis (A is not non-A) for his concept of dialectic truth (the thesis-antithesis-synthesis process), in which concept syntheses continue to emerge from the process of conflict between opposing theses and antitheses and in which concept truth is to be found only at the ultimate end of the process, his own philosophy is untrue because it is only a part of the unfinished dialectic process. In other words, if Hegel's philosophy is true, it is false! And when Kierkegaard abandoned the biblical concept of truth for his concept of truth as unresolvable theses and antitheses, he gave up all possibility of ever identifying a real truth statement anywhere. Accordingly, these philosophers have abandoned rationality for irrationality and are now urging that meaning has nothing to do with thinking rationally. Truth is relative and life's meaning is to be achieved by a "leap of faith" to anything that gives even a momentary *raison d'être*.[11]

All this the Christian eschews in favor of the epistemology graciously given in the fact and propositional content of Holy Scripture. He recognizes that in the fact of Scripture itself he has a truly profound solution to man's need for an infinite reference point if knowledge is to become a reality. He understands that because there is comprehensive knowledge with God, real and true knowledge is possible for man, since God who knows all the data exhaustively in all their infinite relationships and who possesses therefore true knowledge is in the position to impart any portion of that true knowledge to man. The Christian believes that this is precisely what God did when he revealed himself to man propositionally. And he rests in the confidence that it is precisely in and by the Scriptures—coming to him *ab extra* (from "outside the cosmos")—that he has the "Archimedean ποῦ στῶ" that he needs for the buildup of knowledge and the justification of his knowledge claims. Taking all his directions from the transcendent ποῦ στῶ of the divine mind revealed

---

10. See Carl F. H. Henry's critique of Kant's epistemology in *God Who Speaks and Shows,* vol. 1 of *God, Revelation and Authority* (Waco, Tex.: Word, 1976) 387–92.
11. See Francis A. Schaeffer, *Escape from Reason* (Downers Grove, Ill.: Inter-Varsity, 1968), 40–45.

in Holy Scripture, the Christian affirms, first, the created actuality of a *real* world of knowing persons and knowable objects external to these knowing persons. Second, he affirms the legitimate necessity of both sensory experience and the reasoning process in the activity of learning, for the legitimacy of these things are authenticated by the Scriptures themselves. Finally, he happily acknowledges that the divine mind which has revealed something of its knowledge in Scripture is his ποῦ στῶ for universals in order to justify his truth claims. In short, he makes the Word of the self-attesting Christ of Scripture the epistemic basis for all reasoning and knowledge—even when reasoning about reason or about God's revelation.

THE JUSTIFICATION OF MAN'S PERSONAL SIGNIFICANCE

Not only is the Bible man's ποῦ στῶ for the justification of knowledge; it is also his ποῦ στῶ, via its doctrine of creation and God's interpretation of his created state, for human personal significance. It is the biblical doctrine of creation in a unique and profound way that defines who we are—*personal*, significant, covenant-creatures—*unlike* God, true enough, in that we are created, but *like* him in that we are created in his image.

Modern cosmologists who insist that men are the product of an *impersonal* beginning plus time plus chance are really saying that there is no intelligible ground for asserting personal significance for the human race. Shakespeare's Hamlet aptly captures their point:

> What is a man,
> If his chief good and market of his time
> Be but to sleep and feed? A beast, no more.
> (*Hamlet*, IV. iv. 35–37)

But then, if no real distinction exists between man and beast, there is no intelligible base for human morals either. For these theorists to continue to insist on their personal worth and the necessity of morals under such a condition is simply sheer mysticism—the existential leap to an unfounded dogmatic assertion, for if we are only products of chance, why should not the laws of the jungle—only the fit should survive; might is right—prevail?

Modern thought, nevertheless, regards the early chapters of Genesis as at best religious saga, that is, as mythological stories that, while not actually historical, nevertheless intend to convey religious truth. The problem in these chapters for modern men and women, influenced as they are by modern scientism's unfounded dogmatic dictum

THE BIBLE AS THE Ποῦ Στῶ

of cosmic and biological evolution, is the distinctly *supernatural* character of the events which they report—namely, the creation of the universe *ex nihilo* and the creation of man by the direct act of God. Because of the supposed "prescientific" nature of the events that these chapters record, the trend in modern critical thought is to regard the so-called two accounts of creation in Genesis 1 and 2 as ancient Hebrew cosmogonies comparable to the *Enuma Elish* of ancient Babylon, that is, as religious mythology.

But the church must resist this secularistic trend and continue to hold, as it has historically done, to the historical integrity of the early chapters of Genesis. Internal evidence is strong that they are intended historically:

1. The character of the Hebrew itself, employing as it does the *waw* consecutive verb to describe sequential events, the frequent use of the sign of the accusative and the "relative" pronoun, as well as the stylistic and syntactical characteristics of Hebrew narrative rather than Hebrew poetry, indicate that the author (Moses) intended these chapters to be taken as straightforward historical narration of early earth history. (If one wants a sample in this section of Scripture of what the author's poetry—with its parallelism of thought and fixed pairs—would look like, he can consider Gen. 4:23–24.)

2. In Genesis 12–50 the author uses the phrase "These are the generations of . . ." five times to introduce a new patriarch's history, the general history of which is not doubted by contemporary scholarship (see 25:12, 19; 36:1, 9; 37:2). But he also employs the same phrase six times in Genesis 1–11 to introduce new blocks of material (see 2:4; 5:1; 6:9; 10:1; 11:10, 27), the last one of which (11:27) contains the story of Abraham, whose general historicity is no longer questioned by most Old Testament scholars. Does this not suggest that he intended the first five occurrences of the phrase also to introduce blocks of historical record? And does this not suggest that he intended the entirety of Genesis to be viewed under the rubric of the genre of history?

3. In Genesis 1–11 there are 64 geographical terms, 88 personal names, 48 generic names, and at least 21 identifiable cultural terms (gold, bdellium, onyx, brass, bitumen, mortar, brick, stone, harp, pipe, cities, towers), all suggesting that the author was describing the world that we know and not a world belonging to another level of reality or mental conception.

4. Each divine judgment in Genesis 1–11 is followed by an exhibition of divine grace: God's covering of our first parents after he had pronounced judgment upon them; his protection for Cain after he had judged him; and his establishing his covenant with Noah after the judgment of the Flood. But where is God's exhibition of grace after his dispersing of the race into nations in Genesis 11?

Does not God's call of Abraham in Genesis 12, in whom all the dispersed nations of the earth would be blessed, answer to the character of the Babel judgment and thus complete the judgment/grace pattern? It would seem so. Apparently, the author was not aware of the break between Genesis 11 and Genesis 12 brought about by the shift in genre between the two sections (1–11, myth; 12–50, history) that many Old Testament scholars urge must be recognized.

5. Scripture in its entirety regards the Genesis account of man's early beginnings and doings as reliable history. The Genesis account of creation is referred to many times elsewhere in the Old and New Testament Scriptures (including Exod. 20:11; 31:17; Deut. 4:32; Pss. 33:6; 90:2; 136:5–9; 148:2–5; Isa. 40:25–26; 42:5; 44:24; 45:12; 48:13; 51:13; Amos 4:13; Jer. 10:12; Zech. 12:1; Matt. 19:4–5; John 1:2–3; Eph. 3:9; Col. 1:16; 1 Tim. 2:13; Heb. 1:2; 11:3; 2 Pet. 3:5; and Rev. 4:11; 10:6–7). In every instance the Genesis account of creation lies behind these references and is assumed by them to be a reliable record of what God did "in the beginning." To call into question the historical reliability of Genesis 1 and 2 is to call into question the trustworthiness of the entirety of Scripture testimony on the issue of origins. The fall of Adam is referred to in Job 31:33, Isaiah 43:27, Hosea 6:7, Romans 5:12–19, 2 Corinthians 11:3, and 1 Timothy 2:14. Cain's murder of Abel is referred to in Matthew 23:35, Luke 11:51, Hebrews 11:4, 1 John 3:12, and Jude 11. Finally, the Genesis flood is referred to in Isaiah 54:9, Matthew 24:37–39, Luke 17:26–27, Hebrews 11:7, 1 Peter 3:20, and 2 Peter 2:5, 3:6. To call into question the historicity of Genesis 3–11, then, is to call into question the trustworthiness of a great deal of later Scripture testimony.

6. The genealogies in 1 Chronicles 1 and Luke 3 regard Adam as the first human being. Neither genealogy gives the slightest impression that one should realize that he is on reliable historical ground back to the time of Abraham but that the names of Abraham's ancestors given in Genesis 5 and 11 are historically shaky and untrustworthy. These early genealogies, in fact, are treated by the Chronicler and by Luke as being as reliable as the later Genesis genealogy of Abraham, Isaac, and Jacob, or the genealogy of David in Ruth 4:18–20.

7. Finally, the integrity of our Lord's own teaching is at stake, for in Matthew 19:4–5 and Mark 10:6–8 he refers to the creation of man in such a way that it is beyond question (1) that he had Genesis 1:27 and 2:24 in mind, and (2) that he viewed these so-called two diverse accounts of creation as a trustworthy record of what took place at the beginning of human history. He also refers to the "blood of Abel" (Matt. 23:35) and to the Genesis flood (Matt. 24:37–39). To question the basic historical authenticity and integrity of Genesis 1–11 is to assault the integrity of Christ's own teaching.

Therefore the church not only may but also must regard the Genesis account of creation as a reliable record of the origin of the universe, a record preserved from error by the superintending oversight of the Holy Spirit (2 Pet. 1:20–21; 2 Tim. 3:15–7). We may encounter difficulties in interpreting some of the details of Genesis 1 and 2 simply because we are working exegetically and hermeneutically with highly circumscribed, greatly compressed, nontechnical narrative accounts of the beginning of the universe, but these interpretive difficulties are infinitely to be preferred to the scientific and philosophical difficulties which confront those modern interpreters who propound nontheistic solutions to the question of the origin of the universe.

Modern man has found basically only two ways to live without the one living and true God as the base for science and morals:

1. *By ignoring the implications of his declared atheism.* While still insisting on the sanctity of his personal significance and rights, he may entirely refuse to face the implications of his atheism and become thereby a mere "technician" in his daily labors, leaping then—however irrational such a leap may be (and it *is* irrational; see the "meaninglessness" theme of the Teacher of Ecclesiastes) and even though his leap may actually finally destroy him physically—to anything that will even temporarily make him *feel* significant, such as the acquisition of material things, love of the arts, sexual promiscuity, drugs, and therapy, these things having now become his "gods."

2. *By justifying his declared atheism by his sciences.* Modern man may also make a studied effort to argue by means of his physical and biological sciences that no personal God created the universe out of nothing but, to the contrary, that the universe spontaneously "created" (and is continuing to "create") itself and everything in it. In fact, he may argue that there is no infinite, personal Creator. That is, capitalizing the "c" of the word "cosmos," he makes it the cause and end both of itself and of all things in it, including himself, and without acknowledging that he is doing so offers up to the now-deified cosmos the worship and service he as "religious man" *(homo religiosus)* should reserve for his Creator. Tragically, in both cases modern man, in his flight from God and right reason, destroys himself as a person who makes truly significant and meaningful decisions, for he abandons the only base for justifying, first, what he believes in his heart of hearts is true about himself, namely, that he is individually and personally significant, and, second, his conclusions in science and morals.

I must say something more about this second path since it gives the appearance of being the more "learned" and therefore the more "respectable" of the two, since more and more scientists are giving it credence by calling it "scientific fact," and since what is one person's "scientific fact" today becomes mankind's "religion" tomorrow.

There has always been one nonnegotiable, absolutely necessary idea for science. It is the *sine qua non*—the "without which nothing"—of all scientific inquiry. This controlling idea is expressed by the Latin dictum *ex nihilo nihil fit*—"out of nothing, nothing comes." This axiom is universally accepted and everywhere assumed. As

Maria sang in *The Sound of Music* upon learning that Captain von Trapp loved her: "Nothing comes from nothing, nothing ever could; so somewhere in my youth or childhood, I must have done something good." Her theology here is wretched, but her science and logic are impeccable—"Nothing comes from nothing, nothing ever could." Science is hemophiliac at this point. Simply scratch this absolute axiom and modern science will bleed to death, since all experimental science will then have to reckon with the real possibility, regardless of the controls erected around its experimentation, that at any moment a totally "new beginning" may spontaneously intrude itself into the control area. Indeed, it can never be sure in any experiment that a totally "new beginning" has not spontaneously intruded itself undetected into its results and skewed its conclusions. Nevertheless, to avoid what they refer to as the "God-hypothesis," modern cosmologists are increasingly willing to ignore this self-evident truth and to espouse some form of spontaneous generation out of nothing as the explanation for the universe.

The June 13, 1988, issue of *Newsweek* magazine documented this ever-widening trend in an article entitled "Where the Wild Things Are." Reflect upon the following quotations from this article: "Cosmologists are no longer content to invoke the deity" as the ultimate explanation behind the universe.[12] To what do they now look? "For better or worse [they] have cast their lot with the laws of physics and not with Einstein's friend, the Old One, the Creator."[13] "In the greatest leap of imagination, *most [!] cosmologists now believe that the universe arose from nothing, and that nothing is as certain to give rise to something* as the night is to sire the dawn."[14] Alan Guth, a brilliant MIT cosmologist, declares that the universe is a "free lunch," that is, it came from nothing—that there was nothing, not God, not energy, not matter, simply nothing (but wait, he says; there was "possibility"!)—and then suddenly and spontaneously the void of nothing gave rise to, no, "decayed" into all the matter and energy the universe now has. He contends that the universe, "not with a bang so much as with a pfft, . . . ballooned *accidentally* out of the endless void of eternity, from a stillness so deep that there was no 'there' or 'then,' only possibility."[15] Guth, of course, is fudging here; there could not even be possibility, a mathematical concept, if there was nothing. More technically, he has proposed (with refinements from others) that an infinitely dense, infinitely (note the use of a term traditionally reserved as a description of the infinite, personal God) hot point called a "singularity" (he does not explain why or how this infinite singularity got "there"; apparently it spontaneously "decayed" from nothing) spontaneously exploded, that within a

---

12. "Where the Wild Things Are," *Newsweek* (June 13, 1988), 60.
13. Ibid., 65.
14. Ibid., 60, emphasis supplied.
15. Dennis Overbye, "The Universe According to Guth," *Discover* (June 1983), 93, emphasis supplied.

ten-millionth of a quadrillionth of a sextillionth (a 1 preceded by point 42 zeros) of a second later the universe was about the size of a grain of dust, that one-hundred thousandth of a quadrillionth of a quadrillionth (a 1 preceded by point 34 zeros) of a second later it had doubled in size, that—well, the reader gets the point—it has been expanding and forming quarks and leptons (the building blocks of matter), then (possibly) cosmic "strings" (the seeds for galaxies), then protons and neutrons (the building blocks of atomic nuclei), then atoms and galaxies (in that order) ever since. All this supposedly began about fifteen billion years ago, with our own sun and solar system emerging from all this about five billion years ago.

Edward P. Tryon, professor of physics at the City University of New York, proposes that the universe created itself "spontaneously from nothing (*ex nihilo*) as a result of established principles of physics."[16] Alex Vilenkin, a Tufts University cosmologist, explains all this this way: "The universe as a young bubble had tunneled like a metaphysical mole from somewhere else to arrive in space and time. That someplace else was 'nothing.'"[17] Edward Kolb of the Fermi National Accelerator Laboratory near Chicago, explains this by informing us that "even when you have nothing, there's something going on"![18] These descriptive explanations of the universe's origin, I think one must agree, sound like something written, if not by college freshmen who flunked their introductory course in logic, at best by romantic poets, rather than deliverances issued by serious scientists.

Carl Sagan, the David Duncan professor of astronomy and space sciences and director of the Laboratory for Planetary Studies at Cornell University, uses different words, but his view is no more scientifically demonstrable or logically respectable. "The cosmos," he dogmatizes "prophet-like" in his best seller, *Cosmos*, "is all that is or ever was or ever will be"—an assertion that goes far beyond *scientific* statement and that enters deeply into metaphysics, speculative philosophy, religion, even eschatology. Apparently, he believes that the material cosmos, if it has not existed forever in some form (a credo, by the way, which is not without its own philosophical difficulties and ambiguities), "created" and is continuing to "create" itself.

Furthermore, he explains what he calls the "beauty and diversity of the biological world," the "music of life," by the concept of evolution brought about through the occasional beneficial mutations of "natural selection."[19] For Sagan, this conception,

---

16. Edward Tryon, "What Made the World?" *New Scientist* 101 (March 10, 1984), 14.
17. Overbye, "Universe According to Guth," 99.
18. "Wild Things," 62.
19. Oxford biologist Richard Dawkins states that Darwin's theory of natural selection "makes it possible to be an intellectually fulfilled atheist." And the National Association of Biology Teachers has explicitly declared that all life is the outcome of "an unsupervised, impersonal, unpredictable,

over against the so-called personal God hypothesis, is "equally appealing, equally human, and far more compelling."[20]

But how can one speak *meaningfully* or *intelligently* of impersonal matter "selecting" anything? "Selection" suggests the intelligent choice of one end or course of action rather than a less intelligent end or course of action. But what produces the so-called beneficial mutations of Sagan's "natural selection"? Said another way, what are the "causal powers" within the evolutionary process upon which Sagan suspends the origin of all things? Does Sagan believe that intelligence governs the powers of nature? No, he does not. So I ask again, what then are the "causal powers" within the evolutionary process? *Accident, randomness, fate, chance!* All these words are synonyms for "chance." And what is chance? *Chance* is a word we use to

---

and natural process." But the findings of molecular biology fly in the face of this presumption. Michael J. Behe, *Darwin's Black Box: The Biochemical Challenge to Evolution* (New York: Free Press, 1996), a Roman Catholic molecular biologist, argues that molecular systems in the cells are irreducibly complex—chemical "machines" made up of finely calibrated interdependent parts—which means they cannot have originated by a gradual step-by-step process. They all had to be there in the cell from the start—doing their thing—or life would never have been. In sum, our stunningly complex cell systems must have originated all at once in order to function at all, thus suggesting that an Intelligence is the cell's originator. The professional scientific literature to date is completely silent on this subject, stymied by the complexity and elegance of the cell—the foundation of all life!

Phillip E. Johnson, author of *Darwin on Trial* (Downers Grove, Ill.: InterVarsity Press, 1991), in "Shouting 'Heresy' in the Temple of Darwin," *Christianity Today* (Oct. 24, 1994): 26 emphasis supplied, pinpoints the Achilles' heel of the entire evolutionary enterprise when he writes:

Michael Ruse, a leading academic defender of Darwinism, gave a talk about me at the 1993 annual meeting of the American Association for the Advancement of Science. The talk was supposed to be an attack, but Ruse actually conceded the main point at issue between us. Darwinism is founded upon a naturalistic picture of reality, he conceded. That concession will be fatal if the evolutionary scientists agree to make it, because the Darwinian version of evolution has hitherto been presented to the public as value-free fact. Biologists have authority to tell us facts that they know from the study of biology, but they have no intellectual or moral authority to order us to adopt a particular philosophy that they happen to prefer. *Once the crucial influence of philosophy is admitted, nonbiologists and even ordinary people must be allowed to decide whether to believe what the biologists are saying.*

Darwinian scientists have not observed anything like [natural selection creating new organs or . . . a step-by-step process of fundamental change consistently recorded in the fossil record]. What they have done is to *assume as a matter of first principle* that purposeless material processes can do all the work of biological creation because, *according to their philosophy*, nothing else was available. They have defined their task as finding the most plausible or least implausible—description of how biological creation could occur in the absence of a creator. The specific answers they derive may or may not be reconcilable with theism, but the manner of thinking is profoundly atheistic.

20. Carl Sagan, *Cosmos* (New York: Random House, 1980), 15–19.

describe mathematical possibilities, but *chance cannot be a cause of anything because chance is not a thing*—not being, not energy, not mass, not power, not intelligence, not an entity. It is only a mathematical concept. Once we see this, it is clear that Sagan is asking us once again to believe that "nothing" selected something—including you and me—to be, that out of nonintelligence we have risen, that out of impersonal being we have emerged! But how can we, on these grounds, continue to think of ourselves as significant persons? Why is it not now, on these grounds, just as appropriate to think of ourselves as a mere "accident of nature" (as did Sir James Jeans in his *The Mysterious Universe*) or as "the gruesome result of nature's failure to take antiseptic precautions" (as did Sir Arthur Eddington in his *New Pathways in Science*)? And why is it not just as appropriate to regard the elephant as a more advanced stage of the evolutionary process since it has a thicker skin than man? Or the dog since it has a keener sense of smell? Or the horse since it can run at greater speeds? And why is it not also appropriate to conclude, since man seeks to prey upon, tame, imprison, and put to his own use all of the other creatures on earth, that he among all the living species is the *greatest* predator of them all and therefore the *lowest* stage of evolutionary development to date?

These views of the new cosmologists are not "equally appealing, equally human, and far more compelling" than the "personal God view." To prefer the notion that "nothing" is the final reality to the concept of the opening words of Genesis, "In the beginning God created," represents the nadir of theoretical thought. These views leap over reason into the sea of absurdity. And why? Because to become truly God-conscious is to become truly covenant-conscious, and to become truly covenant-conscious is to become sin-conscious. And this situation they want to avoid at all costs, even to their own hurt. For in their denial of God, they also destroy their own significance as human beings.

What is ironic is that the creationist view of origins cannot be taught in the public-school systems of our land and is not tolerated in the physics, geology, and biology departments of our state universities because it is judged to be a purely religious concept, even though it best conforms to the *ex nihilo nihil fit* foundation principle of science and answers the two ultimate philosophical questions of being: Why is there something instead of nothing? and, Why is there cosmos (order) instead of chaos (disorder)? R. C. Sproul observes in this connection:

> Reason demands that . . . if something now exists, then something has always existed. To postulate that something comes from nothing is to substitute mythology for science.
>
> Classical Christianity asserts the doctrine of creation *ex nihilo*. That means creation out of nothing. This, however, does not mean that once there was nothing and now there is something. *Ex nihilo* creation means that the eternal

self-existent God (who is *something*) brought the universe into existence by the power of creation.[21]

These new cosmologists are advocating rank mysticism and sheer intellectual madness! The theological significance of biblical creationism is not only that it addresses and satisfies our intellectual need for a rational explanation of the universe and ourselves, but it also defines who we are as men and women and leaves us with great worth and dignity. It also provides the theistic context necessary for moral absolutes. Without the doctrine of creation we are left with nonanswers in these areas.

Two men named Francis both saw quite clearly the futility of the world's nonanswers and the vacuousness and meaninglessness of a universe without God at its base, and who accordingly described the threat to human personal significance intrinsic to the two basic paths that modern man takes to avoid God. The first, an English poet of the Victorian Age, is Francis Thompson (1859–1907), who immortalized the futility of life without God in his stirring poem, *The Hound of Heaven*. Poetically cataloging his own flight from God and his search for an alternative refuge in human love, in a careless life of indolent leisure, even in the innocent smiles of children, he then begins to elaborate what he discovered from his attempt to find lasting fulfillment in the study and mastery of the mysteries of the material universe. He concludes:

> But not by that, by that, was eased my human
>   smart.
> In vain my tears were wet on Heaven's grey
>   cheek.
> For ah! we know not what each other says,
>   These things and I; in sound *I* speak—
> *Their* sound is but their stir, they speak by silences.
> Nature, poor stepdame, cannot slake my drouth;
>   Let her, if she would owe me,
> Drop yon blue bosom-veil of sky, and show me
>   The breasts o' her tenderness:
> Never did any milk of hers once bless
>   My thirsting mouth.

To live life and to try to understand oneself and the material universe without the God who made all things, Francis Thompson learned, is to live in futility.

---

21. R. C. Sproul, "Cosmos or Chaos," *Table Talk* (August 25, 1988), 7.

THE BIBLE AS THE Ποῦ Στῶ

The second is Francis A. Schaeffer of recent and revered memory. No man in our time has proven to be more perceptive or expressed himself more profoundly about these matters. The entire ministry of his L'Abri Fellowship was committed to exposing the hollowness of modern man's declared atheistic world-and-life-view. The following words he dictated to his wife, Edith, from his hospital bed a few days before his death May 15, 1984. She tells us that they were to become his "last written page, ending the books he had written, set[ting] forth once again the basic foundation he felt so important as a base for life, a world view."[22] We would be well advised to listen to his last dictated words.

For a long time now, it has been held, and universally accepted, that the final reality is energy which has existed forever in some form and energy which has its form by pure chance. In other words, intelligence has no basic place in the structure of the universe from the Enlightenment onward. Therefore, we are to accept totally the basic structure of the universe as impersonal.

This means, therefore, that neither religion nor intelligence are in the universe. The personality issue does not enter into *what* the universe is, nor into *who* people are in this theory. Under this theory, there is no place for morals, nor for there being any meaning to the universe. And the problem here is that [this description of things] is simply not what we observe about the universe—nor especially about man himself. In spite of this, modern man continues to press on, saying that this is what the universe is, and especially what the individual is. In other words, we have been told that in faith we must insist blindly on what the universe is and what man is. In other words, man is simply a mathematical thing—or formula—even though it brings him sorrow.

This is simply mysticism in its worst form, and the final denial of rationality. With understanding, one sees the proud egotism of holding this basic philosophic concept against what comes to man from every side.

What would we do with any other theory that postulated such a theorem? Certainly it would be put aside. Why do we continue to hold this theorem as to what reality is, when in any other area we would simply throw it out?

The answer is clear that it is simply a mystical acceptance. In other words, man is so proud that he goes on blindly accepting that which is not only intellectually inviable, but that which no one can live with in government or personal life, and in which civic life cannot live.

To go back and accept that which is the completely opposite—that the final reality is an Infinite Personal God who created the world—is rational, and returns us to intelligent answers, and suddenly opens the door. It not only gives answers, but puts us once more in a cosmos in which people can live, breathe, and rejoice.

---

22. Edith Schaeffer, *Forever Music* (Nashville, Tenn.: Thomas Nelson, 1986), 62.

If modern man would only be honest, he would say that it is his theory which is in collapse.[23]

Schaeffer is correct. The Bible and right reason roundly condemn as willful moral perversity both the practical atheism of the modern hedonist and the atheistic affirmations of modern cosmologists, the Bible insisting to the contrary that the one living and true God alone has eternally existed, and that the universe began as the result of his creative activity.

Only the biblical response to the question of human origin makes sense, and only the theistic context behind it (1) defines men and women in such a way that they possess genuine worth and dignity, (2) provides the human sciences with an intelligent base for predication and human morality systems with the necessary base for just moral decisions, and (3) saves men and women from becoming caught up in the surd of "chaos and eternal night" (Milton), a meaningless cipher drowning in a meaningless sea of ciphers.

Genesis 1 and 2 are the bedrock of this teaching. The church has traditionally understood Genesis as teaching a divine creation *ex nihilo,* and more particularly, the creation of man in his own image by a direct act of God. In this doctrine is the ground for personal significance and the justification of knowledge and an ethic men can live with. The church cannot afford to abandon this absolutely fundamental teaching of Scripture, for it is indeed the only ποῦ στῶ, *pou stō,* for man's personal significance, his knowledge claims and a just universal ethic. The church will do so only at great cost to herself and to the people she seeks to win to faith and to a home in heaven, because only as human beings are his creatures do they have personal significance, and only as they are God's creatures are they capable of justifying their truth claims and able to see themselves as *responsible* moral beings who make significant moral decisions.

---

23. Ibid., 61–62.

PART TWO

God and Man

CHAPTER SIX

Introduction to the Doctrine of God

THE ACQUISITION of a systematic theology of the doctrine of God that will pass the muster of Scripture is surely one of the most demanding intellectual enterprises man will ever undertake. The "vast deeps" of the Ultimate Subject of theology, who is "infinite, eternal, and unchangeable, in His being, wisdom, power, holiness, justice, goodness, and truth" (Westminster Shorter Catechism, Question 4), will often stretch the creature's understanding beyond his powers of comprehension and humble him as nothing else can or will. He will often find himself exclaiming with Paul:

> Oh, the depth of the riches of the wisdom and knowledge of God!
> How unsearchable his judgments,
> and his paths beyond tracing out!
> Who has known the mind of the Lord?
> Or who has been his counselor? (Rom. 11:33–34)

In Exodus 3 Moses' immediate reaction to the burning bush was to say, "I will go over and see this strange sight," and then to approach it. But God immediately opposed his resolution: "Do not come any nearer. Take off your sandals, for the place where you are standing is holy ground" (Exod. 3:5). We should learn from the divine announcement, as Donald Macleod writes, that

> God is not simply a great sight, the object of speculative curiosity. The revelation of His glory and the whole theological process which legitimately follows from it is holy ground. We cannot stand as superiors over God or His Word. We may not coldly and detachedly analyse and collate the great self-revealing deeds and

utterances of Jehovah. We may not theologise without emotion and commitment. The doctrine must thrill and exhilarate. It must humble and cast down.... Theology has lost its way, and, indeed its very soul, if it cannot say with John, "I fell at his feet as dead" (Rev. 1:17).[1]

THE ONE TRUE GOD

Responding to its fifth question, "Are there more Gods than one?" the Westminster Shorter Catechism declares: "There is but one only, the living and true God." The Catechism derives its description of God here from Jeremiah 10:10: "But the Lord is the true God; he is the living God, the everlasting King." Its monotheistic assertion is expressly supported and everywhere assumed by both the Old and New Testaments:

Deuteronomy 6:4: "Hear, O Israel, the Lord our God, *the Lord is one* [יהוה אֶחָד, *yhwh 'eḥāḏ*]."

Isaiah 45:5: "I am the Lord, and *there is no other* [אֵין עוֹד, *'ēyn 'ôḏ*]; apart from me there is no God."

Zechariah 14:9b: "In that day *the Lord will be one* [יִהְיֶה יהוה אֶחָד, *yihyeh yhwh 'eḥāḏ*], and his name one."

Mark 12:29: "Hear, O Israel, the Lord our God, *the Lord is one* [κύριος εἷς ἐστιν, *kyrios heis estin*]."

Romans 3:30: "*There is only one God* [εἷς ὁ θεός, *heis ho theos*], who will justify the circumcised by faith and the uncircumcised through that same faith."

1 Corinthians 8:4: "We know that an idol is nothing at all in the world and that *there is no God but one* [οὐδεὶς θεὸς εἰ μὴ εἷς, *oudeis theos ei mē heis*]."

1 Timothy 2:5: "*For there is one God* [εἷς γὰρ θεός, *heis gar theos*], and one mediator between God and men, the man Christ Jesus."

James 2:19: "You believe that *there is one God* [εἷς ἐστιν ὁ θεός, *heis estin ho theos*]. Good! Even the demons believe that—and shudder."

Holy Scripture teaches that the one true and living God created the universe (Gen. 1–2; Heb. 1:2; 11:3) not because of an ontological need to complement him-

---

1. Donald Macleod, *Behold Your God* (Ross-shire, Scotland: Christian Focus Publications, 1990), 39.

[130]

self (Isa. 40:12–31; Acts 17:25), for he was ontologically exactly the same after his creative activity as before (Ps. 90:2), but solely because he willed to do so (Rev. 4:11) and for the purpose of glorifying himself (Isa. 43:6–7). He needs nothing outside of himself in order to be fully God. In sum, the God of Scripture is *self-contained* and *self-sufficient,* in no way ontologically correlative to his creation.

After creating the universe, unlike the god of Deism, the infinite personal God of Scripture continues to preserve and to govern all his creatures and all their actions (Pss. 103:19; 104:24; 145:17; Matt. 10:29–30; Heb. 1:3). All that he does and all that occurs in heaven and on earth is determined by his eternal decree (Ps. 115:3; Dan. 4:17, 25, 35; Acts 2:23; 4:27–28; Rom. 9:11–23; Eph. 1:3–14; 1 Pet. 1:20).

In the following discussion I intend by the word *God* this one living and true Creator God of Holy Scripture. It is the existence of this God alone that I confess. With reference to the claimed existence of any other god as the true God, I am not simply agnostic, I am a convinced atheist. I deny that any other gods exist save as idolatrous creations in the minds of sinful men who have "exchanged the truth of God for a lie, and worship and serve the creature rather than the Creator—who is forever praised. Amen" (Rom 1:25).

WHY I BELIEVE IN THE GOD OF THE BIBLE

A word is in order about why I begin at the place I do and not with a discussion of the value of the traditional "proofs" or arguments for God's existence (unlike many other Reformed systematic theologies, including Francis Turretin's *Institutes of Elenctic Theology,* Charles Hodge's *Systematic Theology,* Robert Lewis Dabney's *Lectures in Systematic Theology,* and Louis Berkhof's *Systematic Theology).* I start where I do because I do not commend these arguments, as I have stated in *The Justification of Knowledge,*[2] because they are fundamentally unsound, and because Christians should neither use unsound arguments nor urge unbelievers to place their confidence in them. I believe God is "really there," of course, because he has revealed himself to all men *generally* by creation and providence, that is to say, all men already have an awareness of God *(sensus deitatis)* by virtue of his divine image within them and his revelation of himself both in nature and in his providential dealings with his world, *propositionally* in the Scriptures of the Old and New Testaments,[3] *personally* in his Son, the Lord Jesus Christ, and *savingly* through the

---

2. Robert L. Reymond, *The Justification of Knowledge* (Phillipsburg, N.J.: Presbyterian and Reformed, 1984).
3. See part one for my reasons for believing that God has spoken to us in the Old and New Testament Scriptures.

work of his Word and Spirit.[4] And I believe he is "really there" because, without him as the universe's final Reality, there would be no intelligibility anywhere. But I do *not* confess his existence on the basis of the traditional theistic arguments, whether ontological or empirical.

The Ontological Argument

The ontological argument, set forth by Anselm (1033–1109) in the form of a prayer in his *Proslogion* (1078), contends that the very concept of God in the understanding as "the being than which no greater can be thought" *(aliquid quo nihil maius cogitari possit)* necessitates his existence because such a concept conceives of the most perfect being that can be imagined as necessarily existing. But, he continues,

> suppose it exists in the understanding alone: then it can be conceived to exist in reality, which is greater.
>
> Therefore, if that than which nothing greater can be conceived exists in the understanding alone, the very being than which nothing greater can be conceived is one than which a greater can be conceived. But obviously this is impossible. Hence there is no doubt that there exists a being than which nothing greater can be conceived, and it exists both in the understanding and in reality.
>
> And it assuredly exists so t y that it cannot be conceived not to exist. For it is possible to conceive of a being which cannot be conceived not to exist; and this is greater than one which can be conceived not to exist. Hence if that than which nothing greater can be conceived, can be conceived not to exist, it is not that than which nothing greater can be conceived. But this is an irreconcilable contradiction. There is then so truly a being than which nothing greater can be conceived

---

4. While I believe that God has revealed himself to me in these four ways, I do not believe that I came to know him savingly by means of these four modes of revelation in the order in which I just presented them. Before my conversion, while I "knew" God and his righteous ordinances from general revelation (Acts 17:23; Rom. 1:20, 21, 32; 2:14–15), I suppressed this knowledge (Rom. 1:18). I came to know him first and savingly only when the Holy Spirit, working by and with his propositional revelation, regenerated me and revealed Christ to me. Only then, and not before then, did I understand aright the revelational evidence for him (which was there all the time) in creation and providence. I totally agree with Calvin's comment: "Just as old or bleary-eyed men and those with weak vision, if you thrust before them a most beautiful volume, even if they recognize it to be some sort of writing, yet can scarcely construe two words, but with the aid of spectacles will begin to read distinctly; so Scripture, gathering up the otherwise confused knowledge of God in our minds, having dispersed our dullness, clearly shows us the true God" (*Institutes*, I.vi.1; see also I.xiv.1).

to exist, that it cannot even be conceived not to exist; and this being Thou art, O Lord, our God.[5]

... Why then has the fool said in his heart, there is no God, since it is so evident, to a rational mind, that Thou dost exist in the highest degree of all? Why? except that he is dull and a fool!

As a prayer this argument presupposes the existence of Anselm's God but, as has been often noted, this argument as pure argument at best only proves that people are incapable of holding the concept of a perfect God in the mind that does not include his existence in reality. But their *concept* of God existing in reality and the *actual* existence of such a God are not the same; the former no more establishes the objective reality of its corresponding entity than a merchant's writing zeroes in his ledger increases his actual wealth (so Kant). Gaunilo, a French monk of Marmoutier and Anselm's contemporary, in his rejoinder, *On Behalf of the Fool*, said in effect: "I have an idea of an island than which no more perfect can be conceived, an idea which therefore includes the island's existence, but my idea of such an island does not mean the island really exists for such an island really does not exist."

Not without some justification has this argument been described as the attempt to define God into existence. It is essentially a tautology which merely defines God as a necessarily existing perfect being without supplying any reasons beyond the definition itself for thinking that such a being actually exists. But human thought *per se* imposes no necessity on things.[6]

J. Oliver Buswell Jr. attempts to validate the ontological argument in an inductive form (which he declares he found in Descartes) by supplying some reasons beyond the definition itself. He writes: "Of course we do not hold that every idea corresponds to an ontological existent. What we do hold is that every idea in human culture has some cause."[7] He offers an illustration of what he means:

> If we should discover a tropical island, apparently flat, and if we should find that the people on such an island had a language quite distinct from any other

---

5. For some Eastern religions the ascription to God of existence would not be an ascription of greatness or perfection but of imperfection. For instance, in Hinayana Buddhism *nirvana*, the state of perfection and the goal to be achieved by all *arhats*, is nonbeing since to be at all is to suffer, while in Mahayana Buddhism, *nirvana* is neither existent nor nonexistent: it is simply thusness or void. This shows that Anselm's ontological argument is presupposing the Western, that is Christian, concept of perfection.
6. See Alister McGrath, *Christian Theology: An Introduction* (Oxford: Blackwell, 1994), 130–32, for a brief but helpful assessment of Anselm's argument.
7. J. Oliver Buswell Jr., *A Systematic Theology of the Christian Religion* (Grand Rapids, Mich.: Zondervan, 1962), 1:99.

known to us, and if we should discover that these people on this apparently flat tropical island had a word for a snow-capped mountain, we should find it necessary to make inquiries as to the source of their idea. We should conclude that either there was a snow-capped mountain far in the interior of their island, or that they had migrated from some region containing high mountains, or that some traveler had told them of snow-capped mountains. From the data of a flat tropical island natives could not build up the idea of a snow-capped mountain.[8]

His point here is that our idea that a perfect being exists is the effect of a cause. This cause (and here is the induction) is the data of the universe from which men infer their idea that a perfect being exists who is the ultimate cause of the universe.

Buswell's island illustration, however, ignores the fact that not every idea men may have can or must be traceable to an empirical datum. Men have very active imaginations (recall our modern "sci-fi" novels and horror movies), even delusions, and every culture has developed its own mythology. Any one of these nonempirical causes could be the original source of the word for a snow-capped mountain for these flat-landers. Similarly, an active imagination or a cultural mythology could account for the idea of a perfect being that exists. Buswell's attempt to validate the ontological argument does not persuade me.

The Ligonier apologists advance an ontological argument in their *Classical Apologetics* which is worth mentioning. They assert, following Jonathan Edwards:

> We have an idea of being and we cannot have even an idea of nonbeing. "That there should be nothing at all is utterly impossible." . . .
>
> Therefore, we cannot think of being not being ever or anywhere. . . . Consequently, this eternal, infinite being must necessarily exist because we cannot think of it not existing; and the only ultimate proof of the existence of anything is that we cannot think of it not existing, ever.[9]

This necessary being, they conclude, is God. The first and simplest thing to say regarding their argument is that I and, I suspect, a good many others as well can do precisely what they insist is impossible, namely, "have an idea of [in the sense of 'imagine'] nonbeing." Apparently they themselves also have some idea of what nonbeing is; otherwise the word as they use it is a meaningless term. John Frame raises another objection:

---

8. Ibid., 1:99–100.
9. R. C. Sproul, John Gerstner, Arthur Lindsley, *Classical Apologetics* (Grand Rapids, Mich.: Zondervan, 1984), 106.

However infinite being may be, our idea of being extends to finite being as well. Therefore, if "being" is divine, then finite beings are part of that divine being. In other words, without some modifications, the argument proves pantheism. And the argument fails to draw any distinction between the kind of "infinity," "eternity," "omnipresence," etc. attributable to a pantheistic god, and the very different (but similar-sounding) attributes revealed concerning the God of Scripture.[10]

The Empirical Arguments

Neither do I confess God's existence on the basis of the empirical or inductive arguments of methodological natural theology. Following Aristotle's lead, Thomas Aquinas set forth his famous "five Ways" in his *Summa theologica*, I, 2, 3, and *Summa contra Gentiles*, I, XIII. By it he attempted to demonstrate from sense data alone without any *a priori* equipment the existence of God. For the following reasons his arguments are invalid:

1. One simply cannot begin with the existence of sensory data and proceed by formal laws of logic to the existence of a nonsensory conclusion.

2. Aquinas believed that the mind, prior to sense impressions, is a *tabula rasa*, a blank slate. But a *tabula rasa* epistemology is freighted with insurmountable obstacles to the build-up of knowledge, for if all the mind has to work with are sense-perceptions as reports of what is going on in the external world, knowledge can never rise to the universal and the necessary since from flux only flux can come. In other words, Aquinas's denial of innate ideas of God or of anything else makes the build-up of knowledge impossible.

3. In order to arrive at a first unmoved mover, Aquinas argues that the series of things moved by other things in motion cannot regress to infinity since such a regress would rule out a first mover. Of course an infinite series of moving causes is inconsistent with a first unmoved mover, but if the argument is designed to demonstrate the existence of the latter, the latter's existence cannot be used ahead of time as one of the premises in the argument. This is a blatant "assertion of the consequence."

4. Aquinas's arguments require that the universe as a whole be an effect. But no one has ever seen the universe as a whole, and no observation of the

---

10. John M. Frame, "Van Til and the Ligonier Apologetic," *Westminster Theological Journal* 47 (1985): 296.

observed parts of the universe gives this necessary assumption. There is no demonstrable reason why the universe as a whole might not be made up of interdependent contingencies which, operating together, sustain and support each other.[11]

5. Because Aquinas was convinced that nothing can be predicated of creation in the same sense that it is predicated of God, when he argues from the "existence" of the world to the "existence" of God, he uses the word *existence* in two different senses and thereby commits the logical fallacy of equivocation.

6. Granting, for the sake of argument, the validity of the cause and effect relationship, if it is valid to conclude from observed effects the existence of their cause(s), it is not valid to ascribe to their cause(s) any properties beyond those necessary to produce them. All the existence of a finite world would demand is the existence of a finite cause sufficiently powerful to cause it, a far cry from the omnipotent Creator of the Bible. Moreover, since much of what one observes involves what Christians call moral evil, a strict application of the cause and effect relation would require the conclusion that the ultimate cause of these effects is not completely morally good.

7. Granting, again for the sake of argument, that Aquinas demonstrated from motion the existence of an unmoved mover, yet when he adds, "And everyone understands this to be God," we may demur. The argument taken at face value would prove the existence merely of an unmoved cause of physical motion. But such a mover has no qualities of transcendent personality. It is highly significant that the terms Aquinas employs to denote the God he believes he arrives at by this method are all neuter: *ens perfectissimum, primum movens,* etc. In other words, if his arguments were valid, since there is nothing transcendent or supernatural about Aquinas's first cause, they would be destructive of Christianity with its infinite, personal God.[12]

---

11. See Buswell, *Systematic Theology,* 1:80.
12. See Carl F. H. Henry's rejection of natural theology in favor of a "revelational alternative" on similar grounds in his *God Who Speaks and Shows,* vol. 2 of *God, Revelation and Authority* (Waco, Tex.: Word, 1976), 104–23. See also Karl Barth's opposition to the theistic arguments in *Church Dogmatics,* ed. and trans. G. W. Bromiley (Edinburgh: T. & T. Clark, 1957), 2:1, 79ff.

INTRODUCTION TO THE DOCTRINE OF GOD

All of the empirical arguments of natural theology (construed methodologically)[13] for God's existence may be reduced to the cosmological argument or variations of it.[14] This argument assumes at least five things which should not and cannot be assumed but rather must be demonstrated if the argument is to be accepted:

1. the validity of the epistemological theory of empiricism;
2. an empirical criterion to screen out unwanted sense data;
3. the "effect" character of the universe;
4. the validity of the cause and effect relationship; and
5. the impossibility of an infinite causal regress.

To validate and demonstrate these matters (and there are many other issues that would have to be addressed along the way) will require the Christian's engagement in endless and intricate argumentation which if wrong at any single point in his chain of reasoning nullifies his entire intellectual enterprise. I will explain.

First, the validation of the epistemological theory of empiricism, it seems to me, would require that it be done *empirically*. Empiricists, as I noted in the last chapter, believing that a world of real "brute facts" are "really there" to be studied, comprehended and "rationalized," urge that knowledge is to be gained through the inductive method of the scientist—observing, forming hypotheses, experimenting, and inferring conclusions from that experimentation. They are satisfied that such a procedure provides man with a program for the achieving of knowledge. But aside from the fact of myriad *a priori* assumptions (shall I say presuppositions?) that are implicit in the inductive method, one who would consistently follow the empirical approach to knowledge must either surrender many claims to knowledge that he would otherwise make without hesitation or find some way to overcome the objections, posed by John Frame and many others, that

---

13. There is a legitimate sense in which the awareness of God that all people have by virtue of their being created in his image and by virtue of his inescapable revelation of himself to them in nature (Rom. 1:20) may be called "natural theology." With this use of the term I have no problem; indeed, I wholeheartedly endorse it. But when I refer to "methodological natural theology" I am referring to that theological method whereby a "first floor" philosophical prolegomenon is first built by natural reason working independently with what is portrayed as "neutral data" upon which a "second floor" set of beliefs derived from special revelation is later placed. In this kind of "natural theology," the Christian revelation, not intended to displace or to function as the ground of the philosophical prolegomenon, presupposes the philosophical prolegomenon and presumably confirms and supplements it. I argue against "natural theology" in this latter sense in *The Justification of Knowledge*.
14. See my *The Justification of Knowledge*, 118–30.

empiricism cannot justify a general proposition, such as "all men are mortal," . . . cannot justify any statements about the future, . . . cannot justify any statements about ethical values [for one can never move from "is-ness" to "oughtness"—author] Therefore empiricism cannot justify empiricism. For empiricism is a view of how one *ought* (an ethical "ought") to justify his beliefs, and on an empiricist basis, we cannot justify from sense-experience the proposition that we *ought* to justify our beliefs in that way.[15]

Then, too, if God's being is resistant to empirical checking procedures, as he, being spirit, most assuredly is (he cannot be seen, touched, tasted, smelled, heard, measured in any way), the Christian evidentialist must demonstrate how his empiricism does not rule out arriving at any and all claims to a knowledge of the Christian God at the outset.

Second, the Christian evidentialist must also face the fact, once he makes his initial appeal to raw sense data as evidence for God's existence, that no sense datum can be excluded from consideration unless he can provide an empirical criterion to screen out the sense data he does not want to consider. I have never seen such a criterion offered. Sense data *per se* include a nature which is not only seemingly at war with mankind in the latter's survival efforts but also "red in tooth and claw" relative to itself. Sense data also include the evils of history. Hitler gassed several million Jews and Christians, Stalin murdered a larger number of Ukrainians. Mao slaughtered thirty or possibly fifty million Chinese and virtually annihilated the Tibetans. And, of course, there were Genghis Khan, Ivan the Terrible, and Attila the Hun, not to mention the world's recurring natural disasters such as floods and droughts, hurricanes and fires, and the birth of congenitally deformed and diseased infants. In other words, sense data intrude the problem of evil into the discussion. But add *these* sense experiences to the "effect" of Aquinas's motion of a marble (see his "first way") and see what happens to the argument that attempts to prove the one true God's existence on the basis of empirical data alone.

The great Puritan pastor and theologian, Jonathan Edwards, who is something of a "patron saint" to the Ligonier apologists in their effort to resurrect the evidentialist apologetic in our time, clearly saw the futility of human reason, working independently from special revelation, trying to prove by sense data alone the existence of God precisely because of this fact of the presence of evil in the universe:

I cannot tell whether any man would have considered the works of creation as effects, if he had never been told they had a cause. . . . But, allowing that every

---

15. John M. Frame, *The Doctrine of the Knowledge of God* (Phillipsburg, N.J.: Presbyterian and Reformed, 1987), 117–18.

INTRODUCTION TO THE DOCTRINE OF GOD

man is able to demonstrate to himself, that the world, and all things contained therein, are effects, and had a beginning, *which I take to be a most absurd supposition,* and look upon it to be almost[16] impossible for unassisted reason to go so far; yet, *if effects are to be ascribed to similar causes, and a good and wise effect must suppose a good and wise cause, by the same way of reasoning, all the evil and irregularity in the world must be attributed to an evil and unwise cause.* So that either the first cause must be both good and evil, wise and foolish, or else there must be two first causes, an evil and irrational, as well as a good and wise principle. Thus man, *left to himself,* would be apt to reason, "If the cause and the effects are similar and conformable, matter must have a material cause; there being nothing more impossible for us to conceive, than how matter should be produced by spirit, or anything else but matter." The best reasoner in the world, endeavoring to find out the causes of things, *by the things themselves,* might be led into the grossest errors and contradictions, and find himself, at the end, in extreme want of an instructor.[17]

Third, the "effect" character of the universe must be demonstrated without first assuming that it is an effect, since this feature of the universe is a major part of the issue under debate. That is to say, the Christian evidentialist must first prove empirically, that is, from raw sense data, that the world as a whole had a first moment before he can begin to inquire about its cause. But, to be quite frank about it, no empiricist has ever seen the world *as a whole* and observation of only parts of the world cannot give this necessary datum since the world as a whole could be essentially different from the sum of its constituent parts.

Fourth, the cosmological argument, it seems to me, commits the logical fallacy of *petitio principii* ("begging the question") (1) by simply ruling out at the outset infinite causal regress as an impossibility since this would leave no room for a first cause, and then (2) by "affirming the consequent," namely, by asserting or positing—not demonstrating—the existence of God as the first cause to account for every lesser cause. It commits another logical fallacy when it insists that the essence of this first cause is altogether different (infinite, supernatural, uncaused, nonempirical) from the essence of all of the second causes upon which its existence is made to rest (finite, natural, caused, empirical) since it is a violation of logic to ascribe to a cause any properties beyond those necessary to account for the effects.

---

16. Edwards could have spared his reader this "almost," since no one has ever observed the "all things" that the world contains in order to demonstrate their "effect" character.
17. Jonathan Edwards, "Observations on the Scriptures;—their authority—and necessity," *Miscellaneous Observations* from *The Works of Jonathan Edwards* (Edinburgh: Banner of Truth, 1974), 2:476, emphasis supplied.

Fifth, the cosmological argument, as traditionally framed, is in form an inductive argument and as such claims to be a probability argument.[18] (Of course, apart from Christian theism the world is a world in which Chance is ultimate, rendering the very concept of probability meaningless.) In actuality, it is only a *possibility* argument which falls short of apodictic proof or certainty and does not do justice to the evidential data, which the Christian knows to be theistic, revelational data pointing *incontrovertibly* to God. And an argument that reduces revelational data to "brute data" pointing at best to the possibility of God's existence is a totally inadequate, even apostate, argument that Christians should not use or endorse.

As with the ontological argument, the Ligonier apologists offer their own version of the cosmological argument which, they claim, overcomes this possibility (or probability) problem. They begin by asserting that every effect, by definition, has an antecedent cause. The world is neither an illusion nor is it self-created. If it is self-existent, that is, noncontingent, then *it* is in effect transcendent and we have found "God." If the world, however, is contingent, since an infinite regress of contingent prior causes (they aver) is inconceivable, it must be the effect of a self-existent, that is, noncontingent being, and once again we have proven God.[19]

Frame has something to say about this argument as well:

> What is most notable to me is that . . . the authors fail clearly to rule out the pantheistic alternative, namely that the universe is its own god. About all I can find in the book responding to this objection is one sentence: "(God) is personal because He is the pervasive cause of all things including the purpose and the personal" [123]. But it is by no means obvious that a being must itself be personal in order to be the cause of personality.[20]

---

18. Benjamin B. Warfield affirms the "probability" character of his apologetic method in his article, "The Real Problem of Inspiration," in *The Inspiration and Authority of the Bible* (Phillipsburg, N.J.: Presbyterian and Reformed, 1948), 218–19. But while his method purports to provide a probability argument, it does not really do so. By "probability" in this context is normally meant the degree of verifiability that can be attributed to a religious hypothesis or belief. But for any religious belief, regardless of the number of confirming or favorable test instances, there are an indefinite, if not an infinite, number of possible test consequences, which simply means that it is not possible to calculate mathematically the probability of that belief. Indeed, if the number of possible test consequences is infinite, the probability of that belief can never rise above zero. It is meaningless, therefore, to speak of a given religious belief, on the basis of empirical testing, as "probable" or "highly probable." In fact, apart from Christian theism this world is a world of chance in which the very concept of probability is meaningless.
19. Sproul, Gerstner, Lindsley, *Classical Apologetics*, pp. 111, 116–23.
20. Frame, "Van Til and the Ligonier Apologetic," 296.

Moreover, it is simply not the case that an infinite chain of contingent prior causes is inconceivable. There is nothing illogical about such a conception. Buswell, who places great value on the theistic arguments in his *Systematic Theology*, rightly acknowledges as much:

> We must reject the notion that an infinite regress of causes is impossible to conceive. Rather, it is the case that it is difficult to conceive of the opposite. To argue that since every event has a cause, therefore there must be some event at the beginning which has no cause, is clearly a fallacy.
> ... There is no ground for saying that an infinite chain of contingent beings could not have existed. ...
> That the conditional demands that which is absolute and unconditioned is ... a fallacy. ... There is no logical reason why the entire universe might not be made up of inter-dependent contingencies.[21]

The Ligonier scholars insist that they eschew a Christianity that is only probably true fully as much as presuppositional apologists do (Christianity must be *certainly* true; otherwise, men have an excuse for unbelief). But since they do not want to be "presuppositional" and appeal to special revelation for this desired certainty, they appeal, as the ground for their natural theology, to certain "universal and necessary assumptions," namely, the law of noncontradiction, the "law of causality," and "the basic reliability of sense perception," which, they contend, "no one denies ... regularly and consistently,"[22] and which, for them apparently, are more non-negotiably certain at the beginning of their quest for God and truth than God himself is.[23] These assumptions, they say, along with any and all of their implications (one of

---

21. Buswell, *Systematic Theology*, 1:79–80. John M. Frame, *Apologetics to the Glory of God* (Phillipsburg, N.J.:Presbyterian and Reformed, 1994), 112, argues that if there is no first cause at the beginning of the chain of causes, then there is no "cognitive rest" for human reason. While he represents his argument here as an epistemological argument, Frame is too intelligent not to recognize that his is more an emotive than a probative argument.
22. R. C. Sproul, John Gerstner, and Arthur Lindsley, *Classical Apologetics*, 72. Of course, this universal negation is not true. Many scientists and philosophers of science today regularly deny the law of causality (for evidence of this, see Gordon H. Clark's review, "Classical Apologetics," in *Against the World: The Trinity Review, 1978–88*, ed. John W. Robbins [Hobbs, N.M.: Trinity Foundation, 1996]: 190–91.
23. These assumptions, as their beginning point, reflect the Ligonier apologists' conviction that Christian apologetics "must start with the person who is making the intellectual journey" (*Classical Apologetics*, 212): "From time immemorial all people have assumed that they must begin their thinking with themselves for there is no other place where *they* can begin. *Christian and non-Christian thinkers alike, being human,* have found no starting point but in the human subject" (ibid., emphasis supplied). But are we to make no distinction here between Christian

which, they attempt to show, is the existence of the Christian God), must be regarded as certain.

But when Christian certainty is grounded in assumptions which are regarded as "religiously neutral" and not distinctively Christian, and, in the case of sense perception, can be and often is very unreliable, how can such assumptions logically imply and compel the Christian worldview? Can it be that some unwitting presupposing of the Christian worldview is occurring along the way? While these scholars claim that their argument for God here is, in a sense, "transcendental," that is to say, they are positing assumptions that they claim are necessary for life and knowledge to be possible,[24] and whose ultimate implication, they say, is God, I believe that their conclusions are still freighted with the problem of uncertainty which empirical apologetic systems have never been able to overcome because of the limitations of empirical epistemology and because sense perception in particular is not always dependable, indeed, is often unreliable.

Sixth, the entire approach of natural theology as a method treats people (some, at least) as though they are "neutral" about the fact of God's existence, "simply operat[ing] according to human nature,"[25] and as though they are open to having—indeed, need (at least some of them) to have—the existence of God proven to them. But Holy Scripture teaches otherwise—that human beings do not need to have

---

and non-Christian thinkers (see Exod. 20:3; Prov. 1:7; 1 Cor. 10:31)? For these apologists, apparently not. But does this reflect a doctrine of depravity worthy of Calvinists? Moreover, since every datum of the universe is in some way related to every other datum, how can they be certain, beginning with themselves in their finiteness, that they have interpreted even the first datum, namely themselves, correctly?

Apart from the fact that their universal negative is patently untrue, for neither Euclid nor Aquinas nor Spinoza began with himself, and presuppositional apologists certainly do not begin with themselves, when the Ligonier apologists admit in their attempt to justify their appeal to "the basic reliability of sense perception," "How can we be sure that our senses are even basically reliable and not totally distortive? We cannot. That is why we are left with the common sense necessity of assuming it" (87), they are placing their faith in an unsubstantiated assumption, and thus reveal their own "fideism."

Their assumptions, of course, actually cannot even exist or have any meaning apart from the Christian worldview. The beginning of the buildup of certain knowledge with "this-worldly" assumptions that are viewed as "religiously neutral" appears to deny the theistic origin of these assumptions and to put the "creaturely" ahead of the Creator.

24. In private correspondence dated April 3, 1996, Frame described the Ligonier transcendentalism as "at best" an *ad hominem:* "They hope the unbeliever will concede these assumptions. Perhaps most unbelievers will. Then the Ligoniers get busy drawing assumptions. But you do run into some skeptics who won't grant any initial assumptions."

25. So the Ligonier apologists, *Classical Apologetics,* 233. Frame rightly asks: "Seriously now: is this a doctrine of depravity worthy of Calvinists?" ("Van Til and the Ligonier Apologetic," 292).

their Creator's existence proven to them, because (1) *he has revealed himself to them* through natural revelation (Ps 19:1; Rom. 1:19–20) and (2) they *understand* (νοούμενα, *nooumena*) that revelation because it is clearly seen (καθοράται, *kathoratai*) by them (Rom. 1:20–21, 32; 2:14–15). Nevertheless, they neither glorify Him as God nor are they thankful to Him and are therefore without excuse before Him (Rom. 1:20).[26] And, far from being neutral, they are doing everything they can in their sinfulness, because it is now their nature to do so, to suppress that knowledge, bringing God's wrath down upon them as the result (Rom. 1:18).

All this means that there is no such thing among mankind as an actual atheist. There are only theists, some of whom *claim* to be atheists. But God's Word declares that these "atheists" are not real atheists; they only attempt to live as though there is no God. But they know in their hearts that He is "there" and that He will someday judge them for their sin. As we have said, they are theists who hate, and attempt to do everything they can to suppress, their innate theism. Their "intellectual problems" with Christianity are in reality only masks or rationalizations to cover up their hatred of God and their love of and bondage to sin. These "practicing atheists" insist that the burden of proof lies with the theist to prove God's existence to them. But the burden of proof actually is theirs to prove that the physical world is the only reality and that no supernatural spiritual being anywhere exists. This, of course, they cannot do. Thus their "atheism" is their unproven "grand assumption"—an assumption, by the way, with which they cannot consistently live!

Seventh, the God of Scripture calls upon human beings to begin with or "presuppose" him in all their thinking (Exod. 20:3;[27] Prov. 1:7). But beginning as the

---

26. Some theologians have argued on the basis of the aorist (punctiliar) tense of the participle γνόντες (*gnontes*, "knowing") in Romans 1:21 that, while the entire race may have known God at some point in the past, that knowledge has not continued into the present and therefore the aorist participle does not describe everyone today. John Frame has responded to this argument in his *Apologetics to the Glory of God*, 8, fn. 12:

> Paul's purpose in this passage . . . is to show that all have sinned . . . . How can [Gentiles] be held responsible without access to the written law? Because of the knowledge of God that they have gained from creation. If that knowledge were relegated to the past, we would have to conclude that the Gentiles in the present are not responsible for their actions, contrary to 3:9. The past form is used (participially) because the past tense is dominant in the context. That is appropriate, because Paul intends to embark on a "history of suppressing the truth" in vv. 21–32. But . . . he clearly is using this history to describe the present condition of Gentiles before God. Therefore, the aorist *gnontes* should not be pressed to indicate past time exclusively. As the suppression continues, so does the knowledge that renders the suppression culpable.

27. Westminster's Larger Catechism, Question 106, informs us that the words "before me" in the first commandment are intended, among other things, "to persuade us to do as in His sight whatever we do in His service." This includes apologetics.

Christian evidentialist does in his quest for knowledge, not with God as his ultimate standard and basic reference point for all human predication (in order to "avoid circular reasoning at all costs"), but either with no criteria at all or with the "provisional" criteria of the non-Christian and with "the facts" viewed simply as "brute, uninterpreted facts," he

> posits an exception to 1 Cor 10:31: that when you are just beginning your quest for knowledge, you do not need to think "to the glory of God"; you can justifiably think to the glory of something/someone else.[28]

Such a beginning is out of the question for the Christian for whom "the fear of the Lord is the beginning of knowledge." Benjamin B. Warfield is a leading example of those who begin their apologetic for Christianity at the wrong place when, in his introductory note to Francis R. Beattie's *Apologetics,* he writes:

> *Before we draw it from Scripture,* we must assure ourselves that there is a knowledge of God in the Scriptures. And, *before we do that,* we must assure ourselves that there is a knowledge of God in the world, And, *before we do that,* we must assure ourselves that a knowledge of God is possible for man. And, *before we do that,* we must assure ourselves that there is a God to know.[29]

Here Warfield calls for a very complete natural theology to be erected by human reason. It would be very interesting to learn from him how he intended to prove, without presupposing the truthfulness of all that the Scriptures affirm about such matters, that the one living and true God exists, that man is natively able to know him, that there is a knowledge of God in the world, and that this God has made himself uniquely known propositionally at the point of the Hebrew/Christian Scriptures, and to prove all of this before he draws any of it from the Scriptures. Frankly, if men could assure themselves of all this on their own, and assure themselves of all this before they draw any of it from Scripture, it may be legitimately asked, would they need Scripture revelation at all? And would not their "religion" be grounded in their labors, a monument to their own intelligence? With greater insight into man's need to reason "presuppositionally," Jonathan Edwards wrote:

> Ratiocination, *without . . . spiritual light,* never will give one such an advantage to see things in their true relations and respects to other things, and to things in

---

28. Frame, "Van Til and the Ligonier Apologetic," 287.
29. Benjamin B. Warfield, "Introductory Note" to Francis Beattie, *Apologetics* (Richmond, Va.: Presbyterian Committee of Publication, 1903), 24, emphasis supplied.

general. . . . A man that sets himself to reason *without divine light* is like a man that goes in the dark into a garden full of the most beautiful plants, and most artfully ordered, and compares things together by going from one thing to another to feel of them all, to perceive their beauty.[30]

For Christian evidentialists such reasoning smacks of circularity, of course, and circular reasoning is the big "bugbear" for them—to be avoided at all costs. It is also their major criticism of what is known today as "presuppositional apologetics." Presuppositionalists, they declare, "presuppose" rather than prove the conclusions which they hold and insist that the unbeliever should presuppose them as well. Thus, according to evidentialists, the church is left with no defense of its beliefs.

The evidentialist concern not to leave the church defenseless is certainly legitimate and commendable. But presuppositionalists do not believe that they leave the church in that state. To the contrary, they believe (1) that it is the evidentialist who leaves the church defenseless in that the church is left on evidentialist grounds with no absolutely certain authority,[31] and (2) that it is the presuppositional apologetic alone which offers a sound defense of the Christian faith which does not at the same time compromise the "Godness" of God and the self-authenticating character of Scripture. A word of explanation about this apologetic approach is in order.

At bottom, it is really quite simple. As presuppositionalists employ the word, "presupposition" can be used both objectively and subjectively. Employed objectively, it refers to the *actual* transcendental foundation of universal meaning and intelligibility, namely, the triune God. Used subjectively, it refers to a person's most basic personal heart commitment, this commitment having (1) the greatest authority in one's thinking, being the least negotiable belief in one's network of beliefs, and (2) the highest immunity to revision. In matters of ultimate commitment then, if one is consistent, the intended *conclusion* of one's line of argument will also be the *standard* or presupposition which governs one's manner of argumentation for that conclusion—or else the intended conclusion is not one's ultimate commitment at all. Something else is. For the Christian presuppositionalist, "the two concepts coincide, for his basic commitment is allegiance to the One who really is the foundation of all universal intelligibility."[32]

Believing that "the fear of the Lord is the beginning of knowledge" (Prov. 1:7), that "all the treasures of wisdom and knowledge are hidden in Christ" (Col. 2:3),

---

30. Jonathan Edwards, "Miscellanies #408," in *The Philosophy of Jonathan Edwards*, ed. H. G. Townsend (1955; reprint, Westport, Conn.: Greenwood, 1972), 249, emphasis supplied.
31. See part one, chapter three, pp. 74–78, for my discussion and assessment of the Ligonier apologists' argument for the authority of the Bible.
32. From private correspondence to me from John M. Frame, dated May 6, 1996.

and *therefore* that the triune God (and/or the self-attesting Christ) is the *transcendental*, necessary ground of all meaning, intelligibility and predication, the presuppositional apologist maintains that the truth of God's self-authenticating Word should be presupposed from start to finish throughout one's apologetic witness. Accordingly, while the presuppositionalist values logic he understands that apart from God there is no reason to believe that the laws of logic correspond universally to objective reality. While he values science he understands that apart from God there is no reliable basis for doing science. While he values ethics he understands that apart from God moral principles are simply changing conventions and today's vices can become tomorrow's virtues. While he affirms the dignity and significance of human personhood he understands that apart from God man is simply a biological machine, an accident of nature, a cipher. And while he values the concepts of purpose, cause, probability and meaning he understands that apart from God these concepts have no real basis or meaning. Therefore, he thinks the Christian evidentialist is being untrue to his own faith when he grants to the unbeliever the hypothetical possibility of this being a non-theistic world that can successfully function and be rightly understood in terms of the laws of logic and the human sciences. And to suggest that the law of noncontradiction, the "law of causality," and "the basic reliability of sense perception" are more non-negotiably certain in this world than God himself is to deny the existence of the sovereign God of the universe "for whom and through whom and to whom are all things" (Rom. 11:36). To do so is also to abandon the Christ who "is before all things, in whom all things consist" (Col. 1:17), "in whom are hidden all the treasures of wisdom and knowledge" (Col. 2:3), and without whom man can do nothing (John 15:5). He reminds the evidentialist that it is not God who is the felon on trial; men are the felons. It is not God's character and word which are questionable; men's are (Job 40:1, 8; Rom. 3:4; 9:20). And it is not the Christian who is the unauthorized intruder in this world. This is his Father's world, and the Christian is "at home" in it.

It is not then the Christian primarily who must justify his Christian presence in the world but the non-Christian who must be made to feel the burden of justifying his non-Christian views.

By presupposing the Triune God of the Christian Scriptures and the Scriptures of this God, with all of its truth statements, the presuppositionalist does not have to begin by developing intricate in-depth arguments to justify his employment of the law of noncontradiction, the law of causality, and the general reliability of the senses, for the Scriptures as God's certain Word justify these matters for him.[33] To

---

33. Every fact that is is a theistically-justified fact. There is no such thing as a "brute," that is, uninterpreted, fact anywhere in the universe. Every fact that is enjoys its "thatness" by virtue of some activity of God and thus already carries His "interpretation" within it. For a man truly

illustrate, the Scriptures justify the legitimacy of the law of noncontradiction, first, by its assertion that every person, because he is the image of God, innately possesses the laws of reason as the bestowment of the divine Logos himself (John 1:3, 9), second, by the fact that the God of truth employs the Hebrew, Aramaic and Greek languages—which presuppose the laws of reason—to communicate his truth to the human mind, and third, by its many uses of various kind of logical argument and logical inference. It justifies the idea of causality with its employment of such words as כִּי, *ki*, יַעַן כִּי, *ya'an kî*, the preposition עַל, *'al*, with the infinitive, ὅτι, *hoti*; γάρ, *gar*; διά, *dia*, with the accusative case, and the causal participle. And it attests to the general reliability of the senses by declaring that all of man's senses are of divine origination (Ex. 4:11; Ps. 94:9; Prov. 20:12), and these are represented in Scripture as playing a regular role in the acquisition and build-up of knowledge (Luke 24:36–43; John 20:27; Rom. 10:14–17; 2 Pet. 1:16–18; 1 John 1:1–3; 3:14).[34]

The presuppositional apologist believes that his propagation and defense of the faith should be worked out then in a way which is consistent with his most fundamental commitment lest it become incoherent and ineffective. Accordingly, he does not believe that he can improve upon the total message that God has commissioned him to give to fallen men. Taking very seriously all that the Scriptures say about the inability of fallen man to understand the things of the Spirit (1 Cor. 2:14; see also Rom. 8:7–9; Eph. 4:17–18),[35] he speaks God's message, not to the

---

to know any fact would mean then that his interpretation of a given datum of this world would have to agree with God's prior interpretation of it. Such knowledge, as Van Til declares, would be "receptive reconstruction," that is, thinking God's thoughts after Him, rather than "creative construction," that is, placing meaning on "brute" facts for the first time by means of human intellection.

34. The laws of reason and even ever-reliable senses would by themselves still not give men certain knowledge, for with the aid of these learning apparatus alone, the most learned scholar in the world could not know for sure that the entire universe had not sprung into being five minutes ago with starlight already reaching the earth, trees complete with rings, humans with navels, ideas we call memories, etc. In addition then to these apparatus, men need an infinite reference point—an Archimedian ποῦ στῶ, *pou stō*, outside the universe—providing certain knowledge to them from which to launch their effort to justify their claims to knowledge and meaning. The Christian finds this transcendent ποῦ στῶ, *pou stō*, in the Triune God's comprehensive and certain knowledge of all things, a part of which knowledge God has condescended to share with us in Scripture. And men also need the self-attesting Christ, the one great Teacher (διδάσκαλος, *didaskalos*) (Matt 23:8) and providential governance over them, guiding and governing their employment of the laws of reason and sensation, if they are ever going to come to the least knowledge about anything.

35. Richard B. Gaffin points out in "Some Epistemological Reflections on 1 Cor. 2:6–16," *Westminster Theological Journal* 57 (1995): 122–23:

[W]here we might most expect [1 Cor. 2:6–16] to be treated [in *Classical Apologetics*], there is nothing, not even a parenthetical reference. Most remarkably, v. 14 (the inability of

so-called rational, neutral man who claims to be standing before him (this is fallen man's erroneous presupposition about himself), but to the spiritually blind, spiritually hostile, and spiritually dead person who God says is standing before him. And he does this with the confidence that God's Spirit, working by and with God's Word, will regenerate the elect and call them to himself. Should the evidentialist object that the presuppositionalist is only "throwing gospel rocks at the unbeliever's head" when he insists that the unbeliever must accept his biblical criteria for truth verification, the presuppositionalist, undaunted, will respond that he must continue to follow this approach just as the psychiatrist must continue to reason with a mental patient even though the latter lives in his own dreamworld and believes that it is the therapist who is out of his mind.

In his argumentation with the unbeliever the presuppositionalist is happy to employ all the biblical data and their implications for nature and history as (divinely preinterpreted) *evidence* for the truthfulness of the Christian position (and it is powerful evidence indeed).[36] But he is unwilling to answer the "biblical fool" (that is, the unbeliever) according to his folly, that is, he will not argue the case for Christian theism utilizing the tests for truth of the unbeliever's world-and-life-view, lest "he become like the fool" (Prov. 26:4). When he does "answer the fool according to his folly," he does so only as an *ad hominem,* to show him the unintelligibility of this world without God and the dire results of living consistently with his godless world-view (of course, no unbeliever, as Francis Schaeffer consistently argued

---

the unbeliever to understand) and the antithesis in vv. 14–15 are not even mentioned, much less addressed. . . . Apparently the authors of *Classical Apologetics* consider the passage irrelevant. Then they at least need to show us how that is so: for example, . . . how the cognitive inability of unbelievers in v. 14 does not exclude the rational competence to arrive at a sound natural theology, or how the "all things" of v. 15 must be circumscribed and does not include the truths of such a theology.

Ephesians 4:17-18 is also not cited.

36. See, e.g., part one, chapters one through three, for my argument for the divine origin of Scripture, part one, chapter five, for my argument for the Genesis creation, and part three, chapter fifteen, for my argument for the supernatural Christ. See also John Calvin, *Institutes,* I.8, a careful reading of which much-discussed chapter (which, in my opinion, would be better titled, "Evidences from Scripture for the Credibility of Scripture") will show that Calvin is in the main presenting biblical data in favor of the Bible's truthfulness. Virtually all of his argumentation for the credibility of Scripture ("the heavenly character of its doctrine," its "very heavenly majesty," "the beautiful agreement of all the parts," its "incontestable miracles" and "confirmed prophecy") is drawn from the Bible. What little evidence he adduces not drawn directly from Scripture (the indestructibility of Scripture through the ages, its wide acceptance by the nations, martyrs willing to die for it; I.8.12, 13) is not the main thrust of his chapter and is not compelling (the same could be said of other books such as the Koran). To the degree that he used these external evidences Calvin compromised his own *sola Scriptura* principle.

through the years, is living or can live consistently with his anti-theistic world view), and the presuppositionalist does so in order to keep the unbeliever from "becoming wise in his own eyes" (Prov. 26:5).

In conclusion, the presuppositionalist wishes the evidentialist would recognize that he too has his presuppositions as do all other people, and that he too reasons circularly.[37] For instance, though the evidentialist will not permit the Bible to be self-authenticating, he presupposes (wrongly) that sensory data (cosmic, historical, archaeological, etc.) are self-authenticating,[38] and thus he is as much a "dogmatist" on sensory experience as the presuppositionalist is on revelation. Hence the objection of circularity that the evidentialist levels against the presuppositionalist applies to himself with equal force. But his method, starting where it does, namely, with "uninterpreted" brute sensory data, is rendered logically invalid for the reasons stated in this introduction and thus can never arrive at the one living and true God or get the facts either.

Eighth, the Bible declares that human beings (and this includes Aristotle and Aquinas later who sought to demonstrate the existence of the unmoved Mover) have never been able, beginning with themselves, to reason themselves to God (1 Cor. 1:21), and their very attempt to do so is badly misguided.[39] Edwards writes:

> He that thinks to prove that the world ever did, in fact, by wisdom know God, that any nation upon earth or any set of men ever did, *from the principles of reason only without assistance from revelation,* find out the true nature and true worship of the deity, must find out some history of the world entirely different from all the accounts which the present sacred and profane writers do give us, or his opinion must appear to be a mere guess and conjecture of what is barely possible, but what all history assures us never was really done in the world.[40]

Ninth, by the evidentialist method the base of Christian belief is shifted and made to rest in doctrines certified by the declared "probability" of massed evidence, and more ultimately in the skill, craft and art of the human amasser of the evidence and not in the truth of God's Word and the work of God's Spirit. That is,

---

37. See Frame, *The Doctrine of the Knowledge of God,* 130–33.
38. See Warfield's admission, cited in part one, chapter five, p. 113, fn. 6.
39. If men can do and have done so, then Paul is wrong when he declares: "... in the wisdom of God the world through its wisdom did not know him." But if Paul is right, then we must conclude that all of the theistic arguments launched from earth toward heaven, even if we are not able to pinpoint any of their fallacies, fail to accomplish what their advocates claim for them.
40. Jonathan Edwards, "Miscellanies #986," in *The Philosophy of Jonathan Edwards,* 213, emphasis supplied.

the ultimate ground of faith becomes the work of man and not the Word of God.[41] But Paul expressly rejects such a ground:

> My message and my preaching were not with wise and persuasive words, but with a demonstration of the Spirit's power, so that your faith might not rest on men's wisdom, but on God's power. (1 Cor. 2:4–5)

Finally, methodological natural theology does not square with the actual apologetic activity of the early church as we find it depicted in the book of Acts. The natural theologian maintains that it is not right to ask skeptics to believe in Christ on the basis of scriptural authority before they have had a chance to consider the evidence supportive of the Christian claims. But does the unbeliever possess some independent criterion of verification which can *and should* authenticate the truth of Christian revelation in advance of faith? I think not. Otherwise, we must conclude that Dionysius the Areopagite, who believed in Christ simply on the basis of Paul's testimony prior to any investigation into what Paul proclaimed, was the biggest fool on Mars' Hill that day in A.D. 50 (Acts 17:22–34), and that the most intelligent men there were those who determined to hear Paul again on some subsequent occasion! No, the missionary efforts of Peter, Stephen, Philip and Paul never urge lost men to do anything other than to repent of sin and bow in faith before Jesus Christ. When they debate, they draw their arguments from the Scriptures (Acts 17:2; 18:28). They never imply that their hearers may legitimately question the existence of the Christian God, the truth of Scripture, or the historicity of the death and resurrection of Jesus Christ prior to personal commitment. Never do they suggest by their appeal to the evidence for God's presence and benevolence (Acts 4:9–10; 14:17; Rom. 1:20–21) that they are endeavoring to erect a "probability construct." They went forth into the world not as professional logicians and philosophical theologians but as preachers and witnesses, insisting that repentance toward God and faith in Jesus Christ are the sinner's only proper responses to the apostolic witness. They went forth with complete confidence that their message, as to its truthfulness, was incontrovertible and unassailable, and as to its effect, either the fragrance of life to those who were being saved by it or the stink of death to those who were refusing to bow before its claims (2 Cor. 2:15–16), rendering them culpable, by their refusal, of "making God a liar" (1 John 5:10). They were confident that, though for some their Christ

---

41. A classic example of this shift may be seen in Warfield's defense of inspiration in his "The Real Problem of Inspiration," in *The Inspiration and Authority of the Bible* (Phillipsburg, N.J.: Presbyterian And Reformed, 1948), 169–226. See my critique, "Warfield: A Case Study in Traditional Apologetic Methodology," *The Justification of Knowledge*, 47–70.

would be a cause of stumbling and for other foolishness, yet for the effectually called He would be both the power and wisdom of God.

As we have seen, the theistic proofs are invalid as logical arguments. But though they are invalid as logical arguments, some Christian apologists contend that they are still useful as "testimonies" to the existence of God. One is reminded here of Alasdair C. MacIntyre's remark:

> One occasionally hears teachers of theology aver that although the proofs do not provide conclusive grounds for belief in God, they are at least pointers, indicators. But a fallacious argument points nowhere (except to the lack of logical acumen on the part of those who accept it). And three fallacious arguments are no better than one.[42]

I must conclude that their use is the employment of shabby tools as means to win men to Christ. The defects in the arguments are many and apparent. Is not the apologist, then, leaving himself open to being humiliated should his auditor have the ability to point out the defects in them? And is there not something suspect—even dishonest and dishonoring to the self-attesting God of Scripture who sovereignly commands men everywhere to repent and bow before his Christ—about one's position when one attempts to win people to faith in Christ through the use of what one knows are specious intellectual arguments?

J. I. Packer has written concerning the theistic arguments:

> All arguments for God's existence, all expositions of the analogy of being, of proportionality and of attribution, as means of intelligibly conceptualizing God, and all attempts to show the naturalness of theism, are logically loose. They state no more than possibilities (for probabilities are only one kind of possibility) and can all be argued against indefinitely. They cannot be made watertight, and if offered as such they can be shown not to be watertight by anyone who knows any logic. This will damage the credit of any theology that appears to be building and relying on these arguments.[43]

I concur with Packer and affirm that I believe in the existence of the Christian God because I am a Christian by the grace of God and because of *the incontrovertible evidence* which the Christian faith entails, grounded as that faith is in the truthfulness and history of the Scriptures of the Old and New Testaments. In sum, mine is a Christian commitment and an apologetic attempting to be based upon the Bible alone. And let

---

42. Alasdair C. MacIntyre, *Difficulties in Christian Belief* (New York: Philosophical Library, 1960), 63.
43. J. I. Packer, "Theism for Our Time," in *God Who Is Rich in Mercy* (Grand Rapids, Mich.: Baker, 1986), 13.

no one—certainly no Christian, especially no Reformed Christian committed to the Westminster standards—brand such a faith commitment as simply sheer "fideism," that is, a faith founded on nothing, for my faith as a Christian in the Christian God and the self-attesting Christ of the New Testament is the result of the regenerating work of the Spirit of God which he wrought in my heart by and with the objective, revealed truth of the self-evidencing, self-validating Word of God.[44]

Accordingly, we will not begin our study of the doctrine of God with the question, "Does God exist?" Of course God exists. As Gordon H. Clark has argued repeatedly, anything that has any faint meaning at all "exists."[45] But it makes a great deal of difference whether God is a dream, a mirage, the square root of minus one, or the infinite personal God of sacred Scripture. Consequently, I will begin this study of the doctrine of God where the Shorter Catechism begins, namely, with the question, "What is God?" and set forth the nature of the God who, according to Romans 1:20–21, all men already know because he has revealed himself to them. Apologetically speaking, it is the existence of this God—the Triune God of Holy Scripture—that provides the only viable answers to the most perplexing questions respecting the origin and nature of the world and mankind and the titanic issues of life and death!

---

44. Christians committed to the theology of the Westminster standards believe that "the authority of the Holy Scriptures, for which it ought to be believed, and obeyed, dependeth not upon the testimony of any man, or church; but wholly upon God (who is truth itself) the author thereof: and therefore it is to be received, because it is the Word of God" (Westminster Confession of Faith, I/iv). They also believe that the Holy Scripture "doth abundantly *evidence itself* to be the Word of God" (I/v) by clear incontrovertible "arguments" such as "the heavenliness of the matter, the efficacy of the doctrine, the majesty of the style, the consent of all the parts, the scope of the whole (which is to give all glory to God), the full discovery [disclosure] it makes of the only way of man's salvation, the many other incomparable excellencies, and the entire perfection thereof" (I/v).

45. See Gordon H. Clark, *Three Types of Religious Philosophy* (Jefferson, Md.: Trinity Foundation, 1989), 43–44. Merely to say that a thing "exists" is to predicate of it an idea without meaningful content:

> Stars exist—but this tells us nothing about stars; mathematics exists—but this teaches us no mathematics; hallucinations also exist. The point is that a predicate, such as existence, that can be attached to everything indiscriminately tells us nothing about anything. A word, to mean something, must also not mean something. . . . [But] since everything exists, *exists* is devoid of information [since it does not "distinguish anything from something else"].
> ("Atheism," in *Against the World: The Trinity Review, 1978–1988*, ed. John W. Robbins [Hobbs, N.M.: Trinity Foundation, 1996], 135.)

CHAPTER SEVEN

The Names and Nature of God

OUR KNOWLEDGE of God is totally dependent on revelation (1 Cor. 2:11). All men know something of God's character because of the light of nature within them (John 1:9; Rom. 2:14–15) and natural revelation about them (Ps. 19:1; Rom. 1:20), but due to their fallen condition, they suppress this knowledge and pervert its message (Rom. 1:18, 23, 25, 28). Therefore, if men are to know what God is really like, they must turn to God's revelation of himself in Holy Scripture, where they can behold him aright. God's character is revealed in Scripture both in what he says about himself and in what he does. We shall consider two such areas of self-revelation in this chapter—God's names and God's nature.

THE SIGNIFICANT TITLES AND NAMES OF GOD

To the Western mind very little (if any) significance is attached today to the meaning of a child's given name, the determining factors most often being the parents' personal preference or its phonetic compatibility with the family name. But this was not the case in the ancient Middle East. A given name often commemorated some great historical or religious event or denoted the parent's hope for or assessment of a child's character (see, e.g., Gen. 4:1; 4:25; 5:29; 10:25; 17:5, 15; 1 Sam. 25:25). In keeping with this last instance, that is, where a name reflects a person's character, God in his revelation in Scripture progressively selected titles and names reflecting aspects of his divine character. These titles and names are too numerous to discuss them all in detail, but in this section we will briefly discuss ten of the more significant ones.

God (אֵל, 'ēl)

אֵל, 'ēl, the Qal participle of אוּל, ('ûl, "to be strong"), used 217 times in the Old Testament for the true God, means etymologically something on the order of "Mighty One" or "Powerful One," and is translated in English by the term "God."[1]

God (אֱלוֹהַּ, ʾelôah)

אֱלוֹהַּ, ʾelôah, from the root אָלָה ('ālâh, "to fear or reverence") means "revered one." Found 57 times in the Old Testament, it is occasionally used as a designate of the one true God of Scripture, but mainly in poetry (e.g. Deut. 32:15, 17; Pss. 18:32; 50:22; 114:7; 139:19; Job 3:4 and 41 other times in Job; Prov. 30:5; Isa. 44:8; Hab. 3:3; Neh. 9:7).[2]

God (אֱלֹהִים, ʾelōhîm)

אֱלֹהִים, ʾelōhîm, found 2570 times in the Old Testament, is also used to designate the one true God. Like אֵל, 'ēl, it is more a title than a proper name (although usage treats it like a proper name at times) since it often takes the article, something which a proper name can never do in Hebrew. Most likely אֱלֹהִים, ʾelōhîm, is to be related back to אֵל, 'ēl, ("Mighty One") or to the root אָלָה, 'ālâh, which some scholars suggest may be related with a passive meaning to the Arabic root of the same consonants meaning "to run to and fro in perplexity and fear," hence, "He who is to be feared" (see Gen. 31:42).[3] In form it appears to be the numerical plural (see the ים ending) of אֱלוֹהַּ, ʾelôah, but to construe the ים ending as a numerical plural would require that the word be translated "gods," a polytheistic conception. Its virtually uniform usage with singular verbs and modifiers, when referring to the one true God of Israel, would indicate rather that the title is to be construed as a singular noun, its plural *appearance* to be understood then, according to *Genesius' Hebrew Grammar*, as really a denotation of the abstract notion of majesty:

> The *pluralis excellentiae* or *maiestatis* . . . besides possessing the secondary sense of an *intensification* of the original idea [of the abstract plural], . . . is thus closely related to the plurals of amplification . . . which are mostly found in poetry. So especially אֱלֹהִים ['elōhîm] Godhead, God. . . . That the language has entirely rejected the idea of numerical plurality in אֱלֹהִים ['elōhîm] (whenever it denotes *one* God),

---

1. See Brown, Driver, and Briggs, *Hebrew and English Lexicon of the Old Testament* (Oxford: Clarendon, 1966 reprint), 42.
2. Ibid., 41, 43.
3. Ibid., 41, 43.

is proved especially by its being almost invariably joined with a singular attribute. Hence אֱלֹהִים [*'elōhîm*] may have been used originally not only as a numerical but also as an abstract plural (corresponding to the Latin *numen*, and our *Godhead*), and, like other abstracts of the same kind, have been transferred to a concrete single god (even of the heathen).[4]

Thus אֱלֹהִים, *'elōhîm*, means something like "mighty [or majestic] one," and hence, when referring to the God of Scripture, just "[the one true] God."

God Most High (אֵל עֶלְיוֹן, *'ēl 'elyôn*)

This title is formed by the conjunction of the noun אֵל (*'ēl*, "God") and the qualifying noun עֶלְיוֹן (*'elyôn*, "high"), the latter deriving from the verb עָלָה, *'ālâh*, meaning "to ascend, to mount up."[5] The qualifying noun's superlative signification as "*most* high" or "*most* exalted" may be inferred (1) from its connection with אֵל, *'ēl*, (2) from the appositive phrase, "Owner of heaven and earth," with which it is found in Genesis 14:19, 22, and (3) from its usage with יהוה, *yhwh*, in Psalms 7:18 and 47:3 and with אֱלֹהִים, *'elōhîm*, in Psalms 57:3 and 78:56.

Lord, Master (אָדוֹן, *'ādôn*)

אָדוֹן, *'ādôn*, derives from אָדַן (*'ādan*, "to rule over"), and is translated accordingly as "Ruler, Lord, Master." It is found as a compound with יהוה, *yhwh*, in Genesis 15:2 (אֲדֹנָי יהוה, *"donāy yhwh*, "my Lord, Yahweh") and in Psalm 110:1 it is placed over against Yahweh to designate a second distinct person seated upon Yahweh's throne, a verse often quoted in the New Testament in support of Jesus' messianic investiture. Its many plural occurrences referring to the one true God are to be explained as intensive plurals emphasizing God's exalted lordly ranking.[6]

God All-Sufficient (אֵל שַׁדַּי, *'ēl šadday*)

Much has been written on the meaning of אֵל שַׁדַּי, *'ēl šadday*, God's title particularly identified with the Patriarchal Age (Exod. 6:3). A few scholars trace the qualifying noun שַׁדַּי, *šadday*, to the root שָׁדַד, *šādad*, meaning "to deal violently with, to despoil," and urge that the title denotes God as the Destroyer. This is

---

4. *Gesenius' Hebrew Grammar*, 124g, 398–99.
5. See BDB, 751.
6. *Gesenius' Hebrew Grammar*, 124i, 399.

highly doubtful. If contextual considerations in Genesis are given their due, the more probable root is שָׁדַד, *šāḏaḏ*, from the more original שָׁדָה, *šāḏâh*, meaning "to moisten" or "to breastfeed" (שַׁד, *šaḏ*, means "breast"), hence "God the Blesser, the Nourisher, or Provider." In Genesis 17:1–8 God reveals himself as אֵל שַׁדַּי, *ʾēl šadday*, to Abraham, who had not as yet received the son of promise, and announces that, in keeping with his covenant, he would make Abraham exceedingly fruitful, with nations and kings coming forth from him. In 28:3 it is God in his character of אֵל שַׁדַּי, *ʾēl šadday*, whom Isaac invokes to bless Jacob and to make him fruitful. In 35:11 it is in his character as אֵל שַׁדַּי, *ʾēl šadday*, that God admonishes Jacob, "Be fruitful and multiply; a nation and a company of nations shall come from you, and kings shall spring from you." In 43:14 Jacob uses this same name to speak of the God who would grant mercy to his sons. In 48:3 he declares that it was אֵל שַׁדַּי, *ʾēl šadday*, who appeared to him and promised that he would make him fruitful and bring forth from him a great company of people. Finally, in 49:25 Jacob blesses Joseph with the declaration that אֵל שַׁדַּי, *ʾēl šadday*, would bless him with "blessings of the womb." Clearly, in Genesis אֵל שַׁדַּי, *ʾēl šadday*, is not God the Destroyer but God the Blesser or Succorer—able to subdue nature to his covenant purposes and to grant to the barren woman children innumerable. We see God here in his character of אֵל שַׁדַּי, *ʾēl šadday*, as the God who is able to succor his people and to supply their every need.

Yahweh (יהוה, *yhwh*)

If it is appropriate to say that the Old Testament God has a proper name, it is the tetragram יהוה, *yhwh*. It is pointed in the Hebrew Bible with the vowels of אֲדֹנָי, *ʾaḏōnāy*, (the Qere, "what was to be read"), yielding the hybrid word יְהֹוָה, *yᵉhôwâh*, from which the impossible "Jehovah" is derived. Its revelation, according to Exodus 6:3, while not totally unknown in previous ages (see, e.g., Gen. 9:26; 15:2), belongs to and is characteristic of the Mosaic period and beyond. Some critics have argued from this text that all of the references to Yahweh in Genesis are evidence of a J document distinguishable from an E source, but the Exodus statement must not be construed in an absolute way to suggest that the name had not been known before. As Geerhardus Vos writes:

> It is *a priori* improbable that Moses should have been sent to his brethren, whom he had to recall from forgetfulness of the God of their forefathers, with a new, formerly unknown, name of this God on his lips. Then there is the fact that Moses' mother [actually probably an ancestress—author] bears a name compounded with Jehovah, in its abbreviated form "Jo," viz., "Jokhebed." . . . Closely looked at, Ex. 6:3 does not require absolute previous unknownness of the word. The statement need mean nothing more than that the patriarchs did not as yet

possess the practical knowledge and experience of that side of the divine character which finds expression in the name.[7]

The name itself—occurring some 6000 times in the Hebrew Bible[8]— according to most current opinion would have been originally pronounced "Yahweh" (יהוה, *yâhweh*). This is affirmed on the basis of (1) the contracted poetic form יה, *yâh* (which occurs 50 times, e.g., Exod. 15:2; Isa. 38:11), (2) the יהו, *yâhû*, of compound Hebrew proper names, and (3) the Greek transliteration Ιαουαι, *Iaouai*, found in Clement of Alexandria (*Stromata*, 5.6.34) and 'Ιαβε, *Iabe*, found in Theodoret and Epiphanius.[9]

In apppearance the name seems to be an archaic Qal imperfect[10] from the verb הוה, *hawâh*, a rarer form of היה, *hayâh*, "to be." The name would then mean "he is," "he exists," or "he is present." Thus when God referred to himself, after Moses asked for his name, he said, "I am who I am." Say to the people of Israel, 'I Am' [אהיה, *'ehyeh*] has sent me to you" (Exod. 3:14–15). But when he gave his people a name by which they might know him, he named himself "he is" or "he exists," alluding to his self-existence and "faithful presence."[12] R. Laird Harris has argued on the basis of the evolution of Hebrew phonetic orthography that there is a problem with the pronunciation "Yahweh" because the ending *eh* is probably a post-Davidic form inasmuch as ל"ה verbs (which יהוה, *yhwh*, is said to be based upon) originally ended with a י, *y*, and because "if the word were spelled with four letters in Moses' day, we would expect it to have had more than two syllables, for at that period there were no vowel letters. All the letters were sounded." He also states that the word is of unknown origin and that we do not know what the pronunciation was, and concludes that "we are safer if we find the character of God from his works and from the descriptions of him in the Scripture rather than to depend on a questionable etymology of his name."[13] I concur but would suggest, on the basis of its connection with אהיה, *'ehyeh*, in Exodus 3:14, that *yhwh* is related to *hayâh*.

---

7. Geerhardus Vos, *Biblical Theology* (Grand Rapids, Mich.: Eerdmans, 1948), 130; see Exodus 6:6, 7.
8. 6823 times according to BDB, 217–18, and 5321 times according to TDNT, 3:1067.
9. BDB, 217–18.
10. Because it appears to be linguistically connected to אהיה, *'ehyeh*, which is a Qal form in Exodus 3:14, many scholars urge that *yhwh* should be construed as a Qal and not a Hiphil form.
11. Some scholars have suggested that by this statement God was refusing to tell Moses his name. But as God does proceed to give Moses his name this view is untenable.
12. So J. Barton Payne, *The Theology of the Older Testament* (Grand Rapids, Mich.: Zondervan, 1962), 147–48.
13. R. Laird Harris, *Theological Wordbook of the Old Testament*, ed. Harris, Gleason Archer, and Bruce Waltke (Chicago: Moody, 1980) 1:210–11. See also his article "The Pronunciation of the Tetragram," in *The Law and the Prophets*, ed. J. H. Skilton (Nutley, N.J.: Presbyterian and Reformed, 1974), 215–24.

Because this name for God is characteristic of the Mosaic age (Exod. 6:3) and beyond, during which time God spoke much about his covenant character (Exod. 33:19), it appears that God in his *Yahwistic* character is the self-existent, self-determining, faithful God of the covenant. Geerhardus Vos concurs and urges that the name

> gives expression to the self-determination, the independence of God, that which, especially in soteric associations, we are accustomed to call His *sovereignty*. . . . The name . . . signifies primarily that in all that God does for His people, He is from-within-determined, not moved upon by outside influences.[14]

The Christian should also be aware of the fact that the Old Testament Yahweh is also the tripersonal God of the New Testament, the name being used in some Old Testament contexts to designate specifically the Father (Pss. 2:7; 110:1), in other contexts to designate the Son (Isa. 6:1; see John 12:41), and in still other contexts to designate the Holy Spirit (Ps. 95:7–11; see Heb. 3:7–9).

Yahweh of Hosts (יהוה צְבָאוֹת, *yhwh sᵉbā'ôt*)

Concerning this title of God, Vos states: "This is a specifically prophetic name of God, which does not appear in the Pentateuch, Joshua, or Judges. We meet with it first in Samuel and Kings, next in eight Psalms, in all four of the early prophets, in all the other prophets, except Joel, Obadiah, Jonah, and Ezekiel. Finally, it occurs in three passages in Chronicles."[15] In other words, at the time Israel assumed its monarchical character, Yahweh revealed himself by this name as a Monarch—the "Lord of Hosts"—indeed, the true Monarch of Israel.

Because proper names—in this case יהוה, *yhwh*, ("Yahweh")—cannot stand in the construct state, most likely יהוה צְבָאוֹת, *yhwh sᵉbā'ôt*, is an abbreviation for יהוה אֱלֹהֵי צְבָאוֹת, *yhwh 'ᵉlôhêy sᵉbā'ôt* "Yahweh, God of Hosts." With these basic observations there is general agreement among scholars. But who are the "hosts" here? Four proposals have been advanced: the sum total of all created beings, the starry host, the human armies of Israel, and the angelic spirits.

Each of these options has merit, and certain Scripture verses might be cited in support of each. For example, Genesis 2:1 might be cited in support of the first view, but there is not much evidence beyond this one verse for such a construction. The second view has those passages favoring it which speak of "the host of heaven," such as Deuteronomy 4:19; 17:3; Jeremiah 8:2; 19:13; and Zephaniah 1:5; but

---

14. Vos, *Biblical Theology*, 134.
15. Ibid., 258; see also κύριος Σαβαώθ, *kyrios sabaōth*, in Romans 9:29 and James 5:4.

against it is the fact that the stars are uniformly called the "host" of heaven in the singular and not "hosts" in the plural, and they are never called "the host of Yahweh." The third view has more in its favor than the first two inasmuch as the expression under consideration actually seems to be explained by "the God of the armies of Israel" in 1 Samuel 17:45, and Israel's war-machine is called "our [Israel's] hosts" in Psalms 44:9; 60:10; 108:11. But the fourth view is the oldest and most widely held view because of the passages where the title is associated with angelic beings (1 Sam. 4:4; 2 Sam. 6:2; Isa. 6:2–3; 37:16; Pss. 89:5–8; 103:19–21). It is entirely possible that the original referent of "hosts" was the armies of Israel, but with the ever-increasing apostasy that developed in Israel and thus the ever-increasing "unworthiness of national Israel to be considered as the hosts of Yahweh,"[16] the prophets of the divided monarchy came more and more to transfer the honor of being God's fighting force from Israel on earth to the angels in heaven.

This name, with its warlike flavor, seems to be God's "royal name," designating him as the almighty King over both general human history and redemptive history (see Isa. 6:5; 24:23; Jer. 46:18; 48:15; 51:57).

The Name (שֵׁם, *šēm*)

In light of the fact that many facets of God's character were reflected in his titles and the Tetragram (יהוה, *yhwh*), the word for "name" in the singular (שֵׁם, *šēm*) was occasionally employed as a sufficient representation in itself of his titles and name, as in Leviticus 24:11: "The Israelite woman's son blasphemed the Name" (see also Exod. 20:7; Ps. 76:2). "In such cases 'the name' stands for the whole manifestation of God in His relation to His people, or simply for the person, so that it becomes synonymous with God."[17]

God (Θεός, *theos*)

In the Greek Septuagint, used widely by the early church, Θεός, *theos*, was regularly employed to translate אֵל, *'ēl*, אֱלוֹהַּ, *'elôah*, and אֱלֹהִים, *'elōhîm*. So it was natural that Θεός, *theos*, became the common term for "God" in the New Testament. It is used almost entirely in reference to God the Father, though there are some eight or nine places where it is employed to refer to God the Son (John 1:1, 18; 20:28; Acts 20:28; Rom. 9:5; Tit. 2:13; Heb. 1:8; 2 Pet. 1:1; 1 John 5:20).[18]

---

16. J. Barton Payne, *The Theology of the Older Testament* (Grand Rapids, Mich.: Zondervan, 1962), 150.
17. Louis Berkhof, *Systematic Theology* (Grand Rapids, Mich.: Eerdmans, 1932), 47.
18. See Murray J. Harris, *Jesus as God* (Grand Rapids, Mich.: Baker, 1992), for studies of each of these verses.

SYSTEMATIC THEOLOGY

Lord (Κύριος, *kyrios*)

In the LXX κύριος, *kyrios*, was regularly employed to translate the divine names יה, *yh*, and יהוה, *yhwh*. Very interestingly, while it is common for the New Testament writers to reserve θεός, *theos*, for the Father, they employed κύριος, *kyrios*, for Jesus Christ. Evidently sensitive to the possible charge of teaching a belief in two gods, they generally followed the literary convention of employing the title θεός, *theos*, when referring to the Father, and the covenant name of God in the Septuagint, *kyrios*, to refer to Christ.

THE NATURE OF GOD

The Westminster Confession of Faith declares:

> There is but one only, living, and true God, who is infinite in being and perfection, a most pure spirit, invisible, without body, parts, or passions; immutable, immense, eternal, incomprehensible, almighty, most wise, most holy, most free, most absolute, working all things according to the counsel of His own immutable and most righteous will, for His own glory; most loving, gracious, merciful, long-suffering, abundant in goodness and truth, forgiving iniquity, transgression, and sin; the rewarder of them that diligently seek Him, and withal, most just, and terrible in His judgments, hating all sin, and who will by no means clear the guilty.
>
> God hath all life, glory, goodness, blessedness, in and of Himself; and is alone in and unto Himself all-sufficient, not standing in need of any creatures which He hath made, nor deriving any glory from them, but only manifesting His own glory in, by, unto, and upon them. He is the alone fountain of all being, of whom, through whom, and to whom are all things; and hath most sovereign dominion over them, to do by them, for them, or upon them whatsoever Himself pleaseth. In His sight all things are open and manifest, His knowledge is infinite and infallible, and independent [that is, not dependent] upon the creature, so as nothing is to Him contingent, or uncertain. He is most holy in all His counsels, in all His works, and in all His commands. To Him is due from angels and men, and every other creature, whatsoever worship, service, or obedience He is pleased to require of them. (II/i-ii)[19]

---

19. Some commentators on the Confession, e.g., James Benjamin Green, suggest that these two paragraphs depict respectively what God is *ontologically* in himself (*in se*) and what he is *economically* for us (*pro nobis*). But while there appears to be some basis for this observation, it must be acknowledged, as John Murray observes, that "so inclusive and yet so compressed are the two sections dealing with the being, attributes, and counsel of God that *it is difficult if not impossible to discover the order of thought followed.*" Green himself recognizes that the division

The Westminster Shorter Catechism (Question 4), which the same Assembly prepared for the church's children, reduces all of this to the following: "God is a spirit, infinite, eternal, and unchangeable, in His being, wisdom, power, holiness, justice, goodness, and truth"—which statement Charles Hodge has characterized as "probably the best [extrabiblical] definition of God ever penned by man."[20] This Shorter Catechism definition will therefore be employed here as the skeletal framework for our discussion about God.

The Relation Between God's Nature and God Himself

By the term *nature* I refer to the complex of attributes or characteristics that belongs to or inheres in any given entity and makes it to be what it is in distinction from everything else. Sometimes God's attributes are represented as standing in relation to God in the same sense that pins are related to a pin cushion. This is erroneous thinking in the extreme. While a pin, which has a nature all its own, may be added or removed from a pin cushion, which also has a nature all its own, without changing in any way the essential nature of the pin cushion, the attributes of God are essential to the nature of God. They comprise the characteristics of God which distinguish him as God. It is precisely in the sum total of his attributes that his essence as God finds expression. With them he is distinguished as God from all other entities. Without them, either collectively or singly, he would simply cease to be God.

Sometimes the effort is made to isolate out of the sum total of God's nature some "primary" attribute which is then said to constitute his "being" or "essence"—a *substantia* which "stands under" and unites all the other varied and multiple "secondary"

---

which he draws between the two paragraphs cannot be rigidly maintained, for he asks rhetorically: "Does not the second section repeat some ideas expressed in the first section?" Donald Macleod, professor of systematic theology in the Free Church of Scotland College in Edinburgh, even states that the Confession "is content [in these paragraphs] with an almost haphazard list of the perfections ascribed to God in the Bible." Perhaps the Westminster divines intended the first paragraph to describe what God is in himself, his reactions toward human beings being brought in at the end of the paragraph only to provide a more complete listing of those attributes which describe what God is in himself, and the second paragraph to advance upon the first *in the sphere of authority* by emphasizing God's sovereign dominion over all his works, including angels and men, having the right as the one divine Sovereign to require of them whatever worship, service, or obedience he pleased. The Confession certainly makes no attempt to classify in any irrefutably distinguishable manner the attributes of God, not even in the manner most favored by Reformed theologians, namely, that of "communicable" and "incommunicable" attributes.

20. Charles Hodge, *Systematic Theology* (Grand Rapids, Mich.: Eerdmans, n.d.), 1:367.

attributes in one unified entity. "Spirit" is the attribute most commonly selected in this regard. For example, Gordon R. Lewis writes: "The attributes are essential to distinguish the divine Spirit from all other spirits. The divine Spirit is necessary to unite all the attributes in one being."[21] But the Bible does not seem to endorse the notion that we can isolate some single primary attribute that binds all of the others together, that is, some single "metaphysical" attribute upon which all of the others (the "nonmetaphysical") depend for their unity. The Bible suggests the identification of God's essence with all of his attributes. That is to say, God's nature is his "essence" (what he is) and his "essence" is his nature. True, the Bible does say, "God is spirit" (John 4:24). It is doubtless this statement which leads those who choose God's "spirit" as the "substance" underlying all the rest to insist that this is his *metaphysical* attribute and that all of his other attributes inhere in this single "metaphysical" attribute. But when we say that God is "spirit," we are only using theological shorthand for saying that God is personal and noncorporeal—two of his other attributes. Furthermore, the Bible says: "God is light" (1 John 1:5), "God is love" (1 John 4:8, 16), and "God is a consuming fire" (Heb. 12:29). Is God more fundamentally "spirit," that is, personal and noncorporeal, than he is, say, "love"? It is contended, of course, that there is a difference in the four statements—that the statement "God is spirit" is a metaphysical statement and that the other three are ethical statements. But it is significant, as Morton H. Smith observes,

> that the same kind of predication is used of both areas. Though these are the only four attributes that are placed in such a proposition in the Bible, they are sufficient for us to conclude that similar statements could be made regarding any of His attributes. "Every attribute is identical with His being. He is what He has. Whatever God is He is completely and simultaneously" (H. Bavinck, *Doctrine of God* [Grand Rapids, Mich.: Baker, 1951], 121). Through this doctrine Christian theology is kept from falling into the error of regarding God's attributes as separate from or independent of His essence [the error of the medieval hyperrealists who conceived of God as composed of *real* "universals" or parts—author].[22]

This is a valuable insight and it suggests that the temptation to distinguish between God's "metaphysical essence" and his "nonmetaphysical nature," and to make the former more primary than the latter, should be resisted.

---

21. Gordon R. Lewis, "God, Attributes of," in *Evangelical Dictionary of Theology* (Grand Rapids, Mich.: Baker, 1984), 451.
22. Morton H. Smith, "God, The Attributes of," in *The Encyclopedia of Christianity*, ed. Philip E. Hughes (Marshallton, Del.: National Foundation for Christian Education, 1972), 4:367. See also Robert L. Dabney, *Lectures in Systematic Theology* (1878; reprint, Grand Rapids, Mich.: Zondervan, 1972), 178.

On the other hand, it is equally necessary, when we declare that God's being is identical with his attributes, to resist the error of some medieval nominalists, who held that God's attributes are nothing more than words (Lat. *nomina*), so that the distinctions which they suggest are not really present in the one divine essence. For surely God's eternality is no more identical with his knowledge, his knowledge no more identical with his power, his power no more identical with his omnipresence, and his omnipresence no more identical with his holiness than is our knowledge identical with our power or our goodness identical with our finite extension in space. God's attributes are real, distinguishable characteristics of his divine being.

Classifications of the Attributes

Theologians, both medieval and Reformed, have rather uniformly drawn up their lists of divine attributes and then have classified them under either natural and moral, absolute and relative, original and derived, active and inactive, intransitive and transitive, or—and these are the most common classifications—incommunicable and communicable attributes.[23] Regardless of the preferred rankings, such choices appear to me to be highly scholastic in nature. Donald Macleod writes:

> None of these [classifications] has much to commend it and certainly none is to be regarded as authoritative. Scripture nowhere attempts a classification. . . . All the suggested classifications are artificial and misleading, not least that which has been most favoured by Reformed theologians—the division into communicable and incommunicable attributes. The problem here is that the qualities we refer to as incommunicable adhere unalterably to those we refer to as communicable. For example, God is "infinite, eternal and unchangeable" (*The Shorter Catechism*, Answer 4) and these are deemed to be incommunicable properties: and God is merciful, which is deemed to be a communicable property. But the mercy itself is "infinite, eternal and unchangeable" and as such is incommunicable. The same is true of all the other so-called communicable attributes such as the love, righteousness and faithfulness of God. On the other hand, to speak of omnipotence, omniscience and omnipresence as incommunicable is equally unsatisfactory. If we remove the prefix *omni* we are left simply with power, knowledge and presence, all of which have analogies in our own human existence.[24]

---

23. John Calvin is a notable exception, hardly treating God's attributes, which he speaks of as *virtutes*, at all anywhere in his *Institutes*. The nearest thing to a treatment is in *Institutes*, I.x.2, but even there his treatment is neither systematic nor developed but rather concentrated not on what God is in himself but on what he is for us.
24. Donald Macleod, *Behold Your God* (Fearn, Ross-shire, Scotland: Christian Focus Publications, 1990), 20–1.

Berkhof, while employing the incommunicable/communicable classification himself, stating that it has "always been rather popular in Reformed circles," acknowledges that "it was felt from the very beginning, however, that the distinction was untenable without further qualification." He goes on to say, in order to justify his continuing use of the distinction, that

> if we . . . remember that none of the attributes of God are incommunicable in the sense that there is no trace of them in man, and none of them are communicable in the sense that they are found in man as they are found in God, we see no reason why we should depart from the old division which has become so familiar in Reformed theology.[25]

But these very words give the reason for *not* using this classification and illustrate the qualifications that have to be introduced into every classification the theologian might select. Therefore we will simply discuss God's revealed attributes in a convenient, orderly manner by considering the Shorter Catechism definition.

Analysis of the Shorter Catechism Definition

The Shorter Catechism begins by employing the phrase "a spirit" to describe God—he is "a spirit." This phrase is then qualified by three adjectives—"infinite, eternal, and unchangeable." A prepositional phrase introduced by "in" then modifies the three adjectives; its seven nouns are in turn each qualified by the three adjectives. What this representation intends to show is this: that God is a personal (see the "his"), noncorporeal Being who is infinite, eternal, and unchangeable in his being; infinite, eternal, and unchangeable in his wisdom; infinite, eternal, and unchangeable in his power; infinite, eternal, and unchangeable in his holiness; infinite, eternal, and unchangeable in his justice; infinite, eternal, and unchangeable in his goodness; and infinite, eternal, and unchangeable in his truth. This may be depicted as:

	Transcendent Adjectives	*Condescendent Nouns*	*Summary Referent*
		being	
	infinite	wisdom	
		power	
spirit	eternal	holiness	GLORY
		justice	
	unchangeable	goodness	
		truth	

---

25. Berkhof, *Systematic Theology*, 55–6.

THE NAMES AND NATURE OF GOD

Three observations are necessary: First, it is important to note that it is not the first noun *per se* that distinguishes God absolutely from the creature; angels too are noncorporeal personal beings (Heb. 1:14). Nor is it the last seven nouns that distinguish God from the angels or from the human creature; again, they have, or can have, these same characteristics to a certain degree. It is the three adjectives "infinite, eternal, and unchangeable" that distinguish God in the absolute sense from the angels and from the human creature who bears his image; only God possesses these several characteristics in the infinite, eternal, and unchangeable sense.

Second, it is important to underscore the truth that when we speak of God's "infinite, eternal, unchangeable" being, etc., we are speaking of those attributes that comprise what the Scriptures intend when they speak of God's *glory*. That is to say, *God's glory is the sum total of all of his attributes as well as any one of his attributes.* For the creature to deny to him any one of his attributes is to attack the very glory of God and to deny him that without which he would no longer be God. Or to ascribe to him any attribute which he himself does not expressly claim to have, which ascription can only cancel out some attribute which he does claim to have, is again to represent him as something less than he is and thus is to attack his glory. For this reason it is imperative to listen carefully to God's description of himself in Scripture.

Third, it should be continually borne in mind that what we affirm here about God we are affirming not only about God the Father but also and equally about God the Son and God the Holy Spirit. In other words, the Shorter Catechism definition of God should be viewed as a description of the *Triune* God—Father, Son, and Holy Spirit—and not just a description of God the Father.

Excursus on God's Glory

The Hebrew word translated by our English word "glory" is כָּבוֹד, *kābôd*, which comes from the verb root meaning "to be heavy." Apparently, in the Hebrew mind a person's importance was thought of in terms of "weightiness." The Greek word translated "glory" is δόξα, *doxa*, from the verb root meaning "to think," referring to the opinion a person holds about himself or to what others think about him, that is, his reputation.

In the Bible, both terms refer basically to the importance of a person. In the case of men this importance is determined usually by their wealth, and it is fleeting. Jacob's wealth is called his "glory" (Gen. 31:1), while Joseph's position in Egypt is called his "glory" (Gen. 45:13). When Job lost his wealth, he complained that God had "stripped his glory" from him (Job 19:9). The nobility of Israel is referred to as the nation's "glory" (Isa. 5:13). And the Psalmist reminds us that when the wealthy man dies, "his glory [that is, his wealth] shall not descend after him" (Ps. 45:16–17).

The Bible, however, mainly speaks of God's glory. When it does it refers to what God is in his essential being or nature. That is to say, God's glory is simply the inescapable "weight" of the sheer intrinsic Godness of God, inherent in the attributes essential to him as the Deity. As an application of this idiom, the Bible often substitutes the word "glory" for a specific attribute of God, the attribute intended having then to be determined from the context. A few examples will illustrate this:

Exodus 33:19: When Moses asked the Lord to show him his glory (כָּבוֹד, *kābôd*), the Lord replied: "I will cause all my goodness to pass in front of you, and I will proclaim my name, the LORD, in your presence. I will have mercy upon whom I will have mercy, and I will have compassion on whom I will have compassion." Then the Lord declared that his glory would pass by. Apparently, by his "glory" in this context God intended his goodness (that is, his mercy and compassion), but a mercy and compassion which he sovereignly administers as he wills.

1 Samuel 15:29: "He who is the Glory [נֵצַח, *nēsah*] of Israel does not lie or change his mind." The word "Glory" here is a synonym for God as truthful and faithful.

Psalm 19:1: "The heavens declare the glory [כָּבוֹד, *kābôd*] of God." By "glory" here we should no doubt think of God's majesty, wisdom, and power (see the occurrences of "glory" in the contexts of Pss. 8:1–3; 104:24–31; Rom. 1:20–22).

Isaiah 6:3: The seraphs' antiphonal cry, "Holy, holy, holy is the LORD Almighty; the whole earth is full of his glory [כָּבוֹד, *kābôd*]," probably intends to declare that God's majestic holiness is present and manifest throughout the whole earth.

Romans 3:23: In the sentence "All sinned and are falling short of the glory [δόξα, *doxa*] of God," the word "glory" refers particularly to God's righteousness.

Romans 6:4: The sentence "Christ was raised from the dead through the glory [δόξα, *doxa*] of the Father," speaks particularly of God's power and his love and faithfulness to his Son.

Ephesians 1:6, 12, 14: Because Paul speaks of "the praise of the glory of his grace" in Ephesians 1:6, he most likely intends by his expression, "the praise of his glory" in 1:12 and 1:14 the same idea. If so, "glory" refers specifically in these latter verses to God's grace.

The Shorter Catechism definition then is really a catechetical description of the glory of the Triune God.

God Is Spirit

The Catechism description of God as "a spirit" is based upon the Greek text of John 4:24: πνεῦμα ὁ θεός, *pneuma ho theos*, literally, "spirit [is] the God." The first thing that must be addressed is the intent of the anarthrous πνεῦμα, *pneuma*. Leon

Morris wisely urges that we should omit the indefinite article in our English translation.[26] Jesus is not saying, "God is one spirit among many"; rather, he intended to underscore the truth that God's essence is of the nature of *spirit*.

What does Jesus teach about the essential nature of God when he describes God as "spirit"? The first point is that God is personal, that is, self-conscious and self-determining, living and active. This is the basis upon which the Catechism answer can employ the pronoun "his" a few words later. (The fact that the Bible ascribes to him such attributes as wisdom, knowledge, a will, and goodness also indicates that God is personal.) The God of the Bible is anything but inert impersonalness: he is the living and active Creator and Architect of the universe, beneficent Provider of the creature's needs, Advocate of the poor and the oppressed, Freedom-fighter, just Judge, empathetic Counselor, suffering Servant, and triumphant Deliverer. His personalness should not be taken to mean, however, that God is *one* person; for while it is true that God prefers as a literary convention to speak in his revelation to people as an "I" (see the "I Am" of Exod. 3:14), only rarely speaking as a plural subject employing the first person plural "we" or "us" (see Isa. 6:8 and Jesus' statements in John 10:30 and 14:23), yet in the "fullness" of his own being he speaks within himself as a plural subject for he is actually *tripersonal* (see Gen. 1:26; 3:22; 11:7; Isa. 6:8). Accordingly, Berkhof observes: "In view of the fact that there are three persons in God, it is better to say that God is personal than to speak of Him as a Person."[27]

The second thing God's *spiritual* nature means is that he is noncorporeal. This may be demonstrated from Luke 24:36–43, where, in response to the disciples' assessment that he was "a spirit," Jesus said: "Look at my hands and my feet. It is I myself! Touch me and see; for a spirit does not have flesh and bones, as you see I have" (v. 39). But what does it mean for God, as spirit, to be noncorporeal? It means that *no* property of matter may be ascribed to him. He has no extension in space, no weight, no mass, no bulk, no parts, no form, no taste, no smell. He is invisible (1 Tim. 1:17; 6:16) and, being one in essence and without parts, is indivisible (this last term denotes what some theologians refer to as his "simplicity").

It is this fact of his *spiritual* essence that underlies the second commandment, which prohibits every attempt to fashion an image of him. Moses reminded the nation of Israel: "You saw no form of any kind the day the LORD spoke to you at Horeb out of the fire. Therefore watch yourselves very carefully, so that you do not become corrupt and make for yourselves an idol, an image of any shape" (Deut. 4:15–16). The result of every effort to fashion such an image is a distortion and is thus an idol. God is *spirit*, and they who worship him must worship him *in spirit*

---

26. Leon Morris, *The Gospel of John* (Grand Rapids, Mich.: Eerdmans, 1971), 271.
27. Berkhof, *Systematic Theology*, 85.

and in truth. So the Christian must ever be solicitous never to think of God in his spiritual essence as having any material characteristic.

Infinite, Eternal, and Unchangeable in His Being

We have affirmed that God as spirit is a substantive entity who is personal and noncorporeal. But this description, while it may distinguish God from the corporeal human creature, fails to distinguish God from angels who are also noncorporeal, personal entities. (This fact illustrates the point that no word is self-defining; every word must be sufficiently qualified to distinguish its referent from other things.) So the next thing that the Catechism says about God as personal and noncorporeal is that he is "infinite, eternal, and unchangeable in his being." What does this mean?

INFINITE IN HIS BEING

In the context of the Catechism answer it is apparent that by "infinite in his being" the Westminster divines intended to assert that God is omnipresent, that is to say, that God transcends all spatial limitations and is immediately present in every part of his creation, or (what amounts to the same thing) that everything and everybody are immediately in his presence.

Some have inferred God's attribute of omnipresence from his attribute of omnipotence and omniscience. For example, Richard Swinburne has argued:

> A person who is omnipotent is able to bring about effects everywhere by basic actions. One who is omniscient at a certain time has justified true beliefs about things which are going on anywhere at any time.... An omniscient being does not depend for his knowledge on the correct functioning of intermediaries. Hence an omnipotent and omniscient person ... is of logical necessity an omnipresent spirit.[28]

While such reasoning has value in that it demonstrates the coherence of God's attributes, one is not shut up to an inference as the ground for the Christian assertion of God's omnipresence. It is directly taught in Scripture:

Psalm 139:7–10: "Where can I go from your Spirit? Where can I flee from your presence [מִפָּנֶיךָ, *mippāneykā*]? If I go up to the heavens, you are there. If I

---
28. Richard Swinburne, *The Coherence of Theism* (Oxford: Clarendon, 1977), 222.

make my bed in the depths, you are there. If I rise on the wings of the dawn, if I settle on the far side of the sea, even there your hand will guide me, your right hand will hold me fast."

1 Kings 8:27: "But will God really dwell on earth? The heavens, even the highest heaven, cannot contain you. How much less this temple I have built!"

Proverbs 15:3: "The eyes of the LORD are everywhere [בְּכָל־מָקוֹם, b^ekol-māqôm], keeping watch on the wicked and the good."

Amos 9:2–4: "Though [apostate Israel should] dig down to the depths of the grave, from there my hand will take them. Though they climb up to the heavens, from there I will bring them down. Though they hide themselves on the top of Carmel, there I will hunt them down and seize them. Though they hide from me at the bottom of the sea, there I will command the serpent to bite them. Though they are driven into exile by their enemies, there I will command the sword to slay them." (See also Obad. 4)

Jeremiah 23:23–24: " 'Am I only a God nearby,' declares the LORD, 'and not a God far away? Can anyone hide in secret places so that I cannot see him?' declares the LORD. 'Do not I fill heaven and earth?' declares the LORD."

Ezekiel 8:12: "[The Lord] said to me, 'Son of man, have you seen what the elders of the house of Israel are doing in the darkness, each at the shrine of his own idol? They say, "The LORD does not see us; the LORD has forsaken the land." ' "

Acts 17:27–28: "God . . . is not far from each one of us. For in him we live and move and have our being."

Two words of caution: First, the doctrine of God's omnipresence should not be construed so as to identify God with the universe, as in pantheism. Nor should it be construed, as does the panentheistic process theologian, so as to identify God with the impersonal moving force in the world, with the world as his "body." God's "personalness" and the fact of a real creation will not tolerate such a construction. While God is everywhere present and active in his universe (Christian theism's doctrine of divine immanence), he as *uncreated* ontologically stands off over against the universe that he created and is essentially distinct from it (Christian theism's doctrine of divine transcendence). The biblical teaching on the Creator/creature distinction is the guardian doctrine against all pantheistic and panentheistic reconstructions of the biblical God.

Second, the fact of God's omnipresence precludes taking the biblical depictions of God's "ascending" and "descending" and "comings" and "goings" literally. God, being everywhere present, does not literally "come" or "go" to or from specific places. Where such language is employed (for example, Gen. 11:5; Isa. 64:1–2), it must be recognized for what it is—metaphorical language indicating or invoking a *special manifestation* of God's working either in grace or judgment. Furthermore, since all that we say about God's nature *per se* is equally true of each of the persons of the Godhead, this conclusion has major implications with regard to the meaning of both the Incarnation and the Holy Spirit's "coming" into the world at Pentecost. Being omnipresent himself, God the Son did not literally "come" into the world in the sense that he came to a place where he was not before. The event of the Incarnation should not be interpreted to mean that God the Son literally "left heaven" and "came into the world" and "confined" himself to the earthly body of Jesus. This would mean that he in some way divested himself of his omnipresence. It intends rather to convey the fact that the Son of God uniquely manifested himself to the world and to men in and by human flesh. It intends to affirm that God the Son, through the instrumentality of the virginal conception, took into union with himself our human nature in such a real and vital sense that we properly declare that Jesus of Nazareth was God manifest in the flesh. But we do not for a moment intend to suggest that the Son of God somehow divested himself of his omnipresence when he became a man. Cyril of Alexandria, who led the orthodox opposition to Nestorius at the Council at Ephesus in A.D. 431, in a letter to Nestorius wrote:

> [The eternal Word] subjected himself to birth for us, and came forth man from a woman, without casting off that which he was; . . . although he assumed flesh and blood, *he remained what he was, God in essence and in truth*. Neither do we say that his flesh was changed into the nature of divinity, nor that the ineffable nature of the Word of God was laid aside for the nature of the flesh; for he is unchanged and absolutely unchangeable, being the same always, according to the Scriptures. For although visible and a child in swaddling clothes, and even in the bosom of his Virgin Mother, *he filled all creation as God,* and was a fellow-ruler with him who begat him, for the Godhead is without quantity and dimension, and cannot have limits.[29]

Twenty years later, in A.D. 451, the Council of Chalcedon, whose creedal labors produced the christological definition that fixed the boundaries of all future discussion, declared that Jesus possessed

---

29. From "The Epistle of Cyril to Nestorius with the XII Anathematisms," in *A Select Library of Nicene and Post-Nicene Fathers of the Christian Church* ed. Philip Schaff and Henry Wace (Grand Rapids, Mich.: Eerdmans, 1956 [second series]), 14:202, emphasis supplied.

two natures without confusion [ἀσυγχύτως, *asynchytōs*], without change [ἀτρέπτως, *atreptōs*], without division [ἀδιαιρέτως, *adiairetōs*], without separation [ἀχωρίστως, *achōristōs*], the distinctiveness of the natures being by no means removed because of the union, but the properties of each nature being preserved.

Calvin was hardly being heterodox, then, as the Lutherans sarcastically charged by their *extra-Calvinisticum* ("that extra-Calvin thing")[30] when he wrote:

> Another absurdity . . . namely, that if the Word of God became incarnate, [he] must have been confined within the narrow prison of an earthly body, is sheer impudence! For even if the Word in his immeasurable essence united with the nature of man into one person, we do not imagine that he was confined therein. Here is something marvelous: the Son of God descended from heaven in such a way that, *without leaving heaven*, he willed to be born in the virgin's womb, to go about the earth, to hang upon the cross, yet *he continuously filled the earth even as he had done from the beginning!*[31]

The *Heidelberg Catechism* grants explicit Reformed creedal status to this position when it declares in Question 48:

> Since [Christ's] Godhood is illimitable and omnipresent, it must follow that it is beyond the bounds of the human nature it has assumed, and yet none the less is in this human nature and remains personally united to it.

This is also true of the Holy Spirit's "coming" at Pentecost. He did not "come" into the world in the sense that would suggest that he left some earlier location and came to a place (the upper room) where he had not been before. Rather, his presence was simply uniquely manifested in the upper room at Pentecost.

---

30. In the interest of their doctrine of consubstantiation Lutherans believe that in the union of natures in the one person of Jesus Christ, our Lord's divine nature communicated its attributes to his human nature, resulting in his human nature becoming "ubiquitous" or everywhere present. If this were so, then of course our Lord's divine nature would never be *extra* ("outside of") his human nature since the latter would be everywhere. (Lutherans also believe that our Lord's human nature "emptied" itself of its ubiquity during the earthly days of his flesh but assumed it again at his resurrection.) The Reformed world views the Lutheran doctrine of the *communicatio idiomatum* as a blatant Eutychian rejection of Chalcedon's great adverbs ἀσυγχύτως, *asynchytōs* ("without confusion") and ἀτρέπτως, *atreptōs* ("without change").
31. Calvin, *Institutes*, II.xiii.4, emphasis supplied.

ETERNAL IN HIS BEING

By "eternal in His being" the Catechism intends to teach God's eternality in "both directions," that God has always existed in the past and always will exist in the future. He never began to be, knows no growth or age, nor will he ever cease to be. The following verses underscore this attribute of God:

Genesis 21:33: "Abraham planted a tamarisk tree [a small *ever*green] in Beersheeba, and there he called upon the name of the Lord, the Eternal God."

Psalm 29:10: "The LORD sits enthroned over the flood; the LORD is enthroned as King forever."

Psalm 45:6: "Your throne, O God, will last for ever and ever." (See Heb. 1:8, where the writer applies this passage to the Son of God, and Heb. 13:8, where the writer says of Jesus Christ: "Yesterday and today [he is] the same [ὁ αὐτός, *ho autos*], even forever [καὶ εἰς τοὺς αἰῶνας, *kai eis tous aiōnas*].")

Psalm 48:14: "For this God is our God for ever and ever; he will be our guide even to the end."

Psalm 90:2, 4: "Before the mountains were born or you brought forth the earth and the world, from everlasting to everlasting you are God . . . a thousand years in your sight are like a day that has just gone by, or like a watch in the night." (See also 2 Pet. 3:8: "With the Lord a day is like a thousand years, and a thousand years are like a day.")

Psalm 102:25–27: "In the beginning you laid the foundations of the earth, and the heavens are the work of your hands. They will perish, but you remain; they will all wear out like a garment. Like clothing you will change them and they will be discarded. But you remain the same, and your years will never end. (See Heb. 1:10–12, where the writer applies this passage to the Son of God.)

Isaiah 40:28: "The LORD is the everlasting God, the Creator of the ends of the earth."

1 Timothy 1:17: "Now to the King eternal [τῷ δὲ βασιλεῖ τῶν αἰώνων, *tō de basilei tōn aiōnōn*], immortal [ἀφθάρτῳ, *aphthartō*], invisible [ἀοράτῳ, *aoratō*], the only God [μόνῳ θεῷ, *monō theō*], be honor and glory for ever and ever. Amen."

These verses clearly ascribe everlastingness to God. But what is not so clear is whether his everlasting existence should be understood, with most classical Christian thinkers (for example, Augustine, Anselm, Aquinas), as also involving the notion of *timelessness*.

In his discussion of God's eternality Berkhof makes, I think, a highly significant observation: "The form in which the Bible represents God's eternity is simply that of duration through endless ages."[32] But he immediately aborts the significance of his statement with the remark: "We should remember, however, that in speaking as it does the Bible uses popular language, and not the language of philosophy." But it is sheer dogmatism to assert that the Bible is using "popular language" here, implying that the real truth of the matter is something else and that to arrive at the real truth one must appeal to philosophical categories. How does Berkhof know this?

His comment, of course, reflects the influence of Augustine and others who argue that *time is the succession of ideas in a finite mind*,[33] and since God being omniscient can have no such succession in his mind, therefore, he is "timeless," which "timeless eternity" is to be viewed as qualitatively separate and distinct from time. Gordon H. Clark, also following Augustine, explains:

> If there is a succession of ideas in God's mind, then the ideas that succeeded today were not present yesterday, and presumably some of yesterday's ideas have now passed by. But this means that God did not know all things yesterday, neither is he omniscient today.
>
> Is it not clear that a temporal succession of ideas in God's mind is incompatible with omniscience? Man is not omniscient precisely because his ideas come and go. Man's mind changes from day to day; God is omniscient, immutable, and therefore eternal.[34]

Aside from the fact that the Augustinian view seems to make God's "eternality," viewed in terms of timelessness, more an inference from God's attribute of immutable omniscience (note Clark's "therefore") than an attribute of God's essential being as such (where any longer in his definition of God's eternality, so understood, is God's "everlastingness" which the Bible speaks so much about?), it seems to me to be sheer dogmatism to declare, because God is omniscient (which I do not deny), that there can be no consciousness of successive duration in his mind. And it is a *non sequitur* to conclude from the fact of God's omniscience that God has no *idea of succession,* that is, that relative to his own existence he has no knowledge of a past, present, and future applicable to his own existence. This is to confuse the notion of *the succession of ideas,* which is surely *not* true of God if one means by this

---

32. Berkhof, *Systematic Theology,* 60.
33. Augustine's analysis of time, urging its subjectivity, may be found in his *Confessions,* book eleven, chapters 11–30. Denying that time is "the motion of a body," he declares that it is "extendedness" *(distentionem)* existing in the finite mind. He concludes: "It is in you, O mind of mine, that I measure the periods of time. Do not shout me down that it exists [objectively]. . . . In you, as I said, I measure the periods of time" (chap. 27).
34. Gordon H. Clark, "Time and Eternity," *Against the World. The Trinity Review, 1978–1988* (Hobbs, New Mexico: Trinity Foundation, 1966), 79.

notion that God learns new facts, with the notion of *the idea of succession* which I submit God surely has. Robert Lewis Dabney observes:

> If . . . the divine consciousness of its own existence has no relation to successive duration, I think it unproved, and incapable of proof to us. Is not the whole plausibility of the notion hence; that divines . . . infer: Since all God's thoughts are ever equally present with Him, He can have no succession of His consciousnesses; and so, no relation to successive time. But the analysis is false and would not prove the conclusion as to God, if correct. . . . In all the acts and changes of creatures, the relation of succession is actual and true. Now, although God's knowledge of these as it is subjective to Him, is unsuccessive [I take him to mean here that God does not first learn about them as the creature thinks and acts these changes—author], yet it [his knowledge] is doubtless correct, i.e., true to the objective facts. But these [the objective facts] have actual succession. So that the idea of successive duration must be in God's thinking. Has He not all the ideas we have; and infinitely more? But if God in thinking the objective, ever thinks successive duration, can we be sure that His own consciousness of His own subsistence is unrelated to succession in time?[35]

I concur with Dabney's analysis. Not to do so and to insist that God is timeless, that is to say, that the distinctions of time and hence existence with succession have no reference to him, lies behind much theological mischief. For example, Charles Hodge, who stands in the classical tradition, writes that "with [God] there is *no distinction* between the present, past, and future, but *all things are equally and always present to Him*. With Him duration is an *eternal now,*" that "to Him there is neither past nor future . . . the past and the future are always and equally present to Him [*as* an eternal now (or present)]," and that "to Him there is neither past nor future, neither before nor after."[36]

But such words seem to go too far, first, in that, if taken literally, they reduce to zero significance the temporal reference in every finite Hebrew, Aramaic, and Greek verb form God employed in his revelational description to us of his thoughts, words, and actions, and virtually transform them all into timeless participles.

Second, they also reduce to zero significance the prepositions בְּטֶרֶם (*b'terem*, "before") in such verses as Psalm 90:2 and Jeremiah 1:5 and אַחַר (*'ahar*, "after") in such

---

35. Dabney, *Lectures in Systematic Theology*, 40.
36. Hodge, *Systematic Theology*, 1:385 (emphasis supplied), 386, 538. This topic was apparently somewhat troublesome to Hodge, for when he writes later about God's knowledge he makes this better statement: "God knows all things as they are, . . . the past as past, the present as present, the future as future. Although all things are ever present in his view, yet he sees them as successive in time" (1:397).

verses as Joshua 24:5 and Jeremiah 12:15, as well as the significance of the preposition πρό, *pro*, in "foreknow" (προγινώσκω, *proginōskō*) and "predestine" (προορίζω, *proorizō*) in Romans 8:29 and in the expression, "He chose us in him *before* [πρὸ, *pro*] the creation of the world" (Eph. 1:4; see also John 17:24). Does not God inform us in these verses that he had a plan (his "eternal purpose") *before* he created the world? Does this data not mean that *before* the creation of the world God could have said, indeed, would have had to say as the God of truth if an angel had asked him about the "when" of the world's creation: "I have not yet created the world. Its creation is still in the future"? And does he not now have to say as the God of truth: "I have created the world; its creation is *no longer* in the future, it is *now* in the past"? It would certainly seem that the past is past for God, the present is present for God, and the future is future for God as surely as they are for us! And while he certainly and infallibly *knows* the future because he ordained it, it is still as the *future* that he knows it. It is odd, to say the least, to argue as does E. L. Mascall that all of God's acts are dipolar, and that a given act at the creature's end is temporal (either past, present, or future), while at the Creator's end *the same act is timeless*.[37] If God's "time-words" to us respecting his plans and actions do not mean for God the same as they mean for us, then *for him* the creation of the world may not have actually occurred yet, *for him* Christ's first coming may still be only a thing of predictive prophecy, *for him* Christ's second coming may be a thing of the past, *for him* the Christian may still be in his sin and still under divine condemnation, or *for him* these things and everything else may be past, present, and future all at the same time. In short, if God is timeless and if all of his acts are for him timeless acts, then we can have no true and certain knowledge of anything except perhaps pure mathematics.

Third, there seems to be an inherent contradiction in saying that a *timeless* person lives in the "eternal present" because the referent of the word "present" has significance only in the ordering category which includes past and future as well. Nicholas Wolterstorff points out:

> In order for something to be timeless, none of these ordering relationships [past, present, or future] can be applicable to that being. If a being is truly timeless, it should be impossible for it to exist simultaneously with anything else, or before anything else, or after anything else. Once it is established [or argued, as Hodge does—author] that a being does occupy one of the ordering relations, then that being is clearly temporal.[38]

---

37. E. L. Mascall, *The Openness of Being* (Philadelphia: Westminster, 1971), 166.
38. Paraphrased by Ronald H. Nash, *The Concept of God* (Grand Rapids: Zondervan, 1983), 81. For Wolterstorff's own words, see his "God Everlasting," in *God and the Good*, ed. C. Orlebeke and Lewis Smedes (Grand Rapids, Mich.: Eerdmans, 1975), 181–203.

For these three reasons it would seem that the ascription to God of the attribute of timelessness (understood as the absence of a divine consciousness of successive duration with respect to his own existence) cannot be supported from Scripture nor is it self-consistent. At best, it is only an inference (and quite likely a fallacious one) from Scripture. These reasons also suggest that the Christian should be willing to affirm that the ordering relationships (before, now, after) that are normally represented as relationships of time *are* true for God as well as for man.

On the other hand, the Christian should not endorse, without careful qualification, the idea that time is an aspect of God's eternity. It all depends on how time is defined. For example, if time be thought of as "the *objective* succession of moments existing apart from minds" and applied to God's being, it would suggest that God's being would indeed be undergoing an "ageing process." Also, something independent of God (that is, time itself) would seem to be moving history forward and thus a shadow is cast upon God's sovereign lordship over time and history. But if a definition such as that of J. Oliver Buswell Jr. were adopted, where time is the "mere abstract [that is, ideational] possibility of the before and after relationship in sequence,"[39] that is to say, if time is defined as the *idea* in a knowing mind (note: not simply in a *finite* mind but a knowing mind which includes God's mind as well) of the "before and after" relationship in durational succession, there is no problem in urging that time eternally resides in the mind of God and is descriptive, on the one hand, of the relationship between his thoughts and his creative actions (the former preceding the latter in durational sequence) and, on the other hand, of his knowledge of the relationship between any single divine action and a second divine action (one divine act preceding or following another in durational sequence).[40] This would mean that, for God, while he himself ever remains *ontologically* unaffected by durational sequence (that is, his consciousness of his sequential duration in no way impinges negatively upon his "Godness") and while his thoughts themselves (that is, his wisdom and knowledge) are eternally intuited, comprehensive, and teleologically ordered and *not* arrived at chronologically through the discursive process, nevertheless, the concept or idea of the possibility of "before" and "after" in durational sequence or succession is a distinct *epistemo-*

---

39. J. Oliver Buswell Jr., *A Systematic Theology of the Christian Religion* (Grand Rapids, Mich.: Zondervan, 1962), 1:47.
40. The evangelical philosophical theologian Ronald H. Nash concludes his discussion of God's "eternity" in *The Concept of God* with the words: "Is God a timeless or an everlasting being? At this time, I don't know . . . the jury is still out and presently I see no reason why theism cannot accommodate itself to either interpretation" (83). I am more inclined to view God's eternity in terms of everlastingness.

logical category applicable to him as it is to us. Consequently not only does he know the creature's past, present, and future as past, present, and future but he also knows his own *thoughts* on the one hand and his *actions* on the other as related to each other, the former to the latter, in "the 'before and after' relationship in durational sequence" (see here, for example, "He chose before he created" in Eph. 1:4). And he knows as well that his actions stand related to each other in durational succession (for example, he knows that he created angels sequentially before he created men—a legitimate inference, I would submit, from Job 38:4–7).

Affirming this allows the Christian to hold that the everlasting God, though he is at any and every given moment immanent in his world, is still the sovereign Creator and Lord over it, that the world (including its future) is in no sense foreign or unknown to him, and that history—past, present, and future—is the product of his eternal plan, creative activity, providential preservation, and common and special grace.

UNCHANGEABLE IN HIS BEING

Here the Catechism affirms the unchangeable nature or character of God (referred to in the theological vocabulary as his immutability). This doctrine affirms that God, ontologically and decretally speaking, does not and cannot change. Such verses as the following provide the basis for this classic Christian conviction:

> Numbers 23:19: "God is not a man, that he should lie, nor a son of man, *that he should change his mind* [וְיִתְנֶחָם, *wᵉyitnehām*]. Does he speak and then not act? Does he promise and then not fulfill?"
>
> 1 Samuel 15:29: "The Glory of Israel does not lie or *change his mind* [וְלֹא יִנָּחֵם, *wᵉlō' yinnāḥēm*]; for he is not a man, that he should change his mind."
>
> Psalm 102:26: "[The earth and the heavens] will perish, *but you remain* [וְאַתָּה תַעֲמֹד, *wᵉ'attâ taʿᵃmōd*]; they will all wear out . . . *but you remain the same* [וְאַתָּה־הוּא, *wᵉ'attâ hû'*]."
>
> Malachi 3:6: "For I, the LORD, *do not change* [לֹא שָׁנִיתִי, *lō' šānîtî*]; therefore you, O sons of Jacob, are not consumed."
>
> 2 Timothy 2:13: "If we are faithless, *he remains* [μένει, *menei*] faithful; for he cannot deny himself."
>
> Hebrews 6:17–18: "Because God wanted to make *the unchangeable character of his purpose* [τὸ ἀμετάθετον τῆς βουλῆς αὐτοῦ, *to ametatheton tēs boulēs autou*] very clear to the heirs of what was promised, he confirmed it with an oath [see Gen. 15:8–18]. God did this so that, by two *unchangeable things* [πραγμάτων ἀμεταθέτων, *pragmatōn ametathetōn*] in which it is impossible for God to lie, we may be greatly encouraged."

James 1:17: "Every good and perfect gift is from above, coming down from the Father of the heavenly lights, who does not change like shifting shadows [παρ' ᾧ οὐκ ἔνι παραλλαγὴ ἢ τροπῆς ἀποσκίασμα, *par hō ouk eni parallagē ē tropēs aposkiasma*]."

These verses emphasize the *constancy* of his being (or nature or character) and purpose, which constancy in turn guarantees that he remains always one and the same true God, faithful to himself, his decrees, and his works.

By what they have said about his immutability, as a consequence of their understanding of God's eternality as involving timelessness, classical theists have sometimes portrayed God as One virtually frozen in timeless immobility or inactivity (this is one example of the theological mischief which accrues to the ascription of timelessness to God). These theists correctly argue that since God is a perfect being, he is incapable of any ontological change, since any change must be either for the better or for the worse. He cannot change for the better since he is already perfect, and he cannot change for the worse since that would result in his becoming imperfect. The same holds true, it is incorrectly argued, with regard to any motion or activity on his part. Any movement must either improve his condition or detract from it. But neither is possible for a perfect Deity. Therefore, he remains in an "eternally frozen pose" (Packer's characterization) as the impassible God. But this is not the biblical description of God. The God of Scripture is constantly acting into and reacting to the human condition. In no sense is he metaphysically insulated or detached from, unconcerned with, or insensitive or indifferent to the condition of fallen men. Everywhere he is depicted both as One who registers grief and sorrow over and displeasure and wrath against sin and its ruinous effects and as One who in compassion and love has taken effective steps in Jesus Christ to reverse the misery of men. Everywhere he is portrayed as One who can and does enter into deep, authentic interpersonal relations of love with his creatures, and as a God who truly cares for his creatures and their happiness. In sum, as W. Norris Clarke declares, God is a " 'religiously available' God on the personal level."[41] To say then that God is unchangeable, that is, "immutable," must not be construed to mean that he cannot and does not act. The God of the Bible is portrayed as acting on every page of the Bible! He is not static in his immutability; he is dynamic in his immutability. But his dynamic immutability in no way affects his essential nature as God (that is, his "Godness"); to the contrary, he would cease to be the God of Scripture if he did not will and act in the ways the Bible ascribes to him. But he always wills and acts, as Isaiah

---

41. Clarke, "A New Look at the Immutability of God," in *God, Knowable and Unknowable*, ed. Robert J. Roth (New York: Fordham, 1973), 44.

declared, in faithfulness to his decrees: "In perfect faithfulness you have done marvelous things, things planned long ago" (Isa. 25:1). Berkhof correctly concludes:

> The divine immutability should not be understood as implying *immobility*, as if there is no movement in God. . . . The Bible teaches us that God enters into manifold relations with man and, as it were, lives their life with them. There is change round about Him, change in the relations of men to Him, but there is no change in His Being, His attributes, His purpose, His motives of actions, or His promises.[42]

Thus whenever divine impassibility is interpreted to mean that God is impervious to human pain or incapable of empathizing with human grief it must be roundly denounced and rejected. When the Confession of Faith declares that God is "without . . . passions" it should be understood to mean that God has no *bodily* passions such as hunger or the human drive for sexual fulfillment. As A. A. Hodge writes: "we deny that the properties of matter, such as bodily parts and passions, belong to him."[43]

We do, however, affirm that the creature cannot *inflict* suffering, pain, or any sort of distress upon him *against* his will. In this sense God *is* impassible. J. I. Packer says this well:

> Insofar as God enters into experience of that kind, it is by empathy for his creatures and according to his own deliberate decision, not as his creatures' victim. . . . The thought of God as *apathetos*, free from all *pathos*, characterized always by *apatheia*, represents no single biblical term, but was introduced into Christian theology in the second century: what was it supposed to mean? The historical answer is: not impassivity, unconcern, and impersonal detachment in face of the creation; not insensitivity and indifference to the distresses of a fallen world; not inability or unwillingness to empathize with human pain and grief; but simply that God's experiences do not come upon him as ours come upon us, for his are foreknown, willed and chosen by himself, and are not involuntary surprises forced on him from outside, apart from his own decision, in the way that ours regularly are. In others words, he is never in reality the victim whom man makes to suffer; even the Son on his cross . . . was suffering by his and the Father's conscious foreknowledge and choice, and those who made him suffer, however free and guilty their action, were real if unwitting tools of divine wisdom and agents of the divine plan (see Acts 2:23; 1 Pet. 1:20).[44]

---

42. Berkhof, *Systematic Theology*, 59.
43. A. A. Hodge, *A Commentary on the Confession of Faith* (Philadelphia: Presbyterian Board of Publications, 1869), 73–4.
44. Packer, "Theism for Our Time," ed. Peter T. O'Brien and David G. Peterson, *God Who Is Rich in Mercy* (Grand Rapids, Mich.: Baker, 1986) 7, 16–17.

An objection often raised against God's decretal immutability is this: if God always acts in accordance with his own foreknown eternal purpose, which is unalterably fixed, if he is ever constant in his fidelity to his own eternal decree, how do we explain the fact that the Scriptures will speak of God as being "grieved" over some prior action on his part or of his "changing his mind" and expressing a willingness to chart a course of action other than the one he is on? Are his "grief" and his "changing his mind" also aspects of his dynamic immutability, and if so, what then does "immutability" mean? And how does this square with the unalterable fixity of his eternal decree? This objection is based upon such verses as:

1. Genesis 6:5–7: "The LORD saw how great man's wickedness on the earth had become, and that every inclination of the thoughts of his heart was only evil all the time. The LORD was grieved that he had made man on the earth, and his heart was filled with pain. So the LORD said, 'I will wipe mankind, whom I have created, from the face of the earth . . . for I am grieved that I have made them.'"

How, it is asked, could God be grieved over man's evil—so grieved, in fact, that he could express regret over having made man—if he already knew that man would come to this and if all of this was according to his eternal decree?

2. Exodus 32:9–10: "I have seen these people [Israelites who sinned in worshiping the golden calf]," the Lord said to Moses, "and they are a stiff-necked people. Now leave me alone that my anger may burn against them and that I may destroy them. Then I will make you into a great nation."

By threatening to destroy Israel and to make Moses who was from the tribe of Levi (Exod. 2:1) into a great nation, does not God imply by his words that he was considering declaring null and void his promise that the Messiah would come through the line of Judah (Gen. 49:10)? And if so, does this not mean that God can "change his mind" at any time and thus alter his eternal plan and all subsequent history?

3. 1 Samuel 15:11: "I am grieved that I have made Saul king, because he has turned away from me and has not carried out my instructions."

How, it is asked again, could God grieve that he had made Saul king if he already knew that Saul would do the things he did and if all of this was according to his divine purpose?

4. Jonah 3:3–5, 10: "Jonah . . . went to Nineveh . . . and he proclaimed: 'Forty more days and Nineveh will be destroyed.' The Ninevites believed God. They declared a fast, and all of them, from the greatest to the least, put on sackcloth. . . . When God saw what they did and how they turned from their wicked ways, he had compassion and did not bring upon them the destruction he had threatened."

Did not God alter his course away from his earlier unconditional declaration of judgment? And if so, where then is his immutability?

A fourfold response may be given to these questions. First, where, upon a superficial reading, the biblical text seems to suggest that God did *in fact* alter his course of action away from a previously declared course of action, one should understand that his "new course" is only his settled, *immutably certain* response—in keeping with the principles of conduct respecting himself which he himself enunciates in Jeremiah 18:7–10—to a change in the human response to his holy laws:

> If at any time I announce that a nation or kingdom is to be uprooted, torn down and destroyed, and *if that nation I warned repents of its evil,* then I will relent and not inflict on it the disaster I had planned. And if at another time I announce that a nation or kingdom is to be built up and planted, and *if it does evil in my sight and does not obey me,* then I will reconsider the good I had intended to do for it. (emphases added)

In other words, God *always* acts the same way toward moral evil and the same way toward moral good. In his every reaction to men's responses to him, the *immutable* moral fixity of his character is evident. If men and women alter their relations to him, he will always respond in a manner consistent with his immutably holy character. This being true, God does not deem it necessary to attach to every promise he makes or to every prediction of judgment he issues the conditions for human weal or woe. They are always to be understood as in force, though they may be unstated. They are always operative so that whatever men do, God responds accordingly. And if the biblical interpreter does not realize this—that these conditions are operative even though unstated—he may conclude that God has broken a promise or has failed to carry out a predicted judgment.

A case in point is his dealings with Nineveh through the preaching of Jonah. While the message he instructed Jonah to proclaim to Nineveh appears to be unconditionally absolute in its declaration of judgment ("Forty more days and Nineveh will be destroyed"), the fact that the judgment was not to fall for forty days implies that if during that period of time Nineveh repented of its evil, the "promised" judgment would be withheld. In other words, the full import of Jonah's message was: "You have forty days to repent. If you do not, Nineveh will be destroyed. If you do, God will not afflict you with his threatened judgment." This is precisely the point that God himself enunciates in Jeremiah 18:7–10. We may be sure that God will *always* relate to his creatures with a moral fixity grounded in perfect justice. As the Psalmist declared: "To the faithful you show yourself faithful, to the blameless you show yourself blameless, to the pure you show yourself pure, but to the crooked you show yourself shrewd. You save the humble but bring low those whose eyes are haughty" (Ps. 18:25–27).

Does this mean that God's relationship to his creation is to be viewed always and only as cast in a *reactionary* mode, that is to say, that his actions are always and only penultimate *reactions* to man's more original and ultimate *actions?* No. As I will argue in chapter ten, God "from all eternity, did, by the most wise and holy counsel of His own will, freely, and unchangeably ordain whatsoever comes to pass" (Westminster Confession of Faith, III/i), having decreed nothing "because He foresaw it as future" (WCF, III/ii) and having decreed nothing with respect to the creature's weal because of "any foresight . . . of faith, or good works, or perseverance in either of them, or any other thing in the creature, as conditions, or causes moving Him thereunto" (WCF, III/v).[45] That is to say, he decreed nothing in *reaction* to some foreseen ultimate action of the creature. Accordingly, in keeping with his eternal purpose he grants or withholds repentance as he pleases, "having mercy on whom he wants to have mercy, and hardening whom he wants to harden" (Rom. 9:18), this granted or withheld mercy *as it comes to reality and is reflected in the life of the creature* causing him joy or grief respectively.

What I have said here is simply taking seriously the character of God who *as holy* can never approve of evil and who must always recoil against it even though he decreed its existence; who *as just* must always approve of obedience, pronounce it good, and rejoice over it even though, where it actually exists in the creature, he is the ultimate author of it; and who, simply because he is *good,* must always respond to the sinner's evil with grief and to the sinner's repentance with delight. In other words, the Bible simply will not endorse any theological construction that permits the eternal decree of God to loom so large and so to dominate everything else in it that God himself is represented within the construction as unmoved by the *actual* sin and/or *actual* repentance of his creature. Rather, we must be willing to say that God has willed all the actual conditions of the world in order to accomplish the particular ends he has determined, even though some of those conditions (because he is good) would offend and grieve him.

Second, God being not only the God of infinite holiness but also the God of infinite goodness and compassion, we should not be surprised to read that, in reaction to the evil of those who refuse to obey him, he could be grieved that he had made them. In fact it would be strange if we did not hear him say that their sin and evil were a source of great grief to him. God himself declared, "I take no pleasure in the death of the wicked, but rather that they turn from their ways and live" (Ezek. 33:11). Just as, because of his holiness, God cannot look upon man's sin with acceptance (Hab. 1:13), so also, because of his compassion, he cannot look upon the

---

45. The words "foresaw it as future" and "foresight" in these articles of the Confession suggest that God saw the future as future. But he did not decree the future on the basis of his foresight.

sinner's doom with pleasure (Ezek. 33:11). The creature's obedience *always* brings him joy; the creature's sin *always* grieves him, even to the point that he can declare that he regrets that he made those who disobey him. Buswell poignantly captures this point:

> God's immutability is the absolutely perfect consistency of His character in His actual relationships, throughout history, with His finite creation. Does ever a sinner repent, there is always joy in the presence of the angels (Luke 15:7, 10). Does ever a child of God, "sealed" by the Spirit, fall into sin, the Holy Spirit is [always] "grieved" (Eph. 4:30).[46]

Third, with regard to God's threat to destroy Israel and to "begin anew" with Moses, while God's anger against Israel was in no sense feigned, he knew that his threat to destroy Israel and to make Moses into a great nation was in no danger of ever being actualized. His words to Moses, "Leave me alone that . . . ," indicate that from God's perspective Moses stood before him as Israel's mediator. And God knew, because he had made Moses and had decretally determined to give him his "mediator" character, that Moses would certainly intercede on Israel's behalf and that he himself in response to Moses' mediation would set aside his "threat" toward Israel for Moses' sake. By allowing his response to Israel's sin to turn upon Moses' mediation—as just one instance of biblical mediation (see also, for example, Gen. 18:22–33; 19:29; Exod. 17:9–13; Job 1:4–5; Ezek. 22:30)—God intended to teach that he always relates himself to men salvifically through a mediator. When Moses made his appeal on Israel's behalf to God's own covenant promises to Abraham, Isaac, and Israel (Exod. 32:13) and, in order to "make atonement" for Israel's sin, declared that if God did not forgive Israel he wanted God to blot him out of the book which he had written (Exod. 32:30–32), he by his mediation was signifying the central redemptive principle of salvation through mediation, and in so doing Moses' mediation became by divine design an Old Testament type of Christ's mediatorial work. So what many assert is an example of the *mutability* of God's purpose is in actuality a remarkable example of God's *fixed purpose* to relate himself to sinful men on the basis of the intercession of an appointed Mediator.

Fourth, to those who would respond by asking why God, if he is a God of compassion, made men in the first place if he knew beforehand (not to mention decreed) that some of them would insult him and cause him grief, resulting in his own eternal hostility toward them and in their eternal hurt, I say that before they find fault with God's wisdom and love *vis à vis* the world that actually exists, they must be able to show that another world in which evil could not come to

---

46. Buswell, *Systematic Theology*, 1:57.

actuality would be richer in moral and spiritual values, would better accomplish his same ends, and would more accord with the entire range of his divine attributes. In light of the ultimate end God has wisely determined to accomplish, namely, the glorification of his beloved Son as the "Firstborn" among many brothers (Rom. 8:29) and thereby to glorify himself, it appears impossible that any such imagined world could meet these criteria and thus justify itself.

Infinite, Eternal, and Unchangeable in His Wisdom

God is all-wise—eternally and unchangeably so. His wisdom is reflected both in his eternal plan and in all his ways and works. He has wise reasons for his determined ends even though those reasons may not always be apparent to the creature. The Catechism here also obviously intends to include within the category of wisdom the category of knowledge, since it is not mentioned elsewhere in the definition. In other words, God knows all things and all true propositions (omniscience), always has and always will know all things, and cannot learn more or forget anything he knows. The Scriptures are replete with such teaching:

> 1 Samuel 2:3: "Do not keep talking so proudly or let your mouth speak such arrogance, for the LORD is a God who knows, and by him deeds are weighed."
>
> 1 Samuel 16:7: "Man looks at the outward appearance, but the LORD looks at the heart."
>
> Job 37:16: "Do you know how the clouds hang poised, those wonders of him who is perfect in knowledge?"
>
> Psalm 33:13: "From heaven the LORD looks down and sees all mankind; from his dwelling place he watches all who live on earth—he who forms the hearts of all, who considers everything they do."
>
> Psalm 94:9–11: "Does he who implanted the ear not hear? Does he who formed the eye not see? Does he who disciplines nations not punish? Does he who teaches man lack knowledge? The LORD knows the thoughts of man; he knows that they are futile."
>
> Psalm 104:24: "How many are your works, O LORD! In wisdom you made them all."
>
> Psalm 139:1–4, 15–16: "O LORD, you have searched me and you know me. You know when I sit and when I rise; you perceive my thoughts from afar. You discern my going out and my lying down; you are familiar with all my ways. Before a word is on my tongue you know it completely, O LORD. . . . My frame was not hidden from you when I was made in the secret place. When I was woven together in the depths of the earth, your eyes saw my unformed body. All the days ordained for me were written in your book before one of them came to be."

Proverbs 8:22–23, 27–30: "The Lord brought me [that is, wisdom] forth as the first of his works, before his deeds of old; I was appointed from eternity, from the beginning, before the world began. . . . I was there when he set the heavens in place . . . and when he marked out the foundations of the earth. Then I was the craftsman at his side."

Proverbs 15:3: "The eyes of the Lord are everywhere, keeping watch on the wicked and the good."

Isaiah 40:13–14: "Who has understood the Spirit of the Lord, or instructed him as his counselor? Whom did the Lord consult to enlighten him, or who taught him the right way? Who was it that taught him knowledge or showed him the path of understanding?"

Isaiah 40:27–28: "Why do you say, O Jacob, and complain, O Israel, 'My way is hidden from the Lord; my cause is disregarded by my God'? Do you not know? Have you not heard? The Lord is the everlasting God, the Creator of the ends of the earth. He will not grow tired or weary, and his understanding no one can fathom."

Isaiah 46:10: "I make known the end from the beginning, from ancient times, what is still to come."

Romans 11:33–36: "Oh, the depth of the riches of the wisdom and knowledge of God! How unsearchable his judgments, and his paths beyond tracing out! Who has known the mind of the Lord? Or who has been his counselor?"

Romans 16:27: "To the only wise God be glory forever through Jesus Christ! Amen."

Hebrews 4:13: "Nothing in all creation is hidden from God's sight. Everything is uncovered and laid bare before the eyes of him to whom we must give account."

1 John 3:20: "God is greater than our hearts, and *he knows everything* [γινώσκει πάντα, *ginōskei panta*]."

Thus the all-wise God is at every moment cognizant of everything that ever was, now is, or ever shall be. And it has never been otherwise. He necessarily knows himself exhaustively, and he necessarily knows his creation exhaustively—and both instantaneously, simultaneously, and everlastingly. His knowledge of himself and of all other things is absolutely comprehensive and eternally "intuited," that is, he has never learned anything because he has always known everything. He "never receives from some other source or from his own inventive genius an idea he never previously had" (Clark). God's knowledge is coextensive with all that is. All created things fall within the compass of God's knowledge, indeed, are what they are by virtue of God's prior knowledge (his prescience) and determinate counsel (his eternal plan). Every fact in the universe has meaning (may I say an interpretation?) by virtue of its place in the knowledge and plan of God. There is no such thing as a "brute," that is, uninterpreted, entity upon which man by his wisdom and knowledge places meaning for the first time. Since man's knowledge is then "receptively reconstructive and never creatively constructive" (Van Til), it follows that if a man learns a fact to any degree, his knowledge of that fact must accord with God's prior knowledge of it. And God has said something about everything in his inspired Word. God's knowledge, revealed in Holy Scripture, is then the criterion of validity for all human predication. It is only in God's light that we see light (Ps. 36:9).

A few early theologians questioned whether God bothers himself with a knowledge of earthly trivia (that is, "singularities"). Jerome, for example, thought it "unworthy of the divine majesty to let it down to this, that it should know how many gnats are born or die every moment, [or the] number of cinches and fleas on earth."[47] But the Scriptures explicitly affirm for God just such knowledge, declaring that he determines the number of the stars and calls them each by name (Ps. 147:4), and that "nothing in all creation is hidden from God's sight. Everything is uncovered and laid bare before the eyes of him to whom we must give account" (Heb. 4:13). Jesus said that not a sparrow is forgotten by God (Luke 12:6), and that "even the very hairs of your head are all numbered" (Matt. 10:29, 30).

A very significant implication of God's attribute of absolutely comprehensive, all-encompassing knowledge has to do with his infallible knowledge of *future* events. The Bible teaches that God infallibly knows the future, and this because he has decreed the future. And he himself declares that one distinction between himself and all the false gods of this world is his infallible ability to predict the future. God's knowledge of the future is spoken of in the following verses:

> Isaiah 41:22–23, 25–27: "Bring in your idols to tell us what is going to happen.... Declare to us the things to come, tell us what the future holds, so we may know that you are gods.... I have stirred up one from the north, and he comes—one from the rising sun who calls on my name.... Who told of this from the beginning, so we could know, or beforehand, so we could say, 'He was right'? No one told of this, no one foretold it, no one heard any words from you. I was the first to tell Zion, 'Look, here they are!' "

> Isaiah 42:8–9: "I am the LORD; that is my name! I will not give my glory to another or my praise to idols. See, the former things have taken place, and new things I declare; before they spring into being I announce them to you."

---

47. Jerome, *Commentary on Habakkuk*, on 1:13, 14. See also here Thomas Aquinas, *Summa theologica*, I, Q. 23, Art. 7: "Although God knows the total number of [corrupt] individuals, yet the number of oxen, flies, and such-like, is not in itself pre-ordained by God."

Isaiah 43:11–12: "I, even I, am the Lord, and apart from me there is no savior. I have revealed and saved and proclaimed—I, and not some foreign god among you."

Isaiah 44:7–8: "Who then is like me? Let him proclaim it. Let him declare and lay out before me what has happened since I established my ancient people, and what is yet to come—yes, let him foretell what will come. Do not tremble, do not be afraid. Did I not proclaim this and foretell it long ago? You are my witnesses. Is there any God besides me? No, there is no other Rock; I know not one."

Isaiah 44:24–28: "This is what the Lord says—your Redeemer, who formed you in the womb:

> I am the Lord,
>
> > [A] who [1] has made all things,
> >
> > > who [2] alone stretched out the heavens,
> > >
> > > who [3] spread out the earth by myself, [these three clauses refer to God's *creative* activity in the distant past]
> >
> > [B] who [1] foils the signs of false prophets and makes fools of diviners,
> >
> > > who [2] overthrows the learning of the wise and turns it into nonsense,
> > >
> > > who [3] carries out the words of his servants and fulfills the predictions of his messengers, [these three clauses refer to God's *revelatory* activity which he was then performing in Isaiah's day]
> >
> > [C] who says [1] of Jerusalem, 'It shall be inhabited,' of the towns of Judah, 'They shall be built,' and of their ruins, 'I will restore them,'
> >
> > > who says [2] to the watery deep, 'Be dry,' and 'I will dry up your streams,'
> > >
> > > who says [3] of Cyrus, 'He is my shepherd' and 'He will accomplish all that I please; he will say of Jerusalem, "Let it be rebuilt," and of the temple, "Let its foundations be laid." ' "[48] [these three predictive clauses refer to God's *redemptive* activity which he was to accomplish in the distant future]

Isaiah 45:18–21: "For this is what the Lord says . . .

> "I am the Lord,
>
> > and there is no other.
>
> I have not spoken in secret,
>
> > from somewhere in a land of darkness;
>
> I have not said to Jacob's descendants,
>
> > 'Seek me in vain.'

---

48. See O. T. Allis, *The Unity of Isaiah* (Philadelphia: Presbyterian and Reformed, 1950), 62–80, for a full discussion of this Isaianic "hymn of transcendence."

> I, the LORD, speak the truth;
>   I declare what is right.
> "Gather together and come;
>   assemble, you fugitives from the nations.
> Ignorant are those who carry about idols of wood,
>   who pray to gods who cannot save.
> Declare what is to be, present it—
>   let them take counsel together.
> Who foretold this long ago,
>   who declared it from the distant past?
> Was it not I, the LORD?
>   And there is no God apart from me,
> a righteous God and a Savior;
>   there is none but me."

Isaiah 46:10–11:

> "I make known the end from the beginning,
>   from ancient times, what is still to come.
> I say: My purpose will stand,
>   and I will do all that I please.
> From the east I summon a bird of prey [Cyrus];
>   from a far-off land, a man to fulfill my purpose.
> What I have said, that will I bring about;
>   what I have planned, that will I do."

Isaiah 48:3–7:

> "I foretold the former things long ago,
>   my mouth announced them and I made them known;
>   then suddenly I acted, and they came to pass.
> For I knew how stubborn you were. . . .
> Therefore I told you these things long ago;
>   before they happened I announced them to you
> so that you could not say,
>   'My idols did them;
>   my wooden image and metal god ordained them.'. . .
> From now on I will tell you of new things,
>   of hidden things unknown to you.
> They are created now, and not long ago;
>   you have not heard of them before today.
> So you cannot say,
>   'Yes, I knew of them.'"

Now all of this is very troublesome for some people, chiefly because of the implications God's knowledge of the future has for the "freedom of indifference" (freedom from all necessity) that they desire to ascribe to men. They quite correctly observe that if God knows all things, then it would seem that he must infallibly know the future. If he infallibly knows the future, then he must infallibly know all of the future acts of men. If he infallibly knows all of the future acts of men, then these acts must be certain of occurrence. But if their acts are certain of occurrence, then men are not free to choose and to act as they want. Accordingly, they conclude that divine omniscience is incompatible with human freedom.

To avoid this problem the Jesuits (Fonseca, Lessius, and Molina), against the opposition of the Dominicans, invented (and Socinians, Lutherans, and Arminians later adopted) the notion of a "middle knowledge" in God *(scientia media)*[49] by which God knows absolutely what men will freely do without having specifically decreed their actions, "since [He] knows what any free creature would do in any situation, [and thus] can, by creating the appropriate situations, bring it about that creatures will achieve his ends and purposes and . . . will do so freely."[50] But absolutely arbitrary (or contingent) future actions of men are not knowable, even granted previous divinely created and determined conditions, because these conditions, on this view, never *determine* human arbitrary actions. In sum, human indeterminism excludes divine middle knowledge.[51] Moreover, not only are such contingencies not knowable to God, but also such "future, free contingencies" *do not and cannot even exist* because they do not exist in God's mind as an aspect of the universe whose every event he certainly decreed, creatively caused and completely and providentially governs. In sum, created forces cannot be independent forces and independent forces cannot be created forces. What these thinkers refuse to realize is that if there were one square inch of this entire universe not under his sovereign governance, God is neither absolutely sovereign nor omniscient since that one square inch would have equal claim to its own sovereignty to do as it willed, with the authority even to set up a sign saying to God, "Keep out!" This theological construction allows billions upon billions of these sovereign human "inches" to exist throughout God's universe, all denying by their own sovereign

---

49. "Middle," that is, between what was called God's "necessary knowledge" of himself and all possible things because he is *necessarily* omniscient and his "free knowledge" of all actual things, past, present, and future, because he *freely* willed these things.

50. This view is now known as "Molinism" after the Jesuit scholar L. Molina (1536–1600). For a sympathetic introduction to the notion of "middle knowledge" in God by an evangelical, I would recommend William Lane Craig, *The Only Wise God* (Grand Rapids, Mich.: Baker, 1987), 127–51, from which this quotation is taken (135).

51. John M. Frame, in his review of Paul Helm's *The Providence of God* (*Westminster Theological Journal* 56 [Fall 1994]: 440), states that he "cannot understand why so many . . . sophisticated philosophers have failed to see this point."

right his sovereignty over them.[52] This construction cannot be squared with the biblical passages that teach that God did in fact foreordain whatever comes to pass, knows all things infallibly, and providentially governs all his creatures and all their actions to bring about his own holy ends (see, e.g., Acts 2:23; Rom. 9:16; Eph. 1:11; Phil. 2:13).

Other theologians have insisted that God simply limits his knowledge so that he does not know what men will do until they do it.[53] But according to Isaiah this ranks God with idols and makes him no better than a fortuneteller or a soothsayer, and his prophecies, at best, wishful thinking.

Still other theologians like Buswell simply assert an incompatibility between unabridged divine omniscience on the one hand and unqualified human freedom on the other and insist that we must learn to live with the incompatibility:

> We have called attention to theologians who on the basis of God's omniscience have denied the possibility of free actions. We have also called attention to philosophical writers who on the basis of the assumption that some actions are free, have denied the possibility of omniscience. Here we stand in our simplicity positively denying both conclusions.

---

52. For further helpful analytical discussions and refutations of this teaching of "middle knowledge," I would recommend Francis Turretin, *Institutes of Elenctic Theology* (Phillipsburg, N.J.: Presbyterian and Reformed, 1992), 1:212–18; Paul Helm, *The Providence of God* (Downers Grove, Ill.: InterVarsity Press, 1993); David Basinger, "Divine Control and Human Freedom: Is Middle Knowledge the Answer?" *Journal of the Evangelical Theological Society* 36, no. 1 (1993): 55–64; and David M. Ciocchi, "Reconciling Divine Sovereignty and Human Freedom," *Journal of the Evangelical Theological Society* 37, no. 3 (1994): 395–412.

53. See Clark H. Pinnock, "God Limits His Knowledge," *Predestination and Free Will*, ed. David and Randall Basinger (Downers Grove, Ill.: InterVarsity Press, 1986), 156–57. See also Richard Rice, *God's Foreknowledge and Man's Free Will* (Minneapolis: Bethany, 1985), 39, 54, and Clark Pinnock, Richard Rice, John Sanders, William Hasker, and David Basinger, *The Openness of God* (Downers Grove, Ill.: InterVarsity Press, 1994).

Ronald H. Nash notes that Pinnock's belief here clashes head-on with his belief that God, desiring the salvation of all, must make his salvation accessible to all. Writes Nash:

> I do not see how Pinnock's God can possibly do that, given his ignorance about the innumerable people and events and relationships involved. We all know how human beings are conceived. Presumably most of those conceptions occur as the result of voluntary human behavior [though the genetic code of the child is beyond the control of the parents, and Pinnock's God will not determine such matters—author], that is, the kind of future human acts Pinnock's God cannot know. It would seem to allow that Pinnock's God cannot then know what human beings will exist in the future. Much of the access that these humans will have to salvation would, it seems, depend upon the voluntary actions of themselves and others. But Pinnock's God must be largely ignorant about this as well. (*Is Jesus the Only Savior?* [Grand Rapids, Mich.: Zondervan 1954], 131.)

To the question then of how God can know a free act in the future, I reply I do not know. . . . God's knowledge of free events in the future is only one more mystery, revealed in the Scripture.[54]

Buswell follows here the path of agnosticism and simply asserts unabridged divine omniscience on the one hand and the fact of human freedom on the other.

Many Christian thinkers, for example, Augustine, Luther, Calvin, Edwards, Turretin, Charles Hodge, A. A. Hodge, and Berkhof, have been unwilling to endorse these solutions to the problem. They have denied that men have the freedom of indifference, that is, the freedom to choose either of incompatible courses of action with equal ease and out of no necessity, or the freedom to act in a way contrary to their nature. They have, however, acknowledged that men have the freedom of spontaneity, that is, that men normally can choose and act as they want *(lubentia rationalis)*, which means that as long as their acts are expressions of what they want to do, then their acts are to be viewed as free even if what they will is in some way determined.[55]

Of all these approaches this last seems the proper course to take. Suffice it to say here that the reason that God knows and can predict all future events is because he has sovereignly decreed them.[56]

Infinite, Eternal, and Unchangeable in His Power

According to the Catechism, God is all-powerful (omnipotent), and his power can be neither increased (since it is already infinite) nor diminished. This means that "God is able to do whatever he wills in the way in which he wills it."[57] That he is not subject to another's dominion but is King and Lord of all is a legitimate inference from his attribute of omnipotence. Again, the Scripture verses to these effects could fill several pages, the following among them:

Genesis 18:14: "Is anything too hard for the LORD? I will return to you at the appointed time next year and Sarah will have a son."

Psalm 115:3: "Our God is in heaven; he does whatever pleases him."

---

54. Buswell, *Systematic Theology*, 1:60–61. Buswell strangely introduces here an irreconcilable paradox between divine foreknowledge of future acts on the one hand and human freedom on the other, something he eschews earlier at 1:19–23.
55. This view is known, philosophically, as "soft determinism."
56. See further my discussion in chapter ten on the decree of God.
57. Gordon R. Lewis, "God, Attributes of," *Evangelical Dictionary of Theology*, 457–58.

Jeremiah 32:17, 26–27: Jeremiah prayed: "Ah, Sovereign Lord, you have made the heavens and the earth by your great power and outstretched arm. Nothing is too hard for you." . . . Then the word of the Lord came to Jeremiah: "I am the Lord, the God of all mankind. Is anything too hard for me?"

Luke 1:34, 37: To Mary's question, "How will this be since I am a virgin?" Gabriel replied: "Nothing is impossible with God!"

Ephesians 1:19–20: "His incomparably great power . . . like the working of his mighty strength, which he exerted in Christ when he raised him from the dead."

Revelation 19:6: "The Lord God omnipotent [ὁ παντοκράτωρ, *ho pantokratōr*, lit. "the Almighty One"] reigns."

In addition to these didactic statements, the Holy Scriptures consistently and repeatedly represent God's works of creation (Rom. 1:20), providence (Heb. 1:3), and redemption (Rom. 1:16; Eph. 1:19) to be effects of his almighty power.[58]

When we speak of divine omnipotence, however, *we do not mean that God can do anything*. The first thing God cannot do is whatever is metaphysically or ethically contrary to his nature. For example, he cannot lie (Heb. 6:17–18; Tit. 1:2), break his promise (2 Cor. 1:20), disown himself (2 Tim. 2:13), or change (Num. 23:19; 1 Sam. 15:29). Such divine "cannots," far from detracting from God's glory, "are his glory and for us to refrain from reckoning with such 'impossibilities' would be to deny God's glory and perfection."[59]

It should be apparent, second, that God cannot do the irrational, that is, the self-contradictory—what George Mavrodes calls "pseudo-tasks"—nor would he even try, because contradictories are *eternal* disruptions of his rationality. He cannot make two and two equal five, or create adjacent mountains with no valley between them, or make a stone too heavy for him to lift, or make a four-cornered triangle or a square circle. As Buswell rightly observes, all one has to do is to ask himself: "How much power would it take to accomplish the self-contradictory, for example, to make a wrong answer in arithmetical calculation, without changing it, the right answer?" to realize that such "irrationalities" belong to the domain of logic (and are condemned by it) and not to the domain of power at all.[60]

Third, it is inherently impossible for God to exhaust his power, that is, to exercise all of it at any given moment. To say that he can places a finite limitation upon his power. The fact of the matter is, nothing that we can point to is the evident effect of his *omni*potence—only his divine potence. He did not exhaust his power

---

58. H. Bavinck, *The Doctrine of God* (Grand Rapids, Mich.: Baker, 1977), 242–43.
59. John Murray, *Redemption—Accomplished and Applied* (Grand Rapids, Mich.: Eerdmans, 1955), 13.
60. Buswell, *Systematic Theology*, 1:63–64.

when he created the finite universe.[61] There is no reason to believe that he could not have made more stars or more land and sea creatures or more varieties of *flora* if he had willed to do so. In fact, he was not "exercised" by his creative activity in the slightest degree. He merely spoke and it was done (Ps. 33:9). Job speaks of the universe and its workings as "but the outer fringes of his works," a "faint whisper" of his might. "Who then," he asks, "can understand the thunder of his power?" (Job 26:5–14).

What the Scriptures intend then when they ascribe omnipotence to God is that God has the power to do whatever it takes power to do. He has the power to do even that which he does not will to do, and the only reason he does not exercise his power in this area is that he does not will to do so (this truth points up the fact that God has full authority over his power at all times; it is ever under the governance of his eternal plan and wise control). But whatever he wills to do he has the power to do. In other words, *God can do, and does, all his holy will.* But God does not will to do all that he has the power to do. God has the power, for example, to rid the world of all evil right now, but for wise and holy reasons, determined from all eternity, he does not will to do so.

This then is the conception of God's omnipotence as Christian theism has perceived it: God has the power to do everything that he has determined that he will do, and even the power to do that which is noncontradictory which he does not will to do. The Christian should have no problem accepting this since there is nothing in the conception, when properly explained, that is self-contradictory. As J. L. Mackie declares:

> Once we have decided that omnipotence is not to include the power to achieve logical impossibilities—and it must not include this, if it is to be discussable—there cannot be any contradiction within the concept itself.[62]

Infinite, Eternal, and Unchangeable in His Holiness

God is holy—infinitely, eternally, and unchangeably so. The Hebrew root (קָדַשׁ, *qādaš*) and the Greek root (ἁγιάζω, *hagiazō*) expressive of this idea both have the basic meaning of "separation." When used to describe God this "separateness" is not in the first instance to be construed as the attribute of moral "separateness from sin,"

---

61. It is precisely for this reason—because the universe is finite—that the natural theologian, beginning with an (assumed) "effect" which is finite, cannot move to and thus prove the existence of the infinite personal God of Scripture. All that a finite effect requires as the explanation of its existence is a cause sufficiently powerful to cause it, but a cause that is simply sufficiently powerful to effect a thing is not the "infinite God" of Scripture.
62. Mackie, "Omnipotence," *Sophia* 1 (1962): 24–25.

that is, what we normally characterize as moral purity. The Hebrew root-group, it is true, because of it basic idea came to be employed to describe God's moral purity as well, but more basically, it is descriptive of God's intrinsic "unapproachableness," that is, his majestic transcendence as the Deity over the creature. One sees this transcendent dimension of God's holiness reflected in one significant detail of Isaiah's vision of God in Isaiah 6:1–3. Isaiah writes:

> In the year that King Uzziah died, I saw the Lord seated on a throne, high and exalted, and the train of his robe filled the temple. Above him were seraphs, each with six wings: With two wings they covered their faces, with two they covered their feet, and with two they were flying. And they were calling to one another: "Holy, holy, holy is the Lord of Hosts; the whole earth is full of his glory."

John, who tells us that it was upon the preincarnate Son of God in all his glory that Isaiah was gazing (John 12:40–41), had a similar vision, and he gives us additional information about these seraphs and their antiphonal singing:

> In the center, around the throne, were four living creatures, and they were covered with eyes, in front and in back. The first living creature was like a lion, the second was like an ox, the third had a face like a man, the fourth was like a flying eagle. Each of the four living creatures had six wings and was covered with eyes all around, even under his wings. Day and night they never stop saying: "Holy, holy, holy is the Lord God Almighty, who was, and is, and is to come." (Rev. 4:6–8)

Now when Isaiah saw this awesome scene and heard these four creatures singing, he was immediately struck with his moral impurity (see the reference to his "unclean lips"). But what is often overlooked is that the seraphs are *sinless* creatures, and yet in the presence of God the Son they feel it necessary continually to cover themselves all over by their wings. Clearly, *for them* his "holiness" was his "separateness" from them due to his transcendence over against their creatureliness. It is also probably God's transcendent holiness which is being celebrated in the following contexts, as evidenced by the sustained emphasis upon his uniqueness among the gods and among men:

> Exodus 15:11: "Who among the gods is like you, O Lord? Who is like you—majestic in holiness, awesome in glory, working wonders?"
>
> 1 Samuel 2:2: "There is no one holy like the Lord; there is no one besides you; there is no Rock like our God."
>
> Isaiah 8:13: "The Lord Almighty is the one you are to regard as holy, he is the one you are to fear, he is the one you are to dread."

Isaiah 57:15: "For this is what the high and lofty One [same two Hebrew words as in 6:1] says—he who lives forever, whose name is holy: 'I live in a high and holy place, but also with him who is contrite and lowly in spirit.' "

Hosea 11:9: "I am God and not man—the Holy One among you."

Geerhardus Vos concludes in regard to God's transcendent or majestic holiness:

> Taking the divine holiness in this form, we can easily perceive that it is not really an attribute to be coordinated with the other attributes distinguished in the divine nature. It is something co-extensive with and applicable to everything that can be predicated of God: he is holy in everything that characterizes Him and reveals Him, holy in His goodness and grace, no less than in His righteousness and wrath.[63]

God is also ethically distinct from sinful men. And as we have already noted, the Scriptures employ the same word-groups that it uses to describe his majestic holiness to attest to his ethical holiness (Lev. 11:44–45; 19:2; 1 Pet 1:15–16). For just as he as the Creator is transcendentally "separate" from men as creatures, so also he is ethically "separate" from them as sinners. He is morally pure—infinitely, eternally, and unchangeably so—with regard to his character, his thoughts, and his actions. There is not the slightest taint of evil desire, impure motive, or unholy inclination about him. The Scriptures are replete with this representation of God:

> Psalm 5:4–6: "You are not a God who takes pleasure in evil; with you the wicked cannot dwell. The arrogant cannot stand in your presence; you hate all who do wrong. You destroy those who tell lies; bloodthirsty and deceitful men the Lord abhors."

> Psalm 11:5–7: "The Lord examines the righteous [and acquits them], but the wicked and those who love violence his soul hates. On the wicked he will rain fiery coals and burning sulfur; a scorching wind will be their lot. For the Lord is righteous, he loves justice; upright men will see his face." (See also Pss. 15; 33:5)

> Habakkuk 1:13: "Your eyes are too pure to look on evil; you cannot tolerate wrong."

> 1 John 1:5: "God is light; in him there is no [moral] darkness at all."

Because God is both majestically transcendent and ethically pure, "it becomes important to draw a circle of holiness around Him, which shall bar out the 'profane.' "[64] Accordingly, heaven is called holy, the mountain of the Lord upon which his temple rests is holy, his temple and its services are holy, his commandments are

---

63. Vos, *Biblical Theology*, 266; see also Berkhof, *Systematic Theology*, 73.
64. Vos, *Biblical Theology*, 268.

called holy, and the sabbath is holy. And if men are to live in his presence at all they must not wantonly seek to stray across the holy barrier between them and him or transgress his holy laws delineating this barrier. Specifically, if men are to live in his presence they must obey the laws he regards as essential to the protection of his majestic and ethical holiness from all profanation, which laws God as their Creator has written on their hearts and revealed at Sinai. Those who obey his laws he judges to be ethically "holy." But those who transgress his holy laws (all but one) he regards as mounting an assault upon the glory of his own divine transcendence and moral purity and treats them accordingly as transgressors and sinners.

Infinite, Eternal, and Unchangeable in His Justice

Closely related to his ethical holiness is God's infinite, eternal, and unchangeable justice by which the Christian understands the Scriptures to declare that God is necessarily *righteous* (Heb. צַדִּיק, *ṣādîq*; Gr. δίκαιος, *dikaios*) in his judgments, always rewarding all his rational creatures directly proportional to their works, showing partiality to none (Deut. 10:17) but always acquitting the righteous and always condemning the guilty (Exod. 23:7). As the Judge of all the earth he is righteous in all his ways and judgments (Gen. 18:25). As Moses declared, the Lord "is the Rock, his works are perfect, and all his ways are just. A faithful God who does no wrong, upright and just is he" (Deut. 32:4). But whereas judges among men are righteous judges if and when they adhere to the law *above* them, God as righteous Judge knows no standard of law above him in conformity to which he must render his judicial decisions. The criteria of justice to which he must conform his righteous standards of judgment are his own holy and righteous truth. Accordingly, the creature need have no fear that he will be judged according to an arbitrary fiat; he may rest assured that God's justice is grounded in his infinite wisdom and knowledge, his commitment to truth, and the demands which his own ethical holiness imposes upon him, and thus is and will be unassailably right and just. His judgments will, in sum, be according to the criteria of his own holy and just nature.

His justice is represented in Scripture both as *retributive* and *remunerative*. Retributively, he judges the wicked in righteousness:[65]

---

65. The following four verses—three in the Old Testament and one in the New—have often been cited against the idea that God deals in strict justice with man:
    Isaiah 40:2: "Speak tenderly to Jerusalem, and proclaim to her that her hard service has been completed, that her sin has been paid for, that she has received from the Lord's hand double [כִּפְלַיִם, *kiplayim*] for all her sins."
    Jeremiah 16:18: "I will repay them double [מִשְׁנֶה, *mišnêh*] for their wickedness and their sin."

Psalm 7:11: "God is a righteous judge, a God who expresses his wrath every day."

Psalm 9:7–8: "The Lord reigns forever; he has established his throne for judgment. He will judge the world in righteousness; he will govern the peoples with justice."

Psalm 96:10–13: "Say among the nations, 'The Lord reigns.'. . . . He will judge the peoples with equity. . . . He will judge the world in righteousness and the peoples in his truth."

Isaiah 5:16: "But the LORD Almighty will be exalted by his justice, and the holy God will show himself holy by his righteousness."

Daniel 9:14: "The LORD our God is righteous in everything he does."

Romans 2:5–6: "You are storing up wrath against yourself for the day of God's wrath, when his righteous judgment will be revealed. God 'will give to every person according to what he has done.'"

Romans 3:5–6: "What shall we say? That God is unjust in bringing his wrath on us? . . . Certainly not! If that were so, how could God judge the world?"

2 Thessalonians 1:5–7: "God's judgment is right. . . . God is just: he will pay back trouble to those who trouble you and give relief to you who are troubled."

But although it is true that the Scriptures cast God's righteousness in a retributive role, Herman Bavinck quite properly notes that the punishment of the wicked "is usually derived from God's wrath," with God's righteousness "usually represented as the principle of the salvation of God's people," that is, as the "attribute by virtue of which God justifies [acquits] the righteous, and exalts them to glory and honor."[66] Accordingly, in the Old Testament, God's people

---

     Jeremiah 17:18c: "Bring on them the day of disaster; destroy them with double [מִשְׁנֶה, *misneh*] destruction."

     Revelation 18:6b–c: "Pay her back double [διπλώσατε τὰ διπλᾶ, *diplōsate ta dipla*] for what she has done. Mix her a double [διπλοῦν, *diploun*] portion from her own cup."

     Do these verses not affirm that God can and does exact double jeopardy against the sinner? Do they not suggest an "imbalance in the scales of divine justice, with two talents of punishment loaded on one side for each talent of sin on the other," to use the words of Meredith G. Kline ("Double Trouble," *Journal of the Evangelical Theological Society* 32, no. 2 [1989]: 171–79)? What should one say about this apparent ethical problem? Simply that there has been a mistranslation. Kline has demonstrated that the Hebrew and Greek words translated "double" in these contexts really mean "equivalent" or "matching," as when we speak of something being the "double" of something else. So instead of denying the strict justice of God, these verses affirm that God's dealings with human beings are according to strict justice.

66. Bavinck, *The Doctrine of God*, 216, 217. Vos (*Biblical Theology*, 271) speaks of God's righteousness in this connection as "a righteousness of vindication, and a righteousness of salvation."

long for the future, for the Messiah, who will be the *righteous* Branch, Jer. 23:5, who will be righteous, Zech. 9:9; and who will not judge after the sight of the eyes, but with righteousness, Is. 11:3–5; and whose judgment, therefore, will consist in this: that "he will have pity on the poor and needy (who were now neglected and suppressed), and the souls of the needy he will save," Ps. 72:12–14. Hence, exercising righteousness would consist especially in delivering the needy; doing justice becomes with reference to these needy ones a deed of grace and compassion, as it were.[67]

Accordingly, as the righteous Judge, God

> grants salvation to the pious, because he establishes them, Ps. 7:9; helps them, 31:1; answers them, 65:5; hears them, 143:1; delivers them, 143:11; revives them, 119:40; acquits them, 34:22; grants unto them the justice due unto them, 35:23; etc.; while the wicked do not come into his righteousness, 69:27, 28. Hence, Jehovah's righteousness is not contrasted with his lovingkindness, as is his anger, Ps. 69:24 ff.; but it is synonymous with lovingkindness, Ps. 22:31; 33:5; 35:28; 40:10; 51:15; 89:14; 145:7; Is. 45:21; Jer. 9:24; Hos. 2:18; Zech. 9:9. The manifestation of God's righteousness is at the same time the showing forth of his grace, Ps. 97:11, 12; 112:4; 116:5; 119:15–19. Even the forgiveness of sins is due to God's *righteousness*, Ps. 51:15; 103:17; I John 1:9. Hence, the revelations of that righteousness are deeds of redemption, deeds of salvation and deliverance, Judg. 5:11; I Sam. 12:7; Ps. 103:6; Is. 45:24, 25; Mic. 6:5.[68]

How it is that the righteous Judge of all the earth can in righteousness *forgive* and *show compassion* toward sinners is to be traced to the fact that, while his children are guilty of all manner of iniquity, they nevertheless

> favor a righteous cause, they trust in the Lord, and they expect that he will grant them justice [righteousness], that he will fight their battle, and will give unto them the victory of salvation, Ps. 17:1 ff; 18:20, 21; 34:15; 103:6; 140:12. This salvation [consists] especially in this, that God grants unto his people forgiveness of sins, that he pours his Spirit into their hearts, that he grants unto them a new heart, and that he writes his law in their hearts, so that they walk perfectly before his countenance ..., Is. 43:25; Is. 31:33, 34; 32:39, 40; 33:8; Ezek. 11:19; 36:25; Joel 2:28 ff. [They are sinful, but they realize that] no one else than Jehovah can deliver [them] from this sin; "only in Jehovah ... is righteousness and strength," Is. 45:24.[69]

---

67. Bavinck, *The Doctrine of God*, 217.
68. Ibid., 218.
69. Ibid., 218.

They recognize that only as the Lord is righteous in his *faithfulness* to his covenant, that only "in the LORD all the descendants of Israel will be found righteous" (Isa. 45:25), that it is only as the Lord brings his righteousness near to them that salvation will not be delayed (Isa. 46:13).

These principles of righteousness, operative in the Old Testament, were also preparatory to the New Testament revelation of the righteousness of God in Christ. In the gospel a righteousness of God is revealed that is by faith and to faith (Rom. 1:17; 3:21). By virtue of Christ's righteousness God is able to forgive and to grant Christ's righteousness to believers who "are justified freely by his grace through the redemption that came by Christ Jesus" (Rom. 3:24). Ultimately the atoning work of Christ is the ground upon which God the righteous Judge "passed over [that is, forgave] sins committed beforehand [by the elect in the Old Testament]" as that work demonstrates God's justice in the present age, making it possible for him ever to be both just and the justifier of the one who has faith in Jesus (Rom. 3:25-26).

Infinite, Eternal, and Unchangeable in His Goodness

God has always been and always will be infinitely good (Heb. טוֹב, *tôb*; Gr. ἀγαθός, *agathos*), the Catechism teaches, ascribing thereby to him that perfection of the divine nature which prompts him to deal bountifully and kindly with all his creatures.[70] If it is God's attribute of majestic holiness that emphasizes his *transcendence over* his creation, it is God's attribute of goodness that underscores his *condescendence toward* his creation. For just as the Catechism subsumes God's knowledge under the rubric of his wisdom, so also the Catechism intends this beautiful word as the general category within which God's love, grace, mercy, pity, compassion, long-suffering, kindness, and other such expressions of his tender and fatherly character are to be placed. Among the Scriptures which testify to these characteristics of God's nature are:

> Exodus 33:19: "I will cause all my goodness to pass in front of you, and I will proclaim my name, the Lord, in your presence. I will have mercy on whom I will have mercy, and I will have compassion on whom I will have compassion." Note how God defines his goodness here in terms of sovereign mercy and compassion.
>
> Psalm 73:1: "Surely God is good to Israel, to those who are pure in heart." God's goodness here is saving goodness.
>
> Psalms 103 and 104 in their entirety.

---

70. See Berkhof, *Systematic Theology*, 70–71.

Psalm 106:1, 44–46: "Give thanks to the LORD, for he is good; his love endures forever. [In spite of Israel's great sin and rebellion], he took note of their distress when he heard their cry; for their sake he remembered his covenant and out of his great love he relented. He caused them to be pitied by all who held them captive."

Psalm 107 in its entirety.

Psalm 118:1, 29: "Give thanks to the LORD, for he is good; his love endures forever." The body of this psalm expands upon his goodness and concludes as it begins with the refrain: "Give thanks to the Lord, for he is good; his love endures forever."

Psalm 145:7–9, 13, 15, 16: "[The generations of your people] will celebrate your abundant goodness and joyfully sing of your [remunerative] righteousness [note here how God's goodness is explicated in terms of his grace and compassion]. The LORD is gracious and compassionate, slow to anger and rich in love. The LORD is good to all; he has compassion on all he has made . . . the LORD is loving toward all he has made. . . . The eyes of all look to you, and you give them their food at the proper time. You open your hand and satisfy the desires of every living thing."

Ezekiel 33:11: "As surely as I live, declares the Sovereign Lord, I take no pleasure in the death of the wicked, but rather that they turn from their ways and live. Turn! Turn from your evil ways! Why will you die, O house of Israel?"

Micah 7:18: "Who is a God like you, who pardons sin and forgives the transgression of the remnant of his inheritance? You do not stay angry forever but delight to show mercy."

Matthew 5:45, 48: "[Your heavenly Father] causes his sun to rise on the evil and the good, and sends rain on the righteous and the unrighteous. . . Be all-inclusive in your love [τέλειοι, *teleioi*], therefore, as your heavenly Father is all-inclusive in his." (Author's translation. See Luke 6:35–36 for support for so understanding τέλειοι, *teleioi*. God's goodness here is his common goodness extended to all his creatures.)

Mark 10:18: "No one is good—except God alone."

Acts 14:17: "He has shown kindness by giving you rain from heaven and crops in their season; he provides you with plenty of food and fills your hearts with joy." Here again God's goodness is his common goodness extended to all his creatures.

Romans 8:28: "In all things God works for the good [conformity to Christ's image] of those who love him."

1 John 4:8: "God is love [ὁ θεὸς ἀγάπη ἐστίν, *ho theos agapē estin*]."

These and the myriad other passages that speak of God's goodness to all—the just and the unjust (designated by theologians as his "common grace"), and his love for the world which moved him to give even his own Son for it (John 3:16), his tender and rich mercies which prompt him to relieve with the succor of a mother and the care of a father human misery and distress (Eph. 2:4; 2 Cor. 1:3–4), and his grace—that unmerited favor of God which moves him to extend forgiveness to the undeserving guilty sinner (designated by theologians as his special grace)—all affirm in their own way the infinite goodness of God. And even when he does what many of his rational creatures would contend is the ultimate misdeed of condemning the unjust man to hell, he is not being bad to him. He is simply being retributively just. It is simply impossible for him to be bad or to take pleasure in the horrible end of the unrighteous.

Infinite, Eternal, and Unchangeable in His Truth

By affirming that God is infinitely, eternally, and unchangeably "true," the Catechism declares that he is logically rational, ethically reliable, and covenantally faithful, and that he always has been, is, and always will be unchangeably so.

When Scripture declares that God is the "true" God, it intends to affirm, first, that God is, *metaphysically* speaking, the only God who is "really there" (Jer. 10:10; John 17:3 [referring to the Father]; 1 John 5:20 [referring to the Son]) over against the gods of the nations whom Scripture designates as "lies" (Pss. 96:5; 97:7; 115:4–8; Isa. 44:9–10, 20; Jer. 10:2–16; Amos 2:4; Jon. 2:9).[71] Then because he is *rational*, neither in his own understanding nor in what he declares is there any inherent contradiction. In other words, as the God of truth, for him the laws of logic, which are the *laws of truth*, are intrinsically valid because they are intrinsic to his nature. I would even contend, with John M. Frame, that "logic is an attribute of God."[72]

Therefore, he is ethically *reliable*, that is, there always has been, is now, and always will be a precise equivalency between *what he thinks and what he says*—what he says inerrantly reflects what he thinks and what he thinks is infallibly reflected in what he says: his Word is truth and therefore it is reliable. Consequently, he declares things and relationships to be as they actually are; he cannot lie (Num. 23:19; Rom. 3:4; Heb. 6:18; Titus 1:2). He will not go back on his declared purpose.

Because he is ethically reliable, God is covenantally *faithful*, that is, there is a precise equivalency between *what he says he will do and what he actually does*: "All the

---

71. See Vos, *Biblical Theology*, 255.
72. John M. Frame, *The Doctrine of the Knowledge of God* (Phillipsburg, N.J.: Presbyterian and Reformed, 1987), 253.

ways of the Lord are loving and faithful for those who keep the demands of his covenant" (Ps. 25:10). His covenantal faithfulness is the saint's ground of confidence, the foundation of his hope, the cause of his rejoicing, and the source of his courage: "If we are faithless, he will remain faithful, for he cannot disown himself" (Titus 2:13).

* * * * *

"Non-corporeal, (tri)personal Being—infinite, eternal, and unchangeable in His being, wisdom, power, holiness, justice, goodness, and truth"—this is the Reformed, indeed, the Christian theist's view of the God of Holy Scripture, as confessed in Walter Chalmers Smith's great hymn:

> Immortal, invisible, God only wise,
>   In light inaccessible hid from our eyes,
> Most blessed, most glorious, the Ancient of Days,
>   Almighty, victorious, Thy great name we praise.
>
> Unresting, unhasting, and silent as light,
>   Nor wanting, nor wasting, Thou rulest in might;
> Thy justice like mountains high soaring above,
>   Thy clouds which are fountains of goodness and love.
>
> Great Father of Glory, pure Father of light,
>   Thine angels adore Thee, all veiling their sight;
> All praise we would render; O help us to see
>   Tis only the splendor of light hideth Thee!

This view of God is also expressed in a moving hymn by Frederick W. Faber. The fact that Faber was a Roman Catholic only highlights the broad common ground concerning the nature of God that exists between Roman Catholics and Protestants who believe the Scriptures:

> My God, how wonderful Thou art,
>   Thy majesty how bright!
> How beautiful thy mercy seat,
>   In depths of burning light!
>
> How dread are Thine eternal years,
>   O everlasting Lord,
> By holy angels, day and night,
>   Incessantly adored!

How wonderful, how beautiful,
    The sight of Thee must be,
Thine endless wisdom, boundless power,
    And aweful purity!

No earthly father loves like Thee,
    No mother half so mild
Bears and forebears, as Thou has done
    With me, Thy sinful child.

O how I fear Thee, living God,
    With deepest, tend'rest fears;
And worship Thee with trembling hope,
    And penitential tears.

Yet I may love Thee too, O Lord,
    Almighty as Thou art;
For Thou has stooped to ask of me
    The love of my poor heart.

Father of Jesus, love's reward,
    What rapture will it be
Prostrate before Thy throne to lie
    And gaze, and gaze, on Thee!

CHAPTER EIGHT

God as Trinity

> In the unity of the Godhead there be three persons, of one substance, power, and eternity: God the Father, God the Son, and God the Holy Ghost: the Father is of none, neither begotten, nor proceeding; the Son is eternally begotten of the Father; the Holy Ghost eternally proceeding from the Father and the Son. (Westminster Confession of Faith, II/iii)

IN CONFORMITY with Western dogmatic tradition going all the way back to before Augustine, the last chapter treated the issue of God's attributes without specific reference to those matters which relate to the doctrine of the Trinity, explicating God's nature *as God*. This chapter takes up the dogma of God *as Trinity*, with the full awareness that all that has been said about God as such, if Triune Godhead there be, must be equally true of the three Persons of the Godhead, which is to say that the Father as divine spirit is infinite, eternal, and unchangeable, the Son as divine spirit is infinite, eternal, and unchangeable, and the Holy Spirit as divine spirit is infinite, eternal, and unchangeable, and yet the three are not three Gods but one God.[1]

Three propositions (or doctrines) are essential to the Christian doctrine of the Trinity: (1) there is but one living and true God who is eternally and immutably indivisible (the doctrine of monotheism); (2) the Father, the Son, and the Holy Spirit are each fully and equally God (the doctrine of the three Persons' "sameness

---

1. Theologians routinely distinguish between the *ontological* Trinity and the *economical* Trinity, intending by the former what God as Trinity is in himself and by the latter what God as Trinity is for or toward his creation. In this chapter we are primarily concerned with the doctrine of the ontological Trinity, some evidence for which is drawn from the scriptural teaching on the economical Trinity as it was revealed in the progressive unfolding of the redemptive process.

in divine essence")[2]; and (3) the Father, the Son, and the Holy Spirit are each distinct Persons (the doctrine of the three Persons' "distinctness in subsistence)."[3] These three concepts represent in capsule form the biblical doctrine of the Trinity.[4]

THE DOCTRINE'S REVELATIONAL GROUND

The word "Trinity" does not occur in the Bible, and neither do the expressions "sameness in substance" and "distinctness in subsistence." Nevertheless, the church from the third century on found such expressions helpful when explicating the teaching of Scripture on the tripersonality of the Godhead, being convinced, as Benjamin Warfield states in a somewhat startling fashion, that "it is better to preserve the truth of Scripture than the words of Scripture."[5] Which is just to say, contrary to what Unitarians would think and say, that the church has propounded its distinctive view of the tripersonality of the one true God, not because it became enamored of Greek thought or followed a spurious hermeneutic but because it was convinced that the Trinity is a *revealed* doctrine—not in the sense that it lies before us on the pages of Scripture as a "formulated definition" but in the sense that it appears therein in the form of "fragmentary allusions"; accordingly,

> when we assemble the *disjecta membra* into their organic unity, we are not passing from Scripture, but entering more thoroughly into the meaning of Scripture. We may state the doctrine in technical terms, supplied by philosophical reflection, but the doctrine stated is a genuinely Scriptural doctrine.[6]

Where is the doctrine revealed in Scripture? The answer to this question will occupy a major portion of this chapter, but it will not be superfluous to sketch out here its revelational *modus* before considering its revealed details.

---

2. In the Latin *substantia*, literally "that which stands under," was used to designate God's "essence." This doctrine is also referred to as the doctrine of the *homoousia* (Gk., ὁμοούσια, literally "sameness in essence").
3. In the Latin *subsistentia*, literally "standing or remaining under," came to mean "substance viewed as individualized essence." Other words which were employed to refer to the distinct Persons of the Godhead were the Latin *persona* ("character"), the Greek *prosopon*, "face," and later *hypostasis*, "actual being."
4. To deny the first proposition is to fall into the error of tritheism; to repudiate the second is to embrace some form of essential subordinationism within the Godhead; to reject the third is to embrace some form of modalism.
5. Benjamin B. Warfield, "The Biblical Doctrine of the Trinity," in *Biblical and Theological Studies* (Philadelphia: Presbyterian and Reformed, 1952), 22; F. Turretin concurs (see *Institutes of Elenctic Theology* [Phillipsburg, N.J.: Presbyterian and Reformed, 1992], 1:263).
6. Warfield, "Biblical Doctrine of the Trinity," 22.

THE HISTORICAL NATURE OF ITS REVELATION

It is unlikely that anyone familiar with or reading only the Old Testament today, with no knowledge of the New Testament, would conclude that within the inner life of the divine being resides a real and distinct personal manifoldness. This is not to suggest, however, that the Old Testament is not "Trinitarian," for it is—to the core. Nor is it to suggest that the saints of the Old Testament who had the benefit of enlightened prophets of God living among them and who could therefore consult them respecting the meaning of their writings were *totally* ignorant of a personal manifoldness in God. It is just taking seriously the fact that the Old Testament revelation *per se*, as a written corpus—to use Warfield's delightful metaphor—is like

> a chamber richly furnished but dimly lighted; the introduction of light brings into it nothing which was not in it before; but it brings out into clearer view much of what is in it but was only dimly or even not at all perceived before. The mystery of the Trinity is not revealed in the Old Testament; but the mystery of the Trinity underlies the Old Testament revelation, and here and there almost comes into view. Thus the Old Testament revelation is not corrected by the fuller revelation which follows it, but only perfected, extended and enlarged.[7]

The New Testament writers—thoroughly "Trinitarian" in their theology—evidently saw no incongruity between their doctrine of God and the monotheism of the Old Testament. Accordingly, it is quite proper to suggest that the following phenomena are all to be viewed as adumbrations of the doctrine of the Trinity in the Old Testament:

1. the plural cohortative "Let us make" and the plural pronoun "our" in Genesis 1:26: "Let *us* make man in *our* image" (see also Gen. 3:22; 11:7; Isa. 6:8);[8]

2. those close juxtapositions of some title for God which differentiate God in one sense from God in another sense, as in

> Psalm 45:6–7: "Your throne, O God, will last for ever and ever . . . You love righteousness and hate wickedness; therefore, God, your God, has set you above your companions" (see Heb. 1:8);

---

7. Ibid., 30.
8. As was discussed in the last chapter, אֱלֹהִים, *'lōhîm*, is not to be construed as a numerically plural noun and advanced as evidence for the Trinity: to construe it as such would necessitate that it be translated "Gods," and the Christian church has never believed in three Gods. This noun is consistently employed with singular verbs and modifiers, showing that it is to be taken as a singular noun. Its *–îm* ending should probably be understood as a majestic plural.

Psalm 110:1: "The Lord (יהוה, *yhwh*) says to my Lord (אֲדֹנִי, *ªdōnî*): 'Sit at my right hand until I make your enemies a footstool for your feet'" (see Matt. 22:41–45; also Num. 6:24; Isa. 33:22; Dan. 9:19);

3. the "angel of the Lord" who is both *identified* as God and yet *differentiated* from God (Gen. 16:7–13; 22:1–2, 11–18; 24:7, 40; 28:10–17 and 31:11–13; 32:9–12, 24–30; 48:15–16; Exod. 3:2–6; 13:21 and 14:19; 23:20–23 and 33:14; 32:34; Josh. 5:13–15; Judg. 6:11–24; 13:3–22; 2 Sam. 24:16; Hos. 12:4; Zech. 12:8; and Mal. 3:1).

4. those passages which depict God's Word and Spirit as virtually co-causes with God of his work, as in

Genesis 1:2: "and the Spirit of God hovered over the face of the waters";

Psalm 33:6: "By the word of the Lord were the heavens made, their starry host by the breath of his mouth" (see John 1:1–3; also Isa. 42:1; 43:9-12; Hag. 2:5–6);

5. those passages which tend to "personalize" God's Word, as in

Psalm 107:20: "He sent forth his Word and healed them" (see also Gen. 1:3; Ps. 33:6; 147:15–18; Isa. 55:11);

and which tend to do the same with God's Spirit, as in

Isaiah 63:10: "they rebelled and grieved his Holy Spirit" (see also Isa. 48:16; Ezek. 2:2; 8:3; Zech. 7:12);

6. those passages in which the Messiah as a divine Speaker refers to the Lord and/or the Spirit as having sent him, as in

Isaiah 48:16: "From the first announcement I have not spoken in secret; at the time it happens I am there. And now the sovereign Lord has sent me, with his Spirit";

Isaiah 61:1: "The Spirit of the sovereign Lord is on me, because the Lord has anointed me to preach good tidings to the poor" (see Luke 4:16–18);

Zechariah 2:10–11: " 'Shout and be glad, O Daughter of Zion. For I am coming, and I will live among you,' declares the Lord. 'Many nations will be joined with the Lord in that day and will become my people. I will live among you and you will know that the Lord Almighty has sent me to you' ";

7. those passages in which the prophet speaks of the Lord, the Angel of his presence, and his Holy Spirit as virtually distinct Persons, as in

Isaiah 63:9–10: "In all their distress he too was distressed, and the angel of his presence saved them. In his love and mercy he redeemed them; he lifted them up and carried them all the days of old. Yet they rebelled and grieved his Holy Spirit. So he turned and became their enemy and he himself fought against them";

8. and finally, those passages in which a plural noun is employed to refer to God (these could be plurals of intensification, however, on the analogy of אֱלֹהִים, *ᵉlōhîm*), such as

Psalm 149:2: "Let Israel rejoice in his Maker [בְּעֹשָׂיו, *bᵉʿōśayw;* lit., "Makers"]; let the people of Zion be glad in their King";

Ecclesiastes 12:1: "Remember your Creator [בּוֹרְאֶיךָ, *bôrʾeykā;* lit., "Creators"] in the days of your youth";

Isaiah 54:5: "For your Maker [עֹשַׂיִךְ, *ʿōśayik;* lit., 'Makers'] is your husband [בֹּעֲלַיִךְ, *bōʿᵃlayik;* lit., 'husbands']—the LORD Almighty is his name."

On the other hand, when we turn to the pages of the New Testament we find the doctrine of the Triune character of God everywhere *assumed* (see Matt. 28:19; Mark 1:9–11; John 14:16–26; 15:26; 16:5–15; 1 Cor. 12:3–6; 2 Cor. 13:14; Eph. 1:3–14; 2:18; 4:4–6; Gal. 4:4–6; Rom. 8:1–11; 2 Thess. 2:13–14; Titus 3:4–6; 1 Pet. 1:2; Jude 20–21; Rev. 1:4)—not struggling to be born but already on the scene and fully assimilated into the thought forms of the Christian community. That is to say, in the New Testament the doctrine is not in the making through rigorous debate and theological reflection but already made (Warfield). How do we account for the fact that the Old Testament seems to have been written "before" its revelation while the New Testament seems to have been written "after" its revelation? To cite Warfield:

> The revelation itself was made not in word but in deed. It was made in the incarnation of God the Son, and the outpouring of God the Holy Spirit. The relation of the two Testaments to this revelation is in the one case that of preparation for it, and in the other that of product of it. The revelation itself is embodied just in Christ and the Holy Spirit.[9]

It has been often said, as the reason lying behind the determination of the divine wisdom to reveal the fact of the Trinity in this manner, that it was the task of the Old Testament "to fix firmly in the minds and hearts of the people of God the great fundamental truth of the unity of the Godhead; and it would have been dangerous to

---

9. Warfield, "Biblical Doctrine of the Trinity," 33.

speak to them of the plurality within this unity until this task had been fully accomplished."[10] But, as Warfield argues, it is more likely that the full revelation of the Godhead's personal manifoldness was necessarily tied to the unfolding of the *redemptive* process, and that as that process materialized the revelation of the Trinity necessarily was disclosed as its corollary:

> the revelation of the Trinity was . . . the inevitable effect of the accomplishment of redemption. It was in the coming of the Son of God in the likeness of sinful flesh to offer Himself a sacrifice for sin; and in the coming of the Holy Spirit to convict the world of sin, of righteousness and of judgment, that the Trinity of Persons in the Unity of the Godhead was once for all revealed to men. Those who knew God the Father, who loved them and gave His own Son to die for them; and the Lord Jesus Christ, who loved them and delivered Himself up an offering and sacrifice for them; and the Spirit of Grace, who loved them and dwelt within them, a power not themselves, making for righteousness, knew the Triune God and could not think or speak of God otherwise than as triune. The doctrine of the Trinity, in other words, is simply the modification wrought in the conception of the one only God by His complete revelation of Himself in the redemptive process. It necessarily waited, therefore, upon the completion of the redemptive process for its revelation, and its revelation, as necessarily, lay complete in the redemptive process.
>
> The fundamental proof that God is a Trinity is supplied thus by the fundamental revelation of the Trinity *in fact*: that is to say, in the incarnation of God the Son and the outpouring of God the Holy Spirit. *In a word, Jesus Christ and the Holy Spirit are the fundamental proof of the doctrine of the Trinity.* This is as much as to say that all the evidence of whatever kind, and from whatever source derived, that Jesus Christ is God manifested in the flesh, and that the Holy Spirit is a Divine Person, is just so much evidence for the doctrine of the Trinity; and that when we go to the New Testament for evidence of the Trinity we are to seek for it, not merely in the scattered allusions to the Trinity as such, numerous and instructive as they are, but primarily in the whole mass of evidence which the New Testament provides of the Deity of Christ and the Divine personality of the Holy Spirit.[11]

Louis Berkhof agrees:

> The Old Testament does not contain a full revelation of the trinitarian existence of God, but does contain several indications of it. And this is exactly what might be expected. The Bible never deals with the doctrine of the Trinity as an abstract

---

10. Ibid., 33–34.
11. Ibid., 33, 35, emphasis supplied.

truth, but reveals the trinitarian life in its various relations as a living reality, to a certain extent in connection with the works of creation and providence, but particularly in relation to the work of redemption. *Its most fundamental revelation is a revelation given in facts rather than in words.* And this revelation increases in clarity in the measure in which the redemptive work of God is more clearly revealed, as in the incarnation of the Son and the outpouring of the Holy Spirit. And the more the glorious reality of the Trinity stands out in the facts of history, the clearer the statements of the doctrine become. The fuller revelation of the Trinity in the New Testament is due to the fact that the Word became flesh, and that the Holy Spirit took up His abode in the Church.[12]

It was, in sum, the two great objective redemptive events of the Incarnation and Pentecost which precipitated and concretized the modification in the thinking of the first Christians about the one living and true God. Because they were convinced that men had been confronted by nothing less than the unabridged glory of God in the person of Jesus Christ (2 Cor. 4:6) and that the Holy Spirit possessed a personal subsistence with the Father and the Son, the first Christians were given the impetus to formulate their understanding of God in Trinitarian terms.

The evidence for the Trinity, then, since the deity and personal subsistence of the Father may be viewed as a given,[13] is just the biblical evidence for the deity of Jesus Christ and the distinct personal subsistence of God the Holy Spirit. Said another way, whatever biblical evidence, wherever expressed in Holy Scripture, which can be adduced in support of the deity of Christ and the personal subsistence of the Holy Spirit is evidence for the doctrine of the Trinity. Accordingly, the larger portion of the remainder of this chapter will be devoted to the adduction of the biblical evidence for the deity of Christ and the Holy Spirit's personal subsistence.

THE DEITY OF THE SON

The biblical evidence for the deity of the Son includes (1) the Old Testament adumbrations and predictions of a divine Messiah, (2) Jesus' self-testimony in both words and deeds, (3) his resurrection, (4) the New Testament writers' united witness, and (5) specifically, the nine New Testament passages in which "God" (θεός, *theos*) is used as a title for Christ.

---

12. Louis Berkhof, *Systematic Theology* (Grand Rapids, Mich.: Eerdmans, 1932), 85, emphasis supplied.
13. For a treatment of the Father's "Godness," see Benjamin B. Warfield, "God Our Father and the Lord Jesus Christ," in *Biblical and Theological Studies* (Philadelphia: Presbyterian and Reformed, 1992), 60–78.

Old Testament Predictions of a Divine Messiah

The Old Testament's testimony to the deity of the promised Messiah is so pervasive that only a few of its highlights can be listed:[14]

1. A careful study of the references to the "angel of the Lord" will disclose that he is *differentiated from God* as his messenger by the very title itself as well as by the fact that God refers to him or addresses him (see Exod. 23:23; 32:34; 2 Sam. 24:16). And yet in his speeches the angel lays claim to divine prerogatives and powers, indeed to *identity with God* (see Gen. 31:11–13), thus establishing the pattern present in such Old Testament passages as Psalms 2:7, 45:6–7, and 110:1 and such New Testament passages as John 1:1, 18, Hebrews 1:8, and 1 John 5:20. Geerhardus Vos states that the only way to do justice to both features—the differentiation and the identity—is to

> assume that back of the twofold representation there lies a real manifoldness in the inner life of the Deity. If the Angel sent were Himself partaker of the Godhead, then He could refer to God as His sender, and at the same time speak as God, and in both cases there would be reality back of it. Without this much of what we call the Trinity the transaction could not but have been unreal and illusory.

He notes further that the angel's declarations of identity with God (which he terms God's "sacramental" intent) underscores God's desire to be present with his people in order to support them in their frailty and limitations; but without the angel's differentiation from God (which he terms God's "spiritual" intent), the real spiritual nature of the Deity would have been threatened. Hence, the angel speaks of God in the third person. From this analysis Vos concludes:

> In the incarnation of our Lord we have the supreme expression of this fundamental arrangement. . . . The whole incarnation, with all that pertains to it, is one great sacrament of redemption. And yet even here special care is taken to impress believers with the absolute spirituality of Him Who has thus made Himself of our nature. The principle at stake has found classical expression in John 1:18: "No man has seen God at any time; God only begotten, who is in the bosom of the Father, He has declared Him."[15]

2. David, in Psalm 2:7, identifies the Messiah as God's unique Son, a title in this context carrying implications of deity, according to the writer of Hebrews, for all the angels of God are ordered to worship Him (Heb. 1:5–6). Moreover, when the

---

14. See Benjamin B. Warfield, "The Divine Messiah in the Old Testament," in *Biblical and Theological Studies* (Philadelphia: Presbyterian and Reformed, 1952), 79–126.
15. Geerhardus Vos, *Biblical Theology* (Grand Rapids, Mich.: Eerdmans, 1948), 85–89.

GOD AS TRINITY

writer explicates the content of this "more excellent name," he does so by ascriptions to Christ of the supreme titles of θεός, *theos*, and κύριος, *kyrios*—not new names additional to the title "Son," but explications of the content of the more excellent "Son" title itself of Psalm 2.

3. In Psalm 45:6–7 the Messiah is called "God": "Your throne, O God [אֱלֹהִים, *'ĕlōhîm*], is forever and ever" (see Heb. 1:8).

4. In Psalm 102:25–27 the Messiah bears as his name the sacred Tetragram (יהוה, *yhwh*), possessing accordingly the attributes of creative power and eternity (see Heb. 1:10–12).

5. In Psalm 110:1 the Messiah bears the title of אֲדֹנִי (*'ădōnî*, "my Lord"), a title again carrying implications of deity since the One who bears this title sits on the right hand of Yahweh, a supra-angelic position (Heb. 1:13). Some angels are privileged to stand before God (Luke 1:19), but none are ever said to sit before him, much less sit upon his throne. The One who so sits *with* God must surely share in the divine reign as being himself divine.

6. In Isaiah 7:14 the virginally conceived Messiah is "God with us" (עִמָּנוּ אֵל, *'immānû 'ēl*) (see Matt. 1:23).

7. In Isaiah 9:6 the Messiah is the bearer of the "four wonderful titles": "Wonderful Counselor," "the Mighty God" (אֵל גִּבּוֹר, *'ēl gibbôr*), the "Everlasting Father," and "the Prince of Peace."

8. In Daniel 7:14 the Messiah is the "manlike Figure," *manlike* only to distinguish his kingdom in character from the four "beast" kingdoms preceding his, but himself *divine* as evidenced by (a) his free access to the Ancient of Days, (b) his "coming on clouds" (employed as a descriptive metaphor only of deity; see Nahum 1:3), (c) the universal and everlasting kingdom which the Ancient of Days bestows upon him, and (d) the worship which the peoples and nations of the world offer him.

9. In Malachi 3:1 the Messiah, the Messenger of the Covenant, before whom his own messenger ("Elijah") goes in order to prepare his way, is Yahweh of Hosts (see the "before me").[16]

10. If we include John the Baptist among the Old Testament prophets as the "Elijah who was to come" (see Matt. 11:13–14), then we have John's testimony to (a) the Messiah's preexistence (John 1:15, 30),[17] and (b) the Messiah's divine Sonship (John 1:34). In regard to this latter testimony, Vos notes:

---

16. For extended expositions of Psalms 2:7; 45:6–7; 102:25–27, 110:1; Isaiah 7:14; 9:6; Daniel 7:14; and Malachi 3:1, see Robert L. Reymond, *Jesus, Divine Messiah: The Old Testament Witness* (Ross-shire, Scotland: Christian Focus, 1990).

17. See Vos, *Biblical Theology*, 347: " . . . 'protos' with the imperfect of the verb signifies absolute anteriority as to mode of existence; it relates to the eternal existence of the Lord, usually called his preexistence."

That [the title "Son of God"] cannot be lower in its import than the same title throughout the Gospel [of John] follows from the position it has as the culminating piece of this first stage of witnessing, when compared with the statement of the author of the Gospel (20:31). According to this statement the things recorded of Jesus were written to create belief in the divine sonship of the Saviour. With this in view a series of episodes and discourses had been put in order. Obviously the John-the-Baptist section forms the first in this series, and therein lies the reason, why it issues into the testimony about the Sonship under discussion. That it carried high meaning also appears from [John's declaration in John 1:15, 30], in which nothing less than the preexistence of the Messiah had already been affirmed.[18]

Here then are several lines of Old Testament evidence for the coming of a Messiah who would be divine in nature. The stage was thus set for the appearance to his world of the virginally conceived divine Messiah who gave testimony concerning his deity in many unmistakable ways.

Jesus' Self-Testimony to His Deity

THE TITLE "SON OF MAN"

A truly vast literature has grown up around the Son of Man title in the Gospels, and only a brief discussion can be given here.

The title itself (ὁ υἱὸς τοῦ ἀνθρώπου, *ho huios tou anthrōpou,* anarthrous only in John 5:27, but this anomaly is accounted for by Colwell's rule)[19] occurs sixty-nine times in the Synoptics, appearing in all four of the alleged earlier documentary sources (*Ur-Markus,* Q, M, and L), and thirteen times in the Fourth Gospel, for a total of eighty-two occurrences in the Gospels. The Son of Man sayings themselves depict the Son of Man figure in three distinct situations: that of his current ministry, that of his suffering at the hands of men (maltreated, betrayed, executed, and buried), and that of his rising and appearing in glory on the clouds of heaven. Who is this Son of Man, or are these situations so disparate that we must more accurately speak of more than one Son of Man?

---

18. Ibid., 351.
19. See E. C. Colwell, "A Definite Rule for the Use of the Article in the Greek New Testament," *Journal of Biblical Literature* 52 (1933): 12–21. Some New Testament scholars (e.g., Nigel Turner, D. A. Carson) have expressed reservations concerning this "rule," though Bruce Metzger endorses its *general* validity in "On the Translation of John 1:1," *The Expository Times* 63 (1951–52): 125–26, and "The Jehovah's Witnesses and Jesus Christ," *Theology Today* (April 1953): 75, as do Leon Morris (*Gospel According to John* [Grand Rapids, Mich.: Eerdmans, 1971], 77, n. 15) and C. F. D. Moule, *An Idiom Book of New Testament Greek* (Cambridge: Cambridge University Press, 1953), 115–16.

Assuming the authenticity of these sayings as containing the *ipsissima vox Jesu*, the church has traditionally understood the phrase "Son of Man" as the title Jesus chose as a self-designation precisely because, although assuredly messianic (see Dan. 7:13), the title was ambiguous in meaning to the current popular imagination. This enabled him to claim to be the Messiah with little danger of the current erroneous views being read into it before he had the opportunity to infuse it with the full-orbed content of the messianic task which was foreshadowed in and predicted by the Old Testament.

Furthermore, according to the church's traditional understanding, Jesus spelled out his messianic task as the Son of Man precisely in terms of the three situations of serving, suffering, and glory and applied these situations to himself, the former two being fulfilled in connection with his first Advent, the last to be fulfilled first in the "lesser (typical) coming in judgment" in the destruction of Jerusalem in A.D. 70 (to which most probably Matt. 10:23; 24:27, 30 and perhaps others refer), and second in his grand and final apocalyptic revelation in eschatological glory.

That the church was correct when it understood the title as a self-designation of Jesus and when it applied these situations of the Son of Man to Jesus is evident from the following four lines of evidence:

1. Where Matthew (5:11) reads "on account of me," Luke (6:22) reads "for the sake of the Son of Man"; where Matthew (10:32) has "I," Luke (12:8) has "the Son of Man." Where Mark (8:27) and Luke (9:18) have "I," Matthew (16:13) reads "the Son of Man," but where Mark (8:31 and 8:38) and Luke (9:22 and 9:26) have "the Son of Man," Matthew (16:21 and 10:33) correspondingly reads "he" and "I." Clearly the title, at least at times, was simply a periphrasis for "I" or "me," demonstrating that Jesus intended himself as its referent. And always standing in the background was the eschatological figure of Daniel 7.

2. When Judas kissed Jesus, according to Luke 22:48 (see also Matt. 26:23-24, 45), Jesus asked: "Judas, are you betraying the Son of Man with a kiss?"

3. As Royce G. Gruenler argues:

> Matt. 19:28 is especially instructive on the matter of who the glorified Son of man is, for Jesus promises his disciples with the authoritative "Truly, I say to you" that "in the new world, when the Son of man shall sit on his glorious throne, you who have followed me will also sit on twelve thrones judging the twelve tribes of Israel." Surely Jesus, whom they have followed and in terms of whom they shall reign, will not be excluded from reigning with them. Are there then to be two enthroned central figures? The sense of the passage exegetically would imply that only one central person is assumed, namely, Jesus the Son of man.[20]

---

20. Royce G. Gruenler, "Son of Man," *Evangelical Dictionary of Theology* (Grand Rapids, Mich.: Baker, 1984), 1035–1036.

He argues further:

> It is likely that non-supernaturalist assumptions lie behind the refusal to allow that these sayings [which portray the Son of Man as a glorified divine being] are Jesus' own prophetic vision of his vindication and glorification in the coming judgment. Certainly there is no suggestion elsewhere in the Gospels that he anticipated any other figure to appear after him. In fact, among the Marcan sayings ... 9:9 [Matt 17:9; see also Mark 8:31 (Luke 9:22; 24:7); 9:31 (Matt 17:22–23); Mark 10:33–34 (Matt 20:18–19; Luke 18:31–33)] clearly refers to his own rising as the Son of man from the dead, and 14:62, the scene before the high priest, couples his "I am" confession that he is the Christ, the Son of the Blessed, with the surrogate for "I," the Son of man, "sitting at the right hand of Power, and coming with the clouds of heaven."[21]

4. When Jesus asked the man born blind, whom he had just healed: "Do you believe in the Son of Man?"[22] the man asked "Who is he, Lord? Tell me, that I may believe in him." Jesus replied: "You have now seen him; in fact, he is the one speaking with you" (John 9:35–37).

Thus it is clear that all four Evangelists intended their readers to understand that Jesus is the Son of Man in the roles both of suffering Servant "who came to seek and to save that which was lost" (Luke 19:10), who also came "not to be served, but to serve and to give his life a ransom for many" (Mark 10:45; Matt. 20:28), and of coming Judge and eschatological King.

As for its background, both the evangelical and the growing critical consensus is that Daniel 7:13–14 is the primary source.[23] A common objection that is raised against Daniel's "manlike figure" being made the source of Jesus' "Son of Man sayings" is the alleged absence of the motif of suffering in the description of this figure in Daniel 7 while the idea of suffering is often attached to the title in Jesus' usage. This problem has been adequately answered by evangelical New Testament

---

21. Ibid., 1035.
22. See Bruce M. Metzger, *A Textual Commentary on the Greek New Testament* (New York: United Bible Societies, 1971). 228–29, for his note on this textual variant.
23. Delbert Burkett, in his "The Son of Man in the Gospel of John," *Journal for the Study of the New Testament*, Supplement Series 56 (1991), basing his thesis on his own translation, argues that the background to the "Son of Man" sayings in John is Proverbs 30:1–4, in which oracle the character who designates himself as "the Man" is actually God, describing himself in supernatural terms to his son Ithiel. Jesus is said to see himself as the antitypical Ithiel and so by his use of the title "Son of Man" to be claiming to be the Son of God. The thesis is intriguing but has little data to support it. Why would God the Father identify himself as "the Man"? Who is Ucal, God's second son? And why ignore the more plentiful evidence from the Synoptics that it is Daniel 7:13–14 that provides the background for Jesus' self-designation, "the Son of Man"?

scholarship.[24] When Jesus employed the title he was self-consciously claiming to be the Danielic Son of Man and hence the Messiah, uniting within the one Old Testament figure both the motif of suffering (the work of Isaiah's suffering servant) and the motif of his apocalyptic coming to judge the earth and to bring the Kingdom of God to its consummation.

Commenting upon the significance of the "Son of Man" title, Geerhardus Vos writes:

> In close adherence to the spirit of the scene in Daniel from which it was taken, it suggested a Messianic career in which, all of a sudden, without human interference or military conflict, through an immediate act of God, the highest dignity and power are conferred. The kingship here portrayed is not only supernatural; it is "transcendental."[25]

Even a cursory examination of Jesus' Son of Man sayings will bear out all that Vos asserts here and more. For example, this title in the Fourth Gospel "connotes the heavenly, superhuman side of Jesus' mysterious existence,"[26] expressing what is commonly called his preexistence (John 3:13; 6:62). As the Son of Man, Jesus in the Synoptics claimed to have the authority to forgive sins (Matt. 9:6; Mark 2:10; Luke 5:24) and to regulate even the observance of the divine ordinance of the Sabbath (Matt. 12:8; Mark 2:28; Luke 6:5)—clearly prerogatives of deity alone. To speak against the Son of Man, he said, although forgivable, is blasphemy (Matt. 12:32). As the Son of Man the angels are his (Matt. 13:41), implying thereby his own superangelic status and lordship over them. As the Son of Man he would know a period of humiliation, having no place to lay his head (Matt. 8:20; Luke 9:58) and finally even dying the cruel death of crucifixion; but he, the Son of Man, would suffer and die, he declared, only to the end that he might ransom others (Matt. 20:28; Mark 10:45). A man's eternal destiny would turn on his relationship to the Son of Man, he taught, for unless the Son of Man gives a man life, there is no life in him (John 6:53). As the Son of Man, he would rise from the dead and "sit at the right hand of power," and "come in clouds with great power and glory" (Matt. 24:30; Mark 13:25; Luke 21:27)—coming with all his holy angels in the glory of his Father, true enough (Matt. 16:27; Mark 8:38), but coming in his *own* glory as well (Matt. 25:31). And when he comes, he declared, he would come with the authority

---

24. See my *Jesus, Divine Messiah: The New Testament Witness* (Phillipsburg, N.J.: Presbyterian and Reformed, 1990), 60–1.
25. Geerhardus Vos, *The Self-Disclosure of Jesus* (1926; reprint, Phillipsburg, N.J.: Presbyterian and Reformed, 1978), 254.
26. Ibid., 239.

to execute judgment upon all men precisely because (ὅτι, *hoti*) he is the Son of Man (John 5:27). Clearly the Son of Man sayings embodied Jesus' conception of Messiahship, and its associations were supernatural, even divine, in character. Warfield does not overstate the matter then when he writes:

> It is . . . in the picture which Jesus Himself draws for us of the "Son of Man" that we see His superhuman nature portrayed. For the figure thus brought before us is distinctly a superhuman one; one which is not only in the future to be seen sitting at the right hand of power and coming with the clouds of heaven . . . ; but which in the present world itself exercises functions which are truly divine,—for who is Lord of the Sabbath but the God who instituted it in commemoration of His own rest (2:28), and who can forgive sins but God only (2:10, see verse 7)? The assignment to the Son of Man of the function of Judge of the world and the ascription to Him of the right to forgive sins are, in each case, but another way of saying that He is a divine person; for these are divine acts.[27]

THE TITLE "SON (OF GOD)"

Jesus claimed, as the Son of God, essential divine oneness with God in the Synoptic Gospels in Matthew 11:27 (Luke 10:22); 21:37–38 (Mark 12:6; Luke 20:13); 24:36 (Mark 13:32); and 28:19; and in the Gospel of John in (at least) 5:17–29; 6:40; 10:36; 11:4; 14:13; 17:1. To these must be added those instances in the Fourth Gospel when he claimed that God was his Father in such a unique sense that the Jewish religious leadership correctly perceived that he was claiming a Sonship with God that constituted essential divine oneness and equality with God and thus, from their perspective, was the committing of blasphemy (John 5:17–18; 10:24–39, especially verses 25, 29, 30, 32–33; 37, 38; see also 19:7).

The Four Great Parallels

In Matthew 11:25-27 (Luke 10:21–22), judged by Vos to be "the culminating point of our Lord's self-disclosure in the Synoptics,"[28] Jesus draws four parallels between God as "the Father" and himself as "the Son" of 1 Chronicles 17:13; Psalm 2:7; Isaiah 9:6, and Matthew 3:17 (Mark 1:11; Luke 3:22). The unique and intimate nature of the Father-Son relationship asserted here by Jesus finds its expression in terms of these parallels.

---

27. Benjamin B. Warfield, *The Lord of Glory* (1907; reprint, Grand Rapids, Mich.: Baker, 1974), 41.
28. Vos, *Self-Disclosure*, 143.

The first parallel has to do with the exclusive, mutual knowledge that the Father and the Son have of each other. Jesus declares in Matthew 11:27: "No one *knows* [ἐπιγινώσκει, *epiginōskei*] the Son except the Father, and no one *knows* [ἐπιγινώσκει, *epiginōskei*] the Father except the Son." Jesus puts emphasis upon the exclusiveness of this mutual knowledge ("no one knows except"). But just as striking is the inference that the nature of this knowledge which Jesus claims to have lifts him above the sphere of the ordinary mortal and places him "in a position, not of equality merely, but of absolute reciprocity and interpenetration of knowledge with the Father."[29] Vos observes:

> That essential rather than acquired knowledge is meant follows . . . from the correlation of the two clauses: the knowledge God has of Jesus cannot be acquired knowledge [it must, from the fact that it is God's knowledge, be direct, intuitive, and immediate—in a word, divine—author]; consequently the knowledge Jesus has of God cannot be acquired knowledge either, [it must be direct, intuitive, and immediate—author] for these two are placed entirely on a line. In other words, if the one is different from human knowledge, then the other must be so likewise.[30]

The only conclusion to be drawn is that God has this exclusive and interpenetrating knowledge of the Son because he is the Father of the Son, and that Jesus has this exclusive and interpenetrating knowledge of God because he is the Son of the Father. And inasmuch as the knowledge Jesus here claims for himself could not possibly have resulted from the investiture of the messianic task but must have originated in a Sonship which, of necessity, would have been *antecedent* to his messianic investiture, it is plain that Jesus' Sonship and the messianic task with which he had been invested are not descriptive of identical relationships to the Father—the former must have logically preceded the latter and provided the ground for it.

The second parallel, which rests upon the first, involves Jesus' assertion of the mutual necessity of the Father and the Son to reveal each other if men are ever to have a saving knowledge of them. This parallel may be seen in Jesus' thanksgiving to the Father, Lord of heaven and earth, that he—the Father—had *hidden* (ἔκρυψας, *ekrupsas*) the mysteries of the kingdom which are centered in the Son (for it was he whom that generation [11:19] and the cities of Korazin, Bethsaida and Capernaum [11:20–24] were rejecting) from the "wise" (that is, spiritual "know-it-alls") and had *revealed* (ἀπεκάλυψας, *apekalypsas*) them to "babies" (that is, to men like Peter; see

---

29. Benjamin B. Warfield, "The Person of Christ According to the New Testament," in *The Person and Work of Christ* (Philadephia: Presbyterian and Reformed, 1950), 65.
30. Vos, *Self-Disclosure*, 149.

Matt. 16:17) (11:25), and his later statement that "no one knows the Father except the Son and those to whom the Son wills *to reveal* [ἀποκαλύψαι, *apokalypsai*] him" (11:27). The reason that the messianic task was invested in the Son becomes even plainer from this parallel: not only does the Son alone know the Father with sufficient depth (that is, to infinity) to give a faithful revelation of him, but also, and precisely because he alone has such knowledge, the Son alone can be the revelatory channel of salvific blessing to the Father (John 14:6). Therefore, the Messianic investiture had to repose in him.

The third parallel is evident in the mutual absolute lordship each is said to possess, the Father's expressed in the words, "Lord of heaven and earth," the Son's in his declaration: "All authority is given to me."

The fourth parallel is that of the mutual absolute sovereignty each exercises in dispensing his revelation of the other. The Father's sovereignty is displayed in Jesus' words: "for this was your *good pleasure*" (εὐδοκία, *eudokia*) (11:26), the Son's in his words: "to whomever the Son *wills to reveal*" (βούληται ἀποκαλύψαι, *bouletai apokalypsai*) (11:27).

A higher expression of parity between the Father and the Son with respect to the possession of the divine attributes of omniscience and sovereignty in the dispensing of saving revelation is inconceivable. Warfield writes concerning this "in some respects the most remarkable [utterance] in the whole compass of the four Gospels":

> in it our Lord asserts for Himself a relation of practical equality with the Father, here described in most elevated terms as the "Lord of heaven and earth" (v. 25). As the Father only can know the Son, so the Son only can know the Father: and others may know the Father only as He is revealed by the Son. That is, not merely is the Son the exclusive revealer of God, but the mutual knowledge of Father and Son is put on what seems very much a par. The Son can be known only by the Father in all that He is, as if His being were infinite and as such inscrutable to the finite intelligence; and His knowledge alone—again as if He were infinite in His attributes—is competent to compass the depths of the Father's infinite being. He who holds this relation to the Father cannot conceivably be a creature.[31]

Such a parity with the Father is the basis upon which our Lord grounds his invitation to the weary that follows this utterance—an invitation to come not to the Father but to himself as the Revealer of the Father—an unholy usurpation of divine place and privilege if he were not himself deity. And it is not without significance that his invitation, in its all-encompassing comprehensiveness ("all you who are

---

31. Warfield, *Lord of Glory*, 82–83.

weary and burdened") and the absolute certainty of its unqualified promise of blessing ("I will give you rest"), parallels in form the divine invitation in Isaiah 45:22, as is plain if one only places the two invitations in their several parts beside each other as follows:

> Isaiah 45:22: "Turn to me, all the ends of the earth, and be saved [that is, I will save you]."
>
> Matthew 11:28: "Come to me, all you who are weary and burdened, and I will give you rest."

Clearly, by his promise to succor all who come to him, Jesus was asserting for himself a place of power and privilege as the Son of the Father altogether on the level of deity.

The Parable of the Wicked Farmers

In the parable of the wicked farmers recorded in Matthew 21:33-39 (Mark 12:1-11; Luke 20:9-15), Jesus tells the story of a landowner who leased his vineyard to some farmers. When the time arrived for him to receive his rental fee in the form of the fruit of the vineyard, he sent servant after servant to his tenants, only to have each one of them beaten, stoned, or killed. Finally, he sent his son (Luke: his "beloved son"; Mark: "yet one [other], a beloved son" which evokes the earlier words of the Father from heaven [1:11; 9:7]), saying: "They will respect my son." But when the tenants saw him, they said: "This is the heir; come, let us kill him and take his inheritance." This they did, throwing his body out of the vineyard. When the landowner came, he destroyed the tenants and leased his vineyard to others.

The intended referents of the parable are obvious: the landowner is God, the vineyard the nation of Israel (Isa. 5:7); the farmers the nation's leaders, the servants the prophets of the theocracy (Matt. 23:37a); and the son is Jesus himself, the Son of God. The central teaching of the parable is also obvious, just as it was to its original audience (Matt. 21:45): God, the true Owner of Israel, after having sent his prophets repeatedly to the nation and its leaders to call it back to him from its rebellion and unbelief, only to have them rebuffed and often killed, had in Jesus moved beyond sending mere servants. In Jesus God had finally sent his beloved (that is, his "one and only") Son who was to be similarly rejected. But *his* rejection, unlike the rejections of those before him, was to entail, not a mere change of politico-religious administration, but "the complete overthrow of the theocracy, and the rearing from the foundation up of a new structure in which the Son [the elevated Cornerstone] would receive full vindication and supreme honor."[32] The

---

32. Vos, *Self-Disclosure*, 162.

parable's high Christology—reflecting Jesus' self-understanding—finds expression in the details of the story, as Vos explains:[33]

1. By virtue of his Sonship, Jesus possesses "a higher dignity and a closer relation to God than the highest and closest official status known in the Old Testament theocracy." This is apparent from the highly suggestive "beloved" attached to the title "Son," not to mention the title "Son" itself over against the word "servant."

2. The Son's exalted status in the salvific economy of God is apparent from the *finality* of the messianic investiture which he owns. From the word ὕστερον (*hysteron*, "finally") (see Mark's "He had yet one other" and his ἔσχατον [*eschaton*, "finally"]; also Luke: "What shall I do?"), it is clear that Jesus represents himself as the last, the final ambassador, after whose sending nothing more can be done. "The Lord of the vineyard has no further resources; the Son is the highest messenger of God conceivable" (see Heb. 1:1–2).[34]

3. The former two points cannot be made to answer merely to a functional "messianic sonship," as some theologians claim. This is apparent from the two facts that Jesus represents himself as the Son *before* his mission and that he is the "beloved Son" *whether he be sent or not!* "His being sent describes . . . His Messiahship, but this Messiahship was brought about precisely by the necessity for sending one who was the highest and dearest that the lord of the vineyard could delegate. . . . The sonship, therefore, existed antecedently to the Messianic mission."[35] And because he was, as the Son, the "heir" (in all three Synoptics; see also Psa. 2:8; Heb. 1:2, where the Son is the Heir of all things prior to his creating the world), his Sonship is the underlying ground of his messiahship.

There is a strong suggestion here of Jesus' preexistence with the Father as the latter's "beloved Son." And his divine station in association with his Father prior to his messianic commitment in history is confirmed. The "Son" in this parable of Jesus, a self-portrait one may say with ample justification, is clearly divine.

The Ignorant Son

Already in his 1901 article, entitled "Gospels," appearing in *Encyclopaedia Biblica*, Paul Wilhelm Schmiedel had included Mark 13:32 among his infamous nine "foundation-pillars for a truly scientific life of Jesus," meaning by this entitlement that they "prove that in the person of Jesus we have to do with a completely human being," and that "the divine is to be sought in him only in the form in which it is

---

33. Ibid., 161–63.
34. This parable clearly rules out as false any later religion's claim to being a higher revelation of God than Jesus, such as Islam's claim regarding Mohammed.
35. Vos, *Self-Disclosure*, 161–63.

capable of being found in a man."[36] For Schmiedel, these nine passages (Mark 3:21; 6:5; 8:12, 14–21; 10:17; 13:32; 15:34; Matt. 11:5; 12:31) could serve as a base for "a truly scientific life of Jesus" because each in its own way affirms of him something which would be appropriate to a human Jesus but which would be impossible for a divine Jesus. The reason for his inclusion of Mark 13:32 among these nine is Jesus' admission of his ignorance of the day and hour of his return in glory. But does this passage show that Christ could not have been divine?

It would be facile to assume, as did Schmiedel, that the passage places the Son entirely within the category of the merely human. This fails to take into account Jesus' clear claim in Matthew 11:27 to a knowledge all-encompassing in character—equal to that of the Father himself.[37] But it is equally facile simply to declare, as does the Roman Catholic decree, *Circa quasdam propositiones de scientia animae Christi* (1918), that Christ does not mean here that as man he did not know the day of judgment, that the idea of any limitation to the knowledge of Christ cannot possibly be taught in view of the hypostatic union of the two natures. Clearly it is dogmatic bias that is governing Roman Catholic exegesis here. How then is one who is really interested in "hearing" the text to understand this passage?

That Jesus speaks here as one with a divine self-consciousness is apparent for three reasons: first, this is the connotation of the simple "the Son" when it is associated as it is here with "the Father," as we have already had occasion to observe in Matthew 11:27 and will observe when we treat Matthew 28:19; second, it is of his coming as the Son of Man in glory that Jesus speaks in this passage (and in 25:31), which Danielic figure is supernatural, even divine in character; and third, coming as the phrase "not even the Son" does after his reference to angels, Jesus places himself, on an ascending scale of ranking, above the angels of heaven, the highest of all created beings, who are significantly marked here as supramundane (see Matthew's "of heaven," Mark's "in heaven"). Clearly, he classifies himself with the Father rather than with the angelic class, inasmuch as elsewhere he represents himself as the Lord of the angels, whose commands they obey (Matt. 13:41, 49; 24:31; 25:31; see Heb. 1:4–14). And if this be so, and if for these two Synoptists, Jesus is not merely superhuman but superangelic, "the question at once obtrudes itself whether a superangelic person is not by that very fact removed from the category of creatures."[38]

---

36. Schmiedel, "Gospels," *Encyclopaedia Biblica*, ed. T. K. Cheyne and J. Sutherland Black (New York: Macmillan, 1914), 1881.

37. The fact that this claim is found in Matthew 11:27 might explain why a scribe would have omitted "not even the Son" from Matthew 24:36 (see ℵ¹, K, L, W, Δ, 33, and some Fathers), but would have allowed it to remain in Mark 13:32 since Mark does not contain the "thunderbolt from the Johannine heaven" (Matt. 11:27).

38. Warfield, *Lord of Glory*, 37.

But if Jesus is speaking here out of a divine self-consciousness, as we believe we have just demonstrated is the case, how can he say of himself that he is ignorant of the day and hour of his coming in glory? In response, I would submit that Jesus' language reflects a theological construction concerning himself which is also quite common in the language of the New Testament writers when they speak about him. The theological construction to which I refer is this: because of the *union* of the divine and human natures in the one divine person, Christ designates himself here and is occasionally designated by others elsewhere in Scripture in terms of what he is by virtue of one nature when what is then predicated of him, so designated, is true of him by virtue of his other nature. As the Westminster Confession of Faith says:

> Christ, in the work of mediation, acts according to both natures, by each nature doing that which is proper to itself; yet, by reason of the unity of the person that which is proper to one nature is sometimes in Scripture attributed to the person denominated by the other nature. (VIII/vii)

This means that, regardless of the designation which Scripture might employ to refer to him, it is always the *person* of the Son and not one of his natures who is the subject of the statement. To illustrate: when what is predicated of Christ is true of him by virtue of all that belongs to his person as essentially divine and assumptively human, for example, "that he might become a . . . high priest" (Heb. 2:17), it is the person of Christ, as both divine and human, and not one of his natures, who is the subject. Again, when what is predicated of Christ, designated in terms of what he is as human, is true of him by virtue of his divine nature, for example, he is "the man [ἄνθρωπος, *anthrōpos*] from heaven" (1 Cor. 15:47–49) and "a man [ἀνήρ, *anēr*] who . . . was before [John]" (John 1:30), it is still his person and not his human nature who is the subject. Finally, when what is predicated of Christ, designated in terms of what he is as divine, is true of him by virtue of his human nature, for example, Elizabeth's reference to Mary as the "mother of my Lord" and Paul's "they crucified the Lord of Glory" (1 Cor. 2:8), again it is his person and not his divine nature that is the subject.

So in Mark 13:32 we find Christ designating himself in terms of what he is as divine ("the Son" of "the Father"), but then what he predicates of himself, namely, ignorance as to the day and hour of his return in heavenly splendor, is true of him in terms of what he is as human, not in terms of what he is as divine. As the Godman, he is simultaneously omniscient as God (in company with the other persons of the Godhead) and ignorant of some things as man (in company with the other persons of the human race). So what we have in Mark 13:32, contrary to Schmiedel's "pillar for a truly scientific life of Jesus" as a mere man, is as striking a witness by our Lord himself as can be found anywhere in Scripture (1) both to his supremacy as God's Son over the angels—the highest of created personal entities (2) and at the same time to his creaturely limitations as a man, (3) as well as to the union of both complexes of attributes—the divine and the human—in the one personal subject of Jesus Christ. I conclude that in this saying which brings before us "the ignorant Son," Jesus, as "the Son," places himself outside of and above the category even of angels, that is, outside of and above creatures of the highest order, and associates himself as the divine Son with the Father, while testifying at the same time to his full, unabridged humanity.

The "Son" of the Triune Name

Sometime between his resurrection and his ascension, our Lord gathered with his eleven disciples and commissioned them to "go and make disciples of all the nations" (Matt. 28:19).

As a prelude to the Great Commission itself, our Lord declared that all authority in heaven and on earth had been given to him, words reminiscent of Daniel 7:13–14, claiming thereby an all-encompassing, unrestricted sovereignty over the entire universe. In his postlude to it, he declared he would be with his church ("I am with you"), words reminiscent of the Immanuel title of Isaiah 7:14 and Matthew 1:23, implying that the attributes of omnipresence and omniscience were his. In the additional words ("always, even to the end of the age"), he implied his possession of the attribute of eternity. Between the prelude and the postlude—both pregnant with suggestions of deity—comes the Commission itself (Matt. 28:19–20a). In its words, "all nations . . . teaching them to observe all that I have commanded you," his universal lordship is affirmed. Sovereignty, omnipresence, omniscience, eternity, and universal lordship—all demonstrating that the risen Christ claimed to be divine.

Particularly interesting is the precise form of the baptismal formula. Jesus does not say, "into the names [plural] of the Father and of the Son and of the Holy Spirit," or what is its virtual equivalent, "into the name of the Father, and into the name of the Son, and into the name of the Holy Spirit," "as if," to quote Warfield, "we had to deal with three separate Beings."[39] Nor does he say, "into the name of Father, Son, and Holy Spirit" (omitting the three recurring articles), again citing Warfield, "as if 'the Father, Son, and Holy Ghost' might be taken as merely three designations of a single person." What he does say is this: "into the name [singular] of the Father, and of the Son, and of the Holy Spirit," first "[asserting] the unity

---

39. Warfield, "Biblical Doctrine of the Trinity," 42.

of the three by combining them all within the bounds of the single Name, and then [throwing up] into emphasis the distinctness of each by introducing them in turn with the repeated article."[40]

To comprehend fully the import of Jesus' statement, one must appreciate the significance of the term "the Name" for the Hebrew mind. In the Old Testament, the term does more than serve as the mere external designation of the person. Rather, it refers to the essence of the person himself. Warfield writes, "In His name the Being of God finds expression; and the Name of God—'this glorious and fearful name, Jehovah thy God' (Deut. xxviii. 58)—was accordingly a most sacred thing, being indeed virtually equivalent to God Himself" (see Isa. 30:27; 59:19). "So pregnant was the implication of the Name, that it was possible for the term to stand absolutely . . . as the sufficient representation of the majesty of Jehovah" (see Lev. 24:11). Warfield concludes:

> When, therefore, our Lord commanded His disciples to baptize those whom they brought to His obedience "into the name of . . ." He was using language charged to them with high meaning. He could not have been understood otherwise than as substituting for the Name of Jehovah this other Name "of the Father, and of the Son, and of the Holy Ghost," and this could not possibly have meant to His disciples anything else than that Jehovah was now to be known to them by the new Name, of the Father, and the Son, and the Holy Ghost. The only alternative would have been that, for the community which He was founding, Jesus was supplanting Jehovah by a new God; and this alternative is no less than monstrous. There is no alternative, therefore, to understanding Jesus here to be giving for His community a new Name to Jehovah and that new Name to be the threefold Name of "the Father, and the Son, and the Holy Ghost."[41]

What are the implications for his person of a saying that places Jesus as "the Son," along with the Father and the Holy Spirit and equally with them, "even in the awful precincts of the Divine Name itself"?[42] The answer is obvious: Jesus is affirming here his own unqualified, unabridged deity! And that this is his intent may be seen still further from an analysis of that portion of the saying that precedes the mention of "the Son," namely, the phrase "the name of the Father." Clearly, in this abbreviated expression, the phrase "the name" must carry the highest connotation, even that of deity itself, inasmuch as it is the Father's name and thus the Father's nature which is so designated. But it is precisely this same "name" which also governs the genitives "of the Son" and "of the Holy Spirit," and to which the Son (along with the Holy

---

40. Ibid., 42.
41. Ibid., 43–44.
42. Warfield, *Lord of Glory*, 156.

Spirit) stands related, evincing his equality with the Father insofar as his deity is concerned.

Thus the significance of the title, "the Son," for the Synoptic Evangelists is consistent and pervasive: as "the Son" of "the Father" Jesus Christ is deity incarnate. And when we press our investigation of the meaning of Jesus' "Son [of God]" sayings into the Fourth Gospel, we find no new doctrinal content in them respecting his person but rather only a more pervasive testimony to the same doctrine of Jesus' divine Sonship which we find in the Synoptic Gospels.

While it is true that the Synoptic Gospels only infrequently report Jesus' use of "the Son" as a self-designation, preferring to preserve for the church the memory that Jesus favored the title "Son of Man" as his public self-designation (which fact, of course, John does not ignore, as for example, in 1:51; 3:13; 5:27; 6:62; and 9:35, and which, as we have seen, connotes through its association with the Danielic "Son of Man" a divine Messiah), John informs us that our Lord employed with great frequency and as a self-designation the title "the Son" in direct association with "the Father." Jesus also uses "the Father" by itself some seventy additional times and "my Father" by itself almost thirty more times.

The Divine Son

That the title "the Son of God" is, for John, messianic is borne out from its appearance in his Gospel alongside the clearly messianic titles of "the King of Israel," "the Christ," and "he who was to come into the world" (1:49; 11:27; 20:31). But that it connotes more than the messianic office *per se* is also apparent in several of Jesus' discourses recorded in John. In John 5:17–29, after healing the lame man on the Sabbath day, Jesus justified his act before the offended religious hierarchy by claiming both the ability and the prerogatives of "seeing" and "doing" as "the Father" does: "My Father is working still, and I am working" (5:17); "The Father loves the Son, and shows him all that he himself is doing" (5:20); therefore, he said: "The Son does . . . what he sees the Father doing" (5:19a). Indeed, "Whatever he [the Father] does, that the Son does likewise [ὁμοίως, *homoiōs*]" (5:19b). Furthermore, as "the Son," Jesus claimed to have the "Father-granted" sovereign right to give life: "The Son gives life to whom he is pleased to give it" (5:21b). There are no limitations here: both spiritual and physical life is intended; for as spiritually dead men hear the voice of "the Son of God," they "live" (5:24–25; see also 6:40a), and as physically dead men someday hear his voice, they will come forth from their graves (5:28–29; see also 6:40b). And when they do the latter, he declared, they do so only to stand before him in the Judgment because the Father has committed all judgment to him (5:22–27). These are clearly activities within the province and powers of deity alone;

Jesus claimed, as "the Son," to be coordinate with "the Father," the Sovereign of life, of salvation, of the resurrection, and of the final judgment. But perhaps his most emphatic claim to equality with the Father comes in 5:23 when he makes one's honoring of "the Father" turn on the issue of whether one honors "the Son," that is, himself. With these words Jesus laid claim to the right to demand, equally with the Father, the honor (that is, the devotion and worship) of men![43] Is it any wonder, given the assumption of the religious leaders that he was only a man, that they thought him, under Jewish law (Lev. 24:16), to be worthy of death: by the unique relationship he was claiming with the Father, he was making himself "equal [ἴσον, *ison*] with God" (5:18).

In view of Jesus' express statements that "the Son can do nothing by himself; he can do only what he sees his Father doing" (5:19), and "by myself I can do nothing" (5:30), and his later declaration that "the Father is greater than I" (14:28; see also 1 Cor. 15:28), Unitarians have concluded that the charge that he was making himself "equal with God" was unfounded and one which Jesus himself expressly disavowed. It is true that in making these statements, our Lord was asserting in some sense a subordination to the Father. But in what sense—in an essential, covenantal, or functional sense? Warfield sensitizes us to the problem and offers words of caution here:

> There is, of course, no question that in "modes of operation," as it is technically called—that is to say, in the functions ascribed to the several persons of the Trinity in the redemptive process, and, more broadly, in the entire dealing of God with the world—the principle of subordination is clearly expressed.... The Son is sent by the Father and does His Father's will (Jn. vi:38).... In crisp decisiveness, Our Lord even declares, indeed: 'My Father is greater than I' (Jn. xiv.28).... But it is not so clear that the principle of subordination rules also in "modes of subsistence," as it is technically phrased; that is to say, in the necessary relation of the Persons of the Trinity to one another. The very richness and variety of the expression of their subordination, the one to the other, in modes of operation, create a difficulty in attaining certainty whether they are represented as also subordinate the one to the other in modes of subsistence. Question is raised in each case of apparent intimation of subordination in modes of subsistence, whether it may not, after all, be explicable as only another expression of subordination in modes of operation. It may be natural to assume that a subordination in modes of operation rests on a subordination in modes of subsistence; that the reason

---

43. Christians do not worship the human nature of Christ—that would be idolatry, since it would involve worshiping the creature. In worshiping Christ we understand that we worship the Second Person of the Holy Trinity, God the Son, who by the Incarnation became man for us and for our salvation.

why it is the Father that sends the Son . . . is that the Son is subordinate to the Father. . . . But we are bound to bear in mind that these relations of subordination in modes of operation may just as well be due to a convention, an agreement, between the Persons of the Trinity—a "Covenant" as it is technically called—by virtue of which a distinct function in the work of redemption is voluntarily assumed by each. It is eminently desirable, therefore, at the least that some definite evidence of subordination in modes of subsistence should be discoverable before it is assumed.[44]

In the context we are considering it is not at all evident that, in "subordinating" himself to "the Father," Jesus was denying that he was in essence one with the Father. When the charge of blasphemy for making himself "equal with God" was leveled against him, a charge which hounded him to the very end of his life and which became finally the basis for the judgment of death against him (see 8:58–59; 10:33; 19:7; in the Synoptics, Matt. 26:65–66; Mark 14:61–62; Luke 22:70–71), he said nothing to allay the suspicions of the religious leaders concerning him, but followed their charge with the very discourse we have been considering in which he laid claim to the powers and privileges which belong to deity alone.

THE UNITY OF THE SON AND THE FATHER

In his Good Shepherd discourse in John 10:22–39, Jesus asserted that the security of his sheep is grounded in their being kept by both himself and the Father (John 10:28, 29). Then our Lord explained that this *coordinated* keeping on his and the Father's part was based on the essential oneness of "the Father" and "the Son": "I and the Father *are one* [ἕν ἐσμεν, *hen esmen*]," he declared (John 10:30; see also 12:45; 14:9, 23). Concerning this declaration B. F. Westcott writes:

> It seems clear that the unity here spoken of cannot fall short of unity of essence. The thought springs from the equality of power *(my hand, the Father's hand)*; but infinite power is an essential attribute of God; and it is impossible to suppose that two beings distinct in essence could be equal in power.[45]

When Jesus was then confronted by the religious leaders who took up stones to kill him, charging him again with blasphemy (John 10:33), if they were hoping that some word from him would relieve their suspicions, they were to be disappointed,

---

44. Warfield, "Biblical Doctrine of the Trinity," 54.
45. B. F. Westcott, *The Gospel According to St. John* (1881; reprint, Grand Rapids, Mich.: Eerdmans, 1958), 159.

for instead of declaring that they had misunderstood him, to the contrary, arguing *a minori ad majus* ("from lesser to greater"), he insisted that if human judges, because they had been made recipients of and were thus the responsible administrators of the justice of the Word of God, could be called "gods" (see Ps. 82:6), how much greater right did he—"the One whom the Father sanctified and sent into the world" (John 10:36)—have to call himself "the Son of God." The fact that Jesus' claim to be "the Son of God" both here (10:36) and earlier (5:25) invoked on both occasions the same response from the Jewish opposition, namely, the charge of blasphemy, points up how wrong the modern popular perception is that concludes that Jesus' claimed "Sonship" intended something less than the claim of deity. "He was not claiming to be God; he was only claiming to be the Son of God," the saying goes. Such a perception completely overlooks the fact that the religious leadership of his day understood his claim to involve the claim to deity. And that Jesus' answer intended the claim to deity is evident also from the fact, as Vos notes with respect to the word order of "sanctified" and "sent" in Jesus' explanation of his right to the title "the Son of God," that "He places the sanctifying before the sending into the world, because it preceded the latter, and a suggestion of pre-existence accompanies the statement."[46] Jesus asserts here that he is not "the Son" because he was sent, but rather was "the Son" and was "sanctified" (that is, was "set apart" and invested with the messianic task) before he was sent; and he was sent precisely because only One such as himself as "the Son" could complete the task which the messianic investiture entailed.

THE SON'S ETERNAL PREEXISTENCE

This last observation of Vos catapults us into the center of a controversy that is raging around the person of Christ: Did Jesus claim for himself preexistence, and if so, in what sense: in the ontological (essential) or in the ideal ("foreknown") sense? The Gospel of John witnesses that Jesus claimed eternal preexistence: "Glorify me, Father," Jesus prayed, "with yourself, with the glory which I had with you before the world was" (John 17:1, 5), indeed, with "my glory which you have given me because you loved me before the foundation of the world" (17:24). This claim on Jesus' part to an eternal preexistence with his Father is not an aberration, for he speaks elsewhere, though in somewhat different terms, of that same preexistence:

> John 3:13: "No one has ascended into heaven but he who descended from heaven, even the Son of Man."

---

46. Vos, *Self-Disclosure*, 198.

John 6:38: "I have come down from heaven, not to do my own will, but the will of him who sent me." (See also 6:33, 50, 58)

John 6:46: "[No one] has seen the Father except him who is *from* [παρά, *para*, with genitive; that is, from the side of] the Father."

John 6:62: "What if you were to see the Son of Man ascending where he was *before* [τὸ πρότερον, *to proteron*]?"

John 8:23: "You are from below, I am from above; you are from this world, I am not from this world."

John 8:38: "I speak of what I have seen with the Father."

John 8:42: "I came out and came forth *from* [ἐκ, *ek*, with genitive] God."

John 16:28: "I came *out from* [ἐκ, *ek*, παρά, *para*] the Father, and have come into the world" (see also 9:39; 12:46; 18:37).

But perhaps the greatest assertion to eternal preexistence is to be found in Jesus' "I am" saying of John 8:58. Most of his "I am" sayings, it is true, are supplied with a subjective complement of some kind, such as:

"I am the Bread of Life" (John 6:35, 48, 51);

"I am the Light of the World" (8:12; 9:5);

"I am the Door of the Sheep" (10:7, 9);

"I am the Good Shepherd" (10:11, 14);

"I am the Resurrection and the Life" (11:25);

"I am the Way, the Truth, and the Life" (14:6); and

"I am the Vine" (15:1, 5).

But according to D. A. Carson, "two are undoubtedly absolute in both form and content . . . and constitute an explicit self-identification with Yahweh who had already revealed himself to men in similar terms (see esp. Isa. 43:10-11)."[47] The two sayings Carson refers to are in John 8:58 and 13:19, but there could well be others such as his "I am" usage in John 6:20; 8:24, 28; and 18:5-8. In John 8:58, standing before men who regarded him as demonic, Jesus declared: "Before Abraham was, I am," invoking not only the term which Yahweh in the Old Testament had chosen as his own special term of self-identification, but claiming also a preexistence (see "before Abraham was") appropriate only to one possessed of the nature of Yahweh. His meaning was not lost on his audience, for "they took up stones to

---

47. D. A. Carson, " 'I Am' Sayings," in *Evangelical Dictionary of Theology* (Grand Rapids, Mich.: Baker, 1984), 541.

throw at him" (8:59). They understood that Jesus was claiming divine preexistence for himself and was thus making himself equal with God. In the case of his "I am" in 13:19 Jesus himself explicated its implications for his unity with the Father and in turn his own Yahwistic identity when he declared in the following verse: "he who receives me receives him who sent me." In 6:20, by his "I am" in "I am; be not afraid," Jesus admittedly might have been simply identifying himself to his terrified disciples, but as Carson notes: "Yet not every 'I' could be found walking on water." Then in 8:24, following immediately as it does his declaration that he was "from above" and "not of this world," Jesus' "I am" in his statement, "If you do not believe that I am, you will die in your sins," surely carries with it divine implications. Finally, in the case of his "I am" in 18:5–8, as soon as he uttered these words, his would-be captors "drew back and fell to the ground." John surely intended to suggest by this that his readers were to recognize in Jesus' acknowledgement that he was Jesus of Nazareth also his implicit self-identification with Yahweh.

JESUS' ACTS

In addition to his mighty miracles ("powers") which were designed to authenticate his messianic claim (Matt. 11:2–6; John 5:36; 10:25; 38; 14:11; Acts 2:22) and to reveal his glory (John 2:11), instances of Jesus' exercise of other divine prerogatives (like his public claims to deity itself, as we have seen) occur with sufficient frequency to warrant our taking note of them.

Forgiving Sins

Jesus claimed, as the Son of Man, to have the authority to forgive sins (Matt. 9:6; Mark 2:10; Luke 5:24) and, in fact, forgave men of their sins against God as evidenced not only by the spoken word (Matt. 9:2; Mark 2:5; Luke 5:20; 7:48) but also by his willingness to eat meals with sinners (Luke 15:1–2). This authority, as the teachers of the law who were present on the occasion of Jesus' healing of the paralytic rightly judged, is the prerogative of God alone. The one factor which they did not recognize but which would have explained his act to them is the factor of his deity. It is true, of course, that a man may forgive the transgressions of another man against him, but Jesus forgave men of their sins *against God!* Only One who is himself divine has the right to do that.

Hearing and Answering Prayer

Jesus declared that he will answer the prayers of his disciples (John 14:13), but equally significant for our purpose, he represents himself as One to whom prayers may properly be addressed. In verse 14, Jesus stated again that he himself will answer his disciples' prayers—surely an implicit claim to deity since one would have to be divine to hear, in all the languages of the world, the myriads of prayers being offered up to him at any one moment and then wisely to answer each prayer. While many other examples might be cited, the instances of prayer addressed to Jesus in Acts 1:24, 7:59, 9:10–17, 2 Corinthians 12:8, 1 Thessalonians 3:11, and 2 Thessalonians 2:16 bear out the literalness with which the disciples understood Jesus' promise, and reflect the immediacy on their part of the recognition of his divinity.

Receiving Men's Adoration and Praise

Immediately after his triumphal entry into Jerusalem, when asked by the indignant chief priests to silence the children who were praising him (Matt. 21:16), Jesus defended their praise of him by appealing to Psalm 8:2 (Heb. 8:3), which speaks of children praising God. Concerning Jesus' appeal to Psalm 8:2, Carson writes:

> God has ordained praise for himself from "children and infants." . . . Jesus' answer is a masterstroke. . . . 1. It provides some kind of biblical basis for letting the children go on with their exuberant praise. . . . 2. At the same time thoughtful persons, reflecting on the incident later (especially after the Resurrection), perceive that Jesus was saying much more. The children's "Hosannas" are not being directed to God but to the Son of David, the Messiah. Jesus is therefore not only acknowledging his messiahship but justifying the praise of the children by applying to himself a passage of Scripture applicable only to God.[48]

After his resurrection, Jesus accepted Thomas's adoring ascription of him as his "Lord and God." There can be no doubt, in light of these clear instances when Jesus accepted and approved the adoration and praise of men, that he was endorsing the notion of his own deity.

The Object of Men's Faith

In the familiar saying of John 14:1, whether the two occurrences of πιστεύετε εἰς (*pisteuete eis*, "believe in [with unreserved trust]") are both to be rendered indicatively ("you believe in") or imperatively ("believe in"), or whether the former is to be translated indicatively with only the latter to be rendered imperatively, makes no difference relative to our present purpose; Jesus places himself on a par with the Father as the proper object of men's trust. If Jesus was not in fact divine, such a

---

48. D. A. Carson, *Matthew, Expositor's Bible Commentary* (Grand Rapids, Mich.: Zondervan, 1984), 443.

saying would constitute blasphemy. The only ground upon which his goodness may be retained in the light of such teaching is to affirm his Godness. He cannot be a mere man and at the same time good while teaching men to trust him as they would trust the Father.

JESUS' DIVINE ATTRIBUTES

Jesus, in addition to exercising divine powers and claiming divine prerogatives, claimed to possess divine attributes as well. We have noted the attribute of preexistence; other divine attributes of Jesus include:

Sovereignty and Omnipotence

In claiming the authority to reveal the Father to whomever he chooses (Matt. 11:27) and to give life to whomever he chooses (John 5:21); in claiming both the prerogative and the power to call all men someday from their graves (5:28–29) and the authority to judge all men (John 5:22, 27); in claiming the authority to lay down his life and the authority to take it up again (John 10:18); in declaring he would return someday "in power and great glory" (Matt. 24:30); in claiming that all authority in heaven and on earth had been given to him by the Father (Matt. 28:18), our Lord was claiming, implicitly and explicitly, an absolute sovereignty and power over the universe—claims, were they to be made by any other man, deserving only the judgment of madness, but made by him deserving our adoration and our praise.

Omnipresence

When Jesus promised that "where two or three gather together in my name, there am I with them [ἐκεῖ εἰμι ἐν μέσῳ αὐτῶν, *ekei eimi en mesō autōn*]" (Matt. 18:20), and when he promised "*I am with you always* [ἐγὼ μεθ᾽ ὑμῶν εἰμι πάσας τὰς ἡμέρας, *egō meth hymōn eimi pasas tas hēmeras*] (Matt. 28:20), not only was Jesus invoking the language of the Immanuel title but he was also claiming that he is himself personally always with his own, not just in the power and presence of his Holy Spirit but present himself as the omnipresent Savior.

Omniscience

When Jesus surprised Nathaniel with his comment: "I saw you while you were still under the fig tree before Philip called you" (John 1:48), Jesus was revealing a level of knowledge not available to the sons of men and above that of the merely human. And when Jesus claimed for himself the prerogative to hear and to answer the prayers of his disciples, he was making an implicit claim to the possession of omniscience. One who can hear the innumerable prayers of his disciples, offered to him night and day, day in and day out throughout the centuries, keep each request infallibly related to its petitioner, and answer them in accordance with the divine mind and will would need himself to be omniscient. And when Jesus claimed to have not only an exclusive knowledge of the Father, but also a knowledge whose object is just God the Father himself in all the infinite depths of his divine being (Matt. 11:27), he was again claiming to be in possession, as "the Son," of a degree of knowledge falling nothing short of omniscience itself.

JESUS' TEACHING

Other indications that Jesus' self-understanding entailed the perception of his own deity are (1) the authoritative manner in which he expounded the Law of God to his contemporaries, (2) the manner in which he related himself to the Kingdom of God, and (3) his reference to two other Persons and his special employment at times of plural verbs.

His Authoritative Exposition of the Law

Jesus claimed to know the will and true intention of God which lay behind the Law (see his "I say to you"—Matt. 5:22, 28, 32, 34, 39, 44, and his many sayings introduced by ἀμήν [amēn, "Truly"]—Matt. 6:2, 5, 16). In speaking the way he did, writes I. Howard Marshall, Jesus

> made no claim to prophetic inspiration; no "thus says the Lord" fell from his lips, but rather he spoke in terms of his own authority. He claimed the right to give the authoritative interpretation of the law, and he did so in a way that went beyond that of the prophets. He thus spoke as if he were God.[49]

His Perception of His Relation to the Kingdom of God

Another indication, although indirect, that Jesus' self-understanding included the self-perception of deity may be discerned in his teaching concerning the Kingdom of God. According to Jesus, while the kingdom or rule of God will come some day in the future in power and great glory in conjunction with his own παρουσία,

---

49. I. Howard Marshall, *The Origins of New Testament Christology* (Downers Grove, Ill.: InterVarsity Press, 1976), 49–50.

parousia (Matt. 25:31–46, particularly v. 34), it had already invaded history in the soteric/redemptive sense (its "mystery" form) in his own person and ministry (see Matt. 11:2–6 against the background of Isa. 35:5–6; Matt. 12:28; 13:24–30, 36–43). In him God's Kingdom had invaded the realm of Satan, and he had bound the "strong man" himself (Matt. 12:29; Mark 3:27), a claim clearly carrying messianic implications. But Jesus was equally explicit that the Kingdom of God is both supernatural in nature and *supernaturally* achieved. George Ladd explains:

> As the dynamic activity of God's rule the kingdom is supernatural. It is God's deed. Only the supernatural act of God can destroy Satan, defeat death (I Cor. 15:26), raise the dead in incorruptible bodies to inherit the blessings of the kingdom (I Cor. 15:50ff.), and transform the world order (Matt. 19:28). The same supernatural rule of God has invaded the kingdom of Satan to deliver men from bondage to satanic darkness. The parable of the seed growing by itself sets forth this truth (Mark 4:26–29). The ground brings forth fruit of itself. Men may sow the seed by preaching the kingdom (Matt. 10:7; Luke 10:9; Acts 8:12; 28:23, 31); they can persuade men concerning the kingdom (Acts 19:8), but they cannot build it. It is God's deed. Men can receive the kingdom (Mark 10:15; Luke 18:17), but they are never said to establish it. Men can reject the kingdom and refuse to receive it or enter it (Matt. 23:13), but they cannot destroy it. They can look for it (Luke 23:51), pray for its coming (Matt. 6:10), and seek it (Matt. 6:33), but they cannot bring it. The kingdom is altogether God's deed although it works in and through men. Men may do things for the sake of the kingdom (Matt. 19:12; Luke 18:29), work for it (Col. 4:11), suffer for it (II Thess. 1:5), but they are not said to act upon the kingdom itself. They can inherit it (Matt. 25:34; I Cor. 6:9–10, 15:50), but they cannot bestow it upon others.[50]

Jesus viewed himself as the One upon whom rested the responsibility of bringing in this supernatural kingdom. But "if Jesus saw himself as the one in whom this kind of Kingdom was being inaugurated, then such a perception is a Christological claim which would be fraudulent and deceptive if Jesus was ignorant of his Godness."[51]

His Reference to Two Other Persons and His Special Employment of Plural Verbs

Christ spoke *directly* and unmistakably of *two* other Persons, alongside himself,

---

50. George Ladd, "Kingdom of God, Heaven," *Evangelical Dictionary of Theology* (Grand Rapids, Mich.: Baker, 1984), 609.
51. David F. Wells, *The Person of Christ* (Waco, Tex.: Crossway, 1984), 38.

within the Godhead. In the following passages observe the reiterative references to "I," "the Father," and "the Spirit," and specifically the use of *plural* verbs:

> John 14:16–26: "I will ask the Father, and he will give you *another* [ἄλλον, *allon*] Counselor to be with you forever—the Spirit of truth. . . . If anyone loves me, he will obey my teaching. My Father will love him, and *we will come* [ἐλευσόμεθα, *eleusometha*] to him and *we will make* [ποιησόμεθα, *poiēsometha*] our home with him . . . the Counselor, the Holy Spirit, whom the Father will send in my name, will teach you all things and will remind you of everything I have said to you."
>
> John 15:26: "When the Counselor comes, whom I will send to you from the Father, the Spirit of truth who goes out from the Father, he will testify about me."
>
> John 16:5–15: "I am going to him who sent me. . . . It is for your good that I am going away. Unless I go away, the Counselor will not come to you; but if I go, I will send him to you. . . . But when he, the Spirit of truth, comes, he will guide you into all truth. He will not speak on his own; he will speak only what he hears. . . . He will bring glory to me by taking from what is mine and making it known to you. All that belongs to the Father is mine. That is why I said the Spirit will take from what is mine and make it known to you.

Thus not only in the specific titles that he employed, but also in the explicit claims he made and the deeds he did, Jesus showed that he believed himself to be in possession of attributes and prerogatives that are the property of God alone, and in this way he was claiming to be God incarnate.

Paul's Christology

Paul reveals his assessment of Jesus as divine in many ways. For example, he (1) prayed to Christ (2 Cor. 12:8–9), (2) declared "the name of our Lord Jesus Christ" to be the name to be "called upon" in the church (1 Cor. 1:2; Rom. 10:9–13), (3) coupled "the Lord Jesus Christ" with "God our Father" as the co-source of those spiritual blessings of grace, mercy, and peace that God alone can grant (Gal. 1:3; Rom. 1:7; etc.), (4) applied to Christ the title κύριος, *kyrios*, which in the Septuagint is employed to translate the sacred name of Yahweh, (5) applied directly to Christ Old Testament passages in which Yahweh is the subject (for example, Isa. 45:23 and Phil. 2:10), and (6) implied Christ's preexistence as God's Son (Rom. 8:3; 2 Cor. 8:9; Gal. 4:4; Phil. 2:6–7; Col. 1:15–16; Eph. 4:8–9).

But there are eight specific pericopes where Paul makes explicit his view of Christ—Romans 1:3–4; 9:5; Titus 2:13; Colossians 1:15–20, 2:9; Philippians 2:6–11; and 1 Timothy 1:15 and 3:16.

ROMANS 1:3–4

While all of the New Testament writers know of and apply the significance of Christ's resurrection to the believer in one way or another, it is particularly Paul who highlights the significance of Jesus' resurrection for his divine Sonship.

In the early verses of Paul's theological treatise to the church at Rome, he informs us of certain characteristics of the gospel. He tells us that it is *God's* gospel, that it had been *promised in the Old Testament Scriptures,* and that it "concerned his Son." It is what he then says in 1:3–4 concerning Jesus as "God's Son" that concerns us here. A literal rendering of these verses would be:

> concerning his Son,
> > who *became* [or "came to be," that is, "was born"] of the seed of David, according to the flesh,
> > who *was marked out* the Son of God in power, according to the spirit of holiness, by the resurrection from the dead,
>
> Jesus Christ, our Lord.

The "Bracketing" Phrases

Note that the two participial clauses (indented in the translation above for easy identification; the participles are italicized) are "bracketed" between the two phrases "his Son" and "Jesus Christ, our Lord"; and were it the case that Paul had omitted the intervening participial clauses entirely, we would still have here the highest kind of incarnational Christology. The former phrase ("his Son") indicates both the relationship in which Jesus, as God's Son, stands with God the Father and what he is in himself, while the latter phrase ("Jesus Christ, our Lord") designates what he is, as such, to us. In view of several contexts where Paul employs the title "Son," specifically those in which he speaks of God "sending [πέμψας, *pempsas*] his own Son" (Rom. 8:3), "sparing not his own Son" (Rom. 8:32), and "sending forth [ἐξαπέστειλεν, *exapesteilen*] his Son" (Gal. 4:4), it is clear that for Paul the Son enjoyed an existence with God the Father prior to his being sent, and that in this preexistent state he stood in a relation to the Father as the Father's *unique* Son (see also Col. 1:13, 16–17 where the Son is said to be "before all things"). The reflexive pronoun and possessive adjective respectively in Romans 8:3 and 8:32 (ἑαυτοῦ, *heautou*, and ἰδίου, *idiou*), in the words of John Murray, also highlight

> the uniqueness of the sonship belonging to Christ and the uniqueness of the fatherhood belonging to the Father in relation to the Son.... In the language of Paul this corresponds to the title *monogenes* ["only one of a kind"] as it appears in John (John 1:14, 18; 3:16, 18; 1 John 4:9). It is the eternal sonship that is in view and

to this sonship there is no approximation in the adoptive sonship that belongs to redeemed men. The same applies to the fatherhood of the first person. In the sense in which he is the eternal Father in relation to the Son he is not the Father of his adopted children.[52]

This being so, Murray is justified when he also writes concerning the phrase "his Son" in Romans 1:3:

> There are good reasons for thinking that in this instance the title refers to a relation which the Son sustains to the Father antecedently to and independently of his manifestation in the flesh. (1) Paul entertained the highest conception of Christ in his divine identity and eternal preexistence (*see* 9:5; Phil. 2:6; Col. 1:19; 2:9). The title "Son" he regarded as applicable to Christ in his eternal preexistence and as defining his eternal relation to the Father (8:3, 32; Gal. 4:4). (2) Since this is the first occasion in which the title is used in this epistle, we should expect the highest connotation to be attached to it. Furthermore, the connection in which the title is used is one that would demand no lower connotation than that which is apparent in 8:3, 32; the apostle is stating that with which the gospel as the theme of the epistle is concerned. (3) The most natural interpretation of verse 3 is that the title "Son" is not to be construed as one predicated of him in virtue of the process defined in the succeeding clauses but rather identifies him as the person who became the subject of this process and is therefore identified as the Son in the historical event of the incarnation. For these reasons we conclude that Jesus is here identified by that title which expresses his eternal relation to the Father and that when the subject matter of the gospel is defined as that which pertains to the eternal Son of God the apostle at the threshold of the epistle is commending the gospel by showing that it is concerned with him who has no lower station than that of equality with the Father.[53]

C. E. B. Cranfield concurs:

> It is clear that, as used by Paul with reference to Christ, the designation, "Son of God" expresses nothing less than a relationship to God which is "personal, ethical and inherent," involving a real community of nature between Christ and God. The position of the words τοῦ υἱοῦ αὐτοῦ [*tou huiou autou*, "his Son"]— . . . . they are naturally taken to control both participial clauses—would seem to imply that the One who was born of the seed of David was already Son of God before, and independently of, the action denoted by the second participle.[54]

---

52. John Murray, *Romans* (Grand Rapids, Mich.: Eerdmans, 1960), 1:279.
53. Ibid., 1:5.
54. C. E. B. Cranfield, *Romans* (Edinburgh: T. & T. Clark, 1975), 1:58.

The latter phrase ("Jesus Christ, our Lord") Paul obviously intends as explanatory of the former phrase. That is to say, he who stands in relation to God the Father as his own unique Son and who is in himself the preexistent Son of God is also as to his historical identity just "Jesus" of Nazareth, who because of his antecedent Sonship received the messianic investiture ("Christ") and as such is not only "Lord," the One who has been exalted to the Father's right hand (Ps. 110:1; Phil. 2:9–11) and who exercises there all authority in heaven and on earth (Matt. 28:18), but also "*our* Lord," the One to whom we owe absolute obedience and who properly exercises such lordship over the creature as is the prerogative only of One who is himself the divine Creator.

The two bracketing phrases are thus a summary statement of Paul's Christology: for Paul, the Son, in his preexistent state, is both equal with the Father as God and distinguishable from the Father as his Son. This One, in keeping with the terms of his messianic investiture, became man, and by virtue of his work as the incarnate Son was exalted to the highest place of honor in the heavens and was given a name above every name ("Lord"), "that at the name of Jesus, every knee should bow, in heaven and on earth and under the earth, and every tongue confess that Jesus Christ is Lord, to the glory of God the Father" (Phil. 2:10–11).

The "Bracketed" Clauses

As we turn to the participial clauses between the bracketing phrases, it is imperative that we keep constantly in mind that what the apostle now tells us about Christ is thrown up against the background of his deity implicit in the "bracket" phrases. This backdrop must be allowed to serve as a governing control over all of our subsequent exegesis. For example, we should realize immediately that something is amiss in our exegesis if, in determining the meaning intended by the second participle, we conclude that Paul teaches that at his resurrection Jesus was "constituted" or "appointed" as "Son of God." Such an adoptionistic Christology is precluded at the outset by Paul's representation of his Subject as *being* the Son of God prior to and independently of either his "being born" of the seed of David or his being "marked out" as the Son of God. Whatever one makes of Paul's second clause, the "bracket" phrases preclude any form of adoptionism.

There is little dispute regarding the meaning of the first clause, "who became [that is, 'came to be' or 'was born'] of the seed of David, according to the flesh." Paul simply intended that his reader understand that in one sense, that is, "according to the flesh," the Son of God had a *historical beginning* as the Son of David. He says essentially the same thing in Galatians 4:4: "When the time had fully come, God sent forth his Son, born [the same word as in Rom. 1:3] of a woman," only in

Romans 1:3 he specifies the lineage out of which he came, namely, the Davidic line. By making specific mention of Jesus' Davidic lineage, Paul intended to make it clear that Jesus, standing as he did in the Davidic line on his human side, was the promised Messiah and king.

Note that Paul does not simply say that Jesus was born of the seed of David but adds the qualifying phrase "according to the flesh." What does he intend by this additional thought? As in Romans 9:5, the phrase intends a specificity and limits the sense in which it may be said that Jesus had a historical beginning as the seed of David. There can be no question that the word "flesh" denotes Christ's human nature in its entirety. In New Testament usage, σάρξ (*sarx,* "flesh"), when applied to Christ (see John 1:14; 6:51; Rom. 8:3; 9:5; Eph. 2:14; Col. 1:22; 1 Tim. 3:16; Heb. 5:7; 10:20; 1 Pet. 3:18; 4:1; 1 John 4:1; 2 John 7), denotes not simply the material or physical aspect of his human nature over against the nonmaterial aspect, that is, over against his human spirit. Rather, it uniformly refers to him in the totality of his humanness as a man. Accordingly, when Paul says that Jesus had a historical beginning "according to the flesh," he intends, as Cranfield states,

> that the fact of Christ's human nature, in respect of which what has just been said is true, is not the whole truth about Him. "Son of David" is a valid description of Him so far as it is applicable, but the reach of its applicability is not coterminous with the fullness of His person.[55]

The sense in which the lineal description of Jesus as the Son of David ceases to be applicable as a full description has already been implicitly stated in the first of the "bracket" phrases—Jesus is not only David's son but also "his ['God's'] Son." Paul makes this explicit in the second participial clause. It reads: "who was marked out the Son of God in power according to the spirit of holiness by the resurrection from the dead." This clause has proven to be difficult for exegetes, but it seems that, whereas the former clause speaks of Jesus' historical beginning as "the Son of David" on his human side, this latter clause speaks of Jesus' *historical establishment,* by his resurrection from the dead, as the Son of God on his divine side. My reasons for this conclusion follow.

The participle ὁρισθέντος, *horisthentos,* the aorist passive of ὁρίζω, *horizo,* I suggest, should be translated "was marked out," "was delineated," or "was designated." The verb is used in the Septuagint in the sense of "fixing" or "marking out" or "delineating" boundaries (see Num. 34:6; Josh. 13:27; 15:12; 18:20; 23:4), and the noun ὅρια, *horia,* is used in both the Septuagint and the New Testament for

---

55. Ibid., 1:60.

"boundaries" or "borders" (see Matt. 2:16; 4:13; 8:34; 15:22, 39; 19:1; Mark 5:17; 7:24, 31; 10:1; Acts 13:50).

In accordance with its uniform usage as a periphrasis for the adverb "powerfully" (see Mark 9:1; Col. 1:29; 1 Thess. 1:5; 2 Thess. 1:11), I would construe the phrase ἐν δυνάμει (*en dynamei,* "in power"), in concert with Meyer, Hodge, Sanday and Headlam, H. Alford, F. Godet, and Warfield, with the participle rather than with "the Son of God," and translate the participle and the prepositional phrase by "was powerfully marked out" or "was powerfully delineated."

The preposition ἐκ, *ek,* introducing the phrase "the resurrection from [ablative use of the genitive] the dead," has a different nuance from the ἐκ, *ek,* in the former clause. Whereas the preposition ἐκ, *ek,* in the former clause, after the participle of "begetting," clearly denotes "origin," that is, "came to be [or "was born"] *out of* [or *"from"*] the seed of David," in the second clause, after the passive participle "was marked out," it denotes "instrumentality" or even "result" (on the analogy of its use in Heb. 11:35). Accordingly, I would render the last phrase of the clause by "through the instrumentality of [or "as the result of"] the resurrection from the dead." This can, of course, and probably should be, be reduced to the simpler *"by the resurrection from the dead."*

The final phrase to be discussed is "according to the Spirit of holiness." It is universally agreed that the phrase stands in contrast to "according to the flesh" in the first clause. Since "flesh" in the former clause denotes Christ's humanity *in its totality,* including both corporeal and noncorporeal aspects of his human nature, "spirit" in the latter clause cannot refer to the human spirit of Jesus. His human spirit is already included within the Davidic "flesh" which he assumed at his birth. Its referent must be sought outside of his humanity. Many, if not most, modern commentators assume that the phrase refers to the Holy Spirit, but I would disagree. On every occasion in the New Testament where the word "holy" is attached to the noun "spirit" to refer to the Holy Spirit, the adjective ἅγιος, *hagios,* is employed. But here, precisely to avoid reference to the Holy Spirit, I would suggest, Paul employs the genitive form of the noun ἁγιωσύνη, *hagiōsynē:* "the Spirit of holiness."

If "Spirit" does not refer to Christ's human spirit or to the Holy Spirit, then to what does it refer? I suggest that it refers to Christ's divine nature, to what he is, as the Son of God, on his divine side. There are two reasons for this: first, because the phrase stands in contrast to "flesh" in the former clause which refers to what Christ, as the Son of David, is on his human side, the implication is that "Spirit" in the latter clause must also refer to something intrinsically inherent in Christ. But standing as it does in such close correlation to the title "the Son of God" in the same phrase which denotes Christ in terms of his Godness, it follows that its referent here is to what he is, as the Son of God, on his divine side, that is, to his deity.

Second, in the same letter, some chapters later (9:5) Paul refers again to Christ as "from the fathers, specifically according to the flesh," intimating that something more can and must be said about him. In this later context, what this "something more" is, Paul himself provides us in the phrase "who is over all, God blessed forever." In other words, in Romans 9:5 Paul declares that Christ is "of the fathers according to the flesh," but in the sense that he is not "of the fathers" and not "flesh" he was and is "over all, God blessed forever." Similarly in Romans 1:3–4 Paul informs us that Christ is "of David, according to the flesh," but in the sense that he is not "of David" and not "flesh," he was and is, as the Son of God, "the Spirit of holiness" (see 1 Cor. 15:45), that is, divine Spirit, intending by this phrase what he explicitly spells out in the later Romans 9:5 context. Warfield explains:

> [Paul] is not speaking of an endowment of Christ either from or with the Holy Spirit. . . . He is speaking of that divine Spirit which is the complement in the constitution of Christ's person of the human nature according to which He was the Messiah, and by virtue of which He was not merely the Messiah, but also the very Son of God. This Spirit he calls distinguishingly the Spirit of holiness, the Spirit the very characteristic of which is holiness. <u>He is speaking not of an acquired holiness but of an intrinsic holiness</u>; not, then, of a holiness which had been conferred at the time of or attained by means of the resurrection from the dead; but of a holiness which had always been the very quality of Christ's being [see Luke 1:35; 5:8; John 6:69].[56]

Thus the entire clause can be paraphrased as "who was powerfully marked out the Son of God in accordance with his divine nature by his resurrection from the dead."

John Murray (Cranfield as well) is persuaded that the verb ὁρίζω, *horizo,* means "appoint" or "constitute" in this context and connotes, as does the former clause, a new "historical beginning" of some kind commencing with the resurrection. Accordingly, he regards the two clauses as depicting the "two successive stages" of *humiliatio* and *exaltatio* in the historical process of Jesus' incarnate messianic state. He carefully avoids what would otherwise be an adoptionist Christology by affirming that in the second of the two stages what was "constituted" was not Jesus as the Son of God *per se* but Jesus as the Son of God "in power." This addition, he writes, "makes all the difference."[57] The successive stages stand in Murray's construction in a certain kind of *antithesis* to each other, the former clause denoting

---

56. Warfield, "The Christ That Paul Preached," 87–88; so also Charles Hodge, *Systematic Theology* (Grand Rapids, Mich.: Eerdmans, n.d.) 1:472, and Robert Lewis Dabney, *Lectures in Systematic Theology* (1878; reprint, Grand Rapids, Mich.: Zondervan, 1972), 208.
57. Murray, *Romans,* 1:10.

what Jesus was *before* his resurrection, the latter clause denoting what he was *after* his resurrection. In other words, in the former stage, having been "born of the seed of David according to the flesh," Jesus, as the Son of David, was in a state of apparent *weakness;* but with his resurrection, Jesus entered a new stage of messianic existence, one of powerful "pneumatic endowment" (according to Murray this is the meaning of "according to the spirit of holiness") commensurate with his messianic lordship, a lordship "all-pervasively conditioned by pneumatic powers."[58] He writes, "The relative weakness of his pre-resurrection state, reflected on in verse 3, is contrasted with the triumphant power exhibited in his post-resurrection lordship."[59] But the traditional view that what Paul intended to teach is that Jesus was powerfully marked out as the Son of God in accordance with what he is on his divine side by his resurrection seems to have stronger arguments on its side.

Murray's view, representing the two clauses as "successive stages," injects a contrast between the clauses (what Jesus was *before,* and what he was *after* his resurrection) which is not in the text. Murray implies that being "the Son of David according to the flesh" meant a certain state of lowliness and weakness, this former clause needing to be read, at least to a degree, depreciatingly or concessively ("although he was born . . ."). But as Warfield says of the former clause:

> To say "of the seed of David" is not to say weakness; it is to say majesty. It is quite certain, indeed, that the assertion "who was made of the seed of David" cannot be read concessively, preparing the way for the celebration of Christ's glory in the succeeding clause. It stands rather in parallelism with the clause that follows it, asserting with it the supreme glory of Christ.[60]

In other words, while there is the intimation of the idea of a second successive stage within the second clause itself simply because of the mention of the resurrection, it is not the dominant idea in the passage. As for succession between the clauses, it is absent from the context. The two clauses, as is evident from the parallelism of the two genitive participles (τοῦ γενομένου, τοῦ ὁρισθέντος, *tou genomenou, tou horisthentos*) with no connecting particle, stand parallel to one another as together representing all that the Son of God is in his incarnate state. This is also made clear by Paul's similar statement in 2 Timothy 2:8, where he writes, as an encouragement to Timothy: "Remember Jesus Christ, having been raised out of the dead, is of the seed of David, according to my gospel." Clearly Christ's descent from David, was, in Paul's mind, a truth which should cause the beleaguered Christian to rejoice, for it speaks of Christ's messianic majesty. It in no way speaks of weakness

---

58. Ibid., 1:11.
59. Ibid.
60. Warfield, "The Christ That Paul Preached," 81.

and it is not to be set off over against his state inaugurated by his resurrection, for it is precisely Jesus Christ as the One who "has been raised" (the same theme as in Romans 1:4) and who "is of the seed of David" (the same theme as in Romans 1:3) who is in *both* aspects to be remembered by the Christian in distress. The relation of the second participial clause to the first in Romans 1:3–4 is not then one of opposition or contrast but rather one of climax, not one of *supersession* but one of *superposition*. This is obvious from the fact that Jesus did not cease to be either "the Son of David" or "flesh" at his resurrection; indeed, the resurrection insured that he would continue to be both (a fact which Murray recognizes). So what Paul is saying by the first clause is that the Son of God was born as the Davidic Messiah with all the glories that such an investiture entails; what he is saying by the second clause is that

> the Messiahship, inexpressibly glorious as it is, does not exhaust the glory of Christ. He had a glory greater than even this. This was the beginning of His glory. He came into the world as the promised Messiah, and He went out of the world as the demonstrated Son of God. In these two things is summed up the majesty of His historical manifestation.[61]

Thus Paul offers us in these two verses a magnificent Christology: the eternal Son of God, who was born of the seed of David according to his manhood, was also the Son of God according to his deity. And this latter fact was powerfully marked out or displayed by his resurrection from the dead, as not only he himself exercised that divine power which he had displayed in raising others from the dead by raising himself from the dead (John 2:19; 10:18), but also his Father placed his stamp of approval on all that his Son had done by raising him from the dead "in accordance with the working of the might of his strength which he exerted in Christ when he raised him from the dead" (Rom. 4:24; 6:4; 8:11; Eph. 1:19–20).

Thus Romans 1:3–4, which may well be a portion of an early Christian confession, teaches us that Jesus' resurrection from the dead was both his and his Father's powerful witness to the fact that Jesus of Nazareth was God incarnate and not simply a man.

ROMANS 9:5

This verse reads: "from whom came the Messiah according to the flesh, who is over all, God blessed forever. Amen." The debate surrounding this verse arises not from a divergence of opinion over textual variants or the meaning of words but

---

61. Ibid., 80.

rather over the question of punctuation. The most natural way to punctuate the verse is to place commas after both "flesh" and "all" and a period after "forever," as above. This punctuation is supported by both the context and the grammatical and implicatory demands of the verse itself.

No one expresses the significance of the context for the meaning of Romans 9:5 with greater depth of insight that E. H. Gifford:

> St. Paul is expressing the anguish of his heart at the fall of his brethren: that anguish is deepened by the memory of their privileges, most of all, by the thought that their race gave birth to the Divine Saviour, whom they have rejected. In this, the usual interpretation, all is most natural: the last and greatest cause of sorrow is the climax of glory from which the chosen race has fallen.[62]

As for the grammatical demand of the verse, it can hardly be denied that the most natural way to handle "who is" (ὁ ὤν, *ho ōn*, the definite article and present participle) is to view the phrase as introducing a relative clause and to attach it to the immediately preceding ὁ Χριστός, *ho Christos*.

The implicatory demand of the verse flows from the presence of the words τὸ κατὰ σάρκα (*to kata sarka*, "insofar as the flesh is concerned"). This expression naturally raises the question: in what sense is the Messiah not from the patriarchs? The second half of the implied antithesis is supplied in the words which follow: "who is over all, God blessed forever." This treatment of the verse ascribes full, unqualified deity to the Messiah, and has enjoyed the support of many early Fathers, the large majority of commentators, and also the AV (1611), RV (1881), ASV (1901), NASV (1971), NIV (1978), and the NKJV (1982).

Because they judge that to refer to Christ as "God" is an un-Pauline locution, opposing scholars (see RSV [1946] and NEB [1970]) have proposed two alternative punctuations, the first detaching the last expression, θεὸς εὐλογητὸς εἰς τοὺς αἰῶνας, *theos eulogētos eis tous aiōnas*, and construing it as a doxology, from the preceding, the second detaching the entire expression after σάρκα, *sarka*, from the preceding, again construing the clause as a doxology.

As for the objection itself, it is a clear case of "begging the question" to declare a reference to Christ as God "un-Pauline" in a Pauline letter where all the syntactical evidence indicates that this may well be the very time that he has done so. Can a writer never express a theological *hapax legomenon* ("said one time")? And to assert that he does so nowhere else requires the additional judgment that Titus 2:13 is at best "deutero-Pauline," that is, non-Pauline in authorship though "Pauline-like" in

---

62. E. H. Gifford, *Romans* (London: John Murray, 1886), 168–69.

style and essential substance. Furthermore, it is to ignore the words of Colossians 2:9, not to mention the profusion of exalted terminology throughout Paul's writings which ascribe deity to Jesus.

And what about the two alternative proposals? The first, as we indicated, suggests that the last words of the verse should be construed as a disconnected doxology ("May God be blessed before!"). But Bruce M. Metzger certainly seems to be correct when he writes: "Both logically and emotionally such a doxology would interrupt the train of thought as well as be inconsistent with the mood of sadness that pervades the preceding verses."[63]

Furthermore, if this detached clause is a doxology to God, it reverses the word order of every other such doxology in the Bible (over thirty times in the Old Testament and twelve times in the New), where the verbal adjective always *precedes* the noun for God and never follows it (as here). It is difficult to believe that Paul, whose ear for proper Hebraic and Hellenistic linguistic and syntactical formulae was finely tuned, would violate the established form for expressing praise to God which even he himself observes elsewhere (Eph. 1:3; 2 Cor. 1:3).

Finally, if this clause is an ascription of praise to God, it differs in another respect from every other occurrence of such in Paul's writings. Invariably, when Paul would ascribe blessedness to God, he connects the expression either by some grammatical device or by direct juxtaposition to a word which precedes it. There is, in other words, an antecedent reference to God in the immediately preceding context. For example, he employs ὅ ἐστιν, *ho estin* (Rom. 1:25), ὁ ὤν, *ho ōn* (2 Cor. 11:31), ᾧ, *hō* (Gal. 1:5; 2 Tim. 4:18), αὐτῷ, *autō* (Rom. 11:36; Eph. 3:21), and τῷ δὲ θεῷ, *tō de theō* (Phil. 4:20; 1 Tim. 1:17) to introduce ascriptions of praise to God. In the cases of Ephesians 1:3 and 2 Corinthians 1:3, even here there is an antecedent reference to God in the immediately preceding contexts. Thus all of Paul's doxologies to God are connected either grammatically or juxtapositionally to an immediately preceding antecedent reference to God. Never is there an abrupt change from one subject (in this case, the Messiah in 9:5a) to another (God in 9:5b) as suggested by this proposal.

The second proposal is the one preferred by most of the scholars who reject the idea that Paul is referring to Christ as God, and it is commended by the *Greek New Testament* (United Bible Societies), the RSV, and the NEB. But not only do the objections against the former proposal tell equally against it as well, but an additional objection may be registered. By disconnecting everything after σαρκα, *sarka*, and construing the disconnected portion as an independent ascription of praise, it denies to the participle ὤν, *ōn*, any real significance. Metzger highlights this failing:

---

63. Bruce M. Metzger, "The Punctuation of Romans 9:5," in *Christ and Spirit in the New Testament* (Cambridge: Cambridge University Press, 1973), 108.

If . . . the clause [beginning with ὁ ὤν, *ho ōn*] is taken as an asyndetic [unconnected] doxology to God, . . . the word ὤν [*ōn*] becomes superfluous, for "he who is God over all" is most simply represented in Greek by ὁ ἐπὶ πάντων θεός [*ho epi pantōn theos*]. The presence of the participle suggests that the clause functions as a relative clause (not "he who is . . ." but "who is . . ."), and thus describes ὁ Χριστός [*ho Christos*] as being "God over all."[64]

Nigel Turner also points out that detaching the words beginning with ὁ ὤν, *ho ōn*, from the preceding clause "introduces asyndeton and there is no grammatical reason why a participle agreeing with 'Messiah' should first be divorced from it and then be given the force of a wish, receiving a different person as its subject."[65] It is strange that some scholars can recognize the presence and natural force of the relatival ὁ ὤν, *ho ōn*, in 2 Corinthians 11:31, where we find precisely the same syntactical construction ("God . . . , who is blessed forever"), and yet fail to recognize it in Romans 9:5.

There can be no justifiable doubt that Paul in Romans 9:5, by his use of θεός, *theos*, as a christological title—surrounding it with the particular descriptive phrases that he does, ascribes full deity to Jesus Christ who is and *abides as* (the force of the present participle) divine Lord over the universe, and who deserves eternal praise from all.

TITUS 2:13

The debate surrounding this verse is whether Paul intended to refer to one person (Christ) or to two persons (God the Father and Christ) when he wrote: "while we wait for the blessed hope, even the appearing of the glory [or, glorious appearing] of the great God and Savior of us, Jesus Christ" (author's translation). There are five compelling reasons for understanding Paul to be referring to Christ alone throughout the verse and thus for translating the relevant phrase as "the appearing of our great God and Savior, Jesus Christ."

First, it is the most natural way to render the Greek sentence, as numerous commentators and grammarians have observed. Indeed, more than one grammarian has noted that there would never have been a question as to whether "God" and "Savior" refer to one person if the sentence had simply ended with "our Savior." Second, the two nouns both stand under the regimen of the single definite article preceding "God," indicating (according to the Granville Sharp rule, formulated in

---

64. Ibid., 105–6. Metzger's discussion of Romans 9:5 in *Textual Commentary on the Greek New Testament* (New York: United Bible Societies, 1971), is an excellent treatment of the issue.
65. Nigel Turner, *Grammatical Insights into the New Testament* (Edinburgh: Clark, 1965), 15.

1798, which states that when two nouns of the same case are connected by *kai*, a single article before the first noun denotes conceptual unity, whereas the repetition of the article with both nouns denotes particularity) that they are to be construed as one, not separately, that is to say, that they have a single referent. If Paul had intended to speak of two persons, he could have expressed this unambiguously by inserting an article before "Savior" or by writing "our Savior" after "Jesus Christ." Third, inasmuch as "appearing" never refers to God the Father but is consistently employed to refer to Christ's return in glory, the prima facie conclusion is that the "appearing of the glory of our great God" refers to Christ's appearing and not to the Father's appearing. Fourth, the terms θεός καὶ σωτήρ (*theos kai sōtēr*, "god and savior") were employed in combination together in the second and first century B.C. secular literature to refer to single recipients of heathen worship. James H. Moulton, for example, writes:

> A curious echo [of Titus 2:13] is found in the Ptolemaic formula applied to the deified kings: thus GH 15 (ii/B.C.), τοῦ μεγάλου θεοῦ . . . καὶ σωτῆρος . . . , *tou megalou theou . . . kai sōtēros*. . . . The phrase here is, of course, applied to one person.[66]

And Walter Lock writes in the same vein:

> The combination σωτὴρ καὶ θεός [*sōtēr kai theos*] had been applied to Ptolemy I, θεὸς ἐπιφανής [*theos epiphanēs*] to Antiochus Epiphanes, θεὸν ἐπιφανῆ καὶ...σωτῆρα [*theon epiphanē kai . . . sōtēra*] to Julius Caesar [Ephesus, 48 B.C.].[67]

It is very likely in light of this data that one impulse behind Paul's description of Christ here was his desire to counteract the extravagant titular endowment that had been accorded to human rulers. Fifth, contrary to the oft-repeated assertion that the use of θεός, *theos*, as a christological title is an "un-Pauline locution" and thus the noun cannot refer to Christ here, our exposition of Romans 9:5 has demonstrated that this is not so. Grammatically and biblically, the evidence would indicate that Paul intended in Titus 2:13 to describe Christ as "our great God and Savior."

If we could look no further for Paul's Christology than to these two texts—Romans 9:5 and Titus 2:13—we would have to conclude that his was a Christology of the highest kind. The One who had identified himself to Paul on

---

66. James H. Moulton, *A Grammar of New Testament Greek* (Edinburgh: T. & T. Clark, 1930), 1:84.
67. Walter Lock, *The Pastoral Epistles*, International Critical Commentary series (London: T. & T. Clark, 1928), 145.

the Damascus Road as "Jesus of Nazareth" (Acts 22:8), who as his Lord had called Paul to himself and whom Paul now served, was "over all things, the ever-blessed God" (Rom. 9:5, author's translation) and his "great God and Savior" (Titus 2:13). And considering the extensiveness of Paul's missionary travels and the significance of the church (Rome) and the man (Titus) to whom he wrote these letters, this same high Christology would have become widely held and regarded as precious by all those who accepted Paul's apostolic authority. Paul and his churches would have held to a high, ontological, incarnational Christology.

COLOSSIANS 1:15–20

In this hymnic pericope, beginning in 1:15 with the words "who is," the antecedent of which is "the Son of his [that is, "the Father's"; see 1:12] love" in 1:13, Paul gives us a magnificent description of the person of our Lord:

Lord of the Natural Creation:
   Who is the Image of the invisible God,
     the Firstborn of all creation,
   because by him were created all things in heaven and earth,
     things visible and things invisible—
     whether thrones or dominions,
     whether rulers or authorities—
   [because] all things through him and for him have been created,
     and he is before all things, and all things by him endure.

Lord of the Spiritual Creation:
   And he is Head of the body, the church,
     who is the Beginning,
      the Firstborn from the dead, in order that he might come to have first place in all things,
   because in him he [the Father] willed all the fullness to dwell, and
   [because] through him [the Father willed] to reconcile all things for him,
     by making peace through the blood of his cross—
     through him,
     whether things upon earth,
     or things in heaven. (author's translation)

The first thing that Paul tells us is that Christ, as the Father's Son, is "the Image of the invisible God." What does he mean by this? In view of Paul's equation of "the light of the gospel of the glory of Christ, who is the Image of God" (2 Cor. 4:4) with "the light of the glory of God [imaged] in the face of Jesus Christ" (2 Cor. 4:6), it appears that he is saying that in Jesus Christ the glory of God, indeed God himself, becomes manifest. When one recalls, in addition, that the writer of Hebrews (Paul?) also described God's Son as "the radiance of God's glory and the exact representation of his being" (1:3), and that James described "our Lord Jesus Christ" as "the Glory" of God (2:1; see Zech. 2:5), there can be little doubt that Paul, with the New Testament writers in general, intended to assert that Jesus Christ is the invisible God made visible.

This understanding—that Paul intended here to assert Jesus' divine nature—receives further support by the hymn's accompanying descriptions of him. That the Son enjoyed preexistence with the Father, prior to the creation of the universe, Paul explicitly affirmed when he tells us that (1) the Son is ("exists") "before all things" (1:17; see John 1:15, 30; 8:58), and (2) that God created "all things in heaven and on earth—things visible and things invisible—whether thrones or dominions, whether rulers or authorities" by (ἐν, *en*) him, through (διά, *dia*) him, and for (εἰς, *eis*) him (1:16). (3) The Son's divine character is also apparent in Paul's declaration that "all [created] things" are dependent upon him for their continuance in existence: "all things by him endure [or "hold together"]" (1:17; see Heb. 1:3). (4) Finally, Paul's description of Christ as "the Firstborn of all creation," in light of the entire context, is to be understood, as in Romans 8:29, in the Hebraic sense of an ascription of priority of rank to the firstborn son who enjoys a special place in the father's love.[68]

The recent attempts of some scholars to empty Paul's description of all references to the Son's *personal* preexistence and to make his words mean nothing more than that the power that God exercised in creation is now fully revealed and embodied in Christ fall far short of the passage's full import. Furthermore, Paul's intention behind his description of Jesus as "the Firstborn of all creation" is a universe away from the Arian interpretation of the Jehovah's Witnesses that would insist that the word shows that the Son was the "first" of all *other* created things; the entire context demands that the term is to be understood in the Hebraic sense as an ascription of that priority which the firstborn son enjoyed in the father's love.

That the Son is also preeminent over the church is stated in Paul's description of him as "the Head of the body, the church," "the Beginning [of the new humanity]," "the Firstborn from the dead, that he might come to have first place [as the Father's exalted Son] over all things" (1:18a, b, c; see Rom. 8:29) and the One through whose peacemaking cross work God is finally to reconcile all things for his (Christ's) glory (1:20).

It is difficult to find any biblical passage that more forthrightly affirms the full and unabridged deity of Jesus Christ than Colossians 1:15–20, spelling out as it does

---

68. See Robert L. Reymond, "Firstborn," in *Evangelical Dictionary of Theology*, ed. Walter A. Elwell, 2d ed. (Grand Rapids, Mich.: Baker, 1998).

on a scale of cosmic dimensions his role in creating and preserving all things and his divine preeminence over all created things as Creator and Redeemer. Here Paul explicitly declares that Jesus Christ, as God's Son, was existing with the Father prior to the creation of the universe, was himself God's Agent in creation, and as the Image of the invisible God, that is, as God himself, by his incarnation made the invisible God visible to men. Then, as the exalted "Firstborn from the dead," his eschatological preeminence is implied in Paul's assertion that God willed to reconcile all things for Christ's glory (εἰς αὐτόν, *eis auton*) which is finally to be fulfilled in the "Eschaton."

COLOSSIANS 2:9

I postponed the discussion of the phrase in 1:19, "all the fullness," to this point, because Paul uses the phrase in 2:9 with even greater clarity of meaning and the phrase almost certainly means the same thing in both contexts.

In Colossians 1:19, Paul wrote: "In him [God] willed all the fullness to dwell." Here in 2:9 Paul says virtually the same thing, but he specifies the nature of the "fullness" and the manner in which the "fullness" dwells in Jesus. To see this, let us follow his thought. In the last verses of Colossians 1 Paul discussed the "mystery" of God, which, he says, is "Christ in you, the hope of glory" (1:27). A few verses later, Paul affirmed again that God's "mystery," only recently fully revealed (it had been anticipated in the Old Testament revelation), is Christ (2:2) "in whom all the treasures of wisdom and knowledge are deposited" (2:3). This highlights the uniqueness of Christ as the sole true repository and integrating point of all knowledge. Paul then gives the reason why his readers are to "walk" in Christ and to "be on guard" that no one should take them captive through the pursuit of the knowledge that springs from human philosophy and tradition. Translated literally, 2:9 reads: "because in him [Christ] dwells all the fullness of deity bodily."

To assess Paul's intention here, it will be necessary to give some attention to three of his words. By "fullness" (πλήρωμα, *plērōma*), which is perhaps an example of his employment of his (pre-Gnostic?) opponents' terminology, Paul means plainly and simply "completeness," "totality," or "sum-total." To insure that no one would miss his intention, Paul qualifies this noun with "all," that is, "*all* [not just some of] the fullness."

If it is an allusion to his opponents' language, this phrase already carries overtones of "fullness of deity," but Paul clarifies his intention by the following defining genitive "of deity." The word for "deity" here is θεότης, *theotēs*, the abstract noun from θεός, *theos*, meaning "the being as God," or "the being of the very essence of deity." Putting these two words together, Paul is speaking of the "totality of all that is essential to the divine nature." Concerning this "totality of divine essence" Paul affirms that it "dwells [permanently]" (for this is the force of the preposition κατά, *kata*, prefixed to the verb and the present tense of the verb κατοικέω, *katoikeō*) in Jesus.

Precisely how it is that this "totality of the very essence of deity" permanently "dwells" in him, Paul specifies by the Greek adverb σωματικῶς, *sōmatikōs*. Some scholars suggest that the word means "essentially" or "really" (as over against "symbolically"; see the contrast in 2:17 between "shadow" and "reality" [σῶμα, *sōma*]), but much more likely it means "bodily," that is, "in bodily form," indicating that the mode or manner in which the permanent abode of the full plenitude of deity in Jesus is to be understood is in incarnational terms. In short, Paul intends to say that in Jesus we have to do with the very "embodiment" or incarnation of deity. Christ is God "manifest in the flesh" (1 Tim. 3:16). Here we have the Pauline equivalent to the Johannine "the Word became flesh" (John 1:14). Finally, to underscore Jesus' uniqueness as such, Paul throws the "in him" forward in the sentence to the position of emphasis, implying by this, against his opponents' claim that "fullness" could be found elsewhere, that "in him [and nowhere else]" permanently resides in bodily form the very essence of deity!

To interpret Paul so is clearly in keeping with his earlier "hymn" to Christ in 1:15–20, as virtually every commentator acknowledges. This view alone coincides with the rich language of the hymn where, as we have seen, Christ is described as the "Image of the invisible God," who was "before all things" and by, through, and for whom God created all things, and in whom all things "hold together."

Some modern scholars believe that Paul's language should be construed, both in 1:15–20 and in 2:9, as functional language, but such an interpretation fails to take seriously the nature of the salvation envisioned in 2:10, its import only being meaningful if the Savior who effects it is the One in whom resides the fullness of deity. Here, then, is another context in which Paul asserts Christ's full divine status.

PHILIPPIANS 2:6–11

What we may actually have preserved for us in this famous pericope is portions of *two* early Christian hymns—the first comprising 2:6–8 and based on Genesis and Isaianic material, the second comprising 2:9–11 and based mainly on Isaianic material. I would submit the following structural arrangement of the two proposed hymns, which arrangement leaves the text as it comes to us in Paul's letter intact and allows the content of the material to govern the strophic arrangement and division. The "first hymn" I would arrange as follows:

Who [refers antecedently to "Christ Jesus" in 2:5],
    Strophe 1:

> though in the form of God existing,
>> did not regard equality with God a thing to be seized,
>> but himself he poured out,
> having taken the form of a servant.

It should be noted that there are four lines in this strophe, the first and the fourth being participial clauses, separated by the second and third lines ("did not regard . . ." and "but poured out . . ."). That the first and fourth lines appear to belong together strophically is evident from the occurrence of μορφή, *morphē* ("form") in both, and the occurrence of participles in both, suggesting also that they are to be viewed as "bracketing" clauses, tying these lines together.

Strophe 2:

> In the precise likeness of men having been born,
>> and having been found by external appearance to be a man,
>> he humbled himself,
> having become obedient unto death—

Climactic addendum:

> even the death of the cross."

Postponing for the moment any discussion of the climactic addendum, which may have been an original short choral refrain at the end of the hymn or Paul's own addendum intended to highlight the shameful character of the death which our Lord died, I would point out that again we have a strophic arrangement of four lines, and again the first and the fourth are participial clauses separated by the second and third lines ("and having been found . . ." and "he humbled . . ."). That these four lines appear to form a natural and single strophe is evident from the fact that the participles in the first and fourth lines are the same in both (γενόμενος, *genomenos*), though it is true that their nuance of meaning is different and that they appear in inverted word order—in last place in the first line, in first place in the last line. Again, I would suggest that these participial clauses serve as "brackets" to set the strophe apart from the preceding strophe and those which follow. Further evidence that these lines are to be construed together strophically is the climactic parallelism of thought between the first and second lines and the occurrences of the word for "man" in the first and second lines (though it is true that they differ in number, being plural in the first line and singular in the second line).

Note now the parallels between the two strophes that suggest that they form a single hymn:

1. The two strophes have the same number of lines.
2. Both first lines begin with the preposition ἐν (*en*, "in"), which is then followed in each case with a dative noun, then a genitive noun, concluding with a participle.
3. The first lines of the two strophes contain an antithetic parallelism: "form of God" and "likeness of men."
4. The third line in both strophes ascribes to Christ a reflexive action, the relation of the reflexive pronoun ἑαυτόν (*heauton*, "himself") to the verb appearing in inverted order—in the former, "himself he poured out," in the latter, "he humbled himself." This striking similarity suggests that the two actions mean essentially the same thing, a possibility that receives further support from the likelihood that the former phrase has Isaiah 53:12 as its background while the latter phrase echoes the thought of Isaiah 53:8 (LXX), which is quoted in Acts 8:33 ("In his humiliation he was deprived of justice"), both Isaianic statements, of course, describing the suffering Servant.
5. Postponing the reason for my interpretation until later, but assuming its validity here for the sake of grouping together the several parallels between the strophes, the hymn moves from the idea of "death" ("poured himself out") in strophe 1, line 3, to "servitude" ("he humbled himself") in strophe 2, line 3; but it moves in reverse order from the idea of "servitude" ("the form of servant") in strophe 1, line 4, to "death" ("obedient unto death") in strophe 2, line 4.
6. In strophe 1 the word "God" occurs in the first and second lines; in strophe 2 the word "man" occurs in the first and second lines, suggesting an antithetic parallel between these lines of the two strophes.
7. Both strophes deal with the same subject, namely, Jesus' state of humiliation.

The "second hymn" is to be arranged as follows:

Therefore [in light of Christ's "servant work" depicted in the first hymn],
Strophe 1

>God has highly exalted him,
>and he has given to him the name,
>>the "above everything" name,

These lines are separated both from the preceding hymn by the "therefore" preceding them and from the lines that follow them by the following purpose particle "in order that," which introduces the purpose behind the divine action of this strophe. Further evidence that these lines are to be distinguished from the preceding strophes is the shift in the subject of the actions from Christ in the earlier strophes to the Father here. But the most obvious indication that these lines may be *hymnically* distinguished from the previous two strophes is the fact that in this strophe we find only three lines, as over against four in the previous strophes. The three lines here follow the pattern of "independent line, independent line, dependent (or modifying) line."

As evidence that these lines are to be construed together strophically, we may cite the undeniable synonymous parallelism in thought between the first two lines, and the three internal lexical parallels, namely, the repeated "him" (αὐτόν, *auton*, and αὐτῷ, *autō*) in lines 1 and 2 (in both cases in the emphatic position), the repeated preposition ὑπέρ (*hyper*, "above") in lines 1 and 3, and the repeated reference to "the name" in lines 2 and 3.

in order that
   Strophe 2

> at the name of Jesus
> every knee should bow in heaven and on earth and under the earth,
> and every tongue should confess that Jesus Christ is Lord—

Climactic addendum

> to the glory of God the Father!"

Postponing again for the time being any discussion of the climactic addendum, we are immediately conscious that we have again only three lines to consider. But it is also immediately apparent that in strophe 2 the structural arrangement is the precise reverse of strophe 1: where earlier we had the arrangement "independent line, independent line, dependent line," here we find the arrangement "dependent (or qualifying) line, independent line, independent line." Within the strophe itself, again we have an undeniable synonymous parallelism in thought between lines 2 and 3. This parallelism is underscored by the presence of the word "every" in both lines, the aorist subjunctive verb form in both lines, and the adverbial modifying phrase in both lines, the former anticipating the question "where?" or "whose?" and the latter anticipating the question "what?" There is also a lexical connection between lines 1 and 3 through the repetition of the proper name "Jesus," found here and nowhere else in the hymn.

Having distinguished between the two strophes, we may now note the following parallels between them:

1. The phrase "the name" is found in the dependent line of both strophes.
2. The word "every" is found in line 3 of both strophes.
3. Both strophes are concerned with the same subject, namely, Jesus' state of exaltation, the former stating the fact itself, and the latter stating the Father's design behind the fact.

Concerning now the climactic addenda, "even the death of the cross" and "to the glory of God the Father," which may have been either original to both hymns or Pauline additions to both: it is apparent that a marked antithesis lies between them, each of them capturing the mood of its respective hymn. The former, by designating the particular kind of death Christ died, underscores the depth of the *humiliation* that Christ voluntarily underwent. The latter highlights the Father's glory that Christ's *exaltation* entailed. The former concentrates our attention on the death of Jesus; the latter focuses our attention on the glory of the Father. The former brings the first hymn to a close by focusing on the cross; the latter brings the second hymn to a close by focusing on the glory that followed. These addenda neatly summarize for us the essential flow of the apostle's thought: from humiliation to exaltation, from cross to crown.

The very first line of the first strophe is directly related to the concern of this present study. What does Paul mean when he declares that Christ Jesus was "existing in the form of God"? Those who are advocates of what is called Adam Christology insist that this is the equivalent to the Genesis description of Adam as created in the image of God—meaning that Christ, like Adam, was truly a man. Now it is true that the two Greek words εἰκών (eikōn, "image") and μορφή (morphē, "form") are both employed to translate the same Semitic root in the Septuagint, εἰκών, eikōn, translating the Hebrew noun צֶלֶם, selem, in Genesis 1:26 and μορφή, morphē, translating the Aramaic noun צְלֵם, sᵉlem, in Daniel 3:19. But this is hardly sufficient evidence to warrant the conclusion that they are interchangeable or synonymous, and μορφή, morphē, is not the word used in the Septuagint to render either צֶלֶם, selem, or דְּמוּת, dᵉmût, in Genesis 1:26–27. Moreover, this ignores the occurrence of μορφή, morphē, three lines later, for clearly Jesus did not assume the mere "image" of a servant but became in very fact the Servant of Yahweh. Thus the denotative connection between Adam as the "image of God" and Christ as the "form of God" cannot be made on the basis of such slim linguistic evidence.

Others urge that the meaning of μορφή, morphē, should be established on the basis of its usage in the Septuagint, but the problem here is that it is only used four times in the Septuagint, and each time as the translation of a different Hebrew word (see Judg. 8:18; Job 4:16; Isa. 44:13; and Dan. 3:19). At best, taken together, the idea of μορφή, *morphē*, in the Septuagint seems to be that of "visible form," but the number of samples is just too small and too diverse to draw any hard and fast conclusions. Besides, if it means "visible form," it is questionable whether this meets the conditions of the first occurrence in Philippians 2:6, for there Christ is not said to be "*the* μορφή, *morphē*, of God" but "*in the* μορφή, *morphē*, of God." But "in the 'visible form' of God" would be scripturally inappropriate inasmuch as God is "invisible," as Colossians 1:15 reminds us.

Still others maintain that μορφή, *morphē*, in 2:6a is equivalent in meaning to δόξα (*doxa*, "glory"), but it can hardly be argued that this same equivalency is appropriate in the phrase "form of a servant" three lines later.

In light of these problems, it appears that the weight of linguistic evidence is still on the side of J. B. Lightfoot, who demonstrated from a study of both its usage throughout the history of Greek thought and the occurrences of the μορφ- root in the New Testament that μορφή, *morphē*, refers to the "essential attributes" of a thing, and that Christ's being *in* the form of God, while not the linguistic equivalent, is the connotative equivalent to the Pauline description of Christ in 2 Corinthians 4:4 and Colossians 1:15 as the "[essential] image of the [invisible] God."[69] Warfield concurs:

> "Form" is a term which expresses the sum of those characterizing qualities which make a thing the precise thing that it is. Thus, the "form" of a sword (in this case mostly matters of external configuration) is all that makes a given piece of metal specifically a sword, rather than, say, a spade. And the "form of God" is the sum of the characteristics which make the being we call "God," specifically God, rather than some other being—an angel, say, or a man. When our Lord is said to be in "the form of God," therefore, He is declared, in the most express manner possible, to be all that God is, to possess the whole fulness of attributes which make God God.[70]

Murray agrees,[71] and David F. Wells declares that it "appears inescapable that by 'form' we are to understand that Paul meant the essence or essential characteristics of a thing."[72] This understanding of the term fits both occurrences in 2:6: "form of God" and "form of servant." When then the force of the present participle is also

---

69. J. B. Lightfoot, *Philippians* (1868; reprint, Grand Rapids, Mich.: Zondervan, 1953), 110.
70. Warfield, "The Person of Christ According to the New Testament," *The Person and Work of Christ*, 39.
71. John Murray, *Collected Writings of John Murray* (Edinburgh: Banner of Truth), 3:359.
72. Wells, *Person of Christ*, 64.

taken into account which conveys the idea of "continually subsisting," which in turn excludes the idea that this mode of subsistence came to an end when he assumed the form of servant, we have here a bold and unqualified assertion of both the preexistence and the full and unabridged deity of Jesus Christ.

The classical evangelical interpretation of the entire pericope contends that these verses depict a great parabola, starting with God the Son in the glory of his preexistent condition of sharing the divine essence with God the Father ("in the form of God existing"), then tracing his "downward" movement by means of the Incarnation ("himself he emptied") to his "cross work" as the Father's Servant, and then recording his "upward" movement by means of the Father's exaltation through resurrection and ascension to his present session at his Father's right hand as "Lord." No evangelical will take exception either to the sentiment behind or to the high Christology itself which is thus extracted from these verses by such an exposition. Certainly I do not. Nor do I for a moment have any intention of denying to our Lord in the slightest degree his rightful claim to full unqualified deity or to equality with the Father in power and glory. This I have already shown from my exposition of 2:6a. Nor do I dispute the fact that the New Testament does set forth the work of Christ precisely in terms of "descent-ascent" (κατάβασις, *katabasis*-ἀνάβασις, *anabasis*) in some contexts. But it is precisely this "descent-ascent" motif that has created for evangelical scholars in this particular context a major difficulty, or rather two difficulties.

The first difficulty is this: if we understand the beginning point of the "flow" of the passage, as the classical view does, to be the preincarnational state of the Son of God ("in the form of God being") and take the phrases, "himself he emptied, taking the form of a servant," as the metaphorical allusion to the "downward" event of the Incarnation, it is only with the greatest difficulty, because of the intervening clause, that the conclusion can be avoided that the "emptying" involved his surrender of the "form" ("very nature"—NIV) of God. I grant that the verb κενόω, *kenoō*, may have a metaphorical meaning, as in its other occurrences in the New Testament (Rom. 4:14; 1 Cor. 1:17; 9:15; 2 Cor. 9:3), and that it need not be literally rendered "emptied" in Philippians 2:6. (I too in the end attach a nonliteral meaning to it.) But even a metaphor has a literal meaning when it is divested of its metaphorical "wrapping." What does this metaphor mean literally when it is "unpacked" in the interest of interpretation? The ready answer of those who hold the classical view is that it refers to the event of the Incarnation ("He made himself of no reputation, by means of taking the form of a servant"). But it is just here that the difficulty arises. For according to the classical view, the intervening clause ("He did not regard . . ."), in the "flow" of the hymn, has to mirror an attitude in the *preexistent* Son that prevailed on the "prior side" of the event of Incarnation. But if this clause describes what the preexistent Son of God as God the Son "thought" (ἡγήσατο, *hēgēsato*) of his equality with God, it does not matter, I would suggest, whether ἁρπαγμὸν, *harpagmon* (from the root ἁρπάζω, *harpazō*, meaning "to seize") is construed *res rapta*, that is, "a thing to be held onto," or *res rapienda*, that is, "a thing to be seized"—neither is appropriate as a description of what the Son "thought" with regard to his "equality with God." The former is theologically heretical for it implies that the Son was willing to and did in fact divest himself of his deity ("the form of God") when he took the "form of a servant," for that is what "equality with God" means lexically, contextually, and according to John 5:18 and 10:28–33. The latter is also theologically suspect for it suggests that the Son did not already possess equality with God. But this introduces confusion into the passage in light of the fact that it is clearly affirmed in the first clause of 2:6, as we have seen, that the Son was God and was thus as such "equal with God."

If one should reply that the reason it is said that the Son did not "grasp after" equality with God is because he already had it as the first clause affirms, I would respond that this now introduces a certain theological barrenness, if not an exegetical inanity, into the text at the very point where, obviously, a highly significant insight is intended, for one does not need to be informed of the obvious—that the Son did not seek after something which was already in his possession. Accordingly, I would submit, from the perspective of the classical interpretation of the pericope, that it is only the *res rapta* interpretation of ἁρπαγμὸν, *harpagmon*, that circumvents this barrenness of meaning, but then it is only with the greatest difficulty that the evangelical scholar can escape, if escape at all, the conclusion that the Son is represented, by the implication of his willingness to forego his "equality with God," that is, his essential divine attributes, as having divested himself of his "very nature" character of God when he became a man. (We are not debating at this moment what all admit is the impossibility of One who is God doing such a thing. We are only concerned here with interpreting the text in a grammatical fashion.) One has only to peruse the evangelical literature on these verses to see what hermeneutical contortions are resorted to to affirm, on the one hand, that the Son did not regard equality with God ("the form of God") a thing to be held onto, and that he accordingly "emptied himself" (or, "made himself nothing") by becoming a man, and yet, on the other hand, that he still retained all that he essentially is and was from the beginning. For example, it is said: "He did not divest Himself of His divine attributes, but only the independent use of His attributes." But when did the Son ever exercise his attributes independently from the Trinity? Or, "He did not divest Himself of His deity, but only the glory of His deity." But is not his "divine glory" just the sum and substance of his deity? And how does one square this interpretation with John 1:14 and 2:11? Or, "He did not divest Himself of His deity, but only His rights as deity."[73] But what rights did he forego as God when he became a man? While I do not agree with the "kenotic" theologians who teach that the Son, according to the teaching of this passage, divested himself of at least something that was essentially his as God when he became a man, I can understand, if it is assumed that the passage begins with the preexistent Son, how they come to this conclusion.

The second difficulty is this: if the flow of the passage commences with God the Son in his preexistent state, what meaning can his later exaltation possibly have had for him? Exaltation must involve elevation to a state not in one's prior possession. But such an elevated state is simply nonexistent with regard to God the Son as God. If one should reply that his later exalted state involved his being elevated, as the second hymn declares, to the position of lordship over all things, I must ask whether the Scripture will permit us to believe that God the Son, often identified by Scripture itself as the God and Yahweh of the Old Testament, was not already *de jure* and *de facto* Lord over creation, nature, religious institutions such as the Law and the Sabbath, and, most significantly, over the lives of men, prior to the exaltation spoken about in Philippians 2:9–11. Does not careful reflection on simply what is entailed in being God the Son force one to conclude that the Son as God the Son continued ever, even during the days of his earthly ministry, to be the same Lord he was from the beginning? So what meaning can be attached to an exaltation of One who cannot be exalted more highly than he already is? It is only with the greatest difficulty that the evangelical scholar can escape the conclusion, if he insists that the exaltation was indeed the exaltation of the preexistent Son of God *per se*, that the Son's former state was lower in dignity than his latter state, and that the Son's latter state elevated him to a state which was above the state which he enjoyed when "existing in the form of God" prior to his incarnation. But Scripture and right reason simply will not permit such a conclusion.

These two difficulties ought to make us willing to consider another interpretation that avoids both problems and at the same time affirms the *vere deus vere homo* (truly God, truly man) doctrine of classical Christology.

---

73. Even Larger Catechism, Question 46, teaches that "the estate of Christ's humiliation was that low condition, wherein, he, for our sakes, emptying himself of his glory, took upon him the form of a servant. . . ." The allusion to Philippians 2:7 here is clear on the face of it and in fact is one of the supporting references given by the Catechism for its assertion here.

The Catechism is not urging, of course, any divestiture of attributes on the Son's part in His act of becoming incarnate as is evident from its explanation in Question 47, but I would counsel against using such language to describe the incarnational act itself for that is not what Paul intended by his term "emptying," and it could be very misleading.

The key to the solution of both of these difficulties and to the proper interpretation of these verses is to recognize that it is not God the Son in his preincarnate state as the Second Person of the Holy Trinity who is the subject of the first two strophes and to whom reference is made by the "him" in verse 9 of the third strophe, but rather "Christ Jesus" (see 2:5 and references to "Jesus" and "Jesus Christ" in 2:10–11 respectively)—God the Son certainly, for this is the meaning of "though in the form of God existing," but God the Son *already* incarnately present with men as himself the God-man.[74] The hymn begins with "Christ Jesus" and affirms that, as the God-man, he refused to follow an alternative path to glory to the one which his Father had charted for him. Nor does it refer to the "downward" movement (the κατάβασις, *katabasis*) of the Incarnation event itself, so vital a part of the classical view, save as an event that had already taken place, presupposing it in its affirmation that he "though existing as God," had "taken the form of servant." By this construction, all that is said of him is said of him as the Messiah, the Son-already-dispatched-on-his-mission. It is possible, and this is only a conjecture, that the first hymn has been "decapitated," and that a previous strophe dealt with his pure preexistent state as God the Son and eternal Son of the eternal Father.

How does this elimination of the Son's preexistent state and his incarnational "descent" from the hymn's "flow" circumvent the two difficulties just mentioned? The answer is that now we are no longer interacting at the point of Philippians 2:6 with the Incarnation as a future event, but with the Incarnation as from the outset the God-man's existing state of being. Accordingly, the clauses under discussion may now be interpreted *within* the context of the Incarnation as a *fait accompli* and not within the context of the Incarnation as a *fait anticipé*. But are meaningful interpretations ready at hand? To this I would reply in the affirmative. With respect to the clause, "He did not regard equality . . . ," I would urge that it may now be construed *res rapienda*, that is, "He did not regard equality with God a thing to be seized," and that it should be interpreted against the background of his temptation recorded in Matthew 4. We know that Paul is willing to contrast Adam and Christ in Romans 5:12–19 and 1 Corinthians 15:45–49, actually referring to Christ in the latter passage as the Last Adam and the Second Man. Here the Philippians hymn draws a further contrast between the respective temptations of Adam and Christ. Unlike Adam, the first man, who did "regard equality with God [τὸ εἶναι ἴσα θεῷ, *to einai isa theō*] a thing to be seized,"[75] Christ, the Last Adam and Second Man,

---

74. I do not deny that in other contexts, for example, 1 Timothy 1:15, "Christ Jesus," as a titular description, does designate the Son of God in his preincarnate state.

75. See Genesis 3:5, where the Serpent's temptation is framed in the words "you will be *like* [כְּ, *kᵉ*, translated by *isa* in the LXX at Deut. 13:6; Job 5:14; 10:10; 13:28; 27:16; 29:14; 40:10; Isa. 51:23] God, knowing good and evil."

when urged to demonstrate his equality with God (see Matt. 4:3, 6: "Since you are the Son of God, . . .") refused to take matters into his own hands and assert his rights as the Son. He steadfastly resisted the Tempter's suggestion to "seize equality," that is, to walk no longer in the path of the Servant of the Lord and to achieve "lordship" over "all the kingdoms of this world" (Matt. 4:8) by a route not charted for the Servant in the economy of salvation.

There is another Old Testament motif, beyond the Adam-Christ contrast that assists us when we address the meaning of "himself he emptied," and that is the "Servant" motif of Isaiah's "Servant Songs." In what I have called the second hymn, clearly lines 1 and 2 of strophe 1 borrow a sentiment from Isaiah 42:1–8, and lines 2 and 3 of strophe 2 directly reflect the language of Isaiah 45:23. And in what I have called the first hymn, Paul's references to the "servant" in strophe 1, line 4, and to Christ's "self-humbling" and "obedience unto death" in lines 3 and 4 of strophe 2 are general allusions to the "servant" motif of Isaiah's songs (see Isa. 53:8 [LXX] and Acts 8:33). (Paul also relates Christ to both Adam and the "servant" motif in Romans 5:12–19.) Some Old Testament scholars have therefore suggested that the phrase "himself he emptied" is Paul's Greek dynamic equivalent to the Isaianic expression "He poured his soul out unto death" (which means, "He voluntarily died") in Isaiah 53:12, climactically descriptive of the Suffering Servant's self-sacrificing work so often referred to elsewhere in the New Testament (see, for example, Matt. 8:17; Luke 22:37; Acts 8:32–35; 1 Pet. 2:21–25). The phrase, thus interpreted, derives its meaning against the incarnational backdrop of the high-priestly ministry of our Lord rather than against the backdrop of his preexistence, referring to the sacrifice of his life and not to a "self-emptying" which occurred in and by his incarnation. I would suggest then that the aorist participle λαβών, *labōn*, in the first hymn, strophe 1, line 4, is to be construed as a participle denoting antecedent action,[76] thus placing Christ's "self-emptying" subsequent in time to the "taking." That is to say, the participle does not explain the means of the "self-emptying" ("emptied by taking") but rather denotes a prior action that was the necessary precondition to the "self-emptying." The following paraphrase of the first strophe will assist the reader in understanding this suggestion:

> Though Christ Jesus was and still is God [now, of course, God incarnate],
> He did not regard equality with God a thing to be seized [at his temptation by a self-willed exercise of power],

---

76. "Having taken." Contrary to what some grammarians urge, an aorist participle following a main verb in the aorist tense can express antecedent action, as Moulton, *Grammar of New Testament Greek,* 1:132, acknowledges.

> But "poured himself out" [unto death],
> Having taken the form of the Servant [of Isaiah 53].

By this construction we have both precluded at the outset a kenotic christological interpretation and the first difficulty I mentioned earlier, and have been able to give substantive meaning to 2:6–7b, something the classical view is able to do only with the greatest exegetical ingenuity.

But we are now also in a position to give substantive meaning to the act of exaltation asserted in the second hymn, for now we may refer it, not to God the Son *per se* but to God the Son in his incarnate state as the Messiah. It is, in other words, the divine-human Messiah, Christ Jesus, who is exalted. And because we are compelled by the historical fact itself to describe the Son, now incarnately existent in Jesus Christ, as "the divine-human Messiah," we can boldly say, without fear of denigrating his divine honor, that the Father's exaltation of Jesus Christ entailed for the Son, as the Messiah, a new and genuine experience of exaltation. Precisely because we must use the word "human" as part of our description of him now, we can also say that something truly new and unique occurred at the resurrection and ascension of Jesus Christ: the man Christ Jesus—the Last Adam and Second Man—assumed *de facto* sovereignty over the universe, over all of the principalities and powers in heavenly places, and over all other men, demanding that they submit to the authority of his scepter. That King's name is Jesus, at the mention of whose office some day every knee will bow and every tongue confess that Jesus Christ—the divine-human Messiah—is Lord!

In conclusion, this pericope ascribes deity to "Christ Jesus." It does so in three ways: first, by its description of Jesus as "in the form of God [continually] being"; second, by its tacit ascription to him of "equality with God" when it affirms that he did not "seize" this station in the sense that at the time of his temptation he did not assert himself in a self-willed show of power commensurate with his divine station; and third, by the very nature of his delegated lordship, the entail of his exaltation. It is true that this lordship was "delegated" to him, in his role as Messiah, as the result of his labors (see the "because" of Isa. 53:12 and the "therefore" of Phil. 2:9). But this lordship, described as it is in terms of Isaiah 45:23, where it is declared to be Yahweh's prerogative alone, has a covenantal basis upon which it was determined that this One should "receive" this specific kind of lordship as the Messiah upon the completion of his suffering by right of his own divine Sonship, the antecedent condition to his messianic investiture. Said another way, it is because he was, as the Messiah, "obedient unto death, even the death of the cross" that he was exalted to lordship, but it is also because he is "in the form of God" and "equal with God," as the *divine* Messiah, that the lordship he was delegated could assume the proportions which it does and involve the universal obligation upon men to worship him.

I TIMOTHY 1:15

In Paul's statement in 1 Timothy 1:15: "Christ Jesus came into the world—sinners to save" (author's translation)—the first of the five "faithful sayings" in his pastoral letters—again Christ's preexistence is implied and, as a corollary to his preexistence, his divine Sonship as well.

It is true, just as the "he ascended" in Ephesians 4:8 does not in itself require a prior descent, that the phrase "came into the world" does not necessarily contain within itself the notion of preexistence *per se* (see Rom. 5:12; 1 Tim. 6:7). But as George W. Knight III observes at this point:

> It is one thing to point out that the phrase ἦλθεν [ἔρχεσθαι] εἰς τὸν κόσμον [ēlthen (erchesthai) eis ton kosmon] itself does not imply preexistence and it is another to make this evaluation of the phrase when it is used by Christians with Christ Jesus as the subject. Is it not, as a matter of fact, evident that the uniform usage of that phrase *with* reference to Christ Jesus is to both his preexistence and also his incarnation?[77]

He then proceeds to show from an analysis of the six occurrences of the phrase in John's Gospel (1:9; 3:19; 11:27; 12:46; 16:28; 18:37)—the only other book of the New Testament where the expression is found—that when the phrase is applied to Christ Jesus, it "demands the understanding of preexistence as well as incarnation."[78]

I TIMOTHY 3:16

With the aid of a succinct compendium of the great "mystery of godliness" (that is, the "revealed secret" of the faith, even Jesus Christ; see Col. 1:27; 2:2–3) in the form of a quotation from an early Christian hymn, Paul elaborates his Christology—the Great Mystery—in six phrases:

> who [that is, Christ Jesus]
>   was manifested in the flesh,
>   was vindicated in the spirit,
>   was seen by angels,
>   was proclaimed among the nations,
>   was believed on in the world,
>   was taken up in glory. (author's translation)

---

77. George W. Knight III, *The Faithful Sayings in the Pastoral Letters* (Nutley, N.J.: Presbyterian and Reformed, n.d.), 36–37.
78. Ibid., 38.

As with the other christological hymns we have considered, this one has undergone considerable analysis with regard to its strophic arrangement. Some see strict chronological progression throughout the six lines, with each line therefore receiving independent treatment. Others see two strophes of three lines each (or two strophes of two lines and a refrain). And still others—the majority view today—divide the quotation into three couplets.

The hymn appears to be a finely crafted piece of poetry with not one but two patterns of internal relationships that bind the six lines together in a remarkable literary unit. There are first the six dative nouns—flesh, spirit, angels, nations, world, and glory—which almost certainly are intended to be construed both antithetically and chiastically, that is to say, the hymn moves from that which is earthly ("flesh") to that which is heavenly ("spirit"), then from that which is heavenly ("angels") back to that which is earthly ("nations"), then back again from that which is earthly ("world") to that which is heavenly ("glory"). This being so, it seems that the poet was thinking in terms of the couplets following an a/b, b/a, a/b pattern, with the hymn's movement being not primarily chronological but spatial, emphasizing the truth that both the earthly and the heavenly spheres find their center in Christ.

Robert H. Gundry has observed that when the six lines are considered individually in their entirety, there seems also to be a synthetic parallelism between lines 2 and 3—"vindicated, seen"—and lines 4 and 5—"proclaimed, believed on," both of which are framed between line 1 commemorating the Lord's "descent" and line 6 commemorating the Lord's "ascent."[79] The first of these synthetic parallels (lines 2 and 3) takes place in the realm *invisible* to men; the second of these parallels (lines 4 and 5) takes place in the realm *visible* to men, while the third (lines 1 and 6) begins in the *visible* realm and passes into the *invisible*. The pattern here would be a, bb, aa, b. This strophic analysis or one very similar to it has a wide currency today. Turning to a consideration of the individual lines themselves, we note the following:

Line 1: "was manifested in the flesh." It is commonly acknowledged that "was manifested in the flesh" refers to the Incarnation, and by the constative aorist speaks of Christ's entire incarnate life as a revelation of the divine Son "in the sphere of human being." That it has reference to the Incarnation, implying as well Christ's preexistence as the Son of God, is evident not only from the fact that we do not speak this way about an ordinary man, but also from the fact that the New Testament speaks elsewhere of Jesus' incarnate life in terms of "manifestation" (John 1:31; Heb. 9:26; 1 Pet. 1:20; 1 John 1:2; 3:5, 8; see John 1:14; Col. 2:9).

---

79. Robert H. Gundry, "The Form, Meaning and Background of the Hymn Quoted in 1 Timothy 3:16," in *Apostolic History and the Gospel*, ed. Gasque and Martin (Exeter, U.K.: Paternoster, 1970), 230.

Line 2: "was vindicated in the spirit." Opinions vary concerning the meaning of this line. Because σάρξ (*sarx*, "flesh") in the preceding line has reference to Christ's human nature in its entirety, including his human spirit (see exposition on Romans 1:3–4), it is most unlikely (contra Gundry) that his human spirit is the intended referent of πνεῦμα (*pneuma*, "spirit") here. The choice lies between understanding the referent to be the Holy Spirit or Christ's divine nature. Are there any indications as to which is intended? If it refers to the Holy Spirit, the preposition ἐν, *en*, must be construed instrumentally ("by"), and while this is certainly possible, it does violence to the symmetry present in the uniform locative sense of all of the other occurrences of ἐν, *en*. Therefore, since Paul has instructed us in Romans 1:3–4 that Christ was "powerfully marked out the Son of God according to the Spirit of holiness [his own holy divine spirit] by the resurrection from the dead," his resurrection there clearly being represented as a *vindicating* event, I would urge that the verb "was vindicated" here refers to that same vindicating event, and that "in the spirit"—as the antithesis to "in the flesh," that is, "in the sphere of *human* being"—means "in the sphere of *divine* being." A paraphrase of the line would then be "was vindicated [as the Son of God by the resurrection] in the sphere of [his divine] spirit."

Line 3: "was seen by angels." Since this line contains no ἐν, *en*, "angels" is probably to be construed as a true rather than an instrumental dative. This means in turn that ὤφθη, *ōphthē*, which "nearly always means the *self*-exhibition of the subject" (Gundry), quite probably means "appeared" rather than "was seen." The upshot of these two points is that the phrase means something on the order of "appeared to angels," which is not substantively different from the traditional translation. There is little question that this line refers both to Christ's triumph over the angelic forces of evil by his cross and to his exaltation over all the angelic powers at his ascension (see Eph. 1:21; Col. 2:15; Phil. 2:9–11; Heb. 1:4–14; 1 Pet. 3:22; Rev. 5:8–14). It certainly implies his superangelic dignity.

Lines 4, 5, and 6. There is little substantive disagreement among scholars over the meanings of lines 4, 5, and 6. Line 4, "was proclaimed among the nations," reflects the church's conviction that Christ is properly the Subject of worldwide proclamation and also the fact that the church was in the process of proclaiming him as such. Line 5, "was believed on in the world," reflects the church's confidence in the outcome of that proclamation—the nations of the world will become his disciples. And line 6, "was taken up in [not "into"] glory," brings the hymn to a close with the imagery of Jesus' ascension to heaven *in* the glory attendant upon him on that occasion (see the "glory cloud" in Acts 1:9; see also Acts 1:11 and Matt. 24:30; 26:64; Mark 14:62).

From beginning to end this hymnic confession of faith (see the adverb ὁμολογουμένως, *homologoumenōs*, "by common confession," in Paul's prefatory introduction to the hymn) extols Christ—the preexistent Son who became "enfleshed," who was then "vindicated" as the divine Son of God by his resurrection from the dead, who, having "ascended," is properly the acknowledged Lord among the "angels" and the "proclaimed" Lord in the world of men. Thus the Christology found in the confessional framework of this early Christian hymn is in accord with that high Christology found throughout the Pauline corpus which confesses a Messiah who is Deity incarnate.

Thus Paul portrays Christ as the preexistent Creator and Yahweh of the Old Testament (Col. 1:15–17) and the Co-source with the Father of all spiritual blessings, whose name is to be called upon in the church, at whose name every knee is to bow and every tongue is to confess that he is Lord (Rom. 10:12–13; Phil. 2:9–11). As the Son of God incarnate, he is the visible "Image of the invisible God" (Col. 1:15), who "being in the form of God," possesses all the essential attributes of God and is "equal with God" (Phil. 2:6–7). "In [Christ] dwells all the fullness of deity bodily" (Col. 2:9), the result of the Son of God having become "enfleshed" within the royal line of David as a man like other men (Rom. 1:3; Phil. 2:7; 1 Tim. 3:16), who as a man died for other men's sins and was buried, but who rose on the third day and ascended to the right hand of God, assuming mediatorial sovereignty over the universe. He is, for Paul, Lord "over all, God blessed forever" (Rom. 9:5) and "our great God and Savior" (Titus 2:13).

While it is undoubtedly true that some of Paul's descriptions of Jesus are to be viewed as "functional" (for example, Christ, Servant, Head of the church, even Lord in the mediatorial sense), many are not (for example, Son, Son of God, Lord in the Yahwistic sense, Image of the invisible God, and God). And even the functional descriptions of Jesus derive their power to evoke our religious interest and devotion ultimately from the ontological descriptions of Christ which surround them and lie behind them.

It will not satisfy all of the data to acknowledge on the one hand that Jesus was for Paul both *vere deus* and *vere homo,* but to assert on the other that his Christology was an anomaly in the thinking of the first-century church. As Warfield wrote:

> Paul is not writing a generation or two [after the generation of those who had companied with Jesus in His life], when the faith of the first disciples was a matter only of memory, perhaps of fading memory; and when it was possible for him to represent it as other than it was. He is writing out of the very bosom of this primitive community and under its very eye. His witness to the kind of Jesus this community believed in is just as valid and just as compelling, therefore, as his testimony that it believed in Jesus at all. In and through him the voice of the primitive community itself speaks, proclaiming its assured faith in its divine Lord.[80]

---

80. Warfield, *Lord of Glory,* 257.

Since Warfield wrote these words even more evidence has come to light that this is true, for there is a general consensus today among both critical and evangelical scholars that in Colossians 1:15–20, Philippians 2:6–11, and 1 Timothy 3:16 we have in hymnic form reflections of the primitive Christology of the early church that may very well antedate the letters of Paul in which they appear. Then in 1 Corinthians 15:3–5 and Romans 1:3–4 we have what may well be reflections of primitive church confessions, while in 1 Timothy 1:15 we have an early church confession in the form of a non-Pauline "faithful saying" which Paul endorsed by declaring it to be "worthy of acceptance." All of these pericopes reflect the highest kind of Christology in which Jesus is regarded as the divine, preexistent Son of God who through "descent" became "flesh" for us men and for our salvation and who through "ascent" assumed mediatorial Headship over the universe and the church. And in the case of 1 Timothy 1:15 it is significant that here we have the spokesman of the so-called Pauline community commending what is now commonly recognized as a piece of teaching framed in the wording of the "Johannine community." So instead of there being *competing* communities in the early church, each headed up by a specific apostle and each vying with one another for the minds of the masses, here is indication that the primitive church, at least that majority portion of it which followed the lead of the apostles and for whom the apostles were authoritative teachers in the church, was one in its essential understanding of Christ. When one also takes into account that the Jerusalem apostles approved Paul's gospel (which surely would have included an account of who Jesus was for Paul) when he informed them of it on his second visit to Jerusalem (Gal. 2:2, 6–9), plus the fact that for both the (Palestinian?) Aramaic-speaking and (Hellenistic?) Greek-speaking Christians in the primitive church Jesus was "Lord" (see the occurrence of both κύριος [*kyrios,* "Lord"] and Μαρανα θα [*Marana tha,* Aramaic, meaning either "Our Lord has [or will] come" or "Our Lord, come"] in 1 Cor. 16:22), we must conclude that such strict distinctions as have been drawn by some modern scholars between an early Christology of the Jewish Palestinian church, a later Christology of the Jewish Hellenistic church (or mission), and a still later Christology of the Hellenistic Gentile church (or mission) (all stages of development before Paul) exist more in the minds of those who espouse them than in the actual first-century church itself. Paul's testimony, reflected throughout his letters, gives evidence of the fact that for Christians generally who lived at that time, Jesus was, as Warfield writes:

> a man indeed and the chosen Messiah who had come to redeem God's people, but in His essential Being just the great God Himself. In the light of [Paul's] testimony it is impossible to believe there ever was a different conception of Jesus prevalent in the Church: the mark of Christians from the beginning was

obviously that they looked to Jesus as their "Lord" and "called upon His name" in their worship.[81]

The Non-Pauline New Testament Witness

JAMES'S CHRISTOLOGY

Among modern critical scholars who support a pre-Pauline date for James's letter, the opinion is commonly expressed that his "unobtrusive Christology"—A. M. Fairbairn spoke in 1893 of "the poverty of [James's] Christology"[82]—reflects "an important type of Christianity overshadowed by and misinterpreted through the figure and influence of Paul."[83] The fact that he makes no mention of Jesus' death and resurrection, for example, is interpreted to mean that "the author did not realize the importance of them."[84] For those scholars who urge that James was written contemporaneously with the Pauline corpus, the same silence respecting Jesus' death and resurrection is interpreted to mean that its author wrote "to provide a counterblast to Pauline Christianity in the interests of Judaistic Christianity."[85]

But James's Christology is neither "ante-Pauline" nor "anti-Pauline." J. Adamson notes:

> Evidence such as that from the Dead Sea and Nag Hammadi has almost miraculously revealed or confirmed . . . the continuity preserved in the distinctive Jewish character, thought, and language of early Christian theology. We can now see that the Jewish first Christians had grown up in a wealth of ancient but lively tradition of messianic Christology, so that James, writing to Jewish converts who had accepted the Christian message, "This is he," was able to give most of his Christian letter not to Christian theology but to Christianity in everyday life.[86]

In other words, James took for granted the great events that centered in the historical person of Jesus as he set about the task of writing his guide to Christian behavior. Whatever reasons lay behind his decision not to speak directly of Jesus' death and resurrection (and any number of other things could also be mentioned, such as his supernatural conception in Mary's womb, his mighty miracles, his

---

81. Ibid., 255–256.
82. A. M. Fairbairn, *The Place of Christ in Modern Theology*, 10th ed. (London: Hodder and Stoughton, 1902), 328.
83. E. M. Sidebottom, *James, Jude and 2 Peter* (Camden, N.J.: Thomas Nelson, 1967), 24.
84. Ibid., 24.
85. G. R. Beasley-Murray, *The General Epistles* (Nashville: Abingdon, 1965), 21.
86. J. Adamson, *The Epistle of James* (Grand Rapids, Mich.: Eerdmans, 1976), 23.

ascension, and his present session at the right hand of his Father), it certainly goes beyond the evidence to conclude that James was unaware of these things and their significance—witness his own response in faith to Jesus' resurrection appearance to him—or that he opposed Paul's Christology—witness his approval of Paul's gospel in Galatians 2:9 and his judgment at the Jerusalem council after listening to the testimonies of Peter and Paul. In fact, if we had no more than his one letter to draw upon, we would still have to conclude that James's Christology in no way contradicts and in every way is consistent with the Christology of Jesus' self-testimony and of the other New Testament writers.

There are sufficient parallels between the Sermon on the Mount and James's letter to suggest that James had heard Jesus preach on numerous occasions.[87] And while it is true that he speaks of Jesus by name only twice (1:1; 2:1), on both occasions he not only speaks of him as "the Lord Jesus Christ"—designations of reverence, speaking of both his messiahship and lordship—but also in each case this exalted designation is enhanced by a contextual feature that places him on a par with God the Father. In the former case (1:1), James describes himself as a "servant of God and of the Lord Jesus Christ"—a genitival coordination of God and Jesus that implies the latter's equality with God. In the latter case (2:1), James appositionally describes Jesus as, literally, "the Glory" (τῆς δόξης, *tēs doxēs*),[88] undoubtedly intending by this term not only to ascribe to him the glory attendant upon his resurrection and ascension but also to describe him as the manifested or "Shekinah" ("dwelling") Glory of God (see John 1:14; 2 Cor. 4:4; Heb. 1:3; Rev. 21:3). As Warfield observes:

> The thought of the writer seems to be fixed on those Old Testament passages in which Jehovah is described as the "Glory": e.g., "For I, saith Jehovah, will be unto her a wall of fire round about, and I will be the Glory in the midst of her" (Zech 2:5). In the Lord Jesus Christ, James sees the fulfillment of these promises: He is Jehovah come to be with His people; and, as He has tabernacled among them, they have seen His glory. He is, in a word, the Glory of God, the Shekinah: God

---

87. See James 1:2 and Matthew 5:10–12; James 1:4 and Matthew 5:48; James 1:5 and Matthew 7:7–8; James 1:17 and Matthew 7:11; James 1:20 and Matthew 5:22; James 1:22–27 and Matthew 7:21–23; James 1:22–24 and Matthew 7:24; James 1:23 and Matthew 7:26; James 2:13 and Matthew 6:14ff.; James 2:5 and Matthew 5:3; James 2:13 and Matthew 5:7; James 2:14 and Matthew 7:21–23; James 2:15–16 and Matthew 6:11; James 3:2 and Matthew 12:36, 37; James 3:10–13 and Matthew 7:16; James 3:17–18 and Matthew 5:9; James 4:3 and Matthew 7:7; James 4:4, 8 and Matthew 6:22, 24; James 4:11–12 and Matthew 7:1; James 4:13–14 and Matthew 6:34; James 5:2–3 and Matthew 6:19; and James 5:12 and Matthew 5:34–37.
88. J. B. Mayor's exposition of *tēs doxēs* is still the fullest and finest in English; see his *The Epistle of James* (London: Macmillan, 1913), 79–82.

manifest to men. It is thus that James thought and spoke of his own brother who died a violent and shameful death while still in His first youth![89]

James also speaks of Jesus as "the Lord" (which title from New Testament usage elsewhere presupposes his resurrection and ascension) who, as such, is the One in whose name Christians are to pray and who answers their prayers (5:13–14), who heals and forgives (5:14–15), and whose coming Christians are patiently to await (5:7–8). And while it is true that James also refers to the Father as "the Lord" (see 1:7; 4:15; 5:10–11), precisely because he can pass back and forth between the Father and Jesus in his use of κύριος, *kyrios,* he implies the fitness of thinking of Jesus in terms of equality with God. There is even sound reason for believing that it is Jesus who is before his mind when he speaks in 4:12 of the Lawgiver and Judge (see particularly 5:9).

Then, as Jesus' half-brother, James surely knew of Jesus' death. And as he had experienced firsthand an encounter with the glorified Christ (1 Cor. 15:7), he knew of and believed in Jesus' resurrection. From his references to Christ as "Lord" and to Christ's coming (παρουσία, *parousia*) in 5:7–8, we may surmise that James was also aware of his ascension and present session at the Father's right hand. Therefore, it is not going beyond the available data to insist that James knew about and accepted the great objective central events of redemption.

So while James's declared Christology is hardly an exhaustive Christology, what he does say about Jesus is explicit and exalting, falling nothing short of implying what would come to be known later as the metaphysically divine Sonship of Jesus.

THE CHRISTOLOGY OF HEBREWS

The Christ of Hebrews is as fully and truly human as everywhere else in Scripture—he shared our humanity (Heb. 2:14), was made like his brothers in every way (2:17), was a descendant of Judah (7:14), could sympathize with human weakness, having been tempted in every way like we are (2:18; 4:15), and who "in the days of his flesh" offered up prayers and petitions with loud crying and tears (a reference to Gethsemane?) (5:7) as he "learned obedience from the things which he suffered" (5:8). And he was finally put to death outside Jerusalem (13:12). All this points to a genuinely human life and death.

But the Christ of Hebrews is divine as well. While the usual New Testament designations of Christ may be found scattered throughout the letter,[90] the author's

---

89. Warfield, *Lord of Glory,* 265.
90. See the simple "Jesus" (Heb. 2:9; 3:1; 6:20; 7:22; 10:19; 12:2, 24; 13:12), "[the] Christ" (3:6, 14; 5:5; 6:1; 9:11, 14, 24, 28; 11:26), "Jesus Christ" (10:10; 13:8, 21), "[the] Lord" (1:10; 2:3; 7:14; perhaps 12:14; the first two instances are clearly intended in the Yahwistic sense), "Lord Jesus" (13:20), and "Jesus, the Son of God" (4:14).

favorite title for Jesus is "[the] Son" (1:2, 5 [twice], 8; 3:6; 5:5, 8; 7:28) or its fuller form "[the] Son of God" (4:14; 6:6; 7:3; 10:29). Indeed, it is as God's Son in the preeminent (divine) sense of that title that the author of Hebrews first introduces Jesus to his readers (1:2).

As God's "Son" he is the highest and final form of revelation to men, and as God's "Son" he is higher than the greatest representatives of God on earth, that is, the prophets of the Old Testament (1:1–2), higher even than Moses, who in comparison was only a servant in God's house (3:5–6). Finally, his name as "Son," the Bearer of which is represented as (1) the Heir of all things, (2) God's cooperating Agent in the creation of the world, (3) the Radiance of God's glory, (4) the very Image of his nature, (5) the Sustainer of all things, (6) the Purifier from sin, and (7) the Lord (of Ps. 110:1) sitting at the right hand of the Majesty on high (1:2–3), is "more excellent" even than that of the highest of creatures, that of "angel" (1:4), whose bearers are only "ministering spirits" (1:14), and whose duty it is to worship him (1:6).

As explications of the content of that superangelic "more excellent name" of "Son," and *not* simply new names adduced in addition to that of "Son," he is the "God" (θεός, *theos*) of Psalm 45:6–7 and "the Lord" (κύριος, *kyrios*), that is, the Yahweh, of Psalm 102:25–27.

When he wrote, "To the Son, on the other hand, [God says], 'Your throne, O God, will last for ever and ever'" (1:8), the author of Hebrews, as did Thomas, Paul, Peter, and John, uses θεός, *theos*, as a title for Christ. The controversy surrounding this verse is over whether ὁ θεός, *ho theos*, is to be construed as a nominative (if so, it may be a subject nominative: "God is your throne for ever and ever," or a predicate nominative: "Your throne is God for ever and ever") or a vocative, which would yield the translation given above. With the "overwhelming majority of grammarians, commentators, authors of general studies, and English translations,"[91] I believe that the writer applies Psalm 45:6 to Jesus in such a way that he is addressed directly as God in the ontological sense of the word. This position requires (1) that ὁ θεός, *ho theos*, be interpreted as a vocative, and (2) that the theotic character ascribed to Jesus be understood in ontological and not functional terms.

The fact that the noun ὁ θεός, *ho theos*, appears to be nominative in its inflected form means nothing. The so-called articular nominative with vocative force is a well-established idiom in classical Greek, the Septuagint, and New Testament Greek. So the case of the noun in Hebrews 1:8 must be established on other

---

91. See Murray J. Harris, "The Translation and Significance of ὁ θεός [*ho theos*] in Hebrews 1:8–9," *Tyndale Bulletin* 36 (1985): 146–48; see fns. 56, 57, 58, 59. Also see Harris, "The Translation of אלהים ['lhym] in Psalm 45:7–8," *Tyndale Bulletin* 35 (1984): 65–89.

grounds than its case form, and that it is vocatival is apparent for the following reasons: first, the word order in Hebrews 1:8 most naturally suggests that ὁ θεός, *ho theos*, is vocatival. A vocative immediately after "Your throne" would be perfectly natural. But if ὁ θεός, *ho theos*, were intended as the subject nominative ("God is your throne"), which Nigel Turner regards as a "grotesque interpretation,"[92] it is more likely that ὁ θεός, *ho theos*, would have appeared before "your throne." If it were intended as a predicate nominative ("Your throne is God"), which Turner regards as "only just conceivable,"[93] it is more likely that ὁ θεός, *ho theos*, would have been written anarthrously, appearing either before "your throne" or after "for ever and ever." Second, in the LXX of Psalm 45, which the writer is citing, the king is addressed by the vocative δύνατε, *dynate* ("O Mighty One"), in 45:4 and 45:6. This double use of the vocative heightens the probability, given the word-order, that in the next verse ὁ θεός, *ho theos*, should be rendered "O God." Third, although "about" or "concerning" is probably the more accurate translation of the preposition πρός, *pros*, in Hebrews 1:7 (given the cast of the following quotation), it is more likely that πρός, *pros*, in verse 8 should be translated "to" in light of the second-person character of the quotation itself and on the analogy of the formula in Hebrews 1:13, 5:5, and 7:21. This would suggest that ὁ θεός, *ho theos*, is vocatival. Fourth, the following quotation in Hebrews 1:10–12 (from Ps. 102:25–27) is connected by the simple καί, *kai*, to the quotation under discussion in verses 8–9, indicating that it too stands under the regimen of the words introducing verses 8–9. In the latter verses the Son is clearly addressed as κύριε, *kyrie* ("O Lord"). These five textual and syntactical features clearly indicate that ὁ θεός, *ho theos*, should be construed vocatively, meaning that the writer of Hebrews intended to represent God the Father as addressing the Son as "God."

But what did the writer intend by this address? Opinions run from Vincent Taylor's comment that "nothing can be built upon this reference, for the author shares the same reluctance of the New Testament writers to speak explicitly of Christ as 'God,'"[94] to Oscar Cullmann's comment that "the psalm is quoted here precisely for the sake of this address,"[95] and declaration that "Jesus' deity is more

---

92. Turner, *Grammatical Insights into the New Testament*, 461.
93. Nigel Turner, *A Grammar of New Testament Greek* (Edinburgh: T. & T. Clark, 1965), 3:34.
94. Vincent Taylor, *The Person of Christ in New Testament Teaching* (London: Macmillan, 1958), 96. Raymond E. Brown commented: "We cannot suppose that the author did not notice that his citation had this effect" of addressing the Son of God ("Does the New Testament Call Jesus God?" *Theological Studies* 26, no. 4 [1965]: 563).
95. Oscar Cullmann, *The Christology of the New Testament* (London: SCM, 1980), 310.

powerfully asserted in Hebrews than in any other New Testament writing, with the exception of the Gospel of John."[96]

I would urge from the context of Hebrews 1 itself that the Son is addressed as God in the ontological sense. This may be seen from the fact that, as a "Son-revelation" and the final and supreme Word of God to man (Heb. 1:2), he is the Heir of all things and the Father's Agent in creating the universe. He *abides* as (see the timeless ὤν, *ōn*, in v. 3) the "perfect Radiance of God's glory" and the "very Image of his nature" (v. 3). As God's Son, he is superior to the angels, such that it is appropriate that they be commanded to worship him (v. 6). He is the Yahweh and the Elohim of Psalm 102, who eternally existed before he created the heavens and earth (Heb. 1:10), and who remains eternally the same though the creation itself should perish (1:11–12; see 13:8). Because he is all these things, it is really adding nothing to what the writer has said to understand him as describing the Son as God in the ontological sense in 1:8.

E. C. Wickham and others have suggested that if ὁ θεός, *ho theos,* is really ascribing ontological deity to the Son, the climax of the argument would come at verse 8, since nothing higher could be said about him. Since in fact the author goes on in verse 10 to describe the Son as κύριος, *kyrios,* this further development of the Son's character becomes the climax, indicating that the former description cannot be construed ontologically. But this objection fails to apprehend the significance of the two terms. While θεός, *theos,* is indeed a term of exalted significance when used ascriptively of the true God, it speaks only of his divine essence. It is κύριος, *kyrios,* coming to us out of the Old Testament citation here, that is God's personal name. In the covenantal sense, it is the more sacred of the two! So actually the writer's argument, even though it ascribes ontological deity to the Son in 1:8, does not reach its climax until it ascribes the character of Yahweh himself to the Son, indicating by this ascriptive title that the Son is not only the Creator but the covenant God as well. The writer truly can say nothing higher than this.

Two of the descriptive phrases above deserve further comment. In addition to ascribing to him the divine work of creating and sustaining the universe, the writer

---

96. Ibid., 305. Cullmann is, however, a "functional Christologist" and writes: "We must agree with Melanchthon when he insists that the knowledge of Christ is understood only as a knowledge of his work in redemptive history. . . . All speculation concerning his natures is . . . unbiblical as soon as it ceases to take place in the light of the great historical deeds of redemption" (*Christ and Time,* trans. Floyd V. Filson [Philadephia: Westminster, 1950], 128). He also says: "We come to the conclusion that in the few New Testament passages in which Jesus receives the title 'God,' this occurs on the one hand in connection with his exaltation to lordship . . . and on the other hand in connection with the idea that he is himself the divine revelation" (*Christology,* 325). In other words, for Cullmann Jesus is not God in himself but only God in *Heilsgeschichte* ("holy-" or "salvation-history").

describes the Son as "the radiance [ἀπαύγασμα, *apaugasma*] of God's glory [δόξα, *doxa*]" and "the very image [χαρακτήρ, *charaktēr*] of his nature [ὑπόστασις, *hypostasis*]." In the former expression, with God's "glory" denoting his nature under the imagery of its splendor, as his "radiance" (from ἀπαυγάσω, *apaugasō*, "to emit brightness"), Jesus is pictured as the personal "outshining" of God's divine glory as the radiance shining forth from the source of light. In the latter expression, with God's *hypostasis* denoting his "whole nature, with all its attributes" (Warfield), his "real essence" (F. F. Bruce), or his "very essence" (P. E. Hughes), as his χαρακτήρ, *charaktēr* (from χαράσσω, *charassō*, "to engrave, to inscribe, to stamp"), Jesus is described as God's "very image," by which is meant "a correspondence as close as that which an impression gives back to a seal" (Warfield), his "exact representation and embodiment" (Bruce), or the "very stamp" (Hughes) of God. Clearly such descriptions intend the ascription of divine status to the Son. Accordingly, it is altogether likely, inasmuch as the Son is the Yahweh of Psalm 102:25–27 who remains forever the same (1:11–12) and who in the person of Jesus Christ is "the same yesterday, today, and forever" (13:8), that he is also the subject of the doxology in 13:21, to whom eternal glory is ascribed. Certainly, the collocation of the relative pronoun and the title "Jesus Christ" in 13:21 favors such an interpretation.

J. A. T. Robinson, however, has urged that all of these exalted descriptions are true of Jesus as "God's Man," with only his functional relationship to God as God's "son" being "decisively different" from the relationship that obtains between God and other men.[97] He adduces in support of his view (1) the supposed derivation of the descriptions of 1:3 from Philo and Wisdom 7:26 and (2) what he terms "adoptionist" terminology in 1:2, 4, 9, 13; 2:9, 10, 12f, 16; 3:2f; 5:1–6, 8, 10; 7:28.[98] James D. G. Dunn also insists (1) that "there is more 'adoptionist' language in Hebrews than in any other NT document,"[99] and (2) that "the element of Hebrews' christology which we think of as ascribing pre-existence to the Son of God has to be set within the context of his indebtedness to Platonic idealism and interpreted with cross-reference to the way in which Philo treats the Logos," that is to say, "what we may have to accept is that the author of Hebrews ultimately has in mind an *ideal* pre-existence [of the Son], the existence of an idea [of the Son] in the mind of God,"[100] and this within a strict monotheism in which the concept of preexistent Sonship is "perhaps more of an idea and purpose in the mind of God than of a

---

97. John A. T. Robinson, *The Human Face of God* (London: SCM, 1973), 156.
98. Ibid., 156–61.
99. James D. G. Dunn, *Christology in the Making: A New Testament Inquiry into the Origins of the Doctrine of the Incarnation* (London: SCM, 1980), 52.
100. Ibid., 54.

GOD AS TRINITY

personal divine being."[101] In sum, for Dunn, Hebrews views Jesus in terms of Wisdom language, so that "the thought of pre-existence is present, but in terms of Wisdom Christology it is the act and power of God which properly speaking is what pre-exists; Christ is not so much the pre-existent act and power of God as its eschatological embodiment."[102]

I concur with I. Howard Marshall's assessment that this impersonal construction of the doctrine of divine Sonship in Hebrews is "very alien to the biblical understanding of God as personal, quite apart from imposing a very artificial interpretation upon the biblical text."[103] For while it is true that the Son "*was appointed*" Heir of all things (1:2), and "sat down on the right hand of the Majesty on high, *having become* by so much better than the angels, as he has *inherited* a more excellent name than they" (1:4), this need not be "adoptionist" language. Rather it is language that envisions the glory which became the Son's following the conclusion of his humiliation in his role as Messiah and Mediator (see Heb. 2:9; Ps. 2:8). Philip E. Hughes concurs that this is how the so-called adoptionist language should be construed, writing on 1:4:

> It is true, of course, that by virtue of his eternal Sonship he has an eternal inheritance and possesses a name which is eternally supreme—*the name* signifying, particularly for the Hebrew mind, the essential character of a person in himself and in his work. But our author at this point is speaking of something other than this: the Son who for our redemption humbled himself for a little while to a position lower than the angels has by his ensuing exaltation *become* superior to the angels (2:9 below), and in doing so has achieved and retains the inheritance of a name which is *more excellent than theirs*.[104]

And if he is said to have "inherited" the name of "Son," as Bruce declares,

> this does not mean that the name was not His before His exaltation. It was clearly His in the days of His humiliation: "Son though He was, He learned obedience by the things which He suffered" (Ch. 5:8). It was His, indeed, ages before His incarnation: this is the plain indication of the statement in Ch. 1:2 that God has spoken to us "in his Son, . . . through whom also he made the worlds."[105]

---

101. Ibid., 56.
102. Ibid., 209.
103. I. Howard Marshall, "Incarnational Christology in the New Testament," in *Christ the Lord: Studies in Christology Presented to Donald Guthrie*, ed. H. H. Rowdon (Leicester: Inter–Varsity Press, 1982), 11, fn. 25.
104. Philip E. Hughes, *A Commentary on the Epistle to the Hebrews* (Grand Rapids, Mich.: Eerdmans, 1977), 50.
105. F. F. Bruce, *Commentary on the Epistle to the Hebrews* (Grand Rapids, Mich.: Eerdmans, 1964), 8.

All of the so-called adoptionist language urged by Robinson and Dunn can be similarly explained; none of it requires that the Son's personal preexistence has to be forfeited in deference to an ideal, impersonal preexistence in the mind of God. And even if the writer's language is that of Philo and the Book of Wisdom, Bruce points out that,

> his meaning goes beyond theirs. For them the Logos or Wisdom is the personification of a divine attribute; for him the language is descriptive of a man who had lived and died in Palestine a few decades previously, but who nonetheless was the eternal Son and supreme revelation of God.[106]

Martin Hengel even declares that

> the divine nature of the "Son" in Hebrews is . . . established from the beginning. The approach . . . is the same as in the hymn [Phil 2:6–11] which Paul quotes; the difference is that [in Hebrews] it is made more precise in terms of the metaphysical substantiality of Christ.[107]

Viewed, then, from the scriptural perspective of the *humiliatio-exaltatio* paradigm, the supposed "adoptionist" passages in Hebrews are not "adoptionist" at all, and the letter to the Hebrews throughout supports the full deity of the Son.

PETER'S CHRISTOLOGY

We find Peter's Christology in his Gospel utterances, in Acts, and in his epistles.

Peter's Gospel Utterances

Luke 5:8: Peter's Confession of Jesus as "Lord."

On one occasion after Jesus had addressed the crowds from Peter's boat (Luke 5:1–11), he invited Peter to put out into deep water and to let down his nets for a catch. Although Peter mildly protested that it would do no good inasmuch as he had been fishing all night and had caught nothing, nevertheless, addressing Jesus as his "Master" (Ἐπιστάτα, *Epistata*), he agreed to do as he was instructed. Immediately upon carrying out Jesus' order, he caught so many fish that his nets began to

---

106. Ibid., 5.
107. Martin Hengel, *The Son of God* (Philadelphia: Fortress, 1976), 87.

break, and when the second boat came alongside to render assistance, the catch was so plentiful that both boats began to sink!

Because certain details in the story resemble the miracle in John 21:1–14, Bultmann and his school have urged that Luke has antedated a post-Easter story, but C. H. Dodd has shown that the account lacks the essential "form" of a resurrection story and must be placed in the preresurrection period. The mere fact that the two accounts of the two incidents resemble one another in some details does not necessarily mean that they both reflect one original story in the "tradition." There are numerous examples in the Gospels of pairs of similar but distinct incidents (see Matt. 9:27–31 and 20:29–34; Luke 7:37–38 and John 12:1–3). There is no reason to deny either the historicity or the authenticity of the Lukan account.

At this display of Jesus' supernatural knowledge and power, overcome with an awareness of his own sinfulness in the presence of Jesus' holiness, Peter fell at Jesus' knees, crying: "Depart from me, because I am a sinful man, O Lord!" Although Marshall states that "no precise connotation (e.g., of divinity) can necessarily be attached to [Peter's use of κύριος, kyrios, 'Lord'],"[108] Peter's act of prostrating himself at Jesus' knees, accompanied by an acknowledgement of his sinfulness, can only be viewed as an act of religious worship. Whereas godly men and angels always rejected such prostration as an act of misplaced devotion, indeed, as an act of idolatry (see Acts 10:25–26; 14:11–15; Rev. 19:9–10), Jesus issued no such prohibition to Peter. To the contrary, he endorsed Peter's adoration by calling him to follow him as a "fisher of men." Concerning Peter's address of Jesus as "Lord" here, Warfield remarks that it

> seems to be an ascription to Jesus of a majesty which is distinctly recognized as supernatural: not only is the contrast of "Lord" with "Master" here expressed (see v. 5), but the phrase "Depart from me; for I am a sinful man" (v. 8) is the natural utterance of that sense of unworthiness which overwhelms men in the presence of the divine [see Job 42:5–6; Isa 6:5; Dan 10:16; Luke 18:13; Rev 1:12–17], and which is signalized in Scripture as the mark of recognition of the divine presence.[109]

John 6:69: Peter's Confession of Jesus as "the Holy One of God"

If the last few days prior to this confession had been a period of acute significance for the disciples with regard to the question of Jesus' person, all the more so had they been for Peter, since it had been he who had actually walked with Jesus on

---

108. Marshall, *Gospel of Luke*, 204.
109. Warfield, *Lord of Glory*, 142.

the Sea of Galilee. Now on this occasion, presumably only some hours or days later, certainly not weeks (see John 6:22), Peter had just listened to his Lord's discourse on the Bread of Life, in which Jesus had claimed that he had come down from heaven (John 6:33, 38, 51, 62), was the Giver of eternal life to the world (6:33, 40, 50, 51, 53, 54, 57, 58), and was the Lord of resurrection (6:39, 40, 44, 54). Because of these exalted, exclusive, and universal claims and Jesus' insistence on man's inherent inability to believe on him (6:44–45, 65), many of his followers departed and no longer followed him. At this defection, Jesus turned to the Twelve and asked: "You do not want to leave too, do you?" Although the question was put to all of them, it was Peter who answered for the group: "Lord, to whom shall we go? You have words of eternal life. And we have believed and we know that you are the Holy One of God" (John 6:68–69).

Since there is no miracle in this pericope, most critical scholars concede the general authenticity of Peter's remarks. Some, however, insist that this is the Fourth Gospel's variant account of Peter's confession at Caesarea Philippi, taken out of its historical setting and placed here against the betrayal that was growing in Judas' heart (see John 6:70–71). Against such an identification, however, may be arrayed the differences of place, Jesus' approach, the circumstances, and the wording of the confession itself, and I will approach this as a separate, distinct, and earlier confession on Peter's part.

In light of the several indications in the Gospels of Peter's growing appreciation of the deity of Christ, though it is true that his term of address here ("Lord") "could mean much or little" in itself, in this context, Morris writes, "there can be no doubt that the word has the maximum, not the minimum meaning" of the ascription of deity to Jesus.[110]

As for his statement "You are the Holy One of God," while it is certainly a messianic title, several things can also be said in favor of viewing it as including the further affirmation, by implication, of Jesus' divine origin and character. The first factor is Peter's growing appreciation of who Jesus was. We noted earlier his confession of Jesus as his "Lord" (and that in the divine sense) on the occasion of his call to become a "fisher of men" in Luke 5 when, awed by Jesus' supernatural knowledge and power over nature, he acknowledged his own sinfulness over against the majestic and ethical holiness of Jesus. We noted that his title of address there and here ("Lord") suggests deity, and, once a man has begun to apprehend that Jesus is divine, no title (with the exception of those that clearly mark him out as true man) he ever employs in referring to him can be totally void of intending the ascription of deity.

---

110. Leon Morris, *The Gospel According to John* (Grand Rapids, Mich.: Eerdmans, 1971), 389.

Second, while this title ("the Holy One of God") is applied to Jesus on only one other occasion, leaving little room for extensive comparative study of the title, that one other occasion does cast some light on its meaning here. The title occurs in the mouth of the demoniac in the synagogue at Capernaum, clearly revealing the demon's awareness of who Jesus was (Mark 1:24; Luke 4:34). The demon was obviously fearful of Jesus and implied that he had the power to cast it into hell, suggesting thereby that Jesus possessed divine authority and power as "the Holy One of God."

Third, the stress on holiness in the title is significant. It reminds us of the frequently occurring title for God, "the Holy One of Israel," in the Old Testament. In this connection, Morris writes: "There can be not the slightest doubt that the title is meant to assign to Jesus the highest possible place. It stresses his consecration and his purity. It sets Him with God and not man."[111]

Finally, C. H. Dodd calls attention to the similarity between Peter's words here, "we have *believed* and we have come to *know*" and Yahweh's words, "that you may *know* and *believe* that I am he" (LXX, Isa. 43:10). Dodd writes:

> The combination [in Peter's confession] πιστεύειν καὶ γινώσκειν [*pisteuein kai ginōskein*] follows Isaiah closely; but for ὅτι ἐγώ εἰμι [*hoti egō eimi*, "that I am"] is substituted ὅτι σὺ εἶ ὁ ἅγιος τοῦ θεοῦ [*hoti su ei ho hagios tou theou*, "that you are the Holy One of God"]. The content of knowledge is the unique status of Christ Himself, which is an equivalent for knowledge of God.[112]

For these reasons it appears likely that Peter's confession, stressing as it does Jesus' inward character of holiness, marks him out not only as the Messiah, but also, by virtue of his possessing a majestic and ethical holiness identical to that of God himself (see Luke 5:8), as being divine himself. And again Jesus accepted Peter's tacit assessment of him as the Messiah and his implied identification of him as divine.

Matthew 16:16: Peter's Confession of Jesus as "the Christ, the Son of the Living God"

At Caesarea Philippi, Jesus through questioning the disciples drew from Peter his great confession: "You are the Christ, the Son of the living God" (Matt. 16:16; see Mark 8:29; Luke 9:20).

---

111. Ibid., 390.
112. C. H. Dodd, *The Interpretation of the Fourth Gospel* (Cambridge: Cambridge University Press, 1953), 168.

Bultmann regarded the whole episode as a legend of the early church intended to undergird its "Easter faith" in Jesus' messiahship, and R. H. Fuller regards Matthew 16:17–19 as a "Matthean expansion" and thus "clearly secondary" and Mark 8:30–32 as both Marcan redaction and later tradition, the end result being that Jesus is represented as positively rejecting all claims to messiahship as a "diabolical temptation." But there is no legitimate ground to question either the historicity of the event or the authenticity of Jesus' recorded response.

Given the fact that all three Synoptic Evangelists report that Peter confessed faith in Christ's messiahship (Matthew and Mark: "You are the Christ"; Luke: "You are the Christ of God"), and that in Matthew Jesus gives express approval and in Mark and Luke tacit approval to this confession, I conclude that here is a clear and incontrovertible instance when Jesus claimed to be the Messiah.

But Matthew reports Peter's confession as containing a second part: "[You are] the Son of the living God." We have no way of knowing why Mark and Luke do not report this second part; we can only assume that it did not serve their respective purposes. It has been suggested that the second part is only a further elucidation or synonym for Peter's "the Christ," and that the two Evangelists saw no need for the elucidation. But there are four cogent reasons for believing that Peter intended to go beyond the ascription to Jesus of messianic investiture and to confess him as God's Son both as to nature and origin.

First, in the disciples' earlier act of worship in Matthew 14:33, their united confession of Jesus as "truly the Son of God" ascribed divine Sonship to him.[113] The title, "the Son of the living God" in 16:16 can hardly carry lower import on this later occasion than the same phrase did on the former occasion. In fact, the additional word "living" in this latter expression, if anything, adds weight to the import of Peter's confession, in that it particularizes the God whose Son Jesus is and by extension particularizes him as well.

---

113. The disciples' act of worship we may deduce from the Matthean word προσεκύνησαν, *prosekynēsan*, "they [fell down and] worshiped, did obeisance to, prostrated before, reverenced." At the very least the word connotes an attitude of reverence, but because of the character of the miracle itself (see Pss. 89:9; 106:9; 107:23–30, which Jewish fishermen must surely have known by heart), the word should be given its full meaning of "worship." Their earlier question, "What kind of man is this? Even the winds and the waves obey him!" (Matt. 8:27) receives here its answer: "You are truly the Son of God!" This can only mean that they believed that they were in the presence of One who was supernatural, indeed divine. Vos remarks that in its dissociation from the idea of messiahship, the confession of Matthew 14:33 stands even higher than Peter's confession, "for through it, the disciples for a moment caught a vision of this [superhuman] character of Jesus as such, apart from its reflection in the Messiahship" (*Self-Disclosure of Jesus*, 178–79).

Second, if the second part of Peter's confession does not intend *more* than the ascription of messiahship to Jesus, then it follows that all that Peter was confessing here is just Jesus' messiahship. But such a confession, expressed both by Peter and others on other occasions (see John 1:41, 49; 6:69), hardly explains Jesus' unusual response to Peter's confession here. Why would Peter's confession of the mere fact of Jesus' messiahship on this occasion elicit Jesus' declaration that Peter's confession was the effect of a special, supernatural revelation when "the ordinary means of self-disclosure during our Lord's long association with Peter would have sufficed for the basis of a mere confession of Jesus' messiahship."[114] The question cannot be intelligently answered on the assumption that Peter's confession entailed simply the recognition of Jesus' messiahship.

Third, the two facts—(1) that the two Evangelists who do not report the second part of Peter's confession do not report Jesus' response to Peter either, whereas Matthew reports both, and (2) that Jesus referred to God in his response to Peter not as "God," which would have been appropriate in light of Peter's reference to "the living God," but as "my Father"—strongly suggest that Jesus' benediction was not primarily a response to the first part (although the first part cannot be divorced from the universe in which Jesus' response is to be interpreted) but was rather his response primarily to the second part. Now if it is true that *any* correct assessment of Jesus must be finally traced to the Father's "teaching" (John 6:45), especially is it true that the Father's "teaching" is necessary with respect to the essential Sonship of Jesus. Jesus expressly declared this to be so in Matthew 11:25–27: "No one knows *the Son* except *the Father,*" he said, and if one is to know "the Son," he also stated, it will be through the Father's act of revelation and by his good pleasure. Now Jesus declares Peter's confession to be the result of a supernatural revelation (16:17); and by his reference to "my Father" in 16:17, it is apparent (1) that Jesus regarded Peter's confession of his Sonship as just such an instance of the revealing activity by the Father which he had spoken of in 11:25–26, and (2) that the disclosure made to Peter had reference to the paternal ("Father") and filial ("Son") relationship between God and Jesus and not simply to the messianic investiture *per se.*

Fourth, the juxtaposition of the two occurrences of σὺ εἶ (*su ei,* "you are") in this context should not be overlooked: Peter's "*You are* the Christ, the Son of the living God" (v. 16), and Jesus' "*You are* Peter (or "a rock")" (v. 18). They are very significant in determining the intent of Peter's confession, the correspondence between them being highlighted by Jesus' words: "And I, on my part, say also to you" (16:18). The import of Jesus' "You are" lifts Peter, as an apostle confessing the Father's revelation, by his title as "a rock" to an altogether *new* and *higher* category,

---

114. Vos, *Self-Disclosure of Jesus,* 180.

the confessing representative of all of the apostles and thus the very foundation of the church which Jesus was erecting (Eph. 2:20; Rev. 21:14; see Gal. 2:9). The correspondence, then, between Peter's "You are" and Jesus' "You are" suggests that Peter's prior confession be construed similarly as elevating Jesus beyond a purely *official* interpretation, to a supramessianic ascription in which his anterior supernatural nature and origin receive special stress. And as a matter of historical record, it is a fact that the church which Jesus erected on the foundation of (the doctrine of) the apostles and prophets has never confessed Jesus simply as the Messiah but has also declared him to be the divine Son of God with respect to both nature and origin.

For these reasons I would urge that by his confession Peter self-consciously intended, as the result of the Father's revelatory activity, to affirm full, unabridged deity to Jesus as "the Son" of "the Father," and that Jesus, by declaring him in making such a confession to have been directly blessed by his Father, tacitly claimed to be God incarnate.

Peter's Witness to Jesus in his Pentecost Sermon

E. Zeller, A. Loisy, and E. Haenchen view the event of Pentecost recorded in Acts 2 as the dogmatic construct of Luke's theological genius, that is, as his own redactional adaptation of an early Jewish legend in which God's voice is divided into seventy languages at the time of the law-giving at Sinai, which adaptation Luke intended as an explanation of the origin of the church. Without giving a detailed refutation of this view here, suffice it to say that there is no evidence to support it and every reason to believe that Luke, as a historian, was simply reporting under inspiration an incident with roots deep in the earliest common Christian tradition concerning the first days of the church after Christ's resurrection and ascension.

As for the popular hypothesis associated with the name of E. von Dodschütz that the Pentecost event is actually a variant account of the resurrection appearance to the five hundred brethren which Paul mentions in 1 Corinthians 15:6, but stripped of its appearance features by Luke in order to highlight the distinctive significance of Pentecost, here again the power of imagination has been at work!

Regarding the source-critical analysis of the event that urges that Luke (or his source) took an account of an experience of ecstatic glossolalia from the primitive church and, under the influence of the Babel story or his own desire to portray symbolically the church's universal embrace, transformed it into a miracle of speaking foreign languages, it must be said again that this approach lacks evidence, is highly subjective, and appears to be an attempt to explain on rationalistic grounds what Luke intended as a supernatural event of deep and abiding significance.

Finally, the modern attempts to explain the Acts account psychologically on the basis of what is known about the modern Pentecostal movement reverses the true order of things by making the modern movement the norm for determining the nature of the Pentecost event, rather that making the Acts account the norm for evaluating the validity of the current occurrences of glossolalia.

I therefore propose to take the Acts account as a straightforward narrative rendition of what actually occurred and set forth the evidence in it for Peter's view of the divine nature of Christ.

The Contextual Setting of Pentecost

The events that occurred on the Day of Pentecost are set in the context of Jesus' statement, made just prior to his ascension, that he would baptize his disciples with the Holy Spirit "in a few days" (Acts 1:5). In light of the teaching of Matthew 3:11, Mark 1:8, Luke 3:16, 24:49, and John 1:33, there can be no doubt that Jesus' statement "you will be baptized" (Acts 1:5) means "I will baptize you." This fact—that *Jesus* baptized his church on that occasion—provides the hermeneutical paradigm for understanding the event of Pentecost.

The Meaning of Pentecost

While the facts of Pentecost are described clearly enough in Acts, what is often misunderstood is the *meaning* of this event. People have tended to concentrate their attention either on the Holy Spirit who was "poured [or "breathed"] out" and/or on the empirical phenomena accompanying his "out-pouring," rather than on the "Baptizer" himself, the One who did the "pouring." But Peter explained the meaning of the event in his sermon that responded to the people's query "What does this mean?" (Acts 2:12).

For the disciples the "Spirit-filling" meant their "empowering" as witnesses, as we know from our Lord's statements in Luke 24:49 and Acts 1:8, and from Peter's sermon itself, which classically illustrates this effect. But from the perspective of the history of redemption, it meant something else, and it is this that Peter brings out in his sermon.

Peter begins by citing Yahweh's promise in Joel 2:28-32a that in the last days he would pour out his Spirit on all kinds of "flesh"—sons and daughters, young men and old men, and men and women servants (Acts 2:16-21). By his "This is what was spoken of by the prophet Joel" (2:16), Peter identified the events of Pentecost as the (initiatory phase[?] of the) fulfillment of that prophecy. Then he argues from the events of Pentecost for the lordship and messianic investiture of Jesus Christ. The argument concludes and culminates in 2:36: "Therefore, let all the house of Israel know for certain that God has made him both Lord and Christ—this Jesus whom you crucified." Further indication that Peter intended his remarks as an apologetic of Jesus' lordship and messiahship may be seen in his reference to God's having accredited Jesus by doing authenticating miracles through him and in his insistence that his audience knew of Jesus' mighty works. These features indicate that Peter's remarks prior to his 2:36 "therefore" are to be regarded as an argument intended to buttress this conclusion.

In Acts 2:24 Peter remarks that God had raised Jesus from the dead. Why had God done this? "Because," Peter says, "it was impossible for death to keep its hold on him." And why not? Because David had prophesied concerning Jesus' resurrection in Psalm 16:8–11. Peter argued that David was speaking of the Messiah rather than of himself, because David died and his body did decay, and because as an inspired prophet, David had been informed of the Messiah's resurrection and heavenly enthronement (2:29–31).

In Acts 2:33, with Psalm 110 in mind, Peter describes Jesus' exaltation to the right hand of God. But how do we know that David was speaking of the Messiah in Psalm 110? Because, Peter says, "David did not ascend to heaven"(2:34)—employing the same form of argument from history he had used earlier. So David was not speaking of himself in Psalm 110:1 but of the Messiah, who would be exalted to the right hand of God, every detail of which prophecy had been accomplished in Jesus.

To this point Peter has demonstrated that David had foretold all that had come to pass with respect to "this Jesus," that he would be raised from the dead and would be exalted to God's right hand and would pour out his Spirit. But why did Peter use the Pentecost event to argue for the messiahship of Jesus? The answer is that for Peter Pentecost was to be viewed as one more concrete miraculous self-attestation on Jesus' part that he was the Messiah, and so he concludes his remarks with a strong "therefore"—"therefore . . . let all the house of Israel know for certain that God has made him both Lord and Christ—this Jesus whom you crucified."

Thus for Peter the meaning of the event was not primarily in the fact that the Holy Spirit had been manifested in a unique and striking fashion, but rather in the fact that Jesus, the exalted Lord and Messiah, by this further display of his authority, had attested once again to his divine lordship and messiahship by "breathing upon" ("baptizing") his disciples.

Because men's minds have tended to focus on the empirical phenomena of Pentecost rather than on the Baptizer himself, the church's understanding of the significance of Pentecost has become warped and distorted. The point of emphasis has shifted away from viewing the miracle as a self-attestation to Israel of Christ's divine lordship and has come to rest upon the person and work of the Holy Spirit. The framers of the Westminster Confession of Faith were more perceptive when they wrote:

> To all those for whom Christ hath purchased redemption, *he doth certainly and effectually apply and communicate the same,* making intercession for them, and revealing unto them, in and by the Word, the mysteries of salvation; effectually persuading them by his Spirit to believe and obey; and governing their hearts by his Word and Spirit; overcoming all their enemies by his almighty power and wisdom, in such manner and ways as are most consonant to his wonderful and unsearchable dispensation. (VII/viii; emphasis supplied)

The Westminster divines are here only stating in a different fashion what they confess elsewhere when they affirm that Christ executes the offices of Prophet, Priest, and King, not only in his estate of humiliation but also in his estate of exaltation (Shorter Catechism, Questions 23-28).

Here then is the real significance of Pentecost in the history of redemption: It was Jesus' self-attestation to the truth that he was Israel's Lord and Messiah. And the nonrepeatable "Samaritan Pentecost" (Acts 8:14–17) and the non-repeatable "Gentile [or "ends-of-the-earth"] Pentecost" (Acts 10:44–46) are to be viewed in the same light: both were Jesus' self-attestations to the church and to the people involved, at the critical junctures of the missionary endeavor that he had delineated in Acts 1:8, of his messiahship and saving lordship over the nations (see 8:14; 11:17–18).

Pentecost's Implications for Christ's Nature

In explaining the meaning of Pentecost, Peter also said certain things that carry implications with respect to Jesus' divine nature.

First, the very fact of his ascension and of his session at the Father's right hand suggests that Jesus is divine. F. F. Bruce comments

> The most exalted angels are those whose privilege it is to "stand in the presence of God" like Gabriel (Luke 1:19), but none of them has ever been invited to sit before Him, still less to sit in the place of unique honor at His right hand.[115]

To the divine Son alone this honor has been accorded (Heb. 1:4, 13).

Second, the fact that it was the ascended *Jesus* who poured out the Spirit (2:33)

---

115. Bruce, *Commentary on the Epistle to the Hebrews,* 24.

moves in the same direction, for the connection between what Peter emphasizes in 2:17 by his insertion of the words "God says" into the Joel prophecy (" 'In the last days,' *God says,* 'I will pour out my spirit' ") and his later statement in 2:33 (*He* [the ascended Jesus] *has poured out this which you now see and hear*" cannot have been unintentional. Peter connects the God and Yahweh of Joel 2 who promised to pour out his Spirit to the ascended Jesus who poured out the Spirit.

Third, the fact that the authority to apply the benefits of his redemption by his Spirit to whomsoever he pleases in his role as Baptizer of men by his Spirit (salvation) and by fire (judgment) means that the prerogatives and functions of deity are his to exercise, and therefore that he himself is God.

Fourth, when Peter, in response to his listeners' query "Brothers, what shall we do?" urged them to repent and be baptized *in the name of Jesus Christ*" (2:38), it appears that he was urging them to follow the way of salvation Joel had spoken of: "And everyone who calls on *the name of the Lord* will be saved" (Acts 2:21). So for Peter Jesus was the Lord of Joel 2:32a (see Rom. 10:9–13), the Yahweh who spoke through Joel.

Peter's Epistolary Witness to Jesus

As we turn to Peter's letters, we should bear in mind that from the numerous experiences he had as one of the original twelve disciples he had gained firsthand insight into the character and work of his Lord. And he was among the disciples in the upper room who confessed to Jesus: "You know all things and do not need to have anyone ask you questions [in order for you to know what is on his mind]. This makes us believe that you came from God" (John 16:30).

In addition to seeing the miracles which Jesus performed publicly, Peter was also among that inner circle of disciples who witnessed his transfiguration and heard the Father's attestation to his unique Sonship (Matt. 17:2–6). He was also the private beneficiary of one of Jesus' postresurrection appearances (he probably was the first apostle to see him) (Luke 24:34; 1 Cor. 15:5), and he saw him on several other occasions, hearing Thomas's confession of Jesus as "Lord and God" during one of them (John 20:28). He witnessed Jesus' ascension into heaven, and it was Peter who preached the sermon on the Day of Pentecost in which he acclaimed both the messiahship and mediatorial lordship of the divine Jesus. We should not overlook the fact, finally, that Peter was surely aware of Paul's Christology and was approving in his assessment of it (Gal. 1:19; 2:1–9; 2 Pet. 3:15–16). Consequently, one should not be surprised to find Peter espousing the highest kind of Christology "from above" in his letters.

1 Peter

In his first letter Peter refers to Jesus as "[the] Christ"—his most common designation for him (1 Pet. 1:11, 19; 2:21; 3:15, 16, 18; 4:1, 13, 14; 5:1, 10, 14), "Jesus Christ" (1:1, 2, 3, 7, 13; 2:5; 3:21; 4:11), "[the] Lord" (2:3, 13; 3:15; perhaps also in 1:25; 3:12), and "our Lord Jesus Christ" (1:3). What Peter says about Jesus in these contexts reveals a fully developed incarnational Christology. He implies his preexistence with the Father (1:20a), affirming that it was Christ's Spirit who had inspired the prophets in Old Testament times (1:11) and that he had been "manifested" in these last times (1:20b). In accordance with Old Testament prophecy (1:11), as our sinless substitute (2:22, a citation of Isa. 53:9) he suffered death vicariously on the cross (1:2, 11, 19; 2:21, 23, 24; 3:18; 4:1, 13; 5:1), was raised from the dead (1:3, 21; 3:18, 21), ascended to the right hand of God and to glory (1:11, 21; 3:22), and will be revealed in the Eschaton (1:7, 13; 5:1, 4). He is the Mediator between God and man (1:21; 2:5; 4:11; 5:10, 14) and the One in whom men must trust for salvation (2:6).

Not only does Peter place Christ in the Trinitarian context of the Father and the Spirit (1 Pet. 1:2, 3, 11; 4:14), but three times he refers to Old Testament passages in which Yahweh is the subject and uses them of Christ in a way that suggests that Christ is to be equated with the Yahweh of the Old Testament Scriptures. In 2:3, alluding to Psalm 34:8 ("Taste and see that the Lord is good"), he writes with reference to Christ: "if you tasted that the Lord is good." In 2:8, citing Isaiah 8:14b, he equates the Lord of Hosts there, who would become "a stone that causes men to stumble, and a rock that makes them fall" with Christ, the "stone laid in Zion" (2:6, citing Isa. 28:16), and the "stone the builders rejected [who] has become the capstone" (2:7, citing Psa. 118:22). And in 3:14–15, alluding to Isaiah 8:12–13, he equates the Lord of Hosts who is to be sanctified with Christ ("Sanctify Christ as Lord in your hearts").

Finally, Peter provides us with two pastoral descriptions of Christ: "the Shepherd and Overseer of your souls" (1 Pet 2:25) and the "Chief Shepherd" (5:4).

2 Peter

In his second letter Peter refers to Jesus as "Jesus Christ" (2 Pet. 1:1), "[the] Lord" (3:8, 9, 10, 15; perhaps 2:9), "the Lord and Savior" (3:2), "our Lord and Savior Jesus Christ" (1:11; 2:20; 3:18), and finally, "our God and Savior Jesus Christ" (1:1).

This last reference is very important, for now we find Peter—like Thomas, Paul, and the author of Hebrews before him—employing θεός, *theos,* as a christological title. This assertion has not gone unchallenged, the alternative suggestion being that by θεός, *theos,* Peter intended to refer to the Father. As earlier with Titus 2:13, the issue turns on the question whether by the phrase, "the righteousness of our God and Savior Jesus Christ," Peter intended to refer to two persons (God the Father and Jesus) or to only one person, Jesus alone. It is my opinion, as well as that of the KJV, RV, RSV, NASV, NEB, NIV, and the NKJV, that Peter intended to refer only to Christ. I would offer the following six reasons for this:

First, it is the most natural way to read the Greek sentence. If Peter had intended to speak of two persons, he could have expressed himself unambiguously to that effect, as he does in the very next verse ("knowledge of God and of Jesus our Lord"), by placing "our Savior" after "Jesus Christ" or by simply inserting an article before "Savior" in the present word order. Charles Bigg rightly observes: "if the author intended to distinguish two persons, he has expressed himself with singular inaccuracy."[116]

Second, both "God" and "Savior" stand under the regimen of the single article before "God," linking the two nouns together as referents to a single person. Bigg again rightly states: "It is hardly open for anyone to translate in I Pet. 1.3 ὁ θεὸς καὶ πατήρ [ho theos kai patēr] by 'the God and Father,' and yet here decline to translate ὁ θεὸς καὶ σωτήρ [ho theos kai sōtēr] by 'the God and Saviour.'"[117]

Third, five times in 2 Peter, including this one, Peter uses the word "Savior." It is always coupled with a preceding noun (the other four times always with κύριος, kyrios) in precisely the same word order as in 1:1. Here are the last four uses in their precise word order:

1:11: "kingdom of the Lord of us and Savior Jesus Christ"
2:20: "knowledge of the Lord of us and Savior Jesus Christ"
3:4: "commandment of the Lord and Savior"
3:18: "knowledge of the Lord of us and Savior Jesus Christ"

In each of these four cases, "Lord" and "Savior," standing under the regimen of the single article before "Lord," refer to the same person. If we substitute the word θεός, theos, for κύριος, kyrios, we have precisely the word order of verse 1: "righteousness of the God of us and Savior Jesus Christ." In other words, the phrases in these verses are perfectly similar and must stand or fall together. The parallelism of word order between the phrase in 1:1 and the other four phrases, where only one person is intended, puts it beyond all reasonable doubt that one person is intended in 1:1 as well.

---

116. Charles Bigg, *A Critical and Exegetical Commentary on the Epistles of St. Peter and St. Jude* (Edinburgh: T. & T. Clark, 1902), 251.
117. Ibid., 251.

Ernst Käsemann's opinion is that "our Lord and Savior" in the four occurrences reflects a "stereotyped" christological formula, and that therefore the employment of θεοῦ, *theou*, in 1:1 stands outside of the stereotype, the phrase thus referring to two persons.[118] But there is no reason why a variant of a stereotyped formula could not occur, and here the grammar clearly indicates that it has occurred.

Fourth, the doxology to "our Lord Jesus Christ" in 3:18 ascribes "glory both now and forever" to him, an ascription suggesting a Christology in which Christ may be glorified in the same manner in which God is glorified. There would be, then, nothing incongruous in describing Christ as God in 1:1.

Fifth, Peter was surely present on the occasion of Thomas's confession of Jesus as both Lord and God (John 20:28), which confession had received Christ's approval. The memory of that confession, not to mention his own confession in Matthew 16:16, would have dissolved any reticence on Peter's part to refer to Jesus as θεός, *theos*, and a description of Jesus here as God is in line with those earlier confessions.

Sixth, since Peter was almost certainly aware of the content of Paul's letter to the Roman church—he seems to allude to it in 2 Peter 2:19 and 3:15 (compare 2:19 with Rom. 6:16, and 3:15 with Rom. 2:4; 9:22-23, 11:22-23)—he would most likely have been aware that Paul in Romans 9:5 had referred to Christ as "over all, the ever-blessed God" (author's translation). According "scriptural status" to Paul's letters as he does (2 Pet. 3:16), he would have seen nothing inappropriate or "unscriptural" about his own description of Christ as God, just as his "dear brother Paul" had done some years earlier.

We conclude then that 2 Peter 1:1 takes its place alongside Romans 9:5, Titus 2:13, and Hebrews 1:8 as a verse in which Jesus is described as God by the use of θεός, *theos*, as a christological title.

While Peter's Christology in 2 Peter is not as full with respect to detail as in his first letter, it is still the same high Christology. That Jesus is God incarnate is attested by Peter's description of him as "our God" (2 Pet. 1:1), and by his being, with the Father, the Co-source of grace and peace (1:2). Divine power (τῆς θείας δυνάμεως, *tēs theias dynameōs*), divine essence (θείας φύσεως, *theias physeōs*), and divine majesty (μεγαλειότητος, *megaleiotētos*) are assigned to him (1:3, 4, 16). His is an eternal kingdom (1:11), into which Christians will be welcomed when he comes in power (1:16) on his "Day" (3:10), which is "the Day of God" (3:12), to destroy the heavens and earth with fire (3:10-12). He is the Owner (δεσπότην, *despotēn*) of men (2:1), whose commands they are to obey (3:2), and through the knowledge

---

118. Ernst Käsemann, "An Apologia for Primitive Christian Eschatology," in *Essays on New Testament Themes* (London: SCM, 1964), 183.

of whom all spiritual blessing and Christian virtue come (1:2, 8; 2:20; 3:18). Finally, to him is directed the doxology in 3:18 ("To him be the glory both now and forever"), a doxology not unlike those addressed both to him (2 Tim. 4:18; Heb. 13:20–21; 1 Pet. 4:11; Rev. 1:5b–6) and to the Father (1 Pet. 5:11; Jude 24–25) elsewhere. And yet he is distinct from his Father as the Son of the Father, who in his mediatorial role receives honor and glory from his Father (1:17). All of this agrees with what we have seen elsewhere in the Petrine witness to Jesus and adds the weight of its testimony to the New Testament's depiction of the deity of Jesus Christ.

THE SYNOPTISTS' CHRISTOLOGY

It was most likely during the seventh decade of the first century—the decade in which several of the New Testament letters were written and also in which Peter and Paul were martyred—that the Synoptists wrote their Gospels. In their accounts of Jesus' life and ministry not only did they report Jesus' witness concerning himself but also they revealed what they themselves believed regarding Jesus. Thus it can be said that Jesus' reported *self*-witness reflects also *their* understanding of him—that for all three authors Jesus was the divine Son of God who, being equal to the Father as to his deity, was dispatched on the messianic errand and thus became man and died for man's sins, but who then rose from the dead and who now sits at the right hand of God, awaiting the time when he will return in power and great glory to judge the world. But there are authorial distinctions between the Evangelists, and these are also important to note.

Mark's Christology

It is true that Matthew and Luke are in some ways more explicit than Mark regarding their views of Christ. But it is still the case that Jesus is for Mark divine: "Son of God" as a christological title occurs in Mark 3:11 and 15:39, with the variants "Son of the Most High God" and "Son of the Blessed" occurring in 5:7 and 14:61 respectively. Beside these stand the simple "a son" (12:6), "the Son" (13:22), and "my Son" (1:11; 9:7). In each of these instances the title intends the ascription to Jesus of a unique filial relationship to the Father, this unique Sonship being ultimately grounded in his transcendent coessentiality with the Father.

Mark's "Son of Man" sayings also indicate that, although Jesus as the Danielic "Son of Man" would suffer and be betrayed into the hands of sinners and be killed (8:31; 9:31; 10:33–34; 14:21, 41), he is, as that same Son of Man, also a superhuman, superangelic figure of transcendent dignity who does mighty works, is the Lord of the Sabbath (2:28), has the authority to forgive sins (2:10), actually *gives* his life as a ransom for many (10:45) in accordance with the prophetic Scriptures (14:21), but rises from the dead (8:31; 9:9, 31; 10:34), sits on the right hand of the Mighty One (14:62), and will return in clouds with the holy angels and with great power and glory to judge the world (8:38; 13:26–27).

E. Lohmeyer correctly declares that, as the Son of God, Jesus for Mark is

> not primarily a human but a divine figure.... He is not merely endowed with the power of God, but is himself divine as to his nature; not only are his word and work divine but his essence also.[119]

And William L. Lane notes that "it is widely recognized that the figure of Jesus in Mark's Gospel is altogether supernatural."[120]

Matthew's Christology

For Matthew, as for Mark, Jesus is the Son of God (Matt. 2:15; 3:17; 4:3, 6; 11:27; 14:33; 16:16; 17:5; 21:37–38; 22:2; 24:36; 26:63–64; 27:54; 28:19), by which title he intends all that Mark means by it—that Jesus stands in a unique filial relationship to the Father because, as the Father's Son, he is divine. But Matthew makes explicit at some points what Mark takes for granted. Matthew reports Jesus' supernatural entrance into the world as "Immanuel," "God with us" (1:18–25). In the "embryonic Fourth Gospel" in 11:27, he brings out the truth that Jesus' knowledge of the Father is on a par with the Father's reciprocal knowledge of him, and his sovereign disposition of that knowledge to people is also on a par with the Father's reciprocal sovereign disposition of his knowledge of the Son (11:27). And it is in Matthew's account of the Great Commission that we see Jesus placing himself even in the "awful precincts of the divine Name" (Warfield) as the One who shares with the Father and the Spirit the one ineffable Name or essence of God (28:19).

As the messianic Son of Man, Matthew's Jesus undergoes a period of humiliation as he serves men (20:28) and suffers all kinds of indignities—even death—at their hands (12:40; 17:12, 22–23; 20:18–19, 28; 26:2, 24, 45). But as the same Son of Man he possesses the authority to forgive sins (9:6) and is the Lord of the Sabbath (12:8). Although he is killed, according to Matthew his death was a self-sacrifice—"a ransom for many" (20:28)—in accordance with prophetic Scripture (26:24), but he rises from the dead (12:40; 17:9, 23; 20:19), assumes authority at the right hand of the Mighty One (26:64), and will return on the clouds with *his* angels (16:27; 24:31) in power and great glory to judge the nations of the world (19:28; 24:27, 30, 39, 44; 25:31–46; 26:64).

---

119. E. Lohmeyer, *Das Evangelim des Markus* 12th ed., (Göttingen: Vandenhoech and Ruprecht, 1953), 4 (author's translation).
120. William L. Lane, *The Gospel According to Mark* (Grand Rapids, Mich.: Eerdmans, 1974), 44, fn. 23.

Luke's Christology

Luke's witness to Jesus' divine Sonship is as clear as that of the other Synoptists (Luke 1:32, 35; 3:22; 4:3, 9, 41; 8:28; 9:35; 10:22; 20:13; 22:70). With Matthew he reports Jesus' supernatural birth and claim to a knowledge of the Father equivalent in every way—complete, exhaustive, and unbrokenly continuous—to the Father's knowledge of him, by virtue of which he is the only adequate Revealer of the Father to men, just as the Father is the only adequate Revealer of the Son to men (10:21–22). With the other Synoptists, Luke's Jesus, as the Danielic Son of Man, suffers for a time at the hands of men "in order to seek and to save that which was lost" (9:22, 44; 18:31–32; 19:10) as it had been predicted in Scripture (18:31; 22:22). But then he rises from the dead (9:22; 18:33; 24:7), ascends to the right hand of the Mighty God (22:69), and will return in a cloud with power and great glory (9:26; 21:27) to determine the destinies of men—certainly a divine prerogative and function (9:26; 12:8; 21:36). Again, as in the other Synoptic Gospels, Luke's Jesus as the Son of Man is a figure of transcendent proportions.

But Luke's Gospel contains a feature that is absent from the other Synoptic Gospels. Though it is true that Jesus is also for Mark and Matthew "the Lord" (see Mark 1:3; Matt. 3:3), Luke makes this characterization of Jesus explicit through his recurring narrative use of "the Lord" (Luke 7:13, 19; 10:1, 39, 41; 11:39; 12:42; 13:15; 17:5, 6; 18:6; 19:8; 22:61; 24:3; see the numerous occurrences of the same feature in Luke's Acts), no doubt reflecting the terminology of the early church.[121] As for the significance of Luke's usage, after noting that "what was in the OT [LXX] the name of God has been applied to Jesus," and that ὁ κύριος (*ho kyrios*, "the Lord") "is used of both God and Jesus quite indiscriminately [in Acts], so that it is often hard to determine which Person is meant," Marshall declares that in his Gospel Luke

---

121. Vos writes on this Lukan feature in his *The Self-Disclosure of Jesus*, 119:

> In [the case of Luke using the title "the Lord" of Jesus] we have, of course, nothing but an instance of the custom which generally prevailed at the time the Gospels were written, of referring to Jesus as "the Lord." The Evangelist must have followed this custom in his daily speech, and no reason can be discovered why he should have refrained from following it in writing, even though it should have been, strictly speaking, an anachronism. For not only the Evangelist, but also the readers for whom he proximately wrote, daily so expressed themselves. Grammatically analyzed . . . the language means simply this: "He, whom we now call the Lord. . . ."

employs it particularly to introduce authoritative statements by Jesus and concludes that "Jesus . . . is for Luke the Lord [in the Yahwistic sense] during his earthly ministry,"[122] although Luke is careful not to place the title with that significance on the lips of the disciples in an indiscriminate, anachronistic way.

JUDE'S CHRISTOLOGY

In this short letter of only twenty-five verses, Jude refers to Jesus six times by name and always in conjunction with one or more additional titles: "Jesus Christ" (Jude 1 [twice]), "our Lord Jesus Christ" (vv. 17, 21), "Jesus Christ, our Lord" (v. 25), and "our only Master and Lord, Jesus Christ" (v. 4). All ascribe to Jesus both the messianic investiture and lordship, while the contexts in which they occur suggest that for Jude Christ's station was not below the Father himself insofar as divine status is concerned. For if it is in God the Father that the called are loved, it is in or for Jesus Christ that they are kept (v. 1). If they are to keep themselves in the Father's love, they are no less to wait for the mercy of our Lord Jesus Christ to grant them eternal salvation (v. 21). If it is the Father who is to be glorified for the final salvation of the called, it is through Jesus Christ, our Lord, that such praise is to be mediated (v. 25). If it is the Father who is the "only God" (v. 25), it is Jesus Christ who is "our only Master and Lord" (τὸν μόνον δεσπότην καὶ κύριον, *ton monon despotēn kai kyrion*, v. 4). And if Jude sees himself as a servant, it is as a servant of Jesus Christ (v. 1) precisely because it is Jesus Christ who is "our only Master and Lord" (v. 4).

There is some debate, it must be admitted, as to whether the full title in verse 4 refers only to Christ ("our only Master and Lord, Jesus Christ") or to both God the Father ("the only Master") and to Jesus ("our Lord Jesus Christ"). Many commentators argue that the latter is the more likely interpretation, but two factors militate against this view. First, both nouns ("Master" and "Lord") stand under the regimen of the single article before "Master," suggesting that they are to be construed together as characterizations of the same person. While it is certainly true that κύριος (*kyrios*, "Lord") does not require the article, it is also true that had Jude intended to refer both to God the Father and to Jesus, he could have made that intention explicit either by placing "our Lord" after "Jesus Christ" as he does in verse 25, or by employing a second article before "our Lord Jesus Christ" as he does in the other two places where he refers singly to Jesus by that title (vv. 17, 21). Second, 2 Peter 2:1, reflecting this phrase here, evidently understood Jude 4 to refer to Jesus as the Master. Thus Jude intended to describe Jesus as both our Master and our Lord.

---

122. I. Howard Marshall, *Luke, Historian and Theologian* (Exeter, U.K.: Paternoster, 1970), 166–67.

Since it is doubtful that the two titles are a pleonasm or tautology, what did Jude intend to imply by the former title? In addition to the fact that Jesus is "our Lord," Jude by this title highlights the fact that Jesus is the "Owner" of Christians by virtue of his messianic work, with the right that inheres in such ownership to command his followers and to expect their immediate and humble response.

But Jude implies still more. In addition to the six direct references to Jesus by name, there is reason to think that he had Jesus in mind when he refers to "the Lord" in verses 5 and 14. Consider the latter context first. Regardless of who the referent is in 1 Enoch 1:4–9, it seems that Jude intended to refer to Jesus when he wrote: "Behold, the Lord will come [ἦλθεν, *ēlthen,* an aorist with prophetic (future) intention] with his myriad holy ones" (see Matt. 16:27; 25:31; Mark 8:38; Luke 9:26; 1 Thess. 3:13; 2 Thess. 1:7–10). In light of consentient Christian testimony, no other referent will suffice. But then, this being so, Jude here ascribes the divine prerogative of eschatological judgment to Jesus.

In the former verse (Jude 5), apart from the fact that "Jesus" may well be the original reading instead of "Lord," there is every reason to believe that Jesus may still have been Jude's intended referent. Consider the following facts. First, there is no question that Jude employed "Lord" to refer to Jesus four times (vv. 4, 17, 21, 25). Second, we have just seen that the almost certain referent of "Lord" in verse 14 is Jesus. And third, this occurrence of "Lord" in verse 5 comes hard on the heels of Jude's certain reference to Jesus in the immediately preceding verse as "our only Master and Lord, Jesus Christ." So it is not only possible but also virtually certain that it is to Jesus, in his preincarnate state as the Yahweh of the Old Testament, that he ascribes, first, the deliverance of Israel from Egypt and then the destruction of those within the nation who rebelled; second, the judgment of the angels at the time of their primeval fall; and third, the destruction of Sodom and Gomorrah. And if this is so, Jude was clearly thinking of Jesus Christ in terms that encompass the Old Testament Deity. But however one interprets this last verse, it is apparent from the others that, for Jude, Christ was the sovereign Master and Lord of men, who at his coming will exercise the prerogative to dispense eschatological salvation and judgment as the Savior and Judge of men. There can be no doubt that for him Christ was divine.

JOHN'S CHRISTOLOGY

John's Christology is set forth in his Gospel utterances, his epistles, and the Revelation.

John's Gospel Christology

Sometime during the last four decades of the first century (it is impossible to be more specific), John the Apostle wrote his Gospel, the Christology of which is explicitly incarnational, as even the most radical critics recognize.

John 20:28

Even though the occurrence of θεός, *theos*, as a christological title in Thomas's great confession is not John's direct and personal confession, its incorporation in his Gospel shows that it reflects his own christological thinking.

The verse in which Thomas's confession occurs, in the words of Raymond E. Brown, is a critically secure text "where clearly Jesus is called God."[123] As such, Thomas's confession of Jesus as his "Lord [κύριος, *kyrios*] and God [θεός, *theos*]" is the "supreme christological pronouncement of the Fourth Gospel."[124] Here within a week of Jesus' resurrection, in the presence of the other disciples who would surely have learned from Thomas's words and Jesus' favorable response the appropriateness of doing so, a disciple for the first time employs θεός, *theos*, as a christological title. This demonstrates that there is no basis in fact for the view of some form-critical scholars that the church only gradually came to the view of an incarnational Christology. Christians virtually from the beginning believed that in Jesus they had to do with God incarnate.

No modern scholar has shown any interest in following the opinion of Theodore of Mopsuestia (c. A.D. 350–428) that Thomas's words do not refer to Christ "but having been amazed over the wonder of the resurrection, Thomas praised God who raised the Christ."[125] This opinion was rejected by the Second Council of Constantinople in A.D. 553. The closest one comes to finding this idea expressed today is in the insistence of Jehovah's Witnesses that the first title was addressed to Jesus while the second was addressed to Jehovah. But Bruce M. Metzger is justified when he writes:

> It is not permissible to divide Thomas' exclamation. . . . Such a high-handed expedient overlooks the plain introductory words, "Thomas said *to him*: 'My Lord and my God!'"[126]

---

123. Brown, "Does the New Testament Call Jesus God?" 561.
124. Raymond E. Brown, *The Gospel According to John XIII–XXI*, Anchor Bible Series (Garden City, N.Y.: Doubleday, 1970), 1047.
125. See H. Denzinger and A. Shönmetzer, *Enchiridion Symbolorum* (Freiburg: Herder, 1976), 150, sec. 434.
126. Metzger, "The Jehovah's Witnesses and Jesus Christ," 71, n. 13.

Moreover, the fact that both appellations appear to be nominative in form should occasion no difficulty for the view that the terms are addressed to Jesus. The articular nominative with vocative force is a well-known idiom in classical, Septuagint, and New Testament Greek.

Thomas's confession is all the more amazing when one reflects, first, on the incongruity of a confession of this magnitude coming from probably the least likely of the Twelve to utter it—a man given to melancholy and gloom (John 11:16) and to theological dullness (John 14:5), and, second, on the fact that it is Thomas who "makes clear that one may address Jesus in the same language in which Israel addressed Yahweh" (see Pss. 35:23; 38:15, 21).[127] John doubtless intended his report of Thomas's ascent from skepticism to full faith in Jesus as Lord and God, under the impact of the historical reality of the resurrection, to illustrate what he thought should be the response of everyone when provided the evidence for Jesus' resurrection.

Two contextual features of Thomas's confession are also worthy of note. The first is that only a week earlier Jesus in his conversation to Mary had spoken of his Father as "My God," using precisely the same words that Thomas used later of him. He also said on that occasion that *his* God was also his disciples' God. And yet now, only a week later, he accepts Thomas's description of *himself* as his disciple's God! Clearly in Jesus' mind there was a personal manifoldness in the depth of the divine being which would permit his Father to be regarded as their God and also himself to be regarded as their God.

The second interesting contextual feature is that Thomas's confession is followed immediately by a statement of John's intention in writing his Gospel, namely, that his readers "may believe that Jesus is the Christ, the Son of God" (20:31). If John had intended by the title "Son of God" something other than or less than an ascription of full deity to Jesus, it is odd that he would have brought this lesser title into such close proximity to Thomas's confession of Jesus' full, unabridged deity. Clearly, the only adequate explanation for the near juxtaposition of the two titles is that, while "Son of God" distinguishes Jesus as Son from the Father, it does not distinguish him as God from God the Father. To be the Son of God in the sense John intended it of Jesus is just to be God the Son.

John 1:1

John begins his Gospel with a powerful statement concerning the Logos (ὁ λόγος, *ho logos*)—a term, according to his usage, meaning "[the independent, personalized] Word [or Wisdom] [of God]." He deliberately repeats the term three

---

127. Brown, *The Gospel According to John XIII–XXI*, 1047.

times in verse 1 to refer to the Son of God—against the background of the first-century forms of pre-Gnostic and Stoic theology—in order to warn his readers against all of the false forms of the Logos doctrine.[128] Translated literally, verse 1 reads:

> In the beginning was the Word,
>   and the Word was with God,
>   and God was the Word.

The term occurs in each clause, each time in the nominative case (subject nominative), and three times ἦν, *ēn,* the imperfect of εἰμί, *eimi,* occurs, expressive in each case of continuous past existence.

In the first clause, the phrase "In the beginning," as all commentators observe, is reminiscent of the same phrase in Genesis 1:1. What John is saying is that "in the beginning," at the time of the creating of the universe, the Word "[continuously] was" already—not "came to be." This is clear not only from the imperfect tense of the verb but also from the fact that John declares that the Word was in the beginning with God and that "all things were made by him, and without him nothing was made which has been made" (John 1:3). In short, the Word's preexistent and continuous *being* is antecedently set off over against the *becoming* of all created things.

---

128. The Logos idea goes back to Heraclitus (sixth century B.C.), who taught that in the midst of all the constant ebb and flow in the universe there is an eternal principle of order—the Logos—that makes the world a "cosmos," that is, an ordered whole. The Stoics, faced with the common Greek dualism of form and matter, employed the notion of a seminal Logos that pervades all things to solve the problem of dualism and to provide them the basis for a rational moral life. Philo of Alexandria employed the Logos as a means of mediation between God, who is absolutely transcendent and separate from the material universe, and the universe itself. For him the Logos was both the divine pattern of the world and the power that fashioned it. In Jewish wisdom literature one may find Wisdom personified in Proverbs 8:22–31. All this led C. H. Dodd to conclude in his *The Interpretation of the Fourth Gospel* (Cambridge: Cambridge University Press, 1953), 280:

> The opening sentences . . . of the [Gospel] Prologue are clearly intelligible only when we admit that the Logos, though it carries with it the association of the Old Testament Word of the Lord, has also a meaning similar to that which it bears in Stoicism as modified by Philo, and parallel to the idea of Wisdom in other Jewish writers. It is the rational principle in the universe, its meaning, plan or purpose, conceived as a divine hypostasis in which the eternal God is revealed and active.

George Eldon Ladd in *A Theology of the New Testament* (Grand Rapids, Mich.: Eerdmans, 1974) notes, however, that never is the Logos *personalized* or is it *incarnated* in these earlier usages of the concept: "the theological use John makes of the Logos . . . can be paralleled neither in Hellenistic philosophy nor in Jewish thought" (241). Leon Morris concurs in *The Gospel According to John* (Grand Rapids, Mich.: Eerdmans, 1971), 115–26, esp. 116, 123–25.

In the second clause, the Word is both coordinated *with* God and distinguished in some sense *from* God as possessing an identity of its own. The sense in which the Word is distinguishable from God may be discerned by comparing the phrase in 1:1, ἦν πρὸς τὸν θεόν, *ēn pros ton theon*, with its counterpart in 1 John 1:2, where we read that "the Word," which was "from the beginning" (v. 1), "was with the Father" (ἦν πρὸς τὸν πατέρα, *ēn pros ton patera*). This shows that John intends by "God" in John 1:1b God the Father. The Word which stands coordinate with and yet distinguishable from God as *Father* is by implication then the preexistent Son, which means that John is thinking of the Word in personal terms. This thought is reminiscent of Hebrews 1:8–9, where the Son is both identified as himself God but distinguished from God the Father.

In the third clause, John now asserts the obvious: "And the Word was God" (KJV, RV, ASV, RSV, NASV, NIV, NKJV). That ὁ λόγος, *ho logos*, is the subject with θεός, *theos*, as the predicate nominative is evident from the fact that the former is articular while the latter is anarthrous. But the fact that θεός, *theos*, is anarthrous does not mean that it is to be construed qualitatively, that is, adjectively ("divine," as Moffatt's translation suggests) or indefinitely ("a god," as the Jehovah's Witnesses' *New World Translation* suggests). No standard Greek lexicon offers "divine" as one of the meanings of θεός, *theos*, nor does the noun become an adjective when it "sheds" its article. If John had intended an adjectival sense, he had an adjective (θεῖος, *theios*) ready at hand. That the anarthrous noun does not connote indefiniteness is evident from the recurring instances of the anarthrous θεός, *theos*, throughout the Johannine Prologue itself (John 1:6, 12, 13, 18), where in each case it is definite and its referent is God the Father.

That θεός, *theos*, is to be construed as definite in meaning is suggested by its position in the clause before the copula ἦν, *ēn*, in accordance with E. C. Colwell's observation. But that John wrote θεός, *theos*, anarthrously is also due most likely to his desire to keep the Word hypostatically distinct from the Father to whom he had just referred by τὸν θεόν, *ton theon*. If John had followed 1:1b by saying, "and ὁ θεός [*ho theos*] was the Word" or "and the Word was ὁ θεός [*ho theos*]," he would have implied a retreat from, if not a contradiction of, the clear distinction which he had just drawn in 1:2b, and thus fallen into the error later to be known as Sabellianism. Ladd concurs:

> If John had used the definite article with *theos*, he would have said that all that God is, the Logos is: an exclusive identity. As it is, he says that all the Word is, God is; but he implies that God is more than the Word.[129]

---

129. Ladd, *A Theology of the New Testament*, 242.

Here then John identifies the Word as God *(totus deus)* and by so doing attributes to him the nature or essence of deity. When John further says in 1:2 that "This One [οὗτος, *houtos*, the One whom he had just designated "God"] was in the beginning with God," and in 1:3 that "through him all things were created," the conclusion is that as God his deity is as ultimate as his distinctiveness as Son, while his distinctiveness as Son is as ultimate as his deity as God.

When John then declares that the Word, whom he had just described as eternally preexistent, uncreated, personal Son and God, "became flesh," he not only goes beyond anything in the first-century pre-Gnostic theology but also ascends to an incarnational Christology. Marshall has observed:

> the prologue of the Gospel comes to a climax in the statement that the Word who had been from the beginning with God and was active in the work of creation and was the light and life of men became flesh and dwelt among us. It is noteworthy that the subject of the passage is the Word or Logos. It is the career of the Logos which is being described, and not until verse 17 is the name Jesus Christ used for the first time, thereby identifying the Word who became flesh with the historical figure of that name. From that time onwards John ceases to use the term Logos and writes about Jesus, using his name and a variety of Jewish messianic titles to refer to him.
>
> For John, then, Jesus is undoubtedly the personal Word of God now adopting a fleshly form of existence. When we talk of incarnation, this is what is meant by it, for it is here that the New Testament offers the closest linguistic equivalent to the term "incarnation": *ho logos sarx egeneto*.[130]

John 1:18

In this verse we face a problem which we have not faced before in our appraisal of verses in which Jesus is either described or addressed as θεός, *theos*. Here any conclusions we reach must be made on the basis of determining the original reading in the Greek text. Did the original text of John 1:18 read (1) ὁ μονογενής, *ho monogenēs*, (2) ὁ μονογενὴς υἱός, *ho monogenēs huios*, (3) μονογενὴς θεός, *monogenēs theos*, or (4) ὁ μονογενὴς θεός, *ho monogenēs theos*?

The first reading, although it has in its favor the fact that it is the shortest, may be dismissed because it has no Greek manuscript support whatever. The second reading has in its favor the support of the Greek uncials A, the third corrector of C, K, a later supplement to W, X, D, Q, 063, and many late minuscule manuscripts from the Byzantine tradition. It is also found in the Old Latin, the Latin Vulgate, the

---

130. Marshall, "Incarnational Christology in the New Testament," 2–3.

Curetonian Syriac, the text of the Harclean Syriac, and the Armenian version. It is also found in about twenty church fathers. In addition, it has in its favor the fact that, apart from John 1:14 where it stands alone, in the other three places where μονογενής, *monogenēs*, occurs in the Johannine literature, it appears in a construction with υἱός, *huios* (John 3:16, 18; 1 John 4:9). But this reading has three strikes against it. First, on the basis of the text-critical canon that "manuscripts are to be weighed, not counted," the textual support for this reading, in comparison with the two remaining readings, is not impressive, being found mainly in inferior and late manuscripts. Second, the fact that it is found in some significant church fathers is not a substantive argument in its favor, inasmuch as the Ante-Nicene Fathers tended to "follow the analogy of the versions," υἱός, *huios*, being "one of the numerous Ante-Nicene readings of the 'Western type' . . . [which fail to] approve themselves as original in comparison with the alternative readings."[131] Third, while it can be readily understood, if θεός, *theos*, were the original reading, how υἱός, *huios*, could have arisen, namely, through the scribal tendency to conform a strange reading to a more common one (in this case, to the formula in John 3:16, 18, and 1 John 4:9), it is difficult to explain why a scribe would have changed υἱός, *huios*, to θεός, *theos*.

The two remaining readings, both supporting an original θεός, *theos*, differ only in that the former omits the article while the latter retains it before μονογενής, *monogenēs*. The manuscript support for the former is Bodmer Papyrus 66, the original hand of ℵ, B, the original hand of C, and L, plus the Syriac Peshitta, the marginal reading of the Harclean Syriac, the Roman Ethiopic, the Diatesseron, and about seventeen church fathers, including the heretical Valentinians and Arius. The manuscript evidence for the latter is Bodmer Papyrus 75, the third hand of ℵ, the Greek minuscule 33 (the best of the cursives), and the Coptic Bohairic. Of these two, the former has the better manuscript support. But the *combined* weight of both lends exceedingly strong support for the originality of θεός, *theos*, in John 1:18. It has also in its favor the fact that it is the harder reading (the *lectio difficilior*). Because the nature of the problem calls for a judgment of evidence, the final decision will always have an element of uncertainty about it, but the evidence is weighty that θεός, *theos*, is the original reading. Indeed, if it were not for the christological

---

131. F. J. A. Hort, *Two Dissertations* (Cambridge: Macmillan, 1876), 7–8. Hort's dissertation laid the groundwork for virtually all subsequent text–critical work on John 1:18 and provided the single greatest impulse toward the conclusion that θεός, *theos*, is the original reading. What is most telling as an indication of his careful scholarship is that Hort did his work without the advantage of having the two great Bodmer papyri 66 and 75, the later discovery of which vindicated his conclusion. Bruce Metzger writes: "With the acquisition of p[66] and p[75], both of which read θεός, *theos*, the external support of this reading has been notably strengthened" (*Textual Commentary*, 198).

implications in the reading itself ("[the] only [Son], [himself] God") one suspects that the evidence would be sufficient to carry the field of scholarly opinion. Even so, there is a trend in modern translations to adopt θεός, *theos*, as the original reading (NASV, NIV). Therefore, I would suggest that John 1:18 be translated as follows:

> God no man has seen at any time;
> the only [Son], [himself] God,
> who is continually in the bosom of the Father—
> that One revealed him.

The present participle ὁ ὤν, *ho ōn*, in the third line indicates a continuing state of being: "who is continually in the bosom of the Father." Leon Morris comments:

> The copula "is" expresses a continuing union. The only begotten is continually in the bosom of the Father. When the Word became flesh His cosmic activities did not remain in abeyance until the time of the earthly life was ended. There are mysteries here that man cannot plumb, but we must surely hold that the incarnation meant the adding of something to what the Word was doing, rather than the cessation of most of His activities.[132]

Thus very probably here in John 1:18 we have another instance of θεός, *theos*, as a title for Christ, and the context clearly shows that John regarded Jesus as God the Son incarnate.

Miscellanea

John's Gospel explicates Jesus' self-understanding particularly in his "Son of God" sayings (see John 5:17–26; 10:30, 36), his "Son of Man" sayings (see 3:13; 6:62), and his "I am" sayings (see 8:24, 58). There is also corroborative evidence supporting Christ's deity in John's record of his "works" and his report of Jesus' disciples' testimonies respecting him (see 1:34, 49; 6:69; 11:27; 16:30; 20:28). Now in that John incorporated these data in his Gospel, we may assume that they reflect his own Christology as well, for he expressly declares that he wrote what he did in order to bring his readers to faith in Jesus as "the Christ, the Son of God" (John 20:31). Surely, for example, the high incarnational Christology in his Prologue reflects his personal Christology. But there are three other features in John's Gospel which we have not yet treated in any direct way that afford still further insight into his personal Christology.

---

132. Morris, *The Gospel According to John*, 114.

First, there are the two paragraphs in John 3:16–21 and 3:31–36, which may be in their contexts continuing remarks by Jesus and by John the Baptist respectively (the NIV seems to construe them as such), but which may be reflections by John the Evangelist himself on the themes touched upon by Jesus and the Baptist. If the latter case is correct, we have in both instances discourses by John upon the transcendent nature and origin of Jesus. In 3:16–21, he speaks of Jesus as God's "unique Son" (ὁ υἱὸς ὁ μονογενής, *ho huios ho monogenēs*, 3:16, 18), whom God "sent into the world" (3:17), who himself, as the Light, "has come into the world" (3:19), and through faith in whom eternal life is mediated (3:16, 18). In 3:31–36, the same themes are advanced: Jesus is God's Son whom God "sent" (3:34) and who may be thus characterized as himself "the One who comes from above" (3:31a) and "the One who comes from heaven" (3:31b). What Jesus declares is what he himself has seen and heard in heaven (3:32). He is "over all" (3:31) in that his Father "has given all things into his hand" (3:35), including the Spirit without limit (3:34). And, as in the former paragraph, the destiny of men and women turns upon their relation to him (3:36). These features—the "descent" of Christ from the supernal world, the experiential character of his knowledge of the things of heaven, his identification with God so that to hear him is to seal the veracity of God, his all-comprehensive authority in the sphere of revelation, the function of faith in him as mediating eternal life while unbelief results in exclusion from life and permanent abiding under the wrath of God—these feature all underscore both the preexistence and the absolutely transcendent character of Jesus Christ.

Second, when this perception of Jesus is coupled with John's citation of Isaiah 6:10 in 12:40, bringing out the divine sovereignty in salvation and reprobation, and concerning which citation John declares: "These things Isaiah said because he saw his [the preincarnate Son's] glory, and spoke concerning him," one must conclude that the transcendent character of Jesus Christ is the transcendence of Yahweh himself, for it was "Yahweh, seated on a throne, high and exalted" (Isa. 6:1; see 57:15) whom Isaiah reports that he saw. As Leon Morris remarks:

> John sees in the words of the prophet primarily a reference to the glory of Christ. Isaiah spoke these things "because he saw his glory." The words of Isaiah 6:3 refer to the glory of Yahweh, but John puts no hard and fast distinction between the two. To him it is plain that Isaiah had in mind the glory revealed in Christ.[133]

This being so, it should not go unnoticed that it was the preincarnate Christ who commissioned and sent Isaiah on his prophetic mission, a fact which Jesus himself noted in Matthew 23:34 (see Luke 11:49) and to which Peter alludes in 1 Peter 1:11.

---

133. Ibid., 605.

Third, since for John the glory of Christ is equivalent to the glory of Yahweh himself, it is highly probable that when John refers to Christ as "the Lord" (ὁ κύριος, *ho kyrios*) in the narrative of his Gospel (see 4:1; 6:23; 11:2; 20:20; 21:12), he intends the title, used as it is in the Septuagint to translate the divine name Yahweh, in its most eminent, that is to say, in its divine, Yahwistic sense.

There can be no doubt that John's Gospel Christology is incarnational in the highest conceivable sense, Jesus Christ being true God and true man. No view of John's Christology which would claim otherwise can claim to be exegetically sound.

John's Epistolary Christology

It is immediately evident from even a cursory reading of John's letters that "the same concept of incarnation which one finds in the Gospel is present in 1 and 2 John, and indeed it is the principal Christological idea in these Epistles."[134] This is plain from the fact that John defends (1) the dual confession that Jesus is both the Christ (1 John 2:22; 5:1) and the Son of God (1 John 2:22–23; 4:15; 5:5; see 1:3, 7; 2:24; 3:8, 23; 4:9, 14; 5:9, 11, 12, 13, 20), and (2) the incarnational prerequisite that God the Father "sent" his Son into the world (1 John 4:9, 10, 14), and that, having been "sent," the Son was "sent" in such a way that he "came in the flesh" (1 John 4:2; 2 John 7; see 1 John 5:6, 20) and thus was "manifested" to men (1 John 1:2 [twice]; 3:8) in such a way that, while still "the Eternal Life, which was with the Father" from the beginning (1 John 1:1–2), he could be heard, seen with the human eye, gazed upon, and touched by human hands. So intense is John's conviction regarding the necessity of a real incarnation that he makes the confession, "Jesus Christ has come in the flesh," a test of orthodoxy—to confess the same is to be "of God"; to deny it is to be "not of God" but "of Antichrist" (1 John 4:2–3). The incarnate Christ was also sinless (3:5).

1 John 5:20

One verse in 1 John requires special notice, for in it John quite likely intends to employ θεός, *theos,* as he does in John 1:1, 18, and 20:28, as a christological title. Translated literally, 1 John 5:20 reads:

> And we know that the Son of God has come, and he has given us understanding in order that we may know the True One. And we are in the True One in his Son Jesus Christ. This is the true God and eternal life.

---

134. Marshall, "Incarnational Christology in the New Testament," 5.

The issue is to determine who it is that John had in mind when he wrote, "This is the true God and eternal life," the Father or the Son. I am personally persuaded that a better case can be made for understanding θεός, *theos*, as referring to the Son.

The case for the Father being the referent of "the true God" highlights the following features in the verse. First, reference to the Father is indirectly but clearly present in the genitives "of God" and the "his" following the two occurrences of "the Son." Second, it is likely that the two occurrences of "true One" (τὸν ἀληθινόν, τῷ ἀληθινῷ, *ton alēthinon, tō alēthinō*) both refer to the Father because (1) it would be a harsh rendering to interpret John as saying that "he [the Son] has given us understanding that we may know the true One [that is, himself]"; (2) the Father clearly seems to be the referent of the second occurrence of "true One" because of the αὐτοῦ, *autou*, in the phrase immediately following it, "in *his* Son" (the NIV rendering, "even in his Son," implies the presence of a καί, *kai*, before the prepositional phrase, but there is no καί, *kai*, in the Greek text); (3) it is truer to Johannine thought to represent the Son's messianic mission as a revelation of the Father than as a revelation of himself (see John 1:18; 17:3–4). These features, it is urged, since it is highly unlikely that John would have referred to two different persons so closely in the same verse by the one adjective "true," point to the Father as the referent of John's phrase "the true God." This would accord with John's clear reference to the Father as "the only true God" in John 17:3. Accordingly, John's assertion at the end of 5:20, "This is the true God and eternal life," it is urged, has as its referent the Father. Both exegetically and theologically, this interpretation is possible, and it has been espoused by Brooke (ICC), Westcott, and Dodd. Murray J. Harris also urges this interpretation in his *Jesus as God*.[135]

But there are four grammatical or exegetical considerations which tell against this interpretation. First, the nearest possible antecedent to οὗτός, *houtos*, ("This One") is the immediately preceding phrase "Jesus Christ," and it is a generally sound exegetically principle to find the antecedent of a demonstrative pronoun in the nearest possible noun to it unless there are compelling reasons for not doing so. There are no such reasons here, as there are in the oft-cited counter examples of 1 John 2:22 or 2 John 7, which would require that one go further forward in the sentence to "his" or to "true One" or to "God." (The suggestion of some critics that "in his Son, Jesus Christ" is a gloss and should therefore be omitted, this being suggested in order to make "the true One" the nearest antecedent, has no manuscript support and is a mere expediency.)

Second, to choose the more distant antecedent—that is, the Father, injects a tautology into the verse, for one does not need to be informed that the Father, who

---

135. Murray J. Harris, *Jesus as God* (Grand Rapids, Mich.: Baker, 1992), 239–53.

has just been twice identified already as the "true One," is "the true God," whereas John advances the thought and avoids the tautology if he is saying that Jesus Christ is "the true God." It is true that Jesus describes the Father as "the only true God" in John 17:3, but there the Father has not been previously identified as the "true One."

Third, both the singular οὗτός, *houtos,* and the fact that "true God" and "eternal life" both stand under the regimen of the single article before "God," thereby binding the two predicates closely together on the pattern, for example, of "the true God who is (also for us) eternal life" (unless both are *titles* of a person, which seems preferable for this avoids placing a person and an abstract concept under the regimen of a single article) indicate that *one* person is before the mind of the apostle. This eliminates the suggestion of some that the first title refers to the Father and the second refers to the Son. And while it is true that the Father has life in himself (John 5:26; 6:57) and gives to men eternal life (1 John 5:11), he is nowhere designated "the Eternal Life" as is Jesus in 1 John 1:2 (see also John 1:4; 6:57; 11:25; 14:6). "This predicate fits Jesus better than it fits God," writes Raymond E. Brown.[136] But then if Jesus Christ is the referent of "Eternal Life," and if both titles refer to one person, it would follow that he is also the referent of "the true God."

Fourth, while John reports that Jesus describes the Father as "the only true God" (John 17:3), he himself either describes or records that Jesus describes himself as "the true Light" (John 1:9; 1 John 2:8; see John 1:14, 17), "the true Bread" (John 6:32), "the true Vine" (John 15:1), "the true One" (Rev. 3:7; 19:11), "the true Witness" (Rev. 3:14), and "the true Sovereign" (Rev. 6:10). We have already established that John is not at all reticent about designating Christ as "God" (see John 1:1, 1:18, 20:28). So just as "the true One" can refer as a title both to the Father (1 John 5:20) and to the Son (Rev. 3:7), there is nothing that would preclude John from bringing together the adjective "true," which is used of Jesus elsewhere, and the noun "God" which he himself has used of Jesus, and applying both in their combined form as "the true God" to Jesus Christ. These considerations make it highly probable that 1 John 5:20 is another occurrence of θεός, *theos,* as a christological title. Athanasius, Cyril of Alexandria, Jerome, Bede, Luther, and Calvin in earlier times, and Charles Hodge, Bengel, R. L. Dabney, B. B. Warfield, Raymond E. Brown, F. F. Bruce, R. Bultmann, I. H. Marshall, John Murray, Olshausen, Schnackenburg, and the translators of the NIV, to name only a few in more modern times, have so interpreted John here.

Portraying Jesus Christ, the Son of the Father, then, as just "the true God and Eternal Life" (1 John 5:20) and the Co-source with the Father of the blessings of

---

136. Raymond E. Brown, *The Epistles of John,* Anchor Bible (Garden City, N.Y.: Doubleday, 1982), 626.

grace, mercy, and peace (2 John 3), who "came in the flesh" and who also came "through water and blood, not with the water only but with the water and with the blood," John asserts a "real and lasting union between the Son of God and the flesh of Jesus"[137] from the very beginning of Jesus' life and throughout his ministry, including even the event of his death. Presupposing the same concept of incarnation as is found in John 1:1–3, 14, John leaves no room for a docetic or an adoptionist Christology. Only the real incarnation of the Son of God satisfies all the doctrinal affirmations of these letters.

There is no explicit Christology in 3 John, the only allusion to Christ being the reference to "the Name" in verse 7. But about this term Westcott writes: "From the contexts it is evident that 'the Name' is 'Jesus Christ' . . . , or, as it is written at length, 'Jesus Christ, the Son of God' (John xx.31; I John iv.15). This 'Name' is in essence the sum of the Christian Creed. . . . When analyzed it reveals the triune 'Name' into which the Christian is baptized, Matt. xxviii.19."[138]

John's Christology in the Revelation

The nature of the Revelation as "apocalyptic," being unique within the New Testament corpus, one should not be surprised to find its Christology to be more "marvelous," if not more "other-worldly," than elsewhere in the New Testament. But this is not to suggest that its representation of Christ differs in any essential way from the Christology of Christ himself or of Paul, or of the Synoptic Evangelists, or of the writers of the General Epistles, or of that of the rest of the Johannine corpus. But it must be acknowledged that its Christology is more consistently "advanced," to use Beasley-Murray's term,[139] in that it portrays Christ almost singularly from the perspective of his state of exaltation.

The customary names and titles for Jesus are still present—"Jesus" (1:9 [twice]; 12:17; 14:12; 17:6; 19:10 [twice]; 20:4; 22:16), "Christ" (20:4, 6; see also "his [the Lord's] Christ," 11:15; "his [God's] Christ," 12:10), "Jesus Christ" (1:1, 2, 5), "Lord" (11:8; probably 14:13; see also "the Lord of lords," 17:14; 19:16; and "the Lord's Day," 1:10), "Lord Jesus" (22:20, 21), "a son of man," meaning "a man" (1:13; 14:14; see Dan. 7:13–14), "the Son of God" (once, in 2:18; but see "My Father," 2:27; 3:5, 21; and "his God and Father," 1:6), and "the Word of God" (19:13). But by far, the most common (twenty-eight times), almost personal, "new" name which John (1:1, 9; 22:8) uses for the

---

137. Marshall, "Incarnational Christology in the New Testament," 5.
138. B.F. Westcott, *The Epistles of St. John*, 3d ed. (London: Macmillan, 1892), 238–39; see also Warfield, *Lord of Glory*, 274.
139. G. R. Beasley-Murray, *The Book of Revelation* (London: Oliphants, 1974), 24.

glorified Christ is "the Lamb" (ἀρνίον, arnion, 5:6, 8, 12, 13; 6:1, 16; 7:9, 10, 14, 17; 12:11; 13:8; 14:1, 4 [twice], 10; 15:3; 17:14 [twice]; 19:7, 9; 21:9, 14, 22, 23, 27; 22:1, 3), a representation found elsewhere in the New Testament only at John 1:29, 36, and 1 Peter 1:19 (see Acts 8:32) where the word is ἀμνός, amnos. What is remarkable about this title in the Revelation is the fact that, while "the Lamb" is identified as "the Lamb that was slain" (5:6, 9, 12; 13:8), with allusions to his death in such an expression as "the blood of the Lamb" (7:14; 12:11), and while the term itself, as Warfield notes, always carries the "implied reference to the actual sacrifice,"[140] never is the One so designated still a figure of meekness in a state or condition of humility. Isbon T. Beckwith observes:

> [Lamb] is the name given to him in the most august scenes. As the object of the worship offered by the hosts of heaven and earth, chapts. 4–5; as the unveiler of the destinies of the ages, chapts. 5–6; as one enthroned, before whom and to whom the redeemed render the praise of their salvation, 7:9ff.; as the controller of the book of life, 13:8; as the Lord of the hosts on mount Zion, 14:1; as the victor over the hosts of Antichrist, 17:14; as the spouse of the glorified Church, 19:7; as the temple and light of the new Jerusalem, 21:22f.; as the sharer in the throne of God, 22:1,—Christ is called the Lamb. Nowhere in the occurrence of the name is there evident allusion to the figure of *meekness and gentleness* in suffering.[141]

In other words, if Jesus is "the Lamb" in the Revelation, it is as the "Lamb glorified" that he is depicted. And it is this depiction of Christ as the glorified Lamb which is dominant throughout the Apocalypse.

Of course, he is certainly a *human* Messiah still, as the "male child" (Rev. 12:5, 13), the "Lion of the tribe of Judah" (5:5), and the "Root and Offspring of David" (5:5; 22:16) who is capable of dying, but who by his exaltation is the "Firstborn from the dead" (1:5), and thus the "Ruler of the kings of the earth" (1:5), indeed, the "King of kings and Lord of lords" (19:16; see 17:14). But while he is set off over against God in that he is the Son of God (2:18) and the Word of God (19:13), and in the sense that God is his Father (1:6; 2:27; 3:5, 21; 14:1), indeed, even in the sense that God is his God (1:6; 3:2, 12; see 11:15; 12:10) who gives to him both the authority to rule (2:27) and the Revelation itself to show to his servants (1:1), he is represented as being himself divine. Beckwith observes again in this connection:

> Nowhere else are found these wonderful scenes revealing to the eye and ear the majesty of Christ's ascended state, and these numerous utterances expressing in

---

140. Warfield, *Lord of Glory*, 290.
141. Isbon T. Beckwith, *The Apocalypse of John* (1919; reprint, Grand Rapids, Mich.: Baker, 1967), 315.

terms applicable to God alone the truth of his divine nature and power. He is seen in the first vision in a form having the semblance of a man, yet glorified with attributes by which the Old Testament writers have sought to portray the glory of God; his hair is white as snow, his face shines with the dazzling light of the sun, his eyes are a flame of fire, his voice as the thunder of many waters; he announces himself as eternal, as one who though he died is the essentially living One, having all power over death, 1:13–18. He appears in the court of heaven as coequal with God in the adoration offered by the highest hosts of heaven and by all the world, 5:6–14. He is seen coming forth on the clouds as the judge and arbiter of the world, 14:14–16. Wearing crowns and insignia which mark him as King of kings and Lord of lords, he leads out the armies of heaven to the great battle with Antichrist, 19:11–21. In keeping with these scenes, attributes and prerogatives understood to belong to God only are assigned to him either alone or as joined with God; he is the Alpha and Omega, the first and the last, the beginning and the end, 22:13, 1:17, 2:8—a designation which God also utters of himself, 1:8, see Is. 44:6, 48:12; worship is offered to him in common with God, 7:10, 5:13—a worship which angelic beings are forbidden to receive, 19:10; doxologies are raised to him as to God, 1:6; the throne of God is his throne, the priests of God are his priests, 3:21, 22:1, 20:6; life belongs essentially to him as to God, compare 1:18 with 4:9, 10.[142]

In this same regard H. B. Swete writes:

> What is the relation of Christ, in His glorified state, to God? (i) He has the prerogatives of God. He searches men's hearts (2:23); He can kill and restore to life (1:18; 2:23); He receives a worship which is rendered without distinction to God (5:13); His priests are also priests of God (20:6); He occupies one throne with God (22:1, 3), and shares one sovereignty (11:15). (ii) Christ receives the titles of God. He is the Living One (1:18), the Holy and the True (3:7), the Alpha and the Omega, the First and the Last, the Beginning and the End (22:13). (iii) Passages which in the Old Testament relate to God are without hesitation applied to Christ, e.g., Deut. 10:17 (Apoc. 17:14), Prov. 3:12 (Apoc. 3:19), Dan. 7:9 (Apoc. 1:14), Zech. 4:10 (Apoc. 5:6). Thus the writer seems either to coordinate or to identify Christ with God. Yet he is certainly not conscious of any tendency to ditheism, for his book . . . is rigidly monotheistic; nor, on the other hand, is he guilty of confusing the two Persons.[143]

Beasley-Murray likewise affirms:

---

142. Ibid., 312–13.
143. H. B. Swete, *The Apocalypse of St. John*, 3d ed. (London: Macmillan, 1911), clxii.

Constantly the attributes of God are ascribed to Christ, as in the opening vision of the first chapter, which is significantly a vision of Christ and not of God. The lineaments of the risen Lord are those of the Ancient of Days and of his angel in the book of Daniel (chs. 7 and 10). Christ is confessed as Alpha and Omega (22:13), as God is also (1:8). The implications of the claim are drawn out in the book as a whole. . . . In the closing vision of the city of God . . . God and the Lamb are united as Lord of the kingdom and source of its blessedness. It is especially noteworthy that John depicts the throne of God and the Lamb as the source of the river of water of life in the city, thereby conveying the notion of a single throne, a single rule, and a single source of life. He adds, 'his servants shall worship him; they shall see his face, and his name shall be on their foreheads' (22:3f.). In the context it is difficult to interpret the pronoun 'his' as meaning anything other than 'God and the Lamb' as a unity. The Lamb remains the mediator . . . , yet he is inseparable from the God who enacts his works . . . through him.[144]

John's Revelation thus unites its "other worldly" witness to the prior consentient testimony of the entire New Testament in support of the full and unabridged deity of the Son of God.

Old Testament Yahweh Passages Applied to Jesus

The New Testament writers show no hesitancy in applying to Christ Old Testament descriptions and privileges that are reserved specifically for Yahweh. For instance, (1) Moses' description of Yahweh as "King of kings" (Deut. 10:17) John applies to Christ (Rev. 17:14; 19:16); (2) the author of Hebrews applies the entirety of Psalm 102:25–27 to him (1:10–12); (3) Proverbs 18:10 provides the background for Peter's assertion in Acts 4:12; (4) Joel's summons to trust in Yahweh (2:32) Paul employs to summon men to faith in Christ (Rom. 10:13); (5) when Isaiah looked upon Yahweh (Isa. 6:1–3), according to John he was beholding the glory of the preincarnate Son of God (John 12:40–41); (6) Isaiah's call to sanctify Yahweh in the heart (8:12–13) Peter applies directly to Christ—he is the one who is to be sanctified as Lord in the heart (1 Pet. 3:14–15); (7) Isaiah's representation of Yahweh as a stone that causes men to stumble and a rock that makes them fall (8:14) Paul applies to Christ (Rom. 9:32–33); (8) Yahweh, whose coming would be preceded by Yahweh's forerunner (Isa. 40:3; Mal. 3:1; 4:5), is equated with Christ (Matt. 3:3; 11:10; Mark 1:2–3; Luke 1:16–17; 3:4; John 1:23); (9) Jesus himself employs Yahweh's words in Isaiah 43:10 and 45:22 to summon men to be his witnesses and to rest in him (Acts 1:8; Matt. 11:28); (10) Isaiah's description of Yahweh as "the first and the last" (44:6) John employs to describe the

---

144. Beasley-Murray, *Revelation*, 24–25.

glorified Christ (Rev. 2:8; 22:12–13); (11) Yahweh, "before whom every knee shall bow and by whom every mouth shall swear (Isa. 45:23), Paul identifies as Christ (Rom. 14:10; Phil. 2:10); and (12) Yahweh, the pierced One upon whom men would look and mourn (Zech. 12:10), John tells us is the Christ (John 19:37).

A Summary of Θεός, *Theos,* as a Christological Title

In light of this overwhelming amount of evidence for Jesus' full, unabridged deity, it is not at all surprising, as noted, that upon occasion the New Testament writers actually refer to him as θεός, *theos,* the title normally reserved for the Father. For example,

1. Exactly one week after Jesus' resurrection, in the presence of the other ten disciples, Thomas worshiped him by his acclamation: "[You are] my Lord and my God" (John 20:28).

2. In his letter to the Romans Paul speaks of him as "over all, the ever-blessed God" (Rom. 9:5).

3. In his letter to Titus Paul speaks of Christ as "our great God and Savior" (Titus 2:13).

4. In his farewell address to the Ephesians elders at Miletus, Paul charged: "Be shepherds of the church of God which he bought with his own blood" (Acts 20:28).

5. In his second letter Peter refers to him as "our God and Savior Jesus Christ" (2 Pet. 1:1).

6. In the Letter to the Hebrews God himself is represented as referring to the Son as "God" (Heb. 1:8).

7. In the first verse of his Gospel John informs us: "In the beginning was the Word, and the Word was with God, and the Word was God," and then he writes: "And the Word became flesh, and dwelt among us" (John 1:14).

8. In John 1:18, the closing verse of his prologue, John writes: "No one has seen God at any time. But his only [Son, himself] God, who is in the bosom of the Father, he has made him known."

9. In 1 John 5:20, John writes: "we are . . . in his Son, Jesus Christ. This One is the true God and Eternal Life."

Thus the New Testament intends to teach that Jesus Christ is divine in the same sense that God the Father is divine.

THE DEITY AND PERSONAL SUBSISTENCE OF THE HOLY SPIRIT

The third person of the Godhead is referred to in Scripture in many striking ways. In the Old Testament, in addition to the numerous references to him simply as "the Spirit of God" (Gen. 1:2 *et al.*) and "the Spirit of Yahweh" (Judg. 3:10 *et al.*), he is designated "the Spirit of the Lord God" (Isa. 61:1), God's "good Spirit" (Neh. 9:20), God's "Holy Spirit" (Ps. 51:11), Yahweh's "Holy Spirit" (Isa. 63:10, 11), "the Spirit of wisdom and of understanding" (Isa. 11:2), "the Spirit of counsel and of power" (Isa. 11:2), "the Spirit of knowledge and of the fear of the Lord" (Isa. 11:2), and "the Spirit of grace and supplication" (Zech. 12:10).

In the New Testament, in addition to the numerous references to him as "the Spirit of God" (Matt. 3:16 *et al.*), he is designated as "the Spirit of the living God" (2 Cor. 3:3), "the sevenfold Spirit of God" (Rev. 1:4; 3:1; 4:5; 5:6; see Isa. 11:2), "the Spirit of your Father" (Matt. 10:20), "the Spirit of him who raised Jesus from the dead" (Rom. 8:11), "the Spirit of [God's] Son" (Gal. 4:6), "the Spirit of Christ" (Rom. 8:9; 1 Pet. 1:11), "the Spirit of Jesus Christ" (Phil. 1:19), "the Holy Spirit" (Luke 11:13), "the Holy Spirit of promise" (Eph. 1:13), "the eternal Spirit" (Heb. 9:14), "the Spirit of truth" (John 14:17; 15:26 16:13), "the Spirit of sonship [or adoption]" (Rom. 8:15), "the Spirit of life" (Rev. 11:11), "the Spirit of grace" (Heb. 10:29), "the Spirit of wisdom and revelation" (Eph. 1:17), "the Spirit of glory and of God" (1 Pet. 4:14), and the "Counselor [or Comforter]" (John 14:16, 26; 15:26; 16:7).

In several other ways, in addition to these titles, the Scriptures affirm the full, unabridged deity of the Holy Spirit:

1. He is identified as God: according to Peter, when Ananias "lied to the Holy Spirit," he was "lying to God" (Acts 5:3–4).

2. He is identified as the Yahweh of the Old Testament: (a) what Isaiah reports that Yahweh said in Isaiah 6:9–10, Paul asserts that the Holy Spirit said (Acts 28:25–27), (b) what the Psalmist puts in the mouth of Yahweh in Psalm 95:7–11, the author of Hebrews puts in the mouth of the Holy Spirit (Heb. 3:7–9), and (c) where Leviticus 26:11–12 foretells Yahweh's "dwelling with his people," Paul, citing the Leviticus passage, speaks of the church in 2 Corinthians 6:16 as the antitypical "temple of the living God" with whom Yahweh dwells. And how does Yahweh dwell in his church? In the person of the Holy Spirit (who, according to Romans 8:9, is also both the Spirit of God and the Spirit of Christ).

3. Though distinguished from them, he is represented as equal with the Father and the Son in the great Trinitarian passages of the New Testament (Matt. 3:16; 28:19; 1 Cor. 12:4–6; 2 Cor. 13:14; Eph. 2:18; 4:4–6; 1 Pet. 1:2). In Matthew 28:19 he is, along with the Son, brought into and included within the divine Name itself, surely divine since it is the "name" of the Father.

4. He possesses divine attributes: he is eternal (Heb. 9:14; see also "with you forever" in John 14:16), omnipresent (Ps. 139:7–10), omnipotent (Ps. 104:30; Rom. 15:19), omniscient (Isa. 40:13–14; 1 Cor. 2:10–11), and sovereign (John 3:8).

5. He comes from the Father (John 15:26), and is sent by the Father and the Son (John 16:7; 14:26; see also John 14:18; Acts 2:33; 16:7; Rom. 8:9–10).

6. Accordingly, he does divine works: he creates (Gen. 1:2; Job 26:13a; 33:4; Ps. 104:30a), regenerates (Ezek. 37:1–14; John 3:5–6; Titus 3:5), resurrects (Ezek. 37:12–14; Rom. 8:11), and exercises divine authority in Christ's church (Acts 13:2, 4; 15:28; 16:6–7). More specifically, he effected Mary's virginal conception (Matt. 1:18–20; Luke 1:35), he anointed and empowered Christ throughout his earthly ministry and in the hour of his death (Isa. 11:1–2; 42:1–3; 61:1–2; Matt. 12:28; Luke 4:1–18; John 1:32–33; 3:34; Acts 10:38; Heb 9:14), glorifies Christ (John 16:13–14), inspired the Scriptures (John 14:26; 16:13–14; Eph. 6:17; 1 Pet. 1:11; 2 Pet. 1:20–21), convicts the world of sin, righteousness, and judgment (John 16:8–11), invites men to come to Christ (Rev. 22:17), builds the church (Eph. 2:22), "comes upon" and indwells believers as the "seal," the "down payment," and "firstfruits" of their full inheritance (Joel 2:28; Ezek. 36:24–27; John 7:38; Acts 2:17; 8:15–17; 10:44–45; 11:15; Rom. 8:9–11, 23; 2 Cor. 1:22; Eph. 1:13–14; 4:30), baptizes (that is, regenerates; John 3:8), which leads to faith in Christ (1 John 5:1), dominion over sin (1 John 3:9; 5:18), works of righteousness (1 John 2:29), and love for others (1 John 4:7), induces believers to their perception of Jesus as Lord (1 Cor. 12:3) and to their filial consciousness of God as their Father (Rom. 8:15–16; Gal. 4:6), empowers believers to boldness, love, and self-discipline (Acts 4:29; 2 Tim. 1:7), sanctifies (1 Cor. 6:11; Rom. 15:16; Gal. 5:16–18), produces holy fruit in the believer (Gal. 5:22–23), gives "gifts" to the believer (1 Cor. 12:1–11), intercedes for them in their ignorance (Rom. 8:26–27), and raises them to glory from the dead (Rom. 8:11).

Thus the Holy Spirit is represented in Holy Scripture as fully divine. The more pertinent issue relative to the Holy Spirit and the doctrine of the Trinity is whether Holy Scripture represents the Holy Spirit not only as personal but also as a person distinct from the persons of the Father and the Son. This I believe it does, for the following reasons:

1. Personal pronouns are used of him (John 15:26; 16:13–14; see particularly Acts 10:19-20: "the Spirit said to him, 'Simon, three men are looking for you. . . . I have sent them' " (see 11:12); Acts 13:2: "the Holy Spirit said, 'Set apart for me Barnabas and Saul for the work to which I have called them.' ");

2. Personal properties are ascribed to him, such as understanding or wisdom (Isa. 11:2; 1 Cor. 2:10–11), will (1 Cor. 12:11; John 3:8), and power (Isa. 11:2; Mic. 3:8; Acts 10:38; Rom. 15:13; Eph. 3:16).

3. Personal activities are ascribed to him: he speaks (Mark 13:11b; Acts 13:2; 21:11; 1 Tim. 4:1; Heb. 3:7; 10:15), he reveals (Luke 2:26; 1 Pet. 1:11), he guides into all truth (John 16:13), he teaches (Luke 12:12; John 14:26), he comforts, counsels, helps, and loves the believer (John 14:16, 26; 15:26; 16:7; Rom. 15:30; James 4:5), he encourages (Acts 9:31), he warns (1 Tim. 4:1), he appoints to office (Acts 13:2; 20:28), he may be grieved (Isa. 63:10; Eph. 4:30), may be lied to (Acts 5:3), may be resisted (Acts 7:31), and may be blasphemed (Matt. 12:31–32).

These data show that the Holy Spirit is, like Christ, a divine Person. Thus we have to do with three divine Persons in the Godhead—God the Father (for whose deity we have offered no separate argument since it has never been seriously questioned in the church), God the Son, and God the Holy Spirit.

★ ★ ★ ★ ★

Today many modern "doctors of the church" would seek to liberate the church from its "bondage to all arcane models of vertical transcendence." But the Christian need have no doubts that the biblical evidence for the doctrine of the Trinity is on his side: the Bible knows no other God than the one living and true God who has eternally existed as the Father, the Son, and the Holy Spirit—*tres personae in una substantia*. It was his recognition of this fact that lay behind the statement of Gregory of Nazianzus (c. 329–c. 389): "I cannot think of the One, but I am immediately surrounded with the splendor of the Three; nor can I clearly discover the Three, but I am suddenly carried back to the One."[145] John Calvin also declared that God "so proclaims Himself the sole God as to offer Himself to be contemplated clearly in three Persons. Unless we grasp these, only the bare and empty name of God flits about in our brains, to the exclusion of the true God" (*Institutes,* I. xiii, 2). Moreover, if the triune Personhood of God is given its proper place in biblical soteriology, the several aspects of salvation, as we shall see, fit together "hand in glove" and form one glorious and harmonious whole; if one rejects the triune Personhood of God, both Old and New Testament salvation—particularly the latter—is left in total confusion. And one loses all but an empty perception of God to boot.

The church of Jesus Christ, accordingly, has gladly included within its hymnody such beloved hymns as Reginald Heber's

> Holy, Holy, Holy, Lord God Almighty!
>   Early in the morning our song shall rise to thee;
> Holy, holy, Holy! Merciful and Mighty!
>   God in three Persons, blessed Trinity!

and the anonymous hymn:

> Come, thou Almighty King, Help us thy Name to sing,
>   Help us to praise:
> Father, all glorious, O'er all victorious,
>   Come and reign over us, Ancient of Days.

---

145. Gregory of Nazianzus, *Oratio* 41, *Patrologia Graeca*, ed. by J.P. Migne (Paris, 1857–1866), 36, 417.

Come, thou Incarnate Word, Gird on thy mighty sword,
    Our prayer attend:
Come, and thy people bless, and give thy Word success;
    Spirit of Holiness, On us descend.

Come, Holy Comforter, Thy sacred witness bear
    In this glad hour:
Thou who almighty art, Now rule in every heart,
    And ne'er from us depart, Spirit of pow'r.

To the great One in Three Eternal praises be,
    Hence evermore.
His sovereign majesty May we in glory see,
    And to eternity Love and adore.

CHAPTER NINE

The Trinity in the Creeds

ANALYSIS OF THE NICENE CREED AND ITS CHRISTOLOGY

IT WAS IN LIGHT of such biblical data as we have surveyed in the previous chapter that the Christians of the first three centuries—as monotheistic in their outlook as the ancient Israelites, and who in fact believed that they were worshiping the God of Israel when they worshiped God the Father, the Lord Jesus Christ, and the Holy Spirit—began to formulate their doctrine of God in Trinitarian terms. That is to say, the early church's Trinitarianism was a deduction from its conviction that Jesus Christ and the Holy Spirit were both divine persons. The formulating process itself, precipitated in the first three centuries particularly by the emergence of second-century Gnosticism and the Logos Christology, by third-century Sabellianism and early fourth-century Arianism, brought the church to a basic but real crystallization of the doctrine in the Nicene Creed of A.D. 325. That creed of the First Ecumenical Council reads as follows:

> We believe in one God the Father, Almighty, Creator of all things visible and invisible;
> And in one Lord Jesus Christ, the Son of God, begotten of the Father, only begotten, that is, *from the essence of the Father* [ἐκ τῆς οὐσίας τοῦ πατρός, *ek tēs ousias tou patros*], God from God, Light from Light, true God from true God, begotten not created, *of the same essence of the Father* [ὁμοούσιον τῷ πατρί, *homoousion tō patri*], through whom all things came into being, both in heaven and in earth; Who for us men and for our salvation came down and was incarnate, becoming human. He suffered and the third day He rose, and ascended into the heavens. And He will come to judge both the living and the dead.
> And [we believe] in the Holy Spirit.

But those who say, Once He was not, or He was not before His generation, or He came to be out of nothing, or who assert that He, the Son of God, is of a different *hypostasis* or *ousia,* or that He is a creature, or changeable, or mutable, the Catholic and Apostolic Church anathematizes them.

Its Major Affirmations

The council affirmed, first, that the church would continue to be a Trinitarian church (see the "Trinitarian" form of the earlier Old Roman Symbol). Its Trinitarian commitment is evident in the very cast of the Creed itself: "We believe in one God the Father, Almighty, Creator of all things visible and invisible, and in one Lord Jesus Christ . . . , of the same essence of the Father, through whom all things came into being, both in heaven and in earth . . . , and in the Holy Spirit."

Second, by confessing faith in the ὁμοούσια (*homoousia*, "same essence") of the Son with the Father, which is an essential part of the doctrine of the Trinity, and describing him as "true God," the council affirmed the church's continuing commitment to the full deity of the Son of God.

Third, confessing its faith in the terms that it did, the council, with its doctrine of the ὁμοούσια, *homoousia*, distanced the church from all forms of polytheism, tritheism, and Arianism.

Fourth, by distinguishing between the Father and the Son the way it did (the Father eternally begets the Son; the Son is being eternally begotten of the Father), the council distanced the church from all forms of Sabellianism.

Fifth, by confessing that the one Lord Jesus Christ, who as "true God" and "of the same essence of the Father," "for us men and for our salvation came down and became flesh, becoming man, suffered and rose the third day, ascended into heaven, and is coming to judge the living and the dead," the council certified that the church would continue to see itself as a redeemed community with a message of redemption, at the center of which message stands the real Incarnation of God in the person of the Son, the result of which event is the divine-human Lord Jesus Christ.

In sum, the council declared that the church would continue to retain at the heart of its faith, as the centerpiece of its doctrinal life and devotional piety, the truth of the one living and true God (its monotheism being assured by the "same essence" clause), who eternally subsists as three distinct self-conscious Selves in the one divine unity who stand in "I-you" relation each to the other (the doctrine of *tres personae in una substantia*). The church, it determined, would also continue to confess that the Triune Godhead revealed itself in the Incarnation of the Son through the power of the Spirit for redemptive purposes.

THREE ISSUES

This conciliar description of the God of Christian theism raises three issues with regard to the orthodox doctrine of the Trinity: (1) the meaning of "person" in the Trinitarian construction, (2) the relationship of the three Persons to the one divine essence, and (3) the legitimacy of the doctrinal instrument which the Nicene Fathers employed to distinguish between the Father and the Son, namely, the Father's eternal generation of the Son. Each of these requires comment.

The Meaning of "Person"

What is the meaning of *person* in the orthodox representation of the Trinity? Etymologically, the word is from the Latin *persona*, from *per*, "through," and *sono*, "speak," hence, "speak through" and thus the "mask" through which the Roman actor spoke, and hence the specific "character" he portrayed. The word, it is true, does not appear in the Nicene Creed *per se*. But it has a history of doctrinal usage that went back as far as Tertullian and which eventually came to be universally used by the church to designate the Three in the One God and to distinguish them from the one divine essence which each is as God.

Today it is commonly understood by orthodox theologians to refer in the Trinitarian context to a "conscious self or ego," that is, a "center of self-consciousness." But it is often alleged that *persona* did not mean in the fourth and fifth centuries what it means today, that it originally referred only to "roles" which God assumed, and that it has only been since the days of R. Descartes and J. Locke that "person" has been defined as a self-conscious center of individuality, and that, therefore, because of its modern divergence in meaning away from its first and original intention, the word "person" has lost its usefulness as a theological term and should be abandoned. What are we to say in response? Here we need to be reminded of Calvin's opinion that all such words as the church finds useful after the close of the canon to aid in the understanding of Scripture are admissible provided they attest to what Scripture itself actually teaches. There is nothing sacrosanct about the word "person," and if the church were to discover another word that more accurately conveyed the intention of Scripture, I would welcome it. Indeed, John Calvin speaks for every Christian when he writes:

> I could wish they [that is, such words as ὁμοούσια, *homoousia*, οὐσία, *ousia*, πρόσωπον, *prosōpon*, *substantia*, *persona*] were buried, if only among all men this faith were agreed on: that Father and Son and Spirit are one God, yet the Son is not the Father, nor the Spirit the Son, but that they are differentiated by a peculiar quality.[1]

---

1. Calvin, *Institutes*, I.xiii.5.

John Murray also warns:

> We must jealousy avoid the danger of attaching the formulation of the doctrine of the Trinity to certain terms of merely human device if these terms are shown to be inadequate or misleading, and we must not allow the doctrine of the Trinity to be prejudiced by the fluctuations of meaning to which words are subjected in different periods of thought.[2]

But having issued these caveats, Murray also writes:

> With reference to the word "person" . . . , it does not appear . . . that the alleged change since the time of Descartes and Locke has ruled out the propriety of the use of the word "person" . . . with reference to the distinctions and differentiations that are immanent and eternal in God . . . why should we have any hesitation in thinking of "self-consciousness" as predicable of each of the persons of the Godhead? Why should we have difficulty in viewing each person as "a distinct centre of consciousness"? . . . Does not the Scripture represent the Father as addressing the Son as "Thou" and the Son the Father as "Thou"? . . . And the same must hold true of the Holy Spirit if trinitarian distinction applies to him as well as to the Father and the Son. And does not the Scripture teach us to address the persons of the Trinity in their distinctiveness as well as in their unity? If we are to address the Father in his distinctiveness as the Father in heaven, his "Thou" must be distinct from the "Thou" of the Son and of the Spirit. It undermines the biblical witness to the elements of the doctrine of the Trinity to plead the unity . . . of essence as in any way impinging upon or inconsistent with the reality of the distinctive self-consciousness of the persons in reference to one another. . . . One can hardly avoid the suspicion of a unitarian bias in the failure to appreciate distinguishing self-consciousness in the three persons of the Godhead.[3]

I concur and would urge, in spite of the reservations which some modern theologians have expressed regarding the term, that until another term comes along which serves the church better, the church should continue to employ "persons" to distinguish between the Father, the Son, and the Holy Spirit as real and distinct self-conscious Egos within the Godhead.

The Relation of the Three to the One

What is the relation of the three Persons in the Godhead to the one divine essence? This is admittedly an extremely complex question, the answer to

---

2. John Murray, *Collected Writings of John Murray* (Edinburgh: Banner of Truth, 1982), 4:278.
3. Ibid., 4:278–79.

which requires that we reflect upon the nature of unity (the "one") and the nature of multiplicity (the "many") as they relate to each other. Gordon H. Clark has offered helpful insights into this "one and many" problem. He begins with a short discussion of one aspect of metaphysical Realism, then applies his conclusions to the relation of the three Persons in the Godhead to the one divine essence. He writes:

> Suppose we have a lot of dice of various sizes. They all have the same shape. Now, this shape is something real. Even though the shape comes in different sizes, it is the same identical shape. If sensory objects alone were real, there could be no idea of similarity or identity, for none of the individual dice is itself similarity. Nor is any one of the dice *cube*. If one of the dice were the cube, and if only sense objects are real, then no other die could be cube. Hence, there is a real object of knowledge, the cube. It is not a sense object, not only for the preceding reason, but also because this cube exists in many places at once, as no sense object can. . . .
>
> Without this part of the theory [of Realism], viz., the assertion of [the reality of] non-sensory intellectual objects, it is hard to see how an understanding of the Bible would be possible. To begin with, God himself is a non-sensory object. So is the idea of justification by faith, and man, as well as animal and cube. . . .
>
> Now, when we face the subject of the Trinity, the common unity in the three Persons, may we not say that the three Persons share or communicate the common characteristics of omnipotence, omniscience, and so forth, and so constitute one essence. The [Realist] point of view makes this essence a reality, as truly as Man and Beauty are real. Were the essence not a reality, and the Persons therefore the only realities, we should have tritheism instead of monotheism.[4]

What Clark is saying here, in other words, is that if three Persons (distinguished as Persons by distinguishing "personal properties") are absolutely identical in all the attributes of deity, they are really and essentially one God; their one identical divine essence is as real as the distinguishable properties of the Persons. Three Persons with the same omnipresence would have one omnipresence. Three Persons with the same omniscience would have one omniscience. Three Persons with the same omnipotence would have one omnipotence. Three Persons with the same all-encompassing purpose would have one purpose. Three Persons identical in divine essence would be, in a word, one God. This means that while we must affirm, if we would be faithful to Scripture, that each Person is a distinct Person, nevertheless, because of the reality of their sameness in divine essence (the famous Nicene ὁμοούσια, *homoousia*), we can never properly think of the three Persons as existing

---

4. Gordon H. Clark, "The Trinity," *The Trinity Review* 9 (November 1979), 1.

independently of each other. God the Father is eternally "the Father of the Son," and God the Son is eternally "the Son of the Father," while God the Holy Spirit is eternally "the Spirit of God" and "the Spirit of Christ."

Describing then the oneness of the Trinity, that oneness pertaining to their divine essence, we should speak of the sameness of their "substance," "essence," "being," or "nature." That is to say, each Person possesses the one divine substance, essence, being, or nature. For example, each Person is *essentially* omniscient, that is, each knows all things (Father, 1 John 3:20; Son, Matt. 11:27; Holy Spirit, 1 Cor. 2:11). But designating the distinctions between the self-conscious Egos themselves, we should employ "persons" (or "hypostases") to underscore the truth that there are real self-conscious, subjective *differentia* in the depth of the one divine Being that correspond to the titles Father, Son, and Spirit. This means, if we may continue with the example of their co-omniscience, that while each of the Persons of the Godhead knows all things, each one knows these things in the way peculiar to his own person, that is to say, he knows them *subjectively*. Both the Father and the Spirit, for example, knew the *objective* fact that the Son would die on the cross but neither ever thought, "I will die on the cross." Only the Son *subjectively* thought that. Both the Father and the Son knew the *objective* fact that by the Spirit's overshadowing and empowering Mary would virginally "conceive the Son" in her womb, but neither ever thought, "I will overshadow Mary and empower her to virginally conceive." Only the Holy Spirit *subjectively* thought that. Both the Son and the Holy Spirit knew the *objective* fact that the Son's righteous life would provide the ground for the believer's justification, but neither ever thought, "I will justify the believer on the ground of Christ's righteousness." Only the Father *subjectively* thought that. This means, therefore, that while there is one *objective* omniscience in the Godhead, that is to say, *each Person knows all there is to know* (hence, one omniscience), there are also three *subjective personal apprehensions* in the Godhead of all there is to know, which apprehensions cannot be reduced to one personality, that is to say, *each Person knows all there is to know in the manner distinctly peculiar to his own Person*. Far then from being less personal than we sinful personal beings are, the Persons of the Trinity are even more personal, if personhood be judged by true *subjective* self-awareness, sensitivity, and responsiveness to all that is *objectively* nonself.

To the objection of Hodge and Berkhof that the unity in the Godhead cannot be the unity of a species or a genus, that is to say, "the three Persons are one in a stricter, deeper, more inexplicable sense than the sense in which three or thirty men are one,"[5] Clark responds:

---

5. Charles Hodge, *Systematic Theology* (1871; reprint, Grand Rapids, Mich.: Eerdmans, 1952), 2:59; see Louis Berkhof, *Systematic Theology* (Grand Rapids, Mich.: Eerdmans, 1932), 88.

Whether this objection is plausibly true or not depends on the sense in which men are one and the sense in which the Trinity is one. Those who make this objection should define the two senses (if indeed there are two) and point out the distinction. Unless we know how the Persons [of the Godhead] are one and how men are one, we cannot tell whether the unity is the same or different. But the objectors hardly define specific unity and disclaim ability to define divine unity....

Hodge ... wrote (II, p. 59), "The whole nature or essence [of God] is in the divine person [each one], but the human person [each one] is only a part of the common human nature." This is a confusing sentence. To fit the argument it ought to read, "The whole nature or essence [of God] is in the divine person, but only a part of the common human nature is in the human person." If the sentence is not so interpreted, the antithesis Hodge wants to assert, the antithesis between the unity in God and the unity in men, vanishes. Yet this interpretation, the only one that preserves the antithesis, makes the second half of the sentence false; for if a part of human nature were lacking in an object, if the definition of that object did not include every part of the definition of man, if the man did not participate in the whole Idea [of man], that object would not be an individual man. A man is a man only because the entire definition [of man] fits.[6]

Clark is quite correct in his observation. Simply to assert that the divine unity is different from the specific unity of three men is not sufficient. One must spell out the nature of each "unity" if one is to insist that they are different. It seems to me that Clark's solution satisfies all the biblical data. In presenting his view I have attempted to say *multum in parvo,* but it appears to allow the Christian to affirm both the *reality* of the three Persons, thereby avoiding the empty perception of God as an undifferentiated Monad, and the *reality* of the one essence, thereby avoiding tritheism.

But does this representation of the Trinity avoid tritheism? Some critics have urged that it does not, contending that if there are in fact three "centers of self-consciousness" within the one God, tritheism cannot be avoided.[7] But is their criticism sound? I think not, for every form of real tritheism requires three *separable* and *distinguishable* gods, that is to say, one could be eliminated without impinging upon the "godness" of the others in any way. But if any one of the three "centers of self-consciousness" within the Trinity were to be eliminated from the Godhead, that elimination would immediately and directly necessitate eliminating data from the knowledge of the other two, which in turn would impinge upon their omniscience

---

6. Clark, "The Trinity," 1–2.
7. See Cyril Richardson, *The Doctrine of the Trinity* (New York: Abingdon, 1958), 94.

which is immutable. Simply the immutable, shared omniscience possessed by the three Persons of the Godhead means that all tritheistic separability is out of the question. We affirm again then that there is only one divine essence, and insist that each Person of the Godhead possesses this one real divine essence. Accordingly, we confess the existence of the one living and true God who eternally exists as the one God in Trinity and as Trinity in Unity.

To those who would insist that the early doctrine known as the περιχώρησις, (*perichōrēsis;* Lat. equivalent, *circumincessio;* the doctrine of the *ontological* "interpenetration of persons" between or mutual coinherence or indwelling of the three Persons within the Godhead)—thought to be taught by Jesus in his declaration: "The Father is in me, and I [am] in the Father" (10:38; see 14:10, 11; 17:21)—is a characteristic of the divine unity which is not true of the specific unity of three men, I say that it is not at all clear that our Lord intended to speak of an ontological interpenetration between the persons of the Father and the Son when he said this. If the same language in John 14:20 and 17:21 is taken into account where he described the relationship between the Father and himself on the one hand and his disciples on the other, which is surely *not* ontological but spiritual (see "I am in my Father, and you are in me and I am in you," and "in order that they all may be one, just as You, Father, are in me and I am in you, in order that also they may be in us"), he could have intended and likely did intend simply to say that he and the Father were in *vital* union one with the other, that is, shared the same divine life and purpose, and nothing more (see also here the Pauline expressions Χριστὸς ἐν ὑμιν, *Christos en hymin,* and ἐν Χριστῷ, *en Christō*).

The Father's Eternal Generation of the Son

We come now to the question concerning the legitimacy of distinguishing between the Father and the Son by means of Origen's doctrine of eternal generation, which Louis Berkhof defines approvingly as "that eternal and necessary act of the first person in the Trinity, whereby he, within the divine Being, is the ground of a second personal subsistence like his own, and puts this second person in possession of the whole divine essence, without any division, alienation, or change."[8]

We must begin by making clear what the Nicene Fathers intended by their phrases "begotten out of the Father," "out of the *being* [οὐσίας, *ousias*] of the Father" and "God *out of* [ἐκ, *ek*] God, Light out of Light, very God out of very God." From personal investigation, I have discovered that many evangelical pastors who use the expression "very God of very God" from their pulpits as a description of Christ

---

8. Berkhof, *Systematic Theology,* 94.

believe that the phrase is simply a literary convention, on the analogy of the phrases "King of kings" and "Lord of lords," to denote the superlative degree. However if this were the intention of the phrase, the second occurrence of "God" would have to be plural with a lower case "g," making then the attached "very" inappropriate. Since this is not the way the phrase is turned, it should be obvious that the phrase is not intended merely to exalt the Son above all the false gods which men fashion and worship.

When the Nicene Fathers employed the phrase, they did so in order to distance the church from Sabellianism. They were saying that the Father and the Son possess distinguishing properties (ἰδιότητες, *idiotētes*) which will not allow "Father" and "Son" simply to be revelational modes by which the "one undifferentiated divine Monad" manifested himself to his creation. The Father is alone unbegotten, they said. The Son, however, is begotten by the Father and that by an act of eternal generation on the part of the Father but in such a sense that the Son is "begotten, not made." What does all this mean precisely? It means that these Fathers taught that the Son derives his essential being or existence as God from the Father (see their "out of the being of the Father") through an "always continuing and yet ever complete" act of begetting on the Father's part.[9] In sum, the Father alone has being from himself; the Son eternally derives his being from the Father.

In both Nicene and post-Nicene times, this doctrine of the Father's eternal generation of the Son was supported by four main arguments: (1) the very titles "Father" and "Son" were said to imply that the Father generates the Son; (2) the term μονογενής (*monogenēs*; John 1:14, 18; 3:16; 1 John 4:9) was thought to teach that the Father begat the Son; (3) John 5:26, expressly declaring that the Father who has life in himself "gave to the Son also to have life in himself," was thought to teach that the Father communicates the divine essence to the Son; and (4) 1 John 5:18b—"the one who was begotten by God keeps him"—was said explicitly to teach that the Son was generated by the Father.[10] With regard to the first argument, the titles "Father" and "Son" must not be freighted with the Western ideas of source of being and superiority on the one hand and of subordination and dependency on the other. Rather, they should be viewed in the biblical sense as denoting sameness of nature, and in Jesus' case, equality with the Father with respect to his deity (see John 10:30–36).

---

9. Ibid., 93.
10. Francis Turretin in his *Institutes of Elenctic Theology*, ed. James T. Dennison Jr. (Phillipsburg, N.J.: Presbyterian and Reformed, 1994), third topic, question 29, argues that the doctrine is also taught in and proven by Psalm 2:7; Proverbs 8:22–31; Micah 5:2; Colossians 1:15; and Hebrews 1:3. His exegesis, however, is at every point more assertive than argumentative and probative, more scholastic than biblical.

Regarding the second, it is the general consensus among twentieth-century scholars that μονογενής, *monogenēs*, does not mean "only begotten," alluding to some form of generation, but rather "one and only" (see Luke 7:12; 8:42; 9:38) or "only one of a kind" or "unique." Warfield, for example, writes: "The adjective 'only begotten' conveys the idea, not of derivation and subordination, but of uniqueness and consubstantiality: Jesus is all that God is."[11] Third, a consensus has by no means been reached among theologians and commentators that the words of John 5:26 refer to an ontological endowment. It is entirely possible, indeed, much more likely, that they refer to an aspect of the *incarnate* Son's messianic investiture. John 5:22–23 refers to his designated authority to judge, which is clearly an aspect of his messianic role, and so is the similar thought of 5:27. Accordingly, 5:26, paralleling 5:27, seems to be giving the ground upon which the Son is able to raise the dead, namely, it is one of the prerogatives of his messianic investiture.[12] Finally, it is not at all certain that 1 John 5:18b teaches that the Father eternally generates the Son. Raymond E. Brown, for example, discusses five interpretations that have been proposed by scholars, opting himself for the idea that "the one who was begotten of God" refers to the Christian whom God enables to keep himself.[13] Even those who contend that the phrase refers to Jesus (the majority view) must and do acknowledge that it is not certain that John had an essential begetting in mind or that he was referring to the eternal generation of the Son. Thus Scripture provides little to no warrant for the speculation that the Nicene Fathers made the bedrock for the distinguishing properties of the Father and the Son. In fact, when they taught that the Father is the "source" (ἀρχή, *archē*, Lat. *fons*), "fountain" (πηγή, *pēgē*) and "root" (ῥίζα, *rhiza*) of the Son and that the Son in turn is God *out of* (ἐκ, *ek*) God, that is, out of the being of the Father, they were virtually denying to the Son the attribute of *self-existence*, an attribute essential to deity, and were implying that the same divine essence, paradoxically, can be both "unbegotten" and "begotten" depending upon whether it is the Father or the Son which is being considered.

No doubt the Nicene Fathers were satisfied that they had carefully guarded the full deity of the Son by their affirmation of the *homoousia* and by their insistence that the Son was "begotten not made." But their utilization of the language, if not also in some measure the thought modes, of the earlier Origen, regardless of these Fathers' commendable intention to distance the church from Sabellianism by it,

---

11. Benjamin B. Warfield, *Biblical Doctrines* (New York: Oxford, 1929), 194; see also Dale Moody, "God's Only Son: The Translation of John 3:16 in the Revised Standard Version," *Journal of Biblical Literature* 72 (1953): 213–19, and BAGD, *A Greek-English Lexicon of the New Testament*, 527. See also the NIV translation of the relevant passages.
12. Hodge, *Systematic Theology*, 1:470–71.
13. Raymond E. Brown, *The Epistles of John*, Anchor Bible (New York: Doubleday, 1982), 620–22.

suggests the Son's subordination to the Father not only in modes of operation but in modes of subsistence as well. Nonetheless, in spite of these deficiencies, the church continues to employ the Nicene terminology to this very day.

In the sixteenth century, John Calvin contended against the subordinationism implicit in the Nicene language,[14] if not also in its theology (without mentioning the work of the council *per se*), in his debates with a contemporary, one Valentinus Gentilis who contended that the Father alone is αὐτόθεος, *autotheos*—"God in himself," and with Michael Servetus the Unitarian. Citing Augustine, Calvin writes:

> Christ with respect to Himself is called God; with respect to the Father, Son. Again, the Father with respect to Himself is called God; with respect to the Son, Father. In so far as He is called Father with respect to the Son, He is not the Son; in so far as He is called the Son with respect to the Father, He is not the Father; in so far as He is called both Father with respect to Himself, and Son with respect to Himself, He is the same God.

Calvin then concludes from this:

> Therefore, when we speak simply of the Son without regard to the Father, we well and properly declare Him to be *of Himself*; for this reason we call Him the sole beginning. But when we mark the relation that He has with the Father, we rightly make the Father the beginning of the Son. (*Institutes*, I.xiii.19, emphasis supplied)

What Calvin affirms here is that the Son with reference to himself is God in himself, but in relation to his Father, he derives his Sonship from the relationship in which he stands to the Father. In this *relational* sense, Calvin is willing to speak of the Father's "begetting" the Son (see *Institutes*, I.xiii.7, 8, 18, 23, 24). Calvin also declares, in that the New Testament employs the divine name Yahweh as a titular ascription of Christ, that all that is implied in this name, including self-existence, is true no less of the Son than of the Father (*Institutes*, I.xiii.23). Furthermore, while Calvin will say that the term "God" is sometimes applied to the Father "because He is the fountainhead and beginning of deity—and this is done to denote the simple unity of essence"

---

14. So different from Nicene Trinitarianism was the view of the Protestant Reformers, especially Calvin, pertaining to the Trinity that Gerald Bray believes their vision was "fundamentally different from anything which had gone before, or which has appeared since," and he mentions, among other things, their belief that "the persons of the Trinity are equal to one another in every respect," a position he says which had been qualified in the medieval tradition when the Father was viewed as the source of divinity in a way that the other two Persons were not (*The Doctrine of God* [Downers Grove, Ill.: InterVarsity Press, 1993], 197, 200).

(*Institutes*, I.xiii.23), he explains later that what he means by "the beginning of deity" is "not in the bestowing of essence, as fanatics babble, but *by reason of order*" (*Institutes*, I.xiii.26, emphasis supplied). Therefore, he will "admit that in respect to order ... the beginning of divinity is in the Father" (*Institutes*, I.xiii.24). So there is no question that Calvin does distinguish between the Father and the Son as to order.

But in the very contexts in which he underscores the order between the Father and the Son, granting the relational order of priority to the Father, he also asserts:

> Certain rascals . . . indeed confessed that there are three persons; but they added the provision that the Father, who is truly and properly the sole God, in forming the Son and the Spirit, infused into them His own deity. Indeed, they do not refrain from this dreadful manner of speaking: the Father is distinguished from the Son and the Spirit by this mark, that He is the only "essence giver." (*Institutes*, I.xiii.23)

Realizing that such a representation of the intra-Trinitarian relationship between the Father and the Son detracts from the glory of the Son and wounds the doctrine of the Trinity at its heart, Calvin asks concerning the Son:

> How will the Creator, who gives being to all, not have being from Himself, but borrow His essence from elsewhere? For whoever says that the Son has been given His essence from the Father denies that He has being from Himself. But the Holy Spirit gives the lie to this, naming Him Yahweh. (*Institutes*, I.xiii.23)

He also writes:

> The essence of God, if these babblers are to be believed, belongs to the Father only, inasmuch as He alone is, and is the essence giver of the Son. (*Institutes*, I.xiii.24)
>
> ... even though we admit that in respect to order ... the beginning of divinity is in the Father, yet we say that it is a detestable invention that essence is proper to the Father alone, as if He were the deifier of the Son. (*Institutes*, I.xiii.24)
>
> ... we teach from the Scriptures that God is one in essence, and hence that the essence of the Son and of the Spirit is unbegotten—but inasmuch as the Father is first in order. . . . He is rightly deemed the beginning and fountainhead of the whole of divinity. (*Institutes*, I.xiii.25)
>
> ... we say that deity in an absolute sense exists of itself; whence likewise we confess that the Son since He is God, exists of Himself, but not in respect of His Person; indeed, since He is the Son, we say that He exists from the Father. Thus His essence is without beginning; while the beginning of His Person [with respect to order] is God Himself. (*Institutes*, I.xiii.25)

He concludes his treatment of the doctrine of the Trinity by declaring the ancient doctrine of "eternal generation" to be "of little profit," unnecessarily "burdensome," "useless trouble," and "foolish":

> While I am zealous for the edification of the church, I felt that I would be better advised not to touch upon many things that would profit but little, and would burden my readers with useless trouble. For what is the point in disputing whether the Father always begets? Indeed, it is foolish to imagine a continuous act of begetting, since it is clear that three persons have subsisted in God from eternity. (*Institutes*, I.xiii.29)

Warfield summarizes the entire history of this doctrine in the following words:

> The determining impulse to the formulation of the doctrine of the Trinity in the church was the church's profound conviction of the absolute Deity of Christ, on which as on a pivot the whole Christian conception of God from the first origins of Christianity turned. . . .
>
> In the nature of the case the formulated doctrine was of slow attainment. . . . In the second century the dominant neo-Stoic and neo-Platonic ideas deflected Christian thought into subordinationist channels, and produced what is known as the Logos-Christology, which looks upon the Son as a prolation of Deity . . . ; meanwhile, to a great extent, the Spirit was neglected altogether. A reaction . . . , under the name of Monarchianism, identified the Father, Son, and Spirit so completely that they were thought of only as different aspects or different moments in the life of the one Divine Person, called now Father, now Son, now Spirit. . . . In the conflict between these two opposite tendencies the church gradually found its way, under the guidance of the Baptismal Formula elaborated into a "Rule of Faith," to a better and more well-balanced conception, until a real doctrine of the Trinity came to expression, particularly in the West, through the brilliant dialectic of Tertullian. It was thus ready at hand, when, in the early years of the fourth century, the Logos-Christology, in opposition to dominant Sabellian tendencies, ran to seed in what is known as Arianism, to which the Son was a creature, though exalted above all other creatures as their Creator and Lord; and the church was thus prepared to assert its settled faith in a Triune God, one in being, but in whose unity there subsisted three consubstantial Persons. Under the leadership of Athanasius this doctrine was proclaimed as the faith of the church at the Council of Nicea in 325 A.D., and by his strenuous labors and those of "the three great Cappadocians," . . . it gradually won its way to the actual acceptance of the entire church. . . . The language [of the later so-called Athanasian Creed] still retains elements of speech which owe their origin to the modes of thought characteristic of the Logos-Christology of the second century, [and which are] fixed in the nomenclature of the church by the Nicene Creed of 325 A.D., though

carefully guarded there against the subordinationism inherent in the Logos-Christology, and made the vehicle rather of the Nicene doctrines of the eternal generation of the Son and procession of the Spirit, with the consequent subordination of the Son and Spirit to the Father in modes of subsistence as well as of operation.... It has been found necessary ... from time to time, vigorously to reassert the principle of equalization, over against a tendency unduly to emphasize the elements of subordinationism which still hold a place thus in the traditional language in which the church states its doctrine of the Trinity. In particular, it fell to Calvin, in the interests of the true Deity of Christ—the constant motive of the whole body of Trinitarian thought—to reassert and make good the attribute of self-existence (*autotheotes*) for the Son. Thus Calvin takes his place, alongside of Tertullian, Athanasius, and Augustine, as one of the chief contributors to the exact and vital statement of the Christian doctrine of the Triune God.[15]

Finally, John Murray also says of Calvin's rejection of the ancient doctrine of the Father's eternal generation of the Son:

Students of historical theology are acquainted with the furore which Calvin's insistence upon the self-existence of the Son as to his deity aroused at the time of the Reformation. Calvin was too much of a student of Scripture to be content to follow the lines of what had been regarded as Nicene orthodoxy on this particular issue. He was too jealous for the implications of the *homoousion* clause of the Nicene creed to be willing to accede to the interpretation which the Nicene fathers, including Athanasius, placed upon another expression in the same creed, namely, 'very God of very God' (θεὸν ἀληθινὸν ἐκ θεοῦ ἀληθινοῦ [*theon alēthinon ek theou alēthinou*]). No doubt this expression is repeated by orthodox people without any thought of suggesting what the evidence derived from the writings of the Nicene fathers would indicate the intent to have been.[16] This evidence shows that the meaning intended is that the Son *derived* his deity from the Father and that the Son was not therefore αὐτόθεος [*autotheos*]. It was precisely this position that Calvin controverted with vigour. He maintained that as respects personal distinction the Son was of the Father but as respects deity he was self-existent (*ex se ipso*). This position ran counter to the Nicene tradition. Hence the indictments levelled against him. It is, however, to the credit of Calvin that he did not allow his own more sober thinking to be suppressed out of deference to an established pattern of thought when the latter did not commend itself by conformity to Scripture and was inimical to Christ's divine identity.[17]

---

15. Benjamin B. Warfield, "The Biblical Doctrine of the Trinity," in *Biblical and Theological Studies* (Philadelphia: Presbyterian and Reformed, 1952), 58–59.
16. See Athanasius's *Expositio fidei* and his *De Decretis Nicaenae Synodi*, paragraphs 3 and 19.

ANALYSIS OF THE NICENO-CONSTANTINOPOLITAN CREED'S PNEUMATOLOGY

Consumed as the Nicene Council was with working out the doctrine of the person of the Son over against the claims of the Arians, it said nothing about the Holy Spirit beyond the simple declaration that the church believed in him. It was but natural that until the church had settled the issue of the deity and personal subsistence of the Son it could not make much progress regarding the doctrine of the Holy Spirit. This lack was addressed at the Council of Constantinople in A.D. 381, when, in addition to addressing the teaching of Apollinaris (or -ius) which damaged the full humanity of Christ, it declared against the Arian and semi-Arian parties who were teaching that just as the Father had created the Son so also the Son had created the Spirit,[18] that the church believes "in the Holy Spirit, the Lord, the Giver of life, who proceeds from the Father [τό ἐκ τοῦ πατρὸς ἐκπορευόμενον *to ek tou patros ekporeuomenon*], who, with the Father and Son, is worshiped and glorified, who spoke through the prophets." By the phrase "who proceeds from the Father" (the word "proceeds" comes from the Latin Vulgate which had translated the Greek with *qui a Patre procedit*) the council intended to point out the unique property (ἰδιότης, *idiotēs*) of the Spirit which distinguished him from the Father and the Son, and by this confession it meant to say that just as the Son is essentially, necessarily, and eternally generated by the Father, so also the Spirit essentially, necessarily, and eternally proceeds from the Father. The later doctrine that the Spirit proceeds also from the Son—the "double procession"—can be traced back to Hilary, Ambrose, Jerome, and Augustine and was current at Rome in the fifth century, with Pope Leo I declaring it an aspect of the orthodox faith.[19] It is also reflected in the *et Filio* in verse 23 of the fifth-century Athanasian Creed. Accordingly, the Third Council of Toledo in Spain in A.D. 589 proclaimed it a tenet of orthodoxy and may have had the words "and the Son" (Lat. *filioque*) inserted in the third article of the Creed, reflecting Western Christianity's anti-Arian theology by announcing in the fact of the Spirit's procession from both the Father *and* the Son the latter's

---

17. John Murray, "Systematic Theology," *Westminster Theological Journal* 25 (May 1963): 141. See also Morton Smith, "God, the Persons of," in *The Encyclopedia of Christianity* (Marshallton, Del.: National Foundation for Christian Education, 1972), 4:379.
18. Philip Schaff, *History of the Christian Church* (1910; reprint, Grand Rapids, Mich.: Eerdmans, 1960), 3:663.
19. In a letter to the Spanish bishop Turibius of Asturica, *Quam laudabiliter*, dated July 21, 447, Leo I, following an earlier Latin tradition, declared that he wanted to see the doctrine of the double procession of the Spirit affirmed at a council to be held in Toledo. See *Enchiridion Symbolorum*, ed. Denzinger and Schönmetzer, 284.

co-equality with the Father.[20] Louis Berkhof approvingly defines the Holy Spirit's "spiration" as "that eternal and necessary act of the first and second persons in the Trinity whereby they, within the divine Being, become the ground of the personal subsistence of the Holy Spirit, and put the third person in possession of the whole divine essence, without any division, alienation or change."[21]

Although the Constantinopolitan Council intended to set forth the unique property of the Spirit that distinguished him from the Father and the Son, in fact its assertion of the Holy Spirit's eternal procession from the Father (later, from the Father and the Son, or from the Father through the Son) is another instance of the early fathers going beyond Scripture in their effort to explain how it is that the Holy Spirit is the Spirit of God and of Christ. In so doing, they subordinated the Spirit to the Father and the Son not only in modes of operation but in essential and personal subsistence as well and, as Nicaea did with the Son earlier, denied thereby to the Holy Spirit the attribute of autotheotic self-existence.

The New Testament teaches that the Father and the Son "send" (John 14:26, πέμψει, *pempsei*; 15:26; 16:7) the Holy Spirit, and that the Son "breathed" (John 20:22, ἐνεφύσησεν, *enephysesen*) and "poured out" (Acts 2:17, ἐκχεῶ, *ekcheo*; 33, ἐξέχεεν, *execheev*) the Holy Spirit on the day of Pentecost. But these expressions are descriptive of the Father's and the Son's soteric activity as well as the Spirit's submission to them *in the economy of redemption* and not of an inscrutable mysterious process transpiring eternally within the Trinity. In fact, only one verse in the entire New Testament even remotely approaches such a teaching, namely, John 15:26, which contains the phrase, "who is coming forth [παρὰ . . . ἐκπορεύεται, *para . . . ekporeuetai*] from the Father."[22] But even here, the much more likely meaning, in accordance with John 14:26, is that the Spirit "comes forth from the Father" *into the world* on his salvific mission of witnessing to Jesus Christ. B. F. Westcott, for instance, declares:

---

20. The *filioque* clause has continued to this day to be a major difference between Western Christendom and the Eastern churches. The latter reject it because it was added by the Third Council of Toledo without the aid of a broader ecumenical gathering and because the Patriarch Photius of Constantinople (864–867 and 880–886) added after the words "and the Father" the word "alone" in his exposition of the Cappadocian theology. This difference contributed to the prevention of a reunion of the churches in 1274 and 1439.
21. Berkhof, *Systematic Theology*, 97.
22. Calvin's lengthy treatise of the Trinity in his *Institutes*, I, xiii, does not contain a single mention of the doctrine of the Spirit's procession from the Father. Turretin in his *Institutes of Elenctic Theology*, Third Topic, Question XXXI, advances even less biblical evidence for this doctrine than he did for the Father's eternal generation of the Son, referring to John 15:26; 16:7, 13–15; 20:22; Galatians 4:6. His exegesis is slight and at every point assumes the position he wishes to prove. The Spirit's coming forth or being sent in these verses actually has reference to his salvific mission in this world and not to relationships within the Trinity.

The original term ἐκπορεύεται [ekporeuetai] may in itself either describe proceeding from a source, or proceeding on a mission. In the former sense the preposition out of (ἐκ [ek]) would naturally be required to define the source (Rev. i.16, etc.); on the other hand the preposition from (παρά [para]) is that which is habitually used with the verb to come forth of the mission of the Son, *e.g.* xvi.27, xvii.8. The use of the latter preposition (παρά [para]) in this place [15:26] seems therefore to show decisively that the reference here is to the temporal mission of the Holy Spirit, and not to the eternal Procession. . . . it is most worthy of notice that the Greek Fathers who apply this passage to the eternal Procession instinctively substitute ἐκ [ek] for παρά [para] in their application of it.[23]

Alfred Plummer concurs:

It seems best to take this much discussed clause as simply yet another way of expressing the fact of the *mission* of the Paraclete . . . there seems to be nothing in the word [ἐκπορεύεσθαι, ekporeuesthai] itself to limit it to the Eternal Procession. On the other hand the παρά, *para,* is strongly in favour of the reference being to the mission.[24]

J. H. Bernard writes:

Here [in John 15:26 ἐκπορεύεσθαι, ekporeuesthai] is used . . . of the Spirit "coming forth" from God in His mission of witness. To interpret the phrase of what is called "the Eternal Procession" of the Spirit has been a habit of theologians. . . . But to claim that this interpretation was present to the mind of Jn. would be to import into the Gospel the controversies and doctrines of the fourth century. [The clause] does not refer to the mysterious relationships between the Persons of the Holy Trinity, but only to the fact that the Spirit who bears witness of Jesus Christ has come from God.[25]

H. R. Reynolds declares:

[John 15:26] is the great text on which the Western Church and the Greeks have alike relied for their doctrine concerning the "procession of the Spirit," the timeless, pre-mundane relations among the Personalities of the Godhead. . . . There

---

23. B. F. Westcott, *The Gospel According to St. John* (1881; reprint, Grand Rapids, Mich.: Eerdmans, 1962), 224–25.
24. Alfred Plummer, *The Gospel According to St. John* (1882; reprint, Grand Rapids, Mich.: Baker, 1981), 288–89.
25. J. H. Bernard, *A Critical and Exegetical Commentary on the Gospel According to St. John* (Edinburgh: T. & T. Clark, 1928), 2:499.

are those . . . who urge that these passages do not bear at all upon the internal relations of the Godhead, but simply refer to the temporal mission of the Holy Spirit . . . and much may be said in favour of this view. If this verse does not furnish the basis of an argument, there is no other which can be advanced to establish the view either of the Eastern or Western Church.[26]

Raymond E. Brown concurs with this view, as do F. F. Bruce, Leon Morris, J. I. Packer,[27] and D. A. Carson, who points out that:

> it is almost certain that the words "who goes out from the Father," set in synonymous parallelism with "whom I will send to you from the Father," refer not to some ontological "procession" but to the mission of the Spirit.[28]

Benjamin B. Warfield, commenting approvingly on Calvin's doctrine of the Trinity, writes:

> The principle of his doctrine of the Trinity was not the conception he formed of the relationship of the Son to the Father and of the Spirit to the Father and the Son, expressed respectively by the two terms "generation" and "procession"; but the force of his conviction of the absolute equality of the Persons. *The point of view which adjusted everything to the conception of "generation" and "procession" as worked out by the Nicene Fathers was entirely alien to him.* The conception itself he found difficult, if not unthinkable; and although he admitted the facts of "generation" and "procession," he treated them as bare facts, and refused to make them constitutive of the doctrine of the Trinity. He rather adjusted everything to the absolute divinity of each Person, their community in the one only true Deity; and to this we cannot doubt that he was ready not only to subordinate, but even to sacrifice, if need be, the entire body of Nicene speculation.[29]

He states further:

> It was . . . a very great service to Christian theology which Calvin rendered when

---

26. H. R. Reynolds, *The Gospel of John* (reprint of The Pulpit Commentary, vol. 17, Grand Rapids, Mich.: Eerdmans, 1962), 2:276.
27. Raymond E. Brown, *The Gospel According to John (XIII–XXI)* (Garden City, N.Y.: Doubleday, 1970), 29a, 689; F. F. Bruce, *The Gospel of John* (Grand Rapids, Mich.: Eerdmans, 1983), 316; Leon Morris, *The Gospel According to John* (Grand Rapids, Mich.: Eerdmans, 1971), 683, and *New Testament Theology* (Grand Rapids, Mich.: 1986), 265, fn. 18; J. I. Packer, *Knowing God* (Downers Grove, Ill.: InterVarsity Press, 1973), 59.
28. D. A. Carson, *The Gospel According to John* (Grand Rapids, Mich.: Eerdmans, 1991), 528–29.
29. B. B. Warfield, "Calvin's Doctrine of the Trinity," *Calvin and Augustine* (Philadelphia: Presbyterian and Reformed, 1956), 257.

he firmly asserted for the second and third persons of the Trinity their αὐτοθεότης, *autotheotēs* ["self-deity"].[30]

Warfield declares that Calvin's position

> roused opposition and created a party. But it did create a party: and that party was shortly the Reformed Churches, of which it became characteristic that . . . in the doctrine of the Trinity they laid the stress upon the equality of the Persons sharing the same essence, and thus set themselves with more or less absoluteness against all subordinationism in the explanation of the relations of the Persons to one another.[31]

Accordingly, Warfield expresses great astonishment "at the tenacity with which [Calvin's] followers cling to all the old speculations."[32]

Loraine Boettner, a contemporary "follower of Calvin," does indeed follow Calvin here, rejecting the doctrine of the Spirit's eternal procession from the Father and the Son as without biblical warrant:

> In the original Greek [of John 16:28] the phrase "came out from," which is here used of Jesus, is stronger than the "proceedeth from" [in 15:26], which is used of the Spirit; yet the context of John 16:28 makes it perfectly clear that what Jesus said of Himself had reference to His mission and not to what is commonly termed His eternal generation; for His coming forth from the Father into the world is contrasted with His leaving the world and going back to the Father. We are, of course, told that the Holy Spirit is sent by the Father and by the Son; but the mission as He comes to apply redemption is an entirely different thing from the procession. It seems much more natural to assume that the words of John 15:26, which were a part of the Farewell Discourse, and which were, therefore, spoken within the very shadow of the cross, were not philosophical but practical, designed to meet a present and urgent need, namely, to comfort and strengthen the disciples for the ordeal through which they too were soon to pass.
>
> . . . Hence, John 15:26, at best, carries no decisive weight concerning the doctrine of the procession of the Spirit, if, indeed, it is not quite clearly designed to serve an entirely different purpose.[33]

J. Oliver Buswell Jr., another twentieth-century follower of Calvin, asserts that "the ancient church incorrectly understood the words of John 15:26" when it "took

---

30. Ibid., 273.
31. Ibid., 251.
32. Ibid., 279.
33. Loraine Boettner, *Studies in Theology* (Phillipsburg, N.J.: Presbyterian and Reformed, 1985), 123.

this passage of Scripture as teaching a doctrine of the 'eternal procession' of the Holy Spirit within the Trinity." While he says that the doctrine's only value "is that it gives us a vehicle for conceiving of the relationship between the Spirit and the Father and the Son," he also states that the word "procession" is "a hindrance rather than a help. The Scripture certainly does not teach the 'procession' of the Holy Spirit as a mode of expression of his eternal relationship within the Trinity."[34]

With all this I concur, but I do not intend to deny that the three Persons of the Godhead do have distinguishing, incommunicable properties which are real, eternal, and necessary. Indeed, without them there would be no Trinity. The distinguishing property of the Father is paternity *(paternitas)* from which flow "economical" activities in which the Son and Spirit do not share; the Son's is filiation *(filiatio)* from which flow "economical" activities in which the Father and Spirit do not share; and the Holy Spirit's is spiration *(spiratio)* from which flow "economical" activities in which the Father and the Son do not share, all descriptions which can be justified by Scripture.

We must be extremely cautious, however, in asserting what these distinguishing properties mean lest we go beyond Scripture. There can be no question that in his paternity the Father is the Father of the Son. But *we must not attempt to define, beyond the fact of the clearly implied order, a modal "how" of the Father's paternity.* And there can be no question that the Son is the Son of the Father. We know that his Sonship means that he is equal with the Father with respect to deity (John 5:18; 10:33–36), and we also know that as the Son he is to be distinguished from the Father with respect to his personal property of filiation (John 1:1–3, 18). We know also that his Sonship implies an order of relational (not essential) subordination to the Father which is doubtless what dictated the divisions of labor in the eternal Covenant of Redemption in that it is unthinkable that the Son would have sent the Father to do his will. But beyond this we dare not go. *We must not attempt to define, beyond the fact of the clearly implied order, a modal "how" of the Son's filiation.* It is enough to know that the Scriptures affirm that the titles "Father" and "Son" speak of a personal, differentiating manifoldness (that is, "subjective conscious selves") within the depth of the divine Being. Finally, there can be no question that the Holy Spirit is a divine Person who is the Spirit of God and of Christ (Rom. 8:9), and that he "proceeded" or "came forth from" the Father and the Son (John 14:26; 15:26; 16:7; 20:22) at Pentecost on his salvific mission. But *we must not attempt to define, beyond the fact of the clearly implied order, a modal "how" of the Spirit's spiration.* It is enough to know that the Scriptures affirm that this title distinguishes a third subjective conscious self in the depth of the divine Being.

---

34. J. Oliver Buswell Jr., *A Systematic Theology of the Christian Religion* (Grand Rapids, Mich.: Zondervan, 1962), 1:119–20.

In conclusion, I would say that it was not in their concern to distinguish between the persons of the Godhead that the Nicene and post-Nicene fathers made their mistake. That task had to be undertaken in the face of the Sabellian heresy which denied any real personal distinctions between them. Where they made their mistake was in their attempt to explain *how* it is that the Son becomes the Son of the Father and *how* it is that the Spirit is the Spirit of God and of Christ. The explanations they offered have the Son *acquiring* his essence and personal subsistence from the Father through an eternal act of being begotten and the Spirit *acquiring* his essence and personal subsistence from the Father and the Son through an eternal act of proceeding. But in doing so they went beyond Scripture and concluded to formulations that in effect make God the Father alone autotheotic and the cause and "deifier" of the Son—the very opposite effect to the dominant intention which governed them throughout their labors—and the Father and the Son the co-causes and "co-deifers" of the Spirit.

Yet in spite of the paucity of Scripture evidence for the eternal generation and eternal procession doctrines, advocates of these aspects of the Nicene theology, in order to protect the Trinitarian faith from a "perceived tritheistic tendency" and the Christian life from a "perceived soteric fragmentation," still attempt to find ways to delineate the ontological relationship between the Father and the Son and the ontological relationship between the Father and the Son on the one hand and the Spirit on the other that will resemble if not replicate the theology of Nicaea. Usually, with Origen they urge that we should infer from the fact that the Father sent the Son into the world through the virginal begetting, and from the fact that the Father and the Son sent the Spirit into the world at Pentecost through their "pouring" Him out that these events effected by the economical Trinity on the finite level reflect an eternal generation and an eternal procession existing within the ontological Trinity. I would caution against such an approach, when clear scriptural warrant for it is slim to none, because it is a pretentious metaphysical speculation and as such faces the particular prospect of being discredited or ignored which every such speculation always faces.

Of course, it might be argued that it is quite appropriate—indeed, necessary—to assume that events reflecting a kind of relational subordination in modes of operation on the part of the Godhead rest on a prior and eternal kind of relational subordination in modes of subsistence within the Godhead. But we should bear in mind that the relational subordination in modes of operation may just as readily be traced to that theological convention the Reformed community has designated the eternal "covenant of redemption," for which there is a large amount of biblical support and thus requires no speculation (see Chapter Thirteen), and by virtue of which these distinct activities in the work of redemption at the finite level are voluntarily assumed by each. That is to say, in keeping with that eternal agreement the Son freely and willingly agreed to be sent by the Father, and the Spirit freely and willingly agreed to be sent by the Father and the Son. To look elsewhere for the warrant for these proposed ontological relational subordinations within the Godhead, that is to say, to press back behind the eternal covenant of redemption and to attempt to think about the ontological Trinity "behind" and "apart from" all redemptive considerations, is to think about the Trinity bereft of all content save for only its barren existence. But the covenant of redemption, properly construed (see chapter thirteen), will not permit even Genesis 1 and the doctrine of God as Creator to be considered apart from redemptive considerations. It is eminently desirable, therefore, that definite exegetical evidence for these proposed eternal relational subordinations within the Godhead in modes of subsistence be offered before the church is asked to accept them.

WESTMINSTER'S TRINITARIANISM: NICENE OR REFORMED?

Given the fact that the Westminster Confession of Faith employs the language of Nicea as well as that of the Athanasian Creed in II/iii, does not the Confession of Faith affirm the very doctrines—the Son's eternal begottenness and the Spirit's eternal procession—which this present study has called into question, and is it not then Nicene rather than Reformed in its Trinitarian perspective?

When one considers the confessional treatment of the Trinity, one cannot help but be impressed by the restraint which the Confession observes when it states the doctrine. It says everything it wants to say in one or two sentences (depending upon how one punctuates the Article). John Murray observes:

> [Chapter II, Article III's] brevity is striking and its simplicity is matched only by its brevity. Both surprise and gratification are evoked by the restraint in defining the distinguishing properties of the persons of the Godhead. It had been Nicene tradition to embellish the doctrine, especially that of Christ's Sonship, with formulae beyond the warrant of Scripture. The Confession does not indulge in such attempts at definition. Later generations lie under a great debt to Westminster for the studied reserve that saved the Confession from being burdened with such speculative notions as commended themselves to theologians for much more than a thousand years, but to which Scripture did not lend support. Hence all we find on this subject is the brief statement: 'the Father is of none, neither begotten, nor proceeding; the Son is eternally begotten of the Father; the Spirit eternally proceeding from the Father and the Son.' "[35]

Since there is nothing in the minutes of the Assembly's proceedings to adopt the second chapter of the Confession of Faith as its official view and thus to indicate that Calvin's insights concerning Christ's autotheotic character were being expressly upheld,[36] it is possible that the framers of the Confession simply leaped back over Calvin and assumed the theological accuracy of the Nicene and Athanasian Creeds. Certainly the language, brief as it is, is that of these earlier creeds. And the majority of Westminster divines apparently would have approved of the language, if not also the theology, of the Nicene Creed, having committed themselves to it when they subscribed to the Thirty-nine Articles upon their ordination to the Church of England (see the Eighth Article, which states: "The Nicene Creed . . . ought thoroughly to be received and believed: for [it] may be proved by most certain warrants of Holy Scripture"). It would also appear that the debates on God's attributes and the doctrine of the Trinity specifically consumed less than a week of the Assembly's time, commencing in Session 472, meeting on Friday, July 18, 1645, and concluding (since there was no meeting on the following Monday) in Session 473, meeting the following Wednesday.

But I would immediately point out that if this short span of time in July 1645 should appear to be a cavalier "rush to judgment" respecting these all-important doctrines, it should not be forgotten that the Assembly had earlier engaged itself in lengthy debates about these matters during its first weeks of assembly (July 8 to October 12, 1643) in connection with its efforts to revise the Thirty-nine Articles, which debates, as Alex F. Mitchell writes, "could not fail to prepare the way for a more summary mode of procedure in connection with the Confession of Faith."[37] And I would also note, as Warfield reminds us, that

> when during the first weeks of its sessions, the Westminster Assembly was engaged on the revision of the Thirty-nine Articles, and Article viii. on the Three Creeds came up for discussion, objection was made to the ἐκ θεοῦ, [ek theou], clauses. It does not appear that there was any pleading for the subordinationist

---

35. John Murray, "Systematic Theology," in *Collected Writings of John Murray* (Edinburgh: Banner of Truth), 4:248.
36. We know nothing of the deliberations of the eleven-man committee appointed to prepare a Confession for the Assembly's deliberations (William Maxwell Hetherington, *History of the Westminster Assembly of Divines* [1856; reprint, Edmonton, Can.: Still Waters Revival Books, 1993], 345). Hetherington noted that "almost an entire harmony" prevailed throughout the Assembly's consideration of the committee's work and that there were differences of opinion on only two subjects—the doctrine of election and the first proposition in the chapter "Of Church Censures."
37. Cited by B. B. Warfield, *The Westminster Assembly and Its Work* (New York: Oxford, 1931), 77.

position: the advocates for retaining the Creeds rather expended their strength in voiding the credal statement of any subordinationist implications.[38]

So if it is true, as Alex F. Mitchell declares, that "the so-called Athanasian Creed is shrunk up into the single sentence: 'The Father is of none, neither begotten nor proceeding; the Son is eternally begotten of the Father; the Holy Ghost eternally proceeding from the Father and the Son,' " it is equally true, as Mitchell also states, that the "rash speculations respecting the mode of the Sonship, which the Irish divines were blamed for inserting, were passed over by the Westminster divines."[39] So I say again that there is virtually no speculation in the confessional statement with respect to the Trinity, and certainly no reference is made to Christ as "God from [ἐκ, ek] God."

So while it is just possible that the Westminster divines intended to stand with the Nicene and Athanasian Creeds and affirm the ancient church doctrines of the Father's eternal generation of the Son and the Spirit's eternal procession from the Father and the Son, notwithstanding Calvin's later and (I believe) better insights regarding the difficulties attending these affirmations (which insights we know the Westminster divines were surely aware of), it is also quite possible—I would even suggest, much more likely—that these men wanted their Trinitarian statement, clearly shorn of much Nicene "speculation," to be understood, *in keeping with Calvin's better insights,* as an expression denoting only "order" in the Godhead.[40]

Bringing this chapter to a conclusion, I would contend that the three basic propositions given at the beginning of the preceding chapter are sufficient to express the orthodox doctrine of the Trinity. When the church went beyond these three in its conciliar deliverances and added the two additional propositions that the

---

38. Warfield, "Calvin's Doctrine of the Trinity," 279, fn. 137.
39. Mitchell is referring here to Article 9 of *The Irish Articles of Religion* (1615), which reads: "The essence of the Father does not beget the essence of the Son; but the person of the Father begetteth the person of the Son, by communicating his whole essence to the person begotten from eternity." Alex F. Mitchell, *Minutes of the Sessions of the Westminster Assembly Divines* (Edinburgh: William Blackwood and Sons, 1874), li.
40. Certain English churchmen of the period, such as George Bull and John Pearson, did write defenses of the Trinitarian statements of the Nicene Creed, but I find it difficult to believe that the framers of the Confession simply leaped back over Calvin's treatment of the Trinity as if it were nonexistent and returned uncritically to the theology of Nicea with its subordination in essential subsistence of the Son to the Father (and later of the Spirit to the Father and the Son). Orthodox American Presbyterian theologians, such as Charles Hodge, Benjamin Warfield, Loraine Boettner, J. Oliver Buswell Jr., John Murray and Morton H. Smith, have generally followed the Reformers' insistence that the Second and Third Persons of the Trinity are both autotheotic.

Son's essence is eternally generated by the Father and that the Spirit eternally and essentially proceeds from the Father and the Son, I would urge that it went beyond the deliverances of Scripture and that these last two propositions should not be made elements of Trinitarian orthodoxy.

CHAPTER TEN

The Eternal Decree of God

God, from all eternity, did, by the most wise and holy counsel of His own will, freely, and unchangeably ordain whatsoever comes to pass: yet so, as thereby neither is God the author of sin, nor is violence offered to the will of the creatures; nor is the liberty or contingency of second causes taken away, but rather established.

Although God knows whatsoever may or can come to pass upon all supposed conditions, yet hath He not decreed anything because He foresaw it as future, or as that which would come to pass upon such conditions. (Westminster Confession of Faith, III/i–ii)

EVERY CHRISTIAN will have either a God-centered or a man-centered theology. The Christian who gives the Bible its due will learn that, just as the chief end of man is to glorify God and to enjoy him forever, so also the chief end of God is to glorify and to enjoy *himself* forever. He will learn from Scripture that God loves himself with a holy love and with all his heart, soul, mind, and strength, that he himself is at the center of his affections, and that the impulse that drives him and the thing he pursues in everything he does is his own glory! He will learn that God created all things *for his own glory* (Isa. 43:7, 21), more specifically, in order that he might show forth through the church his "many splendored" wisdom to the principalities and powers in heavenly realms (Eph. 3:9–10), that he chose Israel for his renown and praise and honor (Jer. 13:11), that it was for his name's sake and to make his mighty power known that he delivered his ancient people again and again after they had rebelled against him (Ps. 106:7–8), and that it was for the sake of his name that he did not reject them (1 Sam. 12:20–22), spared them again and again (Ezek. 20:9,14, 22, 44), and had mercy upon them and did not pursue them with destruction to the uttermost (Isa. 48:8–11). He will learn too that Jesus came the first time

[343]

to glorify God by doing his Father's will and work (John 17:4, 6), that every detail of the salvation which Jesus procured and which he himself enjoys God arranged in order to evoke from him the praise of his glorious grace (Eph. 1:6, 12, 14), and that Jesus is coming again "to be glorified in his saints on that day, and to be marveled at among all who have believed" (2 Thess. 1:9–10).

Thus the believer should not hesitate to declare that that same concern—*to glorify himself*—is central to God's eternal plan. In the words of the Westminster Confession of Faith, "God from all eternity did, by the most wise and holy counsel of His own will, freely and unchangeably ordain whatsoever comes to pass" (III/i), and

> by the decree of God, *for the manifestation of His own glory,* some men and angels are predestinated unto everlasting life, and others foreordained to everlasting death. (III/iii, emphasis supplied)

Without controversy, this is surely one of the "deeps" of the divine wisdom.[1]

Concerning those of mankind predestinated unto everlasting life, the Confession states that

> God, before the foundation of the world was laid, according to His eternal and immutable purpose, and the secret counsel and good pleasure of His will, hath chosen, in Christ, unto everlasting glory, out of His mere free grace and love, without any foresight of faith, or good works, or perseverance in either of them, or any other thing in the creature, as conditions, or causes moving Him thereunto; and *all to the praise of His glorious grace.* (III/v, emphasis supplied)

Concerning "the rest of mankind," the Confession teaches that

> God was pleased, according to the unsearchable counsel of His own will, whereby He extendeth or withholdeth mercy as He pleaseth, *for the glory of His sovereign power over His creatures,* to pass by; and to ordain them to dishonor and wrath for their sin, *to the praise of His glorious justice.* (III/vii, emphasis supplied)

These two groups do not arrive at their divinely determined destinies arbitrarily with no interest on God's part in what they would believe or how they would behave before they got there, for

> as God hath appointed the elect unto glory, so hath He, by the eternal and most free purpose of His will, foreordained all the means thereunto (III/vi),

---

[1]. The issue of the order of the decrees is addressed in part three, chapter thirteen, "God's Eternal Plan of Salvation."

such as his beloved Son's atoning work, his own effectual calling of the elect, the Spirit's regenerating work by which repentance and faith are wrought in the human heart, and his own act of justification and his work of sanctification. And, while it is true that God's determination to pass by the rest of mankind (this "passing by" is designated "preterition" from the Latin *praeteritio*) was grounded solely in the unsearchable counsel of his own will, his determination to ordain those whom he had determined to pass by to dishonor and wrath (condemnation) took into account the condition which alone deserves his wrath—their sin.

This eternal plan or purpose (Eph. 3:11) God began to execute by his work of creation (Shorter Catechism, Question 8). In fact, since the creation of the world to this present moment God has continued to execute his eternal purpose to bring glory to himself through his providential exercise of his almighty power, unsearchable wisdom, and infinite goodness, his providence extending itself to all his creatures and all their actions—

> even to the first fall, and all other sins of angels and men; and that not by a bare permission, but such [permission] as hath joined with it a most wise and powerful bounding, and otherwise ordering, and governing of [all the sins of angels and men], in a manifold dispensation, *to his own holy ends*. (V/iv, emphasis supplied)

Adam's sin "God was pleased, according to His wise and holy counsel [which counsel eternally existed in its perfection before the creation of the world], to permit, *having purposed to order it to his own glory*" (VI/i, emphasis supplied). By his sin Adam fell from his original state of righteousness (*status integritatis*)—a state in which it was possible for him to sin or not to sin (*posse peccare aut posse non peccare*)—and so "became dead in sin, and wholly defiled in all the parts and faculties of soul and body" (*status corruptionis*) (VI/ii)—a state in which it was *not* possible for him *not* to sin (*non posse non peccare*). And, because Adam was the covenantal (federal) representative head of his race by divine arrangement, his first sin with its corruption was imputed to all mankind descending from him by ordinary generation (VI/iii). Accordingly, all mankind (with the sole exception of Christ who did not descend from Adam by ordinary generation) God regards as sinners in Adam. And because of their representation in Adam and also their own sin and corruption all men are continually falling short of the ethical holiness of God and the righteous standards of his law (Rom. 3:23), and thus are under his sentence of death.

But in accordance with his gracious elective purpose God is pleased to save his elect and to save them forever by Christ's atoning death in their behalf and in their stead and by the Holy Spirit's application of the benefits of Christ's redeeming virtues to them. And though the elect do assuredly believe in Christ to the saving of their souls, yet they contribute nothing *ultimately* determinative of that salvation. All that they bring to their salvation is their sin and moral pollution from which they need to be saved. Salvation from beginning to end belongs ultimately and wholly to the Lord (Jonah 2:10), *to the praise of his glorious grace* (Eph. 1:6, 12, 14).

THE DEBATE OVER DIVINE SOVEREIGNTY AND HUMAN FREEDOM

Opponents of the Reformed faith, both within and without the church, insist that if all of this is true, a horrible and insoluble problem emerges. Specifically, if God himself has foreordained whatever comes to pass, the only conclusion that one may logically draw is that men are not really free; and if men are not really free when they are faced with incompatible courses of action but rather are divinely determined to make the choices they do, then their sinful choices must ultimately be traced to God. And if this is so, how can God escape the charge of being the "author of sin," and how can he justly hold men responsible for their unbelief and disobedience?

Arminian theologians have argued that this problem alone ought to be sufficient to show the unbiblical character of Reformed thinking. J. Kenneth Grider, citing Arminius, argues that Reformed thinking in these regards is "repugnant to God's wise, just, and good nature, and to man's free nature," and "makes God 'the author of sin.' "[2] In his bibliography Grider commends to the reader a widely acclaimed volume of essays, edited by Clark Pinnock, entitled *Grace Unlimited,* which espouses Arminian theology.[3] Pinnock himself is convinced that God cannot justly hold men responsible for their sins under such conditions as those described by Reformed theologians. In the chapter he contributes to the volume, entitled "Responsible Freedom and the Flow of Biblical History," he presents a sustained rejection of any form of predestination that infringes on human freedom. Since his position on these matters is representative of Arminian thinking in general, I will employ Pinnock's article as a foil and analyze it.[4]

---

2. J. Kenneth Grider, "Arminianism," in *Evangelical Dictionary of Theology* (Grand Rapids, Mich.: Baker, 1984), 79–81.
3. Clark Pinnock, ed., *Grace Unlimited* (Minneapolis: Bethany, 1975). All of the page references from Pinnock that follow are from this title.
4. Since the publication of *Grace Unlimited,* Clark Pinnock has coauthored, along with Richard Rice, John Sanders, William Hasker, and David Basinger, a book entitled *The Openness of God* (Downers Grove, Ill.: InterVarsity Press, 1994). In this volume the authors contend for the same basic position Pinnock espoused in his earlier contributions to *Grace Unlimited,* namely, that the God of Scripture, having restricted himself at creation with respect to his sovereignty (viewed in terms of domination and control) and omniscience, can be surprised:

Pinnock's Thesis

Repudiating by name the insights of such notable Reformed scholars as Loraine Boettner, J. I. Packer, and John H. Gerstner (101), Pinnock marshals alongside of his own interpretation of the scriptural data in support of his position the opinions of Mortimer J. Adler, Gordon D. Kaufman, Walther Eichrodt, Antony Flew, Karl Barth, and Karl Rahner, none of whom unfortunately are even evangelical, not to mention Arminian, in their doctrinal outlook. (This fact alone ought to make his readers somewhat wary of Pinnock's conclusion.) But supported by such men,

---

God is delighted by something that happened or made angry by it; sometimes he relates to such events by repenting or changing his mind. So we [the authors of *Openness*] think that God is monitoring everything that happens and that he knows the future in great detail, but that surprises happen in history and God's own knowledge takes account of them when they happen rather than before. We see the future as not totally settled, and that, of course, relates to the risks that God faces in the future. Our assurance comes not from believing that God knows everything exhaustively (a view we question biblically), but from believing he has the wisdom to handle any surprises that arise. We understand predestination to mean not that God creates a blueprint of all that will ever happen, but that God has predestined purposes and goals which God is pursuing.... [God] voluntarily limits his own power so that the creature is able to decide things, even things that God disapproves of. (Pinnock, "Does God Relate?" *Academic Alert,* IVP's book bulletin, 3, no. 4 (1994); see also Pinnock, "God's Sovereignty in Today's World," *Theology Today* 53, no. 1 (1996), 15–21.

In *The Openness of God* Pinnock argues that the God of Scripture has freely limited his power for the sake of unabridged human freedom (112–13). He views God's sovereignty as open and flexible, a sovereignty of "infinite resourcefulness in the subtle use of power" rather that a sovereignty that "dominates, manipulates, coerces and tyrannizes" people. According to Pinnock, God's knowledge does not include a complete knowledge of the future, for if it did "the future would be fixed and determined" and human freedom would be an illusion (121). He writes "More power and wisdom are required for God to bring his will to pass in a world that he does not control than in one that he did control" (124).

The book as a whole, with its revisionist view of God as self-limiting and its authors' Arminian noncompatibilist notion of human freedom, fails adequately to answer three basic questions: (1) Can a risk-taking, self-limiting God who rarely if ever intervenes in the free choices and actions of human agents know that history will end the way he envisions and predicts *without having to rob creatures of their freedom?* (2) Can this God who does not know the future hold false views about the future? (3) Why should Christians pray to such a God for the salvation of absolutely free agents? It also shows a lack of familiarity with the historical roots of the orthodox doctrine of God and the evangelical tradition. To illustrate, Robert B. Strimple, "What Does God Know?" in *The Coming Evangelical Crisis,* ed. John H. Armstrong (Chicago: Moody, 1996), argues that *The Openness of God* proposal of a self-limiting God is not really Arminianism at all, as it claims, but just the old Socinian heresy that the church rejected centuries ago.

For four critical reviews of *The Openness of God,* see Roger Olson, Douglas F. Kelly, Timothy George, and Alister McGrath, "Has God Been Held Hostage by Philosophy?" *Christianity Today* (Jan. 9, 1995): 30–34.

Pinnock maintains throughout his chapter that men are free moral agents undetermined by the divine will. He regards human freedom to be "one of the deepest of all human intuitions" (95) and a "fundamental self-perception." He states that "universal man almost without exception talks and feels *as if* he were free" (95, emphasis original), and furthermore that "human freedom is the precondition of moral and intellectual responsibility" (95). Pinnock is persuaded that "when a theory comes along, whether philosophical, theological, or psychological, which endeavors to deny this intuition of freedom, it is up against a basic human self-perception that will eventually overwhelm it" (96).

Pinnock's Proposal

In order to have the real picture of God's dealings with the human race "borne home to us in a fresh way," Pinnock proposes that we "retell the biblical story and allow it to create its own impression upon us" (97). When we do this, all determinism, fatalism, and what Pinnock (following Kaufman) calls "blueprint-predestination" will "fall away" and "the clear biblical witness to significant human freedom" will impress itself upon us (97).

Now as incredible as it may seem, it is nonetheless true that Pinnock's "retelling the biblical story" fails to include any references at all to the numerous didactic passages scattered throughout Scripture where divine predestination in general and divine sovereignty in salvation in particular are clearly taught in so many words. Rather, he restricts his exposition of Scripture to Genesis 1–12, and more specifically only to a brief consideration of four themes he finds therein: (1) the creation of man, (2) Adam's fall, (3) what he calls "the cycle of cumulative degeneration" which pervaded mankind after Adam's fall, and (4) God's "counteractive grace."

With respect to his first theme—man's creation—Pinnock is certain, because of man's image-bearing character, that man "has been made ... capable ... of self-determination," and that man as *imago Dei* is a "creature who through the exercise of his freedom would be able to shape his own future" (98). According to Pinnock, Genesis portrays Adam as "enjoying free will in the fullest sense, acting without any coercion" (98).

The entrance of sin into mankind—Pinnock's second theme—resulted when Adam misused his divinely given freedom (100). By his willful rebellion, writes Pinnock, Adam "vetoed God's will" and contravened God's purpose for him (101). In no sense, Pinnock insists, can one suggest that God predestinated man's fall without blaspheming God (102). To the contrary, Pinnock asserts that Adam's fall sprang *wholly* from his own free choice to disobey God. *In no sense* was man's rebellion against God the result of God's sovereign will.

The question now arises, did Adam's sin in any way affect his descendants? Certainly not in any biological or legal sense, writes Pinnock (104). The "cumulative degeneration" following upon Adam's sin—Pinnock's third theme—he explains as the result of the "warped social situation" which now confronts every man with the temptation to misuse his freedom (104–5) and which invariably perverts all men. According to Pinnock, this is the *only* construction of the doctrine of original sin which the Bible will tolerate (104).

Into the arena of man's "cumulative degeneration," the result solely of man's misuse of his moral freedom, God injects his "counteractive grace" (illustrated by God's call of Abraham in Genesis 12) as his response to man's misuse of his freedom (107). Elucidating his view of God's gracious activity, Pinnock declares that God does not have a secret plan "according to which he only desires to save some" (105). Rather, he wills the salvation of all men (105), and "it was for the whole world that [Christ] was delivered up" (106). However, God's will is not always done, Pinnock continues, because he will not force his grace upon any man. Hence, "people perish because they reject God's plan for them ... and *for no other reason* (106, emphasis supplied). Pinnock considers it blasphemy to assert that man's rebellion against God is "*in any sense* the product of God's sovereign will or primary causation" (102, emphasis original).

This then is the theological construction advanced by Pinnock to explain the presence of human sin and to ground the basis upon which God may justly hold men responsible for their transgressions against his holy laws. By way of summary, Pinnock urges that God has created men with free wills and hence with the power to choose with equal ease between incompatible courses of action. God also determined to permit them to choose the way of death if they so desire. Of course, he urges men to choose life and is delighted when some do so, but the decision is wholly theirs. Therefore, when men do disobey him, concludes Pinnock, God may justly hold them responsible for their sin.

While not every Arminian will agree with every detail of Pinnock's exposition, the general conclusions he draws reflects the classic Arminian position, which uniformly grounds human responsibility in *freedom* to sin on man's side and *permission* to sin on God's side. It is important that the reader clearly see that these two tenets form the heart of the Arminian doctrine of human responsibility.

Clearly, the Reformed or Calvinistic position and the Arminian position are antithetical visions of God's relationship to human actions and cannot both be correct. The former traces all things ultimately to God (hence we speak of a "God-centered" theology); the latter relates God to human actions only in a "permissional" way, every choice for or against Christ ultimately springing from the "free" human will (hence we speak of a "man-centered" theology). Which position does the Bible endorse?

Pinnock's Proposal Analyzed

From several different perspectives Pinnock's proposal (and Arminianism to the degree that Pinnock accurately reflects it) is markedly unbiblical and therefore untrustworthy. This does not mean that Pinnock intentionally sets out to mislead: his passionate concern to teach truth is obvious in every paragraph. And one can only admire the tenacious way in which he rigidly applies the law of noncontradiction when he writes:

> It is surely a *real* contradiction . . . to assert (1) that God determines all events, and (2) that man is free to accept or reject his will. Fortunately Scripture does not require us to attempt logical gymnastics of this kind. It does not teach that God "determines" all things. (109, fn. 17)

He also correctly attacks the oft-heard evangelical pronouncement that the propositions, "God is sovereign and man is free," both said to be equally true and equally ultimate, simply present us with a "paradox" or "antinomy" (101). It really is regrettable that some Reformed theologians have not perceived as clearly as Pinnock that these propositions entail a *real* contradiction and not just an *apparent* contradiction which God demands that we believe to be true. It does men little good to be informed that this contradiction is only "apparent and not real" (how their informant is able to distinguish between the two is not at all clear) since it is still a contradiction which they are told they must believe. And, of course, once they believe that contradictories can both be true at the same time, they can never detect a real falsehood. These observations by Pinnock are on the plus side. But Pinnock is in error—seriously so—in his understanding of what the Bible teaches concerning the significant issues he addresses. The following critical evaluation will demonstrate why it is that Pinnock's construction totally fails as a truly Christian understanding of God's relation to human events.

FAILURE TO SOLVE THE PROBLEM

As we have seen, Pinnock believes, with Arminian thought in general, that unless one postulates on God's part a *laissez-faire* posture toward man's choices and actions and on man's part the complete freedom to choose one from two or more incompatible courses of action, God becomes the responsible cause of sin and thus renders himself incapable—at least in justice—to call men to account for their sins. Pinnock's counter-construction, however, assuming its correctness for the sake of argument, does not accomplish what it claims to do, namely, distance God from all involvement in man's choices. This may be demonstrated from two different perspectives.

First is the *legal* perspective. Consider the following illustration: If I, knowing my minor son's intention beforehand, *permitted* him to commit a violent crime with the gun and the training I gave him, claiming as the ground for my own exoneration from all responsibility that, though I knew of his intention and did not prevent him, I warned him of the penalty for wrongdoing and that it was he, exercising his freedom (which I granted him), who chose the unlawful course of action, legal consensus would hold, on the ground of my knowledge of his planned course of action and my failure to restrain him by all lawful force, that I am an "accessory before and during the fact." So in the case of God: If he determined that he would permit his rational creatures, using the gifts he gave them, to sin if they want to, and determined too that he would do nothing to interfere with their God-given freedom to do so, knowing however even before he created them—as he knows all other things as well in accordance with his all-comprehending prescience—that if he created them and permitted them to do so Adam and all other men would certainly sin, again legal consensus could rightly conclude that his *informed* creation of men who he knew would in fact sin makes God an "accessory before and during the fact," that he is "in this sense" responsible for their sin, and accordingly that he must be judged "culpable" along with them.

In his recent writings, as we noted in connection with our discussion of God's infinite knowledge in part two, chapter seven, Pinnock circumnavigates this objection by *denying* that God knows before men act what they will do! But this—the rejection of divine omniscience with regard to human actions which are still future—is indeed a bold step to take, and one totally beyond the boundaries of Scripture.[5] It also illustrates the extreme measures that Pinnock is willing to take to preserve the freedom of man.

---

5. In spite of such statements as Isaiah 42:8–9; 44:8; 45:21; 46:9–10; 48:4–6; and Acts 15:18, in his chapter in *The Openness of God*, Pinnock cites six verses as evidence that God does not possess a complete knowledge of the future (Gen. 22:12; Deut. 13:3; Jonah 3:10; Jer. 26:3; 32:25; Ezek. 12:3) (121–22). Space forbids a detailed refutation of his handling of these texts, but suffice it to say that in each case a less radical interpretation can be placed on the Lord's words. For example, Calvin writes about God's words "Now I know . . ." in his commentary of Genesis 22:12:

> But how can any thing become known to God, to whom all things have always been present? Truly, by condescending to the manner of men, God here says that what he has proved by experiment, is now made known to himself. And he speaks thus with us, not according to his own infinite wisdom, but according to our infirmity.

Gordon J. Wenham offers an alternative interpretation: "the mention of God knowing is used more in the sense of confirming his knowledge" (*Word Biblical Commentary, Genesis 16–50*, in loc.). The same may be said about Deuteronomy 13:3. Jonah 3:10 has been discussed under God's immutability (see p. 181).

Again, the Lord's use of "perhaps" in Jeremiah 26:3 and Ezekiel 12:3 need not mean that God did not know what the men described in these verses would do; rather, as Calvin notes in his commentary on Jeremiah 26:3, God simply made use of a common mode of speaking.

> God indeed has perfect knowledge of all events, nor had he any doubt respecting what would take place. . . . [But by saying "perhaps"] He . . . strengthens His prophet; for he might from long experience have been led to think that all his labour would be in vain; therefore God adds this, that [the Prophet] might not cease to proceed in the course of his calling; for what seemed incredible [to him] might yet take place beyond his expectation.

The same may be said about God's words in all other such statements in Scripture: God is speaking *anthropomorphically* to benefit his people.

Second, there are the *theological* problems implicit in Pinnock's quasi-deistic description of God's relationship to human actions as being that of "bare permissionism." Gordon H. Clark has noted that *bare permission* to do evil, as opposed to *positive causality*, does not relieve God of involvement *in some sense* in man's sin, inasmuch as it was God, after all, who made the world and man with the ability to sin in the first place.[6] On grounds which the Arminian demands for him, God could have made both the world and man differently, or on these grounds, at the very least he could have made mankind with the freedom to do only good (as is the condition of the glorified saints in heaven).[7] On these same grounds, an omniscient, omnipotent God could have found some way to prevent mankind from sinning without inhibiting them. It is clear then that if the Creator God simply permits a man to sin, he is still not totally unrelated to the event when that man does sin. John Calvin, responding to theologians in his day who were seeking to make the same distinction as does Pinnock between God's decretive will and his mere permission, would have none of it. He writes:

> They have recourse to the distinction between will and permission. By this they would maintain that the wicked perish because God permits it, not because he so wills. But why shall we say "permission" unless it is because God so wills? Still, it is not in itself likely that man brought destruction upon himself through himself, by God's mere permission and without any ordaining. As if God did not establish the condition in which he wills the chief of his creatures to be! I shall not hesitate to confess with Augustine that "the will of God is the necessity of things," and that what he has willed will of necessity come to pass.[8]

This is already serious enough to illustrate the inadequacy of Pinnock's solution to the problem of human sin. But there is a second factor that Pinnock has failed to face. As Clark declares:

> The idea of permission is possible only where there is an independent force [beyond the permitter's control]. But this is not the situation in the case of God and the universe. Nothing in the universe can be independent of the Omnipotent Creator, for in him we live and move and have our being [a fact not even Pinnock

---

6. Gordon H. Clark, *Religion, Reason and Revelation* (Philadelphia: Presbyterian and Reformed, 1961), 205.
7. I say "On grounds which the Arminian demands for him . . ." because, according to the Westminster Confession of Faith, III/i, "God, from all eternity, did by the most wise and holy counsel of his own will, freely, and unchangeably ordain whatsoever comes to pass." By "freely" here, the Confession intends to say that God decreed what he did with no external coercion.
8. Calvin, *Institutes*, III.xxiii.8.

would wish to deny, for Clark is merely citing Scripture]. Therefore, the idea of [bare] permission makes no sense when applied to God.[9]

Furthermore, if God only "permits" people to make the choices they do, he does it either willingly or unwillingly. If he permits them *unwillingly,* then one can only conclude that something is more powerful than God and thus one "loses" God altogether, or rather he places the more powerful thing that countermands God's will on God's throne in his stead. But if God *willingly* permits men to make the choices they do, *knowing* as he knows all things that they *will* make sinful choices, and refuses to prevent them from making those choices, then Pinnock's assertion of divine permission as half of the solution to the problem of sin does not provide the solution it is supposed to yield. Indeed, if *God* knows they will make wrong choices before they do so, then their future acts are certain and can be nothing other than certain, and again "bare permission" is shown to be an inadequate irrelevancy.

Finally, there are problems in his claim that men have free wills (understood as the ability or power to choose any one of numerous incompatible courses of actions). There simply is no such thing as a will which is detached from and totally independent of the person making the choice—suspended, so to speak, in midair and enjoying some "extra-personal vantage point" from which to determine itself. The will is the "mind choosing" (Edwards). Men choose the things they do because of the complex, finite persons that they are. They cannot will to walk on water or to flap their arms and fly. Their choices in such matters are restricted by their physical capabilities. Similarly, their moral choices are also determined by the total complexion of who they are.[10] And the Bible informs us that men are not only finite but

---

9. Clark, *Religion, Reason and Revelation,* 205.
10. For this reason one cannot answer the question "Do people have free will?" with a simple yes or no. The answer must take into account the specific state of humankind which the inquirer has in mind. In his state of innocency, Adam "had freedom, and power to will and to do that which was good and well pleasing to God; but yet, mutably, so that he might fall from it" *(posse non peccare et posse peccare).* In the state of sin, humankind has "wholly lost all ability of will to any spiritual good accompanying salvation; so as, a natural man, being altogether averse from that good, and dead in sin, is not able, by his own strength, to convert himself, or to prepare himself thereunto" *(non posse non peccare).* In the state of grace, the converted sinner, freed by God from his natural bondage to sin, is able "freely to will and to do that which is spiritually good; yet so, as that by reason of his remaining corruption, he doth not perfectly, nor only, will that which is good, but doth also will that which is evil" *(posse non peccare sed non prorsus et posse peccare).* Finally, in the state of glory, the will of the glorified saint "is made perfectly and immutably free to good alone" *(non posse peccare).* See also Westminster Confession of Faith, "Of Free Will," IX/ii–v, and Thomas Boston, *Human Nature in Its Fourfold State* (1850; reprint, London: Banner of Truth, 1964).

are *now* also sinners, who by nature *cannot* bring forth good fruit (Matt. 7:18), by nature *cannot* hear Christ's word that they might have life (John 8:43), by nature *cannot* be subject to the law of God (Rom. 8:7), by nature *cannot* discern truths of the Spirit of God (1 Cor. 2:14), by nature *cannot* confess from the heart Jesus as Lord (1 Cor. 12:3), by nature *cannot* control the tongue (James 3:8), and by nature *cannot* come to Christ (John 6:44, 45, 65). In order to do any of these things, they must receive powerful aid coming to them *ab extra*. So there simply is no such thing as a free will which can always choose the right.

But assuming, again for the sake of argument only, that man's will is *normally* free, even Pinnock will not deny that causes unknown to them can influence and even force people to choose one rather than another course of action. The weather—at least sometimes unknown to us—affects how we feel, for instance, which in turn influences our choices.[11] Diseases present in our body of which we are unaware (for example, brain tumors) can cause us, while we presume all the while our sanity, to make irrational decisions. Parents long dead, through their teaching and example in our formative years, often now without our being aware of it, still wield a powerful determining influence upon us in our adult years (Prov. 22:6). The problem that arises is this: How can any man know for sure, when he has chosen a specific course of action, that he was completely free from all such external or internal causation?

> The conclusion is evident, is it not? In order to know that our wills are determined by no cause, we should have to know every possible cause in the entire universe. Nothing could escape our mind. *To be conscious of free will therefore requires omniscience.* Hence there is no consciousness of free will: what its exponents take as consciousness of free will is simply the unconsciousness of determinism.[12]

Finally, the right that Pinnock claims he and others would have, if God has in fact decreed all things, to make God the chargeable cause of sin applies with equal

---

11. Sallie Tisdale ("Weather's Unseen Power," *Outside* [December 1995]), notes studies in biometeorology, the study of the weather's power over living things, that have found that (1) temperature has an effect on bone density, (2) warm fronts increase gum inflammation, (3) katabatic winds increase the likelihood of stroke and heart attacks, (4) low atmospheric pressure is associated with heart attacks and bleeding ulcers, as well as misbehavior in schools, (5) sunspots and solar flares influence rainfall and geomagnetic forces which in turn seem to increase intraocular pressure in healthy persons and contribute to increased numbers of heart attacks and epileptic seizures (solar activity is also linked to growth-producing hormones) and (6) the end of the eleven-year sunspot cycle seems to produce a drop in human immunoglobulin levels. These weather conditions, many of which we are unaware at the time, affect our choices and our behavior.
12. Clark, *Religion, Reason and Revelation*, 229, emphasis supplied.

force, though for a different reason, against his *laissez-faire* view of things: if God determined he would *not* control his rational creatures' thoughts and actions but give them the freedom to think and to do as they please, then these same people, being the sinners that they are, will blame him in the judgment for their sin because he did not prevent them from falling into the sin that damned them.[13] Warfield makes this point well:

> A God who . . . would make a creature whom he . . . would not control . . . would . . . cease to be a moral being. It is an immoral act to make a thing that we . . . will not control. The only justification for making anything is that we . . . will control it. If a man should manufacture a quantity of an unstable high-explosive in the corridors of an orphan asylum, and when the stuff went off should seek to excuse himself by saying that he [had determined that he would not] control it, no one would count his excuse valid. What right had he to manufacture it, we should say, unless he [had determined to] control it? . . .
>
> To suppose that God had made a universe—or even a single being—the control of which he renounces, is to accuse him of similar immorality. What right had he to make it, if he . . . will not control it? It is not a moral act to perpetuate chaos.[14]

These facts point up the inadequacy and irrelevancy of Pinnock's (and Arminianism's) solution to the problem he sets out to solve, namely, how God can hold men responsible for their deeds. Divine *permission* and human *freedom* simply do not resolve the difficulties which Pinnock presumes that they do.

A FAULTY NORM FOR THEOLOGICAL CONSTRUCTION

Pinnock is apparently little bothered by the idea of deriving his doctrine of human freedom from what *people* think, say, and feel about themselves. Because they have the intuition that they are free, apparently for Pinnock not only must they be free, but also this perceived freedom, so he thinks, is an "important clue" to the very nature of reality itself (65). But it is an exceedingly dangerous approach to base any doctrine on human intuition rather than on God's authoritative Word. Many people think of themselves as basically good as well as free, as having been, so to

---

13. Adam, it should be recalled here, in response to God's question, "Have you eaten from the tree that I commanded you not to eat from?," by implication laid the blame for his sin on God by saying "The woman you put here with me—she gave me some fruit from the tree, and I ate it" (Gen. 3:12).
14. Benjamin B. Warfield, "Some Thoughts on Predestination," in *Selected Shorter Writings of Benjamin B. Warfield*, ed. John E. Meeter (Nutley, N.J.: Presbyterian and Reformed, 1970), 1:104.

speak "immaculately conceived"—and not as the sinful transgressors the Scriptures declare them to be. Are we to conclude that they are essentially good because they have this intuition about themselves? Even a cursory reading of the Bible will disclose how far from the truth is this "human intuition," this "fundamental self-perception" about themselves (see Gen. 6:5; Ps. 58:3; Jer. 17:9; Luke 11:13; Rom. 3:10–18, 23; Gal. 5:19–21; Eph. 2:1–3; 4:17–19). And just as they are in error with regard to their claim to native goodness, so people are equally far from the truth, as we shall now see from Scripture, when they affirm (1) that they are free agents in no sense determined by God's eternal decree or under the governance of God's sovereign providence, and (2) that their unqualified freedom is and can be the "only precondition" of moral responsibility.

The Biblical Perspective

The Bible nowhere suggests that men are free from God's decretive will or providential governance. In fact, everywhere it affirms just the contrary. It teaches that God's purpose and his providential execution of his eternal purpose determine all things. This is why Calvin wrote:

> *God's will is, and rightly ought to be, the cause of all things that are.* For if it has any cause, something must precede it, to which it is, as it were, bound; this is unlawful to imagine. For God's will is so much the highest rule of righteousness that whatever he wills, by the very fact that he wills it, must be considered righteous. When, therefore, one asks why God has so done, we must reply: because he has willed it. But if you proceed further to ask why he so willed, you are seeking something greater and higher than God's will, which cannot be found.[15]

This is in accord with the plain teaching of Scripture. In fact, it is amazing how willing the Bible is to affirm the fact of God's all-encompassing decretive will and his "holy, wise, and powerful preserving and governing all His creatures and all their actions." Certainly the Bible is more willing to do so than those theologians who altogether deny such things, thinking when they do so that they do God service.

The one living and true God, the Bible says, is the absolutely sovereign Ruler of the universe (Pss. 103:19; 115:3; 135:6). Beside the fact that it is God who created the universe according to his eternal purpose in the first place, the Bible teaches that by his providence he oversees both it and all things in it. He works *all* things after the counsel of his will (Eph. 1:11). He causes *all* things to work together for good (conformity to Christ's image) for those who love him, for those who are called accord-

---

15. Calvin, *Institutes*, III.xxiii.2, emphasis supplied.

ing to his purpose (Rom. 8:28). From him and through him and to him are *all things* (Rom. 11:36; 1 Cor. 8:6)—from the raising up and deposing of earthly kings to the flight and fall of the tiny sparrow (Dan. 4:31–32; Matt. 10:29), from the determination of the times and boundaries of the earth's nations to the number of hairs on a man's head (Acts 17:26; Matt. 10:30). Long ago King David recognized these truths when, blessing God, he exclaimed:

> Yours, O Lord, is the greatness and the power and the glory and the majesty and the splendor, for everything in heaven and earth is yours. Yours, O Lord, is the kingdom; and you are exalted as head over all. Wealth and honor come from you; you are the ruler of all things. In your hands are strength and power to exalt and give strength to all. Now, our God, we give you thanks, and praise your glorious name. But who am I, and who are my people, that we should be able to give as generously as this? Everything comes from you, and we have given to you only what comes from your hand. (1 Chron. 29:11–14)

King Jehoshaphat likewise declared God the absolute Sovereign: "O Lord, God of our fathers, are you not the God who is in heaven? You rule over all the kingdoms of the nations. Power and might are in your hand, and no one can withstand you" (2 Chron. 20:6).

The Scriptures are filled with illustrations of God's sovereignty over all creation, relating his divine purpose and predetermination to all the events of the world—to the evil no less than to the good—tracing them all back to God's eternal, wise, and good design to glorify his Son and ultimately himself (Eph. 3:11; Acts 2:23; Rom. 8:29; 1 Cor. 15:28). As the reader reflects upon the following examples, he should bear in mind the helpful distinction Geerhardus Vos draws between the divine decree as it comes to expression in the Old Testament and as it comes to expression in the New:

> Both election and preterition are by preference viewed in the Old Testament as they emerge in the actual control of the issues of history. It is God acting in result of His eternal will rather than willing in advance of His temporal act that this stage of revelation describes to us. Keeping this in mind, we perceive that preterition is as frequently and as emphatically spoken of as its counterpart [election], not only in national and collective relations, but also with reference to individuals. In the New Testament, while the historical mode of viewing the decree as passing over into realization is not abandoned, the eternal background of the same, as it exists above all time, an ideal world in God, is more clearly revealed.[16]

---

16. Vos, "The Biblical Importance of the Doctrine of Preterition," *The Presbyterian* 70, no. 36 (1900), 9–10. See also H. Bavinck, *The Doctrine of God* (Grand Rapids, Mich.: Baker, 1977), 339–44.

OLD TESTAMENT ILLUSTRATIONS

1. All of the main characters of Genesis—Noah, Abraham, Isaac, Jacob, and Joseph—God, according to his gracious purpose, chose to their positions of blessing (Gen. 6:8; 12:1–3; 17:19–21; 21:12–13; 25:23; 45:7–8; see Neh. 9:6–7).

2. Are we to believe that it was only an accident that brought Rebekah to the well to welcome Abraham's servant (Gen. 24:12–27), or that guided Pharaoh's daughter to the ark in which the infant Moses lay (Exod. 2:1–10)?

3. Joseph declared that the wicked treatment he had received at the hands of his brothers had been an essential part of the divine plan to save the family of Jacob during the intense famine which was to come some years later:

Genesis 45:7 "God sent me ahead of you [his brothers] to preserve for you a remnant on earth and to save your lives by a great deliverance."

Genesis 50:20: "You [his brothers] intended to harm me, but God intended it for good to accomplish what is now being done, the saving of many lives."

4. Job, living most likely during the patriarchal age, affirms God's sovereignty over men and all of life when he responds to his "worthless physician" friends in Job 12:10–23:

In his hand is the life of every creature and the breath of all mankind. . . . To God belong wisdom and power; counsel and understanding are his. What he tears down cannot be rebuilt. . . . To him belong strength and victory; both deceived and deceiver are his. He leads counselors away stripped and makes fools of judges. He takes off the shackles put on by kings. . . . He silences the lips of trusted advisors and takes away the discernment of elders. He pours contempt on nobles and disarms the mighty. . . . He makes nations great, and destroys them; he enlarges nations, and disperses them.

5. According to Job 36:32, the Lord "commands [even the lightning] to strike its mark." And the some seventy to eighty questions God later addresses to Job in chapters 38–41 are staggering in their depth of penetration, and the number of spheres over which he claims to exercise his sovereignty is awesome (see Job 42:2).

6. During the events leading up to the exodus from Egypt God represented himself as the One who makes man "dumb or deaf, or seeing or blind" (Exod. 4:11). He also arranged every detail of the exodus event to highlight the great salvific truth that it is he who must take the initiative and save his chosen people if they were to be saved at all, because they were incapable of saving themselves. During his conversation with Moses before Israel's exodus from Egypt, God declared that he would harden Pharaoh's heart throughout the course of the ten plagues precisely

in order to (see the לְמַעַן, *lᵉma'an,* "in order to," in Exod. 10:1; 11:9) "multiply" his signs so that he might place *his* sovereign power in the boldest possible relief, so that both Egypt and Israel would learn that he is God. This repeated demonstration of God's sovereign power, the text of Exodus 3–14 informs us, God accomplished through the means of his repeatedly hardening Pharaoh's heart.

In order to claim that God's hardening activity in this story is to be viewed only as a reactionary, *conditional,* and *judicial* hardening rather than a more ultimate, *discriminating,* and *distinguishing* hardening, some theologians have argued that God hardened Pharaoh's heart only *after* Pharaoh had already hardened his own heart. A careful assessment of the biblical data will show, however, that there is nothing in the entire Exodus context to suggest that this is the proper approach to this *crux interpretum.*[17] It is true, of course, that Pharaoh would already have had a sinner's heart prior to the event, and it is also true that three times we are informed that Pharaoh hardened his heart,[18] but these facts alone do not require that we must say that Pharaoh would necessarily have hardened his heart against Israel after the first confrontation (Exod. 7:6–13). He could just as easily and readily, in God's providence, have been convinced by the first confrontation that the better part of wisdom dictated his letting Israel go. A careful examination of the biblical text will show not only that ten times is it said that God hardened Pharaoh's heart,[19] but also that God twice declared to Moses, even before the series of confrontations between Moses and Pharaoh began, that he would harden Pharaoh's heart "and [thereby] multiply my signs and wonders in the land of Egypt" (Exod. 4:21; 7:3). The first time then that it is said that Pharaoh's heart was hard, the text expressly declares that it was so "just as the LORD had spoken" (Exod. 7:13), clearly indicating that Pharaoh's hardness of heart had came about due to God's previous promise to harden it. And the first time it is said that Pharaoh "made his heart hard," again we are informed that it was so "just as the LORD had spoken" (8:15; see also 8:19; 9:12, 35). Paul would later declare in Romans 9 that in his hardening activity God was merely exercising his sovereign right as the Potter to do with his own as he pleased (Rom. 9:17–18, 21). In the Exodus context, God, in fact, declared to Pharaoh that the reason behind his raising Pharaoh up and placing him on the throne of Egypt (or "preserving him" upon the throne, as some translators construe the Hebrew) was in order to show

---

17. See G. K. Beale, "An Exegetical and Theological Consideration of the Hardening of Pharaoh's Heart in Exodus 4–14 and Romans 9," *Trinity Journal* 5 (1984): 129–54.
18. Exodus 8:15, 32; 9:34. The other verses that are cited as evidence that Pharaoh hardened his heart (Exod. 7:13, 14, 22; 8:19; 9:7, 35) simply declare that Pharaoh's heart "was hard," leaving the question of who did the hardening unanswered.
19. Exodus 4:21; 7:3; 9:12; 10:1; 10:20; 10:27; 11:10; 14:4; 14:8; 14:17; see also Deuteronomy 2:30; Joshua 11:20; Psalm 105:25; Romans 9:18.

by him his power and in order to proclaim his own name throughout the earth (Exod. 9:16; see also Rom. 9:17). It is evident from both Exodus and Romans that Pharaoh and Egypt were at the disposition of an absolute Sovereign.[20]

7. God declared that he would so control the hearts of men that none would desire an Israelite's land when the latter appeared before him three times a year (Exod. 34:24).

8. During the conquest of Transjordan, Moses again represented God as the hardener of kings' hearts: "Sihon . . . was not willing for us to pass through his land; for the LORD your God hardened his spirit and made his heart obstinate, in order to deliver him into your hands" (Deut. 2:30).

---

20. In his *Divine Election* (Grand Rapids, Mich.: Eerdmans, 1960) G. C. Berkouwer addresses the matter of the hardening of Pharaoh's heart (212–16; 244–53). In keeping with his larger concern, namely, the avoidance of the equal ultimacy of election and reprobation in the divine decree, he declares that "we must beware that *no deterministic interpretation* is attached to [God's sovereignty in hardening the heart of the nonelect]" (249; emphasis supplied), and also that "hardening is not the result of a fateful decree but an act of God which manifests its judgment upon man's sinful *self*-determination" (251; emphasis supplied). But these assertions simply fail to come to grips with such passages as those in the Exodus story itself, Luke 22:22, Acts 2:23, 4:27, 28; 17:26, Romans 9:10–24; 11:5–10, and Ephesians 1:4–11, which unmistakably speak of the predeterminate counsel of the purposing God which embraces the differentiation that exists between elect and nonelect men as well as sin and evil. Berkouwer is blinded to the obvious by his determination to view the teachings of all these passages as in no way related to a divine decree but rather as restricted only to the history of salvation (212–13) and thus to an "either-or" only in connection with Christ and his salvation. As if the history of salvation and the "either-or" of the gospel are not to be related to God's eternal decree!

While we must insist on the equal ultimacy of election and reprobation in the divine decree, we must not speak of an exact identity of divine causality behind both. For while divine election is alone the root cause of the sinner's salvation, divine reprobation takes into account the reprobate's sin, apart from which his condemnation must never be conceived and for which God is in no way the chargeable cause (see Confession of Faith, III/vii). John Murray rightly cautions:

> The necessary distinctions which must be observed, in respect of *causality*, between election unto life . . . and "reprobation" unto death . . . do not in the least interfere with the truth which is the real question at issue, to wit, the pure sovereignty of the differentiation inhering in the counsel of God's will. . . . The "equal ultimacy" is here inviolate. God differentiated between men in his eternal decree; *he* made men to differ. And, ultimately, the only explanation of the differentiation is the sovereign will of God. (*Collected Writings of John Murray* [Edinburgh: Banner of Truth], 4:330.)

Finally, when Berkouwer urges, over against H. Hoeksema, that heart-hardening is not the purpose of preaching to the nonelect, I concur, in the sense that it is not the only purpose. But it is one purpose. Many Scriptures affirm that heart-hardening is an effect, and thus one purpose, of preaching to the nonelect (see Isa. 6:9–13; Mark 4:11–12; John 9:39; 12:38–40; 2 Cor. 2:15–16).

9. On the eve of Canaan's conquest, Moses informed Israel that God had chosen them to be a people for his own possession by an election (see Amos 3:2) based not upon Israel's merit but upon God's condescending love and grace:

Deuteronomy 4:37: "Because he loved your forefathers and chose their descendants after them, he brought you out of Egypt by his Presence and his great strength."

Deuteronomy 7:6–8: "The LORD your God has chosen you out of all the peoples on the face of the earth to be his people, his treasured possession. The LORD did not set his affection on you and choose you because you were more numerous than other peoples, for you were the fewest of all peoples. But it was because the LORD loved you and kept the oath he swore to your forefathers that he brought you out with a mighty hand."

Deuteronomy 9:4–6: "After the LORD your God has driven them out before you, do not say to yourself, 'The LORD has brought me here to take possession of this land because of my righteousness.' No, it is on account of the wickedness of these nations that the Lord is going to drive them out before you. It is not because of your righteousness or your integrity that you are going in to take possession of their land; but on account of the wickedness of these nations, the LORD your God will drive them out before you, to accomplish what he swore to your fathers, to Abraham, Isaac and Jacob. Understand, then, that it is not because of your righteousness that the LORD your God is giving you this good land to possess, for you are a stiff-necked people."

Deuteronomy 10:15: "The LORD set his affection on your forefathers and loved them, and chose you, their descendants, above all the nations, as it is today."

10. During the conquest of Canaan, "there was not a city which made peace with the sons of Israel except the Hivites living in Gibeon; they took them all in battle. For it was of the LORD to harden their hearts, to meet Israel in battle in order that he might utterly destroy them, just as the LORD had commanded Moses" (Josh. 11:19–20). Here again the hardness of people's hearts is traced to the Lord's providence.

11. Samson's infatuation with the Philistine woman of Timnah "was from the LORD, who was seeking an occasion to confront the Philistines" (Judg. 14:4).

12. Eli's wicked sons did not listen to their father's sage advice which would have saved them, "for it was the LORD's will to put them to death" (1 Sam. 2:25).

13. During Absalom's rebellion against David, although Ahithophel's counsel to Absalom was militarily superior to Hushai's, Absalom nonetheless decided to follow Hushai's advice, "for the LORD had determined to frustrate the good advice of Ahithophel, in order to bring disaster on Absalom" (2 Sam. 17:14).

14. According to Proverbs 8:22–31, God, acting under the guidance of his eternal wisdom which "he possessed in the beginning of his work," framed "from everlasting" an all-inclusive plan embracing all that is to come to pass, in accordance with which plan he governs his universe down to the least particular so as to accomplish his perfect and unchangeable purpose.

15. Rehoboam's failure to heed the people's plea for relief from the yoke of heavy taxation and oppressive labor resulted in the division of the united kingdom, and "this turn of events was from the Lord" (1 Kings 12:15).

16. Amaziah of Judah did not heed the warning issued to him by Joash of Israel "for it was from God, that he might deliver them into the hand of Joash because they had sought the gods of Edom" (2 Chron. 25:20).

17. Such passages as the above illustrate the truth of Proverbs 21:1: "The king's heart is in the hand of the Lord; he directs it like a watercourse wherever he pleases." (See Judg. 7:22; 9:23; 1 Sam. 18:10–11; 19:9–10; 2 Chron. 18:20–22; Ezra 1:1–2; 7:27.)

18. The Psalmist declares that the number of a man's days is ordained by God before he is born (Pss. 31:15; 39:5; 139:16).

19. The Psalmist traces the blessings of salvation to divine election when he sings: "Blessed is the man you choose and bring near to live in your courts" (Ps. 65:4).

20. The Psalmist also exclaims: "Our God is in the heavens; he does whatever he pleases" (Ps. 115:3). Again, he declares: "The Lord does whatever pleases him, in the heavens and on the earth, in the seas and all their depths" (Ps. 135:6).

21. The wise man of Proverbs 16 acclaimed God's sovereign rule over men when he declared: "To man belong the plans of the heart, but from the Lord comes the reply of the tongue" (Prov. 16:1); again, "The Lord has made everything for himself, even the wicked for the day of evil" (v. 4); yet again, "In his heart a man plans his course, but the Lord determines his steps" (v. 9); and finally, "The lot is cast into the lap, but its every decision is from the Lord" (v. 33). See also in the same vein the following statements:

Proverbs 19:21: "Many are the plans in a man's heart, but it is the Lord's purpose that prevails."

Proverbs 20:24: "A man's steps are directed by the Lord. How then can anyone understand his own way?"

Proverbs 21:30: "There is no wisdom, no insight, no plan that can succeed against the Lord."

22. Isaiah declared God's awesome sovereignty over Assyria when he wrote that under God's sovereign governance Assyria would come against Israel because of the latter's transgressions, even though Assyria "does not intend nor does it plan so in its heart" (Isa. 10:6–7).

23. The same prophet declared that all things happen in accordance with God's eternal and irresistible decree:

> Isaiah 14:24, 27: "Surely, as I have planned, so it will be, and as I have purposed, so it will stand.... For the Lord Almighty has purposed, and who can thwart him?"
>
> Isaiah 46:10, 11: "I make known the end from the beginning, from ancient times, what is still to come. I say: My purpose will stand, and I will do all that I please.... What I have said, that will I bring about; what I have planned, that will I do."

24. Through the same prophet God declared that it is he, the Lord, who forms and creates darkness: "I bring prosperity and create disaster; I, the Lord, do all these things" (Is. 45:7).

25. Echoing the same theme, Amos rhetorically queried: "When disaster comes to a city, has not the Lord caused it?" (Amos 3:6).

26. Through Habakkuk God revealed to Judah that he was going to bring the Neo-Babylonians into the land to chasten Judah for her sins (Hab. 1:5–6), again pointing up his sovereign governance of the hearts of kings and of nations.

27. Daniel informed Nebuchadnezzar on the basis of a heavenly vision (Dan. 4:17) that "the Most High is ruler over the realm of mankind; and bestows it on whomever he wishes" (4:31–32). Then after his humbling experience, the chastened Babylonian king blessed the Most High with the following words: "His dominion is an everlasting dominion, and his kingdom endures from generation to generation. And all the inhabitants of the earth are accounted as nothing, but he does according to his will in the host of heaven and among the inhabitants of the earth; and no one can ward off his hand or say to him, 'What have you done?'" (vv. 34–35).

28. Perhaps no declaration sums up the attitude of the Old Testament witness to God's awesome sovereignty over men and nations more majestically than Isaiah 40:15, 17, 22, 23:

> Surely the nations are like a drop in a bucket;
>   they are regarded as dust on the scales;
> He weighs the islands as though they were fine dust....
> Before him all the nations are as nothing;
>   they are regarded by him as worthless
>   and less than nothing....
> He sits enthroned above the circle of the earth,
>   and its people are like grasshoppers....
> He brings princes to naught
>   and reduces the rulers of this world to nothing.

These Old Testament statements make it abundantly clear that God is absolutely sovereign in his world, that his sovereignty extends to the governance of all his creatures and all their thoughts and actions, and that his governance of people in particular down to the minutest detail is in accord with his most wise and holy purpose for both the world and the rational creature whom he created.

NEW TESTAMENT ILLUSTRATIONS

The New Testament is even more didactically explicit than the Old in its insistence upon God's sovereignty over life and salvation:

1. Jesus teaches that the minutest occurrences are directly controlled by his heavenly Father. It is he who feeds the birds of the air (Matt. 6:26) and clothes the fields with flowers (Matt. 6:28). Not a sparrow is forgotten by God or falls to the ground apart from his will, and the very hairs of our heads are all numbered (Matt. 10:29–30).

2. Immediately after being rejected by certain cities of Galilee, Jesus prayed: "I praise you, Father, Lord of heaven and earth, because you have hidden these things from the wise and learned, and revealed them to little children. Yes, Father, for this was your good pleasure" (Matt. 11:25–26).

3. He also said: "Every plant that my heavenly Father has not planted will be pulled up by the roots" (Matt. 15:13).

4. On another occasion Jesus expressly taught that no one can come to him unless the Father savingly acts first in his behalf:

John 6:44–45: "No one can come to me unless the Father who sent me draws him. . . . It is written in the Prophets: 'They will all be taught of God.' Everyone who listens to the Father and learns from him comes to me."

John 6:65: "No one can come to me unless the Father has enabled him."

5. In the same vein Jesus declared in his high-priestly prayer in John 17:

John 17:2: "For you [Father] granted him [the Son] authority over all people that he might give eternal life to all those you have given him."

John 17:6: "I have revealed you to those whom you gave me out of the world."

John 17:9: "I am not praying for the world, but for those you have given me, for they are yours."

John 17:12: "None has been lost except the one doomed to destruction so that Scripture would be fulfilled."

6. John traced Israel's rejection of Jesus to God's work of blinding and hardening: "For this reason they could not believe, because . . . 'He has blinded their eyes

and deadened their hearts, so they can neither see with their eyes nor understand with their hearts, nor turn" (John 12:37–40; see Isa. 6:9-10; Mark 4:11-12; Rom. 9:18-24; 11:32). Here we see in the New Testament the same "hardening" doctrine that we noted in the Old Testament.

7. Again, Jesus said: "You did not choose me, but I chose you to go and bear fruit—fruit that will last" (John 15:16). And on another occasion he said: "Many are invited, but few are chosen" (Matt. 22:14).

8. Before Pilate Jesus declared: "You could have no authority against me, except it were given you from above" (John 19:11).

9. Peter declared unequivocally that the treatment and death by crucifixion perpetrated on the Son of God by wicked men were in accordance with "the predetermined plan and foreknowledge of God" (Acts 2:23)—evidence from Scripture that God's eternal decree included the foreordination of evil (see also in this connection Matt. 18:7; 26:24; Mark 14:21; Luke 17:1; 22:22.)

10. The entire early church in Jerusalem gladly affirmed God's sovereignty over all of life, and specifically reaffirmed that all that Herod, Pilate, the Roman soldiers, and the Jewish religious leaders had done to Jesus was "what your power and will had decided beforehand should happen" (Acts 4:28).

11. Three times in Acts Luke points to the election and prevenient work of God in the salvation of individual Gentiles:

Acts 13:48: "And all who were appointed for eternal life believed."

Acts 16:14: "The Lord opened her heart to respond to Paul's message."

Acts 18:27: "On arriving, [Apollos] was a great help to those who by grace had believed."

Accordingly, Luke ascribes the church's growth to the hand of the Lord (Acts 11:21) or to the direct act of God (Acts 14:27; 18:10).

12. James notes that God, the source of "every good and perfect gift," "chose to give us birth through the word of truth, that we might be a kind of firstfruits to all he created" (James 1:17–18) and "chose those who are poor in the eyes of the world to be rich in faith and to inherit the kingdom he promised those who love him" (James 2:5).

13. In the extended passage in Romans 8:28–39 Paul traces all redemptive blessing ultimately to God's sovereign foreknowledge (to be understood as God's covenantal love, not mere prescience) and predestination: "those whom God foreknew [foreloved], he also predestined. . . . Who will bring any charge against those whom God has chosen?"

14. In Romans 9, in view of Israel's high privileges as the Old Testament people of God and the lengths to which God had gone to prepare them for the coming of the Messiah, Paul addresses the anomaly of Israel's official rejection of Christ. He

addresses this issue at this point for two reasons: first, he is aware that, if justification is by faith alone (as he had argued earlier), with race being irrelevant, one could ask: "What then becomes of all of the promises which God made to Israel as a nation? Have they not proven to be ineffectual?" He knows that, unless he can answer this inquiry, the integrity of the Word of God would be in doubt, at least in the minds of some. This in turn raises the second possible question: "If the promises of God proved ineffectual for Israel, what assurance does the Christian have that those divine promises implicit in the great theology of Romans 3–8 and made to him will not also prove to be finally ineffectual?" Accordingly, he addresses the issue of Israel's unbelief. His explanation in one sentence is this: *God's promises to Israel have not failed, because God never promised to save every Israelite; rather, God promised to save the elect (true) "Israel" within Israel* (Rom. 9:6). He proves this by underscoring the fact that from the beginning not all the natural seed of Abraham were accounted by God as "children of Abraham"—Ishmael was excluded from being a child of promise by sovereign elective divine arrangement (9:7–9).

Now few Jews in Paul's day would have had much difficulty with the exclusion of Ishmael from God's gracious covenant. But someone might have urged for the sake of argument that Ishmael's rejection as a "son" of Abraham was due both to the fact that, though he was Abraham's seed, he was also the son of Hagar the servant woman and not the son of Sarah, and to the fact that God knew that he would "persecute him that was born after the Spirit" (Gal. 4:29; see Gen. 21:9; Ps. 83:5–6). In other words, it could be argued, God drew the distinction between Isaac and Ishmael not because of a sovereign divine election of the former, but because they had two different earthly mothers and because of Ishmael's (divinely foreknown) subsequent hostility to Isaac. The fact of two mothers is true enough, and indeed this fact is not without some *figurative* significance, as Paul himself argues in Galatians 4:21–31.[21] But Paul sees clearly that the principle which is operative in Isaac's selection over Ishmael is one of sovereign divine discrimination and not one grounded in human circumstances. Lest the elective principle which governed the choice of Isaac (and all the rest of the saved) be lost on his reader, Paul fortifies his position by moving to a consideration of Jacob and Esau. Here there were not two mothers. In their case there was one father (Isaac) and one mother (Rebekah) and, in fact, the two boys were twins, Esau—as Ishmael before him—even being the

---

21. In the Galatians passage Hagar and Sarah symbolize respectively salvation by works or law-keeping and salvation by grace through faith. Paul's purpose is to argue that it is not enough merely to be a child of Abraham. The Judaizers, who were attempting to be children of Abraham through law-keeping, needed to be reminded that Abraham had *two* sons and that the one who was his son by the "ordinary way" (that is, by human effort) was a slave and not really a son of Abraham at all.

older and thus the one who normally would be shown the preferential treatment reserved for the firstborn son. Moreover, the divine discrimination was made *prior to their birth*, *before* either had done anything good or bad. Note Romans 9:11–13:

> Before the twins were born or had done anything good or bad—in order that God's purpose according to election might stand: not by works but by him who calls—she was told, "The older will serve the younger." Just as it is written: "Jacob I loved, but Esau I hated."

Clearly, for Paul both election ("Jacob I loved") and reprobation ("Esau I hated") are to be traced to God's sovereign decree of discrimination among men.[22]

Because Romans 9:13 is a quotation from Malachi 1:2, 3, which was written at the end of Old Testament canonical history, the Arminian theologian contends that God's election of Jacob and his rejection of Esau are treating of nations here and are to be traced to God's prescience of Edom's sinful existence and despicable historical treatment of Israel (Ezek. 35:5). But for the following three reasons this interpretation introduces the element of human merit that is foreign to Paul's entire argument in Romans 9 and totally distorts his point.

a. The Malachi context is against it. The very point the prophet is concerned to make is that after his election of Jacob over Esau God continued to love Jacob, in spite of Jacob's (Israel's) similar history to that of Esau (Edom) as far as his covenant faithfulness is concerned, and to reject Esau because of his wickedness.

b. To inject into Paul's thought here to the slightest degree the notion of human merit or demerit as the ground for God's dealings with the twins is to ignore the plain statement of Paul: "before the twins were born or had done anything good

---

22. Berkouwer denies that Romans 9–11 can be used to establish "a *locus de praedestinatione* as an analysis of individual election and rejection" (*Divine Election*, 210) or should be used to discover therein "a system of cosmology in which everything is deduced from God as prime cause" (211). In particular, on the unfounded presumption that such passages as Romans 9:22 are to be restricted in their design to showing "the acts of the electing God through the course of history" (214), he disputes Calvin's exposition of this passage that says that "the predestination of Pharaoh to ruin" is "to be referred to the past and yet hidden counsel of God" (213). His dialectical hermeneutic, which governs his whole discussion, comes to the surface in such comments as "the objects of wrath—against their will and in the wrath of God—are subject to God's majestic and merciful acts. . . . Thus Romans 9:22, which seems to carry such a strong suggestion of parallelism, actually negates this parallelism and points out to us the freedom of God's acts, *opening windows in all directions* [shades of Barth!]." I am not persuaded that Berkouwer's conclusions do justice to Paul's teaching. Calvin is the better exegete here.

or bad—in order that God's purpose according to election might stand: not by works but by him who calls—she was told...."

c. To inject into Paul's thought here the notion of human merit or demerit as the ground of God's dealings with Jacob and Esau is also to make superfluous and irrelevant the following anticipated objection to Paul's argument which he captured in the questions: "What then shall we say? Is God unjust?" No one would even think of accusing God of injustice if he had related himself to Jacob and Esau strictly on the basis of human merit or demerit. But it is precisely because Paul had declared that God related himself to the twins not on the basis of human merit but solely in accordance with his own elective purpose that he anticipated the question: "Why does this not make God unjust and arbitrarily authoritarian?" It is doubtful whether any Arminian will ever be faced with the question that Paul anticipates here simply because the Arminian doctrine of election is grounded in God's prescience of men's faith and good works. It is only the Calvinist who insists that God relates himself to the elect "out of his mere free grace and love, without any foresight of faith or good works, or perseverance in either of them, or any other thing in the creature, as conditions, or causes moving him thereunto; and all to the praise of his glorious grace" (WCF, III/v) who will face this specific charge that God is unjust.

We also learn from Romans 9:11–13 that the *elective* principle in God's eternal purpose serves and alone comports with the *grace* principle which governs all true salvation. Note Paul's expression, "in order that God's purpose according to election might stand: not according to works but according to him who calls." Here we see the connection between God's grace and his elective purpose dramatically exhibited in God's discrimination between Jacob and Esau, which discrimination, Paul points out, occurred "before [μήπω, *mēpō*] the twins were born, before either had done anything good or bad" (see Gen. 25:22–23). Paul then explains the reason for the divine discrimination with the words: "not by [ἐκ, *ek*] works but by [ἐκ, *ek*] him who calls [unto salvation]" (Rom. 9:12).[23] This is equivalent to saying "not according to works but according to electing grace." Paul teaches here that God's elective purpose is not, as in paganism, "a blind unreadable fate" which "hangs, an impersonal mystery, even above the gods," but rather that it serves the intelligible purpose of "bringing out the *gratuitous* character of grace."[24] In fact, Paul refers later to "the election of grace" (Rom. 11:5). The upshot of all this is just to say: "If unconditional election, then grace; if no unconditional election, then no grace!"

---

23. BAGD, *A Greek-English Lexicon of the New Testament and Other Early Christian Literature*, 2d ed. (Chicago: University Press, 1958), 235, 3, i, for support for this reading of *ek*.
24. Geerhardus Vos, *Biblical Theology* (Grand Rapids, Mich.: Eerdmans, 1954), 108, 110.

THE ETERNAL DECREE OF GOD

Stated another way: To say "sovereign grace" is really to utter a redundancy, for to be gracious at all toward the creature undeserving of it *requires* that God be sovereign in his distributive exhibition of it.

In Romans 9:15–18 and 9:20–23 Paul responds to two objections to his teaching on divine election which he frames in question form: (a) "What then shall we say? Is God unjust?" (9:14)—the question of *divine justice* (or fairness)—and (b) "One of you will say to me: 'Then why does God still blame us? For who resists his will?'" (9:19)—the question of *human freedom*. In response to both objections he simply appeals to God's absolute, sovereign right to do with men as he pleases in order to accomplish his own holy ends.

In Romans 9:15–18, in response to the first question (the question of divine justice or fairness), contrasting Moses—his example of the elect man in whose behalf God had sovereignly determined to display his mercy (v. 15; see also v. 23)—and Pharaoh—his example of the nonelect man whom God had sovereignly determined to raise up in order to (ὅπως, *hopōs*) show by him his power and to publish his name in all the earth (v. 17; see also v. 22), Paul first declares: "[Salvific mercy] does not depend on man's will or effort, but on God who shows mercy" (9:16). By this remark Paul makes it clear that God's salvific dealings with men are grounded in decretive, elective considerations with no consideration given to human willing or working (see also John 1:13). Then Paul concludes: "Therefore God has mercy on whom he wants to have mercy, and he hardens whom he wants to harden" (v. 18), answering the question concerning the justice of God in view of his elective and reprobative activity (see 9:11–13) by a straightforward appeal to God's sovereign right to do with men and women as he pleases in order that he might exhibit the truth that all spiritual good in man is the fruit of his grace alone.

Then in Romans 9:20–23, in response to the second question (the question of human freedom), after his rebuke: "Who are you, O man, to talk back to God," Paul employs the familiar Old Testament metaphor of the potter and the clay (see Isa. 29:16; 45:9; 64:8; Jer. 18:6) and asks: "Does not the potter have the right to make out of the same lump of clay [mankind viewed generically] some pottery for noble purposes and some for common use?"

Paul, of course, expects an affirmative response to this rhetorical question. He is teaching (1) that the *potter* sovereignly makes both kinds of vessels, and (2) that he makes *both* out of the *same* lump of clay. The metaphor clearly implies that the determination of a given vessel's nature and purpose—whether for noble or for common use—is the potter's sovereign right, *apart from any consideration of the clay's prior condition*. This suggests in turn that God sovereignly determined the nature and purpose of both the elect and the nonelect in order to accomplish his own holy ends, apart from a consideration of any prior condition which may or may not have

[369]

been resident within them (see 9:11–13 again). Proverbs 16:4, in my opinion, aptly expresses the intention of the metaphor: "The LORD has made everything for his own purpose, even the wicked for the day of evil." So here Paul simply appeals again to God's sovereign right to do with men and women as he pleases in order to accomplish his own holy ends. And Paul registers his appeal to God's sovereignty without qualification even though he fully understands that the "man who does not understand the depths of divine wisdom, nor the riches of election, who wants only to live in his belief in the non-arbitrariness of his own works and morality, can see only arbitrariness in the sovereign freedom of God."[25] This feature of the potter metaphor then lays the stress on the divine will as the sole, ultimate, determinative cause for the distinction between elect and nonelect.

God's Word has not failed regarding Israel, Paul argues in sum, because God's dealings with men are not ultimately determined by anything they do but rather by God's own sovereign discriminating purpose. Therefore, Christians too may be assured that, God having set his love upon them from all eternity by his sovereign purposing arrangement, nothing will be able to separate them from the love of God which is in Christ Jesus our Lord (Rom. 8:28–39).

For many people, even Christians, this teaching raises the question of arbitrariness in God. Even Geerhardus Vos, commenting on Romans 9:11–13, acknowledges "the risk of exposing the divine sovereignty to the charge of arbitrariness"[26] which Paul was willing to run in order to underscore the fact that the *gracious* election of Jacob (and the corresponding reprobation of Esau) was decided before (indeed, eternally before) the birth of the brothers, before either had done good or bad. Arminian theologians would spare Vos's readers the words "risk of" and simply charge that the Reformed understanding of election does in fact expose God to the charge of arbitrariness in his dealings with men. What may be said in response to this charge? Does the Reformed understanding of election (which we would insist is the Pauline understanding of election as well) impute arbitrariness to God when it affirms that God discriminated between man and man before they were born (is this not what Paul says?), completely apart from a consideration of any conditions or causes (or the absence of these) in them (is this not what Paul means by his "not by works" and his "before either had done good or bad"?)?

As Paul would say (9:14): "Not at all!" *God's dealings with men are never arbitrary* if Arminians mean by the word "arbitrary" to choose or to act one way at one time and another way at another, that is to say, willy-nilly or inconsistently, or to choose or to act without regard to any norm or reason, in other words, capriciously. Reformed thinkers deny that they impute such behavior to God. They insist that God

---

25. Berkouwer, *Divine Election*, 109.
26. Vos, *Biblical Theology*, 109.

always acts in a fashion consistent with his prior, settled discrimination among men, and that his prior, settled discrimination among men was wisely determined *in the interests of* the grace principle (see Rom. 9:11–12; 11:5). Because Paul recognized that the degree, however small, to which an individual is allowed to be the decisive factor in receiving and working out the subjective benefits of grace for his transformation "detract(s) in the same proportion from the monergism of the divine grace and from the glory of God,"[27] he calls attention to God's "sovereign discrimination between man and man, to place the proper emphasis upon the truth, that *his grace alone* is the source of all spiritual good to be found in man."[28] Which is just to say that if God chose the way he did, out of the infinite depth of the *riches of his wisdom and knowledge* (11:33), in order to be able to manifest his *grace* (9:11), *then he did not choose arbitrarily or capriciously.* In other words, the condition governing the reason for his choosing the way he did does not need to lie in the creature. (Indeed, from the very nature of the case the condition could not lie in the creature. If it did, the creature would be the determining agent in salvation and become thereby, for all intents and purposes, God.) If there was a wise reason in himself for choosing the way he did (and there was, namely, that he might make room for the exhibition of his grace as alone the source of all spiritual good in men), then he did not choose capriciously. Of course, "there may be many other grounds [that is, reasons] for election, unknown and unknowable to us," it is true. But, as Vos reminds us, "this one reason we *do* know, and in knowing it we at the same time know that, whatever other reasons exist, they can have nothing to do with any meritorious ethical condition of the objects of God's choice."[29]

Paul concludes his discourse on predestination by saying "For from him and through him and to him are all things" (Rom. 11:36).

15. In another context Paul writes: "By [God's] doing you are in Christ Jesus" (1 Cor. 1:30), which effectual work he views as the outworking of divine election (1:23–28).

16. Paul enunciated God's sovereignty over and predestination of men unto adoption as sons in doxological form in Ephesians 1:3–14:

> Blessed be the God and Father of our Lord Jesus Christ, who has blessed us with every spiritual blessing in the heavenly places in Christ, just as *he chose us in him before the foundation of the world,* that we should be holy and blameless before him. In love *he predestinated us* to adoption as sons through Jesus Christ to himself, according to the kind intention of his will, *to the praise of the glory of his grace,* which he freely bestowed upon us in the Beloved. . . . In him also we have obtained an inheritance, *having been predestinated according to his purpose who works*

---

27. Ibid., 108.
28. Ibid., 110, emphasis supplied.
29. Ibid.

all things after the counsel of his will, in order that we . . . might be *for the praise of his glory.* (emphasis supplied)

17. Paul insists still further that "God has chosen [the Christian] from the beginning for salvation" (2 Thess. 2:13), and that God saved the Christian "not according to works, but according to his own purpose and grace which was granted [the Christian] in Christ Jesus from all eternity" (2 Tim. 1:9).

18. As a final example, Peter contrasts those who disobey, "unto which disobedience," he says, "they were appointed," with those who believe, whose faith he traces to the fact that they are "a chosen generation" (1 Pet. 2:8–9).

Scores of other examples could be cited (e.g., 2 Thess. 2:11; Rev. 17:17) all to the same effect, showing that God is represented in Scripture as both the sovereign Ruler over the world and all its creatures and the sovereign Savior of sinners.

Thus it is clear that Pinnock in particular and Arminianism in general are in grave error when they reject the Calvinist view of predestination that teaches that God's sovereign decree determines human actions and destinies. The Bible teaches that God, for the manifestation of his glory, predestined some men and angels to everlasting life and foreordained others to everlasting death.

Why God Is Not the Author or Chargeable Cause of Sin

If God has decreed all that comes to pass, and if God, by his most holy, wise, and powerful providence, governs all his creatures and all their actions in order to accomplish his own holy ends, how is one to understand all this so that God is not made the author of sin and man is left responsible?

If we are to be biblical, it is important at the outset to affirm with no equivocation that God has ordained whatever comes to pass. As the Westminster Confession of Faith declares, God is the sole ultimate "First Cause" of all things (V/ii). With Calvin we must confess that God's will "is, and rightly ought to be, the cause of all things that are."[30] But God is neither the author of sin nor the chargeable cause of sin. And we must insist upon this for three reasons. The first is simply this: The Bible teaches that "God is light; in him there is no darkness at all" (1 John 1:5) and that he tempts no one to sin (James 1:13). The second reason is this: While he certainly decreed all things, God decreed that all things would come to pass *according to the nature of "second causes,"* either (1) *necessarily,* as in the case of planets moving in their orbits, (2) *freely,* that is, voluntarily, with no violence being done to the will of the creature, or (3) *contingently,* that is, with due regard to the contingencies of

---

30. Calvin, *Institutes,* III.xxiii.2.

future events, as in his informing David what Saul and the citizens of Keilah *would* do to him *if* David remained in the city of Keilah (1 Sam. 23:9–13). Therefore, *whatever sinfulness ensues proceeds only from men and angels and not from God.* Warfield observes in this connection:

> That anything—good or evil—occurs in God's universe finds its account . . . in His positive ordering and active concurrence; while the moral quality of the deed, considered in itself, is rooted in the moral character of the subordinate agent, acting in the circumstances and under the motives operative in each instance. . . . Thus all things find their unity in His eternal plan; and not their unity merely, but their justification as well; even the evil, though retaining its quality as evil and hateful to the holy God, and certain to be dealt with as hateful, yet does not occur apart from His provision or against His will, but appears in the world which He has made only as the instrument by which He works the higher good.[31]

Far from God's decree violating the will of the creature or taking away his liberty or contingency, God's decree established that what they would do they would (normally) do freely (Westminster Confession of Faith, III/i; V/ii, iv). The occurrence of the word "freely" here may surprise some readers. How can the Reformed Christian speak of man's "freedom" if God has decreed his every thought and action? The solution is to be found in the meaning of the word. Reformed theology does not deny that men have wills (that is, choosing minds) or that men exercise their wills countless times a day. To the contrary, Reformed theology happily affirms both of these propositions. What Reformed theology denies is that a man's will is ever free from God's decree, his own intellection, limitations, parental training, habits, and (in this life) the power of sin. In sum, there is no such thing as the *liberty of indifference;* that is, no one's will is an island unto itself, undetermined or unaffected by anything.

Furthermore, Reformed theology is not opposed to speaking of man's "free will," "freedom," or "free agency" (the phrases may be found in the Westminster Confession of Faith and in the writings, for example, of A. A. Hodge, John Murray, and Gordon Clark, whose Reformed convictions are unquestioned), provided the Arminian construction of free will as the liberty of indifference is not placed upon the phrases. According to Reformed theology, if an act is done *voluntarily,* that is, if it is done *spontaneously* with no violence being done to the man's will, then that act is a *free* act.[32] This is happily acknowledged in order to preclude the conclusions

---

31. Benjamin B. Warfield, "Predestination," in *Biblical and Theological Studies* (Philadelphia: Presbyterian and Reformed, 1952), 283–84.
32. See A. A. Hodge, *Outlines of Theology* (Edinburgh: Banner of Truth, 1972), 287–88.

of a Hobbesian or a Skinnerian determinism that would insist that man's will is mechanistically, genetically, or chemically forced or determined to good or evil by an absolute necessity of nature. What all of this means is this: If at the moment of willing, the man *wanted* to do the thing being considered for reasons sufficient to him, then Reformed theology declares that he acted *freely*. There is, Reformed theology would affirm in other words, a *liberty of spontaneity*. It is in this sense that I used the term "freely" earlier. To illustrate: Was Adam aware of God's prohibition and warning respecting the tree of the knowledge of good and evil at the moment he ate its fruit? Reformed theology says yes. Did Adam have the capacity and power to do God's *preceptive* will respecting the fruit? Reformed theology says yes. Did Adam, *for reasons sufficient to him,* come to the place cognitively where he *wanted* to eat the fruit? Reformed theology says yes again. (Reformed theology would also insist at this point, over against Arminianism, precisely because Adam had his reasons, that he was not exercising an "indifferent" will.) Was Adam forced to eat the fruit against his will? Reformed theology would say no. Therefore, because Adam acted knowingly, willingly, spontaneously, for reasons sufficient for him, with no violence being done to his will, Reformed theology insists that he was a free agent in his transgression. But if someone should ask: Was Adam totally free from God's eternal decree, Reformed theology would say, of course not. Could Adam have done differently? Again, from the viewpoint of the divine decree, the answer is no. To answer these questions any other way is simply to nullify the Scripture's teaching to the effect that God, who works everything in conformity with his eternal purpose (Eph. 1:11), purposed before the foundation of the world to save a multitude of sinners who would fall in Adam (see Westminster Confession of Faith, V/iv; VI/i; IX/ii). Henry Stob says this succinctly and superbly:

> Calvinists are not "free willists." They assert indeed that man is free—that he is a moral agent not caught up in the wheel of things or determined by mere natural antecedents. But they apprehend that this is something else than freedom of the will. Man is free, i.e., he can under ordinary circumstances do what he wills to do. But the will is not free, i.e., there is no extra-volitional vantage point from which the will can determine itself. Man's will responds to his nature, which is what it is by sin or by the sovereign grace of God. All of which leaves responsibility fully grounded, for *nothing more is required for holding a man accountable than his acting with the consent of his will, however much this may be determined.*[33]

Thus because God decreed that all things would come to pass *according to the nature of second causes*, which means that in the case of men they would act

---

33. Henry Stob, *Ethical Reflection* (Grand Rapids, Mich.: Eerdmans, 1978), 152, emphasis supplied.

freely and spontaneously, whatever sin they commit proceeds from them and not from God. He does not sin, nor is he the author of sin. Only self-conscious, self-determining, rational second causes sin.

For yet a third reason it is clear that God is not the chargeable cause of sin and that man alone is responsible for his sin. This may be shown by a careful analysis of the *meaning of* and *necessary condition for* responsibility, a word which every theologian uses but whose meaning very few bother to think much about.

As the main element of the word suggests, *responsibility* has reference to the obligation to give a response or an account of one's actions to a lawgiver. To illustrate, when a judge hears a case concerning an auto accident involving two cars, he attempts to determine who is "responsible," that is, which one of the two drivers bears the obligation arising from a traffic violation to give an account to the traffic court. In short, a man is a *responsible* moral agent if he can and will be required to give an account to a lawgiver for any and all infractions he commits against the law imposed upon him by the lawgiver. Whether or not he has free will in the Arminian sense of that term (the liberty of indifference) is irrelevant to the question of responsibility. To insist that without free will a man cannot lawfully be held responsible for his sin completely fails to appreciate the meaning of the word. *Free will has nothing to do with the establishment of responsibility.* What makes a person "responsible" is whether there is a lawgiver over him who has declared that he will require that person to give an account to him for his thoughts, words, and actions. Hence, if the divine Lawgiver determined that he would require every human being to give a personal account to him for his thoughts, words, and actions, then every human being is a "responsible" agent whether free in the Arminian sense or not. In other words, *far from God's sovereignty making human responsibility impossible, it is just because God is their absolute Sovereign that men are accountable to him.* If the sovereign God has determined that men shall answer to him for their thoughts, words, and actions, then that determination makes them responsible to him for their thoughts, words, and actions.

A full biblical treatment of all of the grounds of human responsibility would also include treatments of (1) man's innate knowledge of God's law, and (2) the doctrine of original sin. Men are chargeable causes of the sins they commit if they *know* to do the good but do not do it, even if they are unable to do it (Luke 12:47; Rom. 8:7). God has also determined that men are responsible for Adam's sin by the principle of representative headship and legal imputation (Rom. 5:12–19). Clearly, free will is in no sense the precondition of responsibility for imputed sin, but accountable to God for Adam's sin men are nonetheless, Paul teaches. Thus free will in the Arminian sense is not the necessary precondition of a man's responsibility for his sin. A lawgiver is the necessary precondition of responsibility.

It should now be evident from the above analysis of the precondition of responsibility why God cannot be the chargeable or responsible cause of sin. Men are responsible for their thoughts, words, and actions because there is a Lawgiver over them who will call them to account (Rom. 14:12). But God is not "responsible" for his thoughts, words and actions because there is no lawgiver over him to whom he is accountable. Contrary to what some might think, he is not obligated to keep the Ten Commandments as the human creature is. The Ten Commandments are his revealed precepts for men. They do not apply to him as the ethical norm by which he is to live. He cannot worship another God because there is none. He cannot dishonor his father and his mother because he has no parents (we are not considering at this moment the Incarnation), he cannot murder because all life is his to do with as he pleases, he cannot steal because everything already belongs to him, he cannot lie because his nature disallows it, he cannot covet anything that does not belong to him because, again, everything is his already. And because he is the absolute Sovereign over the universe, he cannot be called to account by a more ultimate lawgiver (there is no such being) for anything he does or ordains someone else to do. Because he is sovereign, whatever he decrees and whatever he does in accordance with his eternal decree are proper and right just because he is the absolute Sovereign. Did he decree the horrible crucifixion of Christ? The Bible says he did. Then it was proper and right that he did so. Did he predestine some men in Christ before the foundation of the world to be his sons while he foreordained others to dishonor and wrath for their sins? The Bible says he did. Then it was proper and right that he did so. Did he determine that he would call men to account for their transgressions against him. The Bible says he did. Then it is proper and right that God should regard us as the chargeable, responsible causes of our sin.

We have now elucidated the reasons why Reformed theologians believe they can unhesitatingly affirm God's predestination of all things in general and his sovereignty in salvation in particular and yet deny at the same time that God is the Author of sin and that people have free wills in the Arminian sense of the term. The first is simply the clear biblical teaching (see the many illustrations cited) that God has in fact decreed and is in control of all things but does not sin in doing so. The second is that God ordained that all things would come to pass according to the nature of second causes, either necessarily, freely, or contingently, with no violence being done to the will of the creature. The third is the meaning of responsibility and the clear Reformed perception that divine sovereignty, far from being an impediment to human responsibility as the Arminian imagines, is ultimately the necessary precondition for it.

A Biblical Theodicy

Given the fact that God decreed as part of his eternal plan that all men would sin

(Rom. 11:32–36) and that only some men would be redeemed from the effects of Adam's fall, *why did he do it?* And a second question might be, *Is there any way we can justify his actions before men?*

I would suggest the following as the only possible direction in which to look for a biblical and thus a defensible theodicy: *The ultimate end which God decreed he regarded as great enough and glorious enough that it justified to himself both the divine plan itself and the ordained incidental evil arising along the foreordained path to his plan's great and glorious end.* But is there, indeed, can there be, such an end? Yes, indeed there is such an end. Paul can declare: "I consider that our present sufferings [which are ordained of God; the reader is referred to 2 Cor. 11:23–33 and 12:7–10 for a sampling of Paul's sufferings] are not worth comparing with the glory that will be revealed in us"; and again: "our light and momentary troubles are achieving for us an eternal glory that far outweighs them all" (Rom. 8:18; 2 Cor. 4:17; 1 Cor. 2:7). And what is that anticipated and destined end for us? It is this: Someday the elect will be conformed to the image of Christ—our *highest* good according to Romans 8:28–29. But our conformity to Christ's likeness is not the "be all and end all" of God's eternal purpose. We have not penetrated God's purpose sufficiently if we conclude that *we* are the center of God's purpose or that his purpose terminates finally upon us by accomplishing *our* glorification. Rather, our glorification is only the means to a higher, indeed, the *highest* end conceivable—"that God's Son [N.B.: *not* Adam] might be the Firstborn [that is, might occupy the place of highest honor] among many brothers" (Rom. 8:29), and all to the praise of God's glorious grace (Eph. 1:6, 10, 12, 14; 2:7).

The point of mentioning Adam in the above sentence is this: from the comparison which Paul draws between Adam and Christ in Romans 5:12–19 as representative heads of two covenant arrangements, it is necessary to insist that had Adam successfully passed his probation in the garden, he would have been *confirmed* in holiness, passing from the state of being able to sin *(posse peccare)* to a state of not being able to sin *(non posse peccare),* and all his descendants would have received by legal imputation *his* righteousness. But then his descendants—you and I—learning of the outcome of his test, would have needed gratefully to look to Adam, still living among us, as our "Savior" from sin and death and as "our righteousness." God would then have been required eternally to share his glory with the creature, and his own beloved Son would have been denied the mediatorial role which led to his messianic lordship over men and to his Father's glory which followed (see Phil. 2:6–11). Accordingly, God decreed to "permit [the fall], having purposed to order it to His own glory" (Westminster Confession of Faith , VI/i).

As for "the others," someday the nonelect, irrevocably hardened in their rebellion against God, will endure God's wrath for their sin in eternal perdition, and this "to the praise of His glorious justice." Consider: Of Pharaoh, who is the Old Testament type and Pauline example of the nonelect man, God declares: "I raised you up for this very purpose, that I might display my power in you and that my name might be proclaimed in all the earth" (Exod. 9:16; Rom. 9:17). It is evident from this divine declaration that Pharaoh, the enemy of God and of God's people, served the divine purpose in being instrumental to the display of God's power and his ultimate exaltation in the earth, and also in providing the backdrop against which God could, by contrast, "make the riches of his glory [that is, his grace and mercy] known to the objects of his mercy, whom he prepared in advance for glory" (Rom. 9:23).

Consider another example: In the Revelation (19:1–4), after eschatological "Babylon the Great," the symbolic epitome of Satanic and human evil, is destroyed, heaven is filled with the exultant shout of a great multitude:

> Hallelujah! Salvation and glory and power belong to our God, for true and just are his judgments. He has condemned the great prostitute who corrupted the earth by her adulteries. He has avenged on her the blood of his servants.

And again they shout:

> Hallelujah! The smoke of her goes up for ever and ever.

Here we have the *ultimate end* of all things in heaven and on earth: The unabridged, unqualified *glorification of God himself* in the praises of his saints for his judgment against their enemies and for his stark, contrasting display to them—who equally deserved the same judgment—of his surpassing great grace in Christ Jesus. And *that* end God regards as sufficient reason to decree what he has, including even the fact and presence of evil in his world!

A Critique of Pinnock's Specific Errors

It only remains to direct some final criticisms to Pinnock's understanding of the four themes he extracted from Genesis, thus defending the case for God's glorious decree determining all things.

ADAM'S CREATION AND FALL

Pinnock is entirely correct, of course, when he affirms forthrightly both the real creation and fall of Adam. In a day when the historicity of these events is being denied on every hand such forthrightness is refreshing indeed. Pinnock is to be given high marks for his faithfulness to the biblical witness relating to these events. But with respect to the former event, except for the obvious fact that God sovereignly asserted his right to determine all of the details of the creation and to impose the restrictions that he did upon Adam, the Genesis record does not enter into the question of divine determinism in any didactic fashion one way or the other. Whether or not the first pair were free from divine determinism must be decided on the basis of a statement of God on the matter. This the Bible does give to us in its general didactic statements concerning God's sovereign determination of all things, not in Genesis it is true, but in many other places, as we have already seen (see, for example, Rom. 11:32–36; Eph. 1:11). Pinnock's contention that Adam was entirely free from all divine influence, deriving this perception from the *imago Dei* character of man, begs the question. He offers not one word of exegesis to sustain his declaration that the *imago* is to be defined in terms of freedom *from* God's decretive will.

What Pinnock refuses to face anywhere in his chapter is the fact that the Fall of man, not to mention the creation of man as well, was preceded—indeed, eternally so—by salvific decision-making on God's part (see Eph. 1:3–4). By this decision-making, referred to by Reformed thinkers as "the covenant of redemption," God determined before the creation of the world, in keeping with his eternal purpose (Eph. 3:11), to effect an atonement for the elect by Christ Jesus which would directly address the effects of the historical Fall. Since this is so, it follows necessarily that the Fall of man was an integral and essential aspect of the eternal and immutable purpose of God. Not to affirm so is either to permit contradictory propositions to stand unresolved in our theological thinking ("The decree of God knows nothing of a Fall of man" and "God decreed to save the elect from the Fall") or to reduce to zero the meaning of the preposition *pro* ("before") in the great *pro*-verbs ("foreknow," "predestine") in the passages that teach eternal election.

MAN'S CUMULATIVE DEGENERATION

In this area, as we have seen, Pinnock denies the legal imputation of Adam's sin to the race. But Romans 5:12–19 expressly teaches precisely this fact.[34] While it is certainly true that a "warped social situation" is a contributing factor in man's universal morass of sin, that factor alone hardly suffices as the sole explanation of the biblical description of the condition of man since the fall (see Rom. 1:18–32; 3:10–18; 1 Cor. 2:14; Eph. 2:1–3; 4:17–18). If all that Adam's act of disobedience did

---

34. The reader may consult John Murray's treatment of these verses in *The Epistle to the Romans* (Grand Rapids, Mich.: Eerdmans, 1959), 1:178–206, for a full exposition, but suffice it to say here that any interpretation of these verses which rejects the legal imputation of Adam's sin to his race calls into question the legal imputation of Christ's righteousness which is the other half of Paul's comparison.

was to open up by way of a bad example an alternative path for men to follow which would take them away from God's purpose for them (Pinnock's explanation), this is hardly an adequate explanation of the fact that *all men have followed his example.*

GOD'S COUNTERACTIVE GRACE

The Bible is quite explicit regarding what the sinner's response to God's overtures of grace would be if it were left to the sinner to determine it. He would adjudge such overtures foolishness (1 Cor. 2:14) and would refuse to submit to them (Rom. 8:7). And a form of grace that would only place salvation before lost men, God knowing all the while that as sinners they are incapable of receiving it apart from powerful divine aid that he would not extend, is no grace at all. It would be a charade and a mockery of man's helpless condition. But God's grace not only makes salvation available; it also actually saves men! Salvation is from the Lord (Jonah 2:9)—this is the united and consistent theme of Scripture. Man contributes nothing that is ultimately determinative of his salvation—*not good works* (Eph. 2:8–9; 2 Tim. 1:9; Tit. 3:5) because he has none that will commend him savingly to God's favor (Isa. 64:6; Rom. 3:10–18, 23), *not faith* (Acts 11:18; 13:48; 16:14; 18:27; Phil. 1:29) because he has a mind that *"does not* subject itself to the law of God [this is depravity], *neither is it able* to do so [this is inability]" (Rom. 8:7; 1 Cor. 2:14), *not the exercise of will* (John 1:12–13; Rom. 9:16) because his unregenerate will is in bondage to sin (Rom. 6:17, 19, 20; 7:14–25) and is dead toward God (Eph. 2:1). From beginning to end the Scriptures teach that men, when they come to God savingly, come because God effectually calls them to himself: "Blessed is the man whom you choose and cause to approach unto you, that he may dwell in your courts" (Ps. 65:4). Men do not come, as Pinnock would teach, because *they* will to do so; they come because *God* wills that they should will to do so. The Triune God alone saves men, and to God alone rightly belongs all the glory, just as it has been written: "Let him who boasts, boast in the Lord" (1 Cor. 1:31).

★ ★ ★ ★ ★

I began this chapter by saying that if the Scriptures are given their due, a person's theology will be God-centered because God's glory is central to himself. I believe that I have shown that the sovereign God has foreordained whatever comes to pass for his own glory, and that he governs all his creatures and all their actions for his own glory in order to accomplish his own wise and holy ends. I believe that I have shown just as plainly that he is the only Savior of men. Though men make choices and initiate actions that either honor or violate God's revealed preceptive will for them, never is God's decretive will thwarted, his wise design frustrated, or his eternal purpose checkmated. And while unbelieving men and many sincere but mistaken Christians would deny to God his sovereign right to decree all things or would seek to share his glory with him, the Christian mind informed by Scripture will humble itself before the God of Scripture and sing:

> I sought the Lord, and afterward I knew
>   He moved my soul to seek him, seeking me.
> It was not I that found, O Saviour true,
>   No, I was found of thee.
>
> Thou didst reach forth thy hand and mine enfold;
>   I walked and sank not on the storm-vexed sea,—
> 'Twas not so much that I on thee took hold,
>   As thou, dear Lord, on me.
>
> I find, I walk, I love, but, O the whole
>   Of love is but my answer, Lord, to thee;
> For thou wert long beforehand with my soul,
>   Always thou lovedst me.

CHAPTER ELEVEN

God's Works of Creation and Providence

GOD's "eternal purpose, according to the counsel of His will, whereby, for His own glory, He hath foreordained whatsoever comes to pass" (Shorter Catechism, Question 7), he "executes in His works of creation and providence" (Question 8).[1]

GOD'S WORK OF CREATION

It pleased God the Father, Son, and Holy Ghost, for the manifestation of the glory of His eternal power, wisdom, and goodness, in the beginning, to create, or make of nothing, the world, and all things therein whether visible or invisible, in the space of six days; and all very good.

After God had made all other creatures, He created man, male and female . . . after His own image. (Westminster Confession of Faith, IV/i-ii)

The Historical Integrity of Genesis 1–11

Because the first eleven chapters of Genesis figure so significantly in biblical teaching on the origin and nature of the universe, biblical anthropology, and salvation itself, it is necessary to say something about their integrity as reliable, trustworthy history over against the modern view which treats them at best as religious *saga*, that is, as a mythical story which, while not actually historical, nevertheless intends to convey religious truth.

---

1. God's providence here should be understood as including both "His most holy, wise, and powerful preserving and governing all His creatures and all their actions" in and throughout *general* human history (Shorter Catechism, Question 11) and his special acts of providence in and related to *salvation* history *(Heilsgeschichte)*.

[383]

The problem in these chapters for many scholars, simply put, is the distinctly *supernatural* character of the events which they report, such as the following:

1. The creation of the universe *ex nihilo* and, as a special aspect of that general creation of all things, more specifically the creation of man by the direct act of God. (Because of the supposed "prescientific" nature of the events that Genesis 1 and 2 record, the trend in modern secularistic intellectual life, influenced as it is by modern scientism's unfounded dogmatic dictum of cosmic and biological evolution, is to regard the so-called two accounts of creation in Genesis 1 and 2 as ancient Hebrew cosmogonies comparable in nature to the mythological *Enuma Elish* of ancient Babylon.)
2. God's covenant arrangement with Adam.
3. Adam's fall with its resultant effects on the race (in connection with which event we read of a serpent who speaks, two trees the fruit of which impart life and death respectively, and cherubim who guard the tree of life with a flaming sword).
4. The extraordinary longevity of the antediluvian patriarchs.
5. The universal deluge.
6. The tower of Babel incident.

The reader is referred to the seven exegetical reasons in part one, chapter five (pp. 117–18), for the historical integrity of the first eleven chapters of Genesis. It is vital that the church resist the current secularistic trend and continue to insist that the first eleven chapters of Genesis are reliable history, preserved from error by the superintending oversight of the Holy Spirit (2 Pet. 1:20–21; 2 Tim. 3:15–17). Certainly we may encounter difficulties in interpreting some of the details of Genesis 1–11, because we are working exegetically and hermeneutically with highly circumscribed, greatly compressed, nontechnical narrative accounts of the beginning of the entire universe, but these interpretive difficulties are infinitely to be preferred to the scientific and philosophical difficulties which confront modern interpreters who propound nontheistic responses to the issues of the origin of the universe, the presence of evil in the world, and man's spiritual and moral ills.

Creatio Ex Nihilo?

The traditional Christian doctrine of an original creation *ex nihilo*, based upon Genesis 1 and 2 and particularly upon the first three verses of Genesis, has been attacked in recent years from a quarter in addition to that of the scientific community. Increasingly, modern translations of Genesis (e.g., NEB, NRSV), representing the consensus of Old Testament scholarship, have rejected the traditional translation found in such versions as the KJV, RV, ASV, NIV, and NKJV, and have replaced it by a translation that does away, in the proverbial single stroke of the pen, with the doctrine of *creatio ex nihilo* in the first and second chapters of Genesis. Of course, this doctrine is not taught only in Genesis; it is affirmed scores and scores of times throughout the Scriptures, but it does place the theological integrity of these other verses in jeopardy if the one account which deals explicitly with the creation of the universe allows for, if it does not in fact teach, the eternality of matter. Accordingly, I intend to consider a couple of typical translations in order to make clear the reasons for their replacement translation, and set forth the case again for the traditional understanding of Genesis 1:1–3.

THE NEW JEWISH VERSION (NJV)

The first of the translations is a distinctly Jewish publication. In 1955 the Jewish Publication Society of America appointed a committee of seven scholars to prepare a new English translation of the Hebrew Scriptures, the first such translation to be sponsored by the Society since 1917. Late in 1962 the first part appeared under the title, *The Torah, the Five Books of Moses: A New Translation of the Holy Scriptures According to the Masoretic Text*. This New Jewish Version (NJV) translates the first three verses of Genesis as follows:

> 1 When God began to create the heaven and the earth—2 the earth being unformed and void, with darkness over the surface of the deep and a wind from God sweeping over the water—3 God said, "Let there be light"; and there was light.

A footnote on verse one reads "Or 'In the beginning God created' " and a second footnote on verse two says "Others 'the Spirit of.' " A careful examination of the two footnotes reveals that the first footnote does acknowledge the traditional translation as a possibility by the introductory word "Or." By the word "Others" in the second footnote, the editor-in-chief, Harry M. Orlinsky, explains that the traditional reading was "excluded altogether as an alternate rendering."[2] It is not my purpose at this time to defend the traditional translation of רוּחַ אֱלֹהִים, *rûaḥ ʾĕlōhîm*, by "the Spirit of God," but two reasons for the traditional translation may be noted in passing:

---

2. Harry M. Orlinsky, "The New Jewish Version of the Torah," *Journal of Biblical Literature* 82 (1963): 252–53.

1. Everywhere else the phrase occurs in the Old Testament, it refers to the Spirit of God and never to a mighty wind. (See, for example, Exod. 31:3; Num. 24:2; 1 Sam. 10:10; 2 Chron. 24:20; Ezek. 11:24).

2. The participle מְרַחֶפֶת, m‛rahepet, traditionally rendered "moved" and describing the action of רוּחַ אֱלֹהִים, rûah ’elōhîm, does not describe the action of wind. In Deuteronomy 32:11 a verb from the same root describes the action of an eagle hovering over her young. The idea in Genesis 1:2 is that of the Holy Spirit, as an active Agent in creation, hovering over the uninhabited earth, ready to carry out the divine fiat. It is a most revealing fact that in his defense of the NJV translation Orlinsky says not one word about the participle used with רוּחַ אֱלֹהִים, rûah ’elōhîm, but rather collects ancient testimony in support of his translation.[3] In every case, this testimony may be discounted as weak and unconvincing or simply indicating that "wind" rather than "Spirit" enjoyed some acceptance among Jewish scholars. More than likely, this Jewish rendering simply reflects sectarian bias against the phrase since it does provide support for the Christian's Trinitarian view of God. Consequently, I would submit that the traditional translation of the phrase as "the Spirit of God" should be retained.

Let us return to the problem raised by the Jewish construction of the first three verses and the variant translation suggested in the first footnote. Orlinsky's explanation points up the fact that the traditional translation—recognized in the footnote by the word "Or"—is at least grammatically possible in the opinion of the translators. Or at least they thought so in 1962, for in a 1965 revision of the NJV the footnote is altered to read "Others" instead of "Or," indicating, according to Orlinsky in the above-mentioned article, "a traditional rendering no longer considered tenable, but worth mentioning because of its familiar and sometimes significant character" (xiv). Such a change points up, if nothing else, the state of flux in which modern scholarly opinion lives and moves and has its being. But be that as it may, the body of the revision suffered no essential change. It still regards verse 1 as a temporal clause, verse 2 as three circumstantial clauses, and verse 3 as the main clause of the opening statement of Genesis. This means, of course, that the first two verses are subordinated grammatically and syntactically to verse 3. The implication of this rendering is obvious. The verses now say absolutely nothing about a creation out of nothing or about the beginning of matter. To the contrary, they imply the pre-existence, if not the eternality, of matter. The effect of such teaching on Christian theology hardly needs to be stated. Ultimately, it would alter all Christian thought—in the areas of dogmatics and Christian experience no less than in biology and science.

---

3. Harry M. Orlinsky, "The Rage to Translate: The New Age of Bible Translations," in *Genesis* (New York: Harper, 1966).

THE ANCHOR BIBLE (AB) GENESIS

Ephraim A. Speiser's *Genesis* (AB), published in 1964, also calls for a change in the traditional rendering of Genesis 1:1–3. This translation too opens with the words:

> 1 When God set about to create heaven and earth—2 the world being then a formless waste, with darkness over the seas and only an awesome wind sweeping over the water—3 God said, "Let there be light." And there was light.

Once again, and even in a heightened sense due to the purely arbitrary introduction of the "then" in verse 2, the first two verses are subordinated to the third verse grammatically and syntactically.

This handling of these verses is not entirely new. With minor variations this "subordination [of the first two verses to the third] view" was suggested by Rashi, the Jewish expositor, in the eleventh century, by Heinrich Ewald in the nineteenth century, and by other scholars in our time. For instance, Theophile J. Meek adopted this construction.[4] *The Westminster Study Edition of the Holy Bible* (1948) states in a footnote its preference for this construction over the traditional one. Moffatt's translation follows suit. And the *Revised Standard Version* (RSV), though it follows the traditional translation in the text, inserts the footnote "Or *When God began to create.*" Even Merrill F. Unger feels compelled to say that the first three verses of Genesis say nothing about an original creation out of nothing, escaping the implications of his assertion by affirming that a period of time should be posited *before* Genesis 1:1 during which the Bible student should place the original creation and the fall of the angels. In other words, Genesis 1:1–3 describes a later re-creation.[5]

Reasons for such a radical alteration of the meaning of these verses away from the traditional one certainly must be compelling. What are they? Basically two: the *cultural* and the *grammatical*.

The Cultural Reason

The Genesis account of creation, it is argued, being an ancient Near Eastern cosmogony, must be placed within its cultural milieu. When this is done a remarkable similarity is seen to exist between its account of creation and other ancient Near Eastern cosmogonies, particularly in that they all agree on the preexistence of

---

4. See Meek's translation of Genesis for *The Bible: An American Translation* (Chicago: University of Chicago Press, 1931).
5. See Merrill F. Unger, "Rethinking the Genesis Account of Creation," *Bibliotheca Sacra* 115 (Jan. 1958): 28, and his *Unger's Bible Handbook* (Chicago: Moody, 1966), 226.

matter at the time of the first creative act. Specifically, (1) the Babylonian account, popularly entitled *Enuma Elish,* and (2) the so-called second account of creation in Genesis 2:4b–25 are cited as proofs of this fact. (Unger does not affirm this cultural reason.)

It is true that *Enuma Elish* does begin with a temporal clause—"When above the heavens had not [yet] been named, [and] below the earth had not [yet] existed as such"—and it is equally true that lines 3–8 may be construed either as another temporal clause (or possibly two) or as circumstantial thoughts with the main clause introduced at line 9: "Then were the gods created." It is also true that similarities between Genesis 1 and *Enuma Elish* do exist. But are these similarities sufficient reason to insist that the Genesis account recognizes, as does *Enuma Elish,* the preexistence of matter? May not these similarities be due to a common source of original information originating from an actual occurrence? Classic Christian theism believes that Moses was enabled by the inspiration of the Spirit of God to record the true account of creation accurately, purged of all the crude mythological and polytheistic incrustations found in the other accounts. Certainly one cannot find a primitive polytheism in the Mosaic record. Why then insist that the Mosaic record must teach the preexistence of matter? Perhaps those who do ought to admit that they do so, not on an empirically established, objective basis founded on careful exegesis, but rather on the a *priori* assumption that the Genesis account of creation is *not* unique among ancient cosmogonies, that it is *not* an inspired account of what actually occurred at the beginning of earth history but rather the literary reconstruction of an ancient story by the so-called Priestly School of late Israelite history.

Regarding the use of Genesis 2:4b–25 as an illustration of *another* creation account within the Scriptures themselves that begins with a temporal clause, followed by circumstantial thoughts, the main clause being introduced at verse 7, this passage should not and cannot be employed as a parallel to Genesis 1:1–3 for three reasons: First, such a view assumes at the outset that Genesis 2:4b–25 is a second account of creation, an assumption far from being proved or universally accepted; rather, the content of Genesis 2 suggests that far more likely it is a more detailed account of the sixth creative day of Genesis 1.

Second, the division of Genesis 2:4 into two parts is both arbitrary and hermeneutically suspect. The first part (2:4a) is made to serve as a subscription to the creation account of Genesis 1:1–2:3, and the second part (2:4b) is construed as the opening temporal clause of the second account of creation—a division which is absolutely essential to the view that Genesis 2:4bff. is a precise parallel to Genesis 1:1–3. But the division is made only in the interest of having a second parallel account of creation in Genesis 2. It is hermeneutically suspect in that, if the phrase in 2:4a–"These are the generations of the heavens and the earth"—be construed as a postscript to the preceding passage, it is the *only* time out of the eleven times that it is used in Genesis where it is appended to a preceding passage rather than allowed to serve as a superscription to a following passage!

Third, the syntax in the two accounts actually differs, with Genesis 2:4b containing a Hebrew infinitive construct in a very crucial place whereas Genesis 1:1 contains a finite verb in the same crucial place, a fact which makes all the difference in the way the two verses are to be translated. In any translation 2:4b must be regarded as a subordinate clause because of the presence of the infinitive construct, whereas Genesis 1:1 may be rendered as an independent statement, a fact which the first footnote of the NJV (1962) on Genesis 1:1 readily recognized.

I conclude that the cultural reason for the "subordination view" of Genesis 1:1–2 is not compelling. But what about the grammatical reason? The reason for accepting or rejecting the proposed translation of any passage of Scripture must ultimately be based on sound grammatical and exegetical considerations found in the passage itself. Therefore, we need to look at the grammatical reason for the proffered change in translation.

The Grammatical Reason

The particular form of the first word-group in Genesis 1:1 (בְּרֵאשִׁית, $b^e r\bar{e}'\hat{s}\hat{\imath}t$, taken to be in the construct state) is said to demand that the verse be translated as a temporal clause, literally, "In the beginning of God's creating," which normally is then smoothed to "When God began to create"; and the clauses of verse 2, taken as noun or circumstantial clauses, are said to require a rendering which shows the circumstances which they speak of as existing at the time of the divine fiat of verse 3.

Nothing is wrong with the translation of verse 3 in either of the modern translations mentioned earlier. (Verse 3 is not really germane to the problem before us.) Nor is it a problem that the three clauses of verse 2 are construed as noun or circumstantial clauses which are subordinated to the third verse ("Now the earth being empty and formless, with darkness upon the face of the deep, and the Spirit of God hovering over the face of the waters, God said, 'Let there be light, and there was light.' ") But the treatment of verse 1 is the problem.

The entire issue of whether to render Genesis 1:1 as "In the beginning God created the heaven and the earth," or as a temporal clause meaning "When God began to create the heaven and the earth," turns on the first word-group in Genesis, traditionally translated "In the beginning." This word is composed of the preposition בְּ, b^e, meaning "in," and the noun רֵאשִׁית, $r\bar{e}'\hat{s}\hat{\imath}t$, meaning "beginning." The noun is anarthrous, having no article, and as far as its form is concerned could be in either the absolute or the construct state. Now admittedly, when a definite noun is in the construct state, it is anarthrous and derives its definiteness from the following definite noun or verbal idea. Hence, it is argued by modern scholars that since

בְּרֵאשִׁית, *bᵉrē'šît*, is anarthrous, (1) it is standing in relation to what follows, (2) it is thus made definite by the following verbal idea, and (3) it is accordingly to be translated literally: "In the beginning of God's creating," which resolves itself quite naturally into the temporal thought: "When God began to create." (A noun in the construct state is normally followed, it is true, by another noun while here it is followed by the finite verb בָּרָא, *bārā'*; but it must be admitted that such a construction is also a genuine Semitic usage, as evidenced by the occurrence of this construction in Exod. 4:13; 6:28; Lev. 14:46; Deut. 4:15; 1 Sam. 5:9; 25:15; Pss. 16:3; 58:9; 81:6; Isa. 29:1; Hos. 1:2.)

But does the omission of the article in בְּרֵאשִׁית, *bᵉrē'šît*, demand that the noun be construed as standing in a construct relation to the following finite verb? Not necessarily, for in Isaiah 46:10 this very word is anarthrous, and yet it is clearly in the absolute state: "the One declaring from [the] beginning the end." Thus the mere absence of the article is not sufficient evidence, standing alone, for determining the state of the noun רֵאשִׁית, *rē'šît*. The decision must be made in the light of other considerations, and for these I am indebted to Edward J. Young's following exegetical insights:[6]

1. In the Hebrew text בְּרֵאשִׁית, *bᵉrē'šît*, is accented with a disjunctive accent, indicating that the word has its own independent accent and was thus construed by the Masoretes as an absolute noun.

2. Without exception the ancients versions regarded בְּרֵאשִׁית, *bᵉrē'šît*, as an absolute.

3. In the Old Testament when a construct noun precedes a finite verb, the fact of constructness is apparent, either from the form of the noun in construct or from the demands of the context that the noun be so taken. Neither of these conditions is present in Genesis 1:1. In fact, the context, specifically the finite verb בָּרָא, *bārā'*, favors the absolute state, for while the verb is frequently employed with the accusative of the *product* produced, it is *never* employed in a context where an accusative of the *material* employed in the creative act is mentioned, which would be the case here if בְּרֵאשִׁית, *bᵉrē'šît*, were construed as a construct noun. Even Gerhard von Rad, the form-critical Old Testament scholar, feels obliged to write: "Since pre-existent matter is never mentioned in connection with this activity [denoted by בָּרָא, *bārā'*], the idea of *creatio ex nihilo* is connected with it."[7]

It is preferable, therefore, to view בְּרֵאשִׁית, *bᵉrē'šît*, as an absolute noun on the analogy of Ἐν ἀρχῇ, *en archē*, in John 1:1, and to construe verse 1 as a grand summary statement of the creation of the universe out of nothing—as it has been traditionally rendered.

---

6. Edward J. Young, *Studies in Genesis One* (Philadelphia: Presbyterian and Reformed, 1964), 5–7.
7. Gerhard Von Rad, *Old Testament Theology*, trans. by D. M. G. Stalker (New York: Harper & Row, 1962), 1:142.

Why regard verse 1 as a "grand summary statement" of all that follows? First, because the phrase "the heavens and the earth" is what is known as an "antonymic pair" in Hebrew idiom, standing in for our "universe," but more than that, for the "well-ordered universe." Second, because in the verses that follow verse 1, the reader actually sees God's consecutive acts whereby he created "the well-ordered universe" of verse 1. Admittedly, this view of the matter, in the words of Edward J. Young, sees, regarding verse 2, "no explicit statement of the creation of the primeval matter from which the universe we know was formed,"[8] but we have every reason to infer its origination from the hand of God by an *ex nihilo* act from the summary statement of verse 1.

The following paraphrase of Genesis 1:1–3 gathers together the several points and nuances which were noted throughout the exposition:

> 1 In the beginning God created the well-ordered universe. 2 Now with respect to the earth, being originally created by God empty and formless, with darkness upon the face of the deep and the Spirit of God hovering over the face of the waters, 3 God said, "Let there be light." And there was light.

Some object that this construction has God originally creating a "chaos"—an ascription insulting, it is said, to the divine nature. But such an objection is based on an unwarranted *a priori* perception of what God should or should not do in keeping with the perfections of his nature. The objection presumes that an originally unformed earth as a first creative act on his part is unbecoming to his character. But this cannot be demonstrated and therefore must not be assumed. The emphasis of Genesis 1 itself appears to be not so much on God's *power* to create—this is assumed and everywhere displayed—but on his creative ability as an Architect to "build" from originally created material, supplemented with subsequently created material, a beautiful world capable of sustaining created life.

In light of this exposition we may reaffirm the historic Christian conviction that the Triune God created the universe out of nothing and that the Son and the Spirit were the Father's Coagents in creating the universe. The Son's involvement in the original creative activity is declared in these Scriptures:

> John 1:2–3: "[The Word] was with God in the beginning. Through him all things were made; without him nothing was made that has been made."

> Colossians 1:16: "By [the Son] all things were created: things in heaven and on earth, visible and invisible, whether thrones or powers or rulers or authorities; all things were created by him and for him."

---

8. Young, *Studies in Genesis One*, 11.

Hebrews 1:2: "[God] has spoken to us by his Son . . . through whom he made the universe."

The Scriptures teach that the Holy Spirit was involved in the creation work as well:

Genesis 1:2: "And the Spirit of God was hovering over the waters" in a state of readiness to carry out the divine fiats of the Logos of God as they were issued.
Job 26:13: "By his Spirit the skies became fair." (See also Ps. 104:30)

Finally, the writer of Hebrews declares plainly that God created the universe out of nothing: "the universe was formed at God's command, so that what is seen was not made out of what was visible" (Heb. 11:3).

The Days of Creation

Much has been written about the length of the days of creation, whether they were ordinary days of around twenty-fours hours duration, long ages, some combination of days and ages, or simply a nonhistorical literary framework or mnemonic device intended to serve as the means whereby information about the divine activity in creation might be presented in an aesthetically pleasing and helpful fashion. I can discern no reason, either from Scripture or from the human sciences, for departing from the view that the days of Genesis were ordinary twenty-four-hour days.[9] The following points favor this view:

---

9. It is often said, as does Hugh Ross in *The Fingerprint of God,* 2d ed. (Orange, Calif.: Promise, 1991), that "many of the early church fathers and other biblical scholars interpreted the creation days of Genesis 1 as long periods of time. The list includes . . . Augustine, and later Aquinas to name a few" (141). Andrew Dickson White is much closer to the truth when he states that "down to a period almost within living memory [in 1896], it was held, virtually 'always, everywhere, and by all,' that the universe, as we now see it, was created literally and directly . . . in an instant or in six days" (*A History of the Warfare of Science with Theology* [New York: D. Appleton, 1896], 60). In fact Augustine said repeatedly that God created the universe *ex nihilo* and that the "days" of Genesis, as Ernan McMullin summarizes his view in *Evolution and Creation* (Notre Dame: University Press, 1985), were "stages in the angelic knowledge of creation," the "days" themselves occurring in "an indivisible instant, so that all the kinds of things mentioned in Genesis were really made simultaneously" (11–12). Augustine was even willing to say that "from Adam to the flood there were 2,262 years according to the calculation data in our versions of the Scriptures" (*The City of God,* book 15, chapter 8)—not a chronology in keeping with an evolutionary view of the origin of the universe. As for Aquinas, nowhere does he explicitly declare for the days as being ages; in fact he states, "The words *one day* are used when day is first instituted, to denote that one day is made up of twenty-four hours" (*Summa theologica,* Question 74, Article 3).

1. The word "day" (יוֹם, yôm), in the singular, dual and plural, occurs some 2,225 times in the Old Testament with the overwhelming preponderance of these occurrences designating the ordinary daily cycle. Normally, the preponderate meaning of a term should be maintained unless contextual considerations force one to another view. As Robert Lewis Dabney states with respect to the meaning of יוֹם, yôm, in Genesis 1: "The narrative [of Genesis 1] seems historical, and not symbolical; and hence the strong initial presumption is, that all its parts are to be taken in their obvious sense.... The natural day is [yôm's] literal and primary meaning. Now, it is apprehended that in construing any document, while we are ready to adopt, at the demand of the context, the derived or tropical meaning, we revert to the ordinary one, when no such demand exists in the context."[10] No such contextual demand exists in Genesis 1.

2. The recurring phrase, "and the evening and the morning [taken together] constituted day one, etc." (1:5, 8, 13, 19, 23, 31), suggests as much. The qualifying words, "evening and morning," attached here to each of these recurring statements occur together outside of Genesis in 37 verses (e.g., Exod. 18:13; 27:21). In each instance these words are employed to describe an ordinary day.

3. In the hundreds of other cases in the Old Testament where יוֹם, yôm, stands in conjunction with an ordinal number (first, second, third, etc.), e.g., Exodus 12:15; 24:16; Leviticus 12:3, it never means anything other than a normal, literal day.

4. With the creation of the sun "to rule the day" and the moon "to rule the night" occurring on the fourth day (Gen. 1:16–18), days four through six would almost certainly have been ordinary days. This would suggest that the seventh would also have been an ordinary day.[11] All this would suggest in turn, if we may

---

While Luther and Calvin construed the days of Genesis as ordinary days, it is true that some later conservative theologians such as Charles Hodge and Benjamin B. Warfield were willing to interpret the days of Genesis as periods of indefinite duration.

See Jack Lewis, "The Days of Creation: An Historical Survey of Interpretation," *Journal of Theological Studies* 32, no. 4 (1989): 433–55, for a survey of what the church fathers said about the days of Genesis 1.

10. Robert Lewis Dabney, *Lectures in Systematic Theology* (1878; reprint, Grand Rapids, Mich.: Zondervan, 1972), 254–55.

11. An oft-repeated argument for the days of Genesis 1 to be construed as long periods of time is that, since the biblical account does not employ for the seventh day the concluding phrase "and the evening and the morning were the seventh day," the seventh-day Sabbath is still continuing. I would suggest that because the divine activity on the Sabbath day differed in character from that on the first six days (rest over against work), a different concluding formula was appended to indicate not only the end of the seventh day but also the end of the creation week: "and by the seventh day God ended his work which he had made; and he rested on the seventh day from all his work which he had made" (author's translation). These words suggest an end of the seventh day as surely as do the words "and the evening and the morning were the first day."

assume that the earth was turning on its axis at that time, that days one through three would have been ordinary days as well.

5. If we follow the *analogia Scripturae* principle of hermeneutics enunciated in the Westminster Confession of Faith to the effect that "the infallible rule of interpretation of Scripture is the Scripture itself: and therefore, when there is a question about the true and full sense of any Scripture (which is not manifold, but one), it must be searched and known by other places that speak more clearly" (I/ix), then the "ordinary day" view has most to commend it since Moses grounds the commandment regarding seventh-day Sabbath observance in the fact of the divine Exemplar's activity: "In six days the Lord made the heavens and the earth, the sea, and all that is in them, but he rested on the seventh day. Therefore the Lord blessed the Sabbath day and made it holy" (Exod. 20:11; see also 31:15–17).

6. In the 608 occurrences of the plural "days" (יָמִים, *yāmîm*) in the Old Testament (see Exod. 20:11), their referents are always ordinary days. Ages are never expressed by the word יָמִים, *yāmîm*.

7. Finally, had Moses intended to express the idea of seven "ages" in Genesis 1 he could have employed the term עוֹלָם, *'ôlām*, which means "age" or "period of indeterminate duration."

The Age of the Universe

A related question has to do with the age of the universe. Some evangelical scholars have urged that by simply determining the birth date for Abraham and then totaling up the ages of the patriarchs listed in the genealogies of Genesis 5 and 11 at the time each fathered his successor, one may determine when Adam was created and accordingly (assuming that the days of Genesis are ordinary days) when the universe itself was created. This procedure has yielded a date for the creation of the universe of around 4004 B.C. (Usher's date). But the issue cannot be settled so simply for several reasons:

1. The ancestral connections between people in Scripture are often abridged. For example, Matthew 1:1 represents Abraham as the father of David and David as the father of Jesus, both halves of this portion of Jesus' genealogy omitting many generations. In Matthew 1:8 we read that "Joram begat Uzziah," but this omits three generations, namely, Ahaziah, Joash, and Amaziah. Then we read in Exodus 6:20

Another argument urges that the seventh day of Genesis 2:1–3 is represented in Psalm 95:7–11 and Hebrews 4:3–6 as an open-ended (but finite) day of rest. But these passages may just as easily be interpreted as referring to the believer's *eschatological* rest, of which the Sabbath-day rest is the type (which is the reason why Christians should observe the fourth commandment today).

that Amram (by Jochabed) fathered Aaron and Moses, giving the impression that Amram was Moses' immediate father. But from Numbers 3:17–19, 27–28, we learn that in the days of Moses the Amramites, together with the families of Amram's three brothers (Izhar, Hebron, and Uzziel), numbered 8600 males, 2630 of whom were between 30 and 50 years of age (Num. 4:35–36). Rather clearly, Amram was an ancestor of Moses and Aaron, separated from them by a span of some 300 years—unless we want to conclude that Moses had over 8500 living male first cousins!

2. The total number of years for the several patriarchs is not totalled in either Genesis 5 or Genesis 11. This suggests that the genealogical lists are not complete, particularly when we note that Moses did add together the two numbers which are given in connection with each antediluvian in Genesis 5.

3. The name and years of Cainan (Luke 3:36) must be placed between Shelah and Arphaxad in the Genesis 11 list.

4. With the addition of Cainan's name in Genesis 11, the genealogies of Genesis 5 and 11 both list ten patriarchs, the tenth in each case having three sons. This symmetry suggests that the principle of selectivity rather than completeness governed the compilation of the lists.

5. Information is given which is irrelevant to a strict chronology. The additional information is given primarily to impress upon us "the vigor and grandeur of humanity in those old days of the world's prime."[12]

6. The postdiluvian patriarchs could not have been contemporaries of Abraham. But if the strict interpretation of Genesis 11 is correct, *all* the postdiluvian patriarchs, including Noah, would still have been alive when Abraham was fifty years of age. *Three* of those who were born before the earth was divided by the Babel incident (Shem, Shelah, and Eber) would have outlived Abraham. And Eber, the father of Peleg, not only would have outlived Abraham but also would have lived for two years after Jacob arrived in Mesopotamia to work for Laban. But why then would Genesis 10:25 declare that the Babel incident took place in Peleg's day if all of the postdiluvian patriarchs to that time were still alive? And why would Genesis 25:8 say of Abraham who died at 175 years of age that he "died at a good old age, an old man and full of years," if the three ancestors who outlived him lived respectively to be 600, 433, and 434 years old?

7. The strict interpretation of Genesis 11 would place the Flood in the year 2459 B.C., 292 years before the birth of Abraham (assuming that 2167 B.C. was Abraham's birth date). But there is good evidence that Near Eastern cultures have a continuous archaeological record (based upon occupation levels and pottery chronology)

---

12. See Benjamin B. Warfield, *Biblical and Theological Studies* (Philadelphia: Presbyterian and Reformed, 1952), 244.

back to at least the fifth millennium B.C. It seems impossible to fit a third millennium B.C. universal flood into such a framework.

Thus the Bible gives us no basis for determining the precise date for the creation week of Genesis. The genealogical formula employed in Genesis 5 and 11 should be understood as: "X lived x number of years, and begot [the ancestral father that begot] Y. And X lived after he begot [the ancestral father that begot] Y x number of years, and begot [other] sons and daughters."

On the other hand, there is no reason to believe that the universe and the earth in particular are billions of years old either, as many astronomers and geologists insist. A real creation would of necessity require that some aspects of the universe would have come from the hand of its Creator with an appearance of age. For example, Adam in the very hour he was created would have appeared to be a mature man of some years. Then the geological upheaval at the time of the Flood (see Gen. 7:11; 2 Pet. 3:6) could also account for much of the geologist's "evidence" for an ancient earth which is exhibited in his "geological column" (which actually exists as such only in geology textbooks and nowhere in the actual earth record itself). Moreover, the various scientific methods (e.g., carbon-14 dating, potassium-argon dating, thermoluminescent dating) employed for fossil and pottery dating are suspect, being imprecise and contradictory in their findings. Consequently, we simply cannot discover the age of the earth or of man on the basis of any evidence we have to date. But the tendency of Scripture, limiting the *known* gaps in its genealogies to tens and hundreds of years and not thousands and millions of years, seems to be toward a relatively young earth and a relatively short history of man to date.

The Purpose of the Created Universe

The created universe exists as a matchless display of the glory of God. David declared in Psalm 19:1–4:

> The heavens are declaring the glory of God,
>   The vast expanse displays his handiwork.
> Day after day they "pour forth speech";
>   Night after night they display knowledge.
> They have no speech, there are no words;
>   No sound is heard from them.
> Their "voice" goes out into all the earth,
>   Their words to the ends of the world. (author's translation)

The Hebrew word translated in verse 1 as "are declaring" is מְסַפְּרִים, *mᵉsappᵉrîm*, the Piel masculine plural participle from the root סָפַר, *sāpar*, meaning literally, according to W. Gesenius, "to scratch, scrape, hence, to inscribe or to write," according to Brown, Driver, and Briggs, "to count, recount, number," and according to Koehler-Baumgartner, "to recount, make known." The idea of "inscribing" or "recounting" seems to be intrinsic to the word and here it is ascribed figuratively to the heavens. The heavens and the sheer vastness of space are eagerly (force of the Piel) and continually (force of the participle) "writing out" without the use of words (19:3) the glory of God, that is, the inescapable weight of the sheer Godness of God.

Then in Romans 1:20 Paul declares: "God's invisible attributes—even his eternal power and deity—since the creation of the world are clearly seen, being understood by the things which he made." Here again the Scriptures testify to God's revelation in nature to mankind of certain of his attributes.

Nowhere do we find any warrant in Scripture to conclude that God ever intended creation to provide the basis for the efforts of methodological natural theology to erect a philosophical prolegomenon on top of which it would then place other beliefs derived from revelation.[13] J. I. Packer is absolutely right when he insists (1) that we do not need natural theology for information about God, (2) that we do not strengthen our biblical position by invoking natural theology, (3) that all of its arguments for the existence of God are logically loose and can be endlessly debated, (4) the speculative method for building up a theology is inappropriate, and (5) there is always a risk (I would even say that it is an inescapable fact) that the foundations that natural theology lays will prove too narrow to build all the emphases of Scripture upon.[14]

In his eternal purpose God intentionally integrated both the purpose of creation as such as well as the ordinances of creation into the more primary redemptive plan which he accomplished in Christ. Indications of this are (1) the fact that God's seventh-day creation rest is made the symbol of the Sabbath rest which the redeemed

---

13. To justify their effort to erect an empirical "first floor" for their revealed "second floor" theology, advocates of methodological natural theology always cite Romans 1:19–21 as scriptural support. But Paul is not employing the empiricist's cosmological argument (which moves from things to God) for God's existence in Romans 1. Rather, moving from God to man, he *declares* that God has *revealed* himself to people in and by the creation of the world and that they so "clearly see" the evidence for him that, when they suppress it as they do and fail to worship and serve him (1:18), they are guilty before him. Never does Paul (or any other biblical writer) represent the created universe as only probable evidence for God's existence. The natural theologian overlooks the fact that, given mankind's spiritual blindness and hardness of heart since the Fall, it is only "by faith," which is a gift from God, that we can "understand that the universe was formed at God's command, so that what is seen was not made out of what was visible" (Heb. 11:3).

14. J. I. Packer, "Theism for Our Time," in *God Who Is Rich in Mercy*, ed., Peter T. O'Brien and David G. Peterson, (Grand Rapids, Mich.: Baker, 1986), 12–14.

people of God will enter upon at the Eschaton (Gen. 2:2; Heb. 4:4–11), (2) later Sabbath observance, based upon God's creation rest, commemorated the exodus-redemption (Deut. 5:15), (3) the fact that God intended the original marriage ordinance from the beginning as an earthly representation of the relationship between Christ and his redeemed church (Gen. 2:24; Matt. 19:4–6; Eph. 5:30–32), and (4) the fact that God "subjected creation to frustration" specifically because of human sin (Gen. 3:17–18), determining that in empathy with the redeemed it would "groan as in the pains of childbirth right up to the present time," and that, for "its own liberation from bondage to decay," it would have to "wait in eager expectation for the revelation of the sons of God" at the time of their physical resurrection when their bodies will be redeemed, at which time creation too "will be brought into the glorious freedom of the children of God" (Rom. 8:19–23). Creation then was intended as the stage on which God's redemptive design is enacted and fulfilled; it was not intended to provide the speculative mind with neutral data on the basis of which the unbeliever may conclude that some undefined entity possibly lies behind it. Paul viewed the purpose of creation much differently, writing: "God created all things in order that the many-splendored wisdom of God might now be made known, *through the church,* to the principalities and powers in the heavenly realms" (Eph 3:9–10). Creation's *raison d'être* then is to serve the redemptive ends of God.

GOD'S WORKS OF PROVIDENCE

God the great Creator of all things doth uphold, direct, dispose, and govern all creatures, actions, and things, from the greatest even to the least, by His most wise and holy providence, according to His infallible foreknowledge, and the free and immutable counsel of His own will, to the praise of the glory of His wisdom, power, justice, goodness, and mercy.

Although, in relation to the foreknowledge and decree of God, the first Cause, all things come to pass immutably, and infallibly; yet, by the same providence, He ordereth them to fall out, according to the nature of second causes, either necessarily, freely, or contingently.

God, in His ordinary providence, maketh use of means, yet is free to work without, above, and against them, at His pleasure.

The almighty power, unsearchable wisdom, and infinite goodness of God so far manifest themselves in His providence, that it extendeth itself even to the first fall, and all other sins of angels and men; and that not by a bare permission, but such as hath joined with it a most wise and powerful bounding, and otherwise ordering, and governing of them, in a manifold dispensation, to His own holy ends; yet so, as the sinfulness thereof proceedeth only from the creature, and not from God, who, being most holy and righteous, neither is nor can be the author or approver of sin.

As the providence of God doth, in general, reach to all creatures; so, after a most special manner, it taketh care of His Church, and disposeth all things to the good thereof. (Westminster Confession of Faith, V/i–iv, vii)

His Ordinary Works of Providence

The Lord is good to all;
    He has compassion on all he has made.
The Lord is faithful to all his promises
    and loving toward all he has made.
The eyes of all look to you,
    and you give them their food at the proper time.
You open your hand
    and satisfy the desires of every living thing.
The Lord is righteous in all his ways
    and loving toward all he has made. (Ps 145:9, 13, 15–17)

What the Psalmist declares here the Bible everywhere else endorses, namely, that with prudent *foresight* God "provides for," upholds, sustains, and governs his creation—every part of it (see, e.g., Neh. 9:6; Acts 17:25, 28; Heb. 1:3). While the word "providence" (Lat. *providentia*, "foresight, forethought") is not a biblical word *per se*, the idea that it conveys is everywhere present in the *ad hoc* statements of Scripture to this effect (see Ps. 136:25). A corollary insistence of Scripture is that the entire universe is dependent upon the sustaining power and care of its Creator.

With the Confession of Faith—indeed with Scripture itself—the church must draw a distinction between God's "ordinary [or "general"] providence" and his "special providence" (V/iii, vii), meaning by the former, for example, what the Psalmist extols God for in Psalm 145—that in love and tender compassion he sustains and cares for all his creatures (theologians speak of this as God's "common grace"), and by the latter those specific divine activities looking directly to the salvation of his elect (that is, his "special grace"). But one must be careful, when distinguishing between his ordinary ("common" or "general") and special providence, not to interpret these "kinds" of providence to mean that God is conducting *two* works alongside each other with no relationship between them. Scripturally, this simply is not so. Since I will be working with the schema, I should explain how it is that God's "ordinary" providence is related to his "special" providence and serves it. I begin with the caveat of T. H. L. Parker:

> We must resist the temptation to think about providence generally and independently of Christ. It would be possible to draw on certain Psalms and the

Sermon on the Mount, for example, to make up a doctrine of God's relationship to his creation that had nothing to do with Jesus Christ. But since it is in Christ that this relationship is established, an attempt to understand it apart from him would be a misinterpretation from the start. In Jesus Christ, God has set up the relationship between himself and his creatures, promising to carry through his purpose in creation to its triumphal conclusion. The primal relationship with Adam, renewed with Noah (Gen. 6:21–22), is no less *in Christo* than is the covenant with Abraham or Moses. The Mediator who is the incarnate Word establishes this relation, and in him God becomes the God of men and they become his people. (The Mediator must also be regarded as setting up the relationship between God and his creatures other than man.) As their God, he will take up the responsibility for their earthly existence.[15]

I wholeheartedly concur with Parker, and would submit that one must never sever any aspect of God's providence away from the ἐν Χριστῷ, *en Christō*, relationship that exists between God and his creation, since all of God's dealings with his creation are mediated through the Christ. To do so provides the natural theologian the ground he needs to conduct his theological enterprise with no thought, at least at first, of Christ the Creator and Sustainer of all things. The Scriptures will not permit such an enterprise, however, insisting that Christ is not only the Co-Creator with the Father and the Spirit of the universe, but its Sustainer as well:

> John 17:2: "For you [the Father] granted him [the Christ] authority over all people [general providence] that he might give eternal life to all those you have given him [special providence]."
>
> Colossians 1:16–17: "All things were created by him and for him. He is before all things, and in him all things hold together [συνέστηκεν, *sunestēken*, that is, have their orderly integration]."
>
> Hebrews 1:3: "While upholding [φέρων, *pherōn*] all things by the word of his power, he made [ποιησάμενος, *poiēsamenos*] purification for sins and sat down on the right hand of the Majesty in heaven." (Here is a beautiful merging of Christ's providential governance of general human history and redemption's "holy history." Even while hanging on the cross as our Redeemer, he continued still as the world's Sustainer.)

This means then, to cite Parker again, that

---

15. T. H. L. Parker, "Providence of God," in *Evangelical Dictionary of Theology* (Grand Rapids, Mich.: Baker, 1984), 890.

the creation is the stage on which are enacted God's dealings with mankind. Providence is God's gracious outworking of his purpose in Christ which issues in his dealings with man. We . . . are saying that from the beginning God has ordered the course of events toward Jesus Christ and his incarnation. From the biblical point of view world history and personal life stories possess significance only in the light of the incarnation. The squalid little story of lust in Judah's dealings with Tamar (Gen. 38) falls into its place in the genealogy of the Messiah (Matt. 1:3). Caesar Augustus was on the throne in Rome for the sake of the unknown baby in its manger.[16]

Jesus taught that God "causes his sun to rise on the evil and the good, and sends rain on the righteous and the unrighteous" (Matt. 5:45), and Paul declared that God "has not left himself without testimony: he has shown kindness by giving you rain from heaven and crops in their seasons; he provides you with plenty of food and fills your heart with joy" (Acts 14:17), and also that "he himself gives all men life and breath and everything else . . . and he determined the times set for them and the exact places where they should live, that men should seek for him and find him, though he is not far from each of us. For in him we live and move and have our being" (Acts 17:25–28). God's wise and kind providential care, benefiting the heathen physically and materially as it does and witnessing thereby to God's presence among them ultimately serves redemptive ends, and according to Romans 1:18–23, also renders men "defenseless" when they fail to acknowledge him as God and to worship him (see Rom. 1:20: εἰς τὸ εἶναι αὐτοὺς ἀναπολογήτους, *eis to einai autous anapologētous*).[17] So at this point too, as Parker notes, "providence is included in the doctrine of reconciliation."[18]

The Bible also says that God gives not only to mankind but also to all living things the necessities for the sustaining of life. For example, according to Psalm 104:10–30, God provides not only for mankind but for all other living things as well:

> He makes springs pour water into the ravines;
>   it flows between all the mountains.
> They give water to all the beasts of the field;
>   The wild donkeys quench their thirst;

---

16. Ibid., 890–91.
17. See also John Murray's comment in his article "Common Grace," *Collected Writings of John Murray* (Edinburgh: Banner of Truth, 1977), 2:106, to the effect that "just because they are good gifts and manifestations of the kindness and mercy of God . . . the abuse of them brings greater condemnation and demonstrates the greater inexcusability of impenitence."
18. Parker, "Providence of God," 891.

> The birds of the air nest by the waters;
>> they sing among the branches. . . .
> He makes grass grow for the cattle, . . .
>
> The lions roar for their prey
>> and seek their food from God. . . .
> These all look to you
>> to give them their food at the proper time.
> When you give it to them,
>> they gather it up;
> when you open your hand,
>> they are satisfied with good things.

In Matthew 6:25–34 the disciples are reminded (by their Creator himself!) of these very truths, that "the birds of the air neither sow nor reap nor store away in barns, and yet your heavenly Father feeds them," and that God "clothes the grass of the field—which is here today and tomorrow is thrown into the fire—with lilies." From these providential relationships which the Father faithfully maintains with birds and lilies of the field under his beneficent care, Jesus immediately draws the lesson for his disciples that the heavenly Father also knows the needs of his sons and daughters who have trusted his Son—who are "much more valuable in his sight than birds and flowers"—and that he will provide for them as well. So once again, God's general providence is drawn into the arena of redemptive considerations and made to serve them. Along the same line, Paul urges Christians to be content with their food and clothing, since "God, who gives life to *everything* . . . richly provides *us* with everything for our enjoyment" (1 Tim. 6:8, 13, 17; see also Rom. 8:32). In sum, God's "ordinary" works of providence disclose to men, whether they acknowledge it or not, that they are not ruled by chance or by fate but by the God who finally "lays bear his purposes of providence in the incarnation of his Son."[19]

In a real sense, then, given the fact that he now has to do with a *fallen* world, what we are calling God's "ordinary" works of providence are one manifestation of his common grace to undeserving sinners and a world under his curse. John Murray, in fact, discusses this aspect of divine providence under the rubric of common grace.[20] But here again, we have only exchanged one idiom for another while the substance remains the same, for common grace as well serves the purposes of special grace. In this latter regard Murray writes:

---

19. Ibid., 891.
20. Murray, "Common Grace," 104–6.

The redemptive purpose of God lies at the centre of this world's history. While it is not the only purpose being fulfilled in history and while it is not the one purpose to which all others may be subordinated,[21] yet it is surely the central stream of history. It is however in the wider context of history that the redemptive purpose of God is realized. This wider context we have already found to be a dispensation of divine forbearance and goodness. In other words, it is that sphere of life or broad stream of history provided by common grace that provides the sphere of operation for God's special purpose of redemption and salvation. This simply means that this world upheld and preserved by God's grace is the sphere and platform upon which supervene the operations of special grace and in which special grace works to the accomplishment of his saving purpose and the perfection of the whole body of the elect. Common grace then receives at least one explanation [Murray does not hazard a guess regarding another explanation] from the fact of special grace, and special grace has its precondition and sphere of operation in common grace. Without common grace special grace would not be possible because special grace would have no material out of which to erect its structure. It is common grace that provides not only the sphere in which, but also the material out of which, the building fitly framed together may grow up into a holy temple in the Lord. It is the human race preserved by God, endowed with various gifts by God, in a world upheld and enriched by God, subsisting through the means of various pursuits and fields of labour, that provides the subjects for redemptive and regenerative grace. . . . To conclude . . . common grace provides the sphere of operation of special grace and special grace therefore provides a [I would say "the"] rationale of common grace.[22]

Once again we are reminded that God's ordinary works of providence do not stand unrelated to his special works of providence but in fact find their *raison d'être* in the service which they render his special works of providence. Stated biblically, "in all things [his general providence] God works for the good of those who love him, who have been called according to his purpose [an act of his special providence]" (Rom. 8:28).

---

21. With the sole exception of the end which redemption itself serves—the glory of God—which both Murray and I recognize, I would dispute this statement. In fact, Murray himself cites Isaiah 1:9 and Matthew 13:28–29 (and I could add such verses as Gen. 18:23–33; 39:5, and John 17:2) as biblical evidence that common grace appears to be extended to unregenerate men precisely because of the special grace principle. He also admits that "what the other ends promoted by common grace may be it might be precarious to conclude," offering no suggestions at all as to what they might be.
22. Murray, "Common Grace," 2:113, 116.

His Special Works of Providence

In addition to his ordinary works of providence whereby he sustains all things generally in order that he might have the world arena essential to the accomplishment of his salvific ends and the human pool from which his elect would emerge, God has related himself to mankind throughout history under two covenant arrangements—the covenant of works and the covenant of grace—for the *special* purpose of executing his salvific work and on the basis of which his elect actually realize their "so great salvation."

Before the Westminster Confession of Faith describes these two covenants separately and individually, it offers this introductory comment on the covenant concept as such:

> The distance between God and the creature is so great, that although reasonable creatures do owe obedience unto Him as their Creator, yet they could never have any fruition of Him as their blessedness and reward, but by some voluntary condescension on God's part, which He hath been pleased to express by way of covenant. (VII/i)

What is instructive about this statement is, first, its insight that men owe God their obedience simply on the basis of the Creator-creature relationship existing between them. This points up the truth that it is *not* on the basis of the covenant of works which God established with Adam, as some might think, that mankind acquired the obligation to serve God. Even if he had done nothing more for them than to sustain them by his ordinary providence and to tell them what they had to do to please him, Adam and his descendants would still have been under obligation to him as their Creator to render to him all due obedience as his rational creatures. Accordingly, and second, the introductory statement highlights the truth that the purpose of God's condescension toward them *covenantally* is strictly and solely in order that mankind "could have fruition of Him as their blessedness and reward." This underscores the truth that *both* covenants were intended, each in its own way, for the ultimate benefit and blessedness of his elect.

THE COVENANT OF WORKS

The twelfth question of the Shorter Catechism asks: "What special act of providence did God exercise toward man in the estate wherein he was created?" Its answer is revealing in that, responding as it does to a question concerning God's special providence, it specifically places the covenant of works within the arena of God's special providence: "When God had created man, He entered into a covenant of life with him, upon condition of perfect obedience; forbidding him to eat of the tree of the knowledge of good and evil, upon pain of death." The Confession of Faith, in fact, is not as clear on this specific point as is the Shorter Catechism, stating only that "The first covenant made with man was a covenant of works, wherein life was promised to Adam; and in him to his posterity, upon condition of perfect and personal obedience" (VII/ii; see also XIX/i). A comparison of the two statements shows that the Westminster divines spoke of the first covenant as both a covenant of life and a covenant of works, the former designation emphasizing man's "blessedness and reward" for obedience, the latter emphasizing his obligation to obey under the terms of the covenant.

In the plan of God "our first parents, being left to the freedom of their own will, fell from the estate wherein they were created by sinning against God" (Shorter Catechism, Question 13), Adam under the terms of the covenant thereby corrupting not only himself but also all mankind descending from him by ordinary generation (Rom. 5:12–19; see also Shorter Catechism, Questions 14–19). The fall of Adam made the establishment of that second covenant—the covenant with which biblical history is mainly concerned, the covenant of grace—both necessary and possible.[23]

THE COVENANT OF GRACE AND "HEILSGESCHICHTE"

After man, by his fall, had made himself incapable of life by the covenant of works, and because God had from all eternity elected some men to everlasting life, the Lord "was pleased to make a second, commonly called the covenant of grace,"

---

23. Some contemporary Reformed thinkers have called into question the existence and presence of a covenant of works in Genesis 2–3. John Murray prefers to speak simply of the "Adamic administration," urging that (1) the term *covenant of works* is "not felicitous, for the reason that the elements of grace entering into the administration are not properly provided for by the term 'works,'" and (2) "it is not designated a covenant in Scripture.... Covenant in Scripture denotes the oath-bound confirmation of promise and involves a security which the Adamic economy did not bestow" ("The Adamic Administration," in *Collected Writings of John Murray* [Edinburgh: Banner of Truth, 1977], 2:49). But Murray fails to make clear what the "Adamic adminstration" is an administration *of*. Moreover, it is debatable whether "elements of grace" intrude themselves at the critical point of the "administration," namely, at the point of Adam's decision-making. Finally, it is clear from Hosea 6:7 that the relation between God and Adam should be construed as one of covenant ("Like Adam, they have broken the covenant"). Therefore, Murray presumes the very thing that needs to be proved when he says that *covenant* is always used only in reference to a provision that is redemptive.

W. Wilson Benton Jr., in his article, "Federal Theology: Review for Revision" (*Through Christ's Word* [Phillipsburg, N.J.: Presbyterian and Reformed, 1985], 180–204), argues that the two-covenant schema of federal theology in general and the Westminster Confession of Faith in particular is not biblical but is traceable primarily to the *political* thought of the period, to a renewed interest in the history of revelation, and to the influence of Ramist logic, with its stress on the deductive method and the dichotomizing of ideas. But these influences alone cannot account for federal theology or show how federal theology produces the dire effects Benton sees federal theology producing.

in order to deliver the elect "out of the estate of sin and misery, and to bring them into an estate of salvation, by a Redeemer" (Shorter Catechism, Question 20). Under the terms of the covenant of grace, God "freely offereth unto sinners life and salvation by Jesus Christ; requiring of them faith in Him, that they may be saved, and promising to give unto all those that are ordained unto eternal life His Holy Spirit, to make them willing, and able to believe" (Westminster Confession of Faith, VII/iii).

That the Westminster divines had a real sensitivity to the Bible's *Heilsgeschichtliche* ("history of salvation") character under the covenant of grace is evidenced by their accompanying descriptions of the covenant of grace "under the law" and "under the gospel." They were aware that though God's redemptive plan was initially disclosed with the divine *protevangelium* of Genesis 3:15, its fuller revelation was progressively unfolded on "the principle of successive Berith- [covenant-]makings, as marking the introduction of new periods" of "salvation history."[24] In other words, the one overarching "covenant of grace" was historically advanced and administered after Genesis 3:15 by God's historical covenants with Noah (Gen. 6:18; 9:8–17), Abraham (Gen. 12:1–3; 15:18; 17:7–14; 22:15–18), Israel (Exod. 19:5; 24:6–8; Deut. 29:1), David (2 Sam. 7:11–16; 1 Chron. 17:10–14), and finally through the administration of the New Covenant (Jer. 31:31–34; Luke 22:20; 2 Cor. 3:6; Heb. 8:8–13), Jesus Christ himself being the Mediator of the New Covenant between God and his elect (Heb. 9:15). Accordingly, the Confession of Faith summarizes the historical development and unfolding of the covenant of grace in the following words:

> This covenant was differently administered in the time of the law, and in the time of the gospel: under the law, it was administered by promises, prophecies, sacrifices, circumcision, the paschal lamb, and other types and ordinances delivered to the people of the Jews, all foresignifying Christ to come; which were, for that time, sufficient and efficacious, through the operation of the Spirit, to instruct and build up the elect in faith in the promised Messiah, by whom they had full remission of sins, and eternal salvation; and is called the Old Testament.
>
> Under the gospel, when Christ, the substance, was exhibited, the ordinances in which this covenant is dispensed are the preaching of the Word, and the administration of the sacraments of Baptism and the Lord's Supper: which, though fewer in number, and administered with more simplicity, and less outward glory, yet, in them it is held forth in more fulness, evidence and spiritual efficacy, to all nations, both Jews and Gentiles; and is called the New Testament. There are not therefore two covenants of grace, differing in substance, but one and the same, under various dispensations. (VII/v–vi)

---

24. Geerhardus Vos, *Biblical Theology* (Grand Rapids, Mich.: Eerdmans, 1949), 25.

All of this means that God's special works of providence as they relate to the covenant of grace include such great historical events as the provision of a covering for our first parents (Gen. 3:21), the preservation of Noah and his family at the time of the Flood (Gen. 6:8), the call of Abraham, the exodus-deliverance of Israel from Egypt (*the* Old Testament type of redemption), God's preservation of his chosen nation Israel throughout her history in spite of her many failings, the sending of his only Son into the world as the New Testament antitype of the Old Testament paschal lamb, the building of the church, Christ's cross work, his resurrection from the dead and ascension to the Father's right hand, the Spirit's manifestation at Pentecost, the conversion of Saul of Tarsus, Christ's second advent, the raising of all men from the dead in the Eschaton, the judgment of the living and the dead, and the ushering in of the new heaven and new earth.

THE REVELATORY PROCESS AND MIRACLES

The final feature of special providence to be considered here is (1) God's revelatory activity, accompanying his redemptive activity, which produced the Holy Scriptures, and (2) the miracles of power which provided the organs of revelation along the way their authenticating credentials as spokesmen from God.

The Revelatory Process

The revelatory process which produced the Holy Scriptures is not represented in Scripture as an end in itself. Rather, it served the more primary redemptive purpose of God. In Ephesians 1:8–9 Paul indicates that God has blessed the church not only redemptively but revelationally as well. In Christ, he writes, "we have redemption, even the forgiveness of trespasses, according to the riches of his grace which he has lavished upon us in all wisdom and understanding, *making known to us the mystery of his will,* according to his good pleasure which he purposed in Christ." It is striking how Paul moves easily from God's redemptive work to his revelatory work as the means of explaining the former. Geerhardus Vos elucidates the revelatory process's bearing on the redemptive process in the following words:

> Revelation does not stand alone by itself, but is (so far as Special Revelation is concerned) inseparably attached to another activity of God, which we call *Redemption*. Now redemption could not be otherwise than historically successive, because it addresses itself to the generations of mankind coming into existence in the course of history. Revelation is the interpretation of redemption; it must, therefore, unfold

itself in instalments as redemption does. And yet it is also obvious that the two processes are not entirely co-extensive, for revelation comes to a close at a point where redemption still continues. In order to understand this, we must take into account an important distinction within the sphere of redemption itself. Redemption is partly objective and central, partly subjective and individual. By the former we designate those redeeming acts of God, which take place on behalf of, but outside of, the human person. By the latter we designate those acts of God which enter into the human subject. We call the objective acts central, because, happening in the center of the circle of redemption, they concern all alike, and are not in need of, or capable of, repetition. Such objective-central acts are the incarnation, the atonement, the resurrection of Christ. The acts in the subjective sphere are called individual, because they are repeated in each individual separately. Such subjective-individual acts are regeneration, justification, conversion, sanctification, glorification. Now revelation accompanies the process of objective-central redemption only, and this explains why redemption extends further than revelation. To insist upon its accompanying subjective-individual redemption would imply that it dealt with questions of private, personal concern, instead of with the common concerns of the world of redemption collectively. Still this does not mean that the believer cannot, for his subjective experience, receive enlightenment from the source of revelation in the Bible, for we must remember that continually alongside the objective process, there was going on the work of subjective application and that much of this is reflected in the Scriptures. Subjective-individual redemption did not first begin when objective-central redemption ceased; it existed alongside of it from the beginning.[25]

In other words, according to Vos, because the objective-central events of redemption have been sufficiently and fully explained by the Old and New Testament writers, there is no further need for special revelation (see 2 Tim. 3:16–17). However, because subjective-individual redemption was occurring simultaneously with the objective-central events of redemption and was treated accordingly in the full elucidation of redemptive realities by the biblical writers, since our own individual experiences are not and cannot be dissimilar to the experiences of the saints in Scripture, we are instructed to appeal to the scriptural representation of their experience for authoritative direction respecting our own daily walk (see, e.g., Heb. 11).

Vos's insistence that special revelation has come to a close should disturb no one, especially when it is recalled that even the revelatory process that produced our Bible did not flow uninterruptedly. Between Genesis 49:1–27 and Exodus 3:4 there was a "blackout" of divine communication for over four hundred years. Then with the passing of Malachi, another four-hundred year "blackout" ensued before the

---

25. Vos, *Biblical Theology*, 14–15.

angel Gabriel appeared to Zechariah the priest. These prior revelational "blackouts" show the naturalness of the revelational "blackout" that has been in place since the close of the New Testament canon.

We have suggested to this point, therefore, a relational schema between the revelatory process and the redemptive process, namely, that special revelation primarily serves the nonrepeatable, objective, historical events of redemption as the explication of the latter to men.

Authenticating Miracles

The second element in this special providence which we are now considering, which must be related to the revelatory process, is the Bible's "miracles of power" such as Jesus' changing water into wine, stilling storms, healing the incurable, and raising the dead (in distinction from current supernatural acts of grace such as God's regenerating the lifeless souls of sinners or answering their prayers).

I have no sympathy with the contention of many theologians that miracles of power are simply interventions of God into human affairs in ways which run counter to *known or observable* processes but which do not really violate the laws of nature. Some may be such, but others are clearly *contrary to* the laws of nature, such as Jesus' changing of water into wine, and it seems to me that it is catering too much to modern man's hostility to the whole idea of the supernatural so to define biblical miracles that they are emptied of their supernatural uniqueness. I believe that the Confession of Faith more accurately reflects the true situation when it states: "God, in His ordinary providence, maketh use of means, yet *is free to work without, above, and against them,* at His pleasure" (IV/iii, emphasis supplied).

The biblical "miracles of power" do not occur haphazardly, for no rhyme or reason, in salvation history. To the contrary, the Bible suggests that they served the revelatory process by authenticating the credentials of the human organs of special revelation who brought to men the redemptive truth of God. This fact has been observed by many Reformed scholars. For example, John Calvin writes:

> [Our adversaries] do not cease to assail our doctrine and to reproach and defame it with names that render it hated or suspect. They call it "new" and "of recent birth." They reproach it as "doubtful and uncertain." They ask what miracles have confirmed it. . . . First, by calling it "new" they do great wrong to God, whose Sacred Word does not deserve to be accused of novelty. Indeed, I do not at all doubt that it is new to them, since to them both Christ himself and his gospel are new. But he who knows that this preaching of Paul is ancient, that "Jesus Christ died for our sins and rose again for our justification," will find nothing new among us.

That it has been long unknown and buried is the fault of man's impiety. Now, when it is restored to us by God's goodness, its claim to antiquity ought to be admitted just as the returning citizen resumes his rights.

The same ignorance leads them to regard it as doubtful and uncertain. This is precisely what the Lord complains of through his prophet, that "the ox knew its owner, and the ass its master's crib; but his own people did not know him." But however they may jest about its uncertainty, if they had to seal *their* doctrine in their own blood, and at the expense of their life, one could see how much it meant to them. Quite the opposite is our assurance, which fears neither the terrors of death nor even God's judgment seat.

In demanding miracles of us, they act dishonestly. For we are not forging some new gospel, but are retaining *that very gospel whose truth all the miracles that Jesus Christ and his disciples ever wrought serve to confirm.* But, compared with us, they have a strange power: even to this day they can confirm their faith by continual miracles! Indeed, they allege miracles which can disturb a mind otherwise at rest—they are so foolish and ridiculous, so vain and false! And yet, even if these were marvelous prodigies, they ought not to be of any moment against God's truth, for God's name ought to be always and everywhere hallowed, whether by miracles or by the natural order of things.

Perhaps this false hue could have been more dazzling if Scripture had not warned us concerning the legitimate purpose and use of miracles. For Mark teaches that those signs which attended the apostles' preaching were set forth to confirm it [Mark 16:20]. *In like manner, Luke relates that our "Lord . . . bore witness to the word of his grace," when these signs and wonders were done by the apostles' hands* [Acts 14:3]. *Very much like this is that word of the apostle: that the salvation proclaimed by the gospel has been confirmed in the fact that* "the Lord has attested it by signs and wonders and various mighty works" [Heb. 2:4]. *When we hear that these are the seals of the gospel, shall we turn them to the destruction of faith in the gospel? When we hear that they were appointed only to seal the truth, shall we employ them to confirm falsehoods?* . . . And we may also fitly remember that Satan has his miracles, which, though they are deceitful tricks rather than true powers, are of such sort as to mislead the simple-minded and untutored. Magicians and enchanters have always been noted for miracles. Idolatry has been nourished by wonderful miracles, yet these are not sufficient to sanction for us the superstition either of magicians or of idolaters.

The Donatists of old overwhelmed the simplicity of the multitude with this battering-ram: that they were mighty in miracles. We, therefore, now answer our adversaries as Augustine then answered the Donatists: the Lord made us wary of these miracle workers when he predicted that false prophets with lying signs and divers wonders would come to draw even the elect (if possible) into error. And Paul warned that the reign of Antichrist would be "with all power and signs and lying wonders." But these miracles, they say, are done neither by idols, nor by magicians, nor by false prophets, but by the saints. As if we did not understand that to "disguise himself as an angel of light" is the craft of Satan! . . . What shall

GOD'S WORKS OF CREATION AND PROVIDENCE

we say except that it has always been, and ever will be, a very just punishment of God to "send to those" who have not received the love of truth "a strong delusion to make them believe a lie." We, then, have no lack of miracles [he refers to the New Testament ones], sure miracles, not subject to mockery. On the contrary, those "miracles" which our adversaries point to in their own support are sheer delusions of Satan, for they draw the people away from the true worship of their God to vanity.[26]

In the same way Warfield approaches the purpose of biblical miracles. He speaks of "the inseparable connection of miracles with revelation, as its mark and credential; or more narrowly, of the summing up of all revelation, finally, in Jesus Christ." Miracles, he writes,

> do not appear on the pages of Scripture vagrantly, here, there, and elsewhere indifferently, without assignable reason. They belong to revelation periods, and appear only when God is speaking to His people through accredited messengers, declaring His gracious purposes.[27]

This perception of miracles as the authenticating credentials of bearers of revelation[28] receives striking verification in the Scriptures themselves. For example, in the Old Testament, the great period of special revelation known as Mosaism (Exodus through Deuteronomy) arose in connection with and as a result of the great (typical) redemptive event of the exodus-redemption of the people of God from Egypt. Moses—himself the central conduit of that revelation—received attestation to his authenticity as God's spokesman from all the miracles of the exodus itself (see Exod. 4:1–9) and from the miracles recorded in Numbers (see Num. 12:1–11; 17:1–8; 21:5–9). The subsequent body of revelation known as Prophetism, which spanned Israel's history from the conquest under Joshua down to postexilic times, should not be construed as unrelated or detached from the former body of revelation, inasmuch as Prophetism, dealing as it does by its revelational material both historically and hortatorily with the Mosaic community founded at the exodus, continued to explain and unfold the implications of the earlier Mosaic redemption (see, for example, Josh. 1:5–17;

---

26. Calvin, *Institutes*, "Prefatory Address to King Francis I of France" (emphasis supplied).
27. Benjamin B. Warfield, *Miracles: Yesterday and Today* (Grand Rapids, Mich.: Eerdmans, n.d.), 25–26. See also Richard B. Gaffin Jr., "A Cessationist View," in *Are Miraculous Gifts for Today?* ed. Wayne A. Grudem (Grand Rapids, Mich.: Zondervan, 1996), 25–64; Robert L. Saucy, "An Open But Cautious View," 103–12, and Richard B. Gaffin, "A Cessationist Response to Robert L. Saucy," 149–51, in the same volume.
28. This perception is unfortunately and inaccurately called today the "Warfield View." We have already seen that Calvin espoused it, and he did so on the same basis that Warfield did—the teaching of Scripture.

2:10–11; 4:23; 9:24; Ezek. 23; Mal. 4:4). The miracles of Prophetism in turn served to authenticate the revelatory organs of Prophetism. Consider the following examples:

> 1 Kings 17:17–24: After Elijah raised the widow's son from the dead, she exclaimed: "Now I know that you are a man of God and that the word of the Lord from your mouth is the truth."
>
> 1 Kings 18:36–39: In his later conflict with the prophets of Baal on Mount Carmel, Elijah prayed: "O Lord, God of Abraham, Isaac and Israel, let it be known today that you are God in Israel and that I am your servant and have done all these things at your command. Answer me, O Lord, answer me so these people will know that you, O Lord, are God.... Then the fire of the Lord fell and burned up the sacrifice, the wood, the stones and the soil, and also licked up the water in the trench."
>
> 2 Kings 1:10: "Elijah answered the captain, 'If I am a man of God, may fire come down from heaven and consume you and your fifty men!' Then fire fell from heaven and consumed the captain and his men." (see also 1:12; 20:8–11; Dan. 2)

Old Testament *revelation*, when rightly viewed, is then essentially unitary in its concern to explicate Old Testament *redemption*, both principially and typically, and thereby to prepare the way for its antitypical fulfillment in the New Testament age. *And the miracles of the Old Testament age authenticated Moses and the prophets as men of God.*

All of this accords with the New Testament's representation that Old Testament redemption foreshadowed by its revealed principles, and pointed forward to, its grand climactic New Testament antitype—the objectively historical redemption accomplished by Christ in his incarnation. Then the entire New Testament corpus of revelation, related to the Old Testament corpus as fulfillment is related to promise, provided the climactic special revelatory explanation of the New Testament complex of historical redemptive events. *And the miracles of the New Testament age authenticated in turn Christ and his apostles as the bearers of this new corpus of revelation.* Consider this New Testament testimony:

> John 5:36: "I have testimony weightier than that of John. For the very work that the Father has given me to finish, and which I am doing, testifies that the Father has sent me."
>
> John 10:38: "Even though you do not believe me, believe the miracles [ἔργοις, *ergois*], that you may learn and understand that the Father is in me, and I in the Father."
>
> Acts 2:22: "Men of Israel, listen to this: Jesus of Nazareth was a man accredited by God to you by miracles, wonders, and signs, which God did among you through him, as you yourselves know."
>
> Acts 14:3: "So Paul and Barnabas spent considerable time there, speaking boldly for the Lord, who confirmed [μαρτυροῦντι, *martyrounti*] the message of his

grace by enabling them to do miraculous signs and wonders [σημεῖα καὶ τέρατα, *semeia kai terata*]."

2 Corinthians 12:12: "The things that mark an apostle—signs, wonders and miracles [σημείοις τε καὶ τέρασιν καὶ δυνάμεσιν, *semeiois te kai terasin kai dynamesin*]—were done among you with great perseverance" (see here Rom. 15:18–19).

Hebrews 2:3–4: "This salvation, which was first announced by the Lord, was confirmed to us by those who heard him. God also testified to it by signs, wonders and various miracles, and gifts of the Holy Spirit distributed according to his will."

It is now possible to enlarge the redemption-revelation schema earlier proposed to the paradigm of redemption-revelation-miracle. If what we have suggested is correct, the paradigm means that post-Fall special revelation serves the nonrepeatable historical events of redemption as the latters' explanation (see Vos's explanation above), while miracles of power in turn serve the organs of special revelation by becoming the latters' authenticating credentials (see Warfield's statement above). It is nonrepeatable historical events of redemption which call forth special revelatory explanation; it is special revelation in turn which calls forth miraculous authentication. Where the first is absent, there is no necessity for the second; where the second is absent, there is no necessity for the third. When the first had been sufficiently and permanently interpreted (in inscripturated form) by the second, and the second sufficiently authenticated by the third, there was no further need for the continuation of either the second or the third, and in fact the revelatory process and the occurrence of authenticating miracles of power have ceased (see Westminster Confession of Faith, I/i).[29] Conversely, once the second and the third had occurred, the events of redemption took their place in the world as explicated, authenticated incontrovertible facts of world and human history.[30]

* * * * *

---

29. Charismatic theologians have urged that Jesus' statement, "Anyone who has faith in me will do what I have been doing. He will do even greater things than these, because I am going to the Father" (John 14:12), guarantees the continuation of miracles of power in the church throughout this age. But as Leon Morris writes in *The Gospel According to John* (Grand Rapids, Mich.: Eerdmans, 1971), 645, fn. 29, 646:

> Notice that ἔργα [*erga*] is not repeated with μείζονα [*meizona*]. . . . Jesus is not speaking of the doing of miracles, but of service of a more general kind. . . . What Jesus means we may see in the narratives of the Acts. There are a few miracles of healing, but the emphasis is on the mighty works of conversion. On the day of Pentecost alone more believers were added to the little band of believers than throughout Christ's entire earthly life. There we see a literal fulfillment of "greater works than these shall he do."

30. For further discussion, see Robert L. Reymond, *What About Continuing Revelations and Miracles in the Presbyterian Church Today?* (Phillipsburg, N.J.: Presbyterian and Reformed, 1977).

In the foregoing pages we have surveyed God's works of creation and providence. We emphasized both the *ex nihilo* origin of the universe, insisting that according to Genesis 1:1–3 "the universe was formed at God's command, so that what is seen was not made out of what was visible" (Heb. 11:3), and that man owes his existence to a direct act of God (Gen. 2:7). We have shown too that according to the consentient witness of Scripture the entire universe is dependent at every single moment upon its Creator to sustain it. God, who alone is self-contained and self-sufficient, "gives to all men life and breath and everything else" (Acts 17:25; 1 Cor. 4:7).

In this chapter I also urged that *redemptive* considerations ultimately lie behind all of God's activities pertaining to the created universe, which activities include both the work of creation itself and his works of providence. In his eternal purpose God determined that his Son would have a Bride conformed to his image (Rom. 8:29), and that he would have a special people residing in the glorified "new heaven and new earth" state, all to the praise of the glory of his grace (Eph. 1:6, 12, 14). And *that* purpose he executed in and by his works of creation and providence.

Many theologians teach that God had a more original purpose for his universe, which purpose had to be set aside—because of his vicegerent's fall from his created state of integrity (*status integritatis*)—in favor of that purpose which he ultimately did pursue and which has led to the creation of the church in the world. But I fail to find this taught anywhere in Scripture. I find Paul, rather, declaring that God "created all things *in order that* [ἵνα, *hina*] now, through the church, the manifold wisdom of God should be made known to the rulers and authorities in the heavenly realms, according to his eternal purpose which he accomplished [or purposed] in Christ Jesus our Lord" (Eph. 3:9–10). I find him expressing the same thought in different words when he speaks of the "mystery of [God's] will according to his good pleasure, which he [eternally] purposed in Christ, to be put into effect when the times will have reached their fulfillment—to bring all things in heaven and on earth together under one head, even Christ" (Eph. 1:9–10). Every other divine purpose (and there are countless other lesser divine purposes), every other divine motivation, is subordinate to God's accomplishing his one overarching determination to glorify his Son both as "the Firstborn among many brethren" and as the Lord of the church, and in the process ultimately to glorify himself (Phil. 2:11; 1 Cor. 15:28). Never for a moment has his work of creation *per se* or any work of providence ever had a purpose independent of or rivaling in significance God's redemptive purpose in Christ, and all this to his own glory.

CHAPTER TWELVE

The Biblical View of Man

After God had made all other creatures, He created man, male and female, with reasonable and immortal souls, endued with knowledge, righteousness, and true holiness, after His own image; having the law of God written in their hearts, and power to fulfil it: and yet under a possibility of transgressing, being left to the liberty of their own will, which was subject to change. Beside this law written in their hearts, they received a command not to eat of the tree of the knowledge of good and evil; which while they kept, they were happy in their communion with God, and had dominion over the creatures. (Westminster Confession of Faith, IV/ii)

Our first parents being seduced by the subtilty and temptation of Satan, sinned in eating the forbidden fruit. This their sin God was pleased according to his wise and holy counsel to permit, having purposed to order it to his own glory.

By this sin they fell from their original righteousness and communion with God, and so became dead in sin, and wholly defiled in all the faculties and parts of soul and body.

They being the root of all mankind, the guilt of this sin was imputed, and the same death in sin and corrupted nature conveyed to all their posterity, descending from them by ordinary generation. (Westminster Confession of Faith, VI/i-iii)

WHAT IS MAN? Simply the "outcome of accidental collocations of atoms"?[1] The highest evolutionary stage to date of the primate? Is he among world species primarily *homo sapiens*? According to the Bible, none of these popular current ideas captures what man is *essentially*. Rather, man is a *creature* of God, indeed, the crowning work of God's creative activity; uniquely the "image of God" with whom

---

1. So Bertrand Russell, "A Free Man's Worship," in *Why I Am Not a Christian,* ed. Paul Edwards (New York: Simon and Schuster, 1957), 107.

[415]

God has entered into covenant, and as a covenant creature man is accordingly *homo religiosus* before he is *homo sapiens*. But as a book written about and for covenant breakers, the Bible also tells us about Adam's Fall from his original "golden age" of created integrity and about the dire condition in which all men find themselves in their raw, natural state as the result of his Fall, a condition which can only be reversed by redemption through Jesus Christ and the work of the Holy Spirit.

MAN AS COVENANT CREATURE OF GOD

Genesis 1:26–27 and 2:5–25 together comprise the biblical account of the creation of man. The Bible definitely teaches the creation of man by a direct act of God. There is not a hint that he is the product of either naturalistic or theistic evolution. But what is man's place in the creation arrangement of things? Is he just one more created entity—along with stars and animals—or does he occupy a very special place in God's creation? The biblical witness is that man occupies a position of the very highest significance in the creation order, as shown by the following details of the Genesis narrative:

1. Man's creation occurs as the last major event of the sixth day of the creation week, as the climax of God's activity. Clearly, God intended all that he had done prior to man's creation to be preparatory to the creation of man.

2. The very pattern of expression introducing the details of the consecutive acts of creation—quite uniform until the account reaches the creation of man—undergoes a noticeable change at 1:26. Instead of the "And God said: 'Let there be'" formula (1:3, 6, 9, 14, 20, 24), we are confronted with the new expression "And God said [not 'Let there be man' but]: 'Let us make man'"—suggesting almost a pause in the divine activity for the purpose of solemn divine counsel.

3. It is man alone who is described as having been created in the image of God (Gen. 1:26–27).

4. Man is granted dominion over God's creation as God's vicegerent (1:26–28; 2:19–20). Of man as God's vicegerent David exclaimed in Psalm 8:3–8:

> When I consider your heavens,
>   the work of your fingers,
> The moon and the stars,
>   which you have set in place,
> what is man that you are mindful of him,
>   the son of man that you care for him!
> You made him [only] a little lower than the angels
>   and crowned him with glory and honor.

> You made him ruler over the works of your hands;
> you put everything under his feet:
> all flocks and herds,
> and the beasts of the field,
> the birds of the air, and the fish of the sea,
> all that swim the paths of the seas.

These verses should not be read so as to infer the insignificance of man before the fathomless reaches of the heavenly universe. To the contrary, David, contemplating the magnificence of the heavens, is awed by the exalted status God has bestowed upon man and expresses his awe by the breathless question of 8:4. David's inspired commentary on Genesis 1–2 even suggests that God views man as his *crowning* act of creation.

5. The creation of man receives special attention in Genesis 2:5–25, which is *not* a "second account" of creation differing in many details from the account in Genesis 1, but a more detailed account of God's creative activities on day six of Genesis 1. Genesis 1 as it were gives an overview of the creation week as a whole, then concentrates in Genesis 2 on the creation of man.

6. Man is distinguished from the animals in a very special way in Genesis 2. Not only is he made their ruler in the Genesis 1 narrative, but also *into man's nostrils alone* does God breath the "breath [נְשָׁמָה, *nᵉšāmâh*] of life (Gen. 2:7). The one context where some expositors contend that the נְשָׁמָה, *nᵉšāmâh*, is identified with animals as well is Genesis 7:21–22, but a careful reading of the text will disclose that the נְשָׁמָה, *nᵉšāmâh,* of 7:22 has for its referent "mankind" at the very end of 7:21, that is to say, the verses should be read "and all mankind—all on dry land [which excludes the occupants of the ark] in whose nostrils was the נְשָׁמָה, *nᵉšāmâh,* of life died." With the gift of the נְשָׁמָה, *nᵉšāmâh,* of life, God imparted more to man than the mere physical life principle, which animals equally possess. Along with the human life principle (see Job 33:4: "The Spirit of God has made me; the נְשָׁמָה [*nᵉšāmâh*] of the Almighty has given me life"), God imparted to man through his gift of the נְשָׁמָה, *nᵉšāmâh,* of life at least two other things that clearly distinguish man from animals:

a. Spiritual comprehension of God and his moral law. Job 32:8 reads: "There is a spirit in man, and the נְשָׁמָה, *nᵉšāmâh,* of the Almighty gives them understanding [תְּבִינֵם], *tᵉbînēm*." In light of the debate going on throughout the book of Job in which Job and his "miserable counselors" are attempting to analyze the ways of God with men, the youthful Elihu clearly intends by his word "understanding" *spiritual* comprehension, which, according to Paul, includes not only an awareness of God but also the works of his moral law "written in the heart":

When the nations who do not have law [that is, the benefit of the special revelation of law] do *by nature* [φύσει, *physei*] the precepts of the law, these, though they do not have law, for themselves are law, who show *the work of the law written in their hearts*. (Rom. 2:14–15a)

b. Conscience. Proverbs 20:27 reads: "The נְשָׁמָה, *nᵉšāmâh*, of man is the Lord's [inner] 'lamp'; it searches out his inmost being." Clearly the נְשָׁמָה, *nᵉšāmâh*, here, as indicated by its "searching" activity, is conscience, that human sense of moral oughtness and the capacity to distinguish between moral right and moral wrong. By his innate knowledge of God and his moral law and his sense of moral good and moral evil, man is clearly superior to the animals.

7. It is to man that God gives the capacity of rational speech. Indeed, it is to man that God himself speaks, thereby ennobling him and honoring him above the animals.

8. Finally, it is with man that God enters into covenant. Though the Hebrew word for "covenant" (בְּרִית, *bᵉrît*) does not occur until Genesis 6:18, (1) the elements of a covenant between God and man are present in Genesis 1–2 (two parties, a condition laid down, the blessing of eternal life promised for obedience, the penalty of death declared for disobedience) and (2) Hosea 6:7 clearly speaks of a covenant with Adam ("Like Adam, they have broken the covenant"). More will be said about the covenant of works later.

The Constituent Elements of Human Nature

Man, uniquely situated among the various created orders, is also unique as to his nature. He is material or body, true enough, in the sense that he possesses a physical body. But the witness of Scripture is that man is more than simply a material body. Christians have interpreted this witness in several different ways.[2]

Monism ("Whole Man")

I will begin with G. C. Berkouwer's view of the "whole man."[3] Berkouwer argues that "humanness" in the Bible is always defined in terms of *relation* (*relationis*) and not *being* (*entis*). That is to say, what it is specifically about man that holds the Bible's interest is neither his "soul" nor his "heart" understood as an immaterial *substantia* but

---

2. John Murray's two articles, "The Nature of Man" and "Trichotomy," in *Collected Writings of John Murray* (Edinburgh: Banner of Truth, 1977), vol. 2, comprise an extremely insightful treatment of this whole issue.

3. G. C. Berkouwer, *Man: The Image of God* (Grand Rapids, Mich.: Eerdmans, 1962), 194–233.

rather simply man *in relation to* God. According to Berkouwer, Scripture *always and only* views man as a total "one" before God, and it has no interest in either trichotomy or dichotomy. Such terms as "soul" and "spirit," Berkouwer argues, are interchangeable, flexible, and imprecise, and are not intended

> to give to a scientific anthropology the status of church doctrine or biblical teaching. They only wish to underscore man's inescapable God orientation, to say that man is more than the chemical components of his flesh. Man as he is constituted, as he exists in himself abstracted from his relationship to God, does not interest the Bible and therefore is not a proper object of theological concern.[4]

Berkouwer recognizes that his rejection of the notion of the human soul as an ontic entity separable from the body "runs hard against the pious belief that at death the soul departs to be 'with the Lord.'" But he insists that

> we must think of the future of man, not in terms of the part of man that is with Christ, but in terms of the victory of Christ over sin and death, of total resurrection, of the glorious acts of God still awaited in the coming of Christ to establish the New Earth. The state of man in the "between times" we must leave as one of the hidden things. Scripture itself "gives us no help in a search for an analyzable anthropological conclusion."[5]

We shall shortly see, to put it bluntly, that this is nonsense, but we should acknowledge now that his view is motivated by the very proper concern that any analysis that distinguishes between "constituent parts" within the "whole man" runs the risk of making the soul the valuable and God-like part of man while the body is that which drags the soul down to sin and corruption. Such a notion must be rejected out of hand as completely unbiblical. Both ontological entities are valuable and significant to God. But Smedes rightly asks a series of questions:

> [O]n the profoundly difficult subject of man, has Berkouwer adequately faced the question of whether . . . his quarrel is not with an antiquated psychology, and whether therefore it may be unnecessary to reject the old ontology of body and soul once it is separated from the old psychology? . . . is it not possible that the classic ontological distinction between soul and body still best fits the religious and redemptive portrayal of man? . . . given the fact that man, after death, is at home with the Lord while his body is rotting in the grave, and given

---

4. Lewis B. Smedes, "G. C. Berkouwer," in *Creative Minds in Contemporary Theology* (Grand Rapids, Mich.: Eerdmans, 1966), 84.
5. Ibid.

the fact that the Bible speaks of a separation of the soul from the body, is it not possible that the older notion best fits both pious hope and biblical suggestion? And, after we clear our minds of the expendable psychology that was appended to the body-soul distinction, what would be wrong with assuming that man is a substantial soul, and that the man with whom the Bible is concerned is the whole man, body and soul, in their mysterious but indivisible unity? Berkouwer [elsewhere] insists that the "unmixed and unconfused" natures of Christ do not impede their genuine unity in the One Christ. Why should not man be a unity—a different kind and level than that of Christ's unity, indeed—between two distinct ontological realities? Could we not have both, the "whole man" in dynamic relationship with God *and* the whole man in a unity of ontologically distinct entities, body and soul?[6]

It should be clear from Smede's comments that whatever else one might say, the Bible will not permit us to view man simply as the "whole man" in relationship to God. He is either a dichotomous (body/soul) or trichotomous (body/soul/spirit) creature in relationship to God.

Trichotomy

The trichotomist must admit, along with the dichotomist and in agreement with Berkouwer, that there is a certain "imprecision" at times in the Bible's use of the relevant terminology. One has only to consider the several New Testament quotations of Deuteronomy 6:5, for example, to see this. Where Luke 10:27 reads that we should love God with all our heart (καρδία, *kardia*) and soul (ψυχή, *psychē*) and strength (ἰσχύς, *ischys*) and mind (διάνοια, *dianoia*), Matthew 22:37 reads that we should love God with all our heart and soul and mind, omitting strength, while Mark reports in 12:30 that we should love God with all our heart and soul and mind and strength (reversing the order of the last two Lukan words), and in 12:33 that we should love God with all our heart and understanding (συνέσεως, *syneseōs*) and strength, using another word for "mind" and omitting "soul" altogether. In all, five different words are employed without even mentioning the body. Surely, no one would insist, on the basis of these series of words connected by "and," that each of these words refers to an immaterial, ontologically distinct entity, and that therefore Luke was a quintchotomist, Matthew was a quadchotomist, and Mark was a sexchotomist. With Berkouwer we must all admit that these parallel admonitions are simply saying that we are to love God with our entire or total being. Similarly I would urge that the three passages that trichotomists regularly advance in support

---

6. Ibid., 93–94.

[420]

of trichotomy do not really draw an ontological distinction between "soul" and "spirit, as the following expositions will demonstrate:

> 1 Corinthians 15:44: "[The body] is sown a natural [ψυχικόν, *psychikon*] body, it is raised a spiritual [πνευματικόν, *pneumatikon,* that is, a supernatural] body. If there is a natural body, there is also a spiritual [that is, a supernatural] body."

Here the trichotomist urges that to assert that there is no difference between "soul" and "spirit" is to assert that there is no distinction between the preresurrection body and the resurrection body. But precisely because it is evident that there is a difference between these two bodies, he continues, it is equally clear that there is an ontological distinction between soul and spirit.

I would note, however, that the implied subject of both verbs ("sown," "raised") is the *same* subject, the body, and that the same word σῶμα, *sōma,* is used in both instances, suggesting that it is the *same* body numerically that is sown and raised. If the two words really intended totally distinct ontological entities, then the body that is raised is not the same body that is sown. Paul doubtless intended simply to say that the "soulish body," that is, the body whose attributes fit it for life in this *natural* world during this age, will be so transformed that, as the "spiritual body," it will fit the life which the person who is associated with the risen Christ will live in the *supernatural* New Earth situation.

> 1 Thessalonians 5:23: "May the God of peace himself sanctify you wholly [ὁλοτελεῖς, *holoteleis*] and may your whole [ὁλόκληρον, *holoklēron*] spirit and soul and body be preserved blameless in the coming of our Lord Jesus Christ."

The trichotomist insists that the conjunction "and" between "spirit" and "soul" intends that they be viewed as separate entities. But I would urge, first, that it is no less precarious to argue that "spirit" and "soul" refer here to separate, immaterial entities on the basis of the "and" between them than it is to argue that heart and soul and strength and mind in Luke 10:27 refer to separate immaterial entities because of the repeated "and" there. Second, the adverb "wholly" and the adjective "whole" in the verse strongly suggest that the emphasis of the verse is on the Christian man viewed here in his entirety as the "whole man."

> Hebrews 4:12: "Sharper than any two-edged sword, [the Word of God] penetrates even to 'dividing' of soul and spirit . . . and is the judge of the thoughts and intents of the heart."

Here the trichotomist insists, since the soul can be "divided" from the spirit, is evidence that they are two separate and distinct ontological entities. But this is to ignore the fact that "soul" and "spirit" are both genitives governed by the participle "dividing." The verse is saying that the Word of God "divides" the soul, *even* the spirit. But it does not say that the Word of God divides *between* soul and spirit (that would require some such word as μεταξύ, *metaxu*) or divides the soul *from* the spirit. The verse no more intends this than it intends, when it goes on to say that the Word is the judge of *thoughts* and of *intents* of the heart (again, two genitives governed by the noun "judge"), that thoughts and intents are ontologically distinct things. Clearly, intents are simply one kind of thought. What the verse is actually saying is that the Word of God is able to penetrate into the deepest recesses of a man's spirit and judge his very thoughts, even the secret intentions of his heart.

While these verses offer no support to the trichotomous view, this erroneous view of man's constituent make-up has been made the base for the espousal of other erroneous views both in Christology (Apollinarianism) and in the area of sanctification (the view that it is the Christian's spirit which is regenerated, his soul remaining unregenerate, and that it is this condition which accounts for the struggle within him to live either righteously or unrighteously).

Dichotomy

The dichotomist affirms that the Bible teaches that man's constituent elements are the material body and the immaterial soul (or spirit)—two ontologically distinct entities—which are in a mysterious, vital union and interact in what Berkhof calls the "union of life."[7] In other words, he is neither pure matter alone nor pure spirit alone but a wonderful duality-in-unity and unity-in-duality. The scriptural support for this view includes the following verses:

> Genesis 2:7: "the Lord God formed man from the dust of the ground and breathed into his nostrils the breath [נְשָׁמָה, *n⁽e⁾šāmâh*] of life, and man became a living being."
>
> Ecclesiastes 12:7: "The dust returns to the ground it came from, and the spirit returns to God who gave it." (This seems to be a commentary on Genesis 2:7.)
>
> Matthew 10:28: "Do not be afraid of those who kill the body but cannot kill the soul. Rather, be afraid of him who can destroy *both* soul and body in hell" (emphasis added).

Here our Lord makes it plain that a person has an entity that men may kill. He calls it the body (σῶμα, *sōma*). But he has another entity that men cannot kill. He calls

---

7. Louis Berkhof, *Systematic Theology* (Grand Rapids, Mich.: Eerdmans, 1932), 195.

it the soul (ψυχή, *psychē*). By his use of the καί . . . καί, *kai . . . kai*, construction in the second half of the verse, which grammatically means "both . . . and," Jesus clearly teaches that man's constituent parts are *two*, namely, "body" and "soul." This is the reason he could say to the dying thief, "I tell you the truth, today *you* will be with me in paradise" (Luke 23:43; emphasis added).

> 2 Corinthians 5:1–10: "Now we know that if the earthly tent [the body] we live in is destroyed, we have a building from God [that is, the resurrection body] . . . we groan, longing to be clothed with our heavenly dwelling, because when we are clothed, we [that is, our souls] will not be found naked. . . . as long as we are at home in the body we are away from the Lord. . . . we would prefer to be away from the body and at home with the Lord. So we make it our goal to please him, whether we are at home in the body or away from it."

> Philippians 1:21–24: "For to me, to live is Christ and to die is gain. If I am to go on living in the body, this will mean fruitful labor for me. Yet what shall I choose? I do not know! I am torn between the two: I desire to depart and be with Christ, which is far better; but it is more necessary for you that I remain in the body."

Because of this evidence, the Reformation creeds all adopt the dichotomous view of man. Again, the Westminster Confession of Faith will be sufficient to illustrate the point.

> The bodies of men, after death, return to dust, and see corruption: but their souls, which neither die nor sleep, having an immortal subsistence, immediately return to God who gave them: the souls of the righteous . . . are received into the highest heavens. . . . And the souls of the wicked are cast into hell. . . . Besides these two places, for *souls separated from their bodies,* the Scripture acknowledgeth none. (XXXII/i; emphasis supplied)

It is clear that the Confession of Faith views people as having one ontological entity which permits them to die and to see corruption. The Scripture calls this entity the body. But men *are* another ontological entity, and have thereby an immortal subsistence that neither dies nor sleeps when it leaves the body at death. The Bible calls this entity the soul or spirit. It is plain that the Confession of Faith in accordance with the Scriptures clearly teaches here the dichotomous view of man.

This is not to suggest that Holy Scripture *never* intends any distinction in its usage of "spirit" and "soul." H. D. MacDonald has nicely captured the nuancial distinction between "spirit" and "soul" when he writes:

> However used, *both terms refer to man's inner nature* over against flesh or body, which refers to the outer aspect of man as existing in space and time. In reference, then,

to man's psychical nature, "spirit" denotes life as having its origin in God and "soul" denotes *that same life* as constituted in man. Spirit is the inner depth of man's being, the higher aspect of his personality. Soul expresses man's own special and distinctive individuality. The *pneuma* is man's nonmaterial nature looking Godward; the *psyche* is *that same nature* of man looking earthward and touching the things of sense.[8]

The Origin of the Soul

Before we leave this subject entirely, something must be said about the origin of the human soul. With virtually unanimous rejection of the idea of the preexistence of souls put forward by Plato, by Origen, and by other Alexandrian Fathers, because it is devoid of scriptural support, the church has, throughout the history of dogma, framed the issue of the soul's origin in terms either of "creationism" or of "traducianism."

The creationist view, emphasizing the *vertical* nature of the acts of God, contends that the soul of each human being is *immediately created* by God and united to the body either at conception, at birth, or at some time between these two events. It relies primarily on five texts: Genesis 2:7, Ecclesiastes 12:7, Isaiah 57:16, Zechariah 12:1, and Hebrews 12:9.

The traducianist view (Lat. *tradux*, "branch" or "shoot"), urging that God carries out his "vertical" work primarily in and through *horizontal* or *mediate* means, holds that after the immediate creation of Adam both body and soul of each individual are immediately formed and propagated together by the natural generation effected by the sexual union of the human male and female. It appeals primarily to four texts: Genesis 2:2, 21 (interpreted by 1 Cor. 11:8), Romans 5:12, and Hebrews 7:9–10.

Berkouwer concludes his treatment of the controversy by declaring that the entire issue is illegitimate since it concentrates on the origin of the soul, whereas the Bible is concerned only with the origin of the "whole man before God."[9] He urges total rejection of the dilemma. While I concur with Kuyper and Bavinck that Scripture does not give us sufficient data to conclude decisively either way, and also that neither view helps us understand the nature of man in a way that the other does not, I myself am drawn to the traducianist view for the following reasons:

1. It appears to be everywhere assumed by Scripture that through conception human parents "father" and "mother" not just a physical body but the entire offspring, body and soul. When Charles Hodge, himself a staunch creationist, to avoid

---

8. H. D. MacDonald, "Man, Doctrine of," in *Evangelical Dictionary of Theology*, ed. Walter A. Elwell (Grand Rapids, Mich.: Baker, 1984), 678; emphasis supplied.
9. Berkouwer, *Man: The Image of God*, 284, 292, 295, 307.

the conclusion that God creates sinful souls, declares: "we do not know how the agency of God is connected with the operation of second causes, how far that agency is mediate, and how far it is immediate," and then admits in his later discussion of original sin: "It is moreover a historical fact universally admitted, that *character, within certain limits, is transmissible from parents to children*. Every nation, separate tribe, and even every extended family of men, has its physical, mental, social, and moral peculiarities which are *propagated from generation to generation*,"[10] he has abandoned his creationism, for if God does *immediately* create souls at conception or at birth, the mental and moral characteristics of parents cannot be *propagated*.

2. Creationism allows for only the physical or corporeal connection between Adam and his offspring and has to explain how human souls, immediately created by God and not by biological parents, become evil, whereas traducianism has a ready answer for why the individual is guilty of Adam's sin and is thus corrupt: Adam's "sin was imputed; and the same death in sin, and corrupted nature [were] *conveyed* to all [his] posterity descending from [him] by *ordinary generation*" (Westminster Confession of Faith, VI/iii).

Whatever one finally concludes about this matter, it is quite clear that Berkouwer's reductionist view of man's nature as simply the "whole man before God" is unscriptural and cannot be safely followed.

Man as the *Imago Dei*

The Bible's answer to the questions, "Is mankind distinct from all other animate life, and if so, in what way?" may be framed in one sentence: "Man and man alone is the very image of God (*imago Dei*)." But what is this "image" and how has the church understood this "image" that makes man distinct from all other animate life?

THE BIBLICAL DATA AND THEIR SYNTACTICAL SIGNIFICANCE

The idea first appears in Genesis 1:26, where we read that God in solemn counsel with himself said, "Let us [a probable reflection of the trinity of persons in the divine essence] make man in our image [בְּצַלְמֵנוּ, *bᵉsalmēnû*], according to our likeness [כִּדְמוּתֵנוּ, *cidmûtēnû*]." Quite early in Christian thinking a distinction was drawn between the two terms, due perhaps to the LXX rendering, εἰκόνα καὶ ὁμοίωσιν (*eikōna kai homoiōsin*, "image *and* likeness"), which also is reflected in the Latin Vulgate's *et* between the phrases. Irenaeus and Tertullian saw the former term (צֶלֶם,

---

10. Charles Hodge, *Systematic Theology*, 2:69, 253.

ṣelem) as referring to bodily traits and the latter (דְּמוּת, d*ᵉmût*) to the spiritual nature of man. Clement of Alexandria and Origen, rejecting this understanding of the issue, urged that "image" denotes the characteristics of man *qua* man, while "likeness" refers to qualities not essential to man's "manness" but which may be cultivated or lost. Athanasius, Ambrose, Augustine, and John of Damascus in their own times were persuaded that the latter view was correct. Scholastics of the Middle Ages continued to urge this distinction between the nouns, conceiving of the former as including the intellectual powers of reason and freedom, and the latter as original holiness and righteousness (*dona superaddita*). Accordingly, in Roman Catholic theology, in and by the fall man lost the "likeness" while still retaining as man the image of God. Thus fallen man is essentially *deprived* of the "superadditional gifts" of holiness and righteousness but not morally *depraved* throughout the whole man. Indeed, he is not even in a state of sin but only in the state of a *tendency* to sin.[11]

The Reformers rejected the distinction between the two terms and regarded righteousness as belonging originally to the very nature of man. Luther regarded the image exclusively in terms of original righteousness and concluded, therefore, that the image of God was entirely lost in the Fall (Lutherans, out of loyalty to Luther, have generally followed their namesake). Calvin disagreed, viewing the image as lying primarily in the understanding or in the heart, that is, in the soul and its powers, but he also suggested that "no part of man, not even his body," is not adorned in some sense with some rays of its glory. In other words, the image included, for Calvin, both natural endowments and the spiritual qualities of original righteousness (knowledge, righteousness, holiness). The whole image, according to Calvin, has been affected by the Fall, with only original righteousness being completely lost. This is the explication of the image that has become generally acceptable in the Reformed tradition. Today it is quite common to see the image defined *formally*

---

11. The *Catechism of the Catholic Church* (1994) declares: "[Original sin] is a sin . . . transmitted by propagation to all mankind, that is, by the transmission of a human nature *deprived of original holiness and justice*" (par. 404, emphasis supplied). It also states that "original sin does not have the character of a personal fault in any of Adam's descendants. It is *a deprivation of original holiness and justice,* but human nature has not been totally corrupted: it is wounded in the natural powers proper to it: subject to ignorance, suffering, and the dominion of death; and inclined to sin—an inclination to evil that is called 'concupiscence' " (par. 405, emphasis supplied). Thus, according to Roman Catholic theology, man's fallen state is a *relapse* back to the state of pure nature (*status naturae purae*) which is not a state of sin, but only the state of a tendency to sin. The *Catechism* goes on to state that Rome's teaching "was articulated in the sixteenth century [at the Council of Trent], in opposition to the Protestant Reformation," whose first leaders "taught that original sin has radically perverted man and destroyed his freedom" (par. 406).

in terms of personality (rationality, emotion, and moral responsibility) and *materially* in terms of a true knowledge of God. The Fall brought about great weakness in the former (liability to error in thinking, depression in emotion, misjudgment in moral responsibility) and a serious distortion (but not a total demolition) of the latter. But sufficiently horrible was the Fall's effects in both areas of the image that Paul can justifiably describe men as "dead" in their sins in the sense that they are spiritually dead toward God and love of righteousness.

Were the Reformers right in rejecting all distinctions between "image" and "likeness"? I would affirm that they were, and for the following reasons:

1. There is no *waw* conjunctive (and) between the phrases in the Hebrew. As we noted already, it is true that the LXX and the Vulgate insert a καί, *kai,* and an *et* respectively, which may be part of the reason for early efforts to find a distinction between them.

2. Both Genesis 1:27 and 9:6 employ only צֶלֶם, (*selem*, "image"), apparently regarding the one word as sufficient to explain the entire idea.

3. Genesis 5:1 employs only דְּמוּת, (*dᵉmût*, "likeness"), and with the בְּ, *bᵉ*, preposition which was affixed to צֶלֶם, *selem,* in Genesis 1:26. This again suggests that the one word is sufficient to express the entire idea.

4. In Genesis 5:3 both terms are employed, but the verse reverses both the order of the terms and the usage of prepositions found in Genesis 1:26.

5. In Colossians 3:10 (see also 1:15 and 2 Cor 4:4) only "image" (εἰκών, *eikōn*) is found, while in James 3:9 only "likeness" (ὁμοίωσις, *homoiōsis*) is employed, again suggesting that either term sufficiently expresses the original idea.

In light of this data, today the terms are generally viewed as simply stating emphatically or intensively the fact that man uniquely reflects God, that is to say, man as created was the *"very* image" or *"perfect* likeness" of God.

But in what precise way did God intend man to "mirror" him? What is the meaning of this *"very* image"? How was (is) man a "reflection" of God?

THE NATURE OF THE IMAGE

While there is a general consensus among scholars today that no distinction should be drawn between "image" and "likeness," there is no such consensus regarding what the "very image" is or means.

Some scholars (e.g., Buswell)[12] suggest that the image in man (or at least an aspect of it) is his dominion over the creation. But Genesis 1:26 seems to indicate that

---

12. J. Oliver Buswell Jr., *A Systematic Theology of the Christian Religion* (Grand Rapids, Mich.: Zondervan, 1962), 1:233–35.

dominion was to be a bestowment upon God's image bearer, an investiture grounded in and contingent upon the fact that man *is* God's image. Verse 28, where dominion is made a reality by its actual bestowment upon man, follows the action of verse 27 where man is created and already stands before God and the world as God's image. In other words, it is because man *is* God's image that God bestows dominion over the world upon him.

Others (e.g., Barth)[13] urge a christological construction of the image. Citing Colossians 1:15 and 2 Corinthians 4:4, where Christ is referred to as the εἰκὼν τοῦ θεοῦ, *eikōn tou theou*, they teach that Christ is the *true* man, the *real* man, and that his humanity is the "original" and that ours is the "derivative." We participate in *his* humanity, not in Adam's, and not he in ours. Basing his remarks on Romans 5:12–19, Barth writes:

> Man's essential and original nature is to be found . . . not in Adam [for Barth, Adam is not the historical individual of Genesis 1–3 but the *typical* man, that is, we are all Adam] but in Christ. . . . Adam can be interpreted only in the light of Christ and not the other way around.
>
> . . . Human existence, as constituted by our relationship with Adam . . . has no independent reality, status, or importance of its own. . . . [And the relationship between Adam and us is] the relationship that exists originally and essentially between Christ and us.[14]

In addition to the universalistic overtones in such a construction, in light of the verses (1) which represent Adam as the *first* man and Christ the *second* (and last) man (1 Cor. 15:45–49), and (2) which describe Christ in his incarnation as becoming like *us* and taking *our* humanity upon himself (Phil. 2:7b, Heb. 2:14, 17; Rom. 8:3), I would urge that this construction has improperly interpreted the εἰκὼν τοῦ θεοῦ, *eikōn tou theou*. I would suggest that Christ is the "image of God" because he is deity and because as such in his incarnation he took our flesh. As man, then, he is both the realized ideal and the goal of human glory (Rom. 8:29; 2 Cor. 3:18).

More traditionally, Reformed scholars, employing a "restoration hermeneutic," have urged a personal/moral construction of the image. By determining precisely what it is that fallen man is *restored* to through Christ, by a direct "reading back" they have urged that the image of God is true righteousness, holiness, and a true knowledge of God. They appeal to the following two texts in particular:

---

13. Karl Barth, *Christ and Adam*, trans. T. A. Smail (1957; reprint, New York: Macmillan, 1968). See John Murray's critique of Barth's view in "Karl Barth on Romans 5," in *The Epistle to the Romans* (Grand Rapids, Mich.: Eerdmans, 1968), Appendix D, I, 384–90.

14. Barth, *Christ and Adam*, 29–30.

Ephesians 4:21-24: "By him you were taught . . . to put off from yourselves [that which is] in accord with the former manner of life, the old man, the one corrupted in accord with deceitful lusts, and be renewed in the spirit of your mind and put on the new man which in God's image [κατὰ θεὸν, *kata theon*] is created in true righteousness and holiness [δικαιοσύνῃ καὶ ὁσιότητι τῆς ἀληθείας, *dikaiosynē kai hosiotēti tēs alētheias*]."

Colossians 3:10: "Putting on the new man which is being continually renewed unto knowledge [ἐπίγνωσιν, *epignōsin*] according to the image [κατ 'εἰκόνα, *kat eikona*] of the One who created him."

The allusion in these verses to Genesis 1:26–27 is inescapable, and the renewal through Christ is described in terms of true righteousness and holiness in the former verse and in terms of knowledge ("knowledge" is perhaps Colossians' dynamic equivalent to Ephesians' "righteousness and holiness") in the latter verse. The Reformed creeds understand the original image in Genesis 1:26 accordingly to be these "renewed image virtues." For example, the Confession of Faith (IV/ii) states:

After God had made all other creatures, He created man, male and female, with reasonable and immortal souls, *endued with knowledge, righteousness, and true holiness, after His own image*.

Charles Hodge contends that ἐπίγνωσιν (*epignōsin*, "knowledge") refers to (true) knowledge *of God*, since the word has this sense in Colossians 1:6, 9, 27–28; 2:2–3, that δικαιοσύνη (*dikaiosynē*, "righteousness") refers to moral rectitude *toward one's neighbor*, that is, justice, and that ὁσιότητι (*hosiotēti*, "holiness") refers to the Godward relation known as *piety toward God*.[15] This means that these three "renewed image virtues" are not religio/ethical abstractions, but rather are indicative of right relationships with God and neighbor. This in turn affirms that the image must be defined both in terms of *entis* and also in terms of *relationis*. God created man in his image, that is, with a creaturely but true knowledge of God, with justice toward his neighbor (which virtue was originally expressed in Adam's relation to Eve and vice versa), and piety (covenant faithfulness) toward God. When Adam fell, though he still retained the image in the *formal* sense that man is still *homo religiosus/homo sapiens*, the *material* image which he was to "mirror" by justice toward neighbor and covenant faithfulness toward God became terribly marred both in him and in his posterity. The material image is principially restored only through salvation in Christ, the antitypical and ideal "image of God."

---

15. Charles Hodge, *A Commentary on the Epistle to the Ephesians* (Grand Rapids, Mich.: Eerdmans, 1954), 265–66.

THE COVENANT OF WORKS

The first covenant made with man was a covenant of works, wherein life was promised to Adam, and in him to his posterity, upon condition of perfect and personal obedience. (Westminster Confession of Faith, VII/ii.)

The Hebrew word for "covenant" is בְּרִית, *bᵉrît*, and it occurs some 285 times in the Old Testament. The covenant which God originally made with Adam was a divinely arranged suzerainty pact wherein, on the divine side, God bound himself to both promise and threat while, on the human side, Adam was expected to obey the covenantal stipulations which were accompanied by God's promise of blessing for obedience and threat of sanction for disobedience.

The Exegetical Basis for the Presence of a Covenant in Genesis 2

Although the word "covenant" does not occur in Genesis 2, there are four reasons for regarding the arrangement between God and Adam as a covenant as the Westminster Confession of Faith teaches (VII/i, ii):

1. The word בְּרִית, *bᵉrît*, does not have to be actually used at the time a covenant is made in order for a covenant to be present, as is made clear from 2 Samuel 7, where, although the word is not employed, according to Psalm 89:19–37 God *covenantally* promised David that his dynastic house would rule over Israel.

2. Covenant elements (parties, stipulation, promise, and threat) are present.

3. Hosea 6:7, "But they, like Adam, transgressed covenant," states by implication that Adam's sin was a "transgression of covenant." Some commentators suggest that the phrase "like Adam" should be translated "like men," but this is to intrude an inanity into the text, for how else could Hosea's contemporaries transgress than "like men"? Other commentators have wanted to emend the "like Adam" (כְּאָדָם, *kᵉʾādām*) phrase to "in Adam" (בְּאָדָם, *bᵉʾādām*), and then they speak of some transgression which occurred in the town by that name mentioned in Joshua 3:16. But the Scriptures are silent regarding such an event. It seems best to retain the most obvious sense of the phrase.[16]

4. The New Testament parallels between Adam and Christ (Rom. 5:12–19; 1 Cor. 15:22, 45–49) imply that just as Christ was the federal (*foedus*: "covenant") representative of the New Covenant (Luke 22:20; Heb. 9:15), so also Adam acted as a federal representative of a covenant arrangement.

---

16. So also Benjamin B. Warfield, "Hosea vi:7: Adam or Man?" in *Selected Shorter Writings of Benjamin B. Warfield*, ed. J. E. Meeter (Nutley, N.J.: Presbyterian and Reformed, 1970), 1:116–29.

The Nature of the Genesis 2 Covenant

How shall we characterize this covenant between God and Adam? Most commonly today it is called either a covenant of works (Confession of Faith, VII/ii; XIX/i) or a covenant of life (Larger Catechism, Question 20; Shorter Catechism, Question 12), the former characterization emphasizing that the confirmation in righteousness which God would give Adam upon the latter's successful sustaining of his probationary test he would necessarily give to Adam in *justice* and that what Adam would receive he would receive as *reward or merit* for his obedience, the latter characterization specifying the nature of the reward which Adam and his posterity would receive if he obeyed God.

Increasing numbers of biblical scholars today, led by Daniel P. Fuller, are expressing unhappiness with the former characterization, claiming that *whatever* Adam received from the hand of God would have been undeserved and a gift of "grace" (this grace being understood however more in terms of God's goodness in establishing the conditions of the New Covenant than in terms of God's sovereignly applying salvation to the elect).[17] He explicitly refuses to see a works/grace contrast in the divine-human relationship anywhere in history, even before the Fall. In his *Gospel and Law: Contrast or Continuum?* he insists upon a "continuum" of divine "grace" in all of God's dealings with man, including even his pre-Fall dealings with Adam.

The irony in all this is that Fuller declares that this "grace" does its work of justification through what he calls the "work, or obedience, of faith,"[18] insisting that many Scripture passages make good works the *instrumental cause* of justification (he is quick to insist that such good works are not meritorious).[19] Accordingly, a view that insists upon "grace" everywhere winds up with true grace nowhere and a kind of works principle everywhere, with his representation of the relation of works to justification coming perilously close to what late medieval theologians

---

17. Daniel Fuller, *Gospel and Law: Contrast or Continuum?* (Grand Rapids, Mich.: Eerdmans, 1980), 103, 109, 118–20.
18. Daniel Fuller, "A Response on the Subjects of Works and Grace," *Presbuterion* 9, no. 1–2 (1983): 79. This article was a response to O. Palmer Robertson's review of Fuller's book appearing in *Presbuterion* 8, no. 1 (1982): 84–91. See also W. Robert Godfrey's response to the debate in his "Back to Basics: A Response to the Robertson-Fuller Dialogue," and Meredith G. Kline's "Of Work and Grace," both of which appeared in *Presbuterion*, 9, no. 1–2 (1983). See also Kline's more popular "Covenant Theology Under Attack," *New Horizons* (Feb. 1994), 3–5.
19. "Obedience of faith" (ὑπακοὴ πίστεως, *hypakoē pisteōs*) is a Pauline expression, it is true (Rom. 1:5; 16:26). But the genitive should be construed as either a genitive of source and rendered "obedience that flows from faith" or as an appositional genitive meaning "obedience that consists of faith."

would have called works having not condign but congruent merit.[20] One thing is certainly clear from Fuller's representation of this whole matter: he has departed from the *sola fide* principle of the Protestant Reformation.

Meredith G. Kline declares Fuller's construction to be an "error of massive proportions" and insists that justice, *not* grace, is the governing principle and element of continuity in both the pre-Fall and redemptive covenants. He offers the following explanation for his judgment:

> The necessity of affirming the traditional works principle [in Genesis 2] becomes clear if we concentrate on the subject of justification in God's covenantal dealings with Adam and Christ. If the first Adam had obediently fulfilled the stipulations of God's covenant with him, then assuredly he would have been worthy of being declared righteous by his Lord. Adam's justification would have been on the grounds of his works and would have been precisely what those good works deserved. God's declaring Adam righteous would have been an act of justice, pure and simple. In fact, any other verdict would have been injustice. There is absolutely no warrant for obscuring the works character of such an achievement of justification by introducing the idea of grace into the theological analysis of it.
>
> Rejection of the works principle [with reference to Adam] extends in the logic of [this construction] to the Second Adam. [Norman Shepherd] notes that the covenantal relationship is a father-son relationship and from this concludes that parental grace, not any claim of strict justice, accounts for any favorable treatment man receives from God, his Father. But if the elimination of simple justice as the governing principle is thus due to the presence of a father-son relationship, mere justice could no more explain God's response to the obedience of his Son, the second Adam, than it could his dealings with the first Adam. This means that in [the Fuller/Shepherd] theology, consistently developed, the work of obedience performed by Jesus Christ did not merit a verdict of justification from his Father. The justification of the second Adam was not then according to the principle of works in contrast to grace, but rather found its explanation in the operation of a principle involving some sort of grace—a grace required because of the inadequacy of Christ's work to satisfy the claims of justice.[21]

But a rejection of the full meritoriousness of the work of Christ has devastating implications for the doctrine of justification through the imputation of Christ's

---

20. In his *The Harvest of Medieval Theology* (Grand Rapids, Mich.: Eerdmans, 1967), 471–72, Heiko Obermann defines congruent (or "half") merit as "merit meeting the standard of God's generosity," over against condign (or "full") merit, which is merit that deserves the grace it receives.
21. Kline, "Of Works and Grace," 88–89.

righteousness to believers; for if Christ's obedience has no meritorious value, neither has a penal satisfaction been made for our sins nor is there a preceptive righteousness available to be imputed to us.

In order to justify their use of the term "grace" rather than "works" to describe the character of the pre-Fall covenant, advocates of the Fuller approach have urged that the blessing to be bestowed upon Adam for his obedience (eternal life) would have so far exceeded the value of his obedience that the concept of simple justice is inadequate as a description of the ground of the covenantal pre-Fall relationship between God and man. Accordingly, they urge that we can only speak of the ground of this covenant in terms of grace. But, as Kline rightly observes, this alleged disparity in value between the obedience to be rendered and the reward to be bestowed is very debatable, first, since insofar as Adam's obedience would have glorified God and given him pleasure, it would have had *infinite* value. All obedience to God is infinite in its worth. Second, if we allow the factor of relative values to become the judge of justice, we would have to accuse the Father of injustice towards his Son, inasmuch as his Son's atonement was sufficient in its worth for all mankind but he receives from his Father not all men but only the elect. We can avoid such a blasphemous conclusion, Kline writes,

> only if we recognize that God's justice must be defined and judged in terms of what he stipulates in his covenants. Thus, the specific commitment of the Father in the eternal covenant was to give the Son the elect as the reward for his obedience, and that is precisely what the Son receives, not one missing. Judged by the stipulated terms of their covenant, there was no injustice, but rather perfect justice. By the same token, there was no grace in the Father's reward to the Son. It was a case of simple justice. The Son earned that reward. It was a covenant of works, and the obedience of the Son (active and passive) was meritorious.
>
> What was true in the covenant arrangement with the Second Adam will also have been true in the covenant with the First Adam, for the first was a type of the second (Rom 5:14) precisely with respect to his role as a federal head in the divine government. Accordingly, the pre-Fall covenant was also a covenant of works, and there, too, Adam would have fully deserved the blessings promised in the covenant, had he obediently performed the duty stipulated in it. Great as the blessings were to be which the good Lord committed himself, the granting of them would not have involved a gram of grace. Judged by the stipulated terms of the covenant, they would have been merited in simple justice.[22]

---

22. Kline, "Covenant Theology Under Attack," 4.

The Representative Feature of the Covenant of Works

There is one all-important feature of the covenant of works which calls for special treatment, and that is the nature of the relationship between Adam and the race which the covenant entailed, on the basis of which Adam's sin became the sin of the race.

From his analysis of Romans 5:12–19, John Murray concludes that the relationship clearly entailed

> some kind of solidarity existing between the "one" [Adam] and the "all" [the race] with the result that the sin contemplated can be regarded at the same time and with equal relevance as the sin of the "one" or as the sin of "all."[23]

But what is the nature of this "solidarity"? Is it the *natural* union between Adam and his posterity? Or is it the *representative* union between Adam as the federal head of the race and the race itself?

As we begin our own exposition of Romans 5:12–19, we note that the expression διὰ τοῦτο (*dia touto*, "because of this") commencing verse 12 refers back to the expression "in his life" in verse 10. It is plain that the following ὥσπερ (*hosper*, "just as") introduces a protasis. Where is its apodosis? Some expositors have urged that the apodosis is also to be found in verse 12, commencing with the καὶ οὕτως (*kai houtos*, "and so"). But when Paul introduces his apodoses after ὡς, *hos*, or ὥσπερ, *hosper*, he regularly does so, not with καὶ οὕτως, *kai houtos*, but with οὕτως καὶ; (*houtos kai*, "so also"), as in verses 5:15, 18, 19, 21; 6:4; and 11:30. Where then is the apodosis after the ὥσπερ, *hosper*, if not in verse 12? It is the οὕτως καὶ, *houtos kai*, of verse 18 with the original ὥσπερ, *hosper*, clause of verse 12 introduced again in different language by the ὡς, *hos* of verse 18. The thought would then be:

> Verse 12: Because of this [being in Christ], *just as* by one man sin and death entered the world, and death came upon all men in that all sinned—
>
> > (Verses 13–17: An excursus commences [verses 13–14] on the "all sinned" phrase at the end of verse 12 in which Paul makes it clear that he means "all sinned in Adam's transgression"; then a second excursus [verses 15–17] follows in which he shows that while Adam is indeed a "type" of Christ [end of verse 14], Christ and God's gift of grace through him achieve far more than Adam's failure by reversing the operation of divine judgment not only against Adam's sin but also against "many trespasses" [verse 16])—
>
> Verse 18: So then [having disposed of certain questions in the two excurses], *as* through one transgression [judgment came] unto all men [in Adam] unto

---

23. John Murray, *The Imputation of Adam's Sin* (Grand Rapids, Mich.: Eerdmans, 1959), 21.

condemnation [note: this is a rephrasing of the "just as" clause of verse 12], *so also through one act of righteousness, [the free gift came] unto all men [in Christ]*[24] *unto justification of life.*

Verse 19: [Paul now summarizes the whole] For *just as* through the disobedience of the one man [Adam] the many [in Adam] were made sinners, *so also* through the obedience of the one Man [Christ] the many [in Christ] were constituted righteous.

The main point of the passage turns upon the term "one" (εἷς, *heis*), which occurs twelve times. Note in these verses the reiterated point that "in Adam's fall we sinned all," that is to say, for some reason the one (first) sin of the one man Adam God regards as the sin of all:

Verse 12: "Through *one* man sin into the world entered and through that sin [came] death, and so unto all men death came, in that all sinned [in Adam]" (this last bracketed phrase is argued in the excursus of verses 13–14).

Verse 15: "By the trespass of the *one* the many died."

Verse 16: "And not as through *one* who sinned is the gift . . . judgment [arose] out of *one* [trespass] unto condemnation [unto all men]" (the last bracket is from verse 18).

Verse 17: "By the trespass of the *one* death reigned through the *one* [Adam]."

Verse 18: "Through *one* trespass [judgment came] unto all men unto condemnation."

Verse 19: "Through the disobedience of the *one* man, the many were appointed sinners."

Paul could not have made himself clearer respecting the solidarity of the "one man" and "the many." And he could not have been plainer in his insistence that Adam's sin is in some sense the sin of all. Some theologians (Pinnock, for example), it is true, reject the idea that Adam's sin is also the sin of the race and therefore the ground on which the race's condemnation is based. But every effort to force any other meaning on Paul's words both shatters on the rock of rigorous exegesis and

---

24. Soteric universalists and Arminians urge that Paul's second "all men" in Romans 5:18 should be construed as widely and extensively as his first "all men" in the verse, that is to say, they make its referent the entire race. While I concur that both occurrences of πάντας ἀνθρώπους, *pantas anthrōpous*, in 5:18 are to be translated as "all men," I would urge, as my translation above suggests, that they should be interpreted within their "universes" in the passage. The first refers to the "all men" in Adam; the second refers to the "all men" in Christ.

The same insight should apply to Paul's employment of οἱ πολλοί (*hoi polloi*, "the many") in 5:19; the former refers to "the many" in Adam; the second refers to "the many" in Christ.

destroys the ground on which man's salvation is based, even the alien righteousness of Jesus Christ. For consider the corresponding side of the apostle's analogy:

> Verse 14: "Adam, who is a type [with respect to his federal headship] of the Coming One."
>
> Verse 15: "Grace . . . and the gift by grace abounded unto the many which [grace] is of the *one* man Jesus Christ."
>
> Verse 16: "The ones receiving the abundance of grace and the gift of righteousness shall reign in life through the *one* Jesus Christ."
>
> Verse 18: "Through *one* righteous act [the free gift came] unto all men unto justification of life."
>
> Verse 19: "Through the obedience of the *one* [man] the many shall be constituted righteous."
>
> Verse 21: "Grace reigns through righteousness . . . through Jesus Christ our Lord."

Clearly for Paul there is a connection between Adam's sin and the sin and condemnation of the race. How is that connection to be explicated? Warfield classified the more recent explanations which have been offered as follows:[25]

The Agnostic View

This view, held by R. W. Landis, accepts the fact of the transmission of Adam's guilt and depravity to the race but refrains from framing a theory of the mode of transmission or the relation of guilt to corruption.

The Realist View

This view, postulated for example by William G. T. Shedd and James Henry Thornwell, rejects the idea of the imputation of Adam's sin and contends that "human nature" must be viewed generically and numerically as a *single* unit. It proposes that Adam possessed the entire human nature and that all mankind, being present in Adam as generic humanity, corrupted itself by its own apostatizing act in Adam. Individual men are not separate substances, but manifestations of the same generic substance. They are numerically one in nature. The reason that all men are accountable for Adam's sin is because they *actually* (really) sinned in Adam before the individualizing of human nature began.

---

25. Benjamin B. Warfield, "Imputation," in *New Schaff-Herzog Encyclopaedia of Religious Knowledge* (reprint, Grand Rapids, Mich.: Baker, 1977), 5:465–67.

This view, however, cannot explain why Adam's descendants today are held responsible for his *first* sin only (see "that sin" in verse 12; the "one trespass" in verses 16 and 18) and not for all of his subsequent sins as well, not to mention the sins of all the generations of forefathers that followed Adam and that precede any particular man today. Moreover, it destroys the parallel which Paul draws between Adam and Christ (see his *"just as . . . so also"*). Men are not righteous because they themselves *actually do* righteousness in Christ. They are constituted righteous because Christ's righteousness is forensically imputed (reckoned) to them. Paul's parallel would require the correlative conclusion that men are not ultimately unrighteous because they *actually did* unrighteousness in Adam but because Adam's unrighteousness is imputed to them. Not to affirm this destroys the parallel which Paul draws between Adam and Christ. John Murray writes in this regard:

> Since the analogy instituted between Adam and Christ [in Rom. 5] is so conspicuous, it is surely necessary to assume that the kind of relationship which Adam sustains to men is after the pattern of the relationship which Christ sustains to men. To put the case conversely, surely the kind of relationship that Christ sustains to men is after the pattern which Adam sustains to men (see Rom. 5:14).[26]

Murray goes on to argue, and I think correctly, that since *natural* or seminal headship is not and can never be descriptive of Christ's relationship to men, and since the relationship between Christ and the justified, therefore, must be one of vicarious representation, we must assume that the relationship between Adam and his posterity, on the basis of which his *one* (first) sin is imputed, is also one of *vicarious representation*.[27] This is the core contention of the federal view which we will now review.

The Federal (Immediate Imputation) View

This view, held by Charles Hodge and John Murray, appears to be much more in accord with the Pauline analogy between Adam and Christ than the realist view does in that it is the only view that does justice to both halves of that analogy. It does not deny for a moment the natural union between Adam and his posterity, but it urges that the *natural* union only determined the "direction of application" which the governing principle of *representational* union took. Determined to do justice to the representative principle which alone governs the relationship between Christ and the justified, it regards the relation between Adam's first sin and the sin of the

---

26. Murray, *Imputation*, 39.
27. Ibid., 40.

race as also grounded in *federal representation*. In other words, just because Adam was the federal representative of the human race in the covenant of works, in his righteous judgment God imputed Adam's first transgression to the race that was federally related to him. Charles Hodge, an *immediate* imputationist (which view we discuss below), believed, however, that what God imputed was only *reatus poenae*, the judicial obligation to satisfy divine justice, or the liability to punishment, and not *reatus culpae* (the liability to guilt). But it would surely be a violation of simple justice were God to hold a person liable for punishment whom he did not at the same time regard as guilty of the sin being punished. Murray, more consistently I would judge, insists that Romans 5 intends that we understand that both *reatus culpae* and *reatus poenae* and not just the latter were imputed to the race. Indeed, he insists that God imputed to the race, as an implicate of the race's representational solidarity with Adam, both Adam's guilt and Adam's corruption (that is, his disposition to sin). After all, he notes, Paul does not say that God only imputed Adam's liability to punishment but rather that he imputed Adam's *sin* itself (which necessarily entails both guilt and corruption) to the race.

The "New School" (Mediate Imputation) View

This view, held by such men as Josua Placaeus and Henry B. Smith (with variations), denies that Adam's first sin was immediately or directly imputed to his descendants. Rather, it urges that Adam's descendants derive their corruption from him because of their racial solidarity with him, and only then does God, on the basis of this antecedent corruption (or through the *medium* of this corruption), impute to them the guilt of Adam's apostasy. In other words, men are not born corrupt because God imputed Adam's sin to them; rather, God imputed Adam's sin to them because they are corrupt. In sum, "their condition is not based on their legal status, but their legal status on their condition."[28] The *immediate imputationist* insists, on the other hand, that God sovereignly imputed Adam's sin immediately, that is, directly, to his descendants, and that, *as a result* (if one follows Berkhof), God then willed that Adam's corruption would be transmitted to the race, or (if one follows Murray) that God immediately imputed, as an implicate of the race's solidarity with Adam, both Adam's guilt and his corruption to the race.

On the basis of the Pauline analogy in Romans 5, the "immediate imputation" view considered from every vantage point is the correct one, for men are not regarded as righteous in Christ because in some sense they are antecedently righteous. Rather, they are regarded as righteous on the basis of Christ's immediately

---

28. Berkhof, *Systematic Theology*, 243.

imputed righteousness, and it is this punctiliar justification which necessarily leads to their progressive sanctification.

I would urge, in conclusion, that the Adam/Christ parallel in Romans 5 teaches that under the terms of the covenant of works Adam's sin was imputed to the human race solely on the basis of Adam's *federal representation* of the race, and that Adam's first sin *per se*, entailing both the guilt and corruption of that sin, was *immediately* imputed to the human race, with its penalty and corruption being conveyed to all his posterity descending from him by ordinary generation.

The Covenant's Continuing Normativeness

The covenant of works reflects the fact that the most fundamental obligation of man the creature to God his Creator always has been, is now, and always will be obedience to the will of the Creator. As *covenant* creature (and therefore always as either covenant *keeper* or covenant *breaker*), man is always ultimately related to God on a *legal* (covenantal) basis. Accordingly, while the covenant of works is no longer in force as a probationary framework for mankind, it is still normative in the following ways:

1. In the incumbency it places upon man always to render to God perfect obedience to the moral law, it reflects the obligation of the rational creature to obey his Creator, which obedience is always both necessary and appropriate for his approbation.

2. The sentence handed down and the punishment actually meted out in Genesis 3 continues in force; men represented by Adam are still culpable before God and subject to death on the basis of the terms of the original covenant of works (Rom. 5:12-14; 18-19).

3. The principle, "Do and live!" (stated in the New Testament, "To him who overcomes, to him [God] gives the right to eat of the tree of life, which is in the paradise of God"), is still operative (Rev. 2:7; see also Lev. 18:5; Rom. 10:5; Gal. 3:12) in that divine approval of true human righteousness is an eternal principle of divine justice (though since the Fall no one with the exception of Christ in his or her natural state can comply with this condition).

4. Precisely the same obligation of personal, perfect, and perpetual obedience that God laid upon Adam as the federal representative of the race by the covenant of works God laid upon Christ, the "second Man" and "last Adam" (see 1 Cor. 15:45, 47), who by his obedience accomplished

the salvation of the elect represented by him (Rom. 5:18–19). This means that because we as lost men in Adam are no longer in innocence or on probation, *our* character and *our* conduct can no longer be the determinative ground of our approbation before God (it *is* one ground of our disapprobation), but with respect to all those whom Christ represents, *Christ's* character and conduct are the determinative ground of their approbation before God.

It is true that the covenant of works *per se* contained no provision for redemption from sin in the event that Adam should fall, but this fact should not be construed to mean that the covenant of works is no longer in force or was rendered null and void by the entrance of the covenant of grace. Rather, the covenant of grace should be seen as providing the requisite redemptive provision as a second-level "covenantal overlay" upon the covenant of works. What this means is that Christ the "second Man" stepped forward, representing certain *sinners* who could not themselves keep the covenant (it is in *his* representation of these undeserving sinners and in all that this entails for them that the *grace* of the covenant of grace is exhibited), and as the "last Adam" he kept (where Adam had not) all of the requirements of the covenant in their behalf by meeting both the preceptive and penal demands of the covenant of work.

MAN AS COVENANT BREAKER

The Nature of the Fall

Our first parents, being seduced by the subtilty and temptation of Satan, sinned, in eating the forbidden fruit. This their sin, God was pleased, according to His wise and holy counsel, to permit, having purposed to order it to His own glory. (Westminster Confession of Faith, VI/i)

What was the precise nature of Adam's sin according to Genesis 3? As we begin it is important that we remind ourselves that Genesis 3 is Holy Scripture and authentic history. Those critical views which deny to Genesis 3 all historical significance in reference to the sinfulness and depravity of mankind, preferring to see in it everything from aetiological legends (to explain, e.g., why people wear clothes, why snakes go on their belly and why people dislike them, why we die) to ancient Semitic myths (e.g., Adam, the earth god, and his companion, Eve, the earth serpent), in the words of J. Barton Payne, show "utter disregard for the analogy of Scripture."[29]

---

29. J. Barton Payne, *Theology of the Older Testament* (Grand Rapids, Mich.: Zondervan, 1962), 216. See Job 31:33; Hosea 6:7; Romans 5:12–19; 16:20; 2 Corinthians 11:3; 1 Timothy 2:13–14.

The event we are about to consider in the early verses of Genesis 3 was both a probation and a temptation. Geerhardus Vos observes:

> There is a difference between probation and temptation, and yet they appear here [in Genesis 3] as two aspects of the same transaction.... We may say that what was from the point of view of God a probation was made use of by the evil power to inject into it the element of temptation. The difference consists in this, that back of the probation lies a good, back of the temptation an evil design, but both work with the same material. It is, of course, necessary to keep God free from tempting anybody with evil intent (cpr. James 1:13). But it is also important to insist upon the probation as an integral part of the divine plan with regard to humanity. Even if no tempter had existed, or projected himself into the crisis, even then some form for subjecting man to probation would have been found, though it is impossible for us to surmise what.[30]

Turning now to our exposition, we are immediately confronted in 3:1 with the presence of the "serpent" as tempter working at cross-purposes to God. Throughout the history of dogma, this "presence" has consistently been regarded as a literal creature under the control of Satan. Buswell's suggestion that the serpent is not a literal animal but Satan himself designated as "the Serpent"[31] is attractive in that it relieves the interpreter of having to explain to the modern skeptical mind the fact of a talking snake, but such a view seems hardly possible, first, in view of the fact that his "craftiness" is compared with and declared to be superior to the (other) creatures of the field, surely peculiar if the serpent was the archangel Satan, and second, because in 3:14 the curse is depicted in terms applicable to a literal serpent. With regard to the very idea of a "talking snake," it may be that what we have here was really simply a case of ventriloquism—Satan throwing his voice. But if the snake did actually speak, it should be pointed out that this is no stranger than the *other* instance in Scripture of a talking animal—namely, Balaam's ass—who not only *spoke* words of rebuke to Balaam but *saw* the angel of the Lord (Num. 22:28–30). The Balaam incident suggests that all it takes to make an animal talk is simply power sufficient to make it do so. That a demonic power can seize control of another creature's mind and speak through its mouth is clear from the Gospels. Vos makes the interesting observation here: "So far from there being anything impossible in [Satan speaking through the serpent], it finds a close analogy in the demoniacs of the Gospels, through whose mouth demons speak."[32] But however

---

30. Geerhardus Vos, *Biblical Theology* (Grand Rapids, Mich.: Eerdmans, 1949), 43.
31. Buswell, *Systematic Theology*, 1:265–66.
32. Vos, *Biblical Theology*, 44.

we might explain the serpent's ability to talk, we must acknowledge this much—that in this chapter he is represented by implication as being under the control of Satan and as doing his bidding.

In the Hebrew the first clause of 3:1 is a noun clause indicating a condition existent in the serpent at the time of the action of the main verb. That is to say, 3:1 should be translated: "The serpent, being more crafty than any of the other beasts of the field which Yahweh God had made, said...." This suggests that we should expect to find in *what he said* a very subtle, crafty thought. And indeed we do. To see this we must determine whether his remark is a question or a declaration of fact. The issue turns on the meaning of אַף כִּי, *'ap kî*, introducing the serpent's remark. Because אַף, *'ap*, literally "even," is an *intensive* particle, the Brown, Driver, and Briggs *Hebrew Lexicon*, taking the sentence as a question (though a ה, *h*, interrogative is not present), translates: "Has God *really* said ... ?"[33] The Koehler-Baumgartner *Hebrew Lexicon* concurs, translating: "Is it *really*, that he said?"[34] Both lexicons recognize the presence of the intensive particle, but by their renderings one can easily conclude that the implication in the "really" is that the serpent was trying to get Eve to consider whether God had actually said what the serpent quoted him as saying. Of course, God had not said that they could not eat of any of the trees of the garden. But if this was the serpent's intent, that is, to get the woman to consider whether God had actually said what the serpent represented him as saying, one must conclude not only that his question was hardly subtle, but also that he failed in his intention, for Eve, in response, gave a more accurate rendering of what God had said than the serpent had.

Ephraim A. Speiser seems to have captured more accurately the force of the אַף כִּי, *'ap kî*, when he translates: "Even though God has said you shall not eat of any of the trees of the garden...."[35] Note by this construction of the serpent's thought that he states error as though it were fact. It *demands* correction. Note too that his statement is an incomplete sentence, consisting only of a protasis. While we will never know how he was going to finish his sentence since the woman interrupted him to *correct* his premise, no matter what his apodosis would have been (perhaps, "you realize, of course, that you have to eat to live. What are you going to do to meet your need?"), the protasis, as it then stood, would still have required correction because any apodosis would have been based on the contrary-to-fact protasis. Note finally that by such a statement the woman, concentrating on the necessity of

---

33. Francis Brown, S. R. Driver, and Charles A. Briggs, *A Hebrew and English Lexicon of the Old Testament* (1907; reprint, Oxford: Clarendon, 1966), 65, 2.2.
34. Koehler-Baumgartner, *Lexicon in Veteris Testament Libros* (Grand Rapids, Mich.: Eerdmans, 1958), 74, 6.
35. Ephraim A. Speiser, *Genesis* (Garden City, N.Y.: Doubleday, 1964), 21, 23.

correcting the false protasis, would be drawn into the conversation before she would have perhaps realized the anomaly of the creature's speaking. Then, by actually providing the needed correction to the contrary-to-fact premise, the woman was cast immediately in the role of an *authority in matters religious*. She had demonstrated "superior understanding" of the ways of God to that of the serpent, and in so doing she had lost in her felt intellectual superiority over him any sense of fear she might otherwise have felt toward him.

The serpent's cleverly framed exaggeration ("of any tree") forced Eve to an explicit recognition and admission to a third party of her *restricted* status. Payne has correctly noted that "the Tempter was here seeking not man's *question* of God's command, but rather his admission of it!"[36] His misstatement forced her to concentrate on God's prohibition and to recognize that she was restricted by Another. That her restricted status was in the forefront of her mind is apparent from her additional remark, "neither shall you touch it," *her* addition to God's restriction. Vos concurs and comments:

> In the more or less indignant form of this denial there already shines through that the woman had begun to entertain the possibility of God's restricting her too severely . . . still further, in this direction goes the inexact form of her quoting the words of God: "ye shall not eat of it, neither shall you touch it." In this unwarranted introduction of the denial of the privilege of "touching" the woman betrays a feeling, as though after all God's measures may have been too harsh.[37]

Whether Vos is correct when he suggests that Eve was already giving indication that she felt she was being too severely restricted, her response to the serpent's opening statement clearly indicates that she was aware that she was restricted.

The serpent's forcing Eve by his remark to consider the precise wording of God's prohibition reminded her too of God's declared penalty for disobedience ("you shall surely die"). But, having been reminded anew of her restricted status, she apparently felt that if she represented her restricted status as a *benevolent charity* on God's part ("lest you die") she could justify her contentment to live under such restriction and in so doing "save face" with this third party before her, for she would not be acquiescing to sheer *authority* but to benevolent concern. The popular view which suggests that the woman increased the prohibition and *reduced* the penalty for disobedience misses the point of the *"lest* you die." What she actually seems to have done was to "interpret" God's clear prohibition as only the *warning*

---

36. Payne, *Theology of the Older Testament*, 217.
37. Vos, *Biblical Theology*, 46.

of another expert—who might indeed be wrong (see her *"lest* you die")—who was speaking out of benevolence, and not issuing a divine command grounded in sheer authority, one's acquiescence to the latter being impossible to explain to a third party unless one gladly owns his creaturehood and happily acknowledges his delight in living under such authority. It is as if she were saying: "He recommended that we not eat only because he was concerned for our well-being." This much, at least, seems clear: Eve appears to have felt the necessity to defend her acceptance of her restricted status as soon as she was forced to acknowledge it.

Immediately, capitalizing on his perceived advantage gained from both her admission of her restricted status and her expression of willing submission to God's benevolent concern but not necessarily to his authority, the serpent challenged outright God's stated penalty for disobedience on the ground of what, he says, was the real motive behind God's prohibition. "You are in error," he says in effect, "in interpreting the prohibition as a warning; it was indeed intended as a command. The One to whom you have submitted is attempting to extend his authority, with no justifiable warrant, over you. You are equally wrong in interpreting the 'death' statement merely as a reflection of benevolent concern; it was indeed intended as a threat. But you can believe that the prohibition is hollow and the penalty is an idle threat—*you surely shall not die.* God's real motive is a selfish one for he is threatened by *your* potential if you eat of the fruit of the tree of the knowledge of good and evil—even *equality with him.* God knows that in the day you eat of its fruit your eyes will be opened, that is, you will acquire a knowledge of the mysteries of good and evil, and you will accordingly be like God—knowers of good and evil. Since his motive is false, you can believe that his prohibition is also unwarranted and his threatened penalty for disobedience mere words."

What was Eve's response to the serpent's blasphemous imputation of falsehood and evil motive to God? Already embarrassed by the specter of submission to bare authority in the presence of this third party and apparently shaken in her allegiance as a covenant creature to her Creator, Eve failed to defend God's honor as evidenced by her silence. Rather, she actually concluded that the tree was good for food, pleasant to the eye, and "to be desired to make one wise." (The statement in 3:6, "When the woman *saw* that the tree was . . . ," means, "When the woman had come to the conclusion that the tree was . . . .") These words make it clear that the woman had come to the place where she *believed* the serpent's words rather than God's words. Her actions which then followed were simply consistent with her new understanding of the situation: "She took some of its fruit and ate and gave some to her husband also, who was with her, and he ate"—an action on the part of both which was simply the "sign" and "seal" that in their hearts they had already ceased to be covenant keepers and instead had become covenant breakers.

The phrase, "[who was] with her" in 3:6 is significant. It shows that Adam was present throughout the entire conversation between the serpent and his wife and that he had abdicated his headship role over his wife. Although he remained silent, he, no less than Eve, refused to defend God's honor when the serpent attacked his integrity. He allowed his wife to instruct him to ignore God's prohibition (see 3:17) instead of instructing her to resist the serpent's deception.[38] According to Paul (1 Tim. 2:14), while the woman was plainly deceived, Adam transgressed God's prohibition consciously, knowingly, and willingly.

What precisely occurred here? Our first parents permitted Satan to challenge God's word concerning the tree and to give an alternative interpretation. When the pair remained silent in the face of Satan's lie and thus demonstrated their willingness to reject God's authority over them and their unwillingness to take God at his word merely on the basis of his sovereign authority, they in effect permitted Satan to reduce God's word to a mere *hypothesis* at best and a lie at worst, the invalidity of which could be demonstrated by scientific testing. This means, however, that the center of authority for man had shifted away from God to himself. Adam and Eve came to believe that they were to be their own authority, that they had the right to determine for themselves by experimentation what is true and what is false. Of course, the fact that they "experimented" at all makes it clear that at the moment they ate they already believed the serpent's hypothesis concerning the tree to be true, for had they really believed that their experimentation might lead to their deaths they would hardly have tried it. This shows, as Paul says, that men are never truly autonomous, but rather are walking either in obedience to God or according to the prince of the power of the air (Eph. 2:2). But Adam and Eve thought that it was they who were determining the course they would follow, that they were only exercising their autonomous right to determine for themselves the true, the good, and the beautiful. They became, in their understanding, their own authority, and their fallen descendants ever since that time have claimed a similar autonomy from God.

How shallow, then, is the oft-heard mockery of the whole situation in Genesis 3 that ascribes to God a "temper tantrum" merely because someone committed the picayunish act of "eating a piece of apple." The transgression of Adam was far

---

38. People often wonder what God would have done had Eve eaten the fruit but Adam had refused to receive it from her. It is unnecessary to speculate because there never was a moment when Eve was sinful but Adam still sinless, and there was not a chance that Adam would have refused the fruit. His presence with Eve throughout the event involved him in transgression as well. Having abdicated his protective headship over her, he went along with her in her transgression and permitted her to disobey God, thus transgressing himself. In sum, when Eve fell, Adam also fell, indeed had already fallen.

more than that; it was at its core the creature's deliberate rejection of God's authority and an act of willful rebellion against the Creator. It was man claiming the stance of autonomy and freedom from God. It was man believing he had the right to determine for himself what he would be *metaphysically* ("You will be like God"), what he would know *epistemologically* ("like God, knowing good and evil"), and how he would behave *ethically* ("she took and ate . . . her husband ate"). It was man heeding Satan's call to worship the creature rather than the Creator. Authority was the issue at stake, and man decided against God and in his own favor.

Seven Effects of the Fall

By this sin, [our first parents] fell from their original righteousness and communion with God, and so became dead in sin, and wholly defiled in all the parts and faculties of soul and body.

They being the root of all mankind, the guilt of this sin was imputed;[39] and the same death in sin, and corrupted nature, conveyed to all their posterity descending from them by ordinary generation. (Westminster Confession of Faith, VI/ii–iii)

In a real sense one could argue that everything else in Scripture after Genesis 3:1–6, with the exception of the effects of the operations of divine grace, is in one way or another an effect of the Fall—that everything that has occurred and thus contributed to making human history on its evil side what it is, is the result of the Fall. And of course, this is correct. What concerns us here, however, is a determination of the most obvious and immediate effects of Adam's first transgression. I would suggest seven such effects.

1. Our first parents lost their legal/moral innocence and original righteousness and found themselves the subjects of real guilt and moral corruption (what Murray refers to as "internal revolution"). Following upon man's willful transgression, we are informed in verse 6 that "the eyes of both of them were opened," that is, that they now experientially knew their prior created goodness as a memory and the fact of their disobedience as an awareness of real guilt. This awareness of guilt first displayed itself as shame or embarrassment with respect to their own physical nakedness in the presence of each other. This shame, traced in the text to their physical nakedness in the presence of each other, was only the *reflex* of the inner nakedness of the guilty conscience before God working itself out in the sphere of the external. Nakedness

---

39. The Westminster Confession of Faith is not being biblical when it suggests that the sin of the first pair was imputed to their descendants descending from them by ordinary generation. Nowhere in Scripture is Eve's sin said to have been imputed to mankind. It was Adam who was the federal or covenantal head of the race. Consequently everywhere in Scripture it is Adam's sin that is said to have been imputed to the race.

per se is not a reason to be ashamed, since prior to their fall, "both of them, the man and his wife, were naked and were not ashamed" (2:25). Physical nakedness before another in the presence of whom there should be no felt shame becomes a thing of shame only for sin-burdened minds. (Where men and women anywhere today would seem in their sinfulness to experience no shame over their nudity before others where they really should feel shame does not mean that they are not sinners; rather, it means that they have *seared their consciences* with respect to their sinfulness and wrongdoing—an even more dire condition.)

The fig-leaf aprons (3:7) which our first parents manufactured to cover their nakedness represent their efforts to relieve their shame and accordingly to rid themselves of their sense of moral guilt which was expressing itself through their shame over their physical nakedness. Their subsequent act of hiding themselves from God when he came to them also powerfully portrays the fact of their guilt before God. It is true that Adam traced his fear of God to his sense of physical nakedness (3:10), but God "does not permit man to treat the physical as if it were sufficient reason for his sensation [of fear], but compels man to recognize in it the reflex of the ethical."[40] He asked Adam: "Who told you that you were naked?" Aroused conscience, of course, that "lamp of the Lord" in the breast of every man (Prov. 20:27), had so informed him. God then immediately drives him back to the true ground of his fear—the fact of his disobedience: "Have you eaten . . . ?" Disobedience and the sense of real guilt which naturally springs from it is the real root of the "shame/nakedness/fear of God" complex.

That our first parents are now not only really guilty before God but also morally corrupt throughout their entire being is also immediately evident in the fact that their first transgression is immediately followed by a series of transgressions. It is now their *nature* to act in accordance with their new sinful condition. We see Adam and then Eve refusing to acknowledge openly their willful act of disobedience and to take the blame for it. Adam blames his wife and, indirectly, God himself for his situation. Eve then blames the serpent. And in 3:22 God declares that Adam was now of such a state of mind that he would actually try to devise a plan how he might snatch the fruit of the tree of life though he no longer had a right to it. How quickly and completely man corrupted himself! In a word, Adam and Eve are now *sinners*. Accordingly, the Hebrew word for "sin" (חַטָּאת, *haṭṭā't*, meaning "a missing of the mark," Judg. 20:16) occurs quite early in the Genesis record (4:7).

2. The image of God, reflected originally both by Adam and Eve as individuals and by the human community which they comprised in terms of a true knowledge of God and concern for justice for one's neighbor, was immediately fractured and

---

40. Vos, *Biblical Theology*, 53.

distorted (what Murray refers to as "revolution in the human family"). This is apparent in the sense of shame which each of our original parents felt in the presence of the other and in the presence of God. It is also reflected by the selfish concern for his own well-being that each showed at the sound of God's approach. We are informed in 3:8 not that the man and his wife together hid themselves but, as the Hebrew literally reads, that "the man hid himself and the woman herself." It was a case of "every man for himself." Finally, as we have already noted, Adam blamed the woman for his plight (3:12).

This is one of the saddest outcomes of the Fall. God had lost the perfect (created) reflection of himself, the analogue of his own triune character, in his universe. Recall that the man and the woman, according to God's own stated intention for them, were created in a just and holy relationship in order that they might mirror the Creator God to his creation. But see them now, alien and hostile in their attitude not only toward God but also toward each another.

3. Fellowship between God and man was broken. Real alienation now existed between God and man, God's alienation being holy and fully justified, man's alienation being unholy and unjustified. Real alienation from God's side is illustrated by his judicial sentencing of the pair to death and by his expulsion of them from the garden and away from himself (which in point of fact is the essence of death). The way back to the tree of life is rendered forever impossible by the ever-turning flaming sword (the symbol of God's justice) and the cherubim (the guardians of God's holiness (Exod. 25:18–22; 26:1, 31; 36:8, 35; 37:7–9; Num. 7:89; 1 Sam. 4:4; 2 Sam. 6:2; 22:11; Ps. 18:10; Ezek. 1:5–28).

Alienation from man's side toward God is reflected in the pair's hiding themselves from God out of fear, and second, by Adam's tacit imputation of the blame for his fallen condition to God in his explanation: "The woman you put here with me—she gave me some fruit from the tree, and I ate it" (3:12).

4. Man's environment was cursed, and nature's productivity accordingly became impaired by thorns and weeds (what Murray refers to as "cosmic revolution"). To Adam God said: "Cursed is the ground because of you. . . . It will produce thorns and thistles for you" (3:17–18). Bildad would say later that because of human sin—the "fly" in the "ointment of the universe"—even "the stars are not pure in God's eyes" (Job 25:5). And Paul would write later that "the creation was subjected to frustration, not by its own choice, but by the will of the One who subjected it" and that this imposed subjection is reflected in the whole creation's "bondage to decay" and its "groaning as in the pains of childbirth right up to the present time" (Rom. 8:20–22).

Adam accordingly was told that he would eat of nature's productivity "through painful toil all the days of your life" and "by the sweat of your brow" (3:17, 19).

5. The man and the woman were judicially condemned and accordingly punished (what Murray refers to as "disintegration in man's constitution"). Eve was first sentenced. Her punishment consisted in suffering in childbearing and in the desire that would relentlessly work within her driving her to master her husband (see the similar expression in Gen. 4:7 for support for this view). Although it is stated in connection with Adam's sentence as the head of the race, by implication Eve too was sentenced to death—physical with respect to the body, spiritual with reference to the soul—as is evident from the fact that she was driven—along with Adam—away from the "garden of God" (Ezek. 28:13) and away from the tree of life.

Adam's sentence consisted, first, in *painful* labor, not labor *per se* (see 2:15), but labor that would characterize a veritable struggle for subsistence. Second, construing 3:19 ("to dust you will return") as a judicial sentencing, Adam was sentenced to physical death. In this regard, J. Barton Payne comments:

> There was . . . no natural reason why man had to die. Death came rather as punishment for sin. . . . God's words, "Dust thou art, and unto dust thou shalt return" (3:19) can be appealed to as substantiating a "natural" inevitableness of death only by twisting the words from their context. For they constitute a judicial sentence, uttered *as the result* of man's fall; they would lose their very significance as a curse were they to be considered descriptive of man's previous natural state.[41]

Finally, as a third aspect of his judicial curse, and in order to symbolize Adam's estranged state in *spiritual* death, God "banished him from the Garden of Eden to work the ground from which he had been taken" (3:23).

6. By God's forensic imputation of Adam's first transgression to all those descending from him by ordinary generation, "all mankind lost communion with God, are under his wrath and curse, and are so made liable to the miseries of this life, to death itself, and the pains of hell forever." In keeping with the representative principle, which we discovered from our exposition of Romans 5 was an integral aspect of the covenant of work, when Adam sinned, all those descending from him by ordinary generation sinned in him and fell with him in his first transgression.

7. Man's greatest and most immediate need is now divine grace, which God declared he would provide in and by a Redeemer who would himself in and by his own mortal wounding finally destroy Satan's kingdom of evil. By the *protevangelium* of Genesis 3:15 God put into effect the "covenant of grace" which in its Abrahamic form became salvifically definitive for all time to come.

---

41. Payne, *Theology of the Older Testament*, 220.

The Natural State of Fallen Man

From this original corruption, whereby we are utterly indisposed, disabled, and made opposite to all good, and wholly inclined to all evil, do proceed all actual transgressions.

Every sin, both original and actual, being a transgression of the righteous law of God, and contrary thereunto, doth, in its own nature, bring guilt upon the sinner, whereby he is bound over to the wrath of God, and curse of the law, and so made subject to death, with all miseries spiritual, temporal, and eternal. (Westminster Confession of Faith, VI/iv, vi)

We may summarize the Bible's view of the natural state of fallen man under three headings.

Total Depravity

First, man in his raw, natural state as he comes from the womb is *morally and spiritually corrupt in disposition and character*. Every part of his being—his mind, his will, his emotions, his affections, his conscience, his body—has been affected by sin (this is what is meant by the doctrine of *total* depravity). His understanding is darkened, his mind is at enmity with God, his will to act is slave to his darkened understanding and rebellious mind, his heart is corrupt, his emotions are perverted, his affections naturally gravitate to that which is evil and ungodly, his conscience is untrustworthy, and his body is subject to mortality. The Scriptures are replete with such representations of the condition of fallen man, as the following verses will verify:

Genesis 6:5–6: "The LORD saw that . . . *every* inclination of the thoughts of [man's] heart was only evil all the time."

Genesis 8:21: "The LORD . . . said in his heart: '. . . the inclination of [man's] heart is evil from childhood.'"

1 Kings 8:46: Solomon declared that "there is no one who does not sin" against God.

Psalm 14:1–3: "The fool [נָבָל, *nābal*, denotes the spiritually and morally deficient man, which is descriptive of every man outside of Christ] says in his heart, 'There is no God.' They are corrupt, their deeds are vile; there is no one who does good. The LORD looks down from heaven on the sons of men to see if there are any who understand, any who seek God. All have turned aside, they have together become corrupt; there is no one who does good, not even one."

Psalm 51:5 (MT, 51:7): David declared: "Surely I have been a sinner from birth, sinful from the time my mother conceived me."

Psalm 58:3: "Even from birth the wicked go astray; from the womb they are wayward and speak lies."

Psalm 130:3: "If you, O Lord, kept a record of sins, O Lord, who could stand?"

Psalm 143:2: "No one living is righteous before you."

Ecclesiastes 7:20: "There is not a righteous man on earth who does what is right and never sins."

Ecclesiastes 9:3: "The hearts of men . . . are full of evil and there is madness in their hearts while they live."

Isaiah 53:6: "We all [God's elect], like sheep, have gone astray, each of us has turned to his own way."

Isaiah 64:6 (MT, 64:5): "All of us have become like one who is unclean and all our righteous acts are like filthy rags."

Jeremiah 17:9: "The heart is deceitful above all things and beyond [human] cure. Who can understand it?"

Luke 11:13: "You, though you are evil, know how to give good gifts to your children."

John 5:42: "I know that you do not have the love of God in your hearts."

Romans 1:29–32 (see also 1:18–28): Men, Paul asserts, "have become filled with every kind of wickedness, evil, greed and depravity. They are full of envy, murder, strife, deceit and malice. They are gossips, slanderers, God-haters, insolent, arrogant and boastful; they invent ways of doing evil; they disobey their parents; they are senseless, faithless, heartless, ruthless. Although they know God's righteous decree that those who do such things deserve death, they not only continue to do these very things but also approve of those who practice them."

Romans 3:9–23: "Jews and Gentiles alike are all under sin. As it is written [then follows a fourteen-point indictment against the entire human race—all drawn from the Psalms with one exception] . . . *for all sinned* [πάντες γὰρ ἥμαρτον, *pantes gar hēmarton*] and *are continually falling short* [ὑστεροῦνται, *hysterountai*] of the glory [righteousness] of God."

Galatians 3:22: "The Scripture 'shuts up in prison' under sin the whole world." Here we see that the one who disputes the universality of sin's dominion is not arguing with the Christian who asserts such but with the Scripture, the very Word of God.

Ephesians 2:1–3: To the Ephesian believers, Paul writes: "As for you, you were dead in your trespasses and sins, in which you used to live when you followed the ways of this world and of the ruler of the kingdom of the air, of the spirit which is now at work in those who are disobedient. All of us also lived among them at one time, gratifying the cravings of our sinful nature and following its desires and thoughts. Like the rest, we were by nature objects of wrath."

Ephesians 4:17–19: The nations live "in the futility of their thinking. They are darkened in their understanding and separated from the life of God because of the ignorance that is in them due to the hardness of their hearts. Having lost all sensitivity, they have given themselves over to sensuality so as to indulge in every kind of impurity, with a continual lust for more."

1 John 1:8, 10: "If we claim to be without sin, we deceive ourselves and the truth is not in us. . . . If we claim we have not sinned, we make him out to be a liar and his word has no place in our lives."

1 John 5:19: "The whole world lies in the power of the evil one."

From these and many other passages which could be cited, it is clear that the Bible affirms of fallen mankind *total* (that is, pervasive) *depravity*. By this I do not mean that people act as bad as they really are by nature, since they are prevented from doing so by several manifestations of God's common restraining grace such as their innate awareness of God and his judgments (*sensus deitatis*) (Rom. 1:20-21, 32), the works of the law written on their hearts and consciences (Rom. 2:15), and civil government (Rom. 13:1–5). I mean rather that all men are corrupt throughout the *totality* of their being with every part, power, and faculty of their nature—mind, intellect, emotions, will, conscience, body—being affected by the Fall.[42]

With respect to the noetic effects of sin, none of the above is intended to say or to imply that Adam's fall brought him and his progeny to a state of brutish irrationality (that is, the inability to reason). Because of God's common grace extended to them (John 1:9),[43] fallen men are able to mount and to follow a logical argument. Otherwise, the Fall could well have had the effect of bringing men to brutish nonreason. But because of sin's effects on them men now must face the fact that, in spite of the aid from common grace, there are many things hampering them as they construct their sciences—falsehood, unintentional mistakes, lapses in logical reasoning, self-delusion and self-deception, the intrusion of fantasy into the imagination, intentional and unintentional negative influences of other men's minds

---

42. See Berkhof, *Systematic Theology*, 246–47.
43. As we have already noted, the Bible affirms that God has shown and continues to show a measure of favor or undeserved kindness to his creatures in general. He provides the sustenance they need for their physical well-being. He restrains the effects of sin in both individuals and society and enables the unregenerate to perform civic good, that is, to accomplish things that promote the welfare of others. Not the least evidence of his common goodness is his sustaining men in their scientific enterprises and their search for truth about themselves and the physical universe, enabling them to make many very fruitful discoveries. But the efforts of the unregenerate scientist are only successful because he is unwittingly "borrowing capital" from a *Christian-theistic* universe where uniformity in nature and the orderly meaning of facts are guaranteed by God and his plan.

upon their's, physical weaknesses influencing the total human psyche, the disorganized relationships of life, the effect of misinformation and inaccuracies learned from one realm of science upon ideas in other realms, sinful self-interest, the weakening of mental energies, the internal disorganization of life-harmonies, and most importantly their detachment from the ποῦ στῶ, *pou stō*,[44] found only in the revealed knowledge of God which alone justifies human knowledge and from which alone true human predication may be launched. Any and all of these effects of sin can and do bring men and women in their search for knowledge to unrecognized and thus unacknowledged ignorance.

It is evident too from these passages that the Reformers were far more sensitive to the total teaching of Scripture concerning the condition of fallen man than were the Roman Catholic apologists at the Council of Trent and their modern followers.[45]

Total Inability

Second, because man is totally or pervasively corrupt, he is *incapable of changing his character or of acting in a way that is distinct from his corruption*. He is unable to discern, to love, or to choose the things that are pleasing to God. As Jeremiah says, "Can the Ethiopian change his skin or the leopard his spots? Then you also can do good who are accustomed to do evil" (Jer. 13:23). The Bible specifically affirms several "cannots" (οὐ δύναται, *ou dynatai*) of man.

Matthew 7:18: "A bad tree cannot bear good fruit."

John 3:3, 5: "Unless a man is born from above, he cannot see the kingdom of God . . . unless a man is born of water and the Spirit, he cannot enter the kingdom of God."

John 6:44, 65: "No one can come to me unless the Father who sent me draws him . . . no one can come to me unless the Father has enabled him."

John 14:17: "The world cannot accept [the Spirit of truth], because it neither sees him nor knows him."

John 15:4–5: "No [branch] can bear fruit by itself; it must remain in the vine. Neither can you bear fruit unless you remain in me. I am the vine . . . apart from me you can do nothing."

Romans 8:7–8: "The sinful mind . . . does not submit to God's law, nor can it do so. Those controlled by the sinful nature cannot please God."

---

44. By *pou stō* (see part one, chapter five), I intend the ultimate heart commitment of whatever kind from which a person launches all his argumentation and predication. For a Christian it should be the revealed transcendent knowledge of God.
45. See footnote eleven of this chapter.

1 Corinthians 2:14: "The man without the Spirit does not accept the things that come from the Spirit of God, for they are foolishness to him, and he cannot understand them, because they are spiritually discerned."

1 Corinthians 12:3: "No one can say, 'Jesus is Lord,' except by the Holy Spirit."

James 3:8: "No man can tame the tongue."

Revelation 14:3: "No one could learn the song except [those] who had been redeemed from the earth."

These two human conditions demonstrate that man in his natural state is not only *morally and spiritually corrupt* but also *incapable of the understanding, the affections, and the will to act* which, taken together, enable one to be subject to the law of God, to respond to the gospel of grace, to appreciate the things of the Spirit, to do those things which are well-pleasing in God's sight, and to love God.

Two specific objections have been raised against these doctrines of total depravity and total inability.

Objection 1: "The teaching that man is totally corrupt and unable to please God is a counsel of despair to the lost and only encourages them to delay in responding to the gospel."

The opposite is true. It is only when a man knows that he is sinful and incapable of helping himself that he will seek help outside of himself and cast himself upon the mercies of God. Nothing is more soul-destroying than the sinner's belief that he is righteous and/or is capable of remedying his situation himself. And precisely this attitude is fostered by the teaching that man is natively able to do whenever he desires to do so what is good in God's sight. To encourage such a conviction is truly to plunge men into self-deception, and that is indeed a counsel of despair.

Objection 2: "How can the teaching of total depravity and total inability be reconciled with God's commands? Do not the very commands of God presuppose the human ability to do them? Can a man justly be required to do that for which he has not the necessary ability?"

God deals with man according to his *obligation,* not according to the measure of his ability. Before the Fall, man had both the obligation and the ability to obey God. As a result of the Fall, he retained the former but lost the latter. Man's inability to obey, arising from the moral corruption of his nature, does not remove from him his obligation to love God with all his heart, soul, mind, and strength, and his neighbor as himself. His obligation to obey God remains intact. If God dealt with man today according to his ability to obey, he would have to reduce his moral demands to the vanishing point. Conversely, if we determined the measure of man's ability from the sweeping obligations implicit in the divine commands, then we would need to predicate *total ability* for man, that is to say, we would all have to adopt the

Pelagian position, for the commands of God cover the *entire* horizon of moral obligation.

In an exchange I had with Robert H. Schuller in the pages of *Presbuterion: Covenant Seminary Review* over the doctrine of man's sinfulness,[46] Schuller declared that "once a person believes he is an 'unworthy sinner' it is doubtful if he can really honestly accept the saving grace God offers in Jesus Christ." He then wrote:

> I believe that man has total inability—not total depravity. If a person is totally depraved he ought to be shot, gassed in the chamber, or hanged by the neck 'till dead. Total inability means that he is totally incapable of earning his own salvation but is completely dependent upon the grace of God in Jesus Christ and the power of the Holy Spirit for regeneration and sanctification. Total depravity are words that taken literally are irresponsible, unintelligent, and destructive—not redemptive! Furthermore, they are contrived by human theologians and are not scriptural. Total inability contains compassion and fits into the gospel spirit producing persons who become humbly dependent upon the goodness of God and the Grace of our Lord and Savior Jesus Christ.

I felt at the time and still do that these are strange statements indeed, coming as they do from one who claims to stand in the Reformed tradition. So I pointed out to him that according to Jesus' parable of the Pharisee and the tax collector "it was the man who stood at a distance and who would not even look up to heaven and who beat his breast and who cried, 'God, have mercy upon me, the sinner,' who went down to his house justified" (Luke 18:13–14). I went on to say:

> You say that you subscribe to the Canons of Dort with one exception—you reject total depravity in deference to total inability. What you then say about the person you envision as totally depraved makes me wonder if you understand what the Reformed Faith means by the doctrine. Now it goes without saying that this is no minor departure on your part away from the Canons of Dort. In fact, it is, in my opinion, the root problem with your "self-esteem hermeneutic" and the reason that you cannot do justice to the substitutionary atonement. Of course, it is not entirely clear from your stated rejection of total depravity whether it is the adjective "total" or the noun "depravity" at which you take umbrage. If it is only the adjective to which you take exception, the result being that you are willing to affirm that man is *partially* depraved, then, of course, you still have the problems of explaining which part or faculty of man is not depraved, and how it is that man is unaffected by sin in this area—no small task I can assure you. If it is depravity *per se* which you are disavowing, then the only conclusion that I can draw

---

46. *Presbuterion* 10, no. 1–2 Spring/Fall (1984).

is that you must believe that man is essentially good but just psychologically malnourished due to his low self-esteem, and that his total inability to "earn his own salvation" springs from a psychological disorder and not from a nature that is morally corrupt and hostile to God. But in either case you have the problem of squaring your view of man with such Scripture passages as [Ps 14:2–3; Jer 17:9; Rom 3:9–18; Eph 2:1–3; and 4:17–19] which affirm both the corruption and the all-pervasiveness of that corruption throughout the human heart.

I concluded this section of our exchange with the comment that Paul

> portrays depravity and inability as of one piece [that is to say, they do not exist apart from each other] . . . because man is by nature corrupt and wicked (totally depraved), he cannot (total inability) incline himself toward spiritual good. He writes in Romans 8:7: "the sinful mind . . . does not submit to God's law, nor can it do so." The first clause asserts what we mean by depravity, while the second refers to what we mean by inability. But . . . both are condemnatory, . . . both are true.

It must be underscored that it is this biblical doctrine of man's total corruption and inability that makes the Reformed vision of soteriology necessary (of course, it is not only necessary; it is also biblical). It is just because Christians generally do not believe this teaching that they are willing to entertain a synergistic soteriology in which God and man both contribute something to man's salvation, with man even contributing the decisive part. But where sinful men have seen that they are so spiritually corrupt and impoverished that they themselves can do *nothing* to rectify their lost condition, there men revere the Reformed faith, for they understand that they bring to their salvation nothing but their sinfulness from which they need to be saved.

Real Guilt

Third, because of man's corruption and inability to please God, he is deserving of punishment, for his sin is not only real evil, morally wrong, the violation of God's law, and therefore, undesirable, odious, ugly, disgusting, filthy, and ought not to be; it is also the contradiction of God's perfection, cannot but meet with his disapproval and wrath, and *damnable* in the strongest sense of the word because it *dishonors* God. God must react with holy indignation. He cannot do otherwise. And here we come face to face, as John Murray declares,

> with a divine "cannot" that bespeaks not divine weakness but everlasting strength, not reproach but inestimable glory. He cannot deny himself. To be

complacent towards that which is the contradiction of his own holiness would be a denial of himself. So that wrath against sin is the correlate of his holiness. And this is just saying that the justice of God demands that sin receive its retribution. The question is not at all: How can God, being what he is, send men to hell? The question is, How can God, being what he is, save them from hell?[47]

* * * * *

> What a piece of work is a man! How noble in reason! How infinite in faculty! In form and moving how express and admirable! In action how like an angel! In apprehension how like a god! The beauty of the world! The paragon of animals! . . . this quintessence of dust.

This brief description of man from *Hamlet* (2.2.315–22) is breathtakingly beautiful and emotionally moving. Many Shakespeare scholars urge that Shakespeare was giving expression here to the Renaissance Man's new attitude toward the glory of man. This may be the case. But to the degree that these words are poetically descriptive of man as he came fresh from the hand of his Creator at creation, they help us feel something of the crowning glory which man was to God's week of creative activity. But they tell only part of the story. Adam, being left to the liberty of his own will, as we have seen, "transgressed [God's] covenant" (Hos. 6:7) and plunged himself and the entire human race into the estate of sin and misery.

It is this state of affairs that lies behind and makes necessary the work of Jesus Christ. This creation/fall background is the Bible's context for the work of Christ on the cross. To deny either man's original state of integrity or his self-willed fall into the state of corruption and misery is to rob the cross of the only context in which it has any meaning. Accept the Bible's account of man's "golden age" and his later rebellion against God, and the cross fits man's need exactly and perfectly. For this reason, as unpopular as this teaching is today in many quarters, it is imperative that the Reformed Christian continue to proclaim and to teach the doctrine of man's total sinfulness and inability. For if men are not corrupt, they have no need of the saving benefits of the cross! If men are not sinners who are incapable of saving themselves, they have no need of the Savior! If men are not lost, they have no need of the Lord's mercies! It is *only* when men by God's enabling grace see themselves as they truly are—sinful, incapable of saving themselves, and guilty before God—that they will cry with Augustus Toplady:

> Rock of Ages, cleft for me,
>   Let me hide myself in Thee;

---

47. John Murray, "The Nature of Sin," in *Collected Writings of John Murray* (Edinburgh: Banner of Truth), 1977, 2:81–82.

Let the water and the blood,
   From Thy riven side which flowed,
Be of sin the double cure,
   Cleanse me from its guilt and pow'r.

Not the labor of my hands
   Can fulfil Thy law's demands;
Could my zeal no respite know,
   Could my tears forever flow,
All for sin could not atone;
   Thou must save, and Thou alone.

Nothing in my hands I bring,
   Simply to Thy cross I cling;
Naked, come to Thee for dress,
   Helpless, look to Thee for grace;
Foul, I to the Fountain fly,
   Wash me, Saviour, or I die.

PART THREE

Our "So Great Salvation"

CHAPTER THIRTEEN

God's Eternal Plan of Salvation

By the decree of God, for the manifestation of His glory, some men and angels are predestinated unto everlasting life....

These angels and men, thus predestinated, . . . are particularly and unchangeably designed, and their number so certain and definite, that it cannot be either increased or diminished.

Those of mankind that are predestinated unto life, God, before the foundation of the world was laid, according to His eternal and immutable purpose, and the secret counsel and good pleasure of His will, hath chosen, in Christ, unto everlasting glory, out of His mere free grace and love, without any foresight of faith, or good works, or perseverance in either of them, or any other thing in the creature, as conditions, or causes moving Him thereunto; and all to the praise of His glorious grace.

As God hath appointed the elect unto glory, so hath He, by the eternal and most free purpose of His will, foreordained all the means thereunto. Wherefore, they who are elected, being fallen in Adam, are redeemed by Christ, are effectually called unto faith in Christ by His Spirit working in due season, are justified, adopted, sanctified, and kept by His power, through faith, unto salvation.

The doctrine of this high mystery of predestination is to be handled with special prudence and care.... (Westminster Confession of Faith, III/iii–vi, viii)

THE EXPRESSION "God's eternal plan of salvation" is often used in gospel tracts to refer to three or four things God wants the sinner to do in order to be saved, such as: (1) "Acknowledge that you are a sinner and need to be saved," (2) "Believe that Jesus died on the cross for sinners," (3) "Ask God to forgive you of your sins," and (4) "Put your trust in Jesus." While these are things which the sinner must surely do in order to be saved, they hardly constitute the content of God's "*eternal plan* of salvation." And it is only a debased level of theological awareness, but one quite current in our day, that would suggest that it is. What the expression more properly designates is "the order of the decrees"[1] in the mind of God (Eph. 3:11).

It would be an irresponsible if not an irrational God who would create the world and direct its course of events with no prior plan or purpose behind such activity—or who would not direct it at all. The Bible, however, has a great deal to say about the divine purpose governing this world and the men who inhabit it. Benjamin B. Warfield has justly remarked about God's plan:

> That God acts upon a plan in all his activities, is already given in Theism. On the establishment of a personal God, this question is closed. For person means purpose: precisely what distinguishes a person from a thing is that its modes of action are purposive, that all it does is directed to an end and proceeds through the choice of means to that end.... If we believe in a personal God, then, and much more if, being Theists, we believe in the immediate control by this personal God of the world he has made, we must believe in a plan underlying all that God does, and therefore also in a plan of salvation. The only question that can arise concerns not the reality but the nature of this plan.[2]

Before examining the details of this eternal plan of salvation, it is important to first consider the significant biblical evidence for the fact of the eternal plan itself and for the central elements of its content.

THE FACT AND CENTRAL ELEMENTS OF GOD'S ETERNAL PLAN

The reader may have a certain reticence, if not total resistance, toward any discussion of God's decrees which would seek to understand the logical order in which God planned what he did, but a simple rehearsal of some of the basic biblical material about the plan should help to ease his suspicions that we are "rushing in where angels fear to tread."[3] What God has revealed concerning his plan he surely desires people to attempt to understand.

---

1. John Murray explains this term this way: "The distinct elements comprised in the design or plan have often been spoken of as the distinct decrees. If this term is adopted, then the expression 'the order of the decrees' means the same as the order that the various elements of salvation sustain to one another in the eternal counsel of God" ("The Plan of Salvation," in *Collected Writings of John Murray* [Edinburgh: Banner of Truth, 1977], 2:124).
2. Benjamin B. Warfield, *The Plan of Salvation* (Grand Rapids, Mich.: Eerdmans, n.d.), 14–15.

God's Eternal Purpose

In Ephesians 3:11 Paul speaks of God's "eternal purpose [πρόθεσιν, *prothesin*] which he accomplished in the Christ, Jesus our Lord" (author's translation). Five brief comments are in order here:

1. The Greek word translated quite properly here as "purpose," which may also be translated "plan" or "resolve,"[4] is in the singular: God has *one* overarching purpose or plan (of course, with many different parts as we shall see).

2. Paul describes God's purpose or plan as his "eternal purpose" (πρόθεσιν τῶν αἰώνων, *prothesin tōn aiōnōn*; lit., "purpose of the ages"), intending by the adjectival genitive that there was never a moment when God had a blank mind or a time when God's plan with all of its parts was not fully determined. He never "finally made up his mind" about anything. He has *always* had the plan, and within the plan itself there is no chronological factor *per se*. The several parts of the plan must be viewed then as standing in a logical or teleological rather than a chronological relationship one to the other.

3. The person and work of Jesus Christ are clearly central to God's "eternal plan," because Paul says that God "accomplished" or "effected" (ἐποίησεν, *epoiēsen*) it "in the Christ, Jesus our Lord." The closely related earlier statement in Ephesians 1:9 echoes the same truth: Paul states there that "the mystery of [God's] will [θελήματος, *thelēmatos*], according to his good pleasure" he purposed (προέθετο, *proetheto*) to put into effect in Christ—that "purposed good pleasure" being "to bring all things in heaven and on earth under one Head in Christ." Here we learn that God's eternal plan, which governs *all* his ways and works in heaven and on earth, he *purposed* to fulfill in Christ. Christ, as God's Alpha and Omega, is at the beginning, the center, and the end of his eternal purpose.

---

3. Many Christians today desire to suppress all study of the eternal plan of God out of fear that the doctrine of election will destroy the Christian's certainty of salvation or be detrimental to their understanding of man's "free will." Calvin warned against such suppression:

> Scripture is the school of the Holy Spirit, in which, as nothing is omitted that is both necessary and useful to know, so nothing is taught but what is expedient to know. Therefore we must guard against depriving believers of anything disclosed about predestination in Scripture, lest we seem either wickedly to defraud them of the blessing of their God or to accuse and scoff at the Holy Spirit for having published what it is in any way profitable to suppress. . . . But for those who are so cautious or fearful that they desire to bury predestination in order not to disturb weak souls—with what color will they cloak their arrogance when they accuse God indirectly of stupid thoughtlessness as if he had not foreseen the peril that they feel they have wisely met? Whoever, then, heaps odium upon the doctrine of predestination openly reproaches God, as if he had unadvisedly let slip something hurtful to the church. (*Institutes of the Christian Religion*, III.xxi.3, 4)

4. BAGD, *A Greek-English Lexicon* (Cambridge: Cambridge University Press, 1957), 713, 2.

4. This eternal purpose or plan, directly and centrally concerned as it is with Jesus Christ, is accordingly directly and centrally concerned with *soteric* issues as well. In the verses immediately preceding this reference to God's "eternal purpose which he accomplished in the Christ," Paul declares that God "created all things in order that *through the [redeemed] church*, the manifold wisdom of God should be made known to the rulers and authorities in the heavenly realms" (3:9–10). He then follows this statement with the words of 3:11 to the effect that the indicated activity in 3:9–10 was "according to [κατά, *kata*] his eternal purpose which he accomplished in the Christ, Jesus our Lord" (author's translation). *The church of Jesus Christ—the redeemed community—also stands in Jesus Christ at the beginning, the center, and the end of God's eternal purpose.*

This soteric feature of the divine purpose receives support from the other passages where Paul refers to God's purpose. In Romans 8:28 Paul declares that Christians were effectually "called [to salvation] according to [his] purpose." In Ephesians 1:11 he says that Christians "were made heirs [of God], having been predestined according to the purpose of him who works all things according to the purpose of his will." And in 2 Timothy 1:9 Paul affirms that "God saved us and called us with a holy calling, not according to our works but according to his own purpose and grace which was given to us in Christ Jesus from all eternity."

5. Finally, we learn from Romans 9:11–13 that the *elective* principle in God's eternal purpose serves and alone comports with the *grace* principle which governs all true salvation. Paul writes:

> Yet, before the twins were born or had done anything good or bad—in order that God's purpose according to election might stand: not according to works but according to him who calls—she was told, "The older will serve the younger." Just as it is written: "Jacob I loved, but Esau I hated."

Here we see the connection between God's grace and his elective purpose dramatically exhibited in God's discrimination between Jacob and Esau, which discrimination, Paul points out, occurred "*before* the twins were born, before either had done anything good or bad" indeed, eternally so (see Gen. 25:22–23). As we urged in chapter ten, Paul elucidates the *ratio* standing behind and governing the divine discrimination signalized in the phrase, "in order that God's 'according to [κατά, *kata*] election purpose' might stand [that is, might remain immutable]," in terms of the following phrase, "not according to [ἐκ, *ek*] works but according to [ἐκ, *ek*] him who calls [unto salvation],"[5] which is equivalent to saying "not according to works but according to grace." Paul teaches here that God's elective purpose is not, as in paganism, "a blind

---

5. See BAGD, 235, 3, i, for this rendering of *ek*.

unreadable fate" which "hangs, an impersonal mystery, even above the gods," but rather that it serves the intelligible purpose of "bringing out the *gratuitous* character of grace."[6] In fact, Paul refers later to "the election of grace" (Rom. 11:5).

From all this we can conclude that God has a single eternal purpose or plan at the center of which is Jesus Christ and his church. This plan therefore involves also such issues as God's election, predestination, and effectual call of sinners to himself in order to create through them the church, which in turn serves as the vehicle for showing forth, not the glory of man (see Rom. 9:12; 2 Tim. 1:9), but the many sides (πολυποίκιλος, *polypoikilos*) of God's own infinite grace and *wisdom* (Eph. 3:10)—the latter a synonym for the plan itself.

Christ's Cross Work in the Plan

In Luke 22:22 Jesus taught his disciples that "the Son of Man is going [to the cross] in accordance with the [divine] decree [κατὰ τὸ ὁρισμένον, *kata to horismenon*]." Echoing the same truth, in Acts 2:23 Peter proclaimed: "This one, by the determining purpose [τῇ ὁρισμένῃ βουλῇ, *tē horismenē boulē*] and foreknowledge [προγνώσει, *prognōsei*] of God, was handed over, [and] you with wicked hands put him to death by nailing him to the cross." In both Jesus' and Peter's statements the church should find indisputable reason for believing that the cross of Christ was central to the eternal plan of God. Accordingly, in Acts 4:24–28 the entire church confessed to God that Herod and Pontius Pilate, with the Gentiles and leaders of Israel, had done to Jesus "what your hand and your will predestined [προώρισεν, *proōrisen*] should happen." And it is possible that it is God's eternal plan of salvation in and by Christ's cross work which Hebrews 13:20 intends when it speaks of "the blood of the eternal covenant." If this is its referent, then again the cross is represented as a central aspect of God's eternal purpose. One learns from these verses that not only Christ but also his sacrificial death was an integral part of the divine decree.

God's Foreknowledge and Predestination of the Elect in the Plan

From Romans 8:29–30 we learn of other aspects of God's eternal purpose or plan. Paul tells the Christian that "[the ones] whom he [the Father] foreknew [προέγνω, *proegnō*—that is, set his heart upon in covenantal love], he also predestined [προώρισεν, *proōrisen*] to be conformed to the image of his Son . . . , and whom he predestined [προώρισεν, *proōrisen*], those he called [ἐκάλεσεν, *ekalesen*—that is, in history]." Two things are clear from this:

---

6. Geerhardus Vos, *Biblical Theology* (Grand Rapids, Mich.: Eerdmans, 1954), 108, 110.

1. In his eternal plan (note the προ, *pro*, prefixes ["before"] attached to the first two verbs) God "foreknew" (that is, "set his heart upon") certain people and "predestined" their conformity to his Son's likeness. And in this very context (Rom. 8:33) Paul designates those whom God has always so loved as "God's elect."

Why have we interpreted the first verb "foreknew" (προέγνω, *proegnō*) as we have? Reformed theologians have uniformly recognized that the Hebrew verb יָדַע (*yāda'*, "to know"; see its occurrences in Gen. 4:1, 18:19; Exod. 2:25; Pss. 1:6, 144:3; Jer. 1:5; Hos. 13:5; Amos 3:2) and the Greek verb γινώσκω (*ginōskō*, "to know"; see its occurrences in Matt. 7:22–23; 1 Cor. 8:3; 2 Tim. 2:19) can mean something on the order of "to know intimately," "to set one's affections upon" or "to have special loving regard for," and that the verb προέγνω, *proegnō*, in Romans 8:29 intends something approximating this meaning rather than the sense of mere prescience.[7]

Reformed theologians also understand Paul to mean here that God did not set his love upon the elect from all eternity because of *foreseen* faith or good works, or perseverance in either of them, or any other condition or cause in them.[8] To assert that he did, not only intrudes circumstances and conditions into the context but also flies in the face of the teaching of Romans 9:11–13, that election is according to grace and not according to works, of Ephesians 1:4, that God chose us before the creation of the world "that we should be holy" and not because he saw that we *would be* holy, and of 2 Timothy 1:9, that he saved us and called us to a holy life, not because of anything we have done but because of *his own* eternal purpose and grace.

2. We learn also from the tight grammatical construction between the verbs "predestined" and "called" that what God planned in eternity, he executes in this world. So there is a clear connection between his plan and his execution of his plan. He is the Author of both. The former is the "blueprint" of the latter. The latter is the "historical outworking" of the former.

The Election of Men in the Plan

In Ephesians 1:4–5 Paul tells the church that God the Father "chose [ἐξελέξατο, *exelexato*] us in him [Christ] before the creation of the world, that we should be

---

7. For an excellent discussion of the meaning of "foreknew" in Romans 8:29, see David N. Steele and Curtis C. Thomas, *Romans: An Interpretive Outline* (Philadelphia: Presbyterian and Reformed, 1963), Appendix C, 131–37.
8. Even if God had elected men on the basis of their foreseen faith and/or good works, as Arminians contend, since faith in Jesus Christ is not native to the human heart but is a gift from God not given to everyone (Eph. 2:8–9) and since good works are the product of God working in men both to will and to act according to his good purpose (Phil. 2:13), salvation would still be all of God and men would make no decisive contribution to their salvation.

holy and without blame before him, in love having predestinated [προορίσας, *proorisas*] us unto sonship by adoption through Jesus Christ unto himself, according to the good pleasure of his will." In this doxology Paul clearly states that from all eternity God had chosen the Christian to holiness and predestinated him to sonship. And he did so, Paul writes, "according to the good pleasure of his will" (see also in this same regard Eph. 1:9, 11). And "it is to trifle with the plain import of the terms, and with the repeated emphasis" here, writes Murray,

> to impose upon the terms any determining factor arising from the will of man. If we say or suppose that the differentiation which predestination involves proceeds from or is determined by some sovereign decision on the part of men themselves, then we contradict what the apostle by eloquent reiteration was jealous to affirm. If he meant to say anything in these expressions in verses 5, 9, and 11, it is that God's predestination, and his will to salvation, proceeds from the pure sovereignty and absolute determination of his counsel. It is the unconditioned and unconditional election of God's grace.[9]

In 2 Thessalonians 2:13 Paul informs his readers—"brothers who have been loved by the Lord"—that "God chose [εἵλατο, *heilato*] you from the beginning [ἀπαρχὴν, *aparchēn*] unto salvation." This verse, in addition to the previous verses cited, underscores the truth that from all eternity God had determined upon a course of salvific activity which would result in the salvation of his beloved children from sin and death.

From all this it should be clear that no Christian can legitimately doubt the *reality* of God's eternal plan of salvation. When Reformed theologians speak, then, of God's eternal purpose or God's eternal plan of salvation, they refer to this eternal salvific decision-making on God's part concerning Christ and his work on the cross and the election and predestination of men to salvation in him.

THE NATURE OF GOD'S ETERNAL PLAN

With this scriptural data before us, we may now turn to a discussion of the nature of the eternal decree. Before Warfield offered his readers his own opinion respecting this matter in his *The Plan of Salvation,* he developed his treatment of God's salvific plan against the backdrop of the "differing conceptions" of it which have been offered at one time or another in the history of the church.

---

9. Murray, "The Plan of Salvation," 127.

Who Saves Men?

The "deepest cleft" separating people calling themselves Christians, Warfield claimed, is that which distinguishes the "naturalistic" conception of salvation held by some from the "supernaturalistic" conception held by others.[10] The naturalistic vision, which he designates "autosoterism" ("self-salvation") and which the church has designated "Pelagianism," after Pelagius, a late-fourth/early-fifth-century British monk, who proposed it, contends that men can save themselves, that is to say, that *their native powers are such that men are capable of doing everything that God requires of them for salvation.* The supernaturalistic vision, designated "Augustinianism" after Augustine (354–430), bishop of Hippo, who vigorously resisted Pelagius's teaching, insists that *men are incapable of saving themselves and that all the powers essential to the saving of the soul must come from God.* Augustinianism triumphed formally, if not actually, over Pelagianism in A.D. 418 when the latter was condemned at the Sixteenth Council of Carthage. In this conciliar triumph, Warfield notes, "it was once for all settled that Christianity was to remain a religion, and a religion for sinful men, and not rot down into a mere ethical system, fitted only for the righteous who need no salvation."[11] In other words, the church of Jesus Christ, alone among all the religions of the world in this regard, in its best creedal moments is "supernaturalistic" or "Augustinian" in its soteric conception, and every Christian *should be* in this sense "Augustinian" in his soteric beliefs.

I do not mean to suggest that Augustine always held consistently to this supernaturalistic principle, for it is a matter of simple historical record that he did not. In Augustine one can find the doctrine both of salvation by grace through faith and of salvation dispensed through the church and its sacraments.[12] The former may be found expressed, for example, in his *Confessions* when he writes: "You converted me to yourself so that I no longer sought . . . any of this world's promises" (8.12), and again, "By your gift I had come totally not to will what I had willed but to will what you willed" (9.1). Clearly, Augustine understood that his conversion was entirely the work of God's grace. But the latter may also be found in his *Confessions:* "I recognized the act of your will, and I gave praise to your name, rejoicing in faith. But this faith would not let me feel safe about my past sins, since your baptism had not yet come to remit them" (9.4). Augustine then declares that, after Ambrose baptized him, "all anxiety as to our past life fled away" (9.6). Warfield seems quite justified in observing that the Protestant Reformation, especially on the Reformed side, was the revolt of Augustine's doctrine of grace against his doctrine of the church, "a

---

10. Warfield, *The Plan of Salvation*, 16–18.
11. Ibid., 36.
12. See Louis Berkhof, *Systematic Theology* (Grand Rapids, Mich.: Eerdmans, 1941), 559.

revolt . . . against seeing grace channeled through the sacraments . . . a revolt, in all Reformational expressions, against the notion that predestination trickled only through the narrow crevices of church ordinances. It was, by contrast, an affirmation of Augustine's grasp upon human lostness, bondage to what is dark and wrong, the indispensability of grace, the glory of the gospel because of him in whom the Good News took and takes form."[13]

It should also be noted that Pelagianism did not die with its conciliar condemnation in A.D. 418, men and women being born as they are with Pelagian hearts, but rather it only went underground, "meanwhile vexing the Church with modified forms of itself, modified just enough to escape the letter of the Church's condemnation."[14] For example, it reappeared at once in the semi-Pelagian denial of the necessity of *prevenient* grace for salvation. This was opposed by the Second Council of Orange in A.D. 529.[15] But while that Council saved the church from semi-Pelagianism, that same council betrayed the church into the semi-semi-Pelagian denial of the *irresistibility* of that prevenient grace by human free will, which theological vision, in spite of the recurring protests through the centuries of such men as Gottschalk, Bradwardine, Wycliffe, and Hus, eventually an Aquinas was to systematize and the Council of Trent (1545) was to declare the official position of those churches in communion with Counter-Reformation Rome. The Reformers of the sixteenth century, as we just noted, rejected the synergistic stance of Roman Catholic soteriology[16] and returned to the earlier best insights of the later Augustine and to the inspired insights of Paul in his letters to the Romans and the Galatians.

---

13. David F. Wells, *Turning to God* (Grand Rapids, Mich.: Baker, 1989), 84.
14. Warfield, *The Plan of Salvation*, 36.
15. Alister E. McGrath notes that the earlier pronouncements of the Sixteenth Council of Carthage were "vague at several points which were to prove of significance, and these were revised at what is generally regarded as being the most important council of the early church to deal with the doctrine of justification—the Second Council of Orange, convened in 529." He further notes:

    No other council was convened to discuss the doctrine of justification between [529] and 1545, when the Council of Trent assembled to debate that doctrine, among many others. There was thus a period of over a millennium during which the teaching office of the church remained silent on the issue of justification. . . . Recent scholarship has established that no theologian of the Middle Ages ever cites the decisions of Orange II, or shows the slightest awareness of the existence of such decisions. . . . The theologians of the Middle Ages were thus obliged to base their teaching on justification on the canons of the Council of Carthage, which were simply incapable of bearing the strain which came to be place upon them. The increasing precision of the technical terms employed within the theological schools inevitably led to the somewhat loose terms used by the Council of Carthage being interpreted in a manner quite alien to that intended by those who originally employed them. (*Luther's Theology of the Cross* [Oxford: Blackwell, 1985], 11–12)

Because Pelagianism, in whatever form it takes, is a threat to the *solus Christus, sola gratia, sola fide* principle, claiming as it does that man deserves at least some measure of credit for effecting his salvation, if not in its initiation, at least in his cooperation with initiating grace, the church must ever be on guard to insure that this *solus Christus, sola gratia, sola fide* principle of Holy Scripture remains the sole ultimate ground of salvation.

How Does God Save Men?

Among supernaturalists, which is just to say among Christians generally since all Christians agree that it is God who saves men, there is, however, a division over the question of the *means* by which God effects their salvation. The "sacerdotal" churches, for example, the Roman Catholic Church, urge that God deals *mediately* with the soul in that he has imposed "supernaturally endowed instrumentalities" (the sacraments) between himself and the sinner, with the powers essential to the salvation of the soul being mediated *ex opere operato* to the sinner through these instrumentalities. That is to say, the sacraments cause grace to flow to their recipients by the mere administration of them "without any act or movement of the soul in the recipients, accommodating themselves intelligently to the grace signified."[17] I might add in passing that Rome's *ex opere operato* view of the sacraments, which had been worked out in the Middle Ages and at the Council of Trent (see Session 7, Canons 6–8), the Second Vatican Council (1962–1965) did nothing to alter in any substantive way.[18] Rome holds that through the foundational sacrament of baptism the sinner is delivered from the liability of original sin (Aquinas had declared that baptism "opens the gate of heaven"), and through the sacraments of the Mass and of penance the liabilities of postbaptismal sins are removed. The *institutional church* becomes then through its sacramental ministrations the source and conveyer of saving grace to men, or as John Murray says, "the church is the

---

16. Where Protestantism has always placed its "either-or" or *solus* ("alone," as in *sola Scriptura, solus Christus, sola gratia, sola fide, soli Deo gloria*), Roman Catholic theology has continued to place its "both-and" or *et* ("and," as in Scripture *and* tradition, Christ *and* Mary, grace *and* nature, faith *and* works). All of these "ands" are outworkings of Rome's commitment to Aquinas's vision of the "analogy of being" between God and creation, the latter of which Rome regards as being still fundamentally good in spite of the Fall. I agree with Karl Barth when he said: "I regard the *analogia entis* as the invention of Antichrist, and think that because of it one can not become Catholic" (*Church Dogmatics*, trans. G. T. Thomson [Edinburgh: T. & T. Clark, 1936], 1:1, x).
17. Robert L. Dabney, *Lectures in Systematic Theology* (1878; reprint, Grand Rapids, Mich.: 1972), 739.
18. See F. S. Piggin, "Roman Catholicism," in *Evangelical Dictionary of Theology*, ed. Walter A. Elwell (Grand Rapids, Mich.: Baker, 1984), 957.

depository of salvation and the sacraments the media of conveyance."[19] Carried through consistently, the sacerdotal vision urges that *where the church works, there the Spirit works,* and also that *apart from the church's sacramental ministrations of grace there is no salvation.* This sacerdotal vision is essentially semi-Pelagian in that its teaching on penance substitutes a shallow moralism that defines sin as the infraction of rules, which can be compensated for by good works, for the Augustinian understanding of sin as a dishonoring of the eternal and holy God. Warfield objects to the sacerdotal conception of salvation on three additional grounds:

1. The ground of *distantiation:* "the sacerdotal system separates the soul from direct contact with and immediate dependence upon God the Holy Spirit as the source of all its gracious activities. It interposes between the soul and the source of all grace a body of instrumentalities, on which it tempts it to depend; and it thus betrays the soul into a mechanical conception of salvation."

2. The ground of *depersonalization:* "sacerdotalism deals with God the Holy Spirit, the source of all grace, in utter neglect of his personality, as if he were a natural force, operating not when and where and how he pleases, but uniformly and regularly wherever his activities are released."

3. The ground of the *"deification"* of the priesthood: "this obviously involves . . . the subjection of the Holy Spirit in his gracious operations to the control of men . . . the Holy Spirit is made an instrument which the Church, the means of grace, uses in working salvation."[20]

Over against sacerdotalism stands evangelicalism, which all of *consistent* Protestantism espouses, and which insists that the soul must depend on no intermediate instrumentality for its salvation but must ever depend directly and immediately upon God alone. Evangelicalism insists not only that it is God who saves, but that he saves by working *immediately* upon the soul by his Word and Spirit as the gospel is rightly proclaimed and as the gospel mysteries are properly administered. Evangelicalism urges that *where the Spirit works, there the church emerges,* and also that *apart from that church which emerges where the Spirit works there is no salvation.*

In Whom Does God Do His Saving Work?

Organized Protestantism, formally united by the evangelical over against the sacerdotal vision of salvation, has itself suffered division over the issue of the objects of God's saving mercies. The evangelical "universalists" or Arminians, the disciples of James Arminius (1560–1609), contend that "all that God does looking

---

19. Murray, "The Plan of Salvation," 124.
20. Warfield, *The Plan of Salvation,* 66–67. The descriptive terms are mine.

to the salvation of sinful man, he does not to or for individual men but to or for all men alike, making no distinctions."[21] Opposed to this universalistic scheme is the "particularistic" vision of the Reformed or Calvinistic churches. Indeed, its vision of divine particularism in salvation is the hallmark of the theology of the Reformed churches.[22]

The Reformed churches contend that if it is God alone who saves (the supernatural confession), and if he saves by the Spirit's direct and immediate operation by and with the Word upon the soul (the evangelical confession), and if all that he does looking to the salvation of men he does directly to and for all men alike, drawing no distinctions between them (the universalist confession), it seems logical to conclude that all men will be saved. But since neither Scripture, history, nor Christian experience allows this conclusion, it would seem that one of the premises on either side of the evangelical contention must be relaxed—either the supernaturalistic premise or the later premise:

> It must either be held that it is not God and God alone who works salvation, but that the actual enjoyment of salvation hangs at a decisive point upon something in man, or something done by man . . . ; or it must be held that God's gracious activities looking to salvation are not after all absolutely universal . . . ; or else it would seem inevitable that we should allow that all men are saved.[23]

Arminian theologians acknowledge the force of this observation; accordingly, they declare that the reason that some people are saved and that others are lost, despite the fact that God's saving operations go forth to all without exception, is that the former group by the exercise of free will accepts while the latter group—again by the exercise of free will—rejects some aspect(s) of God's saving operations when God extends them. In short, the supernaturalistic premise is relaxed. But this means, as Warfield notes, that at the decisive point it is something that *the man does or becomes* that determines whether he is saved or lost. To preserve the universalist premise, the evangelical universalist

---

21. Ibid., 69. See also Roger R. Nicole, "Arminius, James," in *The Encyclopedia of Christianity* (Wilmington, Del.: National Foundation for Christian Education, 1964), 1:405–11, and J. Kenneth Grider, "Arminianism," in *Evangelical Dictionary of Theology*, 79–81. "Arminianism" as a general term, in its insistence upon the freedom of the will, could be embraced at least at this point by the Roman Catholic, Greek Orthodox, Melanchthonian Lutheran (not Luther himself), Methodist, and many Baptist churches.
22. Warfield, *The Plan of Salvation*, 87.
23. Ibid., 70.

relaxes the original supernaturalistic premise and thus reintroduces at the decisive point the Pelagian or autosoteric principle, the outcome being a "semi-Pelagian" (partly God, partly man), "cooperative" salvation (the reason it should be called "semi-Pelagianism" and not "semi-Augustinianism" is because at the decisive point it is *man's* part that actually determines who is saved and who is not):

> The upshot of the whole matter is that the attempt to construe the gracious operations of God looking to salvation universally, inevitably leads by one path or another to the wreck of . . . the supernaturalistic principle, on the basis of which all Christian Churches professedly unite. Whether this universalism takes a sacerdotal form or a form which frees itself from all entanglements with earthly transactions, it ends always and everywhere by transferring the really decisive factor in salvation from God to man.[24]

To avoid this "wreck" of the supernaturalistic or Augustinian principle and to preserve both the supernaturalistic (fundamentally Christian) and the evangelical (fundamentally Protestant) teachings of Scripture, the Reformed (Calvinistic) side of the Protestant movement contends that the reason that all men are not saved is that God does not work his saving operations in the hearts of all men without exception but in the individual and particular hearts one by one of the elect. In sum, the Reformed churches replace the "universalistic" premise of non-Reformed Protestantism with the "particularistic" premise, and accordingly, they urge that "men owe in each and every case their actual salvation, and not merely their general opportunity to be saved, to him. And therefore, to him and to him alone belongs in each instance all the glory, which none can share with him."[25] In this way the particularistic principle preserves both the supernaturalistic principle which is the bedrock of Christianity as the redemptive religion of God as well as the substitutionary character of Christ's cross work.

For Whom Did Christ Do His Cross Work?

Not only does the evangelical universalist relax the supernaturalistic principle that is the bedrock of Christian theism, but to be consistent he must also reject the substitutionary character of Christ's atoning death in favor of what he terms

---

24. Ibid., 84.
25. Ibid., 23.

the governmental theory of the atonement.[26] This necessarily follows from his recognition that if all that God did looking to the salvation of men he did for all men alike, and if Christ substitutionally atoned for all men's sins (the doctrine of unlimited or indefinite atonement), then all men would be saved. Since, however, he recognizes that all men are in fact not saved, and since in his thinking no one must receive any benefit from Christ's work that all others do not also receive (and those who are finally lost obviously do not receive salvation), he construes the cross work of Christ so that in itself it does not possess, nor was it intended to possess, the intrinsic efficacy actually to save anyone. Accordingly, where there is still talk within the ranks of evangelical universalism of a substitutionary atonement in the sense that Christ's death paid the penalty for sin, it is—as Arminian theologian J. Kenneth Grider acknowledges in his article on "Arminianism" in the *Evangelical Dictionary of Theology*—a "spillover from Calvinism":

> A spillover from Calvinism into Arminianism has occurred in recent decades. Thus many Arminians whose theology is not very precise say that Christ paid the penalty for our sins. Yet such a view is foreign to Arminianism. . . . Arminians teach that what Christ did he did for every person; therefore, what he did could not have been to pay the penalty for sin, since no one would then ever go into eternal perdition. Arminianism teaches that Christ suffered for everyone so that the Father could forgive the ones who repent and believe; his death is such that all will see that forgiveness is costly and will strive to cease from anarchy in the world God governs.[27]

This is the governmental theory of the atonement. Its germinal teachings are in Arminius, but it was his student, the lawyer-theologian Hugo Grotius (1583–1645), who delineated the view in his *De satisfactione Christi* (1617).

Perhaps this is the place to respond to one reason which Grider offers for the Arminian view. He informs us that Arminians

> feel that God the Father would not be forgiving us at all if his justice was satisfied by the real thing that justice needs: punishment. They understand that

---

26. The governmental theory of the atonement denies that Christ's death was intended to pay the penalty for sin (a penal substitution), but rather was simply a penal *example* of sin's dreadful and tragic nature, so that divine pardon ("bypassing" the demand for the sinner's punishment) could be issued without having the effect of weakening the honor or enforcement of God's moral demands in the eyes of the public. The theory's proponents contend that society would not take seriously the need to be morally governed by God unless in the place of punishing sinners God substituted some great measure which was unpleasant and filled with grief.
27. Grider, "Arminianism," 80.

there can be only punishment or forgiveness, not both—realizing, e.g., that a child is either punished or forgiven, not forgiven after the punishment has been meted out.[28]

But such a view—construing punishment and forgiveness as it does as incompatible antitheses—simply fails to recognize that in all true forgiveness—human as well as divine—the offended party is vicariously bearing in himself the offense of and the punishment due to the offending party. To use Grider's illustration, when a parent truly forgives his repentant child and does not inflict judicial punishment upon him, what is taking place is this: the parent is vicariously bearing in himself both the child's offense against him and the punishment which the child's offense deserves, the parent's "vicarious sin bearing" becoming precisely the ground upon which he may justly extend forgiveness to his child. Here punishment and forgiveness are both present; there is no incompatibility between them. Similarly, in the case of divine forgiveness, Christ—who was not a disinterested third party but as the Son of God was himself the offended party (along with the entire Godhead)—bore in himself both the offense and the punishment of those whom the Father gave to him, his "vicarious sin bearing" becoming precisely the ground upon which the Godhead may justly extend forgiveness to those for whom Christ died.

Also in response to Grider, if Christ's death upon the cross was not intended as a sin offering to pay the penalty for anyone's sin but was intended rather, by whatever emotive power it may assert, to illustrate to men what their sins penally deserve at the hands of a just God, then not only is no man's sin atoned for yet but also Christ's death is rendered useless, for it is simply not the case that sinful men conclude from his death that "forgiveness is costly" and that they should "strive to cease from anarchy in the world God governs."

The Amyraldian Scheme

While all Reformed Christians are committed to the particularistic principle in salvation, some Reformed theologians designated "Amyraldians" after Moise Amyraut (Amyraldus) (1596–1664) of the theological school of Saumur in France who developed the scheme (also known as "hypothetical universalists," "post-redemptionists," "ante-applicationists," and "four-point Calvinists," for reasons which will become clear later) unite with evangelical universalists in their view of Christ's cross work and maintain that the Bible teaches that Christ died for all men

---

28. Ibid.

without exception.[29] Here, they maintain, is at least one aspect of the divine activity looking toward the salvation of men which is *universal* in its design. But how can this universalistic aspect of the divine activity be adjusted to the particularistic aspect of the divine activity which, after all, is the hallmark of the Reformed (or Calvinistic) soteriological vision?

Amyraldian theologians resolve for themselves the tension between soteric particularism on the one hand (which they are convinced the Bible teaches) and the universalistic design of Christ's cross work on the other (which they are equally convinced the Bible also teaches) by analyzing God's eternal plan of salvation and by positing a specific arrangement or order for its several parts (or decrees; see fn. 1). This order, they claim, justifies their soteric vision.

The Amyraldian arrangement of the several major elements or decrees of God's eternal plan of salvation is as follows:

1. the decree to create the world and (all) men
2. the decree that (all) men would fall
3. the decree to redeem (all) men by the cross work of Christ
*4. the election of some fallen men to salvation in Christ (and the reprobation of the others)
5. the decree to apply Christ's redemptive benefits to the elect.

Even a cursory analysis of the Amyraldian scheme will show that the first three decrees are universal with respect to their referents (thus my insertion of the word "all" in parentheses), with the last two being particular in regard to their referents, the discriminating decree to elect some men to salvation (marked by the *) having been postponed to the *fourth* position in the scheme, coming *immediately after* the decree to redeem men (hence the scheme's name "post-redemptionism") and *immediately before* the decree to apply Christ's redemptive benefits (hence its name "ante-applicationism").

The decrees of God being so arranged by him, the Amyraldian postulates that in the one "eternal purpose" of God, his first decree pertains to the creation of the world and of *all men* who would populate it. His second decree pertains to the fall

---

29. See Roger R. Nicole, "Amyraldianism," in *The Encyclopedia of Christianity* (Wilmington, Del.: The National Foundation for Christian Education, 1964), 1:184–93. Amyraut's view goes back to his tutor, John Cameron (1580–1626), minister of the Reformed church at Bordeaux, who served in a professorial capacity in the schools of Saumur and Montauban and finally in the University of Glasgow. In his *Eschantillon de la doctrine de Calvin touchant la predestination* (1636), Amyraut claimed that Calvin espoused universal atonement. Contemporary Amyraldians also maintain that their position is essentially that of John Calvin (but see chapter 18, fn. 3).

of Adam and in him of *all men* descending from him by ordinary generation. The third decree pertains to the cross work of Christ, and since no "distinguishing decree" yet appears in the order, the referent of its work is *all men* without exception or distinction. The Amyraldian contends that the biblical passages that ascribe a universal reference to Christ's cross work ("all men"—John 12:32; Rom. 5:18; 8:32; 11:32; 2 Cor. 5:14–15; 1 Tim. 2:5–6; Tit. 2:11; Heb. 2:9; "world"—John 3:16; 1 John 2:2; 2 Cor. 5:19) necessarily reflect an order of the decrees in which the decree to save men by Christ's cross work *precedes* any decree to discriminate among men.

Because some biblical passages also clearly mention the fact of election, however, the Amyraldian acknowledges that the election factor must be given a place in the eternal plan of salvation. Therefore, he quite willingly includes it in his scheme, placing the electing decree which discriminates among men *after* the "cross work decree" (which position, he contends, preserves the cross's "unlimited" design and justifies the presence of the biblical passages that speak of Christ's cross work in universal terms) but *before* the decree concerning its application. Of course, once discrimination is introduced, it must be honored by any subsequent decree. The upshot of the Amyraldian arrangement is that *the actual execution of the divine discrimination comes not at the point of Christ's redemptive accomplishment but at the point of the Spirit's redemptive application.*

While this scheme preserves for the Amyraldian the right to regard himself as "Calvinistic" (since he allows a place for the particularistic principle which is the hallmark of Calvinism), those creedal churches within the Reformed world which have adopted the Belgic Confession, the Heidelberg Catechism, the Canons of Dort, and the Westminster Confession of Faith have uniformly rejected it, for three basic reasons:

1. Amyraldianism is a logically inconsistent form of Calvinism in that its scheme has persons of the Godhead working at cross-purposes with one another: by decree the Son died with the intention to save all men, and by decree the Spirit savingly applies Christ's saving benefits to some men only. Each person's labor cancels out the intention of the other's labor.

2. Because the Son and the Spirit by their respective labors are both simply executing the Father's "eternal purpose" for them, Amyraldianism implies that either a *chronological* element, which in effect cancels the eternity of the divine purpose, or an *irrational* element, which in effect imputes confusion to the divine purpose, resides in the decrees, either element of which assaults the nature of God. Warfield rightly asks:

> How is it possible to contend that God gave his Son to die for all men, alike and equally; and at the same time to declare that when he gave his Son to die, he already fully intended that his death should not avail for all men alike and equally, but only for some which he would select (which . . . because he is God and there

is no subsequence of time in his decrees, he had already selected) to be its beneficiaries?[30]

He answers his own question:

> As much as God is God ... it is impossible to contend that God intends the gift of his Son for all men alike and equally and at the same time intends that it shall not actually save all but only a select body which he himself provides for it. The schematization of the order of decrees presented by the Amyraldians, in a word, necessarily implies a chronological relation of precedence and subsequence among the decrees [or the other alternative which, as we suggested above, is irrationality within the divine mind—author], the assumption of [either of] which abolishes God.[31]

3. When it urges that the Bible teaches that both by divine decree and in history Christ's death, represented by it as unrestricted regarding its referents, was intended to save all men without exception (the doctrine of unlimited atonement), Amyraldianism must necessarily join forces with Arminian universalism which, as we have seen, shares this aspect of its vision[32] and turn away altogether from a real *substitutionary* atonement, "which is as precious to the Calvinist as is his particularism, and for the safeguard of which, indeed, much of his zeal for particularism is due."[33] But this is to wound Christianity as the redemptive religion of God fatally at its heart, for (unless one is prepared to affirm the final universal salvation of all men) one cannot have an atonement of infinite intrinsic saving value and at the same time an atonement of universal extension. One can have one or the other but not both.

If Christ by his death *actually* propitiated God's wrath, reconciled God, and paid the penalty for sin (which is what I mean by an atonement of infinite intrinsic value), and if he *sacrificially* substituted himself for (περί, *peri*), on behalf of (ὑπέρ, *hyper*), for the sake of (διά, *dia*), and in the stead and place of (ἀντί, *anti*) sinners, then it follows that for all those for whom he substitutionally did his cross work he did all that was necessary to procure their salvation and thus guarantee that they will be saved. But since neither Scripture, history, nor Christian experience will tolerate the conclusion that all men have become, are becoming, or shall become Christians, we must conclude that Christ did not savingly die for all men but for some men only—even God's elect.[34]

---

30. Warfield, *The Plan of Salvation*, 94.
31. Ibid., 94.
32. See H. Orton Wiley, *Christian Theology* (Kansas City: Beacon Hill, 1959), 2:246–47.
33. Warfield, *The Plan of Salvation*, 94.
34. See part three, chapter eighteen, "The Divine Design Behind the Cross Work of Christ," for fuller argument.

If, on the other hand, Christ did his work for all men without exception, and if he did not intend its benefits for any one man in any sense that he did not intend it for any and every other man distributively, since again neither Scripture, history, nor Christian experience will allow the conclusion that all men are saved, it necessarily follows that Christ actually died neither savingly nor substitutionally for any man since he did not do for those who are saved anything that he did not do for those who are lost, and the one thing that he did not do for the lost was save them. It also follows necessarily, since Christ by his death *actually* procured nothing that guarantees the salvation of any man, and yet some men are saved, that the most one can claim for his work is that he in some way made all men salvable. But the highest view of the atonement that one can reach by this path is the governmental view. This view holds that Christ by his death actually paid the penalty for no man's sin. What his death did was to demonstrate what their sin deserves at the hand of the just Governor and Judge of the universe, and permits God justly to forgive men if *on other grounds,* such as *their* faith, *their* repentance, *their* works, and *their* perseverance, they meet his demands. This means, of course, that the *actual* salvation of those who are saved is ultimately rooted in and hangs decisively upon something other than the work of him who alone is able to save men, namely, in something that those who are saved do themselves in their own behalf. But this is just to eviscerate the Savior's cross work of all of its intrinsic saving worth and to replace the Christosoteric vision of Scripture with the autosoteric vision of Pelagianism.

THE PRINCIPLE GOVERNING THE ORDER OF THE DECREES

Most Calvinists have followed two other orders, traditionally known as "infralapsarianism" and "supralapsarianism." The first of these orders urges a historical arrangement as best representing the principle governing the divine mind, and the second, a teleological arrangement.

Infralapsarianism: the Historical Principle

The consentient testimony of consistent Calvinism, acutely aware of the pitfalls inherent within Amyraldianism, is that, regardless of the arrangement of the decrees one finally espouses, both the decree to save men by Christ and the decree to apply his saving benefits to them by the Holy Spirit must appear in the order of the decrees *logically* (not chronologically) *after* the distinguishing or electing decree. By this single adjustment all of the difficulties lurking within Amyraldianism are swept away. For now Christ dies for the *elect* and the Spirit applies his benefits to the *elect*, and both are working consistently together to fulfill the Father's single redemptive purpose—to save the *elect*. Accordingly, all consistent Calvinism elevates God's discriminating decree from the fourth position, where it is inserted by the Amyraldian, at least to the third position in the order of decrees (as we shall see, the supralapsarian raises it even higher), as follows:

1. the decree to create the world and (all) men
2. the decree that (all) men would fall
*3. the election of some fallen men to salvation in Christ (and the reprobation of the others)
4. the decree to redeem the elect by the cross work of Christ
5. the decree to apply Christ's redemptive benefits to the elect.

This proposed arrangement represents the Calvinistic scheme known as "sub-" or "infralapsarianism." The terms literally mean "below [*sub*] or after [*infra*] the Fall [*lapsus*]," and denote the position in the order of the decrees which the discriminating decree sustains to the lapsarian (Fall) decree—*immediately after* the decree that man would fall. In agreement with the Canons of Dort (see the Synod's First Head of Doctrine, Articles VII, X),[35] most consistent Calvinists espouse this scheme because

---

35. The Canons of Dort, while practically and substantially infralapsarian, are not so framed, however, as to make it impossible for supralapsarians to subscribe to them honestly and intelligently, as is evident from the fact that Franciscus Gomarus and Gisbertus Voetius, members of the Synod and both staunch supralapsarians, did subscribe to them. The Westminster Confession of Faith is noncommittal—see Benjamin B. Warfield's article "Predestination in the Reformed Confessions," in *Studies in Theology* (New York: Oxford University Press, 1932), 228–30. He writes:

> Some of [the Reformed Confessions] are explicitly Infralapsarian, and none exclude, much less polemically oppose, Infralapsariansm. None of them are explicitly Supralapsarian: many, however, leave the question between Supra- and Infralapsarianism entirely to one side, and thus open the door equally to both; and none are polemically directed against Supralapsarianism.... In view of these facts, it is hardly possible to speak of the Reformed creeds at large as distinctly Infralapsarian.... Some Reformed Confessions explicitly define Infralapsarianism: none assert anything which is not consonant with Infralapsarianism. On the other hand, nothing is affirmed in the majority of the Confessions inconsistent with Supralapsarianism either; and this majority includes several of the most widely accepted documents [such as, according to Warfield, the Heidelberg Catechism, the Second Helvetic Confession, and the Westminster Confession of Faith].

See also John Murray for a similar opinion in "Calvin, Dort, and Westminster on Predestination—A Comparative Study," in *Crisis in the Reformed Churches* (Grand Rapids, Mich.: Reformed Fellowship, 1968), 154–55.

it represents God as distinguishing among men *as sinners,* which, they contend, represents God as both gracious and tender toward the *elect* sinner as well as holy and just toward the *reprobated* sinner. To advance the discriminating decree to any position *before* the decree respecting the Fall, they argue against the supralapsarian ("before [*supra*] the Fall"), depicts God as discriminating among men *as men* rather than as sinners, which in turn makes God appear to be arbitrary, to say the least, if not also the author of sin.

Supralapsarian Calvinists have raised the following six objections against the infralapsarian scheme:

1. The infralapsarian scheme cannot account for the election and reprobation of angels. There are "elect angels" (1 Tim. 5:21), but they were not elected out of a totality of their order viewed as *fallen* as the infralapsarian scheme affirms is true of elect men, inasmuch as the elect angels never fell. Berkhof, who seems (only slightly) to favor the infralapsarian position, acknowledges as much when he writes:

> The predestination of the angels can only be understood as supralapsarian. God did not choose a certain number out of the fallen mass of angels . . . the predestination of the angels would seem to favor the Supralapsarian position, for it can only be conceived as supralapsarian.[36]

Moreover, the angels who did fall, though they are creatures of God as much in need of redemption as are fallen men, will know no divine efforts to redeem them (see Heb. 2:16; 2 Pet. 2:4; Jude 6). Apparently, for reasons sufficient unto himself, God simply by decree granted the grace of perseverance in holiness to some angels and denied it to the others. If God did so relative to the destiny of angels, did he not do so, to use the infralapsarian's word, "arbitrarily" (though the more appropriate, nonpejorative word which should be used here is "sovereignly")? And if he did so, is there any reason why he should not have done so regarding the destiny of men? It is true, of course, that the ground of God's dealings toward one order of his creatures (angels) may not be the same for his dealings toward another order of his creatures (humanity), but if any weight is given to it at all, it is a fact that the analogy between the elect angels and elect men favors more the supralapsarian scheme than it does the infralapsarian scheme.

2. Although the infralapsarian's concern to represent God's reprobation of some sinners as an act of justice (evidenced in his placing the discriminating decree *after* the decree concerning the Fall) issues a proper caution against any depiction of God which would suggest that he acts toward men with purposeless caprice, nevertheless, if he intends by this to suggest that God's reprobation of these sinners is

---

36. Berkhof, *Systematic Theology*, 113, 121.

solely an act of justice (condemnation alone) which in no sense entails also the logically prior sovereign determination to "pass them by" and to leave them in their sin (preterition), then he makes reprobation solely a *conditional* decree, a position in accord with the Arminian contention that God determines the destiny of no man, that he merely decreed to *react* in mercy or justice to the actions of men.[37] But then, as soon as the infralapsarian acknowledges (as he must if he would distance himself from Arminianism) that sin is not the *ultimate* cause of reprobation, and that God who works *all* things according to the counsel of his will (Eph. 1:11) decreed the Fall of man and by his decree of reprobation, which entails both preterition (the "passing by") and condemnation (see Westminster Confession of Faith, III/vii), determined the destiny of the nonelect sinner, his insistence over against the

---

37. Arminians regularly teach that God does not positively bring about moral evil; rather, he merely permits the sinner to act on his own (see James Arminius, *The Writings of James Arminius* [Grand Rapids, Mich.: Baker, 1977], 3:450). John H. Gerstner (*A Predestination Primer* [Winona Lake, Indiana: Alpha Publications, 1980], 7) also seems to assert this when he writes:

> Election is what is called a positive decree, and reprobation is usually regarded as a permissive decree. . . . [By the former] we mean to indicate that God from all eternity foreordains that some actions should be unto eternal life by actually initiating, or instigating, or energizing, or empowering, these actions. . . . This is called "positive" because God actually does something. He actually effects the act in the person. . . . What is meant by the [latter term] is this: according to this decree God predestinates the acts of sinful men by ordaining all the circumstances which lead to the sinner's choice of evil without actually inclining, or disposing or energizing the sinner to do the evil deed. God simply permits the reprobate of himself and his own instigation or inclination to do that which is evil. . . . God in this instance refrains from positive action.

In the same vein, Gerstner writes elsewhere: "It is only the wickedness of the human heart, and not the decree of God, which causes men to reject the overtures of God and His gospel."

But this distinction means that, if not elect sinners, at least reprobate sinners will and act independently of God. The reader is referred to Exodus 4:21, 7:3, Psalm 105:25, and Proverbs 21:1 as a sufficient biblical rebuttal to Gerstner's view of reprobation as a "permissive decree." See also John Calvin, *Concerning the Eternal Predestination of God* (Cambridge: James Clarke, 1961), 174–77, written as a refutation of Albertus Pighius and Georgius of Sicily, for his (and Augustine's) rejection of Gerstner's representation of God's relation to the evil acts of reprobate men.

Gerstner's error here stems at least in part from his insistence that the human will is free: "There is no power with which we are acquainted in this world which can actually force our will . . . The powers of this world can do virtually anything they want to but this one area is invulnerable and impervious to anybody and anything, namely, the sovereignty of our own will . . . Not even Almighty God, once He has given me this faculty of choice, can make me, coerce me, force me to choose" (29). Of course, if this were true, God could not "actually initiate, or instigate, or energize, or empower" the elect sinner to choose the way of eternal life. For they too would be "invulnerable and impervious" to God's advances. But Daniel 4:35, John 6:44, and a host of other verses contradict Gerstner's contention.

GOD'S ETERNAL PLAN OF SALVATION

supralapsarian that the discriminating decree must not be advanced to any position prior to the decree concerning the Fall lest God appear to be responsible for sin and arbitrary in his dealings with men loses all of its force. Why? Because the infralapsarian also must envision God's preterition regarding the nonelect as ultimately being grounded wholly and solely in God's sovereign will, apart from consideration of the fact of their sin.[38] Consequently, the infralapsarian position simply does not relieve the difficulty which it seeks to address. Besides, whether God discriminates among men viewed simply as men (one supralapsarian arrangement admittedly does indeed suggest this) or among men viewed as sinners makes very little difference to every rebellious human objector. To him a God who determines

---

38. Calvin in his *Commentary* on Romans (9:11, 30) states that "the highest cause" (*suprema causa*) of reprobation is "the bare and simple good pleasure of God," while "the proximate cause" (*propinqua causa*) is "the curse we all inherit from Adam." The Westminster Confession of Faith, III/vii, declares:

> The rest of mankind [i.e., the nonelect] God was pleased, according to the unsearchable counsel of His own will, whereby He extendeth or withholdeth mercy, as He pleaseth, for the glory of His sovereign power over His creatures, to pass by; and to ordain them to dishonor and wrath for their sin, to the praise of His glorious justice.

Concerning this statement John Murray writes:

> The precision of the formulation is evident in the distinction drawn between the two expressions "to pass by" and "to ordain them." The former is not modified, the latter is. No reason is given for the passing by except the sovereign will of God. *If sin had been mentioned as the reason, then all would have been passed by* [emphasis supplied]. The differentiation [among men] finds its explanation wholly in God's sovereign will and in respect of this ingredient the only reason is that "God was pleased . . . to pass by." But when ordination to dishonour and wrath is contemplated, then the proper ground of dishonour and wrath demands mention. And this is sin. Hence the addition in this case, "to ordain them to dishonour and wrath for their sin."
>
> . . . It might be alleged that the *Confession* represents judicial infliction and ill-desert as the only factor [*sic*] relevant to the ordaining to dishonour and wrath, that what has been called "reprobation" as distinct from preterition is purely judicial. The *Confession* is eloquent in its avoidance of this construction and only superficial reading of its terms could yield such an interpretation. The earlier clauses, "God was pleased, according to the unsearchable counsel of His own will, whereby He extendeth or withholdeth mercy, as He pleaseth, for the glory of His sovereign power over His creatures," govern "to ordain them to dishonour and wrath" as well as "to pass by." So the sovereign will of God is operative in ordaining to dishonour and wrath as well as in passing by. And careful analysis will demonstrate the necessity for this construction. Why are some ordained to dishonour and wrath when others equally deserving are not? The only explanation is the sovereign will of God. The *ground* of dishonour and wrath is sin alone. But the reason why the non-elect are ordained to this dishonour and wrath when others, the elect, are not is sovereign differentiation on God's part and there is no other answer to this question. ("Calvin, Dort, and Westminster on Predestination," 154–55).

to leave even one man in his sin when he could save him is hardly less arbitrary and cruel than a God who determined some men unto damnation from the beginning. In other words, from the perspective of bare sinful human considerations, God is still "arbitrary" if he was in a position to determine to save every sinner but determined to save only certain sinners and to leave the rest in their sin and then to condemn them for it. Berkhof again rightly observes:

> The Infralapsarian . . . cannot maintain the idea that reprobation is an act of divine justice pure and simple, contingent on the sin of man. In the last analysis, he, too, must declare that it is an act of God's sovereign good pleasure, if he wants to avoid the Arminian camp. . . . [His] language may sound more tender than that of the Supralapsarians, but is also more apt to be misunderstood, and after all proves to convey the same idea.[39]

3. Espousing as the infralapsarian scheme does the view that the *historical* principle governs the order of the decrees, and arranging as it does the order of the decrees accordingly in the order that reflects the historical order of the corresponding occurrences of the events which they determined (as indeed the Amyraldian scheme does also), this scheme can show no purposive connection between the several parts of the plan *per se*. In a single, consistent, purposive plan one assumes that any and every single member of the plan should logically necessitate the next member so that there is a purposive cohesion to the whole. The historical arrangement simply cannot demonstrate, for example, why or how the decree to create *necessitates* the next decree concerning the Fall, or why the decree concerning the Fall *necessitates* the following particularizing decree.

4. Because the infralapsarian scheme can show no logical necessity between the first two decrees (the creation decree and the Fall decree) and the three following soteric decrees, it "cannot give a specific answer to the question why God decreed to create the world and to permit the fall."[40] It must refer these elements to some general purpose in God ("for his general glory as Creator"?) which has no discernible connection to the central redemptive elements in the "eternal purpose" of God, which severance between creation and redemption could be used to justify the dualism of a natural theology.[41] Berkhof registers this objection in these words:

---

39. Berkhof, *Systematic Theology*, 122–24.
40. Ibid., 121.
41. An infralapsarian could justify being a natural theologian by arguing that it is not necessary to take into account either the inabilities of man due to his fallenness or redemptive considerations when assessing the purpose of creation and its revelatory character, since in his schema the decree of creation is unrelated to these following decrees.

The Infralapsarian position does not do justice to the unity of the divine decree, but represents the different members of it too much as disconnected parts. First God decrees to create the world for the glory of his name, which means among other things that he determined that his rational creatures should live according to the divine law implanted in their hearts and should praise their Maker. Then he decreed to permit the fall, whereby sin enters the world. This seems to be a frustration of the original plan, or at least an important modification of it, since God no more decrees to glorify himself by the voluntary obedience of *all* his rational creatures. Finally, there follows the decrees of election and reprobation, which mean only a partial execution of the original plan.[42]

5. The infralapsarian scheme, by espousing a *historical* order of the decrees, reverses the manner in which the rational mind plans an action. The infralapsarian scheme moves from *means* (if, indeed, the earlier decrees can be regarded as means at all, disconnected as they are in purpose from the later decrees) to the *end*, whereas "in planning the rational mind passes from the end to the means in a retrograde movement, so that what is first in design is last in accomplishment"[43] and, conversely, what is last in design is first in accomplishment.

6. The infralapsarian scheme does not come to terms with the teaching of certain key Scripture passages as well as the supralapsarian scheme does. In Romans 9:14–18 and 9:19–24 Paul responds to two objections to his teaching on divine election which he frames in question form: (a) "What then shall we say? Is God unjust?"—the question of divine fairness, and (b) "One of you will say to me: 'Then why does God still blame us? For who resists his will?' "—the question of human freedom. Now if Paul had been thinking along infrapalsarian lines, he would have found it sufficient to answer both questions something like this: "Who are you, O *sinner*, to question God's justice? Since we all fell into sin, God could justly reject us all. As it is, in mercy he has determined to save some of us while leaving the rest to their just condemnation." But this he did not do. As we shall see, in response to both objections he simply appealed to God's absolute, sovereign right to do with his creatures as he pleases in order to accomplish his own holy ends.

In Romans 9:15–18, in response to the first question (divine fairness), contrasting Moses—his example of the elect man in whose behalf God had sovereignly determined to display his mercy (v. 15; see also v. 23)—and Pharaoh—his example of the nonelect man whom God had sovereignly determined to raise up *in order to* [ὅπως, *hopōs*] show by him his power and to publish his name in all the earth (v. 17; see also v. 22), Paul concludes: "Therefore God has mercy on whom he wants to have

---

42. Berkhof, *Systematic Theology*, 124.
43. Ibid., 119.

mercy, and he hardens whom he wants to harden" (v. 18). As we just said, here he responds to the question concerning the justice of God in view of his elective and reprobative activity by a straightforward appeal to God's sovereign right to do with men as he pleases in order that he might exhibit the truth that all spiritual good in man is the fruit of his grace alone (see also Rom. 9:11–13 and chapter ten of this work).

Then in Romans 9:20b–24, in response to the second question (human freedom), after his rebuke: "Who are you, O man, to talk back to God?" Paul employs the familiar Old Testament metaphor of the potter and the clay (see Isa. 29:16; 45:9;[44] 64:8; Jer. 18:6) and asks: "Does not the potter have the right to make out of the same lump of clay [man construed generally] some pottery for noble purposes and some for common use?" Paul teaches here (1) that the *potter* sovereignly makes *both kinds* of vessels, and (2) that he makes *both* out of the *same* lump of clay. The metaphor would suggest that the determination of a given vessel's nature and purpose—whether for noble or for common use—is the potter's sovereign right, *apart from any consideration of the clay's prior condition*. This suggests in turn that God sovereignly determined the number, nature, and purpose of both the elect and the nonelect in order to accomplish his own holy ends, *apart from a consideration of any prior condition which may or may not have been resident within them* (see 9:11–13). So here, as earlier, in response to the second objection to his doctrine Paul simply appeals again to God's sovereign right to do with his creatures as he pleases in order to accomplish his own holy ends. And he registers his appeal without qualification. (It should be noted in passing that no Arminian would ever be asked either of these questions.)

This feature of the metaphor means then, at the very least, that there is no scriptural compulsion to place the discriminating decree in the order of decrees after the decree respecting the Fall. Furthermore, it lays stress on the divine will as the sole, ultimate, determinative cause for the distinction between elect and nonelect, a point that the supralapsarian scheme stresses.

The infralapsarian agrees, of course, that the divine will is the sole determinative cause for the distinction between elect and nonelect, but he insists that the "lump" about which Paul speaks here is mankind already viewed by God as fallen (see, e.g., the commentaries by Hodge and Murray). But if this were the case God would only need to make *one* kind of vessel from the lump—the vessels for noble use. He would not need to make the vessels for common use—they would be already represented by the "sinful" lump. As it is, the metaphor expressly affirms that the potter makes *both* kinds of vessels from the lump, suggesting that the lump has

---

44. Isaiah goes even further than Paul by actually pronouncing a woe against those who would question their Creator's sovereign right to do with his creatures as he pleases.

no particular character beforehand—good or bad—which would necessarily *determine* the potter toward a given vessel's creation for one kind of use or the other. This feature of the metaphor also favors the supralapsarian scheme.

Then, in Ephesians 3:9–10 Paul teaches that God "created all things, *in order that* [ἵνα, *hina*] now through the church the many-sided wisdom of God might be made known to the rulers and authorities in the heavenly realm, according to his eternal purpose which he accomplished in the Christ, Jesus our Lord." Here, supralapsarians urge, Paul teaches that God created the universe, which creative act reflects his prior creation decree, not as an end in itself but as a means to an end. And what end is that? Elsewhere (Rom. 1:20), Paul teaches that by glorifying its Maker's power and "architectural skill" (no work of God, simply by virtue of the fact that it is his work, can avoid doing so), creation serves the condemnatory aspect of the particularizing decree by leaving men who would plead ignorance of God in the final judgment "without excuse [ἀναπολογήτους, *anapologētous*]."[45] But in Ephesians 3:9–10 Paul affirms that the end for which all things were created is not this alone but rather, and more primarily, to provide the arena and all the necessary conditions for God's *redemptive* activity to manifest itself in order that he might show forth, *through the redeemed church,* his many-sided wisdom (or plan) to the rulers and authorities in the heavenly realm.

Further indications that in his "eternal purpose" God integrated the purpose of creation and the creation ordinances into the more primary redemptive plan which he accomplished in Christ, as we noted in chapter ten, are (1) the fact that God's creation rest was the symbol of the Sabbath rest which the redeemed people of God will enter upon at the Eschaton (Gen. 2:2; Heb. 4:4–11), (2) the fact that God intended the original marriage ordinance from the beginning as an earthly representation of the relationship between Christ and the redeemed church (Gen. 2:24; Matt. 19:4–6; Eph. 5:30–32), and (3) the fact that God "subjected creation to frustration" specifically because of human sin (Gen. 3:17–18), determining that in empathy with the redeemed it would "groan as in the pains of childbirth right up to the present time," and that, for "its own liberation from bondage to decay," it would have to "wait in eager expectation for the revelation of the sons of God" at the time of their physical resurrection when their bodies will be redeemed, at which time creation too "will be brought into the glorious freedom of the children of God" (Rom. 8:19–23).

In sum, supralapsarians urge, the infralapsarian scheme (1) implies that God originally intended creation to serve some purpose other than his final redemptive purpose which is history's ultimate end, a theological construction which could be

---

45. See John Murray, *Romans* (Grand Rapids, Mich.: Eerdmans, 1968), in loc.

also used to justify the erection of an unscriptural natural theology, (2) runs the risk of failing to reflect as clearly as it should that God decreed and grounded the predestination and foreordination of men purely and solely on sovereign considerations within himself, and (3) ultimately, as Berkouwer states, "does not solve anything."[46]

Supralapsarianism: the Teleological Principle

In light of these difficulties with the infralapsarian arrangement of the order of the divine decrees, supralapsarians, including such eminent Reformed thinkers as Theodore Beza of Geneva, William Whitaker and William Perkins in the sixteenth-century Church of England, Franciscus Gomarus and Gisbertus Voetius in seventeenth-century Holland, William Twisse, first prolocutor of the Westminster Assembly, and in more recent times Geerhardus Vos, offer another arrangement. But most supralapsarians, after placing the discriminating decree in the first position, for some inexplicable reason then abandon the supralapsarian insight that "in planning the rational mind passes from the end to the means in a retrograde movement" and arrange the remaining decrees not in a retrograde order but in the order in which the events to which they refer occurred historically (the effect of which will become clear as we proceed). Thus the more common (but inconsistent) supralapsarian arrangement is as follows:

*1. the election of some men to salvation in Christ (and the reprobation of the others)
2. the decree to create the world and both kinds of men
3. the decree that all men would fall
4. the decree to redeem the elect, who are now sinners, by the cross work of Christ
5. the decree to apply Christ's redemptive benefits to these elect sinners.

An analysis of this arrangement of the order of decrees will show, because the discriminating decree is placed at the head of all the other decrees with the others then proceeding in the order in which the events to which they refer took place in history, that God at the point of discrimination is represented as discriminating among men simply as men, inasmuch as the decree respecting the Fall does not come until point three.

---

46. G.C. Berkouwer, *Divine Election* (Grand Rapids, Mich.: Eerdmans, 1960), 273.

Other supralapsarians, such as (possibly) Jerome Zanchius (1516–1590),[47] Johannes Piscator (1546–1625), Herman Hoeksema (d. 1965),[48] and Gordon H. Clark (1902–1985),[49] have suggested, with minor variations among them, that the decrees should be arranged in the following order:

*1. the election of some sinful men to salvation in Christ (and the reprobation of the rest of sinful mankind in order to make known the riches of God's gracious mercy to the elect)
2. the decree to apply Christ's redemptive benefits to the elect sinners
3. the decree to redeem the elect sinners by the cross work of Christ
4. the decree that men should fall
5. the decree to create the world and men.

In this latter scheme the discriminating decree stands in the first position with the creation decree standing in the last position. It should also be noted that in this scheme, *unlike the former,* God is represented as discriminating among men viewed as sinners and not among men viewed simply as men. The election and salvation of these elect sinners in Christ becomes the decree that unifies all the other parts of the one eternal purpose of God. This revision of the more common scheme addresses the infralapsarian objection that supralapsarianism depicts God as discriminating among men viewed simply as men and not among men viewed as sinners. How it is that this revised scheme is able to depict God as discriminating among men as sinners, even as the infralapsarian scheme does (but for an obviously different reason), will become clear as we elucidate the two principles which govern this revision of the supralapsarian order.

THE PRIMACY OF THE PARTICULARIZING PRINCIPLE

Because they are persuaded that Scripture places the particularizing grace of

---

47. See Jerome Zanchius, *The Doctrine of Absolute Predestination,* trans. Augustus M. Toplady (Grand Rapids, Mich.: Baker, 1977). Richard A. Muller in *Christ and the Decree* (Grand Rapids, Mich.: Baker, 1986) argues that Zanchius was an infralapsarian (112), but Otto Gründler maintains that he was indeed a supralapsarian (*Die Gotteslehre Girolami Zanchis und irhe Bedeutung für seine Lehre von der Prädestination* [Neukirchen, 1965], 112). See also L. Leblanc, *Theses Theologicae* (London, 1683), 183.
48. Herman Hoeksema, *Reformed Dogmatics* (Grand Rapids, Mich.: Reformed Free Publishing Association, 1966), 161–65.
49. Gordon H. Clark, "The Nature of Logical Order" (unpublished paper presented at the Third Annual Meeting of the Evangelical Theological Society).

God in Jesus Christ, the Alpha and Omega, at the beginning, the center, and the end of all God's ways and works, the supralapsarians who offer the revised, or consistently supralapsarian, order make the particularizing principle the primary and unifying principle of the eternal purpose of God. (All supralapsarians share *this* concern, by the way.) Therefore, these supralapsarians believe it both appropriate and necessary so to arrange the decrees that every decree is made to serve this primary principle. Accordingly, they postpone to the fourth and fifth positions respectively, after the explicitly redemptive decrees, the lapsarian decree and the creation decree in order to make the Fall and even creation itself serve the particularistic purpose of God. Contrary to the infralapsarian assertion that "creation in the Bible is never represented as a means of executing the purpose of election and reprobation,"[50] all supralapsarians insist that the created world must never be viewed as standing off over against God's redemptive activity, totally divorced from the particularizing purpose of God, the ultimate concern of God's "eternal purpose," and as fulfilling some general purpose(s) unrelated to the redemptive work of Christ. They insist so on the ground that such a representation of creation shatters the unity of the one eternal purpose of God and provides a base within the eternal decree itself for the development of an unbiblical natural theology. As we have seen, they are persuaded that Ephesians 3:9–11 expressly affirms that creation's purpose is subservient to God's redemptive purpose and that the same subservience is suggested in Romans 1:20 and 8:19–23. In sum, they are persuaded

1. that God created all things *in order that* he might show forth *through the redeemed community, his church,* the glory of his wisdom and grace in accordance with his eternal purpose which he accomplished in Christ Jesus our Lord;[51]
2. that he determined that creation by its revelation of his "eternal power and divine nature" would condemn the reprobate; and
3. that by its reflexive agony and ecstasy creation would empathize with the church's agony and ecstasy.

TWO EXEGETICAL OBJECTIONS CONSIDERED

First, concerning Ephesians 3:9–10 infralapsarians argue that the ἵνα, *hina,* clause

---

50. Charles Hodge, *Systematic Theology* (Grand Rapids, Mich.: Eerdmans, 1954), 2:318.
51. See Ephesians 1:6, 12, 14; 2:7, where Paul declares that all that God has done for the Christian (in accordance with his eternal purpose) he has done "to the praise of the glory of his grace which he has freely given us in the One he loves" and "in order that he might show in the ages to come the incomparable riches of his grace in his kindness toward us in Christ Jesus."

commencing verse 10 should not be connected syntactically to the immediately preceding participial clause in verse 9, "[in God] who created all things," but to the penultimate participial clause in verse 9, "[the mystery] which was hidden from the ages in God." By this construction they suggest that Paul intended to teach that God hid the administration of the "mystery" of the church from men in ages past in order that he might reveal it to the rulers and authorities in the heavenly realm now in this age through his (and the other apostles') preaching. Infralapsarians marshal to their side in support of this interpretation Paul's earlier teaching in Ephesians 3:4–6.

Supralapsarians, of course, do not deny that Paul's preaching played a part—indeed, a very significant part—in making known through the church "come of age," to a degree to which it could not have been made known by the church "under age" in former times, the many-sided wisdom of God to the rulers and authorities in the heavenly realm. But they insist that infralapsarians commit two errors by rejecting the nearer participial clause in the sentence as the clause to which the ἵνα, *hina,* clause of 3:10 should be attached (which participial clause is clearly the closest possible antecedent clause and the one which grammarians ordinarily would recommend when seeking a following word's antecedent). (1) They reduce the nearer clause, as Gordon Clark points out, to a "meaningless excrescence on the verse."[52] Charles Hodge, for example, writes: "the words 'who created all things,' is entirely subordinate and unessential . . . and might be omitted without materially affecting the sense of the passage."[53] But this leaves the phrase serving no intelligible purpose, since it was hardly necessary for Paul to identify the God about whom he spoke as the God "who created all things" or to teach his readers the *fact* that their God did create all things—surely they would have known *these* things. (2) They in effect divorce the creation from God's *particularizing* purpose in Christ and allow it to have a *raison d'être,* by implication, which moves in a direction other than the redemptive *raison.* But this implies that God has (or had) *two* purposes, not directly related to each other, a general purpose which the creation (which includes unfallen man) was somehow to fulfill (but which purpose had to be abandoned when man, the human part of creation, fell) and a specific redemptive purpose. This in turn implies that God's redemptive purpose was not at first central and primary to his eternal purpose but was even subordinate to the more original general purpose of the creation and man. To avoid these highly questionable implications, supralapsarians urge that it is much better to recognize the presence of the

---

52. Gordon H. Clark, *The Philosophy of Gordon H. Clark* (Philadelphia: Presbyterian and Reformed, 1968), 482.
53. Charles Hodge, *A Commentary of the Epistle to the Ephesians* (Grand Rapids, Mich.: Eerdmans, 1954), 172.

nearer participial clause as the antecedent to the following ἵνα, *hina,* clause, and to give it its full force as the "lead-in" idea to 3:10.

Second, in their alternative interpretation of Paul's teaching in Romans 8:19–23, infralapsarians contend that supralapsarians make too much of the relationship between creation and the church when they interpret creation's "reaction" to the church's redemptive conditions as a "reflexive" one. But the "reflexive relationship" on creation's part cannot be avoided. Surely there is a divinely imposed reflexive relationship between creation and the changing fortunes of the church—Paul expressly affirms it to be so. And he declares that the church does not await creation's liberation from its bondage to decay but the other way around: creation awaits what is expressly said to be the church's full and final "redemption." In other words, creation's "fortunes" are directly dependent on redemptive considerations. So how better to describe creation's relationship to the church than as a "reflexive" one?

THE PURPOSING PRINCIPLE GOVERNING THE RATIONAL MIND

All supralapsarians aver as a second consideration (though only those who affirm the revised scheme offer an order of the decrees consistent with this consideration) that in all purposive planning the rational mind is governed by the principle of determining first the end to be accomplished and then the several appropriate means to attain that end; and in the case of the means in the plan, each of which becomes an "end" of the immediately *following* means, the rational mind determines them in *retrograde* order from the end or goal back through all the means necessary to the accomplishment of that ultimate end. The rational mind recognizes that only in this way is each element of the plan purposive and contributory to the coherence of the entire plan. And God is a purposing planner!

To illustrate: suppose a rational planner decides to buy a car. This is the end that he will pursue. With his end determined, only then does he determine the appropriate means to achieve it. (A rational mind is actually capable of doing both instantaneously; by the phrase "only then" we intend a logical or teleological, not a chronological, order.) Never would a rational car buyer first leave home with twenty thousand dollars in his pocket, understanding his action to be a means to something, and *only then* determine the end which his action was intended to be a means to. *The end always precedes the means in a rational mind.*

The rational planner also realizes, if he would achieve his end, that he must actually *execute* the means he determines are essential to that end in a particular order. For example, suppose the car buyer has determined that between the point where he finds himself—in bed at home and carless—and his determined end of purchasing a car stand five means necessary to his becoming a car owner: (1) getting out of bed, (2) leaving home, (3) arriving at the car dealership, (4) agreeing with the car salesman on the purchase price of the car, and (5) arranging a loan through his bank for that sum. The rational car buyer realizes that he cannot first arrange with the bank for the agreed-upon sum, then agree with the car salesman on the purchase price of the car, then get to the car dealership in order to speak with the car salesman, then leave home, and then get out of bed. Never would a rational car buyer even try to execute the means to his end in a manner that would frustrate his plan and lead to failure.

But there is another aspect to *rational* planning which is not always taken into account. How does the rational mind go about determining the means that are necessary to reach a determined end? Because it recognizes that each means in any purposive chain of means, except for the last one (last, viewed from the point of the determined end), of necessity is the "end" of the means that follows it, and because it is necessary always to pass from the end to the means to the end, the rational mind will not begin from the point where it finds itself and determine first from that point the last means to the end. Rather, the rational mind (in the case of men, it may do this at times without even realizing it; at other times it will be very conscious that it is doing so) will begin from the determined end and in a retrograde movement work back in its planning to the point where it finds itself at the moment. Only in this way does each means answer purposively to the need of the former means. To use our car buyer illustration one more time: The car buyer has determined that he will purchase a car (his ultimate end). But in order to do that (given his present circumstance), he determines, as the first means to his ultimate end (which means becomes the "end" of any second means that he determines would be necessary), that he must arrange a loan with his bank for the agreed-upon sum. But in order to do that, he determines, as the second means to his ultimate end (which second means becomes the "end" of any third means that he determines would be necessary), that he must agree with the car salesman on the purchase price of the car. But in order to do that, he determines, as the third means to his ultimate end (which third means becomes the "end" of any fourth means that he determines would be necessary), that he must get to the car dealership. But in order to do that, he determines, as the fourth means to his ultimate end (which fourth means becomes the "end" of any fifth means that he determines would be necessary), that he must leave home. But in order to do that, he determines, as the fifth means to his ultimate end (which means becomes the "end" of any sixth means that he determines would be necessary, but since in our illustration it is the last means it does not become an "end"), that he must get out of bed. In purposive planning, each element of the plan necessarily answers the need of the preceding element, so that there is purpose in each member and purposive coherence governing the whole plan. This is actually the way the truly rational mind purposes or plans, and one will have no trouble accepting this as so if he will recognize (1) that the purposing mind always determines the end before it determines the means to achieve it, and (2) that each means in any plan necessarily is the "end" of the means that follows it in the plan.

One final point: It is exceedingly important to note that when he finally carries out his plan, the rational planner executes the means (if he acts purposively) in the precise inverse order to the order in which the means he determined upon appear in the plan. *That which is last in design is first in accomplishment and that which is first in design is last in accomplishment.*

All supralapsarians take seriously the biblical truth that God, as a rational God of purpose, must *necessarily* do all that he does purposively. It is inconceivable to them that God would decree to create the world for no purpose or would decree to create it for some purpose unrelated to his one final purpose. Accordingly, in light of their perception of the manner in which the rational mind plans and then executes its plan (and who will deny that God is rational, since the only alternative consistent with such a denial is that he is irrational), the *more consistent* supralapsarians urge that the order of God's eternal plan is the precise inverse to the order in which he executes it. Since God initiated the execution of his eternal purpose by first creating the world, the decree to create the world is the last in design, and since God's eternal purpose culminates with redeemed sinners praising him in the Eschaton for the glory of his particularizing grace made theirs through the cross work of Christ (see 2 Thess. 1:7–10; Rev. 19:1–8; 21:9–27; 22:1–5), the decree to bring that to pass (the end) is the first in design. In other words, while the *execution* of the divine purpose is indeed "infralapsarian" in the sense that God's historical redemptive activity necessarily follows the historical Fall, the *plan itself* is supralapsarian. But while all supralapsarians share the same basic perception of the principles which govern the order of the decrees, many have failed to work out the order of the decrees in a manner consistent with their own perception of things and have done a disservice to their cause as a result. By placing the discriminating decree first and then simply arranging the remaining decrees in the historical order, they abandon the purposing principle of arrangement which alone relates the discriminating decree to the Fall of man, and accordingly they represent God as discriminating among men as men—since they may be regarded as sinners only after the decree concerning the Fall—leaving themselves open thereby to the infralapsarian charge that we have already noted. The consistent supralapsarian, however, submits the following order of the decrees, which reflects, it must be emphasized again, not a chronological but a teleological order within the divine plan:

*1. For the praise of the glory of his grace God elected some *sinful* men (note: in order to reveal the glory of his *grace,* he views these men as transgressors of his law from the outset; how it is that they may be so viewed is determined by the fourth decree) to salvation in Christ (Eph. 1:3–14) and for the praise of his glorious justice reprobated the rest of sinful mankind.[54]

In order to accomplish this end, he determined that

> 2. the Holy Spirit would *apply* Christ's *accomplished* redemptive benefits to elect sinners of the New Testament age and those same redemptive benefits *anticipatively* to elect sinners of the Old Testament age, the necessary first condition to the consummation of the original determined end.

In order to accomplish this means (which necessarily becomes a second "end"), he determined that

> 3. Christ would actually *redeem* elect sinners of both the New and Old Testament ages by his cross work, the necessary second condition if the Holy Spirit was to have Christ's redemptive benefits to apply.

In order to accomplish this means and to provide the context which makes Christ's cross work meaningful (which necessarily becomes a third "end"), he determined that

> 4. men would fall in Adam, their federal head, the necessary third condition if Christ's redemptive benefits were to have any elect referents needing redemption.

In order to accomplish this means (which necessarily becomes a fourth "end"), he determined that

> 5. he would enter into a covenant of works with the first man "wherein life was promised to Adam; and in him to his posterity, upon condition of perfect and personal obedience" (Confession, VII/ii), making him thereby the race's *federal head* as well, and then providentially "permit" the federal head to fall, but this "not by a bare permission, but such [permission] as hath joined with it a most wise and powerful bounding, and otherwise ordering, and governing . . . , in a manifold dispensation, to his own holy ends" (Confession, V/iv; see also VI/i), and yet to bind, order, and govern the entire Adamic temptation in such a way that "the sinfulness thereof proceedeth only from the creature, and not from

---

54. Of course, even here the decree of reprobation is not an end in itself; rather, it serves the decree of election. See Paul's teaching in Romans 9:22–23 that the decree of reprobation serves the end of making known the riches of God's glory (that is, his merciful grace) to the elect, whom he "prepared in advance for glory."

God, who, being most holy and righteous, neither is nor can be the author or approver of sin" (Confession, V/iv; see also III/i), all these features of the plan comprising the necessary fifth condition if men were to experience a moral and ethical fall.

In order to accomplish this means (which necessarily becomes a fifth "end"), that is, in order that a moral "lapse" on man's part could occur, he determined that

> 6. he would create Adam in a condition of holiness *(status integritatis)* but also in a mutable condition *(posse pecarre et posse non pecarre)* "so that he might fall from it" (Westminster Confession of Faith, IX/ii).

In order to accomplish this means (which necessarily becomes a sixth "end"), that is, to provide the necessary arena in which all this could take place, and to do so with such an evident display of his attributes as to leave fallen men who would deny his existence without excuse, he determined that

> 7. he would create the universe (since this is the last means in the plan, it does not become a seventh "end" requiring a following means).

This revision of the more common supralapsarian arrangement, since the first part of the one eternal purpose is teleologically integrated with every aspect following it, allows God from the first to discriminate among men viewed as sinners.

Then, when he put his plan into execution—in inverse order to the order in which the several parts appear in his plan—he created the world and Adam and entered into covenant with Adam, making him the race's federal head. Then Adam fell and all men descending from him by ordinary generation fell in him. Then Christ redeemed the Old Testament elect by his (for them) *anticipated* cross work and the New Testament elect by his *accomplished* cross work, with the Holy Spirit applying *anticipatively* his redemptive benefits to the Old Testament elect and applying his *accomplished* redemptive benefits to the New Testament elect, all leading to God's finally achieving his determined end—enhanced by the reprobation of the nonelect—even the praise of his glorious electing grace in Christ toward undeserving sinners. Each historical occurrence is purposive because it is the execution of an aspect of God's one eternal purpose which answers not chronologically but *teleologically* to the need of the immediately preceding aspect of the plan.

FOUR THEOLOGICAL OBJECTIONS CONSIDERED

In addition to the two exegetical difficulties already considered, infralapsarians, such as Roger R. Nicole, have certain theological difficulties with this supralapsarian vision (though Nicole acknowledges that this arrangement of the several decrees in the one eternal purpose is "very attractive," possessing a "lucid simplicity" about it), *first* among these objections being the contention that since the decree to create human beings appears here in the furthest position from the first, these people—whether viewed as elect and reprobate sinners or simply as elect and reprobate men—can be regarded at the point of their election and reprobation only as "bare possibilities" and not as *real,* that is to say, as nonexistent entities who can be contemplated not as created but *at best* only as potential or creatable men. But how can God determine any particular condition for entities which he has not yet even determined to create? As Charles Hodge, following Francis Turretin, wrote: "Of a *Non Ens* . . . nothing can be determined. The purpose to save or condemn, of necessity must, in the order of thought, follow the purpose to create . . . the purpose to create of necessity, in the order of nature, precedes the purpose to redeem."[55] The supralapsarian response to this objection is twofold:

1. If the infralapsarian is right when he insists that concerning an entity whose existence God has not yet decreed he can determine nothing, then God could not even determine to create the world and human beings (the infralapsarian's first decree), since the decree to create them, which entities would necessarily have to possess some characteristics, would necessarily entail the prior determination of these characteristics, which before he decreed to create them, according to the infralapsarian's prescription, are nonentities about which nothing can be determined. Furthermore, if God must determine to create human beings before he can determine any and every further characteristic about them—for example, whether they would be bad or amoral or good, and if the latter whether they would stay good or become bad, and if the latter whether he would punish them or redeem them, and if the latter whether he would redeem all of them or only some of them (the infralapsarian historical order), then it follows that God does not decree his first act with his last in view, which means that he does not *purposively* decree anything! Therefore, since the infralapsarian must affirm, for the sake of his own order, that God could determine characteristics for the world and human beings as well as actions on their and his part *anticipatory* of his decree to create them, then he should be willing to acknowledge that God could *determine* ultimate ends for people logically prior to his decree to create them. If, however, he persists in his objection that God could determine no purpose for the world and mankind until he had first decreed to create them, then he is saying by implication that God decreed the existence of things for no rhyme or reason, which is to ascribe an inherent irrationality to the decrees of God. And this is to fall away from Christian theism altogether.

---

55. Hodge, *Systematic Theology,* 2:318.

2. While it is true that the creation of human beings was not yet decreed at the point in the purposing order where they were elected or reprobated, yet, since God's decree is eternal with no *chronological* antecedence or subsequence in it, there was never a moment when people, viewed as *created* people, did not *certainly* exist in it. In fact, the first decree as the "end" decree, because it had to do with mankind viewed both as sinful people and as created people, rendered the Fall and creation decrees (teleo)logically necessary. Accordingly, their existence as *created* people was as decretally real and certain in the divine mind at the point of the first decree as it was at the point of the fifth decree.

Second, and it is again Roger Nicole in particular who raises this objection, it is charged that "serious difficulties arise from the attempt to view the order of decrees as the reverse of history." Nicole illustrates his concern this way:

> The relation of the application of salvation by the Holy Spirit to the impetration of salvation by Christ is identical for all the elect. But Abraham and Augustine are not chronologically on the same side of the Cross [his point here is that this would seem to split the decree of application in two, with it appearing both *before* and *after* the decree to provide salvation by Christ—author]! It would appear, therefore, that the historical order is after all not a precise mirror of the logical relationships in the mind of God.[56]

But it is strange that Nicole would register this objection against the proposed scheme for, if nothing more could be said, it applies equally to his infralapsarian order in which the decree to redeem the elect by the cross work of Christ is followed by the decree to apply Christ's redemptive benefits to the elect. Even in this arrangement, if nothing more could be said, the application decree needs to be split in two to effect the salvation of the elect before the cross and the salvation of the elect after the cross. So more can be said and indeed must be said by both the infralapsarian and the supralapsarian. And it is this: there is a certain measure of distortion in speaking of only five decrees as we have with respect to both schemes. As Clark states:

> The distortion occurs, not by splitting the one [eternal divine decree] into four [or five], but by arbitrarily stopping at four [or five or six or seven] and not continuing to enumerate all the particulars of the unitary decree. The ordinary lapsarian discussion refers to the decree of creation. But the first chapter of Genesis uses the verb create to apply to three occasions. Even if the first occurrence is comprehensive of the latter two, there are still two creative acts, and others

---

56. Roger Nicole, "The Theology of Gordon Clark," in *The Philosophy of Gordon H. Clark*, 397.

may be implied in the text. Thus the decree of creation must be subdivided. The fall of man is a fairly unified event, but even the fall can be split into several parts: the approach of Eve, Eve's persuasion of Adam, and the actual disobedience. When now we come to the decree to provide and apply salvation, the decree splits into millions of parts. For the purposes of the lapsarian discussion the application of salvation to the elect has been treated as unitary; but in reality one can speak of the decree to apply salvation to Abraham and the decree to apply it to Augustine. The decree must be split into as many parts as there are persons individually called and saved. That Christ died between the dates of Abraham and Augustine is irrelevant.

The consequence to the lapsarian problem is this. The decree to apply salvation to Augustine is teleologically prior to the decree to apply salvation to Abraham, for the life of Abraham has as one of its purposes the salvation of Augustine: "In thee shall all families of the earth be blessed."[57]

Third, infralapsarians charge that the supralapsarian scheme, in its zeal to place God's particularizing decree at the beginning of all that God planned for men, too severely construes the Fall of Adam, which was an act of rebellion on his part against God and which meant the spiritual ruin and misery of some men at least, as a *necessary* part of the divine plan (indeed, even a "fortunate" event for the elect in that it paved the way for their salvation in Christ). To this objection supralapsarians respond with a series of questions: "Did God, according to your understanding of the order of the decrees, decree the Fall?" The infralapsarian knows, as Warfield—an infralapsarian himself—acknowledges,[58] that if he answers this question in the negative he has fallen away not only from Calvinism but also from genuine Christian theism altogether. When he therefore acknowledges that God decreed the Fall, the supralapsarian has a second question: "Did he have a purpose in mind for it when he did so?" Again, the infralapsarian knows, if he answers in the negative, that he has fallen away from Calvinism as well as Christian theism. When he therefore acknowledges that God decreed the Fall for a purpose, the supralapsarian asks yet a third question: "Did that purpose play a role in God's redemptive plan or in some other plan?" Again, the infralapsarian knows, if he answers: "In some other plan," that he must admit, first, that he knows nothing concerning the content of this other plan, and, second, that this other plan (whatever its content) has been frustrated inasmuch as God's *redemptive* purpose in Christ directly addresses the Fall and the exigencies created by it (which he avers were intended to fulfill a role in another plan). This is plain from the fact that God's *redemptive* purpose reverses the Fall and its effects with

---

57. Gordon H. Clark, "Reply to Roger Nicole," in *The Philosophy of Gordon H. Clark*, 483–84.
58. See Warfield, *The Plan of Salvation*, 111, fn. 81.

regard to elect persons and nature itself (see Rom. 5:12–19; 8:19–23). When he then acknowledges, as he must, that the Fall fulfills a purposive role in God's redemptive plan, the supralapsarian finally asks: "Wherein then do we differ, since neither of us believes that sin *per se* is good, and since we both believe that sin is intrinsically evil and proceeds only from the nature of second causes; since neither of us believes that God is the chargeable cause of sin, and since we both believe that God decreed from all eternity that the redemptive aspects of his particularizing purpose would address the Fall and its effects in behalf of the elect? Must we not both acknowledge then that God decreed the Fall and its effects to provide the condition from which Christ would redeem God's elect? And if so, do we not both stand on precisely the same ground?"

The supralapsarian is deeply committed to the belief that the Fall has significance as a real event of history only as it is allowed to stand in the redemptive history of Scripture as a means to an end in relation to God's one eternal plan of redemption, on the ground (along with the others that have already been offered) that the state of *the elect as children of God in Christ by divine grace* is ultimately a higher, more glorious, and more praiseworthy end than the state of *all men as children of God in unfallen Adam by divine justice.*

Fourth and finally, infralapsarians contend that the supralapsarian scheme is an overly pretentious speculation in its analysis of the manner in which God plans. Better is it, they argue, to be satisfied with the more modest, less pretentious historical order for the decrees. Again the supralapsarian response is twofold:

1. The infralapsarian's charge that the supralapsarian is "pretentiously speculative" because he would attempt to determine the principle which governed the divine mind when God decreed what he did lacks any real force since the infralapsarian too, after analyzing the divine purpose, offers his order of decrees as the order in the divine mind, thereby tacitly suggesting a governing principle. It is simply a case of determining which of the two is the more likely principle—the historical or the teleological, and the supralapsarian is convinced that his conclusion is more biblical over all and reflects more clearly the purposing character of the mind of God.

2. The supralapsarian denies that his arrangement is a "pretentious speculation" or "the invention of unaided human intellection." Rather, he insists that it is simply the result of (1) exegesis of divinely revealed information about the nature and ways of God and (2) legitimate "sanctified" deductions "by good and necessary consequence" (Westminster Confession of Faith, I/vi), based upon the results of that exegetical labor.

In my opinion the supralapsarian vision of God's eternal plan of salvation holds the exegetical and deductive edge. It satisfies better than the infralapsarian vision does the demands of all the pertinent teachings of Scripture, integrates more intelligibly the myriad parts of the one divine purpose to magnify the particularizing grace of God in Jesus Christ, and elucidates better the teleological principle that governs the whole of the order of the decrees of God, who does everything that he does for a purpose and as an aspect of his one, overarching eternal purpose.

Some may feel that the supralapsarian's vision is lacking in evangelical warmth and not conducive to sincere and earnest gospel preaching. But not a single feature of his vision prohibits the supralapsarian from maintaining with infralapsarian Calvinists everywhere that the redemptive activity of God in Christ—which is the beginning, the center, and the end of all his wisdom, ways, and works—must be central to the church's proclamation as well. He glories in the cross as God's special exhibition of grace to sinful mankind, and he recognizes that the proclamation of the gospel, with the Spirit's enabling blessing, is the God-ordained means of reaching lost sinners for Christ. Just as the apostle who wrote Romans 9 and Ephesians 1 could with no contradiction also declare: "I consider my life worth nothing to me, if only I may finish the race and complete the task the Lord Jesus has given me—the task of testifying to the gospel of God's grace" (Acts 20:24) and could also write: "When I preach the gospel, I cannot boast, for I am compelled to preach. For woe to me if I do not preach the gospel" (1 Cor. 9:16), and "Although I am less than the least of all God's people, this grace was given me: to preach to the Gentiles the unsearchable riches of Christ" (Eph. 3:8), so the supralapsarian knows that the same holy burden to be used of God to reach the lost must be his as well. And far from his doctrine of predestination being an impediment to his carrying out the Great Commission, in concert with the infralapsarian he sees it as the guarantee and surety that his ministry will not be in vain. As he preaches the gospel to people everywhere, he knows that God by his Word and Spirit *will* call his elect unto salvation. Before detractors conclude then that their negative judgment is just, due to some fault in the supralapsarian vision itself, perhaps they should examine themselves to see whether their evaluation may not be due to the fact that they are simply uncomfortable with a soteric vision that places God's sovereignty over the lives and destinies of people so manifestly in the forefront of all of his ways and works with them. No doctrine signalizes the *soli Deo gloria* more and no doctrine humbles proud people more than the supralapsarian vision of predestination. It should not surprise even the saintliest Christian to find his heart reacting at first against it.

But whatever one finally decides about these debates (and they should not become a basis of party strife among Calvinists), if a Christian upon examination should discover—and this is the more serious matter by far—that his dissatisfaction is with the particularism of the entire Calvinistic vision due to the desire for a doctrinal system that allows room for men to contribute in some ultimate and decisive way to their salvation, then it must be said with all charity that he has not yet learned the alphabet of Christianity as the redemptive religion of divine grace.

Before we move on to a consideration of the covenant program of God and the execution of God's eternal plan of salvation in history, it only remains to point out in conclusion that Reformed dogmaticians for the most part (e.g., Louis Berkhof) have come to designate this eternal order of the decrees as the *pactum salutis* or "covenant of redemption" to distinguish it from the concrete, tangible execution in history of the specifically redemptive aspects of the same eternal decree, which they designate the "covenant of grace."[59] There seems to be some justification for this designation (1) in the fact that the persons of the Godhead determined before the foundation of the world what role each would fulfill in the redemption of the elect, and (2) in the words of Hebrews 13:20 where the writer speaks of "the blood of the *eternal covenant* [διαθήκης αἰωνίου, *diathēkēs aiōniou*]."

Some Reformed scholars, it is true, have preferred other designations for the order of the decrees. For example, J. Cocceius spoke of it as the "counsel of peace." Warfield was satisfied to refer to it as "the plan of salvation." Murray preferred the designation, "the inter-trinitarian economy of salvation."[60] The Westminster Confession of Faith speaks of it simply as "God's eternal decree" (see the title of chapter three). But regardless of what term is finally adopted, Murray is surely correct when he writes:

> The truth concerned is all-important. For it is not only proper, it is mandatory that in the plan of salvation as eternally designed and as executed in time, we discover the grandeur of the arrangements of divine wisdom and love on the part of the distinct persons of the Godhead, and recognize the distinguishing prerogatives and functions of each person and the distinct relations we come to sustain to each person as we become the partakers of God's grace. After all, our study of the plan of salvation will not produce abiding fruit unless the plan captivates our devotion to the triune God in the particularity of the grace which each person bestows in the economy of redemption, and in the particularity of relationship constituted by the amazing grace of Father, Son, and Holy Spirit.[61]

---

59. The historical Fall that occurred in accordance with the eternal decree is treated within what Reformed scholars call the "covenant of works." For example, the Westminster Confession of Faith declares: "The first covenant made with man was a covenant of works, wherein life was promised to Adam; and in him to his posterity, upon condition of perfect and personal obedience. Man, by his fall, having made himself incapable of life by that covenant, the Lord was pleased to make a second, commonly called the covenant of grace" (VIII/ii–iii).
60. Murray, "The Plan of Salvation," 130.
61. Ibid., 131.

CHAPTER FOURTEEN

The Unity of the Covenant of Grace

"THE DOCTRINE of the covenants is a peculiarly Reformed doctrine." So writes Geerhardus Vos in his major article, "The Doctrine of the Covenant in Reformed Theology."[1] With the Reformation came a general return to the study of Scripture using grammatical/historical/biblical hermeneutics, and the Swiss Reformers in particular returned to the Bible's root idea of the preeminence of God's glory not only in creation but also in salvation. It was natural then that they would develop the biblical concept of the covenants as the instrumentalities whereby God determined to bring glory to himself by the salvation of the elect through the mediatorial work of his Son and the ministrations of his Spirit and Word. Covenant theology, then, emerged on Swiss soil, particularly in Geneva in Calvin's thought and in Zürich in the writings of Ulrich Zwingli (1484–531), who as a result of his debates with the Anabaptists made the covenant the main argument for the Reformed understanding of infant baptism,[2] and in the sermons of Johann Heinrich Bullinger (1504–1575).[3] In his *Of the One and Eternal Testament or Covenant of God*, the first treatise in church history on the covenant as such, Bullinger argues that the entirety of Scripture must be viewed in light of the Abrahamic covenant in which God graciously offers to give himself to men and in turn requires that men "walk before him and be perfect."

---

1. Geerhardus Vos, "The Doctrine of the Covenant in Reformed Theology," in *Redemptive History and Biblical Interpretation: The Shorter Writings of Geerhardus Vos,* ed. Richard B. Gaffin Jr. (Phillipsburg, N.J.: Presbyterian and Reformed, 1980), 234.
2. The common view that "all things Protestant" originated with Martin Luther is quite wrong. William Cunningham rightly observes:
   > The important movement of which Zwingle might be said to be the originator and the head, was wholly independent of Luther; that is to say, Luther was in no way whatever, directly or indirectly, the cause or the occasion of Zwingle being led to embrace the views

Calvin makes extensive use of the covenant idea in his *Institutes* (see, e.g., II.ix–xi), but because he developed his *Institutes* along Trinitarian lines the covenant concept is not the architectonic or governing principle in that work.[4]

The influence of the Geneva Reformer of French-speaking Switzerland and of the Zürich Reformers of German Switzerland was widespread and lasting. They influenced the Heidelberg theologians, Caspar Olevianus (1536–1587) and Zacharias Ursinus (1534–1583), both men having studied with Calvin in Geneva and both having spent time in Zürich as well. Olevianus later wrote *The Substance of the Covenant of Grace Between God and the Elect* (1585), and Ursinus applied the covenant concept in his Larger Catechism (1612).[5] Their ideas respectively of a precreation covenant between God the Father and God the Son for the salvation of men and of a pre-Fall covenant of law between God and Adam that promised life for perfect obedience and threatened death for disobedience resulted in the developed covenant theology of such men as Johannes Cocceius (1603–1669) in the Netherlands.[6]

The Swiss Reformers also influenced the development of covenant theology in England. Many preachers and scholars had fled to Geneva and Zürich during the reign of Queen Mary, and Calvin and Bullinger had maintained correspondence with them. Accordingly, Robert Rollock and Robert Howie in Scotland, Thomas Cartwright, John Preston, Thomas Blake, and John Ball in England, and James Ussher in Ireland all developed and wrote their theologies along covenantal lines.

---

which he promulgated, or to adopt the course which he pursued. Zwingle had been led to embrace the leading principles of Protestant truth, and to preach them in 1516, the year before the publication of Luther's Theses; and it is quite certain, that all along he continued to think and act for himself, on his own judgement and responsibility, deriving his views from his own personal and independent study of the word of God. This fact shows how inaccurate it is to identify the Reformation with Luther, as if all the Reformers derived their opinions from him, and merely followed his example in abandoning the Church of Rome, and organizing churches apart from her communion. Many at this time, in different parts of Europe, were led to study the sacred Scriptures, and were led further to derive from this study views of divine truth substantially the same, and decidedly opposed to those generally inculcated in the Church of Rome. ("Zwingle, and the Doctrine of the Sacraments," in *The Reformers and the Theology of the Reformation* [1862; reprint, London: Banner of Truth, 1967], 213–14)

3   See Bullinger's *Decades,* five books of ten long sermons each, which were structured entirely by the covenant idea.

4.   Paul Helm marshals evidence in his article "Calvin and the Covenant: Unity and Continuity," *Evangelical Quarterly* 55 (1981): 65–81, to show, however, that all the essential features of covenant theology—the covenant of redemption between the Father and the Son, the covenant of works (in elementary form) between God and Adam, and the covenant of grace between God and the redeemed—have clear roots in Calvin's theology.

5.   See Ursinus's *Larger Catechism,* Questions 1, 2, 9, 19, 20, 86, 131, 147, 223.

6.   See Cocceius's *Doctrine of the Covenant and Testaments of God,* published in 1648.

Bullinger's *Decades* were also translated into English in 1577 and made the official theological guide for clergy who had not obtained a master's degree. Influenced as they were by the labors of these men, the framers of the Westminster Confession of Faith placed the concept of the covenant in the foreground of their confessional deliverances, giving creedal status to the covenant of works and the covenant of grace.[7] About the former the Confession states:

> VII/ii. The first covenant made with man was a covenant of works, wherein life was promised to Adam; and in him to his posterity, upon condition of perfect and personal obedience.

The tangible, concrete expression of the specifically redemptive aspects of God's eternal decree (the *pactum salutis* or "covenant of redemption") in creation history the Westminster divines speak of as the "covenant of grace." Of this covenant the Westminster Confession of Faith says the following:

> VII/iii: Man, by his fall, having made himself incapable of life by [the first covenant], the Lord was pleased to make a second, commonly called the covenant of grace;[8] wherein He freely offereth unto sinners life and salvation by Jesus Christ;

---

7. This does not mean that covenant theology is simply "manmade" and appeared on the scene for the first time during the Reformation. The Swiss Reformers knew the early patristic literature well, citing the early fathers extensively, and they found in them many nuances of covenant theology. After the age of Augustine biblical study languished, and as a result the church fathers failed to develop covenant theology. But Vos has rightly noted that once the Reformers turned the church back to a study of Scripture and insisted that God should receive the preeminence in all things, particularly with respect to man and his relation to God,

> [this principle] immediately divides into three parts: 1. All of man's work has to rest on an antecedent work of God; 2. In all of his works man has to show forth God's image and be a means for the revelation of God's virtues; 3. The latter should not occur unconsciously or passively, but the revelation of God's virtues must proceed by way of understanding and will and by way of the conscious life, and actively come to external expression. ("The Doctrine of the Covenant," 242)

> Vos then proceeds to show how this threefold demand was addressed in the doctrine of the covenant, with the eternal *covenant of redemption* becoming the resting place for all three requirements; and the *covenant of works* and the *covenant of grace*, which flows out of the covenant of redemption, each in its own way fulfilling the demands of all three parts. See Vos, "The Doctrine of the Covenant," 242–67. See also Donald Macleod, "Covenant Theology," in *Dictionary of Scottish Church History and Theology*, ed. Nigel M. de S. Cameron (Downers Grove, Ill.: InterVarsity Press, 1993), 214–18, for an excellent overview of the historical development of covenant theology.

8. The New Covenant, while it is for the elect sinner a "covenant of grace," was for Christ, the Mediator and Head of the covenant, the original "covenant of works," requiring of him

requiring of them faith in Him, that they may be saved, and promising to give unto all those that are ordained unto eternal life His Holy Spirit, to make them willing, and able to believe.

Without using the following phrase in so many words, the Westminster Confession of Faith then clearly asserts "the unity of the covenant of grace and the oneness of the people of God in all ages":

> VII/v: *This covenant* was differently administered in the time of the law, and in the time of the gospel: *under the law*, it was administered by promises, prophecies, sacrifices, circumcision, the paschal lamb, and other types and ordinances delivered to the people of the Jews, *all foresignifying Christ to come*; which were, for that time, sufficient and efficacious, through the operation of the Spirit, *to instruct and build up the elect in faith in the promised Messiah,* by whom they had full remission of sins, and eternal salvation; and is called the Old Testament. (emphasis supplied)
> VII/vi: *Under the gospel,* when Christ, the substance was exhibited, the ordinances in which *this covenant* is dispensed are the preaching of the Word, and the administration of the sacraments of Baptism and the Lord's Supper: which, though fewer in number, and administered with more simplicity, and less outward glory, yet, in them, it is held forth in more fulness, evidence, and spiritual efficacy, to all nations, both Jews and Gentiles; and is called the New Testament. *There are not therefore two covenants of grace, differing in substance, but one and the same, under various dispensations.* (emphases supplied)

These descriptions of the covenant of grace expressly make the point that the covenant is one, the covenant after the cross simply being administered (to employ the terms to describe the two administrations as such which are used specifically to describe their respective sacraments) with "more simplicity," "less outward glory," and more fulness, evidence, and spiritual efficacy to all nations. It also underscores the truth that the earlier administration's "promises, prophecies, sacrifices, circumcision, the paschal lamb, and other types and ordinances" all pointed forward to Christ, and were sufficient and efficacious, through the Spirit's operation, to "instruct and build up the elect in faith in *the promised Messiah."* The Westminster Confession of Faith makes this same point later, albeit in a more directly soteric setting and in different words, when it declares:

> Although the work of redemption was not actually wrought by Christ till after His incarnation, yet the virtue, efficacy, and benefits thereof were communicated

---

personal, perfect, and perpetual obedience. As the "last Adam" and "second Man from heaven" (1 Cor. 15:45, 47), he perfectly met the obligations of the covenant of works.

unto the elect, in all ages successively from the beginning of the world, *in and by those promises, types, and sacrifices, wherein He was revealed,* and signified to be the seed of the woman which should bruise the serpent's head; and the Lamb slain from the beginning of the world; being yesterday and today the same, and forever. (VIII/vi, emphasis supplied)

While the influence of the work of the Westminster Assembly was short-lived in England itself, being stifled by the restoration of Charles II to the English throne in 1660, its Confession of Faith and Catechisms were adopted by the Church of Scotland and later by the Presbyterian churches in colonial America. Through these churches the covenant theology of the Assembly has since the 1640s had a growing influence over Protestant theology in general around the world, even in churches which have never formally adopted the Westminster Confession of Faith and Catechisms as their own.

Over against the Westminster representation of the covenant of grace as being one in all ages, through the execution of which is created the one people of God—the church of Jesus Christ—comprising all the elect in all ages, stands the dispensational school's interpretation of salvific history. Classic dispensational scholars uniformly define a dispensation as "a period of time during which man is tested in respect of obedience to some specific revelation of the will of God."[9] For example, Charles C. Ryrie defines a dispensation as "a distinguishable economy in the outworking of God's program" for the world viewed as a household, during which "distinguishable economy" man is responsible "to the particular revelation given at the time."[10] Since these scholars differ widely among themselves over how many such dispensations there are (the *Scofield Reference Bible* finds seven: innocence, conscience, human government, promise, law, grace, and kingdom) and how the Scripture material is correspondingly to be divided between them, it is not possible to present here one dispensational scheme that would represent the opinion of every dispensationalist. But such a list is not necessary since, regardless of which particular scheme a given dispensational scholar may espouse, all would agree with the Doctrinal Statement of Dallas Theological Seminary, the leading dispensational seminary in the United States if not in the world, that

three of these dispensations or rules of life are the subject of extended revelation in the Scriptures, viz., the dispensation of the Mosaic law, the present dispensation of grace, and the future dispensation of the millennial kingdom.

---

9. See note on Genesis 1:28 in both the *Scofield Reference Bible* and the *New Scofield Reference Bible.*
10. Charles C. Ryrie, "Dispensation, Dispensationalism," *Evangelical Dictionary of Theology,* ed. Walter A. Elwell (Grand Rapids, Mich.: Baker, 1984), 322.

Of these three dispensations, the Doctrinal Statement immediately affirms: "We believe that these are distinct and are not to be intermingled or confused, as they are chronologically successive." And while the Doctrinal Statement affirms that "salvation in the divine reckoning is always 'by grace through faith,' and rests upon the basis of the shed blood of Christ," it qualifies this affirmation by declaring

> that it was historically impossible that [Old Testament saints] should have had as the conscious object of their faith the incarnate, crucified Son, the Lamb of God (John 1:29), and that it is evident that they did not comprehend as we do that the sacrifices depicted the person and work of Christ [and] that they did not understand the redemptive significance of the prophecies and types concerning the sufferings of Christ (1 Pet. 1:10–12); therefore, we believe that their faith toward God was manifested in other ways as is shown by the long record in Hebrews 11:1–40 [which manifested faith was] counted unto them for righteousness.

Thus according to classic dispensational teaching, while Old Testament saints (including Moses, David, Isaiah, and all the other great prophets) were saved by grace through faith, they were not saved through a conscious faith in a *suffering* Christ, since (1) "it was historically impossible that they should have had as the conscious object of their faith the incarnate, crucified Son, the Lamb of God," (2) "they did not comprehend . . . that the sacrifices depicted the person and work of Christ," and (3) "they did not understand the redemptive significance of the prophecies and types concerning the sufferings of Christ."

The Doctrinal Statement does not clearly explain why these three things were historically impossible for Old Testament saints, but the *New Scofield Reference Bible* (1967), as did the original *Scofield Reference Bible* before it (1917), provides us with the standard dispensational explanation when it comments on Jesus' proclamation in Matthew 4:17, "Repent, for the kingdom of heaven is at hand":

> The Bible expression "at hand" is never a positive affirmation that the person or thing said to be at hand will immediately appear, but only that *no known or predicted event* must intervene. When Christ appeared to the Jewish people, the next thing, in the order of revelation as it then stood, should have been the setting up of the Davidic kingdom. In the knowledge of God, *not yet disclosed,* lay the rejection of the kingdom and the King, the long period of the mystery-form of the kingdom, the world-wide preaching of the cross, and the out-calling of the Church. But *this was as yet locked up in the secret counsels of God* (Mt.13:11,17; Eph.3:3–12).[11]

---

11. *New Scofield Reference Bible,* 996, emphases supplied.

The Dallas Seminary Doctrinal Statement makes essentially the same point in only somewhat different language when it states: "*in fulfillment of prophecy* [see Scofield's phrase above, "in the order of revelation as it then stood"] [the eternal Son of God] came first to Israel as her Messiah-King, and . . . being rejected of that nation, He, *according to the eternal counsels of God* [see Scofield's phrase, "locked up in the secret counsels of God"], gave His life as a ransom for all" (emphases supplied).

Of course, if no one before the time of Jesus' public ministry knew about the rejection of the Messiah, this present age, the worldwide proclamation of the cross, or the outcalling of the church, because God had disclosed none of these things to men before that time, then the faith of the Old Testament saint could not have been directed toward the person and work of the *suffering* Christ as its saving object. But this has not been the historic confession of the church, which has not hesitated to sing:

> In the cross of Christ I glory,
>   Towering o'er the wrecks of time;
> All the light of sacred story
>   Gathers round its head sublime.

It is difficult to conceive of two evangelical perspectives on Old Testament faith differing more radically. The covenantal perspective stresses the unity and continuity of redemptive history; the dispensational perspective stresses the discontinuity of redemptive history. The former insists that Old Testament saints were saved through conscious faith in the future, anticipated sacrificial work of the promised Messiah in their behalf. The latter insists, since Old Testament saints *did not know* about his future sacrificial work because God had not revealed it to them, that they were saved through a general "faith toward God . . . manifested in other ways." In these regards these two theological systems are mutually exclusive. One may be pardoned if he were to conclude then that these two views advocate *different* Old Testament plans of salvation, the *former* insisting upon the necessity of faith in the person and sacrificial work of the coming Messiah for salvation, the *latter* insisting upon the necessity of a faith in God for salvation that was actually devoid of any conscious awareness that "without the shedding of [Messiah's] blood there is no forgiveness" (Heb. 9:22). But this means, since dispensational scholars happily affirm that the New Testament saint believes unto salvation with a faith which has precisely Messiah's death work as its saving object, that, from the perspective of the saints before and the saints after the cross, there are *at least two* different plans of salvation in Scripture.

I say "*at least two* different plans of salvation" because dispensational scholars actually insist that Old Testament saving faith in God was manifested in "different *ways,*" depending on the dispensation, and to prove the point they refer to the "long record in Hebrews 11:1–40." And they insist that the clearest examples of two different "ways of faith" in the Old Testament record itself by which God related himself to men is, *first,* the "dispensation of promise," lived out under the terms of the Abrahamic covenant, which dispensation came to an end when Abraham's descendants "rashly accepted the law" at Sinai and "exchanged grace for law,"[12] and, *second,* the immediately following "dispensation of law" during which God's "point of testing" the nation of Israel with respect to the issue of their "faith in him" was (1) "legal obedience as the condition of salvation"[13] and (2) a future hope that looked forward to the coming of the Messiah, not as a suffering Savior, but as a conquering Davidic king. According to dispensational teaching, the Messiah as a suffering Savior could not have been a proper object of faith for Israel, just as he as Israel's King "could be no proper object of faith to the Gentiles."[14] In other words, the Mosaic age was a time period during which God expressly *excluded* faith in the Messiah's death as "a proper object of faith"! Accordingly, dispensational scholars teach that the saved of the Mosaic age (Israel "under law") are the earthly people of God bound for one blessed destiny, while the saved of this age (the church "under grace") are the heavenly people of God bound for another blessed destiny. As Ryrie forthrightly affirms in the same article referred to above, dispensationalists

> distinguish God's program for Israel from his program for the church. Thus the church did not begin in the OT but on the day of Pentecost, and the church is not

---

12. *Scofield Reference Bible* (SRB), note on Genesis 12:1. The *New Scofield Reference Bible* (NSRB) does not say this, but it still insists that "as a specific test of Israel's stewardship of divine truth, the dispensation of Promise was superseded, though not annulled, by the law that was given at Sinai" (note on Gen. 12:1). And the NSRB still declares at Exodus 19:5, as did the SRB, "What under law was conditional is, under grace, freely given to every believer. The 'if' of v.5 is the essence of law as a method of divine dealing. . . . To Abraham the promise preceded the requirement; at Sinai the requirement preceded the promise. In the New Covenant the Abrahamic order is followed." But what do such statements mean if they do not mean that under the law, "requirement" (legal obedience) was the condition of the promise of salvation?
13. *Scofield Reference Bible,* note on John 1:17.
14. *Scofield Reference Bible,* note on John 12:23: "A Christ in the flesh, King of the Jews, could be no proper object of faith to the Gentiles, though the Jews should have believed on Him as such. For Gentiles[!] the corn of wheat must fall into the ground and die; Christ must be lifted up on the cross and believed in as a sacrifice for sin, as Seed of Abraham, not David."
15. Ryrie, "Dispensation, Dispensationalism," 322. Using Ryrie, the SRB and the NSRB as I have, I have described what would be generally regarded as the "classic" depiction of dispensationalism (though Darrell L. Bock refers to Ryrie's dispensational vision as a "revised" version of classic dispensationalism).

presently fulfilling promises made to Israel in the OT that have not yet been fulfilled.[15]

Two distinct ages with two distinct contents of faith, and as a result two distinct peoples of God with two distinct destinies, with these two ages and two peoples never to be "intermingled or confused, as they are chronologically successive," lest one fall into the error of "Galatianism" (the intermingling of law and grace, works and faith, which Paul vehemently condemned in his letter to the Galatian churches)—this is the dispensational understanding of the relationship between Old Testament Israel and the New Testament church.[16]

It should be plain from this summary of its interpretation of the Mosaic period and the relationship between that period and this present age that the dispensational school self-consciously repudiates the *unity* of the covenant of grace and the *oneness* of the people of God in all ages. Consequently, it should be equally plain, if the Confession of Faith is right, that dispensationalism is wrong, and if dispensationalism is right, then the Confession of Faith is wrong. I would suggest that the following five lines of argument place beyond all reasonable doubt the Westminster position.

There is a movement today within dispensational circles, termed by its proponents as "progressive dispensationalism," which denies the "offer, rejection, postponement and only-*future*-fulfillment of the kingdom" motif of classic dispensationalism and declares to the contrary that the church is fulfilling spiritual promises made to Old Testament Israel. In short, these dispensationalists place more emphasis on the continuities between the dispensations than did the "classical" dispensationalists. See Robert L. Saucy, *The Case for Progressive Dispensationalism* (Grand Rapids: Zondervan, 1993), and Craig A. Blaising and Darrell L. Bock, *Progressive Dispensationalism* (Wheaton: Victor, 1993).

No one can say, of course, whether "progressive dispensationalism" with its implicit rejection of classic dispensationalism's "keystone" doctrine, namely, its rigid separation of Israel and the church, will forever remain dispensationalism and not become a form of covenant premillennialism (see Walter A. Elwell's assessment, "Dispensationalists of the Third Kind," *Christianity Today* 38/10 [September 12, 1994] p. 28: "The newer [progressive] dispensationalism looks so much like nondispensationalist premillennialism that one struggles to see any real difference."). But at the present time "progressive dispensationalism" is still clearly dispensational in its commitment and declarations and is in no sense covenantal. Al Mawhinney got it right when he commented: "The authors [of *Progressive Dispensationalism*] are not covenant theologians in sheep's clothing. ...They are pursuing significant change within their own tradition."

16. Modern dispensationalists debate among themselves regarding dispensationalism's "basic principle." Most would insist that the first tenet of dispensationalism is that the Bible must be interpreted literally and its meaning must not be "spiritualized." The question arises: Why must the Bible be so interpreted? I suggest that this is the only hermeneutic that allows dispensationalists to draw their needed distinction between Israel and the church, and that behind this distinction, which views Israel as "under law" and the church as "under grace," is the still more ultimate concern to avoid the heresy of Galatianism, that is, the intermingling of law and grace.

FIVE ARGUMENTS FOR THE UNITY OF THE COVENANT OF GRACE

A. Once the covenant of grace had come to expression in the spiritual promises of the Abrahamic covenant, the Abrahamic covenant became salvifically definitive for all ages to come.

Immediately after Adam's tragic transgression of the "covenant of works," which had been sovereignly imposed upon him by his Creator (Gen. 3:1–7; see Hos. 6:7), in the hearing of Adam God said to the serpent, and by extension to Satan himself: "I will put enmity between you and the woman, and between your offspring and hers; he will crush your head, and you will strike his heel" (Gen. 3:15). Theologians have long recognized in these words both the inauguration of the "covenant of grace" and God's first gracious promise to men of salvation from sin. Not without good reason then has this divine promise been designated the "first gospel proclamation" (*protevangelium*). The promise is given in "seed-form," true enough, but God clearly stated that someone out of the human race itself ("the woman's seed"), although fatally wounded in the conflict, would destroy the serpent (Satan).

In accord with this promise, God extended grace to certain antediluvian descendants of Adam, for example, to Abel (Gen. 4:4; Heb. 11:4), to Enoch (Gen. 5:22–23; Heb. 11:5), and to Noah (Gen. 6:8–9; see "my covenant" in 6:18)[17] and to Noah's family (Gen. 6–8). But this period between the Fall and the flood, it must be acknowledged, saw only a minimal demonstration of restraining and saving grace, as evidenced by the fact that the human race came to moral ruin and was judged. This was doubtless in order that the true nature of sin might be disclosed.[18] Nor was the situation much different during the postdiluvian age prior to the call of Abraham. There is some indication of the operations of special or redemptive grace in this period of human history, such as the identity of Yahweh as "the God of Shem" and the implicit promise of divine grace to the descendants of Japheth, who would "dwell in the tents of Shem" (9:26–27), but again the main feature of this period is the divine judgment in the form of the confusion of tongues at Babel (Gen. 11:1–11) and the consequent dispersion of the postdiluvian people over the face of the earth (Gen. 10) as punishment for the race's manifest expression of pride (Gen. 11:4). Human moral declension in this period again underscored sin's power to corrupt. In sum, the two emphases of the first eleven chapters of Genesis are the pervasive fact and power of human sinfulness and God's holy recoil against sin in every form. And

---

17. Although the word "covenant" occurs for the first time in Genesis 6:18, the fact that it occurs with the pronominal suffix and the Hiphil form of the verb קוּם, *qûm*, "establish," rather than כָּרַת, *kārat*, "cut, make," suggests that this covenant was not first made in Noah's day but rather was already in existence and was being extended into the Noahic Age.
18. See Geerhardus Vos, *Biblical Theology* (Grand Rapids, Mich.: Eerdmans, 1954), 56.

while we see evidences of the divine operations of salvific grace in accordance with the covenant of grace, it is equally true that we see it only minimally displayed.

But with the call of Abraham, the covenant of grace underwent a remarkable advance, definitive for all time to come. The instrument of that advance is the covenant which God made with Abraham which guaranteed and secured soteric blessing for "all the families of the earth." So significant are the promises of grace in the Abrahamic covenant, found in Genesis 12:1–3; 13:14–16; 15:18–21; 17:1–16; 22:16–18, that it is not an overstatement to declare these verses, from the covenantal perspective, as the most important verses in the Bible. The fact that the Bible sweeps across the thousands of years between the creation of man and Abraham in only eleven chapters, with the call of Abraham coming in Genesis 12, suggests that the information given in the first eleven chapters of the Bible was intended as preparatory "background" to the revelation of the Abrahamic covenant. Revelation subsequent to it discloses that *all that God has done savingly in grace since the revelation of the Abrahamic covenant is the result and product of it.* In other words, once the covenant of grace had come to expression in the salvific promises of the Abrahamic covenant—that God would be the God of Abraham and his descendants (17:7), and that in Abraham all the nations of the earth would be blessed (12:3; see Rom. 4:13)—*everything that God has done since to the present moment he has done in order to fulfill his covenant to Abraham (and thus his eternal plan of redemption).* This suggests that the divine execution of the soteric program envisioned in the covenant of grace, from Genesis 12 onward, should be viewed in terms of the salvific promises contained in the Abrahamic covenant.[19] This line of evidence demonstrates the unity of the covenant of grace from Genesis 3 to the farthest reaches of the future.

---

19. Undoubtedly, temporal, earthly, promises of a land were given to Abraham and his descendants in the Abrahamic covenant (Gen. 13:15; 15:18; 17:8). But the land promises were never primary and central to the covenant intention, and a literal and complete fulfillment of these promises under Old Testament conditions was never envisioned by God. Rather, the fulfillment of the land promises must be viewed as arising from the more basic and essential soteric promises, and for their fulfillment they will have to await the final and complete salvation of God's elect in the Eschaton (Rom. 8:19–23).

I say this because the Bible declares that Abraham dwelt in the Old Testament land of promise "as in a foreign country, dwelling in tents" (Heb. 11:9) and never possessed it (Acts 7:25), since, as with so many other of God's promises made during the "shadow" days of Old Testament *Heilsgeschichte* (Col. 2:17), he looked forward to this promise's final fulfillment, in the "substance" days of New Testament *Heilsgeschichte,* that is, in the new heaven and new earth of the Eschaton, whose country "is a better one, that is, a heavenly one" (Heb. 11:16), whose "city [the redeemed church; Rev. 21:9–27] has foundations, whose builder and maker is God" (Heb. 11:10), and in which he would be "the heir of the world" (Rom. 4:13).

O. Palmer Robertson, in his *Understanding the Land of the Bible* (Phillipsburg, N.J.: Presbyterian and Reformed, 1996), 7–13, provides a short but helpful study of the land concept in Scripture:

If this representation of the salvific significance of the Abrahamic covenant for the unity of the covenant of grace seems to be an overstatement, the following declarations from later divine revelation should suffice to justify it:

1. It is the Abrahamic covenant and none other that God later confirmed with Isaac (Gen. 17:19; 26:3–4) and with Jacob (Gen. 28:13–15; 35:12).

"Land" as a factor of theological significance begins with "Paradise." . . . In this "land" called "Paradise" man could serve his God and find meaningful purpose for life.

As a consequence of [Adam's rebellion], the first man and woman found themselves ejected from this land of bliss. . . .

But a divine promise gave [fallen man] hope. There was a "land," a land flowing with milk and honey. Somewhere ahead of him he would find it, for God had purposed to redeem man . . . , to restore him to the land of blessing he had lost.

This glimpse of hope found concrete expression in the promise given to Abraham. As a supreme act of faith, the Patriarch abandoned the land of his fathers and became a wandering stranger, always on the move toward a "land" that God had promised.

Abraham arrived at the land but never possessed it . . . he died owning no more than a family burial plot (Gen. 23:17–20). His whole life-experience forced him to look beyond the present temporal circumstances in which he lived to "the city which has foundations, whose builder and maker is God" (Heb. 11:10, NKJV).

. . . Moses and his contemporaries wandered in the wilderness of Sinai for forty years, and Moses died in faith, not having received the promise (Heb. 11:39).

Under Joshua's general leadership the people conquered the land, receiving in a limited fashion the paradise God had promised. But it quickly became obvious that this territory could not be the ultimate paradise. Undefeated Canaanites remained as "hornets." . . . [And because of Israel's sin throughout the monarchy period, finally] the land was devastated, the people banished. Persistently disregarding God's laws, they came to be known as *lo-ammi*, meaning "not-my-people" (Hos. 1:9). The fruitful land took on the appearance of a desert, a dwelling place of jackals, owls, and scorpions. . . . Paradise, even in its old covenant shadow form, was taken from them.

[Even the restoration of the "second commonwealth"] could not be paradise. But the return to "the land" and the rebuilding of the temple point the way. . . . The glory of this tiny temple would be greater than Solomon's grand structure, and the wealth of all nations would flow to it (Hag. 2:9).

All this hyperbolic language—what could it mean?

It meant that God had something better. . . . The promise of the land would be fulfilled by nothing less than a restored paradise. As Isaiah had predicted earlier, the wolf would lie down with the lamb, and a little child would lead them (Isa. 11:6). No more would sin and sorrow reign, nor thorns infest the ground.

When the Christ actually came, the biblical perspective on the "land" experienced radical revision. . . . By inaugurating his public ministry in Galilee of the Gentiles along a public trade route, Jesus was making a statement. This land would serve as a springboard to all nations. The kingdom of God [the central theme of Jesus' teaching] encompassed a realm that extended well beyond the borders of ancient Israel. As Paul so pointedly indicates, Abraham's promise from a new covenant perspective meant that he would be heir of the cosmos (Rom. 4:13).

2. God redeemed Jacob's descendants from Egypt (which redemptive act is *the* Old Testament type of New Testament redemption in Christ) in order to keep his covenant promise to Abraham: "God heard their groanings and he remembered his covenant with Abraham, with Isaac, and with Jacob" (Exod. 2:24; see 4:5).

3. Again and again throughout Israel's history in Old Testament times, the inspired authors trace God's continuing extension of divine grace and mercy to Israel directly to his faithfulness to his covenant promises to Abraham:

> Exodus 32:12–14: "'Turn from your fierce anger; relent and do not bring disaster on your people. Remember your servants Abraham, Isaac and Israel, to whom you swore by your own self. . . .' Then the Lord relented and did not bring on his people the disaster he had threatened."
>
> Exodus 33:1 (said immediately after the golden calf incident): "Leave this place . . . and go up to the land I promised on oath to Abraham, Isaac and Jacob, saying, 'I will give it to your descendants.'"
>
> Leviticus 26:42: "I will remember my covenant with Jacob and my covenant with Isaac and my covenant with Abraham."
>
> Deuteronomy 1:8: "Go in and take possession of the land that the Lord swore he would give to your fathers—to Abraham, Isaac, and Jacob."
>
> Deuteronomy 4:31: "For the Lord your God is a merciful God; he will not abandon or destroy you or forget the covenant with your forefathers, which he confirmed to them by oath." (See Deut. 4:37)
>
> Deuteronomy 7:8: "But it was because the Lord . . . kept the oath he swore to your forefathers that he brought you out with a mighty hand and redeemed you from the land of slavery." (See Deut. 9:5; 10:15)
>
> Deuteronomy 9:27: "Remember your servants Abraham, Isaac, and Jacob. Overlook the stubbornness of this people, their wickedness and their sin."
>
> Deuteronomy 29:12–13: "You are standing here in order to enter into a covenant with the Lord your God, a covenant the Lord is making with you this day and sealing it with an oath, to confirm you this day as his people, that he may be your God as he promised you and as he swore to your fathers, Abraham, Isaac and Jacob."

The radical implications of Jesus' pointing his ministry toward the whole of the world rather than confining himself to the land of Canaan need to be appreciated fully. By setting this perspective on his ministry, Jesus cleared the way for the old covenant "type" to be replaced by the new covenant "antitype." The imagery of a return to a "land" flowing with milk and honey was refocused on a rejuvenation that would embrace the whole of God's created order. It was not just Canaan that would benefit in the establishment of the kingdom of the Messiah. The whole cosmos would rejoice in the renewal brought about by this newness of life.

Joshua 21:44: "The Lord gave them rest on every side, just as he had sworn to their forefathers."

Joshua 24:3–4: "I took your father Abraham from the land beyond the River and led him throughout Canaan and gave him many descendants. I gave him Isaac, and to Isaac I gave Jacob and Esau."

Psalm 105:8–10, 42–43: "He remembers his covenant forever . . . , the covenant he made with Abraham, the oath he swore to Isaac. He confirmed it to Jacob as a decree, to Israel as an everlasting covenant. . . . For he remembered his holy promise given to his servant Abraham. He brought out his people with rejoicing, his chosen ones with shouts of joy."

2 Kings 13:23: "But the Lord was gracious to them and had compassion and showed concern for them because of his covenant with Abraham, Isaac and Jacob. To this day he has been unwilling to banish them from his presence."

1 Chronicles 16:15–17: "He remembers his covenant forever, the word he commanded, for a thousand generations, the covenant he made with Abraham, the oath he swore to Isaac. He confirmed it to Jacob as a decree, to Israel as an everlasting covenant."

Micah 7:20: "You will be true to Jacob, and show mercy to Abraham, as you pledged on oath to our fathers in days long ago."

Nehemiah 9:7–8: "You are the Lord God, who chose Abram and brought him out of Ur of the Chaldeans and named him Abraham. You found his heart faithful to you, and you made a covenant with him. . . . You have kept your promise because you are faithful."

4. Both Mary and Zechariah declared the first advent of Jesus Christ, including the very act of the Incarnation itself, to be a vital constituent part of the fulfillment of God's gracious covenant promise to Abraham:

Luke 1:54–55: "He has helped his servant Israel, remembering to be merciful to Abraham and his descendants forever, even as he said to our fathers."

Luke 1:68–73: "Praise be to the Lord, the God of Israel, because he has come . . . to remember his holy covenant, the oath he swore to our father Abraham."

It should be noted in passing that, whereas Christians today mainly only celebrate the Incarnation of God's Son at Christmas time, Mary and Zechariah, placing this event in its covenant context, saw reason in his coming to celebrate the *covenant faithfulness* of God to his people. In their awareness of the broader significance of the event and the words of praise which that awareness evoked from them we see biblical theology at its best being worked out and expressed!

THE UNITY OF THE COVENANT OF GRACE

5. Jesus, himself the Seed of Abraham (Matt. 1:1; Gal. 3:16), declared that Abraham "rejoiced at the thought of seeing my day; he saw it and was glad" (John 8:56).

6. Peter declared that God sent Jesus to bless the Jewish nation in keeping with the promise he gave to Abraham in Genesis 12:3, in turning them away from their iniquities (Acts 3:25–26).

7. Paul declared that God, when he promised Abraham that "all peoples on earth will be blessed through you" (Gen. 12:3), was declaring that he was going to justify the Gentiles by faith and was announcing the gospel in advance to Abraham (Gal. 3:8). Accordingly, he states that *all* believers "are blessed [by justification] along with Abraham" (Gal. 3:9).

8. Paul also declared that "Christ became [γεγενῆσθαι, *gegenēsthai*] a Servant of the circumcision ... in order to confirm [εἰς τὸ βεβαιῶσαι, *eis to bebaiōsai*] the promises made to the patriarchs so that the Gentiles might glorify God for his mercy" (Rom. 15:8–9).

9. Paul further declared that Christ died on the cross, bearing the law's curse, "*in order that* [ἵνα, *hina*] the blessing given to Abraham might come to the Gentiles in Christ Jesus, *in order that* [ἵνα, *hina*] we [that is, Jews and Gentiles] might receive the promise of the Spirit through faith" (Gal. 3:13–14). The two ἵνα, *hina*, clauses are coordinate, the latter an elaboration of the first. God, having delivered his covenant people among the Jews from the curse of the law through Christ's cross work, by that same cross work is free to deal likewise in grace with the Gentiles, with both Jew and Gentile receiving the promised Spirit through faith.

10. Paul expressly declared also that the Mosaic law, introduced several centuries after God gave his covenant promises to Abraham and to his Seed (Christ), "does not set aside the covenant previously established by God [with Abraham] and thus do away with the promise" (Gal. 3:16–17).

11. Paul also declared (1) that Abraham is the "father of all who believe" among both Jews and Gentiles (Rom. 4:11–12), and (2) that all who belong to Christ "are Abraham's seed, and heirs according to the promise" which God gave to Abraham (Gal. 3:29).

12. Finally, Christ described the future state of glory in terms of the redeemed "taking their place at the feast with Abraham, Isaac, and Jacob in the kingdom of heaven" (Matt. 8:11).

These passages of Scripture make it clear that the promises of God, covenantally given to Abraham, that he would be the God of Abraham and of his (spiritual) descendants after him forever (Gen. 17:7–8) extend temporally to the farthest reaches of the future and include within their compass the entire community of the redeemed. This is just to say that the Abrahamic covenant, in the specific prospect it holds forth of the salvation of the entire church of God, is identical with the

[517]

soteric program of the covenant of grace, indeed, is identical with the covenant of grace itself. It also means specifically that the blessings of the covenant of grace which believers enjoy today under the sanctions of the New Testament economy are founded upon the covenant which God made with Abraham. Said another way, the "new covenant" itself is simply the administrative "extension and unfolding of the Abrahamic covenant."[20] Thus the temporal and spiritual reach of the Abrahamic covenant establishes and secures the organic unity and continuity of the one church of God composed of the people of God living both before and after the cross.

B. The exodus from Egypt—the Old Testament type *par excellence* of biblical redemption—by divine arrangement exhibited the same great salvific principles which governed Christ's work of atonement, both in its accomplished and applied aspects, in the New Testament, thereby teaching the elect in Israel about salvation by grace through faith in the atoning work of Messiah's mediation.

As a major feature of the Old Testament ground for the truth that "everything that was written in the past was written to teach us" (Rom. 15:4; see 1 Cor. 10:1–11, where Paul employs the exodus and certain subsequent wilderness events for this pastoral purpose), the great exodus redemption of the people of God from Egypt (and Moses' inspired record of it) communicated God's redemptive ways to his Old Testament people as it would do later to us, his New Testament people.

That it is not reading too much into the event of the exodus to characterize it as a *redemptive* event is borne out by the fact that the biblical text represents it precisely that way:

> Exodus 6:6: "I will free you from being slaves to them, and I will redeem [וְגָאַלְתִּי, *wᵉgāʾaltî*] you with an outstretched arm and with mighty acts of judgment."
>
> Exodus 15:13: "In your unfailing love you will lead the people you have redeemed [גָּאַלְתָּ, *gāʾaltā*]."
>
> Deuteronomy 7:8: "But it was because the Lord loved you . . . that he brought you out with a mighty hand and redeemed [וַיִּפְדְּךָ, *wayyipdᵉkā*] you from the land of slavery."
>
> Deuteronomy 9:26: "O Sovereign Lord, do not destroy your people, your own inheritance, that you redeemed [פָּדִיתָ, *pādîtā*] by your great power and brought out of Egypt with a mighty hand."

The exodus is also described as "Yahweh's salvation" (יְשׁוּעַת יהוה, *yᵉšûʿat yhwh*, Exod. 14:13), Moses also writing: "That day the Lord saved [וַיּוֹשַׁע, *wayyôšaʿ*] Israel

---

20. John Murray, *Christian Baptism* (Philadelphia: Presbyterian and Reformed, 1962), 46.

from the hands of the Egyptians." (Exod. 14:30). Later Stephen applied the title "redeemer" (λυτρωτής, *lytrōtēs*) to Moses, a type of Christ (Acts 7:35).

Far from their becoming after Sinai a nation living under divinely imposed constraints of *legalism,* the people of the Mosaic theocracy, having been delivered from their slavery as the result of the great redemptive activity of God in the exodus event, became God's "treasured possession," "a kingdom of priests and a holy nation" (Exod. 19:5–6; Deut. 7:6) in order to "declare the praises of him who brought them out of darkness into his marvelous light" (see 1 Pet. 2:9). In the exodus God revealed the following four great salvific principles that regulate all true salvation, taught Israel about faith in Christ, and bind the "soteriologies" of the Old and New Testaments indissolubly together into one "great salvation."

1. The exodus redemption, in both purpose and execution, originated in the sovereign, loving, electing grace of God. This principle is expressly affirmed in Deuteronomy 7:6–8:

> You are a people holy to the Lord your God. The Lord your God *has chosen you* out of all the peoples on the face of the earth to be his people, his treasured possession. The Lord did not set his affection on you and *choose* you because you were more numerous than other peoples, for you were the fewest of all peoples. But it was because the Lord *loved* you and kept the oath he swore to your forefathers [which oath itself was grounded in sovereign electing grace—Heb. 6:13–18] that he brought you out with a mighty hand and *redeemed* you from the land of slavery, from the power of Pharaoh king of Egypt. (emphases supplied)

And it is implied in God's description of the nation as his "firstborn son" in Exodus 4:22–23 (see Deut. 14:1; Isa. 1:2–3; 43:6; 63:16; 64:8; Jer. 3:4; 31:9; Hos. 11:1; Mal. 1:6; 2:10), sonship from the very nature of the case being *nonmeritorious* and all the more so since Israel's sonship was not sonship by nature (only God the Son is a Son of God by nature) but by adoption (Rom. 9:4).

In actual execution of the exodus it is highly significant that there was little religious or moral difference between the nation of Egypt and Jacob's descendants in Egypt: both peoples being *idolatrous* (Exod. 12:12; Josh. 24:14; Ezek. 23:8, 19, 21; but see Deut. 26:7 for evidence that a "remnant" still worshiped Yahweh) and *sinful* (Deut. 9:6–7). Accordingly, it was God himself who had to "make a distinction" between the Egyptians and the Israelites (Exod. 8:22–23; 9:4, 25–26; 10:22–23; 11:7).

2. The exodus redemption was accomplished by God's almighty power and not by the strength of man (Exod. 3:19–20). Every detail of the exodus event was divinely arranged to highlight the great salvific truth that it is God who must save his people because they are incapable of saving themselves. God permitted Moses to attempt Israel's deliverance at first by his own strategy and in his own strength, and

allowed him to fail (Exod. 2:11–15; Acts 7:23–29). Then he sent Moses back to Egypt with the staff of God in his hand to "perform miraculous signs with it" (Exod. 4:17). God himself promised, precisely in order to "multiply" his signs that he might place *his* power in the boldest possible relief and this in order that both Egypt and Israel would learn that he is God, that he would harden Pharaoh's heart throughout the course of the plagues, and he did so (Exod. 7:3; 10:1–2; 11:9; see Rom. 9:17). And the Song of Moses in Exodus 15 has as its single theme the extolling of God for his mighty power to save. There should have been no doubt in anyone's mind after the event whose power had effected Israel's redemption.

3. The exodus redemption, notwithstanding the two previous facts that it sprang from God's gracious elective purpose and was accomplished by the power of God, actually delivered only those who availed themselves of the expiation of sin afforded by the efficacious covering of the blood of the paschal lamb (Exod. 12:12–13, 21–23, 24–27). This truth underscores the fact that biblical redemption is not simply deliverance by power but deliverance by price as well.[21]

That the paschal lamb was a "sacrifice" is expressly declared in Exodus 12:27, 34:25, and 1 Corinthians 5:7. As a biblical principle, wherever the blood of a sacrifice is shed and applied as God has directed so that he stays his judgment, the expiation or "covering" of sin has been effected. Accordingly, the exodus redemption came to its *climax* precisely in terms of a divinely required substitutionary atonement in which the people had to place their confidence if they were to be redeemed. As we will suggest later, Moses could have informed them of the christological significance of the paschal lamb.

4. The exodus redemption resulted in the creation of a new community liberated from slavery in order to serve its gracious new Redeemer and Lord. Again and again God ordered Pharaoh: "Let my people go that they may serve me" (see Exod. 3:18; 4:23; 5:1; 7:16; 8:1, 20; 9:1, 13; 10:3). The Bible knows nothing of a people of God springing into existence as the result of his redemptive activity who then continue to remain under the hostile power of their former master (see Rom. 6:6, 17–22; 7:4–6, 23–25; 8:2–4; 2 Cor. 5:15, 17). Though Pharaoh suggested compromises that would have resulted in something less than complete liberation for Israel (Exod. 8:25, 28; 10:11, 24), Moses would have none of it. Accordingly, Israel left Egypt *completely* (Exod. 12:37; 13:20), becoming a *guided* people (Exod. 13:21–22) and a *singing* people (Exod. 15), who had their *sacraments* (Exod. 14:21–23; 16:4, 13–15; 17:1–6; see 1 Cor. 10:2–4), and whose *perseverance* in their pilgrim struggles was dependent ultimately on the intercession of "the man on top of the hill" and not on their own strength and stratagems (Exod. 17:8–16). And far from Israel "rashly accepting the law" at Sinai and "falling from grace" when the nation promised its obedience to God's

---

21. See part three, chapter seventeen, "The Character of the Cross Work of Christ," for the fuller argument.

law, the very preface of the Ten Commandments (Exod. 20:1–2) places these ten obligations within the context of and represents them as the anticipated outcome of the redemption which they had just experienced. So it was to be through Israel's very obedience to God's commandments that the nation was to *evidence* before the surrounding nations that it was God's "treasured possession," his "kingdom of priests," and "a holy nation"—precisely the same way that the church today evidences before the watching world its relationship to God. Peter informs Christians that they, like Israel in Old Testament times, are a "chosen people, a royal priesthood, a holy nation, a people belonging to God, in order that [ὅπως, *hopōs*] you may declare the praises of him who called you out of darkness into his wonderful light" (1 Pet. 2:9). And Christians, just as Israel was to do through its obedience to God's laws, are to show forth his praises as "aliens and strangers in the world" by "living such good lives among the pagans that . . . they may see your good deeds and glorify God on the day he visits us" (1 Pet. 2:11–12).

C. Moses and the prophets prophesied about the events of the New Testament age, including the death and resurrection of Christ.

The New Testament writers, following the example of their Lord, regularly justified the existence and nature of the church of Jesus Christ by grounding them in Old Testament prophecy. A few of the clearest examples follow:

1. Jesus said: "the [Old Testament] Scriptures . . . testify about me" (John 5:39); he also said: "[Moses] wrote about me" (John 5:46). Jesus teaches here that there are references to him in the Pentateuch, the specific reference in his mind on this occasion probably being the "prophet like unto Moses" of Deuteronomy 18:15.

2. Jesus also declared that Isaiah 53 "must be fulfilled in me, for that [which is written] concerning me is coming to an end" (Luke 22:37; see also Matt. 26:24, 31, 54, 56; Luke 18:31; Acts 8:32–35).

3. Immediately after his resurrection, Jesus said to the Emmaus road disciples: "How foolish you are, and how slow of heart to believe all that the prophets have spoken! Did not the Messiah have to suffer these things and then enter into his glory?" Then Luke reports that "beginning with Moses and all the Prophets, [Jesus] explained [διερμήνευσεν, *diermēneusen*] to them what was said in all the Scriptures concerning himself" (Luke 24:25–27; see John 13:18; 19:24, 28, 36–37; 20:9). Jesus specifically declares here that Moses and the prophets predicted that the Messiah would suffer the very things which he himself had just endured. And he implies that the Emmaus road disciples should have known about these things as a result of Old Testament prophecy.

Christians today often wish that they could have heard Jesus' interpretation of the Old Testament on that occasion. But they can be assured that both the apostles' sermons recorded in Acts—Luke's "second work"—and the apostolic letters themselves, in the very way in which they interpret the Old Testament christologically, reflect major features of Christ's Emmaus road exposition.

4. In addition to the numerous well-known Old Testament citations in his sermons and letters that endorsed his teachings about Christ and his work (see, for example, Acts 2:17–21, 25–28, 34; 1 Pet. 2:6–8, 22), Peter said to a Jewish crowd in Jerusalem: "I know that you acted in ignorance, as did your leaders. But this is how God fulfilled what he had foretold through all the prophets, saying that his Christ would suffer" (Acts 3:17–18), and then, after citing Moses' predictive reference to Christ in terms of the "prophet like me," declared: "Indeed, all the prophets from Samuel on, as many as have spoken, have foretold these [New Testament] days" (Acts 3:22–24).

5. On another occasion, Peter declared: "All the prophets testify about him that everyone who believes in him receives forgiveness of sins through his name" (Acts 10:43). Here Peter teaches that the Old Testament prophets designated the Messiah, described precisely in terms of One who would suffer and rise from the dead in the Acts 10 context, as the object of Old Testament faith.

6. In 1 Peter 1:10–12, Peter wrote that the Old Testament prophets (1) "spoke of the grace that was to come *to you* ['God's elect, strangers in the world']," (2) that they "searched intently and with the greatest care, trying to find out the time and circumstances to which the Spirit of Christ in them was pointing when he predicted the sufferings of Christ and the glories that would follow," and (3) that in response to their searching, "it was revealed to them that they were not serving themselves but you, when they spoke of the things that have now been told you by those who have preached the gospel to you by the Holy Spirit sent from heaven."

It should be noted that according to the Dallas Doctrinal Statement this passage in Peter teaches that the Old Testament saints (this would include the Old Testaments prophets themselves) "did not understand the redemptive significance of the prophecies and types concerning the sufferings of Christ" (see also in this connection the New American Standard Bible's very misleading translation: "what person or time"). But this is not what Peter says. Rather, he says that it was only the time and circumstances (τίνα ἢ ποῖον καιρὸν, *tina e poion kairon*, lit. "which or what kind of time") of the Messiah's sufferings and "the after these things glories" which they investigated intently and with great care, but he certainly does not say that they were ignorant of the Messiah's sufferings as such.[22] In other words, Peter's "'or' is not disjunctive (as if two contrasted questions are referred to) but conjunctive

---

22. BAGD, ποῖος, *poios*, *A Greek English Lexicon*, 691, 1, a, a, translates the phrase "what time or what kind of time," which repetitive expression Blass-Debrunner suggests may be a "tautology for emphasis" (*A Greek Grammar of the New Testament*, 155, sec. 298 [2]).

(one question that could be stated either way): 'What or what kind of period is this?' "[23] This fact is borne out by Peter's description of God's revelatory response which answered to the prophets' intense searching. It dealt only with the *time factor* of messianic prophecy. He revealed to them, not *whose* sufferings they were about which they spoke—this they quite apparently already knew—but *when* the Messiah's sufferings were to occur. His sufferings, they were informed, were to occur not in their own time but in a later age (see, e.g., Dan. 2:44; 9:2, 24–27), at the beginning of this present age in which men preach the gospel by the Holy Spirit sent from heaven.

7. In addition to the many well-known Old Testament citations in his sermons and letters, also too numerous to list here, which endorsed his views of Christ, his death, and justification by faith (see, e.g., Rom. 4:3–8), Paul on his missionary journeys regularly "reasoned with [the Jews] from the Scriptures, explaining and proving that the Messiah had to suffer and rise from the dead" (Acts 17:2–3). For example, in the synagogue at Pisidian Antioch he taught that "the people of Jerusalem and their rulers . . . fulfilled the words of the prophets that are read every Sabbath when they condemned him. . . . When they had carried out all that had been written about him, they took him down from the tree and laid him in a tomb." (Acts 13:27–30). Beyond all doubt the Old Testament prophets wrote about a suffering Messiah.

8. Paul also declared that "the gospel concerning God's Son . . . Jesus Christ our Lord," to which he had been set apart, "God promised beforehand through his prophets in the Holy Scriptures" (Rom. 1:2–3). Paul expressly declares here that the Old Testament prophets wrote about "the gospel concerning God's Son . . . Jesus Christ our Lord."

9. Paul also wrote that "Christ died for our sins according to the Scriptures" and "was raised the third day according to the Scriptures" (1 Cor. 15:3–4). From this passage too we learn that the Old Testament Scriptures spoke about the death and resurrection of the Messiah.

10. While defending himself before Agrippa, Paul testified that he was standing trial only because of his teaching concerning "the hope of the promise made by God to our fathers, to which our twelve tribes hope to attain as they earnestly serve God day and night, concerning which hope I am being accused by the Jews" (Acts 26:6–7). He then explained what he meant by Israel's hope by declaring that throughout his long missionary ministry of some thirty years he had never said anything "beyond what the prophets and Moses said would happen—that the Messiah would suffer and, as the first to rise from the dead, would proclaim light to his

---

23. R. C. H. Lenski, *The Interpretation of the Epistles of St. Peter, St. John and St. Jude* (Minneapolis: Augsburg, 1945), 45.

own people and to the Gentiles" (Acts 26:22–23). From these verses it is clear that Paul believed that the Old Testament hope to which Moses and the prophets witnessed was the Messiah's death, resurrection, and saving ministrations, which "light" the Messiah himself would proclaim both directly and through his apostles to the Jewish people and to the Gentiles (see Eph. 2:17; 4:21).

11. While under house arrest in Rome, Paul told the Jewish leaders: "I am wearing this chain because of the hope of Israel [ἕνεκεν . . . τῆς ἐλπίδος τοῦ Ἰσραὴλ, *heneken . . . tēs elpidos tou Israēl*]" (Acts 28:20), which hope was the death, resurrection, and ministry of Messiah. Then Luke tells us that Paul from morning to evening "explained and declared to them the Kingdom of God and tried to convince them about Jesus from the Law of Moses and from the Prophets" (28:23). It is inconceivable that the author of Galatians and Romans would have talked about Jesus from morning to evening from the Old Testament Scriptures and said nothing about Christ's sufferings (see Acts 13:27–30; 17:2–3; 26:22–23).

12. James, moderating the Jerusalem conference assembled in debate in Acts 15, declared in verse 15 that "the words of the prophets *are in agreement with* [συμφωνοῦσιν, *symphōnousin*]" the missionary activities of the apostles among the Gentiles, and he proceeded to cite Amos 9:11–12 as a summary description of what God had previously revealed in Old Testament times that he would do in behalf of the Gentiles in this present age.

Dispensational scholars have argued that the verb συμφωνοῦσιν, *symphōnousin*, means in this context "are in agreement with," not "speak about," and simply indicates that the missionary policies being observed in connection with Gentile evangelism in the present age are harmonious with the policies to be followed in the future Jewish kingdom age—the real referent of Amos's prophecy. But aside from the fact that such an interpretation imposes an inanity on the text since the Jerusalem assembly hardly needed to be informed that God's prescribed missionary policies throughout history are consistent with each other from age to age, this is a classic example of "theological reaching" in order to avoid the obvious. If there is no connection between the cited "words of the [Old Testament] prophets" and the missionary activity of this present age, beyond the mere fact that the (according to dispensationalists, unpredicted) character of the church's present missionary activity among the Gentiles "fits in with" the (according to dispensationalists, predicted) character of Jewish missionary activity among the Gentiles in the latter half of the dispensationalist's "seven-year tribulation period" just before Christ returns and in their millennium, one is left with no perceivable explanation for James's citation of the Amos prophecy in this context. In fact, by this line of reasoning he is made to introduce an irrelevancy that has no bearing on the issue before the assembly. If the dispensationalist should respond that James cited Amos in order to justify, in light of what allegedly was going to be done in the tribulation period and the millennium, the propriety of the character of Gentile evangelism in the present age, he must acknowledge that James violated one of the cardinal canons of dispensational hermeneutics since, according to dispensational thought, one must never attempt to justify a truth or activity for one dispensation by arguing from the normativity of that truth or activity in another dispensation. To do so is to "confuse the dispensations"—a cardinal sin in dispensational hermeneutics. Furthermore, if James did utilize a kingdom-age practice in order to demonstrate that Gentiles should not be required to be circumcised now, it is not apparent how his conclusion follows from what dispensationalists allege elsewhere will be the practice in the kingdom age, since they argue on the basis of Ezekiel 44:9 that Gentile believers must be circumcised in the kingdom age! If James was really attempting to justify a church-age practice from a future kingdom-age practice, and if he had held the dispensational interpretation of Ezekiel 44:9, he should have drawn the opposite conclusion—that circumcision was essential to Gentile salvation! One can only conclude that the dispensational interpretation does justice neither to James's statement in verse 15 nor to his supporting citation of Amos 9:11–12.

Clearly, according to the inspired writers of the New Testament, Moses and the prophets predicted the ministry and death of the Messiah, this present age, and the worldwide preaching of the gospel, and thereby the out-calling of the church in this present age. The evidence for all this is full and certain, and it is regrettable that some evangelical scholars actually labor to avoid the New Testament witness to this effect.

D. The church of Jesus Christ is the present-day expression of the one people of God whose roots go back to Abraham.

The church of Jesus Christ in its earliest "personnel make-up" was *Jewish* in nature and membership (see Acts 1:8; 2:5–6, 14, 22, 36), and it was only after the passage of some years that this *Jewish* church began to evangelize the nations (Acts 10). But even after Jewish Christians within the church became a minority because of the sheer number of Gentiles who were being converted, the New Testament makes it clear, in conformity to the details of the "new covenant" prophecy in Jeremiah 31:31–34 (see Luke 22:20; 2 Cor. 3:6; Heb. 8:8–13; 9:15), that, when Gentiles became Christians, *they entered into the fellowship of that covenant community designated by the "new covenant" prophecy in Jeremiah 31:31 as "the house of Israel and the house of Judah."*

Because of the great number of Gentiles in the church today, it is very difficult for many Christians to think of the church of Jesus Christ of which they are privileged members (by "church" here I refer to the *true* church, that is, the body of truly regenerate saints) as being God's chosen people, the true (*not* the New) spiritual "Israel." But the New Testament evidence endorses this identification.

1. When Jesus described the man excommunicated from the church which he would build (Matt. 16:18) as "the heathen and the tax collector" (ὁ ἐθνικὸς καὶ ὁ τελώνης, *ho ethnikos kai ho telōnēs*) (Matt. 18:17), it is clear that his assumption was that his church was "Israel."

2. To the Ephesian church, clearly a Gentile church, Paul wrote:

> Remember that formerly you who are Gentiles by birth and called "uncircumcised" by those who call themselves "the circumcision" (that done in the body by the hands of men)—remember that at that time you were [a] separate from Christ, [b] excluded from citizenship in Israel [πολιτείας τοῦ Ἰσραὴλ, *politeias tou Israēl*] and [c] foreigners [ξένοι, *xevoi*] to the covenants of the promise, [d] without hope and [e] without God in the world. But now in Christ Jesus you who once were far away have been brought near through the blood of Christ. (2:11–13)

Paul teaches here that the blessed state to which the Ephesian Gentiles (who formerly were "far away") have now been "brought near" includes *Christ*, from whom they had been separated, and *hope*, and *God*, which had not been their possessions before (the first, fourth, and fifth items in Paul's list). But Paul also says that they had been excluded from citizenship in Israel and that they had been foreigners to the covenants of the promise (the second and third items). Since Paul suggests that the first, fourth, and fifth of their previous conditions had been reversed, it would seem reasonable that he also intends to teach that the second and third conditions had been reversed as well. On what authority may one eliminate these two from Paul's list of five conditions which he says God addressed in Christ in behalf of Gentiles? Accordingly, I would urge that Paul is teaching here that Gentile Christians are now citizens of (the true) Israel and beneficiaries of the covenants of the promise. And he seems to say this very thing in 2:19 when, summing up, he writes: "Therefore you are no longer foreigners [ξένοι, *xenoi*] and aliens [πάροικοι, *paroikoi*] but fellow citizens [συμπολῖται, *sympolitai*] of the saints and members of God's household [οἰκεῖοι τοῦ θεοῦ, *oikeioi tou theou*]."

3. To the Gentile churches in Galatia, Paul described those who repudiate Judaistic legalism and who "never boast except in the cross of our Lord Jesus Christ" as "the *Israel of God*" (6:12–16). (It is possible that Paul intended to refer exclusively to Jewish Christians by this expression, but it is equally possible that he intended to refer to the church of Jesus Christ *per se*, made up of Jews *and* Gentiles.)

4. To the Gentile church at Philippi, Paul described those "who worship by the Spirit of God, who glory in Christ Jesus, and who put no confidence in the flesh" as "the [true] circumcision" (Phil. 3:3), an Old Testament term, as he notes in Ephesians 2:11, which the nation of Israel had come to use as a designation of itself.

5. Paul's metaphor of the two olive trees (Rom. 11:16–24) also reflects this same

perception: olive shoots from a wild olive tree, that is, Gentiles, are being grafted into the cultivated olive tree, that is, Israel, from which latter tree many natural branches, that is, Jews, had been broken off. This tree, Paul says, has a "holy root" (the patriarchs; see Rom. 11:28). Clearly, Paul envisions saved Gentile Christians as "grafted shoots" in the true "Israel of faith." And just as clearly, it is into this same cultivated olive tree (which now includes multitudes of "wild shoots") that the elect "natural branches" of ethnic Israel (Paul speaks of them as "all Israel," Rom. 11:26) are being grafted in again through their coming to faith in Jesus Christ throughout this age.[24]

6. Employing Amos 9:11–12 as he did in Acts 15:16–17, James designates the church to which the "remnant of men," even "all the Gentiles who bear my name," was being drawn through the missionary activity of Peter and Paul as Amos's "fallen tabernacle of David" which God was even then in process of "rebuilding" precisely by means of drawing from the Gentiles a people for himself and making them members of the church of Jesus Christ. But for James to represent the church of Jesus Christ as "the fallen tabernacle of David" which Amos predicted was to be "rebuilt" means that James believed that the prophets did speak of this age and the church of this age, that Gentiles were being drawn into "David's fallen tabernacle"—Amos's picturesque term for spiritual Israel—and that an unbroken continuity exists between God's people in the Old Testament and Christians in the New Testament. It is of this "rebuilding" of David's fallen tabernacle that Haggai speaks when he predicted that God would someday "shake all nations, and the desire of all nations will come,"[25] and . . . fill this house with glory" (2:7).

7. The fact that in the course of their description of the Christian life and the life of the church itself the New Testament writers draw heavily upon Old Testament citations, terminology, and concepts (for example, prior to their salvation, Paul writes, Christians had been in "slavery to sin," the idea of slavery having its roots in the fact of Israel's slavery in Egypt, Rom. 6:17–22; Christ is the Christian's "High Priest" and "Passover lamb," Heb. 9:11–14; 1 Cor. 5:7; Christian baptism is "Christian circumcision," Col. 2:11–12; Christians offer up "sacrifices" of praise and good works, Heb. 13:15–16; Christians live under the rule of "elders," 1 Tim. 3:1–7; Tit. 1:5–9;

---

24. A helpful chart depicting Paul's olive-tree metaphor may be found in David N. Steele and Curtis C. Thomas, *Romans: An Interpretive Outline* (Philadelphia: Presbyterian and Reformed, 1963), 100–1.
25. With NASB and NEB, I would say that the "desire of all nations" here is probably not Christ. The verb "will come" (וּבָאוּ, *ûbā'û*) is plural, making its subject, the collective noun "desire" (חֶמְדַּת, *ḥemdat*) also plural. The phrase should be translated: "The precious things [the persons and wealth of the elect] of all nations will come." For an opposing view, see Walter C. Kaiser Jr., *Hard Sayings of the Old Testament* (Downers Grove, Ill.: InterVarsity Press, 1988), 235–37.

Heb. 13:17) clearly teaches that they saw no such line of demarcation between Israel and the church as is today urged by the dispensational school.

E. The requisite condition for salvation is identical in both the Old and New Testaments: the elect were saved, are saved, and will be saved only by grace through faith in the (anticipated or accomplished) work of the Messiah.

Dispensational scholars maintain that *no* Old Testament saint could have been saved through conscious faith in the Messiah's death work, simply because knowledge of this event was "as yet locked up in the secret counsels of God."[26] The Westminster Confession, on the other hand, affirms that the Holy Spirit employed "promises, prophecies, sacrifices, circumcision, the paschal lamb, and other types and ordinances . . . , *all* foresignifying Christ to come," in his Old Testament saving operations "to instruct and build up the elect in *faith in the promised Messiah,* by whom they had full remission of sins, and eternal salvation" (VII/v, emphasis supplied). The Scriptures alone should decide the issue: I will begin with New Testament data and move back into the Old Testament age.

1. Paul wrote to Timothy that "from infancy you have known the holy Scriptures [the Old Testament], which are able to make you wise for salvation through faith in Christ Jesus" (2 Tim. 3:15). Apparently Paul believed that the Old Testament contained revelational information about "salvation through faith in the Messiah."

2. Paul argued his doctrine of justification by faith alone, apart from all human works, by citing in support of it David's words in Psalm 32:1–2 (Rom. 4:6–7) and the example of Abraham who "believed God, and it was credited to him for righteousness" (Gen. 15:6; Rom. 4:1–3). The last thing that Paul would have wanted anyone to believe is that his was a "new doctrine." In light of these Old Testament examples it would have never dawned on Paul to say: "We know how the New Testament saint is saved—he is saved by grace through faith in Christ, but how was the Old Testament saint saved?" Instead he would have reversed the order of the sentence: "We know how the Old Testament saint was saved—he was saved by grace through faith in Messiah; we had better make sure that we are saved the same way, for there is no other way to be saved."

3. From the beginning of his ministry, during his early Judaean ministry (John 2:13–4:3), Jesus himself spoke of his coming death (John 3:14; by implication also in Matt. 9:15; Mark 2:20; Luke 5:35) and resurrection (John 2:19–22). There is no indication in the Gospels of a shift in Jesus' teaching away from an earlier promise to the Jews of an earthly Jewish kingdom to later pronouncements concerning his own death. He spoke about his death from the beginning. We find rather only a shift in emphasis from fewer to more allusions to his death. Vos writes:

---

26. *Scofield Reference Bible,* 996.

Our Lord simply takes for granted that there will be a breach between His followers and the world. And, since the cause of the breach is placed in their identification with Him, the underlying supposition doubtless is that the same conflict is in store for the Master Himself, only after a more principial fashion. And there is no point in Jesus' life where this mental attitude can be said to have first begun. The "sunny" and untroubled days of "fair Galilee" are, when exploited in such a sense, a pure fiction. *There never was in the life of Jesus an original optimistic period followed later by a pessimistic period.* As the approaching crisis did not render Him despondent towards the end, so neither did its comparative remoteness render Him sanguine at the beginning. The intrusion of such a terrifying thought as the thought of His death, in the specific form belonging to it, must have been, could not have failed to leave behind it the evidence of a sudden shock. But there is no evidence of any such sudden shock in the Gospels.[27]

4. No dispensationalist would represent John the Baptist as a New Testament prophet, and quite rightly so. As the forerunner of Jesus Christ, he was the last of the Old Testament prophets, ministering in the spirit and power of Elijah. Jesus himself said: "all the Prophets and the Law prophesied until John. And if you are willing to accept it, he is the Elijah who was to come" (Matt. 11:9–14). Accordingly, he is most often depicted in the role of the stern prophet demanding repentance of his hearers, baptizing only those who evidenced the fruit of repentance. He was that, but he was also a remarkable evangelical witness to Christ, identifying Jesus, the one coming after him, not only as the *Messiah* (John 3:28) in whose hands reside the prerogatives of both salvation and judgment (Matt. 3:10–12) but also as the *Lamb of God who takes away the sin of the world* (John 1:29)—a clear allusion to Messiah's sacrificial death and one very likely drawn from Isaiah 53:7, 10–12.[28] And what were people to do with him then? "He told the people that they should believe in [πιστεύσωσιν εἰς, *pisteusōsin eis*] the one coming after him, that is, in Jesus" (Acts 19:4). Here is the last of the Old Testament prophets, at the very commencement of his ministry, proclaiming that his hearers should believe in the Christ, who

---

27. Geerhardus Vos, *The Self-Disclosure of Jesus* (1926; reprint, Phillipsburg, N.J.: Presbyterian and Reformed, 1978), 278–79 (emphasis supplied).

28. Many suggestions have been made concerning what John the Baptist would have meant by his identification of Jesus as the "Lamb of God" (see Leon Morris, *The Gospel According to John* [Grand Rapids, Mich.: Eerdmans, 1971], 144–48, for a survey of these suggestions). While Morris is not prepared to pinpoint the Old Testament reference which provided the background for this description of Jesus, he does affirm that John, the Gospel's author, by his citation of the Baptist "is making a general allusion to sacrifice" (147). And we must assume that the author of the Gospel would not have used the Baptist's description in a sense the Baptist had not himself intended.

would die for the sins of the world, for their salvation—the very thing that dispensationalists maintain was "as yet locked up in the secret counsels of God"!

5. While the New Testament evidence indicates that the concept of a suffering Messiah in the first third of the first century A.D. was not widespread, having been overshadowed both in the official theological schools of the day (that had so emphasized particular aspects of messianic prophecy that to a considerable degree they misrepresented the total Old Testament picture) and in the popular imagination that clung to the concept of a nationalistic ruling Messiah, Simeon's *Nunc Dimittis* (Luke 2:29–32), with its phrase "a light for revelation to the Gentiles," alluding to Isaiah 42:6 and 49:6, illustrates that at least one circle within first-century Jewry (the elect) identified the Servant of Isaiah with the Messiah. Moreover, his oracle in Luke 2:34–35, by its prophecy: "This child is . . . to be a sign that will be spoken against. . . . And a sword will pierce your own soul too," intimates that the same circle understood (doubtless from Isaiah 53) that there would be a tragic dimension to the Messiah's ministry.

6. Turning to the Old Testament, in Zechariah 12:10 (and we should note that anything God said about the Messiah *before* Zechariah's day would have assisted the elect of his day better to understand him) Yahweh declared that the house of David and the inhabitants of Jerusalem would someday "look on me, the one they have pierced, and mourn," and again in 13:7 he commanded: "Awake, O sword, against my Shepherd, against the Man who is my Associate! Strike the Shepherd, and the sheep will be scattered." Both of these verses are regarded by the New Testament as prophecies having their fulfillment in the crucifixion of Christ (see John 19:37; Rev. 1:7 and Matt. 26:31; Mark 14:27).

7. Seven hundred years before Christ, Isaiah prophesied the substitutionary, atoning death of the Messiah in Isaiah 53. We may legitimately infer that *what Isaiah wrote about, he doubtless also proclaimed in the marketplace* (see Isa. 20:2–3, Jer. 13:1–11 and Ezek. 4:4–8, 5:1–12, 24:15–24, for vivid examples of the Old Testament prophet's "taking his message" to the people of his own generation). And we may be sure that what he proclaimed in the marketplace the Holy Spirit enabled the elect in Israel (Rom. 11:7), albeit a remnant (Isa. 10:22; Rom. 9:27), to understand and to believe to the saving of their souls.

I am not maintaining that all of the elect of the eighth century B.C. understood as much as the average New Testament saint does about Christ. But aware as I am that what the average Christian today knows about him is shockingly little, I am not denying either that some Old Testament saints may have had a *deeper* understanding of the *things* of Christ than some saints today. Nor am I saying that all of the elect of the eighth century B.C. had equal understanding of these matters. For just as among any given generation of true Christians one may find almost every degree of knowledge and understanding from that of the almost "nonknowledge" of some Christians to that depth of knowledge and insight possessed by a Calvin, so also doubtless there were degrees of comprehension among the elect of the Old Testament period. Some would have possessed only the barest minimum of comprehension of Isaiah's message about the Messiah's substitutionary death—but enough to be saved—while others, lacking only the knowledge of the time and circumstances (1 Pet. 1:10–11), would have clearly perceived that Isaiah was prophesying the suffering and death of the Lord's Servant-Messiah in their behalf.

8. Earlier in the same prophecy (7:14) Isaiah had announced that the Messiah would be born of a virgin and be "God with us"—a prediction of the Incarnation (the reader should recall here that the Dallas Doctrinal Statement contends that the Old Testament saint could have known nothing about the Incarnation). Then he described this marvelous Child who would be *born* to us by the fourfold title, "Wonderful Counselor, Mighty God, Everlasting Father, Prince of Peace" (9:6)—another prophetic allusion to the Incarnation. Again, there is no reason to doubt that the Holy Spirit illumined the elect to understand at least something of the implications in these facts about the Messiah.

9. Three hundred years before Isaiah said what he did about the Messiah (and we should note that anything God said about the Messiah *before* Isaiah would have assisted the elect of Isaiah's day better to understand him), David prophesied that the "kings of the earth . . . and the rulers would gather [in rebellion] against the Lord and against his Messiah" in order to cast off their restraints upon them (Ps. 2:2; see Acts 4:25–28). Accordingly, in Psalm 22:16 David spoke of the Messiah's crucifixion, while in Psalm 16:9–11 he spoke of his resurrection from the dead. What is particularly interesting about the latter Psalm is that Peter, commenting upon it, argues that David could not have been talking about himself in the Psalm since he "died and was buried, and his tomb is here to this day." But, Peter continues, David, seeing what was ahead because he was a prophet, spoke of the resurrection of the Messiah (Acts 2:25–31; see Paul's similar use of Psalm 16:10 in Acts 13:35–37), this resurrection necessarily implying his prior death. In these psalms then, David, Messiah's great royal ancestor, expressed a knowledge of his greater Son's rejection, death, and resurrection. And what he knew under the Spirit's inspiration, David expounded through his inspired psalms to his people in order that they might know as well. Again, there is no reason to doubt that the Holy Spirit used David's teaching about the Messiah, revealed through his psalms, to bring David and other elect men and women to a saving trust in the Messiah's anticipated redemptive work.

10. By the Levitical legislation that Moses had given the nation four hundred years before David (and recall again that anything that God had previously revealed to Israel would have assisted the elect better to understand David), Israel was schooled in the great principle of forgiveness through the substitutionary death of

a perfect sacrifice. Again and again in that body of legislative material, the guilty Israelite is instructed "to lay his hand on the head of the [unblemished] burnt offering, and it will be accepted on his behalf to make atonement for him" (Lev. 1:4; 3:2, 8, 13; 4:4, 15, 24, 29, 33; Num. 8:12). The salvific significance of this ritual was not left to the speculative mind to "unpack" but is clearly explained in connection with the scapegoat of the Day of Atonement: once a year the high priest chose two goats, sacrificed one of them for a sin offering, and then he was "to lay both hands on the head of the live goat and confess over it all the wickedness and rebellion of the Israelites—all their sins—and *put them on the goat's head. He shall send the goat away into the desert in the care of a man appointed for the task. The goat will carry on itself all their sins* to a solitary place; and the man shall release it in the desert" (Lev. 16:21–22). In this ritual the great salvific principle was being taught that salvation comes to the sinner who turns for forgiveness from his own efforts, who approaches God through the sacrificial death of a perfect substitute offered in his stead, and whose sins are imputed to the sacrifice. J. I. Packer quite properly understands the activity regarding the scapegoat as a "dramatization" of what occurred in the sacrifice of the *other* goat:

> The [other] goat is the one that really counts. The action with the scapegoat is only a picture of what happens through the [other] goat. The [other] goat is killed and offered as a sin-offering in the normal way. Thus atonement was made for the people of Israel. The banishing of the scapegoat into the wilderness was an illustrative device to make plain to God's people that their sin really has been taken away.
>
> When the writer to the Hebrews speaks of Christ achieving what the Day of Atonement typified [Heb. 9:11–14]—our perfect and permanent cleansing from sin—he focuses not on the goat that went away into the wilderness but on the animal that was offered in sacrifice once a year by the high priest . . . the blood of Christ [fulfills] the whole pattern of the Day of Atonement ritual.[29]

All this was carried out in connection with the service at the Tabernacle—a structure, it must not be overlooked, which was built "according to the pattern which was shown to Moses in the mount" (Exod. 25:9, 40; 26:30; Acts 7:44), a pattern, the author of Hebrews affirms, that was a copy and shadow of the true, heavenly Tabernacle into which Christ himself entered with his own blood as the redeemed man's High Priest (Heb. 8:2, 5). And when and where was that entrance? *Christ's "entrance into the heavenly sanctuary" occurred when he assumed his high priestly*

---

29. J. I. Packer, "Sacrifice and Satisfaction," in *Our Savior God: Man, Christ, and the Atonement*, ed. James M. Boice (Grand Rapids, Mich.: Baker, 1980), 131–32.

role as Mediator of the new covenant at the incarnation, and the Most Holy Place was his cross! Thus the Levitical system foreshadowed the sacrificial work of Christ who saved the elect in Israel as they placed their faith in him as he was foresignified by the earthly types within that system.

11. Even earlier, at the time of Israel's exodus from Egypt, the same essential lessons were being taught in connection with the blood of the paschal lamb: "The blood will be a sign for you on the houses where you are; and when I see the blood, I will pass over you. No destructive plague will touch you when I strike Egypt" (Exod. 12:13; see 1 Cor. 5:7). Again, we may be confident that the Holy Spirit by such words as these instructed and built up the faith of the elect in Messiah's death, which was symbolically and typically depicted in the death of the Passover sacrifice.

12. But did the nation of Israel even know anything about the Messiah and his death during the Mosaic age in order to understand that the bull or goat which the guilty brought to the altar for slaying foresignified Messiah's sacrificial death? The author of Hebrews expressly declares that Moses, Israel's great leader and lawgiver, "regarded as greater riches than the treasures of Egypt the disgrace of the Christ [τὸν ὀνειδισμὸν τοῦ Χριστοῦ, *ton oneidismon tou Christou*], for he was looking forward to the reward . . . for he saw him who is invisible" (Heb. 11:26–27). And Jesus stated that Moses personally had written about him (John 5:46–47). A faith looking to the future, a faith that wrote about the Messiah, a faith aware of the disgrace which would befall the Christ, and a faith that preferred "the fellowship of sharing in his sufferings" to the glories of his own age—this was Moses' faith. And we can presume that Moses shared his understanding with his people.

13. Of Abraham Christ himself affirmed: "Abraham . . . rejoiced at the thought of seeing my day, and he saw it and was glad" (John 8:56). As with Moses after him, Abraham's faith was directed not only toward God in some general way but also toward the Messiah who was to come. He was not looking toward some temporal blessing to become his in his own time, for as the author of Hebrews says of him: "By faith [anticipating "the day of Christ"] he made his home in the promised land like a stranger in a foreign country . . . , for he was looking forward to [ἐξεδέχετο, *exedecheto*] the city having foundations, whose Builder and Maker is God" (11:9–10). Indeed, of *all* of the elect of that age and of those descending from Abraham (11:12) the author of Hebrews affirms a similar faith that looked to the future, indeed, to heaven itself:

> All these people were still living by faith when they died. They did not receive the things promised; they only saw them and welcomed them *from a distance* [πόρρωθεν, *porrothen*]. And they admitted that they were aliens and strangers on earth. People who say such things show that they are looking for a country of their own. If they had been thinking of the country they had left, they would

have had opportunity to return. Instead, *they were longing* [ὀρέγονται, *oregontai*] for a better country—a heavenly one. Therefore God is not ashamed to be called their God, for he has prepared a city for them. (11:13–16)

14. There are indications of this faith in the Messiah's future deliverance even in pre-Abrahamic times: "Enoch, the seventh from Adam, prophesied . . . : 'Behold, the Lord is coming with thousands of his holy ones' " (Jude 14). The intended referent of the title "Lord" seems rather clearly to be the *Messiah*, as evidenced by its occurrences with "Christ" in verses 4, 17, 21, and 25. And a significant textual variant actually reads ʼΙησοῦς, *Iēsous*, in Jude 5, concerning which variant Bruce M. Metzger writes: "Critical principles seem to require the adoption of ʼΙησοῦς [*Iēsous*] which admittedly is the best attested reading among Greek and versional witnesses."[30] One must conclude that Jude viewed the Messiah as present (in his preincarnate state) and active throughout the history of the Old Testament.

15. Abel showed that he understood the principle of the necessity of substitutionary blood atonement when "by faith he offered a better sacrifice than Cain did" (Gen. 4:3–5; Heb. 11:4). His offering from the flock, its death typifying the "Seed of the woman" (Gen. 3:15) who in crushing the serpent's head would himself be fatally *wounded*, doubtless reflected what the Holy Spirit had taught him through his parents' instructions concerning the significance of the *protevangelium*, his need for a blood "covering" before God, and the relationship between the two.

16. Finally, how did Abel's parents know about the need for a blood "covering" before God? From their observation of God's killing an animal, even before they were banished from the garden of Eden, and making for them covering garments from the skin of the animal (Gen. 3:21) and most likely by his own direct instruction to them. This divine work, coming as it did hard on God's *protevangelium* (Gen. 3:15), according to which the Seed of the woman would destroy the Serpent's power through his own death work, illustrated the "covering" significance of that Seed's death. On God's activity here Meredith G. Kline writes:

> This remedy [clothing Adam and Eve] for the obstacle to their approach to God (*see* 3:10) symbolized God's purpose to restore men to fellowship with him. The sinners' shame, as a religious problem, could not be covered by their own efforts (*see* 3:7). Implied in God's provision is an act of animal sacrifice; what is explicit, however, is not the sacrificial mode but remedial result.[31]

---

30. Bruce M. Metzger, *A Textual Commentary on the Greek New Testament* (New York: United Bible Societies, 1971), 726.
31. Meredith G. Kline, "Genesis," *The New Bible Commentary Revised*, ed. D. Guthrie and J. A. Motyer (Grand Rapids, Mich.: Eerdmans, 1970), 85.

These five lines of argument vindicate the covenant theology of the Reformed faith and show that classic dispensationalism is in error when it denies that the Old Testament saint had any awareness of the future Messiah's suffering in his stead. They clearly demonstrate that salvation has always been of one piece in Scripture, that the covenant of grace is one covenant, and that the people of God are one people.

A DISCLAIMER AND A RESPONSE

I certainly do not intend to suggest that the Old Testament elect were given all the information about Christ that the New Testament contains about his person and work. Vos has rightly observed that "it is unhistorical to carry back into the O.T. mind our *developed* doctrinal consciousness of these matters."[32] On the other hand, it is possible to address the issue of the Old Testament saints' understanding of redemption so one-sidedly from the "biblical-theological" perspective that one permits the hermeneutic of that discipline to overpower the "analogy of faith" principle of systematic theology, and as a result neither the teaching of the Old Testament itself nor what the New Testament writers expressly report or imply that the Old Testament meant and that the Old Testament saints knew about the suffering Messiah and his resurrection from the dead is given its due.[33]

In my opinion, Vos himself commits this error in his chapter on "The Content of the First Redemptive Special Revelation" when he construes "the woman's Seed" in Genesis 3:15 in a collective rather than a personal sense: "As to the word 'seed' there is no reason to depart from the collective sense in either case. The seed of the serpent *must* be collective, and this determines the sense of the seed of the woman."[34] But it does not necessarily follow that, because the seed of the serpent

---

32. Vos, *Biblical Theology*, 64, emphasis supplied.
33. See my interaction with Walter C. Kaiser Jr., *Toward an Exegetical Theology: Biblical Exegesis for Preaching and Teaching* (Grand Rapids, Mich.: Baker, 1981), in part one, chapter two, pp. 51–2 in this regard.
34. Vos, *Biblical Theology*, 54. Very interestingly, after he urges that it is the collective sense that must be placed on the "seed of the woman," Vos writes:
    > indirectly, the possibility is *hinted at* that in striking this fatal blow the seed of the woman will be concentrated in one person, for it should be noticed that it is not the seed of the serpent but the serpent itself whose head will be bruised. In the former half of the curse the two seeds are contrasted; here the woman's seed and the serpent. This suggests that as at the climax of the struggle the serpent's seed will be represented by the serpent, in the same manner [that is, at the climax of the struggle] the woman's seed *may find representation* in a single person. (54–55, emphases supplied)

    But having said this, Vos then reverts back and declares:
    > we are not warranted, however, in seeking an exclusive personal reference to the Messiah here, as though He alone were meant by "the woman's seed." O.T. revelation approaches the concept of a personal Messiah very gradually. (55)

is collective, the seed of the woman must also be collective. I would submit that it was precisely of Christ that God spoke, just as Paul insisted that it was precisely of Christ that God later spoke in his reference to Abraham's "Seed" in Genesis 13:15 and 17:8 (Gal. 3:16). Furthermore, it is inexplicable why Vos makes nothing of the "death wound" which "the woman's Seed" would experience in his conflict with the *Serpent* (note: *not* the Serpent's seed), stating only that the *protevangelium* promised that "somehow out of the human race a fatal blow will come which shall crush the head of the serpent."[35] I would submit, on the basis of the clear allusion to his death in the *protevangelium*, that from the very beginning of redemptive history the saints' everlasting hope was made to rest in the triumphant "conflict work" carried out by "the *mortally wounded* woman's Seed."

Vos also refuses to see the divine institution of expiatory sacrifice in Genesis 3:21, even going so far as to affirm that "the Pentateuch contains no record of the institution of sacrifice either as to its expiatory or as to its consecratory aspect."[36] And when he writes of the content of Abraham's faith, he takes the same position:

> [Abraham's] kind of faith is a faith in the creative interposition of God. It trusts in him for calling the things that are not as though they were [see Rom 4:17–23]. *This does not, of course, mean that the objective content of the patriarch's faith was doctrinally identical with that of the N.T. believer. Paul does not commit the anachronism of saying that Abraham's faith had for its object the raising of Christ from the dead. What he means is that the attitude of faith towards the raising of Isaac and the attitude towards the resurrection [of Christ] are identical in point of faith able to confront and incorporate the supernatural.*[37]

Meredith G. Kline seems to concur with Vos's basic position:

> *Between your seed and her seed.* Beyond the woman, the whole family of the true humanity, becoming her spiritual seed by faith, will stand in continuing conflict with those descendants of fallen Adam who obdurately manifest spiritual sonship to the devil. . . . *He shall bruise your head, and you shall bruise his heel.* The 'you' still contending in the remote future points past the mere serpent to Satan. This focusing on an individual from one side in connection with the eventual encounter suggests that the *he* too is not the woman's seed collectively but their individual champion. ("Genesis," *The New Bible Commentary: Revised* [London: Inter-Varsity Press, 1970], 85)

But if the "he" may be (Vos) or is to be (Kline) construed not collectively but as an individual, why is "the woman's seed" not an individual as well, since it is the antecedent of the "he"? Are we to believe, *contra* the Westminster Confession of Faith, I/ix, that "seed" here has a dual meaning?

35. Vos, *Biblical Theology*, 54.
36. Ibid., 173.
37. Ibid., 99–100.

When one takes into account, however, all the data amassed in this chapter, particularly Jesus' own declaration that Abraham "rejoiced at the thought of seeing my day; *he saw it* and was glad" and the New Testament reiterations that the Old Testament Scriptures ("beginning with Moses and all the Prophets") testified that "the Messiah will suffer and rise from the dead on the third day, and repentance and forgiveness of sins will be preached in his name to all nations" (Luke 24:25–27, 45–47; John 5:39, 46; Acts 3:24; 10:43; 13:27–30; 26:22–23; I Pet. 1:10–12), the obvious conclusion is that Old Testament saints, including Abraham the father of the faithful, knew much more about the Messiah's suffering than is generally credited to them, and infinitely more about it than the dispensationalist would allow, since he insists that they knew nothing at all.

CRITIQUE OF THE DISPENSATIONALISTS' SCRIPTURAL RATIONALE

Dispensationalists cite several passages of the New Testament in which the word "mystery" (μυστήριον, *mystērion*) occurs in order to support their view that the Old Testament saints knew nothing about a suffering Messiah. They maintain that the rejection of the King and his suffering and death were biblical "mysteries," that is, facts the knowledge of which God had kept "locked up in the secret councils of God" until he revealed them to men through Jesus and his holy apostles and prophets. It is true, as BAGD states, that "our lit. uses [μυστήριον, *mystērion*] to mean the secret thoughts, plans, and dispensations of God which are hidden fr. the human reason, as well as fr. all other comprehension below the divine level, and hence must be revealed to those for whom they are intended."[38] The meaning of the word is not in contention between dispensational and Reformed interpreters; it is the *content* of the "mysteries" that is the matter of dispute.

Matthew 13:11, 17, 34–35

In Matthew 13 we find seven of Jesus' "kingdom of heaven" parables—the sower and the four kinds of soil, the wheat and the tares, the mustard seed, the leaven, the treasure hidden in the field, the pearl of great value, and the net. Jesus declared that they revealed certain "mysteries" of the kingdom of heaven (Matt. 13:11), explaining what he meant by "mysteries" by saying that "many prophets and righteous men desired to see what you see, and did not see it; and to hear what you hear, and did not hear it" (13:17). Matthew added that Jesus spoke in parables "so that what

---

38. BAGD, 532.

was spoken through the prophet [Asaph] might be fulfilled, saying, 'I will open my mouth in parables; I will utter things hidden since the foundation of the world' " (13:34–35; see Ps. 78:2). The dispensationalist understands Jesus to mean by these parables that he was revealing for the very first time in history that he and the messianic kingdom would be rejected and that "the long period of the mystery-form of the kingdom," all of which was unknown to the Old Testament prophets, would follow. But I suggest that this is an example of seeing in the passage what one already desires to find there.

The first thing that must be established is the meaning of the phrase "the kingdom of heaven." Classic dispensationalists contend that "the kingdom of heaven" must be distinguished from "the kingdom of God," with the former referring to the literal, earthly, Davidic, millennial kingdom, while the latter refers to the universal reign of God in general. It was the former, these dispensationalists urge, that Jesus proclaimed was "at hand" at his first coming (Matt. 4:17). But these phrases are actually "linguistic variations of the same idea" (Ladd), as evidenced by their identity of meaning in Matthew 19:23–24 and by their parallel usage in the Synoptic Gospels. That is to say, where Matthew says "the kingdom of heaven," Mark and Luke say "the kingdom of God" (see, for example, Matt. 13:11; Mark 4:11; Luke 8:10 and Matt. 19:14; Mark 10:14; Luke 18:17). Both terms refer to the sovereign rule or reign of God, either in grace or in judgment.

Now what was it about the kingdom or rule of God that Jesus declared "had been hidden" from men prior to his coming? From Daniel 2 and other passages the Jews knew already about the kingdom of God. Moreover, the picture Daniel 2:34–35, 44–45 gives concerning the coming of the kingdom of God is one entailing the cataclysmic, eschatological overthrow of all the kingdoms of this world. Daniel 2 taught the Jews that when the kingdom of God came, it would brook no competition. It would crush every earthly power and authority before it, fill the whole earth, and endure forever. Accordingly, it was this very "kingdom in power" which the Jews of the first century by and large were anticipating. And if Jesus in fact had gone around offering this kingdom to the Jews, as these dispensationalists insist, it is inexplicable, particularly in light of his display of his mighty "powers" (δυνάμεις, *dynameis;* see Matt. 11:20–23; 13:54, 58; Luke 10:13; 19:37), why the Jews rejected him. But Jesus, by his kingdom of heaven parables in Matthew 13, revealed that the kingdom of God, which was from the perspective of the Old Testament "an undivided unit," would unfold itself in two stages.[39] The second stage—the eschatological phase—of the kingdom of God, Jesus taught, would indeed come as Daniel had prophesied, manifesting itself with the return of the Son of Man in power and

---

39. See Vos, *Biblical Theology,* 399–411.

great glory (Matt. 25:31–46). But before it came in *power,* Jesus taught by these "mystery" parables, the kingdom had come first in *grace,* also in his own person (see Matt. 13:37), coming gradually, coming largely in the internal, invisible sphere of the spiritual life, and tolerating imperfections in its subjects and even resistance from the world system and the kingdom of Satan. In its "mystery form," as George E. Ladd explains the parables,

> The kingdom has come among men but not with power which compels every knee to bow before its glory; it is rather like seed cast on the ground which may be fruitful or unfruitful depending upon its reception (Matt. 13:3–8). The kingdom has come, but the present order is not disrupted; the sons of the kingdom and the sons of the evil one grow together in the world until the harvest (Matt. 13:24–30; 36–43). The kingdom of God has indeed come to men, not as a new glorious order, but like the proverbial mustard seed. However, its insignificance must not be despised. This same kingdom will one day be a great tree (Matt. 13:31–32). Instead of a world-transforming power, the kingdom is present in an almost imperceptible form like a bit of leaven hidden in a bowl of dough. However, this same kingdom will yet fill the earth as the leavened dough fills the bowl (Matt. 13:33).
>
> The coming of the kingdom of God in humility instead of glory was an utterly new and amazing revelation. Yet, said Jesus, men should not be deceived. Although the present manifestation of the kingdom is in humility—indeed, its Bearer was put to death as a condemned criminal—it *is* nevertheless the kingdom of God, and, like buried treasure or a priceless pearl, its acquisition merits any cost or sacrifice (Matt. 13:44–46). The fact that the present activity of the kingdom will initiate a movement that will include evil men as well as good should not lead to misunderstanding of its true nature. It *is* the kingdom of God; it will one day divide the good from the evil in eschatological salvation and judgment (Matt. 13:47–50).[40]

Jesus taught by the "mystery parables" precisely the opposite of what dispensationalists say! Far from offering to the Jews the kingdom of God in power, he declared that he was proclaiming first to them (and then to other men) the spiritual reign of God in the heart which brings "righteousness and peace and joy in the Holy Spirit" (Rom. 14:17)—a reign which men could resist and which the majority of Jews did in fact reject because of the hardness of their hearts (Matt. 13:13–15). Accordingly, they crucified the Bearer of the gospel of the kingdom as a deceiver and a blasphemer—in fulfillment of the prophecies of the Old Testament!

---

40. George Eldon Ladd, "Kingdom of Christ, God, Heaven," in *Evangelical Dictionary of Theology,* 609–10.

Ephesians 3:2–6, 9; Colossians 1:25–27

Two other passages which classic dispensationalists regularly use to argue that the Old Testament saint could have known nothing of "the rejection of the kingdom and King, the long period of the mystery-form of the kingdom, the world-wide preaching of the cross, and the out-calling of the Church" are Ephesians 3:2–9 and Colossians 1:25–27. These two passages say essentially the same thing, and dispensationalists cite both because of the reference in each to the "mystery" that "was not made known" before the apostles and New Testament prophets revealed it:

> Ephesians 3:2–6, 9: "Surely you have heard about the administration of God's grace that was given to me for you, that is, *the mystery made known to me by revelation,* as I have already written briefly [see Eph. 1:9–10]. In reading this, then, you will be able to understand my insight into *the mystery of Christ, which was not made known to men in other generations as it has now been revealed by the Spirit to God's holy apostles and prophets.* This mystery is that through the gospel the Gentiles are heirs together with Israel, members together of one body, and sharers together in the promise in Christ Jesus . . . to make plain to everyone the administration of *this mystery, which for ages past was kept hidden in God."* (emphases supplied)

> Colossians 1:25–27: "I have become [a] servant [of his body which is the church (see v. 24)] by the commission God gave me to make fully known unto you the word of God—*the mystery that has been kept hidden for ages and generations, but is now disclosed to the saints.* To them God has chosen to make known what is the glorious riches of this mystery among the Gentiles, which is *Christ in you, the hope of glory."* (emphasis supplied)

A careful reading of the Ephesians passage will disclose that the "mystery" which was not disclosed to the generations before Christ as it was revealed to Christ's apostles and prophets was that *Gentiles were to be fellow-heirs, fellow-members of Christ's body, and fellow-partakers with the Jews of the promise in Christ Jesus.* In the latter passage the "mystery" which was not disclosed is *Christ in you, the hope of glory.* Two comments are in order: (1) Paul does not say in the Ephesians passage that the mystery which was not made known in earlier generations was the rejection of the King, or that the mystery had been hidden to previous generations in an absolute sense. The Old Testament did testify concerning the future blessings which the Gentiles would share with the Jews (see Gen. 9:26–27; 12:3 [see Gal. 3:8]; 22:18; 26:4; 28:14; Pss. 67; 72:8–11, 17; 87; Isa. 11:10; 49:6; 54:1–3 [see Gal. 4:27]; 60:1–3; Hos. 1:10 [see Rom. 9:24–25]; Amos 9:11–12 [see Acts 15:13–18]; Mal. 1:11). What was not so clearly revealed in Old Testament times was that the Gentiles would be "on a footing of perfect equality" (Hendriksen) with the Jews in Christ's body, the

THE UNITY OF THE COVENANT OF GRACE

church. (2) It is to stretch the meaning of Paul's words beyond legitimate limit to interpret this statement in Ephesians as teaching that "the rejection of the kingdom and King, the long period of the mystery-form of the kingdom, the world-wide preaching of the cross, and the out-calling of the church" were, until the apostles spoke of them, "as yet locked up in the secret counsels of God." Charles Hodge has insightfully written on Ephesians 3:5–6:

> That the Gentiles were to partake of the blessings of the Messiah's reign, and to be united as one body with the Jews in his kingdom, is not only frequently predicted by the ancient prophets, but Paul himself repeatedly and at length quotes their declarations on this point to prove what he taught was in accordance with the Old Testament; see Rom. 9, 25–33. The emphasis must, therefore, be laid on the word *as*. This doctrine was not formerly revealed as, i.e. not so fully or so clearly as under the Gospel....
>
> The mystery made known to the apostles and prophets of the new dispensation, was ... that the Gentiles *are,* in point of right and fact, fellow-heirs, of the same body, and partakers of this promise. The form in which the calling of the Gentiles was predicted in the Old Testament led to the general impression that they were to partake of the blessings of the Messiah's reign by becoming Jews, by being as proselytes merged into the old theocracy, which was to remain in all its peculiarities. [It was not made so clear then as it has been under the Gospel] that the theocracy itself was to be abolished, and a new form of religion was to be introduced, designed and adapted equally for all mankind, under which the distinction between Jew and Gentile was to be done away. *It was this catholicity of the Gospel which was the expanding and elevating revelation made to the apostles, and which raised them from sectarians to Christians.*[41]

With reference to Paul's somewhat cryptic description of the "mystery" in Colossians 1:27 as "Christ in you, the hope of glory," where again he speaks of the corporate inclusion of Gentiles within the body of Christ, he is doubtless assuming and implying the same basic truths which he elaborated upon in Ephesians 3:2–6, 9. But again, Paul's statements do not teach the radical conclusions which dispensationalists wish to draw from them, namely, that the Old Testament saints did not know that the Messiah would be rejected and suffer or that a distinction must be drawn between Old Testament Israel "under law" and the New Testament church "under grace," and that these people are *two* people of God who are "not to be intermingled or confused, as they are chronologically successive."

---

41. Charles Hodge, *A Commentary on the Epistle to the Ephesians* (Grand Rapids, Mich.: Eerdmans, 1954), 162–63, 164–65, emphasis supplied.

Two Tragic Implications

It is not my intention to enter here into a discussion of dispensationalism's debatable assertions respecting the pretribulation, premillennial rapture of the church, the seven-year tribulation period preceding the millennium, the reestablishment of the Jewish theocracy during the millennium (I am not calling historic premillennialism as such into question here), and the return in that Jewish "kingdom age" to the Old Testament requirements of circumcision and the ceremonialism of animal sacrifices. These are matters more appropriately taken up and addressed in the study of eschatology.[42] But something must be said here about two tragic implications of the dispensational interpretation of Scripture.

DISPENSATIONALISM'S UNWITTING JUSTIFICATION OF THE CRUCIFIXION

We have already noted, in spite of the fact that Jesus himself declared that he had come into the world to proclaim first the gospel of the kingdom of grace (Matt. 13), to "seek and to save that which was lost" (Luke 19:10) and that he had "not come to be served, but to serve, and to give his life a ransom for many" (Mark 10:45), and in spite of the fact that Paul teaches that "Christ Jesus came into the world to save sinners" (1 Tim. 1:15), classic dispensationalists insist that when Christ came the first time to Israel he offered to establish the literal, earthly, material, thousand-year-long Davidic kingdom. If this were actually true, then dispensationalists virtually stand with those (false) witnesses at the time of his trial who accused him of opposing political Rome (Luke 23:1–2). And *Christ would have been justly executed under Roman law as an insurrectionist and a revolutionary!*

Of course, it is in fact not true. When the multitudes sought to make him their king by force he spurned the idea (John 6:15). The kingdom he proclaimed to his generation was the spiritual rule of God in people's hearts. There were two Roman officials in the land at that time formally responsible to determine whether Jesus was attempting to establish an earthly kingdom which would challenge the powers of Rome—Pilate and Herod. But neither charged him with this crime. After examining him and analyzing his claim that, while he was in truth a King, his kingdom was not of this world, Pilate exonerated him of the charge of political insurrection (John 18:33–38). He was, therefore, unjustly and illegally crucified. In spite of all this, dispensationalists continue to maintain that until he was officially rejected by the

---

42. See part five, chapter twenty-five. See also O. T. Allis, *Prophecy and the Church* (Philadelphia: Presbyterian and Reformed, 1945), and Anthony A. Hoekema, *The Bible and the Future* (Grand Rapids, Mich.: Eerdmans, 1979).

Jewish religious leadership, he continued to offer to establish an earthly Jewish kingdom which would overthrow the powers of Rome, which if true made him legally liable as a revolutionary leader to execution under Roman law!

DISPENSATIONALISM'S IMPLICIT SUGGESTION THAT THE CROSS WAS NOT ABSOLUTELY ESSENTIAL TO THE SINNER'S SALVATION

The classic dispensational claim that the next thing that should have occurred when Jesus came—as far as predictive revelation was concerned—was the establishment of the Davidic kingdom, implies that the Old Testament prophets had said nothing about the atoning work of the Messiah. Accordingly, dispensationalists maintain that Jesus, in keeping with the prophecies of Old Testament revelation, first offered the Davidic kingdom to the Jews, and that it was not until the Jewish religious leadership had officially rejected him that he then began to teach that he would die for men (but see John 2:19 and 3:14 where Jesus alludes to his death in his *early* Judaean ministry).

This interpretation implies that Jesus actually taught for a time (and that he also allowed the Jews to believe for a time) that if the nation of Israel would accept him as its King, he would forgive the nation of their sins on the basis of their faith in him as their messianic King and accordingly that he would not need to die for them. God would then have forgiven the Gentiles on some basis other than what we now know as the cross work of Christ. But on what other basis?

Some dispensationalists have suggested that the Old Testament ceremonial system of animal sacrifices would have been made a perpetual obligation for Gentiles—in spite of the fact that the author of Hebrews declares that the blood of bulls and goats can *never* take away sin (10:4) and has value and significance only as it symbolizes and typifies the blood of the antitypical Lamb of God.

Other dispensationalists have contended that Christ would have indeed still died—that if the Jewish nation had received him as their messianic King, then not the Jews but the *Roman* authorities would have moved against him as a rival Jewish "Caesar" and crucified him, thus providing the soteriological base for the establishment of the kingdom of grace for both Jews and Gentiles. But this scenario has its own problems. To begin with, the prophetic Scriptures foretold that it would be the Jews who would reject their Messiah and move to have him crucified (Ps. 2:1–2 [see Acts 4:25–28], Zech. 12:10). Furthermore, nowhere in Scripture is the kingdom of God in power represented as depending for its earthly entrance or establishment upon its reception by any single man or any single group of men. According to Scripture, when *it* comes, it will not ask mankind for permission to manifest itself or feel any obligation to present to mankind its credentials. When it comes, it will sweep away any and all opposition before it. When it comes, it will come like a mighty rock that breaks in pieces all that stands in its way (Dan. 2:34, 44). When it comes, it will come like a sickle comes to the harvest (Mark 4:29). When it comes, it will come as the lightning flash (Matt. 24:27). Daniel 2:44–45, in particular, teaches that when Christ establishes his kingdom in power, it "will never be destroyed, nor will it be left to another people. It will crush all those kingdoms [that went before it] and bring them to an end, but it will itself endure forever." Can one really believe, then, if the Jews had only accepted him as their King and if Christ had then gone about establishing the "kingdom of God in power" (and one must remember that it is not at all evident that such a kingdom was to endure for only a thousand years; Dan. 2:44–45; 7:14, 18, 27; and 2 Pet. 1:11 declare that his is an eternal kingdom), that the Romans would have possessed the military might to seize him against his will and execute him, or that he would have allowed them to crucify him? Scripture nowhere allows such a hypothetical scenario. The dispensational claim that Jesus actually offered to establish the earthly kingdom of God in power at his first coming if only the Jews would receive him as their King is a serious error.

The solution to all the difficulties created by dispensationalism is the glorious doctrine of the unity of the covenant of grace and the oneness of the people of God in all ages, as the Westminster Confession of Faith so clearly affirms. In its representation of the one covenant of grace as salvifically normative for men throughout all time, it avoids the soteriological discontinuities and difficulties of the dispensational system, takes seriously what the New Testament says concerning the faith of the Old Testament saints, and retains faith in the Messiah's atoning work—first in its *anticipated* Old Testament character and then in its *accomplished* New Testament character—as the necessary condition of salvation in all ages.

CHAPTER FIFTEEN

The Supernatural Christ of History

> The Son of God, the Second Person in the Trinity, being very and eternal God, of one substance and equal with the Father, did, when the fullness of time was come, take upon Him man's nature, with all the essential properties, and common infirmities thereof, yet without sin; being conceived by the power of the Holy Ghost, in the womb of the virgin Mary, of her substance....
> ... the Lord Jesus ... was crucified, and died, was buried, and remained under the power of death, yet saw no corruption. On the third day He arose from the dead, with the same body in which He suffered, with which also He ascended into heaven, and there sitteth at the right hand of His Father. (Westminster Confession of Faith, VIII/ii, iv)

"WHEN THE TIME had fully come," that is to say, at God's appointed time—when the Jewish diaspora had spread throughout the Roman Empire and the Old Testament had been translated into Greek, opening the eyes of the Greek world to its theological power and beauty, when the *pax Romana* extended over most of the known world with great roads and the Greek language linking the empire of the Caesars and making travel and commerce possible on a scale formerly impossible, when Greek philosophical thought had atrophied into skepticism, offering no hope in human wisdom to improve the ancient world (1 Cor. 1:19–21), when the so-called civilized world as a result had sunk so low morally (Rom. 1:21–32) that even pagans were crying out for relief from the rampant immorality all around them—in keeping with the Old Testament "promises, prophecies, sacrifices ... and other types and ordinances ..., all foresignifying Christ to come" (Westminster Confession of Faith, VII/v), "God sent his Son, born of a woman, born under law" (Gal. 4:4) as the Messiah and Mediator of the covenant of grace.

Without ceasing to be all that he was and is as the Second Person of the Holy Trinity, the eternal Son of God took into union with himself in the one divine Person that which he had not possessed before—even a full complex of human attributes—and became fully and truly man for us men and for our salvation. Jesus of Nazareth was and is that God-man.[1]

The historicity and true humanity of the man Jesus bar Joseph of Nazareth is rarely called into question today.[2] Our Lord calls himself (John 8:40) and is called by others many times a "man" (ἄνθρωπος, *anthrōpos*) (Matt. 8:27; 26:72, 74; Mark 14:71; 15:39; Luke 23:4, 6, 14, 47; John 4:29; 5:12; 7:46; 9:11, 16, 24; 10:33; 11:47; 18:17, 29; 19:5). Ἀνήρ (*anēr*, "man, male") is also used of him in John 1:30; Acts 2:22; 17:31. The author of Hebrews states that Jesus "shared in [our] humanity" and was "made like his brothers in every way" (Heb. 2:14, 17). His human ancestry is given by Matthew, who traces his lineage back to David and to Abraham (Matt. 1:1–17), and by Luke, who traces it back even to Adam (Luke 3:23–37). Luke informs his readers of an incident in Jesus' life that took place when he was twelve years old (2:41–51) and concludes this section of his Gospel by declaring that "Jesus grew in wisdom and stature, and in favor with God and man" (2:52). His historicity is assured by the fact that we are told that he conducted his earthly ministry during the reign of Tiberius Caesar when Pontius Pilate was governor of Judea, Herod was tetrarch of Galilee, and Annas and Caiaphas were high priests in Jerusalem (Luke 3:1–2). The Evangelists portray him as one who grew weary from a journey, sat down at a well for a moment of respite, and asked for water to quench his thirst (John 4), indeed, as one who could be so weary from a day's labors that he could sleep soundly through a raging storm on the sea (Mark 4:37–38). People knew his father and mother (John 1:45; 6:42; 7:27). He spat on the ground and made a healing mud with his saliva (9:6). He wept over the sorrow Lazarus's death brought to Mary and Martha (11:35) and raged in himself against the death that had brought such sorrow (11:33, 38). He was troubled or perplexed in spirit as he contemplated his impending death on the cross (12:27). Here is clearly a *man* for whom death was no friend, who instinctively recoiled against it as a powerful enemy to be feared and resisted. A crown of thorns

---

[1]. The Incarnation should be viewed as an act of addition and not an act of subtraction. See the next chapter.

[2]. This has not always been so. Jesus' true humanness was questioned early on in the Christian era by the Gnostic sects (and later by the Manichees), who taught that his body was not real but merely phantasmal and a masquerade, only seeming to be real. This view, opposed by the apostles (see 1 John 4:2; 5:6) and by the apostolic father Ignatius in particular, has come to be called "docetism," from the Greek verb δοκέω, *dokeō*, meaning "to seem." At the ecumenical councils in the fourth and fifth centuries, the church had to oppose later docetic tendencies appearing in the forms of Apollinarianism, Eutychianism, and monophysitism, all deriving from the catechetical school of Alexandria.

was pressed down on his head (19:2), and he was struck in the face (19:3). At his crucifixion (surely evidence of his humanity) a special point is made of the spear thrust in his side, from which wound blood and water flowed forth (19:34). And after his resurrection on at least two occasions he showed his disciples the wounds in his hands and side (20:20, 27) and even ate breakfast with them by the Sea of Galilee (21:9–14).

Benjamin B. Warfield also shows that the Gospel narratives depict Jesus as a man who was subject to the full range of (sinless) human emotions—compassion or pity (e.g., Matt. 9:36; 14:14; Mark 1:41; Luke 7:13), mercy (e.g., Matt. 9:27; Mark 10:47–48; Luke 17:13), love (e.g., Mark 10:21; John 11:3, 5, 36), anger (Mark 3:5), indignation or irritation (Mark 10:14), joy (John 17:13), grief (Mark 3:5), perplexity (John 12:27), despondency, horror, and distress (Matt. 26:37, 38; Mark 14:34), and marvel or astonishment (Matt. 8:10; Mark 6:6; Luke 7:9).[3] Here clearly is no docetic Christ.

But while Jesus' true humanness is rarely called into question today, the pervasive supernaturalism which the New Testament ascribes to both his person and his work is regularly explained away as fraudulent mythology.[4] Assuming then that which even the world is willing to grant, namely, the historical existence of the first-century Palestinian rabbi named Jesus of Nazareth, it will be my purpose in this chapter to address the major features of the supernaturalism which the New Testament ascribes to him and demonstrate the legitimacy and propriety of the New Testament portrayal of him. We will consider in order Jesus' virginal conception, his miracles, his transfiguration, his resurrection from the dead, and his ascension into heaven.

THE HISTORICITY OF JESUS' VIRGINAL CONCEPTION

The Biblical Data

In the words of J. Gresham Machen, "it is perfectly clear that the New Testament teaches the virgin birth of Christ; about that there can be no manner of doubt. There is no serious question as to the *interpretation* of the Bible at this point."[5] The biblical teaching is to be found in Isaiah 7:14 ("the virgin will be with child"),[6] Matthew 1:16 ("out of *whom* [fem.] was born Jesus"), 1:18 ("before they came together, she was found to be with child through the Holy Spirit"), 1:20 ("that which has been begotten

---

3. Benjamin B. Warfield, "On the Emotional Life of Our Lord," in *The Person and Work of Christ* (Philadelphia: Presbyterian and Reformed, 1950), 93–145.
4. See, e.g., the work of the Jesus Seminar.
5. J. Gresham Machen, *The Virgin Birth of Christ* (New York: Harper & Row, 1930), 382.
6. See Robert L. Reymond, *Jesus, Divine Messiah: The Old Testament Witness* (Ross-shire, Scotland: Christian Focus Publications, 1990), 23–42, for an exposition of the Immanuel prophecy of Isaiah 7:14.

in her is through the Holy Spirit"), 1:22–23 ("All this happened in order that [ἵνα, *hina*] the utterance [τὸ ῥηθέν, *to rhēthen*] of the Lord through the prophet might be fulfilled: 'Behold, the virgin will be with child . . .' "), 1:25 ("He [Joseph] knew her not until she gave birth to a son"), Luke 1:27 ("to a virgin . . . and the virgin's name was Mary"), 1:34 ("How shall this be, since I know not a man?"), 1:35 ("The Holy Spirit will come upon you, even the Power of the Most High will overshadow you. Wherefore, the One to be born will be called holy—[after all, he is] the Son of God"), and 3:23 ("being the son, so it was supposed, of Joseph"). Note also Mary's musings in Luke 2:19 and 2:51b, the snide intimations in Mark 6:3 that something (illegitimacy?) was unusual about Jesus' birth (see parallels in Matthew 13:55 and Luke 4:22), as well as in the suggestions of John 8:41 and 9:29, and Paul's "made of a woman" reference in Galatians 4:4. The tradition is unanimous that Jesus' conception occurred out of wedlock. We have, in other words, to do with either a virginal conception or an illegitimate conception. And the Bible clearly endorses the former as the ground of the rumors of the latter.

Only two New Testament writers—Matthew and Luke—directly mention the virginal conception of Jesus, but they are the only two to record his birth at all. As to whether other New Testament writers knew of his virginal conception, it certainly seems likely that Paul, working as closely as he did with Luke and being familiar with Luke's Gospel as he was (see 1 Tim. 5:18 and Luke 10:7), would have known about it. And it is also most likely that John, writing his Gospel after Matthew and Luke, would have known about it as well. He certainly understood that "the Word became flesh" (1:14) by human birth (19:37) and that he had a human mother (2:1; 19:25). And in light of his recurring statements that Jesus "came from above" (3:31; 8:23), "came down from heaven" (6:38), "came from the Father into the world" (16:27, 28), and "was sent by the Father" (5:36; 6:57; 10:36), John would have had to believe that some form of supernatural intervention intruded itself at the point of Jesus' human conception if all of these features which he reports about Jesus are to be harmonized. This much is clear: *no New Testament writer says anything which would contradict the Matthean and Lukan testimony.*

Church Testimony

The church has uniformly seen Jesus' literal virginal conception in the Matthean and Lukan birth narratives, as evidenced by the united testimonies of

---

7. For specific references in the writings of these early fathers, see Machen, *Virgin Birth*, 2–43. There were, of course, some sects which dismissed the story of Christ's virginal conception (the Jewish Ebionites, the heretic Marcion), but they clearly understood that the birth narratives intended to report history and not myth.

Irenaeus (Asia Minor and Gaul), Ignatius (Antioch of Syria), Tertullian (North Africa), Justin Martyr (Ephesus and Rome) and the Old Roman Baptismal Symbol in the second century[7] right down through the great creeds of the church to the present day (see the Apostles' Creed, the present Nicene Creed, the Definition of Chalcedon, the so-called Athanasian Creed [*homo est ex substantia matris,* that is, "He is man from the substance [nature] of his mother"], the Augsburg Confession, art. III, the Belgic Confession, art. XVIII, the Westminster Confession of Faith, chap. VIII, and the Thirty-nine Articles, art. II). The current suggestion of some modern scholars that Matthew (in particular) was writing "midrash" (the expansion and embellishment of actual history with the "nonhistorical") is simply unproven. There is, in fact, a real question as to whether midrash was a common literary genre at the time when Matthew wrote. It is clear, at any rate, that the early church fathers did not understand Matthew's birth narrative as a midrash. So when men like E. Brunner, W. Pannenberg, and the Jesus Seminar scholars deny the fact of the virginal conception of Jesus, it is not only the New Testament witness but also twenty centuries of consistent, universal testimony of the church that they reject—no small departure from Christian doctrine on the part of any man in any age. I therefore accept the fact of the virginal conception of Jesus[8] and am simply concerned here to draw out the implications of it for the nature of Jesus' person.

---

8. My reasons for believing in Christ's virginal conception in the womb of the virgin Mary through the power of the Holy Spirit are: first, the *biblical* teaching, which, of course, is paramount; second, the weight of the church's *historical* testimony; third, the *Christian theistic* reason, that is, Jesus' virginal conception is simply one aspect of the total supernaturalism of Scripture and of Christian theism in general; if one can believe, for example, Genesis 1:1, or that God speaks to men in Scripture, or in Jesus' miracles, or that he rose from the dead and ascended to his Father, it is asking very little more to believe that Jesus was virginally conceived; fourth, the *psychological* reason: only the virginal conception can explain Mary's willingness to be included in the company of those who *worshiped* Jesus as the *Son of God* (Acts 1:14); it taxes one's credulity to accept that Mary could have believed that her Son died for her sins and was her *divine* Savior deserving of her worship if she knew in her heart that his origin was like that of every other man and that he had been conceived out of wedlock; fifth, the *theological* reasons: (1) the virginal conception of Jesus is the Bible's explanation for the Incarnation, and (2) while the virginal conception is not necessarily the total explanation for Jesus' sinlessness, it is a fact that if Jesus had been the offspring of the union of a human father and mother, such a natural generation would have entailed depravity (John 3:6) and implicated Jesus in Adam's first sin (Rom. 5:12, 19); and sixth, the *apologetic* or *polemical* reasons: (1) if Jesus was not virginally conceived, then the Bible is in error and ceases to be a trustworthy guide in matters of faith (see Machen, *Virgin Birth,* 382–87); (2) if Jesus was not virginally conceived, serious gaps are left in any effort to understand the person of Christ and the Incarnation (Machen, *Virgin Birth,* 387–95); and (3) if Jesus was conceived like all other men, then he stood under the Adamic curse like the rest of us who descend from Adam by natural generation, and he would not have been an acceptable Savior of men before God. But this would mean in turn the end of Christianity as a

Given then the fact of his virginal conception, what was its purpose relative to Jesus himself?

The Purpose of the Virginal Conception

Perhaps we should begin our answer to this question by underscoring two things that we must *not* say its purpose was. First, we must not understand the birth narratives as teaching that Mary's virginal conception of Jesus was the efficient cause or source of his deity. Geerhardus Vos quite properly declares that while "there is truth in the close connection established between the virgin birth of our Lord and His Deity," it would be "a mistake to suspend the Deity on the virgin birth as its ultimate source or reason." To do so "would lead to a lowering of the idea of Deity itself."[9] What we intend to highlight here is the obvious fact that "neither sinful nor holy human parents could produce an offspring *who is God*. That is beyond their humanity. And neither could a virgin human mother do this!"[10] Another ground exists for believing that Jesus Christ is God, namely, the fact that as God the Son, he was fully and truly God prior to and apart from his virginal conception. Nor did the virginal conception produce a hybrid or a sort of demigod, an offspring of the union between a god (the Holy Spirit) and a human woman, who was neither fully god nor fully man but only half-god and half-man. This is simply mythology for which there is *no* scriptural warrant. Another purpose underlay the virginal conception of Jesus.

Second, the virginal conception of Jesus by Mary through the power of the Holy Spirit was probably not the efficient cause of Jesus' sinlessness (see 2 Cor. 5:21; Heb. 4:15). At the very least, it is most unlikely that Jesus' virginal conception was essential to his sinlessness, as some theologions have alleged, because "original [or race] sin" is transmitted through the *male* line, for women also share in the sinfulness of the human race

---

redemptive religion, since there would then be no one who could offer himself up to God as an acceptable, unblemished sacrifice to satisfy divine justice and to reconcile God to man. I fully realize that this last point assumes a particular doctrine of sin ("original and race sin") and a particular view of the atonement ("satisfaction"), but then it is a fact that the Bible teaches this doctrine of sin (Rom. 5:12–19) and this kind of atonement—the kind that Jesus accomplished by his sinless life and substitutionary death on the cross. The reader is referred to Warfield's article, "The Supernatural Birth of Jesus," *Biblical and Theological Studies* (Philadelphia: Presbyterian and Reformed, 1952), 157–68, for the further argument in behalf of the salvific necessity of the virgin birth of Christ.

9. Geerhardus Vos, *The Self-Disclosure of Jesus*, rev. ed. (Phillipsburg, N.J.: Presbyterian and Reformed, 1978), 191, fn. 15.
10. Kenneth S. Kantzer, "The Miracle of Christmas," *Christianity Today* 28, no. 18 (1984): 15.

and are corrupted by it, and this pervasive sinfulness encompassed Mary as well, who possessed a sinful nature, committed sins, and confessed her need of a Savior (Luke 1:47). All the biblical, not to mention the biological, evidence suggests that the woman contributes equally to the total physical, spiritual, and psychic make-up of the human offspring which comes from natural generation. It is striking, for example, that in his great penitential Psalm, it is specifically his mother whom he mentioned when David traces his sinful deed back to his sinful nature: "With sin," he declares, "did my mother conceive me" (Ps. 51:5). There is reason to assume, therefore, that, except for a special divine work of preservation beyond the virginal conception itself, Mary would have transmitted the human bent to sin to her firstborn. John Calvin was even willing to assert as much:

> We make Christ free of all stain not just because he was begotten of his mother without copulation with man, but because he was sanctified by the Spirit that the generation might be pure and undefiled as would have been true before Adam's fall.[11]

Luke 1:35 also suggests as much, if we construe ἅγιον (*hagion*, "holy") as a predicate and understand it in the moral/ethical sense. John Murray also entertains the same possibility, although with a certain degree of reserve:

> [Jesus' preservation from defilement] may reside entirely in the supernatural begetting, for it may be that depravity is conveyed in natural generation. [Note that he does not place the transmission of racial sin in the male line *per se* here but rather in the "natural generation" that involves the union of male *and* female.] In any case, natural generation would have entailed depravity (John 3:6). Yet it may not be correct to find the whole explanation of Jesus' sinlessness in the absence of natural begetting. So it may well be that preservation from the stain of sin (see Psalm 51:5) required another, supernatural factor, namely, the preservation from conception to birth of the infant Jesus from the contamination that would otherwise have proceeded from his human mother.[12]

Obviously, great care should be expended in any explanation of the ground of Jesus' sinlessness. But until we know a great deal more than we do about natural

---

11. John Calvin, *Institutes of the Christian Religion,* trans. Ford Lewis Battles (Philadelphia: Westminster Press, 1960), II.13.4; 481.
12. John Murray, "The Person of Christ," *Collected Writings of John Murray* (Edinburgh: Banner of Truth, 1977), 2:135; see also J. Oliver Buswell Jr., *A Systematic Theology of the Christian Religion* (Grand Rapids, Mich.: Zondervan, 1962), 1:251; 2:57.

generation and human reproduction, we would be wise to refrain from suspending Jesus' sinlessness simply and solely on the obvious fact that in the virginal conception the male factor had been eliminated in his human generation. In any event, it seems quite safe to say that, even if Jesus' sinlessness is a secondary effect of the virginal conception, his sinlessness was not the effect that his virginal conception was primarily intended to bring about.

What then was the primary purpose of Jesus' virginal conception? Before I respond directly to this question, it is appropriate to point out that Jesus' conception in a *human* mother's womb, although virginal in nature, followed by his normal development in that human mother's womb, and his altogether normal passage from that human womb into the world at birth, as recorded in both Matthew and Luke, are features of his human origination which insure and guarantee to us that Jesus was and is truly and fully human. The Bible is quite adamant that Jesus' full and true humanity was in no way threatened or impaired by the miracle of his virginal conception, but just to the contrary, by being conceived by a human mother he "shared" our humanity (Heb. 2:14), and was "like" us in every way (Heb. 2:17). The objection of some that the virginal conception precludes the possibility of our Lord being truly and fully man is hypothetical and undemonstrable.

When we penetrate to the mysterious and marvelous primary purpose of the Christmas miracle, I think we must conclude that both Evangelists intend that we should understand *before everything else* that, by means of the virginal conception, "the [preexistent] Word became flesh" (John 1:14). Mary's virginal conception, in other words, was the means whereby *God became man*, the means whereby he who "was rich for our sakes became poor, that through his poverty, we might become rich" (2 Cor. 8:9). It is the Bible's answer to the question that naturally arises when one hears that Jesus Christ is the God-man: "How did this occur?" The virginal conception is the effecting means of the "Immanuel event" (Isa. 7:14; Matt. 1:22–23) that made God man with us without uniting the Son of God to a second (human) person, which would have surely been the effect of a *natural* generation. But by means of Mary's virginal conception, God the Son, without ceasing to be what he is—the Second Person of the Holy Trinity, the eternal Son and Word of God, took into union with his divine nature in the one divine Person of the Son our *human nature* (not a *human person*) and so came to be "with us" as "Immanuel." Any other suggested purpose for the virginal conception of Jesus, whatever truth it may contain, pales into insignificance in the glorious light of this clear reason for it. And when this is clearly perceived, one will acknowledge that the Matthean and Lukan birth narratives take their rightful place alongside all the other lines of evidence in the New Testament for the deity of Jesus Christ and thus for the classical doctrine of an incarnational Christology.

THE SUPERNATURAL CHRIST OF HISTORY
THE HISTORICITY OF JESUS' MIRACLES
The Biblical Data

The following specific healing miracles of Jesus, having to do with the alleviation of human suffering, are mentioned in the Gospels: (1) the royal official's son (John 4:46–54), (2) Peter's mother-in-law (Matt. 8:14–17; Mark 1:29–31; Luke 4:38–40), (3) the woman with the hemorrhage of blood (Matt. 9:20–22; Mark 5:25–34; Luke 8:43–48), (4) the centurion's servant (Matt. 8:5–13; Luke 7:1–10), (5) the man suffering from dropsy (Luke 14:1–6), (6) the blind (Matt. 9:27–31; John 9:1–7; Matt. 20:29–34; Mark 10:46–52; Luke 18:35–43), (7) the deaf (Mark 7:31–37), (8) the paralyzed and lame (Matt. 9:1–8; Mark 2:1–12; Luke 5:17–26; John 5:1–15; Matt. 12:9–13; Mark 3:1–5; Luke 6:6–10; 13:10–17), (9) lepers (Matt. 8:1–4; Mark 1:40–45; Luke 5:12–16; 17:11–19), and (10) Malchus's ear (Luke 22:49–51). One must also mention here Jesus' exorcisms of demons, which, in his mastery over the forces of Satan which they demonstrated, signaled in a unique way his divine authority over and messianic assault against the cosmic kingdom of evil and sin (Matt. 8:28–34; Mark 5:1–20; Luke 8:26–39; Mark 1:23–27; Luke 4:33–37; Matt. 15:21–28; Mark 7:24–30; Matt. 17:14–21; Mark 9:14–29; Luke 9:37–43) and the raising again to life of Jairus's daughter (Matt. 9:18–19, 23–26; Mark 5:22–24, 35–43; Luke 8:41–42, 49–56), the widow's son (Luke 7:11–16), and Lazarus (John 11:1–54).

In addition to these specific examples of healing, we have several general narrative statements found in all of the Synoptic Gospels:

> Matthew 4:23–24: "Jesus went throughout Galilee, . . . healing every disease and sickness among the people. News about him spread all over Syria, and people brought to him all who were ill with various diseases, those suffering severe pain, the demon–possessed, the epileptics and the paralytics, and he healed them."

> Matthew 8:16: "When evening came, many who were demon-possessed were brought to him, and he drove out the spirits with a word and healed all the sick."

> Matthew 9:35: "Jesus went through all the towns and villages, . . . healing every disease and sickness.

> Matthew 14:14: "When Jesus landed and saw a large crowd, he had compassion on them and healed their sick."

> Matthew 14:35–36: "People brought all their sick to him and begged him to let the sick just touch the edge of his cloak, and all who touched him were healed."

> Matthew 15:30–31: "Great crowds came to him, bringing the lame, the blind, the crippled, the dumb and many others, and laid them at his feet; and he healed them. The people were amazed when they saw the dumb speaking, the crippled made well, the lame walking and the blind seeing."

All of the above general statements are from Matthew's Gospel alone. Statements to the same effect are also found in Mark 1:32–34, 39; 3:10; 6:56; Luke 4:40; 6:17–19; 9:11.

Matthew and Luke also report Jesus' own general description of his ministry in his response to John the Baptist's query: "The blind receive sight, the lame walk, those who have leprosy are cured, the deaf hear, and the dead are raised" (Matt. 11:4–5; Luke 7:22).

Jesus furthermore declared that if his "powers" that had been done in Chorazin, Bethsaida, and Capernaum had been done in Tyre, Sidon, and even Sodom, those ancient cities would have repented (Matt. 11:20–24; Luke 10:12–13). Even his enemies acknowledged his authority over demons (Matt. 12:22–32; Mark 3:20–30; Luke 11:14–23).

In addition to his own works of healing, Jesus gave to his twelve disciples the authority to "drive out evil spirits and to cure every kind of disease and sickness" (Matt. 10:1), including even the authority to raise the dead (Matt. 10:8); and Mark informs us that "they went out and . . . drove out many demons and anointed many sick people with oil and healed them" (Mark 6:13). Then later, he commissioned seventy(-two) other disciples to go and to do the same thing (Luke 10:1, 9, 17, 19). With pardonable overstatement, Benjamin B. Warfield writes: "For a time disease and death must have been almost banished from the land."[13]

To these "signs and wonders" having to do with the alleviation of human suffering, one must add the so-called nature miracles, such as (1) the changing of water into wine (John 2:1–11), (2) the two miraculous catches of fish (Luke 5:1–11; John 21:1–14), (3) the stilling of the storm (Matt. 8:23–27; Mark 4:35–41; Luke 8:22–25), (4) the feeding of the five thousand (Matt. 14:15–21; Mark 6:34–44; Luke 9:12–17; John 6:5–14), (5) the walking on the sea (Matt. 14:22–27; Mark 6:45–52; John 6:16–21), (6) the feeding of the four thousand (Matt. 15:32–39; Mark 8:1–10), (7) the four-drachma coin in the fish's mouth (Matt. 17:24–27), and (8) the cursing of the fig tree (Matt. 21:18–22; Mark 11:12–14, 20–21).

Critical Responses

If the New Testament record is reliable here, never had any other age of the world witnessed such a dazzling display of "wonders," "signs," "powers," and "works" of God. But much effort has been expended through the centuries to explain away Jesus' works of power, some explanations more speculative, some more rationalistic than others, but all having as their chief aim the reduction of Jesus to

---

13. Benjamin B. Warfield, "The Historical Christ," in *The Person and Work of Christ* (Philadelphia: Presbyterian and Reformed, 1950), 31.

manageable human dimensions. Baruch Spinoza (1632–1677), the Dutch rationalist philosopher, for example, argued in his *Tractatus Theologico-politicus* (1670) that God was a God of such unchangeable order that were he to work a miracle, since that miracle would then be as much God's law as the law of nature it violated, he would violate the unchangeable order he had decreed for the laws of nature and thus contradict himself. David Hume (1711–1776), the Scottish skeptic and empiricist philosopher of the Enlightenment, argued in his "Essay on Miracles," a section of his *Philosophical Essays Concerning Human Understanding* (1748), that the only case in which the evidence for a miracle could prevail over the evidence against it would be that situation in which the falseness or error of the affirming witnesses would be a greater miracle than the miracle which they attest. Friedrich Schleiermacher (1768–1834), often called the father of liberal Protestant theology, contended in his *The Christian Faith* (1821) that Christ's "miracles" were such only for those in respect to whom they were first done but not miracles in themselves, being but the anticipation of the discoveries of the laws which govern in the kingdom of nature. According to Schleiermacher, by the providence of God Christ simply possessed a deeper acquaintance with the laws of nature than any other man before or after him, and was able to evoke from the hidden recesses of nature those laws which were already at work therein and to employ them for others' benefits. Another German theologian of the same period, Heinrich Paulus (1761–1851), in his *Exegetical Handbook Concerning the First Three Gospels* (3 vols., 1830–1833) argued that the Evangelists did not intend their reports to be understood as miracles but only as ordinary facts of everyday experience. Thus Christ

> did not heal an impotent man at Bethesda, but only detected an imposter; He did not change water into wine at Cana, but brought in a new supply of wine when that of the house was exhausted; He did not multiply the loaves, but, distributing his own and his disciples' little store, set an example of liberality, which was quickly followed by others who had like stores, and thus there was sufficient for all; He did not cure blindness otherwise than any skilful occulist might do it;—which, indeed, they [the Evangelists] observe, is clear; for with His own lips He declared that He needed light for so delicate an operation—"I must work the works of Him that sent Me, while it is day; the night cometh, when no man can work" (John 9:4); He did not walk on the sea, but on the shore; He did not tell Peter to find a stater in the fish's mouth but to catch as many fish as would sell for that money; He did not cleanse a leper, but pronounced him cleansed; He did not raise Lazarus from the dead, but guessed from the description of his disease that he was only in a swoon, and happily found it as He had guessed.[14]

---

14. Cited by Richard C. Trench, *Notes on the Parables of Our Lord* (London: SPCK, 1904), 82–83.

Then there was David Strauss (1808–1874), another German theologian, who under the influence of Hegelian thought, in his famous *Life Of Jesus, Critically Examined* (2 vols., 1835–1836), argued that the supernatural elements in the Gospels, including the miracles of Jesus, were simply Hellenistic "myth," created between the death of Christ and the writing of the Gospels in the second century. Rudolf Bultmann also espoused a position not too different in its final conclusion from that of Strauss. And Joachim Jeremias, in his *New Testament Theology* (I) (Eng. trans., 1971), after critical literary and linguistic analyses, comparisons with rabbinic and Hellenistic miracle stories, and form–critical analyses of the individual miracle stories, contends that one is left with only a "historical nucleus" of "psychogenous" healings (exorcisms) and healings through "overpowering therapy"—in short, healings produced by psychic powers. G. Vermes in his *Jesus the Jew* (1973) takes a different approach, categorizing Jesus as a "charismatic" similar to other "Galilean charismatics" such as Honi the Circle-Drawer and Hanina ben Dosa. In *Jesus the Magician* (1978), Morton Smith, as the title of his book suggests, makes Jesus out to be simply a magician. A. E. Harvey's *Jesus and the Constraints of History* (1982) is not as radical in its denials as the former two books, but he reduces the authentic miracles of Jesus to eight in number—those dealing with healings of the deaf, dumb, blind, and lame.

Evangelical Responses

A separate and detailed response in support of the historicity and authenticity of each of Jesus' mighty works would require far more space than is possible here. Suffice it to say that this has been done by such men as R. C. Trench in *Notes on the Miracles of our Lord* (chap. 5, "The Assaults on the Miracles"), J. B. Mozely in *Eight Lectures on Miracles*, J. Gresham Machen in *Christianity and Liberalism* (see chap. 5, "Christ,"), C. S. Lewis in *Miracles*, Bernard Ramm in *Protestant Christian Evidences* (see chap. 5, "Rebuttal to Those Who Deny Miracles"), H. van der Loos in *The Miracles of Jesus*, Norman L. Geisler in *Miracles and Modern Thought*, Craig L. Blomberg in *Gospel Truth: Are the Gospels Reliable History?* (see chap. 3, "Miracles"), and Robert B. Strimple, *The Modern Search for the Real Jesus*. It has been shown time and again that every assessment of the supernatural Christ and his miracles as being spurious or rationally explicable is a result of an a priori judgment about the nature of God and the world.

The Christian, of course, acknowledges that he places the question of the historicity and authenticity of Jesus' miracles, first, within the total context of Christian theism *per se*. "Once admit," Machen writes, "the existence of a personal God, Maker and Ruler of the world, and no limits, temporal or otherwise, can be set to the creative power of such a God. Admit that God once created the world, and you cannot deny that he might engage in creation again."[15] And second, the Christian places the question of the historicity and authenticity of Jesus' miracles in the more narrow context of the specific requisite occasion of the reality of sin and its effects. He realizes that man's only hope of conquest over sin lies in supernatural aid from outside the human condition.[16] He believes this need is fully met in the supernatural Savior who gave evidence of his supernatural origin and character through, among other means, the working of miracles. Grant, in other words, the fact of the infinite, personal God of Scripture and the exigencies for mankind caused by human sin, and no philosophical or historical barrier stands in the way of the historicity of any of the supernaturalism and miracles of Scripture. The distinct likelihood of the miracles of the Gospels follows as a matter of course as a natural aspect of Christian theism.

Their Significance

Now within the context of biblical theism, the weight of Jesus' miracles, separately and collectively, point, according to Jesus' own testimony, to a twofold conclusion. They testified to the coming of the Messianic Age in the person of the Messiah (Matt. 12:28), but they also testified to his own divine character as the Son of God who visited this poor planet on a mission of mercy (Matt. 20:28; Mark 10:45) to seek and to save that which was lost. Consider Jesus' own testimony regarding the significance of his miraculous works:

JOHN 5:36

In the John 5 context, where may be found his most amazing series of claims to equality with God, Jesus said that in addition to John the Baptist's witness (5:33–35), the Father's witness (5:37; doubtless including if not specifically intending the confirmation from heaven at the time of his baptismal "commissioning"), and the witness of the Old Testament Scriptures (5:39, 46), "the very work that the Father has given me to finish, and which I am doing, testifies that the Father has sent me" (5:36). These unique works—unique because they were "works . . . which no one else did" (15:24), unique because they "bear upon them the hallmark of their divine origin"[17]—underscored, he says, his uniqueness as One not of human origin but as One whom "the Father sent" from heaven.

---

15. J. Gresham Machen, *Christianity and Liberalism* (Grand Rapids, Mich.: Eerdmans, 1923), 102.
16. Ibid., 104–106.
17. Leon Morris, *The Gospel According to John* (Grand Rapids, Mich.: Eerdmans, 1971), 328.

JOHN 10:24-25, 37-38

In these verses, in direct response to the demand from the religious leaders, "If you are the Messiah, tell us plainly," Jesus replied: "I did tell you, but you do not believe. The miracles I do in My Father's name speak for me." He then said: "Do not believe me unless I do what my Father does. But if I do it, even though you do not believe me, believe the miracles, that you may learn and understand that the Father is in me and I in the Father." By these remarks, Jesus asserts that his miracles bore testimony both to his messianic investiture and to an intimate spiritual union between the Father and himself.

JOHN 14:11

In his Upper Room Discourse, after making the claims that "anyone who sees me has seen the Father" (John 14:9) and that he and the Father were in personal union one with the other (14:10–11), Jesus urged his disciples to believe him for his own words' sake, but if they had any hesitancy concerning his words, then "at least," he said, "because of the works themselves believe." Again, his works, he declared, testified to his divine nature and mission.

MATTHEW 11:4–5; LUKE 7:22

As confirmation to John the Baptist that he was indeed the "one who was to come," that is, the divine Messiah, Jesus said to John's disciples: "Go back and report to John what you hear and see: the blind receive sight, the lame walk, those who have leprosy are cured, the deaf hear, the dead are raised, and the good news is preached to the poor." Jesus clearly implies that his miracles validated and authenticated the fact that with him the messianic age had arrived.

MATTHEW 9:1–8; MARK 2:1–12; LUKE 5:17–26

On this occasion Jesus vindicated his right to forgive sin—a prerogative of God alone—by healing the paralytic.[18]

---

18. The reader should also note the testimony of John and Peter in this connection. By his first miracle, John informs us in 2:11, Jesus "revealed his glory." And what glory was that? Just "the glory of the one and only [Son] who came from the side of His Father" (John 1:14). What is it, then, that John says this miracle signified but Jesus' glory as the divine Son of God!

  Peter's opening remark (Acts 2:22) in his sermon on the Day of Pentecost is also quite revealing: "Jesus of Nazareth, a man attested to you by God with miracles and wonders and signs

THE HISTORICITY OF JESUS' TRANSFIGURATION

Its Background

Peter's great confession at Caesarea Philippi that Jesus was "the Christ, the Son of the living God" (Matt. 16:16; see Mark 8:29; Luke 9:20) marked the beginning of a new emphasis in Jesus' instruction of his disciples. Now that they were fully convinced that he was the Messiah, Jesus began (ἤρξατο, ērxato) to emphasize the necessity of his death and resurrection[19] (which latter event, as the instrumental means to his enthronement at the Father's right hand, he apparently thought of in "shorthand" fashion for both his resurrection *and* ascension, since he says nothing about the latter event but rather assumes it when later he speaks about his Parousia) (Matt. 16:21; Mark 8:31; Luke 9:22). It was now both possible and needful for Jesus to infuse the messianic concept with the content of the Servant Song of Isaiah 52:13–53:2 and to correct the purely nationalistic associations which lingered in the disciples' minds (see Matt. 16:22–23; Mark 9:32–33; 10:35–37; Luke 9:46). So from that moment on to the end of his ministry, even though his disciples did not understand him (Mark 9:32; Luke 18:34), he kept constantly and prominently before them the fact of his "departure which he was about to accomplish at Jerusalem" (Matt. 17:22–23; 20:17–19, 22, 28; 21:39; 26:2, 11–12, 24, 28; Mark 9:31; 10:32–34, 38, 45; 12:8; 14:8, 21, 24; Luke 9:51, 53; 13:33; 17:11; 18:31–33; 22:20).

But Jesus not only began to speak more often than he had before about *his* suffering and death; in this context he also informed them that his disciple must be prepared to die as well and must never be ashamed of him, else "the Son of Man will be ashamed of him when he comes in his glory and in the glory of his Father and of the holy angels" (Luke 9:23–26; see Matt. 16:24–27; Mark 8:34–37). All of the Synoptic

---

which God performed through him in your midst" (see Acts 10:38–39). Here Peter attests to the authenticating value of Jesus' miracles—they testified to God's approval of the "man" Jesus. But then this means that God approved of his teaching as well, and in that teaching he claimed to be the Son of God, one with the Father, and in possession of the rights and privileges of deity.

19. This incident at Caesarea Philippi should not be regarded as marking the point of emergence of a totally new *doctrine* in Jesus' teaching. Rather, it pinpoints only the beginning of a new *emphasis* upon a doctrine which may be found in his earliest teaching (see John 2:19–22; 3:14; by implication also in Matt. 9:15; Mark 2:20; Luke 5:35).

Evangelists report that following immediately upon this reference to his return in glory (which is in itself an implicit claim to the messianic investiture), our Lord then cryptically declared: "Some who are standing here shall not taste death before they see the Son of Man coming in his kingdom" (Matt. 16:28),[20] words doubtless intended to be words of encouragement to counterbalance the apprehension which his previous words concerning martyrdom must have invoked. This cryptic saying implicitly enjoined them to view his passion and their own persecution against the background of his and (by extension) their own ultimate and eternal glory.

C. E. B. Cranfield summarizes seven suggestions which have been proposed for the fulfilling referent of this saying,[21] any one of which is to be preferred to the widely held view that Jesus mistakenly expected his Parousia to take place within the lifetime of that generation of disciples. For myself, with Cranfield,[22] William L. Lane,[23] and (I would suspect) most evangelicals, I believe that Jesus was referring to his transfiguration, which took place a week later, and which all three Synoptic Gospels place immediately after the saying. Such a fulfillment meets all the requirements of the saying:

1. The phrase "some who are standing here" would refer to his "inner circle" of disciples, Peter, James, and John, who alone were present at the transfiguration.

2. The phrase "shall not taste of death" that is, "shall not die," finds the explanation for its presence in the reference which our Lord had just made to the need for the disciple to "take up his cross" and "lose his life for me." The argument of some

---

20. The other Synoptists report this "Son of Man" saying in essentially the same way. Luke's account reads simply: "until they see the kingdom of God" (9:27), which, because in all the Gospels the Kingdom of God and the person of Jesus as the Messiah are bound together, I take to mean, "until they see the kingdom of the divine Messiah." Mark's account reads: "until they see the kingdom of God having come in power" (9:1), which adds the idea that the Messiah's kingdom will have come with accompanying manifestations indicative of the presence of divine omnipotence. See Royce G. Gruenler, "Son of Man," in *Evangelical Dictionary of Theology*, 1036, for the view that Jesus employs the title in a *corporate* sense both here and in Matthew 10:23.

21. C. E. B. Cranfield, *The Gospel According to Saint Mark* (Cambridge: Cambridge University Press, 1966), 285–288. The seven, briefly, are as follows: (1) Dodd's use of it in support of his view of "realized eschatology"; (2) the view that "shall not taste of death" refers to spiritual death, from which faithful disciples will be exempted; (3) Michaelis's view that the meaning is that there will be some at least who will have the privilege of not dying before the Parousia, but that it is not said when these will live and not implied that they must belong to Jesus' contemporaries; (4) the destruction of Jerusalem in A.D. 70; (5) Pentecost; (6) Vincent Taylor's view that Jesus was referring to a visible manifestation of the Rule of God displayed for men to see in the life of the Elect Community; and (7) the transfiguration.

22. Ibid., 287–88.

23. William L. Lane, *The Gospel of Mark* (Grand Rapids, Mich.: Eerdmans, 1974), 313–14.

that if Jesus' transfiguration is made the fulfilling referent of Jesus' remark, then the "some" in the first phrase would imply that at least some if not all of the others there present *would* die in the next few days is surely a *non sequitur*. For while Jesus' remark implies that the majority of those present would not see this thing themselves in their lifetime, it does not mean that they must necessarily die before *some* did see it.

3. The phrase "before they see" fits well with the sustained emphasis in the transfiguration narrative on this inner circle of disciples *seeing* him in his "unearthly" radiance. (See the phrases "transfigured before them" and "what you have seen" in Matt. 17:2, 9; the phrases "transfigured before them," "there appeared before them," and "what they had seen" in Mark 9:2, 4, 9; and the phrases "they saw his glory" and "what they had seen" in Luke 9:32, 36.)

4. The phrase "the Son of Man coming in his kingdom" (Mark: "with power"), as Cranfield notes, "is a not unfair description of what the three saw on the mount of Transfiguration,"[24] for Jesus' transfiguration was, although momentary, nonetheless a real and witnessed manifestation of his sovereign power and glory which pointed forward, as an anticipatory foretaste, to his Parousia when his kingdom would come "with [permanent] power and glory" (Mark 13:26).

Its Historicity

Bultmann's view that the transfiguration account "is an Easter-story projected backward into Jesus' lifetime,"[25] that is, a legendary resurrection appearance mistakenly displaced and put in the preresurrection material, continues to find support today. But it needs only to be said that G. A. Boobyer[26] and C. H. Dodd[27] have demonstrated that nothing about the transfiguration account resembles the later resurrection appearances. For example, all of the accounts of the resurrection appearances in the Gospels begin with Jesus being absent, while here he is present from the beginning. Again, in all of the accounts of Jesus' resurrection appearances, Jesus' spoken word is prominent, where here he is silent as far as any encouragement or instruction to his disciples is concerned. He speaks, but to Moses and Elijah about *his* future death (Luke 9:31). Then again, the presence of Moses and Elijah here is strange, if this is a resurrection appearance, since no figure from the beyond ever appears at the

---

24. Cranfield, *The Gospel According to Saint Mark*, 288.
25. Rudolf Bultmann, *Theology of the New Testament*, trans. Kendrick Grobel (London: SCM Press, 1952), 1:26, 27, 30, 45, 50.
26. G. H. Boobyer, *St. Mark and the Transfiguration Story* (Edinburgh: T. & T. Clark, 1942), 11–16.
27. C. H. Dodd, "The Appearances of the Risen Christ: An Essay in Form Criticism of the Gospels," in *Studies in the Gospels*, ed. D. E. Nineham (Oxford: Blackwell, 1955), 9–35. See also J. Schiewind, *Das Evangelium Nach Markus* (Göttingen: Vandenhoeck & Ruprecht, 1949), 123.

same time with him in the genuine resurrection appearances. Finally, this account contains none of the features that one might have expected if it is an appearance in the context of which Peter is present as a guilt-ridden disciple (see John 21). Consequently, Dodd concludes:

> To set over against these points of difference I cannot find a single point of resemblance. If the theory of a displaced post-resurrection appearance is to be evoked for the understanding of this difficult *pericope*, it must be without any support from form–criticism, and indeed in the teeth of the presumption which formal analysis establishes.[28]

Against the view of Lohmeyer[29] and others that it is a nonhistorical, symbolical expression of a "theological conviction" concerning Jesus, derived from imagery drawn from the Old Testament Feast of Tabernacles (see Peter's reference to "booths"), Cranfield marshals details in the account which are very strange if the pericope was only a theological statement created by the early church, such as Mark's "after six days" and Peter's use of "Rabbi" and his absurd statement about the "booths." The title of Rabbi and Peter's thoughtless statement are hardly likely to have been put in the mouth of a chief apostle if the post-Easter church was creating a symbolic narrative with a theological statement about Jesus as its purpose.[30] A more objective analysis will conclude that Mark was intending to relate something that really happened.

Finally, Matthew's τὸ ὅραμα, *to horama*, ("the vision"; 17:9), which I would translated by "that which you have seen," need not mean that what is reported here occurred merely in a vision which the disciples had. Three facts register tellingly against the view that Jesus' transfiguration was simply a visionary experience shared by the three disciples. First, a single vision is not shared, at least normally, by a plurality of persons at the same time. Second, ὅραμα, *horama*, may be used of what is seen in the ordinary way (see Deut. 28:34). And third, Luke expressly declares that the disciples "had been very sleepy," but it was when "they became fully awake" that "they saw his glory and the two men standing with him" (9:32).

Everything about the Gospel accounts suggests that the Evangelists intended to report an event that actually happened, that could have been seen by others had they been present; and no argument has been advanced that overthrows the traditional view of the church that represents the transfiguration as an actual occurrence in the life of Jesus and the lives of the three disciples. Therefore, I will presume the historicity of the event and proceed to its exposition.

---

28. Dodd, "The Appearances of the Risen Christ," 25.
29. E. Lohmeyer, *Das Evangelium des Markus* (Göttingen: Vandenhoeck & Ruprecht, 1937), 173–81.
30. Cranfield, *The Gospel According to Saint Mark*, 293–94.

The "Metamorphosis" Itself

The accounts all begin by informing the reader that a week after Jesus' cryptic prophecy,[31] Jesus took Peter, James and John up into a mountain.[32] Luke alone adds, "to pray." And while he was praying, we are told, Jesus was "transfigured" (μετεμορφώθη, *metemorphōthē*) before them. Two aspects of his physical appearance in particular are singled out for comment: his face (but this probably included his entire body as well because of the reference to his garments) and his clothing. While Luke simply states that "the appearance of his face was changed" (9:29), Matthew writes: "his face shone like the sun" (17:2). And while Matthew simply states that "his clothes became as brilliant as the light" (17:2), Mark adds that they became "dazzling white, whiter than any cleaner on earth could bleach them" (9:3), and Luke writes that they were "gleaming as lightning" (9:29). If this transformation took place at night, as some details in the Lukan account suggest (see 9:32, 37), the scene unfolding before the disciples must have been all the more fearsomely awesome (Mark 9:6).

This "transfiguration" in Jesus' appearance Luke characterizes in two words: it was a revelation of "his glory" (9:32), a momentary substantiation of the essence of his prophecy in Luke 9:26 where he makes mention of "his glory." Because Luke declares that Moses and Elijah, whose appearances are mentioned by all three Synoptics, also appeared in "glorious splendor" (9:31), one might at first be disinclined to make too much of Jesus' transfiguration so far as that feature in the accounts indicating anything unique about him is concerned, and conclude that the combined glory of all three is simply indicative of the "supernaturalism" of the occasion. But Peter would declare later that, in seeing what they saw, the disciples were made "eyewitnesses of [Jesus'] μεγαλειότης, [*megaleiotēs*]" (2 Pet. 1:16), that is, his "grandeur," "sublimity," or "majesty." He says nothing about Moses and Elijah. This word is used on only two other occasions in the New Testament—as an attribute of God in Luke 9:43 and of the goddess Diana of Ephesus in Acts 19:27, a word which can and does clearly designate the glory of deity. For Peter the word

---

31. Matthew's and Mark's "after six days" could place the event on the seventh day, especially if it occurred at night after the close of the sixth day, whereas Luke's "some eight days after," by inclusive reckoning, as in John 20:26, also means "on the seventh day." In any event, Luke's ὡσεί, *hōsei*, ("about") suggests that he was conscious that his number of days was an approximation to the figure in the other Gospels.

32. See Walter L. Liefeld, "Theological Motifs in the Transfiguration Narratives," in *New Dimensions in New Testament Study*, R. N. Longenecker and M. C. Tenney (Grand Rapids, Mich.: Zondervan, 1974), 167, fn. 27, for an interesting defense of Mount Meron, rather than the more traditional Mount Tabor or Mount Hermon, as the most likely site of the transfiguration. I mention this fact to underscore the historical character of the transfiguration.

took up into itself the idea also of divine power (see δύναμις, *dynamis,* 2 Pet. 1:16). So Jesus' "metamorphosis" was a visible manifestation, we may safely conclude, of his divine "glory" (Luke 9:32) and "majesty" (2 Pet. 1:16), revealed in "power" (2 Pet. 1:16).

The Voice from the Cloud

In response to Peter's thoughtless statement invoked by this awesome sight ("Rabbi, it is good for us to be here. Let us put up three shelters—one for you, one for Moses and one for Elijah" [Mark 9:5]), in order to remove even the remotest notion that these three "glorious" figures should be regarded in any sense "equal in power and glory," God appeared theophanically in the form of a bright cloud that enveloped them, and a Voice from the cloud said: "This is my beloved Son, in whom I am well pleased. Listen to him" (Matt 17:5–6). Whereas the Father's voice from heaven at his baptism *confirmed to Jesus* his rightful claim to Sonship, here it *attests to his disciples* his unique station as the Son of God. Here, as there, these words signalized Jesus' personal and essential divine Sonship as the antecedent ground and presupposition of his messianic investiture which is alluded to in the final words, "Listen to him," words reminiscent of Deuteronomy 18:15, "The Lord your God will raise up for you a Prophet like me [that is, Moses; recall his presence here on this occasion] from among your brothers. You must listen to him." Peter was later to confirm that the voice was that of God the Father and that the Father's attestation "honored" and "glorified" the Lord Jesus Christ (2 Pet. 1:17). Here, then, in the Father's attestation to his Son, in addition to the feature of the transfiguration itself, do we find the second indication in the transfiguration accounts of Jesus' essential deity.

The Disciples' Question

Coming down from the mountain the next day (Luke 9:27), the disciples asked Jesus: "Why, therefore, do the teachers of the law say that Elijah must come first?" (Matt. 17:10; Mark 9:11). Their mention of Elijah, of course, was prompted by the fact that they had just seen him. But what lay behind their question about him? There can be no doubt that it was something in Malachi's prophecy that now was perplexing them. Malachi had said that "Elijah" would come *before* the Lord came (3:1), *before* the great and terrible day of the Lord (4:5), which they had just seen "in miniature." The implication of their question for the identity of Jesus must not be lost: the disciples saw Jesus as Malachi's "Lord who was to come," the Yahweh of the Old Testament. But the order of the historical appearances—Jesus had first appeared, then Elijah—seemed to them to be the reverse of what Malachi had predicted. This seeming inversion of the prophet's order was creating for them the quandary which provoked their question. Jesus solved their problem by informing them that "Elijah" (in the person of John the Baptist) had indeed come first, whom Jesus had then followed as that "Elijah's" Lord. By his exposition of Malachi's prophecy here, Jesus laid unmistakable claim to being the Lord of hosts, the Messenger of the Covenant, who had promised he would come *after* "Elijah," his messenger, had come.

The entire account of the transfiguration is replete—resplendent might be the more appropriate word—with indications of Jesus' essential divine Sonship. It is not surprising that those who deny his deity are solicitous to reduce this event to legend or myth. But the accounts stand, in spite of the attempts of critical scholarship to make them into something which they are not, and thus they lend their combined voice to the larger witness of Scripture to Jesus' essential divine Sonship in the Godhead.

THE HISTORICITY OF JESUS' RESURRECTION

Jesus was crucified as an insurrectionist by Roman authorities at the instigation of the Jewish religious leaders. Few, if any, would deny this today. But in Paul's words, he "was raised on the third day according to the Scriptures" (1 Cor. 15:4). This quotation highlights what may well be taken as the major theme of both the New Testament and church proclamation.

Christians should admit, given the first-century Jewish milieu in which Christ's resurrection occurred, that it was not at all what the nation of Israel expected. I do not mean to suggest by this comment either that the Old Testament had no doctrine of the resurrection for it surely did (see Dan. 12:2), or that Jews of the first century did not believe in the resurrection of the dead, for it is a well-known fact that many Jews did indeed believe in the resurrection (see Acts 23:6–8). But they believed that the resurrection of the dead would occur in the future at the end of the world. But suddenly, here was a small group of men proclaiming, not in some out-of-the-way place like Azotus but in Jerusalem itself—the politico-religious center of the nation—that God had raised Jesus from the dead. Not only was this very strange teaching to the Jewish ear, it was also exceedingly offensive teaching to the majority of them, including Saul of Tarsus, because Jesus had been executed as a blasphemer on a Roman cross, which meant he had died under the curse of God (Deut. 21:23), with the sanction of the nation's highest court, the Sanhedrin.

The disciples of Jesus believed, however, that there were compelling reasons for such a proclamation, for in spite of threats, bodily persecution, and martyrdom, they continued to preach that he had risen from the dead. What were these reasons? I would submit that two great interlocking strands of evidence convinced them beyond all reasonable doubt that Jesus had risen from the dead just as he said he would.[33] These strands of evidence are the empty tomb and the fact and character of his numerous postcrucifixion physical appearances. Each of these calls for some comment.

The First Strand of Evidence: The Empty Tomb

All four Gospels report that on the third day after Jesus had been crucified and entombed his disciples discovered that his body had disappeared from the tomb in which it had been placed (Matt. 28:6; Mark 16:5–6; Luke 24:3, 6, 22–24; John 20:5–8). Almost immediately, as already noted, the disciples began to proclaim their conviction that Jesus had risen from the dead. Now if the tomb, in fact, had still contained his body—the women and later Peter and John all having gone to the wrong tomb (a most unlikely eventuality in light of Matt. 27:61; Mark 15:47; Luke 23:55)—we may be sure that the authorities, both Jewish and Roman, would have corrected the disciples' error by accompanying them to the right tomb to show them that the tomb still contained his physical remains.

Many critical scholars over the years have felt it necessary to concede that the tomb was undoubtedly empty, but they have blunted the edge of their concession at the same time by advancing such theories as the stolen body theory and the swoon theory to explain why it was empty.

THE STOLEN BODY THEORY

If Jesus' body was removed by human hands, they were the hands of either his disciples, his enemies, or professional grave robbers. Now if his disciples had stolen his body, which was the explanation first concocted to explain his body's disappearance (Matt. 28:12–15), one must still face the question as to how his disciples could have gotten past the Roman guards (who, according to Matthew 27:62–66, had been posted there for the express purpose of preventing his disciples from stealing his body) and how they could have rolled the stone away without being detected. The

---

33. Jesus himself spoke of his resurrection in John 2:19–21, Matthew 12:40, 16:21 (Mark 8:31; Luke 9:22), 17:9 (Mark 9:9), 17:23 (Mark 9:31), 20:19 (Mark 10:34; Luke 18:33) (see also Matt. 27:63; Mark 14:58; Luke 24:6–7). Certainly the veracity of everything that Jesus taught is called into question if he did not rise from the dead as he said he would. Indeed, it is not saying too much to insist that if Jesus rose from the dead as he said he would, the gospel is true; if he did not rise, it is false. And the "faith" that would believe he has risen, if in fact he did not rise from the dead, would be vain and futile (1 Cor. 15:17).

only possible explanation is that the entire Roman watch must have fallen asleep, which again was the first explanation offered.

But it is most unlikely that disorganized, fearful disciples would have even attempted such an exploit. And it is even more unlikely that the Roman guards would have fallen asleep on duty, since to do so would have meant certain and severe punishment. Nevertheless, both of these "unlikelihoods" would have to have occurred simultaneously if this explanation for the fact of the empty tomb is to be sustained. Furthermore any tough-minded hearer would have immediately rejected the guards' later explanation as to what had happened, for if in fact they all had fallen asleep they would not have known who had stolen the body (see Matt. 28:13). There is one more problem: if the disciples had been responsible for his body's disappearance—a most unlikely prospect in light of their reaction to everything that had just happened to Jesus (see John 20:19)—we must then believe that they went forth and proclaimed as historical fact a mere fiction which they knew they had contrived, and that, when thus faced by persecution and threats of execution, as many of them were, not one of them ever revealed that it was all a hoax. This scenario is highly improbable; liars and hypocrites are not the stuff from which martyrs are made.

If Jesus' enemies (the religious leaders) arranged for his body's removal, one must wonder why they did the one thing which would have contributed as much as anything else to the very idea which they were solicitous to prevent from arising (see Matt. 27:62–66). And if they, in fact, had his body in their possession or knew of its whereabouts, one must wonder why they did not produce either it or reliable witnesses who could explain the body's disappearance and prove the disciples wrong when they began to proclaim that Jesus had risen from the dead.

To attribute the fact of the empty tomb to grave robbers is the least likely possibility of all, for it is to intrude into the story an explanation for which there is not a grain of evidence. Moreover, not only would thieves have been prevented from doing so by the Roman guards, but also, even if they could have somehow avoided detection and had proceeded to plunder the tomb, they would have hardly, having first unwrapped it, taken the *nude* body of Jesus with them, leaving his grave wrappings behind and essentially intact (John 20:6–7).

THE SWOON THEORY

As for the swoon theory, if we may accept Albert Schweitzer's judgment (see his *Vom Reimarus zu Wrede* [1906], entitled *The Quest of the Historical Jesus* in the English translation), David Strauss dealt the "death-blow" to this view over one hundred and fifty years ago, but one occasionally hears it advanced as a possibility in discussions today. This theory maintains that Jesus had not actually died on the cross but had only slipped into a coma-like state, and that in the tomb he revived and made his way past the guards to his disciples, who then concluded that he had risen from the dead. He died shortly thereafter.

But to believe this pushes the limits of credibility beyond all acceptable boundaries. It requires one to believe that those responsible for his execution were incompetent both as executioners and as judges of the state of their crucified victims when they performed the *crurifragium* (the breaking of the legs) on them (see John 19:31–33). It also requires one to believe that Jesus—though suffering from the excruciating pain of wounded hands and feet, not to mention the loss of blood, the physical weakness and the shock to his entire system which would have naturally ensued from the horrible ordeal of the crucifixion itself and the lack of human care and physical nourishment—somehow survived the wound in his side, the preparation of his body for burial, and the cold of the tomb, and then pushed the huge stone away from the entrance of the tomb with wounded hands and made his way on wounded feet past Roman guards into the city to the place where his disciples were hiding and there convinced his followers that he—an emaciated shell of a man—was the Lord of life! This scenario is surely beyond all possibility. Such books as Hugh Schonfield's *The Passover Plot* and Donovan Joyce's *The Jesus Scroll* are only variations on this same theme and are not taken seriously by the scholarly community.

But if some critical scholars have acknowledged the fact of the empty tomb and have attempted (unsuccessfully) to offer explanations for it, others have simply declared that the empty tomb was not an essential part of the original resurrection story, that the church only later created the "fact" in order to fortify its stories of the resurrection appearances. This is not true. The empty tomb was part of the church's proclamation from the outset (see Acts 2:31; 1 Cor. 15:4). It is simply erroneous teaching that asserts that the first disciples believed that one can have a real resurrection without an empty tomb. G. C. Berkouwer has correctly observed:

> Not the empty grave but the resurrection of Christ is the great soteriological fact, but as such the resurrection is inseparably connected with the empty tomb and unthinkable without it. It is absolutely contrary to Scripture to eliminate the message of the empty tomb and still speak of the living Lord. The Gospels picture his resurrection in connection with historical data, moments, and places of his appearance. Scripture nowhere supports the idea of his living on independently of a corporeal resurrection and an empty tomb.[34]

---

34. G. C. Berkouwer, *The Work of Christ,* trans. Cornelius Lambregste (Grand Rapids, Mich.: Eerdmans, 1965), 184.

The conclusion is self-evident: the theologian who dismisses the empty tomb as irrelevant to the Christian message but who still speaks of "the resurrection of Jesus" does not mean by his "resurrection" what the New Testament means or what the church has traditionally meant by it. It has become more a saving "idea" than a saving event. But such a view of the resurrection would have been rejected out of hand by the early church as no resurrection at all.

We have defended to this point the fact of the "empty" tomb. But now we must point out that such a description is not entirely accurate, since the tomb was not completely empty. Not only did angels appear to the women in the tomb and announce to them that Jesus had risen (Mark 16:5–7; Luke 24:3–7), but also both Luke (24:12) and John (20:5–7) mention the presence of his empty grave clothes. The strips of linen in which Jesus' body had been wrapped were still there, with the cloth that had been around his head folded and lying by itself, separate from the linen. The empty grave linens suggest that not only had Jesus' body not been disturbed by human hands (for it is extremely unlikely that friend or foe would have unwrapped the body before taking it away), but also that the body which had been bound within the wrappings had simply passed through them, leaving the wrappings behind like an empty chrysalis. It is highly significant that, according to John's own testimony (John 20:3–9), it was when he saw the empty grave wrappings within the empty tomb that he himself came to understand that Jesus had risen from the dead.

The Second Strand of Evidence: Jesus' Postcrucifixion Appearances

The second great strand of evidence, after the fact of the empty tomb, is the many postcrucifixion appearances which our Lord made to his disciples under varying circumstances and in numerous places. The New Testament records at least ten such appearances, five of them occurring on that first Easter day, and the remaining five occurring during the following forty days leading up to and including the day of his ascension.

He appeared first to the women who had left the tomb (Matt. 28:8–10),[35] and then to Mary Magdalene, who had returned to the tomb after telling Peter and John what she and the other women had seen (John 20:10–18). Then he appeared to

---

35. Mark 16:9 states that Jesus "appeared first to Mary Magdalene," and this may well be the case. But appearing as it does in the long ending of Mark 16, there is some question as to the authenticity and veracity of this statement. The appearance accounts, in my opinion, are more easily harmonized if one has Jesus appearing first to the women as they hurried away from the tomb (Matt. 28:8–9), and then to Mary who followed Peter and John back to the tomb after informing them that the tomb was empty (see John 20:1–18). But a harmonization is still possible even if Jesus did appear first to Mary Magdalene.

Cleopas and the other (unnamed) disciple on the road to Emmaus (Luke 24:13–35), and then to Peter, no doubt sometime that same afternoon (Luke 24:34; 1 Cor. 15:5). His last appearance on that historic day was to the "Twelve" (actually ten in number since Judas and Thomas were not present) in the upper room (Luke 24:36–43; John 20:20–28; 1 Cor. 15:5). What is of great significance on this last occasion is the fact that Jesus invited the disciples to touch him in order to satisfy themselves that it was really he who stood among them, and he ate a piece of broiled fish in their presence as proof that his body was materially real and not merely a phantasm.

A week later he appeared again to his disciples, Thomas this time being present with the others (John 20:26–29). Again Jesus encouraged confidence in the reality and factuality of his resurrection, this time by inviting Thomas to put his fingers into the wounds in his hands and side. Then Jesus appeared to seven disciples by the Sea of Galilee—"the third time Jesus appeared to his disciples"—and he prepared and ate breakfast with them (John 21:1–22). Then he appeared to the Eleven on a mountain of Galilee (Matt. 28:16–20), this occasion also quite possibly being the one when he appeared to more than five hundred disciples at one time, many of whom were still alive at the time Paul wrote 1 Corinthians (1 Cor. 15:6). Then he appeared to James, his half-brother (1 Cor. 15:7), and finally to the Eleven again on the occasion of his ascension into heaven (Luke 24:44–52; Acts 1:4–9; 1 Cor. 15:7). We should also note his appearance to Saul of Tarsus some time later.

Viewed as "evidence," it is true, of course, that the fact of the empty tomb alone does not prove that Jesus rose from the dead, but it does indicate that something had happened to his body. The numerous postcrucifixion appearances of Jesus best explain what had happened to his body: *he had risen from the dead.* And the fact that the appearances occurred (1) to individuals (Mary, Peter, James), to a pair of disciples, to small groups, and to large assemblies, (2) to women and to men, (3) in public and in private, (4) at different times of the day, and (5) both in Jerusalem and in Galilee, removes any and all likelihood that these appearances were simply hallucinations. An individual may have a hallucination, but it is highly unlikely that entire groups and large companies of people would have the same hallucination at the same time!

One more highly significant feature about the Gospel accounts of the appearances of Jesus must be noted—they lack the smooth "artificiality" that always results when men of guile have conspired to make a contrived story plausible. One immediately encounters numerous difficulties in harmonizing the four accounts of the several postresurrection appearances. Furthermore, according to the Gospel record it was women who first discovered the empty tomb, and it was to women that Jesus first appeared after his resurrection. Given the fact that the testimony of women was virtually worthless at that time, it is highly unlikely, if the disciples had conspired together to concoct the stories of the empty tomb and Jesus' several appearances, that they would have begun their account with a significant detail which almost certainly would have discredited it at the outset. So in spite of the fact that it might have been more desirable from the disciples' point of view to be able to say that men had first discovered the empty tomb and that it was to men that Jesus had first appeared, this feature as it stands in the Gospel accounts compels the conclusion that it simply did not happen that way, and that, concerned to report what in fact had happened, the disciples reported the event accordingly. This feature of the Gospel record gives the account the ring of truth.

These two great strands of New Testament data—the empty tomb and Jesus' numerous postcrucifixion appearances—put beyond all legitimate doubt, I would urge, the factuality and the historicity of Jesus' resurrection from the dead.

In addition to these two lines of argument, one may also mention, for their inferential value for the historicity of Jesus' resurrection, (1) the disciples' transformation from paralyzing discouragement on the day of his death to faith and certainty a few days after his death, (2) the later conversion of Saul of Tarsus, and (3) the change of the day of worship for Christians from the seventh to the first day of the week, each of these facts requiring for its explanation just such an event behind it as is provided by the resurrection of Christ.

CRITICAL VIEWS CONSIDERED

For many critical scholars today the appearance stories recorded in the Gospels are legends. But what is intriguing is that, while these same scholars are not prepared to admit that Jesus actually rose bodily from the dead, most by far, if not all of them, will acknowledge the historicity of Jesus' death by crucifixion under Pontius Pilate, the subsequent despair of his disciples, their "Easter" experiences which they understood to be appearances to them by the risen Jesus, their resultant transformation, and the later conversion of Saul. In short, for many scholars today, while the resurrection of Jesus is not to be construed as a *historical event,* the disciples, they will admit, had some *subjective experiences* on the basis of which they proclaimed that Jesus had risen from the death and had appeared to them. What should we say to this?

Regarding the contention that the appearance stories are later creations of the church, it is significant that New Testament scholars in increasing numbers are advocating that Paul's statements in 1 Corinthians 15:3–5 (the first written account of the resurrection appearances, since 1 Corinthians was written prior to the canonical Gospels) reflect the contents of a quasi-official early Christian creed much older than 1 Corinthians itself (which letter was written probably in the spring of A.D. 56 from Ephesus) that circulated within the *Palestinian* community of believers.[36] This assertion is based upon (1) Paul's references to his "delivering" to the Corinthians what he had first "received," terms suggesting that we are dealing with a piece of "tradition," (2) the stylized parallelism of the "delivered" material itself (see the four ὅτι, *hoti,* clauses and the repeated κατὰ τὰς γραφάς, *kata tas graphas,* phrases in the first and third of them), (3) the Aramaic "Cephas" for Peter, suggesting a Palestinian milieu for this tradition, (4) the traditional description of the disciples as "the Twelve," and (5) the omission of the appearances to the women from the list. If Paul, in fact, had "received" some of this "tradition," for example, that concerning Jesus' appearances to Peter and to James (referred to in 15:5, 7; see also Acts 13:30–31) directly from Peter and James themselves during his first visit to Jerusalem three years after his conversion (see Acts 9:26–28; Gal. 1:18–19), which is quite likely, then this pericope reflects what those who were the earliest eyewitnesses to the events that had taken place in Jerusalem were teaching on *Palestinian* soil within *five to eight years* after the crucifixion. This clearly implies that the material in 1 Corinthians 15:3b–5 is based on *early, Palestinian* eyewitness testimony and is hardly the reflection of legendary reports arising much later within the so-called Jewish Hellenistic or Gentile Hellenistic communities of faith. There simply was not enough time, with the original disciples still present in Jerusalem to correct false stories that might arise about Jesus, for legendary accretions of this nature to have risen and to have become an honored feature of the "tradition." The presence of this "early confession" strongly suggests that the appearance stories in the canonical Gospels are not legendary stories based upon non-Palestinian sources, as many Bultmannian scholars have insisted.

Now it is significant that virtually all critical scholars today are prepared to admit that the disciples very shortly after Jesus' death underwent a remarkable transformation in attitude, with confidence and certainty suddenly and abruptly displacing their earlier discouragement and despair. Even Bultmann admits the

---

36. Günther Bornkamm, for example, refers to Paul's enumeration of the appearances of the risen Christ in 1 Corinthians 15:3–7 as "the oldest and most reliable Easter text . . . formulated long before Paul." He says of this "old form" that it "reads almost like an official record" (*Jesus of Nazareth* [New York: Harper and Brothers, 1960], 182). See also Wolfhart Pannenberg, *Jesus— God and Man* (Philadelphia: Westminster, 1968), 90–91. Excellent treatments of this generally accepted view may be found in George E. Ladd, "Revelation and Tradition in Paul," in *Apostolic History and the Gospel,* ed. W. Ward Gasque and Ralph Martin (Exeter: Paternoster, 1970), 223–30; Grant R. Osborne, *The Resurrection Narratives: A Redactional Study* (Grand Rapids: Baker, 1984), 221–25; and Gary R. Habermas, *Ancient Evidence for the Life of Jesus* (Nashville: Thomas Nelson, 1984), 124–27.

historicity of their "Easter experience"[37] and concedes that it was this newborn confidence that created the church as a missionary movement. What effected this transformation? If one replies, as some scholars do, that it was their belief that they had seen Jesus alive, I must point out that this is tautological: one in the final analysis is simply saying that their *belief* that they had seen Jesus alive gave rise to their *faith* in Jesus' resurrection. We are still left with the question: What gave rise to their belief that they had seen Jesus alive and in person? Some prior event had to effect their belief that they had seen the risen Lord. What was it? If one replies that a visionary experience, that is, a hallucination, was the event which gave rise to their Easter faith, it must be asked what caused this visionary experience. Opinions vary. Some scholars (G. Lampe, E. Schweizer, and G. Bornkamm, for example) have held that the resurrection appearances were mental images which the spiritual ego of the disembodied Jesus actually communicated back to his disciples from heaven, that the resurrection appearances, in other words, were real activities on the part of a "spiritualized" Jesus in which he entered into genuine personal intercourse with his disciples. Others have held that the experience of seeing Jesus after his crucifixion was a purely natural phenomenon—simply the work of autosuggestion. Bultmann, for example, suggests that Jesus' "personal intimacy" with them during the days of his ministry among them began to nourish such fond memories in them that they began to experience "subjective visions" of him and to imagine that they saw him alive again.[38] Michael Goulder, in the first of his two contributions to *The Myth of God Incarnate,* traces belief in Jesus' resurrection back to Peter who, belonging to that psychological type, he says, whose beliefs are rather strengthened than weakened the more apparently refuted they are, underwent a

---

37. Rudolf Bultmann writes: "The resurrection itself is not an event of past history. All that historical criticism can establish is the fact that the first disciples came to believe in the resurrection" ("New Testament and Mythology," in *Kerygma and Myth,* ed. Hans-Werner Bartsch [London: SPCK, 1972], 1:42). Donald Guthrie, however, is quite right to insist at this point upon an explanation for their "Easter faith":

> The more pressing need at once arises for an explanation of the "event of the rise of the Easter faith." The fact is that the skepticism of Bultmann over the relevance of historical enquiry into the basis of the Christian faith excludes the possibility of a satisfactory explanation of any event, whether it be the actual resurrection or the rise of Easter faith. The one is in no different position from the other. The rise of faith demands a supernatural activity as much as the resurrection itself, especially since it arose in the most adverse conditions. (*New Testament Theology* [Leicester: Inter-Varsity Press, 1981], 183).

38. Bultmann's actual words are as follows: "The historian can perhaps to some extent account for that faith from the personal intimacy which the disciples had enjoyed with Jesus during his earthly life, and so reduce the resurrection appearances to a series of subjective appearances" (*Kerygma and Myth,* 42).

"conversion experienced in the form of a vision" and imagined that he saw Jesus on that first Easter morning. That night he told the other disciples of his experience, and

> so great is the power of hysteria within a small community that in the evening, in [the hypnotic spell (?) of] the candlelight, with [the highly charged emotional situation of] fear of arrest still a force, and hope of resolution budding in them too [but on what ground?], it seemed as if the Lord came through the locked door to them, and away again. So [now note how effortlessly Goulder moves to his conclusion] . . . the experience of Easter fused a faith that was to carry Jesus to divinity, and his teachings to every corner of the globe.[39]

Now in addition to the fact that all such views (1) leave the fact of the empty tomb unexplained and (2) fail to come to terms with the variety of objective details in the several accounts of the appearances themselves, George E. Ladd has quite correctly pointed out that

> visions do not occur arbitrarily. To experience them requires certain preconditions on the part of the subjects concerned, preconditions that were totally lacking in the disciples of Jesus. To picture the disciples nourishing fond memories of Jesus after His death, longing to see Him again, not expecting Him really to die, is contrary to all the evidence we possess. To portray the disciples as so infused with hope because of Jesus' impact on them that their faith easily surmounted the barrier of death and posited Jesus as their living, risen Lord would require a radical rewriting of the Gospel tradition. While it may not be flattering to the disciples to say that their faith could result only from some objectively real experience, this is actually what the Gospels record.[40]

Even Bornkamm, one of Bultmann's most influential students, has to admit that "the miracle of the resurrection does not have a satisfactory explanation in the inner nature of the disciples," for as he himself acknowledges:

> The men and women who encounter the risen Christ [in the Gospels] have come to an end of their wisdom. Alarmed and disturbed by his death, mourners, they wander about the grave of their Lord in their helpless love, trying with pitiable means—like the women at the grave—to stay the process and odor of cor-

---

39. Michael Goulder, "Jesus, The Man of Universal Destiny," in *The Myth of God Incarnate*, ed. John Hick (Philadelphia: Westminster, 1977), 59.
40. George E. Ladd, "The Resurrection of Jesus Christ," in *Christian Faith and Modern Theology*, ed. Carl F. H. Henry (Grand Rapids, Mich.: Baker, 1964), 270-71.

ruption, disciples huddled fearfully together like animals in a thunderstorm (Jn. xx. 19 ff.). So it is, too, with the two disciples on the way to Emmaus on the evening of Easter day; their last hopes, too, are destroyed. One would have to turn all the Easter stories upside down if one wanted to present these people in the words of Faust: "They are celebrating the resurrection of the Lord, for they themselves are resurrected." No, they are not themselves resurrected. What they experience is fear and doubt, and what only gradually awakens joy and jubilation in their hearts is just this: They, the disciples, on this Easter day, are the ones marked out by death, but the crucified and buried one is alive.[41]

He goes on to say that by no means was "the message of Jesus' resurrection . . . only a product of the believing community," and concludes that "it is just as certain that the appearances of the risen Christ and the word of his witnesses have in the first place given rise to this faith."[42] I concur and would insist that the "objectively real experience" of the disciples, of which Ladd spoke earlier, came to them as the result of the "many convincing proofs" (Acts 1:3) of his resurrection given to them by Jesus' numerous material postresurrection appearances to them. Nothing less than his actual resurrection can explain both the empty tomb and the disciples' transformation from doubt and gloom to faith and the martyr's joy. And we neither should nor need look for another explanation as the ground of their Easter faith.

THE HISTORICITY OF JESUS' ASCENSION

The Biblical Data

Both in his Gospel and in Acts, Luke records that Jesus, upon completing his forty-day preascension ministry, bodily "ascended into heaven." He employs three verbs to describe this momentous event: ἀνεφέρετο, *anephereto*, "was led up" (Luke 24:51), ἀνελήμφθη, *anelēmphthē*, "was taken up" (Acts 1:2, 11; see ἀναλήμψεως, *analēmpseōs*, in Luke 9:51), and ἐπήρθη, *epērthē*, "was lifted up" (Acts 1:9). Of the four Gospel writers, Luke alone records the historical account of Jesus' ascension,[43] but he is by no means the only New Testament writer who refers to the event. Peter, Luke reports, referred to it in the upper room shortly after it occurred (Acts 1:22) and

---

41. Bornkamm, *Jesus of Nazareth*, 184–85.
42. Ibid., p.183. The reader should recall, however, that Bornkamm espouses the view that Jesus' resurrection appearances were visions sent from heaven and not physical in nature.
43. The long ending of Mark (16:19–20) records that Jesus "was taken up [ἀνελήμφθη, *anelēmphthē*] into heaven and he sat at the right hand of God." This section is textually suspect, but it does reflect a tradition that accords with the Lukan report. It appears, in fact, to have been based mainly on the Lukan testimony.

mentioned it in his sermons later (2:33–35; 3:21; 5:31); he also writes of it directly in 1 Peter 3:22. Stephen's statement in Acts 7:56 presupposes the past occurrence of it. Paul presupposes its historical actuality in his references to Christ's session at the Father's right hand in Romans 8:34 and Colossians 3:1, alludes to it in his words of Ephesians 1:20–22, 2:6, and Philippians 2:9–11, and expressly mentions it in Ephesians 4:8–10 and 1 Timothy 3:16. The writer of Hebrews presupposes it in 1:3, 13, 2:9, 8:1, 10:12, and 12:2, and expressly refers to it in 4:14, 6:20, and 9:24. John informs us that Jesus himself often alluded to it (John 6:62; 7:33–34; 8:21; 13:33; 14:2, 28; 16:7–10; 20:17), and that he "knew that . . . he had come from God and was returning to God" (13:3). Finally, it is clear that Jesus presupposed it in his testimony before the Sanhedrin at his trial when he said: "you will see the Son of Man sitting at the right hand of the Mighty One" (Matt. 26:64; Mark 14:62; Luke 22:69).

The Bultmann school, not surprisingly, relegates Christ's ascension to the realm of legend, Bultmann himself writing:

> According to 1 Cor. 15:5–8, where Paul enumerates the appearances of the risen Lord as tradition offered them, the resurrection of Jesus meant simultaneously his exaltation; not until later was the resurrection interpreted as a temporary return to life on earth, and this idea then gave rise to the ascension story.[44]

This construction reflects his overarching aversion to the "intrusion" of the supernatural into the realm of earth history, the ascension particularly mirroring for him the so-called mythological (nonscientific) "three-story universe" concept of the ancient world. But as Donald Guthrie states, this is not the construction which should be placed on the ascension data:

> The upward movement [of Jesus' physical figure] is almost the only possible method of pictorially representing complete removal. The OT instances of Enoch and Elijah present certain parallels. Inevitably a spatial notion is introduced, but this is not the main thrust of the Acts description. The focus falls on the screening cloud, precisely as it does in the transfiguration account. . . . The reality of the ascension is not seen in an up-there movement, so much as in the fact that it marked the cessation of the period of confirmatory appearances.[45]

B. F. Westcott, likewise, aids us by sensitively commenting on the nature of the ascension in these words:

---

44. Bultmann, *Theology of the New Testament*, 1:45.
45. Donald Guthrie, *New Testament Theology* (Leicester: Inter-Varsity Press, 1981), 395. See also Gordon H. Clark, "Bultmann's Three-Storied Universe," in *A Christianity Today Reader*, ed. Frank E. Gabelein (New York: Meredith, 1966), 173–76.

[Jesus] passed beyond the sphere of man's sensible existence to the open Presence of God. The physical elevation was a speaking parable, an eloquent symbol, but not the Truth to which it pointed or the reality which it foreshadowed. The change which Christ revealed by the Ascension was not a change of place, but a change of state, not local but spiritual. Still from the necessities of our human condition the spiritual change was represented sacramentally, so to speak, in an outward form.[46]

In other words, the "heavenly places" of Scripture expression are not to be conceived in spatial dimensions as "up there," but in spiritual dimensions to which Jesus' *glorified* corporeal existence was capable of adapting without ceasing to be truly human, in keeping with his activity described in Luke 24:31, 36, and John 20:19, 26. Therefore, Berkouwer quite properly concludes:

Only severe Bible criticism can lead one to a denial of the ascension and even to its complete elimination from the original apostolic *kerygma*. . . . To the Church it has always been a source of comfort to know that Christ is in heaven with the Father. And over against the denial of both the *ascensio* and *sessio* as being contrary to the "modern world conception," the Church may continue on the basis of Holy Scripture to speak of these facts in simplicity of faith.[47]

Still other critical scholars contend that the earliest ascension tradition in the church had Christ ascending to heaven directly from the cross with no intervening resurrection and preascension ministry. Traces of this are purportedly to be found in the early Christian hymn cited by Paul in Philippians 2:6–11, for there Christ's humiliation and exaltation are contrasted with no mention of his burial and resurrection. John's Gospel also is supposed to reflect this "ascension from the cross" teaching in such verses as 12:23 and 13:21, where John quotes Jesus to the effect that his hour of death would also mean his glorification. The author of Hebrews is also said to have favored the idea that Jesus ascended to heaven from the cross, because of such statements as the one in 10:12: "But when this priest had offered for all time one sacrifice for sins, he sat down at the right hand of God." Again, the point is made, there is no mention here of Christ's resurrection or preascension ministry.

Several things may be said about this effort to explain the ascension in nonliteral, nonhistorical terms. First, apparently the operative (but erroneous) canon of exegesis here is this: if a New Testament writer does not mention Christ's resurrection and preascension ministry in every context where he mentions Christ's exaltation or

---

46. B. F. Westcott, *The Revelation of the Risen Lord* (London: Macmillan, 1898), 180.
47. Berkouwer, *The Work of Christ*, 206, 234.

his session at the right hand of his Father, one should conclude that either he himself was unaware of the resurrection and the subsequent preascension ministry or that the tradition he is citing was unaware of these events. But this is a *non sequitur*, and it imposes the highly artificial requirement upon the New Testament writer always to mention the resurrection, preascension ministry, and ascension whenever he mentions Christ's session at the right hand of God. Second, such a contention completely ignores the fact that all of these New Testament writers refer elsewhere—indeed, in the very works where the so-called ascension from the cross is supposedly taught—to the postcrucifixion resurrection of Christ: by Paul, for instance, in Galatians 1:1, 1 Thessalonians 1:10, 4:14, Acts 17:31, 26:23, 1 Corinthians 15:4, 12–20, Romans 1:4, 4:25, 6:4, 5, 9, 7:4, 8:11, 34, Ephesians 1:20, Philippians 3:10, Colossians 1:18, 2:12, 3:1, 2 Timothy 2:8; by John in John 2:19–21, 20:1–29, 21:1–22; and by the author of Hebrews in Hebrews 13:20. Moreover, Paul makes mention of the "many days" intervening between Christ's resurrection and ascension (Acts 13:31). Third, what Berkouwer says in defense of the author of Hebrews, namely, that the only way these critical scholars can interpret the work in this way is to proceed with the following formula: "The glory of Christ in Hebrews minus Hebrews 13:20 equals the ascension 'from the cross,'"[48] may be said in defense of all of the New Testament writers: the only way they can be used to support the idea that Christ ascended to heaven directly from the cross is to ignore all of the references in their writings to Christ's resurrection, his postresurrection appearances, and his preascension ministry. One can only conclude that these scholars have very little confidence in the trustworthiness of the Gospels and epistles.

Its Significance

For the disciples, the ascension of Christ meant his *separation* from them, not "with respect to his Godhead, majesty, grace and Spirit" (*Heidelberg Catechism*, Question 47; see also Question 46), of course, for his spiritual communion with them remains unbroken and undisturbed as a genuine and even enhanced spiritual reality, but only with respect to his physical presence among them. This separation Christ himself spoke about in such places as Luke 5:35; John 7:33; 12:8; 13:33; 14:30; and 16:10 (see also 1 Pet. 1:8; 1 John 3:2).[49]

With respect to Christ himself, the Scriptures virtually exhaust available "triumphalist" language, images, and metaphors, to describe the significance of

---

48. Ibid., 208.
49. Here I am following the Reformed rather than the Lutheran tradition, which latter tradition maintains, because of its peculiar doctrine of the *communicatio idiomatum*, that Christ is, by virtue of the union of the two natures in the one person of Christ, *physically* ubiquitous and therefore physically present "in, with, and under" the elements of the Lord's Supper.

Christ's ascension for him. As his resurrection was the means to his ascension, and so a significant aspect of his total exaltation, so his ascension in turn was the means to his climactic exaltation and enthronement (*sessio*) at the Father's right hand as Holy One, Lord, Christ, Prince, and Savior of the world (Acts 2:27, 33–36; 5:31; Rom. 8:34; Col. 3:1; Phil. 2:9–11; Heb. 1:3). If his ascension was "in glory" (1 Tim. 3:16), exalting him thereby "higher than all the heavens" (Eph. 4:10; Heb. 7:26), he is also now "crowned with glory and honor" (Heb. 2:9), "with angels, authorities, and powers in submission to him" (1 Pet. 3:22), with "everything under his feet," the Father alone excepted (1 Cor. 15:26; Eph. 1:22a), sitting "far above all rule and authority, power and dominion, and every title that can be given, not only in the present age but also in the one to come" (Eph. 1:21). God has also "given" him to be "head-over-everything for the church, which is his body, the fullness of him who fills everything in every way" (Eph. 1:22–23), indeed, who fills "the whole universe" (τὰ πάντα, *ta panta*) with his power and lordship (Eph. 4:10). In sum, he now occupies the "highest place" (Phil. 2:9) of glory and honor (Heb. 2:9) which heaven can afford, and to him belongs *de jure* and *de facto* the titles "Lord of all" (Acts 10:36; Rom. 10:12) and Lord above all other lords (Acts 2:36; Phil. 2:9b; Rev. 19:16), "that at the name of Jesus, every knee should bow in heaven and on earth and under the earth, and every tongue confess that Jesus Christ is Lord" (Phil. 2:10–11a). The nature of his lordship entitles him sovereignly to bestow gifts of every and of whatever kind upon men as he pleases (Eph. 4:7–8, 11).

Thus it is clear that upon his resurrection and ascension (these two events may be construed quite properly together, even though the former preceded the latter by forty days, as the collective two-stage means to his exaltation to Lordship), as the fruit and reward for his labors on earth, Jesus as the Messiah was granted supreme lordship and universal dominion over men. This is also suggested (1) by his own statement in Matthew 28:18: "All authority in heaven and on earth has been given to me," where he speaks of that messianic lordship which he received *de jure* at his resurrection but which he actually began to exercise *de facto* universally from heaven upon his ascension and present session at the Father's right hand (I would suggest that his references in Matthew 11:27 and John 17:2 to a possessed "delegated" dominion should be understood against the background of the covenant of redemption in the councils of eternity); (2) by Peter's statement: "God made [ἐποίησεν, *epoiēsen*: "appointed," "constituted"] him both Lord and Christ" (Acts 2:36) following upon his resurrection and ascension—another declaration of his *de facto* assumption of mediatorial reign as the God-man, since Jesus was obviously both Lord and Messiah by divine appointment from the moment of his incarnation; and (3) by Paul's statement: "because of which [διὸ καί, *dio kai*] [earthly work] God exalted him to the highest place and gave him the name, the 'above everything' name," that is, the title of "Lord" (Phil. 2:9).

It would be a fatal mistake theologically to deduce from any of this that Jesus as the Son of God, who (though in union with our flesh) continued infinitely to transcend all creaturely limitations, became "Lord" only at his exaltation and acquired *as God's Son* only then *de jure* and *de facto* universal dominion. We must never forget that, for Peter, it was "our God and Savior Jesus Christ" who "sprinkles us with his blood" (2 Pet. 1:1; 1 Pet. 1:2). For Paul, likewise, it was "the Lord of Glory" (ὁ κύριος τῆς δόξης, *ho kyrios tēs doxēs*), this expression meaning "the Lord to whom glory belongs as his native right," who was also "God over all" (Rom. 9:5) and "our great God" (Tit. 2:13), who was crucified for us (1 Cor. 2:8). As God the Son, then, Jesus, of course, continued as he always had done to uphold all things by the word of his power (Heb. 1:3) and to exercise the powers and lordly rights which were intrinsically his as the divine Being (see Calvin, *Institutes*, II.13.4). Consequently, when these apostles tell us that Christ Jesus was "appointed" Lord or was "exalted" and "given" authority and the title of "Lord" at his ascension, it is necessary that we understand that these things were said of him in his mediatorial role as the Messiah. It is appropriate to say these things about him but only because he, "the Son," who is intrinsically and essentially "rich," who is "Lord" by right of nature, had *first* deigned to take into union with himself our "flesh," becoming thereby "poor" (2 Cor. 8:9). It was as the divine-human Messiah, then, that he "acquired" or "was given" at his ascension *de facto* authority to exercise mediatorial dominion. It was not then the exaltation but the prior "humiliation" which was the "strange experience"[50] to the Son *as God*. Conversely, it was not the humiliation but the "exaltation" which was the "new experience" to the Son *as the divine-human Messiah*. If we are to take history, and specifically redemptive history, seriously we must say this. We must be willing to say that, in a certain sense, the exaltation entailed for the Son an experience which had not been his before. This "new experience" was universal dominion, not as God *per se*, of course, but as the divine-human Messiah and as the divine-human Mediator between God and man. We even learn elsewhere that this mediatorial dominion is a temporarily delegated authority. When he and his Father have subjugated finally all his and our enemies, then he will yield up to the Father not his Sonship[51] but this delegated authority as the Messiah, and his special mediatorial

---

50. The phrase is Benjamin B. Warfield's (see his *The Lord of Glory* [1907; reprint, Grand Rapids, Mich.: Baker, 1974], 225).
51. Herman Ridderbos observes that "where there is mention of the consummation of Christ's work of redemption, in the words of 1 Corinthians 15:28 (when the Son has subjected all things to the Father, then will he himself be subject to him, that God may be all in all), this cannot mean the end of the Sonship. One will rather have to judge the 'post-existence' of the Son intended here in the light of what is elsewhere so clearly stated of his pre-existence" (*Paul: An Outline of His Theology*, trans. John Richard DeWitt [Grand Rapids, Mich.: Eerdmans, 1975], 69).

dominion will be "reabsorbed" into the universal and eternal dominion of the Triune God (1 Cor. 15:24–28). In sum, the ascension meant for the Son, as the divine-human Messiah, the assumption of the prerogatives of the messianic investiture on a universal scale, rights which were already his by right of nature as God the Son, but which he "won" or was "awarded" as the incarnate Son for fulfilling the obligations pertaining to the estate of humiliation intrinsic to the messianic investiture.

It was this Christ, in precisely the terms of this his glorious lordship, who was made central to all early apostolic preaching. The apostles pointedly drew out the implications of Christ's exclusive lordship over the world for their audiences. There is no mention of religious pluralism in their preaching. For them there was an exclusivity and finality about God's revelation to men in Jesus Christ (Matt. 21:37; Mark 12:6; Heb. 1:1). For them, because of who Christ is, the work he did, the place he presently occupies, and the titles he bears, "salvation is in no one else, for there is no other name given among men by which we must be saved" (Acts 4:12). For them, as Jesus himself said, he alone is the way, the truth and the life (John 14:6). For them, he is the only Mediator between God and man (1 Tim. 2:5). He is also the One who, as Lord, will judge the living and the dead at his appearing (Acts 10:42; 17:31; Rom. 14:9; 2 Tim. 4:1). And he is the One whose once-for-all offering up of himself as a sacrifice to satisfy divine justice is alone acceptable to God the Father, the "legal" representative of the Godhead, in the "great transaction" of redemption and the canceling of sin (Heb. 9:24–26), and whose high priestly intercession alone meets with the Father's approval (Rom. 8:34; Heb. 7:24–25; 1 John 2:1). In light of their exclusive claims for him, it is not surprising that the blessing and power of God rested upon the Apostles' evangelistic efforts.

We have said enough about these reported features of Jesus' life and ministry to conclude that nothing about them warrants their rejection as unhistorical or mythological. Those who do reject them as unhistorical or mythological do so on highly questionable critical and philosophical grounds with which they are simply more comfortable psychologically and religiously. Accordingly, we will turn now to a consideration of what the early church said about the historical Jesus who was virginally conceived, who did mighty works during his days of ministry, who was transfigured before his disciples, who on the third day after death was resurrected, who some days later ascended into heaven, and who is the only way to the Father.

CHAPTER SIXTEEN

The Christ of the Early Councils

AT CAESAREA PHILIPPI Jesus asked his disciples: "Who do men say the Son of Man is?" (Matt. 16:13). Later, on the Tuesday of the Passion Week, after the Pharisees, Sadducees, and teachers of the law had terminated their inquisition, Jesus posed for the Pharisees the questions: "What do you think of the Christ? Whose Son is he?" (Matt. 22:41–46). These pointed questions forced them and later the early church—as they force us—to reflect upon the person of Jesus Christ. Is Jesus the Christ of God? And if so, whose Son is he? Is he only the Son of David or is he also the Son of God? Does a right view of him necessarily entail the ascription to him of inherent, intrinsic, ontological deity?

The Bible—both the Old and New Testaments, but particularly the New—represents Jesus as being both God and man—true God in that he is the real incarnation of the eternal Son of God, true man in that he is the virginally conceived offspring of Mary.[1] Accordingly, Christian dogmatics has quite legitimately addressed the biblical teaching on the person of Christ in two different theological *loci*. His deity is stressed in theology proper as a major aspect of the doctrine of the Trinity. His humanity is stressed in Christology proper as a major aspect of the Incarnation, which historical event in turn is taken up in the *locus* of Soteriology, because it occurred for one reason and one reason only, namely, to accomplish the redemption of the elect of God by Christ's cross work.

In this chapter I want to trace out what the early church did with the biblical data about Christ's person and natures and to analyze its work. Nowhere does the Scripture set forth in a formulaic way *how* it is to be understood and represented to people's faith that Jesus is both God and man at the same time, that is to say, how it is that two metaphysically incompatible things—the infinite and the finite, the

---

1. See part two, chapter eight, for a fuller treatment.

eternal and the temporal, the immutable and the mutable—are truly united in one indivisible Jesus Christ of Nazareth. This question of how the Incarnation is to be understood necessarily thrust itself upon the minds of thinking men in the early church with increasing momentum, the results of their reflections at times being extremely bizarre, dealing as the question does with what is obviously an extremely formidable and highly complex issue. It should come as no surprise that the process of forming an answer to this question took several centuries before a general definition was reached that has come to satisfy that large segment of Christendom which still accords to Scripture its normative role as the rule of faith. This history of doctrinal development leading up to the mid-fifth-century Definition of Chalcedon and to certain later refinements will be briefly surveyed in this chapter.[2]

THE APOSTOLIC FATHERS

The "apostolic fathers" are so named because they lived during the age of the apostles and because they authored the earliest postcanonical Christian writings. The group includes Barnabas of Alexandria, who wrote sometime between A.D. 70 and A.D. 100, Hermas, who wrote most likely in the early part of the second century A.D., Clement of Rome, who wrote around A.D. 97, Polycarp, a presbyter from Smyrna, who died around A.D. 155, Papias of Hierapolis in Asia Minor, who died around A.D. 130, and Ignatius of Antioch, who died around A.D. 107. According to Irenaeus (c. 130–c. 200), Polycarp and Papias were actually disciples of John, and according to Origen (c. 185–c. 254), Clement of Rome is the Clement mentioned in Philippians 4:3, but this latter identification is debatable.

Doctrinally, they may be judged "apostolic" in that they basically reproduced the thought of the apostles. There is little theological reflection moving toward doctrinal definition. With respect to their doctrine of God, they are uniformly monotheistic and write freely of God as Father, Son, and Holy Spirit, and of Christ as both God and man, but they "do not testify to an awareness of the implications

---

2. Further details can be found in *The Ante-Nicene Fathers* and *The Nicene and Post-Nicene Fathers* (reprints; Grand Rapids, Mich.: Eerdmans, 1989), Philip Schaff, *History of the Christian Church*, vols. 1–3 (Grand Rapids, Mich.: Eerdmans, 1882), Reinhold Seeberg, *Text-Book of the History of Doctrines* (1895; reprint, Grand Rapids, Mich.: Baker, 1977), Louis Berkhof, *The History of Christian Doctrine* (1937; reprint, London: Banner of Truth, 1969), Kenneth Scott Latourette, *A History of Christianity* (New York: Harper, 1953), J. N. D. Kelly, *Early Christian Creeds* (New York: D. McKay, 1972) and *Early Christian Doctrines*, rev. ed. (New York: Harper and Row, 1978), Geoffrey W. Bromiley, *Historical Theology: An Introduction* (Grand Rapids, Mich.: Eerdmans, 1978), David F. Wells, *The Person of Christ* (Westchester, Ill.: Crossway, 1984), and Gerald Bray, *Creeds, Councils and Christ* (Leicester, U.K.: Inter-Varsity Press, 1984).

and problems involved."[3] What Seeberg declares of Barnabas may generally be affirmed of them all: they all "preserve(d) the fundamental ideas of the apostolic period in a relatively pure form."[4] Barnabas affirms the preexistence of Christ and his divine creative activity. As the Son of God, he appeared in human flesh and suffered on the cross. He will return some day as Judge in divine omnipotence. For Hermas, Christ is the Son of God who is "prior to all his creation," exalted above the angels, and who upholds the world. He became man in order to purify men. For Clement as well, Christ is the Son of God, exalted above the angels, who came into the world, having been sent from God to deliver us. In his letter to the Philippians, Polycarp assumes that his readers believe that Jesus is divine, that he was sent to earth on a mission of mercy, and that he is now glorified and exalted above heaven and earth. But it is probably Ignatius, a staunch opponent of Gnosticism, who is the most explicit in his christological utterances: Christ is "God" (ὁ θεός, ho theos), "our God," and "my God," "the only Son of the Father," and "the Lord." He existed with the Father before the beginning of time, but became man and is thus "both fleshly yet spiritual, born yet unbegotten." Being from God both eternally and by virginal conception, Christ is "the Son of God." Being from Mary, he is "the Son of Man" (Ignatius is in error here with this understanding of the "Son of Man" title). After completing his work, which included his passion, he "raised himself" (and "was raised") from death and returned to the Father.[5]

There is little, if any, grappling with the problematic implications of their speaking of God as Father, Son, and Holy Spirit, or of Christ as both God and man. While these fathers uniformly speak of Christ as the Son of God, who was already active both in the work of creation and in the Old Testament, who is himself God and who appeared in the flesh in the fullness of time, Seeberg's conclusion about their definitional contribution to the doctrine of God and to Christology seems justified: "we find nothing doctrinally definite [that is, definitive] in regard to [Christ's] pre-existence . . . , his relation to the Father, the method of the incarnation, or the relationship of the divine and the human in his person."[6] This is understandable in that they were not being confronted with such aberrations as were later to afflict the church in the christological controversies of the fourth and fifth centuries. These aberrational developments having had neither the theological provenances nor the historical climate in which to define themselves sufficiently, the earliest fathers simply did not feel the urgent need for deeper theological reflection upon the implications of their teachings.

---

3. Berkhof, *The History of Christian Doctrine*, 40.
4. Seeberg, *Text-Book*, 1:70.
5. Ibid., 1:55–82, gives a detailed description of the theological views of these first church fathers.
6. Ibid., 1:78. See also Bromiley, *Historical Theology*, 4–5, 7.

THE APOLOGISTS

In the second century A.D. opposition began to mount against Christianity from several different quarters. Judaism, both because of its adherence to a strict monotheism in which God is viewed as a single personal Monad and because of its views respecting the necessity of law-keeping and circumcision and the political and nationalistic nature of its messianic hope, continued (as it had in the first century) to reject Christ as a deceiver and blasphemer and to regard Christians as idolaters. It is true, of course, that whatever collective strength Judaism may have had within the nation of Israel prior to A.D. 70 to incite either the nation's or the empire's hostilities against the Christian faith was by the second century A.D. generally dissipated, as the Jews themselves after the destruction of Jerusalem in A.D. 70 and the Bar Kochba Rebellion in A.D. 135 became an increasingly displaced people. This situation, coupled with the fact that the Christian faith was no longer drawing its converts mainly from the Jewish nation but rather from pagan society, meant that Christian apologists had to respond less and less to Judaistic opposition. Instead, in light of the fact that the empire itself was regarding the Christian faith more and more as a separate and distinct religion and not as a Jewish sect, second-century church fathers had to answer state charges and to correct erroneous pagan public opinion.

There was not a total disregard for Jewish opinion, of course. Justin wrote his *Dialogue Against Trypho,* and Irenaeus and others responded to certain loosely "Christianized" Jewish sects such as the Ebionites and the Elkasaites, both of which had rejected Jesus' virginal conception and his deity, doubtless as a concession to Judaism. The Ebionites insisted that Jesus was the son of Joseph and Mary and was endowed with the Spirit of God at his baptism, thereby being appointed to the office of prophet. Through his piety, he became the Son of God, marking out the legalistic pathway to salvation for all men. The Elkasaites, more philosophically speculative (Seeberg describes their thought as "Gnosticism in the sphere of Jewish Christianity")[7] and strictly ascetic, thought of Christ as an angel and as the true prophet, after Adam and Moses, of the one God, but not as God himself. To the Eucharist were attached magical and astrological superstitions, evidencing the sect's syncretistic tendency to absorb into itself both Christian and pagan elements. These sects continued for a time as tiny minorities, never posing much threat to the spread of the gospel.

The same cannot be said about the opposition which began to come from paganism itself. Such writers as Lucian, the pagan satirist, and Celsus, the pagan philosopher, registered blistering attacks against Christianity. And a third pagan writer,

---

7. Seeberg, *Text-Book,* 1:89.

Porphyry the Neoplatonist, was to continue this line of attack in the third century. Lucian regarded Christians as credulous and simplistic, while Celsus

> objected to the exclusive claims of the church. Making his own some of the Jewish objections to Christianity, he criticized much in Biblical history for its miracles and absurdities, and expressed his repugnance to the Christian doctrines of the Incarnation and Crucifixion. Objecting that Christians, by refusing to conform to the State, undermined its strength and powers of resistance, he made an impassioned appeal to them to abandon their religious and political intolerance.[8]

Celsus's attack was to receive its most definitive response from Origen in the next century, but already in the second century, stung by charges that Christians were cannibals in that they "ate the flesh and blood" of even their own children at the Eucharist, and were engaging (since they met in secret at night) in all kinds of sexual orgies, certain fathers—now known as the Apologists—"sought to mollify the temper of the authorities and of the people in general toward Christianity" by refuting the charges leveled against Christians. They attempted to make the Christian faith acceptable to the educated classes by depicting it as "the highest and surest philosophy" and stressing its rationality.[9] In connection with their refutations and philosophical endeavors, they sought also to expose the absurdity and immorality in pagan religion. It is generally agreed that with these fathers—the more important of them being Justin Martyr (c. A.D. 100–165), Tatian (c. A.D. 160), Athenagoras (c. A.D. 170), a pupil of Justin, who in later years founded the Gnostic sect of the Encratites but seems to have been the first to set forth a philosophical defense of the doctrine of God as Three in One, and Theophilus of Antioch (late second century A.D.), the first to use the word *Triad* of the Godhead—postcanonical "Christian theology" was born.

There can be no question that the Apologists desired to be true to Scripture. Unfortunately, in their effort to make the Christian faith acceptable to the cultured pagan, they represented their doctrine of God too largely in Platonic terms and their doctrine of the Logos too largely in Philonic thought form. They drew no clear distinction, moreover, between what people know of God on the basis of natural revelation and what they can only know of him by special revelation. Justin, for example, asserted that certain Greek philosophers (Socrates, Heraclitus) were Christians in that they lived according to the Logos.

---

8. Frank L. Cross, ed., *The Oxford Dictionary of the Christian Church* (London: Oxford University Press, 1958), 256.
9. Berkhof, *History of Christian Doctrine*, 56.

While they were monotheists, their representation of God was such that "the true nature of the living God does not find expression. There is no advance beyond the mere abstract conception that the Divine Being is absolute attributeless Existence."[10] While he is the Creator and Preserver of the world, he is invisible, unbegotten, eternal, incomprehensible, passionless, and *nameless*.

When speaking of the Son, they employed the term *Logos* out of deference to the appeal it would have among the cultured classes. Their perception of him seems more Stoic (or Philonic) than biblical: "To them the Logos, as he existed eternally in God, was simply the divine reason, without personal existence. With a view to the creation of the world, however, God generated the Logos out of his own Being and thus gave him personal existence.... Briefly stated, Christ is the divine reason, immanent in God, to which God gave a separate existence, and through which he revealed himself."[11]

While they spoke of the prophetic or divine Spirit, they did little to explicate his being and person. But there can be no doubt that a divine Triad is definitely an aspect of their religious thinking, and they show some awareness of the problems involved in such a conception—"the apprehension of [this mystery] constitutes for them the profoundest problem."[12] Unfortunately, to the degree that they offered a solution, they seemed to suggest a real and definite subordination of the Logos to God not only in forms of operation but in forms of personal subsistence as well. As a result, Bromiley speaks, for example, of Justin's "confused Trinitarianism."

With respect to the Incarnation, they definitely affirmed that the Logos became man, being born of the virgin Mary, and was thus both God and man, his deity being concealed by the flesh. In this regard, it is interesting to note that Justin will speak of Christ's "two natures." As for the purpose of the Incarnation, like the

---

10. Seeberg, *Text-Book*, 1:113; see also Berkhof, *History of Christian Doctrine*, 58.
11. Berkhof, *History of Christian Doctrine*, 58. Seeberg characterizes this Logos Christology thus:
    Originally God was alone, but by virtue of the reasoning faculty ... belonging to him he had in himself the Logos. By a simple exercise of his will, the Logos sprang forth.... He is the first-born work of the Father.... Of the manner in which the Logos originated, it is said: "This power was begotten from the power of the Father and his counsel; but not by a separation, as though the nature of the Father were distributed ..., and that which is taken away from it appears to be also the same and does not diminish that from which it was taken" [citing Justin, *Dialogue*, 128, 61, 100]. He is not an angel, but divine; divine [θεός, *theos*], but not God Himself [ὁ θεός, *ho theos*]. In respect to the Father, he is something else ... and another ... and is such in number but not in mind.... Christ is, therefore, the Reason immanent in God, to which God granted a separate existence. As the divine Reason, he was not only operative at the creation and in the Old Testament prophets, but also in the wise men of the heathen world. (*Text-Book*, 1:113–14)
12. Seeberg, *Text-Book*, 1:114.

apostolic fathers before them, they have no well-defined, biblically grounded doctrine of salvation, for they depict salvation largely in legalistic and moralistic terms and portray Christ as first and foremost a Teacher who urged a new law and a virtuous life which would be rewarded after the resurrection.

To summarize, in that the Apologists treated, however defectively, the relation of the Logos to God and expressed an awareness of the profound mystery in the affirmation of the existence of one God who exists as a divine Triad, we must conclude that they represent an advance, however faltering, in the church's struggle to come to grips with its doctrine of God in light of the Incarnation and Pentecost. But in that they interpreted the preexistence of the Son largely in terms of a Stoic or Philonic conception of the Logos, thereby subordinating the Son to God the Father in essential and personal subsistence, we must judge their apologetic efforts to be doctrinally unsound and definitionally inadequate, however much we honor them for their attempts to "contextualize" their religious convictions in terms understandable to the "cultured despisers" of their day.

THE ANTIGNOSTIC FATHERS

If there was one "Christian heresy" in the second century A.D. that threatened the doctrinal purity of the church more than any other, it was Gnosticism. We can do no better in our search for a clear definition of this "other gospel" than to cite Bromiley:

> The teachers [for example, Valentinus, Basilides, Hermogenes] usually grouped under the title of "Gnostics" so intermingled Christian teachings with current speculations that nothing distinctly Christian remained. Whether they did this as Christians accommodating the gospel to other concepts or as pagans adopting bits and pieces of the gospel makes little difference in the result....
>
> The Gnostics developed complicated theosophies which varied widely in detail. Some generally shared convictions, however, underlay the individual outworkings. According to them, the true God lies at a great distance from this world, the gap being filled by a strange host of intermediaries. A lesser power, the Demiurge, created the material universe. Spirit and matter, sometimes also identified as good and evil, stand in dualistic antithesis. Man's plight consists in the alienation of his spirit or soul, which is from the true God, in his body, the work of the Demiurge (who is for Marcion the Old Testament God of judgment in contradistinction to the gracious Father of Jesus Christ). The true God sends Christ down to rescue the soul. Christ, however, cannot be truly incarnate [because of the antithesis between spirit and matter]; he either associates himself temporarily with the man Jesus [the heresy of adoptionism] or simply takes the appearance and not the reality of a physical body [the heresy of docetism].

Salvation means rescue from imprisonment in the body and entails a life of asceticism in maximum abstraction from bodily wants, although some Gnostics allow licentiousness on the ground that the body cannot be saved itself, nor can it aVect the redeemed soul. Gnostics view[ed] their own teaching as knowledge *(gnosis)* at a higher stage of faith.[13]

The two great antignostic fathers of the second century A.D. were Irenaeus of Lyons (c. 130–c. 200) and Tertullian of Carthage (c. 160–c. 220), the latter of whom was the first Christian theologian to write in Latin and who is judged by many as one of the two greatest Western theologians of the patristic period (Augustine being the other). He is also the father to whom the church is indebted for the vocabulary of subsequent Trinitarian development, being the first, in his *Against Praxeas,* to apply the term "Trinity" *(trinitas)* to what he referred to as the three divine "persons" *(personae)* in the one divine "substance," "essence," or "nature" *(substantia).*

---

13. Bromiley, *Historical Theology,* 18. Some liberal scholars urge that Gnosticism should be viewed as one of the many valid forms of early Christianity and that it was only because the "orthodox" party was the most powerful of many Hellenized "Gnostic" groups that it was able to categorize Gnosticism as heterodox and oust it from the "authentic" church. But this contention falsely assumes that there was a united "orthodox" party whose spokesmen collaborated against a united Gnostic party. There were no such entities. What no doubt did play a major part in forming a collective hostility against Gnostic thought was the fact that already a fairly uniform Rule of Faith *(regula fidei)* was being used as a baptismal formula. Tertullian alludes several times to a *regula fidei,* which he proceeds to quote in his treatise *On the Veiling of Virgins* (1, 3). Its similarity to what we now know as the Apostles' Creed is striking:

> The rule of faith which is one everywhere and unalterable. . . teaches us to believe in one God almighty, creator of the world, and his Son Jesus Christ, born from the Virgin Mary, crucified under Pontius Pilate, raised on the third day from the dead, taken up into heaven, now sitting on the Father's right hand, destined to come to judge the living and the dead through the resurrection of the flesh.

It seems much more likely that the reason for the church's opposition to Gnosticism is that pastors and theologians recognized that it deviated from the Rule of Faith and rejected it because it and not the Rule of Faith deviated from Scripture (for more on the Rule of Faith see Seeberg, *Text-Book,* 1:82–86, and M. E. Osterhaven, "Rule of Faith," in *Evangelical Dictionary of Theology,* ed. Walter A. Elwell [Grand Rapids, Mich.: Baker, 1984], 961–62).

Furthermore, if the orthodox party were really no more than a larger "Gnostic" party, espousing a philosophy that appealed to the elite in pagan society, there is every reason to think that Christianity would have gone the same way as the Gnostic groups—becoming exclusive and sectarian, and regarded as harmless by the philosophical schools. But "the fact that Christianity expanded at the level of the masses, that it was feared and persecuted as a great popular danger and that the philosophical schools, far from recognizing it as a sister, attacked it to the bitter end as an irrational superstition unworthy of a good intellect, is sufficient refutation of the liberal theory" (Bray, *Creeds, Councils and Christ,* 74).

Both of these fathers vigorously stood against the Gnostic distinction between the true God and the Creator of the world, Irenaeus labeling such a conception as blasphemous, spawned by the devil's guile. For both, there is but one God who is the Creator, Preserver, and Redeemer—an intelligent Spirit, just and good, and knowable not through speculation but only by revelation. This perception of God leads Seeberg to note that, in contrast with Gnosticism, their conception of God "displays again concrete, living features, particularly in Irenaeus. He is the active God, who accomplishes creation and redemption. He is the living God, who is just and merciful . . . , and he is the God historically revealed in Christ."[14]

But these two fathers approach the issues of the tripersonality of God and of Christology differently. In a real sense, Irenaeus went behind the Apologists and returned to the approach of Ignatius (the reason he is judged by some as a dull "establishment" figure), declining to speculate on the origination of the Logos or the mode of the Son's generation. It is enough to know that the Son, as the Logos, existed from all eternity with the Father and has revealed the Father both to angels and to men. And since God can be known only through God, and since the Son alone knows the Father and reveals him, the Son is God the Revealer. The Spirit, as the Wisdom of God, occupies for Irenaeus also a personal position alongside the Son.

Thus Irenaeus consciously perceived of the living God as "triadic" in his spiritual life: "For there are always present to Him the Word and Wisdom, the Son and the Spirit, through whom and in whom He made all things freely and spontaneously," he wrote (*Against Heresies* 4.20.1, 3; see 5.6.1).

Finally, it was clear to Irenaeus that John 1 teaches a true Incarnation, through which, as a historical event, the eternal Logos became the historical Jesus. Jesus Christ, the Word in union with human flesh, is both true God and true man. And against Gnostic teaching he expressly denied that the Christ (Logos) departed from Jesus just prior to his death, insisting to the contrary "that He who was born Jesus Christ is the Son of God, and that the same who suffered arose from the dead" (*Against Heresies* 3.16.5; see 18.5). Thus for Irenaeus a continuing union between the Logos and his flesh existed from his virginal conception throughout the historical existence of Jesus Christ up to, including, and extending beyond his resurrection from the dead.

Tertullian, of the two, is the much more "exploratory" or seminal theologian. While Irenaeus was generally content to affirm the facts of the Faith—the existence of the One God as a Triad, the Incarnation of the Logos in Jesus of Nazareth—Tertullian endeavored to explain the origination of the *personae* of the Son and the Spirit and their relationship to the Father. In doing so, he fell into an

---

14. Seeberg, *Text-Book*, 1:121.

unscriptural subordination of the Son and the Spirit to the Father, but it must be noted that in the process of working out his conception of God he employed terminology which the church found extremely useful in its Nicene theology later.

For Tertullian, the one God is the Triune God—a "Trinity." But it appears that for him the Logos was originally *impersonal* reason in God, for he had a beginning: "There was a time when . . . the Son was not . . . who made the Lord a Father" (*Against Hermogenes* 3, 18). But having been begotten by God with a view to the creation of the world and proceeding from him, he is both a real substance *(propria substantia)*—partaking of the same substance of the Father—and a distinct person *(persona)*, to whom belong word, reason, and power. Similarly, the Spirit as a third *persona* partakes of the same one divine *substantia*: "Everywhere," he writes in *Against Praxeas* (12), "I hold one substance in three cohering." He declares, moreover (*Against Praxeas* 2):

> Not as if the One were thus all things because all things are from the One, but through unity of substance; and yet there is preserved the mystery of the economy which disposes the unity in a trinity, placing in order the Father, the Son, and the Holy Spirit—three, not in condition but in order, not in substance but in form, not in power but in aspect, but of one substance, and of one condition, and of one power, because one God, from whom are derived these orders and forms and aspects in the name of the Father, and the Son, and the Holy Spirit.

Unfortunately, these "orders and forms and aspects" of which Tertullian speaks are depicted "in the crude form of greater and lesser participation" of the persons in the divine substance.[15] For example, he writes: "For the Father is the whole substance, but the Son a derivation and portion of the whole" (*Against Praxeas* 9, 26).

On the Incarnation itself, Tertullian was quite scriptural: the preexistent Logos became man, "assuming flesh" by being born of the virgin Mary. And having determined for himself a manner of speaking of natures as "substances," Tertullian was able to speak of the "enfleshed" Logos as possessing two "substances" in the unity of one "person": "Thus a consideration of the *two substances* presents man and God—here born, there unborn; here flesh, there Spirit; here weak, there mighty; here dying, there living" (*Concerning the Body of Christ* 5, 18), the two substances, "not confused, but *combined in one person*, Jesus, God and man" (*Against Praxeas* 27), acting "separately, each in its own condition [*status*]" (ibid.).

He also spoke of the human "substance" of Christ as itself the union of two other "substances"—the bodily and the spiritual substances. So there can be no doubt that Tertullian did full justice to the true humanity of Christ.

---

15. Berkhof, *History of Christian Doctrines*, 66.

In conclusion, because these fathers lived and labored prior to the struggles leading up to the Council of Nicaea and beyond, their orthodoxy would have been judged in their own time by Scripture as interpreted by the highly circumscribed Rules of Faith used as baptismal formulae, which by the way were being continually standardized in form more and more toward what we now know as the Apostles' Creed. Consequently, although his doctrine of the Logos was subscriptural, Tertullian was judged as "orthodox" by the standards of his day. No doubt he believed that he represented scriptural Christianity. And in the sense and to the degree that his faith was "Trinitarian," affirming as he did the deity of the Son and the Spirit and the fact of the Son's Incarnation, Tertullian was truly Christian. But it must be understood that after the Council of Nicaea, a person espousing his particular form of the Son's subordination to the Father would quite rightly have been judged "heterodox."

ORIGEN OF ALEXANDRIA

Turning now to Origen (c. 185–c. 254), we move not only into the third century A.D. but also back to the East to consider the theological vision originating from one of the great catechetical schools of the Ante-Nicene Period. The third catechist of the school at Alexandria (following Pantaenus and his own mentor Clement), Origen became the greatest biblical scholar (see his *Hexapla* and his commentaries on Scripture) and philosopher-theologian (see his *De principiis*) of his day. But regrettably it must be acknowledged that Origen's writings are seriously flawed due to his commitment to Platonism.

As a Christian theologian, Origen was, of course, monotheistic, but his depiction of God was in some significant respects more Greek than biblical. For him, God is Being (οὐσία, *ousia*) and impassible, beyond want of anything. Origen did affirm that God is personal, the Creator, Preserver, and Governor of the world, and just and good. And in these affirmations his Christian training is evident. And he was Trinitarian, referring freely and often to the Father, the Son, and the Holy Spirit. But his was a defective Trinitarianism that was for centuries to wield a harmful influence in the church.

Origen, following Clement and Philo, believed that the Scriptures should be interpreted at different levels, beginning with its literal (lowest) sense, then the moral/spiritual sense, up to the anagogical sense "according to which the revelation of God on earth corresponded as in a mirror to the reality of God in heaven."[16]

---

16. Bray, *Creeds, Councils and Christ*, 80.

In this we may detect, of course, the Platonic influence upon him. It is at this anagogical level that Origen developed his Trinitarianism. Gerald Bray explains:

> [The anagogical sense of Scripture means that] if the Word became flesh by being born of a virgin, then this fact of birth must have a corresponding reality in heaven. Tertullian and those who had gone before him had not known how to explain the generation of the Son of God outside spacetime categories of thought. Because of this, they had tended to say that the Son (and the Spirit) had been latent in God the Father from all eternity and had emerged only when he desired to create the world.
>
> Origen cut across this problem with his use of anagogy. Birth in time on earth reflected birth in eternity in heaven, therefore the Son was eternally begotten of the Father, and it was wrong to suppose that there was ever a time when the Son had not existed. The Son was the exact replica (Hebrews 1:3) of the Father and therefore shared fully in his eternal nature.[17]

Accordingly, because the Father, by an act of will, eternally generates the Son out of himself, Origen spoke of the Son as being of the same essence (ὁμοούσια, *homoousia*) as the Father. But if he is of the same essence (οὐσία, *ousia*, here in Greek is equivalent to Tertullian's Latin *substantia*) as the Father, he is nonetheless a distinct ὑπόστασις, *hypostasis* (the Greek equivalent in Origen to Tertullian's Latin *persona*): "we worship the Father of truth and the true Son, being two things in ὑπόστασις, *hypostasis,* but one in sameness of thought and in harmony, and in sameness of will" (*Against Celsus* 8.12).

Rounding out his doctrine of the Trinity, Origen affirmed that the Father, reproducing himself in the Son, reproduces himself also, through the Son, in the Spirit.

On the surface, this may appear to be a marked improvement over Tertullian's Trinitarianism in which the Logos and the Spirit seem to be originally impersonal reason (and wisdom) in God. And in one respect it is, in that for Origen, unlike Tertullian, the Son always enjoyed a personal existence with the Father. But only brief reflection will reveal that Origen's Trinitarianism was still defective in another regard. In Origen's construction the one God is primarily God the Father, who alone is "uncaused" and "self-existent," while the Son, deriving his Being eternally from the Father, not *necessarily* but by an act of the Father's will, through an eternal act of begetting, is not *self*-existent and thus is lacking one obvious attribute of deity. The Spirit, eternally reproduced by the Father through the Son, though "uncreated" is lower still and also lacking the attribute of *self-*existence. Furthermore, according to Origen, the Spirit does not operate in creation as a whole, which is the Son's sphere of operation, but only in the saints. This perception is what lay behind

---

17. Ibid., 80–81.

Origen's willingness to refer to the Son as a "second God," and not the absolutely Good and True, but simply "good and true" as an emanation and image of the Father (*De principiis* 1. 2. 13). This is also the reason he is willing to say that "the Holy Spirit is lower [than the Son], extending to the saints alone" (*De principiis* 1. 3. 5, 8).

In yet another way Origen's anagogical sense of Scripture, when applied to the Son, makes the Son essentially dependent upon the Father and denies to him the attribute of aseity. Bray explains:

> Origen also knew that the gospel revelation portrayed Christ as doing the will of his Father, who had sent him. It followed [anagogically] that the Son had always done the Father's will, and this subordination of obedience was likewise part of the Son's eternal nature. He was equal, but in second place, and therefore dependent on the one who had begotten him.[18]

It is clear from all this that Origen's Trinitarian construction was seriously flawed. But if this is so, also flawed was his view of the Incarnation. In keeping with his unbiblical view of the preexistence of all human souls, Origen maintained that Christ's human soul both preexisted and had undergone a complete interpenetration with the Logos. It was this Logos-filled soul which became flesh, and which provided the link between the Logos and the material nature of Jesus. Jesus, for Origen, did actually suffer, die, and rise again, but after the ascension, the humanity was so absorbed into the divine Logos that it was "no longer other than the Logos, but the same with it." As a man he is now "everywhere and pervades the universe" (*De principiis* 2. 11. 6). The true humanity of Christ is obscured if not totally abandoned by this construction.

When one reflects upon Origen's doctrines of God and of Christ, not to mention several other bizarre doctrinal assertions he made, it would be quite easy from the vantage point of a later age to ask why he should not be regarded simply as an early heretic. As a matter of fact, both he and Tertullian were condemned as heretics either at a synod in Constantinople in A.D. 543 or at the Fifth Ecumenical Council (the Second Council of Constantinople) in A.D. 553 (scholars are not sure which). But judged by the standards of his day (the Rules of Faith), he was within the bounds of orthodoxy. And he continues to hold a place in the front ranks of early Christian theologians simply because he is so important to an understanding of the history of Christian doctrine that followed him. After his death in A.D. 254 his theological constructions continued to influence thinking for the next two to three centuries throughout the turmoil of the great christological controversies. Bray observes, in fact, that

---

18. Ibid., 81.

it is seldom appreciated just how much Origen himself was responsible for the problems which arose during [the following two centuries]. When Athanasius struggled against Arius over the correct interpretation of Christ's divinity, they were both following Origen as they each understood him. Athanasius began with the equality implied in eternal generation and argued [I think wrongly—author] that this ruled out any form of subordinationism. Arius, on the other hand, assumed the eternal subordination of the Son to the Father and argued from that that he must have lacked something of the Father's nature and thus could not have enjoyed the status of equality implied in eternal generation.[19]

MONARCHIANISM

Before considering the specific controversies that gave rise to the great conciliar decisions concerning God and Christ, it is necessary to say something about what some theologians would describe as the outstanding heresy of the third-century, namely Monarchianism. It was "in general, an attempt to stress monotheism [Tertullian: "the monarchy of the one God"] against those who would make Jesus Christ, as the incarnation of the Logos, a second God, or [when the action of the Holy Spirit is also introduced] what was in effect tritheism, a belief in three Gods."[20] In sum, it was an indictment of those particular Logos Christologies that were being propounded by Tertullian and Origen (and Justin before them) in which the Logos is depicted as a "second God" or as One who is to be worshiped alongside the Father even though there was a time when he personally was not. In this connection Seeberg writes:

> The learned attempts to define the relation of Christ to the Father (Logos, second God) were, indeed, far from satisfactory. Christ was regarded as "a God," and his human nature was asserted. [And it is true that the] Logos-christology was, in the main, framed [with the intent] to guard the unity of God. But when the Logos, proceeding from the Father, assumes an independent existence, he is then regarded as "the second God," and thus Monotheism is endangered. Monarchianism made an effort to reconcile Monotheism, the most precious treasure of Christianity as contrasted with the heathen world, with the divinity of Christ without resort to the expedient of the "second God."[21]

There were two basic kinds of Monarchianism—what has come to be called "Dynamic" (or "Dynamistic") Monarchianism and "Modalistic" Monarchianism.

---

19. Ibid., 83. See also Latourette, *History of Christianity*, 152.
20. Latourette, *History of Christianity*, 143.
21. Seeberg, *Text-Book*, 1:163.

The former, a form of adoptionism sometimes referred to as Samosatianism, is most commonly associated with Paul of Samosata, bishop of Antioch in the third quarter of the third century. He acknowledged that the Logos was indeed ὁμοούσιος (*homoousios*, "the same essence") with the Father, but insisted that this is because the Logos was merely the impersonal rational power in God and not a separate and distinct person in the Godhead. (The Spirit in his construction is simply a manifestation of the grace of the Father.) By penetrating the man Jesus more and more, the Logos divinized him so that he is worthy of divine honor though not God in the strict sense of the word (a view not greatly dissimilar in its outcome to the later Socinian and Unitarian views). Thus monotheism was maintained, but at the expense of the personal subsistence of the Logos. The Samosatian's views, including the very use of the term ὁμοούσια, *homoousia*, because it was being used in the interest of depersonalizing the Logos, were condemned by a synod at Antioch in A.D. 268.

The second kind of Monarchianism—Modalistic—is known both as Patripassianism, since it teaches that the Father himself in a different form (Son) had become incarnate and suffered, and as Sabellianism, after its most famous exponent Sabellius (early third century). Sabellius, also insisting that the Son was ὁμοούσια, *homoousia*, with the Father in the interest of his brand of modalism, taught that the Father, Son, and Holy Spirit were only different designations of the one personal God corresponding to "different moments in the life of the one Divine Person, called now Father, now Son, now Spirit" (Warfield). That is to say, the one divine Monad (which he named "Father of the Son") revealed himself as Father in the creation and in the giving of the law, as Son as he revealed himself in redemption, and as Spirit as he revealed himself as the giver of grace. In short, the terms describe modes of revelation of the one God. Again, monotheism, as well as the deity of the Logos and the Spirit, is maintained by this construction, but again at the expense of the personal subsistence of the Son and the Spirit.

THE ARIAN CONTROVERSY AND
THE COUNCIL OF NICAEA

Sufficient *theological* antecedents have been reviewed that the stage is now set for a rehearsal of the great conciliar decisions which came out of the conflicts which raged throughout the fourth and fifth centuries A.D. and the events which led up to them. But there is also one *historical* antecedent which figured throughout the christological controversies. Beginning with Nero in the first century A.D. and culminating with Diocletian in the early fourth century A.D., the Roman Empire had launched ten major persecutions against Christianity in its attempt to eradicate it as a religion of the realm. But Constantine became emperor in A.D. 306 (sole emperor in 323). Having received, he believed, divine help from a staff in the form of a cross when he invaded Italy in A.D. 312, he declared a policy of toleration for Christianity in A.D. 313 and more and more came to favor it over the pagan religions of the empire. Accordingly, when doctrinal struggles erupted in the church which threatened to divide not only the church but also the empire, now the emperor himself had a stake in the outcome. Therefore, he and emperors after him began to play an active role in settling church disputes, calling church councils together and actually contributing to the proceedings in an effort to maintain the unity of the church and by extension of the empire. Consequently, though the church had on many occasions met in regional synods prior to the Council of Nicaea in A.D. 325 and had reached significant decisions in them, now the decisions of those church councils took on greater significance in guiding the faithful, both because the emperor convened them and because of their "ecumenical" character. The emperor did not dictate the substance of the decisions—at least most of the time—even though he may have tried. But with the reign of Constantine the ecumenical conciliar decisions took on a new significance for the church in the empire.

The doctrinal crisis which is our current interest erupted forth around A.D. 318 when Arius (c. 250–c. 336), a presbyter of Alexandria, began to expound his view of the person of Christ—really just the Christology of the third century carried to its logical conclusion—in opposition to Alexander, bishop of Alexandria, whom he suspected was a Sabellian.

Arius was familiar with Scripture and believed earnestly that his teachings were in accord with certain proof texts such as Proverbs 8:22, John 14:28, and Colossians 1:15. He knew too that a significant strand of church tradition was on his side. For example, he knew that Justin and Tertullian had taught that there was a time when the Logos had no personal subsistence, and that God the Father had begotten his Word (Son) and his Wisdom (Spirit) with a view to the creation of the world. He knew as well that Origen had taught that the Son was subordinate to the Father not only on earth but also in heaven. He knew also that the Synod at Antioch in A.D. 268 had condemned the use of the term ὁμοούσια, *homoousia,* to describe the Son's relation to the Father. He believed too that if the Son was to be distinguished from the Father, and if the Father was God, and if these other things were true, then the Son could not be God in the same sense. Therefore, he concluded that

> there was [a time] when God was alone, and was not yet Father, and afterward he became Father. The Son was not always. For, all things coming into being from not being, and all things created and made having begun to be, this Logos of God also came into being from things not existing; and there was [a time] when he was not, and he was not before he was begotten, but he also had a beginning of being created. (From his *Thaleia,* as cited by Athanasius)

Accordingly, he taught that the Logos or Son of God, unlike the Father, is not unbegotten. Neither is he a part of the unbegotten One, nor is he a part of something previously existing. Rather, he was created as "the beginning of the Lord's works" (Prov. 8:22); and before he was created or began to be, he was nonexistent. As a created being, though the first and highest of all created beings, he had a beginning and was not of the same Being (ὁμοούσια, *homoousia*) of the Father. Arius also declared that the Logos was given the titles of God and Son of God, "just as all others also," by sharing in grace.

He also denied that there are two undiminished natures in Christ, asserting rather that the nature of the Son took the place of the human soul in the historical Christ. What the Son took into union with himself, in sum, was simply the flesh of the man Jesus.

Arius was immediately opposed by Alexander, who led two synods in Alexandria to condemn him. Arius then sought refuge with Eusebius, bishop of Nicomedia, a friend and supporter. Both Alexander and Arius continued to air their conflicting views ever more widely, until it appeared that the church in that area of the empire would be divided.

Concerned that in such an event the empire could be disrupted as well, Constantine convened the First Council of Nicaea in A.D. 325, with over three hundred bishops in attendance, most from the eastern part of the empire. Between the small competing parties of Arius (two bishops) and Alexander (about thirty bishops) were two other parties about evenly divided, the one with semi-Arian leanings led by Eusebius of Nicomedia, with whom Arius had found shelter, and the other, led by the church historian Eusebius of Caesarea, with semi-Alexandrian and Origenistic leanings.

What took place at the council constitutes one of the most amazing chapters in church history. Eusebius of Nicomedia, representing the Arian cause, presented the Arian confession first. It was roundly defeated, and the document was torn into shreds in the presence of everyone. Then Eusebius of Caesarea presented an "Origenistic confession" (Seeberg), which was so worded that both Arians and Alexandrians could have found their respective positions in it. It read in part:

> We believe ... in one Lord Jesus Christ, the Logos of God, God from God, light from light, life from life, the only-begotten Son, the first-born of all creation, begotten of the Father before all the ages, through whom all things were made.

Unhappy with this compromise document, Alexander and his assistant Athanasius (c. 296–373) proposed an alternative that substituted the word "Son" for "Logos" and the phrase "true God from true God" for "life from life," and which added the phrases "from the substance [οὐσία, *ousia*] of the Father," "not created" after "begotten," "[of] the same substance [ὁμοούσιον, *homoousion*] with the Father," and finally, "things in heaven and things on earth" after the last quoted clause above. The alternative confession then read as follows:

> We believe . . . in one Lord Jesus Christ, the Son of God, begotten from the Father, only begotten, that is, from the substance of the Father, God from God, light from light, true God from true God, begotten, not created, [of] the same substance with the Father, through whom all things were made, things in heaven and things on earth.[22]

They also added the following statement aimed directly at the Arian party:

> But the holy and apostolic church anathematizes those who say that there was [a time] when he was not, and that He was made from things not existing, or from another ὑπόστασις, [*hypostasis*], or οὐσια, [*ousia*], saying that the Son of God is mutable, or changeable.

What then occurred is a remarkable instance of the sovereign providence of God directing his church into all truth, for after considerable debate over whether the council should endorse the term ὁμοούσιος (*homoousios*, "same substance") or the term ὁμοιούσιος (*homoiousios*, "similar substance")—the famed "debate over a Greek *iota*"—as the more suitable description of the relation of the Son to the Father (Constantine favored the former), the council overwhelmingly approved the alternative "Alexandrian" statement, all of the bishops signing it with the exception of Arius and five others, including even the bishop of Nicomedia, who did not, however, approve the condemnatory passage.[23] The holdouts were promptly banished (but only temporarily) from the empire by the emperor.

At Alexander's death in A.D. 328, Athanasius became the bishop of Alexandria and the established leader of the orthodox party, and continued tirelessly to defend the doctrine of the Homoousia of the Son until his death in A.D. 373. Five different

---

22. See part two, chapter nine, for my critical assessment of the Nicene doctrine of the Father's eternal generation of the Son.

23. It is indeed striking that the Nicene fathers were willing to accept the very term that had been condemned earlier by the synod at Antioch in A.D. 268 in its debate with Sabellianism. Sabellius had preferred the condemned term, "same essence," in the interest of denying the personal distinctions within the Godhead. Therefore, in that earlier controversy, in the interest of maintaining Jesus' separate *persona* from the Father, the church insisted upon the "like essence" of Jesus with the Father. But when Jesus' full deity became the issue, the church affirmed his "same essence" with the Father. See Berkouwer, *Person of Christ*, 61–63, for his discussion of this "about-face."

times, for a total of seventeen years, he was banished by fickle emperors, including Constantine himself. But because Athanasius continued steadfast in his defense of the full deity of the Son, sometimes having to stand virtually alone, his name occupies a revered place in the annals of church history as a leading contender for the faith once for all delivered to the saints.[24]

In the years immediately following the Council of Nicaea, Arianism continued to exert an influence in major areas of the empire, spreading even beyond the empire into Arabia, where Mohammed came into contact with its teachings, which explains why he says what he does about Jesus in the Koran. But it is generally conceded that the controversy was settled when the Council of Constantinople meeting in A.D. 381 reaffirmed the Nicene statement. The doctrine of the Homoousia was now a dogma of the church,[25] and was employed thereafter as a test of orthodoxy.

APOLLINARIANISM AND THE COUNCIL OF CONSTANTINOPLE

Arianism died hard after the Council of Nicaea, but in the end, Athanasius, supported by the so-called three Great Cappadocians—Gregory of Nazianzus, Basil of Caesarea, and Gregory of Nyssa, Basil's younger brother—won the war. The Cappadocian theologians were able by their energies to enlist the support of a sufficiently large majority of Eastern bishops so that the First Council of Constantinople, convened at the request of Emperor Theodosius I in A.D. 381, reaffirmed the Nicene statement, in a form not strictly that of the Nicene Council itself but sufficiently close that today it is known as the Nicene Creed. (The more scrupulously accurate scholar refers to it as the Niceno-Constantinopolitan Creed.)[26] By the council's endorsement of the Nicene formula, the Arian cause was irretrievably lost insofar as any hope that its Christology would be adopted and declared to be orthodox was concerned.

But the Nicene formula did not bring to a close all christological debate. Indeed, in one sense, it had only insured that debate would continue, for while it affirmed

---

24. For an excellent summary review of Athanasius's teaching in its entirety, see Seeberg, *Text-Book*, 1:206–15.

25. By a "dogma of the church" I intend any doctrine which the church believes the Scriptures teach and which the church has officially defined. It should be remembered that the church's definition is subordinate to Scripture and must be subject to redefinition should greater understanding of Scripture dictate the need for it.

26. As noted in part two, chapter nine, the Council of Constantinople perhaps had added to the earlier Nicene statement the doctrine of the eternal procession of the Spirit from the Father (only later, in 589, did the Third Council of Toledo adopt the statement that the Spirit proceeds from the Son also).

that Christ was truly God and that he was God incarnate, it left the question unaddressed how it is that he is both God and man. Accordingly, various answers were forthcoming, the first being that of Apollinaris (or -ius) (c. 310–c. 390), bishop of Laodicea, a close friend of Athanasius and a staunch defender of the Nicene doctrine of the Homoousia. As a representative of the "Word-flesh Christology" of the Alexandrian catechetical school,[27] Apollinaris declared that while in all other men body, soul, and spirit coexist in a union (trichotomy), in Christ were only the human body and soul, the divine Logos having displaced the human spirit. Thus while Christ was perfect God, he lacked complete humanity, a condition that Apollinaris did not shrink from declaring. Berkouwer explains the reason for his formulation in the following way: Apollinaris reasoned that

> had the Logos assumed a complete human nature, he would have adopted also human variability and human sin. Since it is certain that Jesus Christ is immutable, it is by that token impossible that he united himself with a variable human spirit. A genuine union is possible only when the Logos, as the principle of self-consciousness and self-determination, *takes the place of,* instead of assuming, the human spirit.... The union in Christ was not, therefore, a union of the Logos with a complete nature but a union accomplished by an interpenetration of the Logos and the human nature. The Logos is the active, moving principle and the human nature is the passive recipient of its action.[28]

The effect of Apollinaris's construction was the reduction of Christ's full humanity to something less than the humanness of other men, and thus it rightly falls into the category of a form of docetism.

The Cappadocian fathers, in reaction, argued that this formula for the unity of the natures in Christ failed to do justice to his complete humanity, and they insisted, in the words of Gregory of Nazianzus, that what "has not been assumed cannot be restored; it is what is united to God which is saved." So in addition to its condemnation of Arianism, the (First) Council of Constantinople also condemned Apollinaris's view, and in doing so, affirmed that Christ was "true man" (see the clause: "came down ... and was incarnate from the Holy Spirit and Mary the Virgin").

Thus the fourth century witnessed two significant ecumenical conciliar decisions regarding the person of Christ: Nicaea affirmed his true deity; Constantinople affirmed his true humanity; and both, taken together, protected the mystery of the

---

27. See Wells, *Person of Christ,* 100–2, 104–6, for a discussion of the Word-flesh Christology and the sense in which Apollinaris exemplified its major tenets. For an in-depth analysis see R. V. Seller, *Two Ancient Christologies: A Study in the Christological Thought of the Schools of Alexandria and Antioch in the Early History of Christian Doctrine* (London: SPCK, 1954).
28. Berkouwer, *Person of Christ,* 64–65.

personal union of the two natures against a monophysitism ("one nature"-ism) which would attempt to move in either direction to the rejection, reduction, or neglect of the other.

NESTORIANISM AND THE COUNCIL OF EPHESUS

Although it is one of the least admirable of all of the ecumenical councils because of the seamy political and personal intrigues that figured so prominently in determining its outcome, the Council of Ephesus, ordered by Emperor Theodosius II in A.D. 431, made a significant doctrinal contribution to the final resolution of the christological struggles of the early church.

The church entered the fifth century facing new problems and controversies. Nestorius (died c. 451), bishop of Constantinople and a firm advocate of both Christ's deity (Nicaea) and his humanity (Constantinople), took sides in a controversy centering in the issue of whether it was appropriate to refer to Mary as θεοτόκος (*theotokos*, literally, "God-bearer," but unfortunately rendered in English by the present popular "Mother of God"). As a representative of the "Word-man Christology" of the Antiochene School,[29] and zealous for the *distinction* between the true deity and true humanity of Christ, Nestorius declared a preference for the term Χριστοτόκος (*Christotokos*, literally, "Christ-bearer"), reasoning that

> the Logos, being as divine absolutely immutable, was not born. This can be said only of his garment, or temple, *i.e.*, his human nature. . . . It is only to the man Christ, therefore, that birth, suffering, and death can be ascribed. The man Jesus was the "organ of the divinity." Hence the Logos as God is strictly discriminated from the man.[30]

Furthermore, while he did not deny the union of the Logos and the human nature of Jesus, Nestorius insisted that in their union in Christ his two natures each retained its own πρόσωπον (*prosōpon*, literally, "mask, face"), by which he meant most likely the idea of "appearance" or "attributes."

Cyril (died c. 444), bishop of Alexandria, who was to become Nestorius's chief antagonist, declared that one must not hesitate to refer to Mary as θεοτόκος, *theotokos*. Concerned for the *unity* of Christ's person, he argued that because the personal subject of the God-man, the Logos, was one and the same in relation to both natures, and that because neither nature expressed itself except in the union

---

29. See Wells, *Person of Christ*, 102–3, 106–8, for a discussion of the "Word-man Christology" and how Nestorius reflected its major interests.
30. Seeberg, *Text-Book*, 1:261.

and in conjunction with the other, it was not only appropriate but also essential to regard Mary as the "God-bearer."

Nestorius understood Cyril as saying that Christ, being one person, possessed only one nature, the result of the fusion of his deity and humanity, which fusion could only mean the truncation of both the divine and human natures—an understanding that gains credence from the fact that Cyril both spoke of "one nature after the union" and resorted to the notion of the *communicatio idiomatum*, the transfer of properties between the two natures, as one means to secure the union of the two natures.

Cyril, on the other hand, charging Nestorius with views which scholars today are not convinced were really his, deduced from the fact that Nestorius would not refer to Mary as the "God-bearer" that he believed her to be the mother of a mere man who was in union with God. Thus the charge was made that he was an adoptionist in the Samosatian tradition. And consistent with this, because he said that each nature had its own πρόσωπον, *prosōpon*, it was said that Nestorius taught that Christ was "two persons," thus destroying the unity of the one person of Christ. If we follow Nestorius, said Cyril,

> we would be redeemed by the sufferings of a mere man . . . ; a man would have become to us "the way, the truth, and the life" . . . ; we would worship a God-carrying man . . . ; when we are baptized into Christ and by him, we would be baptized into a man . . . ; we would in the Lord's Supper partake of the flesh and blood of a man. . . . Thus the Christian world would be robbed by Nestorius of all the treasures which it possesses in the historical Christ.[31]

All of this may appear to the person unschooled in theological subtleties to be simply a matter of irrelevant "theological hairsplitting." But it was anything but that. Without fully realizing it, by his refusal to describe Mary as "God-bearer," Nestorius was raising the vitally important question: Did the θεός, *theos*, prefix in θεοτόκος, *theotokos*, refer to the divine *nature* or to the *person* of the Logos?[32] His response seemed to suggest that Mary could be the mother of neither. Cyril, on the other hand, clearly saw that Mary was the mother of the *person* of the Logos, although it must be said that his exposition of this perception was not unambiguous because he spoke of "one nature after the union." But it was not an unimportant question that these two fathers were debating. "The real point of the controversy," writes Seeberg, "is, whether it was the man Jesus controlled by the Logos, or whether it was God himself, who was born, lived, taught, labored, and died among us."[33]

---

31. Ibid., 1:262.
32. Bray, *Creeds, Councils and Christ*, 155.
33. Seeberg, *Text-Book*, 1:263.

There can be no question in light of Scripture that Cyril's understanding of the θεοτόκος, *theotokos,* matter was the more perceptive. But the debate was not to be settled in a peaceful manner. Because the dispute had been so widely aired, each disputant having appealed to the bishop of Rome for vindication, the emperor called for a council to settle the issue. It was to meet on June 7, 431, in Ephesus. Both antagonists arrived in the city in good time, but for some reason the Eastern bishops were unduly delayed until June 26. After waiting for over two weeks for the Antiochene bishops to arrive, Cyril without authority convened the council himself on June 22, despite the protests of not only Nestorius and sixty-eight bishops but also the imperial commission itself. The council, numbering about two hundred bishops, proceeded to hear charges against "the godless Nestorius," then deposed him as a "new Judas" and condemned his teachings. Four days later, when the Antiochene bishops arrived, they convened their own council under John of Antioch in the presence of the imperial commissioner, and though only forty-three in number, deposed Cyril. The emperor's commission also annulled the decision which Cyril's assembly of bishops had handed down concerning Nestorius. Three delegates from the bishop of Rome, having arrived by this time with instructions to stand with Cyril, learned of the conciliar actions. John of Antioch reported that he would have no intercourse with deposed and excommunicated persons (Cyril); therefore, Cyril's council, now in the presence of the legates from Rome, convened again on July 10 and condemned Nestorius's views again. With events having gone badly awry and his hopes of a peaceful settlement frustrated, in August the emperor ordered the bishops home, deposed both Cyril and Nestorius, and ordered their arrest. Cyril eluded arrest and returned home to Alexandria, claiming victory inasmuch as a majority of bishops had upheld his position twice. Nestorius voluntarily confined himself to a monastery and lived out the remainder of his life a broken man, believing that he had been terribly wronged and writing extensively in his own behalf.

Two years after the Ephesus Council, in A.D. 433, Cyril and John of Antioch worked out a *Formulary of Reunion* that granted for the most part what Cyril had sought but walked lightly over the subject of the communication of attributes between the natures. Affirming that Christ was "perfect God and perfect man, consisting of a rational soul and body," the *Formulary* declared that in him

> there has been a union of two natures; wherefore we confess one Christ, one Son, one Lord. In accordance with this conception of the unconfused union, we confess the holy Virgin to be Theotokos, because the divine Logos was incarnate and made man, and from the very conception united to himself the temple that was taken from her.

John received by this statement the recognition of the full humanity of Christ and the distinction of the two natures; Cyril, the one person, the union of the two natures, and the θεοτόκος, *theotokos*. Moreover, John agreed to recognize Cyril's assemblies at Ephesus as "the Council of Ephesus." With peace at hand, Sixtus III, bishop of Rome, then ratified the decisions of Cyril's council. Even more significant, the Council of Chalcedon, meeting only a few years later, certified Cyril's council as the third ecumenical council and endorsed some, though not all, of Cyril's letters against Nestorius.

Cyril's central insistence on the one person and the undivided union of the two natures had been finally upheld, and rightly so, in spite of the "violent means" (Hodge) he employed to have his way. The final outcome indicates that the church wished to say that in the one person of Christ there is to be no separation of the two natures. They are never to be divided.

A christological definition for the church was now taking definite and discernible form: Christ is both God and man, but in the one person of Christ his two natures are to be undivided. Whatever else the church would say about the person of its Lord, these were the boundary lines within which it had to work.

EUTYCHIANISM AND THE COUNCIL OF CHALCEDON

The dust had hardly settled after the adoption of the *Formulary of Reunion* before Eutyches (c. 378–454), the head of a monastery in Constantinople, began to denounce the *Formulary* as Nestorian and propagated the view, not so dissimilar in sound from that of Cyril himself, that "our Lord was of two natures before the union [that is, the Incarnation], but after the union . . . [there was] only one." Here was the advocacy of a strict monophysitism,[34] the one resultant nature being the confusion of the divine and human natures.

At a synod at Constantinople in A.D. 448, over which Flavian, bishop of Constantinople presided, Eutyches was deposed from office and excommunicated. He appealed this decision to the emperor and to several bishops, including the bishop of Rome. Flavian, in his own defense, also wrote Rome. The bishop of Rome at this time was Leo I "the Great" who, according to Latourette, was "one of the ablest men who have ever sat on the throne of Peter."[35] Supporting Flavian's position, he wrote his now-famous *Tome* (known also as the "Dogmatic Epistle"), in

---

34. Bray, *Creeds, Councils and Christ*, 158, points out that Eutyches' problem was the result of the "terminological confusion" that had always dogged Cyril, as reflected in his dictum: "Out of two natures, one nature."
35. Latourette, *History*, 171. I do not endorse Latourette's description of the Roman bishopric.

which, basing his remarks particularly on Tertullian and Augustine, he expounded "with remarkable clarity, precision, and vigour the Christological doctrine of the Latin Church."[36] When Dioscurus, bishop of Alexandria, sided with Eutyches and requested that the emperor convoke a council, the Emperor Theodosius II ordered a council to be held at Ephesus in A.D. 449. Dioscurus dominated the council with "brutal terrorism"[37] and refused even to allow Leo's *Tome* to be read. Attended mainly by monophysite bishops, the council restored Eutyches and deposed Flavian. Dioscurus then excommunicated Leo and appointed an Alexandrine bishop to take his place as the bishop of Rome. The emperor accepted the decision of this "Second Council of Ephesus," but Dioscurus's ascendancy was cut short when the emperor died the following year. Acceding to Leo's request for a new council to countermand the actions of the so-called "Robber Council" of A.D. 449, the newly crowned Emperor Marcian ordered it to be held at Chalcedon in A.D. 451. The emperor's commission presided, with the emperor himself personally attending the sixth session. It was the largest assemblage of bishops up to that time, with around six hundred in attendance. John Leith writes of its constituent make-up:

> The Christological settlement at Chalcedon illustrates the catholicity of the theology of the ancient church. Three major schools of theology had been involved in the Christological controversies and were represented at Chalcedon: Alexandria, Antioch, and Western Christianity. The final result could have been produced by none of these schools of thought alone. Chalcedon was truly catholic in the very great degree in which it was the result of the shared theological wisdom of the church.[38]

The first action of the council was the reaffirmation of the Nicene Creed in both its original form ("the Creed of the Three Hundred and Eighteen Holy Fathers at Nicaea") and its Constantinopolitan form ("the Niceno-Constantinopolitan Creed"). It also declared the Cyrillian Council at Ephesus in 431 to be the third ecumenical council and adopted both Cyril's synodical letters against Nestorius as a refutation of Nestorianism and Leo's *Tome* as a refutation of Eutychianism. It is

---

36. "The Tome of Leo," in *The Oxford Dictionary of the Christian Church*, ed. Frank Cross, 1366.
37. Seeberg, *Text-Book*, 1:268. Leo's delegates, for example, were imprisoned and many delegates from Antioch were beaten up.
38. John H. Leith, ed., *Creeds of the Church*, rev. ed. (Atlanta: John Knox, 1973), 34. Leith also quotes Albert C. Outler to the effect that Chalcedon is the place in "the history of Christian thought where the New Testament was explicated in exact balance so as to discourage the four favorite ways by which the divine and human 'energies' of the Christ event are commonly misconstrued" (35). In light of Outler's insightful comment one can only gasp at his willingness to refer to Christ as "the Christ event" and his natures as "energies."

interesting to note in passing that the council did not declare Leo's *Tome* a dogma of the church as he had wished, doubtless lest it give too much authority to the Roman bishopric. It then wrote a new creed, justifying the need for such by an appeal to the rise of the heresies of Apollinarianism, Nestorianism, and Eutychianism. The Definition of Chalcedon remains to this day "the touchstone of Christological orthodoxy" and "the supreme expression of an orthodox, biblical faith."[39] It reads as follows:

> In agreement, then, with the holy [Nicene] Fathers, we all unanimously teach [Christians] to confess one and the same Son, our Lord Jesus Christ: the same perfect in deity and the same perfect in manness, truly God and truly man, the same of a rational soul and body, consubstantial with the Father according to the deity and the same consubstantial with us according to the manness, like us according to all things except sin; begotten of the Father before the ages according to the deity and in the last days the same, for us and for our salvation, [born] of Mary the Virgin, the God-bearer, according to the manness, one and the same Christ, Son, Lord, Only-begotten, being made known *in two natures* [ἐν δύο φύσεσιν, *en duo physesin*] without confusion [ἀσυγχύτως, *asunchytōs*], without change [ἀτρέπτως, *atreptōs*], without division [ἀδιαιρέτως, *adiairetōs*], without separation [ἀχωρίστως, *achōristōs*], the distinction of the natures being by no means removed because of the union but rather the property of each nature being preserved and concurring *in one person* [εἰς ἓν πρόσωπον, *eis hen prosōpon*] and one subsistence [μίαν ὑπόστασιν, *mian hypostasin*], not parted or divided into two persons but one and the same Son and Only-begotten, God, Word, the Lord Jesus Christ. As the prophets of old [declared] concerning him, and the Lord Jesus Christ himself has taught us, and the [Nicene] Creed of our Fathers has handed down.

Analysis of the Definition of Chalcedon and Its Christology

As an *apologetical* statement, the Definition addressed every problem that had plagued the church with regard to the person of Christ.

1. Against the Docetists it declared that the Lord Jesus Christ was perfect in manness, truly man, consubstantial (ὁμοούσιον, *homoousion*) with us according to the manness, and born of Mary.

---

39. Bray, *Creeds, Councils and Christ*, 151, 163. See also Joseph H. Hall ("Council of Chalcedon" in *Evangelical Dictionary of Theology*) who describes the Definition of Chalcedon as "the standard for Christological orthodoxy" (204), and G.C. Berkouwer (*The Person of Christ*) who declares it to be "a compass to the church in later ages" (69).

2. Against the Samosatian adoptionists it insisted upon the personal subsistence of the Logos "begotten of the Father before the ages."

3. Against the Sabellians it distinguished the Son from the Father both by the titles of "Father" and "Son" and by its reference to the Father having begotten the Son before the ages.[40]

4. Against the Arians it affirmed that the Lord Jesus Christ was perfect in deity, truly God, and consubstantial with the Father.

5. Against the Apollinarians, who had reduced Jesus' manness to a body and an "animal soul" (ψυχὴ ἄλογος, *psychē alogos*), it declared that Jesus had a "rational soul" (ψυχὴ λογική, *psychē logikē*), that is, a "spirit."

6. Against the Nestorians it both described Mary as θεοτόκος, *theotokos*, not in order to exalt Mary in the slightest, but in order to affirm Jesus' true deity and the fact of a real incarnation, and spoke throughout of *one* and the *same* Son and *one* person and *one* subsistence, not parted or divided into two persons and whose natures are *in union* without division and without separation.

7. Finally, against the Eutychians, it confessed that in Christ were *two* natures without confusion and without change, the property of each nature being preserved and concurring in the one person.

As an *ecumenical* statement, it declared to the "Word-flesh Christologists" of the Alexandrian school, who tended to be monophysitic, that they would have to make peace with two natures in Christ, the divine and the human, and that the one person of the Son, who was and is divine from and to all ages, took into union with his divine nature in the one divine person a human nature, without confusion, without change. And to the "Word-man Christologists" of the Antiochene school, who tended to make too much of the distinction between the natures, it declared that they would have to come to terms with the fact that the Lord Jesus was *one and the same* Son, *one and the same* Christ, Son, Lord, Only-begotten, and *one and the same* Son and Only-begotten, God, Word, the Lord Jesus Christ, who is *one* person and *one* subsistence, not parted or divided into two persons, whose natures are without division, without separation.

Finally, as a *clarifying* statement, it drew a line of demarcation between a "person" as a self-conscious substantive entity and a "nature" as a complex of attributes, and settled the meaning of the somewhat fluid terminology which, because of its elusiveness, had long been the source of misunderstanding and division in the church. Bray writes:

> The council made it clear that *person* and *hypostasis* were the same thing, not different as Nestorius had said. It also stated that the *person/hypostasis* was a

---

40. See part two, chapter nine, for my critique of Nicea's doctrine of the eternal gernation.

principle in its own right, not to be deduced from the nature. It further maintained that in Christ there was only one *person/hypostasis*, that of the divine Son of God. The human nature of Jesus did not have a *hypostasis* of its own, which in simple language means that Jesus would not have existed had the Son not entered the womb of Mary. There was no "man" apart from this divine action.[41]

This construction of Christ's person as "one person with two natures," with the person being that of the Son of the intra-Trinitarian Unity, has brought the charge from some modern quarters that the Definition is docetic or at least reductionistic in that it denies to the human nature a human personality. This charge requires a response.

While it is true that the Definition denies that the Son of God, already a person within the Trinity, took into union with himself a human person, insisting rather that he took into union with himself a full complex of human attributes (the doctrine known as the *anhypostasia*, literally, "no person"), these fathers would never for a moment have thought of Jesus, as a man, as being an impersonal human being. Jesus was personal, as a man, by virtue of the union of his manness in the person of the Son. In other words, as a person, the Son of God gave personal identity to the human nature which he had assumed without losing or compromising his divine nature. Never for a moment did *the man* Jesus exist apart from the union of natures in the one divine person, but then this means as well that *the man* Jesus from the moment of conception was personal by virtue of the union of the human nature in the divine Son. Wells puts it this way:

> The Definition asserted that it was to a human nature . . . rather than a person . . . that the divine Word was joined. This means that all of the human qualities and powers were present in Jesus, but that the ego, the self-conscious acting subject, was in fact a composite union of the human and the divine.[42]

This explanation of the personality of the human nature of Jesus has come to be known as the doctrine of the *enhypostasia*, and is traced to the formal theological reflections of Leontius of Byzantium (c. 485–c. 543) (or Leontius of Jerusalem—there is some uncertainty here) and John of Damascus (c. 675–c. 749), who maintained that in the incarnate Christ the humanity of Christ which was indeed personal from the moment of the virginal conception, as we have said, derived its

---

41. Ibid., 161.
42. Wells, *Person of Christ*, 108.

personality from the person of the Son.[43] But the same construction was surely implicit, before these later fathers wrote their theologies, within the Definition of Chalcedon itself by its declaration that Jesus Christ was one person with two natures, not two persons each with his own corresponding nature.

One further implication must be drawn from the "one person" teaching of the Definition. It means that there were not two "*self*-consciousnesses" within Jesus. Prior to the Incarnation the Son was *self*-consciously divine, but after and by virtue of the Incarnation, the one Son was still self-consciously divine and now consciously human as well. No theologian in the Christian and Reformed world has given more careful expression to the Chalcedonian doctrine of the *anhypostasia* than John Murray. He writes:

> The catholic [universal] doctrine [of the person of the Son] has been to the effect that the human nature was not itself hypostatic, that is, personal. There was only one person and this person was divine. This has been known as the Chalcedonian tenet of the *anhypostasia* of the human nature. . . . Does the *anhypostasia* do justice to [the emphasis of Scripture that Jesus was a man]? Is not all that belongs to human personality necessarily involved in such designations [of Jesus as ἀνήρ, *anēr*, and ἄνθρωπος, *anthrōpos*]? Two remarks are in order: First, it may not be possible for us to give adequate expression in our formulae, and particularly in the formulae of Chalcedon, to all that is involved in our Lord's humanness. This is to say, we may not be able to devise a precise formula that will guard the unity of his person, on the one hand, and the integrity of his humanity, on the other.
>
> Second, it may be that the term "person" can be given a connotation in our modern context, and applied to Christ's human nature, without thereby impinging upon the *oneness* of his divine-human person. In other words, the term "nature" may be too abstract to express all that belongs to his humanness and the term "person" is necessary to express the manhood that is truly and properly his.
>
> At the same time there appears to be a great truth in the Chalcedonian insistence on one person. We do not find our Lord speaking or acting in terms of merely human personality. In the various situations reported to us in the Gospel record, it is a striking fact that he identifies himself as one who sustains to the Father his unique relationship as the only-begotten Son, as the one whose self-identity, whose self, is conceived in such terms. It is indeed true that he speaks and acts as one who is human and intensely aware of his human identity. He shows the limitations inseparable from this identity, and also the limitations prescribed by the task given him to fulfil in human nature. But it is highly significant

---

43. F. LeRon Shults, "A Dubious Christological Formula: From Leontius of Byzantium to Karl Barth," *Theological Studies* 57 (September 1996): 431–46, arguing that the error is traceable to Friedrich Loofs's influential misunderstanding of Leontius of Byzantium, declares that this specific theological formulation originated from Protestant Scholasticism and not from Leontius.

that in situations where his human identity, and the limitations incident to this identity and to his commission, are most in evidence, there appears the profound consciousness of his filial relationship and of his divine self-identity (see Matt. 24:36; 26:39, 42, 53; John 12:27. See also John 5:26, 27; 17:1; Rom. 1:3; Heb. 5:7–9; I John 1:7). In such contexts the experiences that were his, in virtue of being human, are conspicuously in the forefront in all the intensity of their being. But just then the consciousness of his intradivine Sonship is in the foreground as defining the person that he is. And the inference would seem to be that our Lord's *self*-identity and *self*-consciousness can never be thought of in terms of human nature alone. Personality cannot be predicated of him except as it draws within its scope his specifically divine identity. There are two centres of consciousness but not of self-consciousness.

In this same connection it is worthy of special attention to observe how, in connection with the sacrifice of Christ which he offered in human nature, it is always he who is represented as offering himself, and in the contexts he is identified and defined in terms of what he is as divine (John 10:17, 18; 17:4; Rom. 8:32–34; Phil. 2:6–8; Heb. 1:3).

The Son of God did not become personal by incarnation. He became incarnate but there was no suspension of his divine self-identity. In these terms his self must be defined. Jesus was God-man, not, strictly speaking, God and man.[44]

In another place he writes:

> Catholic orthodoxy has maintained that the human nature of our Lord was not hypostatic or personal. In the language of the Symbol of Chalcedon, the properties of each nature concurred "in one person and one subsistence, not parted or divided into two persons, but one and the Same Son, and only-begotten, God the Word, the Lord Jesus Christ." . . .
>
> [W]e must be alive to the danger that may inhere in a transfer to our modern context of the terms used in the formulations and defence of the *anhypostasia* in the 5th century; we must be ever alert to maintain the true and full humanity of our Lord and use those terms provided by present-day usage which are best fitted for this purpose. Nevertheless, to the present writer it is not at all apparent that we are required to speak in terms of the "human personality" of Jesus, nor is it apparent that the development of thought and language is such that we need to abandon the language or intent of the Chalcedonian Symbol. It would seem, rather, that the kernel interest and insistence of Chalcedon are sufficiently apparent and that they need to be preserved. This necessity might be viewed from several angles. The basic consideration, however, is biblico-theological.

---

44. John Murray, "The Person of Christ," in *Collected Writings of John Murray* (Edinburgh: Banner of Truth, 1977), 2:137–38.

In the various situations of the Gospel record in which we find our Lord disclosing himself there appears a very striking and relevant fact. It is that he recognizes himself as sustaining a unique relationship to the Father as the eternal and only-begotten Son. More precisely to the point of our present discussion, he speaks and acts as one whose very *Self*, whose *self*-identity is to be defined in such terms. It is, of course, true that he speaks and acts as one who is truly human and as one aware, therefore, of his human identity. He shows thereby not simply the reality of his human nature but also the intense consciousness of the meaning and purpose of his human identity. But even in those situations in which the limitations inseparable from his human identity are most apparent, and particularly the limitations prescribed by the specific task that was given him to perform in human nature, it is exactly then that there shines through the profound consciousness of his intradivine *self*-identity. This type of evidence would indicate that the centre of his *self*-consciousness was his specifically divine Sonship. This is not, however, by any means to say that the divine Sonship or *hypostasis* took the place of his human centre of consciousness in his human life.... It is simply that when his human consciousness in the reality of its intrinsic limitations and in the reality of the limitations imposed by the exigencies of his work is thrust into the foreground, even then the consciousness of his intradivine Sonship is likewise in the foreground as defining the Person that he is. Such considerations as these should constrain, to say the least, hesitation in diverging from the Chalcedonian formula. To the present reviewer it would appear that the Catholic doctrine of *anhypostasia* rests upon New Testament data and evinces a rather profound insight into the implications of our Lord's own self-witness. The *anhypostasia* would simply mean that however integral to the *incarnate* Son is his human nature and however impossible it is to think of his person in abstraction from his human nature, yet to predicate "personality" of his human nature would run counter to the evidence that *self*-identity in his case can never be conceived of or defined in terms of human nature alone. This could not be expressed by saying that his human personality can never be conceived of apart from his divine personality. It is rather that the very notion of personality can never be predicated of him except as it draws within its scope his specifically divine identity. And if this is so, it is not feasible to speak of his "human personality."[45]

To conclude, in my opinion, as an apologetical, ecumenical, and clarifying statement regarding the person of Christ, the Definition of Chalcedon remains unsurpassed. No other human creed has ever been written that captures as well as it does the exact balance of Scripture and permits all that the Scripture says about God the

---

45. John Murray, review of D. M. Baillie, *God Was in Christ*, in *Collected Writings of John Murray* (Edinburgh: Banner of Truth, 1982), 3:342–43.

Son incarnate to be given their just due. Certainly the Definition of Chalcedon is infinitely to be preferred to those modern christological constructions that refuse to reflect the entirety of the Scripture witness to Christ, and which speak accordingly of him as perhaps a very special instance of the human species but when all is said and done still just a mere man.

Not everyone in Christendom has shared or shares today my opinion. In fact, almost immediately after the council itself had adjourned, the Monophysites, located mainly in the Eastern church, disapproved of its inclusion of the phrase "in two natures." And the Second Council of Constantinople, convoked by Emperor Justinian I in A.D. 553, while it did not repudiate the Definition of Chalcedon, did attempt by its Twelve Anathemas to make the Definition more palatable to the Alexandrian interpretation. But when the monophysite heresy ran to seed in the monothelite heresy ("one will"), though its advocates denied the implication that their view bordered on monophysitism and thus endangered the full and true humanity of Christ, the Third Council of Constantinople, convoked by Emperor Constantine IV in A.D. 680, reaffirmed the Definition of Chalcedon and then added a statement affirming that in Christ are two wills (θελήματα, *thelēmata*) and two operations (ἐνέργεται, *energetai*), with the human will and operation at every moment subject to the divine will and operation. Moreover, what is most intriguing about this addition is that it twice invoked the very language of the Chalcedonian statement—"without confusion, without change, without division, without separation"—to define the relationship between these two wills and two operations in the Lord Jesus Christ. The monophysite and monothelite controversies in the two centuries following the Council of Chalcedon must be judged, then, to be at heart relapses into contradictions that Chalcedon had already substantially overcome. And while, of course, there was continuing discussion of the Chalcedonian formula throughout the Middle Ages and the Reformation Period, no significant challenge was mounted against its Christology until the so-called European Enlightenment (*Die Aufklärung*) of the eighteenth century which, of course, opposed all supernatural religion. In sum, the fifth-century Definition of Chalcedon was to become the touchstone of christological orthodoxy in catholic Christendom for the next fifteen hundred years, surviving even the division of the church into Eastern and Western churches in A.D. 1054 and then in Western Christendom the division of that church into Roman Catholic and Protestant churches in the sixteenth century. It has continued to claim the allegiance of the church universal to this very day. Indeed, today, in the creeds that lie at the base of most confessional churches may be found in the articles treating the person of Christ the doctrine and language of the Chalcedonian Definition.

Departures from the Definition

Catholic Christendom has not always and everywhere remained faithful to what it confessed at Chalcedon. In the Lutheran churches, for example, a form of Eutychianism emerged that serves that church's peculiar view of the relationship of Christ's body to the physical elements of the Lord's Supper. This may be seen in the Lutheran representation of the *communicatio idiomatum* ("communication of attributes"), whereby our Lord's divine nature at his virginal conception virtually "divinized" his human nature by communicating its attributes to the human nature. Thus the latter is ubiquitous, Lutherans insist, and is really physically present "in, with, and under" the elements of the sacrament of the Lord's Supper. But such a christological construction, in the words of Charles Hodge, "form(s) no part of Catholic Christianity."[46]

Even those who are most zealous to defend the altogether transcendent mystery of the Incarnation and the true deity and the true humanity of Christ as these truths are defined by Chalcedon have not always done so with doctrinal consistency. For example, when many evangelical pastors and laymen describe the effect which his assumption of human nature had upon the Son of God, all too often they unwittingly employ a "kenotic" formula. The kenosis theory was first propounded formally by Gottfried Thomasius (1802–1875), a German Lutheran theologian, and has been perpetuated, with variations on the theme, by A. M. Fairbairn, F. Godet, C. Gore, A. B. Bruce, H. R. Mackintosh, O. Quick, V. Taylor, and many others. Millard J. Erickson is a contemporary kenotic Christologist.[47] The

---

46. Charles Hodge, *Systematic Theology* (1871; reprint, Grand Rapids, Mich.: Eerdmans, 1952), 2:418. Hodge's entire discussion and critical analysis of the Lutheran view of the person of Christ may be found on 407–18. In brief, the Lutheran view affirms that the human nature of Christ, after assuming divine dimensions by virtue of the communication of divine attributes to it in the union of natures in the one divine person, either hid or divested itself of its divine dimensions (a form of kenosis pertaining only to the "divinized" human nature) during the days of Christ's earthly ministry. But at Christ's resurrection, Lutherans argue, his human nature manifested its divine dimensions. The Reformed churches prefer to speak of a *"communion* of attributes" between the natures and the person of Christ. It is the person of Christ who is both divine and human, the natures communicating their attributes to his person but not to each other. This view more closely accords with the Definition of Chalcedon.
47. In his *Christian Theology* (Grand Rapids, Mich.: Baker, 1984), 2:735, Erickson argues that the Son of God emptied himself, not of the form of God, but of his equality with God, accepting "certain limitations upon the functioning of his divine attributes." For example, though the Son "still had the power to be everywhere . . . he was limited in the exercise of that power by possession of a human body." He argues similarly in his later *The Word Became Flesh* (Grand Rapids, Mich.: Baker, 1991), asserting that in the Incarnation the Son voluntarily decided to "restrict the independent exercise of some divine attributes."

theory in general advocates the view that God the Son "emptied" (ἐκένωσεν, *ekenosen;* see Phil. 2:7) or divested himself of certain of his divine attributes, such as omnipresence and omniscience, or of the use of one or more of them, in assuming human flesh. Consider for a moment the effects of this view on the Son's attribute of omnipresence. On several occasions I have asked evangelical pastors the question: "After the Incarnation had occurred, did the Second Person of the Trinity still possess the attribute of omnipresence or was he confined to the human body which he had assumed?" Many have opted for the latter construction, the necessary implication being that in the Incarnation God the Son divested himself of his attribute of being always and everywhere immediately present in his created universe. But divine attributes are not characteristics that are separate and distinct from the divine essence so that God can set them aside as one might remove a pin from a pincushion and still have the pincushion. Rather, the divine essence is expressed precisely in the sum total of its attributes. To hold that God the Son actually emptied himself in his state of humiliation of even one divine characteristic is tantamount to saying that he who "enfleshed" himself in the Incarnation, while perhaps more than man, is now not quite God either. But as Bishop Moule once wrote, a Savior not quite God "is a bridge broken at the farther end."

The uniform representation of the New Testament and Chalcedonian Christology is that the Incarnation was an act of addition rather than subtraction. Without ceasing to be what he eternally is as God, the Son of God took into union with himself what he was not, making our human nature his very own. And during the days of his earthly ministry, though he displayed all of the characteristics of men generally, sin excepted, he also claimed on numerous occasions to be the eternal God (John 8:58), claiming omnipresence for himself in Matthew 18:20 and

---

He declares that the restrictions imposed upon Christ's divinity by his human body meant that he could be in only one physical location at a time. He made a voluntary decision to limit the exercise of his omnipresence for a certain period of time. This is not to imply that he could have overridden the decision at any moment. He had willed that from approximately 4 B.C. to A.D. 29 he would not have the free use of his omnipresence. *It was not that he was pretending that he could not use it; he really could not.* In like manner, when Jesus asked how long a child had suffered from a disease, or when he professed that he did not know the time of his second coming, *he was not pretending. He had chosen to subject his omniscience to the veiling or cloaking effect of humanity.* For the time being, he gave up his intuitive knowledge of many of the things which God knows. (549, emphases supplied)

He acknowledges that the view he is introducing is "a species of kenotic theology" (551). But see the argument in part two, chapter eight, of this work, where it is demonstrated that there is no exegetical basis in Philippians 2:6–7 for thinking that in the Incarnation Christ "emptied" himself of anything. His "emptying" refers, not to his Incarnation, but to his "pouring himself out" in death as our high priest. Erickson's entire argument is thus based on faulty exegesis.

28:20, giving evidence of omniscience in John 1:47, 2:25, 4:29, and 11:11–14, and exercising divine power, for example, in the calming of the storm (Mark 4:39) and divine authority to forgive sins (Mark 2:10). John informs us that the disciples beheld his glory, the glory of the unique Son, himself God, who is in the bosom of the Father (John 1:14–18). And the author of Hebrews declares that, even while offering himself up for our sins on the cross, he was at the same time also upholding all things by the word of his power (Heb. 1:3).

While we must not ascribe to church fathers, councils, or creeds the same authority that we ascribe to Holy Scripture, it can at least be demonstrated that kenotic Christology was never a part of christological orthodoxy. For example, Cyril of Alexandria, who led the orthodox opposition against Nestorius at the Council of Ephesus, wrote in a letter to Nestorius:

> [The eternal Word] subjected himself to birth for us, and came forth man from a woman, *without casting off that which he was;* but although he assumed flesh and blood, *he remained what he was, God in essence and in truth.* Neither do we say that his flesh was changed into the nature of divinity, nor that the ineffable nature of the Word of God was laid aside for the nature of flesh; for *he is unchanged and absolutely unchangeable, being the same always,* according to the Scriptures. For although visible and a child in swaddling clothes, and *even in the bosom of his Virgin Mother, he filled all creation as God,* and was a fellow-ruler with him who begat him, for the Godhead is without quantity and dimension, and cannot have limits.[48]

And as we have also seen, the Definition of Chalcedon declares that Jesus Christ possesses "two natures without confusion, without change, without division, without separation, the distinction of the natures being by no means removed by the union, but rather *the properties of each nature being preserved*" (emphasis supplied).

It is clear, then, from both Scripture and church history, that kenotic Christology cannot claim to be an orthodox christological formula. Rather, it is a blemish on the face of historic Christology and should be repudiated as a reductionistic heterodoxy respecting Christ's deity.

Another example of doctrinal imprecision among those who would be the most zealous to maintain a biblical and Chalcedonian Christology relates to Jesus' human knowledge. While most Christians are very eager to contend for the full, unabridged deity of Jesus Christ, it has been my experience that they are not as zealous to safeguard his full, unabridged humanity. While they would

---

48. From "The Epistle of Cyril to Nestorius with the XII Anathematisms," in *A Select Library of Nicene and Post-Nicene Fathers of the Christian Church,* ed. Philip Schaff and Henry Wace, Second Series (Grand Rapids, Mich.: Eerdmans, 1956), 14:202, emphasis supplied.

never affirm, as do the Lutherans, that the Son of God, in the union of the divine and human natures in the one divine Person, communicated the attributes of the former to the latter so that the human nature is physically ubiquitous, I have heard many of them attribute the "deification" of his knowledge to other media, namely, to Christ's resurrection from the dead and to his ascension.

Specifically, I have heard it said many times that while our Lord, it is true, did not know all things *as a man* during the days of his earthly ministry—he himself said as much in Mark 13:32—he surely knows everything *now* as a man in his state of exaltation since his resurrection and ascension. But such a representation grants powers to Christ's resurrection and ascension which they simply do not have and were never intended to have. His glorification in no sense altered the essential manness which was his prior to his resurrection into something other or different from that manness which he assumed at the Incarnation. I grant that he entered into that state of glory that comports with the conditions of the postresurrection existence, but his humanity even in its glorified state did not assume the infinity of God. He was a true man before his resurrection and was and will remain so—all that man is, with all that is involved in being man—through all the ages. If we take the reality of his humanity with its inherent limitations as seriously as did the Definition of Chalcedon when it spoke of Christ's two natures as being "without confusion, without change . . . , the distinction of the natures being by no means removed because of the union, but rather *the properties of each nature being preserved,*" then we must affirm that Christ, as a man, remains finite in knowledge forever. As Warfield writes:

> The Reformed theology which it is our happiness to inherit, has never hesitated to face that fact [that all that man as man is, that Christ is to eternity] and rejoice in it, with all its implications. With regard to knowledge, for example, it has not shrunk from recognizing that Christ, as man, had a finite knowledge and must continue to have a finite knowledge forever. Human nature is ever finite, it declares, and is no more capable of infinite *charismata*, than of the infinite *idiomata* or attributes of the divine nature; so that it is certain that the knowledge of Christ's human nature is not and can never be the infinite wisdom of God itself. The Reformed theology has no reserves, therefore, in confessing the limitations of the knowledge of Christ as man, and no fear of overstating the perfection and completeness of his humanity.[49]

This, of course, means that Christ is *as God* self-consciously infinite in wisdom and knowledge and *as man* consciously finite in wisdom and knowledge, and both

---

49. Benjamin B. Warfield, "The Human Development of Jesus," in *Selected Shorter Writings of Benjamin B. Warfield*, ed. John E. Meeter (Nutley, N.J.: Presbyterian and Reformed, 1970), 1:162.

at the same time. Here, of course, is an element of that altogether transcendent mystery of the Incarnation and an example of the kind of difficulty that has caused some men to stumble at the portrait which the Gospels draw of him. How can one person be both omniscient and yet finite in knowledge at the same time? Some theologians, for example, J. Oliver Buswell Jr., have suggested that the answer lies in the postulation of two "levels" of consciousness in Jesus—a level of active consciousness at which level Jesus as a man developed in wisdom and knowledge as do all other men and at which level he acknowledged ignorance of some things and another (subconscious?) level of awareness at which level as the Son of God he knew all things at the same time. At any moment of his life, theoretically, he could have called up to his active level of consciousness any knowledge datum he desired from the infinite pool of divine knowledge which was his possession. But prior to the Incarnation, in the eternal decree respecting his ministry on earth, it had been determined that he would hold in his active consciousness *only* such information as is available to other Spirit-guided men.[50] I am not totally convinced that this particular construction is the answer, since it does not explain how it is that on many occasions Jesus clearly evidenced a conscious possession of knowledge not normally available even to Spirit-guided men, indeed, even a consciousness that he was divine. Thomas Morris proposes a "two-mind" solution that overcomes this difficulty to some degree, suggesting that the human (limited) mind of Christ did not have access to the content of the divine (unlimited) mind unless the latter permitted the former such access.[51] Probably we will never discover the true solution to this problem. But the one thing we must not do in our concern to relieve the difficulty, if we would be subject to Scripture, is to seize upon one series of representations and make that "our position" and discard the other series. For example, concerning this issue of his knowledge, in the Gospels Jesus

> is represented as not knowing this or that matter of fact (Mark 13:32), [but] he is equally represented as knowing all things (John 20:17; 16:30). If he is represented as acquiring information from without, asking questions and expressing surprise, he is equally represented as knowing without human information all that occurs or has occurred—the secret prayer of Nathaniel (John 1:47), the whole life of the Samaritan woman (John 4:29), the very thoughts of his enemies (Matt. 9:4), all that is in man (John 2:25). Nor are these two classes of facts kept separate—they are rather interlaced in the most amazing manner. If it is by human informants that he is told of Lazarus' sickness (John 11:3, 6), it is on no human information

---

50. J. Oliver Buswell Jr., *A Systematic Theology of the Christian Religion* (Grand Rapids, Mich.: Zondervan, 1963), 2:30.
51. Thomas Morris, *The Logic of God* (Ithaca, N.Y.: Cornell University Press, 1986), 88–107.

that he knows him to be dead (John 11:11, 14); if he asks "Where have you laid him?" and weeps with the sorrowing sister, he knows from the beginning (John 11:11) what his might should accomplish for the assuagement of this grief.[52]

The temptation, confronted as we are by the great incarnational mystery, is to deny one of the two series of Scripture data, and this is precisely what many in our generation have done. Today it is particularly in vogue to deny the divine side of this dual life, to explain it away as first-century mythology. But it is precisely this path of choosing only one series of data, taken by so many in the christological controversies leading up to the Council of Chalcedon, that the fathers of Chalcedon refused to take. As a result the Definition of Chalcedon remains to this day a cherished heritage. This Definition, writes Warfield,

> was not arrived at easily or without long and searching study of the Scripture material, and long and sharp controversy among conflicting constructions. Every other solution was tried and found wanting; in this solution the Church found at last rest, and in it she has rested until our own day. In it alone, it is not too much to say, can the varied representations of the Bible each find full justice, and all harmonious adjustment. If it be true, then all that is true of God may be attributed to Christ, and equally all that is true of man. Full account is taken of all the phenomena; violence is done to none. If it be not true, it is safe to say that the puzzle remains insoluble.[53]

This being so, the characterization of the Definition that one sometimes hears to the effect that with its four adverbs it is essentially negative in its teaching is surely inadequate if not totally erroneous. The Definition is quite positive in what it asserts about Christ, declaring that he is (1) one person who is (2) both truly divine by virtue of his Godness and truly human by virtue of the virginal conception, who is also (3) both consubstantial with the Father according to his deity and consubstantial with us according to his humanity, (4) with the distinction of his two natures being by no means taken away by their union in the unity of his person, but (5) the properties of each nature being preserved and (6) concurring in one person, that is, in one subsistence. The "four great negative Chalcedonian adverbs" are only a small, though certainly not an insignificant part, of the total Definition. And while they do indeed describe the relationship of the natures to one another in the one person in terms designating how the two natures are *not* to be related, they do so for the very positive reason of fending off all attempts to make the divine act of the Incarnation

---

52. Warfield, "Human Development," 1:163.
53. Ibid., 1:165.

"transparent by categories in which the unity [of the Person] must yield to the duality [of the natures] or the duality [of the natures] to the unity [of the Person]."[54]

One final comment: While I hold the Chalcedonian Definition in the highest esteem, I do not intend to suggest that it should have been the "terminal point" in christological reflection in the sense that any and all reflection on the Incarnation since Chalcedon has been and is out of order. Dogma, however much revered and however much it becomes time-honored tradition, must be subject in all of its expressions and in all times to the Word of God, and it is uninterrupted research into Scripture that must ultimately guide the church.[55] In fact, in this present discussion I have noted six areas where further reflection on the person of Christ proved to be exceedingly beneficial to our understanding of him, namely, the *enhypostasia* of Leontius of Byzantium, the dithelitic decision of A.D. 680, the so-called *extra-Calvinisticum* that arose out of the Lutheran-Reformed dialogues, the church's reflective opposition to the kenotic Christologies of the nineteenth and twentieth centuries, Warfield's insistence upon the eternal finitude of the man Jesus, and Murray's suggestion of two consciousnesses but only one *self*-consciousness in Jesus Christ. But these conclusions are all implicit in the Definition, and it is significant that even in these further areas of reflection, each is seeking to be true to the major concern of Scripture that Jesus Christ be regarded as the God-man, the central concern of the Definition itself, and to that degree each reflects the insight of the Definition that the Christ of Scripture is the Word of God become flesh. So the Definition should never be used to stifle continuing reflection upon Scripture. But I would also insist with Berkouwer that

> there is a "halt!" at Chalcedon which will indeed continue to sound against every form of speculation which attempts to penetrate into this mystery [of the divine-human Person] further than is warranted in the light of revelation.[56]

Said another way, the Definition of Chalcedon does mark the terminal point, and legitimately so, of all speculation which would discard either its "one Person" doctrine or its "two natures" doctrine so as to eliminate the supernaturalness of the Incarnation and the incarnate Christ. And history is replete with examples that justify the oft-made declaration that "when one moves beyond the borders of Chalcedon he has decided to choose a heresy."

I believe it is helpful for the Christian to see from the struggles of our spiritual predecessors a way whereby he may systematize the massive amount of data the

---

54. Berkouwer, *Person of Christ*, 95.
55. Ibid., 90, 91.
56. Ibid., 88.

Scriptures contain respecting the person of Jesus Christ. This chapter has traced these struggles through the apostolic fathers, the Apologists, the antignostic fathers, and Origen, and then through the conciliar opposition of the church to Arianism and Sabellianism at Nicaea in A.D. 325, Apollinarianism and Monarchianism at Constantinople in A.D. 381, Nestorianism at Ephesus in A.D. 431, and Eutychianism at Chalcedon in A.D. 451. I have suggested that the Chalcedonian Definition has captured more accurately and more fully than any other single statement all that the Scripture teaches about Christ, the One who stands at the center of the Christian confession. This Definition was the product of a gathering of churchmen from every corner of the empire and represented the three major schools of christological thought, which had struggled together for so long to understand him who was their Lord. I would submit that such lengthy and searching labor must not be discarded cavalierly.

CHAPTER SEVENTEEN

The Character of the Cross Work of Christ

THE CROSS WORK of our Lord Jesus Christ, who is God's Alpha and Omega, stands at the beginning, the center, and the end of God's eternal will and all his ways and works. Christ's cross work is sacred ground. It is the church's "holy of holies." John Murray describes our Lord's cross work as "the most solemn spectacle in all history, a spectacle unparalleled, unique, unrepeated, and unrepeatable" and the site of "the most mysterious utterance that ever ascended from earth to heaven, 'My God, my God, why has thou forsaken me?'" Beholding it,

> we are spectators of a wonder the praise and glory of which eternity will not exhaust. It is the Lord of glory, the Son of God incarnate, the God-man, drinking the cup given him by the eternal Father, the cup of woe and of indescribable agony. We almost hesitate to say so. But it must be said. It is God in our nature forsaken of God. The cry from the accursed tree evinces nothing less than the abandonment that is the wages of sin. . . . There is no reproduction or parallel in the experience of archangels or of the greatest saints. The faintest parallel would crush the holiest of men and the mightiest of the angelic host.[1]

As the Surety of the elect in the eternal plan of salvation, and in fulfillment of God's covenant promises to Abraham (Luke 1:54–55, 68–73; Rom. 15:8–9; Gal. 3:8–9, 13–14), and as the Mediator of the covenant of grace and the only Redeemer of God's elect, the Lord Jesus Christ performed his saving work in their behalf in his threefold office of *prophet* (Deut. 18:15; Luke 4:18–21; 13:33; Acts 3:22), *priest* (Ps. 110:4; Heb. 3:1; 4:14–15; 5:5–6; 6:20; 7:26; 8:1), and *king* (Isa 9:6–7; Pss. 2:6; 45:6; 110:1–2; Luke

---

1. John Murray, *Redemption—Accomplished and Applied* (Grand Rapids, Mich.: Eerdmans, 1955), 77–78.

1:33; John 18:36–37; Heb. 1:8; 2 Pet. 1:11; Rev. 19:16). Theologians refer to these as the three offices of Christ, with all the other christological designations such as Apostle, Shepherd, Intercessor, Counselor, and Head of the church being subsumed under one or more of these three general offices.

Fulfilling his office work of prophet, Christ (1) claimed to bring the Father's message (John 8:26–28; 12:49–50), (2) proclaimed God's message to the people (Matt. 4:17) and to us, his disciples (Matt. 5—7), and (3) foretold or predicted future events (Matt. 24—25; Luke 19:41–44). Still today he continues to exercise his work as prophet in "revealing to us, by his word [John 16:12–15] and Spirit [1 Pet. 1:10–11] the will of God for our salvation" (Shorter Catechism, Question 24) and our edification (Eph. 4:11–13).

Executing his office work of high priest, Christ (1) offered himself up to God as a sacrifice to satisfy divine justice and to reconcile the church to God (Rom. 3:26; Heb. 2:17; 9:14, 28) and (2) makes and continues to make intercession for all those who come unto God by him (John 17:6–24; Heb. 7:25; 9:24).

Performing his office work of king, Christ (1) calls his elect out of the world to become a people for himself (Isa. 55:5; John 10:16, 27), (2) gives them officers, laws, and censures by which he visibly governs them (1 Cor. 5:4–5; 12:28; Eph. 4:11–12; Matt. 18:17–18; 28:19–20; 1 Tim. 3:1–13; 5:20; Titus 1:5–9; 3:10), (3) preserves and supports them in all their temptations and sufferings (Rom. 8:35–39; 2 Cor. 12:9–10), (4) restrains and overcomes all his and their enemies (Acts 12:17; 18:9–10; 1 Cor. 15:25), (5) powerfully orders all things for his own glory and their good (Matt. 28:19–20; Rom. 8:28; 14:11; Col. 1:18), and (6) finally takes vengeance on his enemies who know not God and who obey not the gospel (Ps. 2:9; 2 Thess. 1:8).

This delineation of Christ's three general offices indicates that he exercises them in both the estate of his humiliation and the estate of his exaltation (Isa. 9:6–7; Ps. 2:6; Rev. 19:16). That is to say, one must not think that it was his prophetic and priestly ministries that he exercised before his death and entombment while it is his kingly office that he has exercised since his resurrection; the Scriptures represent him as exercising all three offices in both estates.

In filling these offices Christ meets and fulfills all the needs of men. "As prophet he meets the problem of man's ignorance, supplying him with knowledge. As priest he meets the problem of man's guilt, supplying him with righteousness. As king he meets the problem of man's weakness and dependence, supplying him with power and protection."[2] In this chapter our Lord's office work as priest will be particularly considered.

The cross work of Christ is central to the Christian faith and its proclamation, because of who it was who died on the cross and what it was he did there. With the

---

2. James Benjamin Green, *A Harmony of the Westminster Presbyterian Standards* (Richmond: John Knox, 1951), 65–66.

apostles the church affirms that it was the eternal Son of God, the Word who became flesh, the Lord of glory, who died on Calvary (Rom. 9:5; Titus 2:13; Heb. 1:8; 2 Pet. 1:1; John 1:1, 14; 20:28; 1 Cor. 2:8). Accordingly, in its best moments, the church has "gloried in nothing but the cross" (Gal. 6:14) and has "resolved to know nothing among [the nations] except Jesus Christ and him crucified" (1 Cor. 2:2). It has done so even though it knows that the preaching of the cross is "a stumbling block to Jews and foolishness to Gentiles" (1 Cor. 1:23). It has done so, not only because it knows that "God was pleased through the foolishness of preaching [the message of the cross] to save those who believe" (1 Cor. 1:18, 21), but also because it recognizes that the cross of Christ is "the power of God and the wisdom of God" (1 Cor. 1:24).

For Paul to characterize the cross of Christ the way he did in 1 Corinthians 1:24—"the power of God and the wisdom of God"—implies that God accomplished a truly great salvation through the cross work of the Lord of Glory. One can sketch the momentous outlines of that "so great salvation" simply by surveying what the New Testament epistles affirm about the "body," "blood," "cross," and "death" of Christ, words which taken in their contexts represent that great work in terms of a sacrifice (see also 1 Cor. 5:7; Heb.7:27; 9:26, 28; 10:10, 12, 14).

THE BODY OF CHRIST

The New Testament affirms the following about the accomplishments of Christ's "body," this word referring in the contexts cited to his body offered up in sacrifice to God:

Romans 7:4: Christians *"died* [ἐθανατώθητε, *ethanatōthēte*] to the law through the body of Christ."

Colossians 1:22: God *"reconciled* [ἀποκατήλλαξεν, *apokatēllaxen*] you by the body of [Christ's] flesh through death to present you holy and unblemished and blameless in his sight."

Hebrews 10:10: Christians *"have been made holy* [ἡγιασμένοι, *hēgiasmenoi*] through the offering of the body of Jesus Christ once for all."

1 Peter 2:24: Jesus *"bore* [ἀνήνεγκεν, *anēnenken*] our sins in his body on the tree, in order that we might die to sins and live for righteousness—by whose wounds *you have been healed* [ἰάθητε, *iathēte*]."

THE BLOOD OF CHRIST

The New Testament affirms the following about the accomplishments of

Christ's "blood," the word *blood* in these verses to be construed as theological shorthand for his *sacrificial* death.³

> Acts 20:28: God *"acquired* [περιεποιήσατο, *periepoiēsato*] [the church] through his own blood" (or "through the blood of his own [Son].")
>
> Romans 3:25: God *"publicly set Christ forth* [προέθετο, *proetheto*] as a *propitiation* [ἱλαστήριον, *hilastērion*], through faith in his blood, to demonstrate his justice because of the passing over of sins committed beforehand in God's forebearance." (See also Heb. 2:17; 1 John 2:2; 4:10)
>
> Romans 5:9: Christians *"have been justified* [δικαιωθέντες, *dikaiōthentes*, that is, pardoned and constituted righteous] by his blood."
>
> Ephesians 1:7: Christians "have *redemption* [ἀπολύτρωσιν, *apolytrōsin*] through his blood, the forgiveness of trespasses" (see Col. 1:14, where Paul attaches directly to "redemption," virtually as a synonym, "the forgiveness of sins.")
>
> Ephesians 2:12–13: Gentile Christians "who once were far away *have been brought near* [ἐγενήθητε ἐγγὺς, *egenēthēte engys*] [to Christ, to citizenship in Israel, to the benefits of the covenants of the promise, to hope, and to God himself] by the blood of Christ."
>
> Colossians 1:20: God was pleased through Christ *"to reconcile* [ἀποκαταλλάξαι, *apokatallaxai*] all things to himself, *having made peace* [εἰρηνοποιήσας, *eirēnopoiēsas*] through the blood of his cross."
>
> Hebrews 9:12: Christ "entered the Most Holy Place once for all through his own blood, *having obtained* [εὑράμενος, *heuramenos*] eternal *redemption* [λύτρωσιν, *lytrōsin*]."
>
> Hebrews 9:14: The blood of Christ *"will cleanse* [καθαριεῖ, *kathariei*] our consciences from acts that lead to death, so that we may serve the living God."
>
> 1 Peter 1:2, 18–19: God's elect were chosen "for sprinkling by the blood of Jesus Christ," which figure portrays Christ's death as a sacrificial death in fulfillment of the Old Testament typical system of sacrifice in which the blood of bulls and goats was ceremonially sprinkled on the persons and objects to be cleansed. Furthermore, it is by his "precious blood" that the believers *"were redeemed* [ἐλυτρώθητε, *elytrōthēte*]" from their former empty way of life.
>
> 1 John 1:7: "The blood of Jesus, his Son, *cleanses* [καθαρίζει, *katharizei*] us from all sin."
>
> Revelation 1:5: Christ "loved us and *freed* [λύσαντι, *lysanti*] us from our sins by his blood."

---

3. Alan Stibbs demonstrates that *blood* is "a word-symbol for death" in his *The Meaning of the Word "Blood" in Scripture* (London: Tyndale, 1948), 10, 12, 16, 30.

[626]

THE CHARACTER OF THE CROSS WORK OF CHRIST

Revelation 5:9–10: Christ *"purchased* [ἠγόρασας, *ēgorasas*] for God by his blood men from every tribe and language and people and nation, and *made* [ἐποίησας, *epoiēsas*] them for God a kingdom and priests, and they will reign on the earth."

THE CROSS OF CHRIST

Paul states the following about the accomplishments of the "cross"—again, metaphorical shorthand for Christ's sacrificial death:

Ephesians 2:16: God *"has reconciled* [ἀποκαταλλάξῃ, *apokatallaxē*] both [Jews and Gentiles] in one body to God through the cross, *having put to death* [ἀποκτείνας, *apokteinas*] [God's] enmity by [or "on"] it."

Colossians 1:20: Christ *"made peace* [εἰρηνοποιήσας, *eirēnopoiēsas*] through the blood of his cross."

Colossians 2:14–15: God *"canceled* [ἐξαλείψας, *exaleipsas*] the written code, with its regulations, that was against us and that stood opposed to us; *he took it out of the way* [ἦρκεν ἐκ τοῦ μέσου, *ērken ek tou mesou*], nailing it fast to the cross. Having disarmed [ἀπεκδυσάμενος, *apekdysamenos*] the rulers and authorities, *he exposed* [them] *publicly* [ἐδειγμάτισεν ἐν παρρησίᾳ, *edeigmatisen en parrēsia*], *triumphing* [θριαμβεύσας, *thriambeusas*] over them by it."

THE DEATH OF CHRIST

Finally, the New Testament affirms the following about the accomplishments of the "death" of Christ:

Romans 5:10: "When we were enemies, *we were reconciled* [κατηλλάγημεν, *katēllagēmen*] to God through the death of his Son."

Colossians 1:21–22: "Once you were alienated and enemies in your minds as shown by evil works, but now God *has reconciled* [ἀποκατήλλαξεν, *apokatēllaxen*] you ... through [Christ's] death, to present you holy and unblemished and blameless in his sight."

Hebrews 2:9–10: "We see Jesus, through the suffering of death, being crowned with glory and honor, so that by the grace of God in behalf of all he might taste death. For it was fitting for [God] ... in bringing many sons to glory to perfect the Author of their salvation through suffering."

Hebrews 2:14: Christ "shared in their humanity in order that through his death *he might destroy* [καταργήσῃ, *katargēsē*] the one who has the power of death, that is, the devil, and *free* [ἀπαλλάξῃ, *apallaxē*] those who all their lives were held in slavery by their fear of death."

Hebrews 9:15: "He is the Mediator of a new covenant in order that, by means of death *as a ransom to set them free* [εἰς ἀπολύτρωσιν, *eis apolytrōsin*] from the trespasses under the first covenant, the ones who have been called might receive the promise of the eternal inheritance."

Other verses, without using the noun "death," also speak of what Christ accomplished when he "died":

John 12:24: By "falling into the ground and dying," Christ's dying "produces many seeds."

Romans 5:6: "When we were still powerless, Christ died for the ungodly."

Romans 5:8: "When we were still sinners, Christ died for us."

1 Corinthians 15:3: "Christ died for our sins according to the Scriptures."

2 Corinthians 5:15: "He died for all in order that those who live should no longer live for themselves but for him who died for them and was raised again."

1 Thessalonians 5:10: Christ "died for us . . . in order that we may live with him."[4]

---

4. This sustained emphasis on the atonement being accomplished by Christ at the cross highlights how wrong Karl Barth is when he rejects the distinction the Bible makes between Christ's person and Christ's work and insists that His person *is* His work and His work *is* His person:
> It is in the particular fact and the particular way that Jesus Christ is very God, very man, and very God-man that He works, and He works in the fact and only in the fact that He is this One and not another. His being as this One is His history [*Geschichte*], and His history [*Geschichte*] is His being." (*Church Dogmatics*, trans. Geoffrey W. Bromiley [Edinburgh: T. & T. Clark, 1961], IV/1, 128)

By "actualizing" the Incarnation into an ongoing process, in the interest of interpreting Jesus Christ as "event," Barth erroneously concludes:
> . . . the being of Jesus Christ, the unity of being of the living God and this living man, takes place in the event of the concrete existence of this man. It is a being but a being in history [*Geschichte*]. The gracious God is in this history, so is reconciled man, so both are in their unity. And what takes place in this history [*Geschichte*], and therefore in the being of Jesus Christ as such, is atonement. Jesus Christ is not what He is—very God, very man, very God-man—in order as such to mean and do and accomplish something else which is atonement. But His being as God and man and God-man consists in the completed act of the reconciliation of man with God. (*Church Dogmatics*, IV/1, 126–7)

For Barth Jesus Christ *is* the reconciling act! But according to Scripture, the Word became flesh in order to die a reconciling death, and His mediatorial work of redemption at Calvary was accomplished *once for all time* (ἐφάπαξ, *ephapax*) in history and is now a finished work, remaining only to be applied to God's elect.

For a fuller and more detailed exposition and analysis of Barth's thinking on this matter, see my monograph, *Barth's Soteriology* (Philadelphia: Presbyterian and Reformed, 1967).

CHRIST'S ENTIRE LIFE WORK "ONE RIGHTEOUS ACT" OF OBEDIENCE

It is evident from these diverse characterizations of the accomplishments of Christ's cross work that it was a work of cosmic and eternal proportions, with significance for *God*, for *angels*, both holy and demonic, for *men*, both elect and nonelect, and for *creation itself*. Before considering these accomplishments in detail, it is necessary, first, to note that undergirding all the rich and variegated terminology that the Scriptures employ to describe Christ's cross work, there is one comprehensive, all-embracive, unifying feature of his entire life and ministry, which is so essential to his cross work that without it none of the things that the Scriptures say about it could have been said with any degree of propriety. That feature is *the obedience of Christ* (see Rom. 5:18). Quite correctly did John Calvin write: "Now someone asks, how has Christ abolished sin, banished the separation between us and God, and acquired righteousness to render God favorable and kindly toward us. To this we can in general reply that he has achieved this for us by the whole course of his obedience."[5]

The Biblical Data

The New Testament speaks explicitly of the obedience of Christ only three times (but it is significant that two of the occurrences relate Christ's obedience directly to his suffering and death): (1) "through the *obedience* [ὑπακοῆς, *hypakoēs*] of the one man the many will be made righteous" (Rom. 5:19), (2) "he humbled himself and became *obedient* [ὑπήκοος, *hypēkoos*] to death" (Phil. 2:8), and (3) "He learned *obedience* [ὑπακοήν, *hypakoēn*] from what he suffered" (Heb. 5:8). But the concept is alluded to in many other places, for example, (4) in the several contexts in which Christ is called "servant" (Isa. 42:1; 52:13; 53:11; Phil. 2:7; see also Matt. 20:28; Mark 10:45), (5) in the numerous passages where he declared that his purpose in coming to earth was to do his Father's will (Ps. 40:7; John 5:30; 8:28–29; 10:18; 12:49; 14:31; Heb. 10:7), (6) in his and others' testimony concerning his sinless life (Matt. 27:4, 19–23; Mark 12:14; Luke 23:4, 14–15; John 8:46; 18:38; 19:4–6; 2 Cor. 5:21; Heb. 4:15; 7:26), (7) in the two passages in Hebrews (2:10–18; 5:8–10) where he is said to have been "perfected" through his suffering, and (8) in the passages which affirm his submission to all proper authority and to the divine law itself (Matt. 3:15; Luke 2:51–52; 4:16; Gal. 4:4).

---

5. John Calvin, *Institutes of the Christian Religion*, trans. Ford Lewis Battles (Philadelphia: Westminster Press, 1960), II.xvi.5.

All of this shows that it was as an obedient Son that Christ did all that he did at the cross. It was as an obedient Son that he offered himself up once for all as a sacrifice to satisfy divine justice and to reconcile us to God. It was as an obedient Son that he "gave his life as a ransom for many" (Matt. 20:28; Mark 10:45) and "bore our sins in his body on the tree" (1 Pet. 2:24). And it was as an obedient Son that he "made peace through the blood of his cross" (Col. 1:20). His obedience is the "umbrella" overarching his work in its several biblical characterizations.

The Character of His Obedience

Murray has beautifully captured the character of Christ's obedience in four terms: its inwardness, its progressiveness, its climax, and its dynamic.[6]

By its *inwardness* he means that Christ's obedience always came from his heart as a willing, joyous yielding up of himself to his Father's will and law; never was it merely artificial and outward, executed mechanically and perfunctorily. his entire life was one of delight in doing his Father's will.

By its *progressiveness* he intends what the Scriptures imply when it records that he "grew . . . in favor with God and men" (Luke 2:52), that he was "perfected" (Heb. 2:10; 5:9), and that "he learned obedience" (Heb. 5:8). Since our Lord was always morally pure, this perfecting and learning process must not be construed to mean that he learned obedience in the same way Christians do, moving from a state of disobedience to a state of obedience by means of the sanctifying process. Rather, it means that as he moved in perfect obedience to the will of God from one trial to the next throughout his entire lifetime, his will to obey was made ever more and more resolute, even in the face of stiffer and severer trials, in his determination to do his Father's will. This process was necessary to prepare him to face the final ordeal of the cross.

By speaking of its *climax* Murray seeks to do justice to what is represented by Scripture itself as the heretofore unprecedented testing that Jesus faced in his Gethsemane experience (Matt. 26:36–46; Mark 14:32–42; Luke 22:39–44) and then finally in his cross work itself.

Finally, by its *dynamic* Murray intends to underscore the divinely designed means by which our Lord learned the obedience essential to the full execution of the Messianic task—namely, his suffering (Heb. 2:10; 5:8). His trials, temptations, deprivations, and physical suffering all became the instruments in his Father's hand by which Christ was "perfected" as the Author of salvation, that he might become

---

6. John Murray, "The Obedience of Christ," in *Collected Writings of John Murray* (Edinburgh: Banner of Truth, 1977), 2:151–57.

everything he had to be and endure everything he had to endure in order to bring many sons to glory.

The Purpose of His Obedience

Reformed theologians have interested themselves with the purpose lying behind Christ's obedient life and ministry because they have discerned that both Christ's right to carry out the messianic task as God's Messiah-Savior and as the race's last Adam and the salvation of those he came to save directly depend on his personal, perfect, and perpetual obedience to God's law. To make this clear, they customarily distinguish between the *active* and *passive* obedience of Christ. However, because nothing that he did did he do passively, that is, resignedly without full desire and willingness on his part—for while it is true that he *was offered up* (Heb. 9:28, προσενεχθείς, *prosenechtheis*), it is equally true that he *offered himself up* (Heb. 7:27, ἑαυτὸν ἀνενέγκας, *heauton anenenkas*; 9:14, ἑαυτὸν προσήνεγκεν, *heauton prosēnenken*; see also John 10:18)—these are not satisfactory terms. The terms "preceptive" and "penal" are to be preferred to "active" and "passive" respectively, the former referring to Christ's full obedience to all the prescriptions of the divine law, the latter referring to his willing obedience in bearing all the sanctions imposed by that law against his people because of their transgressions. By the former—his preceptive obedience—he made available a perfect righteousness before the law that is imputed or reckoned to those who put their trust in him. By the latter—his penal obedience—he bore in himself by legal imputation the penalty due to his people for their sin. His preceptive and his penal obedience, then, particularly as the latter came to expression in his cross work, is the ground of God's justification of sinners (see Rom. 5:9), by which divine act they are *pardoned* (because their sins were charged to Christ who obediently bore the law's sanctions against them) and *accepted as righteous* in God's sight (because Christ's preceptive obedience or perfect righteousness is imputed to them through faith). With grateful praise the Christian adores the Savior for his obedience to his Father's will and law. Without it, there would be no salvation!

CHRIST'S CROSS WORK AN OBEDIENT WORK OF SACRIFICE (PRESUPPOSITION: HUMAN SIN AND GUILT)

Many times throughout the New Testament, as we have already noted, Christ's cross work is represented as a *work of sacrifice*. The following verses refer to Christ both as the "high priest" after the order of Melchizedek who offered himself up to God and as the "Lamb of God" who was made a "sacrifice" and an "offering" to God.

His Work as High Priest

Jesus' cross work is represented in Hebrews 7:26–27 and 9:11–14 as the work of a high priest [ἀρχιερεύς, *archiereus*] who offered himself up as a sacrifice to God. To him is also ascribed an unchangeable "priesthood" [ἱερωσύνη, *hierōsynē*] in Hebrews 7:24.

> Hebrews 7:26–27: "Such a high priest meets our need . . . when he once for all offered himself up."

> Hebrews 9:11–14: "When Christ came as high priest . . . , not through blood of goats and calves but through his own blood he entered once for all into the Most Holy Place, having obtained eternal redemption."

His Work as the Lamb of God

Jesus is described both as God's "Lamb" (ἀμνός, *amnos*) who "takes away the sin of the world" (John 1:29; see 1:36), whose "precious blood as a lamb without blemish and defect" has redeemed Christians (1 Pet. 1:19), and the "Lamb" (ἀρνίον, *arnion*) who "with his blood purchased men to God" (Rev. 5:8–9) and in whose blood men "have washed their robes and made them white" (Rev. 7:14).

His Work as a Sacrifice

> 1 Corinthians 5:7: "Our Passover lamb [τὸ πάσχα, *to pascha*] *has been sacrificed* [ἐτύθη, *etythē*]—even Christ." (See Mark 14:12; Luke 22:7 for parallel usage of the same verb root [θύω, *thuō*] in connection with the Passover lamb.)

> Ephesians 5:2: "Christ loved us and gave himself up for us as . . . a *sacrifice* [θυσίαν, *thysian*] to God."

> Hebrews 9:23: "It was necessary, then, for . . . the heavenly things themselves [to be purified] with better *sacrifices* [θυσίαις, *thysiais*] than these."

> Hebrews 9:26: "He has appeared once for all at the end of the ages to do away with sin by the *sacrifice* [θυσίας, *thysias*] of himself."

> Hebrews 10:12: "But when this [priest] had offered up for all time one *sacrifice* [θυσίαν, *thysian*] for sins he sat down at the right hand of God."

His Work as an Offering

> Ephesians 5:2: "Christ loved us and gave himself up for us as *a fragrant offering* [προσφοράν, *prosphoran*] . . . to God."

Hebrews 7:27: "He sacrificed for their sins once for all *when he offered himself* [ἑαυτὸν ἀνενέγκας, heauton anenenkas]."

Hebrews 9:14: "Christ . . . *offered himself up* [ἑαυτὸν προσήνεγκεν, heauton prosēnenken] unblemished to God."

Hebrews 9:28: "Christ once for all *was offered up* [προσενεχθεὶς, prosenechtheis] for many to take away sins."

Hebrews 10:10: "We have been made holy through the *offering up* [προσφορᾶς, prosphoras] of the body of Jesus Christ once for all."

Hebrews 10:12: "But when this [priest] *had offered up* [προσενέγκας, prosenenkas] for all time one sacrifice for sins he sat down at the right hand of God."

Hebrews 10:14: "By one *offering* [προσφορά, prosphora] he has made perfect forever those who are being made holy."

It is because of this pervasive testimony that Murray writes: "It lies on the face of the New Testament that Christ's work is construed as sacrifice."[7] It is also because of this testimony to Christ's death as a sacrifice for sin that the church has embraced so many hymns that speak of Christ's "blood" and his death as a sacrifice, such as that by Isaac Watts:

> Not all the blood of beasts
> On Jewish altars slain,
> Could give the guilty conscience peace,
> Or wash away the stain:
>
> But Christ, the heav'nly Lamb
> Takes all our sins away,
> A sacrifice of nobler name
> and richer blood than they.

The Significance of His Death as a Sacrifice

Because the evangelical ear is accustomed to such language, the assertion that Christ offered himself up to God on the cross as a sacrifice may not appear to be

---

7. Murray, *Redemption—Accomplished and Applied*, 24. See also Benjamin B. Warfield's attack on the attempt to rid the New Testament of the idea of Christ's death as sacrifice: "Christ Our Sacrifice," in *The Person and Work of Christ* (Philadelphia: Presbyterian and Reformed, 1950), 391–426.

very significant. But it is replete with implications. Since the Old Testament sacrificial system is the obvious background to the cross-work material of the New Testament, the New Testament material that speaks of Christ's death as a sacrifice certainly presupposes (1) the sinless *perfection* of Christ, since any sacrifice acceptable to God had to be "without blemish" (Exod. 12:5; 1 Pet. 1:19); (2) the *imputation* or transfer of the sinner's sin to Christ on the analogy of the Levitical legislation (Lev. 1:4; 3:2, 8, 13; 4:4, 15, 24, 29, 33; 16:21–22; Num. 8:12; see Isa. 53:4, 5, 6, 7, 8, 10, 11, 12); (3) the resultant *substitution* of Christ *in the stead and place of* (ἀντί, *anti*—Matt. 20:28; Mark 10:45), *because of* (διά, *dia*—1 Cor. 8:11; 2 Cor. 8:9), *for* (περί, *peri*—Matt. 26:28; Rom. 8:3; 1 Pet. 3:18; 1 John 2:2; 4:10), and *in behalf of* (ὑπέρ, *hyper*—Mark 14:24; Luke 22:19, 20; John 6:51; 10:11, 15; Rom. 5:6, 8; 8:32; 14:15; 1 Cor. 11:24; 15:3; 2 Cor. 5:15, 21; Gal. 1:4; 2:20; 3:13; Eph. 5:2, 25; 1 Thes. 5:10; 1 Tim. 2:6; Titus 2:14; Heb.2:9; 10:12; 1 Pet. 2:21; 3:18; 1 John 3:16) those sinners whose sins had been imputed to him; and (4) the necessary *expiation* or cancellation of *their* sins. As Geerhardus Vos has written: "Wherever [in the sacrificial system] there is slaying and manipulation of blood there is expiation."[8]

These four theological principles, taken together, justify the conclusion, based upon the truth that Jesus' death is portrayed in the New Testament as a *sacrificial* death, that Christ's death procured the juridical removal or expiation of the sins of those for whom he died. It also means, because of the principle of substitution necessarily implicit within the scriptural representation of his death as one of sacrifice, that everything else which Christ did in and by his cross work—turning away God's wrath, removing his hostility, delivering from the condemnation of the law, and freeing from the guilt and power of sin—has necessarily been accomplished for those whom the Father chose in him before the foundation of the world.

A further point must be underscored here. One often hears the liberal church declare that the Bible is opposed to all human sacrifice, and occasionally one may hear the evangelical Christian unthinkingly echo the same thought. But as Vos observes:

> It is well to be cautious in committing one's self to that critical opinion, for it strikes at the very heart of the atonement. The rejection of the "blood theology" as a remnant of a very barbaric type of primitive religion rests on such a basis.... Not sacrifice of human life as such, but the sacrifice of average sinful human life, is deprecated by the O.T.[9]

---

8. Geerhardus Vos, *Biblical Theology* (Grand Rapids, Mich.: Eerdmans, 1948), 135. See his extended discussion of the sacrificial system of Mosaism, 172–90.
9. Ibid., 106–7.

In other words, what the evangelical must clearly understand is that the *entire* sacrificial system of the Old Testament had meaning and value only because it typically pointed forward to a *human* sacrifice—the sacrifice of the sinless Jesus. Indeed, it is not going too far to insist that if the Old Testament sacrificial system had not found its antitypical fulfillment in the death of Christ, if the priestly cultus in Israel was simply reflecting the cultic thinking of the Near East in the mid-second-millennium B.C., then Moses, far from being "the world's great lawgiver," was one of the greatest barbarians who ever lived.

As evidence that God is not opposed *in principle* to all human sacrifice, one has only to recall that it was God himself who "did not spare his own Son but gave him up for us all" (Rom. 8:32) and who willed "to crush him and cause him to suffer" (Isa. 53:10). God is not opposed *in principle* to all human sacrifice but only to *sinful* human sacrifice because such sacrifice will not prevail before him. But it is only because of the sinless *human* sacrifice which the Son of God himself became—which alone prevails before God—that anyone will ever be forgiven and go to heaven when he dies.

CHRIST'S OBEDIENT CROSS WORK OF PROPITIATION (PRESUPPOSITION: DIVINE WRATH)

The category under which we now view Christ's cross work is derived from the ἱλάσκεσθαι, *hilaskesthai*, word-group. Four times the New Testament represents his achievement at the cross by some derivative from this verb:

Romans 3:25: God "publicly displayed [Christ Jesus] as *a sacrifice which would turn aside his wrath, taking away sin* [ἱλαστήριον, *hilastērion*]. . . ."[10]

Hebrews 2:17: Christ "had to be made like his brothers in every way in order that he might become a merciful and faithful high priest in service to God, that he *might turn aside God's wrath, taking away* [ἱλάσκεσθαι, *hilaskesthai*] the sins of the people."

1 John 2:2: "If anyone sins, we have an Advocate with the Father, Jesus Christ the Righteous One, and he is the *sacrifice which turns aside God's wrath, taking away* [ἱλασμός, *hilasmos*] our sins, and not only our sins but also the sins of the whole world."

---

10. Leon Morris argues that ἱλαστηριον, *hilastērion*, does not mean "mercy seat" here, as has often been argued, but rather "a propitiating thing," since not Christ but the cross is the place of sprinkling (*The Apostolic Preaching of the Cross* [London: Tyndale, 1955], 172).

1 John 4:10: God "loved us and sent his Son as *a sacrifice which turns aside God's wrath, taking away* [ἱλασμὸν, *hilasmon*] our sins."

Expiation or Propitiation?

The basic understanding of this word-group as "a sacrifice which turns aside God's wrath, taking away sin" has not gone unchallenged. It was primarily the Cambridge scholar, C. H. Dodd, who led this challenge. Dodd argued in several places that the meaning conveyed by the word-group is that of expiation (the cancellation of sin), *not* that of propitiation (the turning away of the wrath of God).[11] While he acknowledged that it had the meaning of "placating an angry person" in both classical and popular pagan Greek literature, he insisted that this meaning was absent in Hellenistic Judaism, as represented by the Septuagint. His argument is essentially twofold: (1) that the Septuagint sometimes translates words from the Hebrew verb root כָּפַר (*kāpar*, "atone") by Greek words other than ἱλάσκεσθαι, *hilaskesthai*, which mean to "purify" or "cancel," and (2) that the Septuagint sometimes employs ἱλάσκεσθαι, *hilaskesthai*, to translate Hebrew words other than those from כָּפַר, *kāpar*, which mean to "cleanse" or "forgive." Here is his summary: "Hellenistic Judaism, as represented by the LXX, does not regard the cultus as a means of pacifying the displeasure of the Deity, but as a means of delivering man from sin."[12] He concluded that the four New Testament occurrences should be rendered in accordance with the understanding that prevailed within Hellenistic Judaism. He also argued that "the wrath of God" denotes not a hostile attitude on God's part toward sinners but only the "inevitable process of cause and effect in a moral universe" whereby disaster follows sin.[13] Dodd's position also has been espoused by A. T. Hanson[14] and is reflected in the RSV and NEB translations of the verses in question. It has also been followed unwittingly by many at the pastoral level. For example, Robert H. Schuller informs us that it is because "we *fabricate* our own images of God . . . that the unsaved human being *imagines* God to be angry rather than loving." It is due to *our* fears, he writes, that we "have *pictured* [God] as a *threatening* rather than a redeeming figure."[15]

---

11. See C. H. Dodd, "Ἱλάσκεσθαι [*hilaskesthai*]. Its Cognates, Derivatives and Synonyms, in the Septuagint," *Journal of Theological Studies* 32 (1931): 352–60. This article was republished in C. H. Dodd, *The Bible and the Greeks* (London: Hodder and Stoughton, 1935). See also his Moffatt New Testament Commentaries on *Romans* (London: Hodder & Stoughton, 1932) and *The Johannine Epistles* (London: Hodder & Stoughton, 1946).
12. Dodd, *The Bible and the Greeks*, 93.
13. Dodd, *Romans*, 23.
14. A. T. Hanson, *The Wrath of the Lamb* (London: SPCK, 1959), 192.

Several rigorous critiques of Dodd's argument have been registered.[16] Both Leon Morris and Roger Nicole pointed out that Dodd made two basic errors: (1) his extrabiblical evidence was incomplete, and (2) he did not pay enough attention to the biblical teaching.

With respect to his first error, Dodd's assessment of data in the Septuagint ignores the books of the Maccabees, which contain several passages that speak of "the wrath of the Almighty" being averted. He also passed over the fact that the meaning of "placate" for the word-group prevails in the writings of Josephus and Philo. F. Büchsel, they note, demonstrated that in First Clement and the Shepherd of Hermas the word-group plainly means to "propitiate" God.[17] Morris concludes: "Throughout Greek literature, biblical and non-biblical alike, ἱλασμός [hilasmos] means 'propitiation.' We cannot now decide that we like another meaning better."[18] And Nicole judges that if Dodd's theory regarding this word-group usage in the Septuagint and the New Testament is correct, it would mean that these sources "form a sort of linguistic island with little precedent in former times, little confirmation from the contemporaries, and no following in after years!"[19]

With respect to their second criticism, both Morris and Nicole show that the idea of the wrath of God is "stubbornly rooted in the Old Testament, where it is referred to 585 times"[20] by no less than twenty different Hebrew words that underscore God's indignation against sin and evil.[21] They also show that there are numerous times when the verb roots כָּפַר, *kāpar*, and ἱλάσκεσθαι, *hilaskesthai*—employed by the Septuagint to translate כָּפַר, *kāpar*—refer to propitiating the wrath both of men (for example, Gen. 32:20; Prov. 16:14) and of God (for example, see Exod. 32:10 with 32:30, Num. 16:41–50; 25:11–13; see also LXX, Zech. 7:2, 8:22, Mal. 1:9).[22]

---

15. Robert Schuller, *Self-Esteem: A New Reformation* (Waco, Tex.: Word, 1982), 66, emphasis supplied. See my review of Schuller's book in *Presbuterion* 9 (Spring-Fall 1983): 1–2, 93–96, and his response and my reply in *Presbuterion* 10 (Spring–Fall 1984): 1–2, 111–122.
16. See Leon Morris, "The Use of Ἱλάσκεσθαι [hilakesthai] etc. in Biblical Greek," *The Expository Times* 72, no. 8 (1951): 227–33, "The Meaning of HILASTERION in Rom III.25," in *New Testament Studies*, 2:33–43, and his *Apostolic Preaching*. See also Roger R. Nicole, "C. H. Dodd and the Doctrine of Propitiation," *Westminster Theological Journal* 17, no. 2 (1955): 117–57.
17. Friedrich Büchsel, "ἱλάσκομαι [hilaskomai]," in *Theological Dictionary of the New Testament*, ed. Gerhard Kittel, trans. Geoffrey W. Bromiley (Grand Rapids, Mich.: Eerdmans, 1965), 3:300–23.
18. Leon Morris, *The Cross in the New Testament* (Leicester, U.K.: Paternoster, 1965), 349.
19. Nicole, "C. H. Dodd and the Doctrine of Propitiation," 132.
20. Leon Morris, "Propitiation," in *Evangelical Dictionary of Theology*, ed. Walter A. Elwell (Grand Rapids, Mich.: Baker, 1984), 888.
21. Morris, *Apostolic Preaching*, 149. The New Testament follows the Old Testament's lead here, employing ὀργή, *orgē* and θύμος, *thumos* (Matt 3:7; Luke 3:7; 21:23; John 3:36; Rom 1:18; 2:5, 8; 3:5; 4:15; 5:9; 9:22; 12:19; Eph 2:3; 5:6; Col 3:6; 1 Thes 1:10; 2:16; 5:9; Heb 3:11; 4:3; Rev 6:16, 17; 11:18; 14:10–19; 15:1, 7; 16:1, 19; 19:15).

It can be demonstrated that the matter is no different in the New Testament. While one could conceivably argue that the two occurrences in Hebrews 2:17 and 1 John 4:10 simply mean that Jesus canceled or took away sin, the occurrences in Romans 3:25 and 1 John 2:2 will brook no such interpretation. In Romans 1:18–3:20, the section leading up to the section in which the word occurs (3:21–31), Paul argues not only the case for universal human sin but in the process of doing so also directly refers to God's wrath in 1:18 (see its exhibition in 1:24, 26, 28, 32), 2:5 (see 2:16), 8, and 3:5 (see also John 3:36; 1 Thess. 1:10). Morris quite properly concludes: "Wrath has occupied such an important place in the argument leading up to this section [3:21–31] that we are justified in looking for some expression indicative of its cancellation in the process which brings about salvation."[23] And John Murray observes:

> The essence of the judgment of God against sin is his wrath, his holy recoil against what is the contradiction of himself (see Rom. 1:18). If Christ vicariously bore God's judgment upon sin, *and to deny this is to make nonsense of his suffering unto death and particularly of the abandonment on Calvary,* then to eliminate from this judgment that which belongs to its essence is to undermine the idea of vicarious sin-bearing and its consequences. So the doctrine of propitiation is not to be denied or its sharpness in any way toned down.[24]

In 1 John 2:1 the reference to Jesus as our Advocate before the Father when we sin, specifically in his character as the *Righteous One,* implies that the One before whom he pleads our cause—who represents the offended Triune Godhead—is displeased with us. Accordingly, the description of Jesus which immediately follows in 1 John 2:2 surely suggests that it is his advocacy before the Father specifically in his character as our ἱλασμός, *hilasmos,* which removes that divine displeasure. But this means that Jesus' advocacy as our ἱλασμός, *hilasmos,* since its referent is Godward, is propitiatory and not simply expiatory in nature (which latter idea, of course, is not entirely absent from the idea of propitiation). By extension, this provides the interpretive control for the meaning of the same word two chapters later in 1 John 4:10 where the same contextual situation obtains. Clearly, the exegetical evidence points decisively in the direction of the idea of propitiation.

So does the following theological consideration: If this word-group means *only* expiation, the question must be asked and answered, What would be the result for

---

22. See George E. Ladd's discussion in *A Theology of the New Testament* (Grand Rapids, Mich.: Eerdmans, 1974), 429–33.
23. Morris, *Apostolic Preaching,* 169.
24. John Murray, "The Atonement," in *Collected Writings of John Murray* (Edinburgh: Banner of Truth, 1977), 2:145, emphasis supplied.

men if there is no expiation? When they die in their sin, would they not face the divine displeasure? Just so, surely! But is this not just another way of saying that Christ by his death satisfies divine justice and removes God's displeasure, that is, propitiates God? It surely seems so!

We would conclude, then, that there is no warrant to depart from the traditional understanding of this word-group in the New Testament literature as denoting placation or propitiation. To the contrary, we believe that the evidence at every critical juncture supports the traditional understanding. Accordingly, we will proceed to draw our theological conclusions on the assumption that, although the basic idea in the ἱλάσκεσθαι, *hilaskesthai*, word-group is a "complex one," yet "the averting of anger [by an offering] seems to represent a stubborn substratum of meaning from which all the usages can be naturally explained."[25]

The Godward Reference in the Propitiation

All of this means that a major revision is essential in the thinking of Christian minds accustomed to viewing the cross work of Christ as being directed primarily, if not solely, toward men. In light of the fact that Paul and John (and probably the author of Hebrews as well) expressly represent it as a *propitiating* work, it is important to recognize that Christ's cross work had a Godward reference. Indeed, if one reflects even for a moment on the sinful condition of the race vis-à-vis the holy character of God, it will become clear that *its Godward reference was the cross's primary reference*. The Bible plainly teaches the doctrine of the wrath of God. It teaches that God is angry with the sinner, and that his holy outrage against the sinner must be assuaged if the sinner is to escape his due punishment. It is for this reason that a *death* occurred at Calvary. When we look at Calvary and behold the Savior dying for us, we should see in his death not first our salvation but our damnation being borne and carried away by him!

God's wrath, of course, must not be construed in any measure as capricious, uncontrolled, or irrational fury. Nor is God himself malicious, vindictive, or spiteful. God's wrath is simply his instinctive holy indignation and the settled opposition of his holiness to sin, which, because he is righteous, expresses itself in judicial punishment. It is his "personal divine revulsion to evil" and his "personal vigorous opposition" to it.[26] It is his "steady, unrelenting, unremitting, uncompromising antagonism to evil in all its forms and manifestations."[27] In sum, God's instinctive

---

25. Morris, *Apostolic Preaching*, 155.
26. Morris, *The Cross in the New Testament*, 190–91.
27. John Stott, *The Cross of Christ* (Downers Grove, Ill.: InterVarsity Press, 1986), 173.

and vehement revulsion to sin demands, if sinners are ever to be forgiven, that their sins be punished. Accordingly, above everything else, it was this demand in God himself—that his offended holiness (which when confronted with sin must react against it in the wrathful outpouring of divine judgment) must be "satisfied"—that necessitated the cross work of Christ. When Christ died, because of his own infinite worth as the Son of God before the Father who stands as the legal representative of the Triune Godhead, he fully paid the penalty for our sin and thus fully discharged the debt which our sin had accrued before God. In sum, he "did enough" to "satisfy" (Lat. *satis,* "enough," *facere,* "to do") fully the demands of the glory of God's offended holiness and justice. Hence we speak of the "satisfaction view" of Christ atonement. Apart from Christ's death work, God could only have continued in an "unpropitiated" state, and sinners would have had to bear the penalty for their sins in themselves. But since they can never "do enough" to satisfy divine justice, they would have had to bear the penalty for their sins *eternally* in themselves.

Isaac Watts gave hymnic expression to the propitiating character of Christ's cross work in the following beautiful verses:

> Jesus, my great High Priest, offered his blood and died;
> *My guilty conscience seeks no sacrifice beside.*
> His pow'rful blood did once atone,
> *And now it pleads before the throne.*
>
> To this dear Surety's hand will I commit my cause;
> *He answers and fulfils his Father's broken laws.*
> Behold my soul at freedom set;
> *My Surety paid the dreadful debt.*
>
> *My Advocate appears for my defense on high;*
> The Father bows his ears and *lays his thunder by.*
> Not all that hell or sin can say
> Shall turn his heart, his love, away.

Not one word of the exposition above is intended to suggest, however, that it was Christ's death work that rendered God *gracious* toward the sinner. P. T. Forsyth has expressed this point succinctly and well: "The atonement did not procure grace, it flowed from grace."[28] M. A. C. Warren states: "[In the cross] we are to see not an attempt to change God's mind but the very expression of that mind."[29] And

---

28. P. T. Forsyth, *The Cruciality of the Cross* (London: Hodder & Stoughton, 1909), 78.
29. M. A. C. Warren, *The Gospel of Victory* (London: SCM, 1995), 21.

John Stott declares:

> It cannot be emphasized too strongly that God's love is the source, not the consequence, of the atonement. . . . God does not love us because Christ died for us; Christ died for us because God loved us. If it is God's wrath which needed to be propitiated, it is God's love which did the propitiating. If it may be said that the propitiation "changed" God, or that by it he changed himself, let us be clear he did not change from wrath to love, or from enmity to grace, since his character is unchanging. What the propitiation changed was his dealings with us.[30]

It was the same God who demanded satisfaction for sin who in grace provided in his Son the "sacrifice which would turn aside his wrath, by taking away sin" (Rom. 3:25). Never should the atonement be represented so as to suggest that it was the Father who hated the sinner, that it was the Son who loved the sinner, and that his cross work won the Father over to clemency or extorted the Father's gracious attitude toward the sinner from him against his will. Not only does Scripture trace the entire plan of salvation back to the Father's electing love (Eph. 3:11; 1:3–14; Rom. 8:29; 2 Tim. 1:9), not only does Scripture trace the execution of his plan back to the Father's love (John 3:16, "God so loved the world that he gave his only Son"; Rom. 5:8, "God demonstrated his own love for us in this: While we were still sinners, Christ died for us"), but also even in the very passages where Christ's death work is represented as a propitiating sacrifice directed toward the demands of the Godhead in order that divine justice be satisfied, it is the Father's provision and the Father's love that are stressed as the spring from which his propitiatory activity flowed. Consider:

> Romans 3:25: "[God] publicly displayed [Christ Jesus] as a sacrifice which would turn aside his wrath, taking away sin . . . to demonstrate his justice."
>
> 1 John 4:9–10: "Herein the love of God was manifested among us: God sent his only Son into the world in order that we may live through him. Herein is love: not that we loved God but that he loved us and sent his Son as a sacrifice which would turn aside his wrath, taking away our sins."

Regarding Dodd's contention that God's wrath is simply "the inevitable process of cause and effect [working itself out] in a moral universe" and not actual divine hostility toward men, Leon Morris has pointed out that such a process of wrath would be "impersonal" and as such meaningless, for what, he asks, is the meaning of an impersonal process of wrath in a genuinely theistic universe?[31]

---

30. Stott, *Cross of Christ*, 174.
31. Leon Morris, *New Testament Theology* (Grand Rapids, Mich.: Academie, 1986), 63.

Some theologians have objected to the reality of God's wrath by urging that love (which God surely has and is) and wrath in the same person are incompatible. But Murray rightly insists that

> love and wrath are not contradictory. They can coexist in their greatest intensity in the same person at the same time. Wrath is not to be equated with hate. Failure to recognize this simple truth . . . is the capital error of those who make the objection concerned. It is an incomprehensible error. Because of the compatibility of love and wrath as coexisting, the wrath-bearing of the Son of God, pre-eminently upon the accursed tree, the vicarious infliction of the wrath of God against those whom the Father invincibly loves, is not only comprehensible, but belongs to the essence of the doctrine that Christ bore our sins in his own body upon the tree as the supreme manifestation of the Father's love. God's glory is not only love. It is also holiness. And because he is holiness, his holy jealousy burns against sin, and therefore against sinners. For only as characterizing sinners does sin exist. The propitiation which God made his own Son is the provision of the Father's love, to the end that holiness may be vindicated and its demands satisfied. Thus, and only thus, could the purpose and urge of his love be realized in a way compatible with, and to the glory of the manifold perfections of his character. . . . And so we must say that this love of the Father was at no point more intensely in exercise than when the Son was actively drinking the cup of unrelieved damnation, than when he was enduring as substitute the full toll of the Father's wrath. . . . What love for men that the Father should execute upon his own Son the full toll of holy wrath, so that we should never taste it![32]

James Denney has also pointed out in this same connection: "If the propitiatory death of Jesus is eliminated from the love of God, it might be unfair to say that the love of God is robbed of all meaning, but it is certainly robbed of its apostolic meaning."[33]

Of course, I certainly do not intend to suggest that the Father, in order to display *his* love and justice, forced the Son as an unwilling victim to become the propitiating sacrifice. For not only does Scripture inform us that the Son of God "loved me and gave himself for me" (Gal. 2:20), that he "loved us and gave himself for us, an offering and a sacrifice to God" (Eph. 5:2), that he "loved the church and gave himself for it" (Eph. 5:25), and that he "loved us and loosed us from our sins by his blood" (Rev. 1:5; see also John 10:18; Heb. 7:27; 9:14), but also even in Hebrews 2:17 where we are informed that Christ conducted his high priestly work "*in order that*

---

32. Murray, *Collected Writings*, 2:145–47.
33. James Denney, *The Death of Christ* (London: Hodder and Stoughton, 1900), 152.

he might propitiate for [εἰς τὸ ἱλάσκεσθαι, *eis to hilaskesthai*] *the sins of the people,*" the author stresses that Christ did so as "a merciful [ἐλεήμων, *eleēmōn*] high priest."

But it must also immediately be said that Christ's love, though it was as intense as the Father's, "is not in its biblical perspective unless we perceive that it is love *constrained by and exercised in fulfillment of the Father's will,* and the Father's will as the purpose flowing from his invincible love."[34] This is just to say that the Son's love was not so intense and all-determinative of his actions that he would have arranged to die for men even if the Father had not determined to save them! In the economy of salvation, the Son ever acts in accordance with the Father's will. But in the economy of salvation, just because the Father in love determined to save them, the Son in free and willing love agreed to endure vicariously his wrath which their sins deserved. Thus Christ's obedient cross work was a work of willing propitiation.

CHRIST'S OBEDIENT CROSS WORK OF RECONCILIATION (PRESUPPOSITION: DIVINE ALIENATION)

The category under which we now consider Christ's cross work—that of reconciliation—is securely based upon four major passages in which words from the ἀλλάσσω, *-allassō*, word-group are employed, the meaning of which words ("to reconcile") is undisputed.

> Romans 5:10–11: "If, when we were enemies, *we were reconciled* [κατηλλάγημεν, *katēllagēmen*] to God through the death of his Son, how much more, *having been reconciled* [καταλλαγέντες, *katallagentes*], shall we be saved by his life. And not only this, but also we rejoice in God through our Lord Jesus Christ, through whom now we received the *reconciliation* [καταλλαγὴν, *katallagēn*]."
>
> 2 Corinthians 5:17–21: "If anyone is in Christ, he is a new creation. The old has gone; behold, the new has come. All this is from God *who reconciled* [καταλλάξαντος, *katallaxantos*] us to himself through Christ, and gave to us the ministry *of reconciliation* [καταλλαγῆς, *katallagēs*]: that God *was,* in Christ, *reconciling* [καταλλάσσων, *katallassōn*] a world unto himself, not imputing to them their trespasses, and entrusted to us the message *of reconciliation* [καταλλαγῆς, *katallagēs*]. We are therefore ambassadors in Christ's stead, as though God were summoning [men] through us. We implore in Christ's stead: *Be reconciled* [καταλλάγητε, *katallagēte*] to God. God made him who knew no sin to be sin in our stead, in order that we might become the righteousness of God in him."
>
> Ephesians 2:14–17: "[Christ] is our peace, who made both [Jews and Gentiles] one and destroyed the enmity, the dividing wall of hostility, in his flesh, nullifying the

---

34. Murray, *The Atonement,* 2:144.

law of commandments with its regulations, in order that the two he might create in himself into one new man, making peace [between them], and that *he might reconcile* [ἀποκαταλλάξῃ, *apokatallaxē*] both in one body to God through the cross, slaying the enmity [of God] by it. And having come he preached the good news of peace to you who were far off and of peace to those who were near."

Colossians 1:19–22: "God was pleased that in him all the fullness [of deity] should dwell, and through him *to reconcile* [ἀποκαταλλάξαι, *apokatallaxai*] all things unto him(self?), making peace through the blood of his cross, through him whether things on earth or things in heaven. And you were once alienated and enemies in your mind because of evil deeds, but now *he has reconciled* [ἀποκατήλλαξεν, *apokatēllaxen*] you by the body of his flesh through death, to present you holy and unblemished and blameless in his sight." (author's translation)

God's Alienation or Man's?

Because of the repeated references in these passages to Christ's cross work as a reconciling event, this characterization of his death achievement is not disputed. It is acknowledged on all sides that his death work, construed as a reconciling work, presupposed that a state of alienation existed between God and man because of human sin, and that his death removed that alienation or enmity. But what is debated is whose alienation or enmity was it that was addressed and removed by Christ's cross work. Both God and man, it is true, were alienated each from the other—God's alienation from man being, of course, both holy and completely justified because of man's rebellion against him; man's alienation from God being both unholy and completely unjustified, the reflex of his rebellion against God in the area of his personal relationship to God. Now does Christ's cross work viewed as a reconciling act terminate upon God's alienation or upon man's? Does it denote once again a Godward reference of the atonement, viewed now simply from a different perspective from that of propitiation, or have we discovered as such a characterization of the atonement that ascribes a manward reference to it?

It has often been said that, while Christ's death propitiated God, it reconciled man. But did the death of God's Son, even the precious blood of the cross, remove man's enmity against God or alter or change man's attitude toward God? The manner in which this Greek word–group is rendered by the English would seem to suggest so, for never does the English translation say that God was reconciled to man but, just to the contrary, either (active voice) that God *reconciled* the world to himself or (passive voice) that men *have been reconciled* to God. Both history and Christian experience would affirm, however, that men have not terminated their unholy hostility toward God. The race, by and large, either detests the cross and all that it implies about man's moral/ethical condition with unrestrained vehemence and contempt or regards the cross with indifference. Paul said it this way: the cross to the Jew is a stumbling block, to the Gentile it is foolishness! It is hardly true then that men, for the most part, because of Christ's cross work, now love God and live to honor and to glorify him. To the contrary, most men have lived and died hating him, neither glorifying him nor giving thanks to him, preferring to exchange the glory of the immortal God for images made to look like mortal man and birds and animals and reptiles (see Rom. 1:21–23).

For the following exegetical reasons most Reformed theologians have insisted that the English translation of the ἀλλάσσω, -*allassō*, word-group only apparently (not substantively) supports a manward reference and that Christ's cross work as a reconciling act is once again to be construed as having a Godward reference. They urge that by his paying the penalty due to the elect for their sin, thereby expiating sin in their behalf, Christ removed the ground of God's alienation respecting them, effecting peace with God as the result. For example, Charles Hodge writes on Ephesians 2:16:

> Neither the English nor Greek terms ... indicate whether the change effected is mutual or only on one side.... Whether the reconciliation effected by Christ between man and God results from an inward change in men, or from the propitiation of God—or whether both ideas are to be included, is determined *not by the signification of the word, but by the context and the analogy of Scripture.* When Christ is said to reconcile men to God, the meaning is that he propitiated God, satisfied the demands of his justice, and thus rendered it possible that he might be just and yet justify the ungodly. This is plain, because the reconciliation is always said to be effected by the death, the blood, the cross of Christ; and the proximate design of a sacrifice is to propitiate God, and not to convert the offerer or him for whom the offering is made. What in one place is expressed by saying Christ reconciled us to God, is in another place expressed by saying, he was a propitiation, or made propitiation for our sins.[35]

Murray echoes this sentiment:

> When we examine the Scripture ... closely we shall find [that] it is not our enmity against God that comes to the forefront in the reconciliation but God's alienation from us. This alienation on the part of God arises indeed from our sin; it is our sin that evokes this reaction of his holiness. But it is God's alienation

---

35. Charles Hodge, *Commentary on the Epistle to the Ephesians* (Grand Rapids, Mich.: Eerdmans, 1954), 138, emphasis supplied.

from us that is brought into the foreground whether the reconciliation is viewed as action or as result.[36]

The exegetical evidence favoring the view that Christ's reconciliatory work on the cross was primarily Godward in its focus is found in all four passages.

ROMANS 5:10–11

Evidence from this passage includes the following points: (1) The "peace with God" (εἰρήνην πρὸς τὸν θεόν, *eirēnēn pros ton theon*), which stands at the very beginning of this passage as the specific grace into which we were ushered as the effect of justification (5:1–2), comports more closely with the idea of the removal of God's alienation through Christ's death, which becomes then the ground of our peace with him, than with the idea of our laying aside our active hostility toward him. (2) Accordingly, the word "enemies" (ἐχθροί, *echthroi*) in 5:10 most probably should be construed in the passive ("hated by God") rather than the active ("hating God") sense.[37] In other words, the word "enemies" does not highlight our unholy hatred of God but rather God's holy hatred of us.[38] Against the background of Paul's earlier assertion that we now have peace with God, it seems that Paul intended to say: "At the very time when God was alienated from us, that is, felt a holy hostility toward us, we were reconciled to God [which passive verb, when rendered actively, means, "God reconciled us to himself"] through the death of his Son." This construction highlights the truth that Paul enunciates in 5:8 that Christ's death work was a signal demonstration of God's love toward us. That is to say, at the very time when he had every reason to loathe us and in fact felt a holy hostility toward us, yet out of love for us he saved us. It is beyond all possibility that Paul intended to say: "At the very time when we were hostile to God, we were reconciled to God through the death of his Son," meaning thereby that our hostility toward God was removed through the death of God's Son, an operation which in fact did not occur. It is clearly God's active hostility toward men and the means which he provided to remove it rather than men's attitude toward God that is in the forefront of Paul's teaching on reconciliation. (3) Both verb forms ("we were reconciled" and "having been reconciled") are in the aorist tense, suggesting that the specific removal of

---

36. Murray, *Redemption—Accomplished and Applied*, 34.
37. See BAGD, ἐχθρός [*echthros*] in *A Greek–English Lexicon of the New Testament*, 331, for these suggested meanings of the active and passive senses.
38. The occurrence of "enemies" in Romans 11:28, where its parallelism with the passive "beloved" indicates that it is God's enmity toward Israel to which Paul refers, suggests that the reference of the word in 5:10 can be the same divine enmity.

alienation or resultant reconciliation that Paul had before his mind occurred *punctiliarly* with the "death of God's Son" and is now an *accomplished* fact. Such a change of attitude clearly can be true only of God and only with reference to the elect since most men continue in their enmity toward God. (4) The striking parallelism between Paul's "how much more, *having been justified* now by his blood" in 5:9, where the justification in view is clearly objective and forensic (whether Christ's blood be viewed as laying the ground for our justification or as constituting us righteous) and not a subjective change in man is the reference, and his parallel statement, "how more much, *having been reconciled* [through the death of his Son]" in 5:10, suggests that the reconciliation intended in 5:10 also occurred in the objective sphere of the divine judgment and attitude. (5) Finally, the striking parallelism between Paul's "having been justified . . . we shall be saved through him *from the wrath* [of God]" in 5:9, where the reference to our salvation from divine wrath clearly characterizes Christ's death as a propitiating sacrifice and thus Godward in its reference, and his "having been reconciled, we shall be saved [(implied) from the same wrath] by his life" in 5:10 implies that Christ's punctiliar reconciliatory work which shall save us from the divine wrath was also Godward in its reference.

2 CORINTHIANS 5:17–21

Evidence from this passage includes: (1) As in the previous passage, the verb form in the phrase "who reconciled us to himself through Christ" in 5:18 is in the aorist tense, again suggesting that the removal of alienation occurred *punctiliarly* with the death of Christ and is now an *accomplished* fact. But such a description of the effect of Christ's reconciliatory act can be true only with reference to God and only with reference to those for whom Christ died since most men continue to remain at enmity with God. (2) Paul's periphrastic construction in 5:19 ("was . . . reconciling," ἦν...καταλλάσσων, *ēn . . . katallassōn*) places the reconciling activity in the past as an accomplished fact. (3) Paul expounds the character of God's reconciling work in 5:19 expressly in terms of two complementary *forensic* acts, one negative and one positive. God was reconciling the world to himself, Paul says, by *not* imputing their trespasses to men (5:19; I shall argue in the next chapter that the reference here is to the elect) and also by imputing them to Christ (5:21). This means that Paul was viewing the reconciliatory work as a past, objective, and forensic event and not as a subjective ongoing operation in men's hearts. (4) Paul's declaration that God has given to us the "ministry of reconciliation" (5:18) whereby we proclaim God's "message of reconciliation" (5:19) as though he himself were beseeching men (5:20) cannot mean that we are to proclaim to men that Christ *has* removed their active enmity against God by his cross. Rather, we preach to men with the specific hope that Christ, through his sovereign application to them of the benefits of his redemptive work, *may* remove their enmity against God. We are to proclaim to men that Christ's cross work has addressed the exigency of God's enmity toward all those for whom he died, and that he has made it possible for God to lay aside his enmity toward them. (5) Accordingly, the imperative "Be reconciled to God" (5:20) must be understood as God's summons to the elect to avail themselves of *his* reconciled attitude toward them, made possible through Christ's cross work, and not his appeal to them to lay aside their enmity toward him (though in the Spirit's regenerating activity this great work is effected). This is made clear from the one other occurrence in the New Testament where a similar obligation is issued. In Matthew 5:24 Jesus says: "be reconciled [διαλλάγηθι, *diallagēthi*] to your brother." On the surface one might understand the English rendering of Jesus' words to mean that the worshiper was harboring enmity in his heart against his brother, and that he was to put away *his* enmity before he worshiped God. But if this were Jesus' intent, as Murray says, there seems to be no good reason why the worshiper would need to leave the altar in order to do so. The altar is the best place to repent of ill will toward another. The situation Jesus describes in fact depicts the distant brother as alienated from and harboring enmity against the worshiper. Accordingly, it is the brother's enmity which is in the forefront of the reconciliation which Jesus here envisions and which the worshiper's reconciliatory activity must address. Jesus' imperative must mean then something on the order of "Do what is necessary to remove *your brother's* alienation; avail yourself of your brother's offered terms of reconciliation." Jesus' command "Be reconciled," so construed, focuses then not upon the enmity of the person commanded to be reconciled (there may not even have been any) but upon the alienation in the mind of the person with whom the reconciliation is made. Accordingly, Paul's command, "Be reconciled [καταλλάγητε, *katallagēte*] to God," in 2 Corinthians 5:20 by analogy would suggest that the primary intent behind Paul's admonition is not that men should put away their enmity against God (this occurs in the application to them of the benefits of salvation procured by Christ) but rather that they should take advantage of God's reconciled attitude toward men, effected by the reconciliatory work of Christ, and avail themselves of his offered terms of reconciliation (of course, only the elect will do so). That is to say, Paul is saying our message should be, "Receive the offer of reconciliation in Christ which God now extends to you; accept his offer of the olive leaf."

EPHESIANS 2:14–17

The evidence here includes: (1) As in the two previous passages, the verb "might reconcile" in 2:16 is in the aorist tense, indicating that the reconciliation was an accomplished fact, effected by Christ's work on the cross. (2) The "enmity" (ἔχθραν, echthran) in 2:14 describes the mutual hostility which existed between Jews and Gentiles. The work of Christ addressed that mutual hostility "in order that the two he might create in himself into one new man, making peace [between them]." So much for that mutual enmity. Now the ἵνα (hina, "in order that") of 2:15 governs not only the verb of creating in 2:15 but also the verb of reconciling in 2:16. In other words, Paul informs us that Christ did what he did at the cross not only in order to *create* the two—Jews and Gentiles—into one new man but also in order to *reconcile* both to God. The second work was necessary because there was *another* enmity that had to be addressed, namely, God's enmity against both Jews and Gentiles. That Paul alludes to God's enmity when he writes: "[in order that] he might reconcile the two in one body to God through the cross, *having put to death* [ἀποκτείνας, apokteinas] the *enmity* [ἔχθραν, echthran] by it [the cross]" is plain from the context. Since the immediately preceding notion of reconciliation is Godward in its reference (τῷ θεῷ, *tō theō*), clearly it is *God's* enmity which Paul boldly says Christ "put to death" by his death. Hodge comments on this second occurrence of "enmity":

> The *enmity* in this place ... many understand to be the enmity between the Jews and Gentiles. ... It is urged in favour of this interpretation that it is unnatural to make the word *enmity* in this verse and in verse 15 refer to different things. ... It is [they say] the enmity between the Jews and Gentiles and their union of which the apostle is treating. But that idea had just before been expressed. It is perfectly pertinent to the apostle's object to show that the union between the Jews and Gentiles was effected by the reconciliation of both, by [Christ's] atoning death, to God. The former flows from the latter. In this connection the words "having slain the enmity on it," serve to explain the declaration that the cross of Christ reconciled us to God. His death satisfied justice, it propitiated God, i.e. removed his wrath, or his enmity to sinners. ... This view is sustained by the constantly recurring representations of Scripture.[39]

It is as though Paul were saying that there was an "enemy" (ἐχθρός, *echthros*, from the same Greek root as ἔχθρα [*echthra*, "enmity"]) against us in God that needed to be "slain." And in the course of being slain himself, indeed, precisely in his being slain, Paul says, our Savior "slew" or delivered the death-blow to that enemy—God's enmity or holy hostility against us, and *reconciled* both Jews and Gentiles in one body *to* God. Thus Christ's death work, in its reconciliatory character, is here said to have removed God's, not man's, enmity toward the one new man created by Christ. (3) According to 2:17–18, Christ, "having come" to his church after his resurrection, proclaimed peace to both Gentile and Jew. This peace, effected by

---

39. Hodge, *Ephesians*, 139–40.

his death work, is clearly *peace with God* (see Rom. 5:1) "because," Paul declares, "through him we both have access by one Spirit *to the Father.*" These data indicate that Christ's reconciling work is here construed as having wholly a Godward reference.

COLOSSIANS 1:19–22

The evidence in this passage includes: (1) The verbs "to reconcile" and "he has reconciled" in Colossians 1:20–21 are both once again in the aorist tense. (2) God accomplished this reconciliation through Christ, "by making peace [also in the aorist tense] through the blood of his cross" (1:20) and "by the body of his flesh through death" (1:22). Again, it must be noted that it is Christ's *death* that reconciled God to men, but Christ's death *per se* has not removed the unholy alienation that most people have toward God. It was his own alienation toward those for whom Christ died which God himself addressed through Christ, and which he took steps to remove by Christ's death on the cross.

The scriptural data which we have examined indicates that Christ's death work construed as a reconciling work addressed God's alienation toward those for whom Christ died, and that by Christ's paying the penalty due to us for sin God's desire to bless us was realized, as it could not have been apart from that work. While Christ would not have died for us had not God loved us, it is equally true that God "would not be to us what he is if Christ had not died" (Denney). That is to say, God could not have been reconciled to us and could only have continued in his holy hostility toward us had Christ not died for us. Plainly, the cross work of Christ in its reconciliatory character had primarily a Godward reference. And the Christian will delight to sing with Charles Wesley:

> Arise, my soul, arise, Shake off thy guilty fears:
>   The bleeding Sacrifice In my behalf appears:
> *Before the Throne my Surety stands,*
>   My name is written on his hands.
>
> He ever lives above, *For me to intercede,*
>   His all-redeeming love, *his precious blood to plead;*
> His blood atoned for every race,
>   And sprinkles now the throne of grace.
>
> *Five bleeding wounds he bears, Received on Calvary;*
>   *They pour effectual prayers, They strongly plead for me;*
> *Forgive him, O forgive, they cry,*
>   *Nor let that ransomed sinner die!*

My God is reconciled; His pard'ning voice I hear;
   He owns me for his child, I can no longer fear;
With confidence I now draw nigh,
   And "Father, Abba, Father!" cry.

Pagan or Christian?

Is it pagan to insist that God required the cross work of Christ in order that he might be not only propitious toward men but also favorably disposed toward them? Liberal theologians have always thought so. But in all other religions men attempt to propitiate their gods and to win them over to clemency through some activity on their part. Christianity, however, declares that "God was, in Christ, reconciling the world to himself" (2 Cor. 5:19), that even at the time when he had just cause for his alienation from us, he "demonstrated his love for us" by reconciling us to himself through the death of his Son. Accordingly, we have not earned reconciliation with God. We neither could nor do we need to do so, since God has in grace freely bestowed it upon us. As Paul declares: "We have received the reconciliation" (Rom. 5:11). This is *not* paganism. It is the exact opposite of paganism. Whereas every other religion of the world represents men as seeking after their gods, Christianity represents God as seeking after men. Such divine dealing with men is unique among the world religions. It is simply the manner in which the one living and true God, who is love (1 John 4:8), acted in grace toward us. As John declares: "This is how God showed his love among us: He sent his one and only Son into the world that we might live through him. This is love: not that we loved God, but that he loved us and sent his Son as a sacrifice which would turn aside his wrath, taking away our sins" (1 John 4:9–10). "How great is the love the Father has lavished on us, that we should be called the children of God!" (1 John 3:1a)

CHRIST'S OBEDIENT CROSS WORK OF REDEMPTION
(PRESUPPOSITION: SLAVERY OR BONDAGE)

Deliverance by Power or Redemption by Price?

That Christ's cross work is to be viewed as a work of deliverance by great power cannot be legitimately doubted. Paul calls Christ "the Deliverer [ὁ ῥυόμενος, *ho rhyomenos*] out of Zion" (Rom. 11:26). He also declares that Christ "delivered" him from his body of death (Rom. 7:24, ῥύσεται, *rhysetai*) and "delivered" Christians in general from the coming wrath (1 Thess. 1:10, τὸν ῥυόμενον, *ton rhyomenon*). E. F. Harrison has perceptively observed, however, that while Paul "can content himself with the use of ῥύεσθαι [rhuesthai] when setting forth the relation of Christ's saving work for us with respect to hostile angelic powers (Col. 1:13), yet when he passes to a contemplation of the forgiveness of our sins he must change his terminology to that of redemption (Col 1:14)."[40]

Arminian scholars construe this redemptive work of the Lord of Glory purely in terms of deliverance by power *apart from price*. This is an error of tragic proportions. R. W. Lyon, an Arminian theologian who wants nothing to do with a real penal substitutionary atonement, commits precisely this error when he writes: "When the ideas of ransom are linked to the saving activity of God, the idea of price is not present."[41] Lyon then expressly interprets both the great Old Testament type of redemption—the exodus deliverance—and its New Testament antitype—the cross work of Christ—in accordance with this stated principle:

> Most importantly the idea of ransom (redeem) is . . . linked with the deliverance out of Egypt (e.g., Deut. 7:8) and the return of the exiles (e.g., Isa. 35:10). In both settings the focus is no longer on the price paid but on the deliverance achieved and the freedom obtained.
>
> When the NT, therefore, speaks of ransom with reference to the work of Christ, the idea is not one of transaction, as though a deal is arranged and a price paid. Rather, the focus is on the *power* (I Cor. 1:18) of the cross to save. In the famous ransom saying of Mark 10:45 Jesus speaks of his coming death as a means of release for many. The contrast is between his own solitary death and the deliverance of many. In the NT the terms of ransom and purchase, which in other contexts suggest an economic or financial exchange, speak of the consequences or results (I Cor. 7:23).[42]

In his day Warfield spoke of those who urged this interpretation upon the church as "assisting at the death bed of a [worthy] word."[43] Furthermore, in his magnificent study of "The New Testament Terminology of Redemption,"[44] Warfield painstakingly demonstrated, against the contrary opinions of Westcott, Oltramare, and Ritschl specifically, that the λυτρο-, lytro-, word-group always retains its native sense of *ransoming* as the mode of deliverance throughout the whole history of profane Greek literature, the Septuagint (where it is employed to trans-

---

40. E. F. Harrison, "Redeemer, Redemption," in *Evangelical Dictionary of Theology*, 919.
41. R. W. Lyon, "Ransom," in *Evangelical Dictionary of Theology*, 907.
42. Ibid., 907–8. So also F. Büchsel, "λύτρον [lytron]," *Theological Dictionary of the New Testament*, ed. Gerhard Kittel, trans. Geoffrey W. Bromiley (Grand Rapids, Mich.: Eerdmans, 1965), 4:355.
43. Benjamin B. Warfield, "Redeemer and Redemption," in *The Person and Work of Christ* (Philadelphia: Presbyterian and Reformed, 1950), 345.
44. Warfield, *The Person and Work of Christ*, 429–75.

late the Hebrew word-groups of גָּאַל, *gā'al*, פָּדָה, *pādâh*, and כָּפַר, *kāpar*), the New Testament material, and the early Patristic literature. I emphasized in chapter fourteen that *the exodus was a redemptive deliverance effected by the ransom price of the Passover Lamb*. While there can be no doubt that that ancient (typical) deliverance was effected by the power of God, it was also rendered salvifically possible only by the shedding of the blood of the Paschal Lamb and the application of its blood to the doorframes of the homes of the Israelites, thereby expiating the sins of the people. I insist upon the same meaning for the New Testament antitypical work of redemption through Christ. Harrison, with much greater sensitivity to the intention and analogy of Scripture than Lyon, observes:

> The occurrence of numerous passages in the OT where redemption is stated in terms which do not explicitly include the element of ransom has led some scholars to conclude that redemption came to mean deliverance without any insistence upon a ransom as a condition or basis. The manifestation of the power of God in the deliverance of his people seems at times to be the sole emphasis (Deut. 9:26). But on the other hand there is no hint in the direction of the exclusion of a ransom. The ransom idea may well be an assumed factor which is kept in the background by the very prominence given to the element of power needed for the deliverance.[45]

Murray concurs:

> The idea of redemption must not be reduced to the general notion of deliverance. The language of redemption is the language of purchase and more specifically of ransom. And ransom is the securing of a release by the payment of a price.[46]

As we shall now show, the relevant New Testament word-groups (λυτρόω, *lytroō*, ἀγοράζω, *agorazō*, and περιποιέω, *peripoieō* [once]) everywhere support this conclusion.

JESUS' TESTIMONY

Jesus opened up his mind to men concerning his life mission in Matthew 20:28 and Mark 10:45, where he indicated that his earthly ministry would terminate in a self-sacrificing act which would serve as "a ransom for many [λύτρον ἀντὶ πολλῶν, *lytron anti pollōn*]." In this saying he brought out the fact that he viewed his approaching death

---

45. Harrison, "Redeemer, Redemption," 918–19.
46. Murray, *Redemption—Accomplished and Applied*, 42.

[653]

as a *sacrificial* death offered up as a ransom *in the stead of* (ἀντί, *anti*) others. Then at the last Passover with his disciples he underscored the same truth when he instituted the Lord's Supper: "This is my body which is given *for* [ὑπέρ, *hyper*] you," he said, and also, "This cup is the new covenant in my blood which is poured out *for* [ὑπέρ, *hyper*] you [Matt. 26:28—"*for* (περί, *peri*) many for the forgiveness of sins"]" (Luke 22:19–20; see also John 10:11, 15). Moreover, Jesus expressly applied the vicarious death of the Suffering Servant of Isaiah 53 to himself in Luke 22:37. Clearly, Jesus believed and taught that deliverance from sin was not simply an issue for power. It was an issue which required the payment of a price for forgiveness.

PETER'S TESTIMONY

Peter writes: "*you were not redeemed* [ἐλυτρώθητε, *elytrōthēte*, "ransomed"] *with perishable things, such as silver and gold . . . but with the precious blood of Christ, a lamb without blemish or defect*" (1 Pet. 1:18–19). Contrasted as it is with silver and gold, the blood of Christ is here clearly construed as a price paid for forgiveness.

JOHN'S TESTIMONY

John utilizes the ἀγοράζω, *agorazō*, word-group—commercial terminology of the marketplace—to teach the same truth: that redemptive deliverance entails a payment price. He reports that he heard the twenty-four elders in heaven singing before the Lamb: "You are worthy . . . because you were slain and *bought* [ἠγόρασας, *ēgorasas*] [men] for God with your blood" (Rev. 5:9). He heard the throngs of heaven singing later before the Lamb a new song, and he tells us that no one could learn the song except "*the bought ones* [οἱ ἠγορασμένοι, *hoi ēgorasmenoi*]" (14:3), and he says of these bought ones: "These are they who follow the Lamb wherever he goes. These *were bought* [ἠγοράσθησαν, *ēgorasthēsan*] from among men" (14:4).

THE AUTHOR OF HEBREWS' TESTIMONY

This writer also, by the contrast he draws in the context of "ransoming" between the blood of goats and calves and Christ's own blood, underscores the price-character of Christ's blood: "He did not enter by means of the blood of goats and calves; but he entered the Most Holy Place once for all by his own blood, obtaining eternal *redemption* [λύτρωσιν, *lytrōsin*] [thereby]" (Heb. 9:12). He says also in 9:15 that "a death has taken place for *redemption* [ἀπολύτρωσιν, *apolytrōsin*]).

THE CHARACTER OF THE CROSS WORK OF CHRIST

PAUL'S TESTIMONY

It is Paul who gives us the largest development of the doctrine. He taught, in concert with his Savior (Mark 10:45), that Jesus "gave himself as a ransom for all [ἀντίλυτρον ὑπὲρ πάντων, *antilytron hyper pantōn*]" (1 Tim. 2:6; note his interesting employment of both ἀντί, *anti*, and ὑπέρ, *hyper*,—"a ransom in the stead of [and] for the sake of"). And Jesus "gave himself for us in order that *he might redeem* [λυτρώσηται, *lytrōsētai*] [ransom] us from all wickedness" (Titus 2:14). Accordingly, Paul refers to the "redemption" (ἀπολύτρωσις, *apolytrōsis*) which we have through Christ's blood or death seven times.

In Romans 3:24–27, he asks: "Having been justified freely by his grace through the redemption which is by Christ Jesus (whom God displayed publicly as a sacrifice which would turn aside his wrath) through faith in his blood . . . , where then is boasting?" Here in a single context where "redemption" is the governing idea for the whole, Paul speaks of that redemption as "by Christ Jesus" and "in his blood," as a *propitiating* redemption, and as a redemption which purchased our *justification through faith*. This demonstrates that Murray is correct when he writes:

> [The bondage to which our sin has consigned us] is multiform. Consequently, redemption as purchase or ransom receives a *wide variety of reference and application*. . . . We may not artificially separate redemption as ransom from the other categories in which the work of Christ is to be interpreted. These categories are but aspects from which the work of Christ once for all accomplished must be viewed and therefore they may be said to *interpermeate* one another.[47]

In Ephesians 1:7 and Colossians 1:14 Paul states that in Christ "we have redemption through his blood ["through his blood" is omitted in Colossians], the forgiveness of sins." Note should be taken of the interpermeation of redemption and forgiveness here, the latter accruing to the Christian through the procurement of the former.

In four contexts Paul speaks of our redemption eschatologically. In Romans 8:23 he refers to the future "redemption of the body," but "not in the sense that redemption will then be operative for the first time, but that the redemption secured by Christ and applied to the soul's forgiveness is then extended to include the body as well, so that salvation is brought to its intended consummation."[48] In Ephesians 1:14

---

47. Ibid., 43, 48, emphasis supplied. It is in light of this fact that Murray could entitle his book as he did. It is extremely important to note the fact of interpermeation here—that Christ's *redemptive* work at Calvary propitiated, reconciled, and purchased justification by grace through faith—since it will figure prominently in our later discussion of the divine design behind the cross work of Christ.

48. Harrison, "Redeemer, Redemption," 918.

[655]

and 4:30 he refers to our final redemption from all evil, as did Jesus in Luke 21:28, which will occur in the "day of redemption." Here Paul underscores the great truth that Christ's redemption, which procured the Spirit's sealing for all those for whom he died, *secures our final salvation*. Likewise, in 1 Corinthians 1:30, the word order of the three nouns in Paul's declaration that Christ Jesus is our "wisdom from God, that is, our *righteousness, sanctification,* and *redemption,*" almost certainly intends that the third noun be construed as referring to our redemption in the eschatological consummation. Here the apostle affirms that Christ's cross work secured our justification, our sanctification, and our *final* redemption. Again, we must insist that this eschatological redemption is grounded in the redemption secured by Christ at Calvary as many features surrounding these three verses indicate (see Eph. 1:7; 4:32; 5:2; 1 Cor. 1:18–25).

Shifting now to the ἀγοράζω, *agorazō,* word-group, in 1 Corinthians 6:19–20 Paul writes: "You are not your own; for *you were bought with a price* [ἠγοράσθητε τιμῆς, *ēgorasthēte timēs*]," and since this is so, he declares in 7:23: "*With a price you were bought* [τιμῆς ἠγοράσθητε, *timēs ēgorasthēte*]: do not become slaves of men." And in Galatians 3:13 he writes: "Christ *purchased* [ἐξηγόρασεν, *exēgorasen*] us from the curse of the law, by becoming a curse for us," and in 4:4–5 he teaches that God "sent his Son . . . *to purchase* [ἵνα . . . ἐξαγοράσῃ, *hina . . . exagorasē*] those under the law."

Finally, to the Ephesian elders Paul declared that God "purchased [περιεποιήσατο, *periepoiēsato*] the church through his own blood" or "through the blood of his own [Son]" (Acts 20:28).

In conclusion, Christ's cross work is seen in the New Testament material as a *redemptive act,* and in *every* instance, either in the immediate or near context, the ransom price he paid (his blood or death), which is what made his work redemptive in nature, is indicated.[49] And it is only theological perversity that leads men to deny this and to insist rather that redemption and ransom simply speak of deliverance through power.

Redemption's Godward Reference

In the early and medieval church many Fathers—among them such luminaries as Irenaeus, Clement of Alexandria, Origen, Basil, the two Gregories, Cyril of Alexandria, John of Damascas, Hilary, Rufinus, Jerome, Augustine, Leo the Great, and as late as Bernard and Luther—contended that Christ's death as a ransom was paid to Satan who then released his hold upon God's elect.

---

49. I will argue in the next chapter that the occurrence of ἀγοράσαντα, *agorasanta* in 2 Peter 2:1 does not pertain to redemption, because of the absence of any mention of the price paid.

This view, conceiving of Christ's cross work as terminating upon Satan, gradually disappeared for lack of scriptural support. But it does raise the question, to whom then was Christ's death as a "ransom" paid? And the answer must, of course, be: Christ's death as a ransom was paid to God whose holiness and justice had been offended by man's transgression of His law. Anselm saw the fallacy in the patristic view and rightly declared:

> As God owed nothing to the devil but punishment, so . . . whatever was demanded of man, he owed to God and not to the devil.[50]

So once again we must conclude that the cross work of Christ in its redemptive character has a Godward direction.

Redemption's Manward References

Just as we found with Christ's cross work construed as propitiation and reconciliation, so also with his cross work construed as redemption: the New Testament represents Christ's redemptive activity, in its objective character, as an *accomplished* fact. In *every* instance the aorist tense is employed to describe his redemptive work at the cross ("to give"—Matt. 20:28; Mark 10:45; "redeemed"—1 Pet. 1:18–19; "entered once for all . . . , obtaining"—Heb. 9:12; "has taken place"—Heb. 9:15; "gave"—1 Tim. 2:6; Titus 2:14; "publicly displayed"—Rom. 3:25; "bought" or "purchased"—1 Cor. 6:20; 7:23; Gal. 3:13; 4:5; Rev. 5:9; 14:3, 4; Acts 20:28). In short, the passages affirm that when Jesus died, his death actually *redeemed*, it actually *procured or purchased* everything essential to the deliverance or liberation of those for whom he died. But unlike propitiation and reconciliation, which need to be given solely a Godward reference, there is reason to view Christ's death, as a redemptive act, also as having a manward reference. Ransom and redemption presuppose our bondage, and are "directed to the bondage to which our sin has consigned us."[51] What specifically then did his death procure?

With reference to *the law of God*, (1) he redeemed us from the *curse* of the law, that is, from its just *condemnation* of us, by becoming a curse for us, that is, by bearing its just condemnation of us vicariously (Gal. 3:13). This redemptive feature insures that there is no longer any condemnation awaiting those who are in Christ Jesus (Rom. 8:1), that is, it guarantees our justification before God. (2) He delivered the people of God from any further need for the *pedagogical* bondage

---

50. Anselm, *Cur Deus Homo*, trans. Sidney Norton Deane (LaSalle, Illinois: Open Court, 1959), Book II, Chapter XIX, 285–86. See appendix D.
51. Murray, *Redemption—Accomplished and Applied*, 43.

SYSTEMATIC THEOLOGY

implicit in the ceremonialism of the Old Testament salvific economy (Gal. 3:23; 4:2–5; 5:1). This redemptive feature insures our full rights as "mature sons." As Murray writes:

> The grace of the NT [over against the grace of the OT] appears in this: that by redemption accomplished and by faith in Christ (see Gal. 3:26) all without distinction (Gal. 3:28) are instated in the full blessing of sonship, without having to undergo the tutelary preparation corresponding to the pedagogical discipline of the OT period. There is no recapitulation in the individual realm of what obtained in the history of progressive revelation and realization.[52]

(3) He redeemed the Christian from any necessity of obtaining on his own, in order to be saved, a righteousness before God. Christ is our righteousness (1 Cor. 1:30), and he is the end of law-keeping for righteousness for every believer (Rom. 10:4).

With reference to *sin*, a close corollary of the former referent inasmuch as sin is transgression of God's law, (1) he redeemed us from the *guilt* of sin (Matt. 26:28; Eph. 1:7; Col. 1:14; Heb. 9:15), by bearing our sin in our stead. That is, he procured for those whose guilt he bore their deliverance from the law's condemnation. (2) He redeemed us from the *power and fruitlessness* of sin (Rom. 6:21–22; 7:4–6; Titus 2:14; 1 Pet. 1:18–19). This deliverance from the power of sin Murray speaks of as the "triumphal aspect of redemption" as it relates to Christian people.[53] By virtue of the real spiritual union that exists between Christ and all those for whom he died (Rom. 6:1–10; 7:4–6; 2 Cor. 5:14–15; Eph. 2:1–7; Col. 3:1–4), the Scriptures affirm of them that they died to the realm and power of sin and that they live to serve him who died for them. It is this union which secures for the Christian his definitive and progressive holiness.

There is a second exigency which this "triumphal aspect" of Christ's redemptive activity bears upon—the destruction of Satan's kingdom of darkness. This brings us to the final category under which Christ's cross work must be viewed.

CHRIST'S OBEDIENT CROSS WORK OF DESTRUCTION (PRESUPPOSITION: A KINGDOM OF EVIL)

In a striking passage on Satan's role in the rebellion of our first parents against God, Murray writes:

---

52. John Murray, "Adoption," in *The Encyclopedia of Christianity* (Wilmington, Del.: The National Foundation for Christian Education, 1964), 1:71.
53. Murray, *Redemption—Accomplished and Applied*, 48.

Back of all that is visible and tangible in the sin of this world there are unseen spiritual powers. Satan is the god of this world, the prince of the power of the air, the spirit that now works in the sons of disobedience. The arch-foe of the kingdom of God is not the visible powers arrayed against it; for behind these visible agents and manifestations of evil is the ingenuity, craft, malicious design, instigation and relentless activity of the devil and his ministers. It was this of which Paul was fully aware when he said, "We wrestle not against flesh and blood, but against the principalities, against the powers, against the world rulers of this darkness, against the spiritualities of wickedness in the heavenlies" (Eph. 6:12). Because we have given way to the impact of naturalistic presuppositions, and to the anti-supernaturalistic and anti-praeternaturalistic bias, we are far too liable in these days to discount this truth of Christian revelation. We are liable to discard it in our construction and interpretation of the forces of iniquity. To the extent that we do so, our thinking is not Christian.[54]

Satan's Names and Titles

The Scriptures bear out the truthfulness of Murray's insight. Satan, referred to in Scripture by the names Abaddon and Apollyon (Rev. 9:11), Beelzebub (Matt. 12:24; Luke 11:15) and Belial (2 Cor. 6:15), but not Lucifer (Isa. 14:12, KJV), is represented as the accuser of the brethren (Rev. 12:10; see Job 1–2, Zech. 3:1), the ancient serpent (Rev. 12:9), the angel of the abyss (Rev. 9:11), the devil (Rev. 12:9 et al.), our enemy (Matt. 13:25, 28, 39; 1 Pet. 5:8), the evil one (Matt. 5:37; 6:13; 13:19, 38; Eph. 6:16; 2 Thess. 3:3; 1 John 2:13–14; 3:12; 5:18–19), the father of lies and a murderer of men's souls (John 8:44), the prince of demons (Matt. 9:34; 12:24; Mark 3:22; Luke 11:15), the prince of this world (John 12:31; 14:30; 16:11), the ruler of the kingdom of the air (Eph. 2:2), and the tempter (Matt. 4:3; 1 Thess. 3:5).

Satan's Actions

While he does not exercise totally free rein over men because of divinely imposed limitations and restraints (see Job 1:12; 2:6; Matt. 12:29; Rev. 20:2–3), Satan is said nonetheless to rage against men (Rev. 12:12), to prowl around like a roaring lion looking to devour the sons of men (1 Pet. 5:8), to work in the sons of disobedience (Eph. 2:2), to blind the minds of unbelievers so that they cannot see the light of the gospel of the glory of Christ (2 Cor. 4:4), to turn men away from God to serve him (1 Tim. 5:15), to take men captive to do his will (2 Tim. 2:26), to deceive the nations

---

54. John Murray, "The Fall of Man," in *Collected Writings of John Murray* (Edinburgh: Banner of Trust), 2:67–68.

(Rev. 12:9; 20:3, 7), to sow tares in the field of the world (Matt. 13:25), to obstruct world missions (1 Thess. 2 :18), to masquerade as an angel of light (2 Cor. 11:14), to make war against the saints (Rev. 12:17), to throw Christians into prison (Rev. 2:10), to oppress with physical and mental illness (Acts 10:38), to lie and murder (John 8:44), and to hold (under God) the power of death (Heb. 2:14).

Specifically, it was Satan who tempted Adam to sin (Gen. 3:1–5), who accused Job of serving God for profit (Job 1–2), and who afflicted him with physical and mental anguish (Job 2:7), who desired the body of Moses (Jude 9), who incited David to sin (1 Chron. 21:1), who accused Joshua the high priest of sin (Zech. 3:1), who tempted Jesus to sin (Matt. 4:11), who crippled a woman for eighteen years (Luke 13:11, 16), who incited Peter to oppose Jesus' approaching death (Matt. 16:23; Mark 8:33), who requested permission to sift Peter as wheat (Luke 22:31), who put it into the heart of Judas to betray Christ (John 13:2) and who then entered into Judas (John 13:27), who filled Ananias's heart to lie against the Holy Spirit (Acts 5:3), and who tormented Paul with a thorn in the flesh (2 Cor. 12:7).

Power-Aspects of the Kingdom of Darkness

In addition to the many references in the Scriptures to demons, particularly in the Gospels, the Scriptures speak of definite "power-aspects" of Satan's kingdom of darkness, for it refers to the "reign of darkness" (Luke 22:53; see Luke 4:6; Acts 26:18; Col 1:13) and to the "hour of darkness" (Luke 22:52), to principalities and powers (Eph. 6:12; Col. 2:15), to powers of this dark world (Eph. 6:12), and to spiritual forces of evil in the heavenly realm against which the man who lacks the whole armor of God cannot possibly stand (Eph. 6:12–13). Satan devises schemes (Eph. 6:11) and "traps" (2 Tim. 2:26), appoints demonic underlings to oversee his interests among the nations (Dan. 10:11–11:1), is the "father" of many men viewed as his "children" (John 8:44; Acts 13:10), and inspires false religions (1 Cor. 10:20), religious organizations, and worshipers (Rev. 2:9; 3:9).

Christ's Triumphant Kingdom Activity over Satan

Thus there was a need for Christ's redemptive work to conquer Satan's "evil kingdom of power" and nullify its powers and effects. Murray observes: "It is most significant that the work of Christ, which is so central in our Christian faith, is essentially *a work of destruction that terminates upon the power and work of Satan*. This is not a peripheral or incidental feature of redemption. It is an integral aspect of its accomplishment."[55] In this same connection, he writes: "It is surely significant . . .

---

55. Murray, *"Fall of Man,"* 2:68, emphasis supplied.

THE CHARACTER OF THE CROSS WORK OF CHRIST

that the first promise of redemptive grace, the first beam of redemptive light that fell upon our fallen first parents, was in terms of the destruction of the tempter."[56] Accordingly, eight New Testament passages specifically speak of the confrontation between Christ—the "Seed of the woman"—and Satan and his seed, and give some suggestions as to how it came about that in the very act of Satan's "[mortally] striking his heel," Christ "crushed his head."

I JOHN 3:8C

"For this reason the Son of God was manifested in order that *he might destroy* [λύσῃ, *lysē*] the works of the devil." While John gives us little detail beyond the bare fact itself here, he does inform his readers that one basic reason why Christ came was to undo the works of the devil "who has been sinning from the beginning" (1 John 3:8b). It is significant in this connection that this is the first use of the title, "the Son of God," in this epistle, suggesting that John particularly intended to stress the *divine* dignity and authority of him who opposed himself to Satan in the conflict. The verb literally means "might loose," suggesting that Christ's cross work undid the bonds by which the works of the devil had been held together. In other words, he and his ranks have been fragmented or dissipated by the cross.

MATTHEW 12:29; LUKE 11:21–22

On the occasion when he was accused of casting out demons through the power of "the prince of demons" (Matt. 12:22–24), after distancing himself from any such relationship by pointing out the absurdity of such a suggestion (12:25–28), Jesus asked: "How can anyone enter a strong man's house and carry off his possessions unless he first *ties up* [δήσῃ, *dēsē*] the strong man? Then he can *thoroughly plunder* [διαρπάσει, *diarpasei*] his house." Here Jesus declares that, by resisting and rejecting Satan's temptations earlier (Matt. 4:1–11), even though Satan had been "fully armed" (καθωπλισμένος, *kathōplismenos*—Luke 11:21) while he himself had been in a state of physical weakness, he had shown himself to be Satan's superior (ἰσχυρότερος αὐτοῦ, *ischyroteros autou*—Luke 11:22) in spiritual power and had thereby "bound the strong man," that is, had *"overpowered* [νικήσῃ, *nikēsē*] him, taking away his armor in which he trusted" (Luke 11:22) Now, he said, he can "thoroughly plunder his house" or "divide up the spoil" (Luke 11:22). Jesus declares by

---

56. Murray, *Redemption—Accomplished and Applied*, 49.

these remarks that Satan had been *personally* bested in a one-on-one conflict with himself, and that his "powerhold" over the sons of men was unraveling. The demons themselves seem to have realized that they were serving a defeated leader, for they queried Jesus on one occasion: "Have you come here before the time [that is, the appointed time of judgment] to torment us?" (Matt. 8:29).

JOHN 12:31

"In a context that is pregnant with allusions to the necessity and results of the cross,"[57] Jesus said: "Now is the time for judgment on this world; now the prince of this world *will be driven out* [ἐκβληθήσεται ἔξω, *eklēthēsetai exō*]." Our Lord declares that by his cross work he was delivering the decisive blow to Satan's powerhold upon this world with regard to those for whom he died. Satan met his match in Christ the Warrior and only acts today as a defeated enemy. Accordingly, Paul can assure his readers at Rome that "the God of peace will soon crush Satan under your feet" (Rom. 16:20).

JOHN 16:11

In the upper room on the night of his betrayal, Jesus declared that the Holy Spirit would convict the world of the judgment to come because, by his own triumph over sin at the cross and over death at the resurrection, "the ruler of this world, *has been judged* [κέκριται, *kekritai*]."

I CORINTHIANS 15:24–26

Describing Christ's present reign, Paul writes: "[Christ will hand] over the kingdom to God the Father after *he has destroyed* [καταργήσῃ, *katargēsē*] all dominion, authority, and power. For he must reign until he has put all his enemies under his feet." Destruction—here again is the theme that was suggested in Matthew 12:29 and Luke 11:21–22. By his cross work Christ "nullified" or "rendered inoperative" Satan's power over those for whom he died (how his cross work did so Paul magnificently elucidates for us in the following Colossians passage), so that the fear of death no longer enslaves them. Accordingly, Paul represents even death itself as "ours" (1 Cor. 3:21–23), its sting (sin) having been removed (1 Cor. 15:55–56). Quite properly did John Owen speak of "the death of death in the death of Christ."

---

57. Ibid.

THE CHARACTER OF THE CROSS WORK OF CHRIST

COLOSSIANS 2:13C–15

"[God] *graciously pardoned* [χαρισάμενος, *charisamenos*] you of all your trespasses, *having canceled* [ἐξαλείψας, *exaleipsas*] the written code, with its regulations, that was against us and that stood opposed to us—he took it out of the way, by nailing it fast to the cross. *Having disarmed* [ἀπεκδυσάμενος, *apekdysamenos*] [thereby] the powers and the authorities, he exposed them openly, *triumphing* [θριαμβεύσας, *thriambeusas*] over them by the cross." What Paul means is this: When Christ publicly died on the cross for his own, he paid the penalty, endured the curse, and died the death which their sins deserved, meeting fully all the penal sanctions of the law ("the written code, with its regulations, that was against us and that stood opposed to us"). It is the fact that God's own are transgressors of his law that has ever been the sole ground of Satan's accusations against them. But when Christ paid the penalty for their sins, God "disarmed" him of that ground and "triumphed" over Satan's kingdom thereby.

HEBREWS 2:14–15

In this final passage Christ's cross work is depicted, as it was in John 12:31, as a work aimed directly at Satan for the good of his brothers and children: "He shared in their humanity in order that through his death *he might destroy* [καταργήσῃ, *katargēsē*] him who holds the power of death, that is, the devil, and *deliver* [ἀπαλλάξῃ, *apallaxē*] those who all their lives were held in slavery by their fear of death."

Christ's cross work was a redemptive work of destruction and conquest! By it he both proved himself Satan's Victor and secured for his own their victory over Satan. Consequently, living out their Christian experience in union with Christ and protected by the "full armor" of God (truth, righteousness, steadfastness, faith, the hope of salvation, and the Word of God), Christians overcome the kingdom of darkness through their God, the Father of mercies and the God of all comfort, "who always *leads* [them] *in triumphal procession* [θριαμβεύοντι, *thriambeuonti*] in Christ" (2 Cor. 2:14). They do so by resisting him (James 4:7; 1 Pet. 5:9), by the exercise of faith (Matt. 17:20; 1 John 5:4), by prayer (Matt. 9:29), by using "the sword of the Spirit, which is the Word of God" (Eph. 6:17; see Matt. 4:4, 7, 10), by the blood of the Lamb (Rev. 12:11), and in the power of his name (Luke 10:17).

A SUMMARY OF THE SCRIPTURAL CATEGORIES OF CHRIST'S CROSS WORK

The *expiation* of their sins through the obedient *sacrifice of himself* in their stead, the *satisfying* of divine justice and thereby the *propitiation* of divine wrath respecting them, the removal of the divine alienation toward them *(reconciliation)*, their *redemption* from the curse of the law and the power and fruitlessness of sin, and the *destruction of the kingdom of evil* which held them as captives and slaves—these are the accomplishments of Christ's cross work in behalf of all those for whom he died. These are the categories which Scripture employs to characterize his death work, each presupposing, as we have seen, a particular exigency which had to be addressed by that work.

THE ABSOLUTE NECESSITY OF CHRIST'S CROSS WORK

Was all this—Christ's salvific work of sacrifice, propitiation, reconciliation, redemption, and destruction—really necessary if the elect were to be saved? This question, on the surface, might appear to be superfluous: "Of course, it was necessary," someone might respond. "Doesn't the Bible teach that Christ's cross work is the only basis upon which men may be saved?" But such a response fails to address the real issue raised by the question, which is: Could God have saved his elect in any number of *other* ways, or was he bound to save them the way he did, by the work of Christ? Asked another way, was Christ's cross work *absolutely* necessary if God would save the elect, or was it necessary only because of his prior divine determination after deliberation to save some that way?

Augustine,[58] Aquinas,[59] and some early Reformers, including apparently even Calvin,[60] espoused what has come to be known as the "hypothetical necessity" view of the atonement. This view, while not denying that God decreed to save his people by Christ's cross work, contends that "there were other modes of liberation possible to him"[61] beside the vicarious atonement of Christ. Stated another way, "while God *could* save without an atonement, yet, in accordance with his sovereign decree, he actually does not," because "[the cross work of Christ] is the way in which the greatest number of advantages concur and the way in which grace is more marvelously exhibited."[62]

Many Protestant theologians (e.g., F. Turretin, Charles and A. A. Hodge, Robert Lewis Dabney, Louis Berkhof, J. Oliver Buswell, John Murray), however, have con-

---

58. Augustine, *On the Trinity*, 13.10.
59. Thomas Aquinas, *Summa theologica*, III.46.2, 3.
60. Calvin (*Institutes*, II.xii.1) writes: "If someone asks why [the atonement] is necessary, there has been no simple (to use the common expression) or absolute necessity. Rather, it has stemmed from a heavenly decree, on which men's salvation depended. Our most merciful Father decreed what was best for us."
61. F. Turretin, *Institutes of Elenctic Theology* (Phillipsburg, N.J.: Presbyterian and Reformed, 1994), 2:418 (topic 14, question 10).
62. Murray, *Redemption—Accomplished and Applied* 11–12.

tended for what has come to be known as the "consequent absolute necessity" view.[63] Murray explains the expression this way:

> The word "consequent" in this designation points to the fact that God's will or decree to save any is of free and sovereign grace. To save lost men *was not of absolute necessity* but of the sovereign good pleasure of God. The terms "absolute necessity," however, indicate that God, *having elected some to everlasting life out of his mere good pleasure,* was under the necessity of accomplishing this purpose through the sacrifice of his own Son, a necessity arising from the perfections of his own nature. In a word, *while it was not inherently necessary for God to save,* yet, since salvation had been purposed, it was necessary to secure this salvation through a satisfaction that could be rendered only through substitutionary sacrifice and blood-bought redemption. (emphases supplied)[64]

In other words, according to Murray's explanation, the "absolute necessity" is necessary because of God's perfections but only as a consequence of God's free and sovereign *antecedent* determination to save men at all. The antecedent determination itself to save men originated in God's sovereign or "mere good pleasure." This view is urged for the following reasons:

1. Several New Testament passages create a strong presumption favoring an absolute necessity on God's part to save the elect the way he in fact did, namely, by the cross of Christ. The author of Hebrews says it was *fitting* (ἔπρεπεν, *eprepen*), in bringing many sons to glory, for God to perfect the Author of their salvation through suffering, adding that Christ *had to be made like* (ὤφειλεν . . . ὁμοιωθῆναι, *ōpheilen . . . homoiōthēnai*) his brothers (Heb. 2:10,17; see also 7:26). In 9:23 the same writer declares: "It was *necessary* [ἀνάγκη, *anangkē*] for [the wilderness tabernacle] to be purified by [animal sacrifices], but [necessary for] the heavenly things themselves [to be purified] with better sacrifices." That the necessity here spoken of is an absolute necessity appears from the fact that the heavenly things in this context are called the "true" (ἀληθινῶν, *alēthinōn*) sanctuary (9:24)—not true as opposed to "false" or real as opposed to "unreal," but true as opposed to earthly, temporal, and provisional, that is, true in the sense of heavenly, eternal, and final. "When we think

---

63. Ibid., 12. See Turretin, *Institutes,* topic 14, question 10; Charles Hodge, *Systematic Theology* (1871; reprint, Grand Rapids, Mich.: Eerdmans, 1952), 2:486–89; A. A. Hodge, *The Atonement* (1907; reprint, Grand Rapids, Mich.: Baker, 1974), 234–39; Robert Lewis Dabney, *Lectures in Systematic Theology* (1878; reprint, Grand Rapids, Mich.: Zondervan, 1972), 486–99; Louis Berkhof, *Systematic Theology* (Grand Rapids, Mich.: Eerdmans, 1932), 367–72; J. Oliver Buswell Jr., *A Systematic Theology of the Christian Religion* (Grand Rapids, Mich.: Zondervan, 1962), 2:85–88; Murray, *Redemption—Accomplished and Applied,* 9–18.
64. Ibid.

of the sacrifice of Christ as offered in connection with things answering to that characterization . . . , is it not impossible to think of this sacrifice as only hypothetically necessary?"[65]

2. Every sin that a person commits carries with it infinite disvalue, that is to say, every sin, because it violates the holy character of the infinite God, deserves infinite punishment and no compensation given by the sinner to the righteous Lawgiver of the universe would ever make an act of disobedience against him right in his sight in the slightest degree. But if every sin is of infinite disvalue, then the means of retribution for that sin which God's holy nature demands must of necessity be of infinite value, which fact rules out any offering to God's offended holiness other than or less than Christ's own infinitely efficacious work at Calvary.

3. Even the familiar verse John 3:16 suggests that the only alternative to God's giving his Son for sinners was the eternal perdition of sinners.

4. Because of God's inviolable holiness and righteousness, a person to be accepted by him must be perfectly holy and righteous. This fact, however, mandates the Father's act of justifying sinners, since sinners cannot make themselves righteous. Paul expressly declares: "if a law had been given that could impart life, then righteousness would certainly have come by the law" (Gal. 3:21).

5. The Scriptures represent the costly character of the cross work of Christ as the supreme and signal demonstration of God's infinite love for sinners (John 3:16; Rom. 5:8; 1 John 3:1; 4:10). But would the Father have given up his only Son to the death of the cross if it had not been absolutely necessary—if, that is, another way to accomplish the same salvific ends had been possible? And would the cross have been the supreme and signal demonstration of God's infinite love for sinners if there had been no *absolute* necessity for it? Does not the costliness of Christ's death work, if it is really a representation of God's great love, require that it and nothing less was absolutely necessary to the salvation of sinners?

To this point I affirm all the above arguments for the "absolute necessity" of the atonement. My one problem is with Murray's word "consequent," for it suggests that God was perfectly free to save or not to save. It also suggests that there was a moment in the divine decree when God deliberated whether he would save some men or not, and a second moment when he deliberated whether he would save them by this means or by that means. But God's decree is both eternal and immutable. And such issues as whether he would save some men or save them the way he did were eternal and immutable determinations of his decree. Therefore, his eternal and immutable purpose makes *all* things absolutely necessary. To propose that he could have purposed in any other way than he did is to suppose that God's

---

65. Murray, *Redemption—Accomplished and Applied*, 16.

omniscience and his eternal decree could have been other than it is. To propose that anything could have been other than it is is to suppose that God could have been other than he is. But this is impossible because he is the eternal and immutable God. A God who might have determined not to create is simply not the God of Scripture. Likewise, a God who might have determined not to save some men or who might have determined to save them in a way other than he did is not the eternal, immutable God of Scripture. Therefore, God *had* to save the elect because of his eternal, immutable decree, and he *had* to save them the way he did because of the specific perfections of his character. To suppose otherwise is to conclude that God's *eternal* purpose had at some moment a degree of mutability about it which is foreign to the immutable character of God. So I would urge as a sixth, and perhaps, the most telling reason for the absolute necessity of Christ's atonement simply the eternal and immutable decree of God himself. His decree still allows, indeed requires, salvation to be of free and sovereign grace grounded in his sovereign good pleasure since no cause external to him forced him to decree as he did.

Of course, if by "consequent" is meant only *logically* consequent, then I would have no problem with the word, for it would mean that the eternal determination to save men at all is only logically *antecedent* to the eternal determination to save them by Christ. But then, of course, we are positing once again an "absolute necessity," only now, with reference to the decree to save at all, we should speak of "antecedent absolute necessity."

For these reasons I would urge that the cross work of Christ was absolutely indispensable to the salvation of men from sin. Nothing less than the vicarious death of Christ was called for by the eternality and immutability of God's decree, by his own holy character, and by the exigencies of the sinful human situation brought on by Adam's fall.

THE PERFECTION OF CHRIST'S CROSS WORK

Precisely because his was an *actual,* not an imaginary or a hypothetical, sacrificial death in which he vicariously bore their curse, paid their debt, endured their *judicial rejection* by God, as evidenced by his cry of dereliction from the cross, and died their death, Christ *actually* accomplished and procured everything essential to the salvation of the elect. In sum, he did not simply open the way of salvation to all men and promise to aid them if they would also do something to procure it and keep it their own. Nor did he simply make the salvation of the elect possible. Rather, he actually did everything necessary to the infallible securing of the salvation of the elect, his people, his sheep, his own—even those whom the Father gave to him. Murray says here that Christ's atoning work was "so perfect and final that it leaves no penal liability for any sin of the believer."[66]

That "perfection" Murray explicated under four expressions: its historic objectivity, its finality, its uniqueness, and its intrinsic efficacy.[67] By its *historic objectivity* is meant that Christ accomplished an objective work in world history two thousand years ago *completely apart* from "any participation or contribution" on the part of those who are its beneficiaries. This is urged against any view that would suggest that the atonement is to be interpreted "in terms of the ethical effects it is calculated to produce in us" and against neoorthodoxy, which contends that the "atoning event" is always a direct theophany outside of ordinary history in "primal" history (*Urgeschichte*) in which Christ becomes "contemporaneous" to the religious existent.

By its *finality* is intended that Christ's objective work of atonement is "a completed work, never repeated and unrepeatable." This is simply to take seriously Christ's victorious cry from the cross, "It has been finished" (John 19:30; τετέλεσται, *tetelestai*), over against Roman Catholic theology, which teaches that in addition to Christ's work of satisfaction the faithful by their suffering either in this life or in purgatory must also make satisfaction for their sins.

By its *uniqueness* is intended that Christ and Christ alone, as he himself said, is "the way, the truth, and the life. No one comes to the Father but by me" (John 14:6); as Peter said, "Salvation is found in no one else, for there is no other name under heaven given to men by which we must be saved" (Acts 4:12); and as Paul said, "There is . . . one Mediator between God and man, the man Christ Jesus" (1 Tim. 2:4). Because of who he is, the messianic investiture which he bore, and the singular task of saving sinners which he came to do (1 Tim. 1:15), he *alone* could expiate sin, propitiate divine wrath, remove God's alienation, redeem sinners from the curse of the law and the guilt and power of sin, and bring Satan's kingdom to its knees. Understanding this, Calvin affirmed that our every need can and must be met in Christ:

> We see that our whole salvation and all its parts are comprehended in Christ. We should therefore take care not to derive the least portion of it from anywhere else. If we seek salvation, we are taught by the very name of Jesus that it is "of him." If we seek any other gifts of the Spirit, they will be found in His anointing. If we seek strength, it lies in His dominion; if purity, in His conception; if gentleness, it appears in His birth. . . . If we seek redemption, it lies in His passion; if acquittal, in His condemnation; if remission of the curse, in His cross; if satisfaction, in His sacrifice; if purification, in His blood; if reconciliation, in His descent

---

66. Ibid., 51.
67. Ibid., 52–58.

into hell; if mortification of the flesh, in His tomb; if newness of life, in His resurrection; if immortality, in the same; if inheritance of the Heavenly Kingdom, in His entrance into heaven; if protection, if security, if abundant supply of all blessings, in His kingdom; if untroubled expectation of judgment, in the power given to Him to judge. In short, since rich store of every kind of good abounds in Him, let us drink our fill from this fountain, and from no other.[68]

Reformed theology urges the uniqueness of Christ's cross work against the notion of liberal theology that "the principle of self-sacrifice is operative in the breast of every loving and holy being" when confronted with sin, and that every Christian may vicariously "follow in his steps."

Finally, by its *intrinsic efficacy* is meant that Christ's cross work is "intrinsically adequate to meet all the exigencies created by our sin" and that it *procured* all the benefits essential to the full salvation of the elect. This is urged against the Arminian insistence that Christ's death work simply made salvation possible for all men but did not in itself save any man.

The Westminster Confession of Faith (VIII/v) states all that we have been arguing for in this chapter quite simply in the one sentence:

> The Lord Jesus, by His perfect obedience, and sacrifice of Himself, which He, through the eternal Spirit, once offered up unto God, hath fully satisfied the justice of His Father; and purchased, not only reconciliation, but an everlasting inheritance in the kingdom of heaven, for all those whom the Father hath given unto Him.

---

68. Calvin, *Institutes*, II.xvi.19.

CHAPTER EIGHTEEN

The Divine Design Behind
the Cross Work of Christ

As God hath appointed the elect unto glory, so hath He, by the eternal and most free purpose of His will, foreordained all the means thereunto. Wherefore, they who are elected, being fallen in Adam, are redeemed by Christ, are effectually called unto faith in Christ by His Spirit working in due season, are justified, adopted, sanctified, and kept by His power, through faith, unto salvation. Neither are any other redeemed by Christ, effectually called, justified, adopted, sanctified, and saved, but the elect only. (Westminster Confession of Faith, III/vi)

The Lord Jesus, by His perfect obedience, and sacrifice of Himself, which He, through the eternal Spirit, once offered up unto God, hath ... purchased ... an everlasting inheritance in the kingdom of heaven, for all those whom the Father hath given unto Him. (Westminster Confession of Faith, VIII/v)

IN HIS GREAT BOOK *The Cross of Christ*,[1] John R. W. Stott argues that in his death Christ accomplished a real substitutionary atonement by which he paid the penalty, bore the curse, and died the death that our sins deserve, enduring the full *penal* consequences of our sins and satisfying divine justice. In the course of his argument, citing Lutheran scholar Joachim Jeremias on the "many" of Isaiah 53:12 and Mark 10:45 for support, Stott declares that Christ died "inclusively" (that is, "the totality consisting of many"), "not exclusively" (that is, "many but not all"), for the "godless among both the Jews and the Gentiles."[2] This latter declaration, of course,

---
1. John R. W. Stott, *The Cross of Christ* (Downers Grove, Ill.: InterVarsity Press, 1986).
2. Ibid., 146–47. See my review of Stott's book in *Presbuterion: Covenant Seminary Review* XIII, 1 (1987), 59–63.

[671]

is the consentient conviction of Amyraldian, Lutheran, and Arminian Christians, all of whom insist upon an atonement of universal extension, unrestricted in any way in its design.

Over against this widely held view, Christians committed to an internally consistent vision of the Reformed faith believe that Jesus Christ died savingly only for the elect (they customarily say here that Christ's death is *"efficient* only for the elect"—*efficaciter tantum pro electis*).[3] Of course, these Christians happily affirm that Christ's death, with respect to its infinite intrinsic worth, is *sufficient* to save all mankind *had that been its design* (they customarily speak here of Christ's death as *"sufficient* for all"—*sufficienter pro omnibus*). This means that had the persons of the Godhead determined to save more people than they did, Christ would not have had

---

3. The "L" in the Calvinistic acronym TULIP refers to this doctrine of limited atonement. (See appendix E.)

Contemporary "Calvinistic universalists," such as R. T. Kendall, maintain that John Calvin did not teach the doctrine of limited atonement and that their position is essentially Calvin's. While Calvin did not write an explicit treatment of the extent of the atonement, as far as we know he never took issue with the contemporary advocates of limited atonement. That he did hold to a limited or definite atonement seems clear from certain of his statements. For example, commenting on "who wants all men to be saved" in 1 Timothy 2:4, he expressly denies that Paul is speaking here of individual men and states rather that Paul "simply means that there is no people and no rank in the world that is excluded from salvation." Commenting on verse 5, Calvin writes:

> The universal term *all* must always be referred to classes of men, and not to persons; as if he had said, that not only Jews but Gentiles also, not only persons of humble rank, but princes also, were redeemed by the death of Christ.

Commenting on John's clause "and not for ours only" in 1 John 2:2, he states:

> Though . . . I allow that what has been said [by the schoolmen to the effect that Christ suffered sufficiently for the whole world but efficiently only for the elect] is true, yet I deny that it is suitable to this passage; for the design of John was no other than to make this benefit common to the whole Church. Then under the word *all* or *whole,* he does not include the reprobate, but designates those who should believe as well as those who were then scattered through various parts of the world.

Here Calvin explicitly excludes the reprobate from Christ's propitiation and represents the "whole world" as referring to all throughout the various parts of the world, without distinction of race or time, who would through faith partake of salvation.

In his reply to Tilemann Heshusius, a Lutheran defender of the corporeal presence of Christ in the Lord's Supper, Calvin writes:

> I should like to know how the wicked can eat the flesh of Christ which was not crucified for them, and how they can drink the blood which was not shed to expiate their sin? (*Tracts and Treatises* [Beveridge's edition], 2:527)

For a fuller treatment of Calvin's view, see Roger R. Nicole, "John Calvin's View of the Extent of the Atonement," *Westminster Theological Journal* 47 (Fall 1985): 197–225, and Paul Helm, *Calvin and the Calvinists* (Edinburgh: Banner of Truth, 1982).

to do more than he in fact did. (Of course, he could not have done less than he in fact did either, if the Godhead had determined to save fewer sinners.) Reformed Christians also readily acknowledge that nonelect people can and do receive some benefits, short of salvation itself, as the fruits of Christ's saving work. Not only does Christ's atoning death, by virtue of its universal saving sufficiency, ground the legitimacy of preaching the gospel to *every* man, woman, and child without discrimination, as Warfield notes,[4] but also, as Roger R. Nicole points out,

> the fact that Christ has come into this world has provided a certain outpouring of common grace. It has justified the long forbearance of God with mankind and therefore given perhaps a new impetus for this forbearance. There is a reprieve for mankind at large which is the result of the work of Jesus Christ.[5]

What is the scriptural evidence for the doctrine that the atonement was particular and definite rather than universal and indefinite in its design? Stated differently, why do Calvinists believe that Christ died savingly only for particular men and women—the elect of God—and not for mankind in general?

TEN LINES OF EVIDENCE FOR THE DOCTRINE OF PARTICULAR REDEMPTION

The Particularistic Vocabulary of Scripture

The Scriptures themselves particularize who it is for whom Christ died. The beneficiaries of Christ's cross work are denominated in the following ways: "The house of Israel, and the house of Judah," that is, the church or "true Israel" (Jer. 31:31; Luke 22:20; Heb. 9:15); his "people" (Matt. 1:21); his "friends" (John 15:13); his "sheep" (John 10:11, 15); his "body," the "church" (Eph. 5:23–26; Acts 20:28); the "elect" (Rom. 8:32–34); the "many" (Isa. 53:12; Matt. 20:28; 26:28; Mark 10:45); "us" (Tit. 2:14); and "me" (Gal. 2:20).

It is true, of course, that logically a statement of particularity in itself does not necessarily preclude universality. This may be shown by the principle of subalternation in Aristotelian logic, which states that if all S is P, then it may be inferred that some S is P, but conversely, it cannot be inferred from the fact that

---

4. Benjamin B. Warfield, *The Plan of Salvation* (Grand Rapids: Mich.: Eerdmans, n.d.), 31.
5. Roger R. Nicole, "Particular Redemption," in *Our Savior God: Man, Christ, and the Atonement*, ed. James M. Boice (Grand Rapids, Mich.: Baker, 1980), 166–67. See also Francis Turretin, *The Atonement of Christ* (Grand Rapids, Mich.: Baker, 1978), 124–25, and R. B. Kuiper, *For Whom Did Christ Die?* (Grand Rapids, Mich.: Baker, 1982), 82–84.

some S is P that the remainder of S is not P. A case in point is the "me" of Galatians 2:20: the fact that Christ died for Paul individually does not mean that Christ died only for Paul and for no one else.

But it should also be evident that one of these particularizing terms—the "elect"—clearly carries with it the implication that some are excluded from the saving intention and salvific work of Christ. And certain details in the other passages suggest that the designated people for whom Christ died stand in a divinely distinguished gracious relationship to him *different in kind* from the relationship in which other people stand to him, *because of which relationship* he did his cross work for them. For example, Christ declared that he, as the good Shepherd, would lay down his life for his sheep (John 10:11, 15). But how does it come about that one is his sheep? By believing on him? Not at all. Jesus said to the Jews, *not* (as it is often represented): "You are not my sheep because you do not believe," but: "You do not believe because [ὅτι, *hoti*] you are not my sheep. My sheep listen to [believe] my voice; I know them, and they follow me" (John 10:26–27).[6] From this we may infer that unless one is *already* in some sense one of his sheep he does not believe, and also that it is *because* one is *already* in some sense one of his sheep that he believes on him. But if one is already in some sense one of his sheep prior to faith, on the basis of which *prior* "shepherd-sheep" relationship Christ does his cross work for the sheep and the sheep in turn believes on him, then that relationship itself can only be the result of distinguishing grace and thus a relationship different from that which the others sustain to him.

Another example is Ephesians 5:25, where Paul teaches, first, that Christ *loved* the church and *gave* himself for it. From this juxtaposition of these two verbs, it may be inferred both that the church enjoyed a special existence and a standing before Christ such that he "loved" her *prior* to his "giving" himself for it, and that his love for his church was the motivating power behind his "giving" himself *for it*. Second, Paul teaches that the husband is to love his wife *just as* (καθώς, *kathōs*) Christ loved the church and gave himself for it. But if Christ does not love his church in a special way, *different in kind* from the way he loves all other people, and if the husband is to love his wife *just as* Christ loved the church, then the husband is to love all other women in the same way that he loves his wife—surely a grotesque ethic! For Paul's comparison to have any meaning for his readers, Christ's love for his church must be construed as a special particularizing, distinguishing love.

---

6. Note also Jesus' earlier words in John 8:47: "He who is of God [that is, belongs to God] hears the words of God. Therefore, you are not hearing because you are not of God [do not belong to God]." Clearly, "belonging to God" is the prerequisite cause of anyone hearing (believing) God's Word. And this "belonging to God" is the elect relationship.

Hence the particularizing terms can and do indicate an exclusive group for whom Christ died, a fact which proponents of a universal atonement can deny only by ignoring details in the contexts in which the particularizing terms occur.

God's Redemptive Love Not Inclusive of Fallen Angels

It is clear that the Triune God's redemptive love is not unlimited or universal from the undeniable fact that it does not embrace fallen angels (Heb. 2:16). There are "elect angels" (1 Tim. 5:21) who clearly were elected on supralapsarian grounds since they were not chosen from a mass of angels viewed as fallen, and accordingly there are fallen angels concerning whose redemption no divine efforts have been or will be expended, although they are creatures as much in need of redemption as are fallen men (2 Pet. 2:4; Jude 6). It is freely granted that the fallen angels belong to a different creation order from that of humankind and that God has sovereignly determined to deal with (at least some) fallen people differently from the manner in which he has dealt with fallen angels. But the nonredemptive nature of his dealings with fallen angels raises the possibility at least that God's redemptive love for fallen humanity may not necessarily be unlimited and universal either.

The Irreversible Condition of Lost Men Already in Hell When Christ Died

Unless one is prepared to say that Christ gave all the dead a second chance to repent (some would say a "first chance"), it is impossible to suppose that Christ died with the intention of saving those whose eternal destiny had *already* been sealed in death, who were at the time of his death *already* in hell. He clearly did not die with the intention of saving them.

Through erroneous exegesis of Ephesians 4:8–10 and 1 Peter 3:19, some expositors urge that all these dead were given a chance to repent after Christ died, but the author of Hebrews disputes this by the unqualified teaching: "it is appointed unto men once to die and after this [that is, after death] comes the judgment" (Heb. 9:27). Jesus' teaching in his parable of the rich man and Lazarus also strongly suggests that one's destiny after death is *irreversibly* final: a "great chasm has been fixed [ἐστήρικται, *estēriktai*, the perfect passive of στηρίζω, *stērizō*, means "has been firmly fixed and stands permanently so"], in order that . . . none may cross over from there to us" (Luke 16:26). Clearly, the weight of Scripture testimony is against the "second– [or "first–"] chance" doctrine. Accordingly, Christ did not die for everyone.

The Limited Number of People, by Divine Arrangement, Who Actually Hear the Gospel

It is difficult to believe that the Triune God intended Christ's death for every man, woman and child, the blessing of which is enjoyed upon condition that they believe in him, when he has not arranged for everyone to hear the gospel. While it is true that Christ has commanded his church to carry the gospel to the nations, it is equally true that many people throughout the course of the centuries have lived and died in spiritual darkness, never having heard the gospel. And the biblical evidence would indicate that God, by determining as he has the recipients of special revelation and by governing the geographic directions of missionary history, determined that some people would not hear the gospel. For example, throughout Israel's history in the Old Testament, God related himself to that nation in a way which he never did to any of the Gentile nations. He left the Gentile nations "alienated from citizenship in Israel and foreigners to the covenants of promise, without hope and without God in the world" (Eph. 2:12). Throughout Old Testament times he "let all the nations go their own way" (Acts 14:16) and "overlooked their ignorance" in the sense that he did nothing directly to overcome it (Acts 17:30). Exclusively to Israel did God entrust the oracles of God (Rom. 3:1–2). And the Psalmist even evokes praise to the Lord because "he has revealed his word to Jacob, his laws and decrees to Israel. He has done this for no other nation; they do not know his laws. Praise the Lord" (Ps. 147:19–20). Furthermore, God adopted only Israel as his son (Rom. 9:4). As God declared to Israel through Amos: "You only have I known ["loved covenantally"], of all the families of the earth" (Amos 3:2). Accordingly, in their midst alone the Shekinah presence of God dwelt. With them he made his covenants, to them he revealed his law, they alone possessed the temple services which instructed them in the salvific ways of God and the promises of God, and theirs were the patriarchs and from them came the Messiah according to the flesh, who is over all, the ever-blessed God (Rom. 9:4–5). During his earthly ministry Christ praised his Father, the Lord of heaven and earth, that he had *hidden* the gospel mysteries from the wise and learned and had revealed them to "little children" (Matt. 11:25), tracing his Father's actions to his good pleasure (11:26). He also declared that only those to whom he reveals the Father know him (11:27). On his second missionary journey, Paul and his companions "passed through the Phrygian and Galatian region, having been forbidden by the Holy Spirit to speak the word in Asia; and when they had come to Mysia, they were trying to go into Bithynia, and the Spirit of Jesus did not permit them; and passing by Mysia, they came down to Troas" (Acts 16:6–8). As a result the gospel spread westward into Europe and not eastward toward Asia, and many Asians died never having heard of Christ. Clearly, the matter of who hears the gospel is under the providential governance of the sovereign God, and he has so arranged gospel history that many people will never hear about Christ. It is unthinkable to suppose then that God sent his Son to save people who, by the ordering of his own providence, never hear the gospel in order that they may believe and be saved.[7]

Christ's High-Priestly Work Restricted to the Elect

It is highly unlikely that Christ's high-priestly work of sacrifice and intercession, two parts of one harmonious work, would be carried out with different objects in view—the former (the sacrifice) for all mankind, the latter (the intercession) for only some people. Since Jesus expressly declared that his *intercessory* work is conducted *not* in behalf of the world but for the elect ("I am not praying for the world," he said, "but for those you [the Father] have given me," and later he prayed, "My prayer is not for them alone. I pray also for those who will believe in me through their message" [John 17:9, 20; see Luke 22:31–32], that is, for God's elect [see Rom. 8:32–34]), consistency of purpose demands that his *sacrificial* work would be conducted in behalf of the same group for whom he carries out his *intercessory* work. It is difficult to believe that Christ would refuse to intercede for a portion of those for whose sin he, by his blood, made expiation![8]

The Father's Particularistic Salvific Will and Work

It is unthinkable, because of the essential and teleological unity of the Godhead, to suppose that Christ's sacrificial work would conflict with the overall salvific intention of the Father in any way. Christ himself declared that he had come to do the will of the Father (Matt. 26:39; John 6:38; Heb. 10:7). In other words, there is

---

7. See John Owen, *The Death of Death in the Death of Christ* (London: Banner of Truth, 1959), 126–28.
8. R. T. Kendall argues for the opposite position, that Christ died equally for all men but only intercedes for the elect: "The decree of election ... is not rendered effectual in Christ's death but in his ascension and intercession at the Father's right hand" (*Calvin and English Calvinism to 1649* [New York: Oxford University Press, 1979], 16). He reasons that without the belief that Christ died equally for all, there can be no assurance of salvation, for otherwise how can the sinner be sure that Christ died for him? "Had not Christ died for all, we could have no assurance that our sins have been expiated in God's sight" (14). But when Kendall makes not the cross but Christ's intercession the decisive point at which the divine election becomes effectual, he simply moves the problem of assurance from the area of Christ's cross work to that of his intercessory work. For how can the sinner know that Christ is interceding for *him*? He cannot. The consistent Calvinist, however, knows that Christ intercedes for him in heaven because he knows that Christ died for him at Calvary.

Kendall insists that his view was Calvin's view as well (13–14), although no previous Calvin scholar had ever imputed this view to him.

harmony and consistency between the Father's salvific will and work and the Son's salvific will and work. But the Scriptures expressly represent the Father's salvific will and work (for example, foreknowing, predestining, calling, justifying, glorifying) as particular and definite with regard to their objects (see the many passages which declare that God the Father, before the foundation of the world, chose certain persons in Christ unto salvation, such as Rom. 8:28–30, 33; 9:11–23; 11:6–7, 28; Eph. 1:4–5, 11; 2 Thess. 2:13; 2 Tim. 1:9). Harmony between the salvific intention of the Father and the salvific intention of the Son would demand that Christ's purpose behind his cross work be as particular and definite as the Father's salvific purpose, and terminate upon the same objects. This is just to say that Christ's cross work was carried out savingly in behalf of the elect—those whom the Father had given him (John 17:2, 6, 9, 24), whom the Father would draw to him (John 6:44), whom the Father would teach to come to him (John 6:45), and whom the Father would enable to come to him (John 6:65). It is unthinkable to believe that Christ would say: "I recognize, Father, that your election and your salvific intentions terminate upon only a portion of mankind, but because my love is more inclusive and expansive than yours, I am not satisfied to die only for those you have elected. I am going to die for everyone."

The Death to Sin and Resurrection to Newness of Life of All Those for Whom Christ Died

All those for whom Christ died are said in Scripture, by virtue of their spiritual union with him, to have died with Christ and to have risen with him to newness of life (Rom. 6:5–11; 2 Cor. 5:14–15). This definitive breach with the old life of sin affords the basis for the *inevitable* experiential and progressive sanctification which flows out of that same union with Christ (Rom. 6:14, 17–22). But neither Scripture, history, nor Christian experience justifies the conclusion that all mankind in actual fact have lived, do live, or shall live out their lives as victors over the power of sin by virtue of and in the power of that union with Christ of which the Scriptures speak. This victory may be ascribed only to believers in Christ, only to "saints" who "died with him and rose with him to newness of life" (Rom. 6:2–4), who "no longer live for themselves but for him who died for them" (2 Cor. 5:15). Accordingly, it follows that the "all" for whom Christ savingly died are equivalent to God's elect, Christ's "saints," that is, his church, and must be restricted in our thinking to the same.[9]

---

9. See John Murray, *Redemption—Accomplished and Applied* (Grand Rapids, Mich.: Eerdmans, 1955), 69–71.

The Implication in the Particularity of the Gift of Faith, a "Purchased" Blessing, For Christ's Cross Work, the "Procuring" Act

The Bible teaches that faith in Jesus Christ is an absolutely indispensable necessity for salvation. But such faith is not natural to the fallen human heart (see Rom. 8:7; 1 Cor. 2:14). (John H. Gerstner declares: "Alongside getting faith out of a heart that is utterly hostile and unbelieving, making a silk purse out of a sow's ear or getting blood from a turnip is child's play."[10]) To the contrary, Scripture makes it clear that faith in Jesus Christ is a spiritual gift traceable to divine grace (Acts 13:48; 16:14; 18:27; Eph. 2:8–9; Phil. 1:29). Moreover, Scripture makes it clear that "every spiritual blessing in the heavenly realms" that men receive, they receive by virtue of the ἐν Χριστῷ, *en Christō,* relation and Christ's "procuring" work at the cross (Eph. 1:3; Rom. 8:32; 1 Cor. 4:7; Gal. 3:13–14). As the Westminster Larger Catechism, question 57, declares: "Christ, by his mediation, hath procured redemption, with all other benefits of the covenant of grace." We may conclude then that faith in Jesus Christ is one of the saving spiritual graces which Christ's death procured for all for whom he died. But since "not everyone has faith" (2 Thess. 3:2) nor will everyone finally have faith (Matt. 7:22–23; 25:46), and since it is impossible to imagine that God the Father, Christ Jesus himself, or the Holy Spirit would ever refuse to grant to those for whom Christ died any blessing which Christ's death procured for them, we must conclude that Christ did not savingly die for all men. Otherwise, all men would be granted the grace of faith.

But while God has not given to all the gift of faith through which instrumentality alone they may apprehend and make their very own the saving Christ and in him the saving righteousness which he procured, Paul informs us that the "elect," the "remnant chosen by grace," who are surely those for whom Christ died, have received a "righteousness that is by [the gift of] faith" (Rom. 11:6–7—in this context he is referring to elect Jews but the same principle surely extends to elect Gentiles as well [see Rom. 9:30–31]).

This argument applies equally to the gift of repentance which was purchased for particular people but not for all. (Acts 5:31; 11:18; 2 Tim 2:25).

The Intrinsic Efficacy of Christ's Cross Work Necessarily Exclusivistic

The Scriptures make it clear that Christ died not a potentially but an actually *sacrificial* death on the cross (1 Cor. 5:7; Heb. 9:23, 26; 10:24), becoming there both

---

10. John H. Gerstner, "The Atonement and the Purpose of God," in *Our Savior God: Man, Christ, and the Atonement,* ed. James M. Boice (Grand Rapids, Mich.: Baker, 1978), 109.

sin (2 Cor. 5:21) and curse (Gal. 3:13) as the substitute *for* others (περί, *peri*—Rom. 8:3; Gal. 1:4; 1 Pet. 3:18), as the substitute *in behalf of* others (ὑπέρ, *hyper*—Rom. 5:6–8; 8:32; 14:15; Gal. 2:13, 20; 1 Cor. 15:3; 2 Cor. 5:15; Heb. 2:9), as the substitute *for the sake of* others (διά, *dia*—1 Cor. 8:11), and as the substitute *in the stead or place of* others (ἀντί, *anti*—Matt. 20:28; Mark 10:45), thereby paying the penalty, bearing the curse, and dying the death for all those for whom he died. Christ by his death work actually (1) *destroyed* the works of the devil in behalf of (1 John 3:8; Heb. 2:14–15; Col. 2:14–15), (2) *propitiated* God's wrath for (by satisfying the demands of divine justice) (Rom. 3:25; Heb. 2:17; 1 John 2:2; 4:10), (3) *reconciled* God to (Rom. 5:10–11; 2 Cor. 5:18–20; Eph. 2:16; Col. 1:20–21), and (4) *redeemed* from the curse of the law and the guilt and power of sin (Gal. 3:13; Eph. 1:7; Col. 1:14; Tit. 2:14) all those for whom he died as a sacrifice. If he did his cross work for all mankind, then the sins of all mankind have been atoned for. But then all mankind would be saved, for what is it which keeps any single man from heaven but his sin? Unless, that is, God punishes sin twice—once in the person of Christ and again in the person of the unrepentant sinner. But the Scriptures will not permit us to espouse either the universal salvation of all mankind or the enactment of double jeopardy by God. The only conclusion that one may fairly draw is that Christ did not do his cross work for all; he did it rather only for some, and for all the sins of those people. John Owen quite properly argued that

> God imposed his wrath due unto, and Christ underwent the pains of hell for, either all the sins of all men, or all the sins of some men, or some sins of all men. If the last, some sins of all men, then have all men some sins to answer for, and so shall no man be saved; for if God enter into judgment with us, though it were with all mankind for one sin, no flesh shall be justified in his sight: "If the Lord should mark iniquities, who should stand?" Ps. cxxx. 3. . . . If the second, that is it which we affirm, that Christ in their stead and room suffered for all the sins of all the elect in the world. If the first, why, then, are not all freed from the punishment of all their sins? You will say, "Because of their unbelief; they will not believe." But this unbelief, is it a sin, or not? If not, why should they be punished for it? If it be, then Christ underwent the punishment due to it, or [he did] not. If so, then why must that hinder them more than their other sins for which he died from partaking of the fruit of his death? If he did not, then did he not die for all their sins. Let them choose which part they will.[11]

Owen's reasoning is impeccable. It illustrates that a general or universal atonement falls under the weight of logical analysis.

---

11. John Owen, *The Death of Death*, 61–62; see also 137; see also Turretin, *Atonement of Christ*, 159–60.

There is a fourth alternative, which, in my opinion, is blasphemous: it is the view that Christ's death did not pay the penalty for the sins of anyone. This is the path theological liberals have chosen to follow, as have also consistent Arminians, who, for reasons that differ from those of liberalism, deny altogether a *substitutionary* atonement, preferring Grotius's governmental theory, which contends that in his death Christ underwent the *suffering* human sin deserves in order to illustrate what the just Governor of the universe thinks human sin merits and this in turn to maintain God's just governance of the world if and when he forgives men on other grounds (namely, *their* repentance, *their* faith, etc.)—but that in doing so he neither took any man's place nor did he bear either the *penalty* or the *curse* which human sin deserves.[12]

An Atonement of High Value Necessarily Exclusive of an Atonement of Universal Extension

Unless one is prepared to affirm the final universal salvation of all mankind (which is so patently unbiblical that we will altogether ignore it as a possible option), one cannot have an atonement of infinite intrinsic value and also an atonement of universal extension. One can have one or the other but not both.

If the nature of his atoning work is such that by his death Christ *actually* propitiated the wrath of God, removed God's holy sense of alienation, and paid the price for sin that God's offended justice required (which is what we mean when we speak of an atonement of infinite intrinsic worth), and if he did this work *sacrificially,* meaning that he did it for, on behalf of, in the stead of, and in the place of sinners, then it follows that for those sinners in whose stead he did this work, as Charles H. Spurgeon wrote, "Christ so died that he infallibly secured [their] salvation . . . , who through Christ's death not only may be saved, but are saved, must be saved, and cannot by any possibility run the hazard of being anything but saved."[13] But then this requires that we conclude that Christ did not savingly die for everyone—since neither Scripture, history, nor Christian experience will tolerate the conclusion that everyone has been, is being, or shall be saved—but for some people only, even those whom the Father had given to him.

If, on the other hand, Christ did his cross work, whatever it is (and those who advocate an atonement of universal extension must make clear precisely what

---

12. See H. Orton Wiley, *Christian Theology* (Kansas City: Beacon Hill, 1959), 2:246–47; J. Kenneth Grider, "Arminianism," in *Evangelical Dictionary of Theology,* ed. Walter A. Elwell (Grand Rapids, Mich.: Baker, 1984), 80.
13. Cited by J. I. Packer in his introductory essay to Owen, *The Death of Death,* 14.

Christ did do at the cross if he did not actually propitiate, reconcile, and redeem and then must square their view with Scripture), with a view to the salvation of every person without exception, and if he did not do for any one particular person anything which he did not do for every person distributively (which is what we mean when we speak of an atonement of universal extension), we must conclude (1) that Christ died neither savingly nor substitutionally for anyone, since he did not do for those who are saved anything that he did not also do for those who are lost, and the one thing that he did not do for the lost was save them, and (2) that Christ's death actually procured nothing that guarantees the salvation of anyone, but only made everyone in some inexplicable way salvable (which, according to Luke 16:26 and Heb. 9:27, is in actuality manifestly impossible in the case of those who were already in hell), whose actual salvation must of necessity be rooted then ultimately in soil other than Christ's cross work—namely, in the soil of the individual's own will and work. But it should be plain to all that this construction eviscerates Christ's cross work of its intrinsic infinite saving worth, is Pelagianism and makes salvation ultimately turn on human merit. As Warfield insists:

> The things that we have to choose between, are an atonement of high value, or an atonement of wide extension. The two cannot go together. And this is the real objection of Calvinism to [the universalizing] scheme which presents itself as an improvement on its system: it universalizes the atonement at the cost of its intrinsic value, and Calvinism demands a really substitutive atonement which actually saves.[14]

It is often urged by Arminian Christians in response to all this that this particularistic teaching is cold and heartless. But in his sermon on 2 Corinthians 5:14–15, J. Gresham Machen observed:

> People say that Calvinism is a dour, hard creed. How broad and comforting, they say, is the doctrine of a universal atonement, the doctrine that Christ died equally for all men there upon the cross! How narrow and harsh, they say, is this Calvinistic doctrine—one of the "five points" of Calvinism—this doctrine of the "limited atonement," this doctrine that Christ died for the elect of God in a sense in which he did not die for the unsaved!
>
> But do you know, my friends, it is surprising that men say that. It is surprising that they regard the doctrine of a universal atonement as being a comforting doctrine. In reality it is a very gloomy doctrine indeed. Ah, if it were only a doctrine of a universal salvation, instead of a doctrine of a universal atonement, then it would no doubt be a very comforting doctrine; then no doubt it would conform wonderfully well to what we in our puny wisdom might have thought the

---

14. Warfield, *The Plan of Salvation*, 95–96.

course of the world should have been. But a universal atonement without a universal salvation is a cold, gloomy doctrine indeed. To say that Christ died for all men alike and that then not all men are saved, to say that Christ died for humanity simply in the mass, and that the choice of those who out of that mass are saved depends upon the greater receptivity of some as compared with others—that is a doctrine that takes from the gospel much of its sweetness and much of its joy. From the cold universalism of that Arminian creed we turn ever again with a new thankfulness to the warm and tender individualism of our Reformed Faith, which we believe to be in accord with God's holy Word. Thank God we can say every one, as we contemplate Christ upon the Cross, not just: "He died for the mass of humanity, and how glad I am that I am amid that mass," but: "He loved me and gave Himself for me; my name was written from all eternity upon His heart, and when He hung and suffered there on the Cross He thought of me, even me, as one for whom in His grace He was willing to die."[15]

EXPOSITION OF THE ALLEGEDLY UNIVERSALISTIC PASSAGES

The God of eternal purpose (Eph. 3:11) never works to achieve merely general ends but always works to accomplish specific and particular ends. But the Scriptures in many ways indicate that the God of particular ends often accomplishes those particular ends through general means. For example,

1. the God "who richly provides us with everything for our enjoyment" (1 Tim. 6:17), in order that his children might enjoy birds and flowers (his particular end), has populated the earth with birds and flowers with what may be described as "prodigal abandon" (his general means);

2. the God of Jonah, in order to turn him away from Tarshish and back toward Nineveh (his particular end), sent such a great storm that the ship on which he sailed threatened to break up (and any and every other ship on the sea that day would also have been threatened with ruin), and *all* the sailors, moved with fear, threw him overboard (his general means; Jonah 1:4–17);

3. the God of prophecy, in order to get Mary to Bethlehem in time for the birth of Christ in fulfillment of Micah 5:2, which states that the Messiah would be born in Bethlehem (his particular end), moved upon the heart of the pagan Caesar Augustus to issue a decree that a census should be taken of the *entire* Roman world, which census required everyone to return to his own town to register (his general means; Luke 2:1–7);

---

15. J. Gresham Machen, *God Transcendent and Other Sermons*, ed. Ned B. Stonehouse (Grand Rapids, Mich.: Eerdmans, 1949), 136.

4. the God of salvation, in order that Christ "might give eternal life to all those you have given him" (his particular end), "granted him [mediatorial] authority over all flesh" (his general means; John 17:2).

So too, the God of salvation, in order to save his elect (his particular end), has commanded both that the gospel should be proclaimed not simply to the elect but to men everywhere (his general means) and that all men should repent (Acts 17:30). Herein, in this mode of divine operation, lies the explanation of the *universal* character of Christ's Great Commission to his church: as the church of God proclaims the gospel of God concerning the saving work of the Son of God, by *every* legitimate means, on *every* possible occasion, to people *everywhere,* the Spirit of God, working by and with that Word in particular hearts, applies the benefits which Christ procured for them to the hearts of God's elect.

And if one will simply recall that the gospel proclamation offers Christ's salvific blessings to people—whether elect[16] or nonelect—upon condition of true repentance and faith in Jesus Christ, it will become evident that there is no substance to the objection to particular redemption that if Christ died savingly only for the elect, there can be no *sincere* indiscriminate proclamation of gospel benefits to men in general. Not only the church, but God as well, can sincerely assure everyone who hears the gospel that *if* he repents and believes, Christ will save him. In this connection Roger R. Nicole urges that the gospel offer is to be universal with respect to range, time, and distribution. But he shows convincingly by using certain well-known analogies that the "features that some deem indispensable for sincerity in the offer of the gospel," namely, a provision, an expectation, and utmost assistance, all three of which necessarily to be coextensive with the offer, are not in fact indispensable for a sincere offer at all. He concludes that "the essential prerequisite for a sincere offer" is

> simply this: that if the terms of the offer be observed, that which is offered be actually granted. In connection with the gospel offer the terms are that a person should repent and believe. Whenever that occurs, salvation is actually conferred. . . . Far from undermining the sincere offer of the gospel, the doctrine of definite atonement undergirds the call. It provides a real rather than a hypothetical salva-

---

16. We must not forget that the elect, prior to their conversion to Christ, are "like the rest [of mankind] . . . by nature objects of wrath" (Eph. 2:3). That is to say, as G. C. Berkouwer says (*The Triumph of Grace in the Theology of Karl Barth,* trans. Harry R. Boer [Grand Rapids, Mich.: Eerdmans, 1956], 253), for the elect there is a real transition from wrath to grace in history.

Karl Barth, who espouses a kind of salvific universalism, urges that everyone is *already* reconciled to God by Christ's incarnation and only needs to be informed by the evangelist of his reconciled state. But this is to place the "already" at the wrong place. According to John 3:18, those who do not believe are not already "in Christ" but are "condemned already."

tion as that which is offered. It does not expect the fulfillment of an unrealizable condition on the part of the sinner as a prerequisite for salvation.[17]

What about those verses in Scripture which relate the saving work of Christ or the saving will of God directly to "all" men, such as John 12:32; Romans 3:22–24; 5:18; 8:32; 11:32; 2 Corinthians 5:14–15; 1 Timothy 2:4, 6; 4:10; Titus 2:11; Hebrews 2:9; and 2 Peter 3:9? And what about those verses that declare that what Christ savingly did he did for the "world," such as John 3:16; 1 John 2:2; and 2 Corinthians 5:19? And finally, what about those verses that suggest that the one for whom Christ died may perish, such as Romans 14:15b; 1 Corinthians 8:11; and 2 Peter 2:1? Do not these three classes of verses weaken, if not totally overthrow, the particularistic interpretation of the atonement?

The "All" Passages

Regarding the verses which are alleged, by virtue of the presence of some form of the Greek word πᾶς (*pas*, "all" or "every"), to teach either a universal reference for the saving work of Jesus Christ (John 12:32; Rom. 3:22–24; 5:18; 8:32; 1 Cor. 15:22; 2 Cor. 5:14–15; 1 Tim. 2:5–6; Tit. 2:11; Heb. 2:9) or a universal saving will on God's part (Rom. 11:32; 1 Tim. 2:4; 2 Pet. 3:9), it should be noted at the outset of our response that the phrase "all men" is not a self-defining expression; it must always be interpreted within the universe of the discourse in which it occurs. And while it certainly can refer to every individual without exception in some contexts (see, e.g., Rom. 3:23; 5:18a; but even here there is *one* exception), quite often it is apparent that it cannot do so. A survey of a few verses not critical to the present discussion in which πᾶς, *pas*, occurs will illustrate that the word "all" *always* needs to be interpreted sensitively within its context and in light of the *analogia Scripturae* principle.

MATTHEW 10:22

When Jesus informed his disciples that they "would be hated by all men [ὑπὸ πάντων, *hypo panton*] because of my name," he surely did not mean by his "all" that everyone without exception would hate them, but rather that only some non-Christians in all the social strata of life would hate them. Many would not even know them in order to hate them. And, of course, Christians love them.

---

17. Roger R. Nicole, "Covenant, Universal Call and Definite Atonement," *Journal of the Evangelical Theological Society* (September 1995): 403–12.

ACTS 26:4

When Paul declared: "All the Jews [πάντες (οἱ) Ἰουδαῖοι, *pantes (hoi) Ioudaioi*] know the way I have lived ever since I was a child," he surely did not intend to suggest that every Jew in the world knew his life story. Surely he intended by his "all" to refer only to those religious leaders in Israel who had experienced social and formal associations with him.

I CORINTHIANS 15:27

Consider now the "everything" (πάντα, *panta*) in this verse. Because of both the specific situation which was governing the presence of the word "everything" in Psalm 8:6 ("You put everything under his feet") and the point which he himself desired to make, when Paul cited Psalm 8:6 in 1 Corinthians 15:27 he felt it was necessary, in order to correct any who might conclude that "everything" means everything *without exception,* to add this caveat: "Now when it says that 'everything' has been put under him, it is clear that this does not include God himself, who put everything under Christ." In other words, here is Paul quite properly interpreting the word "everything" within the "universe" of Psalm 8:6 and concluding that "everything" does not *necessarily* mean "everything"—God himself in this instance must be excluded. Moreover, here we see Paul doing the very thing—restricting the meaning of an "all" to something less than "all without exception"—that Arminians insist that Calvinists must not do.

JOEL 2:28; ACTS 2:17

Two other examples where the universal term "all" must be sensitively handled are Joel 2:28 and Acts 2:17, the New Testament citation of Joel's prophecy. Even Arminian theologians do not teach that the "all flesh" in these passages means that God will someday pour out his Spirit on all men without exception. When Peter cited Joel 2:28 on the Day of Pentecost, he specifically applied the "all flesh" (πᾶσαν σάρκα, *pasan sarka*) upon whom God's Spirit would be poured most immediately to those in "the whole house where they were sitting" who had just been filled with the Spirit, *in distinction from* all the others in the Jerusalem environs, many of whom would never receive the Spirit.

The context both in Joel and Acts makes it clear that God was promising, by his reference to "all flesh," that he would pour out his Spirit on all kinds of people, who would make up the community of the redeemed (see "your sons and daughters," "your old men and young men," "my servants, both men and women"). In sum, the "all flesh" in the Joel prophecy clearly refers to *all the redeemed without dis-*

tinction, and to make the passage refer to *all people without exception* would be a travesty of Scripture interpretation.

I TIMOTHY 6:10

Again, no responsible interpreter of the phrase, "all the evil" (πάντων τῶν κακῶν, *pantōn tōn kakōn*), in 1 Timothy 6:10 would argue that love of money is a root of *all* the evil that has ever been planned and perpetrated by rational beings. In no sense could love of money have been a cause of Satan's downfall, nor does love of money have anything whatever to do with a lot of the sins that human beings commit. Paul was obviously writing in general nontechnical terms, as modern versions of 1 Timothy recognize when they translate the phrase by "all kinds of evil" (NASB, NIV), which means "many kinds of evil." So here again, the "all" cannot be construed as brooking no exceptions.

JOHN 12:32

Coming now directly to the passages pertinent to the present question, it should be obvious, when the Savior declared in John 12:32 that he by his death would draw "all" (πάντας, *pantas*) to himself, that he was not entertaining the notion that all mankind without exception would come to him. Neither actual history nor statements which Jesus himself makes elsewhere (e.g., Matt. 25:31–46; John 5:28–29; 6:70–71; 17:12) will tolerate such an interpretation. Rather, coming as his remark does immediately after certain Greeks had requested to see him (John 12:20–23), and inspired by their request, Jesus, obviously thinking in *nationalistic* terms, said what he did, intending that not only Jews but Greeks (representing Gentile nations generally) as well would come to know the attraction and benefits of his redeeming love. These features in our Lord's teaching to his disciples doubtless provided the matrix for their own later thinking and teaching, and demonstrates how wrong Joachim Jeremias (whom Stott cites in his *The Cross of Christ*) is when, in his *The Eucharistic Words of Jesus*,[18] he contends that Jesus' "many" in his great ransom saying in Mark 10:45 is "not exclusive ('many, but not all') but, in the Semitic manner of speech, inclusive ('the totality, consisting of many')" of "the godless among both the Jews and the Gentiles."

ROMANS 3:22–24

In this passage the "all" of Romans 3:23 is admittedly universal (excepting God, Christ, and the holy angels, of course) as to its referent. But because it has the appearance of being the antecedent of the present passive participle (δικαιούμενοι,

---

18. Joachim Jeremias, *The Eucharistic Words of Jesus* (Oxford: Oxford University Press, 1955), 228–29.

dikaioumenoi, "being justified") standing at the head of verse 24, the "all" is also said to teach that God's soteric provision in Christ is as universal as the sin of verse 23. The argument goes like this: The redemption and propitiation referred to in 3:24, 25 (being aspects of Christ's cross work) serve as the ground for God's act of justification referred to in 3:24, 26. But because God's justifying activity modifies the "all sinned" of 3:23 (which, in light of the occurrence of the same phrase in Romans 5:12, doubtless includes the imputation of Adam's sin to all mankind descending from him by ordinary generation), it would follow that Christ's cross work is as extensive in its intended provision as man's sinful condition.

The entire force of this argument rests on the assumption that the participle "being justified" in verse 24 is to be related directly back to the "all sinned" of verse 23 ("all sinned and are falling short . . . [the same "all"] being justified"). However, the syntax of this passage is not that "cut and dried." I doubt that any Greek scholar will disagree with John Murray's observation that the participle in verse 24 "does not appear to stand in relation to what precedes in a way that is easily intelligible."[19] Not only does the sense of the passage support Murray's statement but the *actual* soteric universalism that ensues by implication from such a syntactical connection also makes this connection tenuous at best. Accordingly, many commentators, Murray among them, urge that the "being justified" of 3:24 should be connected syntactically to 3:22a ("even a righteousness of God which comes through faith in Jesus Christ to all who believe . . . , being justified . . ."), with 3:22b–23 to be construed as standing parenthetically to the main idea of the sentence. This is possible but in my opinion not likely, inasmuch as the participle "being justified" in 3:24 is in the nominative case while the "all who believe" is in the accusative case.

I would urge, therefore, another syntactical possibility, namely, that a period should be placed at the end of verse 23 and that the participle of 3:24, having been rendered by Paul in the nominative plural due to the attraction of the several plurals in the immediately preceding context and intended by him causally, should commence the protasis of a new sentence. That is to say, it should be translated, "Because we are being justified. . . ." The apodosis of the sentence would then commence at 3:27: ". . . , where then is boasting?" The sentence would then read as follows:

> 3:24: Because we are being justified freely by his grace through the redemption which is in Christ Jesus [from verse 25—"through faith in his blood"],
>
>> [3:25–26: A short excursus elaborating upon God's purpose for Christ's redemptive work now ensues—"whom God 'set forth' as a propitiating sacrifice

---

19. John Murray, *The Epistle to the Romans* (Grand Rapids, Mich.: Eerdmans, 1968), 1:113–14.

... in order to 'evidence' his justice" when he forgave Old Testament saints and "to 'evidence' his justice in the present age, with a view to him being both just and justifier of him who believes in Jesus"],

3:27: where then is boasting [answering to the world's boasting implied in 3:19]? It is excluded. By what law? Of works? No, but through the law of faith.

This arrangement makes perfect sense, removes the syntactical difficulty mentioned earlier, and eliminates both the implied universalism and the universal atonement that the Arminian sees here.

ROMANS 5:18B

From the context it is apparent that just as Paul intended the first occurrence of the "all men" phrase in 18a to refer within its theological universe (the "one trespass" of Adam) to all those "in Adam" who were represented by him (in fact at one time all men, except Christ), so also in 18b he intended by the clause, "by one righteous act [the free gift] unto justification of life [shall come] unto all men [πάντας ἀνθρώπους, *pantas anthrōpous*]," that the second "all men" phrase should refer within its theological universe (the "one righteous act" of Christ and the justification of life to which it leads) not to all men without exception but only to all those "in Christ" (ἐν Χριστῷ, *en Christō*) who are represented by him. The same must be said for Paul's second use of "the many" (οἱ πολλοί, *hoi polloi*) in 5:19 and his statement, "in Christ shall all be made alive," in 1 Corinthians 15:22. In the last case, he clearly means "all men [who are] in Christ" shall be made alive; the only alternative is to conclude that Paul teaches here universal resurrection unto salvation.[20]

ROMANS 8:32

Those to whom Paul refers by his "us all" (ἡμῶν πάντων, *hēmōn pantōn*) in Romans 8:32 are clearly to be restricted by the contextual universe of the passage to those whom God predestines, calls, justifies, and glorifies (8:30), to those whom God has chosen (8:33), to those for whom Christ is interceding (8:34), and to those who shall never be separated by anything from the love of God in Christ Jesus (8:35–39). Clearly, the "all" to whom Paul refers in Romans 8:32 are the elect.[21]

---

20. See Owen, *The Death of Death*, 240–41.
21. See Murray, *Redemption—Accomplished and Applied*, 65–69.

ROMANS 11:32

In this verse Paul writes: "God has bound all over to disobedience in order that [ἵνα, *hina*] he might show mercy to all [τοὺς πάντας, *tous pantas*]." The Arminian alleges that the second half of the verse should be understood to teach that God's reach of mercy is as expansive and all-encompassing as the disobedience of men is said to be in the first half of the verse, which is just to say that God wills his salvific mercy for all men without exception. Two things should be said in response: First, it is incredible that the Arminian would use this verse at all to teach his universalism, for at the same time, in the interest of making room for human freedom as the decisive factor in men's salvation, he must completely ignore its primary lesson, that it is God who is the sovereign subject of both verbs. He is the one who is first credited with sovereignly shutting "all" up to disobedience in order that he may show mercy to all. Where is there any room for the human will as the decisive factor in salvation in this Pauline declaration (see Rom. 9:11–16)? Second, as everywhere else, the double "all" here must be interpreted by the context, and so here I will simply cite Warfield's exposition of the verse:

> We must not permit to fall out of sight the fact that the whole extremity of assertion of the ninth chapter [of Romans] is repeated in the eleventh (xi.4–10); so that there is no change of conception or lapse of consecution observable as the argument develops, and we do not escape from the doctrine of predestination of the ninth chapter in fleeing to the eleventh. This is true even if we go at once to the great closing declaration of xi.32, to which we are often directed as to the key to the whole section—which, indeed, it very much is: "For God hath shut up all unto disobedience, that he might have mercy upon all." On the face of it there could not readily be framed a more explicit assertion of the Divine control and the Divine initiative than this; it is only another declaration that he has mercy on whom he will have mercy, and after the manner and in the order that he will. And it certainly is not possible to read it as a declaration of universal salvation, and thus reduce the whole preceding exposition to a mere tracing of the varying pathways along which the common Father leads each individual of the race severally to the common goal. Needless to point out that thus the whole argument would be stultified, and the apostle convicted of gross exaggeration in tone and language where otherwise we find only impressive solemnity, arising at times into natural anguish. It is enough to observe that the verse cannot bear this sense in its context. Nothing is clearer than that its purpose is not to minimize but to magnify the sense of absolute dependence on the Divine mercy, and to quicken apprehension of the mystery of God's righteously loving ways; and nothing is clearer than that the reference of the double "all" is exhausted by the two classes discussed in the immediate context,—so that they are not to be taken individualistically but, so to speak, racially. The intrusion of the individualistic–universalistic

sentiment, so dominant in the modern consciousness, into the interpretation of this section, indeed, is to throw the whole into inextricable confusion. Nothing could be further from the nationalistic-universalistic point of view from which it was written, and from which alone St. Paul can be understood when he represents that in rejecting the mass of contemporary Jews God has not cast off his people, but, acting only as he had frequently done in former ages, is fulfilling his promise to the kernel while shelling off the husk.[22]

Clearly, "nationalistic-universalistic"—referring to all *elect* Jews and Gentiles—is the sense in which the double "all" must be understood in 11:32 (see the "just as . . . so also" comparison of 11:30–31).[23]

2 CORINTHIANS 5:14–15

I have already demonstrated that the "alls" (πάντων, οἱ πάντες, *pantōn, hoi pantes*) in 2 Corinthians 5:14–15 for whom Christ died cannot refer to all men without exception but refer rather to those who, by virtue of their union with Christ, "no longer live for themselves but for him who died for them (p. 678)." To conclude otherwise and to insist that the Apostle is asserting that Christ died for everyone without exception will require the interpreter also to conclude, as we have already seen, that all men without exception have lived, are now living, and shall live for the honor and glory of Christ.

In his sermon on 2 Corinthians 5:14–15 referred to earlier, J. Gresham Machen inquires into what Paul meant by the word "all" in this passage. He concludes:

> Well, I suppose our Christian brethren in other churches, our Christian brethren who are opposed to the Reformed Faith might be tempted to make the word "all" mean, in this passage, "all men"; they might be tempted to make it refer to the whole human race. They might be tempted to interpret the words "Christ died for all men everywhere whether Christians or not." But if they are tempted to make it mean that, they ought to resist the temptation, since this passage is really a very dangerous passage for them to lay stress on in support of their view.
>
> In the first place, the context is dead against it. . . . All through this passage Paul is speaking not of the relation of Christ to all men, but of the relation of Christ to the Church.
>
> In the second place, the view that "Christ died for all" means "Christ died for all men" proves too much. The things that Paul says in this passage about those

---

22. Benjamin B. Warfield, "Predestination," in *Biblical and Theological Studies* (Philadelphia: Presbyterian and Reformed, 1952), 314–15.
23. Calvin interprets the second "all" of this verse to refer to "classes of men" (*Institutes*, III.xxiv.16).

for whom Christ died do not fit those who merely have the gospel offered to them; they fit only those who accept the gospel for the salvation of their souls. Can it be said of all men, including those who reject the gospel or have never heard it, that they died when Christ died on the cross; can it be said of them that they no longer live unto themselves but unto the Christ who died for them? Surely these things cannot be said of all men, and therefore the word "all" does not mean all men.[24]

I TIMOTHY 2:5–6

Paul's statement "Christ Jesus, who gave himself as a ransom for all [πάντων, *pantōn*]," must be interpreted in harmony with his earlier statement, "God our Savior, who wills [θέλει, *thelei*] all men [πάντας ἀνθρώπους, *pantas anthrōpous*] to be saved" (2:3–4). Paul's earlier statement cannot possibly be construed to mean that God *decretally* wills the salvation of all men without exception, not only because such an interpretation would require the necessary implicate that all men without exception will in fact then be saved, which is denied by such verses as Matthew 7:23 and Matthew 25:46, but also because such an interpretation conflicts with the several Pauline and other New Testament declarations to the effect that before the creation of the world God chose only some men to salvation (see again Rom. 8:28–30; 9:11–23; 11:6–7, 28; Eph. 1:4–5, 11; 2 Thess. 2:13; 2 Tim. 1:9). Nor is it likely that Paul means that God *wishes* or *desires* the salvation of all men without exception, for surely what God *desires* to come to pass, he would have *decreed* to come to pass.[25] Therefore, Paul's earlier statement is best understood to mean that

---

24. Machen, *God Transcendent*, 134–35; see also Owen, *The Death of Death*, 238–40, and Murray, *Redemption—Accomplished and Applied*, 71–72.
25. Some Reformed theologians teach that God can and does earnestly desire, ardently long to see come to pass, and actually work to effect things which he has not decreed will come to pass. Basing his conclusions on his expositions of Deteronomy 5:29, Ezekiel 18:23, 32; 33:11; Matthew 23:37; and 2 Peter 3:9, John Murray states in "The Free Offer of the Gospel," *Collected Writings of John Murray* (Edinburgh: Banner of Truth, 1982), that God represents himself as "earnestly desiring the fulfilment of something which he had not in the exercise of his sovereign will actually decreed to come to pass," that he "expresses an ardent desire for the fulfillment of certain things which he has not decreed in his inscrutable counsel to come to pass," that he "desires . . . the accomplishment of what he does not decretively will," that Christ "willed the bestowal of his saving and protecting grace upon those whom neither the Father nor he decreed thus to save and protect," that "God does not wish that any man should perish. His wish is rather that all should enter upon eternal life by coming to repentance," and finally, that "there is in God a benevolent lovingkindness towards the repentance and salvation of even those whom he has not decreed to save" (4:119, 130, 131–32). John H. Gerstner similarly asserts, but without the requisite scriptural support, in *A Predestination Primer* (Winona Lake, Ind.: Alpha Publications,

God wills (that is, decrees) to save (some from) all *categories* of men but not all men without exception. This interpretation receives support both from the later "all kinds of evil" in 6:10 which we have already considered and from Paul's earlier usage of "all men" (πάντων ἀνθρώπων, *pantōn anthrōpōn*) in 2:1, which is also best taken this way. Not only would "prayers, intercessions, and thanksgivings" in behalf of *all* men without exception be positively evil, for such prayers would then need to be offered for the dead and also for the one who has committed the "sin unto death" which John does not encourage (1 John 5:16), but also Paul's following phrase in 2:2a, "for kings and all those who are in authority," indicates that he was thinking in terms of *categories* of men—that is, all kinds of men—when he urges "prayers, intercessions, and thanksgivings to be made in behalf of all men." In sum, Paul urges that prayers be offered in behalf of all *classes* of men—even kings and governors—because God has willed all *classes* of men—even kings and governors—to be saved. When Paul then declares in 2:5–6 that Christ "gave himself as a ransom for all," he doubtless presumes that he will be understood, against the earlier contextual background, to mean that Christ died for *particular men in all those categories of men* whom God wills to save. Then later, when he describes the living God as the "Savior of all men, that is, believers" (1 Tim. 4:10),[26] he doubtless presumes again that he will be understood, against the earlier contextual background, to mean that God is the Savior of *believers,* who are found among all *categories* of men.[27]

TITUS 2:11

With regard to Titus 2:11, scholars disagree over whether the dative "to all men" (πᾶσιν ἀνθρώποις, *pasin anthrōpois*) should be connected syntactically to the verb

---

1979) 36–37, that God sincerely "strives with men whom He knows and has predestined should perish," that "God, who knows all things, including the fact that certain persons will in spite of all efforts reject and disbelieve, continues to work with them to persuade them to believe," and that "God, who knows the futility of certain endeavors to convert certain persons, proceeds to make these endeavors which He knows are going to be futile."

If one followed this trajectory of reasoning to its logical end, one might also conclude that perhaps Christ, though he knew the futility of his endeavor, did after all die savingly for those whom his Father and he had decreed not to save. But all such reasoning imputes irrationality to God, and the passages upon which Murray relies for his conclusions can all be legitimately interpreted in such a way that the Christian is not forced to impute such irrationality to God. For these other interpretations I would refer the reader to John Gill, *The Cause of God and Truth* (Grand Rapids, Mich.: Sovereign Grace, 1971), 4–6, 22–26, 28, 62.

26. Μάλιστα, *malista,* can bear the sense of further definition ("that is"), according to S. K. Skeat, "'Especially the Parchments': A Note on 2 Timothy IV.13," *Journal of Theological Studies* 30 (1979): 173–77.

27. See Calvin, *Institutes,* III.xxiv.16; Owen, *The Death of Death,* 231–35.

"has appeared" or to the adjectival noun "saving," that is to say, whether Paul meant to say that "the grace . . . [that is] saving has appeared to all men" or "the grace . . . has appeared [that is] saving all men." The latter construction is the more likely possibility because the adjectival noun "saving" immediately precedes the dative "all men." But for the present purpose it makes little substantive difference which construction one prefers since it is evident from Scripture, history, and Christian experience that the grace that has appeared in Jesus Christ is not, in fact, actually *saving* all men without exception nor has salvific grace even *appeared* to all men without exception, much less saved them. It is true, of course, that salvific grace did appear in a very special way when Christ came "for us men and for our salvation," and holds out the prospect of salvation to *all who will believe.* In this respect there is surely a universality about the saving grace of God in Christ. But beyond this sense of universality, for the reasons already stated, most likely not even the Arminian would insist upon pressing the literalness of the "all men" expression here so as to encompass all men without exception. As a matter of fact, as we have already seen elsewhere, because Paul refers in the immediately preceding context to "older men" (2:2) and "older women" (2:3), to "young women" (2:4) and "young men" (2:6), and to "slaves" and "masters" (2:9), most likely he again is thinking in terms of all *categories* of men (including even slaves) and not of everyone without exception (note the connecting γὰρ, *gar,* in 2:11). And it is not an insignificant feature of the passage that the emphasis in the context moves immediately from the "all men" to the redeemed community (see the immediately following "teaching us" and "we should live"), giving again virtually the sense that the "all men" to whom grace has savingly appeared are to be defined in terms of the redeemed community, the church (note: "all men, teaching us . . ."). And of that community envisioned by the "us" and "we," Paul declares that Jesus Christ "gave himself for us that he might redeem us from all lawlessness and to purify for himself a *special* [περιούσιον, *periousion*] people, eager to do what is good" (2:14). So in the very context where some would urge a distributive universality for Christ's atoning work, the *particularity* of the intention behind Christ's cross work and the *speciality* of the redeemed community resulting from that cross work receive the emphasis.

HEBREWS 2:9

The statement in Hebrews 2:9 to the effect that Jesus was made a little lower than the angels "so that by the grace of God he might taste death for everyone [παντὸς, *pantos*]" has been interpreted by proponents of a universal atonement to mean that Christ's death has significance for all men distributively without exception. But this interpretation cannot be exegetically sustained. Those for whom he "tasted death," that is, died, are immediately described as those "many sons" whom

God intended to bring to glory (2:10), the "sanctified" who with the Sanctifier are of the same family (2:11), Christ's "brethren" in whose likeness he was made when he became man (2:11, 12, 17), Christ's "children" whom God had given him (2:13), and "Abraham's seed" whom he came to help (2:16). Nothing in the context would support a universalistic application of Christ's death to all men without exception. To the contrary, the entire context suggests that it is Christ's own who is the referent in the writer's "everyone."[28]

2 PETER 3:9

Finally, there is the statement of 2 Peter 3:9 which the universalist alleges also teaches a universal saving will in God: "[The Lord] is patient with you, because he *does not want* [μὴ βουλόμενός, *mē boulomenos*] any [τινας, *tinas*] to perish, but all [πάντας, *pantas*] to come to repentance." Again, the contextual universe will allow no such conclusion. In 3:8 Peter addresses those to whom he is writing as "Beloved" (ἀγαπητοί, *agapētoi*), a term everywhere acknowledged to be a term for Christians or God's elect. Then to them he says: "[The Lord] is patient with you [ὑμᾶς, *hymas*]" (referring to the Christians he is addressing),[29] offering as his ground for this reassuring promise to these Christians the axiomatic truth: "because he does not want any [of you elect] to perish, but all [of you] to come to repentance." Clearly the referent of his "any" is the Christian elect to whom he has been speaking and his "all" refers to the elect of God in their entirety; and his point is God's concern for the church: the Lord, he says, is delaying his coming in order that he might bring the whole elect of God to repentance. To argue to the contrary, that is,

> to argue that because God would have none of those to perish, but all of them to come to repentance, therefore he hath the same will and mind towards all and everyone in the world (even those to whom he never makes known his will, nor ever calls to repentance, if they never once hear of his way of salvation), comes not much short of extreme madness and folly.[30]

---

28. See Owen, *The Death of Death*, 237–38.
29. *The Greek New Testament* (United Bible Societies) gives the "you" an A rating. Bruce M. Metzger, *Textual Commentary on the New Testament* (New York: United Bible Societies, 1971), 705, writes: "Instead of ὑμᾶς, *hymas* the Textus Receptus, following secondary textual authorities (including K 049 Byz Lect), reads ἡμᾶς, [*hēmas*, "us"]." The doctrine being discussed is unaffected by either reading.
30. Owen, *The Death of Death*, 236. Calvin argues that what Peter means here is that God wills that those be saved whom he brings to repentance, and then he argues that God, in whose hand resides the authority to grant repentance, does not will to give repentance to all men without exception. (*Institutes*, III.xxiv.16).

The "World" Passages

Those who espouse a universal and indefinite atonement also seek to marshal to their side, in addition to the verses above, certain other verses which contain the word "world" (κόσμος, *kosmos*). For example, they allege that John's use of "world" in John 3:16, his reference to "the whole world" in 1 John 2:2, and Paul's use of "world" in 2 Corinthians 5:19 place the correctness of their view beyond all doubt. These advocates must assume, of course, that the word "world" in these verses necessarily refers to men, and indeed, to "all individuals without exception." But does it? As we noted concerning the phrase "all men," the word "world" too is not a self-defining term but can have a variety of meanings.[31] For instance, while it is certainly true that in some verses (for example, Rom. 3:19) "world" refers to all men (but even here there is one exception, even Christ!), in Romans 1:8 and Colossians 1:6 "world" has reference to the "world" of the Roman Empire; in Romans 11:12 "world" refers to the "Gentile world" in contrast to Israel; in John 17:9 "world" refers to other men over against Christ's disciples, the latter being excepted from the group designated the "world"; and in 1 John 2:15 "world" carries an ethical connotation and is synonymous for the evil system that stands over against God and is hostile to all that God is and approves.

JOHN 3:16

Accordingly, when John declares that "God so loved the world that he gave his one and only Son, that whoever believes in him shall not perish but have eternal life" (John 3:16), quite likely he intended by the word "world" what he intended by it in 1 John 2:15. In Warfield's brilliant exposition of John 3:16, after demonstrating that the word "world" cannot meaningfully refer to all men without distinction without bringing disrepute upon the love of God which receives the emphasis in the verse, he offers the following observation on the word "world" as it occurs therein:

> [The term "world"] is not here a term of extension so much as a term of intensity. Its primary connotation is ethical, and the point of its employment is not to suggest that the world is so big that it takes a great deal of love to embrace it all, but that the world is so bad that it takes a great kind of love to love it at all, and much more to love it as God has loved it when he gave his son for it. . . . The passage was not intended to teach, and certainly does not teach, that God loves all men alike and visits each and every one alike with the same manifestations of

---

31. See Owen, *The Death of Death*, 192–93.

his love: and as little was it intended to teach or does it teach that his love is confined to a few especially chosen individuals selected out of the world. What it is intended to do is to arouse in our hearts a wondering sense of the marvel and mystery of the love of God for the sinful world—conceived here, not quantitatively but qualitatively as, in its very distinguishing characteristic, sinful.[32]

1 JOHN 2:2

With respect to 1 John 2:2, where John writes: "he is the propitiation for our sins, and not only for ours but also for the whole world," Murray writes:

> We can find several reasons why John should have said "for the whole world" without in the least implying that his intent was to teach what the proponents of universal atonement allege. There is good reason why John should have said "for the whole world" quite apart from the assumption of universal atonement.
>
> 1. It was necessary for John to set forth the *scope* of Jesus' propitiation—it was not limited in its virtue and efficacy to the immediate circle of disciples who had actually seen and heard and handled the Lord in the days of his sojourn upon earth (*see* I John 1:1–3), nor to the circle of believers who came directly under the influence of the apostolic witness (*see* I John 1:3, 4). The propitiation which Jesus himself is extends in its virtue, efficacy, and intent to all in every nation who through the apostolic witness came to have fellowship with the Father and the Son (*see* I John 1:5–7). Every nation and kindred and people and tongue is in this sense embraced in the propitiation. It was highly necessary that John . . . should stress the ethnic universalism of the gospel. . . .
>
> 2. It was necessary for John to emphasize the *exclusiveness* of Jesus as the propitiation. It is this propitiation that is the one and only specific for the remission of sin. [In other words, if the world has a propitiation at all, Jesus is it. This is the sense, I would submit, in which 1 John 4:14 and John 4:42 also should be taken: when John here and the Samaritans earlier declare that Jesus is "the Savior of the world," they are saying that he and he alone is "the world's Savior." If he is not, then the world has no Savior—author.]
>
> 3. It was necessary for John to remind his readers of the *perpetuity* of Jesus' propitiation. It is this propitiation that endures as such through all ages. . . .
>
> Hence the *scope*, the *exclusiveness*, and the *perpetuity* of the propitiation provided sufficient reason for John to say, "not for ours only but also for the whole world." And we need not suppose that John was here enunciating a doctrine of propitiation that is distributively universal in its extent.[33]

---

32. Warfield, "God's Immeasurable Love," in *Biblical and Theological Studies* (Philadelphia: Presbyterian and Reformed, 1952), 516.
33. Murray, *Redemption—Accomplished and Applied*, 73–74. See also Roger R. Nicole, "The Case for Definite Atonement," *Bulletin of the Evangelical Theological Society,* 10, no. 4 (Fall 1967): 206.

2 CORINTHIANS 5:19

Finally, with respect to Paul's statement in 2 Corinthians 5:19: "God was, in Christ, reconciling a world unto himself, not imputing to them their sins," it is enough simply to note that the "world" before Paul's mind here could not possibly have been all men without exception, because about this "world" of men he immediately says that God was not imputing their sins to them. This is manifestly not true of men distributively in a universal sense. Moreover, the "world" of 5:19 is synonymous with the "us" of 5:18, about whom it is said still further in 5:21 that Christ was made sin for them that they might become the righteousness of God in him—again not descriptive of mankind without exception. Manifestly, the "world" here is the world of pardoned believers who are being declared righteous in God's sight, only for the sake of the righteousness of Christ imputed to them, which they receive through faith alone.[34]

The "Christians Can Perish" Passages

Both Lutheran and Arminian theologians, rejecting the Reformed doctrine of a particular and definite atonement, allege that Romans 14:15b, 1 Corinthians 8:11, and 2 Peter 2:1 conclusively teach that men for whom Christ died can still perish. From their conclusion that those for whom Christ died include men who can finally perish, they infer that Christ's death must have been universal and general in its design and hence *not* intrinsically salvific.

An exhaustive response to this allegation would necessarily take one deeply into a discussion of the doctrine of perseverance, which topic will be addressed toward the end of the next chapter. It must suffice here to say that the Scriptures affirm the doctrine of the perseverance of the saints in many places (e.g., Ps. 73:2, 23–24; John 6:37–39; 10:28–30; Rom. 5:9–10; 8:30, 38–39; 11:29; 1 Cor. 1:8–9; 3:15; Phil. 1:6; 2 Tim. 1:12; 1 Pet. 1:5; Heb. 7:25; 1 John 2:19). Consequently, these verses before us, we may be sure, do not teach that men for whom Christ died may actually and finally perish. What then do they intend to teach?

ROMANS 14:15B; 1 CORINTHIANS 8:11

In both Romans 14 and 1 Corinthians 8 Paul is dealing with essentially the same matter: questions of conscience in the Christian experience of the "weaker brother" in the faith. In the former context he urges the "stronger brother" not to

---

34. See Owen, *The Death of Death*, 227–28; Gary D. Long, *Definite Atonement* (Nutley, N.J.: Presbyterian and Reformed, 1976), 99–107.

become a cause of stumbling to the weaker brother: "Do not by your eating ruin [ἀπόλλυε, *apollue*] that one for whom Christ died" (Rom. 14:15b), and in the latter he says to the "stronger brother": "by your knowledge [which the weaker brother does not have, namely, that what one eats does not commend one to God] the weak, the brother for whom Christ died, is ruined [ἀπόλλυται, *apollytai*]" (1 Cor. 8:11). Arminians urge that by the word ἀπόλλυμι, *apollymi,* in these verses, Paul is teaching that Christians for whom Christ died may ultimately perish eternally. Admittedly, this word does intend perdition in several *other* contexts (for example, Matt. 10:28; 1 Cor. 1:18; 2 Cor. 4:3). But certain considerations render this meaning most unlikely in *these* contexts. In Romans 14:4 Paul declares that the Lord's servant, strong or weak, "will stand, for the Lord is able to make him stand." In 14:8, he declares that "whether we live or die, we [the strong and the weak] are the Lord's." And in 14:15a, just before he issues his admonition to the stronger brother, he says, "If because of food your brother is hurt [λυπεῖται, *lypeitai*], you are no longer walking according to love." In 1 Corinthians 8:12, immediately after he has spoken of the stronger brother, by his knowledge, "ruining" the weaker brother, he speaks of the stronger brother's eating as "sinning against the brothers and wounding [τύπτοντες, *typtontes*] their weak conscience." "Hurting" and "wounding" a weaker brother's conscience are extremely serious matters, no doubt, but these verbs suggest conditions that fall far short of actual perdition. Moreover, in more remote contexts in both letters Paul expressly speaks of the eternal security of the Christian (see Rom. 5:9–10; 8:30, 38–39; 11:29; 1 Cor. 1:8–9; 3:15).

Plainly, Paul regards the stronger brother's flaunting his "liberty" in Christ (1 Cor. 8:9) before the weaker brother as a serious sin—he even uses the strong verb ἀπόλλυμι, *apollymi,* to underscore the effect that his actions will have on the weaker brother, and just as plainly, he regards the injurious effect of the stronger brother's actions upon the weaker brother as a grave matter. But if the issue of eternal destinies was really before Paul here, and if Paul really believed that a Christian for whom Christ died could *finally* perish, one may rightly wonder why he dealt in these contexts only with the potential perdition of the weaker brother, and why he did not warn the stronger brother whose offense could be so influential as to result in the perdition of another brother—making his sin by virtue of his spiritual maturity by far the more heinous—that in comparison he faced an even more horrible end. It is truer to the near and distant contexts to conclude that Paul, acutely aware that all sin is "ruinous" in that it exacts a terrible toll on the Christian man's spiritual growth and testimony if left unchecked, is concerned with the serious problems for the weaker brother's conscience which an insensitive stronger brother could create by an insensitive use of his liberty in Christ. And he appeals to the stronger brother, on the ground that Christ had died for his weaker brother too, to be concerned for the weaker brother's spiritual needs. But there is no warrant to conclude that Paul envisioned the outcome of such an exhibition of insensitivity toward the weaker brother for whom Christ died to be the weaker brother's apostasy from the faith and eventual perdition. Rather, he characterizes the outcome or "ruin" to the weaker brother in both contexts in terms of "stumbling" (πρόσκομμα, *proskomma*, σκάνδαλον, *skandalon*—Rom. 14:13; πρόσκομμα, *proskomma*—1 Cor. 8:9, σκανδαλίζει, *skandalizei*—8:13), terms which suggest that the weak brother is weakened in his walk with Christ, thereby inhibiting his growth in grace and rendering him ineffectual in his walk before the world. These results are serious enough to warrant Paul's use of ἀπόλλυμι, *apollymi*, and his appeal to the death of Christ in the weaker brother's behalf, without alleging the dire end for the weaker brother which Arminian Christians do.

2 PETER 2:1

It is alleged by Arminians that Peter, speaking of "false teachers" who "deny the sovereign Lord [δεσπότην, *despotēn*] who bought [ἀγοράσαντα, *agorasanta*] them, bringing swift destruction upon themselves," clearly teaches that those who have been redeemed by Christ can finally perish, the implication being that Christ's death does not infallibly procure or guarantee the salvation of those for whom he died and hence it has no intrinsic saving efficacy. But Gary D. Long observes with respect to the verb root of the participle ἀγοράσαντα, *agorasanta*, that

> of its thirty occurrences in the New Testament, ἀγοράζω [*agorazō*] is never used in a soteriological context (unless II Peter 2:1 is the exception) without the technical term "price" (τιμῆς, [*timēs*]—a technical term for the blood of Christ) or its equivalent being stated or made explicit in the context (see I Cor. 6:20; 7:23; Rev. 5:9; 14:3, 4).... When it is translated with a meaning "to buy," whether in a soteriological or non-soteriological context, a payment price is always stated or made explicit by the context... in contexts where no payment price is stated or implied, ἀγοράζω, [*agorazō*] may often be better translated as "acquire" or "obtain."[35]

He concludes from an analysis of the two Greek words, taken together, against the background of their usage in the LXX and the New Testament, that what Peter actually intends to say in 2 Peter 2:1, alluding as he does to Deuteronomy 32:6 (in 2:13 he loosely alludes to Deuteronomy 32:5), is that

> Christ, the sovereign Lord, acquired [or "obtained"] the false teachers (spots and blemishes, II Pet. 2:13) in order to make them a part of the covenant nation of

---

35. Long, *Definite Atonement*, 72.

God in the flesh because he had created them, within the mystery of his providence, for the purpose of bringing glory to himself through their foreordainment unto condemnation (see II Pet. 2:12; Jude 4).[36]

If Long is right, then what Arminian Christians allege to be a statement with grave soteriological implications for the particularist turns out in the end not to be a soteriological statement at all! Instead of portraying Christ in his role as Savior, Peter, referring to Christ in his role as their Sovereign Creator, states that these false teachers were denying that Christ was their Creator and Sovereign who owned them.

★ ★ ★ ★ ★

This brief exposition of the major problem passages has demonstrated that, when carefully analyzed, these verses do not teach that Christ's redemptive work is distributively coextensive with the entire human race, nor do they teach that those for whom Christ died may perish; in each instance some consideration in the context limits the scope of his cross work to something less than all men distributively without exception (or eliminates from the context his cross work altogether, as in the case of 2 Peter 2:1). Murray concluded his own treatment of the extent of the atonement with these comments:

> We can readily see . . . that although universal terms are sometimes used in connection with the atonement these terms cannot be appealed to as establishing the doctrine of universal atonement. In some cases . . . it can be shown that all-inclusive universalism is excluded by the considerations of the immediate context. In other cases there are adequate reasons why universal terms should be used without the implication of distributively universal extent. Hence no conclusive support for the doctrine of universal atonement can be derived from universalistic expressions. The question must be determined on the basis of other evidence. . . . It is easy for the proponents of universal atonement to make offhand appeal to a few texts. But this method is not worthy of the serious student of Scripture. It is necessary for us to discover what redemption or atonement really means. And when we examine the Scripture we find that the glory of the cross of Christ is bound up with the effectiveness of its accomplishment. Christ redeemed us to God by his blood, he gave himself a ransom that he might deliver us from all iniquity. The atonement is efficacious substitution.[37]

This entire discussion has demonstrated that there are really only two alternatives. The reader must choose between two mutually exclusive views of the atonement; he

---

36. Ibid., 76–77. Long also refers to Romans 9:20–24 in this connection.
37. Murray, *Redemption—Accomplished and Applied*, 75.

cannot consistently hold to both. Either he will espouse, with consistent Reformed Christians, that behind the cross work of Christ was the divine purpose to effect a particular and definite atonement of infinite intrinsic value capable of reversing, and which does in fact reverse, the effects of the infinite disvalue of the sins of the elect, or he will espouse, with Amyraldian, Lutheran, and Arminian Christians, a universal atonement which, though expansive and all-encompassing in its design, is ineffectual in its accomplishments in that in and by itself it procures the salvation of no one and, in fact, fails to save multitudes for whom it was intended.

It may have come as a shock to the Arminian who espouses the doctrine of universal atonement to have had it suggested to him as I did earlier (p. 681) that his view of the accomplishments of Christ's atoning work is no better than the view of the liberal theologian, but it is a sober fact nonetheless. The liberal theologian, finding the entire idea of substitutionary atonement repulsive, insists that Christ *died for no man*. Accordingly, he contends that a Christian is one who, challenged by the beauty of Christ's pure life and ethical teachings, determines by an act of will that he will follow in Christ's steps. The Arminian who espouses the doctrine of universal atonement, on the other hand, insists that Christ *"died for all men."* Accordingly, the Arminian Christian contends that a Christian is one who, convicted of his sin, determines by an act of will that he will both accept Christ as his Savior and abide in him. But in the view of neither does Christ's death *per se* pay the penalty of anyone's sin! (Some Arminians, inconsistently, espouse a substitutionary atonement that pays sin's penalty.) And in the theological systems of both it is ultimately people themselves who determine whether they will become Christians or not by an act of will on their parts! This is tragic, for Christ's atoning death is emptied of its intrinsic worth by both systems and the Pelagian principle looms large in both—in the Arminian system only slightly less than in the liberal system—in spite of the fact that the former seeks to be self-consciously supernaturalistic in its soteriology while the latter seeks to be self-consciously antisupernaturalistic.

For the glory and honor of Christ, Calvinistic Christians must humble themselves before the sovereign Triune God of salvation—acknowledging their sloth in the task of evangelizing the world and, wherever it exists, the sin of intellectual pride in the fact that it is they whom God has entrusted with these glorious truths—and pray that God by his Word and Spirit (for is it not he, after all, who ultimately gives the increase?) will bring many other Christians to embrace a Savior who really and truly saves, and who will then in turn uncompromisingly proclaim with power among all the nations the infinite, infallible worth of Christ's salvific accomplishments for his people!

CHAPTER NINETEEN

The Application of the Benefits of the Cross Work of Christ

To all those for whom Christ hath purchased redemption, He doth certainly and effectually apply and communicate the same; making intercession for them, and revealing unto them, in and by the Word, the mysteries of salvation; effectually persuading them by His Spirit to believe and obey, and governing their hearts by His Word and Spirit; overcoming all their enemies by His almighty power and wisdom, in such manner, and ways, as are most consonant to his wonderful and unsearchable dispensation. (Westminster Confession of Faith, VIII/viii)

AT THE CROSS, in accordance with the eternal plan of the Triune God and in fulfillment of Old Testament prophecy, our Lord Jesus Christ "execut[ed] the office of a priest, in his once offering up of himself a sacrifice to satisfy divine justice, and reconcile us to God" (Westminster Shorter Catechism, Question 25), purchasing thereby our redemption (Question 29). By this work he *accomplished* the atonement (the *acquisitio salutis*), indicating that he had done so by crying exultantly from his cross: "It has been finished!" The issue before us in this chapter is, *How does the elect sinner become a partaker of Christ's accomplishments at Calvary?* Said another way, Christ's cross work, finished and intrinsically efficacious, stands before mankind. How does the elect sinner "get in on" its virtues and benefits? The response we give here takes us into the area of *application* (here we speak of the *applicatio* or *ordo salutis*) and answers the question, How is the elect sinner made partaker of the redemption purchased by Christ?

Many Christians would respond with the simple Pauline affirmation: "Believe in the Lord Jesus Christ, and you will be saved" (Acts 16:31). And, of course, there can be no question that faith in Christ is absolutely necessary to salvation, and that

[703]

before the sinner can claim any of the benefits of Christ's cross work he must humbly bow before the crucified Lord of Glory, who sits today at his Father's right hand in heaven, and rest upon him alone for salvation. But surely something more must be said, for how can sinners who are dead in their trespasses and sins believe? And why does one sinner believe in Christ and another go to his grave in unbelief?

As a matter of fact, this is not all that Paul and the other New Testament authors say concerning the matter either—not at all! To the contrary, they teach that behind the sinner's faith in Christ, as well as behind every other spiritual grace he exercises, stands the salvific activity of the Triune God. In other words, they teach (1) that "salvation is of the Lord," not only at the point of accomplishment but also at the point of application. Furthermore, they make it clear (2) that the divine application of salvation is not "one simple and indivisible act" but rather comprises a "series of acts and processes."[1] Finally, they make it equally clear (3) that this "series of acts and processes" follows a very definite order, leading Reformed theologians to conclude that they may speak of this series as the "order of salvation" (*ordo salutis*).[2]

SCRIPTURAL WARRANT FOR THE ASPECTS AND THE ORDER OF APPLICATION

No single verse of Scripture mentions every act and process in the *ordo salutis*, but a careful collation of the teachings of several New Testament passages will yield an order of application made up of ten basic aspects or parts.

The Skeletal Framework of the *Ordo* in Romans 8:29–30: Effectual Calling, Justification and Glorification

In the eighth chapter of Romans, where he lays out the reasons for the certain and final glorification of the Christian, Paul affirms the following:

> (28) And we know that with reference to those who love God all things are working together *for good* [εἰς ἀγαθόν, *eis agathon*], with reference to those who are *called* according to his purpose; (29) because those whom he *foreknew*, he *predestinated* to be conformed to the image of his Son, that he might be the Firstborn among many brethren. (30) And those whom he predestinated, those [τούτους, *toutous*—the same group he predestinated, not another group or part of that group] he *called;* and those whom he called, those [τούτους, *toutous*—the same

---

1. John Murray, *Redemption—Accomplished and Applied* (Grand Rapids, Mich.: Eerdmans, 1955), 80.
2. See Louis Berkhof, *Systematic Theology* (Grand Rapids, Mich.: Eerdmans, 1949), 415–17.

group he called, not another group or part of that group] he *justified;* and those whom he justified, those [τούτους, *toutous*—the same group he justified, not another group or part of that group] he *glorified.* (author's translation)

In this passage Paul specifies three acts in the order of application: effectual calling, justification, and glorification. There are also at least five indications in the passage that a fixed sequential order lay before the apostle's mind when he placed them in the order he did:

1. In verse 28 Paul says that the Christian's calling was "according to" God's purpose, clearly suggesting, in light of the fact that God's purpose is explicated in verse 29 in terms of his *fore*knowledge and *pre*destination,[3] that his divine purpose or plan preceded the Christian's call—and that eternally so. To reverse the order from "called [after the creation of the world] according to [a precreation] purpose" to "[precreation] purpose according to [postcreation] call" is to destroy the phrase.

2. In verse 29 "there is a progression of thought from foreknowledge to predestination" which "will not allow us to reverse the elements involved."[4] That is to say, foreknowledge properly precedes predestination inasmuch as foreknowledge, while it "focuses attention upon the distinguishing love of God whereby the sons of God were elected," leaves us uninformed regarding the destiny to which they were appointed.[5] It is precisely this information that the predestination clause provides. The former verb indicates the *ultimate source* of our salvation while the latter verb indicates the *ultimate goal* of our salvation. Clearly, with the same progression evident in Ephesians 1:4–5 ("in love [equivalent to "foreknowing"] having predestined"—ἐν ἀγάπῃ προορίσας, *en agapē proorisas*), the two verbs in verse 29 evince a progression of thought that cannot be reversed.

3. Foreknowledge and predestination in verse 29 are both prefixed with the preposition πρό, *pro* ("before"). These two verbs, components of the one eternal "purpose" of God mentioned in verse 28, obviously precede the three verbs that follow, since none of the three has such a prefix. They speak of God's purpose prior to the creative acts of Genesis 1, while the last three verbs refer to acts which occur after the creation of the world, evidencing the sequential order of "precreation, postcreation."

4. Clearly the order between God's foreknowledge (the first of the five verbs) and the Christian's glorification (the last of the five verbs) reflects a sequential order. To argue that the Christian's actual glorification should sequentially precede God's foreknowledge would again destroy the meaning of the passage.

---

3. The reference point from which the "fore" in foreknowledge and the "pre" in predestination take their meaning is the creation of the world (see Eph. 1:4–5).
4. Murray, *Redemption—Accomplished and Applied*, 83.
5. John Murray, *The Epistle to the Romans* (Grand Rapids, Mich.: Eerdmans, 1968), 1:318.

5. The three postcreation acts in verse 30—effectual calling, justification, glorification—as they relate to one another evince a sequential order, since clearly the Christian's glorification, understood as including his full ethical and moral conformity to the Son of God, can only *follow upon* his effectual summons into fellowship with him (1 Cor. 1:9). His call to fellowship with Christ surely precedes his conformity to his likeness. And because of the evident presence of sequential order everywhere else in the passage, we may assume that Paul also intended that we understand that the Christian's effectual calling precedes his justification as well. In fact, since glorification is the *terminus ad quem* of the *ordo*, we have every reason to presume that Paul was thinking in terms of "extremities" when he mentioned these three postcreation aspects of the *ordo* and hence intended that we regard God's act of calling as the *terminus ad quo* of the *ordo*.

For these five reasons it is safe to conclude that Paul gives us in this passage three acts in the order of application and that their sequential order is that of effectual calling first, justification second, and glorification third. Here then we have a framework, into which may be integrated the remaining aspects of the *ordo*, as follows:

The Position of Repentance Unto Life in the Skeletal Framework

Whereas Paul, in response to the Philippian jailer's question, "What must I do to be saved?" replied: *"Believe* in the Lord Jesus Christ" (Acts 16:31), Peter, in response to the people's question, "What shall we do [in light of the fact that we have crucified the Messiah]?" replied: "Repent (and be baptized in the name of Jesus Christ) for the forgiveness of your sins" (Acts 2:38). In Acts 20:21 Paul reminded the Ephesian elders at Miletus that he had "solemnly declared to both Jews and Greeks *repentance* toward God and *faith* in our Lord Jesus." And the Thessalonians, he writes, "turned [in faith] to God [and in repentance] from idols" (1 Thess. 1:9). Rather clearly there is a coordination or concomitance between repentance and faith such that they are properly to be construed as interdependent graces, each occurring in conjunction with the true and proper exercise of the other. Accordingly, repentance unto life in the *ordo* should appear coordinately with faith in Christ, even though, as we shall see, it is the latter response which alone is the instrumentality leading to justification. Hence, repentance, as a response to God's effectual summons, follows effectual calling and precedes justification. So we have the order: effectual calling, repentance unto life, justification and glorification.

The Position of Faith in Jesus Christ in the Skeletal Framework

The New Testament everywhere makes it plain that faith in Jesus Christ is the instrumental *precondition* of justification before God, but nowhere is this truth more clearly affirmed than in Galatians 2:16:

> Knowing that a man is not justified by the works of the law but *through faith* [διὰ πίστεως, *dia pisteōs*] in Jesus Christ, we also *have believed in* [ἐπιστεύσαμεν εἰς, *episteusamen eis*] Christ Jesus *in order that we may justified by faith* [ἵνα δικαιωθῶμεν ἐκ πίστεως, *hina dikaiōthōmen ek pisteōs*] in Christ and not by the works of the law, because by the works of the law no flesh shall be justified. (see also Rom. 1:17; 3:22, 26, 28, 30; 5:1; Gal. 3:24; Phil. 3:9)

Therefore, faith in Jesus Christ (as a concomitant with repentance unto life) must precede justification as its logical (not chronological) prius.

Furthermore, because of the scores of passages that represent faith in Jesus Christ as the human response to the divine summons to men to believe in Christ (e.g., Acts 16:31) and to enter thereby into fellowship with Jesus Christ (1 Cor. 1:9), the response of faith in the order of application must be positioned in the framework between calling and justification. Thus we have the order: effectual calling, the concomitant responses of repentance unto life and faith in Jesus Christ, justification, and glorification.

The Positions of Adoption and Regeneration in the Skeletal Framework

ADOPTION

The place of adoption in the *ordo salutis* may be derived from an exegesis of John 1:12–13:

> To as many as *received* [ἔλαβον, *elabon*] him, to them he gave the *right* [ἐξουσίαν, *exousian*] to become children of God, even to those who believe in his name, who *were begotten* [ἐγεννήθησαν, *egennēthēsan*], not by blood, nor by the will of the flesh, nor by the will of the husband, but by God.

The first thing that should be noted in this passage is that the *act* of "receiving" Christ (an aorist) and the continuous "believing in his name" (a present participle) both refer to the grace of faith in Jesus Christ, the former viewing faith in Christ as the appointed instrumentality that "appropriates" Christ and his benefits from the perspective of its *inception,* the latter viewing that same faith in Christ as the appointed instrumentality whereby the Christian *continues* to appropriate Christ's benefits throughout his entire Christian experience.

John declares in the clause that immediately *follows* the phrase "as many as received him" (his reference to faith viewed inceptively) that to them Christ "gave the right to become children of God." The phrase, "gave the right [authority] to become children," as is clear from the meaning of the "legal" word "authority" (ἐξουσίαν, *exousian*),[6] refers not to regeneration but to the grace of adoption "whereby we are received into the number, and have a right to all the privileges, of the sons of God" (Westminster Shorter Catechism, Question 34). Clearly, John teaches here that faith in Christ is the necessary logical (not chronological) precondition to adoption, just as it is to justification, and conversely that adoption presupposes faith in Christ as the instrumentality through which the believer procures the benefit of adoptive sonship. But since God would not adopt one into his family whose sins he had not forgiven and who had not been accepted by him as righteous, we have sufficient reason to presume that adoption necessarily follows logically (not chronologically) not only upon faith—the point we just made—but also upon justification. Thus we have the order: effectual calling, repentance unto life and faith in Jesus Christ, justification, adoption into God's family, and glorification.

I will note in passing here and develop later the truth that in conjunction with God's act of adoption, he seals the child of God with the indwelling Spirit of adoption.

REGENERATION

Why do some people repent and respond by faith in Christ to the divine summons to faith while others do not? Concerning those who believe in Christ's name John immediately says in John 1:13: "[These are they] who have been begotten [ἐγεννήθησαν, *egennēthēsan*], not by blood, nor by the will of the flesh, nor by the will of a husband, but by God." By this particular reference to God's "begetting" activity John refers to regeneration, and clearly suggests by his statement that, while faith is the instrumental precondition to justification and adoption, regeneration is the necessary precondition and efficient cause of faith in Jesus Christ. In short, regeneration causally precedes faith.

---

6. See Berkhof, *Systematic Theology,* 516.
7. In every other place where it occurs in the Gospel of John—3:31; 19:11, 23—ἄνωθεν, *anōthen,* means "from above."

[708]

This sequential order of "regeneration as the cause, faith in Jesus Christ as the effect" is supported by Jesus' statements in John 3:3, 5. When Jesus teaches that only those who have been "begotten *from above*" (ἄνωθεν, *anōthen*)[7] can "see" and "enter" the kingdom of God (figurative expressions for "faith activities"), he surely intends that regeneration is essential to faith as the latter's causal prius.

John's statement in 1 John 5:1, "Everyone who believes [πιστεύων, *pisteuōn*] that Jesus is the Christ has been begotten [γεγέννηται, *gegennētai*] by God," also bears out the sequential cause and effect relationship between regeneration as cause and faith as effect. It is true, if one were to restrict his assessment of John's intended meaning to only this one verse, that one could conceivably argue that John, by his reference to regeneration, was simply saying something more, in a descriptive way, about everyone who believes that Jesus is the Christ—that he "has been begotten by God," but that he need not be understood as suggesting that a cause and effect relationship exists between God's regenerating activity and saving faith. But when one takes into account that John says in 1 John 3:9a that "everyone who has been begotten [γεγεννημένος, *gegennēmenos*] by God does not do sin, because [ὅτι, *hoti*] his seed abides in him" and then in 1 John 3:9b that "he is not able to sin, because [ὅτι, *hoti*] he has been begotten [γεγέννηται, *gegennētai*—the word in 5:1] by God," we definitely find a cause and effect relationship between God's regenerating activity as the cause and the Christian's not sinning as one effect of that regenerating activity. Then when he later makes the simple statement in 1 John 5:18 that "everyone who has been begotten [perfect tense] by God sins [present tense] not," though he does not say so in so many words, it is surely appropriate, because of his earlier pattern of speech in 1 John 3:9, to understand him to mean that the cause behind one's not sinning is God's regenerating activity. What is significant in 5:18 for 5:1 is his pattern of speech. When John declares in 5:1 that everyone who *believes* (πιστεύων, *pisteuōn*) that Jesus is the Christ *has been begotten* (γεγέννηται, *gegennētai*) by God, it is highly unlikely that he intended simply to say about the Christian, in addition to the fact that he believes that Jesus is the Christ, that he has also been begotten of God and nothing more. His established pattern of speech would suggest that he intended to say that God's regenerating activity is the *cause* of one's believing that Jesus is the Christ, and conversely that such faith is the effect of that regenerating work.[8]

When one adds to this Paul's insistence in Ephesians 2:1–4 that he and Christians generally had been spiritually dead in their trespasses and sins until God, "who is rich in mercy, because of his great love by which he loved us, even when we were dead in trespasses, made us alive [συνεζωοποίησεν, *synezōopoiēsen*—Paul's term for regeneration] with Christ," the conclusion cannot be avoided that God's regenerating work must causally precede a man's faith response to God's summons to faith.

---

8. See Murray, *Redemption—Accomplished and Applied*, 100–3.

Consequently, regeneration must be positioned before repentance unto life and faith in Jesus Christ in the *ordo salutis* as the cause of both. But since Romans 8:29–30 clearly teaches that glorification is the *last* act in the *ordo*, implying thereby, when Paul speaks earlier of calling, that he intended to teach that effectual calling is the *first* act in the "series of acts and processes" in the *ordo*, we may safely conclude that regeneration either follows upon calling or is the effecting force within calling which makes God's summons effectual (I shall argue the case for the latter possibility later).

Accordingly, we have now established the following order of application: effectual calling, regeneration, repentance unto life and faith in Jesus Christ, justification, adoption, glorification.

The Position of Definitive Sanctification in the Skeletal Framework

While sanctification is generally thought of only as a *progressive* work following upon justification and adoption, the New Testament often represents it as a "once for all" *definitive* act as well (see Acts 20:32—τοῖς ἡγιασμένοις, *tois hēgiasmenois* ["the ones who have been sanctified"]; Acts 26:18—"the ones who have been sanctified by faith in me"]; 1 Cor. 1:2—"having been sanctified in Christ Jesus, called holy ones"]; 1 Cor. 6:11—"you were sanctified"; Eph. 5:26—"to make holy, cleansing"). Therefore, the *ordo salutis* must include a place for definitive sanctification. Being a definitive act following upon faith in Christ (see Acts 26:18, above), it must be positioned in the *ordo* as a concomitant act with justification and adoption (which also follow upon faith in Christ) that precedes progressive sanctification. Hence the order: effectual calling, regeneration, repentance unto life and faith in Jesus Christ, justification, definitive sanctification, adoption, glorification.

The Positions of Progressive Sanctification and Perseverance in Holiness in the Skeletal Framework

Being, as its name implies, a "continuous process rather than a momentary act like calling, regeneration, justification and adoption" that "begins . . . in regeneration, finds its basis in justification, and derives its energizing grace from the union with Christ,"[9] progressive sanctification comes properly after justification and adoption in the *ordo*. A life-long process of dying more and more unto sin and living more and more unto righteousness necessarily begins the moment the sinner is regenerated. And all the while that the Christian is "growing in the grace and knowledge of the

---

9. Ibid., 87.

Lord and Savior Jesus Christ" (2 Pet. 3:18), he is at the same time also by divine enabling *persevering in holiness* (Phil. 3:13–14). Consequently, this persevering in holiness must be positioned in the *ordo* as a concomitant of the sanctifying process.

The Completed Order of Application

From all this, the following order of application has emerged. Concomitant aspects of the order are highlighted by arranging them in vertical columns under five headings indicating which aspects are entirely divine acts and which aspects entail human activity working both in response to and in conjunction with accompanying divinely initiated activity. It should be noted that the first three columns do not reflect chronological occurrences, since the moment the sinner is regenerated, in that moment he repents and places his confidence in Christ's saving work, and in that same moment God justifies, definitively sanctifies, and adopts and seals him. These columns reflect the logical (or causal) connection between the several aspects.

2 Div. Acts	2 Div.-Hum. Activ.	3 Div. Acts	2 Div.-Hum. Activ.	1 Div. Act
		(5) justification		
	(3) repentance unto life		(8) progressive sanctification	
(1) eff. call, thru (2) regeneration		(6) definitive sanctification		(10) glorification
	(4) faith in Jesus Christ		(9) perseverance in holiness	
		(7) adoption (and the Spirit's sealing)		

Note in passing here that this order of application reflects the application of salvation as it is effected within the postcreation world. But in accordance with the principle of purposive planning in the divine mind (see my discussion in chapter thirteen), the order in the eternal plan itself is the precise inverse of its actual execution, moving back from glorification, as the final end, through the several processes and acts (viewed as means) following that determined-upon end in inverse order back to calling as the several means to glorification. Even the two aspects of the divine purpose stipulated in Romans 8:29 should be seen as serving the more ultimate end (see the "in order that he might be,") of glorifying the Son of God as the Firstborn among many brethren.

THE SPECIFIC ACTS AND PROCESSES IN THE ORDER OF APPLICATION

We will now consider each act or process in this series separately and in order, but a brief synopsis of the application of salvation elicited by this order of application may be helpful at the outset.

The application of salvation, purchased in its entirety by Christ's redemptive activity, commences with God the Father's irresistible summons to the spiritually dead elect sinner, normally issued in and by the proclamation of the gospel, to enter into fellowship with Jesus Christ. The Spirit of Christ, working by and with that summons, regenerates the spiritually dead elect sinner, enabling him thereby to repent of his sins and in faith to receive and to rest upon Christ alone for salvation, in which activity he is united to Jesus Christ. The moment he believes in Christ, God forgives him of all his sins and declares him righteous in his sight, definitively sanctifies him, adopts him into his family and seals him to the day of redemption with the indwelling Spirit of adoption. The sinner, now a Christian, begins to experience the lifelong process of progressive sanctification, throughout which time he also perseveres in holiness by the power of the Holy Spirit, with the end and goal of this entire series of acts and processes being his glorification, into which state he is finally brought in the Eschaton at the return of Christ. At that point he will be fully conformed to the image of the Son of God, his *summum bonum*, and Christ will then be in the highest sense possible "the Firstborn among many brethren."

Two Divine Acts

EFFECTUAL CALLING

All those whom God hath predestinated unto life, and those only, He is pleased, in His appointed and accepted time, effectually to call, by His Word and Spirit, out of that state of sin and death, in which they are by nature, to grace and salvation, by Jesus Christ; enlightening their minds spiritually and savingly to understand the things of God, taking away their heart of stone, and giving unto them a heart of flesh; renewing their wills, and, by His almighty power, determining them to that which is good, and effectually drawing them to Jesus Christ: yet so, as they come most freely, being made willing by His grace.

This effectual call is of God's free and special grace alone, not from anything at all foreseen in man, who is altogether passive therein, until, being quickened and renewed by the Holy Spirit, he is thereby enabled to answer this call, and to embrace the grace offered and conveyed in it.

Others, not elected, although they may be called by the ministry of the Word, and may have some common [nonsaving] operations of the Spirit, yet they never truly come unto Christ, and therefore cannot be saved: much less can men, not professing the Christian religion, be saved in any other way whatsoever, be they never so diligent to frame their lives according to the light of nature, and the laws of that religion they do profess. And, to assert and maintain that they may, is very pernicious, and to be detested. (Westminster Confession of Faith, X/i–ii, iv)

These statements express *in nuce* the substance of the biblical doctrine of effectual calling through regeneration.

Its Character and Intention

Carried out in accordance with his eternal purpose (Rom. 8:28–29; 2 Tim. 1:9), God's effectual call is heavenly in its origin (κλήσεως ἐπουρανίου, *klēseōs epouraniou*—Heb. 3:1), holy in its character (κλήσει ἁγίᾳ, *klēsei hagia*—2 Tim. 1:9), irrevocable once issued (ἀμεταμέλητα, *ametamelēta*—Rom. 11:29; see also 1 Cor. 1:8–9; 1 Thess. 5:23–24), and heavenward in its destination (τῆς ἄνω κλήσεως, *tēs anō klēseōs*—Phil. 3:14). By it God summons the elect sinner (see 1 Cor. 1:26–30) into fellowship with Christ (1 Cor. 1:9), calls him out of darkness into his marvelous light (1 Pet. 2:9), calls him into his kingdom and glory (1 Thess. 2:12; 2 Thess. 2:14; 1 Pet. 5:10) and finally to the eschatological marriage supper of the Lamb (Rev. 19:9) and to eternal life (1 Tim. 6:12). By it the Christian is summoned to freedom from the law (Gal. 5:13), to one hope (Eph. 4:4), to holiness (1 Thess. 4:7; see Rom. 1:7; 1 Cor. 1:2), to follow Christ by enduring suffering for well-doing (1 Pet. 2:21; 3:9), and to peaceful human social relations (1 Cor. 7:15; Col. 3:15). In a sentence, Christians are exhorted "to walk in a manner suited [ἀξίως, *axiōs*] to the calling by which [they] were called" (Eph. 4:1).

Its Relation to the External Presentation of the Gospel

Effectual calling, as the initiatory act in the *ordo salutis*, under normal circumstances occurs in conjunction with the external or outward proclamation or presentation of the gospel of Christ (2 Thess. 2:14). I say "under normal circumstances," because there are persons, such as elect infants dying in infancy and the elect mentally retarded, who are incapable of being called by the outward preaching of the Word (Westminster Confession of Faith, X/iii). Since Matthew 22:14 uses the word "call" to describe the general invitation to sinners to enter the kingdom of heaven ("many are called [κλητοί, *klētoi*], few are chosen"), it is appropriate to speak of a general, universal, and outward call. By it both the Spirit and the church say to sinners everywhere, "Come" (Rev. 22:17).

It is simply not correct, as I have occasionally heard expressed, to represent the church as alone the source of the external or outward invitation to salvation. After all, it is *God's* Word which the church proclaims. In other words, it is *God himself*, in the church's proclamation of his Word, who outwardly summons all classes of people to repentance unto life and to faith in Christ (Isa. 45:22; 55:1; Matt. 11:27; Acts 17:30–31; Rev. 22:17). And when the church proclaims the gospel correctly, it will make clear to its hearers that it is the summons of God that it is proclaiming.

[713]

It is important for three reasons to insist not only that the church summons mankind but also that God himself summons mankind in the proclamation of the gospel: (1) the requirement of the many passages which ascribe to God the summons to repentance and faith is thus met; (2) God's claim upon the sinner as his sovereign Lord is maintained and asserted; and (3) God's holiness and righteousness and his goodness and compassion toward sinners are revealed, accentuating thereby the twin truths that, on the one hand, he hates their sin and self-destructive manner of life and will judge them if they persist in them, and that, on the other hand, he calls sinful people to turn from their love of sinning and to seek his forgiveness in Christ.

It is absolutely necessary to recall here, however, that the Bible also makes it clear that the race of mankind to whom God issues his general summons by and through the church is spiritually dead (Eph. 2:1) and corrupt (Ps. 14:1–3), and that its collective mind "does not submit to God's law [this is depravity], nor can it do so [this is inability]" (Rom. 8:7) Accordingly, it is quite understandable that such people would conclude, when they sit under the proclamation of the gospel, that they are listening only to the voice of an irrelevant preacher. But quite often, as the sinner listens to the voice of the preacher, something happens. Mysteriously, imperceptively, he no longer hears simply the voice of the preacher; instead, what he now hears is also the voice of God summoning him into fellowship with his Son, and he responds to Christ in faith. What happened? The Scriptures would say that God had "effectually called" an elect sinner to himself.

It is true that the word "effectual" never occurs in Scripture as an adjective before the noun "call" or as an adverb before the verb. But when Romans 8:29 states that all those whom God calls he also justifies, it is evident that the call here envisioned is not simply the general call that people can resist and reject; his summons is irresistible, because all those whom God calls he justifies, which fact implies that all those whom he calls in the sense intended in Romans 8:29 respond to his summons in faith. This means that, in conjunction with his *external* call to all kinds of people everywhere as the divinely appointed means of bringing them to repentance and faith, God's "irrevocable" (Rom. 11:29), irresistible *effectual* call also goes forth, in his appointed and accepted time, to all those whom he predestinated unto life.

The "Effecting" Force in Effectual Calling

The person of the Godhead to whom the effectual summons to faith in Christ is most commonly attributed is God the Father (Rom. 8:30; 1 Cor. 1:9; Gal. 1:15; Eph. 1:17–18; 1 Thess. 5:23–24; 2 Thess. 2:13–14; 2 Tim. 1:9; 1 Pet. 5:10; and 1 John 3:1). There are perhaps two instances where Christ is said to issue the call (1 Cor. 7:22; 2 Pet. 1:3;

see also Matt. 9:13; Mark 2:17; Luke 5:32). As for people in general, there can be no doubt, in light of their spiritual deadness in trespasses and sins, that they are "altogether passive" with respect to God's effectual call, as the Confession of Faith affirms. Murray is entirely correct, then, when he insists that effectual calling "is not to be defined in terms of the responses which the called yield to this act of God's grace," and that it is an activity in which the pure sovereignty of God's grace, alone operative in the accomplishment of the atonement, is also operative at the inception of the applicatory process. Murray enlarges upon this point:

> The fact that calling is an act of God, and of God alone, should impress upon us the divine monergism in the initiation of salvation in actual procession. We become partakers of redemption by an act of God that instates us in the realm of salvation, and all the corresponding changes in us and in our attitudes and reactions are the result of the saving forces at work within the realm into which, by God's sovereign and efficacious act, we have been ushered. The call, as that by which the predestinating purpose begins to take effect, is in this respect of divine monergism after the pattern of predestination itself. It is of God and of God alone.[10]

Murray is entirely correct, then, when he insists that God's summons "carries in its bosom all the operative efficacy by which it is made effective."[11] That is to say, the divine command "Repent and believe!" with reference to the elect sinner mysteriously and powerfully enables him to do what he was not able to do before. Indeed, God's summons *must* be in some way intrinsically efficacious, since the man being summoned is dead in his trespasses and sins and is unable to do anything to advance his salvation until he is enabled to do so. This intrinsic efficacy in the divine summons is what Peter had in mind when he wrote: "you have been born again [ἀναγεγεννημένοι, *anagegennēmenoi*], not of corruptible seed but of incorruptible, through the living and enduring Word of God" (1 Pet. 1:23). It is what James meant when he wrote: "It having been willed [βουληθείς, *boulētheis*] [by him], he brought us forth [ἀπεκύησεν, *apekuēsen*] by the Word of truth" (James 1:18).[12]

I believe, however, that Murray is too restrictive in his view of what God's summons effects. He insists, but offers no scriptural support for his contention, that it *only* actually unites one to Christ,[13] and that it is from this *actual* union with Christ

---

10. John Murray, "The Call," in *Collected Writings of John Murray*, (Edinburgh: Banner of Truth, 1977), 2:166; see also his *Redemption—Accomplished and Applied*, 93–94.
11. Murray, *Redemption—Accomplished and Applied*, 86.
12. See Berkhof, *Systematic Theology*, 473–76, for the biblical and theological arguments in support of the Reformed view that the Holy Spirit works *immediately* by and with the proclaimed Word in the heart of the elect sinner, over against the Lutheran view that the Holy Spirit works *mediately* through the instrumentality of the proclaimed Word.
13. Murray, *Redemption—Accomplished and Applied*, 93.

that every other inwardly operative saving grace, including regeneration, thereafter flows. Murray conceives of regeneration, not as the effecting force in God's effectual summons as the Confession of Faith plainly does,[14] but as a divine work which comes *after* God's effectual call and *before* the human response, and which "provides the link between the call and the response on the part of the person called."[15]

But is it so that it is effectual calling *per se*, apart from regeneration, that *actually* unites one to Christ? Of course, there can be no question that regeneration is a saving grace flowing from the ἐν Χριστῷ, *en Christō*, relationship; after all, we were "made alive with Christ" (Eph. 2:5) and "are [God's] workmanship, created in Christ Jesus unto good works" (Eph. 2:10). But this is true of *every* other spiritual blessing as well (Eph. 1:3), *including God's effectual summons* (see Gal. 1:6—"who called you by the grace of Christ"; 2 Tim. 1:9—"who called you . . . according to his own purpose and grace which was given you *in Christ* Jesus before eternal times")! The elect sinner is not brought by God's effectual summons into the ἐν Χριστῷ, *en Christō*, relationship for the first time. Rather, it is *because* the elect sinner was "chosen in Christ before the creation of the world" and because he was *in Christ* when Christ died for him that God effectually calls him. Murray himself affirms as much when he writes, in accordance with Ephesians 1:3–4, that "those who will be saved were not even contemplated by the Father in the ultimate counsel of his predestinating love apart from union with Christ," and when he writes, in accordance with Romans 6:2–11 and Ephesians 1:7, that "it is . . . because the people of God were in Christ when he gave his life a ransom and redeemed by his blood that salvation has been secured for them."[16] Murray is certainly correct too when he declares that "we do not become *actual* partakers of Christ until redemption is effectually applied."[17] But neither do we become *actual* partakers of Christ until we have repented of our sins and have placed our trust in him, *which are effects of regeneration*. In other words, *being* in the "in Christ" relationship and *becoming* an actual partaker of Christ are *two different things*: the elect sinner has always been "in Christ," but he does not *actually* become a partaker of Christ (as an effect of the "in Christ" relationship and regeneration) until he trusts him. In sum, if Murray means by "actual union with Christ" simply the "in Christ" relationship, this is surely *not* an effect of God's effectual call. The elect sinner is already encompassed within it—eternally so, which is the very reason for God's summoning him to faith in Christ in the first place. If he means by "actual union with Christ" the actual *partaking* of Christ and all

---

14. See also Berkhof, *Systematic Theology*, 470.
15. Murray, *Redemption—Accomplished and Applied*, 94.
16. Ibid., 162.
17. Ibid., 165

the redemptive benefits in him such as justification, this comes only through the instrumentality of faith, which is one effect of regeneration.

While this means that the Father's effectual summons does not usher the sinner into *actual* union with Christ apart from the Spirit's regenerating activity, it does mean that the Father's effectual summons—only the first of really a countless number of applied redemptive benefits purchased by Christ's cross work for those who are *already* "in him"—is effectual through the regenerating work of the Spirit of God, which the Spirit executes by and with God's summons in the hearts of the elect, to effect faith which does unite the sinner to Christ.[18] The Westminster standards clearly draw regeneration within the compass of effectual calling. Murray is being overly critical when he faults the Shorter Catechism definition because it "construes calling as specifically the action of the Holy Spirit, when the Scripture refers it specifically to God the Father."[19] It *is* God the Father who summons—that is true enough. But, as Murray's own Confession of Faith declares, the Father "is pleased . . . effectually to call, *by his Word and Spirit*" (X/i). And the Shorter Catechism—being just that, a *shorter* catechism for children—simply summarizes the longer confessional statement by referring effectual calling to "God's [that is, God the Father's] Spirit."

But I do not want to leave the impression that the Spirit by whom the Father effectually calls the elect is *his* Spirit alone, and that there is no concurring activity on the Son's part in the regenerating activity of the Spirit. To the contrary, the Scriptures teach that the effectual call of the elect is an activity in which all three persons of the Godhead are engaged, and that the Spirit who regenerates is not only the Father's Spirit, he is *Christ's* Spirit as well (see Rom. 8:9–10; see also Westminster Confession of Faith, XIV/i). The Scriptures testify that it is from Christ that the baptismal (regenerating) work of the Spirit "descends upon" the elect (Matt. 3:11; Mark 1:8; Luke 3:16; John 1:33) and that it was Christ who poured out his Spirit on the Day of Pentecost (John 15:26; Acts 2:33). Nothing is more erroneous than the perception that exists in the popular Christian mind that, save for his present intercessory work at the Father's right hand in behalf of the saints, the risen Christ is relatively inactive today, the Holy Spirit being now the person of the Godhead who is primarily entrusted with the task of applying the benefits of Christ's accomplished cross work to men. Sensitive to all the scriptural material, the Confession of Faith (VIII/viii) depicts the present enthronement work of Christ as including within its scope the *application* of redemption:

---

18. See Morton H. Smith, "Effectual Calling," in *The Encyclopedia of Christianity* (Marshallton, Del.: National Foundation for Christian Education, 1972), 4:23–26. See also J. I. Packer, "Call, Calling," in *Evangelical Dictionary of Theology*, ed. Walter A. Elwell (Grand Rapids, Mich.: Baker, 1984), 184.
19. Murray, "The Call," *Collected Writings*, 2:165.

To all those for whom Christ hath purchased redemption, He doth certainly and *effectually apply and communicate the same;* making intercession for them, and revealing unto them, in and by the Word, the mysteries of salvation; *effectually persuading them by His Spirit* to believe and obey, and governing their hearts *by His Word and Spirit;* overcoming all their enemies by His almighty power and wisdom, in such manner, and ways, as are most consonant to His wonderful and unsearchable dispensation. (emphases supplied)

Here the framers of the Confession are only stating in different words what they say elsewhere when they affirm that Christ executes the offices of prophet, priest, and king, not only in his estate of humiliation but also in his estate of exaltation (Shorter Catechism, Questions 23–28).

Summary of the Doctrine

"Effectual calling is the work of God's Spirit, whereby, convincing us of our sin and misery, enlightening our minds in the knowledge of Christ, and renewing our wills, he doth persuade and enable us to embrace Jesus Christ freely offered to us in the gospel" (Shorter Catechism, Question 31). By the regenerating work of his Spirit, God the Father irresistibly summons, normally in conjunction with the church's proclamation of the gospel, the elect sinner into fellowship with, and into the kingdom of, his Son Jesus Christ. His call is rendered effectual by the quickening work of the Spirit of God the Father and God the Son in the hearts of the elect.

By the Spirit's regenerating work the elect sinner (1) is made spiritually alive, thereby opening and favorably disposing him to the things of the Spirit, which were foolishness to him before (1 Cor. 2:14), (2) is convinced of his sin, (3) is enlightened to the all-sufficiency of the Savior Jesus Christ as he is offered in the gospel, and (4) is renewed in his will, rendering him thereby willing (no sinner is brought to Christ against his will!) and able to embrace Jesus Christ as his Savior and Lord. In other words, the Spirit's work makes the sinner willing and able to repent and to believe, but his repenting and his believing *per se* are not aspects of the effectual call itself. They are his divinely effected responses to God's effectual call which, taken together, are indicative of his conversion.

REGENERATION (NEW BIRTH)

The Biblical Data

The framers of the Westminster standards offer no separate and distinct chapter or questions on regeneration, preferring to treat this doctrine, as we have already noted, within the context of effectual calling. But the Scriptures have much to say about this gracious work of the Spirit. Paul employs the word παλιγγενεσία (*palingenesia*, "regeneration") itself only once with reference to the spiritual renewal of an individual: "Not by works which we have done in righteousness but according to his mercy he saved us through the washing of *regeneration* and renewing of the Holy Spirit" (Titus 3:5). But he elaborates the doctrinal notion elsewhere under the terminology of (1) lifegiving resurrection with Christ (Eph. 2:5—"when we were dead in trespasses, he made us alive with Christ"; Col. 2:13—"when you were dead in trespasses and the uncircumcision of your sinful nature, God made you alive with Christ"; see also Rom. 4:17) and (2) the divine work of new creation (2 Cor. 5:17—"if any man is in Christ, he is a new creation"; Gal. 6:15—"what counts is a new creation"; Eph. 2:10—"we are God's workmanship, created in Christ Jesus"). Peter and James, as we noted in another context, speak respectively of God "begetting anew" (1 Pet. 1:23) and "bringing forth" (James 1:18).

It is particularly John, following the teaching of Jesus himself, however, who is in a unique sense the "theologian of the birth from above." John records Jesus' "birth from above [John 3:3, 7—γεννηθῆναι ἄνωθεν, *gennēthēnai anōthen*] discourse" in John 3:1–15, and refers eleven times to God's "begetting," in John 1:13 ("who were begotten by God"), 1 John 2:29 ("by him he has been begotten"), 3:9 ("the one who has been begotten by God," "by God he has been begotten"), 4:7 ("by God he has been begotten"), 5:1 ("by God he has been begotten," "the One who begot," "the one who has been begotten by him"), 5:4 ("whatever has been begotten by God"), and 5:18 ("the one who has been begotten by God," "the one begotten by God").

Its Effects

By this divine work the sinner is re-created in and to newness of life, has the defilement of his heart cleansed or "washed" away (Ezek. 36:25–26; John 3:5; Titus 3:5), and is enabled to "see" and to "enter" the kingdom of God by faith (John 3:3, 5). He is also enabled to believe in Jesus (John 1:12–13), to believe that Jesus is the Christ (1 John 5:1), to love others, particularly other Christians (1 John 4:7; 5:1); and to do righteousness and to shun the life of sin (1 John 3:9; 5:18).

Its Divine Monergism

Jesus expressly taught the *divine monergism* in regeneration when he declared: "No one can come to me, unless the Father who sent me *draws* [ἑλκύσῃ, *helkysē*] him" (John 6:44), "Everyone who has heard and learned from the Father comes to me" (John 6:45), and "No one can come to me, unless it has been granted [ᾖ δεδομένον, *ē dedomenon*] him from the Father" (John 6:65). From the analogy which he drew between the wind's natural operation and the Spirit's regenerating work (John 3:8), Jesus taught, in addition to the *facticity* ("The wind blows") and the *efficacy* ("and you hear the sound of it") of the latter, both the *sovereignty* ("The wind blows wherever it pleases") and the *inscrutable mysteriousness* ("you cannot tell where it comes from and where it goes") of the Spirit's regenerating work. And while Jesus declares that the birth "from above" is absolutely necessary (δεῖ, *dei*) for faith (John 3:7), he never preaches the "birth from above" in the imperative mood as if his auditor could in his own power produce it. By his metaphor of a "begetting from above" to describe the Spirit's quickening work, Jesus underscored its *divine monergism*. J. I. Packer observes:

> Infants do not induce, or cooperate in, their own procreation and birth; no more can those who are "dead in trespasses and sins" prompt the quickening operation of God's Spirit within them (see Eph. 2:1–10). Spiritual vivification is a free, and to man mysterious, exercise of divine power (John 3:8), not explicable in terms of the combination or cultivation of existing human resources (John 3:6), not caused or induced by any human efforts (John 1:12–13) or merits (Titus 3:3–7), and not, therefore, to be equated with, or attributed to, any of the experiences, decisions, and acts to which it gives rise and by which it may be known to have taken place.[20]

Jesus' metaphor points up how erroneous is Arminianism's synergistic construction of regeneration, which makes man's spiritual renewal dependent on his cooperation with grace, and liberalism's vision of redemption, which denies the need for prevenient grace altogether. *Regeneration is the precondition of repentance unto life and faith in Jesus Christ; it is not dependent upon these for its appearance in the Christian life.*

Summary of the Doctrine

Regeneration is not the *replacing* of the substance of fallen human nature with another substance, nor simply the *change in one or more of the faculties* of the fallen spiritual nature, nor the *perfecting* of the fallen spiritual nature. Rather, it is the subconscious implanting of the *principle* of the new spiritual life in the soul, effecting an instantaneous change in the whole man, intellectually, emotionally, and morally,[21] and enabling the elect sinner to respond in repentance and faith to the outward or public gospel proclamation directed to his conscious understanding and

---

20. J. I. Packer, "Regeneration," in *Evangelical Dictionary of Theology*, 925.
21. Berkhof, *Systematic Theology*, 468.

will. No extra-biblical words have captured better both the divine monergism and the inevitable effects of the Spirit's regenerating work than the following verse from Charles Wesley's great hymn, "And can it be that I should gain":

> Long my imprisoned spirit lay
>   Fast bound in sin and nature's night;
> Thine eye diffused a quick'ning ray,
>   I woke, the dungeon flamed with light;
> My chains fell off, my heart was free,
>   I rose, went forth, and followed Thee.

All this is illustrated in the case of Lydia, about whom Luke writes: "Lydia was listening, whose heart the Lord opened to respond to the things spoken by Paul" (Acts 16:14).

Two Divine-Human Activities (Conversion)

REPENTANCE UNTO LIFE

Repentance unto life is an evangelical grace, the doctrine whereof is to be preached by every minister of the Gospel, as well as that of faith in Christ.

By it, a sinner, out of the sight and sense not only of the danger, but also of the filthiness and odiousness of his sins, as contrary to the holy nature, and righteous law of God; and upon the apprehension of His mercy in Christ to such as are penitent, so grieves for, and hates his sins, as to turn from them all unto God, purposing and endeavouring to walk with Him in all the ways of his commandments.

Although repentance be not to be rested in, as any satisfaction for sin, or any cause of the pardon thereof, which is the act of God's free grace in Christ; yet it is of such necessity to all sinners, that none may expect pardon without it.

As there is no sin so small, but it deserves damnation; so there is no sin so great, that it can bring damnation upon those who truly repent.

Men ought not to content themselves with a general repentance, but it is every man's duty to endeavor to repent of his particular sins, particularly. (Westminster Confession of Faith, XV/i–v)

An Aspect of Evangelical Preaching

Because the wise framers of the Westminster Confession of Faith understood the human proclivity to want to be accepted by others, they realized that the minister of the gospel might be tempted to proclaim faith in Jesus Christ as the sole necessary response to the gospel proclamation, to the neglect of preaching repentance as equally necessary for the forgiveness of sins. They understood all too well that when this is done the "faith in Jesus Christ" which the minister elicits from the sinner is abstracted from the need for salvation *from sin,* the context that gives faith in Jesus Christ its significance. Such "faith," absent the call to and response of repentance, inevitably takes on the dimensions of "easy decisionism," which is no true faith at all. Therefore, even before they define the doctrine of repentance, they remind the minister that preaching repentance is not to be regarded as a foreign or disrupting element in gospel proclamation. To the contrary, they describe it as an aspect of *evangelical* preaching. And they insist that none may hope for pardon without repentance, even though it is not to be rested in as if it were itself a satisfaction for sin or the cause of pardon, for repentance *per se* is and can be neither.[22]

The Biblical Data

What is the biblical ground for the insistence that the minister of the gospel must proclaim repentance unto life along with a summons to faith in Jesus Christ? The Old Testament employs the two verb roots שׁוּב (*šûb,* "turn," "return") and נחם (*nāham,* "repent") when it calls for or speaks of repentance:

> Isaiah 55:7: "Let the wicked forsake [יַעֲזֹב, *ya'azōb*] his way and the evil man his thoughts. Let him turn [וְיָשֹׁב, *w'yāšōb*] to the Lord, and he will have mercy on him, and to our God, for he will freely pardon."
>
> Joel 2:12–13: "Even now, declares the Lord, return שֻׁבוּ, [*šûbû*] to me with all your heart, with fasting and weeping and mourning. Rend your heart and not your garments. Return [וְשׁוּבוּ, *w'šûbû*] to the Lord your God, for he is gracious and compassionate, slow to anger and abounding in love, and he relents from sending calamity."
>
> Ezekiel 33:11: "As surely as I live, declares the Sovereign Lord, I take no pleasure in the death of the wicked, but rather that they turn from their ways and live.

---

22. Zane Hodges, in order to preserve the free grace of the gospel from what he perceives to be legalism, denies that repentance is necessary for salvation. Hodges declares that it is a "mistake" and "an extremely serious matter . . . when repentance is . . . made a condition for eternal life" (*Absolutely Free! A Biblical Reply to Lordship Salvation* [Grand Rapids: Zondervan, 1989], 125, 160). He insists that repentance "is not essential to the saving transaction as such," and that it is only a condition for fellowship with God (*Absolutely Free!* 160). Such teaching is incredible, for it means that the impenitent can receive eternal life and be saved even though they never forsake their sin or have any fellowship with God!

Turn! Turn [שׁוּבוּ שׁוּבוּ, *šûbû šûbû*] from your evil ways! Why will you die, O house of Israel?"

Job 42:5–6: "My ears had heard of you but now my eyes have seen you. Therefore I despise myself and repent [וְנִחַמְתִּי, *w°niḥamtî*] in dust and ashes."

Jeremiah 8:6: "I have listened attentively, but they do not say what is right. No one repents [נִחָם, *niḥām*] of his wickedness, saying, 'What have I done?'"

The word-groups denoting repentance in the New Testament are primarily from μετανοέω, *metanoeō*, (34 times) and μετάνοια, *metanioia*, (22 times), meaning "to change one's mind" and "a change of mind" respectively; and secondarily from στρέφω, *strephō*, and ἐπιστρέφω, *epistrephō*, meaning literally "to turn" and "to turn about" respectively (but both are consistently translated "convert" or "be converted"), and μεταμέλομαι, *metamelomai*, meaning "to become concerned about afterwards."

The glorified Christ placed beyond all doubt that repentance is to be a part of gospel proclamation, when he declared on the evening of his resurrection from the dead: "This is what is written: that the Messiah should suffer and rise from the dead the third day, and that *repentance for* [μετάνοιαν εἰς, *metanoian eis*] forgiveness of sins should be proclaimed [κηρυχθῆναι, *kērychthēnai*] in his name to all nations" (Luke 24:46–47). As did John the Baptist before him (Matt. 3:2, 8, 11; Mark 1:4; Luke 3:3, 8; Acts 13:24; 19:4), Jesus himself preached repentance in the imperative mood (Matt. 4:17; Mark 1:15), characterized the very purpose behind his coming to people in terms of calling sinners to repentance (Luke 5:32), warned that unless sinners repented they would perish (Luke 13:3, 5) and unless they were converted (στραφῆτε, *straphēte*) and became as little children, they would never enter the kingdom of heaven (Matt. 18:3), denounced whole cities that would not repent while commending Nineveh for repenting at the preaching of Jonah (Matt. 11:20–21; 12:41; Luke 10:13; 11:32), and declared that heaven rejoices over one sinner who repents (Luke 15:7, 10). The apostles, on their preaching missions throughout Galilee, "preached that people should repent" (Mark 6:12), and they continued to be true to this aspect of their Lord's commission throughout the Book of Acts (Peter in Acts 2:38; 3:19; 8:22; Paul in Acts 17:30; 20:21; 26:20). The author of Hebrews indicates that "repentance from dead works" is a first principle of the doctrine of Christ (Heb. 6:1).

Its "Gift Character" As Procured by Christ's Cross Work and Effected by Regeneration

As the response to God's sovereign, effectual summons that was procured by Christ's cross work (as is every spiritual blessing the Christian receives) and made effectual by his Spirit's regenerating operations in the soul, repentance unto life is represented in Scripture as a gift of God. The Psalmist prayed: "O God, turn us . . . that we may be saved" (Ps. 80:3, 7, 19) and Ephraim and Jeremiah prayed respectively: "Turn me, O Lord, and I will be turned" (Jer. 31:18; Lam. 5:21). Peter declared that God exalted Christ to his own right hand as Prince and Savior "in order to *give* repentance and forgiveness of sins to Israel" (Acts 5:31, emphasis added). Upon hearing Peter's testimony regarding the conversion of Cornelius's household, the Jerusalem church "glorified God, saying: 'Then to the Gentiles also God *has given* [ἔδωκεν, *edōken*] repentance unto life' " (Acts 11:18, emphasis added). And Paul instructs Timothy that the Lord's servant should gently correct the non-Christian opposition "in the hope that God *may give* [δώῃ, *dōē*] to them repentance leading to a knowledge of the truth" (2 Tim. 2:25, emphasis added).

Its Distinction from Mere "Worldly Sorrow"

Godly sorrow for sin that leads to true repentance, characterized (1) in Acts 11:18 as "repentance leading unto life," (2) in 2 Corinthians 7:10 as "repentance leaving no regrets and leading to salvation," and (3) in 2 Timothy 2:25 as "repentance leading to a knowledge of the truth," must be distinguished from what Paul calls in 2 Corinthians 7:10 "worldly sorrow [that] produces death."[23]

Paul's "worldly sorrow [that] produces death" is amply illustrated by the sorrow of the rich young ruler and of Judas. The rich young ruler, when he heard Jesus' requirements for discipleship, "became very sorrowful" (Luke 18:23). But his was a "worldly sorrow," because, being "a man of great wealth," he regarded his wealth as of greater value than the privilege of following Jesus. So he went away. Again, when Judas saw that Jesus had been condemned, "feeling remorse, he returned the thirty pieces of silver" (Matt. 27:3). But his was a "worldly remorse" because it did not lead to the "repentance leaving no regrets and leading to salvation." Instead, it drove him to suicide. But to the Corinthians Paul writes:

> I now rejoice, not because you were made sorrowful, but because you were made sorrowful to the point of repentance, for you were made sorrowful as God intended. . . . For the sorrow that God intends produces *repentance leaving no regrets and leading to salvation;* but worldly sorrow produces death. For behold what *earnestness* this sorrow that God intends has produced in you, what *eagerness* to

---

23. What Paul calls "worldly sorrow" is designated "attrition" (*attritio*) in medieval scholastic and Roman Catholic theology, meaning thereby imperfect contrition that is not sufficient for forgiveness; what he calls "repentance leading unto life" Roman Catholic theology speaks of as "contrition" (*contritio*).

clear yourselves, what *indignation*, what *fear*, what *longing*, what *zeal*, what *readiness to see justice done*. (emphases supplied)

The Scriptures are clear that men may feel remorse over their sins for any number of reasons. But unless their sorrow for sin is their response to their sense of not only the danger of but also of the filthiness and odiousness of their sins as contrary to the holy nature and righteous law of God, which then compels them so to hate their sins that they turn from them to God with full purpose and endeavor to walk with him in all the ways of his commandments, it must be judged as mere "worldly sorrow that produces death." Godly sorrow, the sinner's response to the Spirit's regenerating work in his soul which normally accompanies the evangelical preaching of the doctrine of repentance, produces "repentance leaving no regrets and leading unto salvation."

Summary of the Doctrine

"Repentance unto life is a saving grace, whereby a sinner out of a true sense of his sin, and apprehension of the mercy of God in Christ, doth, with grief and hatred of his sin, turn from it unto God, with full purpose of, and endeavor after, new obedience" (Shorter Catechism, Question 87). As the root implies in μετανοέω, *metanoeō*, and μετάνοια, *metanoia*, (the most common words for repentance in the New Testament), it entails a radical and conscious change of *view* (the intellect), change of *feeling* (the emotions), and change of *purpose* (the volition) with respect to God, ourselves, sin, and righteousness. We *acknowledge* that we are sinners and that our sin entails *personal* guilt, defilement, and helplessness before God; we *sorrow* with a "godly sorrow" for the sins we have committed against the holy and just God; and we *resolve* to seek pardon and cleansing from God through the blood of Christ which alone satisfies the offended justice of God. So in turning from our sins in repentance we turn to Christ in faith for salvation.

FAITH IN JESUS CHRIST

The grace of faith, whereby the elect are enabled to believe to the saving of their souls, is the work of the Spirit of Christ in their hearts, and is ordinarily wrought by the ministry of the Word, by which also, and by the administration of the sacraments, and prayer, it is increased and strengthened.

By this faith, a Christian believeth to be true whatsoever is revealed in the Word, for the authority of God Himself speaking therein; and acteth differently upon that which each particular passage thereof containeth; yielding obedience to the commands, trembling at the threatenings, and embracing the promises of God for this life, and that which is to come. But *the principal acts of saving faith are accepting, receiving, and resting upon Christ alone for justification, sanctification, and eternal life, by virtue of the covenant of grace.*

This faith is different in degrees, weak or strong; may be often and many ways assailed, and weakened, but gets the victory; growing up in many to the attainment of a full assurance, through Christ, who is both the author and finisher of our faith. (Westminster Confession of Faith, XIV/i–iii, emphasis supplied)

With the Bible the Westminster Confession of Faith is not interested in faith viewed simply as a psychic act but in "saving faith," which as "general saving faith" (*fides generalis*) accepts the Bible as the Word of God and accordingly the Christian religion as true (John 2:22; 4:50; 5:46–47; 12:38; Acts 24:14), and as "special saving faith" (*fides specialis*) looks to Jesus Christ alone for justification, sanctification, and eternal life.[24] It is to the latter that the Shorter Catechism confines itself.

The Nature of "Saving Faith"

According to Scripture, "saving faith" is comprised of three constituent elements[25]: knowledge (*notitia*), assent (*assensus*), and trust (*fiducia*).[26] Warfield explains:

> We cannot be said to believe or to trust in a thing or person of which we have no *knowledge*; "implicit faith"[27] in this sense is an absurdity. Of course we cannot be said to believe or to trust the thing or person to whose worthiness of our belief or trust *assent* has not been obtained. And equally we cannot be said to believe that which we distrust too much to *commit* ourselves to it.[28]

---

24. See Berkhof, *Systematic Theology*, 506.
25. See Benjamin B. Warfield, "On Faith in Its Psychological Aspects," in *Biblical and Theological Studies* (Philadelphia: Presbyterian and Reformed, 1952), 402–3.
26. In typical scholastic manner Francis Turretin (and in his own way Herman Witsius also) adds four additional aspects to the act of faith: the aspect of refuge, the aspect of reception and union, the aspect of reflex, and the aspect of confidence and consolation (*Institutes of Elenctic Theology*, ed. James T. Dennison Jr. [Phillipsburg, N.J.: Presbyterian and Reformed, 1994], 2:561–63). In my opinion the first three of these "aspects" are involved in true *fiducia*. The last one is the result or necessary consequence of saving faith and is not part of the essence of faith as such.
27. The term, "implicit faith" (*fides implicita*), refers to the Roman Catholic teaching that as long as the "faithful" accept as true "what the church believes" it is not absolutely essential that they know the objective contents of that "faith." In other words, implicit faith is a faith that is mere assent without knowledge content. Warfield's judgment is just: such faith is an absurdity for from the biblical perspective it is no faith at all. See Confession of Faith, XX/ii.
28. Warfield, "On Faith in Its Psychological Aspects," 402–3, emphasis supplied.

Each of these elements requires some comment.

1. Knowledge (*notitia*) is the cognitive foundation or base of saving faith. The Bible insists that "faith comes by hearing, and hearing through the word of Christ" (Rom. 10:17), that men must "love the *truth* in order that they may be saved" (2 Thess. 2:10), and it speaks of "repentance leading to a knowledge of the truth" (2 Tim. 2:25). In sum, saving faith is based upon divine testimony. It knows nothing of the modern notion that faith is the enemy of knowledge and that it repudiates all grounding in propositional truth, expressed in such sentiments as "It is when one cannot or does not know that one can or must believe" and "It does not matter what one believes as long as one is sincere." These sentiments, of course, are simply empty superstitions and amount to salvation by ignorance and/or by sincerity, which is no salvation at all. They also fatally wound Christianity in the heart. To the contrary, the Bible glories and delights in knowledge and propositional truth as the foundation of true faith and characterizes "faith" devoid of knowledge as "believing the lie" which leads to condemnation (2 Thess. 2:11–12). Accordingly, the Bible often highlights the knowledge aspect of saving faith by employing the construction πιστεύω ὅτι (*pisteuō hoti*, "believe that"), followed by a propositional truth, to indicate the knowledge content of saving faith:

> Hebrews 11:6: "Without faith it is impossible to please God, for the one coming to God must believe that he exists and is the rewarder of those seeking him."
>
> John 8:24: "If you do not believe that I am, you shall die in your sins."
>
> John 11:42: "I said this for the benefit of the crowd standing here, in order that they may believe that you sent me" (see also 17:8, 21).
>
> John 14:11: "Believe me that I am in the Father and the Father is in me."
>
> John 16:27: "For the Father himself loves you, because . . . you have believed that I came out from the Father" (see also 16:30).
>
> John 20:31: "These things are written that you may believe that Jesus is the Christ, the Son of God, and that by believing you may have eternal life in his name."
>
> Romans 10:9: "If . . . you believe . . . that God raised [Jesus] from the dead, you will be saved."
>
> 1 Thessalonians 4:14: "We believe that Jesus died and rose again."
>
> 1 John 5:1: "Everyone who believes that Jesus is the Christ has been begotten by God."
>
> 1 John 5:4: "Who is it who overcomes the world but he who believes that Jesus is the Son of God?"

In this feature of saving faith "lies the importance of doctrine respecting Christ.

The doctrine defines Christ's identity, the identity in terms of which we entrust ourselves to him. Doctrine consists in propositions of truth."[29]

2. Assent (*assensus*) refers to the intellectual or cognitive conviction that the knowledge one has acquired about Christ is indeed factually true and that the provisions of the gospel of Christ correspond exactly to one's actual (not necessarily "felt") spiritual needs. Without this element faith becomes simply mysticism, for to place one's trust in what one has heard or read about but does not believe to be true is simply an "existential leap" into the abyss of absurdity.

It is important to realize that it is entirely possible for an unregenerate person to know the propositions of the gospel and to have a keen comprehension of how they contribute to the gospel proclamation as a whole and yet still not believe that they are factually true or that they address his deepest spiritual needs. Rudolf Bultmann, for example, had as good an intellectual grasp of the content of the Christian gospel as the most orthodox of theologians, but he denied that Jesus was actually born of a virgin, performed the mighty miracles ascribed to him, died on the cross as a sacrifice for sin, and rose from the dead. He believed rather that the gospel propositions were simply a first-century form of twentieth-century Heideggerian existential anthropology addressing man's "this-worldly" need for "authentic existence."

The New Testament indicates this element in saving faith most often by the construction of πιστεύω (*pisteuō*, "believe") with the dative of the person or proposition to which one's assent is given (see Matt. 21:25, 32; Mark 11:31; Luke 1:20; 20:5; John 2:22; 4:21, 50; 5:24, 38, 46, 47; 6:30; 8:31, 45, 46; 10:37, 38; 12:38; 14:11; Acts 8:12; 16:34; 18:8; 24:14; 27:25; Rom. 4:3; 10:16; 1 Cor. 11:18; Gal. 3:6; 2 Thess. 2:11, 12; 2 Tim. 1:12; Titus 3:8; James 2:23; 1 John 3:23; 4:1; 5:10).

3. With respect to *trust (fiducia)*, "as assent is cognition passed into conviction, so *fiducia* is conviction passed into confidence."[30] And it is particularly this third element of *trust* or confidence that is saving faith's most characteristic act, as the sinner cognitively, affectively, and volitionally transfers all reliance for pardon, righteousness, and cleansing away from himself and his own resources in complete and total abandonment to Christ, whom he joyfully receives and upon whom alone he

---

29. Murray, "Faith," *Collected Writings*, 2:258.
30. Ibid. Gordon H. Clark in *Religion, Reason and Revelation* (Philadelphia: Presbyterian and Reformed, 1961), 88–100, and *Faith and Saving Faith* (Jefferson, Maryland: Trinity Foundation, 1983), basing his conclusion on the fact that the Bible's "heart" is semantically equivalent not to one's emotions but to one's *deepest self* with a preponderant emphasis even here upon the intellect of the self, argues that even *fiducia*, as well as *notitia* and *assensus*, is essentially intellectual. With this I concur, but I would urge that this intellectual *fiducia* includes affective and volitional dimensions, since Paul insists that the saved must not simply know about and believe in but also *love* the Lord Jesus Christ (1 Cor. 16:22).

rests entirely for his salvation. It is essential that faith include this third element. Otherwise, one's faith is the intellectual "faith" of demons who "believe that God is one" (James 2:19) and who believe that Jesus is both the Son of God and their Judge (Matt. 8:29) but who, because they have no cognitive affection for Christ—to the contrary, they cognitively hate him—refuse to trust him.

While the Old Testament employs primarily the root אָמַן, 'āman, in the Hiphil stem to designate this trustful repose (Gen. 15:6; Exod. 14:31; Pss. 106:12; 116:10; Isa. 28:16; 53:1),[31] the New Testament uses primarily the following constructions to express the sinner's trustful reliance upon God's Son for salvation: πιστεύω ἐν (*pisteuō en*, "believe in") with the dative (John 3:15; Acts 13:39), πιστεύω ἐπί (*pisteuō epi*, "believe upon") with the dative (Luke 24:25; Rom. 9:33; 10:11; 1 Tim. 1:16; 1 Pet. 2:6), πιστεύω ἐπί (*pisteuō epi*, "believe upon") with the accusative (Matt. 27:42; Acts 9:42; 11:17), and finally, πιστεύω εἰς (*pisteuō eis*, "believe into") with the accusative (Matt. 18:6; Mark 9:42; John 1:12; 2:11, 23; 3:16, 18 [twice], 36; 4:39; 6:29, 35, 40; 7:5, 31, 38, 39, 48; 8:30; 9:35, 36; 10:42; 11:25, 26, 45, 48; 12:11, 36, 37, 42, 44 [three times], 46; 14:1 [twice], 12; 16:9; 17:20; Acts 10:43; 14:23; 16:31; 19:4; 22:19; Rom. 4:5, 24; 10:14; Gal. 2:16; Phil. 1:29; 1 Pet. 1:8; 1 John 5:10 [twice], 13). The occurrences of πιστεύω, *pisteuō*, with the preposition εἰς, *eis*, are by far the most common construction to express the sinner's complete repose and reliance in Christ alone. But all these expressions of believing "in" or "upon" or "into" Jesus connote, at the very least, that one believes that Jesus always tells the truth and that what the Bible teaches about him is also always true, for saving faith necessarily entails believing propositional truths about him.

Such figurative expressions as *looking* to Jesus (compare Num. 21:9 and John 3:14–15), *eating* his flesh and *drinking* his blood (John 6:50–58; see also 4:14), and *receiving* him and *coming* to him (John 1:12; 5:40; 6:44, 65; 7:37–38) are also descriptive of the activity of faith in Christ.

Its Human Psychic Character

Some neoorthodox theologians, for example, Emil Brunner, Fredrich Gogarten, and Karl Barth, in their zeal to stress the transcendent, *sola gratia* character of faith, have denied that saving faith is a human psychic act at all. Faith "crosses over into the absolutely trans-subjective, is a negation of human activity, . . . falls outside the field of psychology," and "puts both feet on the other side of human experience" (Brunner). Faith "is not a neutral organ that accepts divine revelation; it 'belongs

---

31. See Gesenius-Kautzsch-Cowley, *Gesenius' Hebrew Grammar*, 2d ed. (Oxford: Clarendon, 1910), 145, 53e, which represents the Hiphil of this stem as expressing "the entering into a certain condition and further, the being in the same," and thus renders the verb as "to trust in."

itself to revelation.' It is not a function of 'this side' which takes to itself 'the other side'; 'it is itself something from the other side; it is a miracle' " (Gogarten). "Everything human in faith is 'unworthy of belief' . . . the new man is the *subject* of faith. But who is this subject, this new man? 'This subject is not I; in so far as it is a subject, in so far as it is what it is, namely absolutely objective, it is totally other and everything except what I am.' " "[F]aith is 'not an act of man, but the original, divine believing' " (Barth).[32] In sum, the correlation between faith and justification, for these thinkers, is no longer "human subjectivity (faith)–divine objectivity (justification)." There is only divine subjectivity; God does the believing.

Of course, faith in Jesus Christ is not a *natural* reaction to the gospel; it is not native to the depraved human heart. To this extent, these thinkers were correct. For as we have already urged, faith in Christ is the inevitable Spirit-wrought response by the elect to the gospel, an effect of the Holy Spirit's regenerating activity in conjunction with the ministry of the Word. But so conceived, it is still a human act. Just because man cannot in himself respond in saving faith to God's gracious overtures, the correlation between saving faith and divine promise, between saving faith and justification, between saving faith and sanctification, does not become thereby, in Berkouwer's words, "a divine monologue in which man is a mere telephone through which God addresses himself."[33] *It is the regenerated person, not God, who believes in Christ.* But in this regenerated person's justifying and sanctifying faith in Christ that the Spirit generates in his heart, the sovereignty of salvation's *sola gratia* is not spurned but affirmed. The miracle and the sovereignty of grace are still there.

The Instrumental Function of Faith

The Reformers saw that it is not faith *per se* that saves but Christ who saves through or by the instrumentality of the sinner's faith in him:

> The *saving power* of faith resides . . . not in itself, but in the Almighty Saviour on whom it rests. It is never on account of its formal nature as a psychic act that faith is conceived in Scripture to be saving,—as if this frame of mind or attitude of heart were itself a virtue with claims on God for reward. . . . It is not faith that saves, but faith in Jesus Christ. . . . It is not, strictly speaking, even faith in Christ that saves, but Christ that saves through faith. The saving power resides exclusively, not in the act of faith or the attitude of faith or the nature of faith, but in the object of faith; . . . we could not more radically misconceive

---

32. These citation from Brunner, Gogarten, and Barth are taken from G. C. Berkouwer, *Faith and Justification* (Grand Rapids, Mich.: Eerdmans, 1954), 172–75.
33. Ibid., 178–79.

[the biblical representation of faith] than by transferring to faith even the smallest fraction of that saving energy which is attributed in the Scriptures solely to Christ himself.[34]

The Reformers' clarity of vision respecting the instrumental function of faith with the real repository of salvific power being Christ himself and Christ alone resulted from their recognition that Scripture everywhere represents saving faith as (1) the gift of grace, (2) the diametrical opposite of law keeping with regard to its referent, and (3) the only human response to God's effectual summons which comports with grace. We will look at these characteristics of saving faith now.

Saving Faith's "Gift Character" As Procured by Christ's Cross Work and Effected by Regeneration

As is the case with repentance unto life, faith in Jesus Christ is represented in Scripture as a "saving grace," that is, as a saving *gift*. Saving faith, as with repentance unto life and "every [other] spiritual blessing in the heavenly realms," was divinely provided for in election (Eph. 1:3–4), procured for the elect by Christ's cross work, and actually wrought in them, as a second effect of his Spirit's regenerating activity, in conjunction with the ministry of the Word. The following Scripture verses put the "gift character" of saving faith beyond doubt:

Acts 13:46–48: Paul declared to the Jews of Pisidian Antioch, after they had blasphemed the Word of God: "since you repudiate it, and judge yourselves unworthy of eternal life, behold, we are turning to the Gentiles." Luke then reports that the Gentiles to whom Paul turned "began to rejoice and glorify the Word of the Lord, and as many as *were appointed* [ἦσαν τεταγμένοι, *ēsan tetagmenoi*] unto eternal life believed."

Luke teaches here that, unlike the blaspheming Jews who repudiated the Word of God and *judged themselves unworthy* of eternal life (reflexive action), the reception of the Word of God by the believing Gentiles was due to the fact that they *had been appointed* unto eternal life (passive voice). When this passive voice is interpreted actively, it is apparent that Luke traced the Gentiles' believing reception of the Word of God back to their divine election as the ultimate source from which their faith originated.

Acts 16:14: "The Lord opened [Lydia's] heart to respond to the things spoken by Paul." Clearly, Lydia's heart response to Paul's word was a faith response, but it was prompted by the Lord's regenerating work of "opening" or enlightening her heart to it.

---

34. Warfield, "Faith," in *Biblical and Theological Studies* (Philadelphia: Presbyterian and Reformed, 1952), 424–25.

Acts 18:27: Apollos "helped greatly those who had believed through grace."

Ephesians 2:8–9: To the Ephesians Paul writes: "by grace you have been saved through faith—and this [τοῦτο, *touto*] not of yourselves, it is the gift of God—not of works, lest any man should boast." Even though "faith" is a feminine noun in the Greek and "this" is a neuter demonstrative pronoun, it is still entirely possible that Paul intended to teach that "faith," the nearest possible antecedent, is the antecedent of the pronoun "this," and accordingly that saving faith is the gift of God. It is permissible in Greek syntax for the neuter pronoun to refer antecedently to a feminine noun, particularly when it serves to render more prominent the matter previously referred to (see, for example, "your salvation [σωτηρίας, *sōtērias*], and this [τοῦτο, *touto*] from God"—Phil. 1:28; see also 1 Cor. 6:6, 8).[35] The only other possible antecedents to the τοῦτο, *touto*, are (1) the earlier feminine dative noun "grace" (χάριτί, *chariti*) which hardly needs to be defined as a "gift of God," (2) the nominal idea of "salvation" (σωτηρία, *sōtēria*) implied in the verbal idea "you have been saved," which Paul has already implied is a gift by his use of χάριτί, *chariti*, and like "grace" (χάριτί, *chariti*) and "faith" (πίστεως, *pisteōs*) is also feminine in Greek, or (3) the entire preceding notion of "salvation by grace through faith," which, of course, amounts to saying that faith, along with grace and salvation, is the gift of God.[36] However the text is exegeted, when all of its features are taken into account, the conclusion is unavoidable that faith in Jesus Christ is a gift of God.

Philippians 1:29: To the Philippians Paul writes: "to you *it has been given* [ἐχαρίσθη, *echaristhē*] on behalf of Christ . . . to believe on him."

Saving Faith's Character as the Diametrical Opposite of Law-Keeping

With a gloriously monotonous regularity Paul pits faith off over against all law-keeping as its diametrical opposite as to referent. Whereas the latter relies on the human effort of the law-keeper *looking to himself* to render satisfaction before God, the former repudiates and *looks entirely away from all human effort* to the cross work of Jesus Christ, who alone by his sacrificial death rendered satisfaction before God for men.

---

35. See Abraham Kuyper, *The Work of the Holy Spirit*, trans. H. deVries (Grand Rapids, Mich.: Eerdmans, 1946), chapter 39, 407–14, for his argument supporting this understanding of Ephesians 2:8–9.

36. A. T. Robertson, *A Grammar of the Greek New Testament in the Light of Historical Research* (Nashville, Tenn.: Broadman, 1934), 704, urges that the demonstrative pronoun refers to "the idea of salvation" in the clause before it.

Romans 3:20–22: "No one will be declared righteous in his sight by observing the law.... But now a righteousness from God, apart from law, has been made known.... This righteousness from God comes through faith in Jesus Christ to all who believe."

Romans 3:28: "For we maintain that a man is justified by faith apart from works of the law."

Romans 4:5: "To the man who does not work but trusts God who justifies the wicked, his faith is credited as righteousness."

Romans 4:14: "For if those who are of the Law are heirs [of Abraham], faith has been made void."

Romans 10:4: "For Christ is the end of the Law for righteousness for all who believe."

Galatians 2:16: "A man is not justified by works of the law but through faith in Jesus Christ."

Galatians 3:11: "That by the Law no man is justified before God is evident, because 'The righteous by faith shall live.' "

Philippians 3:9: "Not having my own righteousness which is by the Law but the [righteousness] which is through faith in Christ." (See also Rom. 3:20; 4:2; Gal. 2:20–21; 5:4; Titus 3:5).

From such verses it is plain that Paul taught that justification is by "faith alone" (*sola fide*). The Roman Catholic Church has always objected to the use of this *sola* ("alone") attached to *fide*, contending that nowhere does Paul say "alone" when speaking of the faith that justifies, and that where the Bible does attach *sola* to *fide* when speaking of justification it declares: "You see that a person is justified by what he does and *not* by faith alone" (James 2:24). All this is true enough, but I would insist, as the above citations indicate, that when Paul declares (1) that a man is justified "by faith apart from [χωρὶς, *chōris*] works of the law," (2) that the man "who works not but believes in him who justifies the ungodly" is the man whom God regards as righteous, (3) that a man is "not justified by works of the law but through faith," and (4) that "by the Law no man is justified before God ... because 'The righteous by faith shall live,' " he is asserting the "aloneness" of faith as the "alone" instrument of justification as surely as if he had used the word "alone," and he is asserting it even more vigorously than if he had simply employed μόνος, *monos* ("alone") each time. Martin Luther replied to the criticism that the word "alone" does not appear in Romans:

> Note ... whether Paul does not assert more vehemently that faith alone justifies than I do, although he does not use the word *alone* (*sola*), which I have used. For

he who says: Works do not justify, but faith justifies, certainly affirms more strongly that faith justifies than does he who says: Faith alone justifies.... Since the apostle does not ascribe anything to [works], he without doubt ascribes all to faith alone.[37]

John Calvin too, while acknowledging that μόνος, *monos,* does not appear in Paul's exposition of justification, urges that the thought is nonetheless there:

> Now the reader sees how fairly the Sophists today cavil against our doctrine, when we say that man is justified by faith alone. They dare not deny that man is justified by faith because it recurs so often in Scripture. But since the word "alone" is nowhere expressed, they do not allow this addition to be made. Is it so? But what will they reply to these words of Paul where he contends that righteousness cannot be of faith unless it be free? How will a free gift agree with works? ... Does not he who takes everything from works firmly enough ascribe everything to faith alone. What, I pray, do these expressions mean: "His righteousness has been manifested apart from the law"; and, "Man is freely justified"; and, "Apart from the works of the law"?[38]

Since Paul never represents faith as a good work—indeed, since Paul always sets faith off over against works as the receiving and resting upon what God has done for us in Christ and freely offers to us—then it is by faith alone that sinners are justified.[39]

---

37. Martin Luther, *What Luther Says,* ed. Ewald M. Plass (St. Louis: Concordia, 1959), 2:707–8.
38. John Calvin, *Institutes of the Christian Religion,* trans. Ford Lewis Battles (Philadelphia: Westminster Press, 1960), III.xi.19. For an explanation of James 2:24, see the section on justification.
39. The programmatic statement, "Evangelicals and Catholics Together: The Christian Mission in the Third Millennium," which appeared in the May 1994 issue of *First Things,* marginalizes the many stark theological differences that exist between Protestant Christianity and Roman Catholicism when its authors affirm their agreement on the Apostles' Creed and on the proposition that "we are justified by grace through faith because of Christ" (section one) and then on this "confessional" basis call for an end to proselytizing each other's communicants and for a missiological ecumenism which cooperates together in evangelism and spiritual nurture (section five).

The word "alone" after the word "faith" in the statement's proposition on justification is thundering by its absence. As written, the statement is a capitulation to Catholicism's unscriptural understanding of justification, for never in the debate between Rome and the first Protestant Reformers did anyone on either side deny that sinners must be justified by faith. The whole controversy in the sixteenth century in this area turned on whether sinners were justified by faith *alone* or by faith *and* good works which earned merit before God. The Protestant Reformers, following Paul (compare his entire argument in Galatians), maintained that Rome's understanding was "another gospel which is no gospel at all" and that the path the sinner follows here leads either to heaven or to hell.

Saving Faith's Character as Alone Comporting with Salvation by Grace

Paul is explicit that if salvation is to be effected by God's grace (undeserved favor), it can only be by faith, whose nature as a psychic act looks away from the native human resources of the one believing to the Savior's work of satisfaction.

> Romans 4:16: "[God's promise to Abraham] is of faith, in order that it may be according to grace."
>
> Romans 11:6: "And if [a saved Jewish remnant] is by grace, it is no more by works [which "works" for Paul is opposed to faith]; otherwise, grace is no more grace."
>
> Galatians 5:4: "you . . . who are justified by the Law [which is the diametrical opposite of being justified by faith], from grace you have fallen."

I recall on one occasion hearing a well-known preacher say: "I don't know why salvation is by faith in Jesus Christ. God just declared that that is the way it is going to be, and we have to accept it because God said it." I was shocked, because this preacher should have known why salvation is by faith. He should have known because Paul told him: "[Salvation] is of faith [apart from works], in order that it may be according to grace" (Rom. 4:16). If God were to permit the intrusion of human works into the acquisition of salvation to any degree, salvation could not be by grace alone. Salvation by grace and salvation by works are mutually and totally exclusive. In sum, because salvation is by grace, it must be by faith in Jesus Christ, the nature of which faith is to turn totally away from one's own works to the work of another in one's behalf.

Summary of the Doctrine

"Faith in Jesus Christ is a saving grace, whereby we receive and rest upon him alone for salvation, as he is offered to us in the gospel" (Shorter Catechism, Question 86). Along with repentance unto life, it is the divinely effected human response to God's effectual summons of the elect sinner into fellowship with his Son. It is effected, as is true repentance as well, normally in conjunction with the ministry of the Word of God and by the regenerating operations of God the Holy Spirit in the human spirit.

Because of (1) God's *universal command* issued to all men to repent (Acts 17:30), (2) his *universal invitation* extended to all men to come to him in and by faith (Isa. 45:22;

See R. C. Sproul, "Only One Gospel," in *The Coming Evangelical Crisis*, ed. John H. Armstrong (Chicago: Moody, 1996), 107–17.

Matt. 11:28; Rev. 22:17), and (3) the *all-sufficiency of Christ's cross work* to save sinners, no sinner need fear that Christ will refuse to save him or not be able to save him if he repents and comes to him. In these great gospel verities resides the guarantee that Christ is able and willing to save *every* sinner who repents and believes.

As soon as the sinner, in response to God's effectual summons, turns from his sin and places his confidence in Jesus Christ and his vicarious cross work, "thereby uniting [him] to Christ in [his] effectual calling" (Shorter Catechism, Question 30), God the Father immediately does three things: he justifies him, definitively sanctifies him, and adopts him into his family. Each of these divine acts requires some exposition. But before we discuss the great benefits that "they that are effectually called do in this life partake of" (Shorter Catechism, Question 32), something must first be said about the nature of the Christian's union with Christ through faith.

UNION WITH CHRIST

In connection with the discussion on effectual calling, I urged that through faith in Christ the sinner who was chosen "in Christ" from all eternity is *actually* united to Christ. This comports with the Shorter Catechism statement that "the Spirit applieth to us the redemption purchased by Christ, by working faith in us, and thereby uniting us to Christ in our effectual calling" (Question 30), and provides the rationale for treating our union with Christ at this point in the *ordo*. As we saw there, this is in contradistinction to Murray's insistence that it is effectual calling that *actually* unites one to Christ and that it is this union with Christ which then unites one to the inwardly operative grace of regeneration that enables the sinner to repent and to believe.

Murray is certainly correct, however, when he insists that the "in Christ" (ἐν Χριστῷ, *en Christo*) relationship between Christ and the elect individual does not first come into existence when the sinner places his faith in Christ. Rather, it is an all-embracive relationship in its soteric references, which God takes up into and includes within all that he has done, is doing, and will do in behalf of the sinner (see Eph. 1:3: "every spiritual blessing in the heavenly realms in Christ").

The Biblical Data

We have first the Scripture's own explicit statements to this effect, among which are the following representative texts:

Ephesians 1:4: "[The Father] chose us in him [ἐν αὐτῷ, *en auto*] before the foundation of the world." As Murray observes, this verse teaches that "those who will be saved were not even contemplated by the Father in the ultimate counsel of his predestinating love apart from union with Christ—they were *chosen* in Christ. As far back as we can go in tracing salvation to its fountain we find 'union with Christ'; it is not something tacked on; it is there from the outset."[40]

Though this is true, the Scriptures will not permit us to believe that, because God elected certain people in Christ from all eternity, they have therefore always enjoyed the fullness of his favor in history and that for them there is no transition from wrath to grace in history. The Scriptures take the reality of creation, the historical Fall, and history itself with total seriousness and never stress the eternal election of God to such an extent that it reduces to zero significance the reality of creation and creation's history, which God providentially orders and governs to his own holy ends. To the contrary, though they are eternally loved "according to election," until the elect trust Christ as their Savior, they are *actually* "by nature children of wrath" (Eph. 2:3) and are "separate from Christ . . . without hope and without God in the world" (Eph. 2:12).[41] It is only when they are brought to faith in Christ by their effectual calling that the elect *actually* become partakers of Christ and of the salvific blessings of his cross work. As with the nation of Israel, so all the elect, though "beloved according to election," are God's "enemies according to the gospel" until they repent and trust his Son.

> Romans 6:6: "We know that our old man was crucified with him." Here Paul speaks of the believer's union with Christ in his death.
>
> Romans 6:5: "If we have been united with him in the likeness of his death, we will certainly also be united with him in his resurrection." Here Paul speaks of the believer's union with Christ in his resurrection (see also Eph. 2:6).
>
> Ephesians 1:6–7: "In the Beloved, in whom we have redemption through his blood, even the forgiveness of trespasses." It is "in Christ," Paul announces here, that we have redemption and forgiveness.
>
> Ephesians 2:10: "For we are God's workmanship, created in Christ Jesus." Here Paul relates the genesis of redemption's application to the sinner to the "in Christ" relationship.
>
> Ephesians 1:13: "Having also believed, you were sealed in him with the Holy Spirit of promise."
>
> 1 Corinthians 1:5: "For in him you have been enriched in every way—in all your speaking and in all your knowledge." Here Paul relates the Christian's *sanctification* to the "in Christ" relationship (see also John 15:4; 1 John 2:5–6).

---

40. Murray, *Redemption—Accomplished and Applied*, 162.
41. See Romans 11:28, where Paul can say of the Jewish race that they are both "from the standpoint of election beloved [by God]" and "from the standpoint of the gospel [God's declared] enemies," and both at the same time.

Romans 5:10: "How much more, having been reconciled, shall we be saved in his life." Here Paul relates the Christian's security for both this age and the age to come to the "in Christ" relationship.

1 Thessalonians 4:14, 16: "God will bring with Jesus those who have fallen asleep in him . . . and the dead in Christ will rise first." If anything points up the indissolubility and continuance of the Christian's union with Christ it is the fact that *even in death* his body, "being still united to Christ, rests in Christ in its grave until the resurrection."

1 Corinthians 15:22: "In Christ all will be made alive." It is in Christ that the Christian will be raised from the dead in the Eschaton.

Romans 8:17: "In order that we may be glorified with him." It is with Christ that Christians are finally glorified.

From just these few representative references it is plain that union with Christ "embraces the wide span of salvation from its ultimate source in the eternal election of God to its final fruition in the glorification of the elect. It is not simply a phase of the application of redemption; it underlies every aspect of redemption both in its accomplishment and in its application."[42]

The Scriptures offer several striking *figures* to illustrate the believer's union with Christ, such as (1) the relationship between stones in a building (believers) and the building's chief cornerstone (Christ) (Eph. 2:19–22; 1 Pet. 2:4–5), (2) the relationship between branches of a vine (believers) and the main vine itself (Christ) (John 15:1–8), (3) the relationship between members of a body (believers) and the body's head (Christ) (Eph. 4:15–16), (4) the relationship between a wife (believers) and a husband (Christ) (Eph. 5:22–23), (5) the covenantal (federal) relationship between the race which descended from Adam by ordinary generation and Adam himself (Rom. 5:12–19; 1 Cor. 15:22, 48–49), and (6) even the relationship which exists between the persons of the Godhead (John 14:23; 17:21–23)!

The Reality of the Union

In light of the fact that the believer's union with Christ is eminently "spiritual and mystical" (Larger Catechism, Question 66), which is to say that the bond of that union is of and by the Holy Spirit himself and thus apprehended by the human intelligence only in the Word/faith construct, its reality might be doubted. But the Scriptures make it clear that, though it is spiritual and mystical, this nonmaterial union with Christ is as real as though there were in fact a literal umbilical cord uniting them, reaching "all the way" from Christ in heaven to the believer on earth.

---

42. Murray, *Redemption—Accomplished and Applied,* 165.

Since the Christian's very existence as a Christian as well as his growth in grace (Rom. 6:1–14) and his hope of glory (Col. 1:27) are all grounded in his spiritual union with Christ, from whom he derives all his strength and power to live the Christian life (2 Cor. 12:9), to deny or to ignore one's union with Christ is not only to deny or to ignore a cardinal aspect of the Christian life but also to open the way to soul blight and a stunting of the Christian's growth in grace. On the other hand, sin will not reign as king in the life of the Christian who by virtue of his union in Christ's death to sin self-consciously knows and seriously regards himself as dead to sin and alive to God in Christ Jesus (Rom. 6:10–14). Herein lies the significance of the Christian's union with Christ for the Christian's daily walk.

Summary of the Doctrine

Union with Christ is the fountainhead from which flows the Christian's every spiritual blessing—repentance and faith, pardon, justification, adoption, sanctification, perseverance, and glorification. Chosen in Christ before the creation of the world, and *in the divine mind* united with Christ in his death and resurrection, the elect, in response to God's effectual call, are through God's gift of faith *actually* united to Christ. Their union with Christ is in no sense the effect of human causation. "The union which the elect have with Christ is the work of God's grace, whereby they are spiritually and mystically, yet really and inseparably, joined to Christ as their head and husband" (Larger Catechism, Question 66). By virtue of his actual union with Christ the Husband in his death and resurrection, the Christian, as Christ's "bride," is forgiven of his sin and liberated from the law—his previous "husband"—and made capable of doing that which he could never do before, namely, "bear holy fruit to God" (Rom. 7:4–5). To the degree that the Christian "reckons himself dead to sin but alive to God in Christ Jesus" (Rom. 6:11), that is to say, to the degree that the Christian takes seriously the reality of his Spirit-wrought union with Christ, to that degree he will find his definitive sanctification coming to actual expression in his experiential or progressive sanctification. The holiness of the Christian's daily walk directly depends upon his union with the Savior.

Three Divine Acts

JUSTIFICATION

Those whom God effectually calleth, He also freely justifieth: not by infusing righteousness into them, but by pardoning their sins, and by accounting and accepting their persons as righteous; not for anything wrought in them, or done by them, but for Christ's sake alone; nor by imputing faith itself, the act of believing, or any other evangelical obedience to them, as their righteousness; but by imputing the obedience and satisfaction of Christ unto them, they receiving and resting on Him and His righteousness, by faith; which faith they have not of themselves, it is the gift of God.

Faith, thus receiving and resting on Christ and His righteousness, is the alone instrument of justification: yet is it not alone in the person justified, but is ever accompanied with all other saving graces, and is no dead faith, but worketh by love.

Christ, by His obedience and death, did fully discharge the debt of all those that are thus justified, and did make a proper, real, and full satisfaction to His Father's justice in their behalf. Yet, inasmuch as He was given by the Father for them; and His obedience and satisfaction accepted in their stead; and both, freely, not for anything in them; their justification is only of free grace; that both the exact justice and rich grace of God might be glorified in the justification of sinners.

God did, from all eternity, decree to justify all the elect, and Christ did, in the fulness of time, die for their sins, and rise again for their justification: nevertheless, they are not justified, until the Holy Spirit doth, in due time, actually apply Christ unto them.

God doth continue to forgive the sins of those that are justified; and, although they can never fall from the state of justification, yet they may, by their sins, fall under God's fatherly displeasure, and not have the light of His countenance restored unto them, until they humble themselves, confess their sins, beg pardon, and renew their faith and repentance.

The justification of believers under the old testament was, in all these respects, one and the same with the justification of believers under the new testament. (Westminster Confession of Faith, XI/i–vi)

The doctrine of justification is the heart and core of the gospel, the "good news" that God by grace alone justifies sinners through faith alone in Christ alone apart from the works of the law. This centrality of justification by faith alone is evident by the fact that when Paul begins to elucidate the "gospel of God," declaring that "in the gospel a righteousness from God is revealed, a righteousness that is by faith, from first to last" (Rom. 1:17; see also Gal. 3:8), he does so in terms of justification by faith.[43] Consequently, great care must be taken in teaching this doctrine lest one wind up declaring "another gospel," which actually is not a gospel at all. To illustrate, one occasionally hears justification popularly defined as God "looking at me just as if I'd never sinned." This is an example of a (very) partial truth becoming virtually an untruth,

---

43. The word "Gospels" is used to designate the four inspired "lives of Jesus" which serve (with Acts) as something of a "historical prologue" for the New Testament viewed as a covenant document. These books primarily provide in their inspired portrayals of the life of Christ the *historical* basis for *something else* that the New Testament calls the "gospel of God," namely, the good news to mankind regarding the salvific significance of Christ's life, death, and resurrection.

since nothing is said in such a definition concerning the ground of justification or the instrumentality through which justification is obtained. Much more accurately, the Shorter Catechism defines justification as "an act of God's free grace, wherein he pardoneth all our sins, and accepteth us as righteous in his sight, only for the righteousness of Christ, imputed to us, and received by faith alone" (Question 33).

Thus defined over against Rome's tragically defective representation,[44] justification *per se* says nothing about the subjective transformation that necessar-

---

44. The *Catechism of the Catholic Church* (1994), citing the Council of Trent (Sixth Session, Chapter VII, 1547), declares: "Justification is not only the remission of sins, but also *the sanctification and renewal of the interior man*" (para. 1989, emphasis supplied). It also states: "Justification is conferred in Baptism" and by it God *"makes us inwardly just* by the power of his mercy" (para. 1992, emphasis supplied).

In his review of R. C. Sproul's *Faith Alone: The Evangelical Doctrine of Justification* (Grand Rapids, Mich.: Baker, 1995), which appeared in *Christianity Today* (October 7, 1996) under the title "Betraying the Reformation? An Evangelical Response," Donald G. Bloesch takes issue with Sproul because he "does not appear to have kept abreast of the noteworthy attempts in the ongoing ecumenical discussion to bridge the chasm between Trent and evangelical Protestantism" (54). To illustrate this rapprochement, Bloesch notes that an increasing number of Roman Catholic scholars, especially in biblical studies, are coming to acknowledge the forensic or legal thrust of the New Testament concept of justification while Protestant scholars are now recognizing that justification also has a mystical dimension and is therefore more than bare imputation. (54)

Then he faults Sproul for too-narrowly conceiving the options which are possible in any Roman Catholic-Protestant dialogue. Sproul would allow for only three ways forward in the discussion: (1) evangelicals would abandon *sola fide,* (2) Rome would adopt *sola fide,* and (3) the two sides would agree that *sola fide* is not essential to the gospel. Bloesch writes, "Yet there may be another option: to restate the issues of the past in a new way that takes into account both God's sovereign grace and human responsibility in living a life of obedience in the power of this grace" (55).

But Sproul does in fact make numerous references to the 1994 *Catechism of the Catholic Church,* the most recent *official* Roman Catholic statement on justification. More recent ecumenical discussions have not received official papal approval. And the 1983 document "Justification by Faith," which Bloesch alludes to as showing "new ways of stating the doctrine of justification without compromising the tenets of either Reformation or Catholic faith" (54), fails in my opinion to resolve the tension between the parties over the issue: Is justification by faith in Christ's work alone or is it by faith in Christ's work plus something that the justified man must do? (see *Justification by Faith: Lutherans and Catholics in Dialogue VII,* ed. H. George Anderson, T. Austin Murphy, and Joseph A. Burgess (Minneapolis: Augsburg, 1985).

I would also like to know what the "mystical dimension" in justification is, and I wonder who the evangelical theologians are who represent justification as "bare imputation." Not I, and I think not Sproul either.

Finally, I would concur with Sproul that there are only three options. As soon as Bloesch attempts to suggest a fourth, he misrepresents what the issue dividing Protestantism and Rome really is and brings the doctrine of sanctification into the doctrine of justification, which is to ask Protestantism to abandon its *sola fide* position and to adopt Rome's position.

ily begins to occur within the inner life of the Christian through the progressive infusion of grace that commences with the new birth (which subjective transformation Scripture views as progressive sanctification). Rather, justification refers to God's *wholly* objective, *wholly* forensic judgment concerning the sinner's standing before the law, by which forensic judgment God declares that the sinner is righteous in his sight because of the imputation of his sin to Christ, on which ground he is pardoned, and the imputation of Christ's perfect obedience to him, on which ground he is constituted righteous before God. In other words, "for the one who does not work, but believes in him[45] who justifies the ungodly" (Rom. 4:5),[46] God *pardons* him of all his sins (Acts 10:43; Rom. 4:6–7)[47] and *constitutes* him righteous by imputing or reckoning the righteousness of Christ to him (Rom. 5:1, 19; 2 Cor. 5:21).[48] And on the basis of his constituting the ungodly man righteous by his act of imputation, God simultaneously *declares* the ungodly man to be righteous in his sight. The now-justified ungodly man is then, to employ Luther's expression, *simul iustus et peccator* ("simultaneously righteous and sinner").

The doctrine of justification means then that in God's sight the ungodly man, now "in Christ," has perfectly kept the moral law of God, which also means in turn that "in Christ" he has perfectly loved God with all his heart, soul, mind, and strength and his neighbor as himself. It means that saving faith is directed to the doing and dying of Christ alone (*solus Christus*) and not to the good works or inner experience of the believer. It means that the Christian's righteousness before God is *in heaven* at the right hand of God in Jesus Christ and *not on earth* within the believer. It means that the ground of our justification is the vicarious work of Christ

---

45. It would be wrong to speak of the object of justifying faith as being Christ alone. Both in Romans 4:5 and in Romans 4:24 Paul declares that the object of saving faith is also the Father—the One who justifies the ungodly and who raised Jesus from the dead.
46. On the basis of Paul's statement in Romans 4:5 to the effect that God "justifies the ungodly"—the same Greek phrase used in the LXX in Exodus 23:7 and Isaiah 5:23 of corrupt judgments on the part of human judges which God will not tolerate—J. I. Packer declares that Paul's doctrine of justification is a "startling doctrine" ("Justification," *Evangelical Dictionary of Theology*, 595). For not only does Paul declare that God does precisely what he commanded human judges not to do, but he also declares that he does it in a manner designed precisely "to demonstrate his justice" (Rom. 3:25–26). Paul relieves what otherwise would be a problem of theodicy by teaching that God justifies the ungodly on *just* grounds, namely, that the claims of God's law upon them have been fully satisfied by Jesus Christ's doing and dying in their stead.
47. See Acts 10:43: "everyone who believes in him receives forgiveness of sins," and Romans 4:6–7: "David says the same thing when he speaks of the blessedness of the man to whom God credits righteousness apart from works: 'Blessed are they whose transgressions are forgiven and whose sins are covered.' "
48. See Romans 5:1:"having been justified by faith," and 5:19: "so also through the obedience of the One Man the many shall be constituted righteous" (author's translation).

for us, not the gracious work of the Spirit *in* us. It means that the faith-righteousness of justification is not personal but vicarious, not infused but imputed, not experiential but judicial, not psychological but legal, not our own but a righteousness alien to us and outside of us (*iustitia alienum et extra nos*), not earned but graciously given (*sola gratia*) through faith in Christ that is itself a gift of grace. It means also in its declarative character that justification possesses an eschatological dimension, for it amounts to the divine verdict of the Eschaton being brought forward into the present time and rendered here and now concerning the believing sinner. By God's act of justifying the sinner through faith in Christ, the sinner, as it were, has been brought, "before the time," to the Final Assize and has already passed successfully through it, having been acquitted of any and all charges brought against him! Justification then, properly conceived, contributes in a decisive way to the Calvinistic doctrine of assurance and the eternal security of the believer. Let us now look in greater detail at some of the specific features of justification.

Its Character as a Legal Judgment

The primary Old Testament word-group dealing with justification comes from the verb root צָדַק, *ṣādaq*, and the New Testament word-group comes from the verb δικαιόω, *dikaioō*. Murray demonstrates that "there is a pervasive use of the forensic signification of the root צָדַק [*ṣādaq*] in the Qal, Hiphil, and Piel stems and the one instance of the Hithpael ... is not essentially different,"[49] and that the same is true of δικαιόω, *dikaioō*, in both the Septuagint and the New Testament.[50] Leon Morris points out that "verbs ending in -όω [-*oō*] and referring to moral qualities have a declarative sense; they do not mean "to make___.""[51]

That justification is an objective forensic judgment, as opposed to a subjective transformation, is evidenced, first, by the meaning of the term itself in the following contexts:

> Deuteronomy 25:1: "If there is a dispute between men and they go to court, and the judges decide their case, then they shall justify [Hiphil] the righteous and condemn the wicked." In justifying the righteous man, the judges were not making the

---

49. Murray, "Appendix A: Justification," in *The Epistle to the Romans*, 1:336–62, especially 339. Murray's treatment of justification in this appendix is one of the finest available in English.
50. Ibid., 1:339–40, 351.
51. Leon Morris, *New Testament Theology* (Grand Rapids, Mich.: Academie, 1986), 70. Compare ἀξιόω, *axioō*, "to deem worthy," not "to make worthy"; ὁμοιόω, *homoioō*, "to declare to be like," not "to make like."

man righteous; rather, they were declaring him to be what the evidence presented in the case demanded, and what he in fact was.

Job 32:2: According to Elihu, Job "justified [Piel] himself before God." In Elihu's opinion, Job was arguing his innocence before God, that is, declaring himself righteous before God.

Proverbs 17:15: "He who justifies [Hiphil] the wicked, and he who condemns the righteous, both of them alike are an abomination to the Lord" (see also Exod. 23:7; Isa. 5:23). This is obviously a proverb directed toward the judges of the land. That judge who for bribe (see Prov. 17:23) declared the wicked man to be righteous or the righteous man to be guilty provoked the Lord to anger.

Luke 7:29: "they justified God," that is, they declared or acknowledged God to be just; they quite obviously did not make him so (see also 10:29; 16:15).

That justification is an objective forensic judgment, as opposed to a subjective transformation, is evidenced, second, by the fact that the antithesis of justification is invariably condemnation, which latter term is clearly a juridical or forensic determination; for example:

Deuteronomy 25:1: "They shall justify the righteous and condemn the wicked." (see also Prov. 17:15)

1 Kings 8:32: "Judge your servants, condemning the wicked . . . and justifying the righteous." (see also 2 Chron. 6:23)

Matthew 12:37: "For by your words you shall be justified and by your words you shall be condemned."

Romans 5:16: The judgment arose from one transgression resulting in condemnation, but . . . the free gift arose from many transgressions resulting in justification."

Romans 8:33–34: "God is the One who justifies; who is the one who condemns?"

That justification is an objective forensic judgment, as opposed to a subjective transformation, is evidenced, third, by contextual considerations which place the act of justifying in the context of legal judgments. For example:

Psalm 143:2: "Do not enter into judgment with your servant, for in your sight no man living shall be righteous [that is, shall be justified]."

Romans 3:19–20: "Now we know that whatever the Law says, it speaks to those who are under the Law, that every mouth may be closed, and all the world may become accountable to God; because by the works of the Law no flesh will be justified [that is, declared righteous] in his sight."

Romans 8:33: "Who will bring a charge against God's elect? God is the one who justifies."[52]

This biblical evidence makes it clear that justification is a juridical or forensic determination made by a judge.

The Righteousness of Justification

Some have construed the righteousness contemplated in justification as the psychic act of faith itself in Christ and have insisted that Genesis 15:6 teaches this: "Abram believed the Lord, and he credited it [that is, his faith] to him as righteousness" (see also Rom. 4:3, 5, 9, 22, 23; Gal. 3:6; James 2:23). Never is *our* faith-act, however, represented in the New Testament as the ground or the cause of our righteousness. If this were so, faith would become a meritorious work, an idea everywhere opposed by the Apostle Paul who pits faith in Christ over against every human work. We are said to be justified "by faith" (the simple dative—Rom. 3:28, 5:2), "by faith" (ἐκ, *ek*, with the genitive—Rom. 1:17; 3:30; 4:16 (twice), 5:1; 9:30; 10:6; Gal. 2:16; 3:8, 11, 24; Heb. 10:38), "through faith" (διά, *dia*, with the genitive—Rom. 3:22, 25, 30; Gal. 2:16; Phil. 3:9), "upon faith" (ἐπί, *epi*, with the genitive—Phil. 3:9), and "according to faith" (κατά, *kata*, with the accusative—Heb. 11:7). But never are we said to be justified "because of faith" or "on account of faith" (διά, *dia*, with the accusative). In other words, the psychic act of faith is not the righteousness of justification. That distinction the Scriptures reserve for Christ's God-righteousness alone. Faith in Christ is simply the regenerated sinner's saving response to God's effectual summons, by means of which the righteousness of Christ—the sole ground of justification—is imputed to him. Murray observes in this connection:

> The consideration that appears more relevant than any other [when interpreting the Genesis 15:6 formula] is that the righteousness contemplated in justification is righteousness by faith in contrast with righteousness by works and the emphasis falls to such an extent upon this fact that although it is a God-righteousness yet it is also and with equal emphasis a faith-righteousness. In reality these two features are correlative: it is the righteousness of God brought to bear upon us because it is by faith, and it is by faith that we become the beneficiaries of this righteousness because it is a God-righteousness. So indispensable is this complementation in the justification of the ungodly that the righteousness may be called "the righteousness of God" or "the righteousness of faith" without in the least implying that faith sustains the same relation to this righteousness that God does.

---

52. See Berkhof's discussion, *Systematic Theology*, 510–11.

In like manner in the formula of Gen. 15:6 faith can be regarded as that which is reckoned for righteousness without thereby implying that it sustains the same relation to justification as does the righteousness of God. The righteousness is a God-righteousness and it is a faith-righteousness. But it is a God-righteousness because it is of divine property; it is a faith righteousness because it is brought to bear upon us *by faith*. When faith is said to be imputed for righteousness this variation of formula is warranted by the correlativity of righteousness and faith, and it is in terms of this correlativity that the formula is to be interpreted rather than in terms of equation.[53]

Over against Rome's polemic that the righteousness of justification is to be construed in terms of "sanctification and renewal of the inward man," that is, in terms of the Christian's "being inwardly made increasingly righteous" through the impartation or infusion of sanctifying grace[54] stands the consentient biblical (and Protestant) insistence that the righteousness of justification is neither a righteousness which comes through any efforts on our part nor a righteousness infused or generated in us by the Holy Spirit. Rather, the righteousness of justification, as we have already said, is the objective God-righteousness of Jesus Christ, which God the Father, in the very act of justifying the ungodly, *imputes* to him, thereby *constituting* him legally righteous in his sight (which "constituting" act, of course, no human judge can do when a guilty party stands before him).

That the righteousness of justification is the God-righteousness of the divine Christ himself, which is imputed or reckoned to us *the moment* we place our confidence in him (see justification as a finished act in Rom. 5:1—*"having been justified"*), is amply testified to when the Scriptures teach that we are justified (1) *in Christ* (Isa. 45:24–25; Acts 13:39; Rom. 8:1; 1 Cor. 6:11; Gal. 2:17; Phil. 3:9), (2) *by Christ's death work* (Rom. 3:24–25; 5:9; 8:33–34), (3) not by our own but *by the righteousness of God* (Isa. 61:10; Rom. 1:17; 3:21–22; 10:3; 2 Cor. 5:21; Phil. 3:9) and (4) *by the righteousness and obedience of Christ* (Rom. 5:17–19). In short, the only ground of justification

---

53. Murray, *Collected Writings*, 2:358–59.
54. See Council of Trent, Sixth Session: "Decree Concerning Justification," particularly chapters seven to ten and canons nine to twelve. In accord with the medieval Schoolmen such as Thomas Aquinas, the *Catechism of the Catholic Church* (1994), citing Trent, defines justification as "not only the remission of sins [by baptism] but also the sanctification and renewal of the interior man" (para. 1989), and by justification, the reader is informed, God "makes us inwardly just" (para. 1992); indeed, justification "entails the *sanctification* of [the inner man's] whole being" (para. 1995, emphasis in original).

John H. Gerstner ("Aquinas Was a Protestant," *Tabletalk* [May 1994]: 13–15, 52) has argued that Aquinas held to a Protestant view of justification. For a response to this, see Robert L. Reymond, "Dr. John H. Gerstner on Thomas Aquinas as a Protestant," *Westminster Theological Journal* 59, no. 1 (1997):113–21.

is the perfect God-righteousness of Christ that God the Father imputes to every sinner who places his confidence in the obedience and satisfaction of his Son. Said another way, the moment the sinner, through faith in Jesus Christ, turns away from every human resource and rests in Christ alone, the Father imputes his well-beloved Son's preceptive (active) obedience to him and accepts him as righteous in his sight. And the sinner, now a Christian, may (and as far as his righteousness before God is concerned he must) sing thereafter, in the words of Horatius Bonar:

> Not what my hands have done
>   can save my guilty soul;
> Not what my toiling flesh
>   has borne can make my spirit whole.
>
> Not what I feel or do
>   can give me peace with God;
> Not all my prayers and sighs and tears
>   can bear my awful load.
>
> Thy work alone, O Christ,
>   can ease this weight of sin;
> Thy blood alone, O Lamb of God,
>   can give me peace within.
>
> No other work, save thine,
>   no other blood will do;
> No strength, save that which is divine,
>   can bear me safely through.

And with Nikolaus Ludwig von Zinzendorf:

> Jesus, thy blood and righteousness
>   my beauty are, my glorious dress;
> 'Midst flaming worlds, in these arrayed,
>   with joy shall I lift up my head.
>
> Bold shall I stand in thy great day;
>   for who aught to my charge shall lay?
> Fully absolved through these I am,
>   from sin and fear, from guilt and shame.

Objections to the Protestant Doctrine

The following six objections have been raised against the Protestant teaching that by faith alone in Christ alone, completely apart from the works of the law, God immediately pardons the ungodly person of all his sins and constitutes him righteous in his sight by imputing Christ's righteousness to him: (1) such teaching encourages licentious living and hinders the development of true ethical conduct; (2) James's teaching on justification by faith and works contradicts it; (3) the fact that the final judgment is according to works in which there is a corresponding distribution of rewards to the faithful contravenes it; (4) the fact that the Christian needs to continue to seek God's forgiveness for his sins throughout his life opposes it; (5) justification, so construed, grounds the Christian life in a "legal fiction," a not-according-to-truth "as if"; and (6) the Protestant doctrine carries grave implications for millions of professing Christians within Christendom.

1. With regard to the contention that the teaching of justification by faith alone leads to a lax attitude toward sin, Paul himself had to respond to this objection (see Rom. 3:8), which in itself implies that the Protestant understanding of justification accords with Paul's teaching (a good test of the correctness of one's theology is whether one meets the same objections to it that Paul met). Paul meets this objection head on with his doctrine of the Christian's union with Christ (Rom. 6–7; 2 Cor. 5:14–15; Gal. 3:1–5). He understood that to ground his summons of the Christian to a holy walk in anything other than salvation by grace alone through faith alone would only lead to legalism, self-righteousness, and ultimate frustration. He knew too that the Christian, united by grace to Christ in his death to sin and his resurrection to newness of life (Rom. 6:1-14), will not want to sin, indeed, will in gratitude for his salvation immediately and necessarily desire to live for him who died for him (2 Cor. 5:15).

2. It has been urged by Roman Catholic apologists (see Council of Trent, Sixth Session, chapters seven, ten) that James 2:14–26 is a corrective to the Protestant (not the Pauline) teaching that justification is through faith alone completely apart from works, for it expressly declares: "a man is justified by works, and *not* by faith alone" (James 2:24). But a careful analysis of James's teaching will disclose that "in James the accent [falls] upon the *probative* character of good works, whereas in the Pauline polemic the accent falls without question upon the judicially constitutive and declarative [character of justification]."[55] Paul and James clearly mean something different by "justified," "faith," and "works," and they turn to different events in Abraham's life to support their respective applications of Genesis 15:6.

---

55. Murray, *Epistle to the Romans*, 1:351.

Whereas Paul intends by "justified" the *actual* act on God's part whereby he pardons and imputes righteousness to the ungodly, James intends by "justified" the verdict God *declares* when the *actually* (previously) justified man has *demonstrated* his actual righteous state by obedience and good works.[56]

Whereas Paul intends by "faith" trustful repose in the merits of Christ alone for pardon and righteousness, James is addressing those whose "faith" was tending toward, if it had not already become, a cold, orthodox intellectualism that was devoid of love for the brethren.

Whereas Paul, when he repudiates "works," is referring to "the works of the law," that is, any and every work of *whatever* kind done for the sake of acquiring merit, James intends by "works" acts of kindness toward those in need performed as the fruit and evidence of the actual justified state and a true and vital faith (James 2:14–17).

Whereas Paul is concerned with the question of how a man may achieve right standing before God, and turns to Genesis 15:6 to find his answer, James is concerned with the question of how a man is to *demonstrate* that he is *actually* justified before God and has *true* faith, and turns to Genesis 22:9–10, as the *probative* "fulfillment" of Genesis 15:6 (see Gen. 22:12), to find his answer (James 2:21; see also his δεῖξόν [*deixon*, "show me"] and δείξω [*deixō*, "I will show you"] in 2:18; and his βλέπεις [*blepeis*, "you see"] in 2:22 and ὁρᾶτε [*horate*, "you see"] in 2:24).

And whereas Paul believed with all his heart that men are justified by *faith alone*, he insists as strongly as James that such faith, *if alone*, is not true but dead faith: "For in Christ Jesus neither circumcision nor uncircumcision means anything. [What counts] is faith working through love" (Gal. 5:6), which is hardly different in meaning from James's expression: "faith was working together with [Abraham's] works, and by works his faith was perfected" (James 2:22). Paul can also speak of the Christian's "work of faith [τοῦ ἔργου τῆς πίστεως, *tou ergou tēs pisteōs*]" (1 Thess. 1:3). And in the very context where he asserts that we are saved by grace

---

56. That a distinction must be drawn between God's *actual* act of justification whereby he pardons and constitutes the sinner righteous and his subsequent *declaring* acting of justification whereby he openly acquits the justified sinner before others is borne out by our Lord's actions in connection with the woman who washed his feet in Luke 7:36–50. He openly declares to Simon the Pharisee and to the woman herself that her many sins were forgiven "because she loved much" (vv. 47–48). But it is apparent that she had already been *actually* forgiven on some previous occasion, because her acts of devotion toward the Lord—the fruit and evidence of a lively faith—were due, he states, to her having already had "her debt canceled" (vv. 41–43). The chain of events then is as follows: On some previous occasion Jesus had forgiven her (her *actual* justification). This provoked in her both love for him and acts of devotion towards him. This outward evidence of her justified state evoked from Christ his open declaration that she was forgiven (her *declared* justification).

through faith and "not by works," Paul can declare that we are "created in Christ Jesus for good works, which God prepared beforehand that we should walk in them" (Eph. 2:8–10). In sum, whereas for James "faith without works is dead," for Paul "faith working through love" is inevitable if it is true faith. There is no contradiction between them (see Westminster Confession of Faith, XVI: "Of Good Works").

3. Rome also asserts that the fact that the final judgment is according to works, on the basis of which principle of judgment rewards are distributed to the faithful, is a further indication that a person does not achieve right standing before God by faith alone but by faith and works of satisfaction that are deserving of congruous merit.[57] Now it cannot be denied that the Scriptures uniformly represent the final judgment as a judgment of works (Ps. 62:12; Eccles. 12:14; Matt. 16:27; 25:31–46; John 5:29; Rom. 2:5–10; 1 Cor. 3:13; 4:5; 2 Cor. 5:10; Gal. 6:7–9; 1 Pet. 1:17; see also Westminster Confession of Faith, XXXIII/i), and that they hold forth the promise of rewards for faithful living (Exod. 20:5–6; Prov. 13:13; 25:21–22; Matt. 5:12; 6:1, 2, 4, 16, 18, 20; 10:41; 19:29; Luke 6:37–38; Col. 3:23–24; 2 Tim. 4:7–8; Heb. 11:26). But to assert, on the one hand, that men are justified by faith alone completely apart from the works of the law, and, on the other, that the final judgment is according to works, is to assert two entirely different things that in no way are contradictory to one another. The justified man, justified by faith alone, will produce good works "in obedience to God's commandments [as] the fruits and evidence of a true and lively faith" (Westminster Confession of Faith, XVI/ii). These works, as Murray carefully discerns,

> done in faith, from the motive of love to God, in obedience to the revealed will of God and to the end of his glory are intrinsically good and acceptable to God. As such they will be the criterion of reward in the life to come. . . . We must maintain . . . justification complete and irrevocable by grace through faith and apart from works, and at the same time, future reward according to works. In reference to these two doctrines it is important to observe the following: (i) *This future reward is not justification* and contributes nothing to that which constitutes justification. (ii) *This future reward is not salvation.* Salvation is by grace and it is

---

57. Rome distinguishes between *condign* or full merit (*meritum de condigno*), which imposes an obligation upon God to reward it, and *congruous* or a kind of "half" or proportionate merit (*meritum de congruo*), which, while it does not obligate God, is meritorious enough that it is "congruous" or "fitting" that God should reward it. Aquinas argued that the Christian's works, if viewed only in terms of the Holy Spirit's work within him, could be viewed as entailing condign merit, but when viewed in terms of the individual himself, they should be viewed as entailing only congruous merit, since no human act fully deserves the reward of salvation. The Reformers contended that all talk of merit, save for Christ's, is out of place within the context of the biblical doctrine of salvation by grace.

not as a reward for works that we are saved. (iii) The reward has reference to the station a person is to occupy in glory and *does not have reference to the gift of glory itself.* While the reward is of grace yet the standard or criterion of judgment by which the degree of reward is to be determined is good works. (iv) *This reward is not administered because good works earn or merit reward,* but because God is graciously pleased to reward them. That is to say, it is *a reward of grace.*[58]

Two conclusions are clearly in order. First, the reason why Scripture is willing to affirm a final judgment according to works is that good works being what they are—works (1) done by persons accepted by God through Christ, (2) which proceed from his Spirit, (3) and which are done in faith, (4) from the motive of love to God, (5) in obedience to God's revealed will, and (6) for his glory—*only Christians will manifest such works.*[59] But such works, as "the fruits and evidences of a true and lively faith," only serve to underscore the truth that salvation is not ultimately grounded in good works at all but in the gracious salvific work of the entire Godhead.

As for the works of unregenerate men, whose sacrifice, the Scripture says, is detestable to the Lord (Prov. 15:8), and whose "plowing," that is, entire "husbandry" in life, is sin, according to Proverbs 21:4 (so Heb.), the Westminster Confession of Faith declares that

> although for the matter of them they may be things which God commands; and of good use both to themselves and others: yet, because they proceed not from an heart purified by faith; nor are done in a right manner, according to the Word of God; nor to a right end, the glory of God, they are therefore sinful, and cannot please God, or make a man meet to receive grace from God: and yet, their neglect of them is more sinful and displeasing to God. (XVI/vii)

Second, the reason why Scripture is willing to affirm the distribution of rewards to Christians as an outcome of the final judgment is because they flow, never from any sense of indebtedness on God's part toward Christians as though their labors merited them or placed him in his debt, but always from his mercy and grace toward them. John Calvin sensitively speaks of how God shows his children mercy through the promise of rewards when he writes:

> Scripture leaves us no reason to be exalted in God's sight. Rather, its whole end is to restrain our pride, to humble us, cast us down, and utterly crush us. But

---

58. Murray, "Justification," *Collected Writings,* 2:221, emphases supplied.
59. I am not saying here that non-Christians cannot perform acts of civil righteousness in this life, for indeed they can; but such acts do not constitute those "good works" that in the judgment will be adjudged to be the fruit of a true faith in Christ.

our weakness, which would immediately collapse and fall if it did not sustain itself by this expectation and allay its own weariness by this comfort, is relieved in this way.

First, let everyone consider with himself how hard it would be for him to leave and renounce not only all his possessions but himself as well. Still, it is with this first lesson that Christ initiates his pupils, that is, all the godly. Then he so trains them throughout life under the discipline of the cross that they may not set their hearts upon desire of, or reliance on, present benefits. In short, he usually so deals with them that wherever they turn their eyes, as far as this world extends, they are confronted solely with despair. . . . Lest they fail amidst these great tribulations, the Lord is with them, warning them to hold their heads higher, to direct their eyes farther so as to find in him that blessedness which they do not see in the world. *He calls this blessedness "prize," "reward," "recompense," not weighing the merit of works, but signifying that it is a compensation for their miseries, tribulations, slanders, etc.* For this reason, nothing prevents us, with Scriptural precedent, from calling eternal life a "recompense," because in it the Lord receives his own people from toil into repose, from affliction into a prosperous and desirable state, from sorrow into joy, from poverty into affluence, from disgrace into glory. To sum up, he changes into greater goods all the evil things that they have suffered. Thus also it will be nothing amiss if we regard holiness of life to be the way, not indeed that gives access to the glory of the Heavenly Kingdom, but by which those chosen by their God are led to its disclosure. For it is God's good pleasure to glorify those whom he has sanctified.

. . . How absurd is it, when God calls us to one end, for us to look in the other direction? Nothing is clearer than that a reward is promised for good works to relieve the weakness of our flesh by some comfort but not to puff up our hearts with vainglory. Whoever, then, deduces merit of works from this, or weighs works and reward together, wanders very far from God's own plan. (*Institutes*, III, xviii, 4)

That the saints of heaven recognize that all that they receive from the Lord's hand is out of sheer mercy and never as their just desert is borne out by the picture in Revelation 4:10–11, where we see the twenty-four elders "casting the crowns" they have received from him before God's throne as they sing, "You are worthy, our Lord and God, to receive glory and honor and power." Their symbolic action suggests that all that we receive from God, even our rewards at the Final Judgment, comes to us by grace. Ultimately it is *he* who does the work in and through us, and yet he rewards *us* for it (see Phil. 2:12–13).

4. Rome also declares that if in his act of justifying the ungodly, God instantly pardons every sin—past, present, and future—as the Protestant teaching avers (see Rom. 4:6–8), then there would be no further need for the Christian daily to seek divine forgiveness for his sin, which he is required to do by such passages as

Matthew 6:12 and Luke 11:4. But this objection arises from a failure to distinguish between God's wrath, from which the Christian's justified state delivers him, and God's fatherly displeasure, which the Christian may still elicit by his daily sins and for which he needs to seek forgiveness as he grows in grace. The Scriptures will not permit the Christian to choose between his justification, whereby he has been juridically pardoned and delivered from the wrath to come, and his ongoing sanctification, one necessary aspect of which is seeking pardon for his daily transgressions which grieve the Holy Spirit of God and evoke his heavenly Father's displeasure. *The Christian must affirm both*—the fact that he has been fully pardoned juridically (his justification) and also the fact that his daily sins are an offense to his Father in heaven, whose daily forgiveness he needs if he is to grow in grace as he should (his sanctification). The Westminster Confession of Faith highlights this distinction:

> God doth continue to forgive the sins of those that are justified; and, although they can never fall from the state of justification, yet they may, by their sins, fall under God's fatherly displeasure, and not have the light of his countenance restored unto them, until they humble themselves, confess their sins, beg pardon, and renew their faith and repentance. (XI/v)

5. Rome urges, as do also Sanday and Headlam, that if justification is only forensic, "the Christian life is made to have its beginning in a fiction."[60] But this objection is due to a failure to realize that God does not treat the justified sinner *as if* he were righteous before him when actually he is not. To the contrary, the justified sinner is *in fact* righteous in God's sight because of the "in Christ" relationship in which he stands (2 Cor. 5:21), in which relationship the righteousness of Christ is actually imputed to him.[61] It is Rome's insistence that the righteousness of justification is infused and not imputed that lies at the base of this objection. But Rome's error here is serious, for it makes the very gospel of God itself—the teaching of justification by faith alone—truly a fiction.

6. Finally, the Protestant doctrine calls into question the salvation of millions of Christians throughout history. This argument, made in our time even by some Protestants,[62] against a rigid application of Protestantism's doctrine of justification by faith alone contends that if God justifies only those who self-consciously renounce all reliance upon any and all works of righteousness which they have done

---

60. William Sanday and Arthur C. Headlam, *Romans,* International Critical Commentary (New York: Scribner, 1923), 36.
61. See George Eldon Ladd's exposition of 2 Corinthians 5:21 in *A Theology of the New Testament* (1974; reprint, Grand Rapids, Mich.: Eerdmans, 1987), 466, on this issue.
62. Timothy George, "Letters to the Editor," *Christianity Today,* Vol. 40, No. 9 (August 12, 1996): 8.

or will ever do and trust in Christ's vicarious cross work alone, then one must conclude that the vast majority of professing Christians throughout history were not and are not saved. This vast group would include, we are informed, such church fathers as Athanasius, Augustine, Anselm, and Aquinas who as sacerdotalists believed in baptismal regeneration and, because they confused justification and sanctification, believed also in the necessity of deeds of penance for salvation. Against this Protestant rigidity it is urged that just as God predestinates *by grace alone* Arminians who have a faulty understanding of the doctrine of election, so too He justifies *by faith alone* Roman Catholics, among others, whose understanding of justification differs (that is, it does not affirm justification by "faith alone") from classic Protestantism's doctrine of justification.

This argument, however, is aimed not so much against Protestantism's "rigidity" as it is against Paul's insistence (1) that there is only one gospel—justification by faith alone in Christ's work alone (Rom. 3:27, 28; 4:5; 10:4; Gal. 2:16; 3:10–11, 26; Phil. 3:8–9), (2) that any other "gospel" is not the gospel, (3) that those who teach any other "gospel" stand under the anathema of God (Gal. 1:8–9), and (4) that those who rely to any degree on their own works for their salvation nullify the grace of God (Rom. 11:5–6), make void the cross work of Christ (Gal. 2:21; 5:2), become debtors to keep the entire law (Gal. 5:3), and in becoming such "fall from grace" (Gal. 5:4), that is, place themselves again under the curse of the law.

As for the four church fathers named above—and many others like them[63]—it is neither my nor their defenders' place to assure the Christian world that surely God justified them by faith alone even though they themselves did not hold to a *sola fide* view of justification. To judge an individual's salvation is God's province and His alone. Therefore, I will not speculate one way or the other about their salvation. But I will say that our attitude should, with Paul, ever be: "Let God's truth be inviolate, though *every* man becomes thereby a liar" (Rom. 3:4). What I mean by this in the present context is that the clear teaching of the Word of God should be upheld and we should not look for reasons to avoid it, even if the alternative would force us to conclude that *these* fathers—and *all* others like them—were not saved.

---

63. J. L. Neve, *A History of Christian Thought* (Philadelphia: Muhlenberg, 1946), i, 37–9, carefully documents in the Apostolic Fathers how quickly after the age of Paul—doubtless due to pagan and Jewish influences without and the tug of the Pelagian heart within—the emphasis in their preaching and writings on soteriology fell more and more upon works and their merit and moralism. It is one of the saddest facts of church history that from the post-apostolic age onward the church fell more and more into serious soteriological error, with grace and faith giving way to legalism and the doing of good works as the pronounced way of salvation. Only upon rare occasion, and not even fully in Augustine, was the voice of Paul clearly heard again before the sixteenth-century Reformation. See also J. N. D. Kelly, *Early Christian Doctrine* (London: Adam & Charles Black, 1958), 163–64, 165, 168–69, 177–78, 184.

Summary of the Doctrine

Paul defines the "gospel of God," which is also the "gospel of Christ" (Rom. 1:1, 9), specifically in terms of justification by faith—faith alone—in the accomplishments of Christ's obedience and cross work, completely apart from law-keeping (Rom. 1:16–17; 3:21–22, 27–28; 4:5–8; 5:1, 9, 17–19). And the manner in which he employs the term indicates that he regarded justification as an objective divine acquittal respecting the sinner's status before the condemning law of God and not as the subjective improvement of the sinner through the infusion of sanctifying grace. This was the gospel that Paul preached—"through him forgiveness of sins is proclaimed to you, and through him everyone who believes is justified from all things, from which you could not be justified by the law of Moses" (Acts 13:38–39, author's translation). And he pronounced an anathema[64] upon any and all who would muddy the streams of grace by their legalistic efforts to contribute in any way to their righteousness before God (Gal. 1:6–9; 2:11–21; 3:1–14; 5:1–4; 6:12–16). J. I. Packer says as a summary of the biblical doctrine of justification:

> It defines the saving significance of Christ's life and death by relating both to God's law (Rom. 3:24ff.; 5:16ff.). It displays God's justice in condemning and punishing sin, his mercy in pardoning and accepting sinners, and his wisdom in exercising both attributes harmoniously together through Christ (Rom. 3:23ff.). It makes clear what faith is—belief in Christ's atoning death and justifying resurrection (Rom. 4:23ff.; 10:8ff.), and trust in him alone for righteousness (Phil. 3:8–9). It makes clear what Christian morality is—law-keeping out of gratitude to the Savior whose gift of righteousness made law-keeping needless for acceptance (Rom. 7:1–6; 12:1–2). It explains all hints, prophecies, and instances of salvation in the OT (Rom. 1:17; 3:21; 4:1ff.). It overthrows Jewish exclusivism (Gal. 2:15ff.) and provides the basis on which Christianity becomes a religion for the world (Rom. 1:16; 3:29–30). It is the heart of the gospel.[65]

Quite correctly did Martin Luther declare that the Pauline doctrine of justification by faith alone is the article by which the church stands or falls (*articulus stantis vel cadentis ecclesiae*), with John Calvin declaring it to be "the main hinge on

---

64. "Anathema" (ἀνάθεμα, *anathema*) in Galatians 1:8–9 (see Rom. 9:3; 1 Cor. 16:22) is derived from the preposition ἀνά (*ana*, "up"), τίθημι (*tithēmi*, "to place or set"), and μα (*ma*, a noun ending with passive significance). Hence it means "something set or placed up [before God]," and is simply the New Testament expression of the Old Testament חֵרֶם (*herem*, "devoted") principle of handing something or someone over to God for destruction. See BAGD, Ἀνάθεμα [*anathema*], *A Greek–English Lexicon of the New Testament*, 54, no. 2.
65. James I. Packer, "Justification," in *Evangelical Dictionary of Theology*, 593.

which religion turns" (*Institutes*, 3.11.1).[66] And by expressly rejecting this teaching as it did at the Council of Trent (see Sixth Session, canons nine to twelve), which rejection it has not only never repudiated but also has reaffirmed as recently as its 1994 *Catechism of the Catholic Church*, the Roman Catholic Church testifies to its own apostate condition. And in rejecting this doctrine, Rome has fallen heir to a hundred other evils, including Mariology, the indulgence system, and the doctrine of works of supererogation by "saints" whose "congruent merit" is placed in Rome's "treasury of merit" to be dispensed through papal indulgences.

DEFINITIVE SANCTIFICATION

Sanctification is generally thought of as a process, and there is certainly a sense in which it is. But the New Testament often represents the Christian as one who *has been sanctified*, and therefore as one who has been definitively constituted in some way and on some basis *holy* (see Acts 20:32; 26:18; 1 Cor. 1:2; 6:11; Eph. 5:26; note the perfect tense of ἁγιάζω, *hagiazō* in the first three references and the aorist tense in the last two references, as well as the numerous instances where Christians are called "saints" or "holy ones").

The Biblical Data

Additional evidence for God's definitive sanctification of the believer includes:

Romans 6:2, 6: "We died [ἀπεθάνομεν, *apethanomen*] to sin . . . the old man was crucified [συνεσταυρώθη, *synestaurōthē*] [with him]."

Romans 6:18: "You have been set free [ἐλευθερωθέντες, *eleutherōthentes*] from sin and have become slaves [ἐδουλώθετε, *edoulōthete*] to righteousness."

Romans 7:4–6: "You also were made to die [ἐθανατώθητε, *ethanatōthēte*] to the law . . . we were [ἦμεν, *ēmen*] in the flesh . . . but now we have been released [κατηργήθημεν, *katērgēthēmen*] from the law, having died [ἀποθανόντες, *apothanontes*] to that by which we were bound."

1 Peter 2:24: ". . . That we, having died [ἀπογενόμενοι, *apogenomenoi*] to sins, might live to righteousness."

1 Peter 4:1–2: "Therefore, since Christ suffered [παθόντος, *pathontos*] in the flesh, arm yourselves also with the same mind, because he who has suffered [ὁ παθών, *ho pathōn*] in the flesh [a reference to the Christian who "suffered in the flesh"

---

66. See Luther's exposition of Psalm 130:4 in his *Werke* (Weimar: Böhlar, 1883 to present), 40/3:352,3: ". . . *quia isto articulo stante stat Ecclesia, ruente ruit Ecclesia.*"

when Christ "suffered in the flesh"] is done with sin, with the result that no longer does he live the rest of his time in the flesh to the lusts of men but to the will of God."

The Meaning of these Affirmations

Through its language of death and of liberation from slavery, this biblical material depicts a radical contrast between the believer's pre-Christian existence and the life he lives as a Christian. It affirms that every Christian is definitively sanctified the moment he trusts in Christ (see Acts 26:18—"those having been sanctified by faith which is in me"). He died *to* sin and he has been liberated *from* sin.[67] Accordingly, the Scriptures speak of *every* Christian as a "saint" or "holy one" (ὁ ἅγιος, *ho hagios;* see, e.g., Eph. 1:1; Phil. 1:1; Col. 1:2).

This sustained contrast can only mean that for the Christian there exists

> a cleavage, a breach, a translation as really and decisively true in the sphere of moral and religious relationship as in the ordinary experience of death. There is a once-for-all definitive and irreversible breach with the realm in which sin reigns in and unto death. . . . In respect of every criterion by which moral and spiritual life is to be assessed, there is absolute differentiation. This means that there is a decisive and definitive breach with the power and service of sin in the case of everyone who has come under the control of the provisions of grace.[68]

The Ground of the Christian's Breach with Sin

Just as the ground of the Christian's justification is Christ's imputed obedience, which saving benefit every Christian receives the moment he becomes a partaker of Christ through faith, so also the ground of the Christian's definitive sanctification is his real spiritual union with Christ in his death, burial, and resurrection (Rom. 6:1–14; 2 Cor. 5:14–15), into which saving union every Christian is *actually* brought the moment he becomes a partaker of Christ through faith. In other words, not only is the Christian accounted by God as righteous vis-à-vis the law, he is also *constituted holy* by God vis-à-vis the power and mastery of sin. It is not simply *positional* holiness that is envisioned by definitive sanctification: it is a real *existential* breach with the reign and mastery of sin, which breach is created by the

---

67. See the exodus redemption, by which the people of God were delivered from Egypt once for all and completely. This exodus event is the Old Testament soil in which the New Testament imagery of liberation from sin is rooted.
68. Murray, "Definitive Sanctification," in *Collected Writings,* 2:279–80.

Christian's actual spiritual union with Christ in his death and resurrection, and which is as decisive and definite as are Christ's death and resurrection. Murray speaks of the significance of the vital spiritual union between Christ and the believer for his definitive sanctification:

> So intimate is the union between Christ and his people, that they were partakers with him in [his death and resurrection], and therefore died to sin, rose with Christ in the power of his resurrection, and have their fruit unto holiness, and the end everlasting life . . . the decisive and definitive breach with sin that occurs at the inception of Christian life is one necessitated by the fact that the death of Christ was decisive and definitive. It is just because we cannot allow for any reversal or repetition of Christ's death on the tree that we cannot allow for any compromise on the doctrine that every believer has died to sin and no longer lives under its dominion. Sin no longer lords it over him. To equivocate here is to assail the definitiveness of Christ's death. Likewise the decisive and definitive entrance upon newness of life in the case of every believer is required by the fact that the resurrection of Christ was decisive and definitive. As we cannot allow for any reversal or repetition of the resurrection, so we cannot allow for any compromise on the doctrine that every believer is a new man, that the old man has been crucified, that the body of sin has been destroyed, and that, as a new man in Christ Jesus, he serves God in the newness which is none other than that of the Holy Spirit of whom he has become the habitation and his body the temple.[69]

Summary of the Doctrine

The doctrine of definitive sanctification does not mean that the Christian actually achieves, personally and existentially, sinless perfection the moment he trusts Christ; this would leave no room for progressive sanctification. Besides, entire sanctification awaits the coming of our Lord Jesus Christ (1 Thess. 5:23). And the Christian who says he has no sin is deceiving himself and the truth is not in him (1 John 1:8). But what it does mean is that every Christian, the moment he becomes a Christian, by virtue of his union with Christ, is instantly constituted a "saint", and enters into a new relationship with respect to the former reign of sin in his life and with God himself, in which new relationship he ceases to be a slave to sin and becomes a servant of Christ and of God. And the Christian is to take this breach with sin, constituted by his union with Christ, as seriously as God does and stop "presenting the members of his body to sin as instruments of unrighteousness" and start "presenting himself to God as one alive from the dead, and his members as

---

69. Ibid., 2:289, 293.

instruments [or servants] of righteousness to God" (Rom. 6:13, 19). He has Paul's own assurance that "sin will not lord it over him" (Rom. 6:14).

ADOPTION AND THE SEALING OF THE SPIRIT

All those that are justified, God vouchsafeth, in and for His only Son Jesus Christ, to make partakers of the grace of adoption, by which they are taken into the number, and enjoy the liberty and privileges of the children of God, have His name put upon them, receive the spirit of adoption, have access to the throne of grace with boldness, are enabled to cry, Abba, Father, are pitied, protected, provided for, and chastened by Him, as by a Father: yet never cast off, but sealed to the day of redemption; and inherit the promises, as heirs of everlasting life. (Westminster Confession of Faith, XII)

Adoption

The sinner having been pardoned and constituted righteous in God's sight (that is, justified) and constituted holy through union with Christ (that is, definitively sanctified), God also legally constitutes him his child and adopts him into his family. Whereas the doctrine of justification speaks to the relationship of the Christian to God *as Lawgiver and Judge* (it declares that he has been juridically acquitted of any and all transgressions of the law, and thus delivered forever from the wrath of God), whereas the doctrine of definitive sanctification speaks to the relationship of the Christian to God *as his new Master* (it declares that he is no longer sin's slave and is now the servant of God), so the doctrine of adoption speaks to the filial relationship of the Christian to God *as his Father* (it declares that he is a child of God and that God is his heavenly Father).

The Biblical Data

The terminology with which we are concerned here are the nouns υἱός (*huios*, "son"—2 Cor. 6:18; Gal. 3:26; 4:6–7; Heb. 2:10; 12:5–8; Rev. 21:7), τέκνον (*teknon*, "child"—John 1:12; 11:52; 1 John 3:1, 10; 5:2; Rom. 8:16, 21; 9:8; Eph. 5:1; Phil. 2:15) and παιδίον (*paidion*, "little child"—Heb. 2:13–14), all three indicating the filial relationship the Christian sustains to God the Father by virtue of the Father's *adoptive act* (υἱοθεσία, *huiothesia*—Rom. 8:15, 23; Gal. 4:5; Eph. 1:5 [see also Rom. 9:4]). Although υἱοθεσία, *huiothesia*, is not employed in the Septuagint, nevertheless, because the nation of Israel is viewed as God's "son" in Exodus 4:22, Hosea 11:1, Isaiah 1:2, and elsewhere, Paul speaks of Israel's national "adoption" at the time of the exodus in

Romans 9:4. Then, of the Christian's adoption, arranged in the biblical theological order in which the divine actions occur of which the several verses speak, Paul writes:

> Ephesians 1:4–5: "In love he [the Father] predestinated us to adoption through Jesus Christ unto himself." Here in this one verse Paul informs us of the ultimate root (predestination) and the highest end (sonship) of our salvation. In light of the fact that Paul (1) sounds this "adoption" note at the very beginning of Ephesians, (2) refers to "the Father" at critical junctures in Ephesians (1:2, 3, 17; 2:18; 3:14; 4:6; 5:20; 6:23), (3) represents him as the subject of most of the verbs that speak of the divine activity, and (4) develops the Christian's walk in terms of the walk of a "child" before the Father (5:1, 8), I suggest that just as Romans is Paul's treatise on justification so Ephesians in a special sense is Paul's treatise on the Fatherhood of God and the doctrine of adoption.
>
> Galatians 4:4–6: "But when the fulness of time came, God sent forth his Son, born of a woman, born under law, in order that he might redeem those under law, that we might receive the adoption. And because you are sons [by adoption], God has sent forth the Spirit of his Son [by very nature] into our hearts, crying, 'Abba,[70] Father.'"
>
> Romans 8:15–16: "For you have not received a spirit of slavery again to fear, but you have received the Spirit of adoption, by whom we cry, 'Abba, Father.' The Spirit himself testifies with our spirit that we are God's children."
>
> Romans 8:23: "... we ourselves, having the firstfruits[71] of the Spirit, even we ourselves groan within ourselves, waiting for the adoption, even the redemption of our body."

These four verses, so arranged, provide a biblical theology of the doctrine of adoption: (1) in love the Father predestinated the believer's adoption in Christ before the foundation of the world, (2) the Father sent his Son into the world to do the objective redemptive work necessary both to the salvation of his people from the law's condemnation and to their elevation by adoption away from the tutelary discipline of the Mosaic economy under which they as adopted children had lived in former times, to the status of full, mature sonship (Gal. 4:1–2), (3) the Father sent

---

70. It has become a commonplace among evangelicals to assert that "Abba" means something on the order of our informal "Daddy." This is not the case, however. "Abba," the anglicized transliteration of the Greek Αββα, *Abba*, which in turn is the transliteration of the Aramaic אבא, *'abbā'*, as Paul's translation (ὁ πατήρ, *ho patēr*, "Father") makes clear, means "O Father." The suffixed א, *ā*, attached to אב (*'āb*, "father") is simply the Aramaic article used vocatively.

71. God's gift of his Holy Spirit to his child as the "firstfruits" (τὴν ἀπαρχὴν, *tēn aparchēn*) of the approaching full harvest (with τοῦ πνεύματος, *tou pneumatos*, construed as an appositional genitive), guarantees that the Christian will finally receive his full adoption by receiving his glorified resurrection body (Rom. 8:23).

forth the Spirit of his Son, who is also the Spirit of adoption, into the heart of the believer, subjectively assuring him thereby that he is the Father's child and enabling him to cry "Abba, Father," and (4) the child of God, having received the Spirit of adoption as the firstfruits of his adoption, awaits the final stage of his adoption in the Eschaton, when even his fallen mortal body will be redeemed from its corruption and brought to a state of glory like unto that of his Lord (Phil. 3:21). The biblical theology of adoption, then, encompasses (1) the Father's love from all eternity, (2) redemption from past enslavement, (3) a status and way of life in the present, and (4) a future expectation of glory.

A Legal Action with Eternal Consequences

Both Paul's term υἱοθεσία, *huiothesia*, and John's expression in John 1:12—"gave authority to become children"—indicate that adoption envisions an action on the Father's part that is forensically constituting and not subjectively transforming in character. By adoption the status of sonship is legally bestowed upon the believer, and those theologians (e.g., Murray, Packer) who insist that the Christian's status of which this doctrine speaks is the "apex of redemptive grace and privilege" and the "epitome of grace" are certainly correct. For whereas justification addresses the question of one's relation to the law, and definitive sanctification addresses the question of one's relation to the power of sin, *adoption addresses the question of one's relation to God the Father himself.* Paul himself strongly suggests the exalted status envisioned by adoption when he relates the Christian's adoption in Ephesians 1:5 back to the Father's predestinating love—as Murray says: "Here we have the ultimate source and the highest privilege brought together."[72] Paul does the same when he draws his exposition of the privileged status of believing Jews and Gentiles to a close in Ephesians 2:18–19 with the words: "through him we both have access in one Spirit to the Father. So then you are no longer strangers and aliens, but you are fellow–citizens with the saints, and are *members of the household* [οἰκεῖοι, *oikeioi*] of God." Can Christians enjoy any blessedness or privilege higher than that access to God the Father through his Son and Spirit which as members of his household they enjoy? What blessedness can possibly supersede the blessedness of simply being a child of the holy God? There is none, not justification, not sanctification, however great these privileges are.

As *consequences* of his or her constituted status as a child of God, the following additional privileges immediately accrue to every believer: (1) the Christian has the Father's name placed upon him (Eph. 2:19; 3:14–15), being assured thereby that he has

---

72. Murray, "Adoption," *Collected Writings*, 2:230.

the Father's protection and provision; (2) he is sealed by the Holy Spirit (Eph. 1:13); (3) he or she immediately becomes Christ's brother or sister, Christ being the "firstborn Son [that is, the elder Brother] among many brothers" (Rom. 8:29), and thus he or she becomes an "heir of God, co-heir with Christ" (Rom. 8:17); (4) awaiting him in heaven is his "inheritance, imperishable, and undefiled, which will not fade away" (1 Pet. 1:4); and (5) he is assured that he will come into his inheritance because he is "kept ["guarded, protected"—φρουρουμένους, *phrouroumenous*] by the power of God through faith for [the] salvation ready to be revealed in the last time" (1 Pet. 1:5).

As for his *responsibilities*, (1) as a child beloved the believer is to walk in love (Eph. 5:1–2), (2) as a child of light he is to walk in the light and expose the unfruitful deeds of darkness (Eph. 5:8–11), (3) he is warned that he will experience his Father's chastening love when he goes astray (Heb. 12:6–8); and (4) as a family member in God's household, all other Christians are his brothers and sisters, to be cherished and encouraged in the faith (1 John 4:20–21; 5:1–20; Rom. 15:14).

Summary of the Doctrine

"Adoption is an act of God's free grace, whereby we are received into the number, and have a right to all the privileges of the sons of God" (Shorter Catechism, Question 34). This simple definition reminds us that adoption is (1) the Father's objective determination concerning the believer, determined upon his faith in Christ, (2) bestowed by his free grace (see 1 John 3:1), and (3) the act by which the believer becomes a child of God. Adoption is the highest privilege available to fallen children of Adam, with all its privileges accruing to the one who enjoys the status of being an heir of all the promises of God and of everlasting salvation—access to the Father's throne of grace, his pity, protection, provision, and chastening, and the seal of his Spirit unto the day of redemption.

The Sealing of the Holy Spirit

The Spirit of God's Son, who is also the Spirit of adoption, not only testifies with Christians' spirits that they are children of God but also, as "the guaranteeing pledge [ἀρραβών, *arrabōn*] of their inheritance" (note here the legal sonship terminology),[73] seals them as God's own possession to the day of eschatological redemption (Eph. 4:30; 2 Cor. 5:5).

---

73. In his *The Bible and the Future* (Grand Rapids, Mich.: Eerdmans, 1979), Anthony A. Hoekema writes concerning ἀρραβών, *arrabōn*, the Greek transliteration of the Semitic loanword אֵרָבוֹן, *'arābôn*: "One could perhaps render the word 'down payment' or 'first installment,' if it were not for the fact that, in today's world, a down payment does not guarantee the payment of the entire sum due. Hence the word *arrabon* can better be translated *pledge* or *guarantee*" (62).

The Biblical Data

Paul provides the biblical data regarding the Spirit's sealing in two places:

Ephesians 1:13–14: "After having believed, in him *you were marked with a seal* [ἐσφραγίσθητε, *esphragisthete*] by the Holy Spirit of promise, who is a *deposit guaranteeing* [ἀρραβών, *arrabon*] our inheritance." (author's translation)

Note that the Spirit's sealing, as with justification, definitive sanctification, and adoption, follows the Christian's believing as one of the consequences of saving faith. Note too that this sealing is represented by the aorist tense as an accomplished fact, suggesting that as the Spirit is the witness that the Christian is a child of God and as such an heir of God (Rom. 8:16–17), so the indwelling Spirit of adoption, given in conjunction with God's constituting act of adoption, becomes also at the same time the "guaranteeing pledge" of the believer's full inheritance and the "mark" or "seal" that the believer belongs to God's household to the final day of redemption (see Eph. 4:30; 2 Cor. 5:5).

2 Corinthians 1:21–22: "Now it is God who makes both us and you stand firm in Christ. He anointed us, *set his seal of ownership* [σφραγισάμενος, *sphragisamenos*] on us, and gave the *guaranteeing deposit of the Spirit* [ἀρραβῶνα τοῦ πνεύματος, *arrabona tou pneumatos*] in our hearts."

Note that the tense of the verb of sealing here, as in Ephesians 1:13, is aorist, indicating that for the believer the sealing is an accomplished fact, doubtless occurring at the point of the believer's adoption. Note too that again the indwelling Spirit is God's pledge of ownership (I construe πνεύματος, *pneumatos*, as an appositional genitive), guaranteeing that the believer is a child of God forever.

The Nature of the Spirit's Sealing

From these virtually identical statements we learn that, contingent upon our faith in Christ, God not only justifies us, not only definitively sanctifies us, not only adopts us into his family, but also *seals* us in Christ by the Spirit of God, who is the "first installment" ("guaranteeing deposit") of our final glorious inheritance. What does this mean? The first thing that should be noted is that we are not speaking here about chronologically related events. The Spirit's sealing (as is true of justification, definitive sanctification, and adoption) does not follow upon trust chronologically. That is to say, one does not trust Christ one moment and the Holy Spirit seals him in Christ the next. Rather, we are simply urging that faith in Christ is the instrumental cause of the sealing. That is to say, the moment one trusts

Christ, *that same moment* the Holy Spirit seals him in Christ. But it would be true to say that the Spirit's sealing is contingent upon that trust.

Then it should be noted that the "sealing" *is* the indwelling of the Holy Spirit, who is himself the "seal." Paul teaches that the Holy Spirit, being himself the indwelling "pledge [ἀρραβών, *arrabon*] of our inheritance" (Eph. 1:14; 2 Cor. 1:22; 5:5), becomes—by his "indwelling guarantee" that the indwelt Christian is a child of God forever—both the "seal" marking God's *ownership* of the Christian and the *authenticating down payment* or *first installment* guaranteeing the Christian's full inheritance in the Eschaton of every spiritual blessing in heaven in Christ.

Its Distinction from the Baptism of the Holy Spirit

The Spirit's sealing of the believer in Christ should not be confused with the baptism of the Holy Spirit. The baptism of the Holy Spirit is the work of the glorified Christ and is tantamount to the Spirit's regenerating work. It precedes and is the precondition to faith in Christ, while the Spirit's sealing follows upon faith in Christ. Luke records four "Spirit-baptisms" or "comings" of the Spirit in Acts—Acts 2, Jews; Acts 8, Samaritans; Acts 10, Gentiles; Acts 19, followers of John—marking by them the strategic steps in the extension of the church and teaching thereby that there is but *one* church into which all converts are baptized by the same Spirit—whether Jews, Samaritans, Gentiles, or followers of John.[74] In other words, the four "Pentecosts" in Acts *as events* had revelatory import in the nonrepeatable *heilsgeschichtlich* process. They were intended to teach that there is only "one body and one Spirit—just as you were called to one hope when you were called—one Lord, one faith, one baptism; one God and Father of all, who is over all and through all and in all" (Eph. 4:4–6), regardless of the human mix within it. Therefore, the "Spirit-baptisms" as events in Acts are not to be viewed as continuing and normative occurrences in the history of the church. The glorified Christ made it clear from these *heilsgeschichtlich* "Spirit-baptisms" that people of all races and social backgrounds are "heirs together, members together, and sharers together" in the one church (Eph. 3:6). This being so, there is no further need for the continuance of such *revelatory* events.

But while Luke witnesses to the great truth of the oneness of the people of God by recording these "Spirit-comings," he nowhere expounds their *soteriological* significance. This exposition is provided by Paul, who does it in one sentence: "For

---

74. John's disciples were the one group in the first century that had any ground for thinking that it possessed some legitimacy as a separate and independent sect. In this they were wrong, of course, and by their Spirit-baptism Christ was declaring that this sect had to relinquish its independency and allow itself to be absorbed by the Church of Christ.

we were all baptized [ἡμεῖς πάντες . . . ἐβαπτίσθημεν, *hēmeis pantes . . . ebaptisthēmen*] *by one Spirit into one body—whether Jews or Greeks, slave or free—and we were all given the one Spirit to drink*" (1 Cor. 12:13). What Paul means here is that this "Spirit-baptism"—which is the joint act of both the glorified Christ and the Holy Spirit which *every* Christian has experienced (see Paul's πάντες, *pantes*)—

> joins together into a spiritual unity people of diverse racial extractions [Paul's "whether Jews or Greeks"] and diverse social backgrounds [his "whether slave or free"] so that they form the body of Christ—the *ekklesia*. . . . The fact of the oneness of the *ekklesia* is [according to Paul] the theological meaning of the several extensions of Pentecost in Acts.[75]

The four "Pentecosts" in Acts (Acts 2, 8, 10, 19) should be understood then in the light of Ladd's insight. Theologically, they signalize the Spirit's baptismal work—of which the sacrament of baptism is the sign and seal—whereby racially and culturally diverse people are regenerated, cleansed, and placed in the one spiritual body of Christ.

Its Distinction from the Filling of the Spirit

The Spirit's sealing work should also be distinguished from the Spirit's filling activity. The Spirit's filling activity follows upon the Spirit's sealing work, is ongoing in the life of the Christian, and is involved in and is an aspect of the Christian's progressive sanctification.

The key passages here are Ephesians 5:18–21 and Colossians 3:15–17. In the Ephesians passage Paul introduces his instructions with a command containing two imperatives: "Do not get drunk on wine, which leads to debauchery. Instead, *be filled with the Spirit* [πληροῦσθε ἐν πνεύματι, *plērousthe en pneumati*]." The first thing to underscore is the significance of the second imperative itself. It is a command (an imperative), it is addressed to the whole Christian community (the imperative is plural), the command is to be continually observed (the imperative is in the present tense), and it calls us, not to sectarian techniques or formulas, but to a *believing openness* to the Spirit's working in us (it is in the passive voice, best rendered: "Let the Spirit be continually filling you"). In light of the contrasting imperative, Paul is commanding that we must never come "under the influence" of the "intoxicating spirit" of wine, but rather we must ever live under the "intoxicating

---

75. Ladd, *Theology of the New Testament*, 347.

influence" of the Spirit who, far from taking away from us our self-control (which alcohol as a depressant drug does), actually *stimulates* us for the first time in everything that makes a person behave at his best and highest—*including* self-control (Gal. 5:22).

The Colossian parallel reads, not "Let the Spirit fill you," but "*Let* the word of Christ *dwell in* [ἐνοικείτω, *enoikeitō*] you richly" (Col. 3:16), also a present imperative. These two ideas, both highlighting a divine, *subjective* influence, are practically identical. To be filled with the Spirit is to be indwelt by the word of Christ; to be indwelt by the word of Christ is to be filled with the Spirit. One must never separate the Spirit from Christ's word or Christ's word from the Spirit. The Spirit works by and with Christ's word. Christ's word works by and with the Spirit.

Paul articulates the outworking and evidence of this joint work of the Spirit's "filling" us and Christ's word "indwelling" us by the five present participles that qualify the Spirit's filling in Ephesians 5:19–21:

1. *speaking* (λαλοῦντες, *lalountes*) to one another in psalms and hymns and spiritual songs (this is Christian fellowship);

2. *singing* (ᾄδοντες, *adontes*) and *psalming* (ψάλλοντες, *psallontes*) in your heart to the Lord (this is Christian worship in spirit and truth);

3. *giving thanks* (εὐχαριστοῦντες, *eucharistountes*) always for all things in the name of our Lord Jesus Christ to God the Father (this is Christian gratitude); and

4. *being submissive* (ὑποτασσόμενοι, *hypotassomenoi*) to one another in the fear of Christ (wives and husbands; children and parents; slaves and masters; this is Christian display of the meekness and gentleness of Christ himself in personal relationships).

Paul teaches virtually the same thing in Colossians 3:15–17. After admonishing the Colossians to "let the word of Christ dwell in you richly," he immediately follows his admonition, as he does in Ephesians, with a series of four present participles showing result (evidence):

1. *teaching* (διδάσκοντες, *didaskontes*) with all wisdom and *counseling* (νουθετοῦντες, *nouthetountes*) one another (Christian fellowship);

2. *singing* (ᾄδοντες, *adontes*) with psalms, hymns, and spiritual songs, with grace in your hearts, to God (Christian worship); and

3. *giving thanks* (εὐχαριστοῦντες, *eucharistountes*) to God the Father as you do whatever you do in word or in deed in the name of the Lord Christ (Christian gratitude).

As he did in Ephesians, Paul then follows these participles with commands for wives and husbands, children and parents, and slaves and masters to behave toward each other as Christians should and as their respective stations warrant.

The Christian who evidences these things in his life is "being filled with the Spirit," that is, is "letting the word of Christ dwell in him richly." He does not need to practice certain sectarian techniques or to recite certain sectarian incantations or "Christian mantras" in order to receive the Spirit's filling. He needs only to cultivate these things by remaining humbly and believingly open to the Spirit who works by and with the word of Christ in his heart.

Summary of the Doctrine

The sealing of the Spirit, to be distinguished from the baptism of the Spirit and the filling of the Spirit, is that act of God, performed in connection with his act of adoption, whereby he seals the believer to the final day of redemption by the indwelling presence of the Spirit of adoption, whose indwelling is the guaranteeing "down payment" of the Christian's full and final inheritance.

Two Divine-Human Activities

PROGRESSIVE SANCTIFICATION

They, who are once effectually called, and regenerated, having a new heart, and a new spirit created in them, are further sanctified, really and personally, through the virtue of Christ's death and resurrection, by His Word and Spirit dwelling in them: the dominion of the whole body of sin is destroyed, and the several lusts thereof are more and more weakened and mortified; and they more and more quickened and strengthened in all saving graces, to the practice of true holiness, without which no man shall see the Lord.

This sanctification is throughout, in the whole man; yet imperfect in this life, there abiding still some remains of corruption in every part; whence ariseth a continual and irreconcilable war, the flesh lusting against the Spirit, and the Spirit against the flesh.

In which war, although the remaining corruption, for a time, may much prevail; yet, through the continual supply of strength from the sanctifying Spirit of Christ, the regenerate part doth overcome; and so, the saints grow in grace, perfecting holiness in the fear of God. (Westminster Confession of Faith, XIII/i–iii)

The Biblical Data

The Old Testament word-group specifying the believer's holiness of life comes primarily from the Hebrew root קָדַשׁ, *qādaš*:

Exodus 19:6: "You shall be to me a kingdom of priests and a holy nation."

Leviticus 11:44–45: "For I am the Lord your God. Consecrate yourselves therefore, and be holy; for I am holy. . . . For I am the Lord, who brought you up from the land of Egypt, to be your God; thus you shall be holy for I am holy."

Leviticus 19:2: "Speak to all the congregation of the sons of Israel and say to them, 'You shall be holy, for I the Lord your God am holy.'"

The primary New Testament word-group addressing the same matter comes from the verb ἁγιάζω, *hagiazō*:

John 17:17: "*Sanctify* [ἁγίασον, *hagiason*] them by the truth; your word is truth."

1 Thessalonians 5:23: "May the God of peace himself *sanctify* [ἁγιάσαι, *hagiasai*] you entirely."

Employing the adjective ἅγιος, *hagios*, Peter summons the Christian to holiness and cites the Old Testament command to fortify his demand:

1 Peter 1:15–16: "But like the holy One who called you, be yourselves *holy* [ἅγιοι, *hagioi*] in all your behavior, because it has been written: 'Be holy, because I am holy.'"

A significant noun in this connection is ἁγιασμός, *hagiasmos*. Note the following occurrences:

1 Thessalonians 4:3: "This is the will of God, your holiness, that you abstain from sexual immorality."

1 Thessalonians 4:7: "God did not call us unto impurity but unto holiness."

Hebrews 12:14: "Pursue . . . holiness, without which no man shall see the Lord."

Another significant noun specifying the Christian's obligation to perfect a holy walk is ἁγιωσύνη, *hagiōsynē*:

2 Corinthians 7:1: "Let us cleanse ourselves from all defilement of flesh and spirit, perfecting holiness out of reverence for God."

The Nature of the Sanctified Life

Throughout his life, from the moment of his regeneration and conversion to the moment of his final elevation to heavenly glory, the Christian, by virtue of his union with Christ's death and resurrection and through the power of God's word and Spirit dwelling within him, will necessarily experience progressive sanctification, this process to be understood *negatively* in terms of putting to death the deeds of the flesh which still remain in him and *positively* in terms of growth in all saving graces.[76] Consider first the scriptural warrant for the negative side of progressive sanctification:

> Romans 8:13: "If by the [indwelling] Spirit *you are putting to death* [θανατοῦτε, *thanatoute*] the deeds of the body, you shall live."
>
> Colossians 3:5: *"Put to death* [νεκρώσατε, *nekrōsate*] your earthly members with regard to fornication, uncleanness, passion, evil desire, and greed which is idolatry."

It should be noted that both of these admonitions to put to death the evil deeds of the body follow immediately upon Paul's insistence that the believer *has* died to sin (Rom. 6–7; Col. 3:3). Clearly, Paul expected the Christian to conform his *processive* experience with sin to his *definitive* death to sin.

With respect to the positive side of progressive sanctification one may cite the following verses:

> Romans 12:2: *"Be transformed* [μεταμορφοῦσθε, *metamorphousthe*] by the renewing of the mind."
>
> 2 Corinthians 3:18: "We all, with unveiled face beholding as in a mirror the glory of the Lord, *are being transformed* [μεταμορφούμεθα, *metamorphoumetha*] into the same image from glory to glory."
>
> Ephesians 4:11–16: "[Christ] gave [spiritually gifted men] for the equipping of the saints . . . for the building up of the body of Christ; until *we all attain* [καταντήσωμεν, *katantēsōmen*] to the unity of the faith, and of the knowledge of the Son of God, to a mature man, to the measure of the stature which belongs to the fulness of Christ. As a result, we are no longer to be children . . . but . . . *we are to grow up* [αὐξήσωμεν, *auxēsōmen*] in all aspects unto him, who is the head, even Christ, from whom the whole body, being fitted and held together by that which every joint supplies, according to the proper working of each individual part, *causes the growth* [αὔξησιν . . . ποιεῖται, *auxēsin . . . poieitai*] of the body for the building up of itself in love."
>
> Philippians 1:9: "And this I pray, that your love may abound still more and more, in real knowledge and all discernment."
>
> Philippians 3:13–14: "Brethren, I do not regard myself as having obtained [perfection] yet; but one thing I do: forgetting what lies behind and *reaching forward* [ἐπεκτεινόμενος, *epekteinomenos*] to what lies ahead, *I press on* [διώκω, *diōkō*] toward the goal for the prize of the upward calling of God in Christ Jesus."

---

76. See Berkhof, *Systematic Theology*, 533.

Colossians 1:9–10: "We have not stopped... asking that you may be filled with the knowledge of his will... in order that you may walk worthy of the Lord... *growing* [αὐξανόμενοι, *auxanomenoi*] in the knowledge of God."

1 Thessalonians 3:12–13: "May the Lord *cause you to increase* [πλεονάσαι, *pleonasai*] and to abound in love for one another..., that your hearts may be established unblamable in *holiness* [ἁγιωσύνῃ, *hagiōsynē*] before our God and Father when our Lord Jesus comes."

1 Peter 2:2: "Long for the pure milk of the word, that by it *you may grow* [αὐξηθῆτε, *auxēthēte*] in respect to salvation."

2 Peter 3:18: "*Grow* [αὐξάνετε, *auxanete*] in the grace and knowledge of our Lord and Savior Jesus Christ."

The New Testament quite clearly refuses to endorse a carnal Christian experience as a legitimate status quo. It envisions the Christian life as simultaneously one of dying and one of living—of *dying* more and more unto sin and of *living* more and more unto righteousness.

The Threefold Pattern of the Sanctified Life

The Scriptures do not leave in any doubt the issue of the pattern according to which the Christian is to conform his life. They set forth a distinct and unmistakable threefold standard of holiness according to which he should pattern his Christian walk, namely, the ethical holiness of God, his preceptive will, and Christ himself.

1. Since man was created originally in God's image (Gen. 1:26–27) and, according to Paul, is recreated by grace according to God's image in knowledge and true righteousness and holiness (Eph. 4:24; Col. 3:10), the Scriptures summon the Christian to emulate *the ethical holiness of God himself:* "Be holy, for I am holy" (Lev. 11:44–45; 19:2; 1 Pet. 1:15–16). See also the admonitions: "you are to be perfect [in your mercy], as your heavenly Father is perfect [in his mercy]" (Matt. 5:48; Luke 6:36); "forgiving ... just as God forgave" (Eph. 4:32; Col. 3:13).

2. Revelation defines that likeness to God according to which Christians' lives are to be patterned concretely in terms of conformity to *his preceptive will* for them—the moral law or Ten Commandments (Exod. 20:1–17; Deut. 5:6–21). That is to say, it is the Decalogue which is the ethical norm for the Christian's covenant way of life.

To speak about Christian ethics and law in the same breath for many Christians, however, is to graze the rim of, if not actually to enter into, legalism. This, of course, is a mistaken notion. The proper definition of legalism is given by the *Shorter Oxford Dictionary*: "adherence to law as opposed to the gospel; the doctrine of justification by works, or teaching which savors of it." This historic meaning of the term should be kept in mind, for, as David C. Jones points out in his lecture note on Christian ethics, it is all too common in the twentieth century to find the term being used for "adherence to God's precepts as the norm of morality" which is something altogether different. By such misuse of the term the negative connotations of legalism are transferred to the morality of orthodox Protestantism. The doctrine of justification by faith alone relieves the latter from the charge of legalism. Still, an ethical position might "savor" of legalism if it failed to give adequate attention to union with Christ as the ethical dynamic of the Christian life (see Rom. 6:1–14) and to the enabling work of the Holy Spirit in sanctification. Such is not the case with the Westminster Confession of Faith, which affirms the necessity of "the Spirit of Christ subduing and enabling the will of man to do that freely, and cheerfully, which the will of God, revealed in the law, requireth to be done" (XIX/vii). A truly biblical ethic is concerned with obedience to God's precepts made possible by the Spirit of life in Christ Jesus (Rom. 8:4). It is this "manner of life and behaviour which the Bible requires and which the faith of the Bible produces."[77]

This use of the law for Christian ethics has come to be referred to as the "third use of the law," the other two uses being, first, its moral standards which are to serve as the rule of all true civil righteousness, and second, its "tutorial" work of convicting sinners, through the agency of the Holy Spirit, of their sins and thus driving them to Christ that they may be justified by faith (Gal. 3:24).

Some Lutherans, applying their law-gospel paradigm, reject this third use of the law (though it is clearly taught by Melanchthon and the *Formula of Concord,* Art. VI), fearing that it intrudes legalism into the Christian experience. Dispensationalists, fearing the heresy of "Galatianism," also reject the notion that Christians are under the so-called Mosaic law. For example, Lewis Sperry Chafer declares that Christians are not obligated to obey the Decalogue as such and cites Paul's statement that "we are not under law but under grace" to prove it (Rom. 6:15; see Gal. 3:24–25).[78] These Christians argue that Paul teaches that the law has been fulfilled and hence done away in Christ. They are bound to Christ, they declare, and therefore are obligated only to serve him. But does the New Testament repeal the Decalogue's normative character for Christian life and practice? Because it is

---

77. John Murray, *Principles of Conduct* (Grand Rapids, Mich.: Eerdmans, 1957), 12.
78. Lewis Sperry Chafer *(Systematic Theology,* [1947; reprint, Grand Rapids, Mich.: Kregel, 1993], 4:209) writes: "Must Christians turn to the Decalogue for a basis of divine government in their daily lives? Scripture answers this question with a positive assertion: 'Ye are not under the law, but under grace.' "

Paul in particular who is credited with teaching this, it is important that we consider this matter of Paul's teaching on the Christian's relation to the law.[79]

At the outset, it is striking to note that this great apostle of justification by faith alone completely apart from the works of the law can still speak of the law of God as holy, just, spiritual, and good (Rom. 7:12, 14, 16) and can contend that all the world is accountable to God because all men are "under the law" (Rom. 3:19). He argues that his gospel, far from nullifying the law, rather upholds the law (Rom. 3:31). He makes it clear that obedience is conformity to God's will and that God's will provides the specific norms or standards for Christian obedience. Here, as in the case of the content of the gospel message itself, the norms or standards are sometimes presumed or assumed and not always specifically stated. At times, however, the basis or standard is stated in very significant ways. In *these* places it becomes clear that the foundational character of Paul's ethic is God's revealed preceptive will or law.

The norm or standard in Paul's ethic is, first, the law of God known by all men because they are made in the image of God: "Although they know *the righteous ordinance* [τὸ δικαίωμα, *to dikaiōma*] of God, that those who practice such things [as he lists in 1:29–31] are worthy of death, they not only do the same, but also give hearty approval to them who practice them" (Rom. 1:32). Paul's foundational premise here is that men are aware of the basic moral teaching of God made known through God's general revelation to them (see Rom. 1:26, 27; 2:14ff.; 1 Cor. 11:14). Thus it is that Paul speaks of conscience (συνείδησις, *syneidēsis*)—the self-conscious self-evaluative process of assessing the degree of one's moral success or integrity—within men because they are made in God's image (see Rom. 2:15). This is not to say that man's conscience is an independent norm but only that man's conscience is a scale which registers or reflects within him his own awareness of God's standard. *His conscience bears witness to the presence of God's norm within him.*

Paul does not utilize this perspective very often of Christians, however. Of the latter Paul speaks of informing the conscience by God's Word-revelation. So he does not presume that the conscience of man does not need more instruction. But Romans 1:32 does indicate that at the most rudimentary level of human existence, the ordinance or law of God is understood to be the norm of human ethics or conduct. This aspect of the ordinance or law of God Paul develops from its most rudimentary and implicit presence to an explicit unfolding of the normative character of God's law.

For Paul the moral law of God, which Christians are to obey, is revealed in the Scriptures—especially (but not exclusively) in the Decalogue:

---

79. I am indebted to conversations with George W. Knight III for several of the following insights on Paul's teaching on the Christian's relation to the law. See also Murray, *Principles of Conduct*, chapter 8.

Romans 7:7: "I would not have come to know sin except through the law; for I would not have known about coveting if the law had not said, 'You shall not covet.'"

Romans 8:4–13: The work of Christ and of the Spirit in reference to sanctification and obedience is described in terms *not* of Christ's but of the law's requirements being fulfilled *in* or *by us* (ἐν ἡμῖν, *en hēmin*). Here we see Paul placing ethics in this principial framework: Christ has redeemed us to enable us to obey the moral requirements of the law, and the Holy Spirit is enabling us to walk in the law's requirements. From Paul's statement in 8:7 that the ungodly mind cannot subject itself to the law of God, we should infer that the godly can. All the moral teaching that follows in Romans may in a real sense be seen as a statement of the law's requirements.

Romans 12:1–2: When Paul, beginning in Romans 12, takes up the matter of the moral outworking of justification, he does so by picking up on his earlier emphasis on God's law. Now he does so by speaking of the law under the synonym of "the will of God" (τὸ θέλημα τοῦ θεοῦ, *to thelēma tou theou*), describing God's will here in terms similar to those he had used earlier to describe the law (compare his "good and acceptable and perfect will of God" with his earlier description in 7:13 of the law as "holy and just and good"). Here Paul calls on the Christian to use his renewed mind to discern and to obey God's law.

Romans 13:9–10: Before he turns to the specific problem of meat offered to idols, Paul brings to a conclusion his general section on ethics by quoting most of the second half of the ten commandments: "he who loves his fellowman has fulfilled the law. The commandments, 'Do not commit adultery,' 'Do not murder,' 'Do not steal,' 'Do not covet,' and whatever other commandments there may be, are summed up in this one rule: 'Love your neighbor as yourself.' Love does no harm to its neighbor. Therefore love is the fulfillment of the law." Paul indicates that the four commandments he mentions (the sixth, seventh, eighth, and tenth) do not comprise the whole law by adding the words, "and whatever other commandments there may be." And his appeal to the Decalogue as that which the law of love fulfills demonstrates the permanent and abiding relevance of the law. Paul's specific appeal to the love obligation also reminds the Christian that his (Paul's) standard is the same as Jesus had indicated in his summary of the Ten Commandments: "Love your neighbor as yourself" (Paul quotes Lev. 19:18 in Rom. 13:9; see Mark 12:31; Matt. 7:12). He correlates "love" and "law" by saying in 13:10 that "love is the fulfillment of the law." Paul says again here then that the standard of ethics is the law. The very way in which it may be carried out or fulfilled is by the attitude and action of love. As Paul says in Galatians 5:6, 13, it is out of the Christian's "new life" in Christ that faith works through love. In sum, *the norm or standard of the Christian life is the law, and the motive power to keep it is the new life in Christ, that is, life in the Spirit, which exhibits itself as a life of obedience, that is, of love.*

Love finds its direction and its parameters in the law of God. Love is not contentless or only a warm and undefined feeling, nor is it something that may be set in opposition to the law. The law does not need to be a "dead letter," but neither is it an entity with its own inherent strength. Love expresses the true intent and direction of the law as God's good for man and as the way in which men properly express their love to God and man in the ethical realm.

> 1 Corinthians 7:19: Here Paul exhorts Christians to understand that "circumcision is nothing and uncircumcision is nothing. Keeping God's commands is what counts." He says essentially the same thing in Galatians 5:6: "In Christ Jesus neither circumcision nor uncircumcision has any value. The only thing that counts is faith expressing itself through love" (love being viewed here as the active fulfilling of the commandments). Contrary to what most studies have concluded, by setting circumcision, itself a command of God, in contrast to the "commandments," as he does in 1 Corinthians 7:19, Paul makes a distinction between the ethical and the ceremonial, that is, between the permanent and the temporary aspects of the law.
>
> 1 Timothy 1:8–11: Paul insists here that the purpose of the law, indeed, its continuing purpose, is ethical. It is not to be construed as the false teachers were doing. Thus the law is not "made" for the "righteous," that is, for the obedient man who is already molding his life in accordance with them. In saying this, Paul is not denying the law's relevance for Christians but rather is insisting on its *ethical* dimension. In 1:9–10 he virtually summarizes the Ten Commandments in their Old Testament order,[80] and with the strongest and clearest application—following the example of the Old Testament application in Exodus 21 and elsewhere—states the worst expression of the violation of each commandment to remind the congregation of the focus of these commands, that is, to the sinner. For example, to those whom sin tempts to be immoral in the sexual realm, the command say, "You shall not commit adultery." So Paul reminds his readers of the ethical and lawful use of the law. Therefore, to seek to use this passage in reference to the righteous or obedient man in other than in its ethical significance is quite erroneous. Finally, Paul closes this section by saying that law rules to restrain whatever is contrary to the sound teaching of the gospel (1 Tim. 1:10–11). Thus again we see that the law's ethic and the gospel ethic are essentially one and the same.
>
> Ephesians 6:2–3: Here Paul quotes the fifth commandment that children must honor their parents: "Children, obey your parents in the Lord, for this is right. 'Honor your father and mother'—which is the first commandment with a promise—'that it may go well with you and that you may enjoy long life on the earth.'"

---

80. See George W. Knight III, *The Pastoral Epistles* (Grand Rapids, Mich.: Eerdmans, 1992), 82–87.

He does this with the assumption that the Christian community would recognize and accept the abiding significance of the law. He does not quote the law to make it binding but because it is binding. And he quotes this commandment as part of a whole, one among others (see his "which is the first commandment with a promise") that they would know, recognize, and follow. He quotes the commandments with the same ease and assumption with which he refers to the gospel (which also is not always named by name or repeated but assumed).

The focus of the second table of the Ten Commandments, that is, to sinners, can often be found in Paul's admonitions against sin, for example, against sexual immorality, stealing, coveting, and bearing false witness (see Eph. 4:25, 28; 5:3, 5; Col. 3:5, 9; 1 Cor. 6:9–10), but of course not in a wooden or simply citational way.

The law's focus on sinners Paul also underscores by citing other Old Testament passages to state his ethical teaching (see, e.g., the end of Romans 12, Eph. 4:25–26; 5:31; 1 Cor. 9:8–12; 11:8, 9; 14:34; 1 Tim. 5:17–18). In fact, much of Paul's positive teachings he simply finds in the Old Testament and reiterates for his readers. In this approach he followed Jesus' own teaching (in the Sermon on the Mount, for example) that reflected the standards of his Father and correctly interpreted the law of the Old Testament.

> 1 Corinthians 9:20–21: Here Paul declares that he is "not free from the law of God but under the law of Christ." In terms of its ceremonial requirements Paul was not under the law; in terms of its moral code as the law of God and of Christ, he was under it.
>
> 2 Timothy 3:16–17: Here Paul informs Timothy that the *entirety of Scripture*, in a real sense *the* law *(torah)* of God, is profitable for teaching, rebuking, correcting, and training in righteousness, so that the man of God may be thoroughly equipped for every good work.

Ladd is quite correct then when he concludes that Paul

> never thinks of the Law as being abolished. It remains the [ethical] expression of the will of God. . . . The permanence of the Law is reflected . . . in the fact that Paul appeals to specific commands in the Law as the norm for Christian conduct. . . . [For example, from Rom. 13:8–10 and Eph. 6:2] it is clear that the Law [in its ethical demands] continues to be the expression of the will of God for conduct, even for those who are no longer under the Law. . . . the Law as the expression of the will of God is permanent.[81]

---

81. Ladd, *Theology of the New Testament*, 509–10.

Other New Testament writers also directly cite some of the commandments. For example, James cites the sixth and seventh commandments: "For whoever keeps the whole law and yet stumbles in one point is guilty of breaking all of it. For he who said, 'Do not commit adultery,' also said, 'Do not commit murder.' If you do not commit adultery but do commit murder, you have become a lawbreaker" (James 2:10–11). It is significant to our present purpose that James in verse 10 enunciates the principle of the law's *unitary wholeness*. This certainly implies that if the sixth and seventh commandments are still normative for Christ's church and for society in general, so are the other eight.

In fact, the New Testament writers allude to every commandment in one place or other in their letters to the churches: the *first three* commandments lie behind many of the statements in Romans 1:21–30, 2:22, 1 Corinthians 6:9, Ephesians 5:5, Colossians 3:5, James 2:7, 19, and Revelation 21:7; the *fourth* commandment behind the designation of the first day of the week—the Christian's day of worship—as "the Lord's day" (Acts 20:7, 1 Cor. 16:2, and Rev. 1:10; see Isa. 58:13)[82]; the *fifth* commandment behind statements in Romans 1:30, Ephesians 6:2–3, Colossians 3:20, and 1 Timothy 1:9; the *sixth* commandment behind statements in Romans 1:29, 13:9, 1 Timothy 1:9–10, James 2:11, 1 John 3:15, and Revelation 21:8; the *seventh* commandment behind statements in Romans 2:22, 13:9, 1 Corinthians 6:9, Ephesians 5:3, 1 Thessalonians 4:3, 1 Timothy 1:10, James 2:11, Revelation 21:8; the *eighth* commandment behind statements in Romans 2:21, 13:9, 1 Corinthians 6:10, Ephesians 4:28, 1 Timothy 1:10; the *ninth* commandment behind statements in Romans 13:9, Ephesians 4:25, Colossians 3:9, 1 Timothy 1:10, and Revelation 21:8; and the *tenth* commandment behind statements in Romans 1:29; 7:7–8, 13:9, 1 Corinthians 6:10, Galatians 5:26, Ephesians 5:5, Colossians 3:5, and Hebrews 13:5. In addition, the two great Old Testament love commandments—to love God with all one's heart, soul, mind, and strength and to love one's neighbor as oneself (Deut. 6:5; Lev. 19:18), which are beautifully New Testament as well in scope and concept, are declared to be summary statements of the Ten Commandments (see Matt. 22:37–40; Mark 12:29–31; Rom. 13:8–19). Surely the Christian is to obey these commandments! Indeed, Jesus said to his disciples: "If you love me, you will obey what I command"

---

82. See my extended argument, "Lord's Day Observance: Man's Proper Response to the Fourth Commandment," *Presbuterion: Covenant Seminary Review* 13:1 (Spring 1987): 7–23. See also Richard B. Gaffin Jr., "A Sabbath Rest Still Awaits the People of God," in *Pressing Toward the Mark*, ed. C. G. Dennison and R. C. Gamble (Philadelphia: Committee for the Historian of the Orthodox Presbyterian Church, 1986), 33–51, who argues against the view that the Sabbath commandment has been done away in Christ by showing that the weekly Sabbath is a sign of the future Sabbath rest of Hebrews 3:7–4:13: "to deny this is to suppose that for the writer the weekly sign has ceased, even though the reality to which it points is still future—again, an unlikely supposition. What rationale could explain such a severing, by cessation, of sign and unfulfilled reality?" (47).

(John 14:15), and again, "You are my friends if you do what I command" (John 15:14). And John declared: "We know that we have come to know him if we keep his commandments" (1 John 2:3), and then actually defined love for God in terms of obedience to his law: "This is love for God, that we keep his commandments" (1 John 5:3).

Ernest F. Kevan, British theologian and author of *The Grace of Law*, concurs regarding the continuing normativity of the law:

> There is no hint anywhere in the New Testament that the Law has lost its validity in the slightest degree, nor is there any suggestion of its repeal. On the contrary, the New Testament teaches unambiguously that the Ten Commandments are still binding upon all men.[83]

Reformed Christians deny that "the third use" of the law places the Christian under the law as a covenant of works, insisting rather that

> The moral law doth for ever bind all, as well justified persons as others, to the obedience therefore; and that, not only in regard of the matter contained in it, but also in respect of the authority of God the Creator, who gave it. Neither doth Christ, in the Gospel, any way dissolve, but much strengthen this obligation.
>
> Although true believers be not under the law, as a covenant of works, to be thereby justified, or condemned; yet is it of great use to them, as well as to others; in that, as a rule of life informing them of the will of God, and their duty, it directs and binds them to walk accordingly; discovering [revealing] also the sinful pollutions of their nature, hearts, and lives; so as, examining themselves thereby, they may come to further conviction of, humiliation for, and hatred against sin, together with a clearer sight of the need they have of Christ, and the perfection of his obedience. It is likewise of use to the regenerate, to restrain their corruptions, in that it forbids sin: and the threatenings of it serve to show what even their sins deserve; and what afflictions, in this life, they may expect for them, although freed from the curse thereof threatened in the law. The promises of it, in like manner, show them God's approbation of obedience, and what blessings they may expect upon the performance thereof: although not as due to them by the law as a covenant of works. So as, a man's doing good, and refraining from evil, because the law encourageth to the one, and deterreth from the other, is no evidence of his being under the law; and, not under grace.
>
> Neither are the forementioned uses of the law contrary to the grace of the Gospel, but do sweetly comply with it; the Spirit of Christ subduing and enabling the will of man to do that freely, and cheerfully, which the will of God, revealed in the law, requireth to be done. (Westminster Confession of Faith, XIX/v–vii; see also the extended expositions of the law of God in both the Larger (Questions 91–148) and Shorter (Questions 39–81) Catechisms)

---

83. Ernest F. Kevan, in his Tyndale Biblical Theology Lecture, July 4, 1955.

3. Since Christ was "born under the law" and perfectly fulfilled all of its precepts, and since conformity to the image of Christ is the Father's predestinated end for them (Rom. 8:29), it is little wonder that *Christ himself* is set before the Christian's eyes as the third pattern for Christian living—"the supreme exhibition of that pattern which is the exemplar of sanctification."[84] Christ declares: "I have given you an *example* [ὑπόδειγμα, *hypodeigma*] that you also should do as I have done to you" (John 13:15). Paul enjoins: "Let this mind be in you which was also in Christ Jesus" (Phil. 2:5). And Peter writes: "Christ also suffered for you, leaving you an *example* [ὑπογραμμὸν, *hypogrammon*], that you should follow in his steps" (1 Pet. 2:21). As the Christian, through Christ's enabling grace, "beholds as in a mirror the glory of the Lord, [he] is transformed into the same image from [one stage of] glory to [the next stage of] glory" (2 Cor. 3:18).

The Goal of the Sanctified Life

The last point above underscores for us the truth that first and foremost the goal of progressive sanctification (as is true for every aspect of our salvation—see Eph. 1:6, 12, 14), as we are transformed from glory to glory, is *the glory of God himself*:

> Romans 5:2: "Through [Christ] we have gained access by faith into this grace in which we now stand. And we rejoice in the hope of the glory of God [that is, our final glorification]"
>
> Philippians 1:11: "You . . . having been filled with the fruit of righteousness which comes through Jesus Christ, to the glory and praise of God."
>
> 1 Thessalonians 2:12: "Walk in a manner worthy of the God who calls you into his own kingdom and glory."
>
> 1 Peter 5:10: "The God of all grace, who called you to his eternal glory in Christ, will himself perfect, confirm, strengthen, and establish you."

The Agents and Instruments Effecting the Sanctified Life

Christians can no more sanctify themselves by their own efforts than can sinners justify themselves by their own efforts. The Scriptures insist that it is God who must effect the Christian's sanctification by his own grace and power:

> John 17:17: "Sanctify them by your word." Here it is the Father's aid which Jesus is invoking in behalf of his disciples' sanctification.

---

84. Murray, "The Pattern of Sanctification," in *Collected Writings*, 2:308.

Romans 8:13–14: "If by the Spirit you are putting to death the deeds of the body, you will live. For all who are led by the Spirit of God, these are Sons of God."

1 Thessalonians 5:23: "May the God of peace himself sanctify you entirely" Again the referent of the phrase "the God of peace" is probably the Father.

2 Corinthians 3:18: "We all . . . are being transformed . . . from glory to glory, just as [it comes] from the Lord of the Spirit [or perhaps "the Spirit of the Lord"]." Here the referent of the last phrase is either Christ or the Spirit of Christ.

Although growth in grace is divinely energized, I would not suggest for a moment that the Christian is to be passive in his spiritual growth. To the contrary, *he is to be fully and consciously engaged in his sanctification*. Peter calls upon the Christian to be "diligent to make his calling and election certain" by practicing moral excellence, self-control, perseverance, godliness, and brotherly kindness (2 Pet. 1:5–10), and Paul counsels Christians: "work out [κατεργάζεσθε, *katergazesthe*] your salvation with fear and trembling" (Phil. 2:12). We could fill several pages with passages with this same emphasis (see, for example, Rom. 12:1–3, 9–21; 13:7–14; 2 Cor. 7:1; Gal. 5:13–16; Eph. 4:17–32; Phil. 3:10–17; 4:4–9; Col. 3:1–25; 1 Thess. 5:8–22; Heb. 12:14–16; 13:1–9; James 1:19–27; 2:14–26; 3:13–18; 1 Pet. 1:13–25; 2:11–17; 2 Pet. 3:14–18; 1 John 2:3–11; 3:17–24). But in the very context where Paul urges the Philippian Christian to work out his salvation, Paul reminds him that he does so "because [γάρ, *gar*] it is God who *is working* [ἐνεργῶν, *energōn*] in you, both to will and to work in behalf of his good pleasure" (Phil. 2:13). Murray comments:

> God's working in us is not suspended because we work, nor our working suspended because God works. Neither is the relation strictly one of co-operation as if God did his part and we did ours so that conjunction or coordination of both produced the required result. God works in us and we also work. But the relation is that *because* God works we work. All working out of salvation on our part is the effect of God's working in us, not the willing to the exclusion of the doing and not the doing to the exclusion of the willing, but both the willing and the doing.[85]

Nor may Christians, because their sanctification is ultimately effected by God, "grow negligent, as if they were not bound to perform any duty unless upon a special motion of the Spirit; but they ought to be diligent in stirring up the grace of God that is in them" (Westminster Confession of Faith, XVI/iii). Not only should they in faith be obediently about the business of fulfilling their normal duties and responsibilities as Christian husbands, wives, parents, children, employers, and employees, simply because they know God expects it of them, but also they should

---

85. Murray, *Redemption*, 148–49.

in faith actively avail themselves of the divine help in the special means or instrumentalities which God provides for their spiritual growth, chief among them being the following:

1. The reading and the preaching of the Word of God (see John 17:17—"Sanctify them by the truth; your word is truth"; Acts 20:32—"And now I commend you to God and to the word of his grace, which [word] is able to build you up and to give you an inheritance among all those who have been sanctified"; see also Shorter Catechism, Questions 89–90);

2. The receiving and attendance upon the sacraments of the church (see Gal. 3:27—"as many of you as have been baptized [by the Spirit] into Christ have put Christ on [which spiritual truth is signified by the sacrament of baptism]"; Rom. 6:3, 11—"do you not know that all of us who have been baptized [by the Spirit] into Christ Jesus have been baptized into his death?... Even so [in light of your baptism into Christ's death] consider yourselves to be dead to sin"; 1 Cor. 11:24–25—"This is my body, which is for you; do this in remembrance of me.... This cup is the new covenant in my blood; do this, as often as you drink it, in remembrance of me"; see also Shorter Catechism, Questions 91–97);

3. Prayers of adoration, confession, thanksgiving, and supplication (see Phil. 4:6—"Be anxious for nothing, but in everything by prayer and supplication with thanksgiving let your requests be made known to God"; 1 John 5:14—"And this is the confidence which we have before him, that, if we ask anything according to his will, he hears us"; James 4:2—"You do not have because you do not ask"; see also Shorter Catechism, Questions 98–107);

4. The fellowship of the saints in the gathered assembly (see Acts 2:42, 46—"And they were continually devoting themselves to the apostles' teaching and to fellowship [κοινωνία, koinōnia], to the breaking of bread and to prayer.... And day by day continuing with one mind in the temple, and breaking bread from house to house, they were taking their meals together with gladness and sincerity of heart"; Heb. 10:24–25—"let us consider how to stimulate one another to love and good deeds, not forsaking our own assembling together, as is the habit of some, but encouraging one another; and all the more, as you see the day drawing near"; and finally,

5. All of the providences of life which God works together to perfect in them that which he has predestinated for them, namely, their conformity to the image of his Son (Rom. 8:28–29, 35–39).

Summary of the Doctrine

"Sanctification is the work of God's free grace, whereby we are renewed in the whole man after the image of God, and are enabled more and more to die unto sin, and live unto righteousness" (Shorter Catechism, Question 35). It is plain from Scripture, from beginning to end, that God desires that his people walk in holiness before him. And *his* people will so walk. For just as there is no sanctification that is not preceded by justification, so also there is no justification that is not followed by sanctification. The scriptural demand for and expectation of holiness in the Christian should stir the professing Christian in whom there is no hungering and thirsting after righteousness to examine himself to see if he is actually in the faith (2 Cor. 13:5).

This is not to say that God's people will not experience conflict with sin and temptation. Galatians 5:17 assures them that they will struggle with the flesh.[86] But they are also assured that "through the continual supply of strength from the sanctifying Spirit of Christ, the regenerate [man] doth overcome; and so, the saints grow in grace, perfecting holiness in the fear of God" (Westminster Confession of Faith, XIII/iii). The greatest need of Christian children is to see their parents walking with Christ. The greatest need of a congregation is to see its pastor living in true piety. And the greatest need of the church today is a holy walk before the Lord.

PERSEVERANCE OF THE SAINTS

They, whom God hath accepted in his Beloved, effectually called, and sanctified by his Spirit, can neither totally nor finally fall away from the state of grace, but shall certainly persevere therein to the end, and be eternally saved.

This perseverance of the saints depends not upon their own free will, but upon the immutability of the decree of election, flowing from the free and unchangeable love of God the Father; upon the efficacy of the merit and intercession of Jesus Christ, the abiding of the Spirit, and of the seed of God within them, and the nature of the covenant of grace: from all which ariseth also the certainty and infallibility thereof.

Nevertheless, they may, through the temptations of Satan and the world, the prevalency of corruption remaining in them, and the neglect of the means of their preservation, fall into grievous sins; and, for a time, continue therein: whereby they incur God's displeasure, and grieve his Holy Spirit, come to be deprived of some measure of their graces and comforts, have their hearts hardened, and their consciences wounded; hurt and scandalize others, and bring temporal judgments upon themselves. (Westminster Confession of Faith, XVII/i–iii)

---

86. Romans 7:14–25 is *not* a description of the Christian's struggle with sin. It is Paul's description of himself as the *unconverted* Saul of Tarsus, now aroused from his spiritual torpor and convicted by the reality of his sinfulness, struggling even more than before to please God through his efforts at law-keeping. See Appendix F.

At the same time that his people are growing in holiness through the power of God, they are also *"being kept* [φρουρουμένους, *phrouroumenous*] *by the power of God through faith for [the] salvation ready to be revealed in the last time"* (1 Pet. 1:5). This "keeping" work of God effects the perseverance, or perhaps better, the *preservation* of the saints.

It is extremely important that the reader correctly understand what is meant by the perseverance or preservation of the saints. It does not mean that everyone who *professes* to be a Christian is assured of eternal life. Nor does it mean that everyone who satisfies some examining body of a local church with respect to his eligibility for church membership is secure for eternity. The Westminster Confession of Faith quite properly reminds us that "hypocrites and other unregenerate men may vainly deceive themselves with false hopes and carnal presumptions of being in the favour of God, and estate of salvation (which hope of theirs shall perish)" (XVIII/i). What it does mean is that every *true* child of God, that is, every person whom the Father chose in Christ before the foundation of the world and for whom Christ died, whom the Father effectually called by his Word and Spirit unto repentance toward God and faith in Jesus Christ, and whom he consequently justified and adopted into his family, and who is consequently growing in grace, will never come into condemnation. *That* person can never be finally lost and is eternally secure. By virtue of God's preserving grace, he or she will certainly persevere in the state of salvation and be finally and eternally saved.

The Biblical Data

The biblical testimony is replete with assurances to the child of God that once he is truly and genuinely saved, he is saved forever.

> Psalm 37:23–24: "If the Lord delights in a man's ways, he makes his steps firm; though he stumble, he will not fall, for the Lord upholds him with his hand."

> Psalm 73:1–2, 23: "Surely God is good to Israel, to those who are pure in heart. But as for me, my feet had *almost* slipped, I had *nearly* lost my foothold. . . . Yet I am always with you; you hold me by my right hand."

> John 6:37–40: Jesus said: "All that the Father gives me [a reference to the Father's effectual summons, which in turn is grounded in his eternal election] will come to me [this underscores his summon's irresistibility]; and whoever comes to me I will never drive away [οὐ μὴ ἐκβάλω, *ou mē ekbalō*—note the double negative signifying emphasis]. For I have come down from heaven not to do my own will but to do the will of him who sent me. And this is the will of him who sent me, that I shall lose none of all that he has given me, but raise them up at the last day.

For my Father's will is that everyone who looks to the Son and believes in him shall have eternal life, and I will raise him up at the last day."

A highly significant feature of Jesus' promise here is that he states that he came to do his Father's will, and that his Father's will for him is that he should lose none of all those whom the Father savingly gives him but raise them up in the last day. This means that if the Son should fail either initially to save all whom the Father gives him or finally to consummate their salvation in the Eschaton by raising them up from death to glory, he will have violated his Father's will for him. This, we may be sure, he will never do. Consequently, Jesus teaches here the certainty of the elect's salvation, from its initiation to its consummation.

> John 10:28–29: "And I give to [my sheep who follow me] eternal life, and they shall never perish [again a double negative signifying emphasis], and no one will snatch them out of my hand. My Father who has given them to me [note this reference to the Father's election and effectual summons] is greater than all, and no one is able to snatch them out of the Father's hand."

Lest someone should incorrectly insist that it is *only because* his sheep *continue* to follow him (see v. 27) that they are secure, I must note here what I underscored in chapter eighteen (p. 674), namely, that one does not ultimately become one of Christ's sheep by believing in him. This position Jesus expressly repudiates in John 10:26 when he says: "You do not believe, because you are not my sheep." Rather than saying that men are not his sheep because they do not believe in him, Jesus says that they do not believe in him because they are not his sheep. In other words, the Father must have elected them and summoned them first, that is, they must first be his sheep, before they can come to him, that is, believe in him. Then, concerning those who are his sheep by virtue of the Father's election and effectual summons, Jesus declares: "My sheep [the "my" is emphatic in the Greek] hear my voice, and I know them, and they follow me" (10:27); that is, as their Shepherd, he knows them, and as his sheep, they hear and follow him *as a matter of course*. And of those who are his sheep, Jesus says that they shall *never* perish, and that *no one* will or can snatch them out of his and his Father's hands. Here Jesus affirms the saint's eternal security in terms of that precious Shepherd-sheep relationship which eternally prevails between him and his own.

> Romans 5:8b–10: "While we were still sinners, Christ died for us. Since we have now been justified by his blood, how much more shall we be saved from God's wrath through him. For if, when we were God's enemies, we were reconciled to him through the death of his Son, how much more, having been reconciled, shall we be saved through his life!"

Paul's line of reasoning here takes the form of an *argumentum a fortiori,* urging that if it is true that Christ did what he did for us while we were sinners and enemies of God, *how much more certain,* having been justified and having been reconciled by his cross work, shall we be saved from the wrath to come by his life lived for us! If, while we were unsaved, his death effected our justification and our reconciliation, his life of intercession all the more guarantees our future and final salvation.

> Romans 8:30–39: "whom he predestined, these he also called; and whom he called, these he also justified, and whom he justified, these he also glorified [ἐδόξασεν, edoxasen]."

Here the apostle represents the glorification of those who were predestinated, called, and justified by the aorist tense, proleptically "intimating the certainty of its accomplishment."[87] Respecting their certainty of glorification, Murray quite properly affirms: "If saints may fall away and be finally lost, then the called and the justified may fall away and be lost. But that is what the inspired apostle says will not happen and cannot happen=whom God calls and justifies he also glorifies,"[88] and he goes on to say, again quite properly, that one "could rest the argument for the doctrine of perseverance on this one passage."[89]

In light of the certainty of our final glory and eternal salvation which he enunciates in 8:30, Paul issues a series or five rhetorical questions in verses 31–39: (1) If God is for us, who is against us? Certainly not God, and he is the only One who really counts, for "He who spared not his own Son but delivered him up for us all, (2) how shall he not also with him freely give us all things [necessary to the fulfillment of his purpose for us]?" Note that all of the benefits necessary to the fulfillment of God's purpose for us we receive with Christ, indicating that "so great is that gift [of God's Son], so marvellous are its implications, so far-reaching in its consequences that all graces of lesser proportion are certain of free bestowment."[90] (3) Who will bring a charge against God's elect? Certainly not God, and he is the only One who really counts, since it is he who justified them. (4) Who is he who condemns? Certainly not Christ, and he too is the only One who really counts, since it is he "who died, indeed, more than that, who was raised, who is also at God's right hand, who is also interceding for us." (5) What shall separate us from the love of Christ? Certainly not trouble or hardship or persecution or famine or nakedness or danger or sword (8:35–36), for these are simply some of the "all things" which God is working together for our good (8:28), over which "we are more than conquerors through him who loved us" (8:37). Certainly not death or life

---

87. Murray, *Romans*, 1:321.
88. Murray, *Redemption*, 157
89. Ibid., 158.
90. Murray, *Romans*, 1:326.

or angels or demons or things present or things in the future or powers or heights or depths, for nothing in all creation "will be able to separate us from the love of God that is in Christ Jesus our Lord." The final glorification of God's elect, Paul argues here, is infallibly certain.

> 1 Corinthians 1:8–9: "[God] will confirm you unto the end, blameless in the day of our Lord Jesus Christ. God is faithful through whom you were called into fellowship with his Son Jesus Christ our Lord."
>
> 1 Corinthians 3:15: "If any [Christian's] work is burned up [in the judgment], he will suffer loss; but he himself will be saved, but so as through fire."
>
> Philippians 1:6: "He who began a good work in you will carry it on to completion until the day of Christ Jesus."
>
> Hebrews 7:25: "He is able to save forever those who come to God through him, because he ever lives for the purpose of interceding for them."
>
> 1 Peter 1:5: "[you] are kept by the power of God through faith for the salvation ready to be revealed in the last time."

A Response to Objections

Arminian Christians who believe that Christians can fall from grace and be finally lost have advanced three classes of texts against the ones adduced above for the preservation of the saints. First is that class of passages that suggests that the Christian is secure *only if* he perseveres in the faith to the end. Here one may cite the following verses:

Matthew 24:13: "But the one who endures to the end, he shall be saved." (See also Mark 13:13; Luke 21:19; Rom. 2:7.)

John 8:31: "If you abide in my word, then you are truly disciples of mine."

John 15:6: "If anyone does not abide in me, he is thrown away as a branch, and dries up; and they gather them, and cast them into the fire, and they are burned."

1 Corinthians 9:27: "No, I beat my body and make it my slave so that after I have preached to others, I myself will not be disqualified for the prize."

1 Corinthians 15:1–2: "I am making known to you, brothers, the gospel which I preached to you, which you also received, in which you also stand, through which also you are saved, if you hold fast the word which I preached unto you."

Colossians 1:22–23: "He has now reconciled you by the body of his flesh through death, in order to present you before him holy and blameless and beyond reproach—if indeed you continue in the faith firmly established and steadfast, and not moved away from the hope of the gospel that you have heard."

Hebrews 3:6, 14: "Christ was faithful as a Son over his house, whose house we are if we hold fast our confidence and the hope in which we boast [firm until the end] . . . we have become partakers of Christ, if we hold fast the beginning of our assurance firm until the end."

Hebrews 10:36, 39: "For you have need of endurance, so that when you have done the will of God, you may receive the promise. . . . But we are not of those who shrink back to destruction, but of those who have faith to the preserving of the soul."

These several conditions—endurance to the end, abiding in Christ and his Word, continuing in or holding fast to the faith—are they not essential to one's final salvation? And where they do not exist, can that professing Christian expect to be finally saved? To the first question, the Calvinist would answer emphatically in the affirmative, and to the second, he would respond just as emphatically in the negative. These answers may come as a surprise to some Arminian Christians, but Calvinist Christians, out of genuine concern to oppose the quietism and antinomianism within evangelical circles, are as zealous to insist upon these conditions as means to salvation as are Arminians. Charles Hodge, for example, whose Calvinistic convictions are not in doubt, commenting on 1 Corinthians 10:12 ("let him who thinks he stands take heed lest he fall"), writes:

> This may refer . . . to security of salvation. . . . The false security of salvation commonly rests on the ground of our belonging to a privileged body (the church), or to a privileged class (the elect). Both are equally fallacious. *Neither the members of the church nor the elect can be saved unless they persevere in holiness;* and they cannot persevere in holiness without continual watchfulness and effort.[91]

But where the Arminian contends that the true believer may *in fact not persevere* to the end and be finally lost after all, the Calvinist is convinced that the true believer will *in fact persevere,* and to that end will take seriously the Scripture warnings and conditions for salvation.

"But," asks the Arminian, "if true Christians will in fact persevere to the end anyway, why are these admonitions, which often carry with them the threat of eternal destruction, even issued by the Scripture writers? Aren't they really unnecessary if Christians can't be lost?"

The Calvinist responds: "They are issued for the same reason that Paul, even though God had assured him on the occasion of the impending shipwreck recorded

---

91. Charles Hodge, *A Commentary on the First Epistle to the Corinthians,* (London: Banner of Truth Trust, 1958), 181, emphasis supplied.

in Acts 27 that 'there shall be no loss of life among you, but only of the ship' [27:22, 24, 34], warned the centurion and the soldiers that unless the sailors who were trying to escape in the lifeboat remained in the ship, they who remained in the ship could not be saved [27:31]. Though Paul was assured of their 'salvation,' he knew too that the *means* of their salvation was for all to remain on board the ship. Thus he issued his warning, and it had the desired effect—'the soldiers cut away the ropes of the ship's boat, and let it fall away' and in due course 'they all were brought safely to land' [27:44]." The Calvinist takes seriously the fact that God ordains not only the end but also all the means to the end, and one of the means to his final salvation is the Christian's perseverance in the faith to the end, without which means the end is neither achieved nor is it achievable. The Calvinist clearly perceives that one of the ways whereby God effects this means of perseverance in the elect is to warn them of the consequences of their not persevering to the end.[92] G. C. Berkouwer would never entertain any representation of perseverance that would eliminate the Christian's responsibility to pursue holiness but he too insists that the purpose of scriptural admonition is that of insuring the saints' perseverance. He writes:

> Anyone who sees a contradiction between the [Reformed] doctrine of perseverance and the numberless admonitions of the Holy Scriptures, has abstracted perseverance from faith. *Faith itself can do nothing else than listen to those admonitions and so travel the road of abiding in him.* For admonition distinguishes the true confidence, which looks for everything from grace, and the other "possibility," which is rejected on the basis of Christ and the Church. So admonition is at the same time both remembrance and a calling. It points out the way of error to those who travel the way of salvation, and it exhorts them to keep going only in the true way.... *These admonitions, too, have as their end the perseverance of the Church, which precisely in this way is established in that single direction, which is and which must remain irreversible—the direction from death to life!*[93]

The second class of passages Arminians use as evidence that Christians may finally be lost consists of verses that seem to teach that Christian brothers for whom Christ died may still finally perish (Rom. 14:15; 1 Cor. 8:11). At the end of the last chapter (pp. 698–701) I suggested that, while Paul formally employs the "language of perdition" in these contexts in order to impress upon the stronger brother the serious spiritual harm he may inflict upon the weaker brother if he is not sensitive to the latter's scruples, certain details in these and their more distant contexts demand

---

92. See Berkhof, *Systematic Theology*, 548, D, 3, a.
93. G. C. Berkouwer, *Faith and Perseverance* (Grand Rapids, Mich.: Eerdmans, 1958), 116–17, 121, emphasis supplied.

that we stop short of the conclusion Arminians extract from them. The reader is urged to review the exposition in the previous chapter.

Other ways of interpreting these passages are also possible. Hodge, for example, interprets these passages by appealing to the "shipwreck" passage in Acts 27. Consider Hodge's comments on the latter verse ("And through your knowledge shall the weak brother perish, for whom Christ died?") which would apply equally to the former as well:

> The language of Paul in this verse seems to assume that those may perish for whom Christ died. It belongs, therefore, to the same category as those numerous passages which make the same assumption with regard to the elect. If the latter are consistent with the certainty of the salvation of all the elect, then this passage is consistent with the certainty of the salvation of those for whom Christ specifically died. It was absolutely certain that none of Paul's companions in shipwreck was on that occasion to lose his life, because the salvation of the whole company had been predicted and promised; and yet the apostle said that if the sailors were allowed to take away the boats, those left on board could not be saved. This appeal secured the accomplishment of the promise. So God's telling the elect that if they apostatize they shall perish, prevents their apostasy. And in like manner, the Bible teaching that those for whom Christ died shall perish if they violate their conscience, prevents their transgressing, or brings them to repentance. God's purposes embrace the means as well as the end. If the means fail, the end will fail. He secures the end by securing the means. It is just as certain that those for whom Christ died shall be saved, as that the elect shall be saved. Yet in both cases the event is spoken of as conditional. There is not only a possibility, but an absolute certainty of their perishing if they fall away. But this is precisely what God has promised to prevent.[94]

Perhaps Hodge's interpretation is the correct one; perhaps mine in the last chapter is. But regardless of which is correct, both interpretations demonstrate that the Arminian interpretation is not *required* by the details of the passages. And until some irrefutable datum is forthcoming that *demands* the Arminian construction, these verses must not be allowed to overturn the clear preservation passages of Scripture.

Finally, the third class of passages is comprised of those verses that are said to affirm that Christians either have fallen, may fall, or shall fall away from the estate of salvation and be finally lost:

---

94. Hodge, *First Corinthians*, 149 (on 8:11).

Matthew 24:10, 12: "At that time many *will turn away* [σκανδαλισθήσονται, *skandalisthēsontai*] from the faith.... the love of most *will grow cold* [ψυγήσεται, *psygēsetai*]."

1 Timothy 1:19: "Some... *have shipwrecked* [ἐναυάγησαν, *enauagēsan*] their faith."

1 Timothy 4:1: "The Spirit clearly says that in later times some *will abandon* [ἀποστήσονται, *apostēsontai*] the faith."

2 Timothy 4:10: "For Demas, because he loved this world, *has deserted* [ἐγκατέλιπεν, *enkatelipen*] me."

Hebrews 6:4–6: "It is impossible for those who have once been enlightened, who have tasted the heavenly gift, who have shared in the Holy Spirit, who have tasted the goodness of the word of God and the powers of the coming age, *if they fall away* [παραπεσόντας, *parapesontas*], to be brought back to repentance, because [or while] to their loss they are crucifying the Son of God all over again and subjecting him to public disgrace."

2 Peter 2:20–22: "If they have escaped the corruption of the world by knowing our Lord and Savior Jesus Christ and are again entangled in it and overcome, they are worse off at the end than they were at the beginning. It would have been better for them not to have known the way of righteousness, than to have known it and then *to turn their backs on* [ὑποστρέψαι ἐκ, *hypostrepsai ek*] the sacred commandment that was passed on to them."

What then do these passages teach, if they do not teach that Christians may fall away from the state of salvation and be lost? They teach that there is such a thing as "temporary faith" which is not true faith in Christ at all. The Westminster Confession of Faith speaks of some who "may be called by the ministry of the Word, and may have some common operations of the Spirit," yet who "never truly come unto Christ, and therefore cannot be saved" (X/iv). In his parable of the sower and the four kinds of soil, Jesus informed his disciples beforehand, lest they should become unduly discouraged when it happens, that some to whom they would proclaim the Word of God would "immediately receive it with joy," but then, because "they have no firm root in themselves but are only *temporary* [πρόσκαιροί, *proskairoi*], when affliction or persecution arises because of the Word, immediately they fall away" (Matt. 13:20–21, author's translation). Reflecting on our Lord's words here, Murray writes:

> We must appreciate the lengths and the heights to which a temporary faith may carry those who have it.... [This temporary experience] is brought to our attention in the language of the epistle to the Hebrews when it speaks of those "who were once enlightened and tasted of the heavenly gift and were made partakers of the Holy Spirit and tasted the good word of God and the powers of the age to

come" (Heb. 6:5–6). . . . It is this same [experience] that Peter deals with in 2 Peter 2:20–22 [where] Peter has in view persons who had the knowledge of the Lord and Saviour Jesus Christ, who had known the way of righteousness, and who had thereby escaped the pollutions of the world but who had again become entangled in these pollutions and had turned from the holy commandment delivered unto them so that "it is happened unto them according to the true proverb, The dog is turned to his own vomit again; and the sow that was washed to her wallowing in the mire." The Scripture itself, therefore, leads us to the conclusion that it is possible to have very uplifting, ennobling, reforming, and exhilarating experience of the power and truth of the gospel, to come into such close contact with the supernatural forces which are operative in God's kingdom of grace that these forces produce effects in us which to human observation are hardly distinguishable from those produced by God's regenerating and sanctifying grace and yet be not partakers of Christ and heirs of eternal life.[95]

It needs to be stressed that those persons who have only this temporary faith were never God's elect and were never regenerated, and are therefore not true believers. The greatest single piece of evidence that this is so is the fact that they fall away from the faith. Arminians accuse Calvinists who insist that those who fall away were never truly Christians in the first place of resorting to an unholy subterfuge. But such is not the case. They are only echoing John himself, who wrote of anti-Christ teachers who had defected from the fellowship: "They went out from us, but *they did not really belong to us* [οὐκ ἦσαν ἐξ ἡμῶν, *ouk ēsan ex hēmōn*]. For if they had belonged to us, they would have remained with us; but their going showed that none of them belonged to us" (1 John 2:19).

The Assurance of Salvation

"How then can the Christian have any assurance of salvation?" the Arminian counters. "For if the people described in these passages, who surely *believed* prior to their defection from the faith that they were true Christians, were in fact never really so, on what grounds can any Christian know for certain that he is really saved? How can he be certain that he has not deceived himself and that he will not fall away from the faith like they did?"

These questions raise an issue that pertains to the professing Christian's *state of mind*, namely, the *subjective* assurance that he is in fact a Christian, which, because of the numerous grounds that people resort to in their thinking—some appropriate, some quite inappropriate—as proofs that they are Christians, can become extremely

---

95. Murray, *Redemption*, 152–53.

complex. Furthermore, these questions really should be a matter of concern for Arminian as well as for Calvinist Christians, for they too must admit the possibility that a person may *believe* that he is a Christian when in fact he is not.

In spite of the complexity of this issue, however, the Calvinist insists that certain propositions are still undeniably true. The first is that there is such a thing as *false assurance* (which can flow out of what we have called here temporary faith) that one is in the favor of God and the state of salvation (see Westminster Confession of Faith, XVIII/i). Furthermore he would without hesitation insist that it is this *false* assurance that these people in the verses cited above have. He would also insist that some vital fruit or evidence of genuine salvation was doubtless missing from their "Christian experience" which put to the lie their assurance and, for the discerning, their profession as well. The missing fruit, if they had examined themselves in the light of Scripture, they themselves could most likely have discerned. For example, in the Hebrews 6 case the missing fruit was the total absence of *growth in understanding* of even the "elementary teaching about Christ"—a fruit that surely "accompanies salvation" (see Heb. 5:11–14; 6:9), while in the 2 Peter 2 case the missing fruit was the complete absence in the false teachers of *any holy religious affections* (see Peter's characterization of them in 2:3 as greedy and deceptive, in 2:9 as unrighteous, in 2:10 as following "the corrupt desire of the sinful nature and despise authority," and in 2:10–19 as "slaves of corruption," bold, arrogant, and blasphemous).

But just as surely as he believes that one may entertain "false hopes and carnal presumptions" that he is in a state of salvation, the Calvinist is equally persuaded that "such as truly believe in the Lord Jesus, and love Him in sincerity, endeavouring to walk in all good conscience before Him, *may, in this life, be certainly assured that they are in the state of grace, and may rejoice in the hope of the glory of God, which hope shall never make them ashamed*" (Westminster Confession of Faith, XVIII/i, emphasis supplied). This true and certain assurance, he believes, is given by the Spirit of God, working by and with the Word (Rom. 8:15–16), and lies behind these biblical affirmations:

> Romans 8:38: "*I am convinced* [πέπεισμαι, *pepeismai*] that neither death nor life, neither angels nor demons, neither the present nor the future, nor any powers, neither height nor depth, nor anything else in all creation shall be able to separate us from the love of God which is in Christ Jesus our Lord." (See also the "we know [οἴδαμεν, *oidamen*]" of 8:28.)
>
> 2 Timothy 1:12: "I know [οἶδα, *oida*] whom I have believed and *am convinced* [πέπεισμαι, *pepeismai*] that he is able to guard what I have entrusted to him until that day."
>
> 1 John 2:3: "By this *we know* [γινώσκομεν, *ginōskomen*] that we have come to know him, if we keep his commandments."

1 John 3:14: "*We know* [οἴδαμεν, *oidamen*] that we have passed from death to life, because we love the brothers."

1 John 4:13: "*We know* [γινώσκομεν, *ginōskomen*] that we abide in him and he in us, because he has given us of his Spirit."

1 John 5:13: "These things I have written to you who believe in the name of the Son of God, that *you may know* [εἰδῆτε, *eidēte*] that you have eternal life."

It is the Christian's certain assurance of eternal glory which Augustus Toplady immortalized in the following hymn:

> The work which his goodness began,
>   The arm of his strength will complete;
> His promise is Yea and Amen,
>   and never was forfeited yet.
> Things future, nor things that are now,
>   nor all things below or above,
> Can make him his purpose forgo,
>   Or sever my soul from his love.
>
> My name from the palm of his hands
>   Eternity will not erase;
> Impressed on his heart it remains,
>   In marks of indelible grace.
> Yes, I to the end shall endure,
>   As sure as the earnest is giv'n;
> More happy, but not more secure,
>   The glorified spirits in heav'n.

Such assurance of salvation and of eternal life springs from (1) an intelligent understanding of the nature of salvation (2 Pet. 1:2, 3, 5–6, 8; 3:18), (2) the recognition of the immutability of the gifts and calling of God (Rom. 11:29), (3) obedience to the commandments of God (1 John 2:3), (4) self-examination (2 Cor. 13:5), (5) and the inward witness of the Holy Spirit who "himself bears witness with our spirit that we are children of God" (Rom. 8:15–16; Gal. 4:6).[96]

It is the duty of every true Christian to cultivate such assurance through "the right use of ordinary means [of grace]" (Westminster Confession of Faith, XVIII/iii). Peter urges Christians to "be all the more diligent to make certain about his

---

96. See Westminster Confession of Faith, XVIII/ii. See also Murray, "The Assurance of Faith," *Collected Writings*, 2:270–73.

calling and choosing you" (2 Pet. 1:10). But either because of immaturity in understanding the nature of their salvation or because of weakness of faith due to negligence in cultivating their faith or to disobedience to the commandments of God, worldliness, prayerlessness, or some other sin, some "true believers may have the assurance of their salvation divers ways shaken, diminished, and intermitted" (Westminster Confession, XVIII/iv). In other words, God will not permit *true* believers to persist in their immaturity or their sin and at the same time to continue to enjoy unabated peace of conscience and joy in the Holy Spirit (see Pss. 32:4; 38:2; 51:12). He will chasten his "true children" (Heb. 12:6–8), and his "hand of conviction" will grow ever heavier upon them. In the words of the Westminster Confession of Faith, they will "incur God's displeasure . . . come to be deprived of some measure of their graces and comforts . . . and bring temporal judgments upon themselves" (XVII/iii). If they persist in their waywardness, he will even remove the light of his countenance from them and permit them to lose their *assurance* of salvation, which is surely the emotional state of mind lying behind David's cry: "Do not cast me from your presence, or take your Holy Spirit from me" (Ps. 51:11). And he will not restore the light of his countenance to them "until they humble themselves, confess their sins, beg pardon, and renew their faith and repentance" (Westminster Confession, XI/v). But even in their backslidden state,

> however weak may be the faith of a true believer, however severe may be his temptations, however perturbed his heart may be respecting his own condition, he is never, as regards consciousness, in the condition that preceded the exercise of faith. The consciousness of the believer differs by a whole diameter from that of the unbeliever. At the lowest ebb of faith and hope and love his consciousness never drops to the level of the unbeliever at its highest pitch of confidence and assurance.[97]

To cite the words of the Westminster Confession once more: backslidden Christians are "never utterly destitute of that seed of God, and life of faith, that love of Christ and the brethren, that sincerity of heart, and conscience of duty, out of which, by the operation of the Spirit, their assurance may, in due time, be revived; and by the which, in the mean time, they are supported from utter despair" (XVIII/iv). As he did with backslidden Peter, the Lord will continue to support his wayward children even while he chastens them when they fail to grow or when they fall into sin (Luke 22:31–32, 54–61; 24:34; Mark 16:7; John 21:15–19). But those who only outwardly profess Christ and are not truly saved will know neither the Spirit's inward witness, on the one hand, nor the Father's chastening on the other, but, to

---

97. Murray, "The Assurance of Faith," *Collected Writings*, 2:265.

the contrary, will continue to ground whatever assurances they have that they are in a state of grace in false hopes and carnal presumptions, which hope of theirs shall perish.

Not to affirm the eternal security of the truly saved, and actually to teach, as do Arminians, that those whom the Father elected, called, and justified, and to whom he also freely gives, along with the gift of his Son, all things necessary to their salvation, to teach that those for whom the Son paid the penalty of sin by bearing their curse and dying their death, procuring thereby their salvation, and to teach that those whom the Holy Spirit has regenerated and sealed unto the day of redemption can still finally lose their salvation and never be glorified because of some action on their part is truly an ill-advised counsel of despair. For in addition to the insult which such teaching hurls at the Triune Godhead, it virtually places every Christian beyond the pale of final salvation since it makes his attainment of final salvation turn ultimately upon his own vacillating human will and efforts as he seeks to "keep himself in the faith." But no Christian is capable of keeping himself through sheer force of will in the state of salvation.

Summary of the Doctrine

"True believers, by reason of the unchangeable love of God, and his decree and covenant to give them perseverance, their inseparable union with Christ, his continual intercession for them, and the Spirit and seed of God abiding in them, can neither totally nor finally fall away from the state of grace, but are kept by the power of God through faith unto salvation" (Larger Catechism, Question 79). That the Christian, by virtue of all the salvific provisions of God, will be preserved until his final glorification is beyond doubt. What pastors must understand is that the criterion of true discipleship is *continuance in Jesus' words,* and that the test of a true faith is *perseverance in true piety* to the end. Much of the problem that they have with people in their congregations who profess Christ but who live ungodly, uncommitted lives could be redressed if they would proclaim the lordship of Christ and the nature of true discipleship, and make clear that, while the saint of God will be preserved by the power of God, he *will also persevere in a godly walk* throughout his life unto the end. And where that godly walk in true piety is not forthcoming, no professing Christian has the right to assume that he is in fact a Christian, and no pastor has the right to assure him that he is simply a "carnal Christian." To the contrary, he must be counseled to examine himself to see if he is in the faith, and if he insists that he is, then he must be counseled that he must renew his repentance toward God and his faith in Jesus Christ. For him to refuse to do so is to falsify his profession and should make him subject to the church's discipline.

A Final Divine Act

GLORIFICATION

The bodies of men, after death, return to dust, and see corruption: but their souls, which neither die nor sleep, having an immortal subsistence, immediately return to God who gave them: the souls of the righteous, being then made perfect in holiness, are received into the highest heavens, where they behold the face of God, in light and glory, waiting for the full redemption of their bodies.... Besides [the highest heavens and hell] for souls separated from their bodies, the Scripture acknowledgeth none.[98]

---

98. The Roman Catholic Church teaches the existence of the *Limbus Infantum* where the souls of unbaptized infants go after death, in which state they remain without suffering and yet without the vision of God. There is no foundation in Scripture for such a place. That church also teaches that the great mass of Christians, who are only imperfectly sanctified (i.e., justified) in this life, dying in communion with the church, go to purgatory, where they "undergo purification [by suffering in the fires of purgatory], so as to achieve the holiness necessary to enter the joy of heaven" *(Catechism of the Catholic Church,* para. 1030). This latter teaching, based on 2 Maccabees 12:46 and a very strained exegesis of 1 Corinthians 3:15, 1 Peter 1:7, and Jude 22–23, may be found in seed form in Tertullian, where prayers for the dead are mentioned, in Origen, who speaks of a purification by fire at the end of the world by which all men and angels are to be restored to favor with God, and in Augustine, who did express doubt about some aspects of it. It was specifically Gregory the Great (590–604), "who brought the doctrine into shape and into such connection with the discipline of the church, as to render it the effective engine of government and income, which it has ever since remained" (Charles Hodge, *Systematic Theology,* 3:770). It was finally formulated into and proclaimed an article of faith at the Councils of Florence (1439–1445) and Trent (1545–1563). Protestants quite rightly view the entire dogma of purgatory not only as "another one of those foreign growths that has fastened itself like a malignant tumor upon the theology of the Roman Catholic Church" (R. Laird Harris, *Fundamental Protestant Doctrines* [booklet], V:7) but also as a doctrinal promulgation devised in the interest of sustaining the Roman priesthood and the entire indulgence system, the Catholic Church's chief source of income.

Rome teaches, because "a perennial link of charity exists between the faithful who have already reached their heavenly home, those who are expiating their sins in purgatory and those who are still pilgrims on earth," that Christians living on earth can aid sufferers in purgatory to get to heaven by purchasing "indulgences" (remissions before God of sin) in their behalf. An elaborate doctrinal scheme underlies this teaching. Rome teaches that the church is in possession of a "treasury of supererogatory merit" *(thesaurus supererogationis meritorum)* consisting of the infinite worth of Christ's redemptive work, "the prayers and good works [of supererogation] of the Blessed Virgin Mary," which are "truly immense, unfathomable, and even pristine in their value before God," as well as "the prayers and good works [of supererogation] of all the saints" who by their good works "attained their own salvation and at the same time cooperated in saving their brothers in the unity of the Mystical Body" (see Pope Paul VI's *Indulgentiarum doctrina,* 5). In exchange for the purchase of indulgences the Pope dispenses out of this "treasury of the Church," through the administration of the priests, the merits of Christ, Mary, and the saints in behalf of and for the benefit of the purchaser's loved ones suffering in Purgatory (see *Catechism of the Catholic*

At the last day, such as are found alive shall not die, but be changed: and all the dead shall be raised up, with the self-same bodies, and none other (although with different qualities), which shall be united again to their souls for ever.

... the bodies of the just, by His Spirit, [shall be raised] unto honour; and be made conformable to His own glorious body. (Westminster Confession of Faith, XXXII/i–iii)[99]

God hath appointed a day, wherein He will judge the world, in righteousness, by Jesus Christ, to whom all power and judgment is given of the Father. . . .

The end of God's appointing this day is for the manifestation of the glory of His mercy, in the eternal salvation of the elect; and of His justice, in the damnation of the reprobate, who are wicked and disobedient. For then shall the righteous go into everlasting life, and receive that fulness of joy and refreshing, which shall come from the presence of the Lord; but the wicked who know not God, and obey not the Gospel of Jesus Christ, shall be cast into eternal torments, and be punished with everlasting destruction from the presence of the Lord, and from the glory of His power.

As Christ would have us to be certainly persuaded that there shall be a day of judgment, both to deter all men from sin; and for the greater consolation of the godly in their adversity: so will He have that day unknown to men, that they may shake off all carnal security, and be always watchful, because they know not at what hour the Lord will come; and may be ever prepared to say, Come Lord Jesus, come quickly, Amen. (Westminster Confession of Faith, XXXIII/i–iii)

The Tenses of Salvation

The Scriptures speak of salvation in all three time tenses:

1. The past tense: the Christian has been saved from the guilt and penalty of sin (Luke 19:9—"Today salvation *has come* [ἐγένετο, *egeneto*] to this house"; Eph. 2:8—"For by grace *you have been saved* [ἐστε σεσῳσμένοι, *este sesōsmenoi*] through faith"; 2 Tim. 1:9—[God] *has saved* [σώσαντος, *sōsantos*] us"; Titus 3:5—"according to his mercy *he saved* [ἔσωσεν, *esōsen*] us");

2. The present tense: the Christian is being saved from the power of sin (1 Cor. 1:18—"to us who *are being saved* [σῳζομένοις, *sōzomenois*] [the cross] is the power of God"; 1 Cor. 15:2—"by which *you are being saved* [σῴζεσθε, *sōzesthe*]"; 2 Cor. 2:15—"because we are a fragrance of Christ to God among those who *are being saved* [σῳζομένοις, *sōzomenois*]"), and

---

Church, para. 1471–79). So the Roman Catholic Church officially teaches that salvation is by Christ's merit plus the saints' good works, which also have merit before God—another expression of its philosophy of the *analogia entis* in the sphere of soteriology.

99. The final destiny of the wicked will be addressed in part five, chapter twenty-six.

3. The future tense: the Christian will be completely saved someday from the very presence of sin (see Rom. 5:9, 10—"*we shall be saved* [σωθησόμεθα, *sōthēsometha*] through him from the Wrath"; 13:11—"for our salvation is nearer than when we first believed"; 1 Cor. 3:15—"*he shall be saved* [σωθήσεται, *sōthēsetai*], but as through fire"; 1 Thess. 5:18—"having put on . . . as a helmet, the hope of salvation"; 1 Pet. 1:5—"kept by the power of God through faith for the salvation ready to be revealed in the last time").

For several chapters now we have considered the past and present tenses of salvation. With this final phase of the *ordo salutis*, we turn to the future tense of our salvation—glorification.

The Nature of Glorification

Individual salvation encompasses not only all three tenses of time, but also the whole person—body and soul. God will not be satisfied with his salvific work in our behalf until we stand before him as saved people in Christ, redeemed in spirit and in body; nor will our "so great salvation" be consummated until he has brought our full and final glorification to reality. Consequently, while there is a sense in which death itself now serves the Christian (see 1 Cor. 3:22—"death . . . belongs to you") in that "the souls of believers are at their death made perfect in holiness, and do immediately pass into glory" (Shorter Catechism, Question 37a; see 2 Cor. 5:8; Phil. 1:21–23; Heb. 12:23; Rev. 14:13), it is nonetheless true that "their bodies, being still united to Christ, do rest in their graves till the resurrection" (Shorter Catechism, Question 37b). In other words, while the intermediate state of believers in heaven, brought to pass in his will when God calls his children to himself through death, is a more blessed state than their present one (Phil. 1:21–23), it is not the best and most glorious state. Accordingly, death is not the ultimate experience for which Christians should long. Rather, their blessed hope is the glorious appearing (or the appearing of the glory) of their great God and Savior Jesus Christ (Titus 2:13), at whose coming those who have died in the faith and those who are alive at the time of his coming

> will all be changed—in a flash, in the twinkling of an eye, at the last trumpet. For the trumpet will sound, the dead will be raised imperishable, and we will be changed. For the perishable must clothe itself with the imperishable, and the mortal with immortality. When the perishable has been clothed with the imperishable, and the mortal with immortality, then the saying that is written will come true: "Death has been swallowed up in victory." (1 Cor. 15:51–54).

"At the resurrection, believers, being raised up in glory, shall be openly acknowledged, and acquitted in the day of judgment, and made perfectly blessed in the full enjoying of God to all eternity" (Shorter Cathechism, Question 38). Their state of blessedness, as the consequence of their full and open acquittal in the judgment (their *declared* justification), will be all the more evident by its contrast to the state of the wicked (see Rom. 9:22–23). For while they will enter into everlasting life and receive fullness of joy and refreshing from the presence of the Lord, the wicked who did not know or obey the Lord Jesus will pay the penalty of eternal destruction away from his approving presence and from the glory of his power.

At this point Christians will enter upon their glorified state, the goal toward which the Triune Godhead has been relentlessly driving from the moment of creation, and that ultimate end which was the first of the decrees in the eternal plan of salvation.

The Meaning of Christians' Glorification for Creation

With the arrival of their full "adoption as sons" through the redemption of their bodies at the resurrection (Rom. 8:23), the renewal of creation itself will also occur (Rom. 8:19–21). Creation will be "liberated from its bondage to decay and brought into the glorious freedom of the children of God." Peter describes the world that will then be—the fulfillment of Isaiah 65:17 and 66:22—as "a new heaven and a new earth, in which righteousness dwells" (2 Pet. 3:13). John declares that in the "new heaven and new earth" state, "there will be no more death or mourning or crying or pain, for the old order of things has passed away" (Rev. 21:4). Biblical scholars have debated whether "the new heaven and the new earth" condition involves simply the renewal of the present universe or a complete destruction followed by re-creation *ex nihilo*. The preponderance of evidence suggests the former—a renewal—but the transformation of the universe will be so complete that, for all intents and purposes, it will introduce a radically new order of existence.

At this time and in this way God's "land promise" to Abraham and to his seed will be finally realized.

The Meaning of Their Glorification for Christians Themselves

In their glorified state believers, having received the fullness of their adoption by the resurrection of their bodies from the dead (Rom. 8:23), will be fully conformed to the likeness of the Son of God. For at his coming, the Lord Jesus Christ, "by the power that enables him to bring everything under his control, will transform our lowly bodies so that they will be like his glorious body" (Phil. 3:21). Moreover, believers will then fully reflect the holy character of their Savior (Rom. 8:29), their wills being "made perfectly and immutability free to do good alone, in the state of glory" (Westminster Confession of Faith, IX/v). "This is the highest end conceivable for created beings, the highest end conceivable not only by men but also by

God himself. God himself could not contemplate or determine a higher destiny for his creatures."[100] Murray observes that, though Christ will be the "firstborn" at that time (Rom. 8:29), a term referring to priority and supereminence, his will be a

> supereminence among brethren, and therefore the supereminence involved has no meaning except in that relation. Hence, though there can be no underestimation of the pre-eminence belonging to the Son as the firstbegotten, yet the interdependence is just as necessary. The glory bestowed upon the redeemed is derived from the relation they sustain to the "firstborn." But the specific character involved in being the "firstborn" is derived from the relation he sustains to the redeemed in that capacity. Hence they must be glorified *together*.[101]

Little wonder then that Paul can inform Christians, who were originally called "with the view of obtaining the glory [εἰς περιποίησιν δόξης, *eis peripoiēsin doxēs*] of our Lord Jesus Christ" (2 Thess. 2:14) and who will "be glorified together with [συνδοξασθῶμεν, *syndoxasthōmen*]" Christ (Rom. 8:17), that "our present sufferings are not worth comparing with the glory that will be revealed in us" (8:18), indeed, that "our light and momentary troubles are achieving for us *an eternal glory that far outweighs* [αἰώνιον βάρος δόξης, *aiōnion baros doxēs*] them all" (2 Cor. 4:17).

The Meaning of the Church's Glorification for Christ Himself

Understood in terms of its conformity to Christ's glorious likeness and its arrival at its *summum bonum*, the church's glorification is, however, not the *terminus ad quem* of the divine purpose. For God's determination to conform "a great multitude that no one can count, from every nation, tribe, people and language" (Rev. 7:9) to the likeness of his well-beloved Son was designed as a means to effect a still higher end—the final phase of his glorification of his Son and their Savior and Messianic King. Paul teaches this when he declares that the church's final conformity to Christ is "in order that his Son might become the Firstborn [πρωτότοκος, *prōtotokos*] among many brothers" (Rom. 8:29). Murray writes:

> There is a final end that is more ultimate than the glorification of the people of God. It is the pre-eminence of Christ, and that pre-eminence vindicated and exemplified in the final phase of his glorification. 'Firstborn' reflects on the *priority* and *supremacy* of Christ (see Col. 1:15, 18; Heb. 1:6; Rev. 1:5). The glory of God is always supreme and ultimate. And the supreme glory of God is manifested in the glorifying of the Son. . . . But the glory for the people of God is only

---

100. Murray, "The Goal of Sanctification," *Collected Writings*, 2:316.
101. Ibid., 2:315.

enhanced by the emphasis placed upon the pre-eminence of Christ. For it is *among many brethren* that Christ is the firstborn. That they should be classified as brethren brings to the thought of glorification with Christ the deepest mystery of community. The fraternal relationship is subsumed under the ultimate aim of the predestinating decree. This means that the *pre-eminence* of the Son as the firstborn carries with it the correlative *eminence* of the children of God. The unique dignity of the Son enhances the dignity bestowed upon the many sons who are to be brought to glory....

We thus see how, in the final realization of the goal of sanctification, there is exemplified and vindicated to the fullest extent, an extent that staggers our thought by reason of its stupendous reality, the truth inscribed upon the whole process of redemption, from its inception in the electing grace of the Father (see Eph. 1:4; Rom. 8:29) to its consummation in the adoption (Rom. 8:23; Eph. 1:5), that Christ in all his offices as Redeemer is never to be conceived of apart from the church, and the church is not to be conceived of apart from Christ. There is correlativity in election, there is correlativity in redemption once for all accomplished, there is correlativity in the mediatorial ministry which Christ continues to exercise at the right hand of the Father, and there is correlativity in the consummation, when Christ will come the second time without sin for those that look for him unto salvation.[102]

And so with the church's glorification and the accompanying—yet more ultimate—glorification of Christ himself, we come to that moment in the execution of God's work toward which all of history is moving. God will not be finally satisfied until Christ and his church are fully and finally glorified, to the praise of his Son and his own most holy name (Phil. 2:11), and that to all eternity.

Summary of the Doctrine

Glorification is not to be confused with that benefit which the believer receives at death when his soul is made perfect in holiness and passes immediately into glory (Shorter Catechism, Question 37). Death introduces the believer into what is termed the soul's "intermediate state," which is certainly "gain" and "better by far" than this present state (Phil. 1:21, 23). But the soul's intermediate state is not what Paul has in mind when he speaks of the believers' glorification. Rather, glorification speaks of that final state into which all believers enter together at the resurrection, when being raised up in glory or transformed, they are openly acquitted in the Day of Judgment, and made perfectly blessed, as coheirs with Jesus Christ, in the full enjoying of God to all eternity (Shorter Catechism, Question 38).

---

102. Ibid., 2:316–17.

In light of the surpassing glory that awaits the sons and daughters of God, all the benefits of which they enjoy by grace alone, it is appropriate to conclude this treatment of the application of salvation with the words of Robert Murray McCheyne's great hymn:

> When this passing world is done,
>   when has sunk yon glaring sun,
> When we stand with Christ in glory,
>   looking o'er life's finished story,—
> Then, Lord, shall I fully know,
>   not till then, how much I owe.
>
> When I hear the wicked call
>   on the rocks and hills to fall,
> When I see them start and shrink
>   on the fiery deluge brink,—
> Then, Lord, shall I fully know,
>   not till then, how much I owe.
>
> When I stand before the throne,
>   dressed in beauty not my own,
> When I see thee as thou art,
>   love thee with unsinning heart,—
> Then, Lord, shall I fully know,
>   not till then, how much I owe.
>
> When the praise of heav'n I hear,
>   loud as thunders to the ear,
> loud as many waters' noise,
>   sweet as harp's melodious voice,—
> Then, Lord, shall I fully know,
>   not till then, how much I owe.
>
> Chosen not for good in me,
>   wakened up from wrath to flee,
> Hidden in the Saviour's side,
>   by the Spirit sanctified,—
> Teach me, Lord, on earth to show,
>   by my love, how much I owe.

PART FOUR

The Church

CHAPTER TWENTY

The Nature and Foundation of the Church

THE ENGLISH WORD *church*, as is true of the Scottish *kirk* and the German *Kirche*, is derived from the Greek word κυριακός, *kyriakos*, which means "belonging to the Lord." The Greek phrase τό κυριακόν, *to kyriakon*, came to be used to designate the place where Christians met to worship and in time was transferred also to the people themselves as the "spiritual building" of the Lord.

As a result of this transfer, the word *church* has come to be used in our English Bibles as a translation, not of the Greek word from which it was derived, which by the way occurs only twice in the Greek New Testament and in neither case describes God's people.[1] Rather, *church* is the word that translators now conventionally choose to translate the Greek word ἐκκλησία, *ekklēsia*, ("assembly"), which occurs some 114 times in the Greek New Testament and means something else entirely. Because of this, English translations have lost a rich nuance of Scripture regarding the people of God, which the following discussion will seek to recapture.

THE "ASSEMBLY" IN THE OLD TESTAMENT

In part three, chapter fourteen, I argued for the unity of the covenant of grace and the oneness of the people of God in all ages. There I presented five lines of evidence for the fact of the oneness of God's people—his elect—throughout all time. On the basis of that study we can assert here that the church in Scripture is composed of all the redeemed in every age who are saved by grace through personal faith in the sacrificial work of Jesus Christ, "the seed of the woman" (Gen. 3:15) and suffering Messiah (Isa. 53:5–10).

---

1. See 1 Corinthians 11:20, where it refers to the "Lord's Supper," and Revelation 1:10, where it refers to the "Lord's Day."

The church of God in Old Testament times, rooted initially and prophetically in the *protevangelium* (Gen. 3:15) and covenantally in the Genesis patriarchs (Rom. 11:28), blossomed mainly within the nation of Israel. However this church was not equivalent to the nation of Israel *per se*, for there were always some—and sometimes many, if not most[2]—within that nation who were never more than the physical seed of Abraham, who never possessed more than the outward circumcision of the flesh,[3] and who thus were never the spiritual seed of Abraham. The true church of the Old Testament was the spiritual seed of Abraham, that "Israel" within the nation of Israel about whom the apostle Paul speaks in Romans 9:6–8. The true covenant community of God was then, as it has ever been, the remnant *within* the external community of the nation (Isa. 10:22; Rom. 9:27). But because it was Israel as a nation that God had "adopted" from among all the nations of the world by means of the exodus event (Amos 3:2), and in whose midst he had determined to dwell in his Shekinah glory, and with whom he had entered into covenant, and to whom he had given the law, the temple service, and the promises (Rom. 9:4–5), the Old Testament in charity treats the nation of Israel *per se* as the people of God. But of course to that nation God would also say: "*If* you obey me fully and keep my covenant, *then* out of all nations you will be my treasured possession, for all the earth is mine. And you will be for me a kingdom of priests, and a holy nation" (Exod. 19:5–6; emphases added).

Now in the Hebrew Old Testament, as a result of the exodus–redemption, two words in particular came to be used to designate the people of God: עֵדָה, *'ēdâh*, and קָהָל, *qāhāl*. The former is from the verb יָעַד, *yā'ad*, which means "to appoint" or "to arrange a meeting." Hence the noun עֵדָה, *'ēdâh*, means something on the order of "a gathering by appointment," "assembly," or "congregation," and by usage seems to refer to the congregation of Israel, whether assembled or not. Of the two words it is by far the more common word in Exodus through Numbers, but is found only rarely in the later books of the Old Testament. The latter word, certainly not absent from the Pentateuch but more common in Chronicles, Ezra, and Nehemiah, is from the verb קָהַל, *qāhal*, which means "to assemble." Hence the noun קָהָל, *qāhāl*, means "assembly" or "congregation," and by usage seems to be related more directly to the congregation in actual assembly (see Num. 20:6, 10; Deut. 5:22; 9:10; 10:4; 18:16; 23 passim; 31:30; Josh. 8:35; Judg. 20:2; 21:5, 8; 1 Sam. 17:47; 1 Kgs. 8:14, 22,

---

2. For support of the "most" here, the reader may consult 1 Kings 19:18, where God informed Elijah that he had only seven thousand in the land who had not bowed to Baal. This small remnant of true worshipers is represented in the preceding context, not by the great wind, the earthquake, or the fire, but by the "still small voice."
3. According to Romans 4:11, the outward rite of circumcision signified and sealed a righteousness from God which comes through faith *apart from circumcision*.

55, 65).[4] In a few contexts (e.g., Exod. 12:6; Num. 14:5) we find both employed together (קְהַל עֵדָה, *qᵉhal 'ēdâh*), meaning "the assembly of the congregation ["of Israel," or "of the sons of Israel"]." In Leviticus 16:33 atonement is said to be made for "all the people of the assembly" (כָּל־עַם הַקָּהָל, *kol–'am haqqāhāl*).

This "assembly" at first was governed by Moses, the Levitical priesthood, and the elders of Israel. And even after the establishment of the theocracy under Saul and David, the Levites and elders of Israel still played a significant part in the government of the nation, as evidenced by the many references to them in 1 and 2 Samuel, 1 and 2 Kings, 1 and 2 Chronicles, Ezra, and the writing prophets.[5]

The Septuagint translated עֵדָה, *'ēdâh*, almost universally and קָהָל, *qāhal*, usually in the Pentateuch by συναγωγή, *synagōgē*, ("gathering place" or "place of assembly"). But in Deuteronomy particularly (see, e.g., "the assembly of the Lord," 23:1–3) and the later books of the Old Testament, קָהָל, *qāhal*, was translated by ἐκκλησία, *ekklēsia* (from ἐκκαλέω, *ekkaleō*, meaning "to summon forth [into assembly]," hence "assembly" or "congregation").[6] This last fact is pertinent to our present study inasmuch as it is ἐκκλησία, *ekklēsia*, which the New Testament writers employed as the general term to designate the people of God as both a local and a corporate entity.[7]

The question may be asked as to how such a seemingly "colorless" Old Testament term as קָהָל, (*qāhāl*, "assembly") took on such pregnant theological significance that ἐκκλησία, *ekklēsia*, its Septuagint translation, became the most common term in the New Testament to designate the people of God.

For the answer to this question, it should be recalled that in the history of Israel, just as the redemptive event of the exodus came to be viewed as *the* redemptive

---

4. J. Y. Campbell, "The Origin and Meaning of the Christian Use of the Word Ἐκκλησία [*Ekklēsia*]," *The Journal of Theological Studies* 49 (1948): 133.
5. Günther Bornkamm, " 'Elders' in the Constitutional History of Israel and Judah," *Theological Dictionary of the New Testament* (Grand Rapids, Mich.: Eerdmans, 1968), 6:655–58, writes: "The history of the age of the judges and the monarchy shows what power lay in [the elders'] hands especially in time of war and how advisable it was for ruling kings, or their opposition, to win them over" (657). See also Robert S. Rayburn, "Three Offices: Minister, Elder, Deacon," *Presbuterion: Covenant Seminary Review* 12 (1986): 108–10, for a brief discussion of the eldership in Israel.
6. Stephen employed this word in his defense before the Sanhedrin when he said to Moses: "This is the one who was in *the congregation* [τῇ ἐκκλησίᾳ, *tē ekklēsia*] in the wilderness" (Acts 7:38; perhaps an allusion to Deut. 9:10).
7. See Louis Berkhof, *Systematic Theology* (Grand Rapids: Eerdmans, 1941), 556–57, for several of the more important uses of ἐκκλησία, *ekklēsia*, in the New Testament.

event *par excellence*,[8] so also the assembly of the nation before the face of the Lord at Sinai that issued from that redemptive event was viewed as *the* assembly *par excellence*. According to Moses in Deuteronomy—itself a covenant-renewal document created forty years later between God and Israel on the plains of Moab—that which Israel was to remember forever and teach to succeeding generations was "the day you stood before the LORD your God at Horeb, when he said to me, 'Assemble the people before me to hear my words'" (4:10). The Septuagint translates God's command, "Assemble the people before me," by the words Ἐκκλησίασον πρός με τὸν λαόν, *Ekklēsiason pros me ton laon*. Moreover, the Septuagint adds the words τῇ ἡμέρᾳ τῆς ἐκκλησίας, *tē hēmera tēs ekklēsias*, ("in the day of the assembly") after "at Horeb."[9] In sum, the exodus redemption led to Israel's assembly, and this assembly then became the *definitive* assembly for Israel. It marked the climax of God's redemption. In this assembly the people were to "stand before God," a representation depicting solemnity and worship, in order to hear God's words and receive his law.

The idea of the people of God assembling in the presence of God is also vividly portrayed in the description of the tabernacle as the "tent of meeting." At the door of the tent the people gathered, and there the appointed meeting took place between God and his assembled people.

Other great national assemblies occurred in Israel's history. For example, after Moses' death Joshua summoned and reminded "the whole assembly of Israel" at Mount Ebal of its covenant obligations (Josh. 8:30–35). And just before his own death Joshua again assembled all the tribes of Israel at Shechem and renewed the

---

8. That it is not reading too much into the event of the exodus to characterize it as *the* Old Testament redemptive event *par excellence* is borne out by the fact that the biblical text represents it in precisely that way. Consider the following texts:
   Exodus 6:6: "I will free you from being slaves to them, and I will redeem you with an outstretched arm and with mighty acts of judgment."
   Exodus 15:13: "In your unfailing love you will lead the people you have redeemed."
   Deuteronomy 7:8: "But it was because the LORD loved you . . . that he brought you out with a mighty hand and redeemed you from the land of slavery." (See also 9:4–6)
   Deuteronomy 9:26: "O Sovereign LORD, do not destroy your people, your own inheritance, that you redeemed by your great power and brought out of Egypt with a mighty hand."
   The exodus is also described as Yahweh's "salvation" (Exod. 14:13), Moses writing: "That day the LORD saved Israel from the hands of the Egyptians" (Exod. 14:30). Later Stephen applied the title "redeemer" to Moses (Acts 7:35), who (he says) was "in the ἐκκλησία, *ekklēsia*, in the wilderness" (7:38).
   For a sample index to how the rest of the Old Testament viewed the exodus, see Pss. 77:11–15; 111:9; Isa. 43:1.
9. The phrase is missing in the Masoretic text here, but it occurs in 9:10, 10:4, and 18:16. The Septuagint repeats the phrase in 9:10 and 18:16 but omits it in 10:4.

covenant. David convoked a great assembly to secure Solomon's succession to the throne (1 Chron. 28:2, 8; 29:10). On that occasion, according to the Septuagint, David blessed the Lord "before the assembly [ἐνώπιον τῆς ἐκκλησίας, *enōpion tēs ekklēsias*]" (29:10). Later Solomon dedicated the temple, after convening a vast assembly in Jerusalem (2 Chron. 7:8). Standing on a raised platform made for the purpose, Solomon prayed to the Lord "before all the assembly of Israel" (2 Chron. 6:12). Jehoshaphat, threatened with invasion from Moab and Ammon, convened the "assembly of Judah" at the temple, and there "the Spirit of the LORD came upon Jahaziel . . . in the assembly" (2 Chron. 20:14). When Joash the boy king was crowned, Jehoiada had all the heads of all the Israelite families assemble at the temple, and there "all the assembly of Judah" made a covenant at the house of God with the king (2 Chron. 23:3). When Hezekiah purified the temple and celebrated the Passover, the likes of which festivities had not been seen since the days of Solomon (2 Chron. 30:26), he assembled the people and "all the assembly rejoiced" (2 Chron. 30:25). Joel called for spiritual renewal in his day precisely in terms of "sanctifying the ἐκκλησίαν, *ekklēsian*" (2:16). And after the exile Nehemiah summoned a great assembly and made them promise to obey the law, "and all the assembly said, 'Amen' " (Neh. 5:13; 2 Esdras 15:13).

In addition to these assemblies which were called for covenant renewal, three times a year (at Passover, Pentecost, and the Feast of Tabernacles) the people of Israel were instructed to gather in festal assembly before the Lord and to bring their offerings and worship (Exod. 23:14–17; Lev. 23).

All this shows that Israel was a nation constantly being summoned to assemble before the Lord and/or his representatives in times of covenant renewal and national crisis. These historic national assemblies marking reformation, covenant renewal, and the people's festal assemblies before their covenant God show the importance of the "assembly" on the occasions when they were observed. To "enter into assembly and stand before God" was tantamount to being numbered, externally at least, among the people of God. Indeed, the covenant assembly constituted the people of God and became the visible, external expression of the redeemed "kingdom of God" on earth. As John Murray observes: "The assembly of God's people was not a passing phase of Israel's history; it was not ephemeral . . . it was a permanent feature of Israel's identity."[10]

It is clear then that the Old Testament background of the word ἐκκλησία, *ekklēsia*, is rich with theological meaning. It is the most vivid expression for the redeemed kingdom of God, depicting the sovereign God as One who dwells in the

---

10. John Murray, "The Nature and Unity of the Church," in *Collected Writings of John Murray* (Edinburgh: Banner of Truth, 1977), 2:322.

midst of his people and who summons them to assemble before him. Because he is among them they must meet with him. And the immediacy of his presence convokes the people and evokes their worship. His presence demands that the people of God stand before him, just as the people of an earthly king would be required to do. As Edmund P. Clowney writes: "Their assembling is not one activity among many on the part of an already existing nation. As the people of God they are brought into existence by his redemption and given their identity in covenant assembly."[11]

THE "ASSEMBLY" IN THE NEW TESTAMENT

The Old Testament quite obviously provides the background to the New Testament's representation of the church as God's ἐκκλησία, *ekklēsia*.[12] At this time I want to concentrate on this word—the one word, as we have seen, which expressed more vividly than perhaps any other what it meant in the Old Testament to be both the people and the covenant community of God, namely, God's redeemed possession *assembled before him* to worship and to hear his law.[13]

---

11. Edmund Clowney, *The Biblical Doctrine of the Church* (unpublished classroom syllabus, Westminster Theological Seminary), chapter 1, "The Covenant People of God," 23.
12. The Old Testament background shows the inadequacy of the idea that the basic meaning of ἐκκλησία, *ekklēsia*, in the New Testament is, as its etymology suggests, "called-out ones," that is, people "called out of the world." But called to where? If one says no more here than what the word's etymology suggests, the church is left in an "ungathered" condition.
13. In addition to its most common term ἐκκλησία, *ekklēsia*, the New Testament employs many other figurative expressions to describe the church: one flock (John 10:16), the body of Christ (1 Cor. 12:27; Eph. 1:23; Col. 1:18), the temple of God (or of the Holy Spirit) (1 Cor. 3:16; 2 Cor. 6:16; Eph. 2:21–22; 2 Thess. 2:4), the new Jerusalem (Heb. 12:22), the heavenly Jerusalem (Rev. 21:2), the pillar and ground of the truth (1 Tim. 3:15), the salt of the earth (Matt. 5:13), the light of the world (Matt. 5:14), a letter from Christ (2 Cor. 3:2–3), branches (of the vine) (John 15:5), the olive tree (Rom. 11:13–24), God's field (1 Cor. 3:9), God's building (1 Cor. 3:9), the elect lady (2 John 1), the wife or bride of Christ (Eph. 5:22–31; Rev. 21:9), wearers of wedding garments (Matt. 22:1–14; Rev. 19:7), fellow citizens with the saints (Eph. 2:19), God's house (Eph. 2:19), strangers in the world (1 Pet 1:1; 2:11; Heb. 11:13), ambassadors (2 Cor. 5:18–21), the people of God (1 Pet. 2:9–10), a chosen race (1 Pet. 2:9), a holy nation (1 Pet. 2:9), a royal priesthood (1 Pet. 2:9), the circumcision (Phil. 3:3–11), Abraham's sons (Gal. 3:29; Rom. 4:16), the tabernacle of David (Acts 15:16), the remnant (Rom. 9:27; 11:5–7), Israel (Gal. 6:15–16), God's elect (Rom. 8:33), the faithful in Christ Jesus (Eph. 1:1), a new creation (2 Cor. 5:17), a new man (Col. 3:10), the kingdom of God (or of heaven) (Matt. 13), disciples (Matt. 28:19), the way (Acts 9:2; 19:9, 23; 22:4; 24:14, 22), slaves of God, of Christ, and of righteousness (Rom. 6:18, 22), sons of God (Rom. 8:14), the brotherhood (1 Pet. 2:17; 5:9), and Christians (Acts 12:26), See Paul Minear, *Images of the Church in the New Testament* (Philadelphia: Westminster, 1977), for additional New Testament descriptions and figures of the church.

Jesus' Use of *Ekklēsia*

In the Gospel acccounts Jesus used the term ἐκκλησία, *ekklēsia*, in only two verses: Matthew 16:18 and Matthew 18:17 (twice).[14] Both are quite significant.

MATTHEW 16:18

By this point in Jesus' ministry his teaching had alienated many. The journey to Caesarea Philippi pointed toward the Gentile mission that would commence with Israel's rejection. At this crucial point in his ministry Jesus knew the troubled disciples needed further instruction concerning his approaching death and their own position in the kingdom. Furthermore, if multitudes were rejecting him, what future did his kingdom have? And if the nation's religious leadership opposed him, how could he be the Messiah? Jesus' two questions, "Who do *men* say that I am?" and "Who do *you* [pl.] say that I am?" show Jesus' awareness of the widening poles of opinion concerning him and set the stage for the disciples' additional tutelage. Peter, with the aid of the Father's illumination, responded for the Twelve: "You are the Messiah, the Son of the living God." Because Peter's response placed Jesus above all of the prophets as the divine Messiah, Jesus blessed Peter and then declared, literally, "And I am saying to you that you are Peter [Πέτρος, *Petros*—lit., 'a rock'], and upon this rock [πέτρα, *petra*] I will build my ἐκκλησία, [*ekklēsia*] and the gates of Hades will not prevail against it."[15] Very early in Jesus' ministry, on the occasion when Andrew first introduced Simon to him, Jesus said to Simon, "You are Simon son of John. You shall be called Cephas [Κηφᾶς, or 'a cephas'; Gr. transliteration of the Aram. כֵּיפָא, *kêpā*']." John adds, " which means Peter [Πέτρος, *Petros*, or 'a rock']" (John 1:42; see also Mark 3:16). It is clear, therefore, that when Jesus said on this later occasion at Caesarea Philippi "You are Peter," he was not giving to Peter for the first time a *new* name or title. What he was doing was *explaining* to Simon what his intention behind

---

14. I am assuming here the dominical origination and authenticity of the statements in both verses and would refer the reader to Robert L. Reymond, *Jesus, Divine Messiah: The New Testament Witness* (Phillipsburg, N.J.: Presbyterian and Reformed, 1990), 50–51, 176–78, and to D. A. Carson's commentary on Matthew in *The Expositor's Bible Commentary* (Grand Rapids, Mich.: Zondervan, 1984), 8:366–67, 69, for the discussion and reasons.
15. Jesus doubtless intended a play on the words "Peter" and "rock" here, but I do not think that anything should be made of the fact that in Greek the former is masculine and the latter is feminine. While it is true that πετρος, *petros*, was often used to refer to a free–standing boulder rather than a stratum of rock and πετρα, *petra*, designated the rock on which a building could be built (see Matt. 7:24–25), and while such word usage is precisely what the Greek language would have required, this fine distinction is not possible in Aramaic, which Jesus was probably speaking. In Jesus' original statement, he probably employed the Aramic כֵּיפָא, *kêpā'*, in both places.

[811]

his earlier act of "name-giving" was. Both the immediate previous context and his following words, "and upon this rock I will build my assembly . . . ," explain his intention.

The Roman Catholic Church since the early Middle Ages has contended that Jesus was teaching here that Peter was to be the first pope (of Rome, of course) and as such the supreme leader of Christendom, and that his supremacy would be transmitted to each bishop of Rome who would succeed him. This contention is dramatically captured by the Latin inscription around the entablature just below the great dome of Saint Peter's Basilica in Rome: *Tu es Petrus, et super hanc petram aedificabo Ecclesiam meam.*[16] Accordingly, the Roman Catholic *Baltimore Catechism* states:

> Christ gave special powers in his Church to St. Peter by making him the head of the Apostles and the chief teacher and ruler of the entire Church. Christ did not intend that the special power of chief teacher and ruler of the entire Church should be exercised by St. Peter alone, but intended that this power should be passed down to his successor, the Pope, the Bishop of Rome, who is the Vicar of Christ on earth and the visible head of the Church.[17]

The Roman Catholic Church has employed this dogma to claim for itself the authority to bind men's consciences by its interpretation of Scripture, to add new

---

16. Rome also claims that St. Peter's Basilica is built over Peter's grave site. In his Christmas message delivered on December 23, 1950, Pope Pius XII announced, as a result of excavations carried out in 1939 under St. Peter's Basilica, that "the grave of the Prince of Apostles has been found." But Oscar Cullmann, in his *Peter: Disciple—Apostle—Martyr* (Philadelphia: Westminster, 1953), 153, after carefully examining the written reports of this excavation, concluded:
    > The archaeological investigations do not permit us to answer in either a negative or an affirmative way the question as to the stay of Peter in Rome. The grave of Peter cannot be identified. The real proofs for the martyrdom of Peter in Rome must still be derived from the indirect literary witnesses. . .
17. *Baltimore Catechism. The New Confraternity Edition of the Official Revised 1949 Edition* (New York: Benzinger, 1952), XX. The *Catechism of the Catholic Church* (1994) also states in this same regard:
    > The Lord made Simon alone, whom he named Peter, the "rock" of his Church. He gave him the keys of his Church and instituted him shepherd of the whole flock. "The office of binding and loosing which was given to Peter was also assigned to the college of apostles united to its head." This pastoral office of Peter and the other apostles belongs to the Church's very foundation and is continued by the bishops under the primacy of the Pope.
    > The Pope, Bishop of Rome and Peter's successor, "is the perpetual and visible source and foundation of the unity both of the bishops and of the whole company of the faithful. . . . the Roman Pontiff, by reason of his office as Vicar of Christ, and as pastor of the entire Church, has a power which he can always exercise unhindered." (para. 881–82)

doctrines not taught in the Scripture, and to reinterpret the plain teaching of Scripture. It has done so by first distinguishing Peter from the other apostles and then by claiming that his apostolic authority is continued in the single line of bishops of Rome.

It is true that in the early years of the New Testament era Peter was a leader among the apostles. A case can even be made that he was "the first among equals" (*primus inter pares*)(but with no "primacy of power," *primatus potestates*). There are around 140 references to Peter in the four Gospels, about 30 more than all the references to the other disciples combined. He stands at the head of the list of the twelve apostles in each of the lists given in the New Testament (Matt. 10:2 [note Matthew's "first" here]; Mark 3:16; Luke 6:14; Acts 1:13), and he is included among that "inner circle" of disciples (Peter, James, and John) that alone witnessed certain miraculous events such as Jesus' transfiguration; he is the spokesman for the disciples on many occasions (Matt. 15:15; 17:24–25; 19:27; John 6:68–69); it is he who walked with Jesus on the sea (Matt. 14:28–29); it is he whom Jesus specifically charged to "strengthen your brothers" (Luke 22:32). He was in charge in the selection of the one to take Judas's place in Acts 1; it was he who preached the first "Christian sermon" on the Day of Pentecost in Acts 2, converting many Jews to the Way; it was his activities (along with John's) which Luke recounts in the first half of Acts; it was he whom God chose to be the missionary who would take the special action with regard to Cornelius's household in behalf of Gentile salvation in Acts 10; his was the first testimony to be recounted by Luke at the assembly in Jerusalem in Acts 15; his name appears first in Paul's "official list"[18] of those to whom Christ appeared after his resurrection (1 Cor. 15:5); and Paul even refers to him (along with James and John) as a "pillar" in the church at Jerusalem (Gal. 2:9). But to derive Rome's understanding of Peter's priority from Matthew 16:18 (and a few related verses such as Luke 22:31–32 and John 21:16) forces the verse to say something it does not say. For the verse to bear such heavy doctrinal weight, the Roman Catholic apologist must demonstrate the following things *exegetically* and not simply assert them dogmatically:

1. that by his reference to "this rock" in his explanation Jesus referred to Peter personally and exclusively;

2. that the apostolic authority which belonged to Peter *could* be transmitted to his "papal successors" and was *in fact* transmitted to his successors, while the apostolic authority which the other apostles also possessed could *not* be and in fact was *not* transmitted to their successors;

3. that Jesus intended his promise to Peter to extend to Peter's "papal successors" throughout the entire period of the church to the end of the age; and

---

18. An unabridged list would have included Jesus' appearances to the women as they hurried away from the tomb (Matt. 28:8–9) and to Mary who followed Peter and John back to the tomb after informing them that the tomb was empty (see John 20:1–18).

4. that Jesus' promise to Peter, while it could and should be *chronologically* extended to his "papal successors," cannot be *geographically* extended but must be restricted in its transmissibility to one bishop at a time, the bishop who ministers in *one* particular city among the many cities in which Peter ministered, namely Rome. Calvin made this point this way: "By what right do [the Roman apologists] bind to a place this dignity which has been given without mention of place?" (*Institutes*, IV.vi.11).

The Roman Catholic apologist must also be able to demonstrate *historically* that Peter in fact became the first bishop of Rome and not simply assert it dogmatically. But what are the facts? Irenaeus and Eusebius of Caesarea both make Linus, mentioned in 2 Timothy 4:21, the first bishop of Rome.[19] That Peter died in Rome, as ancient tradition has it, is a distinct possibility (see 1 Pet. 5:13, where "Babylon" has been rather uniformly understood by commentators as a metaphor for Rome), but that he ever actually pastored the church there is surely a fiction, as even some scholars in the Roman communion will acknowledge. Jerome's Latin translation of Eusebius (not Eusebius's Greek copy) records that Peter ministered in Rome for twenty-five years,[20] but if Philip Schaff (as well as many other church historians) is to be believed, this is "a colossal chronological mistake."[21] Paul wrote his letter to the church in Rome in early A.D. 57, but he did not address the letter to Peter or refer to him as its pastor. And in the last chapter he extended greetings to twenty-eight friends in Rome but made no mention of Peter, which would have been a major oversight, indeed an affront, if in fact Peter was "ruling" the Roman church at that time. Then later when Paul was himself in Rome, from which city he wrote both his four prison letters during his first imprisonment in A.D. 60–62 when he "was welcoming all who came to him" (Acts 28:30), and his last pastoral letter during his second imprisonment around A.D. 64, in which letters he extended greetings to his letters' recipients from ten specific people in Rome, again he made no mention of Peter being there. Here is a period of time spanning around seven years (A.D. 57–64) during which time Paul related himself to the Roman church both as correspondent and as resident, but he said not a word to suggest that Peter was in Rome.

Now if Peter was at Rome and was simply ignored by Paul, what are we to conclude about him when Paul declared to the Philippians: "I have no one else [besides Timothy] of kindred spirit who will genuinely be concerned for your welfare. For

---

19. Irenaeus does so in his *Against Heresies* III.iii.3; Eusebius, probably following Irenaeus's lead, does so in his *Church History* III.ii.
20. See Jerome, *Lives of Illustrious Men*, chapter 1, in *Nicene and Post-Nicene Fathers*, ed. Philip Schaff and Henry Wace (Grand Rapids, Mich.: Eerdmans, 1989) III, 361.
21. Philip Schaff, *History of the Christian Church* (1910; reprint, Grand Rapids, Mich.: Eerdmans, 1962), 1:252.

they all seek after their own interests, not those of Christ Jesus" (Phil. 2:20–21)? And when he wrote to Timothy later Paul said: "Only Luke is with me.... At my first defense no one supported me, but all deserted me" (2 Tim. 4:11, 16). Where was Peter then? And what about Paul's statement in Galatians 2:7–8 that Peter had been entrusted with missionary efforts to Jews? Are we to conclude that Peter had been disobedient to that trust and gone to minister in Rome? I think not. For just as Paul wrote several of his letters to churches he had founded, it would appear that Peter, writing from Babylon to dispersed Jewish Christians (see his use of διασπορά, *diaspora*, in 1 Peter 1:1) in Pontus, Galatia, Cappadocia, Asia, and Bithynia, was writing to people he had evangelized in those places. The one glimpse we have from Paul's writings concerning Peter's ministry is found in 1 Corinthians 9:5, where he suggests that Cephas, accompanied by his wife (see Matt. 8:14), was an itinerant evangelist carrying out the trust the other apostles had given him. From this data we must conclude that, if Peter did in fact reach Rome as tradition says, his purpose was probably only to pay the church there not much more than a casual visit, and that he would have arrived there only shortly before his death, which, according to tradition, occurred during the Neronic persecution.

The Roman Catholic apologist must also be able to address the following questions to the reasonable person's satisfaction and in accordance with Scripture:

1. Why do Mark and Luke, while they also recount the Caesarea Philippi conversation between Jesus and Peter, omit all reference to that part of Jesus' conversation which grants to Peter his alleged priority over the other apostles, the point which for Rome is the very heart and central point of our Lord's teaching ministry?

2. Why does the New Testament record more of Peter's errors after the Caesarea Philippi confession than of the errors of any of the other apostles? I am referring to (1) his rejection of Jesus' announcement that he would die, Matthew 16:22–23; (2) his levelling comparison of Jesus with Moses and Elijah on the Mount of Transfiguration, Matthew 17:4–5; (3) his refusal to let Jesus wash his feet and his dictating of the terms according to which Jesus would wash him, John 13:8–9; (4) his sleepiness while Jesus prayed in Gethsemane, Matthew 26:36–45; (5) his precipitous use of the sword, Matthew 26:51–54; (6) his protestation of unfailing faithfulness and then his three denials of Jesus, recorded in all four Gospels; (7) his curiosity about John's future that earned him the rebuke, "That's none of your business," (John 21:21–22); (8) his spirited refusal to eat that which God had declared was pure (Acts 10:10–16); and (9) even after Christ's resurrection, the Spirit's outpouring, and his own Jerusalem ministry, his betrayal of the gospel of pure grace at Antioch by compromising actions that called for Paul's public rebuke, Galatians 2:11–14.

Where is the infallibility and the guarantee of the purity and continuity of the gospel in this man? It will not do to respond that Peter was only infallible in what he taught *ex cathedra* and that these errors on his part only highlight the real oneness of the man with sinful humanity at large. For "actions speak louder than words," and surely in the last-cited instance Peter's action, which more than likely was accompanied by some word of explanation from him to the church at Antioch, betrayed the purity of the gospel of grace.

3. Why can the disciples after the Caesarea Philippi incident still dispute among themselves concerning who was the greatest (Matt. 18:1; 20:20–28; Luke 22:24)? Apparently *they* did not understand that Jesus' statement had given Peter any priority over them. And if Christ had in fact intended by his Caesarea Philippi pronouncement that Peter was to be his vicar and the leader of all Christendom, why did he not clear up the disciples' confusion once and for all by telling them so straightforwardly?

4. If Peter was the head of the church, why was he the one sent to investigate the Samaritan revival, instead of being the one doing the sending (Acts 8:14)?

5. If Peter was in fact the undisputed and infallible head of the church, why did the other apostles and the brotherhood in general feel they could challenge his involvement in the Cornelius incident (Acts 11:1–18)?

6. Why does Paul list Peter as only one of the "pillars" in Jerusalem, and second after James at that (Gal. 2:9)? And why at the Jerusalem Council in Acts 15, over which James quite obviously presided, is Peter merely the first speaker and not the president of that council? Why was the entire matter not simply submitted to Peter rather than to the council, and why did not the decision go forth as a "Petrine" deliverance rather than an "apostolic" decree?

7. Why can Paul say of the Jerusalem leadership (James, Peter, and John), who "seemed to be something": "What they were makes no difference to me; God shows no partiality" (Gal. 2:6)?

8. If Peter was the bishop and pastor of Rome, and if it was Paul's established missionary practice "to preach the gospel where Christ was not known, so that I would not be building on someone else's foundation" (Rom. 15:20; see 2 Cor. 10:16), why does Paul declare that he had longed to come to Rome and had purposed many times to come there "so that I may impart to you some spiritual gift to make you strong" and "in order that I might have a harvest among you, just as I have had among the other Gentiles" (Rom. 1:11–13). Would not such activity among them on Paul's part have been both a denial of his own missionary policy and an affront to Peter's ministry? Do his words not suggest that Paul knew of no apostle having labored in Rome?

9. Why does Peter describe himself as simply "*an* apostle of Jesus Christ," as one among many "living stones," and "the fellow elder" (ὁ συμπρεσβύτερος, *ho sympresbyteros*) with other elders (1 Pet. 1:1; 5:1)?

10. Why, if Peter was the living, earthly head of the church at that time, does he disappear completely from Luke's history after Acts 15, with very few references to him, apart from his own two letters, in the rest of the New Testament?

11. Why in the earliest patristic literature is Paul venerated as often as Peter, a fact admitted by Roman Catholic scholars?

12. Would John, the "beloved disciple" and apostle, who apparently outlived Peter, have been subject to the bishop of Rome (Linus or Clement?) who succeeded to Peter's chair?

13. Why did no Roman bishop before Callistus I (d. c. 223), who by the way countenanced a form of modalism,[22] use the Matthew 16 passage to support the primacy of the Roman bishopric; and when he did, why was he rebuked by such notable contemporaries as Tertullian, who totally rejected the notion that Jesus' saying applied to later bishops at all, and Firmilian, bishop of Caesarea in Cappadocia, who opposed the notion that the Roman bishopric is entitled by succession to the "throne" of Peter?

14. This raises the larger and more principial question, namely, while the church at Rome was no doubt influential,[23] why is there no indication in the first couple of centuries of the Christian era that the rest of the church recognized the Roman church as supreme or acceded to Rome any sovereignty over Christendom?[24]

15. Why did the first four ecumenical councils (whose doctrinal decisions are generally admitted by Christians everywhere, including Protestants, to have been orthodox) neither say nor do anything that affords the slightest endorsement of the claim of the Roman bishop's supremacy but in several instances actually passed decrees or canons that the bishop of Rome (or his agents) opposed, with the first such council to explicitly assert the Roman bishop's supremacy being the Fourth Lateran Council, held under Pope Innocent III in 1215?

16. How does Roman Catholic theology in this entire matter avoid the charge of "asserting the consequence" or of "reasoning in a circle" (*petitio principii*) when it makes a highly questionable dogma, namely, the primacy of the Roman bishop, the

---

22. See J. N. D. Kelly, *Early Christian Doctrine* (London: Adam & Charles Black, 1958), 123–24.
23. John Calvin *(Institutes,* IV.vi.16) offered the following three reasons for the Roman church's early prestige: (1) The opinion became quite prevalent that Peter had founded and shepherded the church at Rome; (2) because Rome was the capital city of the empire, the church's leaders were probably more knowledgeable, skilled, and experienced than other church leaders; (3) because the Western half of the church was not as troubled by doctrinal controversy as the Eastern half, bishops deposed from their offices in the East, Greece, and Africa often sought both haven in Rome and the Roman bishop's endorsement of their cause.
24. The Roman Catholic apologist H. Burn-Murdock admits as much in his *The Development of the Papacy* (London: Faber & Faber, 1954), 130f., when he writes: "None of the writings of the first two centuries describe St. Peter as a bishop of Rome."

basis for its claim that it alone is justified in proclaiming any dogma whatsoever, including the Roman bishop's primacy over the entire church?

Rome's exegesis of Matthew 16 and its historically developed dogmatic claim to authoritative primacy in the Christian world simply cannot be demonstrated and sustained from Scripture itself. This claim is surely one of the great hoaxes foisted upon professing Christendom, upon which false base rests the whole papal sacerdotal system.[25]

While it is true that Jesus said that upon "this rock" he was going to build his "assembly," whether this phrase has for its antecedent Peter and in what sense he was going to build his "assembly" on Peter have been matters of considerable controversy in the church. For example, Origen, making his usual distinction between the letter and the spiritual intention of the text, urged that according to the letter the rock in Jesus' explanation referred to Peter, while the Spirit had in mind everyone who becomes such as Peter was.[26] Tertullian explicitly declared that the power to bind and to loose was given to Peter *personally* then and there and was not passed on to the Roman bishop.[27] Cyprian held that Jesus was addressing the whole body of bishops in speaking of Peter, since, he says, he later endowed all the apostles "with a like partnership both of honour and power." He also contended that Jesus spoke specifically of Peter only to highlight the necessity of the *unity* of the church.[28] Chrysostom, followed by Gregory of Nyssa, Isidore of Pelusium, the Latin father Hilary, and the later Greek fathers Theodoret, Theophanes, Theophylact, and John of Damascus, held that the "rock" in Jesus' explanation was the faith of Peter's confession. The later Augustine believed that the rock was not Peter but Christ himself.[29] During the Middle Ages the passage was regularly used by the Roman bishop to ground Rome's claim to ecclesiastical primacy, as though no other understanding were possible. But Luther returned to Augustine at this point ("The rock is the Son of God, Jesus Christ himself and no one else"), and urged that Peter's "rock–like" characteristic applied not to his person but only to his faith in Jesus who was the

---

25. For a more detailed treatment, see William Cunningham, "The Papal Supremacy," in *Historical Theology* (1862; reprint, Edinburgh: Banner of Truth, 1960), 1:207–26.
26. Origen, on Matthew 16:18: "rock means every disciple of Christ."
27. Tertullian, *On Modesty* xxi.
28. Cyprian, *To the Lapsed,* Epistle 26.1; *On the Unity of the Church,* Treatise 1.4.
29. Augustine, *Exposition on Psalm 61,* para. 3: "But in order that the Church might be built upon the Rock, who has made the Rock? Hear Paul saying: 'But the Rock was Christ.' On him therefore built we have been"; *Sermon 26 on New Testament Lessons,* para. 1: "For seeing that Christ is the Rock (Petra), Peter is the Christian people.... [Christ said,] '... upon this Rock which thou has confessed, upon this Rock which thou hast acknowledged, saying, 'Thou art the Christ, the Son of the living God,' will I build my Church, that is upon myself, the Son of the living God, 'will I build My Church.' I will build thee upon Myself, not myself upon thee." Para. 2: "Peter [was] built upon the Rock, not the Rock upon Peter." See also *On the Trinity* II.17.28.

Rock.[30] Calvin also held that the Rock was Christ and that in addressing Peter as "Rock" Christ was addressing both Peter and all other believers as well, in the sense that the bond of faith in Christ is the basis on which the church grows.[31] Zwingli taught that Peter is only the type of him who believes in Christ as the sole Rock.[32] It can be safely said that all of the Reformers believed that the true Rock of the church is Jesus Christ, with Peter being the "Rock" not in respect to his person but in respect to his being the type of all who trust in Jesus as Messiah and God.[33]

In another work I have argued that by his confession Peter declared his conviction that Jesus was both the long-promised Old Testament Messiah and the divine Son of God.[34] It was in response to Peter's exclamatory declaration, "You are [σὺ εἶ,

30. Martin Luther, *What Luther Says* (Saint Louis: Concordia, 1959), 2:1070, para. 3412: "The pope is the archblasphemer of God in that he applies to himself the noble passage which is spoken of Christ alone. He wants to be the rock, and the church should rest on him. . . . Therefore we must see to it that we stay with the simple meaning, namely, that Christ is the Foundation on which the church is to stand." See Luther's *Works*, 17.II.449f.

31. John Calvin, on Matthew 16:18; *Institutes*, IV.vi.6.

32. Ulrich Zwingli, "On the Lord's Supper," *Zwingli and Bullinger*, vol. 24 of the *Library of Christian Classics* (Philadelphia: Westminster, 1953), 192–93: "The papists might complain that we do not abide by the natural sense when it is a matter of the saying: 'Thou art Peter, that is, a stone, or rock, and upon this rock I will build my church.' Does that mean that we fall into error if we do not abide by the simple or natural sense . . . ? Not at all. For we find that Christ alone is the rock, Christ alone is the Head, Christ alone is the vine in which we are held secure. Therefore Christ himself is the rock upon which the Church is built, and that is the natural sense of the words. As applied to the papacy, the words are not natural."

33. Archbishop Peter Richard Kenrick prepared a paper on this subject to be delivered at Vatican I (1870). His paper was actually not delivered at the council but was published later, along with other insights, under the title *An Inside View of the Vatican Council*, ed. Leonard Woolsey Bacon (New York: American Tract Society, 1871). In it Kenrick noted that five interpretations of the word "rock" were held in antiquity: (1) The first declared that the church was built on Peter, endorsed by 17 fathers. (2) The second understood the words as referring to all the apostles, Peter being simply the primate, the opinion of 8 fathers. (3) The third asserted that the words applied to the faith that Peter professed, espoused by 44 fathers, including some of the most important and representative. (4) The fourth declared that the words were to be understood of Jesus Christ, the church being built upon him, the view of 16 fathers. (5) The fifth understood the term "rock" to apply to the faithful themselves who, by believing in Christ, were made the living stones in the temple of his body, an opinion held only by very few (107–8). These statistics show that the view that eventually became normative for Rome is far from certain and, being held by only about 20 percent of the early fathers, is a long way from being the normative view of the early church. See also W. Griffith Thomas, *The Principles of Theology* (London: Longmans, Green, 1930), 470–71.

See also the address given by Bishop Josef Strossmayer to Vatican I in the closing months of the debate on papal infallibility (see *Against the World: The Trinity Review, 1978–1988* [Hobbs, N.M.: Trinity Foundation, 1996], 225–30).

34. Reymond, *Jesus, Divine Messiah: The New Testament Witness*, 50–51, 176–78.

su ei] the Messiah, the Son of the living God!" that Jesus responded to Peter: "And I am saying to you that you are [σὺ εἶ, *su ei*] Peter [lit., 'a rock']!" It is important to note that in his exclamation Peter did not employ a proper name to designate Jesus; rather, he ascribed to him two titles, the first functional (Messiah), the second ontological (Son of the living God). I would suggest from the parallelism in the two σὺ εἶ, *su ei,* clauses that Jesus may have intended to respond in kind. That is to say, he may not have employed Πέτρος, *Petros,* as a proper name. Rather, he may have likewise ascribed to him only a title: "You are a rock!" And by capitalizing the Greek word Πέτρος, *Petros,* the Greek translation of the Aramaic כֵּיפָא, *kêpā',* which Jesus almost certainly used, the editors of our critical editions of the Greek New Testament may have misled us. Jesus may have intended to say, not "You are Peter," but "You are a rock!" meaning, "You are [truly] a rock [by describing me as you just did]!" If so, when Jesus continued by saying, "and upon *this* rock [note: he does not say "upon *you*"] I will build my 'assembly,' " he may have intended to say that it was upon Peter's "rock-like" *description* of him as the Messiah and the Son of the living God, which understanding the Father had just graciously revealed to him, and not upon Peter *personally* that he would ground his church. This would mean, in sum, that the "bedrock" itself of the church is the fact of Christ's own messianic investiture and his ontological existence as the Second Person of the Godhead, just as Paul would later write: "No man can lay a foundation other than the one which is laid, which is Jesus Christ" (1 Cor. 3:11; see also 1 Cor. 10:4: "and the rock was Christ [ἡ πέτρα δὲ ἦν ὁ Χριστός, *hē petra de ēn ho Christos*]"). In confessing the same Peter was himself "a rock."

But it is entirely possible that Jesus did intend to say that upon Peter he would build his church in some sense (I think sometimes that our "Protestant" reluctance to admit this possibility plays into the hands of the Roman apologist), a possibility that certainly receives support from the next verse, where Jesus declared to Peter: "I will give to you [sing.] the keys of the kingdom of heaven,[35] and whatever you

---

35. The phrase "the keys of the kingdom of heaven" symbolically denotes kingdom authority, so Jesus in Matthew 16 is granting "kingdom-building authority" to Peter. But this authority must not be interpreted one-sidedly—as is occasionally done because of the Matthew 18:17 context—as having reference only to church discipline. The phrase in Matthew 16 follows upon Jesus' positive declaration that he would "build" his church. Moreover, Jesus declares that by these keys Peter would both bind *and* loose. Therefore, the authority to open or close the doors of the kingdom of heaven to men which Jesus grants to Peter here (and to the rest of the disciples in Matthew 18) must be seen to include both the authority to proclaim the liberating gospel and the authority to take disciplinary steps to insure that the church remains pure. By means of both Jesus would "build" his "assembly." There is a polemical side to our Lord's statement here as well, for in giving this "kingdom-building authority" to his church, he was saying that it was not the rabbis who "sit in Moses' seat" but his confessing "assembly" that possesses "the keys of knowledge" (Luke 11:52).

[sing.] bind upon earth shall have been bound in heaven, and whatever you [sing.] loose upon earth shall have been loosed in heaven" (16:19, author's translation).³⁶

Even so, Peter's confession of Jesus as Messiah and Son of the living God cannot be excluded from Christ's reference to Peter as "a rock." That is to say, not Peter personally as the man but Peter as the *confessing apostle*—confessing specifically what he did, namely, the revealed truth about Jesus being the Messiah and the Son of the living God—is the foundation rock of the church:

> This interpretation is demanded by the sequel in the passage which follows (Mt. 16:22–23). There Jesus calls Peter by another name: Satan. Just as Peter had spoken by revelation from the Father, he now becomes the mouthpiece of the devil. In confessing Jesus to be the Christ he was the rock, in tempting Jesus to refuse the cross he is Satan. He is called Satan only in direct reference to his word of seduction. Apart from that expression the designation does not apply. Jesus is not declaring that Peter the man is a Satan in terms of all his personal qualities, nor

---

Geerhardus Vos argues in his *The Teaching of Jesus Concerning the Kingdom of God and the Church* (reprint; Nutley, N. J.: Presbyterian and Reformed, 1972), 81, that the authority to bind and to loose goes beyond the authority to impute and to forgive sin and refers to "the administration of the affairs of the house [of God] in general." When one takes into account that this authority was also given to the other apostles and that their doctrinal teaching became the foundation of the church (Eph. 2:20), Vos's broader construction of Jesus' intent is entirely possible.

36. The "shall have been bound" and the "shall have been loosed" in my translation of the Greek text of Matthew 16:19 (and 18:18) reflect the fact that underlying both is a verbal construction known as the future perfect passive periphrastic. Henry J. Cadbury in "The Meaning of John 20:23, Matthew 16:19, and Matthew 18:18," *Journal of Biblical Literature* 58 (1939): 253, urges that "the simple future seems . . . as adequate as any English translation can be" for this Greek construction. But J. R. Mantey, both in "The Mistranslation of the Perfect Tense in John 20:23, Mt 16:19, and Mt 18:18" in the same journal issue and in "Evidence That the Perfect Tense in John 20:23 and Matthew 16:19 Is Mistranslated," *Journal of the Evangelical Theological Society* 16, no. 3 (1973): 129–38, demonstrates that the translations I have urged above are the only English translations that capture the force of the Greek. Thus if the binding and loosing about which Jesus speaks here pertain respectively to "retaining" and "forgiving" men's sins (see John 20:23; see Rev. 1:5), this can only mean that those whom the church through the proclamation of the gospel brings to faith are those who are already God's elect, and that those who finally spurn the church's message or who are finally excommunicated by the church are those who are already the nonelect.

Rome contends that Jesus was instituting the priestly power of absolution in John 20:22 (*Catechism of the Catholic Church,* para. 976). But the verb "He breathed" is aoristic and has no specified object, suggesting a *single* expulsion of breath upon *all* the disciples present, not just upon some individuals among them. And the apostles were not the only ones who were there on that occasion! This action depicted Jesus' approaching action on the Day of Pentecost; see Acts 1:5, 8; 2:2, 4, 33.

is satanicity a *character indelibilis*. Peter is Satan as he speaks for Satan. [This would require by analogy that we understand that] Peter is the rock as he speaks for God.[37]

Here is the governing exegetical proof that Peter is the rock only in his office as a confessing apostle speaking the Word of God.

Furthermore, it must be noted that several days later Jesus gave to the rest of the apostles the same kingdom authority that he had given to Peter: "Truly I say to you [pl.], whatever you [pl.] bind upon earth shall have been bound in heaven, and whatever you [pl.] loose upon earth shall have been loosed in heaven" (Matt. 18:18, author's translation). He did the same thing on the night of his resurrection when he "breathed on [the disciples] and said, 'Receive the Holy Spirit. Whoever's sins you [pl.] forgive, they have been forgiven; whoever's you [pl.] retain, they have been retained'" (John 20:22–23, author's translation). What should we make of this similar promise to the other disciples? I would suggest that Jesus was inferring what Paul would later state explicitly, namely, that his church would be "built on the foundation of the apostles and prophets, Christ Jesus himself being the cornerstone" (Eph. 2:20; see 1 Cor. 10:4), and what John would later symbolically depict as one aspect of the "bride" of Christ: "And the wall of the city had twelve foundation stones, and on them were the twelve names of the twelve apostles of the Lamb" (Rev. 21:14).

The totality of New Testament teaching admittedly grants a certain priority to Peter among the original Twelve, but this priority, to use Jack Dean Kingsbury's phrase, seems to have been "salvation– [or redemptive–] historical" in nature, that is to say, Peter occupied a *primus inter pares* position during the specific time frame of the "salvation history" in which he lived.[38] The New Testament does not restrict the church's foundation to him alone but founds the church on the entire apostolate, not in regard to their persons as such but in regard to their office in the church as authoritative teachers of doctrine who confess the truth about Jesus.

What then can we say about Jesus' "assembly" on the basis of his words in Matthew 16:18? First, the disciples did not appear to have any difficulty comprehending Jesus' talk about building his ἐκκλησία, *ekklēsia*.[39] This can be traced to the fact that the concept had its roots in the Septuagint's recurring depiction of Israel as God's

---

37. Clowney, *Biblical Doctrine of the Church*, 2:108–09.
38. Jack Dean Kingsbury, "The Figure of Peter in Matthew's Gospel as a Theological Problem," *Journal of Biblical Literature* 98, no. 1 (1979): 67–83.
39. Since Jesus almost certainly was speaking Aramaic on this occasion, he probably used קְהָלָא, *qᵉhālā'*, a loan word from the Hebrew, or קְנִשְׁתָּא *qᵉništā'*, the normal Aramaic equivalent for συναγωγή, *synagogē*. See K. L. Schmidt, ἐκκλησία [*ekklesia*], *Theological Dictionary of the New*

"congregation" or "assembly." Second, it is ultimately Jesus, not men, who "will build" his church. Like a wise master builder who builds a house, so Jesus will build his church. Third, his "building," more specifically his "temple" (Eph. 2:20–21) will be unconquerable: the very gates of Hades (the power of death?) will not prevail against it.[40] Fourth, Jesus would build it upon the "bedrock" of his own person as the Messiah and divine Son of God as this "bedrock" comes to expression in both his and his apostles' authoritative teaching. Fifth, his ἐκκλησία, *ekklēsia*, made up of those who like Peter confess his messianic role and divine Sonship, would be "the assembly [or 'congregation'] of the Messiah." Sixth, his ἐκκλησία, *ekklēsia*, would become the vehicle of authority (see "the keys of the kingdom of heaven") throughout this age for carrying out the predetermined will of heaven by "binding" (that is, "retaining") the nonelect man's sins through the "smell of death" character for him (2 Cor. 2:16) of the gospel proclamation and/or of church discipline, and "loosing" (that is, "forgiving") the elect man's sins through the "fragrance of life" character for him (2 Cor. 2:16) of the same gospel proclamation and/or of church discipline. These two activities on the church's part ("binding" and "loosing" in accordance with the predetermining will of heaven) would become the means through the centuries by which Jesus would "build" his "assembly." Seventh, Jesus' statement suggests that his "assembly" would be a *worldwide* entity, for this appears to be the connotation of the word here. Finally, the fact that the "foundation stones" of his "assembly" were given the keys of the *kingdom of heaven* indicates that there is a direct connection between church and kingdom. In other words, by entrusting oneself in saving faith to the Christ espoused in the apostles' doctrine, one enters Messiah's church, which is also the present redemptive expression of the kingdom of heaven among men. As Paul will write later: "[The Father] delivered us from the domain of darkness, and transferred us to the kingdom of the Son of his love" (Col. 1:13).

Testament, 3:525. Jesus, of course, would have known Greek and could have said ἐκκλησία, *ekklēsia*—he had been a carpenter in and around Nazareth, which would have required him to conduct business in Greek; he spoke to the Syrophoenician woman who was Greek, Mark 7:26; when he spoke of "going to him who sent me," the Jews wondered whether he was going to the Dispersion among the Greeks to teach the Greeks, John 7:35; certain Greeks felt at liberty to request to speak to him, John 12:20; finally, he spoke to Pilate, who likely would not have known Aramaic or Hebrew, and was probably using Greek.

40. Whether κατισχύσουσιν, *katischysousin*, is to be construed in such a way as to make Hades the invading force ("will not conquer") or to make the church the attacking force ("will not stand against") is a matter of some debate among commentators. Given the facts (1) that "gates," as part of a wall, are therefore stationary and not doing the advancing, and (2) that the church without question is to invade a world peopled with children of Satan and "take captive every thought to make it obedient to Christ," I favor the latter interpretation.

MATTHEW 18:17

The one other occasion when Jesus employed ἐκκλησία, *ekklēsia*, in the Gospels is in connection with his instructions to his disciples concerning the appropriate steps to follow in church discipline. If a sinning member of his "assembly" should spurn the reproof of another member and then of two or more members (elders?), Jesus instructed the original reprover (εἰπὲ, *eipe*, is singular) to take the third step: "tell it to the ἐκκλησίᾳ [*ekklēsia*]; and if he refuses to listen to the ἐκκλησίας, [*ekklēsias*] let him be to you [sing.] as the Gentile [ὁ ἐθνικὸς, *ho ethnikos*] and the tax-gatherer [ὁ τελώνης, *ho telōnēs*]."

Jesus' characterization of those who stand outside his ἐκκλησία, *ekklēsia*, is intriguing. If one is relegated through the prescribed steps of discipline to the "outside" of the ἐκκλησία, *ekklēsia*, those within are instructed to regard him in his "outside the church" state as the "Gentile" and the unpopular collector of Roman taxes who more than likely was extorting larger tax sums than were due (see Luke 3:12–13; 19:2–8) and who, if he was a Jew, had become an outcast in Jewish society. In sum, *both characterizations describe the unrepentant excommunicated sinner in terms of what he would be relative to his relationship to Israel*. This means then that Jesus, when he made this statement, was thinking of his ἐκκλησία, *ekklēsia*, in terms of its being the true covenant community of Israel, for according to common Israelite usage of the term, to be an Israelite was the opposite of being a Gentile and to be a Gentile was the opposite of being an Israelite.

Note now two further points. First, the word ἐκκλησία, *ekklēsia*, not only can designate the worldwide entity suggested by Matthew 16:18, but it also can be employed to describe the individual local congregation, as it does here. Second, Jesus' ἐκκλησία, *ekklēsia*, is to viewed not only as Messiah's assembly and the redemptive expression of the kingdom of God, but also as the "Israel of God" (see Gal. 6:16). And Gentiles who come into this ἐκκλησία, *ekklēsia*, as Paul would later declare, "have been brought near" to the "commonwealth [πολιτείας, *politeias*] of Israel" and Israel's "covenants of promise" (Eph. 2:12–13), and in this new relationship have become "the circumcision, who worship in the Spirit of God and glory in Christ Jesus and put no confidence in the flesh" (Phil. 3:3; see also Paul's metaphor of the two olive trees in Rom. 11:16–24), and with elect Jews are God's "new man" (Eph. 2:14–16). Jesus' ἐκκλησία, *ekklēsia*, then is the true New Testament "assembly of the Lord" and thus the continuing expression of that spiritual "Israel" within Old Testament national Israel of which Paul speaks (Rom. 9:6). That is to say, just as there was a true spiritual "Israel" within Old Testament national Israel, so also Jesus' ἐκκλησία, *ekklēsia*, as the Israel of God exists within professing Christendom. And just as Old Testament Israel was God's national theocratic kingdom, so also Jesus' ἐκκλησία, *ekklēsia*, is God's soteric theocratic kingdom with

The *Ekklēsia* in Acts 1–12

Luke employs some form of the word ἐκκλησία, *ekklēsia*, 21 times in Acts to refer to the church: at 2:47 (Western reading); 5:11; 7:38 (of the Mosaic assembly in the Old Testament wilderness); 8:1, 3; 9:31; 11:22, 26; 12:1, 5; 13:1; 14:23, 27; 15:3, 4, 22, 41; 16:5; 18:22; and 20:17, 28. In these verses the singular is used to designate the entire company of believers in one locale (8:1) as well as several congregations in several locales (9:31). The singular is dominant (of believers at Jerusalem, 11:22; 12:1, 5; 15:4, 22; of believers at Syrian Antioch, 11:26; 13:1; 14:27; 15:3; of believers at Caesarea, 18:22; and of believers at Ephesus, 20:17, 28). The plural occurs at 9:31 (possibly); 15:41; and 16:5. The expression κατ' ἐκκλησίαν, *kat ekklēsian*, at 14:23 means "churchwide." A striking usage occurs in Acts 15:22, where the *representatives* of the churches from Antioch and Jerusalem at the Jerusalem Council are referred to as "the whole church" (ὅλῃ τῇ ἐκκλησίᾳ, *holē tē ekklēsia;* see 5:11; see also 2 Chron. 23:3 in this regard). Another particularly striking occurrence is at 20:28, where we read of "the church of God." Of this last usage K. L. Schmidt writes:

> We never find ornamental epithets [attached to ἐκκλησία, *ekklēsia*, in Acts]. The only attribute, if we may call it such, is the genitive τοῦ θεοῦ [*tou theou*]. This genitive is of Old Testament origin. Even when it does not occur, we should understand it, since otherwise the full significance of ἐκκλησία [*ekklēsia*] cannot be appreciated. The congregation or Church of God always stands in contrast and even in opposition to other forms of society. This is clear in the very first reference in Ac. 2:47, which makes prior mention of the λαός [*laos*] or κόσμος [*kosmos*] (D).[41]

Luke speaks of the ἐκκλησία, *ekklēsia*, in Acts 1–12 in several ways. He first introduces his readers to the church under the representation of 120 "brethren" (1:15)[42] whom Jesus had instructed to remain in the city of Jerusalem until they were empowered from on high by his Spirit's baptismal work (Acts 1:5, 8) in order to become his

---

41. K. L. Schmidt, "ἐκκλησία [*ekklēsia*]," *Theological Dictionary of the New Testament*, 3:505.
42. This was not the total number of Jesus' disciples at this time. There were also 500 disciples in Galilee (1 Cor. 15:6). Perhaps Luke mentions the 120 here to relate the Pentecost event to the dedication of the Solomonic temple, where the "assembly" gathered for the dedication was heralded by 120 priests blowing trumpets (2 Chron. 5:12). On both occasions the "temple" was filled with the Spirit of God.

witnesses "both in Jerusalem and in all Judea and Samaria, and even to the remotest part of the earth" (Luke 24:49; Acts 1:8). Messiah's "brethren" lived under the authority of the apostles (Acts 1:13–15) and received the outpouring of his "Breath" on the Day of Pentecost (see John 20:22), which showed him once again to be both Lord and Christ (Acts 2:36) and present by his Spirit with his church as he said he would be (Matt. 28:20). Peter proclaimed the fact of Christ's resurrection and messianic lordship in his Pentecost sermon and called his listeners to repentance and faith in him, which resulted in about three thousand people uniting with Messiah's "brethren." All these people "continually devoted themselves to the apostles' teaching and to fellowship, to the breaking of bread and to prayer" (Acts 2:42), sharing what they had with one another "as anyone might have need" (Acts 2:44–45; see 4:32–37), and "day by day continuing with one mind ... breaking bread from house to house, ... taking their meals together with gladness and simplicity of heart, praising God, and having favor with all the people" (2:46–47). Luke concludes his account at this point: "And the Lord was adding daily [recall here Jesus' "I will build"] to the ἐκκλησία, *ekklēsia*, [the Western reading; but probably should be "to their number"] those who were being saved" (2:47). A short time later, after Peter's healing of a lame man at the temple and in response to his second sermon (Acts 3), the Jerusalem congregation grew to a total of about five thousand people (4:4).

Shortly thereafter, after the Sanhedrin had threatened Peter and John for preaching about Jesus' resurrection, they returned to "their own [τοὺς ἰδίους, *tous idious*]" (Acts 4:23; see 24:23), a delightful Lukan description of the Christian brotherhood.

An awe-inspiring use of the "keys" by Peter in church discipline occurred in connection with the Ananias and Sapphira incident (Acts 5:1–10). Great fear fell upon the "whole church" in Jerusalem and upon all who heard of these things, with amazing results: first, "none of the rest dared to associate with them; however, the people held them in great esteem"; second, "all the more believers in the Lord, multitudes of men and women, were constantly added" to the church (5:11–14; this Lukan note assures us that the judicious use of church discipline in pursuit of purity within the church need not result in smaller numbers but can in fact, when done for the glory of God, fall out to greater blessing for and the numerical enlargement of Christ's church.)

In Acts 6:1–6, with Luke referring to the church at Jerusalem for the first time as "the disciples" (6:1, οἱ μαθηταί, *hoi mathētai*), the church's diaconal ministry takes on formal shape as seven men (ἄνδρας, *andras*) were appointed to oversee the task of caring for neglected widows in the church. Stephen, one of these seven deacons, found himself later accused of blasphemy and was brought before the Sanhedrin. The specific charge against Stephen was that he was speaking against the land, the law, and the temple, declaring that Jesus was going to destroy the temple and alter the customs which Moses handed down. Stephen's defense (Acts 7), longer than any other recorded speech in Acts, is highly significant in the way it prepares for the Gentile mission, for in it he makes the point that the worship of God cannot be tied to one land and one place such as the temple—an idea unthinkable to the Sanhedrin, whose members would have contended that the destruction of the temple would have meant the end of all true worship of God, if not the end of the world (see Matt. 24:2–3).

At the same time that Stephen charged them with always resisting the Holy Spirit, illustrating Israel's "stiffnecked" spirit of rebellion by reviewing the nation's history and showing how their fathers had resisted God's appointed leaders (Acts 7:9, 27–28, 35, 39–43), he pointed out that God had appeared to Abraham in *Mesopotamia* and *Haran,* that he had been with Joseph in *Egypt,* that he had spoken to Moses out of the burning bush in *the wilderness of Sinai* (which God himself declared was "holy ground"), and that Isaiah had even declared that the Most High does not dwell in houses made by human hands, since heaven is his throne and the earth his footstool. Here Stephen was declaring that Messiah's "assembly" cannot be tied to one site but is present wherever the Spirit of God does his creating, regenerating work. In sum, he called for a radical recasting of Jewish life to make Jesus, rather than the traditional holy things of land, law, and temple, the center of Jewish faith, worship, and thought. His ensuing martyrdom precipitated the outbreak of persecution against the Jerusalem church and the resultant scattering of members of that church throughout Judea and Samaria. Philip in particular, another of the seven deacons, proclaimed Christ, not only to Samaria, where a church was planted, but also to the eunuch from Ethiopia, and then from Azotus (Ashdod) on the coast as far north as Caesarea (see Acts 18:22). The Messiah was building his church, just as he had said he would (see Acts 1:8).

Peter then used the keys of the kingdom to "open wide" the doors of Messiah's "assembly" to the Gentile world through the Cornelius incident (Acts 10:1–11:18, particularly 10:45; 11:1, 18).[43]

The *Ekklēsia* in James

Because James occupied such a prominent place in the early church (Acts 12:17; Gal. 1:19; 2:9, 12) and at the council at Jerusalem, and because of the early date of his letter (written almost certainly from Jerusalem before the council itself), this

---

43. I discuss the Cornelius incident in some detail in chapter twenty-six, since it is being used today to illustrate the assertion that people do not need to trust Christ in order to be saved.

seems to be an appropriate place to say something about his doctrine of the church.

James wrote his letter around A.D. 45–48 to "the twelve tribes [that is, Jewish Christians] which are in the Diaspora [those scattered at the time of the "Sauline" persecution of Acts 8?]" (1:1). These Christians are worshiping in their "synagogues," that is, their local Christian "assemblies" (2:2). James's doctrine of the church appears to be of a more spiritual than organizational kind. By referring to Christians as "beloved brethren" (2:5), he clearly understands the church to be a "brotherhood" in the Lord. He says next to nothing about the organized church, though teachers apparently played an important role in the assemblies with which he was familiar (3:1). He also refer to "the elders of the church [τοὺς πρεσβυτέρους τῆς ἐκκλησίας, *tous presbyterous tēs ekklēsias*]" (5:14), counseling them in their pastoral duties to visit the sick and to minister to their spiritual and physical needs.

From his oral summation later at the Jerusalem council in Acts 15 we learn that he grounded his doctrine of the nature and function of the church in the Old Testament Scriptures, declaring that the words of the prophets "are in agreement with [συμφωνοῦσιν, *symphōnousin*]" the missionary activities conducted by Peter, Paul, and Barnabas among the Gentiles. He cited Amos 9:11–12 as a summary description of what God had declared in Old Testament times that he would do in behalf of the Gentiles. Employing Amos's prediction, James designated the assembly to which the "remnant of men," even "all the Gentiles who bear my name," was being drawn as the "fallen tabernacle of David," that is, true spiritual Israel. This tabernacle God was even then in the process of "building again" (recall Jesus' promise to "build" his assembly) by means of drawing from the Gentiles a people for himself and making them members of the church. To represent as he did the church of Jesus Christ as the "fallen tabernacle of David" which Amos predicted was to be "rebuilt" means that James believed (1) that the prophets had spoken of this age and the church of this age, (2) that Gentiles being drawn to "David's fallen tabernacle" thereby contributed to its "reconstruction," and (3) that an unbroken continuity exists between God's people in the Old Testament and Christians in this present age.

The *Ekklēsia* in Acts 13–28

With the conversion of Saul of Tarsus and his missionary labors, the gospel's advance throughout the Roman world was to enjoy unprecedented success. It transformed the church from being a mere sect into a religion for the world. The apostle Paul founded local churches not only in the Nabatean kingdom where he labored immediately after his conversion (Gal. 1:17),[44] in Syria and Cilicia (Gal. 1:21), and in Syrian Antioch, which he established as his missionary headquarters (see Acts 11:26; 13:1; 14:27; 15:3), but throughout Asia Minor, Macedonia, Greece, and even perhaps as far west as Spain (see Acts 14:23; 20:17; Gal. 1:2; 1 Thess. 1:1; 2 Thess. 1:1; 1 Cor. 1:2; 2 Cor. 1:1; Col. 4:16; Philem. 2; Rom. 15:24).

In the course of reporting on Paul's ministry Luke says some striking things about the ἐκκλησία, *ekklēsia*. He writes that with Paul's return to Tarsus after his first visit to Jerusalem three years after his conversion "the ἐκκλησία [*ekklēsia*, sing.] *throughout all Judea and Galilee and Samaria* was having peace, *being built up* [same verb as in Matt. 16:18]; and, going on in the fear of the Lord and in the comfort of the Holy Spirit, it continued to increase" (Acts 9:31). He reports that the ἐκκλησία, *ekklēsia*, at Antioch commissioned Paul and Barnabas and sent them to their work (Acts 13:1–3), that Paul and Barnabas "appointed [χειροτονήσαντες, *cheirotonēsantes*][45] elders churchwide [κατ' ἐκκλησίαν, *kat ekklēsian*]" throughout Galatia (Acts 14:23), that local churches were "sending" and "receiving" bodies, as the ἐκκλησία, *ekklēsia*, at Antioch sent Paul's party to the council at Jerusalem and the ἐκκλησία, *ekklēsia*, at Jerusalem received the Antioch party (Acts 15:3, 4), that Paul traveled through Syria and Cilicia, strengthening the ἐκκλησία, *ekklēsia*, (15:41), and that ἐκκλησίαι, *ekklēsiai*, were increasing in number daily (16:5).

---

44. Sometime during the period denoted by Luke's "many days" in 9:23, Saul journeyed into Arabia (Gal. 1:17). Some say he went there for quietude, in order to reorient his mind theologically in light of his Damascus Road experience; others say that he went to preach Christ. I support the latter view, for two reasons:

   1. Probably his three days of blindness in Damascus had been sufficient for his mind to be reoriented. The implication of his own narrative (in Galatians) relates his Arabian visit rather closely to his call to preach Christ among the Gentiles (see 1:17 and 1:16); the point of his reference to it in writing to his Galatian converts was to underline the fact that he began to discharge this call before he went up to Jerusalem to see the apostles there, so that none could say that it was they (or any other authorities on earth) who commissioned him to be the Gentiles' apostle.

   2. By "Arabia" in this context Paul very likely intended the Nabataean kingdom that was readily accessible from Damascus. At this time it was ruled by Aretas IV (9 B.C.–A.D. 40). It would appear from what he says in 2 Corinthians 11:32–33 that it was not simply a quiet retreat that Paul had sought in Arabia. In this later reminiscence he recalls a humiliating experience: "At Damascus the ethnarch of King Aretas guarded the city of the Damascenes in order to seize me, but I was let down in a basket through a window in the wall, and escaped his hands" (author's translation). Why should the Nabataean ethnarch take this hostile action against Paul if he had simply spent his time in Arabia in quiet contemplation? If, however, he had spent his time there in preaching, he could well have stirred up trouble for himself and attracted the unfriendly attention of the authorities.

45. The verb χειροτονέω, *cheirotoneō*, means "to choose by raising hands" or "to appoint." Because Paul and Barnabas appear to be the subjects of the participial action here, they probably appointed elders in these Galatian cities, but with the concurrence of the congregations.

In connection with Luke's report of the Jerusalem council, it should be noted that once the church, through its representatives, had determined upon the course of action the church should follow with regard to the question of Gentile circumcision (here we see church government by the eldership in action), the council's letter (probably drafted by James) was then sent to the local assemblies (see 15:22–31) and was delivered by Paul and Silas as "decrees" or "commands" (16:4; τὰ δόγματα, *ta dogmata*). Universal congregational compliance was expected because of the mutual submission assumed to exist between the local gatherings of churches.

Perhaps the most pregnant single notice about the nature of the church is Luke's report of Paul's statement to the Ephesian elders in which Paul describes the city-church at Ephesus as a "flock" and the elders themselves as "overseers" (plural of ἐπίσκοπος, *episkopos*, from which our word "bishop" is derived) whom the Holy Spirit had appointed "to shepherd [ποιμαίνειν, *poimainein*] the church of God which he acquired through his own blood [or 'the blood of his own (Son)']" (Acts 20:28). The church belongs to God. He acquired it through the blood of his Son. In character it is like a flock of sheep that needs shepherds because savage wolves (false teachers) will come in to draw disciples away after them. Elders, appointed by the Holy Spirit as overseers, are to be like shepherds in caring for and guarding the church.

The *Ekklēsia* in Paul's Letters

In Paul's mind local congregations of believers, often fellowships which met in homes of wealthy Christians (Rom. 16:5, 23; 1 Cor. 16:19; Col. 4:15; Philem. 2), are "churches," as may be seen by his willingness to use the noun in the plural (Rom. 16:4, 16; 1 Cor. 7:17; 14:33; 2 Cor. 8:18; 11:8, 28; 12:13). He can also speak of the "church" at a certain place, such as at Cenchrea (Rom. 16:1), at Corinth (1 Cor. 1:2; 2 Cor. 1:1), at Laodicea (Col. 4:16), and at Thessalonica (1 Thess. 1:1; 2 Thess. 1:1). He also speaks of the "churches" within entire provinces, such as the churches in Judea (Gal. 1:22; 1 Thess. 2:14), Galatia (Gal. 1:21; 1 Cor. 16:1), Asia (1 Cor. 16:19), and Macedonia (2 Cor. 8:1).

These local and regional gatherings of saints Paul views as making up *the* one church throughout the world (1 Cor. 10:32; 11:22; 12:28), which is the "one body" of Christ (Eph. 1:22; Col. 1:18, 24; Rom. 12:4–5; 1 Cor. 12:12–27; Eph. 4:4) and the "wife" of Christ (Eph. 5:25–27, 31–32). For this reason he believes it entirely appropriate to ask Christians in every church to pattern their lives according to the same standard of conduct (1 Cor. 4:17; 7:17; 14:33), and he expects Christians living in one area who are able to do so to assist poor Christians living in another area (1 Cor. 16:1–3; 2 Cor. 8:1–4).

Finally, he can use the term ἐκκλησία, *ekklesia*, to denote the entire number of Christian faithful who have been or shall be united to Christ as their Savior, both in heaven and on earth—what theologians refer to as the "invisible church" (Eph. 1:22; 3:10, 21; 5:23–25, 27, 32; Col. 1:18, 24).

Paul occasionally attaches an attributive or predicate definition to the noun ἐκκλησία, *ekklēsia*, primarily the genitive τοῦ θεοῦ (*tou theou*, "of God") which is added both to the singular (Gal. 1:13; 1 Cor. 1:2; 10:32; 11:22; 15:9; 2 Cor. 1:1; Acts 20:28; 1 Tim. 3:5, 15) and to the plural (2 Thess. 1:4; 1 Cor. 11:16). But he also speaks of "the churches of Christ [τοῦ Χριστοῦ, *tou Christou*]" (Rom. 16:16), "the churches ... which [are] in Christ [ἐν Χριστῷ, *en Christō*]" (Gal. 1:22), and "the churches of God ... in Christ Jesus" (1 Thess. 2:14). Once he speaks of "the churches of the saints" (1 Cor. 14:33). In his expression "to the church of God which is at Corinth" (1 Cor. 1:2a), which is linked with "all those who in every place call on the name of our Lord Jesus Christ" (1 Cor. 1:2d), there is the intimation that Paul is thinking of the "church of God" here in universalistic terms, with Corinth being only one place where it is manifested.

Another striking characterization of the church is found in 1 Timothy 3:15, where Paul speaks of the "house of God, which is the church of the living God, the pillar and ground of the truth." The church is to "hold high" as on a pillar the absolute truth of Christianity upon which it itself is grounded.

It is specifically in Ephesians and Colossians that we find Paul's most fully developed doctrine of the church. The church is the body of Christ, with Christ as its Head (Eph. 1:22, 23; 2:16; 4:4, 12, 16; 5:30; Col. 1:18, 24; 2:19; 3:15), and the wife of Christ (Eph. 5:22–32).

Paul's three pastoral letters (1 and 2 Timothy and Titus) provide much instruction concerning the government of the church and "how people [both officers and laity] ought to conduct themselves in God's household, which is the church of the living God" (1 Tim. 3:15).

The *Ekklēsia* in Hebrews

For the writer of Hebrews (Paul?) the church is the "house of God" (Heb. 3:6), the "wandering people of God" for whom there yet remains a Sabbath-rest (see the "wilderness" theme in Heb. 3:7–4:13; 11:9, 13; 13:14), and "brethren" of the great High Priest (2:17). His Jewish Christian readers have not assembled at Mount Sinai, as did the Old Testament church (12:18–21), but they have come "to Mount Zion and to the city of the living God, the heavenly Jerusalem, and to myriads of angels in joyful assembly [πανηγύρει, *panēgyrei*], to the assembly of firstborn people [ἐκκλησίᾳ πρωτοτόκων, *ekklēsia prōtotokōn*], whose names are written in heaven, and to God the Judge of all, and to the spirits of righteous ones made perfect [see Heb. 12:1], and to Jesus the mediator of a new covenant and to the sprinkled blood, which speaks a better word than the blood of Abel" (12:22–24, author's translation).

[831]

What does he mean when he says that Christians have come to myriads of angels in joyful assembly, and to the ἐκκλησία, *ekklēsia,* of firstborn ones, whose names are written in heaven?

With reference to the "myriads of angels in joyful assembly," one should recall that when Moses spoke of "the assembly of Jacob" in Deuteronomy 33:4, he prefaced his remarks by declaring that "God came from Sinai . . . with myriads of holy ones" (Deut. 33:2; see also Acts 7:53; Gal. 3:19; Heb. 2:2). Here we see the holy angels and the people of Israel brought together in one great assembly. Again, in Psalm 68, in David's description of Israel's march through the wilderness, we read that God, "the One of Sinai," who chooses to reign from that mountain (Ps. 68:8, 16), "has come from Sinai into his sanctuary" with "tens of thousands and thousands of thousands of the chariots of God" (68:17). In his procession are his people Israel who are commanded: "In the assembly bless God" (68:26). So once again we see God, as King reigning from Sinai, surrounded by the heavenly assembly of angels and summoning the earthly assembly to convene before him at his sanctuary. This same great assembly of heavenly and earthly "holy ones" is now more glorious than ever, because the assembly is before Mount Zion, the seat of God's throne, which the writer of Hebrews has in mind when he says that the Christian church has come to "myriads of angels in joyful assembly."[46]

To come as well to "the ἐκκλησία [*ekklēsia*] of firstborn men whose names are written in heaven" highlights the truth that the church, comprised of "firstborn" ones, stands in the heavenly assembly before the King of that assembly as sole heir with Christ (see Rom. 8:17; Gal. 4:7). The fact that the names of these "firstborn" are said to be written on the assembly roles in heaven indicates that they are *permanent* members and heirs in the kingdom assembly (recall here the enrollment of the assembly taken at Sinai in Numbers 1 and the enrollment of the Gentiles in the assembly described in Psalm 87). Entrance into this assembly follows upon repentance from dead works and faith in God and entails baptism (6:1; see 10:22–23, which also appears to be an allusion to Christian baptism).

While he says little about formal worship in the church, the writer of Hebrews does exhort Christians not to forsake the assembling (ἐπισυναγωγὴν, *episynagōgēn*) of themselves together (10:25). When they do come together, they should do so

---

46. Paul's insistence that women wear veils in the public assembly "because of the angels" (1 Cor. 11:10) almost certainly means that he viewed the church, when assembled, as assembled in the presence of the angels of God, who expect to see everything being done decently and in order. See the *Damascus Document* 4QD[b.] XV:15–17: "Fools, madmen, simpletons and imbeciles, the blind, the maimed, the lame, the deaf, and minors, none of these may enter the midst of the community, for the holy angels [are in the midst of it]."

with the consciousness that Christ himself "will sing God's praise in the midst of the church" (2:12), and for the purpose of mutual encouragement (10:25).

Nothing is said about the government of the church beyond the fact that the church has "leaders" who proclaim the Word of God to those for whom they are responsible, set a godly example of faith before the gathered assemblies, watch over the souls under their care as those who must give account, and who in return are to be obeyed (13:7, 17).

The *Ekklēsia* in Peter's Letters

Peter does not use the word ἐκκλησία, *ekklēsia*, in his letters, which is striking in itself when one recalls that it was to him specifically that Jesus was speaking when he declared that he would build his ἐκκλησία, *ekklēsia*, upon Peter as the "confessing apostle" and his revealed confession. But from his letters it is still quite apparent that he has a highly developed view of the spiritual nature of the church. For him the church is comprised of "God's elect, aliens and strangers in the world . . . who have been chosen according to the foreknowledge of God the Father, through the sanctifying work of the Spirit, for obedience to Jesus Christ and sprinkling by his blood" (1 Pet. 1:1–2, 17; 2:11), "who through the righteousness of our God and Savior Jesus Christ have received a faith as precious as ours," and "grace and peace in abundance through the knowledge of God and of Jesus Christ" (2 Pet. 1:1–2).

As such, the church is the *true temple*—made up of "living stones built into a spiritual house to be a holy priesthood, offering spiritual sacrifices acceptable to God" (1 Pet. 2:5). And because "natural" Old Testament Israel stumbled over the "stone laid in Zion," even over him whom God intended to be the "cornerstone and capstone" of his spiritual temple—not accidentally but providentially (1 Pet. 2:6–8), the church is also the *true Israel of God*—"a chosen people, a royal priesthood, a holy nation, a people belonging to God, that you may declare the praises of him who called you out of darkness into his wonderful light" (1 Pet. 2:9; see Exod. 19:5–6). Peter's readers were once "not a people," but are now "the people of God" (1 Pet. 2:10), "servants of God" (1 Pet. 2:16), "the brotherhood of believers" (1 Pet. 2:17), and "God's flock" (1 Pet. 5:2).

But the church for Peter is not simply a spiritual organism. It is also a tangible, concrete organization in a very real and evil world—a world within which the devil prowls like a roaring lion looking for someone to devour (1 Pet. 5:8), a world which is governed by kings and governors (1 Pet. 2:13–14) and which is populated in general with men hostile to Christians and in particular with false teachers who oppose the truth (2 Pet. 2). In this world the church is comprised of "free men" (1 Pet. 2:16) who are slaves (1 Pet. 2:18), wives who must learn to be submissive even to unbelieving husbands (1 Pet. 3:1–6), husbands who must learn to be considerate to their wives (1 Pet. 3:7), elders (1 Pet. 5:1), and young men (5:5)—all standing under the authority, first, of "the Shepherd and Overseer of your souls" (1 Pet. 2:25), second, of the prophetic Scriptures which are "the living and enduring word of God" (1 Pet. 1:10–12, 16, 23–25; 2:6, 7, 8, 22; 3:10–12, 14–15; 4:18; 5:5; 2 Pet. 1:19; 3:2a), third, of Christ's apostles (1:1; 5:1; 2 Pet. 3:2b), and fourth, of appointed "elders" who are to serve as "shepherds" and "overseers" of God's flock (1 Pet. 5:1–2), but "not [Peter says to the elders] because you must, but because you are willing, as God wants you to be; not greedy for money, but eager to serve; not lording it over those entrusted to you, but being examples to the flock" (1 Pet. 5:2b–3).

He alludes to baptism, employing symbolically the waters of the Genesis flood to elucidate its significance (1 Pet. 3:21; see also the "sprinkling" in 1:1): as the waters of the flood separated the present world order from the old, Peter says, the Christian's "baptism now saves you also—not the removal of dirt from the body but the pledge of a good conscience toward God. It saves you by the resurrection of Jesus Christ."

The *Ekklēsia* in Jude

The word ἐκκλησία, *ekklēsia*, does not occur in the brief letter of Jude, and Jude offers us very little data from which to discern his total ecclesiology. This much is plain: for Jude the church is a *spiritual* entity comprised of those "who have been called, loved by God the Father, and kept by Jesus Christ" (v. 1). The church lives under the sovereignty and lordship of Jesus Christ (v. 4) and the teaching of his apostles (v. 17). His readers have experienced the "mercy, peace, and love" of God in abundance (v. 2). They are bound together by "our shared salvation" (v. 3), are in possession of a fixed body of Christian truth which he labels "the once-for-all entrusted to the saints faith" (v. 3) and they eat love feasts (ταῖς ἀγάπαις, *tais agapais*) together (v. 12). They are to build themselves up in their "most holy faith" and pray in the Holy Spirit (v. 20), are to show mercy to outsiders and keep themselves from corrupt flesh (v. 23), and are to evangelize, "snatching others from the fire" (v. 21). Jude says nothing about church leaders or about the church's organizational structure.

The *Ekklēsia* in John's Letters

By his use of ἐκκλησία, *ekklēsia*, in 3 John 6 and 9, John specifically refers to a local church. He says nothing directly about church organization or church officers in his epistles. But it is apparent that the church, for John, is a distinguishable community, because he urges Christians to love one another and to be willing to lay down their lives for their brothers (1 John 3:16). Another indication that the church for John is a distinguishable community is the fact that false teachers have withdrawn from her company (1 John 2:19; see 4:1). In 3 John 7–9 John states that the church should feel the responsibility to support missionaries because these "brothers" receive nothing from "the pagans" (τῶν ἐθνικῶν, *tōn ethnikōn*), suggesting by the use of this word that the church is God's "Israel." Finally, John very likely addresses a local church in 2 John 1 as "the elect lady and her children," admonishing her to have nothing to do with teaching that "goes beyond" the teaching of Christ (2 John 10–11). Obviously, John is concerned that this community of faith remain distinct and morally pure and not be affected by Gnostic docetism, more particularly by Cerinthianism.[47]

Perhaps John's reference in 1 John 2:20, 27 to "the anointing which you received from the Holy One" is an allusion to the Spirit's regenerating work which baptism signifies. If it refers to the sacrament, we can infer nothing about the rite beyond the fact of the practice itself.

The *Ekklēsia* in John's Apocalypse

The church in John's Apocalypse is manifold and local (see chaps. 2 and 3) and yet one and spiritual. Its unity is represented in the picture of the exalted Christ holding all of the local churches in his right hand (Rev. 1:16), walking in the midst of them (2:1), and addressing them all, counseling them to listen to what the Spirit says to the churches.

We see both the church militant and the church triumphant in the Apocalypse. In the former the words of the Apocalypse were to be read aloud (Rev. 1:3), reflecting the practice of public reading of the Word in the assembled churches, very probably on the Lord's Day (1:10). The church is portrayed as "a kingdom, priests to God" (1:6; 5:10) and as the "true Israel," as seen from the expressions in 2:9 and 3:8 and from its representation as the "twelve tribes of Israel" in Revelation 7 and 14. It is also the Bride of the Lamb (19:7–8; 21:9). By this last reference it is linked to the New Jerusalem, whose twelve gates are named after the twelve tribes of Israel and whose twelve foundations are named after the twelve apostles, symbolism highly suggestive of the Reformed teaching of the oneness of the people of God in all ages.

In the Apocalypse, while that portion of the church which is on earth is a persecuted church, the church in heaven is often seen as a worshiping church, singing

---

47. Cerinthus was a Gnostic heretic who denied the Incarnation of Christ. According to Irenaeus, citing Polycarp, John upon meeting Cerinthus in a public bath refused to remain under the same roof with him lest it should fall down.

and extolling the greatness of God and the Lamb (Rev. 4 and 5) and praising God for the eschatological destruction of Babylon (chap. 19), with the martyred church in heaven crying out for God to "judge and avenge our blood on them that dwell on the earth" (6:10). We see it brought to its full and final glorification as the Lamb's wife under the imagery of the "holy city Jerusalem, coming down out of heaven from God" (21:9–22:5).

★ ★ ★ ★ ★

From this survey we have seen that the church, from the Old Testament perspective, is the redeemed "assembly" standing reverently in the presence of God and his holy angels to worship and serve Yahweh. From the New Testament perspective, the church, also God's "assembly," is specifically founded on Jesus Christ as the Messiah and Son of the living God and on his confessing apostles as his authoritative teachers of doctrine. It is a spiritual communion of saints and a worldwide network of local fellowships under the governance of elders, who meet at local and regional levels to conduct the business of the church at large. The church will be finally glorified as the wife of the Lamb.

CHAPTER TWENTY-ONE

The Attributes and Marks of the Church

THE CHURCH of the New Testament age, essentially one with the church of the old dispensation, came to consist of particular churches throughout the Roman Empire in which true believers in the finished work of the Lord Jesus Christ assembled for worship of the Triune God. From the beginning the church was viewed essentially as the elect of God and a communion of saints living under apostolic authority, and as the body of Christ and the fellowship of the Spirit. In its external "earthly" expression, an admixture of evil people with these true believers was always a possibility and often a reality. Where such admixture became apparent, disciplinary measures were taken to return the church to a state of (relative) purity (see Rom. 16:17–18; 1 Cor. 5:1–5; 2 Cor. 2:5–10; 2 Thess. 3:6; Titus 3:10–11; 2 John 9–11).

After the destruction of Jerusalem in A.D. 70, when the church was no longer viewed as existing within the national life of Israel, it was more and more perceived to have had an independent existence of its own all along, having been kept by the power of God and nurtured by Christ and his Spirit. Through the Cornelius incident all national boundaries were swept aside and the church came into its own as a supranational, multiracial community of believers. In order to fulfill its Sovereign's call for ethnic catholicity (Matt. 28:19–20), it had to become a missionary institution, carrying the gospel of salvation to all the nations of the world. The genesis of this universalizing of the church is preserved for us in Luke's account of the missionary labors of Paul.

The organizational structure of the church in New Testament times was "presbyterian" in government. That is to say, the church, under the lordship and kingship of Christ, was governed by pluralities of elders in individual local assemblies (Acts 11:30; 14:23; 20:17, 18; James 5:14; Phil. 1:1; 1 Tim. 3:1, 2; 5:1, 17, 19; Titus 1:5, 7; 1 Pet. 5:1), who had the responsibility of teaching and ruling, of shepherding and exercising oversight, and of ordaining men to office when meeting in presbytery (πρεσβυτέριον, *presbyterion;* 1 Tim. 4:14; 2 Tim. 1:6), and who would upon occasion meet with other regional presbyteries to settle questions of doctrine troubling the church at large (Acts 15).

THE ATTRIBUTES OF THE TRUE CHURCH (OR ASSEMBLY)

Rapid and apparent doctrinal and organizational declension away from apostolic teaching began to appear almost immediately after the age of the apostles.[1] As a result, early church leaders began to feel the need to determine *attributes* by which the *true* church could be identified. Because this movement tended to concentrate on the outward characteristics of the church, the church rather quickly began to be viewed as an external institution ruled by a bishop who was a direct successor of the apostles, and who accordingly would be (it was presumed) in possession of the true apostolic tradition. Accordingly, by the third century A.D. some church fathers were placing a strong emphasis on the bishopric as an institution. Cyprian, bishop of Carthage (d. 258), "regarded the bishops as the real successors of the apostles" and urged that the bishops together "formed a college, called the episcopate, which as such constituted the unity of the Church. The unity of the Church was thus based on the unity of the bishops."[2] For Cyprian the criterion of church membership was submission to the bishop, and outside of such submission there was no salvation.[3] The maxim is usually cited as *Extra ecclesiam nulla salus* or *Salus extra ecclesiam non est.* Augustine (354–430), who defined the church as the *sancta congregatio omnium fidelium salvandorum* ("the holy assembly of all the faithful who are saved") and as the *fidelium predestinatorum et iustificatorum* (the "faithful who are elect and justified") in his treatise *De unitate ecclesiae,* also adhered to the Cyprianic idea that apostolic authority continued through the succession of bishops. Accordingly, he too taught that he for whom the institutional church with its sacramental grace is not mother has not God as his Father.

In the Old Roman Symbol (given by Rufinus, c. 390), the forerunner of the Apostles' Creed, reference is made simply to "the holy church." The received form of the Apostles' Creed (adopted c. 700) speaks of "the holy catholic church." At the First Ecumenical Council held at Nicaea (A.D. 325), reference was made in that

---

1. Church historians are fairly unanimous in their observation that the church in many areas of the then-known world rather quickly departed from the pure gospel and teaching of the apostles and began to espouse defective views of the Trinity and the person and work of Christ, and to advocate Pelagian and sacerdotalistic versions of salvation.
2. Louis Berkhof, *Systematic Theology* (Grand Rapids: Eerdmans, 1941), 558.
3. See Cyprian's treatise, *The Unity of the Church,* and his *Epistles,* 73.21.

council's creed to "the catholic and apostolic church." The framers of the Niceno–Constantinopolitan Creed (A.D. 381) confessed: "[We believe] *in one holy catholic and apostolic church* [εἰς μίαν ἁγίαν καθολικὴν καὶ ἀποστολικὴν ἐκκλησίαν, *eis mian hagian katholikēn kai apostolikēn ekklēsian*]." Here we observe for the first time the four attributes that increasingly came to be used in the ancient and medieval church to describe the true church—*una, sancta, catholica, apostolica*—being given creedal and conciliar sanction. Viewed biblically, these four attributes are appropriate descriptions of Christ's church.[4]

The Church's Oneness

The church is one by virtue of its union with Christ. All its members are baptized by one Spirit into one body having one Head and one Lord. There is one building with one foundation, one flock under one Shepherd. Dissensions and divisions among Christians obscure the oneness of the body of Christ. Hence, we have various appeals in the epistles for unity through patience and love. The church's "oneness," as both fact and ideal to be achieved, is taught particularly by Jesus and Paul. Jesus declared:

> John 10:14–16: "I am the good shepherd; I know my sheep and my sheep know me—just as the Father knows me and I know the Father—and I lay down my life for the sheep. I have other sheep that are not of this sheep pen. I must bring them also. They too will listen to my voice, and there shall be one [μία, *mia*] flock and one [εἷς, *heis*] shepherd."

And he prayed:

> John 17:20–23: "I pray not for [my disciples] alone. I pray also for those who will believe in me through their message, that all of them may be one [ἕν, *hen*], Father, just as you are in me and I am in you. May they also be in us that the world may believe that you have sent me. I have given them the glory that you gave me, that they may be one [ἕν, *hen*] as we are one [ἕν, *hen*]: I in them and you in me.

---

4. Occasionally one finds expressed a certain dissatisfaction with only these four attributes. H. Bavinck, for example, in his *Gereformeerde Dogmatiek*, trans. William Hendriksen (Kampen: Kok, 1930; reprint, Carlisle, Pa.: Banner of Truth, 1977), 4:308, urges that the attributes of indefectibility and infallibility should be added to these four. While I have no particular zeal to restrict the number of the church's attributes to four, I do believe that adequate reflection on the four universally recognized attributes will entail by implication other essential characteristics of the church as well. For example, are not Bavinck's attributes of "indefectibility" and "infallibility" implied in the church's "apostolicity" when this attribute is properly understood?

May they be brought to complete unity [ἕν, *hen*] to let the world know that you sent me,[5] and have loved them even as you have loved me."

Paul throughout his long ministry labored to insure that Christ's church would be one,[6] everywhere insisting that the Gentile churches should joyfully contribute to the needs of the Jewish church and that the Jewish church should humbly accept the aid of its Gentile benefactors. He writes:

> Romans 15:5–6: "May the God who gives endurance and encouragement give you a spirit of unity among yourselves as you follow Christ Jesus, so that with one heart and mouth you may glorify the God and Father of our Lord Jesus Christ."
>
> Galatians 3:28: "There is neither Jew nor Greek, slave nor free, male nor female, for you are all one in Christ Jesus."
>
> 1 Corinthians 1:10–13: "I appeal to you, brothers, in the name of our Lord Jesus Christ, that all of you agree with one another so that there may be no divisions among you and that you may be perfectly united in mind and thought. . . . One of you says, 'I follow Paul'; another, 'I follow Apollos'; another, 'I follow Cephas'; still another, 'I follow Christ.' Is Christ divided? Was Paul crucified for you? Were you baptized into the name of Paul?" (see also 3:1–9).
>
> 1 Corinthians 12:12–13: "The body is a unit, though it is made up of many parts; and though all its parts are many, they form one body. So it is with Christ. For we were all baptized by one Spirit into one body—whether Jews or Greeks, slave or free—and we were all given the one Spirit to drink."

---

5. Clearly the unity among Christians for which our Lord is praying here is to be a *visible* unity if, as he prays, the *world* is to learn from it that the Father has sent him. G. C. Berkouwer rightly declares that "the Church may not be viewed as a hidden, mystical, mysterious present reality full of inner richness, which the world cannot perceive. . . . To flee here to the continuing sinfulness of the Church as an 'explanation' of her disunity or into the reassurance that a hidden unity can survive in the division does not take Christ's prayer seriously. . . . Because of her function and purpose in relating salvation to the world, one cannot boast here of a solidarity that is sufficient in God's eyes, but one must think of the eyes of the world" (*The Church* [Grand Rapids, Mich.: Eerdmans, 1976], 45).

6. Saul of Tarsus, in the divine wisdom, was certainly the right man to meet the special need facing the first–century church—the bridging of the major cultures in the Roman Empire and the avoidance of an irreconcilable breach between Jewish and Gentile members of Christ's community. He was both willing and able to move among Greeks and pagans, addressing their philosophical questions, and to build churches comprised mainly of Gentiles. But because he was also a fervent Jew, he did not make a ruthless break with Judaic Christianity, even when the question of the relationship between Jew and Gentile in the church made fellowship difficult. Though he was "the apostle to the Gentiles," he remained in the highest sense a Hebrew of the Hebrews to the last (see Rom. 9:1–5).

Ephesians 2:14–16: "For he himself is our peace, who made the two [Jew and Gentile] one and has destroyed the barrier, the dividing wall of hostility, by abolishing in his flesh the law with its commandments and regulations. His purpose was to create in himself one new man out of the two, thus making peace, and in this one body to reconcile both of them to God through the cross, by which he put to death their hostility."

Ephesians 4:3–6: "Make every effort to keep the unity of the Spirit through the bond of peace. There is one body and one Spirit—just as you were called to one hope when you were called—one Lord, one faith, one baptism, one God and Father of all, who is over all and through all and in all."

Philippians 2:2: "Make my joy complete by being like-minded, having the same love, being one in spirit and purpose."

Colossians 3:12–14: "As God's chosen people, holy and dearly loved, clothe yourselves with compassion, kindness, humility, gentleness and patience. Bear with each other and forgive whatever grievances you may have against one another. Forgive as the Lord forgave you. And over all these virtues put on love, which binds them all together in perfect unity."[7]

---

7. Paul is not so unrealistic as to believe that false teachings would never arise in the church. Accordingly, he can say to the Corinthian church, which he summons to unity, that he recognizes that "there have to be differences among you to show which of you have God's approval" (1 Cor. 11:19). This "necessity" is not a necessity of fate but rather simply one expression of the "acts of the sinful nature" (Gal. 5:19–20), which the church must ever guard itself against. See J. Oliver Buswell Jr.'s insightful discussion of 1 Corinthians 11:18–19 in his *Systematic Theology*, 1:426–28, in which he argues that the existence of Christian denominations, no doubt traceable all too often to the "sinful nature" manifesting itself either in the form of false teaching or false practice or both (and in these cases truly a real scandal before God), is not necessarily sinful. Division for the sake of maintaining the purity of the gospel is sometimes necessary and right. Buswell asks: "Shall . . . those who in all simplicity and honesty believe that the truth must be defended and expounded on certain scriptural issues . . . be the ones who are to be blamed for 'dissensions'? . . . No, . . . dissensions are necessary in order that the truth may be vindicated. Those who dissent in the interest of the truth are not the ones who are to be blamed for the dissension" (1:428). Indeed, Paul himself, it must be recalled, commands Christians in 2 Corinthians 6:14–17:

> Do not be yoked together with unbelievers. For what do righteousness and wickedness have in common? Or what fellowship can light have with darkness? What harmony is there between Christ and Belial? What does a believer have in common with an unbeliever? What agreement is there between the temple of God and idols? For we are the temple of the living God. As God has said: "I will live among them and walk among them, and I will be their God, and they will be my people." "Therefore come out from them and be separate," says the Lord. "Touch no unclean thing, and I will receive you."

The Westminster Confession of Faith neatly sums all this up in the following words:

> Saints, by profession, are bound to maintain an holy fellowship and communion in the worship of God, and in performing such other spiritual services as tend to their mutual edification; as also in relieving each other in outward things, according to their several abilities and necessities. Which communion, as God offereth opportunity, is to be extended unto all those who, in every place, call upon the name of the Lord Jesus. (XXVI/ii)

The Church's Holiness

The church is definitively holy in an absolute sense in that it is "in Christ." It is processively holy in a relative sense in that its sanctification is progressive, originating from the inner man and finding expression in the outer life. As Calvin remarks: "The church is holy . . . in the sense that it is daily advancing and is not yet perfect; it makes progress from day to day but has not yet reached its goal of holiness."[8] It is also holy in that it is separated from the world in its consecration to Christ. Listen to Jesus, Peter, and Paul again:

> John 17:15–19: "My prayer is not that you take [my disciples] out of the world but that you protect them from the evil one. They are not of the world, even as I am not of it. Sanctify [ἁγίασον, *hagiason*] them by the truth; your word is truth. As you sent me into the world, I have sent them into the world. For them I sanctify myself, that they too may be truly sanctified."

> 1 Corinthians 3:16–17: "Don't you know that you yourselves are God's temple and that God's Spirit lives in you? If anyone destroys God's temple, God will destroy him; for God's temple is sacred [ἅγιός, *hagios*], and you are that temple."

> 2 Corinthians 6:14–7:1: "Do not be yoked together with unbelievers. For what do righteousness and wickedness have in common? Or what fellowship can light have with darkness? What harmony is there between Christ and Belial? What does a believer have in common with an unbeliever? What agreement is there between the temple of God and idols? For we are the temple of the living God. As God has said: 'I will live with them and walk among them, and I will be their God, and they will be my people.' 'Therefore come out from them and be separate, says the Lord. Touch no unclean thing, and I will receive you.' 'I will be a Father to you, and you will be my sons and daughters, says the Lord Almighty.'

---

8. John Calvin, *Institutes*, IV.i.17.

Since we have these promises, dear friends, let us purify ourselves from everything that contaminates body and spirit, perfecting holiness [ἁγιωσύνην, *hagiōsynēn*] out of reverence for God."

Ephesians 4:24: "[You were taught] to put on the new self, created to be like God in true righteousness and holiness."

Ephesians 5:25–27: "Christ loved the church and gave himself up for her to make her holy, cleansing her by the washing with water through the word, and to present her to himself as a radiant church, without stain or wrinkle or any other blemish, but holy and blameless."

1 Thessalonians 5:23–24: "May God himself, the God of peace, sanctify [ἁγιάσαι, *hagiasai*] you through and through. May your whole spirit, soul and body be kept blameless at the coming of our Lord Jesus Christ. The one who calls you is faithful and he will do it."

1 Peter 1:15–16; 2:9: "But just as he who called you is holy, so be holy in all you do; for it is written: 'Be holy, because I am holy.' . . . You are a chosen people, a royal priesthood, a holy nation."

We argued in part three, chapter nineteen, that holiness, as an aspect of the *ordo salutis* relative to the individual saint, is both definitive and progressive. The same must be said about the true church as the *corporate* assembly of saints—that its holiness is both *definitive,* in the sense that, in union as it is with Christ, a radical breach with sin and uncleanness has occurred with regard to it, and *progressive,* in the sense that, God having declared its justification, its sanctification must and will *inevitably* follow. In other words, just as the individual Christian, who is *simul iustus et peccator* ("at the same time righteous and sinner"), will grow in holiness, so the true church, which is also *simul iustus et peccator,* will grow in holiness and consecration to Christ.

The Church's Catholicity

This third attribute follows from the ethnic catholicity of the gospel mandated by the Great Commission and from the church's character as the visible expression of the reconciling work of Christ before the entire world.

The church's catholicity or "universality" is to be understood not only geographically but also socially and continuously. Churches that are segregationist or exclusivistic in their membership (the current church growth method which seeks to reach only one segment of society is guilty here) contradict this fundamental aspect of the nature of the church and commit the "Petrine fallacy" (see Acts 10:13–15) of requiring for church membership some qualification beyond that which the

Lord of the church himself has stipulated. The following Scripture passages bear on this attribute of the church:

Matthew 28:19: "Go and make disciples of all nations.... And surely I am with you always, to the very end of the age."

Galatians 3:28: "There is neither Jew nor Greek, slave nor free, male nor female, for you are all one in Christ Jesus."

Colossians 3:11: "Here there is no Greek or Jew, circumcised or uncircumcised, barbarian, Scythian,[9] slave or free, but Christ is all, and is in all."

Revelation 5:9–10: "With your blood you have purchased men for God from every tribe and language and people and nation. You have made them to be a kingdom and priests to serve our God, and they will reign on the earth."

Revelation 7:9: "After this I looked and there before me was a multitude that no one could count, from every nation, tribe, people and language, standing before the throne and in front of the Lamb."

The Church's Apostolicity

Karl Barth has rightly stated that to be "apostolic" means to be "in the discipleship, in the school, under the normative authority, instruction and direction of the apostles, in agreement with them, because listening to them and accepting their message."[10] Accordingly, apostolicity must be primarily concerned with faithful adherence to the doctrine of the apostles, which was communicated to them by supernatural revelation and inscripturated through them by supernatural inspiration. Just as the true seed of Abraham are those who walk in the faith of Abraham, irrespective of lineal descent, so also the apostolic church is one which walks in the faith of the apostles, irrespective of the issue of "unbroken succession." Only conformity to the apostles' *doctrine* guarantees the church's apostolicity. Apostolicity can never and must never be viewed merely in terms of organizational succession back to the apostles, since such succession in itself, even if it were demonstrable, does not guarantee doctrinal purity. The following passages speak to this attribute of the church:

Matthew 10:40: "He who receives you [his apostles] receives me."

---

9. The Scythians were a tribe of horse-riding nomads and warriors from Western Siberia who lived in the Black Sea-Caspian area from about 2000 B.C. They became intermediaries in trade from Russia, especially in grain and slaves. The Jews looked upon them as exemplars of the lowest form of barbarians. In the church none are to be so regarded.
10. Karl Barth, *Church Dogmatics* (Edinburgh: T. & T. Clark, 1960), 4/1, 714.

Luke 10:16: "He who listens to you [the appointed seventy-two] listens to me; he who rejects you rejects me."

John 13:20: "I tell you the truth, whoever accepts anyone I send accepts me."

In the above three verses our Lord, who is himself "the Apostle whom we confess" (Heb. 3:1), makes it clear that his appointed apostles were his authorized, empowered representatives and spokesmen, and that to hear or reject his apostles is to hear or reject him.

> John 17:20: "My prayer is not for them alone. I pray also for those who will believe in me through their [the apostles'] message."
>
> Acts 2:42: "They devoted themselves to the apostles' teaching."
>
> Galatians 1:6–9: "I am astonished that you are so quickly deserting the one who called you by the grace of Christ and are turning to a different gospel—which is really no gospel at all. Evidently some people are throwing you into confusion and are trying to pervert the gospel of Christ. But even if we or an angel from heaven should preach a gospel other than the one we preached to you, let him be eternally condemned. As we have already said, so now I say again: If anybody is preaching to you a gospel other than what you accepted, let him be eternally condemned."
>
> Ephesians 2:20: "God's household, built on the foundation of the apostles and prophets, with Christ Jesus himself as the chief cornerstone."
>
> Hebrews 1:1–2; 2:1–3: "In the past God spoke to our forefathers through the prophets at many times and in various ways, but in these last days he has spoken to us by his Son. . . . We must pay more careful attention, therefore, to what we have heard, so that we do not drift away. For . . . how shall we escape if we ignore such a great salvation? This salvation . . . was confirmed to us by those who heard him."
>
> Revelation 21:14: "The wall of the city had twelve foundations, and on them were the names of the twelve apostles of the Lamb."

These verses affirm that the church may rightly claim to be "apostolic" only in the sense and to the degree that it continues to adhere to its original foundation, namely, the apostolic gospel and teachings. So concerned for his church's continuing "apostolicity" was the risen Lord, who in the days of his earthly ministry had warned that false prophets would appear within it (Matt. 24:11, 24; Mark 13:22), that he commended the church at Ephesus because it "tested those who claim to be apostles but are not, and have found them false" (Rev. 2:2). Doubtless the criteria for such testing included those already set forth in the Old Testament—whether the prophet's predictions occurred and whether his declarations accorded with the revealed faith of Israel (Deut. 13:1–3; 18:20–22). To these the New Testament church added the tests of whether the one claiming to be an apostle was a witness with the other apostles of Christ's resurrection (Acts 1:22), whether he proclaimed the same Christ and the same gospel that the other apostles taught (Gal. 1:8–9; 1 Cor. 15:11; 2 Cor. 11:4), whether he taught that Jesus Christ has come in the flesh (1 John 4:1–3), whether he did the things that marked an apostle—signs, wonders, and miracles (2 Cor. 12:12)—and whether he was willing to suffer hardship and persecution for the cause of Christ and his people (2 Cor. 12:13–13:13).[11]

THE PAPAL INTERPRETATION OF THE ATTRIBUTES

For several reasons (none scriptural, as we saw in the last chapter) the bishop of Rome increasingly came to be viewed as the "first among equals" *with* "primacy of power" within the hierarchical structure of the medieval church. The papacy as we know it really began around 590. To Gregory I (c. 540–604), the "father of the medieval papacy," is ascribed the credit for establishing the temporal political power of the papacy within the Holy Roman Empire. The papal resolve to dominate the life of every man in Europe received further support from the forged "Donation of Constantine" (to be dated probably during the eighth or ninth century), in which Constantine reputedly ceded to Sylvester I (314–35) primacy over Antioch, Constantinople, Alexandria, and Jerusalem, and dominion over all Italy, including Rome and the "provinces, places, and *civitates*" of the Western half of the empire. (The document's genuineness was challenged and its falsity demonstrated in the fifteenth century by Nicholas of Cusa and Lorenzo Valla.) The papacy's "golden age" was attained during the so-called papal reigns of Gregory VII (c. 1021–1085), Innocent III (1160–1216) and Boniface VIII (1234–1303). Gregory VII won the struggle against lay rulers for the church's right to make appointments without lay interference. He also claimed complete temporal power in Western Christendom. Innocent III was determined to enforce, extend, and define the *plenitudo potestatis* of the Roman see, even insisting in the bull *Venerabilem* that the

---

11. Some advocates of an unscriptural kind of quietism have urged, on the basis of such verses as 1 Thessalonians 4:9 and 1 John 2:27, that Christians, having all received the Spirit's anointing (τὸ χρῖσμα, *to chrisma*), that is, his indwelling (see "remains in you") at regeneration, do not need to concern themselves with apostolic doctrine because "his anointing [indwelling] teaches you about all things." But this view ignores the Bible's teaching that the indwelling Spirit teaches the church by the apostolic Word. John's statement does not set aside the usefulness and necessity of the Christ-given pastor/teacher (Eph. 4:11) in the church. In fact, he was acting the part of their teacher when he wrote those very words. In its context the verse means that his readers were not at the mercy of the Gnostic teachers who were contending that the church needed to listen to them in order to acquire the knowledge necessary for their advancement in the mysteries of God.

papacy had the "right and authority" to examine the man whom the imperial electors elected as emperor, and that the appointment of an emperor came within the sphere of papal authority "chiefly" and "finally." Boniface VIII, one of the great upholders of the absolute power of the papacy, in his bull *Unam Sanctam*, a defense of the jurisdiction of the pope over all creatures, declared:

> We are obliged by the faith to believe and hold—and we do firmly believe and sincerely confess—that there is one Holy Catholic and Apostolic Church, and that outside this Church there is neither salvation nor forgiveness of sins. . . . Of this one and only Church there is one body and one head—not two heads, like a monster—namely, Christ, and Christ's vicar is Peter, and Peter's successor. . . . Therefore, if the Greeks or others say that they were not committed to Peter and his successors, they necessarily confess that they are not of Christ's sheep, for the Lord says in John, "There is one fold and one shepherd." And we learn from the words of the Gospel that in this Church and in her power are two swords, the spiritual and the temporal. For when the apostles said, "Behold, here" (that is, in the Church, since it was the apostles who spoke) "are two swords"—the Lord did not reply, "It is too much," but "It is enough."

Consequently, the church of the Middle Ages came to be regarded less and less as the *communio sanctorum* and more and more in terms of the external, visible, and temporal hierarchical structure comprised of the concentric circles of priests, bishops, archbishops, and cardinals, all finally headed up by the pope. Rome came to interpret the attributes of the church *institutionally*: that is to say, the church's *unity* was defined in terms of the church's submission to the pope as the one Vicar of Christ in the world;[12] the church's *holiness* was said to be both the holiness of the sacramental grace invested in the sacraments, particularly in the Mass, and conveyed from the altar by the priesthood, and the (semi-Pelagian) works-righteousness of "doing what in you lies" (*facere quod in se est*) which William of Occam and others espoused;[13] the church's *catholicity* was affirmed not only because the church

---

12. So today, according to the *Catechism of the Catholic Church* (1994): "The *Pope*, Bishop of Rome and Peter's successor, 'is the perpetual and visible source and foundation of the unity both of the bishops and of the whole company of the faithful' " (para. 882). The *Catechism* also declares that the unity of the church is "assured by the visible bond of communion" exhibited in "apostolic succession through the sacrament of Holy Orders" (para. 815); and it cites Vatican II's *Lumen gentium* (November 1964, 8, 2) for corroboration: "This sole Church of Christ, . . . constituted and organized as a society in the present world, subsists in the Catholic Church, which is governed by the successor of Peter and by the bishops in communion with him" (para. 816).
13. The *Catechism of the Catholic Church* (1994) declares that it is in the church, united with Christ, that "the fullness of the means of salvation" has been deposited, and that it is by these means that "we acquire holiness" (para. 824).

dominated Europe but also because the church claimed as its possessions wherever the flags of Spain and Portugal, the colonizing sea powers in Europe, were planted in the New World[14]; and finally, the church's *apostolicity*, Rome urged, came to manifest expression in terms of the apostolic authority of the pope which he purportedly gained through direct apostolic succession from Peter by virtue of his sitting on "Peter's throne." Ludwig Ott writes:

> In the unbroken succession of the Bishops from the Apostles the apostolic character of the Church most clearly appears. It is sufficient to point to the apostolic succession of the Roman Church, because the Roman bishop is the head of the whole church and vehicle of the infallible doctrinal power. Consequently the apostolic Church and unfalsified apostolic teaching are where Peter or his successor is.[15]

---

14. Similarly, by its Vatican II pronouncements, Rome has defined its catholicity for modern and future times in such a way that the "Catholic church" virtually and ultimately includes not only those who are in the visible structure ruled by the Roman pontiff and his bishops but also, first, the baptized "separated brethren" of the Orthodox and Protestant churches (*Lumen gentium*, 15), second, Jews, because "the Jewish faith, unlike other non-Christian religions, is already a response to God's revelation in the Old Covenant" (*Catechism*, para. 839), because to the Jews belong all the privileges outlined in Romans 9:4–5 (para. 839), and because with Christians they "await the coming of the Messiah" (para. 840), third, Muslims, because they "profess to hold the faith of Abraham, and together with us they adore the one, merciful God" (*Lumen gentium*, 16), fourth, the religious world at large, because "all goodness and truth found in [the world's religions]" is "a preparation for the Gospel and given by him who enlightens all men that they may at length have life" (*Lumen gentium*, 16; see also its *Nostra aetate*, 2, and Pope Paul VI's Apostolic Exhortation, *Evangelii nuntiandi*, 53), and finally, even those "who, through no fault of their own, do not know the Gospel of Christ or his Church, but who nevertheless seek God with a sincere heart, and, moved by grace, try in their actions to do his will as they know it through the dictates of their conscience—those too may achieve eternal salvation" (*Lumen gentium*, 16; see also Denzinger–Schönmetzer, *Enchiridion Symbolorum*, 3866–72). This is world-wide missionary evangelism effected by redefinition!

15. Ludwig Ott, *Fundamentals of Catholic Dogma* (St. Louis, Mo.: Herder, 1960), 308. It must be said that no systemic change of any consequence has occurred in Roman Catholicism since the Middle Ages. The Council of Trent (1545–1563) condemned all the truths of the Reformation. Vatican I (1869–1870), convoked by Pius IX, stated plainly the infallibility of the Roman Pontiff, declaring his teachings as "irreformable of themselves," and not from the consent of the Church, "when he speaks *ex cathedra*, that is, when in discharge of the office of Pastor and Doctor of all Christians, by virtue of his supreme Apostolic authority he defines a doctrine regarding faith or morals to be held by the Universal Church." Vatican II declared in its *Dogmatic Constitution of the Church* (1964) that "the Roman Pontiff, by reason of his office as Vicar of Christ, namely, and as pastor of the entire Church, has full, supreme and universal power over the whole Church, a power which he can always exercise unhindered" (*Lumen gentium*, 22; *Catechism* [1994], para. 882). Article 25 states that the pope's proclamations of doctrine "of themselves, and not from the consent of the church, are justly styled irreformable."

The *Catechism of the Catholic Church* (1994) also declares:

> The Church is apostolic because "she is founded on the apostles" and "continues to be taught, sanctified, and guided by the apostles until Christ's return, *through their successors* in pastoral office: the college of bishops, "by priests, in union with the successor of Peter, the Church's supreme pastor." (para. 857, emphasis supplied)

THE PROTESTANT "MARKS" OF THE TRUE CHURCH

> This catholic church hath been sometimes more, sometimes less visible. And particular churches, which are members thereof, are more or less pure, according as the doctrine of the gospel is taught and embraced, ordinances administered, and public worship performed more or less purely in them. (Westminster Confession of Faith, XXV/iv)

Warfield was quite justified when he observed that the Protestant Reformation, especially on the Reformed side, was the revolt of Augustine's doctrine of grace against his doctrine of the church, "a revolt . . . against seeing grace channeled through the sacraments . . . a revolt, in all Reformational expressions, against the notion that predestination trickled only through the narrow crevices of church ordinances. It was, by contrast, an affirmation of Augustine's grasp upon human lostness, bondage to what is dark and wrong, the indispensability of grace, the glory of the gospel because of him in whom the Good News took and takes form."[16]

John Wycliffe (c. 1329–1384), the "Morning Star of the Reformation," in his *De potestate papae* maintained that the pope's claims were not grounded in Scripture, that his salvation was no more certain that that of any other man, and that the sole criterion of the rightness of his acts was their conformity to Scripture. He denounced the Roman curia[17] as a "synagogue of Satan" and spurned the Roman Mass as a blasphemy. He began to translate the Bible into English and urged that every man should be free to read and interpret the Scriptures for himself. In his *Tractatus de ecclesia* he defined the church as the *congregatio omnium predestinatorum* ("assembly of all those predestined [to salvation]"). The *prescitum*, that is, those foreknown, or foreordained, to damnation, are not part of the church.

John Hus (c. 1369–1415), the Bohemian "pre-Reformer" and betrayed martyr, came under Wycliffe's influence and in his *De ecclesia* declared that "two righteous

---

16. David F. Wells, *Turning to God* (Grand Rapids, Mich.: Baker, 1989), 84.
17. The Roman curia *(curia Romana)* is the papal court, including all the officials and authorities who assist the pope in the government of the Roman Catholic Church.

persons congregated together in Christ's name constitute, with Christ as the head, a particular holy church.... But the holy catholic—that is, universal—church is the totality of the predestinate—or all the predestinate, present, past, and future."

Martin Luther (1483–1546), in his revolt against the indulgence system, eventually rejected the Roman bishop's claim to apostolic succession from Peter and the infallibility of the church's general councils. He repudiated Rome's notion of a special priesthood which dispenses salvation through the sacraments and returned to the New Testament's vision of the church as primarily a *communio sanctorum* in which every believer is a priest before God (1 Pet. 2:9; Rev. 1:6; 5:9–10). With Luther was born the Protestant Reformation of the sixteenth century, the churches of which became distinctly "Lutheran" in Germany and Scandinavia and decidedly "Calvinistic" in Switzerland, France, Scotland, and England.

Roman Catholic polemicists, working with their understanding of the church's four attributes, responded by declaring that these "Protestant" churches could not possibly be the true church because they did not exhibit the attributes of the church. Not only were they not one with Rome, but also since they both rejected Rome's sacerdotalism and ordained ministers who had no episcopal consecration, they had no grace to dispense and hence could not be holy. Not only were they not catholic, being situated only in northern Europe, but also since they had renounced the authority of the pope they were not apostolic and had thereby unchurched themselves.

The leaders of the Protestant cause felt compelled by the exigencies of this debate, therefore, to define more carefully how the true church was to be identified. This they did by introducing into the debate their concept of the "marks" (*notae*) of the church. Berkouwer explains:

> Surveying the history of the Church, we meet with a striking distinction ... namely, the distinction between the attributes and marks of the Church. At first sight, the distinction is quite unclear, since one might expect that the Church can be known and precisely demarcated by means of her "attributes." However, closer inspections shows that there is an explicit motive underlying this distinction, which played a far-reaching role in the controversy between Rome and the Reformation and was related to the question of how one ought to view the Church's attributes ... the judgment of the Reformation was that one had not yet said everything when one had referred only to the Church's attributes. In speaking of the marks of the Church, the *notae ecclesiae*, the Reformation introduced a criterion by which the Church could be, and had to be, tested as to whether she was truly the Church.
>
> ... The notion of *notae*, with its unmistakable implications of criticism and testing, is directed against every presumption of the presence and verifiability of the attributes—in other words, against every static ecclesiology, in which every-

thing is decided simply from the basis that a church "exists" and that she possesses a number of immediately recognizable, unassailable "attributes." Ultimately, such a static ecclesiology no longer allows room for discussion about the ecclesiastical reality . . . in the Reformation it was precisely the *notae* that took on decisive significance, with the result that it was impossible to use the "attributes" apologetically as an unthreatened and unassailable, aprioristic reality.

. . . it is striking . . . that the four words themselves were never disputed, since the Reformers did not opt for other "attributes." . . . Even after the Reformation, in spite of all the differences in interpretation which appeared with respect to the four words, this usage ["one, holy, catholic, and apostolic"] remained the same. But in the midst of this consonant terminology, the Reformers' notion of the *notae* remained a disquieting element. Via the *notae*, the Reformers wanted to indicate from the Word of God "which is the true Church, since all sects which are in the world assume to themselves the name of the Church" (*Belgic Confession,* Art. 29).[18]

In this same connection Clowney writes:

In response [to Rome's charges] the Reformers did not reject the Nicene attributes of the church. They did reject the way the Roman Catholics tied them all to the institutional Papacy. God's grace is not a commodity to be dispensed. Finding the true church is not a matter of locating the Pope (although even that could be complicated by rival Popes!). There is a catholicity of time as well as of space. The Roman church might claim to be spread throughout the world but it had ruptured its link with the early church by corrupting Christian doctrine.[19]

Consequently, the Reformers, particularly the Lutherans, urged that at least two marks distinguished the true from the false church. Later Reformers were to add a third.[20] Where these are present, there the one holy catholic and apostolic church is present; where they are absent, whatever else the church under consideration might claim to have or in fact has, it is *not* the true church, the *ecclesia vera*. What are these marks?

The True Proclamation of the Word of God

The first mark, and the one the Reformers emphasized the most, was faithfulness to and the pure and true proclamation of the Word of God. They employed such verses as the following to make their point:

---

18. Berkouwer, *The Church,* 13–14.
19. Edmund Clowney, *Living in Christ's Church* (Philadelphia: Great Commission, 1986), 129.
20. See Clowney's helpful discussion of the three "marks" in *Living in Christ's Church,* 130–36.

John 8:31, 47: "If you hold to my teaching, you are really my disciples. . . . He who belongs to God hears what God says."

John 14:23: "If anyone loves me, he will obey my teaching."

Galatians 1:8–9: "But even if we or an angel from heaven should preach a gospel other than the one we preached to you, let him be eternally condemned! As we have already said, so now I say again: If anybody is preaching to you a gospel other than what you accepted, let him be eternally condemned."

2 Thessalonians 2:15: "So then, brothers, stand firm and hold to the teachings we passed on to you, whether by word of mouth or by letter."

2 Timothy 3:16–4:4: "All Scripture is God-breathed and is useful for teaching, rebuking, correcting and training in righteousness, so that the man of God may be thoroughly equipped for every good work. In the presence of God and of Christ Jesus, who will judge the living and the dead, and in view of his appearing and his kingdom, I give you this charge: Preach the Word; be prepared in season and out of season; correct, rebuke and encourage—with great patience and careful instruction. For the time will come when men will not put up with sound doctrine. Instead, to suit their own desires, they will gather around them a great number of teachers to say what their itching ears want to hear. They will turn their ears away from the truth and turn aside to myths."

1 John 4:1–3: "Dear friends, do not believe every spirit, but test the spirits to see whether they are from God, because many false prophets have gone out into the world. This is how you can recognize the Spirit of God: Every spirit that acknowledges that Jesus Christ has come in the flesh is from God, but every spirit that does not acknowledge Jesus is not from God. This is the spirit of the antichrist, which you have heard is coming and even now is already in the world."

2 John 9–11: "Anyone who runs ahead and does not continue in the teaching of Christ does not have God; whoever continues in the teaching has both the Father and the Son. If anyone comes to you and does not bring this teaching, do not take him into your house or welcome him. Anyone who welcomes him shares in his wicked work."

The Right Administration of the Sacraments

For the Reformers the second mark of the true church was the right administration of the sacraments, based on such passages as the following:

1 Corinthians 10:14–17, 21: "Therefore, my dear friends, flee from idolatry. I speak to sensible people; judge for yourselves what I say. Is not the cup of thanksgiving for which we give thanks a participation in the blood of Christ? And is not the bread that we break a participation in the body of Christ? Because there is

one loaf, we, who are many, are one body, for we all partake of the one loaf. . . . You cannot drink the cup of the Lord and the cup of demons too; you cannot have a part in both the Lord's table and the table of demons."

1 Corinthians 11:23–30: "I received from the Lord what I passed on to you: The Lord Jesus, on the night he was betrayed took bread, and when he had given thanks, he broke it and said, 'This is my body, which is for you; do this in remembrance of me.' In the same way, after supper he took the cup, saying, 'This cup is the new covenant in my blood; do this, whenever you drink it, in remembrance of me.' For whenever you eat this bread and drink this cup, you proclaim the Lord's death until he comes. Therefore, whoever eats the bread or drinks the cup of the Lord in an unworthy manner will be guilty of sinning against the body and blood of the Lord. A man ought to examine himself before he eats of the bread and drinks of the cup. For anyone who eats and drinks without recognizing the body of the Lord eats and drinks judgment on himself. That is why many among you are weak and sick, and a number of you have fallen asleep."

The Faithful Exercise of Church Discipline

The Reformers' third mark was the faithful exercise of church discipline. Here they employed such passages as the following:

Matthew 18:17: "If [a sinning brother] refuses to listen to [two or three concerned Christians], tell it to the church; and if he refuses to listen even to the church, treat him as you would a pagan or a tax collector."

Acts 20:28–31a: "Keep watch over yourselves and all the flock of which the Holy Spirit has made you overseers. Be shepherds of the church of God, which he bought with his own blood. I know that after I leave, savage wolves will come in among you and will not spare the flock. Even from your own number men will arise and distort the truth in order to draw away disciples after them. So be on your guard!"

Romans 16:17–18a: "I urge you, brothers, to watch out for those who cause divisions and put obstacles in your way that are contrary to the teaching you have learned. Keep away from them. For such people are not serving our Lord Christ, but their own appetites."

1 Corinthians 5:1–5, 13: "It is actually reported that there is sexual immorality among you, and of a kind that does not occur even among pagans: A man has his father's wife. And you are proud! Shouldn't you rather have been filled with grief and have put out of your fellowship the man who did this? Even though I am not physically present, I am with you in spirit. And I have already passed judgment on the one who did this, just as if I were present. When you are assembled in the name of our Lord Jesus and I am with you in spirit, and the power of our Lord

Jesus is present, hand this man over to Satan, so that the sinful nature may be destroyed and his spirit saved on the day of the Lord. . . . 'Expel the wicked man from among you.'"

1 Corinthians 14:33, 40: "God is not a God of disorder but of peace . . . . everything should be done in a fitting and orderly way."

Galatians 6:1: "Brothers, if someone is caught in a sin, you who are spiritual should restore him gently. But watch yourself, or you also may be tempted."

Ephesians 5:6, 11: "Let no one deceive you with empty words, for because of such things God's wrath comes on those who are disobedient. Therefore do not be partners with them. . . . Have nothing to do with the fruitless deeds of darkness, but rather expose them."

2 Thessalonians 3:14–15: "If anyone does not obey our instructions in this letter, take special note of him. Do not associate with him, in order that he may feel ashamed. Yet do not regard him as an enemy, but warn him as a brother."

1 Timothy 1:20: "Among [those who have rejected a good conscience and have shipwrecked their faith] is Hymenaeus and Alexander, whom I have handed over to Satan to be taught not to blaspheme."

1 Timothy 5:20: "[Elders] who sin are to be rebuked publicly [see Gal. 2:11–14], so that the others may take warning."

Titus 1:10–11: "There are many rebellious people, mere talkers and deceivers, especially those of the circumcision group. They must be silenced, because they are ruining whole households by teaching things they ought not to teach—and that for the sake of dishonest gain."

Titus 3:10: "Warn a divisive person once, and then warn him a second time. After that, have nothing to do with him. You may be sure that such a man is warped and sinful; he is self–condemned."

Revelation 2:14–16a: "Nevertheless, I have a few things against you: You have people there who hold to the teaching of Balaam, who taught Barak to entice the Israelites to sin by eating food sacrificed to idols and by committing sexual immorality. Likewise you also have those who hold to the teaching of the Nicolaitans. Repent therefore!"

Revelation 2:20: "Nevertheless, I have this against you: You tolerate that woman Jezebel, who calls herself a prophetess. By her teaching she misleads my servants into sexual immorality and the eating of food sacrificed to idols."

Of course, while all three marks are proper tests of the true church and extremely important, the three are not really coordinate. While the second and third are necessary for the well-being of the church, they are not necessary for the being of the church. Only the first is really necessary for the being of the church. On this point Berkhof remarks:

Strictly speaking, it may be said that the true preaching of the Word and its recognition as the standard of doctrine and life, is the one mark of the Church. Without it there is no Church, and it determines the right administration of the sacraments and the faithful exercise of Church discipline.[21]

CONFESSIONAL WITNESS TO THE MARKS OF THE TRUE CHURCH

It is quite easy to document the significance of these marks for the Reformers and their churches from the national creeds they wrote. Luther insisted that the church becomes visible, not where the rule of bishops and cardinals and popes is present, but where the Word is properly proclaimed and the sacraments purely administered. He approved of the Augsburg Confession (drawn up by Melanchthon in 1530) which states in part one:

> VII. It is also taught among us that one holy Church is to continue forever. But the Church is the congregation of saints [*congregatio Sanctorum*] in which the Gospel is rightly taught and the sacraments rightly administered according to the Gospel.
>
> VIII. . . . the Church, properly speaking, is nothing else than the congregation of saints and true believers [*congregatio Sanctorum et vere credentium*].

And in the *Apology of the Augsburg Confession* (1531) we read:

> VII/VIII. We concede that in this life hypocrites and evil men are mingled with the church and are members of the church according to the outward associations of the church's marks—that is, Word, confession, and sacraments. . . . (4)
>
> The church is not merely an association of outward ties and rites like other civic governments, however, but it is mainly an association of faith and of the Holy Spirit in men's hearts. To make it recognizable, this association has outward marks, the pure teaching of the Gospel and the administration of the sacraments in harmony with the Gospel of Christ. This church alone is called the body of Christ, which Christ renews, consecrates, and governs by his Spirit. . . . (5–6)

---

21. Berkhof, *Systematic Theology*, 577. Calvin writes in this connection: "this is the abiding mark with which our Lord has sealed his own: 'Everyone who is of the truth hears my voice" [John 18:37]. . . . Why do we willfully act like madmen in searching out the church when Christ has marked it with an unmistakable sign, which, wherever it is seen, cannot fail to show the church there; while where it is absent, nothing remains that can give the true meaning of the church? Paul reminds us that the church was founded not upon men's judgments, not upon priesthoods, but upon the teaching of apostles and prophets" (*Institutes*, IV.ii.4).

Hypocrites and evil men are indeed associated with the true church as far as outward ceremonies are concerned. But when we come to define the church, we must define that which is the living body of Christ and is the church in fact as well as in name. We must understand what it is that chiefly makes us members, and living members, of the church. If we are to define the church as only an outward organization embracing both the good and the wicked, then men would not understand that the kingdom of Christ is the righteousness of the heart and the gift of the Holy Spirit but would think of it as only the outward observance of certain devotions and rituals (12–13).

The Geneva Confession of 1536 states:

> 18. The proper mark by which rightly to discern the church of Jesus Christ is that his holy gospel be purely and faithfully preached, proclaimed, heard, and kept, that his sacraments be properly administered, even if there be some imperfections and faults, as there always will be among men.

John Calvin (1509–1564) also contended that the church is essentially a *communio sanctorum*. And in the French Confession of Faith, which he prepared in 1559, he writes:

> XXVII. . . . we believe that it is important to discern with care and prudence which is the true Church, for this title has been much abused. We say, then, according to the Word of God, that it is the company of the faithful who agree to follow his Word, and the pure religion which it teaches; who advance in it all their lives, growing and becoming more confirmed in the fear of God according as they feel the want of growing and pressing onward. . . .
>
> XXVIII. In this belief we declare that, properly speaking, there can be no Church where the Word of God is not received, nor profession made of subjection to it, nor use of the sacraments. Therefore, we condemn the papal assemblies, as the pure Word of God is banished from them, their sacraments are corrupted, or falsified, or destroyed, and all superstitions and idolatries are in them. . . .[22]

---

22. While Calvin repudiated the papacy as an institution, he was still willing to recognize the presence of God's people in the Roman church. See his oft-cited statement in *Institutes,* IV.iii.12 (the student of ecclesiology would be well advised to read the entire section), where, after a lengthy and heated rejection of the papacy, he writes: "I call them churches to the extent that the Lord wonderfully preserves in them a remnant of his people, however woefully dispersed and scattered, and to the extent that some marks of the church remain, especially those marks whose effectiveness neither the devil's wiles nor human depravity can destroy. But on the other hand, because in them those marks have been erased to which we should pay particular regard in this discourse, I say that every one of their congregations and their whole body lack the lawful form of the church."

XXIX. As to the true Church, we believe that it should be governed according to the order established by our Lord Jesus Christ. That there should be pastors, overseers, and deacons, so that true doctrine may have its course, that errors may be corrected and suppressed, and the poor and all who are in affliction may be helped in their necessities; and that assemblies may be held in the name of God, so that great and small may be edified.

XXX. We believe that all true pastors, wherever they may be, have the same authority and equal power under one head, one only sovereign and universal bishop, Jesus Christ; and that consequently no Church shall claim any authority or dominion over any other.

The Scotch Confession of Faith of 1560 also declared:

XVI. As we believe in one God, Father, Son, and Holy Spirit, so do we most constantly believe that from the beginning there has been, and now is, and to the end of the world shall be one Kirk, that is to say, one company and multitude of men chosen of God, who rightly worship and embrace him by true faith in Christ Jesus, who is the only head of the same Kirk, which also is the body and spouse of Christ Jesus, which church is catholic, that is, universal, because it contains the Elect of all ages, of all realms, nations, and tongues, be they of the Jews, or be they of the Gentiles, who have communion and society with God the Father, and with his Son Christ Jesus, through the sanctification of his Holy Spirit: and therefore it is called the communion, not of profane persons, but of Saints, who as citizens of the heavenly Jerusalem, have the fruition of the most inestimable benefits, to wit, one God, one Lord Jesus, one faith, and one baptism: out of the which Kirk, there is neither life nor eternal felicity. And therefore we utterly abhor the blasphemy of them that affirm that men who live according to equity and justice shall be saved, what religion they ever may have professed. For as without Jesus Christ there is neither life nor salvation, so shall there none be participant thereof, but such as the Father has given unto his Son Christ Jesus, and they that in time come unto him, avow his doctrine, and believe into him, [and this] comprehends the children of faithful parents. This Kirk is invisible, known only to God, who alone knows whom he has chosen, and comprehends as well (as is said) the Elect that be departed, commonly called the Kirk Triumphant, and they that yet live and fight against sin and Satan as shall live hereafter.

The Belgic Confession of 1561 likewise confesses:

XXVII. We believe and profess one catholic or universal Church, which is a holy congregation and assembly of true Christian believers, expecting all their salvation in Jesus Christ, being washed by his blood, sanctified and sealed by the Holy

Ghost. This Church hath been from the beginning of the world, and will be to the end thereof; which is evident from this, that Christ is an eternal king, which, without subjects he can not be. And this holy Church is preserved or supported by God against the rage of the whole world; though she sometimes (for a while) appear very small, and, in the eyes of men, to be reduced to nothing: as during the perilous reign of Ahab, when nevertheless the Lord reserved unto him seven thousand men, who had not bowed their knees to Baal. Furthermore, this holy Church is not confined, bound, or limited to a certain place or to certain persons, but is spread and dispersed over the whole world; and yet is joined and united with heart and will, by the power of faith, in one and the same spirit.

XXVIII. We believe, since this holy congregation is an assemblage of those who are saved, and out of it there is no salvation, that no person of whatsoever state or condition he may be, ought to withdraw himself, to live in a separate state from it; but that all men are in duty bound to join and unite themselves with it; maintaining the unity of the Church; submitting themselves to the doctrine and discipline thereof; bowing their necks under the yoke of Jesus Christ; and as mutual members of the same body, serving to the edification of the brethren, according to the talents God has given them. And that this may be better observed, it is the duty of all believers, according to the Word of God, to separate themselves from those who do not belong to the Church, and to join themselves to this congregation, wheresoever God hath established it, even though the magistrates and edicts of princes be against it; yea, though they should suffer death or bodily punishment. Therefore all those who separate themselves from the same, or do not join themselves to it, act contrary to the ordinance of God.

XXIX. We believe that we ought diligently and circumspectly to discern from the Word of God which is the true Church, since all sects which are in the world assume to themselves the name of the Church. But we speak here not of the company of hypocrites, who are mixed in the Church with the good, yet are not of the Church, though externally in it; but we say that the body and communion of the true Church must be distinguished from all sects who call themselves the Church. The marks by which the true Church is known are these: If the pure doctrine of the gospel is preached therein, if she maintains the pure administration of the sacraments as instituted by Christ; if church discipline is exercised in punishing of sin; in short, if all things are managed according to the pure Word of God, all things contrary thereto rejected, and Jesus Christ acknowledged as the only Head of the Church. Hereby the true Church may certainly be known, from which no man has a right to separate himself. . . .

As for the false Church, she ascribes more power and authority to herself and her ordinances than to the Word of God, and will not submit herself to the yoke of Christ. Neither does she administer the sacraments, as appointed by Christ in his Word, but adds to and takes from them as she thinks proper; she relies more upon men than upon Christ; and persecutes those who live holily according to the Word of God and rebuke her for her errors, covetousness, and idolatry. These two Churches are easily known and distinguished from each other.

The Thirty-nine Articles of the Church of England (1563) declared:

> XIX. The visible Church of Christ is a congregation of faithful men, in the which the pure Word of God is preached, and the Sacraments be duly ministered according to Christ's ordinance, in all those things that of necessity are requisite to the same. As the Church of Jerusalem, Alexandria, and Antioch, have erred; so also the Church of Rome hath erred, not only in their living and manner of Ceremonies, but also in matters of Faith.

The Westminster Confession of Faith (1646) affirms:

> XXV. The catholic or universal Church, which is invisible, consists of the whole number of the elect, that have been, are, or shall be gathered into one, under Christ the head thereof; and is the spouse, the body, the fulness of him that filleth all in all.
>
> The visible Church, which is also catholic or universal under the gospel (not confined to one nation as before under the law) consists of all those, throughout the world, that profess the true religion, and of their children; and is the kingdom of the Lord Jesus Christ, the house and family of God, out of which there is no ordinary possibility of salvation.
>
> Unto this catholic visible Church Christ hath given the ministry, oracles, and ordinances of God, for the gathering and perfecting of the saints, in this life, to the end of the world: and doth by his own presence and Spirit, according to his promise, make them effectual thereunto.
>
> This catholic Church hath been sometimes more, sometimes less visible. And particular churches, which are members thereof, are more or less pure, according as the doctrine of the gospel is taught and embraced, ordinances administered, and public worship performed more or less purely in them.
>
> The purest churches under heaven are subject both to mixture and error; and some have so degenerated as to become no churches of Christ, but synagogues of Satan. Nevertheless, there shall be always a Church on earth to worship God according to his will.
>
> There is no other head of the Church but the Lord Jesus Christ: nor can the Pope of Rome in any sense be head thereof; but is that Antichrist, that man of sin and son of perdition, that exalteth himself in the Church against Christ, and all that is called God.[23]

---

23. The clause beginning "but is that Antichrist . . ." has been eliminated by some Presbyterian denominations, such as the Presbyterian Church in America (PCA).

Finally, we may cite the *Book of Church Order* of the Presbyterian Church in America (PCA):

> Our blessed Saviour, for the edification of the visible Church, which is his body, has appointed officers not only to preach the Gospel and administer the Sacraments, but also to exercise discipline for the preservation both of truth and duty. It is incumbent upon these officers and upon the whole Church in whose name they act, to censure or cast out the erroneous and scandalous, observing in all cases the rules contained in the Word of God. (Preface, II, 3)

It also states:

> All of these [different denominations of professing Christians throughout the world] which maintain the Word and Sacraments in their fundamental integrity are to be recognized as true branches of the Church of Jesus Christ. (2–2)

★ ★ ★ ★ ★

In this chapter we have noted, first, how the early church fathers came to describe the church as "one holy catholic and apostolic" church, second, how the papacy perverted the meaning of these attributes to serve the institutional aims of the Roman church, and third, how the Reformers responded by introducing the "marks" of the church as the proper test for determining how the "one holy catholic and apostolic church" was to be identified.

Applying the Reformers' marks of the church to the ecclesiastical situation, according to the creeds of the Reformation the invisible church is universal and consists of the whole body of the elect of every age both in heaven and on earth, that is, all true believers in the Lord Jesus Christ. In other words, the invisible church is simply the church *as God sees it*. The visible "one holy catholic and apostolic" church is the Christian community throughout the world *as we see it*, represented by the world's many individual local churches where the Word of God is rightly taught, where the sacraments are rightly administered, and where a faithful attempt is made through church discipline to remove the chaff that would impede the free exercise of faithful preaching and the proper administration of the sacraments. Some churches have fallen so far away from apostolic doctrine that they have virtually become no churches at all, as is the case with the churches under the governance of Rome. But even within them, in spite of the institutional papacy, there is a remnant of true believers.

CHAPTER TWENTY-TWO

The Authority and Duties of the Church

THE AUTHORITY OF THE CHURCH

According to Holy Scripture the church of Jesus Christ has authority (ἐξουσία, *exousia*). What is the source of its authority, and what is its nature? And in what ways should the church manifest its authority?

Its Source

Authority is an attribute intrinsic only to sovereignty. The Triune God as the sovereign King (מֶלֶךְ, *melek*, βασιλεύς, *basileus*) of the universe (Pss. 10:16; 24:7–10; 29:10; 47:2, 7; 95:3; Jer. 10:10; 1 Tim. 1:17; 6:15; Rev. 19:16) has ultimate dominion or authority over all things (Pss. 22:28; 145:13; Dan. 7:14). But in the eternal economy of redemption, which we designated in part three, chapter thirteen (p. 502), as the covenant of redemption, the Father entrusted this authority to his Son, the Lord Jesus Christ, as one aspect of his messianic investiture and as the reward for his obedient labor (see Pss. 2:8–9; 8:6 [see 1 Cor. 15:25–27]; 110:1–7). On several occasions the Lord Jesus Christ expressly declared that the Father had endowed him, as the messianic Son of Man, with universal sovereignty:

> Matthew 11:27: "All things have been committed to me by my Father."
>
> Matthew 28:18: "Then Jesus came to them and said, 'All authority in heaven and on earth has been given to me.' " (This is an example of the use of the divine passive and means: "God has given to me all authority in heaven and on earth.")
>
> John 5:22, 27: "The Father judges no one, but has entrusted all judgment to the Son. . . . And he [the Father] has given him [the Son] authority to judge because he is the Son of Man."

[861]

John 17:2: "For you [the Father] granted him [the Son] authority over all people that he might give eternal life to all those you have given him."

Revelation 2:27: "I have received authority from my Father."

By the content of his teaching, his manner of teaching (see Matt. 7:29; Mark 1:22, 27; Luke 4:32), and his mighty miracles, such as his healing of the lame man (Matt. 9:8), his exorcism of demons (Mark 1:27; Luke 4:36), and his stilling the storm (Mark 4:39–41), Jesus personally exemplified and reflected the divine authority that was his both as God and as Messiah.[1] By virtue of his divine nature and his messianic investiture, the Lord Jesus Christ is both the Sovereign of the world and King and Head of his church.

Jesus as the sovereign Head of the church has in turn invested his church as his body with authority to do certain things in his name and in his stead. The following verses speak of the authority which Jesus gave first to the original Twelve:

Matthew 10:1 (Mark 3:14–15; 6:7; Luke 9:1): "[Jesus] called his twelve disciples to him and gave them authority to drive out evil spirits and to heal every disease and sickness." (See the entire chapter in Matthew for his authoritative instructions to his disciples regarding how they were to conduct their ministries in his name.)

Matthew 16:19: "I will give you [Peter] the keys [a symbol of authority] of the kingdom of heaven; whatever you bind on earth shall have been bound in heaven, and whatever you loose on earth shall have been loosed in heaven." (author's translation)[2]

Matthew 18:18: "I tell you the truth, whatever you [disciples] bind on earth shall have been bound in heaven, and whatever you loose shall have been loosed in heaven."

Matthew 28:18–19: "All authority in heaven and on earth has been given to me. Therefore go and make disciples of all nations, baptizing them in the name of the Father and of the Son and of the Holy Spirit, and teaching them to obey everything I have commanded you." Here, flowing out of his universal authority, Jesus authorizes the Twelve (and the church as well) to disciple the nations.

Luke 10:19: "I have given you authority to trample on snakes and scorpions [Jesus is referring here to demonic powers] and to overcome all the power of the enemy; nothing will harm you."

---

1. For more supporting New Testament data, see Robert L. Reymond, *Jesus, Divine Messiah: The New Testament Witness* (Phillipsburg, N.J.: Presbyterian and Reformed, 1990), chapter 2.
2. See chapter twenty, fn. 35, for a discussion of the symbolism of the "keys."

Luke 24:46–48: "[Jesus] told them, 'This is what is written: The Christ will suffer and rise from the dead on the third day, and repentance and forgiveness of sins will be preached in his name to all nations, beginning at Jerusalem. You are witnesses of these things.'"

John 14:26: "The Counselor, the Holy Spirit, whom the Father will send in my name, will teach you all things and will remind you of everything I have said to you."

John 16:13–15: "When he, the Spirit of truth, comes, he will guide you into all truth. He will not speak on his own; he will speak only what he hears, and he will tell you what is yet to come. He will bring glory to me by taking from what is mine and making it know to you. All that belongs to the Father is mine. That is why I said the Spirit will take from what is mine and make it known to you."

John 20:21, 23: "Again Jesus said, 'Peace be with you! As the Father has sent me, I am sending you. . . . If you forgive anyone his sins, they are forgiven; if you do not forgive them, they are not forgiven.'"

Acts 1:8b: "And you will be my witnesses in Jerusalem, and in all Judea and Samaria, and to the ends of the earth."

The Lord Jesus Christ later saved Paul and endowed him also with apostolic authority and commissioned him to take the gospel not only to Israel but also and especially to the Gentiles as well. In addition to the accounts in Acts of Paul's contribution and call by the living Christ, this is borne out by the following verses and passages:

Acts 9:15: "[Paul] is my chosen instrument to carry my name before the Gentiles and their kings and before the people of Israel." (see also Acts 22:10, 15)

Acts 20:24: "I consider my life worth nothing to me, if only I may finish the race and complete the task the Lord Jesus has given me—the task of testifying to the gospel of God's grace."

Acts 26:16–18: Jesus responded to Paul's question: "I have appeared to you to appoint you as a servant and as a witness of what you have seen of me and what I will show you. . . . I will rescue you from your own people and from the Gentiles. I am sending you to them to open their eyes and turn them from darkness to light, and from the power of Satan to God."

Galatians 1:11–12: "I want you to know, brothers, that the gospel I preached is not something that man made up. I did not receive it from any man, nor was I taught it [by men]; rather, I received it by revelation from Jesus Christ."

2 Corinthians 10:8: "For even if I boast somewhat freely about the authority the Lord gave us [the authorial plural] for building you up rather than pulling you down, I will not be ashamed of it."

2 Corinthians 13:10: "This is why I write these things when I am absent, that when I come I may not have to be harsh in my use of authority—the authority the Lord gave me for building you up, not for tearing you down."

The apostles, then, acted as Christ's ambassadors and authoritative agents. And that portion of their teaching that the Holy Spirit deemed it appropriate and necessary to preserve in inspired, inscripturated form "for the better preserving and propagating of the truth, and for the more sure establishment and comfort of the church against the corruption of the flesh, and the malice of Satan and of the world" (Westminster Confession of Faith, I/i) has become authoritative also in the life of the church in matters of belief and behavior (2 Tim. 3:16–4:2; 1 Thess. 5:27; 2 Thess. 3:14; Col. 4:16; Rev. 1:3).

Finally, for the edification of the entire church the Lord Jesus has ordained certain offices to continue in perpetuity in his church and has endowed the holders of these offices with his authority:

Ephesians 4:8, 10–11: " 'When he ascended on high, he led captives in his train and gave gifts to men.'. . . He who descended is the very one who ascended higher than all the heavens, in order to fill the whole universe. It was he who gave . . . some to be evangelists, and some to be pastors and teachers, to prepare God's people for works of service."[3]

Here then is the answer to our first question: The Triune God and Jesus Christ in particular are the sole ultimate source of the church's authority. This means that whatever authority the church has, it has only by virtue of the divine act of investiture. It possesses no intrinsic authority of its own. But with God's authority behind it and empowering it, the church has very real and comprehensive authority behind its teaching and activities when they are in harmony with the Word of God and carried out under the direction of the Holy Spirit.

The preface to the *Book of Church Order* of the Presbyterian Church in America declares:

Jesus Christ, upon whose shoulders the government rests, whose name is called Wonderful, Counselor, the Mighty God, the Everlasting Father, the Prince of Peace; of the increase of whose government and peace there shall be no end; who sits upon the throne of David, and upon His kingdom to order it and to

---

3. By his own divine arrangement Christ has not made the offices of apostle and prophet perpetual offices in the church. As offices forming the foundation of the church, they passed out of the life of the church with the passing of the apostolic age. The church possesses in their stead the authoritative writings of the apostles preserved in the New Testament canon.

establish it with judgment and justice from henceforth, even forever (Isaiah 9:6–7); having all power given unto Him in heaven and in earth by the Father, who raised Him from the dead and set Him at His own right hand, far above all principality and power, and might, and dominion, and every name that is named, not only in this world, but also in that which is to come, and has put all things under His feet, and gave Him to be the Head over all things to the Church, which is His body, the fullness of Him that filleth all in all (Ephesians 1:20–23); He, being ascended up far above all heavens, that He might fill all things, received gifts for His Church, and gave all offices necessary for the edification of His church and the perfecting of His saints (Ephesians 4:10–12).

Jesus, the Mediator, the sole Priest, Prophet, King, Saviour, and Head of the Church, contains in Himself, by way of eminency, all the offices in his Church, and has many of their names attributed to Him in the Scriptures. He is Apostle, Teacher, Pastor, Minister, Bishop and the only Lawgiver in Zion.

It belongs to His Majesty from His throne of glory to rule and teach the Church through His Word and Spirit by the ministry of men; thus mediately exercising His own authority and enforcing His own laws, unto the edification and establishment of His Kingdom.

Christ, as King, has given to His Church officers, oracles and ordinances; and especially has He ordained therein His system of doctrine, government, discipline and worship, all of which are either expressly set down in Scripture, or by good and necessary inference may be deduced therefrom; and to which things He commands that nothing be added, and that from them naught be taken away.

Its Nature

The nature of the church's authority is exclusively spiritual and moral, over against the civil and legislative authority of the state—also a divinely appointed authority (Rom. 13:1–7)—the latter authority often manifesting itself in physically coercive ways against human violence and public disorder. That is to say, the church's authority is strictly ministerial and declarative, not imperial, magisterial, or legislative. The church has no police force or battalions of soldiers. The medieval church was dead wrong when it endorsed, under Innocent IV's bull *Ad extirpanda* (1252), the use of torture to break the will of heretics and to extort recantations from them, and penalized the unrepentant with confiscation of goods, imprisonment, and their surrender to the "secular arm," which meant death at the stake. The Spanish Inquisition in 1479 under Ferdinand V and Isabella, in particular, was aimed at Jews, Muslims, and later Protestants, and under its first Grand Inquisitor, Tomas Torquemada, burned some two thousand people for heresy and expelled from the Holy Roman Empire Jews who refused to be baptized. The church was wrong when in the eleventh through the thirteenth centuries it launched the

Crusades (eight or nine in all) to recover the Holy Land from Islam. Martin Luther was wrong when he called for the German princes to use the sword against the Anabaptists in 1531 and 1536. The Protestant leaders at Geneva, including John Calvin,[4] were wrong when they burned Servetus as a heretic. The English Reformers under Henry VIII, Edward VI, and Elizabeth I were wrong when they employed the secular authority to persecute Roman Catholics. And the theonomic reconstructionists of our day are just as wrong when they call upon the state to execute false prophets, witches, adulterers, and homosexuals.[5]

The church is to address the spiritual and moral needs of men and women who are, prior to their salvation, by nature slaves to sin and Satan, and who are, after their salvation, in need of instruction in the details of living out their most holy faith before a watching world. This is not to say that the church must not speak out against political injustice and moral abuses by the state—it must be willing to speak out against moral abuses wherever they occur. But the church's officers must never resort to physical force in order to establish a beachhead for the church within the human community it seeks to reach for Christ.

This spiritual and ministerial nature of the church's authority is taught in the following passages:

> Matthew 20:25–28: "Jesus called [his disciples] together and said, 'You know that the rulers of the Gentiles lord it over them, and their high officials exercise authority over them. Not so with you. Instead, whoever wants to become great among you must be your servant, and whoever wants to be first must be your slave—just as the Son of Man did not come to be served, but to serve, and to give his life a ransom for many.'" (See parallel in Luke 22:24–26)

---

4. William Cunningham, "John Calvin," in *The Reformers and the Theology of the Reformation* (1862; reprint, London: Banner of Truth, 1967), 314–33, amasses evidence that exonerates Calvin to some degree. But Calvin's action still cannot be defended biblically. As Cunningham himself declares: "No one . . . can defend [Calvin's conduct toward Servetus], unless he is prepared to defend the lawfulness of putting heretics to death" (316).

5. Greg Bahnsen, *Theonomy in Christian Ethics*, 2d ed. (Phillipsburg, N.J.: Presbyterian and Reformed, 1984), *By This Standard: The Authority of God's Law Today* (Tyler, Tex.: Institute for Christian Economics, 1985), *No Other Standard: Theonomy and Its Critics* (Tyler, Tex.: Institute for Christian Economics, 1985), Gary North, *Political Polytheism* (Tyler, Tex.: Institute for Christian Economics, 1992), and Gary Demar, *Ruler of the Nations* (Tyler, Tex.: Institute for Christian Economics, 1987) all desire to see the modern state adopt legislation reflecting the Mosaic patterns. For critical appraisals of their views, see Robert Lewis Dabney, *Lectures in Systematic Theology* (Grand Rapids, Mich.: Baker, 1985), 869–75; William S. Barker and W. Robert Godfrey, eds., *Theonomy: A Reformed Critique* (Grand Rapids, Mich.: Zondervan, 1990), and David W. Hall, *Savior or Servant? Putting Government in Its Place* (Oak Ridge, Tenn.: Covenant Foundation, 1996), 372–76.

Matthew 26:51–52: "One of Jesus' companions reached for his sword, drew it out and struck the servant of the high priest, cutting off his ear. 'Put your sword back in its place,' Jesus said to him, 'for all who draw the sword will die by the sword.' "

Luke 9:54–56: "When the disciples James and John saw [a Samaritan village opposing Jesus], they asked, 'Lord, do you want us to call fire down from heaven to destroy them?' But Jesus turned and rebuked them, and they went to another village."

John 18:36–37: "Jesus said [to Pilate], 'My kingdom is not of this world. If it were, my servants would fight to prevent my arrest by the Jews. But now my kingdom is from another place.' 'You are a king, then!' said Pilate. Jesus answered, 'You are right in saying I am a king. In fact, for this reason I was born, and for this I came into the world, to testify to the truth. Everyone on the side of truth listens to me.' "

2 Corinthians 10:3–4: "Though we live in the world, we do not wage war as the world does. The weapons we fight with are not the weapons of the world. On the contrary, [our weapons] have divine power to demolish strongholds. We demolish arguments and every pretension that sets itself up against the knowledge of God, and we take captive every thought to make it obedient to Christ."

Ephesians 6:11–18a: "Finally, be strong in the Lord and in his mighty power. Put on the full armor of God so that you can take your stand against the devil's schemes. For our struggle is not against flesh and blood, but against the rulers, against the authorities, against the powers of this dark world and against the spiritual forces of evil in the heavenly realms. Therefore put on the full armor of God, so that when the day of evil comes, you may be able to stand your ground, and after you have done everything, to stand. Stand firm then, with the belt of truth buckled around your waist, with the breastplate of righteousness in place, and with your feet fitted with the readiness that comes from the gospel of peace. In addition to all this, take up the shield of faith, with which you can extinguish all the flaming arrows of the evil one. Take the helmet of salvation and the sword of the Spirit, which is the word of God. And pray in the Spirit on all occasions with all kinds of prayers and requests."

1 Peter 5:1–3: "To the elders among you, I appeal as a fellow elder, a witness of Christ's sufferings and one who also will share in the glory to be revealed: Be shepherds of God's flock that is under your care, serving as overseers—not because you must, but because you are willing, as God want you to be; not greedy for money, but eager to serve; not lording it over those entrusted to you, but being examples to the flock."

The Duties of the Church

THE DUTY TO WORSHIP AND TO SERVE GOD

Because man, created in God's image, is *homo religiosus* even before he is *homo sapiens*, the first obligation of every man is to worship and serve the Creator (Rom. 1:18–25). The Westminster Confession of Faith reminds us of this when it declares:

> The light of nature showeth that there is a God, who hath lordship and sovereignty over all; is good, and doeth good unto all; and is therefore to be feared, loved, praised, called upon, trusted in, and served with all the heart, and with all the soul, and with all the might. (XXI/i)

If this is man's first obligation simply because he is God's creature, all the more, in view of the fact that the church has experienced God's redeeming mercies, is it the church's first obligation to worship and serve the Triune God (Rom. 12:1). Peter declares that the church is "a chosen people, a royal priesthood, a holy nation, a people belonging to God, that you may declare the praises of him who called you out of darkness into his wonderful light" (1 Pet. 2:9; see Ps. 145:6; Isa. 43:21). Paul informs us that everything that God has done for us soterically, he did "to the praise of his glorious grace" (Eph. 1:6, 12, 14). Therefore, he declares to the church: "whether you eat or drink or whatever you do, do it all for the glory of God" (1 Cor. 10:31). And he prayed that God would give the church "a spirit of unity among yourselves as you follow Christ Jesus, so that with one heart and mouth you may glorify the God and Father of our Lord Jesus Christ" (Rom. 15:5–6). The church, Peter writes, must also so live before the world as to invoke praise to God from outsiders: "Dear friends, I urge you, as aliens and strangers in the world, to abstain from sinful desires which war against your soul. Live such good lives among the pagans that, though they accuse you of doing wrong, they may see your good deeds and glorify God on the day he visits us" (1 Pet. 2:11; see Matt. 5:16). The church then is to view itself primarily as a "trophy" of God's mercy and grace, and see its first duty to be that of living doxologically before God, praising him in both its belief and its behavior for his superabounding grace.

But if the church is duty-bound to worship and serve God as its first obligation, it is equally true that the church (as indeed is true of all men) must worship as God himself directs. This means

1. that all worship is to be directed to God alone and only through the mediation of Christ alone (Westminster Confession of Faith, XXI/ii);

2. that prayer in such worship will be "made in the name of the Son, by the help of his Spirit, according to his will, with understanding, reverence, humility, fervency, faith, love, and perseverance; and, if vocal, in a known tongue" (XXI/iii), and

only for "things lawful," and when made for men, only for men who are "living, or that shall live hereafter; but not for the dead, nor for those of whom it may be known that they have sinned the sin unto death" (XXI/iv);

3. that "the reading of the Scriptures with godly fear; the sound preaching, and conscionable hearing of the word, in obedience unto God, with understanding, faith, and reverence; singing of psalms with grace in the heart; as also the due administration and worthy receiving of the sacraments instituted by Christ; are all parts of the ordinary religious worship of God" (XXI/v);

4. that "God is to be worshipped everywhere in spirit and in truth; as in private families daily, and in secret each one by himself; so more solemnly in the public assemblies, which are not carelessly or willfully to be neglected or forsaken, when God, by his word or providence, calleth thereunto" (XXI/vi); and finally,

5. that the public worship of God is to include the church's assembling on the Lord's Day, which is to be "kept holy unto the Lord, when men, after a due preparing of their hearts, and ordering of their common affairs beforehand, do not only observe an holy rest all the day from their own works, words, and thoughts, about their worldly employments and recreations; but also are taken up the whole time in the public and private exercises of his worship, and in duties of necessity and mercy" (XXI/vii, viii).

This approach to Christian worship reflects and is governed by what has come to be known as the "regulative principle," which is stated by the Westminster Confession of Faith this way:

> God alone is Lord of the conscience, and *hath left it free from the doctrines of men, which are, in anything, contrary to his Word; or beside it, if*[6] *matters of faith, or worship.* So that, to believe such doctrines, or to obey such commands, out of conscience, is to betray true liberty of conscience: and the requiring of an implicit faith, and an absolute and blind obedience, is to destroy liberty of conscience, and reason also. (XX/ii)
>
> ... The acceptable way of worshiping the true God is instituted by himself, and so limited by his own revealed will, that he may not be worshiped according to the

---

6. Most editions of the Westminster Confession of Faith published today place a comma instead of a semicolon after "Word" and replace the "if" with "in." This is a corrupt version of the original text, traceable to Dunlop's 1719 edition, which implies that the Westminster divines intended to limit freedom of conscience from the doctrines of men that are in anything contrary to God's Word *only* to the spheres of faith and worship. Such a conclusion flies in the face of their conviction that the conscience is ever bound, as an absolute universal principle, to obey God in *every* sphere of life; it is never bound to go contrary to his Word. What they intended to say is that in matters of faith and worship, the conscience is not only free from what is contrary to God's Word but also free from what is "beside" it, that is to say, free from things not stated in the Word nor deducible by good and necessary consequence from it.

imaginations and devices of men, or the suggestions of Satan, under any visible representations, or any other way not prescribed in the Holy Scripture. (XXI/i; see also *Larger Catechism*, Questions 108–9; *Shorter Catechism*, Questions 50–51)

According to the Reformation principle of worship (which is only the Reformers' application in the area of worship of their principial *sola Scriptura* position),[7] true worship may include only those matters which God has either expressly commanded in Scripture or which may be deduced from Scripture by good and necessary consequence (such as infant baptism),[8] while false worship is anything done in worship which God has not expressly prescribed.[9] Over against this Reformation principle of worship stands the Roman Catholic principle that argues that true worship may be conducted not only in the manner God has prescribed but in other ways as well as long as they are not expressly forbidden by God, while false worship is only that which is expressly condemned or forbidden in so many words by him. Thus in Roman Catholic worship many things are done which are not allowed by Scripture, such as the veneration of Mary and other saints who are invoked for help and intercession before God, and the use of pictures, images, and relics as aids in worship. But the Scriptures warn against worshiping God in ways which he has not expressly prescribed. Moses instructed Israel:

> When you have driven [the nations] out and settled in their land, and after they have been destroyed before you, be careful not to be ensnared by inquiring about their gods, saying, "How do these nations serve their gods? We will do the same."

---

7. J. I. Packer rejects the regulative principle on the ground that it is a "Puritan innovation" ("The Puritan Approach to Worship," *Diversity in Unity* [papers read at the Puritan and Reformed Studies Conference, December 1963; available London: *The Evangelical* magazine, 1964], 4–5.) Whatever else one may say about this principle, it must be said that it is *not* a Puritan innovation, Calvin having stated that "whatever is not commanded, we are not free to choose" (*Tracts and Treatises on the Doctrine and Worship of the Church* [reprint; Grand Rapids, Mich.: Eerdmans, 1958], 2:118, 122).
8. Both the "regulative principle" of Scripture and the *Westminster Confession of Faith* (I/vi) permit deductions to be drawn from Scripture by "good and necessary consequence" in matters of faith and practice. Infant baptism is one such "good and necessary" deduction because the New Testament prescribes no repeal of the Old Testament command to give the covenant sign to covenant children.
9. The Reformers acknowledged that "some *circumstances* concerning the worship of God ... [which are] common to human actions and societies ... are to be ordered by the light of nature and Christian prudence, according to the general rules of the word, which are always to be observed" (Westminster Confession of Faith, I/vi), such as the place and time for congregational assembly on the Lord's Day and the order of the several prescribed elements of worship in the worship service.

You must not worship the Lord your God in their way, because in worshiping their gods, they do all kinds of detestable things the Lord hates. They even burn their sons and daughters in the fire as sacrifices to their gods. *See that you do all I command you; do not add to it or take away from it.* (Deut 12:29–32, emphasis added)

Nadab and Abihu were consumed by the fire of the Lord because they "offered unauthorized fire . . . contrary to his command" (Lev. 10:1–2). Korah, Dathan, Abiram, and On were swallowed up in an earthquake because they had insisted on their right to burn incense before God without priestly mediation, after which judgment God instructed Eleazar to take the censers of "the men who sinned" and hammer them into sheets and overlay the bronze altar with them as a sign to Israel that "no one except a descendant of Aaron should come to burn incense before the LORD" (Num. 16:36–40). King Uzziah was smitten with leprosy because he attempted to usurp the priestly privilege to burn incense in the temple (2 Chron. 26:16–19). Israel's sin in building high places and offering her sons on them to Baal was that they were doing "something [God says] I did not command or mention, nor did it enter my mind" (Jer 19:5). Jesus himself declared that when men "let go of the commands of God" and "hold on to the traditions of men" in their worship of God, their worship is "in vain" (Mark 7:7–8). To the Samaritan woman, he spoke of the character of true worship: "You Samaritans worship what you do not know; we worship what we do know, for salvation is from the Jews. Yet a time is coming and has now come when the true worshipers will worship the Father in spirit and truth, for they are the kind of worshipers the Father seeks. God is spirit, and his worshipers must worship in spirit and in truth" (John 4:22–24).[10] And Paul admonishes the Colossians against self-willed asceticism in worship:

Since you died with Christ to the basic principles of this world, why, as though you still belonged to it, do you submit to its rules: "Do not handle! Do not taste! Do not touch!"? These are all destined to perish with use, because they are based on human commands and teachings. Such regulations indeed have an appearance of wisdom, with their self-imposed worship, their false humility and their harsh treatment of the body, but they lack any value in restraining sensual indulgence. (Col. 2:20–23)

G. I. Williamson is entirely justified then when he remarks concerning the regulative principle:

---

10. To worship God "in spirit and in truth" means, according to Leon Morris, that he "must be worshiped in a manner befitting [him as the life-giving Spirit]. Man cannot dictate the 'how' of worship. He must come only in the way that the Spirit of God opens to him" (*The Gospel According to John* [Grand Rapids, Mich.: Eerdmans, 1971], 272).

> If we once admit that true worship is not limited by God's revealed will—if we once allow that man can rightly add even one element to divine worship—it becomes exceedingly difficult to refute the devious arguments and distinctions such as those [offered by Rome] between *latria* and *doulia* and "direct" and "indirect" worship.... There is no safeguard to purity of worship except conscious and persistent adherence to this [regulative] principle: what is commanded is right, and what is not commanded is wrong.[11]

For its own spiritual health and well-being then, the church must continually bear in mind the importance of this regulative principle in all that it does in its worship of God. Accordingly, the Reformed worship tradition has a number of things to say to this generation of Christians about the issue of worship.[12]

First, the Reformed worship tradition should remind every generation of Christians that the worship of God is the most important of all the Christian's tasks. That is the primary reason why the Christian should go to church: to worship God. In today's church climate this is a radical idea. Nevertheless, Christians should go to church, *not* to evangelize, *not* to provide a comfortable "consumer-friendly" setting for the unchurched, *not even* primarily for the benefit which fellowship with other Christians provides, and definitely *not* just for lectures and devotionals, but in order to worship God. Christians should also understand that evangelism and the missionary task are not the most important tasks the church has. Such efforts exist among the nations, as John Piper argues in his *Let the Nations Be Glad*, only because worship of the true God among them does not![13]

Second, Reformed Christians must convince this generation that their tradition's "regulative principle" regarding worship should be the governing principle of all Christian worship, that is to say, that Christians must do in worship only those things which God commands, clearly perceiving that "what is not commanded is forbidden" and just as self-consciously rejecting the dictum that "what is not expressly forbidden is permissible" (see again Gen. 4:4–5; Lev. 10:1–2; Num. 16–17; 2 Chron. 26:16–19; Jer. 19:5; Matt. 15:9; Mark 7:6–13; John 4:22–24; 14:6; Col. 2:20–23). This approach to worship will produce a worship that is biblical, spiritual, simple, weighty, and reverent. It will produce a worship centered upon God, substantial and life-transforming. It will prohibit a worship that is superficial in character, complicated by ritual, stimulated by props, and flippant in tone.

---

11. G. I. Williamson, *The Westminster Confession of Faith for Study Classes* (Philadelphia: Presbyterian and Reformed, 1964), 162.
12. I have drawn the following material dealing with the Reformed worship tradition from the unpublished paper, "Why Plant and Grow PCA Churches," which I coauthored with Terry L. Johnson, pastor of Independent Presbyterian Church, Savannah, Georgia.
13. John Piper, *Let the Nations Be Glad!* (Grand Rapids, Mich.: Baker, 1993).

Anyone who will take the time to study the matter will have to conclude that worship in evangelical churches in this generation is, speaking generally, approaching bankruptcy. There is neither rhyme nor reason, much less biblical warrant, for the order of and much that goes on in many evangelical church services today. The fact of the matter is, much evangelical "worship" is simply not true worship at all. For decades now evangelical churches have been conducting their services for the sake of unbelievers. Both the revivalistic service of a previous generation and the "seeker service" of today are shaped by the same concern—appeal to the unchurched. Not surprisingly, in neither case does much that might be called worship by Christians occur. As a result, many evangelicals who have been sitting for years in such worship services are finding their souls drying up, and they have begun to long for something else. Accordingly, they have become vulnerable to the appeal of the *mysterium* of hierarchical liturgical services. This is why some today are "on the Canterbury trail"[14] or defecting to Greek Orthodoxy and Roman Catholicism. Others who have been simply spectators for years in their worship services are getting caught up in the people-involving worship of charismatic services.

The answer to these problems in contemporary worship will not be found by adopting the style of an ecclesiastical tradition foreign to the Reformed liturgical tradition. But regrettably, some Reformed pastors have seen the above defections as a call to imitate their "successful rivals." So they have adopted the "winning formulae" of these attracting churches. Consequently, when one walks into virtually any Reformed church today in this country on the Lord's Day, one can never know for sure whether he will be asked to worship in a "traditional" or "contemporary," liturgical or nonliturgical, formal or revivalistic fashion. This is regrettable and in the long run damaging to the promulgation of the Reformed faith. The real cure to the problems in contemporary worship will be found in the simple, spiritual, substantial, and serious worship of the Reformed faith and liturgy. The Christian must never forget that in Christ the worshiper enjoys fellowship with the one living and true God who, *even for believers,* according to the author of Hebrews, is a "consuming fire." Consequently, while Christian worship should certainly be joyous and filled with gladness (Ps. 149:2), the author of Hebrews urges that it must be conducted "with reverence and awe" (μετὰ εὐλαβείας καὶ δέους, *meta eulabeias kai deous*) (Heb. 12:28–29). The Triune God of the Reformed faith is an awe-inspiring, absolutely sovereign, infinitely just, and infinitely gracious, incomprehensible Deity. He will not long be known as such or served as such by a people fed rote ritual or revivalistic preaching or emotional choruses and gospel songs. Our God must be worshiped with the mind as well as the heart. Faith in him requires understanding. And the understanding of Christian congregations grows primarily as it is nourished by the singing of

---

14. See Robert E. Webber, *Evangelicals on the Canterbury Trail* (Waco, Texas: Word, 1985).

hymns and psalms and by the prayers and preaching of the public worship services. Therefore, Reformed churches cannot adopt forms of worship that are either simply "liturgical" or theologically shallow and expect to remain for long biblically sound, Reformed, and presbyterian. Reformed theology, like all systems of theology, must have a form of worship through which it is expressed and communicated. Neglect that form of worship and Reformed theology will cease to be meaningful.

What then should Reformed worship include? It will include theologically sound congregational singing. For this I recommend the new *Trinity Hymnal*. It will also include the much-neglected singing of the psalms, which express the full range of human emotions in worship. The biblical psalms are realistic in a way that many hymns are not and that choruses can hardly ever be. They also contrast the righteous and the wicked, highlight the conflict between them, and thereby encourage a bold, militant spirituality such as the Huguenot and Puritan forefathers knew and lived by. For this I recommend, particularly for churches for whom regular psalm-singing would be a new thing, the *Trinity Psalter*.[15]

Reformed worship will emphasize and feature biblically based, hermeneutically sound expository preaching of the Holy Scripture, the only infallible rule of faith and practice, as interpreted by the Westminster Confession of Faith and the two *Westminster Catechisms*.

Reformed worship will also include contemplation of God's holy law in keeping with the law-gospel paradigm in order to aid the worshiper in his understanding of his vileness before God (its second use) and to promote its use as a guide for Christian conduct (its third use). Our carnal and antinomian age is in desperate need of a healthy dose of the law of God. Evangelical Christians have become morally lazy, excuse-ridden, and relativistic. It is the Reformed tradition, above all others, which has given prominence to reading and meditating on the law of God.[16] Regular contemplation of God's holy law in worship would do much to cure this age of its rampant immorality and "carnal Christianity" and to restore true personal piety, parents' and children's responsibilities, and the Protestant work ethic in the world.

What should Reformed worship exclude? It should exclude all that God does not command, all announcements (which can be made prior to the call to worship), and any and all other things which do not contribute directly to the Bible's prescribed worship of God.

The church concerned to reflect these Reformed principles in worship will follow a liturgy ("order of service") that will resemble the following:

---

15. The *Trinity Hymnal* and *Trinity Psalter* are both published by Great Commission Publications, Inc., located in Philadelphia, Pennsylvania.
16. The reader should consult the Westminster Confession of Faith, XVI/i–ii and XIX/v–vi, and the Larger (Questions 97–148) and Shorter (Questions 41–81) Catechisms if he doubts this.

Liturgy of the Word

A suggested order of service omitting the preferred (but optional) Liturgy of the Upper Room.

PREPARATION FOR THE WORD

Call to worship (spoken, using perhaps a Psalm citation, or chorale). (If the liturgy of the upper room is to be observed, the presiding minister may extend the call to worship from the Table, after which he may ascend to the pulpit.)

A hymn or psalm of praise and/or of adoration, or an opening prayer of adoration and of supplication for divine grace and illumination, leading perhaps into the unison praying of the Lord's Prayer. (If the minister prefers that a hymn of praise follow his call to worship, then he should follow the opening hymn with a prayer of invocation in which he adores God and invokes his blessing on the congregation's worship.)

Old Testament lesson which confronts the worshipers with God's sovereign majesty and their sinfulness

.

Prayer of confession and petition for pardon (either pastoral, corporate or responsive)

.

Assurance of pardon

.

Hymn or psalm of thanksgiving for God's grace

.

Offering

.

Prayer of intercession

.

New Testament lesson which offers instruction for the Christian life

PROCLAMATION OF THE WORD

Hymn of preparation of the heart for the reception of God's Word

.

Pastoral prayer for illumination

.

Sermon Scripture reading

Sermon

Prayer for application

Hymn or psalm of response to the proclamation of God's Word

Benediction (if no liturgy of the upper room, which is optional)

Liturgy of the Upper Room
(Optional, following upon the hymn of response)[17]

Invitation to true believers to attend the Lord's Table and the fencing of the table from unbelievers

Hymn of worship and thanksgiving for God's grace in Christ (optional)

Congregational recitation of the Apostles' Creed

Words of institution

Prayer of consecration and of the setting apart of the elements

Distribution of the bread

Distribution of the cup

Prayer of Thanksgiving

---

17. John Calvin resisted the separation of Word and Sacrament into two distinct services, which is reflected in the making of the Liturgy of the Upper Room optional. He contended that the celebration of the Supper should be attached each week to the preached Word to form a natural climax to the Sunday service. Beginning his service from the Table with confession of sin and scripture sentences assuring pardon of sin, during the singing of a metrical psalm and acting in his "prophetic capacity," he ascended to the pulpit and preached, usually no longer than half an hour. Then acting in his "priestly capacity" he returned to the Table, offered to God the congregation's prayers of intercession, and without any interruption, gave the words of institution and a serious exhortation, which included fencing the table from unbelievers, then distributed the elements. After a short admonition, a hymn, a prayer of thanksgiving, and the *Nunc dimittis*, he ended the service with a benediction.

THE AUTHORITY AND DUTIES OF THE CHURCH

Hymn or psalm of praise

Benediction[18]

Reformed worship will also stress Sabbath observance, recognizing that not only does the fourth commandment require it but also, as Charles Hodge says: "If men wish the knowledge of [Jesus' resurrection] to die out, let them neglect to keep holy the first day of the week; if they desire that event to be everywhere known and remembered, let them consecrate that day to the worship of the risen Saviour."[19] Again, it is the Reformed tradition which replaced the church calendar (except for what is called there the five evangelical feast days) with weekly Sabbath observance.[20] Any attempt at recovering a Reformed spirituality would do well carefully to study the best of the Puritan literature on the observance of the Lord's Day. Observance of the Lord's Day not only provides unhurried time for prayer, reading of Scripture and meditation all day long, but also becomes the day around which all the rest of the week is organized. For if one knows he is going to devote a day to spiritual concerns and eliminate all secular distractions, he will also know that he must organize the remaining six days in such a way that his other obligations will be met.

We have been urging that it is precisely in doing only the things God prescribes that we worship him as we ought. Conversely, we will not be worshiping him truly if we do anything for him which he does not prescribe. Therefore, it behooves us to look in greater detail at the specific duties which the Scriptures enjoin the church to do.

---

18. For the reader who is concerned to know more about Reformed worship, I would recommend Nathaniel Micklem, ed., *Christian Worship* (Oxford: Oxford University Press, 1936); John M. Barkley, *The Worship of the Reformed Churches* (Richmond: John Knox, 1967); David Lachman and Frank J. Smith, eds., *Worship in the Presence of God* (Greenville: Greenville Presbyterian Theological Press, 1992); Donald Macleod, *Presbyterian Worship* (Atlanta: John Knox, 1980, revised); William D. Maxwell, *A History of Christian Worship* (1936; reprint, Grand Rapids: Baker, 1982); James Hastings Nichols *Corporate Worship in the Reformed Tradition* (Philadelphia: Westminster, 1968); Robert G. Rayburn, *O Come Let Us Worship* (Grand Rapids, Mich.: Baker, 1980); Hughes Oliphant Old, *The Patristic Roots of Reformed Worship* (Zurich: Theologischer Verlag, 1975), *The Shaping of the Reformed Baptismal Rites in the Sxteenth Century* (Grand Rapids, Mich.: Eerdmans, 1992), and his more popular *Worship That Is Reformed According to Scripture* (Atlanta: John Knox, 1986); and *Leading in Worship: A Handbook for Presbyterian Students and Ministers Drawing upon the Biblical and Historic Forms of the Reformed Tradition*, ed. Terry L. Johnson (Oak Ridge, Tenn.: Covenant Foundation, 1996).
19. Charles Hodge, *Systematic Theology* (1871; reprint, Grand Rapids, Mich.: Eerdmans, 1952), 3:330.
20. See Hughes Oliphant Old, "Rescuing Spirituality from the Cloister," *Christianity Today* 38, no. 7 (June 20, 1994): 28.

THE DUTY TO BEAR WITNESS TO DIVINE TRUTH

The church of Jesus Christ, by the authority invested in it by Jesus Christ himself, has the authority and responsibility, as "the pillar and foundation of the truth" (1 Tim. 3:15), to declare to the whole world beyond it as well as to itself the "Thus says the Lord" of Holy Scripture. Jesus Christ commissioned the church to "preach repentance and forgiveness of sins in his name to all nations" (Luke 24:47; see Matt. 28:18–19). And under inspiration the apostle Paul writes:

> 2 Corinthians 5:20: "We are . . . Christ's ambassadors, as though God were making his appeal through us. We implore you on Christ's behalf: 'Be reconciled to God.' "
>
> 1 Timothy 4:13: "Until I come, devote yourself to the public reading of Scripture, to preaching and to teaching."
>
> 2 Timothy 2:2, 15; 4:2: "The things you have heard me say in the presence of many witnesses entrust to reliable men who will also be qualified to teach others. . . . Do your best to present yourself to God as one approved, a workman who does not need to be ashamed and who correctly handles the word of truth. . . . Preach the Word; be prepared in season and out of season; correct, rebuke and encourage—with great patience and careful instruction."
>
> Titus 2:1, 7–8: "You must teach what is in accord with sound doctrine. . . . In your teaching show integrity, seriousness and soundness of speech that cannot be condemned."

All this means that the church must ever be committed to the study, the preaching, and the teaching of the Word of God.

It also means that the church must reflect deeply on the truth of God's Word and frame what it finds there in symbols and confessions in order better to engender in its members a clear conception of their faith and to convey to outsiders a definite understanding of its doctrines. The New Testament calls our attention again and again to such "confessions," as in 2 Thessalonians 2:15—"the traditions," Romans 6:17—"the pattern of doctrine," Jude 3—"the faith once delivered to the saints," 1 Timothy 6:20—"the deposit," and the "faithful sayings" of Paul's pastoral letters (1 Tim. 1:15; 3:1; 4:8–9; 2 Tim 2:11–13; Titus 3:3–8). These descriptive terms and phrases indicate that already in the days of the apostles the theologizing process of reflecting upon and comparing Scripture with Scripture, collating, deducing, and framing doctrinal statements into creedal formulae approaching the character of church confessions had begun[21] (examples of these creedal formulae may be seen in Rom. 1:3–4; 10:9; 1 Cor. 12:3; 15:3–4 and 1 Tim. 3:16, as well as in the "faithful sayings" of the Pastorals).[22]

All this means too that the church is duty bound to provide for the training of successive generations of its sons as ministers to perpetuate the proclamation of the truth of God's Word. This means in turn that the church must enable its sons and daughters to engage in the intellectual discipline of theological study based upon the Holy Scriptures by founding and supporting training schools and seminaries and then supporting them in their pursuit and propagation of biblical truth.

The church's mandate to witness to the truth also means, of course, that the church has no authority to preach or to teach anything other than God's Word (which includes, of course, that which may be deduced from God's Word by good and necessary inference).

In order to have a "Thus says the Lord" of Scripture to proclaim, the church is responsible to preserve both the Scriptures themselves and the truths of Scripture against all attacks and all perversions of the truth by "contending for the faith that was once for all entrusted to the saints" (Jude 3). As Berkhof writes, the church "has the great and responsible task of maintaining and defending the truth against all the forces of unbelief and error."[23] Thus the church must be willing to engage in biblical and philosophical, scientific and historical apologetics. To his faithful helpers the apostle Paul wrote the following instructions:

---

21. James Benjamin Green writes in the preface to *A Harmony of the Westminster Presbyterian Standards* (Philadelphia: John Knox, 1951):

    > A creed, a system of doctrine, is a necessity. It is a necessity of thought. It is a necessity of character. It is a necessity of instruction. It is a necessity of fellowship and co-operation. A cogent system of doctrine is an intellectual and educational necessity. If the Church would edify her people, unify and mobilize them, she must educate them after a thorough manner in her creed. Some are not of this way of thinking, they decry creeds; they demand a creedless Christianity, a religion without theology. This demand had been called pious nonsense. Leave off the pious—call it simply nonsense. To say of a man that he has no creed is tantamount to saying that he has no intelligence and no character.

    I concur wholeheartedly. In fact, every church has a creed whether it knows it or not. It may be called a Statement of Faith, or it may be unwritten, but there will be a creed—as you will find out if you try to unite with a "creedless" Baptist assembly without agreeing to undergo baptism by immersion. "Creedless" churches also have an elaborate *hermeneutical* method in place that has governed them in their exegesis, although they may have never recognized or articulated it. It seems to me preferable, because more honest, to state clearly the theology one's church espouses than to claim to be "creedless" while actually holding to a complex set of dogmas.

    See also David W. Hall, ed., *The Practice of Confessional Subscription* (Lanham, Md.: University Press of America, 1995).

22. An excellent survey of this material may be found in J. N. D. Kelly, "Creedal Elements in the New Testament," *Early Christian Creeds* (London: Longmans, Green, 1950).

23. Louis Berkhof, *Systematic Theology* (Grand Rapids, Mich.: Eerdmans, 1941), 595.

> 1 Timothy 1:3–4, 7: "As I urged you when I went into Macedonia, stay there in Ephesus so that you may command certain men not to teach false doctrines any longer nor to devote themselves to myths and endless genealogies.... They want to be teachers of the law, but they do not know what they are talking about."
>
> 2 Timothy 1:13–14: "What you heard from me, keep as the pattern of sound teaching, with faith and love in Christ Jesus. Guard the good deposit that was entrusted to you—guard it with the help of the Holy Spirit who lives in us."
>
> 2 Timothy 2:25: "Those who oppose [the Lord's servant] he must gently instruct, in the hope that God will give them a change of heart leading them to a knowledge of the truth."
>
> Titus 1:9–11: "[The elder] must hold firmly to the trustworthy message as it has been taught, so that he can encourage others by sound doctrine and refute those who oppose it. For there are many rebellious people, mere talkers and deceivers, especially those of the circumcision group. They must be silenced, because they are ruining whole households by teaching things they ought not to teach."

And Peter writes:

> 1 Peter 3:15: "In your hearts acknowledge Christ as the holy Lord. Always be prepared to give an answer to everyone who asks you to give the reason for the hope that you have."

THE DUTY TO EVANGELIZE AND TO GROW THE CHURCH

A subset of the preceding duty of the church to bear witness to divine truth is its duty to evangelize and to grow the church. This is implicit in Christ's Great Commission to his church to "make disciples of all nations" (Matt. 28:18–20), to "preach repentance and forgiveness of sins in his name to all nations" (Luke 24:47), and to be his witness "to the ends of the earth" (Acts 1:8). Paul declared that Christ has given evangelists to the church (Eph. 4:11)—Philip being a prime New Testament example—and he instructed Timothy as a pastor to "do the *work of an evangelist* [ἔργον εὐαγγελιστοῦ, *ergon euangelistou*]" (2 Tim. 4:5). In carrying out this duty the church must take care to do so in ways that do not ignore or deny God's sovereignty in salvation. This is just to say that the evangelist's message should be controlled by a Calvinistic theology and that the evangelist himself should avoid all Pelagian and Arminian gimmickry in his evangelistic method.[24]

---

24. See James I. Packer, *Evangelism and the Sovereignty of God* (Leicester, U.K.: Inter-Varsity, 1961).

In this context I want to call attention to the "presbyterian" doctrines of covenant succession and covenant nurture. Robert S. Rayburn is doubtless correct when he claims "that far and away the largest part of the Christian church at any time or place—excepting that historical moment when the gospel first reaches a place and people—are those who were born and raised in Christian families."[25] Accordingly, when the church contemplates its growth, either quantitatively or qualitatively, it cannot afford to ignore its responsibility to its own children. The church must always remember that (1) "it is God's will and declared purpose that his saving grace run in the lines of generations" (Gen. 17:7–9; Exod. 20:6; Deut. 6:6–7; Ps. 103:17–18; Isa. 44:3; 54:13; 59:21; Jer. 32:38–39; Ezek. 37:25; Acts 2:38–39; 16:14–15, 31; 1 Cor. 7:14), and (2) "the biblical paradigm is for covenant children to grow up in faith from infancy" (Pss. 22:9; 71:6; Eph. 6:4; 2 Tim. 3:15). Since their children are members of the covenant community, Christian parents are charged to nurture their children in Christian faith and love, "which nurture when carried out faithfully becomes the divine instrumentality of their awakening to spiritual life." Rayburn is right again when he concludes his discussion by declaring:

> The [church's] appropriation by faith of this divine promise and summons of [covenant succession] is the means appointed to furnish the church with generation after generation of great multitudes of Christian servants and soldiers who reach manhood and womanhood well taught, sturdy in faith, animated by love for God and man, sophisticated in the ways of the world and the Devil, polished in the manners of genuine Christian brotherhood, overshadowed by the specter of the Last Day, nerved to deny themselves and take up their cross so as to be counted worthy of greater exploits for Christ and Kingdom. Currently the church not only suffers a terrible shortage of such other-worldly and resolute Christians, superbly prepared for spiritual warfare, but, in fact, is hemorrhaging its children into the world. Christian evangelism will never make a decisive difference in our culture when it amounts merely to an effort to replace losses due to widespread desertion from our own camp. The gospel will always fail to command attention and carry conviction when large numbers of those who grow up under its influence are observed abandoning it for the world. Recovering our Presbyterian inheritance and inscribing the doctrine of covenant succession upon the heart of family and church must have a wonderfully solemnizing and galvanizing effect. It will set Christian parents seriously to work on the spiritual nurture of their children, equipping them and requiring them to live the life of covenant faith and duty to which their God and Savior called them at the headwaters of life. And, ever conscious of the greater effect of parental example, they will forsake the easy

---

25. Robert S. Rayburn, "The Presbyterian Doctrines of Covenant Children, Covenant Nurture, and Covenant Succession," *Presbyterian* 22/2 (1996): 96, 98, 103, 109.

way, shamelessly and joyfully to live a life of devotion and obedience which adorns and ennobles the faith in the eyes of their children. This they will do, who embrace the Bible's doctrine, lest the Lord on the Great Day should say to them: "You took your sons and daughters whom you bore to Me and sacrificed them to idols."

Reformed doctrinal distinctives are also absolutely essential for *true* church growth.[26] This assertion may sound strange to some ears, since in our time Reformed churches, unfortunately, are known more for their emphasis on doctrine than for their evangelism and church growth. But history itself witnesses to the fact that the vast majority of the great missionaries and evangelists of the past have been Calvinists, including John Bunyan, Richard Baxter and all the Puritans, George Whitefield, Jonathan Edwards, and nearly all the leaders of the Great Awakening (the Wesleys are the exceptions here, being tagged by J. I. Packer for their efforts as "confused Calvinists"), Charles Spurgeon, all the leaders of the modern missionary movement from William Carey and the Baptists in England, Henry Venn and the Church of England, Adoniram Judson and the Americans, and of course the Church of Scotland. The Reformed faith has a God-honored legacy here and much to say to our generation.

The problem in our day, which gives rise to highly questionable church growth methods, is two-fold: On the one hand, *we are seeing a waning confidence in the message of the gospel.* Even the evangelical church shows signs of losing confidence in the convincing and converting power of the gospel message. That is why increasing numbers of churches prefer sermons on family life and psychological health. We are being overtaken by what Os Guinness calls the managerial and therapeutic revolutions. The winning message, it seems, is the one that helps people to solve their temporal problems, improves their self-esteem and makes them feel good about themselves. In such a cultural climate, preaching on the law, sin and repentance, and the cross has all but disappeared, even in evangelical churches. The church has become "user friendly," "consumer oriented," and as a result evangelical churches are being inundated with "cheap grace" (Bonhoeffer). Today's "gospel" is all too often a gospel without cost, without repentance, without commitment, without discipleship, and thus "another gospel" and accordingly no gospel at all, all traceable to the fact that this is how too many people today have come to believe that the church must be grown.[27]

---

26. I have drawn the following material dealing with church growth from "Why Plant and Grow PCA Churches."
27. Christian leaders who want to escape the onslaught of our culture's influence on the American church should read David F. Wells, *No Place for Truth Or Whatever Happened to Evangelical Theology* (Grand Rapids, Mich.: Eerdmans, 1993) and its sequel *God in the Wasteland: The Reality*

On the other hand, *we are seeing a waning confidence in preaching as the means by which the gospel is to be spread.* As a result, preaching is giving way in evangelical churches to multimedia presentations, drama, dance, "sharing times," sermonettes, and "how to" devotionals. Preaching is being viewed increasingly as outdated and ineffective. Business techniques like telemarketing are now popular with the church growth movement. Churches so infected also look to the multiplication of programs to effect their growth. They sponsor conferences and seminars on every conceivable topic under the sun; they subdivide their congregations down into marrieds and singles, single parents and divorced, "thirty-something" and "twenty-something," teens, unemployed, the child-abused and the chemically dependent, attempting to arrange programs for them all.[28] And once a person joins such a church, conventional wisdom has it, the church and the minister must meet his every felt need. Accordingly, ministers have become managers, facilitators, and motivators—everything but heralds of the whole counsel of God—and this all because they have lost confidence in the preaching of God's Word as the primary means for the growth of the church and the individual Christian.

What is the answer? A restored confidence in the Reformed doctrine of the sovereignty of God in salvation! When polished, self-confident preachers draw attention to themselves by using music, or story-telling, or hysteria and hype, or appeal to their viewers' "sense of self-worth" in order to produce "decisions," it is evident that they do not understand the depravity of humanity, either their own or their audience's, or they would not act this way. Why do I say this? Because a biblical, experiential understanding of the depravity of man and the necessity of God's sovereign initiative in salvation produces humility and the very antithesis of human self-confidence, namely, confidence in God alone.

Ministers of the gospel should read 1 Corinthians 1:26–31 carefully and let Paul instruct them anew that the truth of God's election destroys human pride and removes

---

of Truth in a World of Fading Dreams (Grand Rapids, Mich.: Eerdmans, 1994), Os Guinness, No God but God: Breaking with the Idols of Our Age (co-authored with John Seel; Chicago: Moody, 1992) and Dining with the Devil: The Megachurch Movement Flirts with Modernity (Grand Rapids, Mich.: Baker, 1993), Mark A. Noll, The Scandal of the Evangelical Mind (Grand Rapids, Mich.: Eerdmans, 1994), and David W. Hall, "On Not Having a Strategy for the New Decade: A Slightly Contrarian Plea," (Oak Ridge, Tenn.: Covenant Foundation [190 Manhattan Avenue], n.d.), in which Hall urges the contemporary church to readopt as its own the strategy of the apostle Paul, who laid out his "futurist strategy" in his charge to Timothy in 2 Timothy 4:1–5.

28. While there is nothing unseemly in these attempts to meet the needs of these groups as long as these efforts do not diminish the primacy of biblical preaching in the life of the church, one may still wonder if the perception that this is what one *must* do in order to minister effectively at the turn of the millennium is not itself a manifestation of waning confidence in the universal appeal and power of the gospel.

all boast before God. They should be reminded that only God can convert a sinner, that only God can grow a saint, that no one can boast in this matter of salvation because God does it all (see 1 Cor. 3:5–7). Neither the preacher nor the convert can take any credit. Salvation is all God's doing. "It is because of him that we are in Christ Jesus" (1 Cor. 1:30; see Phil. 1:28). Accordingly, they can be reassured that one can preach the simple, unadorned, unglamorized, unglittered gospel message of the cross, knowing that God will use it to save souls and build the church.

Then ministers of the gospel should study 1 Corinthians 2:1–5 and let Paul instruct them anew that preaching does not need to be spruced up by the use of the finest Greek oratorical skills or modern communication methodologies. Neither does the gospel message need Aristotelian arguments or Freudian analyses to make it "relevant." And here I am bold to say that it is Reformed theology alone which supplies the necessary theological underpinning to make true dependence upon God in gospel proclamation possible. When will revival come? I say with some confidence that it will only come when after all their failures to produce revival evangelical ministers stop resorting to and relying upon oratorical skills and clever organizational techniques to force church growth and preach once again with power God's simple pristine Word from another world to men and rely upon God to do his work.

I am not suggesting that Reformed preachers are or should be anti-intellectual. But what I do intend to say is that the Reformed understanding of the gospel with its biblical implicates of human depravity, unconditional election, particular atonement, irresistible grace, and perseverance in holiness must not be ignored or watered down in the interest of church growth, and that it will only be when the church unceasingly and uncompromisingly proclaims the message of "Christ and him crucified" as the cutting edge of evangelism and the whole counsel of God for Christian nurture that true revival will come.

All true revival comes from Christ alone. True revival is not worked up by human effort. The last church in the world to be visited by spiritual renewal will be the church that thinks it can produce it. (I am always saddened by the huge notices I see in front of many churches announcing that they are going to have a revival on such and such a date. They will be disappointed.) In one sense, revival is not even "prayed down," though much effectual prayer has always been behind the great periods of spiritual awakening. No, the source of all true revival is none other than Christ, the Baptizer of his people. It is he and he alone who can revive his church (Isa. 57:15). And all effectual prayer on the part of God's people *before* his outpourings of blessing is only the response of a particular heart attitude that he graciously infuses within them—the attitude of a lowly spirit, a broken and contrite heart. The church of Jesus Christ needs the gale of the reviving Spirit of

Christ sweeping through it at this time, calling it back to the truth, infusing it with boldness and courage, and empowering it to great deeds. And if that gale is not present in the church, it is doubtless because Christians are not asking his forgiveness for forsaking the pristine proclamation of the Cross in the power of the Holy Spirit.

Ministers need to be reminded that God looks not primarily at the outward but at the heart. And what does he see when he looks beyond our fine attire and our best social decorum? Does he see ministerial hearts that have "spent time at Sinai" (to employ an old Dutch Reformed phrase) as well as at Calvary, that have been made conscious that apart from being bathed in God's grace the human heart is deceitful above all things and desperately wicked? Does he see ministerial hearts beating in true humility before him? Does he see ministerial hearts that understand that without him they can do nothing good? Or is it possible that he sees proud and haughty spirits, insisting on doing things their own way? Does he see hearts that have not yet come to the end of themselves? Does he see hearts that are willing to try one more "how to" manual before they will sink in humble desperation before him?

Do evangelical ministers want genuine renewal in their churches and in the American church at large? Surely they do! Then they must continually cry out to God, publicly from their pulpits and privately from their closets, for that brokenness of spirit before him that alone he honors with his animating presence. They should importune heaven for new depths of humility before him that he might regale them with his power from on high! And when his Spirit does empower them, they must be true to the Reformed faith in their church-planting and church-growth methods! Not to do so will incur the divine displeasure for hypocrisy.

THE DUTY TO ADMINISTER THE SACRAMENTS

Because the sacraments will be treated in the chapter on the means of grace nothing here will be said about the sacraments beyond the fact that the church is responsible to administer them and to do so in accordance with God's Word.

THE DUTY TO MINISTER TO THE SAINTS

The church has the high privilege and solemn duty to minister to, that is, to nurture and edify, the saints of God.[29]

---

29. I am indebted to David C. Jones's unpublished classroom lecture on the duties of the church for some insights in this section.

The Nature of Ministry

The root idea in διακονέω, *diakoneō*, the common New Testament verb denoting "ministry," is "to wait at table," "to provide or care for" (often used of the work of women), and more generally, simply "to serve." While "serving" was not very dignified in Greek eyes, "ruling" being considered more proper to a man's station, Hebrew thought found nothing unworthy in "serving," though more and more in Judaism the idea arose that service rendered in behalf of God and one's neighbor was a work of merit.

Jesus, linking his view of service to the Old Testament command of love for one's neighbor, purified the Judaistic concept of service from its legalistic distortions, even making discipleship turn precisely on service, both to him and to others (John 12:26). Reversing in the popular estimation the relation between serving and being served, as H. W. Beyer rightly notes, "[Jesus] sees in [loving service] the thing which makes a man His disciple":[30]

> Luke 22:25–27: "The kings of the Gentiles lord it over them; and those who exercise authority over them call themselves Benefactors. But you are not to be like that. Instead, the greatest among you should be like the youngest, and the one who rules [ὁ ἡγούμενος, *ho hēgoumenos*] like the one who serves [ὁ διακονῶν, *ho diakonōn*]. For who is greater, the one who is at the table or the one who serves? Is it not the one who is at the table? But I am among you as one who serves."

Matthew's account of this saying of Jesus is also very instructive:

> Matthew 20:25–28: "Jesus called [his disciples] together and said, 'You know that the rulers of the Gentiles lord it [κατακυριεύουσιν, *katakyrieuousin*] over them, and their high officials exercise authority [κατεξουσιάζουσιν, *katexousiazousin*] over them. Not so with you. Instead, whoever wants to become great among you must be your servant [διάκονος, *diakonos*], and whoever wants to be first must be your slave [δοῦλος, *doulos*]—just as the Son of Man did not come to be served, but to serve [διακονῆσαι, *diakonēsai*], and to give his life a ransom for many."

The Scope of Ministry

It is striking how large the New Testament draws the circle of activities of Christian ministry. Jesus comprises under the term "to serve" many different activities,

---

30. H. W. Beyer, "διακονέω [*diakoneō*] in the New Testament," *Theological Dictionary of the New Testament*, 2:84. Beyer's observation is a healthy corrective to the oft-heard cliché that "love is the only badge of Christian discipleship."

including giving food and drink, extending shelter, providing clothes, and visiting the sick and those who are in prison:

> Matthew 25:37–40: "Then the righteous will answer him, 'Lord, when did we see you hungry and feed you, or thirsty and give you something to drink? When did we see you a stranger and invite you in, or needing clothes and clothe you? When did we see you sick or in prison and go to visit you?' The King will reply, 'I tell you the truth, whatever you did for one of the least of these brothers of mine, you did for me.'"

The apostles represent preaching and teaching in terms of being a "ministry [διακονία, *diakonia*] of the Word" (Acts 6:4; see 2 Cor. 5:18), even a "priestly duty" (ἱερουργοῦντα, *hierourgounta*), in that by proclaiming the gospel one's converts become "an offering acceptable to God" (Rom. 15:16). Indeed, Peter declares that every χάρισμα, *charisma*, of whatever kind a Christian possesses, is a spiritual gift to be used in service for others:

> 1 Peter 4:10–11: "Each one should use whatever gift he has received to serve [διακονοῦντες, *diakonountes*] others, faithfully administering God's grace in its various forms. If anyone speaks, he should do it as one speaking the very words of God. If anyone serves, he should do it with the strength God provides, so that in all things God may be praised through Jesus Christ."

Paul writes similarly:

> Romans 12:6–7: "We have different gifts, according to the grace given us. If a man's gift is prophesying, let him use it in proportion to his faith. If it is serving, let him serve; if it is teaching, let him teach; if it is encouraging, let him encourage; if it is contributing to the needs of others, let him give generously; if it is leadership, let him govern diligently; if it is showing mercy, let him do it cheerfully."

Then the author of Hebrews urges the following upon his readers:

> Hebrews 10:24–25: "Let us consider how we may spur one another on toward love and good deeds. Let us not give up meeting together, as some are in the habit of doing, but let us encourage one another—and all the more as you see the Day approaching."

> Hebrews 13:1–3: "Keep on loving each other as brothers. Do not forget to entertain strangers, for by so doing some people have entertained angels without knowing it. Remember those in prison as if you were their fellow prisoners, and those who are mistreated as if you yourselves were suffering."

Hebrews 13:15–16: "Through Jesus, therefore, let us continually offer to God a sacrifice of praise—the fruit of lips that confess his name. And do not forget to do good and to share with others, for with such sacrifices God is pleased."

The Westminster Confession of Faith summarizes our point this way:

> Saints, by profession, are bound to maintain an holy fellowship and communion in the worship of God, and in performing such other spiritual services as tend to their mutual edification; as also in relieving each other in outward things, according to their several abilities and necessities. Which communion, as God offereth opportunity, is to be extended unto all those who, in every place, call upon the name of the Lord Jesus. (XXVI/ii)

The Goal of Ministry

The sole purpose and objective behind the Spirit's engifting Christians with various gifts is the edifying of the body of Christ and the building up the saints in love. No spiritual gift should ever be used selfishly to edify only its recipient:

1 Corinthians 14:12, 26: "Since you are eager to have spiritual gifts, try to excel in gifts that build up [πρὸς τὴν οἰκοδομὴν, *pros tēn oikodomēn*] the church.... When you come together, everyone has a hymn, or a word of instruction, a revelation, a tongue or an interpretation. All of these must be done for the strengthening [πρὸς οἰκοδομὴν, *pros oikodomēn*] of the church."

Ephesians 4:15–16: "Speaking the truth in love, we will in all things grow up into him who is the Head, that is, Christ. From him the whole body, joined and held together by every supporting ligament, grows and builds itself up in love, as each part does its work."

THE DUTY TO GOVERN ITS AFFAIRS

The Scriptures make it plain that "God is not a God of disorder but of peace" (1 Cor. 14:33), and that he desires that "everything should be done in a fitting and orderly way" in his church (1 Cor. 14:40). God has given "ordering" authority to his church in the following areas:

Authority to Enforce the Laws of Christ

The point has already been made that the church has been authorized, not magisterially but ministerially, to teach Christians to obey everything Christ has commanded them (Matt. 28:20). This duty in a general way is the duty of every Christian individually toward his brothers and sisters in Christ:

> Romans 15:14: "I myself am convinced, my brothers, that you yourselves are . . . competent to instruct one another."
>
> Colossians 3:16: "Let the word of Christ dwell in you richly as you teach and counsel one another with all wisdom."
>
> 1 Thessalonians 5:11: "Encourage one another and build each other up, just as in fact you are doing."

In a special and official sense is this the duty of the elders of the church:

> Acts 20:28: "Guard yourselves and all the flock of which the Holy Spirit has made you overseers. Be shepherds of the church of God, which he bought with his own blood."
>
> 1 Timothy 3:5: "[The elder must] take care of God's church."
>
> Titus 1:7, 9: "An overseer is entrusted with God's work. . . . He must hold firmly to the trustworthy message as it has been taught, so that he can encourage others by sound doctrine and refute those who oppose it."
>
> Hebrews 13:17: "Obey yours leaders and submit to their authority. They keep watch over you as men who must give an account. Obey them so that their work will be a joy, not a burden, for that would be of no advantage to you."
>
> 1 Peter 5:2: "Be shepherds of God's flock that is under your care, serving as overseers."

Authority to Draw Up Constitutions and Manuals of Church Order

To insure that all things will be done decently and in order, to make known to its membership and to the world what it believes doctrinally, to declare the terms of admission into its communion and the qualifications of its ministers and members, as well as the whole system of its internal government which Christ has appointed, to delineate the proper method of officer investiture, and to promote its own purity and welfare, churches have the right and obligation to draw up "constitutions" for themselves, as long as such constitutions are "according to the general rules of the Word, which are always to be observed" (Westminster Confession of Faith, I/vi). The Constitution of the Presbyterian Church in America consists of its doctrinal standards set forth in the Westminster Confession of Faith, together with the Larger and Shorter Catechisms, and the Book of Church Order, which consists of "The Form of Government," "The Rules of Discipline," and "The Directory for the Worship of God" (*Book of Church Order,* Preface, III).

Authority to Discipline the Unruly and Reprobate

Just as God authorized Israel in its "theocratic" character to place those who committed sins "with a high hand" under the ban (חֵרֶם, *herem*) to be punished with extermination, so also the Lord Jesus Christ has given his church the authority to discipline its unruly and reprobate members in order to promote its purity and well-being (Matt. 16:19; 18:15–18; John 20:23). Just as by the preaching of the Word the wicked are doctrinally separated from the holy, so also by discipline the church authoritatively separates between the profane and the holy.

The exercise of discipline is extremely important for the glory of God and of Christ, the purity of the church, and the reclaiming of disobedient members (Rom. 16:17; 1 Cor. 5:1–5; Gal. 6:1; 2 Thess. 3:14–15; 1 Tim. 1:20; Titus 3:10). However, the authority to discipline that Christ has given his church is for building up and not for destroying (2 Cor. 10:8; 13:10). Therefore, it is to be exercised in mercy and not in wrath (Gal. 6:1). In this the church is to take the part of a tender mother (1 Thess. 2:7), correcting her children for their good, that everyone of them may be presented faultless in the day of the Lord Jesus.

Authority to Separate Itself from Error and Unbelief

Churches are more or less apostolic, that is, doctrinally pure or orthodox, according to the degree the gospel and doctrine of the apostles are taught and embraced by them; and while some churches are more faithful than others in confessing the system of doctrine taught in the holy Scriptures, even the purest churches are subject to error and do indeed err at times.[31]

Error in the church should always be of concern to the Christian, and he should charitably labor to rid the church of error. But a Christian should not lightly repudiate his church even when there is perceived error in it. Differences of opinion over nonessentials should not be made the basis for division in a local congregation or denomination. Such division for light causes is "schismatic," schism being understood here as formal and unjustified separation from the church. Paul speaks against such unjustified separation in 1 Corinthians 1:10: "I appeal to you, brothers, in the name of our Lord Jesus Christ, that all of you agree with one another so that there may be no divisions [σχίσματα, *schismata*] among you" (see also 1 Cor. 11:18; 12:25). If a Christian's church is faithfully proclaiming the Word of God, administers the sacraments according to the institution of Christ, and faithfully exercises discipline, his church is a true church of God, and a repudiation of it is wicked and a denial of God and of Christ, even though it may have some error in it.

---

31. I am indebted to David C. Jones for the insights in this section.

But the Bible recognizes that there are some circumstances that may arise in a church which will compel the Christian to separate himself from his church. The Greek New Testament employs two nouns in the main to describe dreadfully sinful situations in the church: apostasy (ἀποστασία, *apostasia*) and heresy (αἵρεσις, *hairesis*):

> 2 Thessalonians 2:3: "Don't let anyone deceive you in any way, for that day will not come until the rebellion [ἀποστασία, *apostasia*] occurs."
>
> 1 Timothy 4:1: "The Spirit clearly says that in later times some will abandon [ἀποστήσονται, *apostēsontai*] the faith and follow deceiving spirits and things taught by demons."
>
> 2 Peter 2:1: "[False teachers] will secretly introduce destructive heresies [αἱρέσεις, *haireseis*]." (see also 1 Cor. 11:19; Gal. 5:20; and Titus 3:10)

In general usage "apostasy" has come to refer to total renunciation of the Christian faith, with "heresy" being viewed more atomistically as any subversive doctrine professing to be Christian (of course, "systemic" heresy is hardly distinguishable from apostasy).

The New Testament lays down the following principles to protect the church in such a situation and to maintain its doctrinal purity:

1. Elders are charged to guard the church by guarding the truth (Acts 20:28–30; Tit. 1:9; see 1 John 4:2–3). The New Testament is realistic about the problems the church will have with false teachers. The passages cited presuppose that the Christian faith has a definite content, and that there are certain pivotal truths which are absolutely necessary to it.

2. Apostates and heretics ought to leave the church (1 John 2:18–19). It is *not* schismatic, indeed, it is quite appropriate, for antichrists to separate themselves from the Christian church. But more often than not, they set themselves up in the church. What is to be done with them then?

3. Unrepentant heretics who do not leave the church should be disciplined (Rom. 16:17; Tit. 3:10; 2 Pet. 2:1–3; 2 John 10–11; Rev. 2:2, 14–15, 20). As there were false prophets in Israel, so there are and will be false teachers in the church. As the former were subject to discipline, so the latter should be as well, *mutatis mutandis*, that is, by excommunication rather than execution.

4. Separation from one's local church or denomination is appropriate if it will not discipline heretics (2 Cor. 6:14–18). If a church rejects discipline for theological errors that subvert the foundation of the gospel and becomes theologically pluralistic in practice (even though it may retain an orthodox confession by which it promises to be guided), that church has become "heretical" in that it no longer stands under the authority of God, and the orthodox are compelled to separate from it to bear witness to the marks of the church.

THE DUTY TO PERFORM DEEDS
OF BENEVOLENCE AND MERCY

The poor, especially those whose poverty is the result of oppression, occupy a special place in the heart of God (Deut. 15:11; 24:14–15; Pss. 35:10; 113:7; 132:15; 141:12; Prov. 17:5; 19:17). He specifically stipulated that Old Testament judges were to defend the cause of the weak and fatherless, maintain the rights of the poor and oppressed, rescue the weak and needy, and deliver them from the hand of the wicked (Ps. 82:3–4). He pronounced judgment against legislators who would make unjust laws and oppressive decrees "to deprive the poor of their rights and to withhold justice from the oppressed of my people" (Isa. 10:1–2).

One characteristic of the righteous is that they care about justice for the poor (Prov. 29:7; 31:20), while one sin of Samaria and Judah is specifically said to be that "they did not help the poor and needy" (Ezek. 16:49; 22:29). God promised longevity to the king who judged the poor with fairness (Prov. 29:14; see 31:8–9), while Daniel 4:27 suggests that the sin which brought Nebuchadnezzar to humiliation and shame was his deficiency in "showing mercy to the poor." And in a striking statement we read that the Lord anointed the Messiah particularly to preach good news to the poor (Isa. 61:1; see Luke 4:18).

Our Lord reminded the church that "the poor you will always have with you, and you can help them anytime you want" (Mark 14:7). Later, the apostles arranged to have deacons appointed, who were then specifically charged with the responsible and delicate task of performing the work of Christian benevolence with reference to all the church's needy (Acts 6:1–6; see 1 Tim. 3:8–12). James defined the "religion that God our Father accepts as pure and faultless" in terms of "looking after orphans and widows in their distress" (James 1:17). Paul exhorted the Galatian Christians to "do good to all people, especially to those who belong to the family of believers" (Gal. 6:10), urged the Ephesian elders to "help the weak, remembering the words of the Lord Jesus: 'It is more blessed to give than to receive' " (Acts 20:35), admonished the Ephesian believer to do "something useful with his own hands, that he may have something to share with those in need" (Eph. 4:28), and counseled the Corinthian church, as he had previously done to the Galatian churches, to contribute to the needs of the saints in Jerusalem (1 Cor. 16:1–2; 2 Cor. 9). He instructed Timothy that the church should care for widows who are in need (1 Tim. 5:16). John rhetorically asks his readers the stinging question: "If anyone has material possessions and sees his brother in need but has no pity on him, how can the love of God be in him?" He answers his own question by urging the church: "Dear children, let us not love with words or tongue but with actions and in truth" (1 John 3:17–18). Clearly, the church has the diaconal duty to help the poor and needy, first those among itself and then the poor at large. Berkhof rightly remarks:

It is to be feared that this function of the Church is sadly neglected in many of the churches today. There is a tendency to proceed on the assumption that it can safely be left to the State to provide *even for the poor of the Church*. But in acting on that assumption, the Church is neglecting a sacred duty, is impoverishing her own spiritual life, is robbing herself of the joy experienced in ministering to the needs of those who suffer want, and is depriving those who are suffering hardship, who are borne down by the cares of life, and who are often utterly discouraged, of the comfort, the joy, and the sunshine of the spiritual ministrations of Christian love, which are as a rule entirely foreign to the work of charity administered by the State.[32]

* * * * *

In this chapter we have treated the general topics of the church's authority and its duties. We made the point that the church's authority is not natively intrinsic to itself but is the result of Christ's act of authorizing the church to minister in his name and stead. The nature of this authority is ministerial and declarative, not magisterial and physically coercive. We must be ever aware that "the arm of flesh will fail us" and resist every temptation to employ carnal weaponry in accomplishing the Lord's work.

We also noted the church's duties to worship and serve God, to witness to his truth, to evangelize the world, grow the church and nurture its young, to administer the sacraments, to minister to the saints, to govern its affairs, and to perform deeds of benevolence and mercy. From our survey of its duties we can see how extensive is the church's responsibilities before God and the watching world. No servant of Christ is sufficient in himself for these things. With Moses we understand that unless the beauty of the Lord rests upon and establishes the work of our hands, the stink of death arises from it (Ps. 90). With the apostle Paul, we must be keenly aware that because "we have this treasure [that is, our ministry] in jars of clay," our only hope of any fruition from our labors is in the "all-surpassing power from God" which is graciously at work in us (2 Cor. 4:7). But we can minister with the confidence that his grace is sufficient for us, for it is when we are weak that we are strong, for Christ's power is made perfect in our weakness (2 Cor. 11:9).

---

32. Berkhof, *Systematic Theology*, 602.

CHAPTER TWENTY-THREE

The Government of the Church

The Lord Jesus, as King and Head of His church, hath therein appointed a government, in the hand of church officers, distinct from the civil magistrate.
To these officers the keys of the kingdom of heaven are committed; by virtue whereof, they have power [authority], respectively, to retain, and remit sins; to shut that kingdom against the impenitent, both by the Word, and censures; and to open it unto penitent sinners, by the ministry of the gospel, and by absolution from censures, as occasion shall require. (Westminster Confession of Faith, XXX/i-ii)

For the better government, and further edification of the church, there ought to be such assemblies as are commonly called synods or councils: and it belongeth to the overseers [pastors] and other rulers [ruling elders] of the particular churches, by virtue of their office, and the power [authority] which Christ hath given them for edification and not for destruction, to appoint such assemblies, and to convene together in them, as often as they shall judge it expedient for the good of the church.

It belongeth to synods and councils, ministerially to determine controversies of faith, and cases of conscience; to set down rules and directions for the better ordering of the public worship of God, and government of His church; to receive complaints in cases of maladministration, and authoritatively to determine the same: which decrees and determinations, if consonant to the Word of God, are to be received with reverence and submission; not only for their agreement with the Word, but also for the power [authority] whereby they are made, as being an ordinance of God appointed thereunto in His Word.

All synods or councils, since the Apostles' times, whether general or particular, may err; and many have erred. Therefore they are not to be made the rule of faith, or practice; but to be used as a help in both. (Westminster Confession of Faith, XXXI/i-iii)

JESUS CHRIST, as King and Head of his church, has given to his people all the oracles, ordinances, and officers necessary for their edification and maturation in this world. In his messianic office as King, from his throne of glory he rules and teaches his people by his Word and Spirit through the ministry of these designated officers. Moreover, he has ordained for his church, in order that all things might be done decently and in order, a system of government, the details of which are either expressly set forth in Scripture or deducible from it by good and necessary inference.

It has become a commonplace in many church circles to say that Scripture requires no particular form of church government. The form a given church employs, it is said, may be determined on an *ad hoc* or pragmatic basis. Whatever works at any given time in any given place is allowable so long as it promotes peace and purity in the church. But this view does not fit the teaching of Scripture or the evidence from early church history. I do not intend to suggest by this last comment that there is unanimity of opinion on the prescribed form of government the church is to enact, for anyone who knows anything at all about church history will know that four distinguishable forms of church government (with variations and combinations of these) have been proposed over time: the presbyterian form, the episcopal form, the congregational form, and the Erastian form.

Is one of these forms the biblical form, and if so which one? As we consider the four proposed alternatives we would do well to keep before us John Murray's admonition respecting this very important matter:

> The church is the church of God and of Christ, and its aims and functions are prescribed by its head, its constitution determined and its officers designed and appointed by him.
>
> Perhaps no doctrine of the New Testament offers more sanctity to this fact than that the church is the body of Christ which he has purchased with his own blood. That which elders or bishops rule is the blood-purchased possession of Christ, that which cost the agony of Gethsemane and the blood of Calvary's accursed tree. It was that which was captive to sin, Satan, and death, and Christ redeemed it as his own precious possession. It is now his body, and he is the head. How shall we dare to handle that body, how shall we dare to direct its affairs, except as we can plead the authority of Christ. The church as the body of Christ is not to be ruled according to human wisdom and expediency but according to the prescriptions of him in whom are hid all the treasures of wisdom and knowledge.[1]

PRESBYTERIANISM

The word "presbyterian" is the English transliteration of the Greek πρεσβύτερος, *presbyteros*, which can mean "elder" in the sense of office holder (in other contexts it

---

1. John Murray, "Government in the Church of Christ," in *Collected Writings of John Murray* (Edinburgh: Banner of Truth, 1976), 1:265.

can refer simply to an old man). Πρεσβυτέριον, *presbyterion,* found in Luke 22:66, Acts 22:5, and 1 Timothy 4:14, means "council of elders."[2] The Greek word ἐπίσκοπος, *episkopos,* meaning "overseer" or "bishop," is another designation for the elder, as is evident from Paul's usage of the word in Acts 20:17, 28, Titus 1:5, 7, and Philippians 1:1.

Its History

Presbyterianism has a long history in the Bible. Moses, the priests and Levites, the judges, and even the kings of Israel, were all assisted in their governance of the nation, with God's permission, by the "elders of Israel [or most striking, 'elders of the congregation']" (Exod. 3:16, 18; 4:29; 17:5–6; 18:13–27; 19:7; 24:1, 9–11; Lev. 4:15; 9:1–2; Num. 11:14–25; Deut. 5:23; 22:15–17; 27:1; Josh. 7:6; 8:33; Judg. 21:16; 1 Kings 8:1–3; 1 Chron. 21:16; Ps. 107:32; Ezek. 8:1, etc.). This practice continued within Israel into the New Testament era, as is evident from Luke 22:66, where we are informed that Jesus was brought before the Jewish "presbytery" in Jerusalem: "At daybreak the *council of the elders* [πρεσβυτέριον, *presbyterion*] of the people, both the chief priests and teachers of the law, met together, and Jesus was led before them" (see also Acts 22:5).

It is this practice of governance by elders, begun in and present from the days of Mosaism onward, that lay behind Paul's practice of appointing (χειροτονήσαντες, *cheirotonēsantes*)[3] a plurality of elders (Acts 14:23) in every church he planted, to govern and oversee it. He would later instruct Titus to appoint (καταστήσῃς, *katastēsēs*)[4] elders "in every city" (Titus 1:5; see also Acts 11:30; 15:2; 20:17; James 5:14; 1 Pet. 5:1–2). Then with the passing of the apostles from the scene, the churches were to continue being governed by councils of elders chosen by the people, as Paul's lists of qualifications for the eldership in 1 Timothy 3 and Titus 1 imply.

The Duties of the Eldership

Just as their Savior, the Good Shepherd, looked with compassion on the multitudes and saw them as sheep having no shepherd (John 10:11, 14; Matt. 9:36), so also

---

2. In a strange etymological twist πρεσβύτερος, *presbyteros,* is the root of our English word "priest"—strange, I say, because Presbyterian ministers would be about the last officeholders in the church to represent themselves as "priests," although they would happily acknowledge their "priestly duty [ἱερουργοῦντα, *hierourgounta*] of proclaiming the gospel of God, so that the Gentiles might become an offering acceptable to God, sanctified by the Holy Spirit" (Rom. 15:16).
3. The verb χειροτονέω, *cheirotoneō,* literally means "choose, elect by raising hands." The action described here probably means that Paul as an apostle simply appointed elders when he first planted a church, just as missionaries often do today. This "appointing" did not preclude, however, his seeking the church's will in the matter by asking the congregation for a show of hands.
4. The verb καθίστημι, *kathistēmi,* means simply "to appoint."

elders are to "take heed to yourselves and to all the flock, among which the Holy Spirit has made you overseers, *to shepherd* [ποιμαίνειν, *poimainein*] the church of God" (Acts 20:28).[5] Peter likewise instructed elders: "Shepherd the flock of God which is among you, serving as overseers, not by compulsion but willingly, not for dishonest gain but eagerly, nor as being lords over those entrusted to you, but being examples to the flock" (1 Pet. 5:2–3). These verses clearly imply that elders, as shepherds of God's flock, are responsible to:

1. Keep the members of their flock from going astray. This implies instruction and warning. An elder must be able and ready to teach those under his care.[6] This means, of course, that he must faithfully labor to acquire a knowledge of God's Word in order to teach it.

2. Go after their members when they go astray. This implies reproof, correction, and in some cases the exercise of church discipline. Of course, elders should attempt by private instruction and admonition to correct an erring member of their flock at the earliest stage of a spiritual or moral defection, before open and censurable sin breaks forth that would require harsher measures of discipline.

3. Protect their members from wolves teaching false doctrine and evil practice that would enter in among them. This implies meticulous, careful application of the admission requirements for church membership, and a constant effort to cultivate in the people a discerning apprehension of the distinction between truth and error.

4. Lead their flock to the fold and pour oil into their wounds and give them pure water to quench their thirst. This implies pastoral concern and consolation. Elders should be keenly aware of the fact that many of their people will be broken in spirit and wounded for many and varied reasons. They should be ready, whenever the need becomes known, to visit the sick, bind up the broken reed, lift up the fallen hand, strengthen the weakened knee, and fan the smoking flax back into a bright and healthy flame.[7]

---

5. I have often thought that pastors would benefit greatly from reading some books on what sheep are like, what their needs are, and what is involved in shepherding them, for it is a fact that under one man a flock will struggle, starve, and suffer endless hardship, while under another that same flock will flourish and thrive contentedly. I would recommend, first, a careful study of Ezekiel 34, then W. Phillip Keller, *A Shepherd Looks at Psalm 23* (Grand Rapids, Mich.: Zondervan, 1970), and J. Douglas MacMillan, *The Lord Our Shepherd* (Bryntirion, U.K.: Evangelical Press of Wales, 1983).

6. Basing his study on Acts 20:28, Richard Baxter (1615–1691) in *The Reformed Pastor* (reprint; Edinburgh: Banner of Truth, 1974) urges that pastors should diligently catechize not only the children but also all the adults of their flocks who are willing to accept such training.

7. I adapted these four points from Murray, "Government in the Church of Christ," 265–67.

Qualifications of the Eldership

To facilitate faithful shepherd care for the flock of God, Paul lists the qualifications of the elder (overseer, bishop) in 1 Timothy 3:2–7 and Titus 1:6–9. In a word, the elder is to be a godly man. The elder, he insists,

1. must live a life which is above reproach, that is, be blameless, and have a good reputation with nonbelievers (1 Tim. 3:2, 7; Titus 1:6);
2. must be the husband of only one wife (1 Tim. 3:2; Titus 1:6);[8]
3. must be temperate, self-controlled, respectable, hospitable, gentle, upright, holy, and disciplined, and one who loves what is good (1 Tim. 3:2; Titus 1:8);
4. must not be given to drunkenness, or be violent, overbearing, quick-tempered, quarrelsome, a pursuer of dishonest gain, or a lover of money (1 Tim. 3:3; Titus 1:7);
5. must manage his own family well, and see that his children, who are to be believers, obey him with proper respect and are not open to the charge of being wild and disobedient (1 Tim. 3:4; Titus 1:6);
6. must be able to take care of God's church and oversee God's work (1 Tim. 3:5; Titus 1:7);
7. must not be a recent convert (1 Tim. 3:6);
8. must hold firmly to the trustworthy message as it has been taught (Titus 1:9); and
9. must be able to teach and thereby to encourage others by sound doctrine and to refute those who oppose this teaching (1 Tim. 3:2; Titus 1:9).

The Diaconate

Deacons, first chosen to assist the apostles (Acts 6:1–7), were thereafter appointed to assist the elders. Paul's list of qualifications for the deacon are found in 1 Timothy 3:8–12. The deacon, he commands,

---

8. This qualification (1 Tim. 3:2, 12; Titus 1:6; lit., "a one-woman [kind of] man," μιᾶς γυναικὸς ἄνδρα, *mias gynaikos andra*) has been variously interpreted. Some interpreters insist that its intent is to mandate that an officeholder in the church be married. Others declare that it means that an officeholder can only be married once, that is to say, a man who has been widowed or divorced and then has remarried is not to hold office. The most likely design of this qualification is the prohibition of a male polygamist from holding church office.

1. must be worthy of respect and sincere, literally, not "two-faced" (3:8);
2. must not indulge in much wine (3:8);
3. must not pursue dishonest gain (3:8);
4. must be the *husband of one wife* (μιᾶς γυναικὸς ἄνδρες, *mias gynaikos andres*) (3:12), whose wife must also be worthy of respect, not a malicious talker, but temperate and trustworthy in everything (3:11);[9]
5. must manage his children and his household well (3:12);
6. must keep hold of the deep truths of the faith with a clear conscience (3:9); and
7. must be tested before being given the diaconal task (3:10).

Thus Christian churches are to be governed by spiritually qualified councils of elders and served by spiritually qualified deacons chosen by the people.[10]

Presbyterian Connectionalism

Beyond the governance of local churches by elders it is important to note also that New Testament churches were connected or bound together by a common

---

9. Edmund Clowney in *The Church* (Downers Grove, Ill.: InterVarsity Press, 1995), basing his argument on Paul's description of Phoebe in Romans 16:1 as a διάκονον [*diakonon*, 'servant, helper, deacon'] of the church in Cenchrea," and on Paul's reference to "women" in 1 Timothy 3:11, concludes that women may legitimately hold the office of deacon (231–35). Other scholars as well, such as C. E. B. Cranfield (*A Critical and Exegetical Commentary on the Epistle to the Romans* [T. & T. Clark, 1986], 2:781), make the same case.

   But I am not persuaded that these verses endorse the position that women may hold official diaconal office, because Paul expressly states in 1 Timothy 3:12 that deacons are to be "one-woman kind of men" who are to manage their children and households well. I believe that Phoebe was a godly "servant" and "helper" of the church in Cenchrea and that the women referred to in 1 Timothy 3:11 are best understood to be deacons' wives.

10. While Christian men and women both bear the image of God (Gen. 1:26–27) and both are heirs together of the grace of life (1 Pet. 3:7), only men are to be elected to the offices of elder and deacon in Christ's church. This is evident from the following data:

    Elder: First, Paul expressly forbids women to teach or to exercise authority over men; rather, they are to be quiet in the churches (1 Tim. 2:12; 1 Cor. 14:33b–36). Since elders are to carry out these very functions, women necessarily are prohibited from holding this office. Second, the lists of qualifications for the elder in both 1 Timothy 3:2–7 and Titus 1:6–9 assume that elders are going to be men: an elder must be "a one-woman kind of man" and "must manage his own family well and see that his children obey him with proper respect." Third, with only rare exceptions (e.g., Deborah and Huldah; see Judg. 4–5 and 2 Kgs. 22:14–20),

government. The principle of mutual accountability, dependency, and submission among the churches is taught at several places in Scripture, for example, in Acts 8:14, where the Jerusalem church sent Peter and John to investigate Philip's work in Samaria, and in Acts 13:1–3 and 14:27, where missionaries were sent out by the Antioch church who then returned to Antioch and reported on the state of the Gentile churches they had founded. But the primary text in demonstrating the connectional nature of the churches of the early church is Acts 15, where we are informed of the appeal made by the Antioch church to the apostles and elders in Jerusalem, who met with them in a deliberative council and then *together* rendered a decision in the form of a "letter," called in Acts 16:4 τὰ δόγματα (*ta dogmata,* "rules, regulations, laws, decrees").[11] The Jerusalem council sent this letter not just to the church at Antioch that raised the question but to the churches in Syria and Cilicia as well (Acts 15:23), with every expectation that its instructions would be heeded and viewed as church law by all these churches. Clearly, these congregations were not independent and autonomous. Rather, they were mutually submissive, dependent, and accountable to each other.

This connectionalism has worked itself out in Presbyterian church history in terms of a gradation of three (or more) levels of "court jurisdiction": (1) the local council of elders, elected by the congregation and referred to as the session or consistory, which has the oversight of the faith and life of the local congregation;[12]

---

there is a consistent pattern of male leadership among God's people throughout the entire Bible. Jesus himself appointed only men as his apostles. A church that would ordain a woman to the eldership is flying in the face of the consistent testimony of Scripture opposing such an action as well as thirty-five hundred years of biblical and church history.

Deacon: First, when the problem of the equitable distribution of food to widows arose in the early church, the apostles expressly directed the church to choose seven men (ἄνδρας, *andras*) to oversee the distribution of food (Acts 6:1–6). Second, Paul's list of qualifications for the deacon in 1 Timothy 3:8–13 assumes that the deacon is going to a man: he is to be "a one-woman kind of man" and "must manage his children and his household well" (1 Tim. 3:12).

See George W. Knight III, *The Role Relationship of Men and Women*, rev. ed., (Chicago: Moody, 1985) and John Piper and Wayne Grudem, eds., *Recovering Biblical Manhood and Womanhood* (Wheaton: Crossway, 1991), chaps. 9 and 20, for the full argument. See also Benjamin B. Warfield, "Paul on Women Speaking in Church," *The Presbyterian* (Oct. 30, 1919): 8–9, for an unqualified insistence on the necessity of women to be absolutely silent in all of the church's public meetings for worship.

11. John Murray writes in "The Government of the Church," *Collected Writings of John Murray* (Edinburgh: Banner of Truth, 1977), 2:344: "It is all the more striking that the church should have resorted to such deliberation, and to this method of resolving an issue, since it was the era of special revelation."

12. Murray wisely comments in "Government in the Church of Christ," 262:
> While the [elders'] oversight is over the church, it is not over something from which the elders themselves are excluded. Elders are not lords over God's heritage; they are themselves

(2) the presbytery, composed of representatives from the sessions and the ordained ministers of the churches in a prescribed geographic area, which meets at designated times and exercises oversight over, coordinates the work of, and gives advice and counsel to the several local churches in its area of responsibility; and (3) the general assembly, composed of elder representatives and the ordained ministers of all the presbyteries, which meets annually and enables all the churches to have a voice in guiding the spiritual and practical affairs of the church in a region or country.

Within this same Presbyterian history, however, there has been some difference of opinion expressed as to whether church authority resides primarily in the local church session or in the highest court, usually spoken of as the "general assembly." Some Scottish Presbyterians have urged a kind of "aristocratic Presbyterianism" in which authority would seem to be vested in the highest courts and then delegated downward. William Cunningham explains:

> The Presbyterians of this country [Scotland] about the time of the Westminster Assembly, had perhaps somewhat higher and more aristocratic ideas of the power and authority of ecclesiastical office-bearers and church courts than had been generally entertained by the Reformers of the preceding century; not that there was any very marked or definite difference in opinion . . . between them on this subject, but [for these later Presbyterians this "somewhat aristocratic" disposition arose in order] to keep rather at a distance from anything that might seem to favour Congregationalism. Accordingly, there is nothing direct or explicit upon the subject of the place and standing of the people in the general regulation of ecclesiastical affairs . . . nothing, indeed, but the general statement . . . that Christ has given the ministry to the church.[13]

Louis Berkhof (following in the company of William Cunningham and James Bannerman), on the other hand, captures the essence of the more democratic expression of Presbyterian church government, in which authority is vested in the local church Session and then delegated upward, in the following five principles:

1. Christ is the Head of his church and the Source of all its authority;
2. Christ exercises his authority in his church ultimately by means of the Word of God and his Spirit;

---

of the flock and are to be examples to it. The Scripture has a unique way of emphasizing unity and diversity, and in this instance, the diversity which resides in the rule exercised is kept in proper proportion by the reminder that the elders themselves also are subject to the rule which they exercise over others. Elders are members of the body of Christ and are subject to the very same kind of rule of which they are the administrators.

13. William Cunningham, *Historical Theology* (1870; reprint, London: Banner of Truth, 1960), 1:57.

3. Christ has endowed both the ordinary members and the officers of his church with authority, with the officers receiving such additional authority as is required for the performance of their respective duties;

4. Christ has provided for the specific exercise of authority by representative organs (elders) who are set apart for the maintenance of doctrine, worship, and discipline; and

5. The authority of the church resides primarily in the session of the local church, with presbyteries and general assemblies possessing only such authority as are granted them by the several local churches.[14]

Berkhof's first four principles are sound and I give hearty approval to them, but with Berkhof's fifth principle I must take exception. I would urge that each "court" in Presbyterianism, if the "graded court system" is scriptural at all (and Berkhof believes it is), should have and would necessarily have its own intrinsic authority peculiar to itself; for if Christ has indeed authorized graded levels of courts at all, the upper levels possess necessarily and intrinsically precisely the authority he has granted them in their authorization from him to exist. The "general assembly" meeting in Acts 15, to illustrate, did not ask the several local churches in Syria and Cilicia if it might issue a dogmatic letter to them. The Jerusalem assembly believed it had the authority to do so, and accordingly it did so. Samuel Rutherford, though he seems to have favored the more aristocratic construction of Presbyterianism, gives expression to this middle perspective which denies both a descending or an ascending authority between the courts when he wrote:

> To a congregation [Christ] has given, by an immediate influx from Himself, a political Church power intrinsically in it, derived from none but immediately from Jesus Christ, and the object of this power is those things that concern a Congregation; and that same Head and Lord has given immediately an intrinsical power to the Presbytery, in things that are purely classical, and that without either the intervening derivation of either a Congregation that is inferior to the Presbytery, by ascending, or without any derivative flux of a Synodical, national or Catholic visible Church, by descending.[15]

---

14. For his full description and defense of this conception of the presbyterian system of church government, see Louis Berkhof, *Systematic Theology* (Grand Rapids, Mich.: Eerdmans, 1932), 581–92.

15. Samuel Rutherford, *The Due Right of Presbyteries, or, A Peaceable Plea for the Government of the Church of Scotland* (London: E. Griffin, for R. Whittaker and A. Crook, 1644), 383.

Whatever one finally decides with regard to these variant expressions of Presbyterianism (as I indicated above, I myself support the middle position), it is still true that it was the Presbyterian form of church government—one that is both conciliar and connectional—which prevailed until the end of the third century,[16] when under the influence of Cyprian (195–258), bishop of Carthage, episcopal forms began to take over. (Presbyterianism was reinstated by John Calvin in Geneva in the sixteenth century.) But the earliest form of church government was Presbyterian. *If then one is looking for a form of church government which is biblical and apostolic, Presbyterianism is it.*[17]

EPISCOPACY

The episcopal[18] (or prelatic)[19] form of church government may be found today in the Roman Catholic Church, the Greek Orthodox and Russian Orthodox Churches, the Church of England, the Episcopalian Church in the United States, and the United Methodist Church in the United States. This form of church government calls for a distinct category of church officers, generally known as a priesthood, comprised of archbishops, bishops, and rectors (or vicars), to govern the church and to have final authority in decision-making in the local church. (The United Methodist Church is an exception here with respect to the nomenclature.) In the case of the Roman Catholic Church, in addition to these officers the pope of Rome, as the supreme head of that church, periodically appoints "proven" archbishops to his College of Cardinals, who in turn rule over the archbishops, bishops, and local priests throughout the world. And the Orthodox Churches have their Patriarchs, who are similar in authority in their respective churches to the Roman pontiff, though they do not claim infallibility as the pope does. This form of church government is also called a "hierarchical" government,[20] especially when referring

---

16. Ignatius of Antioch (d. c. 107) is possibly the lone dissenting voice during this period in presenting a distinction between the bishop and elder, but "even his writings are arguably nonprelatic" (see Joseph H. Hall, "History and Character of Church Government," in *Paradigms in Polity: Classic Readings in Reformed and Presbyterian Church Government*, ed. David W. Hall and Joseph H. Hall [Grand Rapids, Mich.: Eerdmans, 1994], 5).
17. See Hall, "History and Character of Church Government," Thomas Witherow, "The Apostolic Church: Which Is It?" and "Earliest Textual Documentation," in *Paradigms in Polity*, 3–11, 35–52, 55–61, for bibliographic and biblical support respectively for early presbyterianism.
18. The word *episcopal* derives etymologically from the Greek word ἐπίσκοπος, *episkopos*, meaning "overseer, bishop."
19. *Prelacy* goes back through Middle English to the Latin *praelatia*, from *praefero*, meaning "to set before."
20. The word "hierarchical" derives etymologically from the Greek roots ἱερ- (*hier-* "having to do with 'priestly' things") and ἀρχ- (*arch-* "beginning, first"), and means somewhat literally "the power or authority of the high priest." It alludes to the authority which the priests wield in their descending order of rank.

to the Roman Catholic Church. The officers in these churches claim that they stand in a long line of priestly succession going back to the original apostles themselves.

It is acknowledged even by its advocates that the episcopal or prelatic form of church government is nowhere mentioned in the New Testament. But its advocates urge that episcopacy is not forbidden by the New Testament and is a natural outgrowth of the development of the church. E. A. Litton (1813–1897), for example, declares: "No order of Diocesan Bishops appears in the New Testament," but he then aborts the significance of this concession by adding:

> The evidence is in favour of the supposition that Episcopacy sprang from the Church itself, and by a natural process.... The Presbytery, when it assembled for consultation, would naturally elect a president to maintain order; first temporarily, but in time with permanent authority.... Thus it is probable that at an early period an informal episcopate had sprung up in each Church. As the Apostles were one by one removed ... the office would assume increased importance and become invested with greater power.[21]

Moreover, Litton argues that episcopacy should be maintained since it has (so he says) proven beneficial to the church and since there is benefit in the priest being able to say that his authority, as regards its external commission, has come to him from direct descent from the apostles. The renowned J. B. Lightfoot (1828–1889), also acknowledging that the presbyterian system was the one that prevailed in the New Testament church, contended that "the episcopate was created out of the presbytery" but more as a thing of expediency than of divine right.[22] Charles Gore (1853–1932), a High Church Anglo-Catholic, disagreed with this explanation of the origin of episcopacy, contending that it is of divine right and that local bishops, "like the circle of twelve round their Master," are the successors of the apostles and hence of Christ himself and always had authority over presbyters.[23]

It is enough to say in response that episcopacy receives no support whatever from the New Testament. Whether it has been beneficial or not to the church is highly debatable, depending upon one's view of its development in church history since Cyprian, whose views of episcopacy gave rise eventually in the early medieval

---

21. Edward Arthur Litton, *Introduction to Dogmatic Theology*, ed. Philip E. Hughes (1882, 1892; reprint, London: James Clarke, 1960), 401.
22. J. B. Lightfoot, *The Epistle to the Philippians*, rev. ed. (Grand Rapids, Mich.: Zondervan, 1974), 95, and his dissertation on "The Christian Ministry," 195ff. Edwin Hatch (1835–1889) concurred in his 1880 Bampton Lectures, later published under the title *The Organization of the Early Christian Churches* (London: Longmans, Green, 1901), 39, 99.
23. Charles Gore, *The Church and the Ministry*, rev. ed. (London: Longmans, Green, 1919), 302–03, 348–49.

period to the papacy and to the papacy's many subsequent doctrinal heresies and political and social abuses of power. As for the claim by the Roman Catholic Church and the other episcopal church bodies that their authority has come to them through an unbroken line of succession from the apostles themselves down to the present, it is enough to say, first, that such a claim is simply unsupported by history and not verifiable, and second, that even were such an unbroken succession true in some instance, such episcopal succession *per se* would convey no particular authority or guarantee apostolicity to the one so graced. Mere unbroken apostolic succession is not the New Testament criterion for ministerial authority.

CONGREGATIONALISM

The congregational, sometimes called the independent, form of church government, espoused by such theological worthies as John Owen and Jonathan Edwards, advocates self-rule for every local congregation.[24] Final governing authority resides within the congregation itself, but the issue of just who in the local congregation exercises *final* authority differs from congregation to congregation. Wayne Grudem distinguishes five forms of government within congregationalism: the "single elder (or pastor)" form, the "plural local elders" form, the "corporate board" form, the "pure democracy" form, and the "no government but the Holy Spirit" form (Grudem himself espouses the second of these).[25] Even when, for reasons of expediency, congregational churches enter into communal or "denominational" relationship with one another, any and all actions taken by such associations are regarded only as advisory and are not considered as binding on any particular local church.

The following arguments for the "single elder (pastor)/several deacons" form of government—the system followed by the vast majority of independent churches, certainly the smaller ones—are set forth in Augustus Hopkins Strong's *Systematic Theology*:[26] (1) the New Testament does not require a church to have a plurality of elders, (2) James as the single pastor of the church at Jerusalem (so Strong) provides the pattern churches should follow in governing themselves, (3) 1 Timothy 3:2 and Titus 1:7 refer to "the bishop" (in the singular) whereas, by contrast, 1 Timothy 3:8 reads "deacons" (in the plural), and (4) the "angel" in each of the seven churches in Revelation 2 and 3 is best interpreted as the pastor, which means that each church had not many but only one bishop/elder or pastor.

---

24. The best exposition of Independency is still Robert W. Dale's classic, *Congregational Church Polity* (London: Hodder & Stoughton, 1885).
25. Wayne Grudem, *Systematic Theology* (Grand Rapids, Mich.: Zondervan, 1994), 928–36.
26. Augustus H. Strong, *Systematic Theology* (Philadelphia: Judson, 1907), 914–17.

With regard to Strong's first argument, the reader is urged simply to read Acts 14:23, Titus 1:5, James 5:14, and 1 Peter 5:1, where a plurality of elders appears to be present in every congregation. As for his second, it is enough to call the reader's attention to Acts 15:2, where a plurality of elders is clearly indicated as being present in the Jerusalem church. Regarding his third, it must be noted that 1 Timothy was written to Timothy, who was laboring at Ephesus (1:3), which church, according to Acts 20:17, clearly had a plurality of elders, and even in 1 Timothy 5:17 Paul speaks of "elders." As for the singular "elder" in Titus 1:7, one need only note verse 5, where Paul commands Titus to "appoint elders [plural] in every city." Regarding Strong's fourth point, it is enough by way of refutation to say again that the church at Ephesus in Revelation 2:1–7, according to Acts 20:17, had several elders. So whoever or whatever the "angel" of the church at Ephesus was (the teaching elder?), his or its presence did not preclude a plurality of elders from serving there.

Congregationalism, with its rejection of all meaningful connectionalism between local Christian bodies, is not in harmony with the Word of God. Moreover, as Berkhof notes:

> the theory that each church is independent of every other church fails to express the unity of the Church of Christ, has a disintegrating effect, and opens the door for all kinds of arbitrariness in church government. There is no appeal from any of the decisions of the local church.[27]

ERASTIANISM

Named after Thomas Erastus (1524–1583), a Swiss theologian who set forth his views in his *Explicatio Gravissimae Quaestionis* (1589), Erastianism is the opposite of that theocratic system that held sway in Europe for the thousand years after Constantine, in which the state became more and more subjugated to the church until in many ways the church ruled the state. The advocate of the Erastian form of church government contends that it is the right and function of the state to rule over and govern the church and to exercise ecclesiastical discipline and to excommunicate members. The officers of the church are merely preachers and teachers of the Word, with no authority to rule and govern beyond that which the civil magistrate grants them.

This form of church government is followed in the Lutheran state church of Germany and in England, where the reigning British monarch is regarded as the Head and Protector of the "established" Church of England. (In the case of the Church of

---

27. Berkhof, *Systematic Theology*, 580–81.

England, Erastianism is combined with episcopacy.) Two members of the Westminster Assembly, John Lightfoot and Thomas Coleman, accepted the notion of the "godly civil magistrate" legislating and overseeing the community of faith of which he was a member. And, of course, it is true that the Westminster Assembly itself was convened by and served at the behest of the English Parliament, most of the members of which were strong Erastians who wanted the church's government to depend absolutely on the Parliament.

However, this form of church government, as with episcopacy and congregationalism, fails to receive the support of New Testament teaching. Moreover, William M. Hetherington quite properly notes:

> [Erastianism's] direct aim is the abolition of spiritual courts; and so far as Establishments are concerned, it has succeeded; for that is no spiritual court which either cannot meet without the permission of the civil authority, or where not merely its decisions can be reviewed and reversed by one of a different character, but where the judges themselves can be punished for their conscientious judgments. And since the Lord Jesus Christ instituted a government in his Church, the loss of spiritual courts is the loss of that government, and necessarily the loss of direct union with the Head and King of the Church,—which is, in other and plainer words, the loss of spiritual life and true religion.[28]

In sum, Christ is the King and Head of his church, and he has determined that he will rule his church through a system of spiritual and connectional courts comprised of pluralities of qualified elders.

THE SIGNIFICANCE OF PRESBYTERIAN CHURCH GOVERNMENT

Why is the matter of church government in general and of Presbyterian church government in particular important? Because Presbyterianism is not only the most biblically sound form of church government but also provides the most trustworthy, just, and peaceful way for the church to determine its direction, its principles, its practices and its priorities, and to resolve its differences. Lose balance in church government in one direction and one ends up with episcopal tyranny. Lose balance in the other direction and one has congregational anarchy, followed by the tyranny of the one or the few. Of course, the Spirit of God must always animate Presbyterianism, but the form itself is God-given and important.

---

28. William M. Hetherington, *History of the Westminster Assembly of Divines* (Edmonton, Alberta: Still Waters, 1993), 367.

It is no exaggeration to say that the Christian church in our day is about to self-destruct because of its abandonment of biblical church government. How so? Because on the one hand, in the case of episcopacy, local congregations abound in number which have no recourse when an authoritarian churchman in high places forces his decisions upon them. The apostolic form of church government will deliver these churches from such hierarchical tyranny, for it is nothing short of tyranny when ecclesiastical bureaucrats lord it over local congregations and force unwanted priests or ministers on them or refuse them the priests and ministers they request. (Such practices happen regularly today.) The republicanism of biblical and early church government is the answer to ecclesiastical oppression.

On the other hand, there are too many ministers and too many churches that are accountable to no one today. Large areas of American Christianity are in a state of anarchy because churches and pastors are a law unto themselves, answering to no one. Contemporary hero-worshiping churches, influenced as they have been by this hero-worshiping culture, have elevated talented men to such celebrity status that mortal flesh cannot bear the heights. One should not be surprised then when sexual indiscretions, a divorce rate among ministers as high as the national average, and financial mismanagement on the part of such church leaders follow. Power still corrupts. The pastor (or church) who answers to no one inevitably experiences the warping of priorities under the influence of his (or its) privately held biases. Understandably, scandalous deeds ensue. The collective impact of these almost daily church scandals is all but ruining the Christian witness in our generation. Does the populace really respect the American church? A small percentage does, perhaps, but what the church thinks about moral issues does not really matter to most people. And ministers—how do they fare in the public's opinion?

> In a recent study measuring social prestige, on a scale of one to one hundred, ministers ranked fifty-second, alongside factory foremen and the operators of power stations, far below the medical doctors and lawyers with whom they would like to be confused. In another national poll, *only 16 percent of the public expressed confidence in their religious leadership.*[29]

Is it not vital then that the principle of rule by a plurality of elders who are in turn accountable to other elders be restored in the life of the churches?

Church government is not an irrelevancy. Church ministry and church government cannot be separated. One road to church renewal and church growth,

---

29. David F. Wells, *No Place for Truth* (Grand Rapids, Mich.: Eerdmans, 1994), 113 (emphasis supplied).

therefore, is the restoration of the biblical form of church government in the American church, for representative and connectional church government provides the essential "checks and balances" necessary to keep the church on track and to protect it from tyranny on the one side and anarchy on the other.

CHAPTER TWENTY-FOUR

The Church's Means of Grace

Unto [the] catholic visible church Christ hath given the ministry, oracles, and ordinances of God, for the gathering and perfecting of the saints, in this life, to the end of the world: and doth, by His own presence and Spirit, according to His promise, make them effectual thereunto. (Westminster Confession of Faith, XXV/iii)

THE CHRISTIAN is to grow in grace and in the knowledge of his Lord and Savior Jesus Christ. Just as his physical body requires nutritious food to grow physically, so also he needs spiritual food to grow spiritually. This spiritual "food" that God has provided for the Christian's growth in grace theologians refer to as the "means of grace."

God the Father through the coagency of the Lord Jesus Christ and his Holy Spirit is the ultimate source of all grace. Paul writes:

> Praise be to the God and Father of our Lord Jesus Christ, who has blessed us with *every spiritual blessing* in the heavenly realms *in Christ*. . . . I keep asking that the God of our Lord Jesus Christ, the glorious Father, may give you *the Spirit* of wisdom and revelation, so that you may know him better. . . . For through *him* [Christ] we both [Jew and Gentile] have access to the Father by one *Spirit*. (Eph 1:3, 17; 2:18; emphases supplied)

Now while the Triune God can impart salvific blessings such as regeneration directly and immediately to the human spirit apart from means, normally he "graces" his people by or through "the means of grace." What are these "means" whereby God communicates the benefits of Christ's mediation to us?

The church of Jesus Christ, because it is the only community in the world that possesses the message of grace which Christ and his Spirit use for the ingathering of God's elect and the edifying and building up of Christ's spiritual body, may be viewed as the one *"institutional* means of [special] grace" to the world. Also, since God works everything, including death itself, together in the Christian's life to conform him more and more to a spiritual likeness of Christ (Rom. 8:28–29), God's *providence* may be regarded as a "means of grace" to the Christian. But the expression customarily has been employed in a more circumscribed way.

In the confessional literature of the Westminster Assembly the full expression occurs only one time—in the Larger Catechism, Question 195, where we are informed that we should pray that God will "bestow and bless all means of grace." But the Larger Catechism intends the same when it asks:

> Question 153: What doth God require of us, that we may escape his wrath and curse due to us by reason of the transgression of the law? Answer: That we may escape the wrath and curse of God due to us by reason of the transgression of the law, he requireth of us repentance toward God, and faith toward our Lord Jesus Christ, and the diligent use of the *outward means* whereby Christ communicates to us the benefits of his mediation (see Shorter Catechism, Question 85, for virtually the same answer).

> Question 154: What are the outward means whereby Christ communicates to us the benefits of his mediation? Answer: The outward and ordinary means whereby Christ communicates to his church the benefits of his redemption are *all his ordinances; especially the word, sacraments, and prayer;*[1] *all which are made effectual to the elect for their salvation"* (see Shorter Catechism, Question 88, for virtually the same answer).

Here we are provided the general outline for our present study on the means of

---

1. Because prayer is "a fruit of the grace of God," although, as Berkhof admits, it may in turn become instrumental in strengthening the spiritual life, he prefers to view "only the Word and the sacraments as means of grace, that is, as objective channels which Christ has instituted in the Church, and to which He ordinarily binds Himself in the communication of His grace" (Louis Berkhof, *Systematic Theology* [Grand Rapids, Mich.: Eerdmans, 1932], 604–05). Strictly speaking, Berkhof is correct, and his position receives some support from the Confession of Faith itself when it speaks only of "the preaching of the word, and the administration of the sacraments of baptism and the Lord's supper" as the ordinances in which the covenant of grace are dispensed (VII/vi). But when one considers (1) that prayer "brings us near to God, who is the source of all good," (2) that "fellowship with Him, converse with Him, calls into exercise all gracious affections, reverence, love, gratitude, submission, faith, joy, and devotion" (Charles Hodge, *Systematic Theology* [Grand Rapids, Mich.: Eerdmans, n.d.], 3:708), it seems altogether appropriate to treat prayer, although it surely is a fruit of grace, as itself also a means of grace.

grace. We will treat these means under the headings the Larger Catechism provides us, namely, Word, sacraments, and prayer.

Before we consider these means of grace separately, however, I would like to make three general comments. First, these means of grace are instruments not of *common* but of *special* grace, specifically, of that "grace of God that brings salvation [and that] teaches us to say 'No' to ungodliness and worldly passions, and to live self-controlled, upright and godly lives in this present age" (Titus 2:11–12). Second, these means of grace do *not* work, as Roman Catholic theology contends, *ex opere operato*[2] as long as the recipient places no obstacle (*obex*) to their working in the way. Nor does the Word have in itself the intrinsic power to convert men and to produce holiness in them, as Lutherans contend. To the contrary, God and God alone is the efficient cause of all salvific grace. Accordingly, he must do his saving work by and with these means immediately in the hearts of men if they would in fact become instruments of grace. Third, saving grace is not so integrally or inexorably related to the sacraments that there can be no salvation without them. In no sense is saving grace, either in kind or degree, denied the Christian who in God's providence never has the opportunity to receive baptism or commune with the Lord at his table (see, e.g., the penitent thief on the cross). God can and does convey his saving benefits to men in and by the Word alone, the sacraments being obligatory only in view of the divine precept, and their willful neglect resulting in spiritual impoverishment in the same way that all willful disobedience carries with it destructive effects upon the soul.

THE WORD OF GOD AS A MEANS OF GRACE

The Westminster Assembly addressed the subject of Holy Scripture under two major rubrics in its confessional material: (1) in chapter one of the Westminster Confession of Faith where the Scriptures are treated *theologically* as the sole and fundamental basis and norm (the *principium unicum* and *principium cognoscendi externum*) for all Christian doctrine,[3] and (2) in Questions 155–160 of the Larger Catechism (see also the parallel material in Shorter Catechism, Questions 88–90), where the Scriptures are treated *ministerially* as a means of grace. It is with Scripture as the *most important* of the means of grace available to the church that we are presently concerned.

---

2. Literally, "by the work performed." Ludwig Ott in *Fundamentals of Catholic Dogma*, 5th ed. (St. Louis, Mo.: Herder, 1962), writes: "The formula '*ex opere operato*' asserts, negatively, that the sacramental grace is not conferred by reason of the subjective activity of the recipient, and positively, that the sacramental grace is caused by the validly operating sacramental sign" (130).
3. See part one for my treatment of Scripture as the basis and norm for Christian theology.

The Larger Catechism sets forth the Reformed view of the Word of God as a means of grace in the following questions and answers:

> Question 155: How is the Word made effectual to salvation? Answer: The Spirit of God maketh the reading, but especially the preaching of the Word, an effectual means of enlightening, convincing, and humbling sinners; of driving them out of themselves, and drawing them unto Christ; of conforming them to his image, and subduing them to his will; of strengthening them against temptations and corruptions; of building them up in grace, and establishing their hearts in holiness and comfort through faith unto salvation.
>
> Question 156: Is the Word of God to be read by all? Answer: Although all are not to be permitted to read the word publickly to the congregation, yet all sorts of people are bound to read it apart by themselves, and with their families: to which end, the holy Scriptures are to be translated out of the original into vulgar languages.
>
> Question 157: How is the Word of God to be read? Answer: The holy Scriptures are to be read with an high and reverent esteem of them; with a firm persuasion that they are the very Word of God, and that he only can enable us to understand them; with desire to know, believe, and obey the will of God revealed in them; with diligence, and attention to the matter and scope of them; with meditation, application, self-denial, and prayer.
>
> Question 158: By whom is the Word of God to be preached? Answer: The Word of God is to be preached only by such as are sufficiently gifted, and also duly approved and called to that office.
>
> Question 159: How is the Word of God to be preached by those that are called thereunto? Answer: They that are called to labour in the ministry of the Word, are to preach sound doctrine, *diligently,* in season and out of season; *plainly,* not in the enticing words of man's wisdom, but in demonstration of the Spirit, and of power; *faithfully,* making known the whole counsel of God; *wisely,* applying themselves to the necessities and capacities of the hearers; *zealously,* with fervent love to God and the souls of his people; *sincerely,* aiming at his glory, and their conversion, edification, and salvation [emphasis supplied].
>
> Question 160: What is required of those that hear the Word preached? Answer: It is required of those that hear the Word preached, that they attend upon it with diligence, preparation, and prayer; examine what they hear by the Scriptures; receive the truth with faith, love, meekness, and readiness of mind, as the Word of God; meditate, and confer to it; hide it in their hearts, and bring forth the fruit of it in their lives.

The Efficacy of the Word

These Catechism questions and answers reflect the distinctly Reformed view of the Scriptures as a means of grace. Implicit in this view is the conviction that the Bible in its entirety is the inspired, inerrant Word of the living God, made the possession of the church through divinely governed revelatory and inspirational processes, and thus it is the sole propositional expression of the will of God for his church.

Evangelical Lutherans, who share this view of the nature of Scripture as God's Word, do not endorse the idea, however, that it is the Spirit of God who must, immediately and directly, make the reading and the preaching of the Word effectual unto salvation (see Larger Catechism, Question 155). Following the lead of Luther himself, who declared that the written Word of God possesses an intrinsic power because, as Luther believed, the Spirit of God is never separated from it,[4] Lutheran theologian Robert Preus, urging that the power of the Spirit has been communicated to the Word according to the will of God, writes:

> The written and preached Word of God has the *intrinsic* power to convert all men indiscriminately. . . . Hence by virtue of divine ordination and communication, Scripture and the [preached?] Word of God are *intrinsically* endowed with power to regenerate and convert.[5]

The problem with this Lutheran insistence that the written and preached Word carries intrinsically within itself all the power necessary to convert all men is that this view cannot explain in a way that harmonizes with the Scripture's teaching on salvation why all men who read or hear the Word are not immediately and without exception converted thereby. The Lutheran response must, of course, "resort . . . to the doctrine of the free will of man,"[6] and thus Lutherans deny the irresistibility of the very intrinsic power to convert which they claim for the written and preached Word, as Preus admits:

> The efficacy of the Word extends to all men everywhere. It is always the purpose of God and his Word that all men should be converted and saved. But the efficacy of the Word is not irresistible.[7]

---

4. Martin Luther, *Sämmtliche Schriften*, ed. J. G. Walch (St. Louis: Concordia, 1881–1930), 4:307; 8:288; 18:215, 1811; 51:377–88.
5. Robert Preus, *The Inspiration of Scripture* (Edinburgh: Oliver and Boyd, 1957), 170, 183 (emphasis supplied).
6. Berkhof, *Systematic Theology*, 611.
7. Preus, *Inspiration of Scripture*, 189.

The Reformed church, however, insists that the salvation of men is always under the direct, sovereign governance of God, that salvation is always directly from the Lord, and therefore, that the Holy Spirit must bear witness, immediately and directly, *by and with* the Word in men's hearts if they are to respond in repentance and faith to the Word of God. As the Confession of Faith declares:

> All those whom God hath predestinated unto life, and those only, He is pleased, in His appointed and accepted time, effectually to call, *by His Word and Spirit,* out of that state of sin and death, in which they are by nature, to grace and salvation, by Jesus Christ. (X/i, emphasis supplied)

In short, the Reformed position on the efficacy of the Word as a means of grace is that, even though the Bible is the very Word of God, it is rendered efficacious as a means of special grace, not intrinsically or automatically, but only by the immediate and direct attendant working of the Holy Spirit in the hearts of its readers and hearers.[8] The Reformed church emphasizes that the imparting of spiritual life is ever sovereignly with God the Spirit who is the Giver of life. That is to say, where and when the Spirit effectually works in human hearts by and with the Word of God (and only there and then), the Word is irresistibly efficacious as a means of grace in the salvation of lost men and the building up of the saints in faith.

The Ministry of the Word

It has pleased God, particularly "through the foolishness of *what is preached* [τοῦ κηρύγματος, *tou kērygmatos*], to save those who believe" (1 Cor. 1:21). Because true preaching must be biblically based, the Larger Catechism (Question 159) admonishes the minister of God's Word to preach "sound doctrine." This means, of course, that he must preach the Word of God as God intends it to be preached. The Catechism then uses six adverbs to describe *how* he is to preach this doctrine: diligently, plainly, faithfully, wisely, zealously, and sincerely, and then it provides an explanatory phrase for each adverb.

---

8. Two verses in particular appear to support the Lutheran contention that the Word of God is intrinsically efficacious, namely, James 1:18: "He chose to give us birth *through the word* [λόγῳ, *logō*] of truth," and 1 Peter 1:23: "For you have been born again, not *of* [ἐκ, *ek*] perishable seed, but of imperishable, *through* [διά, *dia*] the living and enduring word of God." There can be no doubt that in both instances the "word" referred to is the preached word of the gospel, but a careful reading of these statements must lead one to the conclusion that in both verses the preached word of God is not the *efficient* but rather the *instrumental* cause of regeneration (see the simple dative of means in James and the διά, *dia*, with the genitive in 1 Peter) employed by God the Holy Spirit in his work of regeneration. It is God, James says, who "gives birth [ἀπεκύησεν, *apekyēsen*]" to men, doing it *through* the word of truth.

He is ever to bear in mind that his authority as a minister is subordinate to the authority of Scripture (1 Pet. 4:11), and that he can claim that his message is authoritative only insofar as it coincides with the truth of Scripture itself.

He must also bear in mind that his authority is ministerial and declarative, not magisterial and legislative. That is to say, his authority is the authority of God himself when he proclaims God's Word and ministers as Christ's ambassador in Christ's stead. But he must not take offense when his auditors examine the Scriptures, as did the Bereans (Acts 17:11), to see if what he is preaching is true. To the contrary, he should encourage them to examine God's written Word for themselves. Nor does he have the authority to enact new laws for men's consciences or to abrogate the laws of Scripture that some may think bind them too severely.

Finally, he must continually keep before him God-honoring goals for his ministry of the Word. Before everything else, he must "do his best to present himself to God as one approved, a workman who does not need to be ashamed and who correctly handles the word of truth" (2 Tim. 2:15). In other words, he must aim to please God. He must proclaim "the whole will of God" (Acts 20:27), and proclaim it in its "due and proper proportion,"[9] that is to say, in keeping with the emphases and the balances of Scripture. Then he must also love the souls of men with a sincere passion and minister the Word to effect their conversion, edification, and final salvation.

THE SACRAMENTS AS MEANS OF GRACE

Sacraments are holy signs and seals of the covenant of grace, immediately instituted by God, to represent Christ and His benefits; and to confirm our interest in Him: as also, to put a visible difference between those that belong unto the Church and the rest of the world; and solemnly to engage them to the service of God in Christ, according to His Word.

There is, in every sacrament, a spiritual relation, or sacramental union, between the sign and the thing signified: whence it comes to pass, that the names and effects of the one are attributed to the other.

The grace which is exhibited in or by the sacraments rightly used, is not conferred by any power in them; neither doth the efficacy of a sacrament depend upon the piety or intention of him that doth administer it: but upon the work of the Spirit, and the word of institution, which contains, together with a precept authorizing the use thereof, a promise of benefit to worthy receivers.

There be only two sacraments ordained by Christ our Lord in the Gospel; that is to say, Baptism, and the Supper of the Lord: neither of which may be dispensed by any, but by a minister of the Word lawfully ordained.

---

9. J. Oliver Buswell Jr., *Systematic Theology* (Grand Rapids, Mich.: Eerdmans, 1962), 1:424.

The sacraments of the old testament in regard of the spiritual things thereby signified and exhibited were, for substance, the same with those of the new. (Westminster Confession of Faith, XXVII/i–v)

Before the Confession treats the sacraments separately, it deals with the sacraments together in a general way, but not because it seeks to analyze "the essence" of a sacrament prior to a consideration of the individual sacraments, "for the nature of the sacraments turns precisely upon the concrete givenness of baptism and the Lord's Supper in the historical revelation in Jesus Christ."[10] The Confession is not interested in some kind of natural theology or "sacramentology" that would precede the concrete sacraments and into which they must be made to fit. It treats them first together only for clarity's sake and in order to address certain questions that have arisen in the history of the church, and all that it says, even then, about the "sacraments" in general it says in light of the biblical statements concerning the two concrete biblical sacraments.

The word "sacrament," for which I have no particular fondness, comes from the Latin *sacramentum*, meaning "sacred thing." It became a term in the medieval church designating baptism and the Lord's Supper (as well as Rome's five false "sacraments") as a result of the Vulgate translation of μυστήριον (*mystērion*, "secret thing") by *sacramentum* in Ephesians 1:9, 3:9, 5:32, Colossians 1:27, 1 Timothy 3:16, and Revelation 1:20, 17:7, even though μυστήριον, *mystērion*, is never used of either baptism or the Lord's Supper in the Greek New Testament.[11]

"The two simplest and most generally accepted [definitions of the word 'sacrament'] are the one by Augustine and the other by Peter Lombard."[12] Augustine, bishop of Hippo (d. 430), defined a sacrament as a "sacred sign" (*sacrum signum*),[13] while Peter Lombard (d. 1164) defined a sacrament as "a visible form of an invisible grace" (*invisibilis gratiae visibilis forma*) and "a sign of the grace of God and the form and cause of an invisible grace" (*signum . . . gratiae Dei et invisibilis gratiae forma . . . et causa existat*).[14]

---

10. G. C. Berkouwer, *The Sacraments*, trans. Hugo Bekker (Grand Rapids, Mich.: Eerdmans, 1969), 9–10.
11. Some commentators think that Paul may have been referring to the sacraments in 1 Corinthians 4:1, where he speaks of himself and Peter as "stewards of the mysteries of God [οἰκονόμους μυστηρίων θεοῦ, *oikonomous mystērion theou*]". But this understanding of μυστήριον, *mystērion*, flies in the face of its uniform meaning in the Pauline corpus to designate a truth that comes to men by divine revelation. The "mysteries" in 1 Corinthians 4:1 refer to the revealed truths of the gospel.
12. Hodge, *Systematic Theology*, 3:486.
13. See Augustine, *The City of God*, X, 5.
14. See Peter Lombard, *Sentences*, IV, I, 4.

According to Roman Catholic theology from earliest medieval times to the present day, the sacraments are "perceptible signs (words and actions) accessible to our human nature" which "make present efficaciously the grace that they signify."[15] The sacraments

> act *ex opere operato* (literally, "by the very fact of the action's being performed"), i.e., by virtue of the saving work of Christ, accomplished once for all. It follows that "the sacrament is not wrought by the righteousness of either the celebrant or the recipient, but by the power of God" [a citation from Aquinas, *Summa theologica,* III.68.8]. From the moment that a sacrament is celebrated in accordance with the intention of the Church, the power of Christ and his Spirit acts in and through it.[16]

And "for believers the sacraments of the New Covenant are *necessary for salvation.*"[17]

The Westminster Assembly defined a sacrament as "an holy ordinance instituted by Christ in his church, to signify, seal, and exhibit unto those that are within the covenant of grace, the benefits of his mediation; to strengthen and increase their faith, and all other graces; to oblige them to obedience; to testify and cherish their love and communion one with another; and to distinguish them from those that are without" (Larger Catechism, Question 162). And although it a sinful thing to deliberately neglect the sacraments, yet grace and salvation are not so inseparably annexed to them that no person can be regenerated or saved without them.

Over against Rome's insistence that there are seven sacraments (baptism, confirmation, the Eucharist, penance, extreme unction, holy orders, and matrimony),[18] the Protestant Reformers and the churches following their lead have insisted that "there be only two sacraments ordained by Christ our Lord in the Gospel; that is

---

15. *Catechism of the Catholic Church* (1994), para. 1084.
16. Ibid., para. 1128.
17. Ibid., para. 1129, emphasis original.
18. See the deliverance of the Council of Florence (1438–1445): "By baptism we are spiritually reborn and by confirmation we grow in grace and are strengthened in the faith; being reborn and strengthened we are nourished with the divine food of the Eucharist. If, by sin, we become sick in soul, penance spiritually heals us; extreme unction heals us in spirit, and in body as well, insofar as it is good for the soul. By holy orders the church is governed and given spiritual growth; by matrimony she is given bodily growth." See also the Council of Trent's first of its Canons on the Sacraments in General (1547): "If anyone says that the sacraments of the New Law were not all instituted by our Lord Jesus Christ; or that there are more or less than seven . . . or that any one of these seven is not truly and intrinsically a sacrament, let him be anathema." The theological student is referred to John Calvin's treatment of Rome's five false sacraments in his *Institutes,* IV.xix.

to say, Baptism, and the Supper of the Lord" (Westminster Confession of Faith, XVII/iv).[19]

Over against Rome's contention that the sacraments work *ex opere operato*, that is to say, without depending in any way upon the recipient they causally infuse supernatural grace into the soul that does not resist it,[20] Protestants in general and the Westminster Assembly in particular declared that the sacraments "become effectual means of salvation, not by any power in themselves, or any virtue derived from the piety or intention of him by whom they are administered, but only by the working of the Holy Ghost ['in them that by faith receive them'—Shorter Catechism, Question 91], and the blessing of Christ, by whom they are instituted" (Larger Catechism, Question 161).

Over against Rome's view that for believers the sacraments of the New Covenant are necessary for salvation, Berkhof, reflecting the consentient testimony of the Reformers, writes:

> That [the sacraments] are not absolutely necessary unto salvation, follows: (1) from the free spiritual character of the gospel dispensation, in which God does not bind His grace to the use of certain external forms [it is debatable whether he ever did—author], John 4:21, 23; Luke 18:14; (2) from the fact that Scripture

---

19. John 13:15 (the Synoptics are silent here, but see 1 Tim. 5:10) should not be construed to mean that footwashing should be a third sacrament observed by the church. Only in the most general way does our Lord's washing his disciples' feet signify his redemptive activity. It is much more likely that his washing of his disciples' feet was intended as an example of humility to teach them (and us) that Christians should be ready, in lifelong service to him, to perform the most menial service for others.

20. See Thomas Aquinas, *Summa theologica*, Question 62, Article 11, and the Council of Trent's sixth, seventh, and eighth Canons on the Sacraments in General:

> 6. If anyone says that the sacraments of the New Law do not contain that grace which they signify, or that they do not confer that grace on those who place no obstacles in its way, as though they are only outward signs of grace or justice received through faith and certain marks of Christian profession, whereby among men believers are distinguished from unbelievers, let him be anathema.
>
> 7. If anyone says that grace, so far as God's part is concerned, is not imparted through the sacraments always and to all men even if they receive them rightly, but only sometimes and to some persons, let him be anathema.
>
> 8. If anyone says that by the sacraments of the New Law grace is not conferred *ex opere operato* [i.e., by the outward rite itself], but that faith alone in the divine promise is sufficient to obtain grace, let him be anathema."

Cited from *Creeds of the Churches*, ed. John Leith, rev. ed. (Richmond: John Knox, 1973), 425–26. The reader is referred to Berkouwer's chapter on "The Efficacy of the Sacraments" in his *The Sacraments*, 56–89, for an excellent discussion from a Reformed perspective of the Roman Catholic *ex opere operato* doctrine.

mentions only faith as the instrumental condition of salvation, John 5:24; 6:29; 3:36; Acts 16:31; (3) from the fact that the sacraments do not originate faith but presuppose it, and are administered where faith is assumed, Acts 2:41; 16:14, 15, 30, 33; 1 Cor 11:23–32; and (4) from the fact that many were actually saved without the use of the sacraments. Think of the believers before the time of Abraham and of the penitent thief on the cross.[21]

I would add that Paul expressly states that Abraham himself was justified by faith some years *before* he was circumcised (Rom. 4:9–10).

Over against Rome's "assumption that the sacraments contain all that is necessary for the salvation of sinners, need no interpretation, and therefore render the Word quite superfluous as a means of grace,"[22] the Westminster Assembly affirms that the grace which is exhibited in the sacraments is conferred by "the work of the Spirit, and the Word of institution, which contains, together with a precept authorizing the use thereof, a promise of benefit to worthy receivers" (Westminster Confession of faith, XVII/v). This statement reflects the Reformed view that, while both the Word and the sacraments (1) have the same Author, (2) the same central content (even Christ), and (3) require faith as the means whereby their content is appropriated, the Word does indeed take priority over the sacraments in that the Word is (1) essential to salvation while the sacraments are not, (2) engenders and strengthens faith while the sacraments only strengthen it, and (3) intended for the whole world, while the sacraments are only for the church.

Over against the popular view of the sacraments, often designated the Zwinglian view (but it is not at all clear that Zwingli himself espoused it),[23] that would urge that their material elements are nothing more than mere "representations" of certain

---

21. Berkhof, *Systematic Theology*, 618–19.
22. Ibid., 616.
23. Geoffrey W. Bromiley writes in *Zwingli and Bullinger*, vol. 24 in *The Library of Christian Classics* (Philadelphia: Westminster, 1953):

> Zwingli had no intention of denying a spiritual presence of Christ in the sacrament [of the Lord's Supper]. . . . This presence certainly means that the communion is more than a 'bare' sign, at any rate to the believing recipient. . . . For in the sacrament we have to do not merely with the elements but with the spiritual presence of Christ himself and the sovereign activity of the Holy Spirit. (179)

And again,

> Zwingli does not dispute that Christ is truly present in the Supper. What he disputes is that he is substantially present, present in the substance of his flesh and blood, present after his human nature . . . he had no wish to deny the presence of Christ altogether, and the reality of the spiritual presence of Christ involves something far more than a bare memorialism. The Supper cannot be merely a commemorative rite when the one commemorated is himself present and active amongst those who keep the feast. (183)

See also Roland Bainton, *Here I Stand* (New York: Abingdon, 1950), 319.

spiritual truths, that they are to be observed only as acts of obedience to Christ who commands their observance, and that the Supper in particular is nothing more than a commemorative ceremony, the Reformed tradition insists that as "signs" and "seals" of the covenant of grace,[24] the sacraments are means of grace in which Christ himself is *really spiritually present* and offers himself and the benefits of his death to Christians who receive him and those benefits in humility and faith.[25] His presence and his offer of grace are objective and are in no way *created* by faith, for where there is no repentance and faith such faithless engagement brings judgment, as 1 Corinthians 11:29–31 states. Where there is repentance and faith the sacraments are efficacious, but only because of "the blessing of Christ, and the working of his Spirit in them that by faith receive them" (Shorter Catechism, Question 91).

This teaching of the real spiritual presence of Christ and his benefits in the sacraments and accordingly of the efficacy of the sacraments as spiritual instrumentalities conferring saving grace is based upon the Reformed insight that there are three aspects to both sacraments: (1) the visible elements and the observable actions that are the external signs and seals of spiritual graces; (2) the spiritual graces themselves (such as the righteousness of faith, the forgiveness of sins, communion with Christ in his death and resurrection, that is, Christ himself in his Passion and all his spiritual riches) that are signified and sealed by the visible elements and observable actions; and (3) the "spiritual relation, or sacramental union" between the signs and seals themselves on the one hand and the spiritual graces they signify and confirm on the other. *It is this spiritual union that constitutes the essence of the sacrament*, and it is because of this union that the sacraments confer grace when they are received in faith. It is also because of this union that the names and effects of the signs and seals are attributed to the spiritual graces and vice versa (Westminster Confession of Faith, XXVII/ii; see Gen. 17:10; Acts 22:16; Rom. 6:3–4; Matt. 26:27–28; 1 Cor 5:7).

Before considering the sacraments separately, it might be helpful to note in what ways baptism and the Lord's Supper are similar and in what ways they are dissimilar. The two sacraments are alike in that both were instituted by Christ (Matt. 28:19; 1 Cor. 11:23–25), both are to be perpetually observed in the church (Matt. 28:20; 1 Cor. 11:26), both entail the active employment of material elements (washing with water, eating bread and drinking wine), both are signs and seals of the covenant of grace and can and do become means of grace to those who receive them, and both

---

24. The Reformed representation of the sacraments as "signs" and "seals" of the covenant of grace is based on Paul's statement in Romans 4:11: "And he received the sign [σημεῖον, *sēmeion*] of circumcision, a seal [σφραγῖδα, *sphragida*] of the righteousness that he had by faith while he was still uncircumcised."
25. See Berkouwer's chapter on "The Real Presence," in *The Sacraments*, 219–43, for an excellent discussion of this subject over against the Romanist and Lutheran views.

serve to delimit the visible church (Rom. 6:3–4; 1 Cor. 10:16–17). They are dissimilar in that "baptism is to be administered but once, with water, to be a sign and seal of our regeneration and ingrafting into Christ, and that even to infants; whereas the Lord's supper is to be administered often, in the elements of bread and wine, to represent and exhibit Christ as spiritual nourishment to the soul, and to confirm our continuance and growth in him, and that only to such as are of years and ability to examine themselves" (Larger Catechism, Question 177). It remains, of course, to demonstrate these features in the treatments which follow.

Baptism

Baptism is a sacrament of the new testament, ordained by Jesus Christ, not only for the solemn admission of the party baptized into the visible Church; but also to be unto him a sign and seal of the covenant of grace, of his engrafting into Christ, of regeneration, or remission of sins, and of his giving up unto God, through Jesus Christ, to walk in newness of life. Which sacrament is, by Christ's own appointment to be continued in his Church until the end of the world.

The outward element to be used in this sacrament is water, wherewith the party is to be baptized, in the name of the Father, and of the Son, and of the Holy Ghost, by a minister of the Gospel, lawfully called thereunto.

Dipping of the person into the water is not necessary; but Baptism is rightly administered by pouring, or sprinkling water upon the person.

Not only those that do actually profess faith in and obedience unto Christ, but also the infants of one, or both, believing parents, are to be baptized.

Although it be a great sin to contemn or neglect this ordinance, yet grace and salvation are not so inseparably annexed unto it, as that no person can be regenerated, or saved, without it: or, that all that are baptized are undoubtedly regenerated.

The efficacy of baptism is not tied to that moment wherein it is administered; yet, notwithstanding, by the right use of this ordinance, the grace promised is not only offered, but really exhibited, and conferred, by the Holy Ghost, to such (whether of age or infants) as that grace belongeth unto, according to the counsel of God's own will in His appointed time.

The sacrament of baptism is but once to be administered unto any person. (Westminster Confession of Faith, XXVIII/i–vii)

Old Testament Background

The Old Testament refers many times to ritual washings. The law prescribed ritual bathing for persons deemed ceremonially unclean (Lev. 14:8–9; 15). Aaron and his sons were ceremonially washed at their ordination to the priesthood (Lev. 8:5–6). Sprinkling of the furniture employed in the tabernacle and temple was also prescribed. These ritual washings led to their symbolic application in prayer for spiritual cleansing (Ps. 51:1–2; 7–10; see Ezek. 36:25–26). John's baptism of repentance in preparation for Messiah's coming (Matt. 3:6, 11; Mark 1:4–5; Luke 3:3), given the fact that his ministry belonged to the preparatory age of the Old Testament (Matt. 11:13), should very probably be viewed as a ceremonial or ritual cleansing (denoting spiritual cleansing) standing in this Old Testament context.[26]

Institution

Our Lord himself instituted the sacrament of baptism on the eve of his ascension when he gave to his disciples the Great Commission: "go and make disciples of all nations, baptizing [βαπτίζοντες, *baptizontes*] them in the name of the Father and of the Son and of the Holy Spirit" (Matt. 28:19). The church has then the sanction of heaven to baptize its members; indeed not to baptize them is disobedience to heaven.

---

26. Many scholars, some more cautious than others, for example, Jean Steinmann (*Saint John the Baptist and the Desert Tradition*, translated by Michael Boyes [New York: Harper, 1958], pp. 58–61), Millar Burrows (*More Light on the Dead Sea Scrolls* [New York: Viking, 1958], pp. 56–63), and Charles H. H. Scobie (*John the Baptist* [Philadelphia: Fortress, 1964] pp. 34–40), contend or concede that there may have been some connection between John the Baptist's baptism of repentance and the baptism of initiation of the Essene sect at Qumran.

While an attractive case can be made—if not for a direct connection between Qumran and John—for at least the influence of Qumran upon John, I would still counsel caution here for, while such an influence is possible, one must not lose sight of the fact that, while John's personal lifestyle was ascetic, perhaps even Naziritic (Matt. 3:4; 11:18; Luke 1:15; 7:33; see Num. 6:1–21; Judg. 13:5, 7; 1 Sam. 1:11), (1) his ministry was essentially prophetic (Matt. 3:1–12; 11:7–14; Mark 1:2–3; Luke 3:2–9; John 1:23–27) while Qumran's was esoteric; (2) he issued a broad, public call to repentance (Matt. 3:2, 8; Luke 3:8) while Qumran was reclusive and monastic in its orientation; (3) he demanded probative evidence of repentance in the affairs of ordinary life (Luke 3:8, 10–14) while Qumran required submission to the rigors of ascetic life; (4) he, as Messiah's forerunner, announced that he had come (John 1:29, 35) while Qumran still awaited his appearance; (5) he had a knowledge of the nature of Messiah and of his work (Matt. 3:11–12; John 1:29–35; 3:27–30) which Qumran did not have; (6) his disciples felt at liberty to leave him and to follow Jesus (John 1:35–37)—indeed, he encouraged them to do so (John 1:29; 35; Acts 19:4)—while Qumran's inhabitants felt no such easy freedom to leave the sect; and (7) his baptism was precisely what the New Testament represents it as being, namely, a "baptism of repentance" by which those who repented of their sins and were baptized became members of the broad public community of faith that awaited the appearance of the Messiah and his twofold baptism while Qumran's baptism of initiation was for its initiates the entryway into that monastic sect which viewed itself as the new Israel. These features of John's ministry suggest that it was distinctly different from the sectarian teachings, expressions and attitudes of Qumran.

The present participle in this verse seems to be a "means" participle. That is to say, Jesus seems to represent baptism here as one of the two outward means whereby the nations are to be made his disciples, "teaching them to obey everything I have commanded" (in the next clause) being the second. I do not mean to suggest that baptism simply as an institution *effects* discipleship. I am thinking of baptism here as the ceremony in connection with which Christians normally and formally publicly declare for the first time their commitment to Jesus Christ.

Import

Following John Murray,[27] I would urge that the import of baptism should be derived from the terms of its institution and from the several references to it in the New Testament. When we take our point of departure from the formula that Jesus used in its institution, namely, "baptizing into the name" (βαπτίζοντες εἰς τὸ ὄνομα, *baptizontes eis to onoma*; see 1 Cor. 1:13, 15—"baptized into the name of Paul"; 1 Cor. 10:2—"baptized into Moses"), it becomes apparent that the formula expresses a relationship to the person into whom or into whose name the person is being baptized.[28] Baptism then basically denotes the fact of a relationship. What kind of relationship? When such passages as Romans 6:3–6, 1 Corinthians 12:13, Galatians 3:27–28, and Colossians 2:11–12 are taken into account (see expositions below), it becomes plain that the nature of the relationship is one of *union with Christ,* more particularly, union with Christ in his crucifixion, death, burial, and resurrection (not just union with him in the last two). Of this basic union baptism is the sacramental sign and seal. But since Jesus speaks of being baptized into the name of the Father, and of the Son, and of the Holy Spirit, baptism also

> signifies union with the Father and the Son and the Holy Ghost, and this means with the three persons of the Trinity, both in the unity expressed by their joint possession of the one name and in the richness of the distinctive relationship which each person of the Godhead sustains to the people of God in the economy of the covenant of grace.[29]

---

27. John Murray, *Christian Baptism* (Philadelphia: Presbyterian and Reformed, 1962), 5.
28. Edmund Clowney in *The Church* (Downers Grove, Ill.: InterVarsity Press, 1995) says in this regard: "Christian baptism is a naming ceremony. The baptized is given a name, . . . the name of the triune God. . . . Baptism gives Christians their family name, the name they bear as those called the children of God (Is. 43:6b–7)" (278). He refers to the Aaronic blessing in Numbers 6:24–27 and to Paul's statement in Ephesians 3:14–15 for support.
29. Murray, *Christian Baptism*, 7.

There is another aspect of the import of baptism that must not be overlooked. Because the ordinance involves the use of the visible element of water and the observable action of applying that water to the person, and in view of the teaching of Ezekiel 36:25–26, John 3:5, 1 Corinthians 6:11, and Titus 3:5 concerning the ceremonial use of water and washing for cleansing, as well as the teaching of Colossians 2:11–12 where circumcision (which is a sign of cleansing from sin's defilement) is related to baptism, baptism signifies more specifically the *cleansing* or purification from sin's defilement and guilt. This cleansing results from the sinner's union with the persons of the Godhead in their respective labors in the *ordo salutis*.

Finally, because the very name of the ordinance is what it is, namely, baptism (βάπτισμα, *baptisma*), it obviously symbolizes the spiritual work given that name in Holy Scripture, namely, Christ's work of baptizing his people with the Holy Spirit (see Matt. 3:11; Mark 1:8; Luke 3:16; John 1:33; Acts 1:5; 2:33; 1 Cor. 12:13), which work unites them to himself and to the other persons of the Godhead in their saving labors of regenerating, purifying, justifying, and cleansing.

Apostolic Baptisms in the New Testament

There are relatively few instances—only eleven—of actual Christian baptisms recorded in the New Testament. This is remarkable, since actual baptisms must have been very frequent in the days of the apostles. The recorded instances are the following:

Actual Baptisms Recorded in the New Testament

1.	Jews	Acts 2:37–41
2.	Samaritans	Acts 8:12–17
3.	The Ethiopian eunuch	Acts 8:35–38
4.	Paul	Acts 9:18; see 22:16
5.	Caesareans	Acts 10:44–48
6.	Lydia	Acts 16:13–15
7.	Philippian jailer	Acts 16:30–34
8.	Corinthians	Acts 18:8
9.	John's disciples	Acts 19:1–7
10.	Crispus and Gaius	1 Corinthians 1:14
11.	Stephanas' household	1 Corinthians 1:16

One interesting thing to note about the baptisms in Acts is that they are administered "upon," "into," or "in" the name of Jesus (Acts 2:38, ἐπὶ, *epi*; Acts 8:16, εἰς, *eis*;

Acts 10:48, ἐν, *en*; Acts 19:5, εἰς, *eis*; see also Gal. 3:27; Rom. 6:3) and not in the name of the Triune God as is specified in the Matthew 28 formula. While some critics believe this proves that Matthew 28:19 is "a later Matthean redaction of a more primitive apostolic commissioning," I would suggest that Luke is simply giving an abbreviated form of the words actually used in the baptismal ceremony, highlighting by his use of Jesus' name alone both the fact that it is through Jesus' mediation that one enters into union with the triune God and the fact that these persons were being admitted to the *Christian* church.

Exposition of the Pauline References to Baptism

The references to baptism in the epistles are also relatively few, with only one non–Pauline instance (1 Pet. 3:21), and none in the Apocalypse.[30] The eight Pauline instances are as follows: Galatians 3:27, 1 Corinthians 1:13–17 (6 times); 10:2; 12:13; 15:29 (2 times); Romans 6:3–4; Ephesians 4:5; and Colossians 2:12.[31]

> Galatians 3:26–27: "For all of you are sons of God through faith in Christ Jesus; for as many as have been baptized into Christ have put on Christ." I believe that Paul has in mind by his statement here Christ's baptismal work of baptizing the elect by his Spirit (for surely not all who have been baptized by water have actually "put on Christ"), by which work they are brought into union with him through faith, their union with him being described here metaphorically as their having "put on Christ" in the sense that one would enrobe oneself in a garment.

> 1 Corinthians 1:13–17; 10:2: The six references to baptism in 1 Corinthians 1 "confirm the apostolic practice of baptism as it is reflected in Acts, and are significant theologically in that they presuppose the relational import of Christian baptism (εἰς τὸ ὄνομα, *eis to onoma*), which is also expressed in 1 Corinthians 10:2 (εἰς τὸν Μωυσῆν, *eis ton Mōysēn*)" (Jones). Jones also notes here the evident primacy of the Word over the sacrament in Paul's statement that Christ commissioned him to *evangelize* rather than to baptize, although he did, of course, baptize some initial converts such as Crispus (see Acts 18:8) and Stephanas (see 1 Cor 16:15).

---

30. I am indebted to David C. Jones's unpublished classroom lecture on baptism for several insights in this section.
31. The paucity of Pauline references to baptism in his epistles should not be construed to mean that Paul held the ordinance in low esteem. Though he will say that Christ did not send him to baptize but to evangelize (1 Cor. 1:17), when he then expounds the significance of baptism he gives it high meaning (Rom. 6:3–4) and places alongside the one body, one Spirit, one hope, one Lord, one faith, and one God and Father, "one baptism" as an additional reason for the unity of the body of Christ (Eph. 4:4–5).

1 Corinthians 12:13: "For we were all baptized by one Spirit [ἐν ἑνὶ πνεύματι, *en heni pneumati*] into one body." I fully concur with Jones here that "there is no reason why the preposition ἐν [*en*] should not be translated 'with' rather than 'by.' Christ is the one who 'baptizes' with the Holy Spirit; he is the agent and the Holy Spirit is the 'element.'" (However, I prefer to highlight in the preposition εἰς, *eis*—"*into* one body"—the relational character of this baptismal work rather than the goal or purpose of this work, as Jones suggests.) I concur too with Jones when he writes:

> That Christ rather than the Holy Spirit is the agent of this baptism is confirmed by the succeeding clause: ". . . and we were all given one Spirit to drink." This passage is thus not a direct reference to water baptism; it refers rather to the outpouring of the Holy Spirit on the day of Pentecost as a definitive historico–redemptive event of which subsequent generations of believers partake as they are incorporated into the body of Christ. Water baptism, of course, is the outward sign of the [cleansing] work of the Holy Spirit in the life of the individual believer, but that does not seem to be the main point of this text.

Jones's point is borne out by both the passive voice and the punctiliar tense of the verb ἐποτίσθημεν, *epotisthēmen*, "we were given to drink."

1 Corinthians 15:29: "Now if there is no resurrection, what will those do who are baptized for the dead [ὑπὲρ τῶν νεκρῶν, *hyper tōn nekrōn*]? If the dead are not raised at all, why are people baptized for [ὑπὲρ] them?" As Jones remarks, the two references in this verse to baptism for the dead are puzzling, to say the least. Many are the suggestions made by commentators as to Paul's meaning here, but no solution presently on the scene is carrying the field.³² Therefore, since it is impossible to know for certain what Paul meant by it, there is no warrant in the text or in the context for Jones's conclusion that "Paul seems to view the practice in a positive light." One can only conclude that, whatever was the practice he alludes to, at the very least he is surely employing it as an *ad hominem* argument for the physical resurrection against those in the Corinthian church who denied it.

Romans 6:3–4: "Or don't you know that all of us who were baptized into Christ Jesus were baptized into his death? We were therefore buried with him through baptism into death." Here Paul teaches that when the believer is united to Christ through Christ's baptism by his Spirit into his body, a decisive change occurs in him, of which the ordinance of baptism is the outward sign and seal, namely, he

---

32. Of the more than two hundred [!] interpretations that have been placed on this verse, John D. Reaume in "Another Look at 1 Corinthians 15:29, 'Baptized for the Dead,'" *Bibliotheca Sacra* 152 (October–December 1995): 457–75, considers the nine most likely views and opts for the view that takes the ὑπέρ, *hyper*, in the sense of "because of": "because of the influence of deceased Christians." See also BAGD, "βαπτίζω [*baptizō*]," 2bg, 132, for other literature.

dies to sin's reign and lives for righteousness. If then the import of water baptism is symbolically that of union with Christ, it follows that baptism confirms, that is, serves as the seal of, our union with him in his crucifixion, death, burial, and resurrection. Murray writes: "the fact of having died to sin is the fundamental premise of the apostle's thought. . . . What [he] has in view is the once-for-all definitive breach with sin which constitutes the identity of the believer [concerning which breach baptism is the sign and seal]."[33]

"In demonstration of his premise," Jones notes, "Paul appeals to the import of baptism. Baptism 'into Christ' signifies union with Christ and participation in all the privileges and blessings that reside in him—union with him in all aspects of his work as Mediator, including his death, of which his burial was the unambiguous confirmation."

Ephesians 4:5: "one Lord, one faith, one baptism." Here Paul's "one baptism" seems to refer to the ordinance of water baptism "inasmuch as the preceding verse has already spoken of 'one body and one Spirit' " (Jones). The significance which the apostle attaches to the ordinance is seen in his willingness to place it within the venue of the church's one body, one Spirit, one hope, one Lord, one faith, and one God and Father of all, who is over all and through all and in all. And his point appears to be that "all who participate in Christian baptism rightly administered are subjects of one and the same ordinance with the same spiritual import. Baptism thus stands [along with the other six 'one' things mentioned] as a witness against disunity in the church" (Jones).

Colossians 2:11–12: In these verses Paul expressly relates the two ordinances of Old Testament circumcision and New Testament baptism: *"In him you were also circumcised* [περιετμήθητε, *perietmēthēte*], in the putting off of the sinful nature, not with a circumcision done by the hands of men but with the circumcision done by Christ, *having been buried with him in [the Spirit's] baptism* and raised with him through faith."

The relation between Old Testament circumcision and New Testament baptism may be seen by simply reading the italicized words: "in him you were also circumcised . . . , having been buried with him in baptism." Clearly, for Paul the spiritual import of the New Testament sacrament of baptism—the outward sign and seal of the Spirit's inner baptismal work—is tantamount to that of Old Testament circumcision.[34] By the authority of Christ and his apostles, the church in

---

33. John Murray, *Romans* (Grand Rapids, Mich.: Eerdmans, 1968), 1:213.
34. Paul King Jewett, a Reformed Baptist theologian, acknowledges as much when he writes: "the only conclusion we can reach is that the two signs [circumcision and baptism], as outward rites, symbolize the same inner reality in Paul's thinking. Thus circumcision may fairly be said to be the Old Testament counterpart of Christian baptism. So far the Reformed argument, in our judgment, is biblical. In this sense baptism, to quote the Heidelberg Catechism, 'occupies the place of circumcision in the New Testament' " (*Infant Baptism and the Covenant of Grace* [Grand Rapids, Mich.: Eerdmans, 1978], 89).

this age administers baptism in lieu of circumcision. But it does so with the understanding that the spiritual significance of baptism as a sign is essentially the same as the former Old Testament ceremony, namely, a covenantal sign of the Spirit's act of cleansing from sin's defilement.

Mode

With the exception of those in the baptistic tradition who regard immersion followed by emersion as the only proper mode of baptism, the catholic (universal) position and practice of the Western church regarding the question of the proper mode of baptism is that "dipping of the person into the water is not necessary; but Baptism is rightly administered by pouring, or sprinkling water upon the person" (Westminster Confession of Faith, XXVIII/iii).[35]

Baptist apologists support their claim by contending that (1) βαπτίζω, *baptizō*, has the root meaning "to dip" or "to immerse,"[36] (2) John 3:23 implies that immersion was the mode of baptism John the Baptist employed from the fact that he was baptizing in Aenon near Salem "because there was plenty of water [ὕδατα πολλὰ, *hydata polla*, literally "many waters"] there," (3) New Testament descriptions of actual acts of baptism (Matt. 3:16; Mark 1:9, 10; Acts 8:36–39) support immersion as the proper mode of baptism, and (4) Romans 6:3–6 and Colossians 2:11–12 explicitly make the burial and resurrection of Christ the pattern for the mode of baptism, that is to say, just as Christ was buried so also to represent his death to sin the baptized party is to be immersed in water, and just as Christ rose from the dead so also to depict his resurrection to newness of life the baptized party is to emerge from water.

None of these contentions can be sustained. With reference to the meaning of βαπτίζω, *baptizō*,[37] while it may sometimes mean "to dip," there are several New

---

35. See Warfield's article, "The Archaeology of the Mode of Baptism," in *Studies in Theology* (1932; reprint, Edinburgh: Banner of Truth, 1988), 345–86.
36. Alexander Carson in his classic treatment, *Baptism in Its Mode and Subjects* (Philadelphia: American Baptist Publication Society, 1845), argues that the root meaning of βαπτίζω, *baptizō*, is to "dip, and nothing but dip," with no intimation in the word itself that the object "immersed" is to be withdrawn from the substance into which it has been immersed. Emersion in the case of the ordinance of baptism necessarily follows simply as a matter of course since the living subject cannot be left in an immersed state in the baptismal water.
37. James W. Dale argues in his monumental four-volume work on baptism (*Classic Baptism, Judaic Baptism, Johannic Baptism,* and *Christic and Patristic Baptism*) that βαπτίζω, *baptizō*, does not mean "to dip" (that is, "to put into [and to remove from]") but rather "to put together so as to remain together," with its import "in nowise governed by, or dependant upon, any form of act" (*Classic Baptism* [1867; reprint, Phillipsburg, N.J.: Presbyterian and Reformed, 1989], 126). He shows that the word in classical Greek means a variety of things, including to plunge, to drown, to steep, to bewilder, to dip, to tinge, to pour, to sprinkle, and to dye! He concludes by saying:

Testament contexts where it *must* mean simply "to wash," with no specific mode of washing indicated. For example, ἐβαπτίσθη, *ebaptisthē,* hardly means "was immersed" in Luke 11:38, where we are informed that a certain Pharisee, "noticing that Jesus did not first *wash* [literally "was not baptized"] before the meal, was surprised." Surely this Pharisee did not expect Jesus (note that Jesus the *person* is the subject of the verbal action and not simply Jesus' hands) to be immersed in water before every meal! Surely his surprise was provoked by Jesus not ritually washing his hands before eating, in keeping with the ceremony referred to in Matthew 15:2 and Mark 7:3–4, most probably by having water poured over them (see the practice alluded to in 2 Kgs. 3:11 and Luke 7:44).

Speaking of Mark 7:3–4, in verse 4 we read: "And [when they come] from the marketplace, except they ceremonially wash [βαπτίσωνται, *baptisōntai,* literally 'baptize themselves'] they do not eat." Surely again, βαπτίσωνται, *baptisōntai,* cannot mean that "the Pharisees and all the Jews" *immersed* themselves every time they returned home from the market.[38] Verse 4 also refers to "ceremonial washing [βαπτισμοὺς, *baptismous*] of cups and utensils and copper bowls," with the Received Text even adding "and beds [κλινῶν, *klinōn*]." While κλινῶν, *klinōn,* is textually suspect, at least it must be acknowledged that this textual tradition saw nothing incongruous about the idea of "baptizing" beds (see Lev. 15), an act which could be carried out quite simply if the beds in question were sprinkled but which would be quite difficult if the beds, sometimes quite elaborate in construction, were immersed.

To say that John 3:23 implies something about the mode of baptism from its notice that there were "many [springs of] waters" at Aenon (which proper name means "springs") where John was baptizing is a stretch of exegesis. The "many springs" would have been necessary to any great gathering of people such as came

---

        Baptism is a myriad-sided word, adjusting itself to the most diverse cases.

        Agamemnon was baptized; Bacchus was baptized; Cupid was baptized; Cleinias was baptized; Alexander was baptized; Panthia was baptized; Otho was baptized; Charicles was baptized; and a host of others were baptized, each differing from the other in the nature or the mode of their baptism, or both.

        A blind man could more readily select any demanded color from the spectrum, or a child could more readily thread the Cretan labyrinth, than could "the seven wise men of Greece" declare the nature, or mode, of any given baptism by the naked help of βαπτίζω, *baptizō*. (353–54)

        Therefore, Jay Adams in his foreword to Dale's *Classic Baptism* rightly declares that "water baptism is an appropriate 'uniting ordinance' that permanently introduces Christians to the visible Church, just as Spirit baptism permanently unites Christians with the invisible Church."

38. A variant reading in ℵ and B actually reads ῥαντίσωνται, *rhantisōntai,* literally, "sprinkle," the thought being: "except they sprinkle [themselves, or what is] from the market place, they do not eat [it]."

to the Baptist to hear him and to receive baptism from his hand, but hardly for baptismal purposes. They would have been necessary for the very sustaining of life! And the streams of Israel which are formed from springs are usually rather shallow.

Then it is often argued that the expressions, "went down into the water" and "came up out of the water," used in connection with Jesus' baptism (Matt. 3:16; Mark 1:9, 10) and that of the Ethiopian eunuch (Acts 8:36–39) indicate that immersion followed by emersion was the mode of baptism practiced in these instances. But a careful reading of the text in each instance will show that the act of baptism, whatever mode was being employed, was a separate act that *followed* upon the going down into and *preceded* the coming up out of the water. It should be noted too, in the case of the eunuch's baptism, that Luke records that both Philip and the eunuch went down into and came up out of the water. Clearly these acts in no way constituted any part of the baptismal act itself. Therefore, nothing can be definitely determined from these expressions regarding the mode of the baptismal act itself which occurred between the acts of going down and coming up.[39] Moreover, never does the New Testament describe the act itself of baptism as going down into or coming up out of water. It is a distinct possibility that what made the Ethiopian eunuch even think of and request baptism in the first place, reading Isaiah 53:7–8 as he had been doing, was his having read just moments before the words of Isaiah 52:15: "So will [my Servant] sprinkle [יַזֶּה, *yazzeh*, that is, cleanse] many nations."[40] (He also may have been familiar with Ezekiel 36:25: "I will

---

39. However, because the Spirit's coming at Pentecost is described in terms of a "pouring out" (Acts 2:17–18, 33), because both John the Baptist (Matt. 3:11) and Jesus (Acts 1:5) call the Spirit's coming at Pentecost a "baptizing" work by Jesus, and because both John and Jesus compare the former's baptismal activity with the latter's baptismal activity, the intimation is that the mode of John's earlier baptismal activity, like the latter's, was by affusion or sprinkling.

40. By his study of יַזֶּה, *yazzeh*, the Hiphil imperfect of נָזָה, *nāzâh*, in Isaiah 52:15, in his *Studies in Isaiah* (Grand Rapids, Mich.: Eerdmans, 1954), 199–206, Edward J. Young demonstrates that the root, which occurs twenty-four times in the Old Testament, is a technical ritual word found mainly in the Levitical legislation (see Lev. 4:6; 6:27; 8:11; 14:7a; 16:14; Num. 19:18) denoting ceremonial sprinkling with oil, oil and blood, or water, and means "will sprinkle" and not "will startle" or "astonish" as the Septaugintal θαυμάσονται, *thaumasontai*, suggests. In light of all the evidence, I concur with Henri Blocher's judgment (*The Songs of the Servant* [London: Inter-Varsity, 1975], 61: "the burden of proof . . . rests with those who would reject 'sprinkle.'"

It should be noted that some Pharisees asked John the Baptist, after he had denied that he was the Messiah, Elijah, or the Prophet, "Why then do you baptize?" (John 1:25). Where did they get the notion that the Messiah would baptize? Without a translation such as "sprinkle" in Isaiah 52:15, there is no other prophecy in the Old Testament that expressly states this. But then this suggests that John's mode of baptizing was by sprinkling, because it was his activity that provoked the Pharisees' question in the first place. They saw him sprinkling, and knowing of the prophecy in Isaiah 52:15, they asked him whether he was the Messiah.

sprinkle [וְזָרַקְתִּי], *wᵉzāraqtî*][41] clean water on you, and you will be clean.") Thus the preponderance of evidence suggests that the eunuch's baptism was accomplished by sprinkling. Finally, it may also be noted that the act of going down into the water, say to the knees or thighs, would have been an appropriate procedure for a baptism by sprinkling or by pouring, making it much easier for the baptizer to raise the water from the water's surface to the top of the subject's head.

In the case of Saul's baptism, the baptism of the household of Cornelius, and that of the household of the Philippian jailer, since each of these acts of baptism was carried out within a home (Acts 9:11; 10:25; 16:32), and in the last case sometime after midnight (Acts 16:33) but before dawn (v. 35), it is virtually certain that these baptisms would not have been by immersion, since few homes in those times would have had facilities for such an act (and again in the last case Paul would have hardly taken the jailer's household to a river after midnight), but most probable that they would have been performed by sprinkling.

Furthermore, the author of Hebrews characterizes all of the ceremonial sprinklings of the Old Testament—the sprinkling (ῥαντίζουσα, *rhantizousa*) of those who were ceremonially unclean with the blood of goats and bulls and the ashes of a heifer (9:13), Moses' sprinkling (ἐράντισεν, *erantisen*) of the scroll and all the people with the blood of calves mixed with water and scarlet wool (9:19), and his sprinkling (ἐράντισεν, *erantisen*) of the tabernacle and everything used in its ceremonies with blood (9:21)—as "baptisms [βαπτισμοῖς, *baptismois*]," that is, as "ceremonial washings" (9:10). Moreover, the same writer immediately thereafter and Peter as well speak of Christians as being "sprinkled" with Christ's blood:

> Hebrews 10:22: "Let us draw near to God with a sincere heart in full assurance of faith, having our hearts sprinkled [ῥεραντισμένοι, *rherantismenoi*] to cleanse us from a guilty conscience and having our bodies washed with pure water." (See Ezek. 36:25)
>
> Hebrews 12:24: "[You have come] to Jesus the mediator of a new covenant, and to the sprinkled blood [αἵματι ῥαντισμοῦ, *haimati rhantismou*] that speaks a better word than the blood of Abel."

---

41. The Hebrew Old Testament employs two verb roots, נָזָה, *nāzâh*, and זָרַק, *zāraq*, both meaning "to sprinkle," when it speaks of ceremonial washings. For the usage of the former, see footnote 40. The latter root seems to denote a heavier sprinkling than the former, executed with the whole hand rather than with the finger (Exod. 9:8; 29:20–21). It occurs thirty-five times, and, like the former root, is found mainly in the Levitical legislation (e.g. Exod. 24:6; Lev. 1:5, 11; 3:2, 8, 13; 2 Kings 16:13, 15; Ezek. 36:25; 43:18). *Combined, the approximately sixty references to various sprinklings in the Old Testament, according to the author of Hebrews, may all be described as "baptisms" (Heb. 9:10)!*

1 Peter 1:2: "who have been chosen . . . for obedience to Jesus Christ and sprinkling [ῥαντισμὸν, *rhantismon*] by his blood." (See Isa. 52:15)

Surely the universe of discourse of the Book of Hebrews would warrant the conclusion that the author would have regarded the Christian's "sprinkling" with Christ's blood—the New Testament fulfillment of the Old Testament typical sacrifice—as a spiritual "baptism" as well. And just as surely, "it would be strange if the baptism with water which represents the sprinkling of the blood of Christ could not properly and most significantly be performed by sprinkling."[42]

Finally, Christ's baptismal work (see Matt. 3:11; Mark 1:8; Luke 3:16; John 1:33; Acts 1:5; 2:33; 1 Cor. 12:13), by which he baptizes the elect by or with his Spirit, is invariably described in terms of the Spirit "coming upon" (Acts 1:8, 19:6), being "poured out upon" (Acts 2:17, 33), or "falling upon" (Acts 10:44; 11:15). Note also Romans 5:5: "God has poured out his love into our hearts by the Holy Spirit." Now what work does the outward ordinance of baptism signify and seal if not the Savior's spiritual baptismal work? After all, no other saving work is termed "baptism" in the New Testament epistles. Therefore, if the ordinance of baptism is to signify Christ's baptismal work, which is uniformly described in terms of affusion, then it follows that the ordinance should reflect the affusionary pattern of Christ's baptismal work.

With reference to the alleged pattern of baptism in Romans 6:2–6 and Colossians 2:11–12 as being that of burial and resurrection, a careful analysis of these passages will show that Paul's basic thesis is the believer's union with Christ in his crucifixion, death, burial, and resurrection as the antidote to antinomianism. Baptism by immersion does not modally reflect our crucifixion with Christ, which is one of the four aspects of our union with Christ which Paul mentions in the Romans passage. Murray is right when he affirms:

> It is arbitrary to select one aspect [of our union with Christ, namely, burial] and find in the language used to set it forth the essence of the mode of baptism. Such procedure is indefensible unless it can be carried through consistently. It cannot be carried through consistently here [since baptism by immersion does not and cannot visually reflect our being hung on the cross with Christ, which is as much an aspect of our union with Christ in the passage as our burial with him] and therefore it is arbitrary and invalid.[43]

---

42. Murray, *Christian Baptism*, 24.
43. Ibid., 31. It should be noted too that Christ was not "buried" at all in the sense that the Baptist mode of baptism requires. That is to say, his body was not placed *under* the ground. Rather, his body was temporarily deposited in a new tomb preparatory to what his disciples thought would be a permanent entombment after the Passover festivities.

We should no more single out our union with Christ in his burial and resurrection and make these two aspects of our union with him the pattern for the mode of baptism than we should appeal to Galatians 3:27 ("For all of you who were baptized into Christ have clothed yourselves with Christ," see also Col. 3:9–14) and argue on the basis of its statement that baptism should be carried out by requiring the new Christian to don a white robe, that is, by a "baptism by donning."

The fact is that *there is not a single recorded instance of a baptism in the entire New Testament where immersion followed by emersion is the mode of baptism.* The Baptist practice of baptism by immersion is simply based upon faulty exegesis of Scripture. The ordinance should not be represented as signifying Christ's burial and resurrection (aspects of the *accomplished* phase of his saving work, which the sacrament of the Lord's Supper memorializes) but rather his baptismal work (the *applicational* phase of his saving work). I would conclude therefore that "dipping of the person into the water is not necessary; but baptism is *rightly* administered by pouring, or sprinkling water upon the person."

Paedobaptism

Jesus' Great Commission mandated his church to make disciples of all nations, to baptize them, and to teach them whatever he has commanded. That all this applies to adults who accept the gospel is certain. But what about the infants and small children of the converts who receive the message of the kingdom?[44] Jones rightly poses the following questions: "Are [these little ones, by virtue of their parents' relationship to Christ,] also brought into a new relationship with Christ even though they are too young intellectually to apprehend the gospel and to appropriate it for themselves in the conscious exercise of repentance and faith? Does their psychological inability to fulfill the conditions required of adult converts render the

---

44. Since this is not a treatise on infant baptism *per se*, I must resist the impulse to write a lengthy exposition and defense of the practice and to answer the numerous objections to it. It must suffice at this time simply to refer the student to the following helpful treatments on the subject: Geoffrey W. Bromiley, *Children of Promise* (Grand Rapids, Mich.: Eerdmans, 1979), James M. Chaney, *William the Baptist* (Richmond, Va.: Presbyterian Committee of Publication, 1877), Joachim Jeremias, *Infant Baptism in the First Four Centuries,* trans. by David Cairns (Philadelphia: Westminster, 1962), Murray, *Christian Baptism,* and Robert G. Rayburn, *What About Baptism?* (St. Louis, Mo.: Covenant College Press, 1957). The following articles are also highly recommended: Herbert S. Bird, "Professor Jewett on Baptism," *Westminster Theological Journal* 31 (1969): 145–61, and John R. DeWitt, "Children and the Covenant of Grace," *Westminster Theological Journal* 37 (1975): 239–55. Finally, Benjamin B. Warfield, "The Polemics of Infant Baptism" in *Studies in Theology* (New York: Oxford University Press, 1932) is a masterful classic opposing the antipaedobaptist argument.

idea of discipleship meaningless so far as infants and small children are concerned? Or, [is their covenant status to be granted and baptism to be administered to them, and] are they to be discipled along with their believing parents, given the solidarity of the family unit?"

These are difficult questions over which sincere Christians strongly differ. Reformed paedobaptists must admit that nowhere in the New Testament can a direct command be found: "Baptize the infants and small children of believing parents and treat them as members of the church."[45] Antipaedobaptists therefore argue that to do so is both unscriptural and presumptuous. But Reformed paedobaptists by way of rejoinder, as Jones notes, register the following three points:

1. Just as there is no direct command to baptize these children and to treat them as "little Christians," so also antipaedobaptists must acknowledge that there is no direct command "Baptize *only* those who themselves make a personal profession of faith." Their restriction of baptism, then, only to those who can and do make a credible profession of faith in Christ is as much a deduction from Scripture as is the paedobaptist's practice. Whether it is a valid deduction remains to be seen.

2. The New Testament instances of baptisms which required or presupposed a credible profession of faith on the part of the person or persons baptized do not *ipso facto* rule out the practice of paedobaptism inasmuch as these instances cannot be made normative for the determination of whether the infant who is outside the context of the evangelistic appeal to adults (which is the customary "universe of discourse" of the subjects of the recorded instances of baptism) is a legitimate recipient of baptism. Such a determination must be made on other grounds.

3. Biblical principles have the force of commands by good and necessary inference; as a biblical principle (and this we will develop) "the sacramental continuity between the testaments is so strong that *not* to baptize children of believers would require some explicit word of repeal."[46]

It is clear therefore that both antipaedobaptists and paedobaptists argue by way of inference from more fundamental theological premises, focused largely on the relationship between the testaments, with the former stressing a dispensational discontinuity at this point in the covenant of grace, the latter stressing the continuity of the covenant of grace respecting this matter. It is my conviction that the paedobaptist position receives the warrant of Holy Scripture on the basis of the following line of reasoning.

---

45. Infant baptism would not be a violation of the regulative principle of worship, however, if it can be shown that it is a valid deduction from Scripture by good and necessary consequence.
46. Jones notes, by way of analogy, that "there is no *direct* biblical evidence for women partaking of the Lord's Supper; their participation is derived by theological inference, which no one seriously questions."

Beyond all controversy, throughout history the people of God have regarded their children as "a heritage from the Lord" (Ps. 127:3) and as a blessing from him (Ps. 128:3–4). In a special sense is this true of adult adherents of the Reformed faith as that faith is defined in the great Reformed creeds. According to these Reformed creeds, not only are believing parents to regard their children as blessings from God, but also they are to regard them as bonafide members of both the covenant of grace and the church of God (see Heidelberg Catechism, Question 74; Westminster Confession of Faith, XXV/ii). Furthermore, precisely because these creeds view these infant children in this light, they mandate that Christian parents are to recognize that certain rights, including the right to baptism,[47] accrue to their children which do not pertain to the offspring of unbelieving parents. These same parents are also to recognize that to deny their children these God-ordained rights is virtually to deny that they possess the status in the kingdom of God which God himself guarantees to them, and is to commit "great sin" against God (Westminster Confession of Faith, XXVIII/v).

The Reformed paedobaptist position is, of course, based upon the unity of the covenant of grace and the oneness of the people of God in all ages. As Murray declares: "The basic premise of the argument for infant baptism is that the New Testament economy is the unfolding and fulfillment of the covenant made with Abraham and that the necessary implication is the unity and continuity of the church."[48]

Old Testament Testimony

The sign and seal of the covenant of grace during its "Abrahamic" administration, we learn from Genesis 17:1–16, was circumcision.[49] By divine direction, under the Abrahamic covenant male infants were to receive the sign of the covenant on their eighth day of life (17:12).[50] Accordingly, Abraham circumcised

---

47. The covenant child's right to baptism is based, not only upon his covenant status, but also upon the covenantal principle, enunciated by Peter in Acts 10:47, that the sign of the covenant should not be denied to those to whom the covenantal thing signified belongs.
48. Murray, *Christian Baptism*, 48. See part three, chapter fourteen, for the biblical case for the unity of the covenant of grace and the oneness of the people of God in all ages.
49. So closely connected is the sign (circumcision) and the spiritual reality it signifies (the verities of the covenant of grace) that Stephen is willing to describe the Abrahamic covenant by its sign. He states that God "gave Abraham the covenant of circumcision" (Acts 7:8).
50. Old Testament circumcision was not simply a badge of ethnic identity; like New Testament baptism it signified and sealed the removal of sin's defilement and the imputation of the righteousness of faith, having as its basic import union with God. This is not simply a Pauline perception (see Rom. 4:11) being read back into the Old Testament. Already in Old Testament times the import of the rite began to be transferred metaphorically into the spiritual realm, and it came to be understood as conveying symbolically the removal of sin's defilement through salvation (Exod. 6:13, 30; Lev. 19:23; 26:41; Deut. 10:16; 30:6; Jer. 4:4; 6:10; 9:25–26; see Rom. 2:25–29; 4:11; Eph. 2:11; Phil. 3:3; Col. 2:11–12).

Ishmael, who was already thirteen years old (17:23–25), and later Isaac at eight days of age (21:4).

It should be noted here that the *ground* of applying the sign of the covenant to infants was simply the divine institution. So it is with infant baptism: "It is one of the ways by which it has pleased God to administer the covenant of grace in the world; it is one of the ordinances by means of which it pleases God to fulfill his covenant purposes from age to age and from generation to generation."[51] The ground of infant baptism is not then presumptive election or presumptive regeneration but rather the covenant relation in which the child stands and the ordinance or command of God. When Reformed paedobaptists are asked: "Upon what ground do you baptize infants," they should understand that it is sufficient to answer: "Because our infants are covenant children, and God has commanded that covenant children receive the sign of the covenant." Just as in the case of adults who are baptized by divine ordinance on the basis of an intelligent and credible confession and not on the basis of the church's judgment to the effect that the person is one of God's elect or is regen-

---

It is often asked why God selected a covenant sign in Old Testament times which could be applied only to male infants. In response, it must be noted that the world of the Old Testament was a patriarchal world. Originally its patriarchy was a perfect patriarchy, reflecting the federal headship of the male in the pre-Fall Edenic condition. After the Fall patriarchal culture continued to prevail by divine design (see Gen. 3:16) but with many injustices toward women occurring due to mankind's fallen state (Gen 6:2; 12:11–20; 16:3; 20:2–18; 26:6–7; Deut. 24:1–4, see Matt. 19:7–9). Nevertheless, God continued to honor the original patriarchal arrangement of Eden, even in its corrupted character, and assigned to the male rite of circumcision the role of being the sign of his covenant with Abraham. It should be noted that the sign of circumcision, by the very limits to its applicability, allowed for the sign that replaced it (baptism in the New Testament age) to signify by its capacity for application to *both* genders the *universality and extension of grace* to all nations and the further enlarging of Christian liberty, the greater boldness of access to the throne of grace, and the fuller communication of the Spirit of God.

How can we explain God's willingness to recognize and adapt himself to a *sinful* patriarchal culture? The answer is to be found in what our Lord said about the hardness of men's hearts (Matt. 19:8). Just as God permitted men to put away their wives for light causes in Old Testament times due to the hardness of men's hearts (which divorces entailed many injustices toward these women), so also he adapted himself, *in form but never in principle*, to the albeit-corrupted patriarchal culture of the Old Testament which wrongly held that it was the male who had superior worth. God as Teacher came to the "students" of the fallen ancient world where he found them, in ethical ignorance, accepted for a time this ignorance because they were not able to bear instantly total and radical change, and began to instruct them in a true ethic and to prepare them for the coming messianic age in which it would be recognized that the man and the woman were all along heirs together of the grace of life. Never being satisfied with where his pupils were, he always insisted that they mature and forsake more and more their evil thoughts and ways and seek more and more his holy thoughts and ways.

51. Murray, *Christian Baptism*, 56.

erate, so the church should baptize its infants because God requires that covenant children be baptized and for no other reason.

Subsequent confirmations of the Abrahamic covenant with Isaac and Jacob indicated that the children within the patriarchal community were to be regarded as standing within the compass of the covenant promise:

> Genesis 26:3–4: "I will be with you and will bless you. For to you and your descendants I will give all these lands and will confirm the oath I swore to your father Abraham. I will make your descendants as numerous as the stars in the sky and will give them all these lands, and through your offspring all nations on earth will be blessed."
>
> Genesis 28:13–14: "I will give you and your descendants the land on which you are lying. Your descendants will be like the dust of the earth, and you will spread out to the west and to the east, to the north and to the south. All peoples on earth will be blessed through you and your offspring."

The seriousness with which God took both the covenant status of children and his insistence upon their receiving the sign of the covenant is made plain by his warning: "Any uncircumcised male, who has not been circumcised in the flesh, will be cut off from his people; he has broken my covenant" (Gen. 17:14). The same divine seriousness is strikingly portrayed when God later "met Moses [on the latter's return trip to Egypt] and was about to kill him" for failing to circumcise his son. "But Zipporah . . . cut off her son's foreskin and touched Moses' feet with it. . . . So the LORD let him alone" (Exod. 4:24–26).

That infants and young children were clearly regarded as members of the Old Testament covenant community is evident in many other Old Testament passages as well. They are specifically mentioned as present in the congregation of Israel on the plains of Moab when Moses reconfirmed the covenant with the second generation after the exodus from Egypt. Here are Moses' words which indicate that children were included in the covenant confirmation at that time:

> Carefully follow the terms of this covenant, so that you may prosper in everything you do. All of you are standing today in the presence of the Lord your God—your leaders and chief men, your elders and officials, and all the other men of Israel *together with your children* and your wives. . . . You are standing here in order to enter into a covenant with the Lord your God, a covenant the Lord is making with you this day and sealing with an oath, to confirm you this day *as his people,* that he may be your God as he promised you and as he swore to your fathers, Abraham, Isaac, and Jacob. (Deut 29:9–13; emphases added)

Thus that entire generation of Israelites was circumcised at Gilgal as soon as it crossed the Jordan into Canaan (Josh. 5:2–9).

When the terms of this covenant were later reviewed at Mount Ebal under Joshua's leadership, in keeping with Moses' requirement (see Deut. 31:10–13), "there was not a word of all that Moses had commanded that Joshua did not read to the whole assembly of Israel, including women *and children*" (Josh. 8:35).

When Jehoshaphat later prayed for Judah's military victory over Moab and Ammon, "all of the men of Judah, with their wives and children and little ones stood before the Lord" (2 Chron. 20:13; see also 2 Chron. 31:18).

And when the prophets called Old Testament Israel to repentance, children and nursing infants were expressly required to be present in Israel's solemn assemblies as a sign of national repentance:

> Joel 2:15–16: "Blow the trumpet in Zion, declare a holy fast, call a sacred assembly. Gather the people, consecrate the assembly; bring together the elders, gather the children, those nursing at the breast."

New Testament Testimony

The Old Testament practice of reckoning children among the covenant people of God and having the covenant sign administered to them in infancy is nowhere repealed in the New Testament. To the contrary,

> since the new covenant is characterized by greater, not lesser, privilege and blessing, one would expect some definite word if the established practice (1900 years in place) was supposed to be discontinued. What one finds instead of repeal are definite indications that God continues to work within the solidarity of the family in covenant relationship. (Jones)[52]

To see this, consider the following data:

---

52. Berkouwer comments: "Against those who asked for a direct scriptural proof in which infant baptism was divinely commanded, the Reformers courageously pointed at the injustice of this question. In response, they asked their critics precisely where the Bible says that this fundamental Covenant relation is broken in the New Covenant" (*The Sacraments*, 175).

    Murray, likewise, queries: "Does the New Testament revoke or does it provide any intimation of revoking so expressly authorised a principle as that of the inclusion of infants in the covenant and their participation in the covenant sign and seal? . . . Has [this practice] been discontinued? Our answer to these questions must be, that we find no evidence of revocation. In view of the fact that the new covenant is based upon and is the unfolding of the Abrahamic covenant, in view of the basic identity of meaning attaching to circumcision and baptism, in view of the unity and continuity of the covenant of grace administered in both dispensations, we can affirm with confidence that evidence of revocation or repeal is mandatory if the practice or principle has been discontinued under the New Testament" (*Christian Baptism*, 52–53).

1. When Jesus' disciples attempted to send parents away who had responded to the message of the kingdom and who were bringing their children ("even the babies" [καὶ τὰ βρέφη, *kai ta brephē*; Luke 18:15]) to him that he might touch them and give them his blessing, Jesus commanded his disciples: "Let *the little children* [τὰ παιδία, *ta paidia*] come to me, and do not hinder them, for the kingdom of God belongs to such as these," belongs, that is, "to little children such as these [who have covenant parents]," not simply to such as are *like* little children but actually to these covenant children themselves! Jesus' pronouncement makes clear that covenant children

> are not to be excluded as a matter of course from the new gathering of the people of God, the household or family of God, the kingdom of our Lord Jesus Christ. Jesus welcomes them . . . and makes the ringing assertion that the kingdom of God belongs to such. (Jones)

Jesus then adds: "I tell you the truth, anyone who will not receive the kingdom of God like a little child will never enter it." Then we read: "He took the children in his arms, put his hands on them and blessed them" (Mark 10:13–16; see Matt. 19:13–15; Luke 18:15–17). Now Jesus' blessing, surely verbal and audible, was hardly comprehended by these infants and children, but this absence of comprehension on their part in no way nullified either the fact of the blessing itself on his part or the reality of their covenantal inclusion in the kingdom of God.[53]

2. On the Day of Pentecost, when the Holy Spirit was uniquely manifested in fulfillment of Joel's great prophecy (Acts 2:1–4; see Joel 2:28–32), in his explanatory sermon concerning this epochal event inaugurating the new dispensation of the covenant of grace Peter affirmed that "the promise [of the Holy Spirit] is for you *and your children* [τέκνοις, *teknois*] and for all who are afar off—for all whom the Lord our God will call" (Acts 2:39). This Petrine declaration assures us that the ancient promise that embraced children along with their parents continues unabated in this age. Murray's comment on Peter's words is pertinent:

> Nothing could advertise more conspicuously and conclusively that this principle of God's gracious government, by which children along with their parents are the possessors of God's covenant promise, is fully operative in the New Testament as well as in the Old than this simple fact that on the occasion of Pentecost

---

53. Clowney (*The Church,* 283) observes: "Blessing is always in the divine name. Since Christian baptism is a naming ceremony, . . . the question about infant baptism compares to the benediction at the end of a worship service [which is also regularly done in the divine name]. Does it include the infants in the arms of the believing parents who hold them?" His extended response is in the affirmative. See here Joel 2:15–16.

Peter took up the refrain of the old covenant and said, "The promise is to you and to your children."[54]

3. At least twice in Acts (16:15, 33, 34; see 11:14; 16:31) and once in 1 Corinthians (1:16) reference is made to what has come to be termed "household baptisms," where the adult who came to faith clearly had his family baptized with him. Luke reports that after Lydia responded to Paul's message, "she and the members of her household were baptized" (16:15). While Luke declares that the Lord opened *her* heart to receive the things spoken by Paul, he says nothing of her household's faith, and yet they were baptized as well.

In the case of the Philippian jailer, there is a sustained emphasis in this pericope (Acts 16:31–34) upon the jailer's faith alone. Luke informs us that, after Paul and Silas had instructed him, "Believe [Πίστευσον, *pisteuson*—first aorist active imperative second masculine *singular*] in the Lord Jesus, and you will be saved—you and your household," they spoke the word of the Lord "to him, with all who were in his house" being present at that time (v. 32). Then after the jailer had washed the prisoners' wounds, "immediately *he and all his family* were baptized, and bringing them up into his house, he set a meal before them and he greatly rejoiced with all his house because *he* had believed [πεπιστευκώς—perfect active participle nominative *singular* used causally] in God." While it is virtually certain that the jailer's entire family heard the gospel, Luke says nothing at all about his family's believing (they may have; we simply do not know). Rather, he pointedly highlights only the jailer's faith, and yet his entire household was baptized as well.[55]

4. Paul expressly declares that the children [τὰ τέκνα, *ta tekna*] of even one Christian parent are holy (ἅγια, *hagia*) (1 Cor. 7:14). Paul's concern in this passage is to show that "mixed" marriages, that is, marriages between a believer and an unbeliever, are "holy," and he proves the sanctifying effect of the believing spouse on the marriage relationship (which was the issue in question) by appealing to the sanctifying effect of the believing parent upon the children of the marriage union (which was not in question). Since the children are "holy," the marriage cannot be regarded as unholy. And since he cannot mean by this exceptional word "holy" that these children are actually saved by the relation which they sustain to the believing parent, Paul doubtless intended to ascribe covenant status to children of parents

---

54. Murray, *Christian Baptism*, 71.
55. I would counsel that the paedobaptist should not put much weight on these "household baptisms," for even if he could convince the antipaedobaptist that in these cases the believer's household was baptized on the basis of the believer's faith, while such a view surely underscores the covenant character of the Christian family, he cannot prove that any of these households had infants or small children in them.

[942]

who are themselves members of the church of Jesus Christ—the New Testament form of the community rooted spiritually in the covenant with Abraham.

5. Paul also presupposes the covenant status of children when he includes them among the "saints" at Ephesus (Eph. 1:1; 6:1).

6. The New Testament speaks of the Genesis flood and the exodus from Egypt as "types" of Christian baptism. Peter notes that Noah and his sons, along with their wives, were "baptized" by the waters of the flood (1 Pet. 3:20–21). And Paul declares that all Israel was "baptized into Moses in the cloud and in the sea" (1 Cor. 10:1–2).[56] In both Old Testament "types" an elect people were delivered from death, and in both the covenant is made not only with individuals (Noah and Moses) but also with their family and people respectively in both of which were included children and others who did not have faith in the God of the covenant (Ham in the case of Noah; the wilderness complainers and idolaters in the case of Moses). As Geoffrey W. Bromiley remarks:

> The point is not merely that in these actions, which are types of baptism, the children share the experience with their parents. It is rather that the covenantal action of God is not with individuals in isolation, but with families, or with individuals in families so that those belonging to the individuals are also separated as the people of God and in a very special sense come within the sphere of the divine covenant.[57]

7. I do not wish to place much weight on early church testimony with regard to this matter since Scripture alone is authoritative for doctrine and since sacerdotalism began to emerge early in church history and doubtless influenced the views of the early fathers, but it is a fact that there is evidence that infant baptism was practiced in the ancient church. Justin Martyr (born in the first century) speaks of those who "were made disciples of Christ [presumably by baptism] from childhood [ἐκ παίδων, *ek paidōn*]."[58] Irenaeus (c. 130–c. 200) affirmed: "[Christ] came to save all through means of himself—all, I say, who through him are born again [his reference to the new birth here almost certainly refers to baptism, since it was a doctrinal commonplace in the early church, as I said, that baptism regenerated the soul] to God—infants, and children, and boys, and youths, and old men."[59] Tertullian (145–220),

---

56. A. A. Hodge in his commentary, *The Confession of Faith* (1869; reprint; Edinburgh: Banner of Truth, 1992), 342–43, wryly comments: "the Egyptians who were immersed were *not* baptized; and the Israelites who were baptized were *not* immersed" and "the very gist of [Noah's family's salvation of which baptism is said to be antitypical] consisted in their *not* being immersed." I might add, Noah's family was "sprinkled" by the rain that fell (Gen. 7:12–13).
57. Bromiley, *Children of Promise*, 16.
58. Justin Martyr, *Apology*, I.15.
59. Irenaeus, *Against Heresies*, II.xxii.4.

while counseling the postponement of baptism for children until "they have become able to know Christ," recognized that infant baptism was commonly practiced in his day. That his counsel here is something of an anomaly may be illustrated by the fact that he also counseled postponing baptism for unwed and widowed people.[60] Origen (185–254) writes: "The church has received a tradition from the apostles [παράδοσις ἀποστολική, *paradosis apostolikē*] to give baptism even to infants."[61] In response to a letter from Bishop Fidus, Cyprian (c. 200–58) in A.D. 253 placed the question of infant baptism before a council of 66 bishops, all of whom agreed that parents should not wait until the eighth day to baptize their infants but should have them baptized as early as the second or third day after birth.[62] Augustine, while he wrongly attached sacerdotal powers to infant baptism,[63] "inferred from the fact that it was generally practiced by the Church throughout the world in spite of the fact that it was not instituted in Councils, that it was in all probability settled by the authority of the apostles."[64] Even the heretic Pelagius (late fourth/early fifth centuries), desiring to insure his opponents of his orthodoxy, declared: "We hold likewise one baptism, which we aver ought to be administered to infants in the same sacramental formula as it is to adults."[65] In light of these early witnesses to the practice, Berkhof appears to be justified in concluding that the legitimacy of the practice of infant baptism "was not denied until the days of the Reformation, when the Anabaptists opposed it."[66]

Thus throughout Old Testament history, the New Testament age, and into the church age itself, children of covenant parents are expressly represented as possessing status in the covenant community. Reformed paedobaptists believe therefore that the baptism of their infants and young children today is a justifiable deduction from three undeniable biblical truths:

1. infant males received the sign and seal of the covenant of grace under its Old Testament administration;

2. the covenant of grace has a continuity and organic unity; the people of God are essentially one in all ages (see again part three, chapter fourteen); and

3. one can find no repeal in the New Testament of the Old Testament command to place the sign of the covenant of grace upon covenant children.

---

60. Tertullian, *On Baptism*, xviii.
61. Origen, *Epistle to the Romans*, V.9.
62. Cyprian, *Epistle LVIII. To Fidus, on the Baptism of Infants*, 2–6.
63. See, for example, his treatise, "On the Merits and Remission of Sins, and on the Baptism of Infants."
64. Berkhof, *Systematic Theology*, 635.
65. Augustine, *On the Grace of Christ*, xxxv.
66. Berkhof, *Systematic Theology*, 635.

A. A. Hodge writes:

> The only ground upon which this conclusion could be obviated would be that Christ in the gospel explicitly turns [believers' children] out of their ancient birth-right in the church.[67]

This, of course, he did not do. Antipaedobaptists, of course, insist that this is precisely what Christ did in the Great Commission (Matt. 28:19), where (so they insist) Christ defines his disciples as *only* those who are baptized and capable of being taught whatever he has commanded. But it is surely theological reaching of gigantic proportions to find in the words of the Great Commission a repeal of the covenant child's covenantal birthrights, for both "means"-requirements of the Great Commission (baptizing and teaching) can be and are regularly carried out in connection with the infant children of paedobaptist communions: they are baptized and from their earliest days are indoctrinated in all that Christ has commanded his disciples to do. In fact, if one wishes to argue from the requirements stipulated in the Great Commission as to which view more faithfully adheres to the Great Commission, it is the paedobaptist view, since antipaedobaptists do not baptize their infant children!

To summarize, because little children, even babes in arms, of covenant parents are covenant children, they are not to be excluded from the church as the kingdom of Christ. And just as the sign of the covenant of grace was placed upon male children of covenant parents in Old Testament times, so also the covenant sign, which is now baptism, should be administered to male and female infants and young children of covenant parents under the New Testament administration of the same covenant. Indeed, not to do so the Westminster Confession of Faith describes as "great sin" (XXVIII/v). And so universally is all this held and taught by the "fathers" of Reformed theology that Geerhardus Vos believes he is justified in writing:

> Just because the promises of God have been given to the assembly of believers, in its entirety, including their seed, this assembly is also a mother who conceives sons and daughters and is made to rejoice in her children by the Lord. The name "mother" signifies this truly Reformed point of view in distinction from other terms such as "institution of salvation."
>
> As far as we can discover, the leading spokesmen of Reformed theology are completely agreed on this. They all recognize that the church has received such promises for her offspring. They equally recognize that the consideration of these promises is the heart of the fruit of comfort which her view of the covenant offers.

---

67. Hodge, *The Confession of Faith*, 317.

SYSTEMATIC THEOLOGY

And they insist that remembrance of the promise must function as an urgent reason for rousing the seed of the church to embrace the covenant in faith. On both sides, parents and children, this conviction provides strength. Strength was provided in the days of old, in the golden age of the churches, a glorious comfort, finding its most beautiful fruition in the doctrine of salvation of the children of the covenant who die in infancy.[68] (See David's words, 2 Sam. 12:21–23)

Because of the practical implications of this theological conviction, however, Jones poses yet another series of question: "What should be the attitude of the church toward covenant children baptized in infancy as they grow to years of discretion? Should the church receive them as members of the body of Christ, having been made disciples in their baptism? Or should the church regard them as outside the body [of Christ] until they are made disciples through evangelism, that is, until such time as they make a credible profession of faith or critical 'decision' for Christ?" Regarding these questions even Reformed theological giants have differed.

Earlier Reformed writers, such as John Calvin (*Institutes,* IV.xvi.17), Theodore Beza, Peter Martyr Vermigli and Amandus Polanus, and some later Reformed thinkers such as Warfield and Murray reject the idea that the significance of paedobaptism is confined to external privilege or legal relationship without any reference to internal spiritual grace and blessing. Beza writes: "It cannot be the case that those who have been sanctified by birth and have been separated from the children of unbelievers, do not have the seed and germ of faith."[69] (If Beza had been more sensitive to the implications in the examples of Ishmael and Esau, he would have shown more caution when he wrote this.) Vermigli writes with greater caution: "We assume that the children of believers are holy, as long as in growing up they do not demonstrate themselves to be estranged from Christ. We do not exclude them from the church, but accept them as members, with the hope that they are partakers of the divine election and have the grace and Spirit of Christ, even as they are the seed of saints. On that basis we baptize them."[70] According to Polanus, children of believers should be baptized "because they have been purchased by the blood of Christ, have been washed from their sins, and possess therefore by the work of the Holy Spirit the thing signified. . . . Because the Holy Spirit is promised to them, they possess the Holy Spirit."[71]

68. Geerhardus Vos, "The Doctrine of the Covenant in Reformed Theology," in *Redemptive History and Biblical Interpretation: The Shorter Writings of Geerhardus Vos,* ed. Richard B. Gaffin Jr. (Phillipsburg, N.J.: Presbyterian and Reformed, 1980), 263.
69. Theodore Beza, *Confessio Christianae Fidei,* IV, 48.
70. Peter Martyr Vermigli, *Loci communes,* IV.8.7.
71. Amandus Polanus, *Syntagma theologiae Christianae* (this was Polanus's systematic theology, and it was published in English in 1595 as *The Substance of Christian Religion*), VI.55. Polanus, too, should have been more sensitive to the implications in the examples of Ishmael and Esau.

Warfield argues that in the case of infants of believers, as in the case of those who make a credible profession of faith, they may be recognized in the judgment of charity as belonging to Christ and received as such.[72] Murray writes: "Baptized infants are to be received as the children of God and treated accordingly."[73]

Other Reformed writers have expressed themselves much more cautiously, being satisfied to affirm merely that there is a seed for the Lord among the seed of believers. Though not denying that covenant children have the right to covenant baptism, James Henley Thornwell and Robert Lewis Dabney, for example, held that children of believers "are to be regarded as 'of the world and in the church,' and 'as unregenerate until their personal faith and repentance are evident' " (Jones).[74]

Where should we stand on this issue? I think I have shown that infants of believing parents are to be viewed as members of and under the governance and protection of Christ's church and should be treated as such. The Westminster Assembly's *Directory for the Public Worship of God* (1645) issues the following declarations on this matter:

> That the promise is made to believers and their seed; and that the seed and posterity of the faithful, *born within the church* have, by their birth, interest in the covenant, and right to the seal of it, and to the outward privileges of the church, under the gospel, no less than the children of Abraham in the time of the Old Testament; the covenant of grace, for substance, being the same; and the grace of God, and the consolation of believers, more plentiful than before . . . :

> That the Son of God admitted little children into his presence, embracing and blessing them, saying, For of such is the kingdom of God:

> That children, by baptism, are solemnly received into *the bosom of the visible church,* distinguished from the world, and them that are without, and united with believers; and that all who are baptized in the name of Christ, do renounce, and by their baptism are bound to fight against the devil, the world, and the flesh:

> That *they are [federally] Christians, and federally holy before baptism,* and therefore are they baptized.

---

72. Benjamin B. Warfield, "The Polemics of Infant Baptism," in *Studies in Theology* (New York: Oxford University Press, 1932), 389–90, 405–06.
73. Murray, *Christian Baptism,* 59. For full historical details, see Lewis Bevens Schenck, *The Presbyterian Doctrine of Children in the Covenant* (Yale: Yale University Press, 1940).
74. See especially James Henry Thornwell, *Collected Writings* (Richmond: Presbyterian Committee of Publication, 1886), 4:333–41, 348. Dabney's treatment may be found in his *Lectures in Systematic Theology,* Lecture LXVI, 792–95.

Neither my own nor the Westminster Assembly's statements should be construed as advocating baptismal regeneration or baptismal salvation, for neither regards the covenant child as necessarily regenerate or saved by virtue of his covenant status or his baptism.[75] Neither should the position I am urging here be made the ground for sloth in regard to the Christian parent's responsibility to rear his child in the one true faith. For the *Directory* goes on to state, as does the Confession of Faith (XXVIII/vi), that the *inward* grace of baptism is not tied to the moment of its *outward* administration (a fact evident in the case of Jacob who was circumcised as an infant but for whom the covenant verities signified and sealed by circumcision did not become personal and real until he wrestled with God many years later at Peniel); rather, "the fruit and power thereof reacheth to the whole course of our life." Accordingly, all present at any and every infant baptism are admonished to "look back to their baptism," to repent of their sins *against the covenant,* and to "improve and make right use of their baptism."[76] Parents are then exhorted in consideration of the great mercy of God to bring up their child "in the knowledge and grounds of the Christian religion, and in the nurture and admonition of the Lord."

Before the child's baptism, according to the *Directory*, the Lord is to be addressed and asked to "join the inward baptism of his Spirit with the outward baptism of water; make this baptism to the infant a seal of adoption, remission of sin, regeneration, and eternal life, and all other promises of the covenant of grace." *After* his

---

75. It is true that some Reformed theologians (e.g., Ursinus, Polanus, Cloppenburg, Voetius, Witsius) have taught that covenant children without distinction, by virtue of their status as covenant children, are regenerated from earliest childhood, are united to Christ, and are therefore entitled to baptism. Other Reformed writers (e.g., Zanchius, Ames, Spanheim, Ussher) hesitate to make any stipulation as to the time of regeneration for covenant children. I count myself among this latter group.

76. Larger Catechism, Question 167, asks: "How is our baptism to be improved by us?" The answer given is:

> The needful and much neglected duty of improving our baptism, is to be performed by us all our life long, especially in the time of temptation, and when we are present at the administration of it to others; by serious and thankful consideration of the nature of it, and of the ends for which Christ instituted it, the privileges and benefits conferred and sealed thereby, and our solemn vow made therein; by being humbled for our sinful defilement, our falling short of, and walking contrary to, the grace of baptism, and our engagements; by growing up to assurance of pardon of sin, and of all other blessings sealed to us in that sacrament; by drawing strength from the death and resurrection of Christ, into whom we are baptized, for the mortifying of sin, and quickening of grace; and by endeavouring to live by faith, to have our conversation in holiness and righteousness, as those that have therein given up their names to Christ; and to walk in brotherly love, as being baptized by the same Spirit into one body.

baptism the Lord is to be asked to "so teach him by his word and Spirit, and make his baptism effectual to him, and so uphold him by his divine power and grace, that by faith he may prevail against the devil, the world, and the flesh, till in the end he obtain a full and final victory." The *Directory* thus envisions, as Jones rightly states, "a dynamic, life-long relationship between [the infant's saving] faith [and Christian walk, on the one hand] and [his] baptism [on the other]."[77] All this means, Jones properly observes, that "the Christian family serves God's purposes of grace, not in any mechanical way, but rather through parental responsibility in providing spiritual nurture so that the child grows up in the knowledge of the Savior" and ratifies by his own personal profession and commitment when he reaches the years of discretion what his baptism signified and sealed from his infancy, becoming thereby a communing member of Christ's church. Jones states further:

> God's purpose to be our God and the God of our children is fulfilled in no other way than by obedience to his command in reliance upon his grace (see Gen. 18:16–18, Deut. 6:4–9). The key for [Christian] parents [with respect to the nurturing of their children in the things of the Lord and his Spirit] is to rely upon [God's] grace, and to place no confidence in the flesh as though the conversion and perseverance of their children were a foregone conclusion.

---

77. Jones observes that

> the Synod of New York and Philadelphia in 1729 adopted the *Westminster Confession of Faith* and *Catechisms* as doctrinal standards, and recommended use of the Westminster *Directory for Worship*. In 1788 the Synod ratified its own *Directory for Worship* [which was later] amended and ratified by the General Assembly in 1821. [This *Directory*] continued in use virtually unchanged into the twentieth century.
>
> The differences between the American *Directory* and that of the [earlier] Westminster Assembly are rather significant. The whole section on the administration of baptism in the American *Directory* is much abbreviated, and this is due not simply to a reduction in wordiness, but to a reduction in content. For example, whereas the Westminster *Directory* gave a full definition of what baptism seals, the American revision simply stated that baptism is a seal of the righteousness of faith. The significance of the element [water] and the action [sprinkling] are not given, and the exhortation to those present to look back to their own baptism is omitted. Prayer is to be offered before and after baptism, but no suggestion is made as to their content. Thus the official instruction given by the Presbyterian church at the time of infant baptism was significantly reduced, both reflecting and contributing to a decline in the significance attached to the sacrament. Moreover, in the instruction that is given, the emphasis subtly shifts from the child to the parent. A later chapter on admission to sealing ordinances introduces the thought that children born within the *pale* of the visible church are *dedicated* to God in baptism. The Westminster *Directory*, by way of contrast, thanked God for daily bringing children into the *bosom* of his church, to be *partakers* of the inestimable benefits purchased by Christ.

They should, in other words, always take their responsibility as covenant parents seriously and feel at liberty to speak to their children about Christ and to urge them to examine themselves to see if in fact they are "in the faith" (2 Cor. 13:5).

Nevertheless, where parents are faithful to the covenant the expectation is to be able to say [to their covenant children] in the words of Paul to Timothy: "From infancy [ἀπὸ βρέφους, *apo brephous*] you have known the holy scriptures which are able to make you wise for salvation through faith in Christ Jesus" (2 Tim. 3:15. See Psa. 22:9–10). (Jones)

In sum, a Christian family, with the support of a God-centered, Bible-believing church, is to be a school of Christ. And as schools, notoriously, include untaught children (that is what schools exist for), so the Christian family is to instruct its "holy" children in the faith once for all delivered unto the saints.

Efficacy

The Larger Catechism (Question 154) states that the sacraments "are made effectual to the elect for their salvation." It also declares (Question 161) that the sacraments "become effectual means of salvation" (see also Shorter Catechism, Question 91). At first blush these statements might appear to be advocating a sacerdotal salvation, but nothing could be farther from the truth. For the Westminster Assembly, when speaking of the sacraments as "effectual means" of salvation, also declared in no uncertain language that the sacraments are such, "not by any power in themselves, or any virtue derived from the piety or intention of him by whom they are administered, but only by the working of the Holy Spirit ["in them that by faith receive them"—Shorter Catechism, Question 91], and the blessing of Christ, by whom they are instituted." This statement clears its authors of the charge of an *ex opere operato* view of the sacraments. For they affirm that there is nothing in the sacraments *per se* that saves and that the piety of their administrator contributes nothing to the sacraments as means of salvation. Rather, the position advocated urges that the sacraments become effectual means of salvation for the elect only as Christ blesses them and as his Spirit works in them who by faith receive them.

Mark 16:16, Acts 2:38, and Acts 22:16 have been cited by sacerdotalists to teach that baptism is essential to the forgiveness of sins or at least to the reception of the gift of the Holy Spirit. So some exposition should be given concerning each of these verses.

Mark 16:16: "Whoever believes and is baptized will be saved, but whoever does not believe will be condemned." It must be noted that this verse appears in the so-called longer ending of the Gospel (16:9–20), which is supported by the Textus Receptus and some other late witnesses but not by the most reliable early manuscripts. It is also called into question by Eusebius and Jerome.[78] Its text-critical precariousness, therefore, makes the verse shaky ground for the advocacy of any form of baptismal salvation.

Acts 2:38: "Repent, and be baptized, everyone of you, in the name of Jesus Christ, for the forgiveness of your sins. And you will receive the gift of the Holy Spirit." I would urge that that part of Peter's admonition pertaining to baptism ("and be baptized, everyone of you, in the name of Jesus Christ") should be construed as a subsidiary adjunct (to be mentally read as if it had parentheses around it) to the main thought, which is "Repent . . . for the forgiveness of your sins." I say this because neither in Luke's account of Jesus' commission to the church in Luke 24:47 nor in Peter's later preaching in Acts 3:19 is anything said about baptism. If baptism were essential to salvation or to the reception of forgiveness and the gift of the Holy Spirit, omission of all reference to it in these contexts on the part of Jesus and Peter respectively would be exceedingly strange if not totally irresponsible (see also Paul's statement in 1 Cor. 1:17, and his insistence upon the need only for heart circumcision, baptism's Old Testament spiritual counterpart, in Rom. 2:26–29). Ned B. Stonehouse writes in this connection:

> In the several contexts where it has been possible to evaluate the question of the possible relation between baptism and the bestowal of the Spirit [Acts 2, 8, 10, 19], it has been unmistakably clear that baptism is not conceived of as conferring the Spirit. The two are intimately associated, and the gift of the Spirit may well be regarded as the normal concomitant of baptism, but it never appears as the inevitable or immediate consequence of baptism. It would therefore be rash to insist that the words, "and ye shall receive the gift of the Holy Spirit," in 2:38 indicate that baptism as such confers this gift.
>
> Moreover, Acts 2:38 itself provides a reason for resisting the conclusion that the gift is conditional upon baptism. For it must be underscored that Peter's basic and primary demand is for *repentance,* and his thought may be that the promise of the Spirit is assured upon the basis of conversion rather than merely as the consequence of baptism. This interpretation is given support by noting Peter's appeal in Acts 3:19: "Repent ye, therefore, and turn again, that your sins may be blotted out that so there may come seasons of refreshing from the presence of the Lord." Repentance will bring refreshing from on high, evidently through the work of the Spirit. But

---

78. See Bruce M. Metzger, *A Textual Commentary on the Greek New Testament* (New York: United Bible Societies, 1971), 122–26, for an explanation as to why this passage is not to be regarded as original to Mark's Gospel.

nothing is said about baptism. Similarly in Acts 2:38 baptism may be subordinated to repentance. That the accent falls more on repentance than upon baptism also gains support from the observation that in Luke 24:47 the gospel to be preached in Christ's name to all nations is summed up in terms of "repentance and remission of sins."[79]

Dana and Mantey[80] suggest a second interpretative approach to this verse, which also removes the sacerdotalism which some purport to see in it. They retain the baptism clause as a major part of Peter's injunction, but they urge that the preposition εἰς, *eis*, governing the phrase "forgiveness of your sins" should be given causal force: "because of the forgiveness of your sins." While this interpretation is a possibility, it should be noted that they offer it in the interest of their shared Baptist conviction that baptism must follow upon forgiveness.

Acts 22:16: "be baptized and wash your sins away." With regard to Paul's citation in Acts 22:16 of Ananias's words to him: "And now what are you waiting for? Get up, be baptized and wash your sins away, calling on his name," I would urge that the participial phrase "calling on his name," modifies the person designated in the second imperative, "wash away," as the nearest antecedent. This means that the instrumental cause of Paul's spiritual "washing" was not his baptism *per se* but his "calling upon the name" of Jesus that accompanied his baptism, which ordinance was in turn the visible sign of his spiritual "washing."

So in what way *does* baptism become an effectual means of salvation? In what way does baptism contribute to the salvation of the elect?[81] The answer is plain and simple. Just as Old Testament circumcision was a sign and seal of imputed righteousness received through faith apart from the rite of circumcision (Rom. 4:11), so also New Testament baptism, circumcision's sacramental successor, becomes effectual for salvation in its character as a sign and seal of the spiritual verities of the new covenant. *As a sign and seal it is a means of grace (1) to "signify" and (2) to "confirm" grace "through faith apart from the rite of baptism."*

---

79. Ned B. Stonehouse, "Repentance, Baptism and the Gift of the Holy Spirit," in *Paul Before the Areopagus and Other New Testament Studies* (Grand Rapids, Mich.: Eerdmans, 1957), 83–4.
80. Dana and Mantey, *A Manual Grammar of the Greek New Testament* (New York: Macmillan, 1927), 103–4.
81. The administration of baptism in the presence of unbelievers has a teaching and witnessing ministry to them when accompanied by the words of institution, as it signifies vividly to the senses of the ungodly their sinful and lost condition, the provisions of the gospel, and the privileges of union with Christ. But we are not concerned at this time with this aspect of baptism's sign and seal character. We are concerned rather with the efficacy of baptism for those who receive the ordinance.

Its Sign Character

Not only does God save the elect by uniting them to Christ through the ministry of his Word and Spirit, but also, with Christ's blessing resting upon the ordinance of baptism and with his Spirit working in them who by faith receive it, God by means of the baptismal act

> advertises that great truth [of their union with Christ] by an ordinance which portrays visibly to our senses the reality of this grace. It is a testimony which God has been pleased to give to us so that we may better understand the high privilege of union with the Father and the Son and the Holy Spirit. This is the purpose of baptism as a *sign*.[82]

Thus his baptism becomes a means (in addition to but not independent of the Word), by and with the blessing of God, of sensitizing the believing Christian mind to the privileged covenantal state in which the elect man stands. Baptism as the covenantal sign also reminds him of the covenant of grace *against which he sins* should he fail to be faithful to the spiritual verities signified by it. Thus his baptism in its sign character becomes an effectual means of sanctification to the Christian man and in this way is a means of grace to him.

Its Seal or "Confirming" Character

Just as God confirmed his promise to Noah by placing the bow in the cloud, just as God confirmed his promise to Abraham by an additional oath (Heb. 6:17–18), so also God confirms, certifies, authenticates, and guarantees the promised verities of his covenant with his people by adding the confirming seal of baptism to it. By adding baptism as an authenticating seal to his covenant promises,

> God provides us [additional certification] so that we may thereby be confirmed in the faith of his grace. He thereby shows more abundantly the immutability of the covenant relation in order that we may have strong consolation.[83]

All this is equally true for the baptized infant. Granting the fact that God does not normally render elect infants psychologically capable of the intelligent exercise of

---

82. Murray, *Christian Baptism*, 87.
83. Ibid.

saving faith in their infancy,[84] the infant's baptism in its "sign" and "seal" character still stands as a witnessing *sign* and confirming *seal* of the covenantal verities it signifies and seals.[85] The efficacy of these covenantal truths, moreover, is not tied necessarily to that moment when baptism is administered but is promised, exhibited, and conferred by the Holy Ghost to such (whether of age or infants) as that grace belongs to, according to the counsel of God's own will, in his appointed time. And as a sign and seal his baptism will either defend him against the charge of, or accuse him of, covenant infidelity in the day of judgment, depending upon whether the infant relates in faith or not to it when he reaches the years of discretion.

It is a cause of great concern to Reformed paedobaptists that multitudes of Christian parents within Christendom, under the influence of antipaedobaptist and dispensational teaching, are totally ignorant of the privileged covenant status that their children possess by virtue of the fact that they—the parents—are Christians. I have heard such parents insist that their children are no different in God's sight than the heathen until they turn to Christ by faith, that the first prayer God will hear from them is the cry: "God, have mercy upon me, the sinner." It is interesting, however, to observe these same parents instructing their children, even before they are able to make a credible profession of faith, to think of God the Father as their heavenly Father and to pray the "Lord's Prayer" with the believing members of the family. Their practice, inconsistently but happily, is better than their theology. Apparently these Christian parents instinctively assume that their children are in some sense special to the Lord even though they do not possess the theological grounding necessary to justify their assumption and their corresponding actions.[86] Reformed paedobaptists possess that theological grounding, namely, their biblically warranted appreciation of the privileged status of these little ones as covenant children born within the covenant community of grace. Therefore, they should do more to educate the larger church with respect to their concept of the unity of the covenant

---

84. I used the word "normally" here because elect infants can be and have been, by the Spirit's enabling, made susceptible to God's gracious work of regeneration and of uniting them to Christ while in infancy. I am thinking of John the Baptist, who was "filled with the Holy Spirit even from his mother's womb" (Luke 1:15), and who "leaped in [Elizabeth's] womb" when his mother heard Mary's greeting (Luke 1:41). See also the Messiah's testimony concerning his relation to the covenant God: "You brought me out of the womb; you made me trust in you even at my mother's breast. From birth I was cast upon you; from my mother's womb you have been my God" (Ps. 22:9–10).
85. Both its "sign" and "seal" character and the covenantal verities themselves which baptism "signifies" and "confirms" are still true and remain unaffected whether the child ever comes to faith or not.
86. Robert Lewis Dabney makes the same point in his *Lectures in Systematic Theology,* Lecture 66, 795.

of grace and the oneness of the people of God in all ages and the implications of these facts for their covenant children.

The Lord's Supper

Our Lord Jesus, in the night wherein He was betrayed, instituted the sacrament of His body and blood, called the Lord's Supper, to be observed in His Church, unto the end of the world, for the perpetual remembrance of the sacrifice of Himself in His death; the sealing all benefits thereof unto true believers, their spiritual nourishment and growth in Him, their further engagement in and to all duties which they owe unto Him; and, to be a bond and pledge of their communion with Him, and with each other, as members of His mystical body.

In this sacrament, Christ is not offered up to His Father; nor any real sacrifice made at all, for remission of sins of the quick or dead; but only a commemoration of that one offering up of Himself, by Himself, upon the cross, once for all: and a spiritual oblation of all possible praise unto God, for the same; so that the popish sacrifice of the mass (as they call it) is most abominably injurious to Christ's one, only sacrifice, the alone propitiation for all the sins of His elect.

The Lord Jesus hath, in this ordinance, appointed His ministers to declare His word of institution to the people; to pray, and bless the elements of bread and wine, and thereby to set them apart from a common to an holy use; and to take and break the bread, to take the cup, and (they communicating also themselves) to give both to the communicants; but to none who are not then present in the congregation.

Private masses, or receiving this sacrament by a priest, or any other alone; as likewise, the denial of the cup to the people, worshipping the elements, the lifting them up, or carrying them about, for adoration, and the reserving them for any pretended religious use; are all contrary to the nature of this sacrament, and to the institution of Christ.

The outward elements in this sacrament, duly set apart to the uses ordained by Christ, have such relation to Him crucified, as that, truly, yet sacramentally only, they are sometimes called by the name of the things they represent, to wit, the body and blood of Christ; albeit, in substance and nature, they still remain truly and only bread and wine, as they were before.

That doctrine which maintains a change of the substance of bread and wine, into the substance of Christ's body and blood (commonly called transubstantiation) by consecration of a priest, or by any other way, is repugnant, not to Scripture alone, but even to common sense, and reason; overthroweth the nature of the sacrament, and hath been, and is, the cause of manifold superstitions; yea, of gross idolatries.

Worthy receivers, outwardly partaking of the visible elements, in this sacrament, do then also, inwardly by faith, really and indeed, yet not carnally and corporally but spiritually, receive, and feed upon, Christ crucified, and all benefits of His death: the body and blood of Christ being then, not corporally or carnally, in, with, or under the bread and wine; yet, as really, but spiritually, present to the faith of believers in that ordinance, as the elements themselves are to their outward senses.

Although ignorant and wicked men receive the outward elements in this sacrament; yet, they receive not the thing signified thereby; but, by their unworthy coming thereunto, are guilty of the body and blood of the Lord, to their own damnation. Wherefore, all ignorant and ungodly persons, as they are unfit to enjoy communion with Him, so are they unworthy of the Lord's table, and cannot, without great sin against Christ, while they remain such, partake of these holy mysteries, or be admitted thereunto. (Westminster Confession of Faith, XXIX/1–viii; see also Larger Catechism, Questions 168–75)

Terminology

The Lord's Supper has come to be referred to in several different ways because of the New Testament terminology associated with it. It is called the "Breaking of the Bread" (Acts 2:42; 1 Cor. 10:16), "[Holy] Communion," because Paul states that "the cup of thanksgiving" and "the bread we break" are "communion" with the blood and body of Christ and with fellow believers (1 Cor. 10:16), the "Table of the Lord" (1 Cor. 10:21), the "Lord's Supper" (1 Cor. 11:20), and the "Eucharist," on the basis of Paul's use of the aorist participle εὐχαριστήσας, *eucharistēsas*, in 1 Corinthians 11:24. It is never called the "Last Supper" in Scripture (strictly speaking, this sacrament was not instituted at the last *supper*; rather, it was instituted at the last *Passover*). Neither does the Roman Catholic term, the "Mass," have any scriptural support whatever, being derived from the Latin *missio*, a term used in the Roman liturgy to dismiss the people (the expression *Ite, missa est* is the regular ending of the Roman rite).

Institution

Just as Jesus personally and expressly instituted the sacrament of baptism (Matt. 28:19), so also he personally and expressly instituted the sacrament of the Lord's Supper. The Synoptics specifically declare that he did it in the setting of the Passover celebration just hours before his crucifixion.

All three Synoptics (Matt. 26:26; Mark 14:22; Luke 22:19) and Paul (1 Cor. 11:24) record that Jesus, on the night he was betrayed, took bread and gave it to his disciples and said: "This is my body." Luke (22:19) and Paul (1 Cor. 11:24) both record that Jesus then said in connection with the bread: "[continually] do this in remembrance of me." Both Matthew (26:28) and Mark (14:24) record that Jesus then took

the cup and said: "This is my blood of the covenant which is poured out for many."
Matthew adds at this point: "for the forgiveness of sins." Luke (22:20) and Paul
(1 Cor. 11:25) state that Jesus said at this point: "This cup is the new covenant in my
blood," and Luke adds: "which is poured out for you." Paul alone records that Jesus
then said: "[continually] do this, whenever you drink it, in remembrance of me"
(1 Cor. 11:25). Though these minor variations exist between the accounts, it is still
quite clear from Jesus' imperatives, "*Continually do this* [this is the force of the
present imperative] in remembrance of me," that he did indeed institute this ordinance and that he intended his church to observe this ordinance after he had
departed from them and had gone back to heaven.

In the interest of showing the direct connection between the Passover and the
Lord's Supper, it is important that we note, not only its "Passover setting," but also
that our Lord used elements already normally employed in the Passover celebration when he instituted the Lord's Supper. R. T. Beckwith correctly observes:

> The only new thing which Christ instituted was his interpretation of the elements, *i.e.* his words of institution; for the thanksgivings, breaking of the bread
> and distributing of the elements took place at any formal Jewish meal, as the
> rabbinical literature shows. There were, indeed, interpretative words at the Passover meal, but they interpreted the elements in relation to the deliverance of the
> exodus, not in relation to the new deliverance through Christ's death. All that our
> Lord instituted needs to be performed, but the distinctive thing is his new interpretative words.[87]

Observance

With regard to the question of frequency, the New Testament does not specify
how often a congregation should observe the Lord's Supper. Paul states that Jesus
simply said: "Do this, whenever you drink it, in remembrance of me" (1 Cor. 11:25).
In the Middle Ages, Rome made the Mass obligatory for people only annually.
Zwingli called for a quarterly observance (Easter, Pentecost, autumn, and Christmas),
while Calvin advocated at least a weekly observance but reluctantly settled for less.

Regarding the liturgy to be followed, while Rome has embellished the ordinance
with a great deal of humanly devised pomp and circumstance, reflecting that
church's transubstantiational theology, Protestant churches, following Christ's and

---

87. R. T. Beckwith, "Eucharist," in *New Dictionary of Theology* (Downers Grove, Ill.: InterVarsity Press, 1988), 236. For further information about the first-century Passover seder (order of service) and its relation to the Lord's Supper, see Ceil and Moishe Rosen, *Christ in the Passover* (Chicago: Moody, 1978).

Paul's examples, have kept their liturgy, generally speaking, quite scriptural and simple. The Westminster Confession of Faith, for example, artlessly instructs the church as follows: "The Lord Jesus hath, in this ordinance, appointed his ministers to declare his word of institution to the people; to pray, and bless the elements of bread and wine, and thereby to set them apart from a common to an holy use; and to take and break the bread, to take the cup, and (they communicating also themselves) to give both to the communicants" (XXIX/iii; see also *Larger Catechism*, Question 169).

As to the ordinance's ministrants, in the Reformed churches the administration of the sacrament is restricted to ministers of the Word, not because it is thought that any sacerdotal power is resident in them by virtue of their ordination, but first, because (on the analogy of the high priest's admission to his office) "no one takes this honor upon himself; he must be called of God" (Heb. 5:4), and second, from the desire to insure good order (Jones).

With regard to the question of who are proper communicants at the Supper, the Scriptures make it clear that the Lord's Supper is not a "converting ordinance." It is for Christians only. The presiding minister must (1) caution all against partaking of the elements *unworthily* (ἀναξίως, *anaxiōs*, 1 Cor. 11:27, 29), which in the Corinthians context probably had reference to that church's factiousness and selfishness, lest they bring judgment upon themselves; (2) caution that all who participate must "recognize the Lord's body" as they commune, that is to say, must view the elements in the context of the ordinance, not as food and drink for the physical body, but as the sign and seal of *spiritual* verities; and (3) summon all to self-examination (δοκιμαζέτω, *dokimazetō*, 1 Cor. 11:28), to insure among other things that those who commune are in the faith (see 2 Cor. 13:5).

I should say in passing that while the classic Reformed position has restricted communion, precisely because of these apostolic admonitions, "only to such as are of years and ability to examine themselves" (Larger Catechism, Question 177), a contemporary Reformed challenge has been mounted against this restriction, primarily on the three grounds of (1) the analogy between the Passover and the Lord's Supper, (2) the analogy between baptism and the Lord's Supper, and (3) the insistence that Paul's summons to self-examination should be restricted to its contextual "universe of discourse," namely, to adults.[88] But because the Lord's Supper seems to require *active* participation on the part of the one receiving the elements (he or she is urged to "take, eat, drink, do this"), while baptism by its very nature requires the recipient to be *passive* (no one, not even an adult, baptizes himself), I would

---

88. See Robert S. Rayburn's "Minority Report" appended to the "Report of the Ad-Interim Committee to Study the Question of Paedocommunion," *Minutes of the Sixteenth General Assembly of the Presbyterian Church in America* (1988), 519–27.

urge that it is appropriate to draw a distinction between the two sacraments in this regard and to include infants and young children in baptism but to require them to mature sufficiently to the point where they are able to examine themselves before they are permitted to come to the Lord's Table.[89]

The Relation of Christ's Presence to the Elements

Seeking to expound upon our Lord's words, "This is my body," dogmaticians have urged four different views of the relation of Christ's presence to the elements in the Lord's Supper.

The Roman Catholic View—Transubstantiation

The Roman Catholic Church teaches that, in the "miracle" of the Mass, while the bread and wine continue to appear to the senses to be bread and wine, during the priest's prayer of consecration the elements actually change in substance into the real physical body and blood of Christ. In other words, the elements retain the *accidents* (that which is incidental to a thing) of bread and wine, while the *substance* (that which is essential to a thing) of the elements becomes the very body and blood of Christ.[90]

The Reformers criticized this view (1) for its lack of stress upon the role of faith in the reception of the ordinance's spiritual benefits; conceived as working *ex opere operato*, its benefits are ingested by the mouth and not by the heart governed by faith;[91] (2) for its implicit attack upon Christ's finished work at Calvary in its character as a "bloodless propitiatory sacrifice," and (3) for its magical character; unlike the visible miracles of Christ and of the New Testament in general which could be seen by believer and unbeliever alike, this "miracle" is not visible to anyone.

---

89. Clowney concurs, writing in *The Church*:
    The decisive difference between the two sacraments is that the Supper requires active and discerning participation. Indeed, communicants who take and eat in remembrance of Christ's death are performing the sacrament as well as receiving it. Paul warns against eating without discerning the meaning of the sacrament (1 Cor. 11:23–24). The Westminster Larger Catechism therefore limits participation to "such as are of years and ability to examine themselves." (284)

90. R.C. Sproul contends that a "twofold miracle" has had to occur in Rome's representation: "it takes a miracle to have the substance of one thing and something else's accidents, and it takes another miracle to have the accidents of something and the substance of something else." ("Into the Sanctuary—Worshiping God in Spirit and Truth," Ligonier Ministries, 1994, the ninth in an audio series of nine messages).

91. See Calvin's chapter on the sacrilege of the Mass in his *Institutes*, IV.xviii.

The Lutheran View—Consubstantiation

While Lutherans do not call their view "consubstantiation" (lit., "with the substance") Lutherans, following Luther who was concerned that the ordinance was being trivialized into an empty symbol by Zwingli, teach that while the bread and wine remain bread and wine, yet Christ, through a real physical union with the elements, is really corporally present "in, with, and under" the bread and wine.[92]

Both the Roman Catholic view and the Lutheran view contend that the communicant is actually feeding upon the physical body and blood of Christ. But since both views advocate that Christ is physically present in the elements, grave theological problems arise relative to the nature of Christ's humanity since both must ascribe the attribute of ubiquity ("everywhere–ness") to his humanity. But this is to destroy the true humanity of Christ and to forsake Chalcedon's Christology.[93]

The Zwinglian View—Symbolic Representation

At the other extreme, Zwinglians (but not necessarily Zwingli himself)[94] teach that the elements are symbolic visible representations of the death of Christ. Christ is said to have intended the elements to invoke in the communicant's mind the recollection of his death in his behalf.

While Luther thought that Zwingli (1) was a rationalist who would not believe Christ when he declared of the bread and wine, "This is my body," "This is my blood," (2) did not stress adequately the gift character of the Supper, and (3) overstressed the deity of Christ in the Supper to the neglect of his humanity, Zwingli in turn was persuaded that Luther's position (1) was "magical," (2) did not give an

---

92. The Augsburg Confession of 1530 was a Lutheran confession, but when Melanchthon, as its original author, amended it in 1540 to reflect the changes in his theological understanding (the *Variata*) and removed from the tenth article on the Lord's Supper the words *vere adsint* ("truly present"), replaced the word *distribuantur* ("distributed") with *exhibeantur* ("exhibited, held forth, displayed"), and added *cum pane* ("with the bread"), having the article teach that *with* the bread and wine the body and blood of Christ are displayed to the communicant, both John Calvin and Martin Bucer in good conscience signed it.

93. Not only is it true that the Lutheran teaching of the ubiquity of Christ's humanity really proves too much, for it suggests that Christ is physically present not just in the Lord's Supper but also everywhere else (what advantages then do the Supper elements have as sacramental points of his presence?), but it is also equally certain that this teaching is a departure from the Definition of Chalcedon, which expressly declares that the two natures of Christ know no confusion (ἀσυγχύτως, *asynchytōs*) and no change (ἀτρέπτως, *atreptōs*), with the "difference of the natures being by no means removed because of the union but the property of each nature being preserved."

94. See footnote 23.

adequate place to faith as the receiving instrument of the Supper's spiritual blessing, and (3) did not do full justice to the fact that Jesus, body and soul, actually went away to heaven in the Ascension and therefore is not here on earth.

The Reformed View—Real Spiritual Presence

In concert in the main with John Calvin, Reformed churches teach, following the Westminster Confession of Faith, that the body and blood of Christ (that is to say, Christ with all the benefits of his atoning death) are "really, but spiritually, present to the faith of believers," so that they "really and indeed, yet not carnally and corporally but spiritually, receive, and feed upon, Christ crucified, and all the benefits of his death" (Westminster Confession of Faith, XXIX/vii). The Lord's Supper becomes then for the "worthy" communicant a means of grace, not automatically, but through the blessing of Christ and the working of the Holy Spirit in him who by faith receives the elements. By them the crucified Christ spiritually gives himself and his atoning benefits to the believer to strengthen and nurture him.

Because he "partakes of one loaf" in the Supper, the Christian also communes with his many brethren who are members of Christ's body with him, thereby renewing his love for and fellowship with them (1 Cor. 10:17).

While Reformed churches generally follow Calvin's lead in his insistence that Christ is "really, but spiritually, present" to believers in the Lord's Supper, not every Reformed theologian follows Calvin's exposition in its every detail. For example, Charles Hodge refers to Calvin's view as "peculiar,"[95] William Cunningham with less restraint charges that Calvin's doctrine is "unsuccessful," "about as unintelligible as Luther's consubstantiation" and "perhaps, the greatest blot in the history of Calvin's labours as a public instructor,"[96] and Robert Lewis Dabney declares that it is "strange" and "not only incomprehensible, but impossible."[97]

Cunningham makes his comments because of what he perceives to be Calvin's "effort to bring out something like a real influence exerted by Christ's human nature upon the souls of believers . . . an effort which, of course, was altogether unsuccessful and resulted only in what was about as unintelligible as Luther's consubstantiation."[98]

Dabney writes that Calvin, in his desire to heal the rift between Lutherans and Zwinglians, taught that "the humanity, as well as the divinity of Christ, in a word, his whole person, is spiritually, yet really present, not to the bodily mouth, but to

---

95. Charles Hodge, *Systematic Theology*, 3:630.
96. William Cunningham, "Zwingli, and the Doctrine of the Sacraments," in *The Reformers and the Theology of the Reformation* (Edinburgh: Banner of Truth, 1979 reprint), 240.
97. Robert Lewis Dabney, *Lectures in Systematic Theology*, 810–11.
98. Cunningham, "Zwingli," 240.

the souls of true communicants, so that though the humanity be in heaven only, it is still fed on in some ineffable, yet real and literal way, by the souls of believers."[99] He goes on to state that the Westminster Assembly, while not repudiating Calvin's phraseology in a marked manner, did "modify all that was untenable and unscriptural about it."[100] He illustrates these modifications by stating that the men of the assembly

> say believers receive and feed spiritually upon Christ crucified and the benefits of His death; not with Calvin, on his literal flesh and blood. Next, the presence which grounds this receiving, is only a presence to our faith, of Christ's body and blood.[101]

Regarding Cunningham's and Dabney's criticisms, it is a fact that Calvin does teach that by the Spirit's empowering, Christ's human nature, although in heaven and not endowed with ubiquity, is nonetheless brought to us (or perhaps better, by faith we are lifted up to it) and that we derive spiritual life from *feeding specifically upon it* by faith:

> since it [the flesh of Christ] is pervaded with fullness of life to be transmitted to us, it is rightly called "life-giving" . . . the flesh of Christ is like a rich and inexhaustible fountain that pours into us the life springing forth from the Godhead into itself. Now who does not see that communion of Christ's flesh and blood is necessary for all who aspire to heavenly life? (*Institutes,* IV.17.9)
>
> Even though it seems unbelievable that Christ's flesh, separated from us by such great distance, penetrates to us, so that it becomes our food, let us remember how far the secret power of the Holy Spirit towers above all our senses, and how foolish it is to wish to measure his immeasurableness by our measure. (*Institutes,* IV.17.10)

Calvin acknowledged that "how this takes place, I shall not be ashamed to confess that it is a secret too lofty for either my mind to comprehend or my words to declare. And, to speak plainly, I rather experience than understand it" (*Institutes,* IV.17.32). But he still believed that the Scriptures declare the literal flesh and blood of Christ to be the Christian's life (John 6:27, 33, 51–59; 1 Cor. 6:15; Eph. 1:23; 4:15–16; 5:30; see *Institutes,* IV.17.9) and that therefore exegetical fidelity required him to accept that "his flesh [is] the food of my soul, his blood its drink (*Institutes,* IV.17.32). And he insisted that our "eating His flesh" and "drinking His blood" is brought

---

99. Dabney, *Lectures,* 810.
100. Ibid., 811.
101. Ibid.

about by faith. Our "eating" Christ, he writes "is no other eating than that of faith, as no other can be imagined.... I say that we eat Christ's flesh in believing, because it is made ours by faith, and that this eating is the result and effect of faith ... for me [this eating] seems to follow from faith" (*Institutes*, IV.17.5).

By urging that Christians feed by faith upon the *literal* flesh and blood of Christ at the Lord's Supper and that by doing so they derive from his *humanity* the "life-giving" virtues which flow into it from the Godhead, Calvin, by his language, though not by intention, comes perilously close to suggesting the Godhead's apotheosizing of Christ's humanity and to transferring, at least in the Lord's Supper, the saving benefits of Christ's atoning death directly to his human nature now localized in heaven. Perhaps if Calvin had been more sensitive to the inappropriateness of using the language of John 6 to expound the Lord's Supper, he would not have written what he did and would have avoided the problem that has troubled these later Reformed thinkers. Calvin does rely in the main on John 6 for the language of "eating Christ's flesh" and "drinking his blood" at the Lord's Table.[102] But it is extremely unlikely that Jesus either intended his words to be construed as eucharistic language or was referring to the Lord's Table at all. I say this for four reasons:

1. The context is against it. Jesus was speaking not to committed disciples (v. 66) but to people, including opponents (vv. 41, 52, 59), who would not have understood that he was referring to an ordinance that he had not yet instituted and about which John himself says nothing in his extended account of the events in the upper room (John 13–17). Leon Morris writes:

> No one has satisfactorily explained why John should want us to believe that it was to such an audience that Jesus gave his teaching about a sacrament that was to be observed by committed Christians only. Nor has anyone explained why Jesus should have taught that audience about a sacrament that had not been instituted. They could not possibly have understood him.[103]

2. "Flesh" (σάρξ, *sarx*) is not the word Jesus later used when he instituted the Lord's Table. There he employed "body" (σῶμα, *sōma*). As Morris notes: "The difference may not be great, but it is there. [The language of John 6] is not the way the early Christians referred to communion."[104] Also, when he instituted the Lord's

---

102. While Calvin expressly denies that the Bread of Life discourse is related to the Lord's Supper (see his comments of John 6:53, 54), he retreats from this judgment somewhat by going on to declare that "there is nothing said here that is not figuratively represented, and actually bestowed on believers, in the Lord's Supper; and Christ even intended that the holy Supper should be, as it were, a seal and confirmation of this sermon."
103. Leon Morris, *New Testament Theology* (Grand Rapids, Mich.: Academie, 1986), 285.
104. Ibid., 286.

Supper never did he speak of "chewing" (ὁ τρώγων, *ho trōgōn;* lit., "he who continually munches [or chews] on," John 6:54, 56, 57, 58) his body or drinking his blood; he spoke rather of eating the bread (1 Cor. 11:26) which, he said, is his body, and drinking the cup, which, he said, is his blood.

3. Jesus' words in John 6 are absolute. Without the specific eating and drinking of which he speaks here one has no life in him (John 6:53). But it is impossible to believe that he was teaching the people here that the observance of a particular ordinance, which he had not yet even instituted and about which John says nothing in his Gospel, is necessary for eternal life.

4. The blessings of eternal life and the eschatological resurrection which he declares result from "eating his flesh" and "drinking his blood" (John 6:53–58), Jesus teaches in this very same passage, also flow from his words (v. 63) and from believing in him (vv. 35, 40, 47). "Coming to him" and "believing in him," Jesus says, relieves one's spiritual hunger and thirst (v. 35). Accordingly, Jesus is not binding eternal life here to a liturgical ordinance. To "eat his flesh," answering to the hunger of 6:35, and to "drink his blood," answering to the thirst of 6:35, is his metaphorical way of urging his auditors to hear his words and to trust with all their heart in his forthcoming atoning death to which he alludes in 6:51: "This bread is my flesh, which I will give for the life of the world."

My difference here with some of the details of Calvin's exposition of the Lord's Supper should not be overdrawn, for I believe that Calvin's interpretation is for the most part biblical and the best over-all guide to the nature of Christ's presence in the Lord's Supper.[105]

Import

The import of the Lord's Supper can be addressed and summarized under the following five headings:

A Commemorative Celebration

Just as the Passover was to be a commemorative celebration of the Old Testament church's redemption from Egypt (Exod. 12:11–14, 24–27; 13:8–10; Deut. 16:1–8), so also the Lord's Supper, its New Testament antitype, is to be a commemorative celebration of the church's redemption which "Christ our Passover" (1 Cor. 5:7; see Exod. 12:46)

---

105. For a defense of Calvin's exposition as still "our best guide to the Supper," see W. Robert Godfrey, "This Is My Body," *Tenth: An Evangelical Quarterly*, ed. James M. Boice (Philadelphia: Philadelphia Conference on Reformed Theology, July 1981), 33–43.

accomplished when he died as our sacrifice at the time of the Passover (John 18:28; 19:36). By it the church looks back to the historical actuality of Christ's cross work and remembers (ἀνάμνησις, *anamnēsis*, 1 Cor. 11:24),[106] *not* reenacts, and proclaims (καταγγέλλετε, *katangellete*, 1 Cor. 11:26) Christ's sacrificial death for the church. Christ's summons to "remember" here is addressing not so much the idea that a man may forget something he has learned as it is the unbelief and ungratefulness in which the heart neglects and "allows to be superseded what should never be superseded."[107]

An Eschatological Anticipation

At the same time that it looks back to the historical reality of Christ's Passion, the Lord's Supper looks forward to the coming of the eschatological kingdom. Jesus specifically linked the Lord's Supper with the eschatological perspective of the kingdom of God when he informed his disciples that he would not eat the Passover again with them "until it finds fulfillment in the kingdom of God" (Luke 22:16), and then, after taking the cup, he gave thanks and said: "I will not drink again of the fruit of the vine until the kingdom of God comes" (22:18). Paul's assertion that "whenever you eat this bread and drink this cup, you proclaim the Lord's death until he comes" (1 Cor. 11:26) also gives to the Lord's Supper an eschatological orientation.

The Lord's Supper is given to the church on its pilgrimage through the world and is intended to enkindle the eschatological hope that *then*, in the Eschaton, the knowledge of the glory of the Lord will cover the earth as the waters cover the places of the sea. The "worthy" communicant also anticipates that glorious time in the Eschaton, at the return of Christ, when the church as the perfected Bride of Christ will sit down with Abraham, Isaac, and Jacob in the kingdom of heaven at the "wedding supper of the Lamb" (Rev. 19:9) and drink anew with Christ of the fruit of the vine in his Father's kingdom (Matt. 26:29; Mark 14:25; Luke 22:18).

A Means of Grace

By his "worthy" participation in the Lord's Supper, the celebrant "communes"

---

106. Joachim Jeremias in his *Die Abendmahlsworte Jesu*, 2d ed. (Göttingen: Vandenhoeck & Ruprecht, 1949) has argued that the "do this in remembrance of me" is not a summons to disciples to recollect but an invoking of God to remember, that is, "so that God will remember" (117). He appeals to Acts 10:4 and Mark 14:9 for support, but his argument fails to come to grips with the biblical meaning of true remembrance (the proper resistance of the heart against the act of neglecting what must never be neglected) and gives a meaning to the institution which simply cannot be meaningfully related to the New Testament.
107. Berkouwer, *The Sacraments*, 194.

by faith with his Lord's slain body and blood, which were offered up for him in death as his sacrifice for sin (John 6:50–58, 63–64; 1 Cor. 10:16), thereby experiencing spiritual nourishment, growth in grace, and renewal of thanksgiving and engagement to God.[108] In other words, the communion envisioned is more than a mere mental bringing to mind of Christ's death; it is a renewed appropriation of the spiritual benefits of Christ's redemption represented by the elements. The Larger Catechism, Question 170, enlarges upon this aspect of the Lord's Supper in the following words:

> As the body and blood are not corporally or carnally present in, with, or under the bread and wine in the Lord's Supper, and yet are spiritually present to the faith of the receiver, no less truly and really than the elements themselves are to their outward senses; so they that worthily communicate in the sacrament of the Lord's Supper, do therein feed upon the body and blood of Christ, not after a corporal and carnal, but in a spiritual manner; yet truly and really, while by faith they receive and apply unto themselves Christ crucified, and all the benefits of his death.

A Demanding Ordinance

The Larger Catechism, Question 171, urges those who would come to the Table to prepare themselves *before* they come to it

> by examining themselves of their being in Christ, of their sins and wants; of the truth and measure of their knowledge, faith, repentance; love to God and the brethren, charity to all men, forgiving those that have done them wrong; of their desires after Christ, and of their new obedience; and by renewing the exercise of these graces, by serious meditation, and fervent prayer.

I should add that those who come should come as though they were coming to a banquet table, and should come with the expectation of being fed the "richest food" available to mankind.

Question 174 admonishes those who are receiving the Lord's Supper *during* the time of its administration, that

> with all holy reverence and attention they wait upon God in that ordinance, diligently observe the sacramental elements and actions, heedfully discern the Lord's body, and affectionately meditate on his death and sufferings, and thereby stir up themselves to a vigorous exercise of their graces; in judging themselves,

---

108. I would strongly recommend the reading of John Calvin's treatment of the Lord's Supper in his *Institutes*, IV.xvii.

and sorrowing for sin; in earnest hungering and thirsting after Christ, feeding on him by faith, receiving of his fulness, trusting in his merits, rejoicing in his love, giving thanks for his grace; in renewing of their covenant with God, and love to all the saints.

Finally, Question 175 urges Christians *after* they have received the sacrament of the Lord's Supper

> seriously to consider how they have behaved themselves therein, and with what success; if they find quickening and comfort, to bless God for it, beg the continuance of it, watch against relapses, fulfil their vows, and encourage themselves to a frequent attendance on that ordinance: but if they find no present benefit, more exactly to review their preparation to, and carriage at, the sacrament; in both which, if they can approve themselves to God and their own consciences, they are to wait for the fruit of it in due time; but if they see they have failed in either, they are to be humbled, and to attend upon it afterward with more care and diligence.

A Vindicating Apologetic

In the life and death struggle between Christianity and theological liberalism, indeed against all antisupernaturalism, the Lord's Supper, both by its sign character (bread broken, fruit of the vine poured out, recipient participation) and by the words of institution ("my body which is *for you*"; "my blood of the new covenant which is poured out *for many for the forgiveness of sin*"), stands as a vindicating apologetic that the evangelical interpretation of the death of Christ as a substitutionary, atoning death by sacrifice (over against the portrayal of his death as that of a martyr in a noble cause or as that of a misguided fanatic) is the only true and proper view of Christ's death work. The Lord's Supper itself preaches the substitutionary atonement and proclaims both the Lord's sacrificial death in our behalf and his final return to judgment.

PRAYER AS A MEANS OF GRACE

Larger Catechism, Question 178: What is prayer?
Answer: Prayer is an offering up of our desires unto God, in the name of Christ, by the help of the Spirit, with confession of our sins, and thankful acknowledgement of his mercies.
Question 179: Are we to pray unto God only?
Answer: God only being able to search the hearts, hear the requests, pardon the

sins, and fulfil the desires of all; and only to be believed in, and worshipped with religious worship; prayer, which is a special part thereof, is to be made by all to him alone, and to none other.

Question 180: What is it to pray in the name of Christ?

Answer: To pray in the name of Christ is, in obedience to his command, and in confidence on his promises, to ask mercy for his sake; not by bare mentioning of his name, but by drawing our encouragement to pray, and our boldness, strength, and hope of acceptance in prayer, from Christ and his mediation.

Question 181: Why are we to pray in the name of Christ?

Answer: The sinfulness of man, and his distance from God by reason thereof, being so great, as that we can have no access into his presence without a mediator; and there being none in heaven or earth appointed to, or fit for, that glorious work but Christ alone, we are to pray in no other name but his only.

Question 182: How doth the Spirit help us to pray?

Answer: We not knowing what to pray for as we ought, the Spirit helpeth our infirmities, by enabling us to understand both for whom, and what, and how prayer is to be made; and by working and quickening in our hearts (although not in all persons, nor at all times, in the same measure) those apprehensions, affections, and graces which are requisite for the right performance of that duty.

Question 183: For whom are we to pray?

Answer: We are to pray for the whole church of Christ upon earth; for magistrates, and ministers, and ourselves, our brethren, yea, our enemies; and for all sorts of men living, or that shall live hereafter; but not for the dead, nor for those that are known to have sinned the sin unto death.

Question 184: For what things are we to pray?

Answer: We are to pray for all things tending to the glory of God, the welfare of the church, our own or others, good; but not for any thing that is unlawful.

Question 185: How are we to pray?

Answer: We are to pray with an awful apprehension of the majesty of God, and deep sense of our own unworthiness, necessities, and sins; with penitent, thankful, and enlarged hearts; with understanding, faith, sincerity, fervency, love, and perseverance, waiting upon him, with humble submission to his will.

(Questions 186–96 then provide an exposition of the Lord's Prayer that closes out the Larger Catechism itself.)

Biblical Vocabulary

In the Old Testament the common Hebrew noun for "prayer" is תְּפִלָּה, *t^epillâh*. Its related verb is הִתְפַּלֵּל, *hitpallēl*, the Hithpael of פלל, *pll*, meaning "to pray." The noun תְּהִלָּה, t‘hillâh, meaning "praise," and its corresponding verb הִלֵּל, hillēl, the Piel of הלל, hll, meaning "to praise," are also commonly used to denote prayer and the act of praying. The noun תְּחִנָּה, t‘hinnâh, meaning "supplication," is also found. Verbs of asking (שָׁאַל, šā'al), groaning (the Niphal of אנח, 'nh), crying (צָעַק, sā'aq), calling upon (קָרָא בְ, qārā' b‘), and weeping (בָּכָה, bācâh) are also used to denote the several forms which prayer takes in the Old Testament.[109]

The New Testament employs several different nouns for prayer. In Philippians 4:6, for example, Paul speaks of "prayer" (προσευχή, proseuchē), "petition" (δέησις, deēsis), "thanksgiving" (εὐχαριστία, eucharistia), and "requests" (αἴτημα, aitēma). In 1 Timothy 2:1 and 4:5 he employs a fifth term, "intercession" (ἔντευξις, enteuxis) for prayer. The verbs corresponding to these five nouns are προσεύχομαι, proseuchomai, δέομαι, deomai, εὐχαριστέω, eucharisteō, αἰτέω, aiteō, and ἐντυγχάνω, entynchanō. John (particularly) employs the verb "to ask" (ἐρωτάω, erōtaō, [the noun ἐρώτησις, erōtēsis is not used in the New Testament]). James employs the noun εὐχή, euchē, and the verb εὔχομαι, euchomai, of prayer in 5:15–16.[110]

Prayer in the Bible

Prayer's first implication is that God is "really there," personal and addressable in worship. Prayer is communication with God in worship according to his revealed will, about which Clowney writes:

> To pray according to God's will means to make God's word the guide for our prayers.... Prayer seeks God's will in faith, believing in his power to answer in His created universe (Mt. 21:21, 22). Faith does not use prayer merely as a technique to alter consciousness [as is often urged by rationalists and some hyper-Calvinists], but as an address to the living God.... In adoration we praise God for what he does and who he is.... God's holiness demands confession of sin; his grace invites supplication for pardon.... In the communion of prayer we express our love for God and offer to him the tribute of our lives.... By prayer the church resists the assaults of Satan (Mt. 26:41; Eph. 6:13–20); receives fresh gifts of grace (Acts 4:31); seeks deliverance, healing and restoration for the saints (Eph. 6:18; Jas 5:15; 1 Jn. 5:16); supports the witness of the gospel (Col. 4:3, 4); seeks the return of the Lord (Rev. 22:20); and, above all, worships him of whom, through whom, and unto whom are all things.[111]

---

109. See J. Herrmann, "Prayer in the Old Testament," under εὔχομαι [euchomai], *Theological Dictionary of the New Testament*, 2:785–800.

110. See H. Greeven, "Prayer in the New Testament," under εὔχομαι [euchomai], *Theological Dictionary of the New Testament*, 2:803–08.

111. Edmund Clowney, "Prayer, Theology of," *New Dictionary of Theology* (Downers Grove, Ill.: InterVarsity Press, 1988), 526–27.

The first reference to prayer in the Bible is in Genesis 4:26: "At that time men began *to call on* [בְ לִקְרֹא, *liqrô' b^e*] the name of the LORD." Prayer is characterized in the patriarchal period by the same expression:

Genesis 12:8: "There [Abraham] built an altar to the LORD *and called on* [בְ וַיִּקְרָא, *wayyiqrā' b^e*] the name of the LORD."

Genesis 21:33: "Abraham planted a tamarisk tree [an evergreen] in Beersheba, and there *he called upon* [בְ וַיִּקְרָא, *wayyiqrā' b^e*] the name of the LORD, the Eternal God."

In all of the legal enactments of the Pentateuch there is nothing about prayer apart from Deuteronomy 26:5–15, in which passage a liturgy is prescribed which ends with the petition in 26:15 (but see 26:10, 13–14):

Look down from heaven, your holy dwelling place, and bless your people Israel and the land you have given us as you promised on oath to our forefathers, a land flowing with milk and honey.

"Prayer is pervasive throughout the historical books of the Old Testament, further evidence of its integral place in the lives of the people of God" (Jones). Some of the more prominent examples from the historical and prophetic books are Hannah's prayers in 1 Samuel 1:9–11 and 2:1–10, David's prayers in 1 Chronicles 16:8–36; 17:16–27; and 29:10–13; Solomon's prayer in 1 Kings 8:22–61; Hezekiah's prayer in 2 Kings 19:15–19; Daniel's prayer in Daniel 9:4–19, and Nehemiah's prayers in Nehemiah 1:1–11; 2:2–8; 9:9–38.

But it is particularly in the Psalms, at least seventy-three of which were composed by David, that the depth of devotion and breadth of subject matter of Old Testament prayer are preserved for us, prayers "still normative for the people of God, guiding the content of all the parts of prayer: adoration, confession, thanksgiving, and supplication. Alongside the prayers appropriate for corporate worship are personal prayers for communion, protection, and all necessary graces" (Jones).

When we turn to the pages of the New Testament, we observe, as Clowney notes, that prayer was a constant part of our Lord's devotional life:

Jesus, the incarnate Son of God, prayed to his heavenly Father in unbroken communion. He began his public ministry in prayer (Lk. 3:21). He prayed in solitude before dawn (Mk. 1:31), and marked the turning points of his ministry with periods of prayer (Lk. 5:16; 6:12; 9:18). Before he went to the cross he agonized in prayer, submitting to his Father's will (Mt. 26:36–44). He who as the Priest prayed for his people (Jn. 17), became the sacrifice to die for them (Heb. 9:24–26). As the heavenly High Priest, the risen Christ lives to make intercession for the saints (Rom. 8:34; Heb. 7:24, 25; 1 Jn. 2:1).[112]

Jesus also taught his disciples that they should pray (Matt. 6:5–13; Luke 11:1–13; 18:1–8). And so we see the New Testament church praying (Acts 4:24–30). Paul's letters contain many of his prayers as well as instruction on prayer. And the persecuted and martyred church in the Revelation continually prays.

Significant Discourses on Prayer in Church History

Origen's *Treatise on Prayer* (Περὶ εὐχῆς; *Peri euchēs*, usually cited by its Latin title, *De oratione*) is one of the first full treatments of prayer in church history.[113] In this treatise Origen did a philological study of εὐχή, *euchē*, and προσευχή, *proseuchē*, discussed the moral prerequisites of effective prayer, that is, recollection of God, preparation of the mind, forgiveness of our enemies, and submissiveness to God; discussed the philosophical issue of prayer in the light of God's foreknowledge, exegeted and expounded the Lord's prayer, and offered advice on various practical aspects of prayer (Jones's summary). He concluded with a summary of the parts of prayer: adoration, thanksgiving, confession, and petition. Each of us, Origen says, should organize our prayer in accordance with them:

> These sections are as follows: according to our ability at the beginning and exordium of our prayer we must address praises to God through Christ, who is praised together with him in the Holy Spirit, who is likewise hymned; and after this each must place thanksgiving, both general—enumerating with thanksgiving God's benefits to the many—and for those things which each has received privately from God; and after thanksgiving it seems to me that one ought to be a bitter accuser of one's own sins before God, and to ask first for healing so as to be delivered from the state that leads to sin, and secondly for remission of what is past; and after confession, in the fourth place it seems to me we must add petition for the great and heavenly gifts for ourselves, and for people in general, and also for our families and friends; and in addition to all this, our prayer ought to end in praise to God through Christ in the Holy Spirit.[114]

---

112. Ibid., 526.
113. In this section I am drawing upon Jones's lecture on prayer.
114. Origen, *De oratione*, XXXIII.1.

Augustine also wrote an exposition of the Lord's Prayer.[115] And Calvin devotes a chapter in the *Institutes* (III.xx.1–51) to the doctrine of prayer, in which he offers a sixfold rationale for prayer:

> Therefore, even though, while we grow dull and stupid toward our miseries, he watches and keeps guard on our behalf, and sometimes even helps us unasked, still it is very important for us to call upon him: *First,* that our hearts may be fired with a zealous and burning desire ever to seek, love, and serve him, while we become accustomed in every need to flee to him as to a sacred anchor. *Secondly,* that there may enter our hearts no desire and no wish at all of which we should be ashamed to make him a witness, while we learn to set all our wishes before his eyes, and even to pour out our whole hearts. *Thirdly,* that we be prepared to receive his benefits with true gratitude of heart and thanksgiving, benefits that our prayer reminds us come from his hand. *Fourthly,* moreover, that, having obtained what we were seeking, and being convinced that he has answered our prayers, we should be led to meditate upon his kindness more ardently. And *fifthly,* that at the same time we embrace with greater delight those things which we acknowledge to have been obtained by prayer. *Finally,* that use and experience may, according to the measure of our feebleness, confirm his providence, while we understand not only that he promises never to fail us, and of his own will opens the way to call upon him at the very point of necessity, but also that he ever extends his hand to help his own, not wet-nursing them with words but defending them with present help.[116]

Of Calvin's treatment of the doctrine of prayer John McNeill declares:

> This thoughtful and ample chapter, with its tone of devout warmth, takes its place in the forefront of historically celebrated discussions of prayer, such as Tertullian's *De oratione;* Origen, περὶ εὐχῆς [*Peri euchēs*]; Gregory of Nyssa, On the Lord's Prayer; and the short treatises of Augustine and of Hugh of St. Victor.[117]

The Westminster Assembly devoted large sections of both the Larger Catechism (Questions 178–96) and the Shorter Catechism (Questions 98–107) to the doctrine of prayer, declaring prayer to be among the "outward and ordinary means whereby Christ communicates to his church the benefits of his redemption" (Larger Catechism, Question 154). "Whereas Calvin's treatment of the doctrine of prayer falls

---

115. See his *Commentary on the Lord's Sermon on the Mount with Seventeen Related Sermons,* trans. Denis J. Kavanagh (New York: Fathers of the Church, 1951).
116. Calvin, *Institutes,* III.xx.3.
117. John T. McNeill, ed., *Calvin: Institutes of the Christian Religion,* vol. 21 of *The Library of Christian Classics* (Philadelphia: Westminster, 1960), 850.

under soteriology, in the Westminster system it is connected with ecclesiology, [constructions, of course, which] are not mutually exclusive" (Jones). Its legitimacy as a means of additional grace, even though it is already a manifestation of grace, is apparent from the fact that prayer is the "first expression and exercise of faith" (Jones): "Everyone who calls upon [ἐπικαλέσηται, *epikalesētai*] the name of the Lord will be saved" (Rom. 10:13). Because of "its instrumental function in progressive sanctification and perseverance," it is thus "coordinate with the Word and sacraments as means of grace" (Jones).

Efficacy of Prayer

In his commentary on John 7:37–39 Calvin says something that most Christians can only read with shame:

> That we lie on earth poor and famished and almost destitute of spiritual blessings, while Christ sits in glory at the right hand of the Father, clothed with the highest majesty of empire, must be imputed to our slothfulness and the narrowness of our faith.

There can be no question where the blame must be placed for our spiritual poverty. Every sin problem reveals a prayer problem. There is no sin that the Christian will ever commit that could not have been avoided by prayer. Jesus instructed his disciples: "Pray that you enter not into temptation" (Mark 14:38), and he taught his disciples to pray that they would be delivered from temptation and from the evil one (Matt. 6:13; Luke 11:4). James declares: "You do not have, because you do not ask God [διὰ τὸ μὴ αἰτεῖσθαι ὑμᾶς, *dia to mē aiteisthai hymas*]" (4:2). The preposition διά, *dia*, with the aorist infinitive in the accusative case has a causal nuance here and teaches that there is a direct cause ("because you do not ask") and effect ("you do not have") relationship in the matter of receiving the things one needs from God.[118] Listed below are some of the key "asking–receiving" texts:

> Matthew 6:5–13: "And when you pray, do not be like the hypocrites, for they love to pray standing in the synagogues and on the street corners to be seen of men. I tell you the truth, they have received their reward in full. But when you pray, go into your room, close the door and pray to your Father, who is unseen. Then your Father, who sees what is done in secret, will reward you openly. And when you pray, do not keep on babbling like the pagans, for they think they will be

---

118. Of course, as James also states (James 4:3), when one does pray one can be asking God for things with entirely wrong motives, in which case one's prayers would go unanswered.

heard because of their many words. Do not be like them, for your Father knows what you need before you ask him. This, then, is how you should pray:

> Our Father in heaven,
> hallowed be your name,
> your kingdom come,
> your will be done
> > on earth as it is in heaven.
> Give us today our daily bread.
> Forgive us our debts
> > as we also have forgiven our debtors.
> And lead us not into temptation,
> but deliver us from the evil one.

Matthew 7:7–11: "Ask and it will be given to you; seek and you will find; knock and the door will be opened to you. For everyone who asks receives; he who seeks finds; and to him who knocks, the door will be opened. Which of you, if his son asks for bread, will give him a stone? Or if he asks for a fish, will give him a snake? If you, then, though you are evil, know how to give good gifts to your children, how much more will your Father in heaven give good gifts to those who ask him."

John 14:13–14: "And I will do whatever you ask in my name, so that the Son may bring glory to the Father. You may ask me for anything in my name, and I will do it."

John 15:7, 16: "If you remain in me and my words remain in you, ask whatever you wish, and it will be given you. . . . the Father will give you whatever you ask in my name."

John 16:23–26: "In that day you will no longer ask me anything. I tell you the truth, my Father will give you whatever you ask in my name. Until now you have not asked for anything in my name. Ask and you will receive, and your joy will be complete."

Romans 8:26–27: "The Spirit helps us in our weakness. We do not know what we ought to pray for, but the Spirit himself intercedes for us with groans that words cannot express. And he who searches our hearts [the Father] knows the mind of the Spirit, because the Spirit intercedes for the saints in accordance with the will of God."

Ephesians 3:20: "Now to him who is able to do immeasurably more than all we ask or imagine, according to his power that is at work within us."

James 1:5–8: "If any of you lacks wisdom, he should ask God, who gives generously to all without finding fault, and it will be given to him. But when he asks, he must believe and not doubt, because he who doubts is like a wave of the sea, blown and tossed by the wind. That man should not think he will receive anything from the Lord; he is a double-minded man, unstable in all he does."

1 John 3:21–22: "Dear friends, if our hearts do not condemn us, we have confidence before God and receive from him anything we ask, because we obey his commands and do what pleases him."

1 John 5:14–15: "This is the confidence we have in approaching God: that if we ask anything according to his will, he hears us. And if we know that he hears us—whatever we ask—we know that we have what we asked of him."

These verses raise two problems which must be addressed before we conclude our treatment of prayer. First, some Christians have contended that to pray *conditionally*, that is, to say to God, "if it be your will," is incompatible with the prayer of faith, but this is a mistake:

> We . . . ask in faith, when we submit to the word of God and acquiesce in his will, and pray to be heard according to the good pleasure of our heavenly Father. For faith submits itself to every word and desire of God.[119]

Second, some Christians think that prayer is incompatible with the sovereignty of God: If he has already ordained everything, then why pray? But this is to overlook the fact that God ordains not only ends but all the means to those end as well. Prayer, simply put, is one of the means he has ordained that his children should use to receive blessings from him. If this is problematic, "this is not a problem unique to prayer," Jones writes, as the following quotation from Charles Hodge seeks to demonstrate:

> It is certain that the Scriptures teach both foreordination and the efficacy of prayer. The two, therefore, cannot be inconsistent. God has not determined to accomplish his purposes without the use of means; and among those means, the prayers of his people have their appropriate place. If the objection to prayer, founded on the foreordination of events be valid, it is valid against the use of means in any case. If it be unreasonable to say, "If it be foreordained that I should live, it is not necessary for me to eat," it is no less unreasonable for me to say, "If it be foreordained that I should receive any good, it is not necessary for me to ask for it." If God has foreordained to bless us, he has foreordained that we should seek his blessing. Prayer has the same causal relation to the good bestowed, as any other means has to the end with which it is connected.[120]

"The classic biblical example" (Jones) of praying for a temporal need which was *not* granted is 2 Corinthians 12:8–9: "Three times I pleaded with the Lord to take it

---

119. Zanchius, *Commentary on the Heidelberg Catechism*, 624.
120. Hodge, *Systematic Theology*, 3:169.

[975]

[Paul's thorn in the flesh] away from me. But he said to me, 'My grace is sufficient for you, for my power is made perfect in weakness.' " Paul's experience highlights the simple yet profound truth that prayer is not the means by which we get from God what *we* want. Rather, "prayer is a means God uses to give us what *He* wants."[121]

We have completed our discussion of the three means of grace, the Word of God, the two divinely instituted sacraments of baptism and the Lord's Supper, and prayer. All three are God's appointed ordinances and ordinary means through which he works his grace in the hearts of sinful people (in the case of his word) and his own children.

Their faithful, worthy employment will strengthen the Christian and equip him for every good work in life. Their willful neglect can only result in spiritual loss. Christians should faithfully attend upon these gracious helps that the wise God has established for their growth and spiritual health.

---

121. W. Bingham Hunter, *The God Who Hears* (Downers Grove, Ill.: InterVarsity Press, 1986), 12.

PART FIVE

Last Things

CHAPTER TWENTY-FIVE

Biblical Eschatology

It pleased God, in His eternal purpose, to choose and ordain the Lord Jesus, His only begotten Son, to be . . . the Prophet, Priest, and King, the Head and Savior of His church, the Heir of all things, and Judge of the world. . . .

On the third day [after death, the Lord Jesus] rose from the dead, with the same body in which He suffered, with which He also ascended into heaven, and there sitteth at the right hand of His Father, making intercession, and shall return, to judge men and angels, at the end of the world. (Westminster Confession of Faith, VIII/i, iv, emphasis supplied)

The visible church . . . is the kingdom of the Lord Jesus Christ. . . . (Westminster Confession of Faith, XXV/ii)

God hath appointed a day, wherein He will judge the world, in righteousness, by Jesus Christ, to whom all power and judgment is given of the Father. In which day, not only the apostate angels shall be judged, but likewise all persons that have lived upon earth shall appear before the tribunal of Christ, to give an account of their thoughts, words, and deeds; and to receive according to what they have done in the body, whether good or evil.

The end of God's appointing this day is for the manifestation of the glory of His mercy, in the eternal salvation of the elect; and of His justice, in the damnation of the reprobate, who are wicked and disobedient. For then shall the righteous go into everlasting life, and receive that fulness of joy and refreshing, which shall come from the presence of the Lord; but the wicked who know not God, and obey not the Gospel of Jesus Christ, shall be cast into eternal torments, and be punished with everlasting destruction from the presence of the Lord, and from the glory of His power.

As Christ would have us to be certainly persuaded that there shall be a day of judgment, both to deter all men from sin; and for the greater consolation of the godly in their adversity: so will He have that day unknown to men, that they may shake off all carnal security, and be always watchful, because they know not at what hour the Lord will come; and may be ever prepared to say, Come Lord Jesus, come quickly, Amen. (Westminster Confession of Faith, XXXIII/i–iii)

In his *Systematic Theology*, J. Oliver Buswell Jr. defines eschatology as the "systematic study of eventualities."[1] This area of theology is the capstone of systematic theology, with every other locus of theology finding its resolution in it. Louis Berkhof, citing Abraham Kuyper, points out that

every other locus left some question unanswered, to which eschatology should supply the answer. In theology [proper] it is the question, how God is finally perfectly glorified in the work of His hands, and how the counsel of God is fully realized; in anthropology, the question, how the disrupting influence of sin is completely overcome; in Christology, the question, how the work of Christ is crowned with perfect victory; in soteriology, the question, how the work of the Holy Spirit at last issues in the complete redemption and glorification of the people of God; and in ecclesiology, the question of the final apotheosis of the church.[2]

In fact, eschatology is so significant for New Testament thought in general that many contemporary New Testament theologians are prepared to argue that New Testament theology *as a whole*, as the theology of the "age of fulfillment," is, if not eschatology *per se*, eschatologically oriented with respect to all of its major soteriological and ethical emphases.[3]

---

1. J. Oliver Buswell Jr., *A Systematic Theology of the Christian Religion* (Grand Rapids, Mich.: Zondervan, 1963), 2:295.
2. Louis Berkhof, *Systematic Theology* (Grand Rapids, Mich.: Eerdmans, 1939), 665.
3. This recent emphasis upon the significance of eschatology for New Testament thought is totally foreign to a vast segment of the evangelical church, which has been taught for years now that there is only one "prophetic book" in the New Testament, namely, the Apocalypse, and that it is to be read literally. Hence, a premillennial eschatology is practically guaranteed to be the outcome of such a narrow eschatological mooring.

    Mentioning as I have here "premillennial" eschatology, perhaps some definitions are in order. The Latinized word "millennium," meaning "a thousand years," derives its theological bearing from the six references in Revelation 20:1–7 to "a [the] thousand years" ([τὰ] χίλια ἔτη, [*ta*] *chilia etē*). Premillennialists argue, then, that between this present age and the eternal state a thousand-year reign of Christ will occur, ushered in by Christ's return. That is to say, Christ's return will occur *before* ("pre") this thousand-year period commences (this view is also known as "chiliasm"). Postmillennialists, on the other hand, contend that the spread of the gospel will eventually "Christianize" the world, ushering in a "golden age of righteousness" on the earth. This golden age, still in the future (which may or may not be literally a thousand years long), is said to be the thousand-year period alluded to in Revelation 20. It will be terminated with the

The biblical material treating this locus of theology has traditionally encompassed both *personal* eventualities, such as death, the state of the disembodied human soul, the resurrection of the body, the final judgment, and the individual's ultimate eternal destiny, and *cosmic* eventualities, such as the return of Christ, the liberation of creation from its bondage to decay, and the new heaven and new earth. While both of these areas are vital to a holistic biblical eschatology, one should not forget that personal eschatology as it issues in the glorification of believers and the reprobation of unbelievers is really an aspect of the second area of eventualities, which issues in the cosmic climax and consummation of God's eternal purpose for the world as we presently know it.

THE DEBATE OVER ESCHATOLOGY

Before we consider the biblical material bearing on our topic, something should be said about the debate that has raged in scholarly circles during the last one hundred and fifty years over New Testament eschatology.

Classic Liberal Eschatology

Classic liberalism of the nineteenth and early twentieth centuries, represented by theologians such as Adolf von Harnack (1851–1930), totally rejected the eschatology of the Gospels. It was said that eschatology did not belong to the authentic teaching of Jesus but was the product of the fervent atmosphere of the first-century church. "The kernel of [Jesus'] real message," from which the husk of such things as apocalyptic must be separated, "consisted of a few universal truths such as the fatherhood of God, the infinite value of the individual soul,

---

great apostasy referred to in 2 Thessalonians 2:3, which apostasy will be addressed by Christ himself at his second coming. In other words, according to postmillennial teaching Christ will return *after* ("post") the "millennium." Amillennialists (Jay Adams, himself one, calls this view "realized millennialism") view the thousand years of Revelation 20 as referring both to this age and to the intermediate state of the souls of martyred Christians during this age between their death and resurrection, which latter event occurs at Christ's return.

A related issue among premillenialists has to do with the relation of the rapture of the church (1 Thess. 4:16–17) to the so-called seventieth week of Daniel, known also as the tribulation period. Pretribulationists contend that Christ will rapture the church out of the world seven years *before* his actual Advent, midtribulationists insist that the rapture will occur in the *middle* of Daniel's seventieth week, while posttribulationists argue that the church will remain here on earth throughout the entire tribulation period and be raptured *after* the tribulation period is over at the return of Christ.

and the ethic of love"[4] by which men could and would build the kingdom. In sum, Jesus was primarily a teacher of morality. This view has been thoroughly discredited, and a variety of alternative approaches to the eschatology of Jesus in particular and of the New Testament in general has been proposed.

Consistent Eschatology

Albert Schweitzer (1875–1965) recognized that the noneschatological pronouncements of the liberal view were simply modernizations, that is, personal projections of the individual scholars who wrote on the subject, rather than the results of sound historical analyses. He endorsed and expanded on the view of Johannes Weiss (1863–1914) that the apocalyptic element in Jesus' teaching was not the husk but the kernel of his teaching,[5] and in his *The Mystery of the Kingdom of God* (1906) and *The Quest of the Historical Jesus* (English trans., 1910) he argued that Jesus was a man of only the first century, not of the nineteenth, and that the genre of Jewish apocalyptic, however uncongenial it might be to the nineteenth-century mind, was essential to Jesus' message. As a "deluded fanatic" who, believing that he was the coming Son of Man, "futilely threw his life away in blind devotion to a mad apocalyptic dream,"[6] Jesus taught that the kingdom of God, wholly future, would come in his lifetime. To understand Jesus one must apply the eschatological motif *consistently* throughout (hence the name). That is to say, Jesus' message was *fundamentally* and *exclusively* eschatological. Jesus' sending out of the Twelve, for example, was for the purpose of giving the "lost sheep of the house of Israel" their last chance to repent before the final crisis and the inbreaking of the kingdom of God. When neither the Parousia nor the "messianic" suffering described in Matthew 10 occurred as he had predicted (see 10:23), Jesus purportedly realized that he had made a mistake (the first "delay of the Parousia"), and so he determined to take upon himself alone the messianic woes as a ransom to "extort" from God the new age. But realizing anew his mistake on the cross, he died a forsaken and utterly disillusioned man (Matt. 27:46), a man who occasioned his own death in the effort to bring about something which God had no intention of doing. In what may well be the most quoted statement from his *Quest* book, Schweitzer describes Jesus' death this way:

---

4. George Eldon Ladd, *The Presence of the Future* (Grand Rapids, Mich.: Eerdmans, 1974), 4.
5. Johannes Weiss, *Jesus' Proclamation of the Kingdom of God*, trans. R. H. Hiers and D. L. Holland (Philadelphia: Fortress, 1971).
6. Ladd, *The Presence of the Future*, 5.

In the knowledge that He is the coming Son of Man [Jesus] lays hold of the wheel of the world to set it moving on that last revolution which is to bring all ordinary history to a close. It refuses to turn, and He throws Himself upon it. Then it does turn, and crushes Him. Instead of bringing in the eschatological conditions, He has destroyed them. The wheel rolls onward, and the mangled body of the one immeasurably great Man, who was strong enough to think of Himself as the spiritual ruler of mankind and to bend history to His purpose, is hanging upon it still. That is His victory and His reign.[7]

Really, of course, a more appropriate word than "strong" in the last sentence, from Schweitzer's point of view, is "crazy" or "deluded." Moreover, in his view the eschatological content of Jesus' teaching, though central to Jesus, has no meaning for us today, though Jesus himself does inasmuch as the religious value of Jesus is independent of historical knowledge of him as a first-century Palestinian Jew. And men may still distill from his noneschatological teaching certain ethical emphases, even though his was an "interim ethic" intended only for the brief period of time prior to the inbreaking of the kingdom. F. Holmström's conclusion is right on target:

> Schweitzer's consequent eschatology is, therefore, a consequent liberal Christology; his formal championing of eschatology actually becomes a liquidation of eschatology; his ethics remain a moralism which is even farther removed from true Christianity than was Ritschl's ethicism.[8]

Realized Eschatology

Realized eschatology is associated primarily with the name C. H. Dodd (1884–1973), the Cambridge scholar. Vigorously reacting to Schweitzer's one-sided "consistent eschatology," Dodd in his *The Parables of the Kingdom* (1935) and *The Apostolic Preaching and Its Developments* (1936) went to the other extreme and contended that biblical eschatology has been realized, that Jesus did in fact bring in the kingdom of God. His ministry, death, resurrection, ascension, and Parousia—a single complex event—*constitute* the actual presence of the kingdom. Jesus, according to Dodd, was not greatly concerned with the future. "Future eschatology" entered the New Testament as the result of the later church reconstructing Jesus' scheme on the basis of Jewish apocalyptic literature when he did not immediately return. Rather

---

7. Albert Schweitzer, *The Quest of the Historical Jesus*, 3d ed. (London: A. & C. Black, 1954), 368–69.
8. F. Holmström, *Das Eschatologische Denken der Gegenwart* (Gütersloh, Germany: Bertelsmann, 1936), 89, Hoekema's translation.

than predicting what was going to happen in some distant future, *Jesus was introducing or inaugurating the kingdom of God then and there.*

Accordingly, eschatology does not deal with last things in any temporal sense. Rather, it is concerned with ultimate things, things of ultimate significance. It concerns not the end of history but the "present of the eternal" in history. Apocalyptic language is merely an ancient expression of this truth. The exegete needs to understand that resurrection, ascension, and Second Coming are three variant expressions of the same truth.

Among Dodd's critics are Joachim Jeremias (*The Parables of Jesus,* 1954) and Oscar Cullmann, who in his *Christ and Time* (1951) gave his famous illustration of D-day, the decisive victory in the death and resurrection of Christ, with V-day to follow. In this way Cullmann preserves the "already" and the "not yet" of New Testament eschatology.

Existential Eschatology

Rudolf Bultmann (1884–1976) in his *Theology of the New Testament* (1951) champions the existentialistic eschatological construct. Advancing the notion that any moment of personal, crucial decision is "eschatological," Bultmann argues that the Eschaton is the *kairos* in which the individual human existent is given opportunity to decide for authentic existence. Eschatology is "realized" then, not as Dodd contended, in the ministry of the historical Jesus who (says Bultmann) was only a Jewish apocalyptic prophet announcing the immanent inbreaking of the kingdom of God, but in the proclamation of the *kerygma,* which, stripped of its apocalyptic mythology, calls for decision here and now:

> The essential thing about the eschatological message is the idea of God that operates in it [and that demands decision] and the idea of human existence that it contains—*not the belief that the end of the world is just ahead.*[9]

A similar view is expressed by Hendrikus Berkhof:

> We happen to live and breathe in a world of endless space and time, the product of an evolution of many millions of years, which is ruled to its farthest corners by the same laws. There is no room for either heaven or hell and even less for somebody who would be descending from heaven to earth on a cloud. And we

---

9. Rudolf Bultmann, *Theology of the New Testament,* trans. Kendrick Grobel (London: SCM, 1971), 1:23 (emphasis supplied).

cannot believe in a sudden, complete change, an invasion from above which would violently destroy the agelong evolution.[10]

Bultmann also urges, as an aspect of his thesis, the demythologizing method of exegesis on the basis of perceived different eschatological strata in the New Testament. He believes that already in the New Testament he sees John "demythologizing" Paul ("For John the resurrection of Jesus, Pentecost, and the *parousia* of Jesus are one and the same event"), which Johannine procedure, he contends, justifies the demythologizing method today.

Dispensational Eschatology

Into this wasteland of views created by these critical scholars in the first half of the twentieth century swept the eschatological views of dispensationalism. Ready for anything that sounded biblical and that taught that Christ was indeed going to come again someday, the evangelical church in Britain and the United States welcomed the pretribulation, premillennial view of this new school of prophetic interpretation, fostered chiefly by the 1909 and 1917 editions of the *Scofield Reference Bible* and the teaching of Dallas Theological Seminary, founded by Lewis Sperry Chafer in 1924.

Classic dispensationalists contend that "when Jesus appeared to the Jewish people, the next thing, in the order of revelation as it then stood, should have been the setting up of the Davidic kingdom." But, they also declare, "in the knowledge of God, *not yet disclosed,* lay the rejection of the kingdom and the King, the long period of the mystery-form of the kingdom, the world-wide preaching of the cross, and the out-calling of the Church."[11] Between the Old Testament prophecies concerning the future blessings of Israel and the church of this present age, dispensationalists urge, there is no connection. The Old Testament simply did not speak about this age. This age is the "grand empty parenthesis" in prophetic time. Therefore, all the Old Testament prophecies about Israel's future blessedness[12] await their fulfillment in a decidedly Jewish millennium which will follow this "parenthetical church age." This millennium will be preceded by a pretribulation rapture of the church, Daniel's "seventieth week" of great tribulation for both Jews and the world, and the second coming

---

10. Hendrikus Berkhof, *Well–Founded Hope* (Richmond: John Knox, 1969), 12. But see 2 Peter 3:4.
11. *New Scofield Reference Bible,* 996, emphasis supplied.
12. See Anthony Hoekema, *The Bible and the Future* (Grand Rapids, Mich.: Eerdmans, 1979), 194–222, for his critique of dispensational premillennialism in general and his handling of Old Testament prophecy in particular. Oswald T. Allis, *Prophecy and the Church* (Philadelphia: Presbyterian and Reformed, 1945), also offers a critique of dispensationalism and its eschatology.

of Christ, who will rule the nations with a rod of iron for a thousand years. After his thousand-year reign he will destroy all remaining hostility to him, officiate at the Great White Throne judgment, and then deliver up his kingdom to the Father that God may be all in all.

With such eschatological confusion running rampant today in scholarly circles, never has the need been greater to return to Scripture and to see what God's Word says concerning this vital, all-important, capstoning locus of theology.[13] In the following pages I have attempted to draw together all the biblical data pertinent to such an investigation in order to assist the reader to reach correct, that is, biblical, conclusions.

OLD TESTAMENT ESCHATOLOGY

Jesus began his public ministry by announcing that "the time has been fulfilled, and the kingdom of God [ἡ βασιλεία τοῦ θεοῦ, hē basileia tou theou] is at hand" (Mark 1:15). Nowhere did Jesus define what he meant by his use of the phrase "the kingdom of God." This would suggest that he assumed, because of Old Testament teaching on the subject, that the idea and something of its content were familiar to his listeners. While the expression "the kingdom of God" does not occur in the Old Testament, the idea is certainly present in the fact that God is frequently referred to as the King both of Israel (Exod. 15:18; Num. 23:21; Deut. 33:5; Ps. 84:3; Isa. 43:15) and of the whole earth (2 Kings 19:15; Pss. 29:10; 47:2, 7; 96:10; 97:1; 99:1–4; 145:11–13; Isa. 6:5; Jer. 10:7; 46:18; Dan. 2:44; 4:34–35).

George Eldon Ladd characterizes the Old Testament concept of the kingdom of God in a general way as (1) a dynamic hope, (2) an eschatological hope, (3) an earthly hope, (4) a historically orientated hope, and (5) an ethical hope:[14]

By *dynamic* hope Ladd means that Israel expected God's "kingdom" (מַלְכוּת, *malkût*), conceived primarily as the reign, dominion, or rule of God, and only secondarily as the realm over which his reign is exercised, to be extended over the world of men and the world itself (Ps. 145:11, 13).

By *eschatological* hope he means that, as Israel apostatized more and more away from God, less and less did the godly look to history as the instrument to produce the "kingdom" and increasingly did the prophets speak of a direct cataclysmic "inbreaking" or visitation of God at the end of history to bring history to a glorious consummation by redeeming his remnant and judging the ungodly and wicked.

---

13. For a fuller treatment of this debate the student should consult Ladd, *The Presence of the Future*, 3–42, and the appendix, "Recent Trends in Eschatology," in Hoekema, *The Bible and the Future*, 288–316.
14. Ladd, *The Presence of the Future*, 45–75.

By *earthly* hope he intends that Israel's eschatological hope of redemption always included the earth as "the divinely ordained scene of human existence" (Isa. 11:9; 35:2, 7, 15; 65:17; 66:22).

By *historically orientated* hope (sometimes referred to as "prophetic foreshortening") he avers that the prophets had a *single,* though complex, hope which encompassed both the more immediate historical future and the ultimate eschatological future at the same time. That is to say, because they lacked full information regarding the time factor in predictive prophecy of future events (1 Pet. 1:10–11), they often intermingled more immediate future events with the ultimate future without regard to strict sequence or chronology (see, e.g., the prophets' concept of the Day of the Lord).

Finally, by *ethical* hope he means that the promise of the future kingdom of God held out hope only for those who were faithful to God, and therefore "a constant ethical demand is laid upon Israel to turn from her sins and to submit to God." Only judgment awaits the unrepentant.

We should add that the Old Testament kingdom concept also included the *messianic* hope. Geerhardus Vos isolates five essential aspects of that vision: (1) the imposition from above of a *rule over men* that requires of them absolute submission (Gen. 49:10; Num. 24:17–19); (2) the element of the *eschatological,* reflected in the idea that the Messiah will be "the great final King, who stands at the close of the present world order and ushers in the coming world," this new world appearing not in the natural course of events but catastrophically through a divine interposition (see Ladd's second characterization) and, when once attained, bearing the stamp of eternity, with the Messiah himself standing at the center of this eschatological complex (Pss. 2:8–12; 45:6; 110:1, 5–6; Isa. 9:2–7; Dan. 2:44; 7:13–14; Mal. 3:2–3; 4:1–5); (3) inseparable from the second, the *supernatural ingredient pervading the whole vision,* as it portends the creation of a new world order different in nature from the present one, in which a return to the paradisiacal state that existed at the beginning of history is brought about (see Ladd's third characterization) (Isa. 11:1–9; 32:15; 65:17–25); (4) the component of the *soteric* in which both a spiritual and martial salvation is accomplished by the Lord through his Messiah who delivers his people from divine judgment and introduces them into the blessedness of the new world to come (see Ladd's second and fifth characterizations) (Isa. 9:4–5; 11:1–16; Mic. 5:4–5a; Zech. 9:9–10); and (5) interwoven through it all, the *specifically religious position that the Messiah himself occupies between God and man,* entailing basically both his right to receive worship and his identification with God.[15]

---

15. Geerhardus Vos, *The Self-Disclosure of Jesus* (1926; reprint, Phillipsburg, N.J.: Presbyterian and Reformed, 1978), 17–31. See also Robert L. Reymond, *Jesus, Divine Messiah: The Old Testament Witness* (Ross-shire, Scotland: Christian Focus, 1990).

Anthony Hoekema summarizes the eschatological outlook of the Old Testament by calling attention to seven specific revelational concepts in which that outlook was embodied. There was, he writes, (1) *the expectation of the coming Redeemer,* revealed first as the "seed of the woman" (Gen. 3:15), then the "seed of Abraham" (Gen. 22:18), then a descendant of the tribe of Judah (Gen. 49:10) and specifically a son of David (2 Sam. 7:12–13), who would in some not completely clear but unique and final way fill the offices of prophet (Deut. 18:15), priest (Ps. 110:4), king (Zech. 9:9), suffering servant of God (Isa. 42:1–4; 49:5–7; 52:13–53:12), and son of man (Dan. 7:13–14); (2) *the anticipation of the kingdom of God* when God's rule would be fully experienced, not just by Israel, but by the whole world (Dan. 2:44–45); (3) *the making of a new covenant* with Israel by which instrument God would forgive his people of their sins and idolatry (Jer. 31:31–34); (4) *the restoration of Israel* from her captivity by hostile nations (Isa. 11:11; Jer 23:3; Ezek. 36:24–28); (5) *the outpouring of the Spirit* upon all flesh (Joel 2:28–32); (6) *the approach of the Day of the Lord* which would mean judgment upon the unbelieving nations and deliverance for the people of God (Obad. 15–16; Joel 1:15; 2:1–17; Isa. 13; Amos 5:18–20; Zeph. 1:7, 14–16; Mal. 4:5); and (7) *the creation of a new heaven and a new earth* (Isa. 11:6–9; 32:15; 35:7; 65:17; 66:22).[16]

In connection with the coming Day of the Lord the Old Testament prophets also envisioned the resurrection of both the righteous and the unrighteous (Job 19:25–27; Ps. 73:24–25; Isa. 26:19; Dan. 12:2; see Matt. 22:29–32; Heb. 11:10, 13–16, 19) and a judgment to follow (Ps. 50:4–6; Eccles. 12:14; Mal. 3:2–5).

All of these things loomed on the horizon for the Old Testament believer who had neither a clear understanding of when these things would come to pass nor a complete blueprint of how these events would all be related temporally to each other. Even the prophets themselves, Peter informs us, "searched intently and with the greatest care, trying to find out the time and circumstances to which the Spirit of Christ in them was pointing when he predicted the sufferings of Christ and the glories that would follow." But Peter also states that at least this much was revealed to them—"that they were not serving themselves but [the faithful of a coming age], when they spoke of the things that have now been told . . . by those who have preached the gospel . . . by the Holy Spirit sent from heaven" (1 Pet. 1:10–12).

NEW TESTAMENT ESCHATOLOGY

New Testament eschatology began precisely where Old Testament eschatology had been suspended (see Mal. 3:1; 4:5–6), with the angel Gabriel's announcements

---

16. Hoekema, *The Bible and the Future*, 3–12.

to Elizabeth and Mary concerning the births of John, son of Zechariah, and Jesus. Concerning John Gabriel declared:

> Many of the people of Israel will he bring back to the Lord their God. And he will go on before the Lord, in the spirit and power of Elijah, to turn the hearts of the fathers to their children and the disobedient to the wisdom of the righteous—to make ready a people prepared for the Lord. (Luke 1:16–17)

Zechariah his father predicted of John:

> And you, my child, will be called a prophet of the Most High; for you will go on before the Lord to prepare the way for him. (Luke 1:76)

Clearly, John was the "Elijah-forerunner" whom the Lord of Hosts (יהוה צְבָאוֹת, *yhwh ṣᵉbā'ôt*) had said he would send before him to prepare the people for his coming, a conclusion Jesus himself bears out in Matthew 11:14 and 17:11–13.[17] Concerning Mary's Son in particular Gabriel announced:

> The Lord God will give him the throne of his father David, and he will reign [βασιλεύσει, *basileusei*] over the house of Jacob forever; his kingdom [βασιλείας, *basileias*] will never end. (Luke 1:32–33)

Both Mary (Luke 1:54–55) and Zechariah (Luke 1:68–75) perceived and celebrated

---

17. In Matthew 11:14 Jesus declared to the crowd: "If you are willing to accept it, [John the Baptist] is the Elijah who was to come." Then coming down from the mountain the day following Christ's transfiguration (Luke 9:27), the disciples asked Jesus: "Why, therefore, do the teachers of the law say that Elijah must come first?" (Matt. 17:10; Mark 9:11). Their mention of Elijah, of course, was prompted by the fact that they had just seen him. But what lay behind their question about him? There can be no doubt that it was something in Malachi's prophecy that now was perplexing them. Malachi had said that "Elijah" would come *before* the Lord came (Mal. 3:1), *before* the great and terrible day of the Lord (Mal. 4:5), which they had just seen "in miniature." The implications of their question for the identity of Jesus must not be lost on the reader. The only conclusion one can draw is that for them Jesus—just attested as such by the glory of his deity shining through his humanity and by the heavenly Voice—was Malachi's "Lord who was to come," the Yahweh of Hosts of the Old Testament, but the order of their historical appearances—Jesus had first appeared, then Elijah—seemed to them to be the reverse of what Malachi had predicted. This seeming inversion of the prophet's order was what was creating for them the quandary which provoked their question. Jesus solved their problem for them by informing them that "Elijah," in the person of John the Baptist, had indeed come first, whom Jesus had then followed as that "Elijah's" Lord. By his exposition of Malachi's prophecy here, Jesus identified John as the promised Elijah of Malachi 4:5 and laid unmistakable claim to being the Yahweh of Hosts, the Messenger of the Covenant, who had promised he would come *after* "Elijah," his messenger, had come.

the births of their respective sons as aspects of God's fulfilling his covenant promise to Abraham, while Simeon (Luke 2:29–32) and Anna (Luke 2:38) later described the infant Jesus as God's "salvation," "a light for revelation to the Gentiles and for glory to your people Israel," and "the redemption of Jerusalem." Simeon also intimated that Jesus' ministry would include a tragic dimension (2:34–35).

John the Baptist's Eschatology

As Jesus' forerunner, John the Baptist summoned the nation of Israel to repentance and to faith in the coming Messiah (see Acts 19:4), saying both "Repent, for the kingdom of heaven [ἡ βασιλεία[18] τῶν οὐρανῶν, *hē basileia tōn ouranōn*] has drawn near [ἤγγικεν, *ēngiken*]" (Matt. 3:2) and "Look, the Lamb of God, who takes away the sin of the world!" (John 1:29). Elaborating upon this basic message, John proclaimed:

> The ax is *already* [ἤδη, *ēdē*] at the root of the trees, and every tree that does not produce good fruit will be cut down and thrown into the fire. I baptize you with water for repentance. But after me will come one who is more powerful than I, whose sandals I am not fit to carry. He will baptize you with the Holy Spirit and with fire. His winnowing fork is in his hand, and he will clear his threshing floor, gathering the wheat into his barn and burning up the chaff with unquenchable fire. (Matt. 3:10–12)

Here we see John declaring that Israel had reached a definitive crisis point in its history ("the ax is already at the root of the trees"), and here we see him ascribing to Jesus the prerogatives both of salvation ("will baptize with the Holy Spirit") and of judgment ("and with fire"; see the occurrences of "fire" at the end of vv. 10 and 12).[19] God had visited his people, and his kingdom had broken into history! *Eschatology, in some sense, had been realized!*

In John's ascription to Jesus of the prerogatives both of salvation and of judgment, while at the same time drawing no time distinction between the manifestations of

---

18. Like the Hebrew מַלְכוּת (*malkût*, "kingdom"), the βασιλεία (*basileia*, "kingdom") of heaven (or of God) should be construed dynamically as referring primarily to the reign, dominion, or rule of God, and only secondarily to the realm over which his reign is exercised. For the evidence, see Ladd, *The Presence of the Future*, 122–48.

19. The occurrence of two nouns—"with Spirit" and "with fire"—with only one verb ("baptize") is an example of what is called in hermeneutics a zeugma, which is a figure of speech which promotes brevity of expression. Usually the first noun directly suits the verb and a second verb which better suits the second noun must be supplied by the interpreter. Here I would submit the verb "judge" better fits "with fire." John's predicted judgment against Israel here saw its fulfillment in the destruction of Jerusalem in A.D. 70.

these prerogatives, we see a classic example of what Ladd refers to as the Old Testament prophet's *historically orientated* single, though complex, hope. This hope encompassed both the immediate historical future and the ultimate eschatological future, viewing the immediate future in terms of the ultimate future without regard to strict sequence or chronology. And this absence of chronology in John's message is doubtless what moved him in prison to dispatch his disciples to ask Jesus: "Are you the one who is to come, or should we expect another?" John's questions posed to Jesus arose, not out of doubt on his part about the veracity of Jesus' messianic claims, but rather out of his prophetic impatience, based upon his limited knowledge, with what he regarded as Jesus' slowness to accomplish what he had announced the Messiah would do when he came—namely, destroy the unrepentant and bring his people to their ultimate salvation. His questions constituted an oblique rebuke of Jesus because he saw no evidence in Jesus' ministry of God's righteous judgment against sinners—the second half of his description of Messiah's work.

Jesus' descriptions of John as "an unswaying reed" and as a man accustomed to difficult circumstances, who under the dire circumstances of imprisonment had not begun to doubt the message he had proclaimed about him, were intended to assure the people—since it was imperative that the people understand that John's witness to Jesus remained intact and had not faltered—that John had not wavered in his conviction about Jesus' messianic role simply because he was in prison.[20]

Jesus' Eschatology

C. H. Dodd argues that it was Jesus' "genuinely creative thinking" that brought together "very diverse [Old Testament] scriptures . . . so that they interpret one another in hitherto unsuspected ways," resulting in turn in "an original, and far-reaching resolution of the tension" which existed between the several features of Old Testament eschatology (e.g., David's victorious Priest–King, Isaiah's Suffering Servant, Daniel's Son of Man) and in "a fresh understanding of the mysterious imagery of apocalyptic eschatology."[21] Dodd is absolutely right. The church needs to recognize anew that Jesus Christ is not only its Savior and Lord but also its chief "prophetic scholar." It is from his eschatological teaching that the church should and must derive the programmatic paradigm within which the remainder of New Testament eschatology should be placed.

---

20. See Geerhardus Vos, *Biblical Theology* (Grand Rapids, Mich.: Eerdmans, 1949), 337–38, for a similar representation of John's questions—asked in impatience, not in doubt.
21. C. H. Dodd, *According to the Scriptures* (London: Nisbet, 1952), 108–10.

When Jesus began his public ministry, he declared, in the same vein as his forerunner but in even sharper terms: "The time *has been fulfilled* [Πεπλήρωται, *Peplērōtai*]. The kingdom of God *has drawn near* [ἤγγικεν, *ēngiken*]."[22] Repent and believe the gospel" (Mark 1:15). Luke's Christ expresses the same idea: "Today this Scripture [Isa. 61:1–2] *has been fulfilled* [πεπλήρωται, *peplērōtai*] in your hearing" (Luke 4:21). Later Jesus would declare: "From the days of John the Baptist *until now* [ἕως ἄρτι, *heōs arti*], the kingdom of heaven *has been forcefully advancing* [construing βιάζεται, *biazetai*, as a middle], and *violent men* [βιασταί, *biastai*] are trying to plunder [that is, subvert] it" (Matt. 11:12; Luke 16:16).[23] To the Pharisees—some of those "violent men"—he declared: "if I drive out demons by the Spirit of God, then the kingdom of God *has come* [ἔφθασεν, *ephthasen*] upon you" (Matt. 12:28; Luke 11:20). Later still, when asked by the Pharisees when the kingdom of God would come, Jesus replied: "The kingdom of God does not come in an observable manner, nor will people say, 'Here it is,' or 'There it is,' because [γάρ, *gar*] the kingdom of God is *within you* [ἐντὸς ὑμῶν, *entos hymōn*; or 'within your reach']" (Luke 17:20–21).[24] To the chief priests and elders of the nation who opposed him Jesus declared: "I tell you that the kingdom of God [which is 'within your reach'] will be taken from you and given to a people who will produce its fruit" (Matt. 21:43). To the experts in the law Jesus declared: "Woe to you . . . , because you have taken away the key to knowledge [Matt. 23:13: 'the kingdom of heaven']. You yourselves have not entered, and you have hindered those who were entering" (Luke 11:52). Finally, at the last Passover meal Jesus declared to his disciples: "I confer on ["give by covenant to"] you a kingdom, just as my Father *conferred* [διέθετό, *dietheto*—"gave by covenant to"] one on me" (Luke 22:29). Clearly, with the coming of Jesus to the nation of Israel the kingdom or rule of God had broken into history and into the lives of his generation in his own person.

---

22. I regard ἤγγικεν, *ēngiken*, the perfect active of ἐγγίζω (*engizō*, "to be near"), as intending here what ἔφθασεν, *ephthasen*, the aorist active of φθάνω (*phthanō*, "to arrive"), intends in Matthew 12:28 and Luke 11:20, that is, "has come." For the debate over the meaning of these two words, see Clarence T. Craig, "Realized Eschatology," *Journal of Biblical Literature* 56 (1937): 17–26, and Kenneth W. Clark, "Realized Eschatology," *Journal of Biblical Literature* 59 (1940): 367–83.

23. George E. Ladd also construes the verb as a middle voice but understands the "violent men" as "keen enthusiasts" who want to lay hold of the kingdom, if necessary, even by radical action (see Mark 9:43, 47; Luke 14:26) (*Theology of the New Testament* [Grand Rapids, Mich.: Eerdmans, 1974], 71), even though BAGD states that the other three uses of βιαστής, *biastes*, are all used in a "bad sense." But even if βιάζεται, *biazetai*, should be construed as a passive ("the kingdom of heaven is being violently attacked" or "the kingdom of heaven is being sought with burning zeal"), the specific point I am making here is still the same, namely, that the kingdom of God arrived with Jesus' coming and was in some sense present then and there in his person and ministry.

24. See G. R. Beasley-Murray, *Jesus and the Kingdom of God* (Grand Rapids, Mich.: Eerdmans, 1986), 97–103, for the argument for this translation of ἐντὸς ὑμῶν, *entos hymōn*.

And yet Jesus also spoke of the kingdom of God as something future as well, which awaited his coming (παρουσία, *parousia*)[25] in glory when the full manifestation of his power would make actual the divine rule throughout the world. For example, he taught his disciples that they should pray, "May your kingdom come" (Matt. 6:10). He then declared:

> Not everyone who says to me, "Lord, Lord," will enter the [future] kingdom of heaven, but only he who does the will of my Father who is in heaven. Many will say to me on that day, "Lord, Lord, did we not prophesy in your name, and in your name drive out demons and perform many miracles?" Then I will tell them plainly, "I never knew you. Away from me, you evil-doers!" (Matt. 7:21–23)

He also affirmed:

> I say to you that many will come from the east and the west, and will take their places at the feast with Abraham, Isaac and Jacob in the kingdom of heaven, but the subjects of the kingdom will be thrown outside, into the darkness, where there will be weeping and grinding of teeth. (Matt. 8:11–12)

To his disciples he promised:

> I tell you the truth, at the renewal of all things [ἐν τῇ παλιγγενεσία, *en tē palingenesia*], when the Son of Man sits on his throne in heavenly glory, you who have followed me will also sit on twelve thrones, judging the twelve tribes of Israel. (Matt. 19:28)

In his Olivet discourse Jesus described his future coming and kingdom this way:

---

25. Παρουσία, *parousia*, is the primary New Testament term denoting the return of Christ. It is derived from πάρειμι (*pareimi*, "to be present, to have come") and can denote "presence" in contrast to "absence" (ἀπουσία, *apousia*), as in Philippians 2:12, or it can denote "coming" in the sense of the *first* stage of being present, as in Philippians 1:26 (BAGD, 629–30). In the Gospels παρουσία, *parousia*, occurs only in Matthew 24:3, 27, 37, 39. Its uses in Paul point us to the classic passages of his eschatology (1 Thess. 2:19; 3:13; 4:15; 5:23; 2 Thess. 2:1; 1 Cor. 15:23). It occurs also as a reference to Christ's return in James 5:7, 2 Peter 1:16, 3:4, and 1 John 2:28. Overall, it seems to emphasize the presence of the Lord which is to be realized at his return to earth.

The other New Testament terms for the Second Advent are ἀποκάλυψις (*apokalypsis*, "revelation"; 2 Thess. 1:7, 10; 1 Pet. 1:7, 13; 4:13) and ἐπιφάνεια (*epiphaneia*, "appearing"; 2 Thess. 2:8; 1 Tim. 6:14; 2 Tim. 1:10 [here it refers to Christ's first coming], 4:1, 8; Titus 2:13). The former implies previous hiddenness (BAGD, 92), the latter speaks of "splendid appearance," "visible manifestation," or glorious exposure (BAGD, 304). The verb φανερόω, (*phaneroō*, "make known, reveal, make evident, appear"), from which ἐπιφάνεια, *epiphaneia*, is derived, is used of both the first and second advents (Col. 3:4; 1 Tim. 3:16; Heb. 9:26; 1 Pet. 1:20; 5:4; 1 John 2:28; 3:2, 5, 8).

When the Son of Man comes in his glory, and all the angels with him, he will sit on his throne in heavenly glory. All the nations will be gathered before him, and he will separate the people one from another as a shepherd separates the sheep from the goats. He will put the sheep on his right and the goats on his left. Then the King [ὁ βασιλεὺς, *ho basileus*, that is, he himself] will say to those on his right, "Come, you who are blessed of my Father, take your inheritance, the kingdom [βασιλείαν, *basileian*] prepared for you since the creation of the world." (Matt. 25:31–34)

Finally, at the last Passover meal Jesus informed his disciples:

"I will not drink from this fruit of the vine from now on until that day when I drink it anew with you in my Father's kingdom." (Matt. 26:29)

Clearly, for Jesus the full and final manifestation of the kingdom of God lay in the future.

In this tension between the "already" and the "not yet" we are faced with what has been referred to by biblical theologians as the New Testament paradigm—traceable to Jesus as its Originator—of "eschatological dualism," that is to say, in one sense the kingdom of God has come; in another sense the kingdom of God is yet to come. What the Old Testament had not clearly distinguished chronologically but had represented more as a single though complex unit, Jesus now distinguishes by speaking of the kingdom's arrival first in grace and later in judgment with cataclysmic power and great glory.[26] This may be seen in Jesus' kingdom of heaven parables.

His Kingdom of Heaven Parables

In Matthew 13 we find seven of Jesus' "kingdom of heaven" parables—the sower and the four kinds of soil, the wheat and the tares, the mustard seed, the leaven, the treasure hidden in the field, the pearl of great value, and the net (Mark 4:26–29 adds an eighth—the growing seed). Jesus declared that these parables revealed certain "mysteries" of the kingdom of heaven (13:11). He explained what he meant by "mysteries" by saying that "many prophets and righteous men desired to see what you see [note the implied presence of the kingdom in what Jesus says here], and did

---

26. Hoekema in *The Bible and the Future* characterizes the nature of New Testament eschatology in three sentences: (1) "In the New Testament we find the realization that the great eschatological event predicted in the Old Testament has happened" (15); (2) "In the New Testament we also find the realization that what the Old Testament writers seemed to depict as one movement must now be recognized as involving two stages: the present Messianic age and the age of the future" (18); and (3) "The relation between these two eschatological stages is that the blessings of the present age are the pledge and guarantee of greater blessings to come" (20).

not see it; and to hear what you hear [note again the implied presence of the message of the kingdom in what Jesus says here], and did not hear it" (13:17, emphasis supplied), with Matthew himself adding that Jesus spoke in parables "so that what was spoken through the prophet [Asaph] might be fulfilled [πληρωθῇ, plērōthē], saying, 'I will open my mouth in parables; I will utter things hidden since the foundation of the world'" (13:34–35; see Ps. 78:2).

The classic dispensational school understands Jesus to mean by these parables that he was revealing, for the very first time in history, that he and the messianic kingdom would be rejected and that "the long period of the mystery-form of the kingdom," all of which was unknown to the Old Testament prophets, would follow. But this is a classic example of hermeneutical "reaching," that is, seeing in the passage what one already desires to find there. The Reformed view is that Jesus was declaring that the kingdom of God had indeed come but had come first in grace (the "already") before it came in power (the "not yet"), a distinction not clearly seen by the Old Testament prophets.

The first thing that must be established is the meaning of the phrase, "the kingdom of heaven." Classic dispensationalists contend that "the kingdom of heaven" must be distinguished from "the kingdom of God," with the former referring to the literal, earthly, Davidic, millennial kingdom, while the latter refers to the universal reign of God in general. It was the former, they urge, that Jesus specifically had in mind when he first proclaimed that the kingdom of heaven was "at hand" (Matt. 4:17). But these phrases are actually linguistic variations of the same idea, as evidenced by their identity of meaning within the compass of the two verses of Matthew 19:23–24 and by their parallel usage in the Synoptic Gospels, that is to say, where Matthew employs "the kingdom of heaven," Mark and Luke will employ "the kingdom of God" (see, for example, Matt. 13:11; Mark 4:11; Luke 8:10 and Matt. 19:14; Mark 10:14; Luke 18:17). Both terms refer to the sovereign redemptive rule of God in these contexts.

Now what was it about the redemptive kingdom or gracious rule of God that Jesus declared "had been hidden" from men prior to his coming? The Jews, on the basis of passages such as Daniel 2, clearly knew already about the kingdom of God. Moreover, the picture Daniel 2:34–35 and 44–45 give concerning the coming of the kingdom of God is one entailing the cataclysmic, eschatological overthrow of all the kingdoms of this world. Daniel 2 taught the Jews that when the kingdom of God came, it would brook no competition. It would crush every earthly power and authority before it, fill the whole earth and endure forever. Accordingly, it was this very "kingdom in power," because of Rome's oppression, which the Jews of the first century by and large were anticipating. If Jesus in fact had gone about offering *this* kingdom to the Jews, as dispensationalists insist, it is inexplicable, particularly in light of the display of his mighty "powers" (δυνάμεις, *dynameis*; see Matt. 11:20–23;

13:54, 58; Luke 10:13; 19:37), why the Jews rejected him. But Jesus, by his kingdom of heaven parables in Matthew 13, revealed that the kingdom of God, which was from the perspective of the Old Testament a complex but "undivided unit," would unfold itself in two stages.[27] The second stage—the consummating phase—of the kingdom of God, Jesus taught, would indeed come as Daniel had prophesied, manifesting itself with the coming of the Son of Man in great power and glory (Matt. 25:31–46). But before it came in *power*, Jesus taught by these "mystery" parables, the kingdom had first come in *grace*, also in his own person (see Matt. 13:37), coming gradually, coming largely in the internal, invisible sphere of the spiritual life, and tolerating imperfections in its subjects and even resistance from the world system and the kingdom of Satan. In its "mystery [that is, previously unclear but *now* unveiled] manifestation," as Ladd explains the parables:

> the kingdom has come among men but not with power which compels every knee to bow before its glory; it is rather like seed cast on the ground which may be fruitful or unfruitful depending upon its reception (Matt. 13:3–8). The kingdom has come, but the present order is not disrupted; the sons of the kingdom and the sons of the evil one grow together in the world until the harvest (Matt. 13:24–30; 36–43).[28] The kingdom of God has indeed come to men, not as a new glorious order, but like the proverbial mustard seed. However, its insignificance must not be despised. This same kingdom will one day be a great tree (Matt. 13:31–32). Instead of a world-transforming power, the kingdom is present in an almost imperceptible form like a bit of leaven hidden in a bowl of dough. However, this same kingdom will yet fill the earth [in this "present evil age"—Gal. 1:4] as the leavened dough fills the bowl (Matt. 13:33). . . .
>
> The coming of the kingdom of God in humility instead of glory was an utterly new and amazing revelation. Yet, said Jesus, men should not be deceived. Although the present manifestation of the kingdom is in humility—indeed, its Bearer was put to death as a condemned criminal—it *is* nevertheless the kingdom of God, and, like buried treasure or a priceless pearl, its acquisition merits any cost or sacrifice (Matt. 13:44–46). The fact that the present activity of the kingdom will initiate a movement that will include evil men as well as good should not lead to misunderstanding of its true nature. It *is* the kingdom of

---

27. See Vos, *Biblical Theology*, 399–411.
28. The parable of the wheat and the tares is especially significant for the study of eschatology, for it appears to describe the course of world history between Christ's earthly ministry and his return. Both the "wheat" and the "tares" will apparently grow until the harvest, excluding the postmillennial vision of a "saved world." But the harvest "at the end of the age" eliminates completely the "tares," excluding both a millennial period and the host of unregenerate people over whom, according to premillennialists, Christ and the saints are supposed to hold temporal rule during that period.

God; it will one day divide the good from the evil in eschatological salvation and judgment (Matt. 13:47–50).[29]

And I might add, in view of Jesus' parable of the seed growing by itself (Mark 4:26–29), the kingdom is God's *supernatural* breaking into history in the person of Jesus, it is heaven's *miracle*, it is *God's* deed! The kingdom will advance—though men "know not how"—all by itself [αὐτομάτη, *automatē*]," "whether [they] sleep or get up," because of its own innate vitality to reproduce itself.

When Jesus' "mystery" parables of the kingdom are rightly interpreted then, it will be seen that Jesus taught by them precisely the opposite of what dispensationalists say he taught. Far from offering to the Jews the kingdom of God in power (which they rejected), he declared that he was proclaiming first to them (and then to other men) the spiritual reign of God's grace within and over the hearts of men which, as Paul says in Romans 14:17, brings "righteousness and peace and joy in the Holy Spirit"—a reign which men could resist and which the majority of Jews did in fact reject. They crucified the Bearer of the gospel of the kingdom as a deceiver and a blasphemer—in fulfillment of the prophecies of the Old Testament!

Jesus' paradigmatic distinction between the present "kingdom of grace" and the future "kingdom of power" is also the foundation for (1) his, and later his apostles', distinction, on the one hand, between "this age" (Luke 16:8; 20:34; Rom. 12:2; Gal. 1:4; Eph. 2:2), "this time" (Luke 18:30), and "the now age" (1 Tim. 6:17; 2 Tim. 4:10; Tit. 2:12), and, on the other, "that age" (Luke 20:35), the "age to come" (Mark 10:30; Luke 18:30; Matt. 12:32), or "the ages to come" (Eph. 2:7); and (2) the New Testament writers' distinction, on the one hand, between their *being* in the "last days" (Acts 2:17; 1 Tim. 3:1; Heb. 1:2; James 5:3; 2 Pet. 3:3; Jude 18), the "last times" (1 Pet. 1:20), and the "last hour" (1 John 2:18), and, on the other, their *anticipation* of the "last day" (John 6:39, 40, 44, 54; 11:24; 12:48), the "last trumpet" (1 Cor. 15:52), and "last time" (1 Pet. 1:5).

Accordingly, Paul can declare that "the end of the ages has come" (1 Cor. 10:11) and yet speak of "the ages to come" (Eph. 2:7), and the writer of Hebrews can assert that Christ has appeared at "the end of the ages" (Heb. 9:26) and yet speak also of "the coming age" (Heb. 6:5) when he "will appear a second time, not to bear sin, but to bring salvation to those who are waiting for him" (9:28).

These distinctions clearly teach that the present age is the *consummating* period of God's *saving* activity and is therefore "eschatological" in the salvific sense. Moreover, Christ's present reign is not simply one reign alongside others. Distinct in its

---

29. George E. Ladd, "Kingdom of Christ, God, Heaven," *Evangelical Dictionary of Theology* (Grand Rapids, Mich.: Baker, 1984), 609–10.

nature from all other kingdoms—as distinct as a man is from beasts (see Dan. 7:2–14)—his kingdom of grace is

> the only kingdom that decisively attests that life is more ultimate than death, that mercy can outreach the arenas of sin and guilt, and that the sphere of God is greater than the realms of hell. It signals the satisfaction of all legitimate human need, the triumph of divine mercy, humanity living life fit for eternity, the homecoming of the renewed community of God. It is the kingdom that cannot be frustrated by the puppet kingdoms of Satan but that explains them for what they really are. It is the enduring kingdom amid others that rise only to have their half day and then perish.
> ... the coming of Jesus of Nazareth advances the prophetic promise of the eschatological kingdom into the sphere of fulfillment—if not total fulfillment, yet nonetheless realization in a crucially significant way....
> Jesus in his own person is the embodied sovereignty of God. He lives out that sovereignty in the flesh. He manifests the kingdom of God by enthroning the creation-will of God and demonstrating his lordship over Satan. Jesus conducts himself as Lord and true King, ruling over human hearts, ruling over demons, ruling over nature at its fiercest, ruling over sickness, conquering death itself. With the coming of Jesus the kingdom is not merely immanent; it gains the larger scope of incursion and invasion. Jesus points to his release of the victims of Satan, and to his own devastation of demons and the demonic, as attesting that "the kingdom of God has come upon you" (Mark 12:28). He reveals God's royal power in its salvific activity.[30]

The age to come, exhibiting as it will God's consummating *judgment* activity and the beginning of the eternal state of the new heaven and the new earth, is "eschatological" in the final, eternal sense. That age will be ushered in by the King at his coming in power and glory:

> He shall come with a retinue of heavenly beings, an entourage of angels, which he refused to summon when he was impaled on the cross but who as God's servants remain at Christ's disposal in this final vindication of the godly and punishment of the wicked.
> To this eschatological climax we are directed not only by the Old Testament prophets but by Jesus of Nazareth as well. The past New Testament fulfillment does not exhaust either the predictions of the prophets or the promises of Jesus on earth or the apostolic teaching. In the present age the Church ... at her best ... only approximates [the kingdom], and at her worst she can even do violence

---

30. Carl F. H. Henry, "Reflections on the Kingdom of God," *Journal of the Evangelical Theological Society* 35, no. 1 (1992): 42.

to it. Jesus Christ himself, and the apostles in agreement, and the Old Testament writers in anticipation, speak in principle and in fact of Christ's second coming and of the kingdom's coming . . . in its complete and consummate manifestation, a kingdom coming on earth as well as existing in heaven, a kingdom temporal and historical . . . that dwarfs all world empires.[31]

His Olivet Discourse (Matt. 24–25; Mark 13; Luke 21:3–36; 17:22–37)

In his Olivet discourse Jesus corrected his disciples' thinking about some aspects of his Second Advent which will terminate the "now age" and usher in the "age to come." In so doing he gave the church its most complete description of that future event and its concomitants.

Its Setting

The Olivet discourse is "prophetic/apocalyptic" literature. In it Jesus addresses in a more sustained way than he does anywhere else events of the future and specifically his Second Advent. To understand our Lord's prophetic oracle here, one must first place it in its contextual setting.

Jesus had been teaching in the temple area and had concluded his time there by pronouncing seven "prophetic woes" (impending judgments) against the teachers of the law and the Pharisees because of their perfunctory religiosity, hypocrisy, and unbelief (Matt. 23:13–32). In his final remarks he declared that God's judgment against the nation's sin, whose sin had been accumulating over the centuries and which at that very moment was in process of culminating in the nation's climactic rejection of its Messiah, would be poured out on *that* generation of Jews:

Matthew 23:32, 35–36: "Fill up, then, the measure of the sin of your fathers! . . . upon you[32] will come all [the guilt of previous generations for] the righteous

---

31. Ibid., 45–46.
32. This is an expression of the divine purpose, either according to the principles enunciated in Genesis 15:16 and Exodus 20:5 or because of the unitary, corporate solidarity of Israel as a nation. Most likely it is reflective of both ideas (see Jesus' "whom you [pl.] murdered"). John A. Broadus, *Commentary on the Gospel of Matthew* (Philadelphia: American Baptist Publication Society, 1886), 476, citing Plumptre, writes: "Men make the guilt of past ages their own, reproduce its atrocities, identify themselves with it; and so, what seems at first an arbitrary decree, visiting on the children the sins of the fathers, becomes in such cases a righteous judgment. If they repent, they cut off the terrible entail of sin and punishment; but if they harden themselves in their evil, they inherit the delayed punishment of their father's sins as well as of their own."

blood that has been shed on earth, from the blood of righteous Abel to the blood of Zechariah . . . ,[33] whom you [pl.] murdered between the temple and the altar. I tell you the truth, all this [ταῦτα, *tauta*, lit. "these things"] will come upon this generation [τὴν γενεὰν ταύτην, *tēn genean tautēn*]."[34]

Jesus then left the temple area. But as he was leaving, his disciples called his attention to the beauty and magnificence of the temple (Mark 13:1; Luke 21:5). Our Lord's response was terse: "Do you see all these things? I tell you the truth, not one stone here will be left on another; every one will be thrown down" (Matt. 24:2). There is no question that here our Lord was predicting the destruction of Jerusalem which took place in A.D. 70.

Peter, James, John, and Andrew (Mark 13:3) came to him privately as he was sitting on the Mount of Olives overlooking the temple and asked him, "When will these things happen, and what will be the sign of your coming [παρουσίας, *parousias*] and of the end of the age?" (Matt. 24:3).[35] The first thing that should be noted is that the disciples seemed to believe that the temple's destruction, Jesus' future coming, and the end of the age would all occur at the same time. Jesus answered their questions in what we now know as his Olivet discourse. And we should assume, I would suggest, that Jesus' answer was not only a *response* to their question concerning the time of the temple's destruction but also a *corrective* to their misconception that the three future events they mentioned would occur simultaneously. That is to say, his answer distinguishes temporally between the soon-to-be destruction of the temple which he had just forecast, and his own coming and the end of the age in the distant future.

---

33. This Zechariah is probably Zechariah, son of Jehoiada, who was stoned to death in the courtyard of the temple during Joash's reign (2 Chron. 24:20–22). The Hebrew canon has Chronicles at the end, so that our Lord seems to suggest that the guilt of all such cases, from Genesis to Chronicles, would culminate upon the heads of His generation. Sinaiticus omits "son of Barachiah."

34. Some dispensational exegetes insist that the Greek words γενεὰν ταύτην, *genean tautēn*, here mean "this race," that is, the Jewish people. But Matthew employs γενεά, *genea*, regularly to mean "generation," that is, a group of people living at the same time (Matt. 1:17, three times; 11:16; 12:39, 41, 45; 16:4; 17:17; see also Luke 17:25). Since what our Lord says here is true—that all the guilt of the sins of their fathers would come upon that first-century generation that was in the process of filling up the measure of the sins of their fathers by committing the *greatest* crime in history—it is little wonder that he declares later regarding the destruction of Jerusalem in A.D. 70: "For then there will be great distress, *unequaled* from the beginning of the world until now—and *never* to be equaled again" (Matt. 24:21).

35. Mark reports the disciples' questions in 13:4 as: "when will these things happen? And what will be the sign that they are all about to be fulfilled?" Luke reports these same questions in 21:7: "when will these things happen? And what will be the sign that they are about to take place?"

A Warning About False Signs

Jesus begins his discourse by issuing a caveat (Matt. 24:4–8). He informs his disciples that they should not be deceived by the appearance of false messiahs, the occurrence of wars and rumors of the wars, nations rising against nations and kingdoms against kingdoms, and famines and earthquakes, into thinking that his predicted judgment upon Israel and the destruction of Jerusalem was imminent. In other words, such things should *not* be regarded as signs that Jerusalem was about to be destroyed. He expressly declares: "the end is still to come. . . . All these things are [only] the beginning of birth pains."

An Admonition to Prepare for Hardship

Jesus then alerts them (Matt. 24:9–14) that they would be persecuted and martyred, that many of his followers would fall away from the faith, and that false prophets would appear and deceive many, all of this presumably to take place before the temple was destroyed. He urges them to remain faithful to the end, and declares that the "end" would not come until the gospel had been preached in the "whole world."

If the "end" referred to in Matthew 24:14 does not refer to the destruction of Jerusalem and the "end" of Israel as a nation in A.D. 70 but rather to the "end" associated with the final Eschaton and the end of this present evil age, that is to say, if Jesus has already arrived in verse 14 at the end of this age, then it must be said that Jesus left unanswered, at least in the Matthean form of his discourse, the disciples' question concerning the time of Jerusalem's destruction. But since the disciples' question specifically pertained to the time of Jerusalem's destruction, we should expect it to be answered. I would submit therefore that Jesus was referring here by "end" to Israel's end as a nation that followed upon the destruction of Jerusalem in A.D. 70.

That the gospel had been proclaimed throughout the "whole [then-known] world" before A.D. 70 is borne out by other New Testament testimony:

> Acts 2:5, 11: "Now there were staying in Jerusalem God-fearing Jews from every nation under heaven." And they declared: "We hear them declaring the wonders of God in our own tongues!"
>
> Romans 1:8: "Your faith is being reported all over the world."
>
> Romans 10:17–18: "Consequently, faith comes from hearing the message, and the message is heard through the word of Christ. But I ask: Did they not hear? Of course they did. 'Their voice has gone out into all the earth, their words to the ends of the world.'"

Colossians 1:6, 23: "All over the world this gospel is bearing fruit and growing. . . . This is the gospel that you heard and that has been proclaimed to every creature under heaven."

The Sign of Jerusalem's Destruction

Through Matthew 24:14 our Lord had given the disciples no indication that some particular sign would signal Jerusalem's impending destruction. But in 24:15–21 he does:

> But when you see standing in the holy place the abomination [that causes] desolation [Τὸ βδέλυγμα τῆς ἐρημώσεως, *to bdelygma tēs erēmōseōs*] . . . then let those who are in Judea flee to the mountains . . . pray that your flight will not take place . . . on the Sabbath, for then there will be great distress [θλῖψις μεγάλη, *thlipsis megalē*], unequaled from the beginning of the world until now, and never to be equaled again."[36]

Here is Jesus' answer to the disciples' earlier "when" question: when they saw the "abomination that causes desolation" standing in the holy place, they could be sure that the temple would soon be destroyed. What is this "abomination that causes desolation [ἐρημώσεως, *erēmōseōs*]"? We are left in no doubt as to its referent since Luke's Jesus interprets it for us: "When you see Jerusalem being surrounded by [Rome's] armies, you will know that its desolation [ἐρήμωσις, *erēmōsis*] is near" (Luke 21:20; see also Luke 19:43–44; 23:28–31). Clearly, the sign of Jerusalem's imminent destruction was the surrounding of the doomed city by Rome's armies, which laid siege to the city in A.D. 67 under Vespasian, whose son Titus breached the walls and destroyed it in A.D. 70.

If one will not allow Luke 21:20 to interpret Matthew's "abomination that causes desolation," insisting that Luke is speaking of the A.D. 70 destruction of Jerusalem while Matthew, though his contextual setting is similar, is speaking of a much later destruction of the city, which is to take place in the "Eschaton," then it seems that all argument from the analogy of Scripture is at an end and the principle of interpreting Scripture by Scripture is being totally rejected.

The Judean milieu of this section should also be noted (see "Judea," "on the roof of his house," "Sabbath"), for it helps to determine the "universe" within which our Lord's words should be understood. The "great distress" alluded to here has to be restricted to the Palestinian region. There is no scriptural warrant

---

36. See Josephus's description of the "tribulation" that the Jews of Jerusalem suffered under Titus's siege of the city (*War of the Jews*, V.x—VI.vi).

to universalize the distress to which Jesus refers here and to apply it to the entire globe. Everything in the discourse to this point restricts the universe of Jesus' remarks to Judea and to the destruction of Jerusalem which took place in A.D. 70.

A Warning About False Messiahs

At this juncture our Lord begins to separate the events that his disciples had wrongly united in their original questions. Because he knew that some would think that the destruction of Jerusalem would herald the Messiah's coming, Jesus expressly warns his disciples that they should not let anyone persuade them so (Matt. 24:23–27), for no one, he declares, will need to tell anyone else that the Messiah has returned or where he may be found when he actually comes again at the end of the world. *His* coming will be as public and conspicuous "as lightning that comes from the east is visible even in the west," yes, as conspicuous and direct as the flight of vultures to a lifeless carcass (Matt. 24:28).

Israel's Downfall and the Jubilee

We now come to what for many is the "stumbling block" pericope (Matt. 24:29–31). Admittedly, it does present some difficulties, although they are surmountable. For instance, because of the "Immediately" (Εὐθέως, *Eutheōs*) at the head of 24:29 and the vivid cataclysmic language of 24:29, many would say that this pericope can only be descriptive of the events of the Eschaton and Christ's Second Advent. But this is to fail to recognize the "prophetic/apocalyptic" character of Jesus' words here, which the Old Testament prophets often employed when they wanted to signal the coming of God's judgment upon a specific nation and herald that nation's ensuing downfall.[37] What Jesus is actually saying here is that immediately after Jerusalem's destruction and as a concomitant of it the nation of Israel as a nation would come to an end. Her glory will have departed!

But if the destruction of Jerusalem and the temple was *not* to be viewed as a sign that the Son of Man had returned to *earth* (see 24:23–27), it *was* to be perceived as

---

37. See Joel 2:10, descriptive of the locust plague in ninth-century B.C. Judah; 2:31, predictive of Israel's downfall (see Acts 2:16–21); 3:15, predictive of the final Day of the Lord against the nations; Isaiah 13:10 against Babylon; 34:4–5 against Idumea; Ezekiel 32:7–8 against Egypt; Zephaniah 1:7, 14–16 against Judah.

the sign that the old dispensation with its earthly temple made with hands had been replaced by the new age with its temple made without hands, and that the Mediator of the new covenant had assumed his messianic reign in *heaven* (see 24:30a, which reads literally: "And then shall appear the sign of the Son of man in heaven," not "And then shall appear in the heaven the sign of the Son of man").

"Then," Jesus declared (24:30b), "all the tribes of the earth [πᾶσαι αἱ φυλαὶ τῆς γῆς, *pasai hai phylai tēs gēs*] will mourn, and they shall see the Son of man coming upon the clouds of heaven with great power and glory." These "tribes," referring to the twelve tribes of Israel spread throughout the then-known world, would mourn because of the fearful vengeance of God upon the nation of Israel (the elect Jews among them would also mourn out of true repentance; see Zech. 12:10). Moreover, these tribes would "see [ὄψονται, *opsontai*] the Son of man coming in the clouds of heaven with great power and glory"—in the same sense that Jesus said the high priest and the council would "see [ὄψεσθε, *opsesthe*] the Son of man sitting on the right hand of power and coming in the clouds of heaven" (Matt. 26:64). That is to say, they would "see," that is, *"experience"* throughout this age his coming in wrath against Israel as a nation for its unbelief (see 1 Thess. 2:14–16).

But if his judgments were to be experienced by the Jews, just as surely the Gentile nations of the world would enjoy (and continue to enjoy) the blessings of the "Jubilee Year."[38] For Jesus declares here that he would "send his messengers [that is, his preachers; ἀγγέλους, *angelous*, can be translated "messengers" as in Matt. 11:10; Mark 1:2; Luke 7:24, 27; 9:52; James 2:25] with a great trumpet [σάλπιγγος, *salpingos*; interestingly, the word for the gospel "proclamation," namely, κήρυγμα, *kerygma*, is from the root κηρύσσω, *kēryssō*, which means "to trumpet or proclaim aloud"], and they will gather his elect from the four winds, from one end of heaven to the other" (24:31). So, in spite of Israel's destruction as a nation, Jesus declared that the church's worldwide mission to evangelize the world would continue unabated!

A Parable

By his parable of the fig tree which now follows (24:32–33), Jesus instructed his disciples that "when you see all these things [see 23:36; 24:34], know that it [i.e., the coming of the kingdom of God in judgment upon Jerusalem—Luke 21:31] is near, even at the door."

The phrase "all these things," here and in the next verse, refers to the worldwide preaching of the gospel and the surrounding of Jerusalem by the Roman army. It

---

38. "Jubilee," from the Hebrew יֹבֵל, *yôbēl*, meaning "ram," came by usage to mean "ram's horn," that is, "trumpet." Hence, the "Jubilee Year" was the trumpet-sounding year of liberty (Lev. 25:8–54; Isa. 27:13; 61:1; Luke 4:17–21).

would be an absurdity to understand Jesus as saying: "When you see the abomination that brings desolation, the worldwide tribulation, the sun darkened, the moon not giving light, the stars falling, the powers of heaven shaken, the Son of man coming in the clouds, all the tribes of the earth mourning, and finally, the ingathering of the elect, know that the kingdom is near," for his Second Coming will have already come and the kingdom of power will have already arrived.

The Crucial "Time Text"

Jesus then concluded this section of his discourse by declaring: "I tell you the truth, this generation will certainly not pass away until all these things have happened" (Matt. 24:34). This "time text" places beyond all legitimate question the propriety of the preceding interpretation of Matthew 24:4–33, however strained it may have appeared at times to the modern reader, particularly in 24:29–31. His disciples had asked him about the "when" of the destruction of the temple to which he had referred in 24:2, and he responded to their query by declaring that it would occur during that generation (see Matt. 23:36 for additional confirmation of this fact), to be preceded by the "sign" of Rome's army—the "abomination that causes desolation"—surrounding Jerusalem.

The Corrective

At Matthew 24:36 Jesus' discourse takes a new direction, as many commentators recognize,[39] which continues all the way to Matthew 25:46: "But of that day and hour [the time of my coming and of the end of the age] no one knows, not even the angels in heaven, nor the Son, but only the Father."[40] Previously he had referred to "those days" in the plural (24:19, 22, 29); now he speaks of "that day" in the singular (24:36, 42, 44, 50; 25:13; see 7:22; 11:22, 24; 12:36). Previously he had exhibited a remarkable awareness of when certain things would occur; now he declares that "only the Father" knew the time of "that day." Clearly a new topic—his parousia—is now before him. From this point on in his discourse, by his admonition to watch and to be prepared—a major point of his parables of the watchful householder (24:43–44), the wise and wicked servants (24:45–51), the ten virgins (25:1–13) and the

---

39. John A. Broadus writes: "From the point we have now reached, the destruction of Jerusalem sinks rapidly out of view . . . throughout this [new] section everything naturally suggests that final coming of Christ to judgment, which is alone brought to view in the closing paragraphs of the great discourse" (*Matthew,* 494).
40. See part two, chapter eight (pp. 222–25), on the Trinity for my discussion of this verse.

talents (25:14–30)—he provides the *corrective* to his disciples' misconception that the destruction of Jerusalem, his Second Coming, and the Eschaton would all occur simultaneously, by distinguishing between the first, which, he said, would be preceded by a sign that would prepare them for it and which would occur during their lifetime, and the latter two, the time of which, he said, "no one knows" except the Father (24:36, 39, 42, 44, 50; 25:13) and in preparation for which he offered no signs, only the admonition to "keep watch" (24:42).

We have concluded our treatment of Jesus' discourse, but I must issue a warning at this juncture. It is becoming increasingly common today to view our Lord's representation here of his coming in glory (Matt. 25:31–46, as well as in Mark 14:62 and elsewhere) not as his parousia *from* heaven but as his exaltation *in* heaven, since in Daniel 7:13 the manlike Figure comes on the clouds to God, who has summoned the angels to assemble in court.[41] But I am convinced that this view is mistaken. Daniel 7:13 occurs in a vision depicting the rise of successive *earthly* empires, culminating in one led by an arrogant king who wars against God's "holy ones" "until the Ancient of Days came"—so it is stated in the explanation (7:22). This is to say, the vision records a theophany or manifestation of God to the scene of the rampages of the antigod king, and hence the manlike Figure comes on the clouds to receive the kingdom that replaces the kingdoms of this world. A theophany in Scripture is usually from heaven to earth, for judgment or salvation, and this one is no exception. Interpreting Jesus' statement in the light of Daniel 7:13–14 (as well as 2:34–35, 44–45), I would contend that Matthew 25:31–46 does indeed speak of the Second Coming and the final judgment.

Did Jesus Miscalculate the Time of His Parousia?

Because of three specific verses in the Synoptics, such New Testament academics as Albert Schweitzer (and his "consistent eschatology" school), Fritz Buri, Martin Werner, Oscar Cullmann, and Werner G. Kümmel assert that Jesus mistakenly believed that his return in power and glory as the Son of Man was to take place very soon, indeed, within his and his contemporaries' lifetime. These so-called imminence verses are the following:

---

41. See T. Colani in *Jesus Christ et les croyances messianiques de son temps* (Strasbourg: Truettel et Wurtz, 1864), 20; M. J. Lagrange, *Evangile selon saint Marc* (Paris: Gabalda, 1922), 403; T. F. Glasson, *The Second Advent: The Origin of the New Testament Doctrine* (London: Epworth, 1945), 64–65; and his "The Reply to Caiaphas (Mark xiv. 62)," *New Testament Studies* 7 (1960), 91; J. A. T. Robinson, *Jesus and His Coming* (New York: Abingdon, 1957), 45; and R. T. France, *Jesus and the Old Testament* (Grand Rapids, Mich.: Baker, 1982), 139–48.

Matthew 10:23: "I tell you the truth, you will not finish going through the cities of Israel before the Son of Man comes."

Mark 9:1 (see parallels in Matt. 16:28; Luke 9:27): "I tell you the truth, some who are standing here will not taste death before they see the kingdom of God come with power."

Mark 13:30 (see parallels in Matt. 24:34: Luke 21:32): "I tell you the truth, this generation will certainly not pass away until all these things have happened."

Two things must initially be underscored in response: First, Jesus expressly stated that he did not know the day or the hour of his return (Matt. 24:36; Mark 13:32). That is to say, he emphatically disavowed knowledge as a man of the "when" of his parousia. Since this is so, then no other statement of his should be interpreted in a way that would force one to the conclusion that he erred in his prediction of the time of the end.

Second, before reaching an affirmative conclusion to the question under consideration here, one must take into account that Jesus' statement to Simon the Leper that "wherever the gospel is preached throughout the whole world, what she [the woman who anointed his head with perfume] has done will also be told, in memory of her" (Mark 14:9) intimates that a period of time—possibly a long period of time—would elapse before his parousia. To the same effect are other of his teachings, such as (1) the parable of the pounds, which Luke introduces with the words: "he went on to tell them a parable, because . . . the people thought that the kingdom of God *was going to appear at once* [παραχρῆμα, μέλλει . . . ἀναφαίνεσθαι, *parachrēma mellei . . . anaphainesthai*]" (19:11), (2) the wicked servant's statement, "My master *is staying away a long time* [Χρονίζει, *Chronizei*]," in the parable of the servants over the master's house (Matt. 24:45–51; see the Lukan parallel in 12:41–48: "My master *is taking a long time in coming* [Χρονίζει . . . ἔρχεσθαι, *chronizei . . . erchesthai*]"), (3) his statement, "The bridegroom *was a long time in coming* [χρονίζοντος, *chronizontos*]," in the parable of the ten virgins (Matt. 25:5), (4) his expression, "after *a long time* [πολὺν χρόνον, *polyn chronon*]," in the parable of the talents (Matt. 25:19), and (5) his parables of the mustard seed and the leaven, both of which suggest that this age would entail a considerable length of time.

Now regarding our Lord's assertion in Matthew 10:23 that the disciples would not have finished going through the cities of Israel with the message of the kingdom before the Son of Man came, the coming to which our Lord alluded could refer (1) to his appearance to his disciples after his resurrection at the time of his issuance of the Great Commission or (2) to the destruction of Jerusalem in A.D. 70, or (3), viewing the disciples as representatives of the entire church on the grounds that Jesus' words to his disciples included instructions concerning activities applicable to his church throughout history (see 10:16–22, 24–25, 26–39), our Lord's statement could refer to the church's ongoing mission obligation to Israel throughout this entire age. I myself prefer the second view.

Regarding our Lord's declaration in Mark 9:1 (and the Synoptic parallels) that some disciples standing before him (which group included a crowd in addition to the Twelve) would not taste death before they saw the kingdom of God come with power, I would suggest, as I have written elsewhere,[42] that Jesus was referring to his transfiguration, which would shortly take place.

As for the third verse (Mark 13:30 and its Synoptic parallels), we have just argued in our treatment of the Olivet discourse that Jesus, by his expression "these things," was referring to the destruction of Jerusalem which took place in A.D. 70.

Suffice it to say then that none of these "imminence verses" requires us to understood that Jesus believed his parousia of the Eschaton would occur within his own and the lifetime of his contemporaries. The entirety of the Synoptic evidence suggests to the contrary that, while he did not know as a man the day or the hour of his coming, he represented it, speaking relatively, as a long way off in the future.

Summary of Jesus' Eschatology

The structure of Jesus' eschatological dualism, may be summarized in three statements:

1. Two ages—this present (evil) age and the age to come—comprehend the remainder of human existence; there is no intermediate period or millennial age in Jesus' eschatology.

2. These two ages are consecutive, that is, they neither overlap nor is there any indication of a gap between them, but the age to come follows immediately upon this present age.[43]

3. The great epochal event that terminates this age and ushers in the age to come is the glorious return of Christ and its concomitants.

One would expect then that all else that falls within the field of New Testament eschatology will align itself with this structure. To an assessment of the rest of New Testament eschatology we will now turn.

---

42. See Robert L. Reymond, *Jesus, Divine Messiah: The New Testament Witness* (Phillipsburg, N.J.: Presbyterian and Reformed, 1990), 158–59, and part three, chapter fifteen, pp. 560–61, of this work.
43. Jesus' statement in Matthew 12:32 that blasphemy against the Holy Spirit will not be forgiven either in this age or in the age to come could not have served as a formula for absolute unforgivableness if a gap existed between the two ages.

James's Eschatology

James's eschatology is that which was promulgated by Jesus—an "eschatological dualism" espousing both the "already" of an "inaugurated eschatology" and the "not yet" of future cosmic eventualities. That James taught the former is evident from his statements that by the divine will the Christian is already born anew by the implanted word, that one is already a redeemed child of God (James 1:18), and that the multiethnic expansion of the church is fulfilling the predicted "rebuilding of the fallen house of David" (Acts 15:13–17). That he taught the latter also is clear from such statements as "the coming of the Lord is at hand" and "the Judge is standing at the door" (James 5:7–9), at which time the saints will inherit the kingdom of God (James 2:5).

In sum, the Lord is coming and he is coming to judge the earth "by the [royal] law that gives freedom" (James 5:9; 2:8, 12–13). Christians, as heirs of the kingdom, are to look forward to the kingdom God has promised to those who love him (2:5). James employs his eschatology as a practical incentive for growth in holiness (see here 1 John 3:2–3; Rev. 22:17)!

He makes no reference or allusion to an intermediate period between this age and the age to come or to a future thousand-year reign of peace on earth.

Paul's Eschatology

Confronted on the Damascus Road by the glorified Messiah who identified himself as Jesus of Nazareth (Acts 9:3–6; 22:6–11), it did not take a man of Paul's native genius very long—three days would have been quite sufficient (see Acts 9:9)—to deduce certain conclusions. The following things became immediately evident to Paul from this encounter:

1. Stephen, whose execution he had been party to, had in fact seen, just as he had declared, "heaven open and the Son of Man standing at the right hand of God" (Acts 7:56), and accordingly his own life-experience as a persecutor of the church had its origin in the execution of an innocent man who was serving the Messiah.

2. The Christian proclamation was indeed correct: Jesus was in fact the long-awaited Messiah, wrongly crucified and divinely exonerated from all wrongdoing and "powerfully shown to be the Son of God" by the resurrection from the dead (Rom. 1:4).

3. Jesus' disciples—not national or ethnic Israel with all its efforts to establish its own righteousness before God—were Messiah's people.

4. If a people who did not observe the law as the Pharisees prescribed were in fact the Messiah's people, then salvation was not by law-keeping. Rather, it was a gift.[44]

---

44. In this connection, Ladd (*Theology of the New Testament*, 368–69) writes:

5. If the messianic salvation was being bestowed on *Jews* through faith apart from law-keeping, then this salvation must be universal and appropriate to *Gentiles as Gentiles* as well.

6. If his persecution of Christians was at the same time a persecution of the Messiah himself, then there must be an intimate union between him and them, on the order, say, of the relationship between a head and its body.

7. In Messiah Jesus' coming the messianic kingdom apparently had also already become, in some sense, a present reality.[45] This last deduction in particular required Saul to revise his Judaistic understanding of redemptive history and to begin to think eschatologically within the framework of what we have already had occasion to describe as "eschatological dualism."[46] To comprehend this more fully, one has to know something about what Saul would have believed about redemptive history as a Pharisee prior to his conversion.

> He continued to look forward [as the prophets had predicted] to the Day of the Lord, the appearance of the Messiah in power and glory, to establish his eschatological Kingdom. Paul does not surrender the Jewish scheme of the two ages and the evil character of the present age (Gal. 1:4 [see also Rom. 12:2; 1 Cor. 1:20; 2:6–8; 2 Cor. 4:4; 2 Tim. 4:10]) . . . from the point of view of nature, history, and culture, the Kingdom of God remains an eschatological hope.[47]

But if Jesus was and is the Messiah and if he had already brought his people his

---

The realization that Jesus really was the Messiah was revolutionizing to Saul's evaluation of the entire meaning of the Law, for it was his very zeal for the Law that had made him hate the Christians and their alleged Messiah. Jesus had not been condemned by irreligious, immoral men, but by conscientious devout Jews who believed they were defending God's Law. It was Judaism at its best that put Jesus on the cross. If Paul's effort to establish righteousness by the Law had itself blinded him to the true righteousness of God in the Messiah (Rom. 10:3), then the Law could not be a way of righteousness. Judaism must be wrong in understanding the Law as the way of righteousness. It was this certainty that brought Paul to the conviction that Christ was the end of the Law as a way of righteousness (Rom. 10:4).

45. If it should appear doubtful that Paul could have inferred all these things from his Damascus Road encounter with Jesus Christ, the reader should note that Ladd is willing to assert that "all the essentials of Paul's theology—Jesus as the Messiah, the gospel for the Gentiles, justification by faith as against works of the Law—are contained in his Damascus Road experience" (*Theology of the New Testament*, 369). F. F. Bruce concurs, writing: "Paul's Damascus-road experience . . . contained within itself the totality of his apostolic message" (*Paul: Apostle of the Heart Set Free* [1977; reprint, Grand Rapids, Mich.: Eerdmans, 1980], 188).

46. Ladd, *Theology of the New Testament*, 369–75, 550. Herman Ridderbos calls this eschatological dualism the "redemptive-historical, eschatological" frame of reference in his *Paul, An Outline of His Theology* (Grand Rapids, Mich.: Eerdmans, 1975), 44–46.

47. Ladd, *Theology of the New Testament*, 369.

messianic salvation, something had changed. Something "new" had injected itself into history. What was now different? Paul came to the conclusion under the Spirit's guidance that while the present evil age obviously continues (Gal. 1:4), the kingdom of God of the Eschaton must already be a present reality (into which his people have been brought, Col 1:13) even if the world cannot see it (see Mark 4:11–12).[48] This is clear from the following affirmations found in his later proclamation (κήρυγμα, *kērygma*) to the pagan world and to the church at large in his letters:

1. Jesus entered upon his messianic reign at his resurrection and ascension (see Acts 13:30–41 [see also here Acts 2:22–36]; 1 Cor. 15:23–25; Col. 1:13). The Messiah, in other words, is reigning now and will continue to reign until he has put all his enemies (including death) under his feet! Moreover, as 1 Corinthians 15:25–26 suggests, Jesus' present reign extends in unbroken continuity from his ascension to the Great White Throne Judgment of Revelation 20.

2. The eschatological resurrection of the dead, which in his thinking as a Pharisee belonged in its entirety to the Age to Come, had already begun in the resurrection of Jesus whose resurrection was the "first fruits" (ἀπαρχή, *aparchē*) of the resurrection of all his people (1 Cor. 15:21–23). Ladd writes: "The important point here is that the resurrection of Christ is the beginning of the resurrection as such, and not an isolated event."[49]

3. The eschatological outpouring of the Spirit, predicted by Joel for the "last days" (2:28–32; see Acts 2:17–21), had already begun with the giving of the Spirit to Christians as the sealing "down payment" (ἀρραβών, *arrabōn*) assuring the consummation of the transaction unto the "day of redemption" (2 Cor. 1:22; 5:5; Eph. 1:14; 4:30).

4. Eschatological "life in the Spirit" had already begun.[50] The author of Hebrews (Paul?) declares in this connection that Christians have already "tasted of . . . the powers of the coming age" (Heb. 6:5).

5. Judicial acquittal, properly the affirmative side of the eschatological judgment by the righteous Judge of all the earth at the end of the age, has already occurred for Christians in the death and resurrection of Christ (Rom. 5:1, 9; 4:25; Gal 2:16).[51]

All these truths comprise the reason that Paul would speak about Christ's person and work as the "revelation of [the] mystery [ἀποκάλυψις μυστηρίου, *apokalypsis mystēriou*]." What does he mean? Earlier we treated Jesus' "mystery of

---

48. Citing Bishop Nygren's illustration on this last point, John Marsh (*The Fulness of Time* [London: Nisbet, 1952]) writes: "Any person who now lives in a world that has been liberated from the tyranny of evil powers either in ignorance of, or in indifference to, what Christ has done, is [living] B.C. in A.D." (156).
49. Ladd, *Theology of the New Testament*, 369–70. See also Vos, *The Pauline Eschatology*, 44–45.
50. Ladd, *Theology of the New Testament*, 370–71.
51. Ibid., 374. See also Vos, *The Pauline Eschatology*, 55.

the kingdom" parables (Matt. 13; see Matt. 19:28; 25:31–46). There we saw that Jesus laid the groundwork for the New Testament's "eschatological dualism" by teaching that the kingdom of God would indeed yet come in power and glory but that it had first appeared in grace, that is, it had *already* come in his own person and ministry (see Mark 1:15; Luke 11:20; 17:20–21). About its particular appearance in grace, Jesus declared (Matt. 13:17): "I tell you the truth, many prophets and righteous men longed to see what you see but did not see it, and to hear what you hear but did not hear it." Matthew then made this comment on Jesus' "mystery of the kingdom" parables (13:34–35): "Jesus spoke all these things to the crowd in parables; he did not say anything to them without using a parable. So was fulfilled what was spoken through the prophet [Asaph, Ps. 78:2]: 'I will open my mouth in parables, I will utter [reveal] things hidden since the creation of the world.'" In other words, a particular kind of "kingdom-coming" which had been "hidden since the creation of the world," that is, had hitherto not been *clearly delineated or distinguished* in prophetic revelation, had occurred *before* the kingdom appeared in power. This "kingdom-coming," as we have seen, assumed a grace modality. Concerning the kingdom of God in its grace modality, Jesus had taught that (1) it can be resisted and rejected ("four soils," Matt. 13:3–9, 18–23), (2) it will tolerate the existence of the opposing kingdom of evil throughout this age ("wheat and tares," Matt. 13:24–30, 36–43), (3) though small and insignificant in its inception, it is not to be despised, for it will someday cover the earth ("mustard seed" and "leaven," Matt. 13:31–33), (4) in its growth it is irresistible, that is to say, that though it will use men in its employ, its growth will not depend in any ultimate sense upon the labor of men ("seed growing of itself," Mark 4:26–29), (5) though despised by the world, it is still the most valuable thing a man can ever obtain ("hidden treasure" and "pearl," Matt. 13:44–45), and finally (6) it will not always tolerate opposition from the kingdom of evil, for the citizens of that kingdom will someday be destroyed (Matt. 13:47–50).

In harmony with his Lord, Paul describes the redemptive events that had dawned with the appearing of Christ as the "revelation of the mystery" of *the kingdom of God in its grace modality*, the "making known" of that which until now was "kept secret" or "hidden." For example:

> 1 Corinthians 2:7–8: "we speak of God's secret wisdom, a wisdom that has been hidden and that God destined for our glory before time began. None of the rulers of this age understood it, for if they had, they would not have crucified the Lord of glory."
>
> Romans 16:25–26: "The proclamation of Jesus Christ, according to the revelation of the mystery hidden for long ages past, but now revealed. . . ."
>
> Ephesians 1:9–10: "He made known to us the mystery of his will according to his

good pleasure, which he purposed in Christ to be put into effect when the times will have reached their fulfillment."

Ephesians 3:3–5: "Surely you have heard about the administration of God's grace that was given to me for you, that is, the mystery made known to me by revelation. . . . In reading this, then, you will be able to understand my insight into the mystery of Christ, which was not made known to men in other generations as it has now been revealed by the Spirit to God's holy apostles and prophets."

Colossians 1:25–26: "By the commission God gave me to present to you the word of God in its fulness—the mystery that has been kept hidden for ages and generations, but is now disclosed to the saints. To them God has chosen to make known among the Gentiles the glorious riches of this mystery, which is Christ in you, the hope of glory."

2 Timothy 1:9b–10: "This grace was given us in Christ Jesus before the beginning of time, but it has now been revealed through the appearing of our Savior, Christ Jesus, who has destroyed death and has brought [eschatological] life and immortality to light through the gospel."

Titus 1:2–3: "God, who does not lie, promised [the hope of eternal life] before the beginning of time, and at his appointed season he brought his word to light through the preaching entrusted to me."

All these truths lie behind the words of Paul: "When the time had fully come, God sent forth his Son" (Gal. 4:4).

All these truths are the reasons that Paul declares: "I tell you, now [that is, during this gracious manifestation of the kingdom of God before the Eschaton] is the time of God's favor; now is the day of salvation" (2 Cor. 6:2).

All these truths are the reasons that Paul—knowing that the very idea of "newness" is eschatological (see "new heavens and a new earth," Isa. 65:17; 2 Pet. 3:11; Rev. 21:1; a "new song" for the redeemed, Isa. 42:10; Rev. 5:9; 14:3; a "new thing," Isa. 43:19)—would later say of the one who is "in Christ": "he is a new creation; the old has gone, the new has come!" (2 Cor. 5:17), and that a "new man" had been created that is comprised of all who are in Christ, whether Jew or Gentile (Eph 2:15). Christians are indeed "people of the Eschaton"!

All these truths are the reasons why Paul would later speak of Christians as those "on whom *the fulfillment* [τὰ τέλη, *ta telē*] of the ages has come" (1 Cor. 10:11), and would represent them as those in whose existence a radical transformation has occurred (see Rom. 6:17, 18, 22; 1 Cor. 6:11)—what John Murray speaks of as their "definitive sanctification."

In sum, with the appearance of Jesus the Messiah in redemptive history, the *eschatological* kingdom of God also appeared "before the time" and is even now present in earth history (see Mark 1:15; Matt. 13; Luke 11:20); *eschatological* (eternal) life is already present in Christ; the *eschatological* resurrection has already begun in Jesus' resurrection; the *eschatological* Spirit has already been given to and is present in and empowering the church; *eschatological* life in the Spirit has already begun; and finally, the verdict of the *eschatological* judgment (acquittal) has already been handed down for all those in Christ, and God has already forensically acquitted his people.

This "passing of the old" for the Christian does not mean, however, the end of this age for everyone. The "old age" which is evil (Gal. 1:4) continues until the παρουσία, *parousia*, at which time, through the cataclysmic overthrow of the kingdom of evil, the knowledge of the glory of the Lord will cover the earth as the waters cover the places of the sea (Isa. 11:9; Hab. 2:14). But it does *not* remain intact and unaffected: the "new age" has broken in upon it, and in Christ men may be delivered from this present evil age (Gal. 1:4; Col. 1:13) and no longer conform themselves to the old age but "be transformed by the renewing of their minds" (Rom. 12:2), and in turn invade this present evil age themselves and "demolish arguments and every pretension that sets itself up against the knowledge of God, and . . . take captive every thought to make it obedient to Christ" (2 Cor. 10:5).

All these truths meant for Paul, following the basic "redemptive-historical, eschatological" structure of Jesus' eschatological dualism (without realizing it perhaps at first), that into the midst of *this* present evil age—this "now"—*before* the dawn of the Age to Come, the salvific aspects of the "not yet" of the Age to Come had already *graciously* intruded themselves "before the time." "In a surprising [totally unexpected] way *visible only to faith* the end of the old aeon and the dawn of the new has come upon the [Christian] community," and Christians are no longer citizens of this age but are already citizens of the Age to Come.[52] They are already subjects in the "kingdom of God and of Christ." "The new world and its salvation are already present, but they are hidden in the midst of the old world."[53] As Ladd writes:

> The events of the eschatological consummation are not merely detached events lying in the future about which Paul speculates. They are rather redemptive events that have already begun to unfold within history. The blessings of the Age to Come no longer lie exclusively in the future; they have become objects of present experience. *The death of Christ is an eschatological event.* Because of Christ's death, the justified man stands already on the age-to-come side of the eschatological judgment, acquitted of all guilt. By virtue of the death of Christ, the believer has already been delivered from this present evil age (Gal. 1:4). He

---

52. Ladd, *Theology of the New Testament*, 372.
53. Ibid., 486.

has been transferred from the rule of darkness and now knows the life of the Kingdom of Christ (Col. 1:13). In his cross, Christ has already defeated the powers of evil that have brought chaos into the world (Col. 2:14f.).

The resurrection of Christ is an eschatological event. The first act of the eschatological resurrection has been separated from the eschatological consummation and has taken place in history. Christ has already abolished death and displayed the life and immortality of the Age to Come in an event that occurred within history (II Tim. 1:10). Thus the light and the glory of the Age to Come have already shined in this dark world in the person of Jesus Christ (II Cor. 4:6)

Because of these eschatological events, the believer lives the life of the new age. *The very phrase describing the status of the believer, "in Christ," is an eschatological term.* To be "in Christ" means to be in the new age and to experience its life and powers. "If any one is *in Christ,* he is a new creation; the old has passed away, behold, the new has come" (II Cor. 5:17). The believer has already experienced death and resurrection [in Christ] (Rom. 6:3–4). He has even been raised with Christ and exalted to heaven (Eph. 2:6), sharing the resurrection and ascension life of his Lord.

Yet the experience of this new life of the Age to Come is not a secular event of world history, it is known only to believers. This good news of the new life is hidden to unbelievers. Their eyes are blinded so that they cannot behold it (II Cor. 4:4 [see also Mark 4:11–12]). They are still in the darkness of this present evil age.

[But precisely because the consummating stage of the Age to Come is still future and has not yet dawned] the believer lives in a tension of experienced and anticipated eschatology. He is already in the Kingdom of Christ (Col. 1:13), but he awaits the coming of the Kingdom of God (I Cor. 15:50). He has already experienced the new life (II Cor. 2:16), but he looks forward to the inheritance of eternal life (Gal. 6:8). He has already been saved (Eph. 2:5), but he is still awaiting his salvation (Rom. 13:11). He has been raised into newness of life (Rom. 6:4), yet he longs for the resurrection (II Cor. 5:4).[54]

Just as from the Old Testament perspective the predicted "last days" were to be the undifferentiated but complex times of the Messiah, and just as Jesus spoke of this age—the Old Testament's predicted *salvific* "last days"—as the age of the kingdom's end–time *salvific* work, with the age to come being the kingdom's consummating and eternal state, so Paul maintained this perspective as well. In fact, as Herman Ridderbos states: "It can be rightly said that Paul does nothing but explain the eschatological reality which in Christ's teaching is called the Kingdom."[55] And, as Vos states, "to unfold Paul's eschatology [in terms of the two ages, namely, this

---

54. Ibid., 551–52.
55. Herman Ridderbos, *When the Time Had Fully Come: Studies in New Testament Theology* (Grand Rapids, Mich.: Eerdmans, 1957), 48–9.

age and the age to come] is to set forth his theology as a whole," not just his teaching on Christ's return.[56] But by his interpreting what is commonly regarded as soteriology eschatologically, Paul without distorting in any way the basic structure of Jesus' eschatological perspective makes it clear that with Jesus' death and resurrection the future age which *will* be fully realized in solid existence has in principle *already* been realized now in heaven with Jesus' present reign and on earth salvifically in the church.[57] I would conclude then that Paul's eschatological paradigm is similar to his Lord's—an eschatological dualism.

The stages or sequences in Paul's eschatology may be indicated by the terms "present state," "intermediate state," and "future state." These stages we will now consider in turn.

The Present State

Paul speaks of Christ's work as accomplishing the final victory, and he speaks of us participating here and now in essential, although not in full, completeness of that final victory. About as completely and compactly as is possible for one verse to do (2 Tim. 1:10), Paul declares that by his action in history Christ has abolished death, the end-time specter, and brought life and immortality to life through the gospel (see Col. 2:14ff).

We, here and now, enter into life and immortality and escape death (see again 2 Tim. 1:10). Our inward man (ὁ ἔσω, *ho esō*) experiences now, in this life, an end-time death" to sin and death and a spiritual resurrection to newness of life (Rom. 6:3–4). Even now we can speak of already having been transferred from the dominion of darkness into the kingdom of God's own beloved Son (Col. 1:13). Paul can speak of our being seated with Christ now in heavenly places—John Murray describes this aspect of "present eschatology" as "projective eschatology"—(Eph. 2:6; see Phil. 3:20, where we are informed that we are citizens of heaven, and Col. 3:3, where we are informed that our lives "are hid with Christ in God").

The reality of the newness of our existence is so tremendous that we may be described as a new creation: "If anyone is in Christ, he is a new creation; the old has gone; the new has come!" (2 Cor. 5:17; see Isa. 65:17; 66:22). The messianic age has come and we are in it, and it has given us new life which will never perish.

But this new life, as wonderful as it is, is not all that we will have or be. There is yet more to come. While our inward man is renewed daily, our outward man (ὁ ἔξω ἄνθρωπος, *ho exō anthrōpos*), the body, and the whole universe await the

---

56. Vos, *The Pauline Eschatology*, 11.
57. Ibid., 38.

resurrection (2 Cor. 4:16–18; Rom. 8:10ff). Neither we nor any other Christians are ruling and reigning now in the way that we shall (1 Cor. 4:8). Thus our perspective must be, on the one hand, that of humble and thankful participation in the victory of the inward man here, and on the other, expectant anticipation of the victory of the body and that of the united body and soul together in the Eschaton in a new heaven and a new earth.

The Intermediate State

Paul has as the hope for himself and all other believers the great triumph of Christ's return and the resurrection. This is the prime and main comfort he extends to those who are sorrowing (1 Thess. 4:13–18). Without diminishing this perspective, he also speaks of the provision for believers between their death and resurrection, and it is this to which we refer as the "intermediate state," so named "simply and only because it is temporary, and it is such both for the just and the unjust."[58] Paul readily admits that the intermediate state is a lesser glory than the final state, and that it has its lacks when compared to the final glory accompanying the complex of events occurring at the return of Christ.[59] But for the Christian it promises "gain" and is "better by far" than his present existence:

> Philippians 1:21–23: "For to me to live is Christ and to die is *gain* [κέρδος, *kerdos*]. If I am to go on living in the body, this will mean fruitful labor for me. Yet, what shall I choose? I do not know! I am torn between the two: I desire to depart and be with Christ, which is *better by far* [πολλῷ μᾶλλον κρεῖσσον, *pollō mallon kreisson*]."

Here Paul speaks of being with Christ at death and he informs us that this state is *very much better* or *better by far* than our present condition (v. 23). Since it is a state "with Christ" and one "very much better" than this one, it must at least have as great an aspect of self-consciousness as we have now or the significance of our being "with Christ" and our being "very much better" would seem to have little or no significance. Cullmann's argument from the "pleasure of dreams" for a state of soul sleep as the condition of the blessed dead is not persuasive.[60]

Second Corinthians 5:1–10 contains the lengthiest and clearest reflective treatment of the intermediate state in the Pauline corpus. Here Paul speaks of "being absent

---

58. John Murray, "The Last Things," in *Collected Writings of John Murray* (Edinburgh: Banner of Truth, 1977), 2:401.
59. See my treatment of the Christian's final glorification in chapter nineteen, 797–800.
60. Oscar Cullmann, "Immortality of the Soul and Resurrection of the Dead," *Harvard Divinity Bulletin*, 21 (1955–56), 5–36.

from the body and being at home with the Lord" (v. 8). This appears to speak of the time between the Christian's death and his resurrection. The *crux interpretum* centers around this phrase in verse 8 and the correlative terms "house," "building," and "eternal in the heavens" (v. 1), and the concepts of "clothed" and "naked" (vv. 2–4).[61]

It is my understanding that the present tense "we have" (ἔχομεν, echomen, v. 1) and the references to "house," "building," and "eternal in the heavens" refer to the resurrection body which we certainly "have" in the sense that it is a promised and sure possession. The terms "desiring to be clothed" (v. 2) and "naked" (v. 3) refer to Christians as being with the Lord with reference to their spirits but without their resurrection bodies. The intermediate state is one then of being with the Lord but without our resurrection bodies. Again the language, "absent from the body" and "at home with the Lord" (v. 8) over against the phrases "absent from the Lord" and "at home in the body" (v. 6) and the note of preference for the former condition over our present earthly existence (v. 8) points to the reality of personal communion with the Lord (versus a state of soul sleep). For if we are now "absent from the Lord" and yet aware of personal communion with him, surely "at home with the Lord" will be in some sense an *enhanced* personal communion with him.

What Paul would most prefer would be that he might be alive at the return of the Lord and be clothed with the resurrection body without laying the mortal body down in death (vv. 2–4). But even the intermediate state is better by far than this present existence, beset as the present is with sin in which we have less direct communion with the Lord (v. 6). Here, in this vale of tears, Christians do not yet love him with unsinning hearts as they will when they are actually in his presence. There they will know more intense joy, greater knowledge of, and closer communion with their exalted Savior and Lord. The love relationship between them and him there will be inexpressibly rhapsodic.

---

61. The United Bible Societies Greek text (fourth edition) reads ἐκδυσάμενοι (ekdysamenoi, "unclothed") in 2 Corinthians 5:3. Textually, it appears to be supported only by the original hand of D, the Old Latin versions a and corrected f, and the Fathers Tertullian and the Speculum Pseudo–Augustine. Bruce M. Metzger (*A Textual Commentary on the Greek New Testament* [New York: United BIble Societies, 1971], 579) informs his readers that a majority of the editorial committee, while acknowledging that on the basis of external attestation ἐνδυσάμενοι (endysamenoi, "clothed"), supported as it is by P⁴⁶, ℵ, B, C, D², ψ, and most versions, has the much stronger external support, opted for the weaker "vivid and paradoxical" reading ("inasmuch as we, though unclothed, shall not be found naked") to avoid what it perceived to be an otherwise banal tautology ("because when we are clothed, we will not be found naked"). They do give their choice, however, a D rating ("very high degree of doubt"). I concur with Metzger's private opinion that "in view of its superior external support the reading ἐνδυσάμενοι [endysamenoi] should be adopted, the reading ἐκδυσάμενοι [ekdysamenoi] being an early alteration to avoid apparent tautology" (580). The NASV, NIV, and NKJV adopt the better attested reading.

BIBLICAL ESCHATOLOGY

The Future State

For Paul "the goal of God's redemptive purpose is the restoration of order to a universe that has been disturbed by evil and sin. This includes the realm of human experience, the spiritual world (Eph. 1:10), and . . . even nature itself. God will finally reconcile all things to himself through Christ."[62]

All creation will then pay homage to Christ. This will involve every knee bowing, in heaven, on earth, and under the earth, and every tongue confessing that Jesus Christ is Lord, to the glory of God the Father (Phil. 2:10–11). This will come about as a result of Christ subduing all his enemies including death itself (1 Cor. 15:25–27). Then, having accomplished his messianic task, he will subject himself, the Son/Messiah, to God the Father, who had himself subjected all things to his Son, that the Triune God may be all in all (1 Cor. 15:28).

Creation will then be set free. This triumph will involve the final liberation of the creation from its state of bondage because of man's sin into the freedom of the glory of the children of God (Rom. 8:19–23).

Immortality will then be introduced by either bodily resurrection or bodily transformation. For the believer the final Eschaton will involve either being resurrected from the dead or being transformed to incorruption while living. In either case it will involve the reception of an immortal body and a glorious state of eternity and glory ever with and in the presence of the Lord (Rom. 8:23; Phil. 3:21; 1 Thess. 4:13–18; 1 Cor. 15:51–54; 2 Cor. 5:4–5).

The unbeliever will then be resurrected also (Acts 24:15). Paul does not make this feature of the Eschaton explicit in his letters. In fact, Acts 24:15 is the only place in the New Testament where Paul is unambiguously credited with believing in a resurrection for the unrighteous as well as the righteous dead (though he implies it in 2 Cor. 5:10). For the wicked the time of consummation will be one of judgment, when Christ, having raised them at his coming, "will punish those who do not know God and do not obey the gospel. . . . They will be punished with everlasting destruction and shut out from the [favorable] presence of the Lord and from the majesty of his power on the day he comes to be glorified in his holy people and to be marveled at among all those who have believed" (2 Thess. 1:8–10). Paul elsewhere declares that "in the day of wrath and revelation of the righteous judgment of God," to those who are self-seeking and who do not obey the truth but obey unrighteousness, that is, to those who do evil, God will render wrath (ὀργή, *orgē*, the objective product or issue in act of a "thumotic" state of mind) and anger (θυμός, *thymos*—the subjective state of mind giving vent to ὀργή, *orgē*), trouble (θλῖψις, *thlipsis*) and distress (στενοχωρία, *stenochōria*) (Rom. 2:8–9).

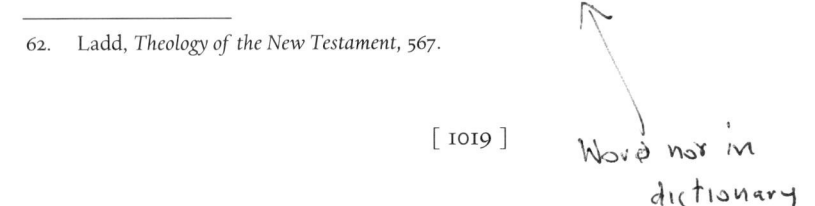

---

62. Ladd, *Theology of the New Testament*, 567.

[1019]

[margin note: Word not in dictionary]

Believers will then be judged according to their works and will receive rewards accordingly.[63] Paul teaches that not only unbelievers but believers as well will be judged in the judgment of the Eschaton (Rom. 14:10, 12; 1 Cor. 3:12–15; 2 Cor. 5:10). To them who, by persistence in doing good, seek glory, honor, and immortality, that is, to them who do good as the fruit of a lively faith in Christ, God will grant eternal life (ζωὴ αἰώνιον, *zōē aiōnion*), glory (δόξα, *doxa*), honor (τιμή, *timē*), and peace (εἰρήνη, *eirēnē*; Rom. 2:7, 10). The *criteria* of this judgment will be their works. With respect to how the apostle's teaching of judgment according to works is compatible with the biblical doctrine of salvation by grace, John Murray declares that:

> (1) The distinction between judgment according to works and salvation on account of works needs to be fully appreciated. The latter is entirely contrary to the gospel Paul preached, is not implied in judgment according to works, and is that against which the burden of [Romans] is directed. Paul does not even speak of judgment *on account of works* in reference to believers. (2) Believers are justified by faith *alone* and they are saved by grace *alone*. But two qualifications need to be added to these propositions. (a) They are never justified by a faith that is alone. (b) In salvation we must not so emphasize grace that we overlook the salvation itself. The concept of salvation involves what we are saved *to* as well as what we are saved *from*. We are saved to holiness and good works (*see* Eph. 2:10). And holiness manifests itself in good works. (3) The judgment of God must have respect to the person in the full extent of his relationship and must therefore take into account the fruits in which salvation issues and which constitute the saved condition. It is not to faith or justification in abstraction that God's judgment will have respect but to these in proper relationship to the sum–total of elements comprising a saved state. (4) The criterion of good works is the law of God and the law of God is not abrogated for the believer. He is not without law to God; he is under law to Christ (see I Cor. 9:21 [see also Rom. 6:14]). The judgment of God would not be according to truth if the good works of believers were ignored. (5) Good works as the evidences of faith and of salvation by grace are

---

63. Christians will have "good works" in this life (Eph. 2:10), but they will not have been perfect works, "because, as they are good, they proceed from [God's] Spirit; and as they are wrought by us, they are defiled, and mixed with so much weakness and imperfection, that they cannot endure the severity of God's judgment. Notwithstanding, the persons of believers being accepted through Christ, their good works also are accepted in him; not as though they were in this life wholly unblamable and unreprovable in God's sight; but that he, looking upon them in his Son, is pleased to accept and reward that which is sincere, although accompanied with many weaknesses and imperfections" (Westminster Confession of Faith, XVI/v–vi). But although their good works will be imperfect, it will be only Christians who have "good works" at the judgment as the fruit and evidence of a lively faith in Christ. And because the Bible takes this fact seriously, it is not hesitant to say that Christians will be judged according to their works.

therefore the criteria of judgment and to suppose that the principle, "who will render to every man according to his works" (2:6), has no relevance to the believer would be to exclude good works from the indispensable place which they occupy in the biblical doctrine of salvation.[64]

James Buchanan certainly would have concurred with Murray's judgment, writing in his work on justification:

> All faithful ministers have made use of both [doctrines—a present Justification by grace, through faith alone, and a future Judgment according to works], that they might guard equally against the peril of self-righteous legalism on the one hand and of practical Antinomianism on the other.[65]

The *issue* to be determined at the final judgment with respect to believers will be, not their justification *per se*, but their rewards for good works as the index to and evidence of their salvation by grace through faith. With respect to this issue of believers' rewards, John Murray writes:

> While it makes void the gospel to introduce works in connection with justification, nevertheless works done in faith, from the motive of love to God, in obedience to the revealed will of God and to the end of his glory are intrinsically good and acceptable to God. As such they will be the criterion of reward in the life to come. This is apparent from such passages as Matthew 10:41; 1 Corinthians 3:8–9, 11–15; 4:5; 2 Corinthians 5:10; 2 Timothy 4:7. We must maintain therefore, justification complete and irrevocable by grace through faith and apart from works, and at the same time, future reward according to works. In reference to these two doctrines it is important to observe the following:
> (i) This future reward is not justification and contributes nothing to that which constitutes justification. (ii) This future reward is not salvation. Salvation is by grace and it is not as a reward for works that we are saved. (iii) The reward has reference to the degree of glory bestowed in the state of bliss, that is, the station a person is to occupy in glory and does not have reference to the gift of glory itself. (iv) This reward is not administered because good works earn or merit reward, but because God is graciously pleased to reward them. That is to say it is a reward of grace. (In the Romish scheme good works have real merit and constitute the ground of the title to everlasting life.) The good works are rewarded because they are intrinsically good and well-pleasing to God. They are not rewarded because they earn reward but they are rewarded only as labour,

---

64. John Murray, *Romans* (Grand Rapids, Mich.: Eerdmans, 1968), 1:78–79; see also Leon Morris, *The Biblical Doctrine of Judgment* (London: Tyndale, 1978), 66f.
65. James Buchanan, *The Doctrine of Justification* (Edinburgh: T. & T. Clark, 1867), 238–39.

work or service that is the fruit of God's grace, conformed to his will and therefore intrinsically good and well-pleasing to him. They could not even be rewarded of grace if they were principally and intrinsically evil.[66]

Some Christians recoil at the thought that they will differ in the eternal state with respect to the degree of rewards meted out, contending that such differences would be the basis for one Christian lording it over another Christian. But this is to forget that glorified saints will be perfected in their love, not only for God, but for one another. The Christian with greater rewards will love the one with less rewards perfectly and will not exalt himself over him. The Christian with less rewards will love the one who has greater rewards also perfectly and will rejoice with him in his blessed state.

The "Triggering Mechanism" of the Future State

For Paul, as for all of the biblical writers, the "triggering mechanism" and beginning point for this future complex of events, this collective eschatology, is the bodily, visible, public return of Christ (1 Thess. 4:13–18; 2 Thess. 1:5–10, esp. v. 7; Phil. 3:20–21; 1 Cor. 15:23). Paul speaks of "the appearing of the glory of our great God and Savior Jesus Christ" as the Christian's "blessed hope" (Titus 2:13). When he comes, he will resurrect the Christian dead, transform the Christian living, and catch both groups up in one body "to the meeting of the Lord" (1 Thess. 4:13–18), these saints then returning immediately with him to earth to participate in the judgment of the resurrected and transformed wicked (1 Cor 6:2).

Two analogies to the saints going up and then returning immediately with Christ to the judgment of the wicked may be seen, first, in the movement of the wise virgins who went out "to meet the bridegroom" and then accompanied him back to the wedding banquet (Matt. 25:1–13), and second, in the movement of the Roman Christians who came "to meet [Paul and his companions]" as they approached Rome and then returned with them (Acts 28:15).

The return of Christ (with its concomitants, namely, the resurrection of the dead, the last judgment, and the final state) is the focal point of Paul's teaching on future eschatology and it must be every Christian's as well. *No other problems, queries, doubts, disagreements, diversities of viewpoint, unresolved questions, and controversies respecting the relation of other events to the advent of Christ in glory can be permitted to set this one great fact aside or blur its significance and centrality for the*

---

66. John Murray, "Justification," in *Collected Writings of John Murray* (Edinburgh: Banner of Truth, 1977), 2:221–22.

Eschaton. Christ is coming, and Christians shall be raised or transformed to imperishability, honor, power, and immortality (1 Cor. 15:42–43)! This knowledge gives us personal comfort concerning both our own future and the future of those who have already died (1 Thess. 4:13ff). It also gives us an ethical perspective to live expectantly and carefully (1 Thess. 5:1–11; 2 Pet. 3:11–12; 1 John 3:2–3). Such is always the by-product of the resurrection hope. It makes for godly living (1 Cor 15:56–58).

The return of Christ is the next important messianic event on the horizon. It overshadows all else. So Paul may speak of all Christians as those who are not only serving the living and true God but as those who also "wait for his Son from heaven" (1 Thess. 1:10).

Did Paul Believe in a Pretribulation Rapture of the Church?

Classic dispensationalists have customarily referred to the rapture or "catching up" of Christians at the return of Christ as the "secret rapture" and have placed its occurrence seven years *before* Christ's actual coming. All kinds of highly dramatic descriptions of the effects of this secret rapture on the world community—all intended to strike fear into the unbeliever and to motivate him to trust Christ—can be found in their books and sermons. But when one takes Paul's description of the rapture within its total biblical context seriously, it is anything but "secret" or "separate" from Christ's coming in power and glory. I say this for three reasons.

First, in order to make their case for pretribulationism, dispensationalists must and do separate Paul's "rapture pericope" (1 Thess. 4:13–18) from the immediately following pericope dealing with the Christian's behavior as "sons of light" in view of the approaching "Day of the Lord" (1 Thess. 5:1–11). The events of the former pericope, according to dispensationalists, occur seven years before the Day of the Lord, which comes later as a thief in the night. But such a chronological division between the pericopes finds no support in the text. The concern which prompted Paul's "rapture pericope" (1 Thess. 4:13–18) in the first place was the issue of the state of the Christian dead, a concern troubling the Thessalonian believers. He begins his pericope by stating: "We do not want you to be ignorant about those who fall asleep [τῶν κοιμωμένων, *tōn koimōmenōn*]" (4:13). Then he treats the Lord's "appearing" (4:15; τὴν παρουσίαν τοῦ κυρίου, *tēn parousian tou kyriou*), a term descriptive of Christ's second coming (2 Thess. 2:8), stating that Christians will be alive and remain on earth "until" (εἰς, *eis*) his "appearing," and assures them that Christ will raise the Christian dead at that time and that they will accompany the living (glorified) Christians into his presence. He then concludes this section by urging his readers to "encourage each other with these words" (4:18). Then with no discernible shift in subject matter, he immediately reminds his readers that "the day of the Lord will come as a thief in the night" (5:2) and urges them until that day to live alert and self-controlled lives as "children of light." He then returns to his original concern and states that Christ "died for us so that, whether we are awake or asleep [καθεύδωμεν, *katheudōmen*], we may live together with him" (5:10). He then repeats his earlier admonition that his readers should "encourage one another and build each other up" (5:11). The unity of this entire section (4:13–5:11) is transparent. Because of the several ideas that parallel each other in these two pericopes, there is no scriptural warrant to rend them apart and make them refer to two separate chronological events.

Second, in 2 Thessalonians 2:1 Paul places the Lord's "coming" (παρουσία, *parousia*) and Christians' "gathering together" unto him under the regimen of the same article, thereby uniting the two ideas and strongly suggesting that the two events occur simultaneously. In Titus 2:13 he places the "blessed hope," customarily construed by dispensationalists as a reference to the rapture, and the "appearing of the glory" of Christ also under the regimen of the same article, again uniting the two ideas and again suggesting that the rapture "hope" and the actual "appearing" are the same event.

Finally, from Paul's declaration that "relief" for the church from its troubles and persecutions will come not seven years before but *"when* the Lord Jesus is revealed [ἐν τῇ ἀποκαλύψει, *en tē apokalypsei*] from heaven with his holy angels with blazing fire" (2 Thess. 1:7, emphasis supplied), which "revelation" he describes only verses later as the "appearing [ἐπιφανείᾳ, *epiphaneia*] of his coming [παρουσίας, *parousias*]" (2 Thess. 2:8), it becomes quite clear that Christ's coming and the ensuing rapture spoken of in 1 Thessalonians 4:15–17 are neither separate events nor is the rapture a "secret, hidden event but a [very visible] breaking into history of the glory of God."[67] The Lord's "loud command," the voice of the archangel, and the trumpet-blast of God—all announcing Christ's coming—make this one of the "loudest" pericopes in the Bible! I say again, Christ's coming and our rapture to him are not separate events nor is the rapture a secret event. It is anything but secret!

When Is the Ingathering of "All Israel" to Take Place?

God has, according to Paul, something of a "love/hate" attitude toward ethnic Israel: "As far as the gospel is concerned, [Jews] are [regarded as his] enemies[68] for

---

67. Ladd, *Theology of the New Testament*, 556. See also Vern S. Poythress, "2 Thessalonians 1 Supports Amillennialism," *Journal of the Evangelical Theological Society* 37, no. 4 (1994): 529–38, especially 529–30.
68. That it is God who is regarding Israel as his enemy for the sake of the gospel and not Israel who is regarding God as its enemy is plain from the parallel thought in Romans 11:28b that it is God who loves Israel as far as election is concerned.

[the salvific sake of Gentiles]; but as far as election is concerned, they are loved on account of the patriarchs" (Rom. 11:28). Today non-Christian ethnic Jews ("the present city of Jerusalem"; ἡ νῦν Ἰερουσαλήμ, *hē nyn Ierousalēm,* Gal. 4:25), because they are Jews "only outwardly" (Rom. 2:28–29), that is to say, because they pursue a righteousness before God "not by faith but as if it were by works" (Rom. 9:31–32; 10:3), are not really sons of Isaac and hence not "Israel" at all (Rom. 9:6–9). Rather, in their unbelief and rejection of Christ "the present city of Jerusalem" is as much the "son of Hagar" as Ishmael himself was (Gal. 4:25)! And just as Ishmael persecuted Isaac (Gen. 21:9; Gal. 4:29), so unbelieving Israelites, Paul writes,

> killed the Lord Jesus and the prophets and also drove us out. They displease God and are hostile to all men in their effort to keep us from speaking to the Gentiles so that they may be saved. In this way they always heap up their sins to the limit. The wrath of God has come upon them at last (1 Thess. 2:15–16).

He says still further that God has given them "a spirit of stupor, eyes so that they could not see and ears so that they could not hear, to this very day" (Rom. 11:8).[69]

Yet Paul also speaks in Romans 11 of a saving ingathering of ethnic Jews of such magnitude that he can speak of "all Israel" being saved (Rom. 11:26). Consider these Pauline statements:

Romans 11:2a: "God did not reject his people, whom he foreknew."

Romans 11:12: "How much greater riches will their fullness [τὸ πλήρωμα, *to plērōma*] bring!"

Romans 11:15: "What will their acceptance [πρόσλημψις, *proslēmpsis*] be but life from the dead?"

Romans 11:23: "And if they do not persist in unbelief, they will be grafted in, for God is able to graft them in again."

Romans 11:24: "How much more readily [than the wild uncultivated branches] will these, the natural [cultivated] branches, be grafted into their own olive tree."

Romans 11:25–26: "Israel has experienced a hardening [only] in part until the full number [τὸ πλήρωμα, *to plērōma*] of the Gentiles has come in. And so all Israel will be saved."

---

69. In this age, while Israel's blindness is not total (elect Jews are exempted, Rom. 9:27–29; 11:5), Israel *as a nation* stands under God's wrath and curse and has *as a nation* no salvific covenant with God. Nevertheless, when "the full number of the Gentiles" has come (Rom. 11:25), the "full number" of Jewish elect will also have been grafted "by faith in Jesus Christ" into the church which is both "the true Israel" and the "covenant people of God," and in that relationship these elect Jews are no longer "Ishmael" but, in the church, are the true "Israel of God."

SYSTEMATIC THEOLOGY

Clearly it is God's design to save the elect in Israel. But when? Throughout this age or at some time in the future *after* the full number of elect Gentiles has been saved?

Classic dispensationalists teach that after the rapture of the church, either during the entire last half of the seven-year tribulation or just before Christ's return at the end of the tribulation or at his return itself, he will save "all Israel" and reign for a thousand years over the restored nation from a throne in Jerusalem. Even some nondispensational scholars, such as George E. Ladd (a historic premillennialist) and John Murray (a postmillennialist), place the time of the gathering of Israel's "full number" in the future, after the "full number" of the Gentiles has been accomplished. Basing his view on Romans 11:12, 15, 26–32, which he describes as the "most relevant passages," Murray asserts:

> Paul envisions a restoration of Israel as a people to God's covenant favour and blessing. In Romans 11:15 this viewpoint is inescapable. The casting away of Israel (*apobole*) is the rejection of Israel as a people collectively (see Matt. 21:43). The rhetorical question which follows implies that there is to be a reception of them again (*proslempsis*), a restoration of that from which they had been rejected. But the same collective aspect must apply to the restoration; otherwise the contrast would lose its force.[70]

Commenting on Romans 11:26, Murray states:

> The apostle is thinking of a time *in the future* when the hardening of Israel will terminate. As the fulness, receiving, ingrafting have this time reference, so must the salvation of Israel have.[71]

As a result of ethnic Israel's future salvation, basing his remarks on Romans 11:12, Murray insists that

> there awaits the Gentiles, in their distinctive identity as such, gospel blessing [which he interprets to mean "the expansion of the success attending the gospel and of the kingdom of God"] far surpassing anything experienced during the period of Israel's apostasy, and this unprecedented enrichment will be occasioned by the conversion of Israel on a scale commensurate with that of their earlier disobedience.[72]

But if the "full number" of the Gentiles, which surely speaks of the totality of the Gentile elect, has already been salvifically realized prior to the "full number" of "all

---

70. Murray, "The Last Things," 2:409.
71. Murray, *Romans*, 2:98, emphasis supplied.
72. Ibid., 79.

Israel," how will Israel's subsequent corporate salvation result in even greater salvific blessing to the Gentiles, which 11:12 and 11:15 seems to envision? Regarding this seeming discrepancy in his interpretation Murray writes:

> It could be objected that [this] interpretation brings incoherence into Paul's teaching. On the one hand, the "fulness" of Israel brings unprecedented blessing to the Gentiles (vss. 12, 15). On the other hand, "the fulness of the Gentiles" marks the terminus of Israel's hardening and their restoration (vs. 25). But the coherence of these two perspectives is not prejudiced if we keep in mind the mutual interaction for the increase of blessing between Jew and Gentile. We need but apply the thought of verse 31 that by the mercy shown to the Gentiles Israel may also obtain mercy. By the fulness of the Gentiles Israel is restored (vs. 25); by the restoration of Israel the Gentiles are incomparably enriched (vss. 12, 15). The only obstacle to this view is the unwarranted assumption that the "fulness of the Gentiles" is the consummation of blessing for the Gentiles and leaves room for no further expansion of gospel blessing. "The fulness of the Gentiles" denotes unprecedented blessing for them but does not exclude even greater blessing to follow. It is to this subsequent blessing that the restoration of Israel contributes.[73]

I am not persuaded that Murray's reasoning here is exegetically sustainable. If unprecedented gospel blessing "far surpassing anything experienced during the period of Israel's apostasy" awaits the Gentile world after the "full number of the Gentiles has come in," the phrase "the full number of the Gentiles," which surely intends the salvific totality of Gentile elect, is emptied of all significance. Murray's exegetical construction appears to be erected in the interest of his postmillennial vision of the conversion of the entire world before Christ's return.

For five reasons I would urge that Paul's intention seems rather to be that just as God throughout this age brings the divinely determined full number (τὸ πλήρωμα, *to plērōma*) of elect Gentiles to faith in Christ and thus into the church, so he is also bringing the divinely determined full number (τὸ πλήρωμα, *to plērōma*) of elect Jews (the "remnant," "all Israel") also to faith in Christ throughout this same age so that both "full numbers" are reached simultaneously.[74]

---

73. Ibid., 95–96.
74. So Berkhof, *Systematic Theology*, 698–700; William Hendriksen, *Israel in Prophecy* (Grand Rapids, Mich.: Baker, 1974), 39–52; G. C. Berkouwer, *The Return of Christ*, trans. James Van Oosterom (Grand Rapids, Mich.: Eerdmans, 1972), 323–58; Herman Ridderbos, *Paul: An Outline of His Theology* (Grand Rapids, Mich.: Eerdmans, 1975), 354–61; Hoekema, *The Bible and the Future*, 139–47; O. Palmer Robertson, "Is There a Distinctive Future for Ethnic Israel in Romans 11?" *Perspectives on Evangelical Theology*, ed. K. Kantzer and S. Gundry (Grand Rapids, Mich.: Baker, 1979), 209–27.

The first reason is the implication of Paul's employment in Romans 11:17–24 of the image of a single cultivated olive tree. The Jewish "cultivated" branches, though "broken off" from this olive tree, can and will be grafted into it again. "Every thought of a separate future, a separate kind of salvation, or a separate spiritual organism for saved Jews is here excluded. Their salvation is here pictured in terms of becoming one with the saved totality of God's people, not in terms of a separate program for Jews!"[75]

Second, the phrase which is rendered "until" (ἄχρις οὗ, *achris hou*) in Romans 11:25 has the force of a *terminus ad quem* with no implication that a prevailing circumstance will then be reversed.[76] What this phrase intends in Romans 11:25 is that the partial blindness of Israel extends to the coming of the fulness of the Gentiles. It implies nothing about a reversal of that condition after that fulness comes.

Third, Paul does not say in Romans 11:25–26 that "Israel has experienced a hardening in part until the full number of the Gentiles has come in. And *then* [τότε, *tote*, εἶτα, *eita*, or ἔπειτα, *epeita*] all Israel will be saved," teaching thereby that the salvation of "all Israel" temporally follows upon the salvation of the full number of elect Gentiles. He says rather in verse 26: "And *so* [οὕτως, *houtos*—"thus," "in this way"; compare the force of same phrase in 5:12] all Israel will be saved," teaching thereby that in and by the remarkable process of calling the full tale of elect Gentiles to himself—which "provokes [the elect Jews] to jealousy"—God also brings them to himself.

Fourth, Paul clearly appears to teach this by his strategic placement of a third "now" in Romans 11:30–31:

> Just as you [Gentiles] who were at one time disobedient to God have *now* received mercy as a result of their [the Jews'] disobedience, so they too have *now*

---

75. Hoekema, *The Bible and the Future*, 139–47.
76. See the use of "until" or "unto" in Matthew 24:38, Acts 22:4, 1 Corinthians 11:26; 15:25, and Hebrews 4:12. The point of the "until" in Matthew 24:38 is not that the eating and drinking, the marrying and giving in marriage going on in the days of Noah were replaced by a different circumstance on the day that Noah entered the ark; rather, the "until" stresses the people's constant practice of these things until the flood came. These things ceased in the destruction of the flood. The point of the "unto" in Acts 22:4 is not that Paul's persecution ceased after the persecuted Christians died; rather, it stresses that Paul's persecution continued to the very point of the Christian's death. The "until" in 1 Corinthians 11:26 does not lay stress on the fact that a day is coming when Christians will no longer celebrate the Lord's Supper; rather, it emphasizes that this celebration will continue right up to the day Christ returns. The "until" in 1 Corinthians 15:25 does not mean that a day will come when the Lord Christ will no longer reign; rather, it stresses that he must continue to reign until he has put all of his enemies under his feet. Finally, the "unto" in Hebrews 4:12 does not mean that the Word's piercing ceases and that another condition will prevail from that time onward; rather, it stresses that the piercing process continues as far as possible.

become disobedient in order that they too may *now* receive mercy as a result of God's mercy to you. (emphases supplied)

The third "now" in this statement, supported by ℵ, B, the original hand (and the third "corrector" hand) of D and several other lesser witnesses,[77] declares that the divine mercy is being shown to elect Jews *now,* throughout *this* age.

Finally, Paul's concluding summary statement in 11:32, "For God has bound all men over to disobedience so that he may have mercy on them all," strengthens the current significance of the gospel for Jew as well as for Gentile.

This view still allows for enough Jewish conversions to Christianity throughout this age to meet the demands of the "riches" (πλοῦτος, *ploutos,* 11:12) and "life from the dead" (ζωὴ ἐκ νεκρῶν, *zōē ek nekrōn,* 11:15) which Paul envisions "all Israel's" salvation will bring to the world.

A final issue is the question of the specific instrumentality that God will employ to bring this ingathering of Israel to pass. Many dispensational scholars urge that the return of Christ itself will be the instrumentality that will effect this ingathering of Jews. For support, they call attention to Paul's statement in Romans 11:26: "The Deliverer will come from Zion; he will turn godlessness away from Jacob." But it is not at all certain that the Deliverer's "coming" here is the second coming of Christ. His first coming is an equally likely—in fact, I think, a more likely—referent. Moreover, it is not at all certain that Zion here is heaven. It could refer to the church (Heb. 12:22), and Paul intimates that *whenever* (ὅταν, *hotan*) God takes away Jacob's sins, he may be said to have "come from Zion" to them and to have kept his covenant with them. The instrumentality of the church's proclamation of the gospel meets all the details of 11:26 as well as or better than the instrumentality of Christ's second coming. Particularly does this appear so when one recalls that when Paul describes the effects of Christ's return elsewhere, he does not represent it as a saving event in the sense that it newly converts men. It is a saving event only in the sense that it delivers those already his own from their final enemies who are judged by him (see 2 Thess. 1:6–10, esp. v. 8: "He will punish those who do not know God and do not obey the gospel of our Lord Jesus").

Then what *is* the instrumentality God is using to bring Israel to himself in this age? On the basis of Moses' prophecy that God would someday make idolatrous

---

77. The Fourth Revised Edition of the UBS *Greek New Testament* places this third "now" (νῦν, *nyn*) in brackets and gives it a C rating, indicating that it "may be regarded as part of the text, but that in the present state of New Testament textual scholarship this cannot be taken as completely certain" (p2*). Metzger in his *Textual Commentary on the Greek New Testament* states that "external evidence and internal considerations are rather evenly balanced" for the retention or deletion of the third νῦν in 11:31 but adjudges that, after all things are considered, "it seemed best to retain νῦν in the text" (527).

Israel "envious by those who are not a people" (Deut. 32:21) and Paul's statements, first, that "salvation has come to the Gentiles to make Israel envious" (Rom. 11:11) and then that the design behind his own ministry to the Gentiles was to "arouse my own people to envy and save some of them" (11:14), I would suggest that the tangible, concrete, visible saving mercies effecting "the full number [τὸ πλήρωμα, *to plērōma*] of the Gentiles" (11:25) is the instrumentality God is using to bring about "the full number [τὸ πλήρωμα, *to plērōma*] of Israel" (11:12; see 11:31). By accomplishing the former (see Paul's καὶ οὕτως, *kai houtōs*—"and accordingly," "and in this way," 11:26), God is making elect Israel "righteously jealous" of the multitudes of saved Gentiles who are enjoying the blessings rightfully and originally theirs, and is thereby quickening their interest in gospel matters—the "mystery" Paul refers to in 11:25—leading also to their "full number" and accordingly to even further blessing for the church at large as they bring their spiritual gifts to the church.

What Should The Christian's Attitude Be Toward Ethnic Israel?

All this—on the one hand, the fact of ethnic Israel's present unbelief and God's wrath exhibited toward them, and on the other, Paul's confident hope of the salvation of the elect portion of Israel and the concomitant blessing elect "all Israel" is bringing to the church—poses a genuine problem for Christians today. What should our attitude be toward these people through whom came not only our Old Testament Scriptures but also our Messiah and Savior according to the flesh (Rom. 9:5), and, indeed, our very salvation (John 4:22)? Should it not be one of gratitude, and should we not do everything in our power to make the lot of the Jew more acceptable to and in the world? And yet, have not the Jewish people for the most part rejected the Savior, declaring him to be only one in a long line of false messiahs, and do not these same Jews, when pressed, have to confess that they regard Christians as idolaters, worshiping as they do a "mere man"?

In response, I would first say that no Christian should advocate anything even remotely resembling discrimination against Jews (or any other race) because of their ethnicity or religion. At the same time, in light of the fact that the only hope for the salvation of the Jews (and for the members of every other ethnic group) resides in the provisions of the gospel, it would be wrong, indeed, unloving, for the Christian to encourage or to support the Jew in any way in the establishment and maintenance of his religious "Jewishness," which for him is the ground of his hope of salvation.[78] Paul denounced every hope for acceptance before God that is

---

78. This is simply taking seriously the uniqueness and finality of Jesus Christ as the only Savior and only hope of the whole world—of every race and every nation.

founded on anything other than the imputed righteousness of Christ, which righteousness is to be received by faith alone in Christ alone. A righteousness pursued through good works and the keeping of the law is futile (Gal. 2:16). Therefore, Paul became convinced that the Jew must forsake his notion of his acceptance by and before God because of his racial connection to the patriarchs and his allegiance to Torah-righteousness (Rom. 2:17–29; Gal. 5:3–4) if he is ever to know genuine conversion to God through repentance toward God and faith in Jesus Christ.

It is indeed a strange twist of thinking, if not outright disloyalty to the gospel, for the Christian to aid or abet the Jew in the retention of these Jewish distinctives which provide him the ground for his hope of salvation, the holding on to which only solidifies him in his unbelief. And yet, in order that the blessing of Genesis 12:3 might be his, and in order that he might escape the threatened curse enunciated in the same verse, many Christians believe that Genesis 12:3 requires them to support Zionist causes and to rejoice over every "Israeli advance" in the world, failing to realize as they do so (1) that as long as they encourage the Jew to continue to hold this unbiblical perception of what constitutes "Jewishness" and (2) that as long as the Jew continues to hold to Judaism as his religion, just so long will he continue to reject him who is the only hope of Israel.

Again, one is often told that in his witness to his modern Jewish friends the Christian may assume that the one to whom he is witnessing *already believes* the Old Testament, and it only remains to show him that Christ Jesus is the one whom the prophets foresaw. This is surely an inaccurate appraisal of the situation. Could one truly believe the Old Testament and not acknowledge Jesus Christ as the Messiah, Savior, and Lord revealed in it? The real truth of the matter is that no one who has heard of Christ and his atoning work and then rejects him really believes the Old Testament. Jesus himself expressly declared: "If you believed Moses, you would believe me, for he wrote of me" (John 5:46). When the modern Jew claims to "believe" and follow Torah, even though he may well say that he sees grace taught therein, he also at the same time believes that he must live a certain way if he is to merit being and remaining a "son of Torah." But this is to deny the saving provision of which Torah speaks.

Christians should love the Jew, surely! But the sooner the Christian realizes that to win the Jew to Christ he must show him the futility of any and every hope for salvation which is related in any way to the fact that he has Abrahamic blood in his veins (Matt. 3:9; John 1:13), and is a circumcised Jew (Rom. 2:25–29; Gal. 5:2–4; 6:15) and a practicing "son of Torah" (Rom. 2:17–24; 3:9; Gal. 3:10; 4:21—5:1), the sooner his witness to the Jew will become more effective.

Thus we must end where we began by echoing God's own verdict. Just as it is true of God that "as far as the gospel is concerned, [Jews] are [regarded as his] enemies [for the salvific sake of non-Jews]; but as far as election is concerned, they are loved on account of the patriarchs" (Rom. 11:28), so it should also be true of Christians that they should love them as those in whom God will fulfill his elective promises to the patriarchs. But Christians must also do everything they can, without being arrogant toward them (Rom. 11:18), to bring them to the place where they will forsake any and every ethnic religious distinctive in which they might rest their hope for salvation. Christians must do this for the sake of the Jews and for the cause of the gospel.

The Apostasy and the Man of Sin

In spite of his expectation of the "blessed hope" of Christ's return, Paul indicates nonetheless that there are certain eschatological events which must occur first, namely, the apostasy and the revelation of the man of lawlessness (2 Thess. 2:1–11), "a distinct personage who will appear on the scene of this world just prior to the advent of Christ."[79] Paul, somewhat cryptically, declares that while the secret power of lawlessness is already at work, the general rule of civil law, that is, civil government, will restrain the power of lawlessness "until [the man of lawlessness] arises out of the midst [of mankind] [ἄρτι ἕως ἐκ μέσου γένηται, *arti heōs ek mesou genētai*]" (2 Thess. 2:7).[80] Then this one—the Antichrist—will be revealed and will oppose and exalt himself over everything that is called God or is worshiped, and even set himself up in God's temple (the church), proclaiming himself to be God.[81] But Christ will slay the lawless one with the breath of his mouth and bring him to an end by the appearance of his coming (2 Thess. 2:8).

How are we to relate the "full number" of saved Gentiles and Jews, and the resultant blessing which the latter's salvation brings to the church (Paul's "world"; Rom. 11:11, 12, 15), with these negative eschatological events? I would respond with this scenario: Through the preaching of the gospel the day will come when the full tale of the Gentile elect will be reached. As this is being accomplished, God's elect

---

79. Murray, "Last Things," 2:410.
80. The traditional translation of this phrase, "until he is taken out of the way," with the "he" being understood by classic dispensationalists as referring to the Holy Spirit, is, in my opinion, highly questionable. Μέσος, *mesos*, clearly means "midst," and γένηται, *genētai*, the aorist middle subjunctive from the deponent γίνομαι, *ginomai*, meaning "be, become, arise, appear," is best rendered by the active voice translation ("he comes" or "he arises") rather than the passive voice translation ("he is taken"). See George E. Ladd, *The Blessed Hope* (Grand Rapids, Mich.: Eerdmans, 1956), 94–95. For an argument for the traditional translation, see Roger D. Aus, "God's Plan and God's Power: Isaiah 66 and the Restraining Factors of 2 Thess 2:6–7," *Journal of Biblical Literature* 96, no. 4 (1977): 537–53, particularly 542–43.
81. The Roman pontiff comes perilously close to doing this, if in fact he does not do it, with his claim to be the infallible vicar of Christ on earth.

"people, whom he foreknew" (Paul's elect "all Israel"), will have also been stirred "in jealousy" to put their trust in their Messiah and will have been grafted into their own olive tree, the church of Jesus Christ (11:23–24), finally achieving thereby their "fulness," which processive grafting in turn will have proved to be a source of still richer blessing to the church at large. But *after* this will occur the apostasy and the appearance of the man of lawlessness, who will assume the role of God in the church, whom Christ will then slay with the breath of his mouth at his coming.

Paul's stress on the expectancy of the return of our Lord might seem on the surface to be contradictory to these negative end-time events. But as a matter of fact Paul wrote about *these* events to correct just such a misconstruction by the Thessalonian Christians, and it should serve the same purpose now. The perspective of expectancy of Christ's return should continue undiminished, but no erroneous deductions, such as the notion that no evil event will precede it, can or should be drawn.

Did Paul Believe in a Millennial Reign?

The concept of a millennial reign *per se* is found only in Revelation 20, a book with extensive symbolism. It is most likely that this Johannine "millennium" should be construed symbolically either of the present *spiritual* reign of Christians with Christ (20:4a; see John 5:24–25; Rom. 5:17; 14:17; Eph. 2:6; Col. 1:13) or of the present reign of the martyred saints in the intermediate state (20:4b), or perhaps even both together, rather than be construed literally as an aspect of the Eschaton (see my discussion of Revelation later in this chapter). Whatever John intended by his teaching, there is certainly no clearly delineated millennial period in Paul's eschatology.

The most appropriate place where Paul might have spoken about it if, in fact, he had advocated a millennial reign of Christ, is the pericope in 1 Corinthians 15:20–26, but he makes no mention of it there. Premillennialists claim that Paul does indeed allude to the millennial kingdom in 1 Corinthians 15:24 by his reference to "the kingdom" and in 15:25 by his phrase, "he must reign." They urge still further, on the basis of what they refer to as the "order" (τάγμα, *tagma*, 15:23) phrases, "Christ the firstfruits" (ἀπαρχή, *aparchē*), "then [ἔπειτα, *epeiata*] those who are Christ's at his coming [παρουσία, *parousia*]," and "then [εἶτα, *eita*] comes the end," that the millennial kingdom occurs between the resurrection of Christ's own at the time of the first "then" and the coming of the "end" (that is, the end of the resurrection) at the time of the second "then." They call attention to the usage of εἶτα, *eita*, and ἔπειτα, *epeita*, in 1 Corinthians 15:5, 7 and the usage of εἶτα, *eita*, in 1 Timothy 2:13 and 3:10 to support the insertion of a gap of one thousand years between 1 Corinthians 15:23 and 15:24.

How does the amillennialist respond to the premillennial interpretation that would insert the millennium of Revelation 20 between verses 23 and 24? Vos observes:

> Much is made of the argument that εἶτα [eita] at the beginning of vs. 24 proves a *substantial* interval between the parousia and "the end." It must be granted that, had the Apostle meant to express such a thought, εἶτα [eita] would have been entirely appropriate for the purpose. But it is not true that εἶτα [eita] is out of place on the [amillennial] view, viz, if Paul means to affirm *mere succession without any protracted interval*. Εἶτα [eita] can be used just as well as τότε [tote] to express *momentary sequence of events*, as may be verified from a comparison with vss. 5, 6, 7 in this same chapter, and with Jno. xiii.4,5. Of course, a brief interval in logical conception at least, must be assumed: "τὸ τέλος [to telos]" comes, speaking in terms of strict chronology, after the rising of οἱ τοῦ χριστοῦ [hoi tou christou]. But that by no means opens the door to the intercalation of a rounded-off chiliad of years.[82]

BAGD also states that "in enumerations [εἶτα, eita] often serves to put things in juxtaposition without reference to chronological sequence," thus becoming "in general a transition word" (e.g., "next," "then").[83] Accordingly, the "order" words as such cannot bear the weight that the premillennialist wishes to place upon them. To those premillennialists who urge that these "order" words are essential as time-sequence words in order to make room for the resurrection of the unjust at the "end" after the millennium, the amillennialist observes that the pericope addresses only the issue of the resurrection of those who are in Christ (see "So in Christ all will be made alive"). But each in his own turn: Christ, the firstfruits of those who have fallen asleep, that is, of Christians (the wicked are not included in this relationship); then, when he comes, those who belong to him.[84]

For those premillennialists who, while not urging that a second resurrection is before the mind of the apostle here, still insist nonetheless that the "kingdom" referred to in 15:24 is the millennial kingdom, the amillennialist notes that according to 15:51–55 Christ destroys death, his last enemy, at his coming by effecting the resurrection. This means that the reign in question in 15:25 occurs *before* his coming (see "he must reign until [ἄχρι, achri] he has put all his enemies [including his last enemy, death] under his feet") and reaches its consummation *with* his coming and

---

82. Geerhardus Vos, *The Pauline Eschatology* (Princeton, N.J.: Princeton University Press, 1930), 243, emphasis added.
83. BAGD, *A Greek-English Lexicon of the New Testament*, 233.
84. Paul is assuming that his readers understand that unbelievers will also be raised at the same time. See his "there will be a [!] resurrection [sing.], both of just and unjust" (Acts 24:15).

the occurring resurrection and the eschatological judgment which immediately ensue, at which time (the εἶτα, *eita,* phrase—"then comes the end") he then delivers up his messianic reign to the Father that the Triune God might be all in all. Careful reflection on the pericope will show that this representation of the relationships of the referred-to events can and will bear the "stringency of Syllogism" (Warfield). Murray shares the same view:

> In verses 54, 55, the victory over death is brought into conjunction with the resurrection of the just, which in turn is at the *parousia* (vs. 24), while in verses 24–26 the bringing to nought of death is at the *telos.* It is not feasible to regard the swallowing up of death in victory (vs. 24), and the destruction of death (vs. 26), as referring to different events.[85]

The reign of Christ which Paul envisions here is a reign of conquest in the sense that it is and will be a spiritual triumph over the forces of evil as it saves and subdues the elect to God and eventually raises them from the dead.

Some premillennialists, acknowledging that the millennium cannot be found anywhere else in the New Testament outside of Revelation 20 (which means by inference that the New Testament, for the most part, is amillennial), nonetheless apply the biblical/theological principle of the progressiveness of revelation to this condition and propose that this important bit of revelation was made to John alone as the last living apostle. But while such a thing is theoretically possible, it is not likely that such a major feature in the eschatological complex as an intervening millennial reign of Christ on earth prior to the new heaven and new earth and the eternal state would have been kept from all of the apostles save one. What would have been the divine purpose behind the keeping of this feature of the Eschaton from the majority of first-century Christians? Furthermore, such an approach requires the much larger "amillennial" stance of the rest of New Testament eschatological teaching to be forced into the narrower, pictorial mold of the highly symbolic vision of the Apocalypse, more specifically, into one ten-verse pericope of that Apocalyptic vision. Still further, this proposal is based upon the unproven and (to date) unprovable conclusion that the Revelation was in fact the last portion of the New Testament to be written. Many scholars dispute the late dating of the Revelation on the basis of external and internal evidence (see, e.g., Rev. 7:1–8; 11:1–2; 13:18;[86] 17:10). Finally, the proclamation of eschatological matters was, as we have seen, a vital, integral aspect of Paul's "gospel," which eschatologically oriented

---

85. Murray, "Last Things," 406. I would urge the students also to read Ridderbos's discussion of premillennialism in his *Paul,* 556–59.
86. See Metzger, *Textual Commentary on the Greek New Testament,* 751–52, on Revelation 13:18.

gospel was also preached, as we will see, by the other apostles, including John (1 Cor. 15:11). These correlative facts suggest that all of the apostles preached essentially the same eschatological vision. For John then to proclaim later a millennial reign of Christ which would precede the eternal "new heaven and new earth" state, which (these premillennialists acknowledge) none of the other apostles taught, could be construed to mean that the other apostles had proclaimed error when they taught that the resurrection of men and the destruction of "the world which is present" immediately usher in, not an intervening kingdom age, but the "new heaven and new earth" state.

Some premillennialists have urged that amillennialists cannot stop with their amillennial stance but are compelled by their line of argument to move all the way to postmillennialism. For if Christ, they argue, is presently reigning and must continue to reign without interruption until he has put all his enemies under his feet, then the world of mankind of necessity must be brought eventually to a state of virtual moral perfection—the major contention of postmillennialism—by the effects of the gospel and by Christ's judgment upon its rejectors *prior* to his return—a representation of world conditions at the time of Christ's return which amillennialists reject. But this line of reasoning does not follow. If it did, it would teach more than the premillennialists themselves would want, for if Paul is referring to the millennial kingdom in 1 Corinthians 15:24 and declares of Christ's reign over it that he must reign until he has put all of his enemies under his feet, then this objection against amillennialism would register with equal force against their own position. For during their alleged millennium Christ would eliminate the very possibility of the apostasy which the premillennialist affirms is to occur after the kingdom age is over (see Rev. 20:7–9). That is to say, by putting all of his enemies under his feet during his reign, Christ would bring the world of mankind to a state of actual moral perfection, excluding thereby the very existence of that "Gog and Magog" (Rev. 20:8), whose numbers are as the sands of the seashore, who allegedly rebel against him. But if the premillennialist admits, as he must if he is to maintain his own view, that sinful opposition to Christ could arise for a short time after the millennium, then his point loses its force and he should acknowledge that Christ could return, not only to resurrect his own, but also (as a related aspect of the eschatological complex of events) to destroy both those who are involved in the great apostasy and the reprobate who have been raised to stand before him in judgment, which is the very point the amillennialist does makes.

The New Heaven and the New Earth

As the final aspect of his vision of the future state, in Romans 8:19–23 Paul speaks of the final redemption (or "re-creation") of the created order. Of this Ladd writes:

> The final state of the Kingdom of God is a new heaven and a new earth. This expresses a theology of creation that runs throughout the Bible . . . a fundamental theology underlies [the Old Testament] expectations, even though they must be clarified by progressive revelation: that man's ultimate destiny is an earthly one. Man is a creature, and God created the earth to be the scene of his creaturely existence. Therefore, even as the redemption of man in the bodily aspect of his being demands the resurrection of the body, so the redemption of the very physical creation requires a renewed earth as the scene of his perfected existence.[87]

As we have noted, after Christ subdues all of his enemies at his coming, with the ushering in of the new heaven and new earth he will deliver up his messianic kingship, with the commission and authority pertaining to it, to the Father. What will his self–subjection to the Father mean for the Son?

> [It will] not mean that from that moment he is really no longer to be spoken of as the Son, or that no power or dominion is any longer due him. . . . Christ's kingly power need not end at the point he transfers to God the subjection of all powers.[88]

After all, as God he is the second person of the Holy Trinity and will continue to be the Son of God forever. While retaining his native divine kingship and lordship, he will transfer his invested *messianic* lordship to the Father that the Triune God might commence "undisturbed dominion . . . over all things."[89] His transference of authority simply "throws light on the fact that Christ has *completed* his task in perfection and that the glory of God, no longer clouded by the power of sin and death, can now reveal itself in full luster."[90]

The redeemed in the eternal state will "be with the Lord forever" (1 Thess. 4:17). This is an important Pauline description of their condition. But Paul employs other phrases as well to "give expression to the content of this life with Christ and the 'all' with which God will fill all in various ways: it is being saved by his life (Rom. 5:10); salvation with eternal glory (2 Tim. 2:10); honor and immortality (Rom. 2:7; 1 Cor. 15:42ff.; 2 Tim. 1:10); eternal glory (2 Cor. 4:17) . . . ; fulfillment of righteousness and peace and joy in the Holy Spirit (Rom. 14:17). All [of these characterizations] are concepts of salvation, descriptions of God's imperishable gift, every one of which has its

---

87. Ladd, *Theology of the New Testament*, 631.
88. Ridderbos, *Paul*, 561–62.
89. Ibid., 561.
90. Ibid., 561, emphasis supplied.

own context, origin, and nuance, and offers its own special contribution *in order to make what is [now] unutterable* (2 Cor. 12:4) nevertheless known even now in part."[91]

Three Final Questions

Did Paul expect Jesus to return in his own lifetime, a dogma of contemporary critical scholarship? Did he teach this in his early letters and change his position in his later letters? What of Paul's expectancy in light of the two thousand years that have transpired since his time (the issue of imminency)?

An Immediate Return?

With respect to the first question, it is true that Paul uses the first person plural "we" in 1 Thessalonians 4:13–18 when he speaks of those who will be alive at Christ's return, and that he uses this "we" in distinction from Christians who are already dead (τοῦ κοιμηθέντας, *tou koimēthentas*). But does this single feature of his writing mean that he expected to be among the living at Christ's coming? Application of this critical method of exegesis to other passages would lead to the opposite conclusion that he expected to be dead at the Lord's return (see 1 Cor. 6:14: "God both raised the Lord and will raise us up"; 2 Cor. 4:14: "he who raised the Lord Jesus will raise us with Jesus"). His "we" is either the "we" that characterizes Paul's manner of speaking by which he identifies himself with his readers and their concerns (e. g., Rom. 3:31; 6:1, 15; 1 Cor. 10:22; Eph. 4:14; 2 Tim. 2:12–13) or the facultative "we" that envisions a condition that may take place under a variety of circumstances. The "we/they" distinction is really just the distinction between the Christian who is alive and the Christian who is dead at the return of Christ. Paul's language cannot be construed to mean that he thought that he and all other Christians who were alive as he wrote would still be alive when they received and read his letter and also when Christ returned. Otherwise, as Ridderbos notes, he would be attributing "a certain immortality to himself and his fellow believers, something that is altogether in conflict with the manner in which he generally speaks of his own life and death and that of his fellow–believers (see, e.g., 1 Thess. 5:10; Rom. 14:7–9; 8:10, 11, to say nothing of such passages as Phil. 1:22ff.; 2 Cor. 4:11; 5:1ff.; 2 Tim. 4:6, in which the possibility, in part even the expectation, of dying before the coming of Christ is explicitly posited)."[92] In sum, his language simply indicates an involvement with his readers which, upon analysis, means "we Christians who are

---

91. Ibid., 562, emphasis supplied.
92. Ibid., 491.

alive, whoever we may be" (see here particularly 1 Thess. 5:10 where Paul can write: "He died for us so that, whether *we* are awake or sleep, *we* may live with him").

A Change of Mind?

With regard to the second and related question, there is no evidence that Paul in his early letters expected an imminent παρουσία, *parousia*, but changed his view in his later letters. Paul wrote 1 Thessalonians 4:15 ("we who are still alive") around A.D. 50 and 2 Corinthians 4:14 ("[He] will also raise us with Jesus") around A.D. 56. No one has explained to date why he held to an imminent return of Christ for about seventeen years (from his conversion around A.D. 33 to 50) and then gave this view up. Leon Morris writes: "[Paul's] letters are too close together for any convincing argument for a major change."[93] Actually, his eschatological expectancy is a feature of his later letters (see Phil. 4:5; Tit. 2:13) as much as it characterizes his earlier ones.

An Erroneous Expectation?

What of his eschatological expectation in light of the passing of these two thousand years since Christ's first coming? Was Paul in error in his expectation? Not at all, since Paul never writes as if nothing at all could transpire between his writing and the return of the Lord. He clearly writes otherwise. For example, he teaches the Thessalonian Christians that something indeed must come to pass—even the apostasy and the appearing of the man of lawlessness—before the coming of the Lord. This does not take away from his admonition to watch in 1 Thessalonians 5:1–10 (especially v. 6). This apostasy and the appearing of the man of lawlessness simply must appear before the coming of the Lord as aspects of the complex of events related to Christ's return. The awareness of the necessity of these events keeps Christians from believing that the Day of the Lord has come. But since these aspects of the eschatological complex may well also come, develop, and transpire quickly without warning, their intervening character does not eliminate the expectancy of the Lord's coming. Because the return of Christ is the next great event in history, and from the believer's perspective the next great act of God, we must be prepared for it. To delay until the time of the apostasy and the appearing of the man of lawlessness to prepare for Christ's return may well be too late.

God was not using Paul or the other apostles to give a timetable or schedule for the believers of the last generation of earth history but rather a perspective on earth history. Thus every generation must be urged to live in the expectancy of

---

93. Leon Morris, *New Testament Theology* (Grand Rapids, Mich.: Academie, 1986), 88, n. 29.

Christ's return. For only in that expectancy does the servant live properly and serve well in the intervening time. Any other perspective gives the nominal Christian the very reason he is looking for to delay activity and obedience (see again 1 Thess. 5:11ff). But it is not only for this reason that a time unknown to any specific man or generation is indicated as the time that Christ will return. The only way for any specific man or generation to be prepared for the coming of the Lord is for every man and generation to be urged to be prepared.

The Eschatology of Hebrews

With the other New Testament authors, the author of Hebrews (Paul?) quite clearly endorses the New Testament's "eschatological dualism" of the "already" and the "not yet" of kingdom appearance. He declares that he and his readers were in the "last days" (ἐσχάτου τῶν ἡμερῶν τούτων, *eschatou tōn hēmerōn toutōn*, 1:2). Christ has come "at the end of the ages [ἐπὶ συντελείᾳ τῶν αἰώνων, *epi synteleia tōn aiōnōn*] to do away with sin by the sacrifice of himself" (9:26), and he has already been crowned with glory and honor (2:9). His messianic reign has begun in that he is already seated at the right hand of the throne of the Majesty in heaven, waiting for his enemies to be made the footstool of his feet (1:3, 8, 13; 8:1; 10:12–13). The day of God's "great salvation" had dawned, the rejection of which leads to just punishment (2:2–3). Christians have already "tasted the powers of the age to come" (6:5), and have already been purified (9:14), sanctified (9:13; 10:10; 13:12), and perfected (7:11; 10:14).

Yet the author of Hebrews speaks also of "the world to come [τὴν οἰκουμένην τὴν μέλλουσαν, *tēn oikoumenēn tēn mellousan*]" (2:5) and of the "coming age [μέλλοντος αἰῶνος, *mellontos aiōnos*]" (6:5), to be ushered in when Christ "will appear a second time, not to bear sin, but to bring salvation to those who are waiting for him" (9:28; see also 10:37). He insists that "there remains a Sabbath rest for the people of God" (4:9) which we must "strive to enter" by obedience (4:11). And he envisions a future cataclysmic cosmic "shaking" of everything that can be shaken down in order that the *one* thing which cannot be shaken down—the eschatological kingdom of God—might remain (12:26–28; see also 1:11–12). Clearly, while Christians already enjoy the benefits of the Messiah's salvation, his parousia will consummate their salvation. Christians are to continue to meet together for mutual encouragement, and all the more so as they see "the Day [of judgment] approaching" (10:25). Those who experience the divine judgment, both after death (9:27) and at Christ's coming, will face God as a "consuming fire" (10:27; 12:29; see Deut. 4:24; 9:3), a God into whose hands it is a fearful thing to fall (10:31).

Nowhere does the author make any reference or allusion to an intermediate period between this age and the world to come, or to a millennium.

One matter pertaining to the author's representation of our Lord's high priestly ministry requires comment in light of his eschatological dualism. In some passages he appears to teach that the Old Testament sanctuary service did not embody ultimate realities, that the Levitical priests served at a sanctuary which was only "a copy and a shadow [ὑποδείγματι καὶ σκιᾷ, *hypodeigmati kai skia*] of the heavenly sanctuary" (8:5), and that Christ at his ascension entered into the "true" Most Holy Place in heaven, taking his own blood (9:12, 24), and *there* purified the heavenly realities with better sacrifices than the animal sacrifices of the Old Testament system, that is, with his own blood (9:23). Some scholars have suggested that this representation reflects a Philonic Platonism.[94] F. D. V. Narborough, for example, writes:

> Whereas Jewish and Christian Apocalyptists envisaged the difference between imperfection and perfection primarily under the categories of *time*, distinguishing between this age and the age to come, the language of Hebrews suggests categories of *space*, distinguishing between this world and the heavenly world of spiritual realities.[95]

J. Hering concurs:

> Like Philo, our author accepts a kind of philosophical and cosmological framework which is more Platonic than biblical. Two successive aeons . . . are replaced by two co-existent, superimposed planes—the suprasensible world and the phenomenal world. The former contains the eternal ideas, which the second one attempts to embody materially. The former is 'heaven' for Philo, as it is in our epistle.[96]

Bruce Demarest writes:

> The writer utilizes Plato's distinction between the ideal form in heaven and the imperfect copy on earth to argue that the levitical sanctuary and sacrifices are mere shadows of the heavenly realities.[97]

And Donald Guthrie states that "there may be here . . . a trace of the background of the Platonic theory of ideas."[98]

---

94. John's Gospel is also often said to reflect a Platonic or Philonic metaphysical dualism. See Ladd, *Theology of the New Testament*, 223–29.
95. F. D. V. Narborough, *Hebrews* (Oxford: Clarendon, 1952), 43.
96. J. Hering, *Hebrews* (London: Epworth, 1970), xii.
97. Bruce Demarest, "Hebrews, Letter to the," *Baker Encyclopedia of the Bible*, 1:947.
98. Donald Guthrie, *New Testament Introduction* (Downers Grove, Ill.: Inter-Varsity Press, 1970), 719.

Accordingly, it has often been suggested that the author of Hebrews has discarded the "horizontal" eschatological dualism of the "already" and the "not yet" found everywhere else in the New Testament, and has substituted in its place a "vertical" Platonic dualism.

In response it must be underscored that the author of Hebrews, completely apart from the question of whether or not he employs a Platonic grid in his argument, has not abandoned the dualism of an "inaugurated" present eschatology (the "already") and an uninaugurated future eschatology (the "not yet"), as we have already seen. Second, as for his alleged "Platonism," I concur with Martin H. Franzmann that the author's

> view and use of the Old Testament never degenerates into mere allegory; that is, the Old Testament figures are never merely symbols of eternal truths, as in the allegorizing interpretation of the Jewish philosopher Philo; rather, the Old Testament history is always taken seriously as history. As such, as history, it points beyond itself to the last days [ushered in at Christ's incarnation].[99]

Ladd is correct that

> it is not accurate to say that Hebrews, like Philo, contrasts the phenomenal world with the noumenal, regarding the former as unreal and ephemeral. Hebrews applies the idea of two worlds primarily to the Old Testament cult. The tabernacle with its priests was a copy and shadow of the heavenly sanctuary. *The real has come to men in the historical life and death of Jesus of Nazareth.* History has become the medium of the eternal. There is nothing ephemeral or transitory about Jesus' life and work. The Christ-event was history with an eternal significance. What Jesus did, he did once for all (*ephapax*, 7:27; 9:12; 10:10).
>
> It is difficult to think that the author of Hebrews conceived of Jesus after his ascension realistically entering a literal Holy Place in heaven. To be sure, he does say, "Thus it was necessary for the copies of the heavenly things to be purified with these [animal] rites, but the heavenly things themselves with better sacrifices than these" (9:23). [But] it is self-evident that the heavenly things experience no defilement or sin and therefore require no cleansing. . . . A statement like this should make it clear that Hebrews is describing heavenly things in earthly, symbolic language. What Christ did on the cross, although an event in space and time, was itself an event in the spiritual world. Eternity at this points intersects time; the heavenly is embodied in the earthly; the transcendental occurs in the historical. Christ's entrance into the Holy Place and [his] sprinkling of his blood to effect cleansing and an eternal salvation occurred when "he . . . appeared once

---

99. Martin Franzmann, *The Word of the Lord Grows* (St. Louis, Mo.: Concordia, 1961), 244–45.

for all at the end of the age to put away sin by the sacrifice of himself" (9:26). . . . Hebrews uses the liturgical language of the Old Testament cult to depict the spiritual meaning of what Jesus accomplished by his death on the cross. Here in history on earth is no shadow, but the very reality itself.[100]

In other words, Christ's "*entrance into the heavenly sanctuary*" *occurred when he assumed his high priestly role as Mediator of the new covenant at the incarnation, and the Most Holy Place was his cross!* What these scholars perceive in the author to be the noumenal category of a Platonic worldview in actuality is the historical "already" of his "inaugurated eschatology" and not Philonic Platonism at all.

Peter's Eschatology

Peter's eschatology is beyond question that eschatological dualism which we have seen in the other New Testament authors. The "already" aspect of his eschatology is evident in the fact that Christ has been revealed "in the end of the times [ἐπ' ἐσχάτου τῶν χρόνων, *ep eschatou tōn chronōn*]" (1 Pet. 1:20), and most important, *his messianic reign has already begun* (1 Pet. 3:22).[101] Christians have already been "redeemed from the empty way of life" (1 Pet. 1:18), have already been "born again" (1 Pet. 1:23), and have already been "called out of darkness into God's marvelous light" (1 Pet. 2:9). They are already "the people of God" (1 Pet. 2:10). They have already returned to the Shepherd and Overseer of their souls (1 Pet. 2:25). And they are already "in the ends of the days [ἐπ' ἐσχάτων τῶν ἡμερῶν, *ep eschatōn tōn hemerōn*]," as evidenced by the fact that the Gnostic enthusiasts who will arise among them deny the coming of Christ (2 Pet. 3:3–4). They have already been given "everything [they] need for life and godliness through [their] knowledge of him who called [them] by his own glory and goodness" (2 Pet. 1:3). Through Christ's "very great and precious promises," they already "participate in the divine nature."[102] They have already "escaped the corruption of the world by knowing our Lord and Savior Jesus Christ" (2 Pet. 1:4; 2:20). They are already "firmly established in the truth you now have" (2 Pet. 1:12).

---

100. Ladd, *Theology of the New Testament*, 574–75.
101. See also Peter's declaration in Acts 5:31: "God exalted [Jesus] to his own right hand as Prince and Savior that he might give repentance and forgiveness of sins to Israel," and Acts 3:21: "He must remain in heaven until the time comes for God to restore everything, as he promised long ago through his holy prophets."
102. Christians do not "participate in the divine nature" in the sense that they are apotheotized—that is, become divine themselves—as the Gnostics taught, but rather only in the contextual sense that they become incorruptible and immortal "in Christ" in his eternal kingdom. In the same vein Paul speaks of our "union with Christ."

Peter's remarks on the Day of Pentecost are a sermonic "apologetic" in behalf of Jesus' present eschatological lordship and messiahship. This is apparent throughout his Pentecost sermon, from his opening remark after quoting the Joel prophecy to his concluding statement in Acts 2:36: "Therefore, let all the house of Israel know for certain that God has made him both Lord and Christ—this Jesus whom you crucified." Peter's remarks prior to this "therefore" are to be regarded as an argument intended to buttress this conclusion. He argues that David was obviously speaking of the Messiah's resurrection in Psalm 16 and not his own because he died and saw corruption and was not raised to life, and because, as an inspired prophet, he had been informed of the Messiah's resurrection and enthronement and thus, under inspiration, had written about these matters. Upon his resurrection the Messiah did not mount the earthly throne of David. Rather, he ascended to heaven and sat down on God's throne. (Of course, in the sense that any throne upon which the messianic Son of David would sit would become by that very act the Davidic throne, God's throne itself has become the "Davidic throne.") David, according to Peter, made it perfectly clear that this heavenly enthronement is what he had in mind, for both in Psalm 16 he has the resurrected Messiah say: "you will fill me with joy in your presence, with eternal pleasures at your right hand" (16:11), and in Psalm 110 he reports that Yahweh said to his Messiah: "Sit at my right hand until I make your enemies a footstool for your feet" (Acts 2:24–25).

Why did Peter use the occasion of Pentecost to argue the case for the reign and messiahship of Jesus? Peter makes the connection very clear: "Having been exalted to the right hand of God, and having received the promise of the Holy Spirit from the Father [note the implication in his reference to "the Father" that the Messiah at the right hand of "the Father" is there as "the Son"], he [that is, Jesus] has poured out this which you now see and hear" (Acts 2:33). When we recall the "accrediting" character of his previous miracles—the point that Peter had underscored at the outset of his discourse—it becomes clear that for Peter Pentecost was a further tangible, concrete, miraculous self-attestation by Jesus that he was now reigning as the Messiah. This is why Peter concluded his remarks with a dogmatic "therefore": "Therefore, [in light of (1) the attesting miracles which God performed through Jesus during his years of earthly ministry, which miracles you, my listeners, can not deny, (2) David's Old Testament prophecies concerning his resurrection from the dead and his present enthronement, and (3) Jesus' miraculous self-attestation from heaven that it is he who is the Spirit-Baptizer of men], let all the house of Israel know for certain that both Lord and Christ God has made him—this Jesus whom you crucified" (author's translation).

So what then is the significance of the event that occurred on the Day of Pentecost? The insight of C. H. Dodd is to the point: "the Holy Spirit in the Church is *the sign of Christ's present power and glory.*"[103] It was the risen Christ who was actively engaged at Pentecost in attesting once again in a grand, climactic way to his saving prerogatives as Israel's Lord and Messiah. And thus Peter believed and taught that the "end of the times" (1 Pet. 1:20) had come and that Jesus was and is *already* reigning as the Messiah.

The "not yet" aspect of his eschatological vision is apparent from the fact that Peter can also speak of God "sending the Christ . . . [who] must remain in heaven until the time comes for God to restore everything" (Acts 3:20–21), of "the salvation ready to be revealed in the last time" (1 Pet. 1:5), of "the grace to be given you when Jesus Christ is revealed" (1 Pet. 1:13), of "the Day God visits you" (1 Pet. 2:12), of "him who is ready to judge the living and the dead" (1 Pet. 4:5) at "the end of all things [which] is near" (1 Pet. 4:7), and of "the about-to-be-revealed glory" (1 Pet. 4:13; 5:1) which will come "when the Chief Shepherd appears" (1 Pet. 5:5), in which eternal glory Christians too will share (1 Pet. 5:10). So there is both an "already" and a "not yet" aspect in Peter's eschatology.

Consistent with this, in 2 Peter 3 Peter divides the whole of cosmic history into three periods: the first period—"the world of that time [ὁ τότε κόσμος, *ho tote kosmos*]"—extended from the beginning of the creation to the Genesis flood (2 Pet. 3:5–6); the second period—"the present heavens and earth [οἱ νῦν οὐρανοὶ καὶ ἡ γῆ, *hoi nyn ouranoi kai hē gē*]"—extends from the flood to the Eschaton (3:7); and the third period—"the eternal kingdom of our Lord and Savior Jesus Christ" in "a new heaven and a new earth [καινοὺς οὐρανοὺς καὶ γῆν καινήν, *kainous ouranous kai gēn kainēn*] in which righteousness dwells"—will extend from the Eschaton on throughout eternity (2 Pet. 1:11; 3:13). Therefore, his readers are to make every effort to make their calling and election sure by adding to their faith the virtues of the Christian life (2 Pet. 1:5–10), and to make every effort to be found spotless, blameless, and at peace with the Lord (2 Pet. 3:14), for they have yet to enter that "eternal kingdom of our Lord and Savior Jesus Christ" (2 Pet. 1:11). The "day of judgment and destruction of ungodly men" yet awaits the unrighteous (2 Pet. 2:9; 3:7). The "Day of the Lord [or, of God] will come like a thief" (2 Pet. 3:10a, 12), at which time "the heavens will disappear with a roar; the elements will be destroyed by fire, and the earth and everything in it will be laid bare" (2 Pet. 3:10). Peter even declares that a major responsibility of his teaching ministry was "to make known the power and [second] coming [παρουσίαν, *parousian*] of our Lord Jesus Christ" (2 Pet. 1:16), the very coming which the false teachers among them had been scoffingly rejecting, saying "Where is this 'coming' he promised?" (2 Pet. 3:3–4). As Paul did before him

---

103. C. H. Dodd, *The Apostolic Preaching and Its Developments* (New York: Harper, 1936), 42, emphasis supplied.

(2 Pet. 3:15–16a; see Rom. 2:4), Peter explains Christ's "delay" in coming, which delay the gnostic teachers interpreted as evidence that he was not coming at all, as actually evidence of the divine patience toward sinners extending to them time to repent and be saved (2 Pet. 3:9, 15).

Peter makes no reference or allusion to an intermediate period between this age and the age to come, or to a millennium. If he had believed in a millennial kingdom following this age, a very appropriate place where he might have made reference to it is in 2 Peter 3, but he makes no mention of it, placing the entirety of earth history within the three time frames which I have just mentioned.

Jude's Eschatology

Jude's eschatology appears to be the same "eschatological dualism" which we find in Jesus, Paul, Hebrews, and Peter, for his readers are living in the "last time" (ἐσχάτου [τοῦ] χρόνου, *eschatou [tou] chronou*) (Jude 18), and yet Jesus, according to Enoch's prophecy, is yet to come (ἦλθεν, *ēlthen*, a prophetic aorist) with "his myriad holy ones" (v. 14).

When he comes, he will bring Christians "without fault" and "with great joy" (v. 24) to their "eternal life" (v. 21). They will then know the fulness of God's "glorious presence" (v. 24). He will also judge with fire both ungodly men (vv. 15, 23), "unto which judgment they had been designated beforehand long ago," and the fallen angels who have been bound in everlasting chains "for the judgment of the Great Day" (v. 6).

Jude makes no reference or allusion to an intermediate period between this age and the age to come, or to a millennium.

John's Eschatology

JOHN'S GOSPEL ESCHATOLOGY

While it is true, as Ladd notes, that the dualism in John's gospel is "primarily vertical: a contrast between two worlds—the world above and the world below" (see John 3:13; 6:62; 8:23),[104] his gospel does contain a "horizontal eschatology"—a contrast between this age and the age to come. This eschatological dualism is exhibited in the following ways: on the one hand, (1) John cites Old Testament prophecies to show that the Old Testament was fulfilled in the events of Jesus' life (John 1:23; 2:17; 6:45; 12:13–15, 38–40; 13:18; 19:24, 36–37); (2) he represents Jesus as

---

104. Ladd, *Theology of the New Testament*, 223.

the Inaugurator of a new era that provides the reality only anticipated in the Old Testament (John 1:17; 8:33–58); (3) he employs the same terms when speaking of Jesus as the Synoptics do—Messiah, King of Israel, Son of Man and Son of God; and (4) he highlights the centrality of Jesus in salvation history by his repeated use of "now" (4:23; 5:25; 12:31; 16:5; 17:5, 13) and "hour" (2:4; 8:20; 12:23) in Jesus' speeches. On the other hand, (1) he sees the church's future Gentile mission in this age (10:16; 11:52) and (2) he can speak of "eternal life" as a blessing in the eschatological future (3:36; 5:39; 12:25).

John makes no reference or allusion to an intermediate period between this age and the age to come, or to a millennium, in his "horizontal" Gospel eschatology.

JOHN'S EPISTOLARY ESCHATOLOGY

With the New Testament authors in general, John's epistolary eschatology may be characterized as simple "eschatological dualism." He teaches his readers, on the one hand, that the "true light is already shining" (1 John 2:8), that Christians already "have passed out of death into [eternal] life" (1 John 3:14), and that they were living in the "last hour," as evidenced by the fact that "even now many antichrists have come" (1 John 2:18; see also 4:3b, where John declares that the spirit of the [future] Antichrist "is already now in the world"). On the other hand, he teaches that this evil world and its desires "are passing away" (2:17), that Jesus will come again (2:28), and that when he does appear (2:28; 3:2), "the day of judgment" will arrive too (4:17). We who have the hope of being like him when he comes will purify ourselves (3:3), and so live that we may be confident and not be ashamed at his coming (2:28).

It is again significant that John makes no reference or allusion to an intermediate period between this age and the age to come or to a millennium in his epistolary eschatology.

THE ESCHATOLOGY OF JOHN'S APOCALYPSE

But what about John's Revelation, also known as the Apocalypse? He refers to the millennium in the Apocalypse, does he not? This question obviously deserves an extended response.

The "Revelation [Ἀποκάλυψις, *Apokalypsis*] of Jesus Christ"—a fitting close to the New Testament's teaching on eschatology but regrettably the first (and pretty much the only) book most lay Christians consider when forming their eschatological point of view—is addressed as an encyclical letter to seven particular churches in the Roman province of Asia (Rev. 1:4, 11; chaps. 2–3). There were more churches than these seven, of course, but the number seven suggests the representative idea of completeness or totality, implying that the Revelation is for the entire church. By its own description, the book claims to be a "prophecy" (1:3; 22:7, 10, 18–19) in the predictive sense of that word (1:1, 19). As such, it is the only book of its kind in the New Testament.

The book is also distinguished from the other New Testament books by its many symbols—numbers, strange beasts, cryptic descriptions—all marking the book as eschatological in nature. Because of its eschatological character, it has proven to be an exceptionally difficult book to interpret.

Methods of Interpretation

Interpreters have followed, in the main, one of the six following approaches to the book, with the first, fourth, and sixth being the most popular today:

1. The preterist (Lat., *praeter*, meaning "past") view. Interpreters advocating this approach argue that, except for the last few chapters, John was speaking of events that were already occurring (the Neronian persecutions) or that would occur in his own time (the destruction of Jerusalem). In other words, the predictions of virtually the entire book have already been fulfilled. Postmillennialists find this approach most to their liking.

2. The historicist view. Interpreters espousing this approach urge that the book is a prophetic forecast of the history of the church from apostolic days to the second advent of Christ and refers to such events in history as the Muslim invasions of Europe, the rise of the papacy, the Reformation, and the French Revolution.

3. The symbolical or idealist view. Interpreters following this approach hold that it was not the purpose of John to predict the future or to foretell precise coming events. Rather, he intended to set forth by symbol basic spiritual principles which govern the life of the church throughout every age of its earthly pilgrimage.

4. The extreme futurist view. Interpreters following this approach contend that after the first three chapters, the remainder of the prophecy sets forth the eschatological events to be fulfilled in the Eschaton. In other words, the predictions of virtually the entire book are yet to be fulfilled. Pretribulation, premillennial dispensationalists adopt this approach.

5. The moderate futurist view. Interpreters following this approach contend that the events beginning with chapter 7 lie in the future and will attend the final disposition of the divine will for human history.

6. The progressive parallelism (or recapitulation) view. Advocates of this view argue that the seven sections of the Revelation cover the period of the church age between Christ's first and second advents from repeated (but in some ways different) perspectives in ascending, climactic order, with special emphasis on the

end times. Amillennialists espouse this interpretation, and it is this approach that I personally take.

Its Author

The author identifies himself once as God's "servant John" (1:1), once as "John, your brother and companion in the suffering and kingdom and patient endurance that is ours in Jesus" (1:9), and twice simply as "John" (1:4; 22:8). There is no reason to assert that this John is someone other than the beloved disciple who authored the Gospel bearing his name and the three letters ascribed to him. Its ultimate author was Jesus himself, who said: "I, Jesus, have sent my angel to give you this testimony for the churches" (22:16).

Its Place of Origin

John saw the visions of the Revelation during his exile on Patmos, a rocky island about five by ten miles in size, situated off the coast of Asia Minor in the Aegean Sea about seventy miles southwest of Ephesus (1:9). John had apparently been exiled there under the Emperor Domitian (A.D. 81–96). He may have written the visions down at that time or shortly afterwards, when he was released.

Its Date of Composition

This is a critical issue (indeed, the *crux interpretum*) in Revelation research, for in determining the Apocalypse's date of composition one also determines certain boundaries for some of his interpretations. If the Apocalypse, as a prophecy, was composed around A.D. 95 or 96, toward the end of the reign of Domitian, then its prophetic utterances cannot find their referents or fulfillment, in any sense, in the events of the mid- or late-60s. But if it was composed around A.D. 65 or 66, during Nero's reign (54–68), before the destruction of Jerusalem in A.D. 70, then the Apocalypse might conceivably include prophetic allusions to the first Roman persecution of Christianity (64–67), the Jewish War with Rome (67–70), the death of Christianity's first imperial persecutor (Nero Caesar, d. 68), the Roman Civil Wars (68–69), and the destruction of Jerusalem and the temple in A.D. 70.

The Late Date Evidence

What is the evidence for the late date of the Apocalypse's composition? First, and, considered by many, weighty to the point of settling the matter, is Irenaeus's reputed testimony—confirmed by Eusebius and Jerome—that it was written toward the end of Domitian's reign. His exact words are:

> if it were necessary that [Antichrist's] name should be distinctly revealed in this present time [c. 180 to 190], it would have been spoken by him who beheld the apocalyptic vision [τὴν ἀποκάλυψιν, *tēn apokalypsin*]. For ἑωράθη [*heōrathē*] no very long time since, but almost in our day, towards the end of Domitian's reign. (*Against Heresies*, 5.30.3)

Late date advocates urge that the subject of the verb which I left untranslated (ἑωράθη, *heōrathē*) is "the apocalyptic vision" of the preceding sentence. Accordingly, they translate the verb "*it* was seen." This view has in its favor the fact that τὴν ἀποκάλυψιν, *tēn apokalypsin*, is the closest possible antecedent to the implied subject in ἑωράθη, *heōrathē*.

Other scholars, however, urge that this does not do justice to the γάρ (*gar*, "for") introducing the sentence. F. J. A. Hort, for example, argues that the γάρ, *gar*, is "syntactically difficult to account for unless it makes reference back to the *main* idea of the preceding statement: 'it [the name of the Beast] *would have been spoken by him*.' "[105] His suggestion is that the subject of the verb is "him who beheld the apocalyptic vision," that is, John, who lived to the time of Trajan (A.D. 98), and that the verb should be rendered "*he* was seen." S. H. Chase explains more fully:

> The statement that the vision was seen at the close of Domitian's reign supplies no reason why the mysterious numbers [666] should have been expounded "by him who saw the apocalypse," had he judged such an exposition needful. If, on the other hand, we refer ἑωράθη [*heōrathē*] to St John, the meaning is plain and simple. We may expand the sentence thus: "Had it been needful that the explanation of the name should be proclaimed to the men of our own day, that explanation would have been given by the author of the Book. For the author was seen on earth, he lived and held converse with his disciples, not so very long ago, but almost in our own generation. Thus, on the one hand, he lived years after he wrote the Book, and there was abundant opportunity for him to expound the riddle, had he wished to do so; and, on the other hand, since he lived on almost into our generation, the explanation, had he given it, must have been preserved to us."[106]

Thus Irenaeus's testimony regarding the time of the Apocalypse's reception by John as being "towards the end of Domitian's reign," while indisputably clear in the

---

105. Kenneth L. Gentry Jr., *Before Jerusalem Fell* (Tyler, Tex.: Institute for Christian Economics, 1989), 50.
106. S. H. Chase, "The Date of the Apocalypse," *Journal of Theological Studies* 8 (1907): 431–32.

opinion of many scholars, is not that evident for others. The latter, however, should acknowledge that the verbal idea in "was seen" more appropriately fits the reception of a "revelation" than an assertion that John "lived" into Domitian's reign.

Second is the contention that the emperor worship alluded to in the Revelation was more widespread in Domitian's than in Nero's day. However this is not as clear–cut as many late date advocates would have their audiences believe.[107]

Third is the argument that the persecutions referred to in the Revelation accord better with Domitian's than with Nero's reign. According to Martin Franzmann, for example, during Domitian's reign "the emperor cult was propagated with great zeal in the province of Asia," which could account for John's banishment to Patmos (1:9), Antipas's martyrdom at Pergamum (2:13), and the souls of men who had been slain for their witness crying aloud for vindication (6:9, 10).[108] Leon Morris explains that while emperor worship was not imposed by the emperors, at least before Domitian, "it was the spontaneous response of the people in the provinces to the peace and good government they owed to the Romans. There was thus a popular demand for emperor-worship and the Christians would have found themselves very much out of step" and thus subjects of persecution.[109] Conversely, Gentry argues that the evidence for an empire-wide persecution of Christians under Domitian is scanty.[110]

The fourth argument is that the seven churches of Asia Minor are given descriptive appearances reflecting a period of development behind them not possible at the time of the Neronic persecution. The evidence presented here is very interesting, but admittedly it is somewhat subjective, the several descriptions of the churches in Revelation 2–3 being open to a given interpreter's interpretation of the known details.[111]

The Early Date Evidence

Early date advocates insist that the book's "self-witness" favors an earlier date for the time of the vision, specifically during Nero's reign, around A.D. 65.

The first, and in my opinion the strongest, piece of evidence is the statement in 17:10 which says that, of the seven kings symbolized by the "seven heads" of the scarlet beast, "the five have fallen, the one is [ὁ εἷς ἔστιν, *ho heis estin*], the other has not yet come; but when he does come, he must remain for a little while." Because "Babylon the Great, the Mother of Prostitutes" is "the great city that rules over the

---

107. Gentry, *Before Jerusalem Fell*, 261–84.
108. Franzmann, *The Word of the Lord Grows*, 270–71.
109. Leon Morris, *The Revelation of St. John* (Grand Rapids, Mich.: Eerdmans, 1969), 36, fn. 1.
110. Gentry, *Before Jerusalem Fell*, 285–99.
111. Ibid., 318–30.

kings of the earth" (17:18), and because the seven heads also represent seven hills upon which the Great Whore sits (17:9), there is little doubt that the "woman" is the city of Rome, capital of the empire. The kings, then, are said to be seven emperors, five of whom have ruled, one who is then ruling at the time of writing, and one who will rule. "All that is required for determining the chronology indicated by Revelation 17:10," writes Gentry, "is that we find a series of seven kings, five of whom 'have fallen,' the sixth of whom 'is' still ruling, and the last of whom was of but a brief reign. The one who 'is' will be the king alive and ruling at the time John wrote Revelation."[112] He suggests that the five kings are Julius Caesar (49–44 B.C.), Augustus Caesar (31 B.C.–A.D. 14; see Luke 2:1), Tiberius Caesar (A.D. 14–37; see Luke 3:1), Gaius Caesar, also called Caligula (A.D. 37–41), and Claudius Caesar (A.D. 41–54; see Acts 11:28; 18:2), the sixth Nero (A.D. 54–68), and the seventh Galba who reigned only from June 68 to January 69. This would suggest that John wrote the Apocalypse during Nero's reign.

This conclusion, Gentry argues, receives support by John's cryptic comment in 13:18: "If anyone has insight, let him calculate the number of the [first] beast, for it is man's number. His number is 666." The one name which fits this number most satisfactorily, Gentry contends, is נרון קסר, *nrôn qsr,* "Neron Caesar"—the very spelling which appears in an Aramaic document from Murabba'at dated to "the second year of the emperor Nero." The numerical value of the name is figured this way, reading from right to left:

$$ ר = 200;\ ס = 60;\ ק = 100;\ ן = 50;\ ו = 6;\ ר = 200;\ נ = 50 $$

It should be noted that a textual variant occurs at 13:18 in manuscript C and in some manuscripts known to Irenaeus and Tyconius that gives the number of the beast as 616. Metzger explains the variant this way:

> When Greek letters are used as numerals the difference between 666 and 616 is merely a change from ξ to ι ($666 = \chi\xi\varsigma$ and $616 = \chi\iota\varsigma$). Perhaps the change was intentional, seeing that the Greek form Neron Caesar written in Hebrew characters (נרון קסר) is equivalent to 666, whereas the Latin form Nero Caesar (נרו קסר) is equivalent to 616.[113]

So what at first seems to overthrow the Nero theory, Gentry writes, "provides a remarkable confirmation of the theory."[114]

---

112. Ibid., 152.
113. Metzger, *A Textual Commentary on the Greek New Testament,* 752.
114. Gentry, *Before Jerusalem Fell,* 203.

It should also be noted that after Nero's suicide on June 9, 68, the empire suffered through the Civil Wars and the usurpation of the imperial throne by three emperors (Galba who reigned from June 68 to January 69; Otho who reigned only from January 15 to April 17, 69; and Vitellius who reigned from January 2 to December 22, 69). The statement in 17:11, "the beast who once was, and now is not, is an eighth king," might seem to require Otho as its referent. But because the phrase, "an eighth king," has no article, Gentry urges that this would allow any subsequent king to be the referent. He believes it refers to Vespasian who reigned from July 1, 69, to June 23, 79, and who restored order and stability to the empire.

William Hendriksen, however, with some biblical justification (see Dan. 2, 7), understands these seven "kings" actually to be seven world empires, and suggests that the first five refer to Ancient Babylon, Assyria, New Babylon, Medo-Persia, and Greco-Macedonia, with the sixth being the Roman Empire and the seventh being "the collective title for all antichristian governments between the fall of Rome and the final empire of antichrist."[115] And he suggests that the eighth is "the final, most terrible dominion of antichrist toward the close of history."[116] He also suggests that the number 666 symbolically means "failure upon failure upon failure," 6 being the number of man, who was created on the sixth day of Genesis 1 and in himself can never attain 7 (the number of perfection).[117]

The second piece of evidence is the suggestion in Revelation 11:1–2 that Jerusalem and the temple are still standing: "I was given a reed like a measuring rod and was told, 'Go and measure the temple of God and the altar, and count the worshipers there. But exclude the outer court; do not measure it, because it has been given to the Gentiles. They will trample on the holy city for 42 months.'" The 42 months are explained as follows: Vespasian, as general, laid siege to Jerusalem in the early spring of A.D. 67; Jerusalem and the temple finally fell to the forces of Titus, his son, in September, A.D. 70—a time approximating the 42 months of 11:2.

While he concedes that John probably did see the Herodian temple in Jerusalem in his vision, Hendriksen quite correctly notes that this piece of evidence is "baseless" as a ground for an early date, since "in a *vision* one can see things which no longer exist in literal reality."[118]

The third bit of evidence to be advanced for an early date are the time indicators that the prophecy stresses relative to the fulfillment of the prophecy's alleged major prediction as understood by many early date advocates, namely, the divine judgment

---

115. William Hendriksen, *More Than Conquerors* (Grand Rapids, Mich.: Baker, 1961), 204.
116. Ibid., 205.
117. Ibid., 182.
118. Ibid., 152.

upon Israel in A.D. 70 for her apostasy from God (1:7). These time indicators translate accordingly:

> Behold, he is coming with the clouds [in judgment],
>   and every eye shall see him,
> even those whose pierced him [the Jewish leadership],
>   and all the peoples of the earth [lit., the tribes of the land, αἱ φυλαὶ τῆς γῆς, *hai phylai tēs gēs*] will mourn because of him.

When does John say the inauguration of the events of this theme verse would commence? Three times in the first chapter of the Revelation, the early date advocates note, we are told that these events would commence *soon*.

> Revelation 1:1: "The revelation of Jesus Christ, which God gave him to show his servants what must *soon* [ἐν τάχει, *en tachei*] take place."
>
> Revelation 1:3: "Blessed is he who reads and those who hear the words of this prophecy, and heed the things which are written in it, for the time is *near* [ἐγγύς, *engys*]."
>
> Revelation 1:19: "Write therefore the things which you have seen, and the things which are, and things which *are about to take place* [μέλλει γενέσθαι, *mellei genesthai*] after these things."

Then three times in the letters to the seven churches Christ declares his soon coming in judgment:

> Revelation 2:16: "Repent therefore; or else I will come to you *quickly* [ταχύ, *tachy*], and I will make war against them with the sword of my mouth."
>
> Revelation 3:10: "Because you have kept the word of my perseverance, I also will keep you from the hour of testing, that hour which *is about to come* [μελλούσης ἔρχεσθαι, *mellousēs erchesthai*] upon the whole world, to test those who dwell upon the earth."
>
> Revelation 3:11: "I am coming *quickly* [ταχύ, *tachy*]; hold fast what you have, in order that no one take your crown."

Finally, five times in the last chapter we are informed of the (purported) temporal immediacy of the prophecy's fulfillment:

> Revelation 22:6: "The angel said to me, "The Lord, the God of the spirits of the prophets, sent his angel to show his servants the things that must *soon* [ἐν τάχει, *en tachei*] take place."

Revelation 22:7: "And behold, I am coming *quickly* [ταχύ, *tachy*]. Blessed is he who heeds the words of the prophecy of this book."

Revelation 22:10: "And he said to me, "Do not seal up the words of the prophecy of this book, for the time is *near* [ἐγγύς, *engys*]."

Revelation 22:12: "Behold I am coming *quickly* [ταχύ, *tachy*], and my reward is with me, to render to every man according to what he has done."

Revelation 22:20: "He who testifies to these things says, 'Yes, I am coming *quickly* [ταχύ, *tachy*].' Amen. Come, Lord Jesus."

It is debatable, however, whether the theme verse can be restricted to Christ's coming in judgment against Israel in A.D. 70, since αἱ φυλαὶ τῆς γῆς, *hai phylai tēs gēs*, can mean "the peoples of the earth." David Chilton's thesis in his *The Days of Vengeance* (following Ray R. Sutton's covenant model in *That You May Prosper: Dominion by Covenant*) that the Apocalypse is God's covenant lawsuit against Israel and prophesies the fall of Jerusalem seems overly restrictive.[119] The judgments foretold throughout the book, even granted the fact that they are explicated in apocalyptic terms, seem to embrace the entire world.[120] Moreover, as H. B. Swete points out, these time indicators "must be interpreted . . . relatively to the Divine measurements of times."[121] And in the progressive parallelism view, these things do begin soon.

The fourth argument to be advanced is the implication from certain statements in the Apocalypse that the *Sitz im Leben* of the Christian community in Asia Minor was one in which it was still operating within Jewish circles and institutions, which was simply not the case after the temple was destroyed in A.D. 70. For example, to the church at Smyrna (2:9) Christ declares, "I know the slander of those who say they are Jews and are not, but are of the synagogue of Satan." And to the church at Philadelphia (3:9) he declares, "I will cause those of the synagogue of Satan, who say that they are Jews, and are not, but lie—behold, I will make them to come and bow down at your feet."

These statements seem to reflect a *Sitz im Leben* when Christians were presenting themselves as the true Jews. Is it credible, Gentry asks, to believe that Christians would have felt the need to do this after the destruction of Jerusalem in A.D. 70?[122]

---

119. David Chilton, *The Days of Vengeance: An Exposition of the Book of Revelation* (Tyler, Tex.: Dominion, 1987). Chilton follows Ray R. Sutton's covenant model set forth in *That You May Prosper: Dominion by Covenant* (Tyler, Tex.: Institute for Christian Economics, 1987).
120. R. Fowler White, "Reexamining the Evidence for Recapitulation in Rev 20:1–10," *Westminster Theological Journal* 51 (1989): 332, notes that Chilton's failure to take into account the fact that both Revelation 6:12–17 and 16:17–21, as descriptions of judgments of cosmic proportions, are parallels to Revelation 20:9–11 (which last passage Chilton acknowledges is descriptive of the eschatological cosmic judgment at Christ's return) makes his overall argument unconvincing.
121. H. B. Swete, *The Apocalypse of St. John* (London: Macmillan, 1922), 2.
122. Gentry, *Before Jerusalem Fell*, 223.

But since Jews would still have been insisting after A.D. 70 that they were the true children of Abraham, Christians could indeed have felt this need. Even today Christians in their witness to their Jewish friends seek to demonstrate that it is they who are the true Israel.

I must conclude that the evidence for the proposed dates is inconclusive. The Apocalypse may have been written around A.D. 65 or 66 before the destruction of Jerusalem in A.D. 70, or it may have been written around A.D. 95 toward the end of Domitian's reign. I am inclined toward the late date because I do not believe that the judgments of the book can be restricted in their applications primarily, if not exclusively, to Israel. But I would suggest that we interpret the Revelation with a certain degree of modesty, gathering its obvious lessons for our schooling in the faith and leaving the more obscure matters for our time of schooling when we see the Revealer himself face to face (22:4).

Its Occasion

Martin Franzmann captures the conditions which occasioned the writing of the Apocalypse in the following words:

> The situation which called forth the writing [of the Apocalypse] is made clear by the writing itself: the churches are being troubled by false teachers (Rev. 2:6, 14, 15), slandered and harassed by Jews, the "synagog of Satan" (Rev. 2:9; 3:9), and are undergoing a persecution (1:9) which has already cost the lives of some faithful witnesses (Rev. 2:13; 6:9, 10) but has not yet reached its height (Rev. 6:11). To these churches John, himself in banishment on the island of Patmos "on account of the word of God and the testimony of Jesus" (1:9), writes the account of the visions vouchsafed to him there, the record of "the revelation of Jesus Christ, which God gave him to show to his servants" (Rev. 1:1). He writes in order to strengthen them in their trials, both internal and external, to hold before them the greatness and the certitude of their hope in Christ, and to assure them of their victory, in Christ, over all the powers of evil now let loose upon the world and, to all appearances, destined to triumph on earth. The book is thoroughly practical, like all the books of the New Testament, designed to be read in the worship services of the churches, as the first of the seven beatitudes [see 1:3; 14:13; 16:15; 19:9; 20:6; 22:7, 14] which the book pronounces shows: "Blessed is he who reads aloud the words of the prophecy, and blessed are those who hear, and who keep what is written therein; for the time is near." (Rev. 1:3)[123]

---

123. Franzmann, *The Word of the Lord Grows*, 270. See also Beckwith, *The Apocalypse of John*, 208–13.

BIBLICAL ESCHATOLOGY

An Outline of Its Content

Before we actually look at the outline[124] it would be helpful to state my reason for holding to the progressive parallelism interpretation of the Apocalypse. A careful reading of the book will disclose that the end of the world (depicted either by the second coming of Christ, cataclysmic cosmic upheaval, the final judgment, or a combination of these) does not occur just one time in the book, namely, in Revelation 20–21, as dispensationalists contend. To the contrary, it is clearly and strikingly depicted in seven visions in the following outline. Again and again the book brings us in striking ways to the end of the world. Consider the following Scripture references:

1. the first vision of the letters to the seven churches, each speaking prophetically and bringing the reader seven times to a contemplation of the final judgment to come and the eternal state: *Ephesus*, 2:7: "To him who overcomes, I will give the right to eat from the tree of life in the paradise of God"; *Smyrna*, 2:11: "He who overcomes will not be hurt at all by the second death"; *Pergamum*, 2:17: "To him who overcomes, I will give . . . him a white stone with a new name written on it"; *Thyatira*, 2:25–27: "Only hold on to what you have until I come. To him who overcomes and does my will to the end, I will give authority over the nations—he will rule them with an iron scepter, he will dash them to pieces like pottery"; *Sardis*, 3:3, 5: "I will come like a thief, and you will not know at what time I will come . . . he who overcomes will . . . be dressed in white. I will never blot out his name from the book of life, but will acknowledge his name before my Father and his angels"; *Philadelphia*, 3:10–12: "the hour of trial that is going to come upon the whole world . . . I am coming soon. . . . Him who overcomes . . . I will write on him . . . the name of the city of my God, the new Jerusalem"; *Laodicea*, 3:14, 21: "I am about to spit you out of my mouth. . . . To him who overcomes, I will give the right to sit with me on my throne";

2. the second vision pertaining to the seals: 6:12–17, especially verse 17: "For the great day of their wrath *has come* [ἦλθεν, *ēlthen*], and who can stand?"; 8:3–5 (note the description of judgment at 8:5, advancing the judgment symbolism of 4:5);

3. the third vision pertaining to the trumpets: 10:7: "But in the days when the seventh angel is about to sound his trumpet, the mystery of God *will be accomplished*"; [ἐτελέσθη, *etelesthē*] 11:15: "The kingdom of the world *has become* [Ἐγένετο, *Egeneto*] the kingdom of our Lord and of his Christ"; 11:18–19: "your wrath *has come* [ἦλθεν, *ēlthen*]. The time has come for judging the dead, and for rewarding your servants the prophets"; and the description of cosmic judgment at 11:19b;

4. the fourth vision pertaining to the woman, the dragon (Satan) and his helpers: 14:14–20, especially verse 15: "the time to reap has come, for the harvest of the earth

---

124. Here I follow rather closely Hendriksen's outline in *More than Conquerors*.

is ripe"; 14:16: "the earth was harvested"; and 14:19: "The angel swung his sickle on the earth, gathered its grapes and threw them into the winepress of God's wrath";

5. the fifth vision pertaining to the seven last plagues: 15:1: "last, because with them the wrath of God *is completed* [ἐτελέσθη, *etelesthē*]"; 16:15–21, especially verse 17: "The seventh angel poured out his bowl into the air, and out of the temple came a loud voice from the throne, saying, '*It is done* [Γέγονεν, *Gegonen*]!' " and, as at 8:5 and 11:19, the description of cosmic judgment at verses 18–21;

6. the sixth vision pertaining to the fall of Babylon: 19:11–21, especially verse 15: "Out of his mouth comes a sharp sword with which to strike the nations. 'He will rule[125] them with an iron scepter.' He treads the winepress of the fury of the wrath of God Almighty";

7. the seventh vision pertaining to the dragon's doom, with Christ and his church the final victors: 20:9–15.

Since this is so, it follows that the Apocalypse should be read as a series of recurring *parallel* or recapitulating visions depicting the terrible judgments awaiting the ungodly and not as a series of visions with each one following its predecessor chronologically.

I suggest therefore the following outline:

I. Introduction, 1:1–8.

A. Superscription, 1:1–3: Jesus announces the Revelation that the Father gave to him to show to his servants. The first blessing is pronounced ("Blessed is the one who reads [aloud] the words of this prophecy, and blessed are those who hear it and take to heart what is written in it.").

B. Greetings from the Triune God to the seven churches, 1:4–5a.

C. Doxology, 1:5b–8. (The book's theme is stated in 1:7.)

II. The church and the world: persecution, vengeance, protection, and victory, chapters 1—11.

A. The first vision, 1:9–3:22: The Christ-indwelt church in the world. This vision, occurring on the Lord's Day, includes a revelation of the exalted Christ (1:12–20)

---

125. Premillennialists interpret this reference to Christ's "ruling" the nations as an oblique allusion to his millennial reign. However, the verb ποιμανεῖ, *poimanei*, says nothing about "ruling" but means rather "He will shepherd." The intended idea is that Christ will "act as a shepherd" toward the enemy nations that threaten his flock by "dashing them to pieces like pottery" (Ps. 2:9; Rev. 2:27).

BIBLICAL ESCHATOLOGY

and his letters to the seven churches of Asia Minor in the midst of which he walks (chapters 2 and 3). It appears to span the entire period between Christ's two advents—from his first coming to shed his blood for his people (1:5) to his coming in judgment (1:7). "Each individual church is, as it were, a type, *not* indicating one definite period in history, but describing conditions which are constantly repeated in the actual life of the various congregations."[126] This is borne out by the recurring refrain at the end of each letter (2:7, 11, 17, 29; 3:6, 13, 22): "He who has an ear, let him hear what the Spirit says to the churches." Christ commends them for their particular strengths and condemns them for their specific weaknesses—these strengths and weaknesses being noted for the benefit of all other churches since then to the end of the age. Each is urged to consider the final judgment and its outcomes.

B. The second vision, 4:1—8:5: The church suffering trial and persecution; the book with the seven seals. This vision too appears to span this age, with a picture both of the Lamb slain (5:6) and of the final judgment (in 6:12–17 and 8:3–5). In this vision we see the heavenly throne room with the four living creatures flying about the throne, the twenty-four elders (angelic beings symbolizing the twelve Israelite patriarchs and the twelve New Testament apostles?) worshiping before the throne, and a seven–sealed scroll resting in the hand of God—"the book of human destiny,"[127] "containing the fixed purposes of God for the future"[128] (4:1–5:5).

Christ, the slain Lamb, is alone worthy to open the scroll and thus receives the praises and adoration of heaven (5:6–14). The Lamb opens the first six seals, which bring in turn false conquering messiahs, wars, famine, death (the so-called four horsemen of the Apocalypse), the prayers of the martyrs in heaven pleading that God would avenge their deaths, and a great earthquake which brings the world to the great judgment day (6:1–17). A brief interlude occurs before the seventh seal is opened to allow the 144,000 saints on earth (the church militant, the number symbolizing completeness—not one of their number is missing) to be sealed and protected from the wrath to come (7:1–8; see note), while the saints in heaven (the church triumphant)—"they who have come out of the great tribulation"—praise God and the Lamb (7:9–17). Then the seventh seal is opened, bringing first a brief silence in heaven, and then an angel, in response to the prayers of the saints, hurls a golden censor of fire to earth, causing "peals of thunder, rumblings, flashes of lightning and an earthquake" (8:1–5), these apocalyptic phenomena graphically depicting the pouring out of the divine wrath on the ungodly. (Observe that the seven seals are divided into two parts, 4 and 3.)

---

126. Hendriksen, *More Than Conquerors*, 22.
127. Morris, *Revelation*, 94.
128. Bruce Metzger, *Oxford Annotated Bible*, 1495.

Note: The 144,000 in 7:1–8 cannot be literal Israel but must be spiritual Israel, the elect of God whether Jew of Gentile, because of three irregularities in the way John describes them, namely, Judah is mentioned first, Dan is omitted altogether with no explanation, and Joseph is mentioned instead of Ephraim.[129]

C. The third vision, 8:6–11:19: The church avenged, protected, victorious; the seven trumpets of judgment that affect the world. From the two facts that John is told that he must continue to prophesy (10:11) and the two witnesses (Moses and Elijah [?], representing all the preachers of the revealed Word of God) also represented as prophesying, this vision seems to span the entire gospel dispensation again, which ends with the completion of the mystery of God and the final judgment (10:7; 11:15, 18–19). In this vision John first hears the first six trumpets sound, the first four of which bringing divine judgments in turn upon the earth, the sea, the rivers, and heavenly bodies (8:6–13), and the fifth and sixth—the first two of the three "woes"—loosing in turn upon the world demons from the Abyss and the four angels of judgment bound at the Euphrates (the eastern border of the Roman Empire) (9:1–10:14).

Before the seventh trumpet is sounded, either as part of the sixth trumpet (the "second woe") or as an interlude to the seventh trumpet (the third "woe"), John is instructed to eat the "little scroll" in a fifth angel's hand. It is sweet because it is the Word of God; it is bitter because it involves God's terrible judgments. He is then told that he must continue to prophesy to the nations, that is, he must report the visions of the second part of the Apocalypse, our chapters 12–22 (10:1–11). He is then instructed to measure the temple and the altar of God and to count the worshipers (Christians), doubtless with a view to their preservation (11:1–2). Then after the two witnesses have prophesied and been killed and raised to heaven (the rapture of the church?), a severe earthquake occurs (11:3–14).

Then the seventh and last trumpet sounds (see the "last trumpet" in 1 Cor. 15:52), and loud voices from heaven declare: "The kingdom of the world has become the kingdom of our Lord and of his Christ, and he will reign forever and ever" (11:15). The twenty-four elders praise God in 11:17–18, but it should be noted that John's earlier acclamation of God in three tenses as the One "who is, and who was, and who is to come (1:4)" is here reduced to the first two tense: "who is and who was." He is no longer the One who is to come; he has come! Then, as occurred at the end of the seventh seal, so here, after the sounding of the seventh and last trumpet, "there came flashes of lightning, rumblings, peals of thunder, an earthquake, and a great hailstorm" (11:19). The "time for the dead to be judged" (11:18) has again come with fiery judgment; and "the mystery of God, as he

---

129. Ladd, *Theology*, 627. See also C. R. Smith, "The Portrayal of the Church as the New Israel in the Names and Order of the Tribes in Revelation 7:5–8," *Journal for the Study of the New Testament* 39 (1990): 111–18.

announced to his servants the prophets, has been completed [ἐτελέσθη, *etelesthē*]" (10:7). (Note again that the seven trumpets are divided into two parts, 4 and 3).

III. Christ and the dragon: persecution and victory. In this section there is noticeable progress in eschatological emphasis.

A. The fourth vision, 12:1–14:20: The woman and the Man-child persecuted by the dragon and his helpers, the beasts and the harlot. This vision clearly spans the age, beginning with Christ's birth (12:5) and closing with a blood-chilling depiction of Christ's second coming (14:14–20). In Ladd's words, it "represents in vivid, picturesque terms an *age-long* battle between Satan and the people of God."[130] In this vision Satan tries to kill the Man-child (Christ; see 12:5) at his birth. Then, having failed in that attempt, he continues his attack on the woman (the church). But the Lord protects the church during her times of persecution (12:1–17). Satan enlists the help of "the beast out of the sea" (the anti-Christian governments of the world; see note 1) and "the beast out of the earth" (the anti–Christian religions and philosophies of the world; see note 2) in his efforts against the church (13:1–18). But the church, the whole number of the faithful symbolized by the 144,000 *now* on Mt. Zion, is protected and preserved (14:1–5). Three angels are sent to warn mankind of the approaching judgment of God (14:6–13; see v. 13: the second blessing of the Apocalypse: "Blessed are the dead who die in the Lord."), which finally falls upon Babylon—representing the world viewed as the great seducer of men's hearts away from God—as Jesus comes, sickle in hand, to the great harvest of the earth (14:14–20). The picture of "blood flowing as high as a horse's bridle for two hundred miles" in 14:20 should not be understood literally, but as contributing to the general effect of the terror of the Eschaton.

Note 1: John's readers would doubtless have seen in his description of the beast out of the sea a reference to the anti-Christian Roman Empire under which they lived, and which, under Nero, launched formal state persecutions against Christians (13:7). The beast's head which "seemed to have had a fatal wound, but the fatal wound had been healed" (13:3, 12, 14; see 17:8, 11) probably has for its background the Nero *redivivus* myth which was prevalent in some parts of the empire after Nero's suicide, but the beast's fatal wound should probably be taken to refer to the Civil Wars which ensued after Nero's death (A.D. 68–69) and its "healing" as referring to the revival of the Roman Empire under Vespasian. First-century Rome would have been then the then–current expression of "the beast out of the sea," which has perpetuated itself in the anti-Christian governments of the world throughout this age.

---

130. Ladd, *Theology of the New Testament*, 625, emphasis supplied.

Note 2: The second beast represents the anti-Christian religions and philosophies of the world, because John later calls it the "false prophet," a *religious* description (16:30; 19:20). It uses its powers to deceive people (13:14) and to enforce the worship of the first beast (13:12) through economic sanctions (13:16–17).

B. The fifth vision, 15:1–16:21: Final wrath upon the impenitent; the seven bowls of wrath. John now sees seven angels with the seven last plagues or bowls of wrath (15:1–8). As with the trumpets before them, as the angels pour out their bowls of divine wrath, the first six plagues come in turn upon the earth, the sea, the rivers, the heavenly bodies, the kingdom of the beast, and the river Euphrates (16:1–12).

As with the seals and trumpets series, there is a very brief interlude before the seventh bowl is poured out in which Jesus announces his coming as a thief and pronounces the third blessing of the Apocalypse (16:15: "Blessed is he who stays awake and keeps his clothes with him, so that he may not go naked and be shamefully exposed").

Then the seventh angel pours out the seventh and last bowl of wrath. Again, as occurred at the end of the seals and trumpets, "there came flashes of lightning, rumblings, peals of thunder, a severe earthquake, and huge hailstones" (16:18–21)—symbolical representations of the wrath of Almighty God being poured out—and "every island fled away and the mountains could not be found" (16:20). Again, the picture of hailstones weighing a hundred pounds each falling upon men in 16:21 should not be understood literally, but as contributing to the general effect of the terror of the Eschaton.

C. The sixth vision, 17:1–19:21: The fall of "Babylon the great, the mother of harlots" ("Rome") and the Scarlet Beast (the "Roman empire"). In this vision John is shown what happens in particular to the great harlot and the beast. The anti-Christian world of seduction and government will pass in due course under the judgment of God until the appearance of the kingdom of Antichrist, the "eighth king which once was, and now is not, who belongs to the seven" (17). But he too "is going to his destruction" (17:11), for in spite of her greatness Babylon will fall (18:1–3). God's people are now warned to "come out of her" (18:4). Then, in a lamentation over the fallen city, the kings, merchants, and mariners of the earth will weep and mourn (18:9–19). An angel through the act of casting a great millstone into the sea symbolizes the total destruction which will come upon "the city of man."

Then heaven rejoices at the news that Babylon will be destroyed and announces in response that the wedding of the Lamb and his bride has come (19:1–10; see the fourth blessing of the Apocalypse in 19:9: "Blessed are those who are invited to the wedding supper of the Lamb"). Christ then returns and crushes the kingdom of Antichrist (19:11–21). Once again, the picture of Christ's robe "dipped in blood" in verse 13 and birds "gorging themselves on the flesh of kings, captains, mighty men, and horses" in verses 18 and 21 should not be understood literally, but as contributing to the general effect of terror.

D. The seventh vision, 20:1–22:5: The dragon's doom; Christ and his church the final victors. This vision begins with Satan's binding, which occurred during our Lord's ministry here on earth (see Matt. 12:29),[131] and ends with the saints in the new heaven and new earth (21:1). In this vision John is shown what happens to Satan. Throughout this age (the "one thousand years")[132] the church militant (20:4a) and the martyred church triumphant reign with Christ, having been regenerated by him, which regeneration is the "first resurrection" of 20:5 (see John 5:24–25; Eph. 2:4–6). The fifth blessing of the Apocalypse is pronounced in 20:6: "Blessed and holy are those who have part in the first [spiritual] resurrection." Though Satan tries to mount a final effort to overthrow the kingdom of Christ through the great apostasy and the man of lawlessness (see 2 Thess. 2), he fails and is cast into hell (20:1–10). Then his kingdom cohorts are brought before the great white throne to be judged and they too are judged and cast into hell (20:11–15).

John then sees in a new heaven and a new earth the holy city, new Jerusalem (the completed church triumphant), coming down from God and prepared as a bride adorned for her husband, in whose midst dwells the enthroned Triune God (21:1–27) and from whose throne flows the river of the water of life for the "healing" of all who live in her. The redeemed "shall see his face [Ladd: "the most

---

131. Premillennialists chide amillennialists for suggesting that Satan is "bound" today. "If he is," they say sarcastically, "he is surely on an exceedingly long chain." But amillennialists interpret Satan's binding to mean only that he is unable in this age to "deceive the nations" as he was able to do in the ancient dispensation. In other words, today his binding, while it is real, is a *relative* thing and not an absolute binding as it will be someday.

  If this interpretation seems to play fast and loose with the words of the text, those who disagree with it must acknowledge that it accords with (1) Jesus' earlier declared binding of Satan (Matt. 12:29) which was not absolute either but a binding only in the sense that his "goods" may now be plundered, (2) Jesus' assurance that by his cross the prince of the world would be "driven out" (John 12:31), not immediately but eventually, as evidenced by the fact that Gentiles were then desiring to "see him," and (3) the author of Hebrew's declaration that Christ "destroyed" him who held the power of death (Heb. 2:14–15), not absolutely yet but in the sense that he cannot hold subject those whom Christ saves.

132. Gerrit C. Berkouwer's judgment appears to be sound when he writes in his *The Return of Christ* (Grand Rapids, Mich.: Eerdmans, 1972):

  Does this vision [of the thousand years] intend to sketch for us a particular phase of history? . . . A choice is inevitable: either one does not tamper at all with any of the facets of this "end-historical" vision, or one accepts the fact that this vision is not a narrative account of a future earthly reign of peace at all, but is the apocalyptic unveiling of the reality of salvation in Christ as a backdrop to the reality of the suffering and martyrdom that still continue as long as the dominion of Christ remains hidden. (307)

important word of all—that which contains every other blessing of the new order"][133] and reign for ever and ever" (22:1–5). What a glorious conclusion to God's redemption of his own and what a blessed hope!

IV. Epilogue, 22:6–21. The angel who showed John these things testifies that what John has seen is true (22:6). Then Jesus promises to come soon and pronounces the sixth blessing of the Apocalypse upon those who heed the words of the prophecy (22:7: "Blessed is he who keeps the words of the prophecy in this book"). Then John testifies that he saw and heard these things (22:8). Jesus again promises to come soon (22:12), pronounces the Apocalypse's seventh and last blessing (22:14: "Blessed are those who wash their robes, that they may have the right to the tree of life and may go through the gates into the city"), and declares that it is he who gave this testimony to the churches (22:16).

The Spirit and the bride (the church) now issue the invitation to drink of the water of life (22:17). John then warns that his verbal revelation of the seven visions is not to be tampered with in any way (22:18). A third time Jesus promises to come (22:20), to which John responds with a simple: "Amen, Come, Lord Jesus" (22:20). He concludes by pronouncing a benediction upon God's people (22:21).

The Apocalypse is a fitting conclusion to the New Testament revelation with its recurring warnings of the end of the world and the final judgment awaiting all mankind. Its dominant theme is the ultimate victory of Christ and his church over *every* enemy. D-day has come; V-day is a certainty!

★ ★ ★ ★ ★

In this chapter I have attempted to demonstrate that Jesus both integrated the teaching of Old Testament eschatology, centering them in Himself, and established the eschatological paradigm for all of the New Testament authors. His "eschatological dualism" embraced both a kingdom of grace, which was inaugurated at his first coming, and a kingdom of power, which will appear when he returns.

Old Testament eschatology pointed forward both to today's "now" (soterically oriented) eschatology and to the "not yet" (consummating) eschatology of the age to come that will commence with Jesus's return, but eschatological clarity awaited Jesus' prophetic insights to distinguish these two ages. All of the New Testament writings project the same eschatological vision; none of them teaches that a millennial age should be inserted between Jesus' "this age" and "the age to come" (Matt. 12:32).

The next great historical event in redemptive history will be the return of Christ, at which time the entire race—the living and the dead—will stand before him in the

---

133. Ladd, *Theology of the New Testament*, 632.

Great Assize to be judged. The true church, having been raised up in glory, will then be "openly acknowledged and acquitted in the Day of Judgement, and made perfectly blessed in the full enjoying of God to all eternity" (Shorter Catechism, Question 38), and the others, having been raised up as well, will experience dishonor and wrath for their sins to all eternity. After he has destroyed all hostile dominion, authority, and power, with all of his enemies being put under his feet, then Christ will hand over the kingdom to God the Father that the Triune God may be all in all. Even so, come, Lord Jesus.

CHAPTER TWENTY-SIX

Downgrade Trends in Contemporary Evangelical Eschatology

A FINAL WORD of caution is in order concerning three disturbing trends in contemporary eschatological studies that are making themselves increasingly felt within certain evangelical quarters.

THE DENIAL OF A LITERAL RETURN OF CHRIST

A kind of realized eschatology is on the rise that, with its peculiar preterist interpretation of the Apocalypse, sees all of the New Testament references to the return of Christ as having been fulfilled by A.D. 70 and consequently denies a literal future return of Christ altogether. In this view only a golden era (Scripture's "kingdom of God") finally awaits the earth and its inhabitants as the gospel of Christ increasingly "Christianizes" the whole earth. The result is a universal reign of peace under the governance of God.

Such a view leaves too many questions unanswered, such as how the saints are finally perfected, how sickness and death are finally overcome, and how the redemption of the body and the glorification of nature are finally achieved. In the words of Donald Guthrie,

> The coming of Christ marks the climax of the history of the ages and forms a fitting conclusion to the redemptive purposes of God in human history. Those who deny the fact of the second coming by attaching to it a wholly spiritual significance are left with a view of human history which has no effective conclusion. A New

Testament theology which finds no place for a second coming of Christ must necessarily be incomplete and unsatisfactory.[1]

ETERNAL PUNISHMENT CONSTRUED AS ANNIHILATION

Just as the Apocalypse gives us a picture of the state of the glorified church in heaven in Revelation 21:1–22:5 that is sheer rapture, so it gives us an equally graphic representation of hell that is sheer horror. In Revelation 14:9–11 John declares that he who has the mark of the beast "will drink of the wine of God's fury, which has been poured full strength into the cup of his wrath," and that he "will be tormented in fire . . . and the smoke of their torment rises for ever and ever.[2] And those who worship the beast . . . have no rest day and night." Here *eternal conscious torment* is said to be the punishment of those who have the mark of the beast. In 19:20 John speaks of "the lake of fire that burns with brimstone," and in 20:15 he declares that "if anyone's name was not found written in the book of life, he was thrown into the lake of fire" which is the "second death." From such Johannine notices as these in the Apocalypse it is clear that the divine judgment awaiting evildoers is certain, just, and eternal.

These features of the eschatological judgment have led some modern evangelical theologians who consider the doctrine of unending conscious torment to be, if not intrinsically unethical, at the very least a reflection upon the gracious side of the divine character, to propound the theory of the impenitent's final annihilation, body and soul.[3] In fact, the Doctrine Commission of the Church of England issued a report in January 1996, entitled "The Mystery of Salvation," that declares:

> Hell is not eternal torment, but the final and irrevocable choosing of that which is opposed to God so completely and absolutely that the only end is total non-being.

---

1. Donald Guthrie, *New Testament Theology* (Downers Grove, Ill.: InterVarsity Press, 1970), 817.
2. John Stott's comment on this passage in David L. Edwards and John Stott, *Evangelical Essentials: A Liberal-Evangelical Dialogue* (Downers Grove, Ill.: InterVarsity Press, 1988), 316, that "it is the smoke (evidence that fire has done its work) which 'rises for ever and ever' " is somewhat facile, for while it is true that it is the smoke that is said to rise, it is also true that it is the smoke of their *torment* that rises forever and ever. It is also said of these people that they experience "no rest day or night"—an expression hardly descriptive of a state of nonexistence.
3. See Edwards and Stott, *Evangelical Essentials*, 312–20. Clark H. Pinnock, in his "The Destruction of the Finally Impenitent," *Criswell Theological Review* 4, no. 2 (1990): 246–47, is unrestrained in his outright rejection of the doctrine of hell as eternal conscious torment:
> I consider the concept of hell as endless torment in body and mind an outrageous doctrine, a theological and moral enormity, a bad doctrine of the tradition which needs to be changed. How can Christians possibly project a deity of such cruelty and vindictiveness

Donald Guthrie is, of course, correct when he states that "the doctrine of eternal punishment is not an attractive doctrine and the desire to substitute for it the view that, at the judgment, the souls of the wicked will cease to exist, is understandable."[4] But, and with this Guthrie would agree, the Bible—which, after all, is our only rule of faith for the doctrine of hell—will not endorse such a substitution. Nor is such a substitution really any more acceptable to the modern mind than the traditional view, for there would still needs come that moment when God would annihilate the sinner by casting him into hell—a notion equally repugnant to the modern mind, which would have God to be a God only of love. Nevertheless, no less an esteemed evangelical than John Stott advances four arguments—related in turn to scriptural language, scriptural imagery, scriptural divine justice, and scriptural universalism—to make the case for the impenitent's annihilation. His first argument makes the basic point that since eternal perdition is often described in Scripture in terms of the sinner's "destruction," "it would seem strange . . . if people who are said to suffer destruction are in fact not destroyed."[5] Second, he contends that the imagery of hell as "eternal fire" suggests—since (he writes) "the main function of fire is not to cause pain, but to secure destruction, as all the world's incinerators bear witness"—that the sinner in hell is to be consumed, not tormented.[6] Third is his contention that a serious disproportion incompatible with the biblical revelation of divine justice would seem to exist between "sins consciously committed in time and torment consciously experienced throughout eternity."[7] Finally, he argues that "the eternal existence of the impenitent in hell would

---

whose ways include inflicting everlasting torture upon his creatures, however sinful they may have been? Surely a God who would do such a thing is more nearly like Satan than like God, at least by any ordinary moral standards, and by the gospel itself. . . . Surely the God and Father of our Lord Jesus Christ is no fiend; torturing people without end is not what our God does.

Millard J. Erickson in his *The Evangelical Mind and Heart* (Grand Rapids, Mich.: Baker, 1993), 152, cautions Pinnock to be more temperate:

If . . . one is going to describe sending persons to endless punishment as "cruelty and vindictiveness," and a God who would do so as "more nearly like Satan than God," and "a bloodthirsty monster who maintains an everlasting Auschwitz," he had better be very certain he is correct. For if he is wrong, he is guilty of blasphemy. A wiser course of action would be restraint in one's statements, just in case he might be wrong.

See my review article on Stott's position, "Dr. John Stott on Hell," *Presbuterion*, 16, no. 1 (1990): 41–59. See also Robert A. Peterson, "A Traditionalist Response to John Stott's Arguments for Annihilation," *Journal of the Evangelical Theological Society* 37, no. 4 (1994): 553–68.

4. Guthrie, *New Testament Theology*, 892; see his entire discussion of hell, 887–92.
5. Edwards and Stott, *Evangelical Essentials*, 316.
6. Ibid., 316.
7. Ibid., 318.

be hard to reconcile with the promises of God's final victory over evil, or with the apparently universalistic texts which speak of Christ drawing all men to himself (John 12:32), and of God uniting all things under Christ's headship (Ephesians 1:10), reconciling all things to himself through Christ (Colossians 1:20), and bringing every knee to bow to Christ and every tongue to confess his lordship (Philippians 2:10–11), so that in the end God will be 'all in all' or 'everything to everybody' (1 Corinthians 15:28)."[8] I will address these arguments in turn.

THE SCRIPTURAL LANGUAGE

The most fruitful way to address the meaning of the scriptural language pertaining to the eternal condition of the impenitent is to cite the relevant passages and to comment upon those whose meaning may not be obvious.

The Old Testament Doctrine of Eternal Punishment

J. A. Motyer correctly observes that while "the Old Testament contains only a suggestion of diversity of destiny for the godly and the ungodly," no sooner does Christ "bring life and immortality to light" than he

> also reveals eternal loss and death, so that even Hades, otherwise equivalent to Sheol, cannot refuse the further significance. This simultaneous maturing of truth concerning eternal gain and loss is ignored by every attempt to divest the New Testament of its grim doctrine of eternal punishment.[9]

What are some of these Old Testament "suggestions of diversity of destiny for the godly and the ungodly"? To begin, as evidence of the Old Testament distinction between the divine deliverance of the godly on the one hand and the divine destruction of the ungodly on the other, one may cite the destruction of Sodom and Gomorrah. Showing righteous Lot mercy (Gen. 19:16), God delivered Lot and his family from Sodom. Then we read:

> The Lord rained down burning sulfur on Sodom and Gomorrah—from the Lord out of the heavens. . . . Early in the morning Abraham looked down toward Sodom and Gomorrah . . . and he saw dense smoke rising from the land, like smoke from a furnace. (Gen. 19:24, 27, 28)[10]

---

8. Ibid., 319.
9. J. A. Motyer, "Destruction," *Baker's Dictionary of Theology* (Grand Rapids, Mich.: Baker, 1960), 260.

Then the intimation of eternal loss respecting the ungodly may be seen in the Old Testament חֵרֶם, *herem*, principle. Recall, for example, that, in conquering Sihon, Israel, Moses wrote, "took all his towns and completely destroyed [וַנַּחֲרֵם, *wannaḥᵃrēm*] them—men, women, and children. We left no survivors" (Deut. 2:34); and that in conquering Og, Israel left "no survivors" (Deut. 3:3), "destroying [הַחֲרֵם, *haḥᵃrēm*] every city—men, women, and children" (Deut. 3:6). Here we see Israel carrying out the חֵרֶם (*herem*, "devoted," and hence "banned") principle—the irrevocable giving over of persons and things to the Lord, often by destroying them.

Liberal theologians and freethinkers have found this principle exceedingly distasteful and repulsive, and accordingly have concluded that the God of the Old Testament is barbaric in the extreme, governed by a sub-Christian ethic, and in no way to be identified with the loving "God and Father of our Lord Jesus Christ." But Meredith G. Kline rightly affirms:

> Actually, the offense taken is taken at the theology and religion of the Bible as a whole. The New Testament, too, warns men of the realm of the everlasting ban where the reprobate, devoted to wrath, must magnify the justice of God whom they have hated. *The judgments of hell are the* חֵרֶם *[herem] principle come to full and final manifestation.* Since the Old Testament theocracy in Canaan was a divinely appointed symbol of the consummate kingdom of God, there is found in connection with it an intrusive anticipation of the ethical pattern that will obtain at the final judgment and beyond.[11]

Supporting this perception, the Preacher of Ecclesiastes declares: "God will bring every deed into judgment, including every hidden thing, whether it is good or evil" (Eccles. 12:14).

Then there are the two explicit Old Testament statements supporting the "diversity of destiny for the godly and the ungodly" found in Isaiah 66:22–24 and Daniel 12:2:

> Isaiah 66:22–24: " 'As the new heavens and the new earth that I make will endure before me,' declares the Lord, 'so will your descendants and your name endure. From one New Moon to another and from one Sabbath to another, all

---

10. Sodom's destruction is significant for it is often cited later as a warning of the divine judgment that will befall those who sin against God (Deut. 29:23; Isa. 1:9, 10; Jer. 23:14; 49:18; Lam. 4:6; Amos 4:11; Zeph. 2:9; Matt. 10:15; Luke 17:29; Rom. 9:29; Rev. 11:8). Particularly instructive are the two references to the destruction of Sodom and Gomorrah found in 2 Peter 2:6–9 and Jude 7.
11. Meredith G. Kline, *Treaty of the Great King* (Grand Rapids, Mich.: Eerdmans, 1963), 68, emphasis supplied; see also Geerhardus Vos, *Biblical Theology* (Grand Rapids, Mich.: Eerdmans, 1949), 141, 143.

[redeemed] mankind will come and bow down before me,' says the Lord. [Note the suggestion of eternal life and blessedness here for God's own.] 'And they will go out and look upon the dead bodies of those who rebelled against me; for their worm will not die, nor will their fire be quenched, and they will be *loathsome* [דֵּרָאוֹן, *dērā'ôn*] to all [redeemed] mankind.'"

In his commentary on Isaiah F. Delitzsch states here that דֵּרָאוֹן, *dērā'ôn*, is the strongest word in Hebrew for "abomination," adding:

It is perfectly obvious that the [picture] itself, as here described, must appear monstrous and inconceivable, however we may suppose it to be realized.... He is speaking of the future state, but in figures drawn from the present world. The object of his prediction is no other than the new Jerusalem of the world to come, and the eternal torment of the damned.[12] (Jesus' later citation of verse 24 in Mark 9:48 [see discussion below] bears out Delitzsch's comment.)

Daniel 12:2: "Multitudes who sleep in the dust of the earth will awake: some to everlasting life [חַיֵּי עוֹלָם, *ḥayyê 'ôlām*], others to shame and *everlasting loathing* [דֵּרָאוֹן עוֹלָם, *dir'ôn 'ôlām*]."

The New Testament Doctrine of Eternal Punishment

What is the evidence supporting what Motyer termed earlier the New Testament's "maturer" doctrine of unending conscious torment for the unrepentant? In addition to John's witness from the Apocalypse, consider the following New Testament data:

John the Baptist

To the multitudes who came to hear him, John the Baptist declared: "[the Messiah] will consume [κατακαύσει, *katakausei*] the chaff with *unquenchable* [ἀσβέστῳ, *asbestō*] fire." (Matt. 3:12)

Annihilationists argue that the action depicted by the verb here is not one of "tormenting" the chaff in unquenchable fire but one of "consuming" the chaff. But this argument ignores the fuller analogy of Scripture and leaves unexplained why John characterizes the fire as "unquenchable." To maintain that the adjective "unquenchable" means that that which is instantly consumed by the fire is consumed

---

12. F. Delitzsch, *The Prophecies of Isaiah* (1877 trans.; reprint, Grand Rapids, Mich.: Eerdmans), 2:517.

forever[13] does not really explain why the fire is described as unquenchable. If the chaff is consumed by the fire, as the annihilationist maintains, there would be no need for it to be unquenchable. Once it had "incinerated" the chaff, it could be put out. I do not mean that hell is necessarily a place of literal flame. Doubtless much of the language of Scripture describing the unseen world must be understood figuratively. But figurative language, if it has any meaning at all (and it does), intends something literal, and it is my contention that the figure of "unquenchable fire" here, in the light of many other Scripture references, intends at the very least unending conscious misery of immeasurable dimensions.

Jesus Christ

It may come as a surprise to some readers that the strongest support for the doctrine of unending conscious torment for the impenitent is to be found in the teaching of Jesus Christ. *The Christian church and Christian pastors are not the authors of this doctrine.* Rather, Jesus, the Redeemer of men, is more responsible than any other person for the doctrine of eternal perdition. It is he, therefore, *more than any other,* with whom the opponents of the doctrine are in conflict. Consider his witness:

> Mark 9:43: "It is better for you to enter life maimed than with two hands to go into hell [τὴν γέενναν, *tēn geennan*], where the fire never goes out."

Jesus' word translated "hell" here is Gehenna, the Aramaic form of "Valley of Hinnom," and it is derived from the Hebrew placename in 2 Kings 23:10, "Topheth [place of spitting?] which was in the Valley of Benei Hinnom," an idolatrous worship center from the time of Ahaz to Manasseh south of Jerusalem where children were burned in fire as an offering to the god Moloch (2 Chron. 28:3). It was destroyed by Josiah and from late Jewish tradition (David Qimchi, c. A.D. 1200) we learn that it was made a refuse dump for the city's garbage. Since fire burned continually in this valley, Gehenna became a symbol of the "unquenchable fire" of hell, a place of perpetual fire and loathsomeness (see Isa. 30:33 for the meaning of Topheth, which became a synonym for the site as a whole: "Topheth has long been prepared; it has been made ready. . . . Its fire pit has been made deep and wide, with an abundance of fire and wood; the breath of the Lord, like a stream of burning sulphur, sets it ablaze.")

> Mark 9:47–48: "It is better for you to enter the kingdom of God with one eye than to have two eyes and be thrown into hell, where 'their worm [that is, their "maggot"] does not die, and the fire is not quenched' "(see Isa. 66:24; Matt. 18:9).

---

13. Edwards and Stott, *Evangelical Essentials,* 316.

Because maggots, the larvae of flies, normally feed upon a corpse's flesh and are finally done with it (Job 21:26; 24:20; Isa. 14:11) whereas here the unrepentant sinner's "maggot" is said never to die, and because hell's fire is said never to be quenched, Guthrie appears to be correct when he states that Jesus' description here of the unrepentant sinner's final state is that of "a state of continuous punishment."[14]

> Matthew 5:22: "Anyone who says, 'You fool!' will be in danger of the fire of hell [τὴν γέενναν τοῦ πυρός, *tēn geennan tou pyros*]" (see vv. 29, 30).
>
> Matthew 7:13: "Wide is the gate and broad is the road that leads to destruction [ἀπώλειαν, *apōleian*, in this context means "[eternal] death," the antithesis of the "life" mentioned in verse 14], and many enter through it."
>
> Matthew 8:12 (see 22:13): "The subjects of the kingdom will be thrown outside, into the darkness, where there will be weeping and gnashing of teeth."

Because this "weeping and gnashing of teeth," suggesting as it does *conscious* anger, pain and woe, exists in hell's "outer darkness," this expression too seems to describe a state of continuous punishment.

> Matthew 10:15: "I tell you the truth, it will be more bearable for Sodom and Gomorrah on the day of judgment than for that town." (see also 11:22, 24; Luke 10:12, 14)

The New Testament teaches that there will be degrees of punishment meted out in the day of judgment to the impenitent, depending on such matters as the sinner's amount of spiritual light and his opportunity to repent and believe. Matthew 10:15 (see Jesus' "more bearable") is one such expression of this teaching. It is difficult, to say the least, to comprehend how this teaching can be adjusted to the annihilationist position if the final outcome of the day of judgment for all the impenitent is the same, namely, annihilation of all, body and soul.

> Matthew 10:28: "Do not be afraid *of those who can destroy* [τῶν ἀποκτεννόντων, *tōn apoktennontōn*] the body but cannot *kill* [ἀποκτεῖναι, *apokteinai*] the soul. Rather, be afraid of the One who can *destroy* [ἀπολέσαι, *apolesai*] both soul and body in hell." (The Lukan parallel in 12:5 reads: "Fear him who, after [μετά, *meta*, with the accusative] the killing of the body, has power to throw you into hell [γέενναν, *geennan*].")

Annihilationists argue that Jesus' terms of destruction here suggest that annihi-

---

14. Guthrie, *New Testament Theology*, 888.

lation is the impenitent's end. But "destruction" does not have to connote annihilation, that is, the cessation of existence. It can also connote a state of *existence*, the precise nature of which to be determined by any and all language qualifying that existence. Accordingly, the impenitent can properly be said to be "destroyed" when he has been cast into hell. And the Lukan parallel (Luke 12:5) suggests precisely this connotation for the Matthean notion of destruction.

> Matthew 13:42, 50: "They will throw them into the fiery furnace, where there will be weeping and gnashing of teeth." (see Luke 13:28)
>
> Matthew 18:8: "It is better for you to enter life maimed or crippled than to have two hands or two feet and be thrown into eternal fire"; (18:9) "... than to have two eyes and be thrown into the fire of hell."
>
> Matthew 23:33: "You snakes! You brood of vipers! How will you escape from the judgment of hell?"
>
> Matthew 25:41: "Then he will say to those on his left, 'Depart from me, you who are cursed, into the eternal fire prepared for the devil and his angels." (see Rev. 20:10)
>
> Matthew 25:46: "Then they [those on his left] will go away to eternal punishment [κόλασιν αἰώνιον, *kolasin aiōnion*] but the righteous to eternal life."

I can find no occurrence of κόλασις, *kolasis*, where it connotes annihilation; rather, it seems in every instance to mean "punishment." Ralph E. Powell correctly notes that in this last reference "the same word 'eternal' is applied to the duration of the punishment in hell as is used for the duration of the bliss in heaven."[15]

> Matthew 26:24: "woe to that man who betrays the Son of Man! It would be better for him if he had not been born." (See Matt. 18:6; Luke 17:2)

But if Judas's final end was to be his soul's annihilation and thus simply nonexistence, how is his final state worse than the nonexistent state which was his prior to his birth?

> Luke 16:23, 24, 28: "In hell, where he was in torment [βασάνοις, *basanois*] ... 'I am in agony in this fire.' ... 'this place of torment [βασάνου, *basanou*].'" (See also 12:5; 13:27)

While one should not press every detail of our Lord's parables, still Jesus surely must have been aware that his listeners would understand him here to teach that,

---

15. Ralph E. Powell, "Hell," *Baker Encyclopedia of the Bible* (Grand Rapids, Mich.: Baker, 1988), 1:954.

following upon physical death, the impenitent sinner endures conscious torment in hell's flames. That literal and intense suffering is the meaning intended by "torment" and "agony" cannot be denied by any reasonable method of exegesis. As annihilationists commonly have done before, Stott interprets this parable to mean that lost men in the *intermediate* state between their physical death and resurrection "will come to unimaginably painful realisation of their fate. But [he continues] this is not incompatible . . . with their final annihilation."[16]

I grant that the parable may be describing most immediately the intermediate state, but there is nothing in the parable which suggests that the intermediate state's "torment" will cease for the lost after their resurrection and judgment. To the contrary, Jesus' description of the "great gulf" between the blessed and the lost (which is doubtless metaphorical language) as "fixed" (ἐστήρικται, *estēriktai*, the perfect passive of στηρίζω, *stērizō*, that is, "has been fixed and continues so") implies the unchanging character of the impenitent's estate in hell.

> John 5:28–29: "Do not be amazed at this, for a time is coming when all who are in their graves will hear his voice and come out—those who have done good will rise to live, and those who have done evil will rise to be condemned."
>
> John 15:6: "If anyone does not remain in me, he is like a branch that is thrown away and withers; such branches are picked up, thrown into the fire and burned."

Demons

> Matthew 8:29: "What have we to do with you, O Son of God? Have you come here before the time to torment us?" (See the references to conscious torment in Luke 16:23, 24, 28.)

It would appear that demons believe that conscious *torment*, not annihilation, awaits them someday.

Paul

Concerning Paul's teaching regarding the judgment of unbelievers, Ridderbos writes:

> Paul declares the certainty of [punitive judgment on unbelievers and the ungodly] in an unmistakable way, in many respects with words that have been derived from

---

16. Edwards and Stott, *Evangelical Essentials*, 317–18.

the Old Testament preaching of judgment. He speaks of it as ruin, death, payment with an eternal destruction . . . ; wrath, indignation, tribulation, anguish. But nowhere is the how, the where, or the how long "treated" as a separate "subject" of Christian doctrine in the epistles of Paul that have been preserved for us.[17]

Here are Paul's statements:

> Galatians 1:9: "If anybody is preaching to you a gospel other than what you accepted, let him be *condemned* [ἀνάθεμα, *anathema*]." Meaning as it literally does, "offered up [to God]," "anathema" brings the Old Testament *herem* principle into the New Testament (see 1 Cor. 16:22).
>
> 1 Thessalonians 1:10: "[Jesus] rescued us from the coming wrath."
>
> 1 Thessalonians 5:3: "Destruction [ὄλεθρος, *olethros*] will come upon them suddenly . . . and they will not escape."

Annihilationists press the word "destruction" here to mean the cessation of existence, but I would urge, on the basis of the analogy of Scripture, that this is playing with words (see my comments on the next verse). This "destruction," coming as Paul says it will upon the ungodly *suddenly*, seems to connote more the general notion of the swift coming upon them of the divine judgment than a specific description of the nature of the end of that judgment.

> 2 Thessalonians 1:9: "They will be punished with everlasting destruction [ὄλεθρον αἰώνιον, *olethron aiōnion*] and shut out from the [approving] presence of the Lord."

This is the only passage in the Pauline corpus where αἰώνιος, *aiōnios*, is explicitly attached to ὄλεθρος, *olethros*. Vos makes some very telling comments on this expression:

> This is the statement most frequently depended upon to tone down the principle of two-sided eternal retribution traditionally ascribed to the Apostle. It not being feasible to modify the eschatologically-constant value of "aionios," the attack has centered upon the noun or nouns to which the adjective is attached. "Olethros" and "apoleia" have been given the sense of annihilation. . . . As concerns the statement in 2 Thess. no one can deny that it posits a strong contrast between the destiny of believers and the end of their persecutors. Only, the question arises, whether the thought of annihilation is fitted to serve as the evil opposite pole in

---

17. Ridderbos, *Paul*, 554.

SYSTEMATIC THEOLOGY

> a contrast so sharply stressed by Paul. It will have to be remembered at the outset that "annihilation" is an extremely abstract idea, too philosophical, in fact, to find a natural place within the limits of the realistic biblical eschatology, least of all, it would seem, in this outburst of vehement indignation against the enemies of the Gospel. Closely looked at it is not a stronger but a weaker concept than that of protracted retribution to threaten with, so that, instead of contributing to the sharpness of the opposition intended, it would to a certain extent obliterate the latter. . . .
>
> The problem of the relation of "olethros" and "apoleia" to existence or non-existence could be solved without much difficulty, were writers willing to test the Pauline statements by reference to the words of Jesus, because the latter on the one hand uses "apoleia" of the state and Gehenna of the place of eternal destruction and on the other hand combines with these the strongest predicates of unceasing retribution; cp. Matt. v. 29; vii. 13; Mk. v. 29, 30; ix. 43, 44, 46, 48; Lk. xii. 5. . . . Could Paul in a matter like this have shown less severity than Jesus?[18]

Vos answers his own question: "In none of [the passages where Paul employs ἀπώλεια, *apōleia*] is there noticeable a lack of pathos, rather the opposite."[19] Moreover, to describe the soul's annihilation in terms of being "shut out from the [approving] presence of the Lord" is a strange phrase, to say the least.

> Romans 2:8–9: "For those who . . . reject the truth and follow evil, there will be wrath and anger; there will be trouble and distress for every human being who does evil."

The last two descriptions here of the sinner's end (trouble and distress) do not comport easily with the notion of cessation of existence.

> Romans 2:12: "All who sin . . . will perish."
>
> Romans 6:21, 23: "[The things you are now ashamed of] result in [physical and spiritual] death . . . the wages of sin is death."
>
> Romans 9:22: "Vessels of his wrath—prepared for destruction."
>
> Romans 14:10–12: "For we will all stand before God's judgment seat. It is written: 'As surely as I live,' says the Lord, 'every knee will bow before me; every tongue will confess to God.' So then, each of us will give an account of himself to God."
>
> 1 Corinthians 3:17: "If anyone destroys God's temple, God will destroy him."
>
> 1 Corinthians 16:22: "If anyone does not love the Lord—a curse [ἀνάθεμα, *anathema*] be upon him."

---

18. Vos, *Pauline Eschatology*, 294.
19. Ibid., 296, fn. 12.

2 Corinthians 5:10: "For we must all stand before the judgment seat of Christ, that each one may receive what is due him for the things done while in the body, whether good of bad."

Philippians 3:19: "Their [the enemies of the cross of Christ] destiny is destruction."

James

James declares: "[The tongue is] a fire [which] sets the entire course of life on fire, and is itself set on fire by hell" (James 3:6). Note that James does not say that the tongue, "set on fire by hell," is annihilated by that fire but rather that it becomes itself a "fire," causing still further damage.

The Author of Hebrews

The author of Hebrews includes among the "elementary teachings" and "foundation" (or "fundamental") doctrines of the Christian faith (the English word, "foundation," the translation of θεμέλιον, *themelion*, here, is from the Latin root from which we also derive our word "fundamental") the doctrine of "eternal judgment" (κρίματος αἰωνίου, *krimatos aiōniou*) (6:2). Of this judgment he writes:

Hebrews 9:27: "Man is destined to die once, and after that to face judgment."

Note that this verse clearly states that men do survive the experience of physical death, *after* which they stand before God in judgment.

Hebrews 10:26–27: "If we deliberately keep on sinning after we have received the knowledge of the truth, no sacrifice for sins is left, but only a fearful expectation of judgment and of raging fire that will consume the enemies of God." (see vv. 28–31)

Annihilationists must place a construction on these words that is not in keeping with the analogy of Scripture.

Hebrews 10:39: "But we are not of those who shrink back and are destroyed."

Hebrews 12:29: "Our God is a consuming fire."

Peter

2 Peter 2:4: "in chains of blackness, consigning [them] to Tartarus [σειραῖς ζόφου ταρταρώσας, *seirais zophou tartarōsas*]."

Tartarus is a classical word for the place of eternal punishment.

Jude

Jude 7: "[The cities of the plain] serve as an example of those who suffer the justice of eternal fire."

John

In addition to the texts already cited in Revelation, note the following words and phrases in John's Gospel: "perish [ἀπόληται, *apolētai*] (John 3:16), "stands condemned already" (3:18), and "God's wrath remains [μένει, *menei*] on him" (3:36). Then John informs us in Revelation 19:20, regarding the destiny of the eschatological beast and the false prophet, that they "were thrown alive into the lake of fire that burns with brimstone."

Of Satan himself, John states:

> Revelation 20:10: The devil, who deceived [the nations], was thrown into the lake of burning sulphur, where the beast and the false prophet had been thrown. They will be tormented day and night for ever and ever.

Stott argues here that, since the beast and the false prophet "are not individual people but symbols of the world in its varied hostility to God" (with which view I am in essential agreement), as symbols they "cannot experience pain."[20] This seems to me to be a desperate attempt to explain away the plain import of the passage. Surely the devil is a person, and if the beast and false prophet are symbols, surely they represent in some sense people hostile to God, about whom John declares, "They will be tormented [βασανισθήσονται, *basanisthēsontai*] day and night for ever and ever."

Finally, John describes the last judgment in the following words:

> And I saw the dead, great and small, standing before the throne, and books were opened. Another book was opened, which is the book of life. The dead were judged according to what they had done as recorded in the books. The sea gave up the dead that were in it, and death and Hades gave up the dead that were in them, and each person was judged according to what he had done. Then death and Hades were thrown into the lake of fire. The lake of fire is the second death. If anyone's name was not found written in the book of life, he was thrown into the lake of fire. (Rev. 20:12–15)

---

20. Edwards and Stott, *Evangelical Essentials*, 318.

The fact that at the final judgment each person will be judged according to what he has done implies that *degrees* of punishment will be meted out by the Judge of all the earth, who will do right by all (Gen. 18:25). This passage also implies that the same destiny awaits the impenitent that awaits the devil, the beast, and the false prophet, namely, torment day and night for ever and ever.

I must conclude from this survey of biblical passages dealing with hell that the only natural meaning of these several texts, interpreted both individually and collectively, is that the retributive infliction of which they speak is unending conscious torment for the impenitent. If these affirmations speak only of the soul's annihilation, none of them intending to teach that the unrepentant sinner consciously suffers eternal torment after the final judgment, then we must conclude that a large majority of the church's scholars for twenty centuries have known little about biblical hermeneutics and have failed to do proper exegesis.

THE SCRIPTURAL IMAGERY

Stott's second argument is that the imagery of hell as eternal fire suggests annihilation since "the main function of fire is not to cause pain, but to secure destruction."[21] It is true that hell is characterized in Scripture primarily in terms of fire. But it goes beyond the evidence to conclude from this fact, as Stott does, that "our expectation [of the effects of this 'fire']" would be the consummation or destruction of the impenitent. Leon Morris concurs:

> Against the strong body of NT teaching that there is a continuing punishment of sin we cannot put one saying which speaks plainly of an end to the punishment of the finally impenitent. Those who look for a different teaching in the NT must point to possible inferences and alternative explanations.[22]

If the New Testament descriptions of hell are to be taken as images at all (and some details are probably to be so construed), then just as any earthly calamity is always more horrible than a word picture can depict it, surely we should understand the realities these biblical passages seek to represent to be *more*—not less—horrible than their word depictions.

SCRIPTURAL DIVINE JUSTICE

Assuming quite properly that scriptural justice insists that the penalty must be

---

21. Ibid., 316.
22. Leon Morris, "Eternal Punishment," *Evangelical Dictionary of Theology*, ed. Walter A. Elwell (Grand Rapids, Mich.: Baker, 1984), 370–71.

commensurate with the evil done, Stott then draws from this what in my opinion is a *non sequitur*, namely, that a serious disproportion incompatible with justice would exist between sins consciously committed in earth history and torment consciously experienced throughout eternity. On this ground God could not even annihilate the sinner for sins "committed in time" since annihilation is certainly eternal in duration.

Moreover, if Stott's argument is sound, then the justice in God's retribution against a whole host of what most people would view as rather insignificant sins recorded in Scripture is also highly questionable. To illustrate what I mean here, consider God's turning Lot's wife into a pillar of salt because she glanced back at Sodom and Gomorrah (Gen. 19:26), God's killing Nadab and Abihu for an irregularity in their priestly duties (Lev. 10:1–2), God's commanding an unnamed man to be stoned to death because he picked up some sticks on the Sabbath (Num. 15:32–36), God's disqualification of Moses entering the promised land because he struck the rock twice rather than speaking to it (Num. 20:11), God's commanding Achan's entire family to be executed because Achan stole something that God had said he wanted (Josh. 7:11, 25), God's killing of Uzziah because he steadied the Ark with his hand (2 Sam. 6:6–7), and his striking down of Ananias and Sapphira for lying to Peter (Acts 5:1–10). But beyond debate, the greatest example of "injustice" from the world's perspective is God's inflicting the entire human race with physical death and condemnation because Adam ate a piece of fruit forbidden him (Gen. 3:5–6; Rom. 5:12–19). The world's justice systems would conclude that in not one of these instances did the divine reaction fit the crime, that these are all only "little sins," if sins at all, hardly deserving the severe retribution God meted out against their perpetrators.

But are these "little sins"? The fact that Stott wants to stress—that men commit such sins in time and not in eternity is irrelevant to the nature and extent of their punishment. The only relevant fact, as David saw, is that such sins—indeed, all sin—are transgressions of the law of God: "Against you, you only, have I sinned and done what is evil in your sight" (Ps. 51:4). Because all sin is finally against God, there is infinite demerit about the "tiniest" sin. Every sin then deserves God's wrath and curse, for the just and holy character of God demands that every sin should receive its just retribution. Thomas Aquinas notes:

> The magnitude of the punishment matches the magnitude of the sin.... Now a sin that is against God is infinite; the higher the person against whom it is committed, the graver the sin—it is more criminal to strike a head of state than a private citizen—and God is of infinite greatness. Therefore an infinite punishment is deserved for a sin committed against him.[23]

---

23. Thomas Aquinas, *Summa theologica*, Ia2ae. 87, 4.

God has certainly given evidence throughout the Old Testament that he will inflict the sinner with conscious *temporal* miseries (see the flood, Sodom and Gomorrah, the plagues of Egypt; the horrible threats of Lev. 26:14–39; Deut. 28:15–68; Hab. 1:5–11; and Mal. 4:1–6). Of this there can be no doubt. If he has made it known by subsequent New Testament revelation that final justice is served only by the conscious *eternal* torment of the impenitent—whose impenitence, we are informed, also continues throughout eternity (since true repentance, which is a gift of God, will not be granted; see Rev. 16:11, 21)—then the creature must acquiesce in his wise and just judgment.

SCRIPTURAL UNIVERSALISM

Stott is not a soteric universalist. He is persuaded that the biblical doctrine of the final judgment which involves "a separation [among men] into two opposite but equally eternal destinies" is too deeply embedded in Scripture to be controverted.[24] One example of this conviction on his part is his total rejection of Pope John Paul II's statement: "Man—every man without exception whatever—has been redeemed by Christ, and . . . with man—with each man without any exception whatever—Christ is in a way united, even when man is unaware of it."[25] Nevertheless, Stott suggests that "the apparently universalistic texts" (Eph. 1:10; Col. 1:20; Phil. 2:10–11; 1 Cor. 15:28) are easier to reconcile with the awful realities of hell if hell means the destruction of the impenitent and not their continuing rebellion against God and God's corresponding continuing infliction of punishment upon them.[26]

The universalist will not be convinced by Stott's reasoning. He will argue that a judgment which eventuates in even the annihilation of one man equally overthrows the import of these universalistic passages. J. A. T. Robinson's words illustrate the universalist's concern:

> Christ, in Origen's old words, remains on the Cross so long as one sinner remains in hell. That is not speculation: it is a statement grounded in the very necessity

---

24. The New Testament alone teaches the ultimate bifurcation of human destiny in more than fifty passages (Matt 7:22, 23; 12:41, 42; 13:40–43; 24:51; 25:41–46; Mark 12:9; Luke 13:25–30; 16:19–28; 21:36; John 5:22–30; 12:47, 48; 15:6; 22–25; 16:8–11; Acts 17:31; 24:25; Rom 1:32; 2:2, 3, 5; 5:16, 18; 14:10; 1 Cor 5:13; 2 Cor 5:10; Gal 6:7; 1 Thes 4:6; 5:1–10; 2 Thes 1:5–10; 2:3–12; 2 Tim 4:1; Heb 4:12; 13; 6:4–8; 10:26–31; James 2:13; 4:12; 1 Pet 2:7, 8, 23; 3:12; 4:17, 18; 2 Pet 2:3–10; 3:7; 1 John 3:7, 8; Jude 4–6, 13, 15; Rev 14:7, 9–11, 17–20; 15:1; 16; 19:1–3, 11–21; 20:11–15; 22:15).
25. Edwards and Stott, *Evangelical Essentials*, 319, 325. For Pope John Paul II's statement, see the papal encyclical *Redemptor Hominis* (1979), para. 14.
26. Edwards and Stott, *Evangelical Essentials*, 319.

of God's nature. In a universe of love there can be no heaven which tolerates a chamber of horrors, no hell for any which does not at the same time make it hell for God.[27]

I am persuaded that the universalist is more consistent here than Stott, for once Stott brings these "apparently universalistic texts" into the debate as part of his argument for annihilation, he can find no exegetical warrant in them for stopping short of the universalist's deduction of the final salvation of all.

I would urge that the doctrine of hell, as historically understood and propounded, is not an infringement upon the notion of God's final victory over evil, nor is it an infringement upon his final joy. Victory over an enemy may be manifested in more ways than one. An enemy's total destruction is one of these ways, to be sure. But his deserved and permanent incarceration at hard labor is equally a manifestation of victory over an enemy and could equally fall out to the praise of the victor's justice. In the case of God and of his Christ, faced as they will be at the judgment with impenitent people guilty of sins of infinite disvalue, the sinner's eternal incarceration in hell will not infringe upon the final divine victory over evil but will in stark lines exhibit the divine triumph over sin. I concur with James I. Packer's judgment that "the holy God of the Bible is praised no less for establishing righteousness by retributively punishing wrongdoers (Rev. 19:1–5) than for the triumph of his grace (Rev. 19:6–10) [and] it cannot be said of God that expressing his holiness in deserved retribution mars his joy."[28]

I must conclude that the doctrines of the final judgment and of hell for the impenitent and the unbeliever are among the *cardinal* doctrines of the Christian faith (see Westminster Confession of Faith, XXXII/i; XXXIII/ii) and that conscious eternal torment awaits the unrepentant sinner. These things are spoken of clearly and plainly in the New Testament. Furthermore, if Christ bore my curse and died my death at Calvary, and if my "eternal punishment" would have been my final and total annihilation, body and soul (a bizarre thing metaphysically even to contemplate), then the annihilationist must be prepared to declare that Christ experienced, body and soul, at least for a time my annihilation, that is to say, nonexistence, a position far more difficult to explicate and to defend than the traditional view that contends that he consciously bore the suffering and separation from God which my sins made me liable to. I would even urge, if the final state of the unrepentant sinner is nonexistence, that we should stop talking about man's need for the work of Christ in any *urgent* sense, for if there is no hell, construed as eternal conscious torment, awaiting the unrepentant sinner, then there is no urgent need for Christ's work, the doctrines

---

27. J. A. T. Robinson, *In the End God* (New York: Harper, 1968), 133.
28. James I. Packer, "Is Hell Out of Vogue?" *Action* (Sept.–Oct. 1989), 11.

of grace, the church as the redemptive community in the world, and the incalculable personal sacrifices that individual Christians and Christian missionaries make to carry the gospel to the ends of the earth. Powell rightly states: "Rejection or neglect of this doctrine will have dire effects upon the true health and mission of the church."[29]

It is just because the Apocalypse takes the fact of an eternal hell seriously that it concludes with the Spirit and the church urging any and all who are thirsty to come and to take the free gift of the water of life (Rev. 22:17). Students of John's Apocalypse have not been sufficiently touched by their study of the book if they have not been moved to take more seriously the evangelization of a world which is on a collision course with God's wrath.

THE NON-NECESSITY OF CONSCIOUS FAITH IN JESUS CHRIST FOR FINAL SALVATION

Others, not elected, although they may be called by the ministry of the Word, and may have some common [nonsaving] operations of the Spirit, yet they never truly come unto Christ, and therefore cannot be saved: much less can men, not professing the Christian religion, be saved in any other way whatsoever, be they never so diligent to frame their lives according to the light of nature, and the laws of that religion they do profess. And, to assert and maintain that they may, is very pernicious, and to be detested. (Westminster Confession of Faith, X/iv)

A third disturbing trend within modern evangelicalism in the area of eschatology is the notion that it is not necessary for people to hear about Christ and consciously to put their faith in him in order to be saved.[30] There was a time in the

---

29. Powell, "Hell," 1:955. Several fine works have been published in recent years upholding the historic teaching on hell as a place of eternal conscious torment, among them being Robert A. Peterson, *Hell on Trial: The Case for Eternal Punishment* (Phillipsburg, N.J.: Presbyterian and Reformed, 1995) and Larry Dixon, *The Other Side of the Good News: Confronting the Contemporary Challenges to Jesus' Teaching on Hell* (Wheaton: BridgePoint, 1992).

30. The Church of Rome has long endorsed this position, stating that those "who, through no fault of their own, do not know the Gospel of Christ or his Church, but who nevertheless seek God with a sincere heart, and, moved by grace, try in their actions to do his will as they know it through the dictates of their conscience—those too may achieve eternal salvation" (*Lumen gentium*, 16; see also Denzinger-Schönmetzer, *Enchiridion Symbolorum*, 3866–72).

Karl Rahner (1904–1984), a leading Roman Catholic inclusivist who coined the phrase "anonymous Christian," by which he meant a non-Christian who gains salvation through faith, hope, and love by the grace of Christ which is mediated imperfectly through his or her own non-Christian religion, writes in his *Theological Investigations* (New York: Seabury, 1966), 1:131, 132:

not-too-distant past when evangelical leaders were in agreement regarding the eternal destiny of the unevangelized. The common view was that people outside of personal faith in Christ are lost, and this belief was one of the main motives driving the entire evangelical missionary enterprise. Accordingly, it was common to evangelical language (one could hear it on all sides) to speak of a "lost and dying world" or an "unsaved world." But today increasing numbers of evangelical spokespersons are stating either that this simply is not so or that the Bible is not clear on these matters.

As an example of the former position, Clark H. Pinnock declares: "We do not need to think of the church as the ark of salvation, leaving everyone else in hell; we can rather think of it as the chosen witness to the *fullness* of salvation that has come into the world through Jesus."[31] Accordingly, he embraces the notion that people from other religions will be saved by Christ without knowing Christ.[32]

Others, while acknowledging that Christ is and always will be man's only Savior, argue that he saves some who have never heard of him through the revelation which is available to them in nature. According to Millard Erickson (a cautious advocate of this position), the essential elements in this "gospel message" in nature are

> 1) The belief in one good powerful God. 2) The belief that he (man) owes this God perfect obedience to his law. 3) The consciousness that he does not meet

---

> Christianity does not simply confront the member of an extra-Christian religion as a mere non–Christian but as someone who can and must already be regarded in this or that respect as an anonymous Christian. . . . The proclamation of the Gospel does not simply turn someone absolutely abandoned by God and Christ into a Christian, but turns an anonymous Christian into someone who now also knows about his Christian belief in the depths of his grace-endowed being by objective reflection and in the profession which is given a social form in the Church.

If Rahner is correct, the world should be seeing large numbers of these gospel-enlightened "anonymous Christians" moving out of their religions and into Christianity because of the spread of the gospel throughout the world via the mass media. But there is little evidence that this is happening. According to John, far from being already "saved" when the gospel comes to them, non-Christians are "already" condemned because they do not have faith in Christ (John 3:18).

31. Clark H. Pinnock, "Acts 4:12—No Other Name Under Heaven," in *Through No Fault of Their Own*, ed. William V. Crockett and James G. Sigountos (Grand Rapids, Mich.: Baker, 1991), 113. He contends for this position more fully in his *A Wideness in God's Mercy* (Grand Rapids, Mich.: Zondervan, 1992).

Arguing the case for classic salvific exclusivism, Ronald H. Nash, *Is Jesus the Only Savior?* (Grand Rapids, Mich.: Zondervan, 1994), provides a thorough exposition and refutation of both John Hick's religious pluralism and Pinnock's and Sanders's soteric inclusivism.

32. In his "Toward an Evangelical Theology of Religions," *Journal of the Evangelical Theological Society* 30, no. 3 (1990): 359–68, Pinnock argues for what he calls the "universality axiom" (God's saving grace is for the entire race, and he desires to save the entire race) and the "particularity axiom" (God's saving grace comes only through Jesus).

this standard, and therefore is guilty and condemned. 4) The realization that nothing he can offer God can compensate him (or atone) for this sin and guilt. 5) The belief that God is merciful, and will forgive and accept those who cast themselves on his mercy.[33]

"May it not be," Erickson asks, "that if a man believes and acts on this set of tenets he is redemptively related to God and receives the benefits of Christ's death, whether he consciously knows and understands the details of that provision or not?"[34]

A spokesman for the agnostic position is John Stott. Stott believes that all men outside of Christ are lost, but with regard to the question of the final annihilation (Stott's view of "eternal punishment") of those who have never heard of Christ, he writes: "I believe the most Christian stance is to remain agnostic on this question. . . . The fact is that God, alongside the most solemn warnings about our responsibility to respond to the gospel, has not revealed how he will deal with those who have never heard it."[35] Timothy Phillips, Aida Besancon Spencer, and Tite Tienou likewise assume an agnostic stance here, stating they "prefer to leave the matter in the hands of God."[36]

These are cited as representative speakers for this "new trend" in order to provide a sampling of what is now being urged by some at the highest levels of academic evangelicalism. But can people be saved through natural revelation? Are the Scriptures silent about the destiny of those who do not hear about and put their trust in Christ? I would reply to both questions in the negative and will give my reasons for these convictions.

General Revelation and Universal Condemnation

According to Holy Scripture, all men outside of Christ are lost in sin—Jews and Gentiles, "good" men and "bad" men, the pagans in the Far East and the pagans in the West. All sinned in Adam and are continually falling short of the glory of God (Rom. 3:23). The wages of their sin is death (Rom. 6:23). In spite of the fact that all peoples and cultures receive general revelation and hence possess an awareness

---

33. Millard Erickson, "Hope for Those Who Haven't Heard? Yes, but . . . ," *Evangelical Missions Quarterly,* 11, no. 2 (1975), 124.
34. Erickson, "Hope for Those Who Haven't Heard?," 125. John Sanders, a Wesleyan thinker, in his *No Other Name: An Investigation into the Destiny of the Unevangelized* (Grand Rapids, Mich.: Eerdmans, 1992) also supports this hope, which he terms "inclusivism," urging that people who never hear about Christ can be saved by exercising saving trust in God as revealed to them by general revelation.
35. John Stott, *Evangelical Essentials,* 327.
36. See *Through No Fault of Their Own,* 259, fn. 3.

both of God's eternal power and divine nature (Rom. 1:19–20) and of sins's deserts (Rom. 1:32), they neither glorify God as God nor are they thankful to him (Rom. 1:21), but pervert their knowledge of him into unspeakable forms of idolatry (Rom. 1:23). The peoples of this world love darkness and hate the light of Christ's gospel because their deeds are evil (John 3:19–20). *Far from saving the world, general revelation becomes the ground of God's just condemnation of the world.* God views the whole world as "under sin": "There is no one righteous, not even one" (Rom. 3:9–10). All are by nature children of wrath (Eph. 2:3). All are already under condemnation (Rom. 3:19). All are alienated from the life of God (Eph. 4:18), ignorant of the truth of God (Rom. 1:25), hostile to the law of God (Rom. 8:7), disobedient to the will of God (Titus 3:3), and subject to the wrath of God (John 3:19).

These statements include the peoples of the world who have never heard the gospel and who have never had a chance to accept or reject Christ. From the biblical perspective there is really no such thing as the "noble savage," Rahner's "anonymous Christian," or the "holy pagan." Such concepts exist only in the minds of unbelieving anthropologists and sociologists and certain Catholic and evangelical inclusivists. Men are lost and under God's judgment, not only because they may have heard about and then rejected Christ at some point in their lives, but also (and more primarily) because they are sinners by nature (they sinned "in Adam") and sinners by practice, and accordingly they have failed to live in accordance with the light of law which they possess. They have sinned against God's revelation without, the works of his law written on the heart within, and their accusing conscience (Rom. 2:14–15).

Inclusivism and the Necessity of Saving Faith in Christ

The Scriptures teach the necessity of faith in Christ for salvation. Jesus Christ declared: "I am the way and the truth and the life. No one comes to the Father except through me" (John 14:6). He also taught that "repentance and forgiveness of sins should be preached in his name to all nations" (Luke 24:46–47). Then Peter emphatically states: "Salvation is found in no one else [not Buddha, not Mohammed, not even Moses], for there is no other name under heaven given to men by which we must be saved" (Acts 4:12). John states emphatically: "No one who denies the Son has the Father; whoever acknowledges the Son has the Father also" (1 John 2:23), and "He who has the Son has life; he who does not have the Son of God does not have life" (1 John 5:12). And Paul declares with equal clarity: "through the obedience of the one man [Jesus Christ] the many will be made righteous (Rom. 5:19b), and "there is one God and one mediator between God and men, the man Christ Jesus" (1 Tim. 2:5). He also writes:

"Everyone who calls on the name of the Lord [in the context, the Lord Jesus Christ] will be saved." How, then, can they call on the one they have not believed in? And how can they believe in the one of whom they have not heard? And how can they hear without someone preaching to them? And how can they preach unless they are sent? As it is written, "How beautiful are the feet of those who bring good news!" (Rom. 10:13–15)

The clear implication of this series of questions is that if missionaries are not sent to preach to those who have not heard about Christ in order that they may believe in him, the unevangelized will not and cannot be saved.

Paul also expressly declared with regard to the destiny of men who do not trust Christ: "All who sin apart from the law will also perish [note: Paul does not say, "can or will be forgiven"] apart from the law, and all who sin under the law will be judged by the law" (Rom. 2:12). John Murray comments here:

> The contrast is . . . between those who were outside the pale of special revelation and those who were within.
>
> With reference to the former the apostle's teaching is to the following effect: (1) Specially revealed law is not the precondition of sin—"as many as have sinned without the law". (2) Because such are sinners they will perish. The perishing referred to can be none other than that defined in the preceding verses as consisting in the infliction of God's wrath and indignation and endurance of tribulation and anguish in contrast with the glory, honour, incorruption, and peace bestowed upon the heirs of eternal life. (3) In suffering this perdition they will not be judged according to a law which they did not have, namely, specially revealed law—they "shall also perish *without the law*."[37]

We should finally note that the fourteen-point judicial indictment inclusive of and applicable to the entire human race in Romans 3:9–20 establishes that all humans—Jew and Gentile—are under the power of sin and will be speechless before the judgment bar of God. Therefore the death of Christ is set forth by Paul in the following verses as the answer to this universal problem of sin. The cross is not one among many ways God deals with sin. It is the only basis on which God justifies any sinner.

In sum, the atoning work of Christ is not merely for Jews or merely for one nation or tribe or language. It is the one and only way for anyone to come into fellowship with God. Christ's death, burial, and resurrection and the need for personal faith in him stand on the "cutting edge" of the mission message in the book of Acts since the

---

37. John Murray, *Romans*, 1:70.

work of Christ is the only basis for salvation. And conscious personal faith in him is everywhere declared as essential to a person's salvation (Rom. 3:26).

Inclusivists question whether conscious faith in Jesus is always essential to salvation. Why do they do this? For three reasons primarily. First, because they believe that Jews in the Old Testament were saved apart from conscious faith in Jesus, that is to say, they had only the "form" of the Christian gospel without its New Testament "content." But this is a false premise, as I demonstrated in part three, chapter fourteen, when I dealt with the unity of the covenant of grace. There I showed that while it is true that the elect of the Old Testament would not have known myriads of details about the Christ of the New (such as the specific time of his coming or the name of his mother), they did understand that the Messiah would die as their substitute and that they had to place their trust in his anticipated death work for them for their salvation.

Second, these inclusivists rely upon what they view as the biblical tradition of "holy pagans" who were saved though they held to religious faiths other that Yahwism and Christianity. They refer here to such people as Melchizedek, Job, the Midianite priest Jethro, Naaman the Syrian, the eastern Magi, and the Roman centurion Cornelius. But these people were hardly "holy pagans." Melchizedek was a priest of the "most high God, owner of heaven and earth," whom Abraham identifies as Yahweh (Gen. 14:22). Melchizedek was certainly a worshiper of Yahweh, as was Job (Job 1:21), and as Jethro (Exod. 18:8–12) and Naaman (2 Kings 5:15–18) came to be. And while the Magi were probably pagan astrologers before their observance in the east of Messiah's "special star," from that point on they gave themselves to the task of finding the "king of the Jews" and worshiping him (Matt. 2:2, 10–12). In each of these instances we may be sure that the Holy Spirit instructed these elect Old Testament saints and directed them to trust the promised Messiah.

Cornelius, described by Pinnock as "the pagan saint par excellence of the New Testament,"[38] is hailed as the prime example of a man who was saved apart from faith in Christ, to whom Peter was sent to inform him that he was forgiven and saved.[39] Does not God say of this "devout [εὐσεβής, *eusebēs*] and God-fearing man" who "gave generously to those in need and who prayed to God regularly" (Acts 10:2) that he had made him "clean" (10:15)? And does not Peter plainly state that "God does not show favoritism but accepts men in every nation who fear him and do what is right" (10:34–35)?

But these statements should not be taken to mean that Cornelius was a saved man. I say this for the following reasons:

---

38. Pinnock, *A Wideness in God's Mercy*, 165.
39. Sanders in *No Other Name*, 254, writes: "Cornelius was already a saved believer before Peter arrived but he was not a Christian believer."

1. To the equally "devout [εὐλαβεῖς, *eulabēs*] men" of Acts 2:5 Peter declared that they had to repent if they were to receive the forgiveness of sins (Acts 2:38; see also 3:19; 13:38–39). So being "devout" in the sense in which Luke employs his terms in these passages should not be construed to mean that those described by them were saved.

2. Peter later states that it was by means of the message that he brought to Cornelius, namely, that "everyone who believes in him receives forgiveness of sins through his name" (see 10:43), that Cornelius was saved (see Peter's "shall be saved," σωθήσῃ, *sōthēsē*, future indicative passive; Acts 11:14).

3. The Jewish Christians of Jerusalem responded to Peter's explanation by saying, "Then God has even granted the Gentiles repentance unto life" (Acts 11:18), this last expression meaning that repentance *leads to* eternal life and that until Gentiles repent and trust Christ they do not have eternal life.

Clearly, then, before Peter came and preached Christ to him, Cornelius was *not* saved. But as surely as this is so, it is equally certain that Cornelius *was* "clean" in the sense that he was not to be viewed any longer as ceremonially "taboo" but as a legitimate candidate for evangelization.[40] This is clearly Peter's own interpretation of his "great sheet" vision in Acts 10:28–29, where we read: "[Peter] said to them: 'You are well aware that it is against our law for a Jew to associate with a Gentile or visit him. But God has shown me [by the vision God had given him] that I should not call any man [ceremonially] impure or unclean [i.e., an "untouchable"]. So when I was sent for, I came without raising an objection." One may legitimately say that the entire event was recorded not only to recount the conversion of Cornelius but also to record the "conversion" of Peter to Gentile evangelism.

Cornelius was also "accepted" (δεκτός, *dektos*) by God (this "accepted" is not the same thing as the earlier "clean," for the "clean" are everyone everywhere, whereas the "accepted" are said to be *in* every nation) in the sense that, since Cornelius was seeking God sincerely and genuinely in God's providence and at the Spirit's prompting, God took steps to get the gospel to him. In sum, he was *accepted* in the sense that he was one of God's *elect* found throughout the world and not just within the nation of Israel. Although he is not as explicit as I that the "accepted" here are God's elect in every nation whom God will reach with the gospel, Everett F. Harrison agrees that Cornelius was not saved prior to Peter's preaching to him:

---

40. In Old Testament times God had "let all the nations go their own way" (Acts 14:16) as he prepared Israel to be the repository of special revelation and the racial originator of the Messiah, and he had "overlooked the nations' ignorance" (Acts 17:23) in the sense that he had taken no direct steps to reach them savingly. But now that Christ has come God commands all people *everywhere* to repent (Acts 17:30) and to put their faith in Christ.

God is prepared to receive those "in every nation" who fear him and work righteousness, the very things which are noted about Cornelius (10:2; see Mt 6:1–2). The meaning [of Peter's statement in 10:34–35] is not that such persons are thereby saved (see Acts 11:14) but rather are suitable candidates for salvation. Such preparation betokens a spiritual earnestness which will result in faith as the Gospel is heard and received.[41]

Cornelius is representative then, not of people who can and are saved apart from faith in Christ (there are none!), but of the unsaved elect in every nation throughout the world who under the Spirit's prompting are "seeking God in an extraordinary way,"[42] that is, who in God's gracious providence are drawn by his cords of electing love to realize (1) that they as desperate sinners must meet someday the one living and holy God with whom all men have to do, and (2) that they are unable to save themselves, and who therefore pray day and night that God in his mercy will somehow find them acceptable in his sight. These God saves through the mission enterprise by getting the good news of Jesus Christ to them, just as he arranged for the gospel to be taken by Peter to Cornelius.

Third (and the previous two reasons grow out of this more fundamental error), evangelical inclusivists believe that "people are saved by faith, not by the content of their theology."[43] Pinnock declares:

Faith in God is what saves, not possessing certain minimum information.... A person is saved by faith, even if the content of faith is deficient.... The issue God cares about is the direction of the heart, not the content of theology.[44]

But surely saving faith must be directed to the true God, the God and Father of our Lord Jesus Christ, and not to an idolatrous or pagan substitute for him. And the content of saving faith must have Christ at its center. Otherwise, such faith is empty and of no value. Moreover, this "faith principle" *per se*, originating as these Arminian thinkers contend in man's determination and will, constitutes a sinful work that cannot save and is everywhere condemned by Scripture. Faith *per se* does not and cannot save. Speaking precisely, it is not even faith in Jesus Christ that saves. It is Jesus Christ who saves the sinner who through faith rests in him.

The Bible intends Christians to understand that the nations are lost, unsaved, perishing without a knowledge of Christ. They are under divine condemnation, not just because they have never heard of Christ but more primarily because they

---

41. Everett F. Harrison, *Acts: The Expanding Church* (Chicago: Moody, 1975), 172.
42. John Piper, *Let the Nations Be Glad* (Grand Rapids, Mich.: Baker, 1993), 146.
43. Pinnock, *A Wideness in God's Mercy*, 157.
44. Ibid., 158.

are sinners by nature and sinners by practice. Christians should pray that God will melt their own hearts and remove all that would blind their eyes that they may see the world as it really is—a world of men on the broad road leading to eternal flame! And then they should pray that God will empower them and send them to that world that is threatened with eternal fire with the message of redeeming love.

Laus Deo!
Soli Deo Gloria!

APPENDIX A

Two Modern Christologies

A CURRENT area of interest in theology that highlights in a striking way the great need for the church to continue to engage itself in the task of *biblical* theologizing is Christology. Just as the central issue of church theology in the book of Acts was christological (see Acts 9:22; 17:2–3; 18:28), so also today Christ's own questions, "What do you think of the Christ? Whose son is he?" (Matt. 22:42), continue to occupy center stage in current theological debate. The conciliar definition of Chalcedon in A.D. 451 espousing a two–natured Christ has come under criticism in the church in our day (see the extreme examples of this in the results of the Jesus Seminar and *The Myth of God Incarnate*).[1] The church dogma that this one Lord Jesus Christ is very God and very man in the full unabridged sense of both of these terms and is both at the same time has been increasingly rejected, not only (it is alleged) on biblical grounds, but also as a contradiction in terms, an impossibility, indeed, a rank absurdity. As a result, it is widely affirmed today that Christology in a way heretofore unparalleled in the history of the church is simply "up for grabs." Christology is a "whole new ballgame."

The Johannine phrase, "the Word became flesh" (ὁ λόγος σὰρξ ἐγένετο, *ho logos sarx egeneto*), is at the center of the modern debate and crystallizes the major issue of the current debate: Is the church's Christology to be a Christology "from below," that is, is it to take its starting point in a human Jesus ("flesh"), or is it to be a Christology "from above," that is, is it to begin with the Son of God ("the Word") come to us from heaven? And in either case, what precisely is the import of John's

---

1. John Hick, ed., *The Myth of God Incarnate* (Philadelphia: Westminster, 1977). The contributors were Don Cupitt, Michael Goulder, John Hick, Leslie Houlden, Dennis Nineham, Maurice Wiles, and Frances Young.

choice of verbs, "became"? It is clear that never has the need been greater for careful, biblically governed, hermeneutically meticulous theological reflection on the perennial question: *Who is Jesus of Nazareth?*

Any response to this question should recall at the outset that the ultimate aim of the early church fathers throughout the decades of controversy over this matter (A.D. 325–451) was simply to describe and to defend the verbal picture that the Gospels and the rest of the New Testament draw of Jesus of Nazareth. Certainly party strife and personal rancor prevailed between some individuals engaged in the debate and made complete objectivity extremely difficult at times. But a faithful reading of the Nicene and post-Nicene Fathers must lead one to the conclusion that neither was it their concern simply to "have it their own way" nor was it the desire to contrive a doctrinal formula so intellectually preposterous that it would be a stumbling block to all but the most gullible that propelled them to speak as they did of Jesus Christ as a two-natured person. Rather, it is apparent that what ultimately underlay their entire effort was simply the faithful resolve to set forth as accurately as words available to them could do what the New Testament said about Jesus. If their creedal terms were sometimes the terms of earlier and current philosophy, those terms nonetheless served the church well in communicating who the Bible declares Jesus to be. If the "four great Chalcedonian adverbs" ("without confusion" [ἀσυγχύτως, *asynchytōs*], "without change [or transmutation]" [ἀτρέπτως, *atreptōs*], "without division" [ἀδιαιρέτως, *adiaretōs*], "without separation" [ἀχωρίστως, *achōristōs*]) describe not so much how the two natures—the human and the divine—are to be related to each other in the unity of the one person of Christ as how they are *not* to be related, again it can and should be said that these negative adverbs were intended to protect what the fathers believed the Scriptures clearly taught about Jesus as well as the mystery of his person, and both at the same time. My own deep longing is that the church today might be as faithful and perceptive in assessing the picture of Jesus in the Gospels for our time as our spiritual forebears were for theirs.

I fear, however, that it is not just a modern dissatisfaction with their usage of Greek philosophical terminology or the belief that the early fathers simply failed to read the Bible as accurately as they might have that lies behind the totally new and different reconstructions of Jesus presently being produced by doctors in the church. Rather, it is a new and foreign manner of reading the New Testament, brought in by the "assured results of Enlightenment criticism"—a new hermeneutic reflecting canons of interpretation neither derived from Scripture nor sensitive to grammatical/historical rules of reading an ancient text—that is leading current scholars to draw totally new portraits of Jesus. The Christ who emerges from these new portraits is no longer one whose purpose was to reverse the effects of the Genesis 3 Fall from an original state of moral integrity and to bring people into the kingdom of God and to eternal life, but rather one who aimed to shock people into an existentially conceived "authentic existence" or into any number of other religio/psychological responses to him.

It is quite in order to ask the creators of these "new Christs": Is the mind-set of modern men really such that they are incapable of believing in the Chalcedonian Christ and the "mythologized proclamation" of the New Testament (so Bultmann)? Is it so that modern science compels the necessity of "demythologizing" the church's proclamation and reinterpreting it existentially? I believe not. In fact, what I find truly amazing is just how many impossible things many modern men are able to believe every day, such as the idea that this present universe spontaneously "decayed" into existence out of nothing, or that man is the product solely of forces latent within nature itself, or that mankind is essentially good and morally perfectible through education and social manipulation, or that justice and morals need not be grounded in theistic ethical absolutes.

It is also in order to ask: Who has better read and more carefully handled the biblical material regarding the person and purpose of Jesus Christ—the ancient or the modern Christologist?

BULTMANN'S CHRIST "FROM BELOW"

Rudolf Bultmann (1884–1976), a New Testament form-critical scholar,[2] in his commentary on John's Gospel, when he comes to John 1:14, writes: "the Logos became flesh! It is the *language of mythology* that is here employed," specifically "the mythological language of Gnosticism."[3] For Bultmann, the emphasis in this statement falls on "flesh" and its meaning, so that "the Revealer is nothing but a man," for that is what "flesh" means.[4] Moreover, the Revealer's glory (δόξα, *doxa*) "is not to be seen ... *through* the σάρξ [*sarx*, "flesh"] ... ; it is to be seen in the σάρξ [*sarx*] and nowhere else."[5]

But John's statement cannot mean that in becoming flesh the Word ceased to be the Word who was in the beginning with God and who was God (John 1:1), because the same Word is also the subject of the following phrase ("and dwelt among us") and because John's sequel to this latter phrase is "and we beheld his glory, glory *as* [ὡς,

---

2. "Form criticism" is an approach to Gospel study that attempts to penetrate behind the written Gospels and even behind the presumed more primitive literary sources underlying them (*Ur-Markus*, Q, M, L) to the still more primitive *oral* Gospel traditions, and to examine and classify the various "forms" or types of traditions discovered there in light of their supposed religious and mythological sources.
3. Rudolf Bultmann, *The Gospel of John* (Philadelphia: Westminster, 1971), 61.
4. Ibid., 62. See too his statement: "It is in his sheer humanity that he is the Revealer" (63).
5. Ibid., 62f., 69.

[1097]

hōs, denoting here not only comparison but also identification] of the unique[6] [Son] of the Father" whom John then further describes in 1:18 as "the unique [Son], God [himself],[7] who is in the bosom of the Father." Bultmann's conclusion is therefore untenable when he claims, using John's "we beheld," that John's assertions are reflecting the perspective of *faith* which has understood that the revelation of God is located precisely in the humanity of Jesus. Bultmann further alleges that John's statements are not statements about the divine *being* of Jesus but rather the mythological shaping of the *meaning* of the man Jesus for faith in light of, not who he is, but what he does to us,[8] and what he does to us is to call us out of our illusory existence in the world to authentic freedom. "In this way," Ridderbos declares, "Bultmann has continued to find in his interpretation of John 1:14 one of the most powerful arguments for an anthropological interpretation of the New Testament kerygma."[9]

The exegete who is not a follower of the highly personal, individualistic, existential school of Bultmann will certainly demur at this perspective. For here there remains not even a kenotic Christ who once was God and divested himself of his deity but only an existential Christ who in *being* never was God but who is only the Revealer of God to faith. But of course the faith in such a construction is devoid of any historical facticity or grounding.

The questions must be squarely faced: Is Bultmann's interpretation preferable to that of Chalcedon? Is it in any sense exegetically sustainable? Is not the language of John 1:14 the language of an *eyewitness* (see John's "we beheld" and his commentary on this phrase in 1 John 1:1–3)? And does John not declare that others (see the "we") as well as he himself "beheld his glory," which glory he then identifies as the glory of

---

6. The word translated "unique" here is μονογενής, *monogenēs*, related to γένος (*genos*, "kind") and γίνομαι (*ginomai*, "to become"), not γεννάω (*gennaō*, "to beget"). It literally means "one of a kind" and highlights the Son's unique sonship.

7. So F. F. Bruce, *The Gospel of John* (Grand Rapids, Mich.: Eerdmans, 1983), 44. With regard to the occurrence of θεός, *theos*, here as a christological title, which is supported by P[66], the original hand of ℵ, B, the original hand of C, P[75], and 33 and given therefore a B rating ("almost certain") in UBS4, Bruce M. Metzger writes: "With the acquisition of P[66] and P[75], both of which read θεός [*theos*], the external support of this reading has been notably strenthened" (*A Textual Commentary on the Greek New Testament* [New York: United Bible Societies, 1971], 198).

8. Bultmann, *John*, 69. See also his *Theology of the New Testament*, trans. Kendrick Grobel (New York: Scribner, 1955), 2: 62.

9. Herman N. Ridderbos, "The Word Became Flesh," in *Through Christ's Word*, ed. W. Robert Godfrey and Jesse L. Boyd III (Phillipsburg, N.J.: Presbyterian and Reformed, 1985), 6. Of course, because, according to Bultmann, faith in the *kerygmatic* Christ cannot be connected with any certainty with the actual earthly life of Jesus of Nazareth nor does it need to be, his Christology as a whole should be classified as a radical Christology "from above." But, as I have said, in his comments on John 1:14 to the effect that "the Revealer is nothing but a man" and that the Revealer's glory (δόξα, *doxa*) "is not to be seen . . . through the σάρξ [*sarx*, "flesh"] . . . ; it is to be seen in the σάρξ [*sarx*] and nowhere else," he reflects a Christology which is moving "from below" to the "above."

the Word's divine being as "unique Son of the Father"? And that Jesus' divine glory was observable is evident on every page of John's Gospel, in every sign-miracle he performed, a glory that neither bystander could overlook nor enemy deny (see 2:11; 3:2; 9:16; 11:45–48; 12:10–12, 37–41; see also Acts 2:22: "as you yourselves know"; and Acts 4:16: "and we cannot deny it").[10] When Thomas the Twin came to faith in Jesus and cried out, "[You are] my Lord and my God" (John 20:28), he did so not because an existential flash bringing a new appreciation of the meaning of the human Jesus for human existence overpowered him, but because his demand to see the print of the nails with his own eyes had been graciously met (see John 20:25, 27, 29) and because the only possible implication of Christ's resurrection appearance for the nature of his being (see Rom. 1:4) made its inescapable impact upon him.

Bultmann's interpretation of John 1:14, only one of many examples of what is designated today as a Christology "from below,"[11] represents one extreme to which faulty theologizing can lead the church—the extreme of portraying the Christ of the Gospels as a mere man and only a man. Of course, this conclusion not only the Fourth Gospel but also the entire New Testament finds intolerable. As we have seen in our discussion of the Trinity (part two, chapter eight), careful exegesis shows that θεός (theos, "God") is employed at least eight or nine times as a christological title in the New Testament (Acts 20:28; Rom. 9:5; Titus 2:13; Heb. 1:8; 2 Pet. 1:1; John 1:1, 18; 20:28; 1 John 5:20; see also Col. 2:9), with Jesus being called scores of times κύριος (kyrios, "Lord"), the Greek word employed in the Septuagint to translate the unpronounced Tetragram (יהוה, yhwh). Old Testament passages spoken by or descriptive of Yahweh, the God of the covenant, are freely applied to Christ in the New (John 12:40–41; Rom. 10:13; Heb. 1:10–12; 1 Pet. 3:14–15). Divine attributes and actions are ascribed to him (Matt. 18:20; Mark 2:5, 8; John 8:58). Jesus' own self-testimony evidences his consciousness of his divine nature (see, for example, the famous so-called "embryonic Fourth Gospel" in Matt. 11:25–28 and Luke 10:21–22). In light of the abundance of New Testament evidence for his deity, it carries one beyond the bounds of credulity to be asked to believe that the several New Testament writers, living and writing under varying circumstances, places, and times were nonetheless all seduced by the same mythology of Gnosticism. All the more is this conclusion

---

10. It is directly germane to our point here to observe in connection with Christ's first sign-miracle (John 2:1–11) that John does not say that the disciples' faith was the pathway to the beholding of Jesus' glory, but to the contrary, that his miracle manifested his glory, and his disciples believed on him *as a consequence*.
11. The most instructive, fully developed example of a "Christology from below" is Wolfhart Pannenberg's *Jesus—God and Man* (Philadelphia: Westminster, 1968), in which he moves from Jesus' resurrection, which he attempts to confirm on the basis of the empty tomb tradition and the appearance traditions, to Jesus' claim to deity, concerning which God demonstrated his approval by raising Jesus from the dead.

highly doubtful in light of the fact that the very fact of a pre-Christian Gnosticism has been seriously challenged by much competent scholarship.[12]

KÄSEMANN'S CHRIST "FROM ABOVE"

Very interestingly, it is one of Bultmann's students, Ernst Käsemann, who argues that the opposite extreme is present in John 1:14—a Christology "from above."[13] In his *The Testament of Jesus*,[14] Käsemann also deals at some length with the meaning of this verse. He argues that the Evangelist intends by σάρξ, *sarx*, here "not the means to veil the glory of God in the man Jesus, but just the opposite, to reveal that glory before every eye. The flesh is the medium of the glory."[15]

According to Käsemann, John's Jesus, far from being a man, is rather the portrayal of a god walking across the face of the earth. Commenting on the expression, "the Word became flesh," he queries: "Is not this statement totally over-shadowed by the confession, 'We beheld his glory,' so that it receives its meaning from it?"[16] Thinking it to be so, Käsemann contends that the Fourth Gospel uses the earthly life of Jesus "merely as a backdrop for the Son of God proceeding through the world."[17] Furthermore, he urges: "the glory of Jesus determines [the Evangelist's] whole presentation so thoroughly from the very outset that the incorporation and position of the passion narrative of necessity becomes problematical,"[18] so problematical, in fact, that "one is tempted to regard it as being a mere postscript [*Nachklappt*] which had to be included because John could not ignore this tradition nor yet could he fit it organically into his work."[19] So great is John's emphasis on the divine glory of Jesus that, according to Käsemann, the Fourth Gospel has actually slipped into a "naïve docetism"[20]:

---

12. See Edwin M. Yamauchi, *Pre-Christian Gnosticism: A Survey of the Proposed Evidence* (Grand Rapids, Mich.: Baker, 1983), particularly chapter 12; C. H. Dodd, *The Interpretation of the Fourth Gospel* (Cambridge: Cambridge University Press, 1955); Raymond E. Brown, *The Gospel According to John I–XII* (Garden City, N.Y.: Doubleday, 1966), LVI; and the articles by W. F. Albright and R. Casey in the Dodd *Festschrift*, *The Background of the New Testament and Its Eschatology*, ed. W. D. Davies and D. Daube (Cambridge: Cambridge University Press, 1956).
13. I am indebted to Ridderbos for calling my attention to this contrast between teacher and student. See his "The Word Became Flesh," *Through Christ's Word*, 3–22, especially 5.
14. Ernst Käsemann, *The Testament of Jesus: A Study of the Gospel of John in the Light of Chapter 17* (Philadelphia: Fortress, 1978), 9–10.
15. Ridderbos, "The Word Became Flesh," 6.
16. Käsemann, *Testament*, 9–10.
17. Ibid., 13.
18. Ibid., 7.
19. Ibid., 7.
20. Docetism, from the Greek root δοκέω, *dokeō*, meaning "to seem" or "to appear," was one of the

TWO MODERN CHRISTOLOGIES

John [formulated who Jesus was and is] in his own manner. In so doing he exposed himself to dangers.... One can hardly fail to recognize the danger of his Christology of glory, namely, the danger of docetism. *It is present in a still naïve, unreflected form.*[21]

In sum, John "was able to give an answer [to the question of the center of the Christian message] only in the form of a naïve docetism,"[22] Jesus' humanity really playing no role as it stands "entirely in the shadow" of Jesus' glory as "something quite non-essential."[23] "In what sense," Käsemann asks, "is he flesh, who walks on the water and through closed doors, who cannot be captured by his enemies, who at the well of Samaria is tired and desires a drink, yet has no need of drink and has food different from that which his disciples seek?... How does all this agree with the understanding of a realistic incarnation."[24] Käsemann seriously doubts whether "the 'true man' of later incarnational theology becomes believable" in John's Christology.[25]

What is one to say about Käsemann's opposite extreme to that of Bultmann's? One can only applaud Käsemann's emphasis on the "very God" character of Jesus, but surely Ridderbos is right when commenting on John 1:14 he writes:

> *Egeneto,* "became," is not there for nothing. It is surely a matter of a new mode of existence. Also, not accidental is the presence of *sarx,* "flesh," which... indicates man in his weakness, vulnerability, and transiency. Therefore, it has been said, not incorrectly, that this statement... certainly approximates the opposite of what one would expect if it were spoken of a docetic... world of thought.[26]

Furthermore, nowhere is Jesus' humanity more apparent in a natural and unforced way than in John's Gospel. Our Lord calls himself (John 8:40) and is called

---

earliest errors in church history. It advocated that Christ did not actually become a man but only seemed or appeared to be such. Cerinthus (c. A.D. 85) is the first known advocate of this teaching. Ignatius, Irenaeus, and Tertullian defended Christ's true humanity against this teaching.

21. Käsemann, *Testament,* 26, 77, emphasis supplied; see also his statement: "The assertion, quite generally accepted today, that the Fourth Gospel is anti–docetic, is completely unproven" (26, fn. 41).
22. Ibid., 26.
23. Ridderbos, "The Word Became Flesh," 9.
24. Käsemann, *Testament,* 9.
25. Ibid., 10.
26. Ridderbos, "The Word Became Flesh," 10. Ridderbos's reference in his "it has been said" here is to the opinions of Rudolf Schnackenburg, *The Gospel According to St John* (New York: Crossroad, 1990), 1:268, and R. E. Brown, *The Gospel According to John I–XII,* 24. But one could add almost indefinitely to this list the names of scholars who view John as self-consciously opposing docetism by his statement in John 1:14, for example, Leon Morris, *The Gospel According to John* (Grand Rapids, Mich.: Eerdmans, 1971), 102, and F. F. Bruce, *The Gospel of John,* 39–40.

by others many times a "man" (ἄνθρωπος, *anthrōpos*) (John 4:29; 5:12; 7:46; 9:11, 16, 24; 10:33; 11:47; 18:17, 29; 19:5). He grows weary from a journey, sits down at a well for a moment of respite, and asks for water to quench his thirst (John 4). People know his father and mother (1:45; 6:42; 7:27). He spits on the ground and makes a healing mud with his saliva (9:6). He weeps (11:35) and is troubled or perplexed (12:27).[27] A crown of thorns is pressed down on his head (19:2) and he is struck in the face (19:3). At his crucifixion blood and water flow from the spear thrust (19:34). And after his resurrection he shows his disciples the wounds in his hands and side (20:20, 27) and even eats breakfast with them (21:9–14). Clearly, in John's Christology we have to do with "flesh"; (see 1 John 1:1–3; 4:2), a man in weakness and vulnerability, a "true man." In Käsemann's interpretation of John's Jesus, while we certainly have to do with a Christology "from above," Christ is so "wholly other" that his humanity is only a costume and no part of a real Incarnation.

Where precisely does the material in the Fourth Gospel lead us? I would urge that a fair reading of John's testimony in its entirety portrays a Jesus who is true man and yet who is at the same time *more than* true man. And in what direction are we instructed to look for the meaning of this "more than"? Clearly, in his being also the divine Son of God who was with the Father in the beginning, who was and is himself God, and who for us men and for our salvation, without ceasing to be God, became man by taking into union with himself our humanness.

What about Käsemann's suggestion that the Fourth Gospel's "theology of glory" (*theologia gloriae*) so overpowers everything in its path that there is really no room in it for a "theology of the cross" (*theologia crucis*), that John brings it in only because he cannot ignore the tradition? I would submit that such a perspective springs from Käsemann's own philosophico-theological vision rather than from straightforward exegesis and objective analysis. The "theology of the cross" fits as comfortably in John's Gospel as it does in the Synoptics or in Paul's thought. It is introduced at the outset in the Forerunner's "Behold the Lamb" (John 1:29, 36) and continues throughout as an integral aspect of John's Christology, for example, in Jesus' early Judaean ministry when he refers to the destruction of his body (2:19, 21) and his being lifted up as the serpent was lifted up in the wilderness (3:14), in the several references to the "hour" that was to come upon Jesus (2:4; 7:30; 8:20; 12:23; 13:1; 17:1), in Jesus' Good Shepherd Discourse where he reveals that he will lay down his life for the sheep (10:11, 15), and in his teaching of the grain of seed which must die (12:24). It must be clearly understood that Käsemann's suggestion that the dogma of a *divine* Christ does violence to a "the-

---

27. See Benjamin B. Warfield, "On the Emotional Life of Our Lord," in *The Person and Work of Christ* (Philadelphia: Presbyterian and Reformed, 1950), 93–145, for a thorough exposition of Jesus' very human emotional life. See also part three, chapter fifteen of this work.

ology of the cross" wounds Christianity as the redemptive religion of God at its very heart, for both Christ's deity and his cross are essential to man's salvation. The implication of Käsemann's point is that one can have a "theology of glory" or a "theology of the cross" but one cannot have both simultaneously. Surely, though, these two stand side by side throughout the New Testament. Paul, whose theology is specifically a "theology of the cross" sees precisely in his cross Christ's glory and triumph over the kingdom of evil (Col. 2:15). The writer of Hebrews affirms that it is precisely by his death that Jesus destroyed the devil and liberated those enslaved by the fear of death (Heb. 2:14–15). Käsemann's construction cannot be permitted to stand unchallenged; it plays one scriptural theme off over against a second, equally scriptural, theme which is in no way intrinsically contradictory to it.

Is there a sense, in the light of these conclusions, in which we may legitimately speak of both kinds of Christology—"from below" and "from above"—in the Gospels? I believe there is, but in the sense clarified by the great Princeton theologian, Benjamin B. Warfield, many years ago:

> John's Gospel does not differ from the other Gospels as the Gospel of the divine Christ in contradistinction to the Gospels of the human Christ. All the Gospels are Gospels of the divine Christ. . . . But John's Gospel differs from the other Gospels in taking from the divine Christ its starting point. The others begin on the plane of human life. John begins in the inter-relations of the divine persons in eternity.
>
> [The Synoptic Gospels] all begin with the man Jesus, whom they set forth as the Messiah in whom God has visited his people; or rather, as himself, God come to his people, according to his promise. The movement in them is from below upward. . . . The movement in John, on the contrary, is from above downward. He takes his start from the Divine Word, and descends from him to the human Jesus in whom he was incarnated. This Jesus, says the others, is God. This God, says John, became Jesus.[28]

In this appendix I have illustrated what I think the theological task is and how it is to be fulfilled today. Our task as Christian thinkers and theologians is simply to

---

28. Benjamin B. Warfield, "John's First Word," *Selected Shorter Writings of Benjamin B. Warfield*, ed. John E. Meeter (Nutley, N.J.: Presbyterian and Reformed, 1970), 1:148–49. Millard Erickson speaks of the effort to integrate the Christologies "from above" and "from below" as the "Augustinian model" ("I believe in order that I may understand"), over against what he terms the "fideistic" and "Thomistic" models respectively, in which one begins with the Christology of the *kerygma* (that is, "from above"), which is then employed to interpret and integrate the data supplied by inquiry into the historical Jesus ("Christology from Above and Christology from Below," *Perspectives on Evangelical Theology*, 54).

listen to and to seek to understand and explicate, whether in sermonic, lecture, or creedal form, what we hear in Holy Scripture in its entirety in order to benefit the church and enhance the faithful propagation of the one true gospel. With humility and the best tools of exegesis we should draw out of Scripture the truth of God revealed therein, being always sensitive to all of its well-balanced nuances. If we are to emulate our Lord, his apostles, and the New Testament church, that and that alone is our task. As we do so, we are to wage tireless intellectual war against every effort of the many hostile philosophies which abound around us to influence the results of our labors.

Will we solve all the problems in the church's doctrine of a two-natured Christ by this method? In my opinion, probably not. Will the theologian solve all the problems which have been raised against Christian theism in general and resolve all of the tensions which men claim to see in it? Probably not. But this should not detract the theologian from the task itself! For it is in his willingness to continue to submit his mind to all of Scripture that the theologian as a student of the Word most emulates the example of his Lord (see Matt. 4:4, 7, 10; 5:17–18; Luke 24:27; John 10:35). And it is in submission to Scripture that the theologian as he goes about his task best reflects that disciple character to which he has by grace been called.

APPENDIX B

The New Testament *Antilegomena*

IN COMPARISON with the writings that the church universally and always regarded as "canonical" (the thirty-nine books of the Old Testament and twenty New Testament books known as the *homologoumena* or "agreed upon" books, bringing to fifty-nine the number of undisputed books out of the total sixty-six canonical writings), the seven books that came to be questioned (known as the *antilegomena* or "disputed" books), namely, James, Hebrews, 2 Peter, 2 John, 3 John, Jude, and Revelation, were not as important, speaking comparatively, as the others. Of these "disputed" books the most important, of course, are Hebrews and Revelation. In the case of Hebrews the objections, primarily in the West and particularly in Rome, were not "original" but arose late, not primarily because its Pauline authorship was doubted but because of the Montanist appeal to Hebrews 6:4.[1] As for the Revelation of John the objections, primarily in the East, were also late and arose as the result of dogmatic antichiliastic considerations.[2] But by the end of the fourth century, traceable to the ecumenical ties which had grown up among the several regions of the church, virtually all the regional doubts respecting these seven books of the New Testament canon had been resolved. And because of the near-universal Christian conviction that the Lord of the church had given the twenty-seven specific New Testament books, and only those books, to His people, the church for the last sixteen hundred years has restricted the New Testament canon to these twenty-seven commonly received New Testament books.

Our discussion of the formation of the canon in chapter three may have appeared to give too much credence to what G. E. Lessing (1729-1781) termed the

---

1. Herman N. Ridderbos, *Redemptive History and the New Testament Scriptures*, second revised edition (Phillipsburg, N.J.: Presbyterian and Reformed, 1988), 44.
2. Ibid.

"ugly ditch of history," that is, that the past by its very nature is at best only indirectly available to later generations, since religious certainty cannot be based upon the shaky foundations of historical research. Without intending in any way to qualify the basic position that I espoused in chapter three, something can, and perhaps should, be said in behalf of the historical evidence for their "apostolic authority" and thus in support of their canonicity.

THE LETTER OF JAMES

James the Just, half-brother of our Lord, most likely authored the letter bearing the name "James." I say this for these reasons: If we ask ourselves which one of the four men named James in the New Testament—*James*, the son of Zebedee and brother of John, one of the Twelve who was martyred by Herod (Matt. 4:21; 10:2; 17:1; Mark 10:35; 13:3; Luke 9:54; Acts 1:13; 12:2); *James* the younger, the son of Alphaeus, one of the Twelve (Matt. 10:3; 27:56; Mark 3:18; 15:40; Luke 6:15; 24:10; Acts 1:13); *James*, the father of Judas "not Iscariot" (Luke 6:16; Acts 1:13); or *James*, the Lord's half-brother (Matt. 13:55; Mark 6:3)—if we ask ourselves, I say, which one of these four could and would expect himself to be recognized and identified when he calls himself simply "James, a servant of God and of the Lord Jesus Christ" and could speak with such massive authority to Judaic Christianity as he does in this writing, reflection on what we know of the first three—which is virtually nothing—should convince us that the last James alone attained the special leadership among Jewish Christians generally which could justify its author making the broad appeal that we find in this letter.

Assuming then that this James is the author, when one recalls, first, that one of Jesus' appearances after His resurrection was specifically to James (1 Cor. 15:7), at which time presumably He called His half-brother to saving faith in Him and to a lifetime of service; second, that James certainly moved in apostolic circles (Acts 15; Gal. 2:9) and doubtless carried apostolic endorsement when he spoke or wrote; third, that Paul speaks of James as an "apostle" and a "pillar" in the church (Gal. 1:19; 2:9); and fourth, that James played a dominant role at the Jerusalem Council attended by Peter and Paul, summarizing the apostolic argument and probably preparing the "Apostolic Decree" himself (Acts 15:13-21), one can hardly doubt that the other apostles clearly recognized that James, as an "apostolic man," was a witness to Jesus' resurrection and a redemptive-historical spokesman to the church of the circumcision. His letter's intrinsic canonicity, accordingly, the Lord led his church to recognize.

THE LETTER TO THE HEBREWS

About the only thing one hears expressed about the question of the authorship of

Hebrews today is Origen's opinion to the effect that God alone knows the real truth of the matter. It is not so commonly recognized that the context of his remark suggests that in his opinion the letter was Pauline—certainly in content if not by the actual pen of Paul. He writes: "If I gave my opinion, I should say that *the thoughts are those of the apostle*.... Therefore, if any church holds that this Epistle is by Paul, *let it be commended* for this. For *not without reason* have the ancients handed it down as Paul's" (cited by Eusebius, *Ecclesiastical History*, 6.25.14).

The letter, admittedly, is anonymous. But whoever the author was, it is clear that the letter's original recipients knew him, for he calls upon them to pray that he would be restored to them shortly (Heb. 13:18-24). Could Paul be the author? In Egypt and North Africa Paul's authorship seems never to have been a matter of serious dispute; in Italy and particularly in Rome, as we have already noted, it was. As evidence of the former, while it is true that Paul in every other instance that we know of indicated his authorship by name, Eusebius (*Ecclesiastical History*, 6.14) informs us that Clement of Alexandria (A.D. 155-215) declared that Paul wrote the letter to Hebrew Christians in Hebrew and that Luke had carefully translated it into Greek and published it among Greek-speaking Christians, and that Paul had omitted his name here out of deference to His Lord whom he looked upon as the real Apostle to the Hebrews (Heb. 3:1; see Rom. 15:8) and also to avoid Jewish prejudice against the letter which would have surely come were they to know that he had authored it. Although it is omitted from the Muratorian Canon (due perhaps to the corrupt state of the text of that Canon), Eusebius himself grouped it with the "fourteen" epistles of Paul (*Ecclesiastical History*, 3.3), this striking notice no doubt reflecting an earlier opinion such as is found (1) in P^{46} (c. 200 A.D.) which places Hebrews between Romans and 1 Corinthians, (2) in the ancestor of Vaticanus which places it between Galatians and Ephesians, and (3) in the majority of ancient Greek copies which place it after 2 Thessalonians, all three positions implying Pauline authorship. Clement of Rome appears to have used it already sometime between 90 and 100 A.D. Furthermore, both Jerome (Jerusalem) and Augustine (North Africa) cite it as Paul's. Internal evidence also supports the legitimacy of suggesting that Paul could have been the author. It is certainly a Paulinism to call upon his readers to pray for him (see Heb. 13:18 and 1 Thess. 5:25; Rom. 15:30-31; Eph. 6:19-20). Moreover, the author's reference to "our brother Timothy" (13:23) surely has a "Pauline ring" about it (see 1 Thess. 3:2; 2 Cor. 1:1; Col. 1:1; Phlm. 1). Furthermore, there is a definite affinity of language between the letter and the recognized Pauline letters (see Heb. 1:4 and Phil. 2:9; Heb. 2:2 and Gal. 3:19; Heb. 2:10 and Rom. 11:36; Heb. 7:18 and Rom. 8:3; Heb. 7:27 and Eph. 5:2; Heb. 8:13 and 2 Cor. 3:11; Heb. 10:1 and Col. 2:17; Heb. 10:33 and 1 Cor. 4:9; Heb. 11:13 and Eph. 2:19; Heb.12:22 and Gal. 4:25, 26). Finally, the person and work of Christ are central here as in the undisputed Pauline epistles.

In my opinion, far too much weight has been given to the statement in Hebrews 2:3 ("... so great salvation, which having first been spoken by the Lord, was confirmed to us by the ones who heard [Him]") as being "the most significant point" *against* Pauline authorship.[3] The statement, by this construction, supposedly teaches that the author was a "second-generation" Christian who had heard the gospel from the Apostles and who was converted as a result of their preaching, thus precluding Paul as the author because he claims in Galatians 1:12 that he received the gospel directly from Christ (see Acts 9:1-9). But Hebrews 2:3 does not say what this construction contends that it says. It does not say that the author had first *heard* the gospel from the Apostles and was converted thereby. Rather, it says that the message of salvation was *confirmed* (ἐβεβαιώθη, *ebebaiōthē*) to him by those who had heard the Lord, implying thereby that the author was already in possession of it at the time of its confirmation to him, an activity which the Apostles could have done for Paul on the occasion of his first or second visit to Jerusalem about which he speaks in Galatians 1 and 2. Certainly the actions of the Apostles, as described by Paul in Galatians 2, give the appearance of being such a "confirming activity."

As for its style, grammar and doctrinal content, I grant that these matters are markedly different in some respects from Paul's other letters to specific churches and individuals, but Hebrews' specific recipients, its very subject matter, its purpose, and Paul's use of an amanuensis (Luke?) could have had much to do with regard to the style and vocabulary of the letter. There is nothing in the content of the letter that Paul could not have written.[4] But whatever the truth of the matter actually is, God led his church to recognize the letter's intrinsic canonicity.

THE LETTER OF JUDE

If the letter of Jude was written by Jude, son of James and one of the original twelve apostles (Luke 6:16; Acts 1:13; probably the "Lebbaeus, whose surname was Thaddaeus," Matt. 10:3), then the letter's apostolic authority is immediately secured.

---

3. Simon J. Kistemaker, *Exposition of the Epistle to the Hebrews* (Grand Rapids: Baker, 1984), 7.
4. I would recommend that the reader consult R. Laird Harris, *Inspiration and Canonicity of the Bible* (Grand Rapids, Mich.: Zondervan, 1957), 263-70, who neatly surveys the patristic evidence and concludes that Hebrews is "a genuine Epistle of Paul using Barnabas as his secretary" (269), though he concedes that another person may have served Paul as an amanuensis (Luke is a strong possibility here). Some think that Barnabas could have been the *original* author, for as a Levite (Acts 4:36) he would have been acquainted with the temple ritual, and as "a son of consolation" (Acts 4:36) he might have written just such a "word of consolation" (13:22). But Donald Guthrie properly concludes that any solid data for Barnabas's authorship is "practically non-existent" (*New Testament Introduction*, fourth edition [Downers Grove, Ill.: InterVarsity Press, 1990], 675).

If, as seems more likely, the letter is from the pen of Jude, James the Just's brother (Jude 1) and younger half-brother of Jesus Himself, since it is improbable, as Salmond writes, that "any forger would have selected a name comparatively so obscure as that of Jude under which to shelter himself,"[5] Jude's blood relationship to Jesus and to James the Just, while such a relationship would not insure the letter's apostolic character in and of itself, would surely have given any letter from him a certain advantage over other letters, insofar as interest is concerned. And as a witness of Christ's resurrection and follower of Christ (Acts 1:14), Jude may have become an "apostle" in a special sense, that is, an "apostolic man."

Regardless of who wrote it, this much we know. Eusebius lists it among the books "spoken against" because not many of the earlier Fathers had mentioned it. He admits, however, that some had done so and that it was regarded as genuine by many in the church (*Ecclesiastical History*, 2.23; 3.25). Jerome reports that it was questioned in some quarters because it seemed to quote from the book of Enoch; "nevertheless, it has acquired authority by antiquity and use, and is reckoned among the sacred Scriptures" (*Catalog of Ecclesiastical Writers*, chap. 4). It is not certain, however, that Jude cites this source, since he may have relied upon the same Jewish tradition that the book of Enoch did. Besides, Paul, whose apostolic authority is unquestioned, also cited uninspired sources without jeopardizing the apostolocity and truthfulness of his teaching.[6] Therefore, the fact that Jude may have cited Enoch should not be used to declare against the canonicity of the book. In any event, God led his church to acknowledge its character as an inspired witness to "the once-for-all-delivered-to-the-saints faith."

THE SECOND LETTER OF PETER

The author identifies himself as "Simon Peter, a servant and apostle of Jesus Christ" (1:1), declares that the Lord had spoken to him about his death (1:14; see John 21:18-19), claims to have been an eye- and ear-witness of Christ's transfiguration (1:16-18), claims to have written his readers a previous letter (3:1), and implies that he knows "our dear brother Paul" (3:15-16). All of this provides exceptionally solid internal evidence for accepting the Petrine authorship of 2 Peter. Nevertheless, 2 Peter was probably the most controverted New Testament book throughout the first three centuries of the Christian era. While there is no evidence that any

---

5. S. D. F. Salmond, "The General Epistle of Jude," *The Pulpit Commentary* (Grand Rapids: Eerdmans, 1950), 22, vi.
6. Paul quotes approvingly Aratus of Cilicia (Acts 17:28), Epimanides of Crete (Titus 1:12), and Menander, author of the Greek comedy, *Thais* (1 Cor. 15:33).

part of the early church ever rejected the letter as "spurious,"[7] it is true that Eusebius (*Ecclesiastical History*, 3.3), while he "makes it clear that the majority [of Fathers] accepted the Epistle as authentic,"[8] classified it among his list of "disputed" books (the *antilegomena*) because it had not been quoted by "the ancient presbyters."

How are we to account for its paucity of quotes by the church fathers? Why was 2 Peter not expressly quoted more than it was during the first centuries of the Christian era? Several things may be said in response. First, the nature and shortness of the letter may partly account for the paucity of quotations from it. As Bigg writes: "It contains very few quotable phrases. It is probably very seldom quoted even in the present day."[9] Second, the church was flooded during the second and third centuries with numerous pieces of pseudonymous Petrine literature. Some questions would naturally rise about any epistle claiming to be Petrine.[10] Third, as Plumptre suggests, "The false teachers condemned in the epistle would make an effort to discredit and suppress it as far as lay in their power."[11] Finally, as Harrison suggests, because it was a general epistle, that is, because it was not addressed to one specific congregation, "no single congregation was committed to...making it more widely known."[12] All these reasons could account for some Fathers' hesitancy in accepting it. But it should be noted that there is reason to believe that Jude used material from it, treating it as though it were authoritative, that the two great third-century Egyptian versions of the New Testament, the *Bohairic* and the *Sahidic*, included it, that P^{72} accepted it as canonical, that Origen cites it at least six times as though it were for him canonical, that Jerome admitted it into the Vulgate, and that the church fathers Athanasius, Epiphanius, Ambrose, Cyril of Jerusalem, Hilary of Poitiers, Gregory of Nazianzus, Basil the Great, and Augustine all received it as canonical.[13]

---

7. Guthrie, *New Testament Introduction*, 819.
8. Guthrie, *New Testament Introduction*, 817.
9. Charles Bigg, *A Critical and Exegetical Commentary on the Epistles of St. Peter and St. Jude* (ICC; Edinburgh: T. & T. Clark, 1902), 211.
10. Guthrie, *New Testament Introduction*, 818.
11. E. H. Plumptre, *The General Epistles of St. Peter and St. Jude* (Cambridge: University Press, 1879), 81.
12. Everett F. Harrison, *Introduction to the New Testament* (Grand Rapids: Eerdmans, 1971), p. 415.
13. I highly recommend Warfield's article, "The Canonicity of Second Peter," *Selected Shorter Writings* (edited by John Meeter; Presbyterian And Reformed, 1973), II, 48-79, E. M. B. Green's *Second Peter Reconsidered* (London: Tyndale, 1961), an admirable monograph of original scholarship which ably combats the contention that 2 Peter is a spurious "pious forgery" (he argues for the priority of Jude over 2 Peter), and Gleason L. Archer, Jr.'s brief but substantive defense of the Petrine authorship of 2 Peter in his *Encyclopedia of Bible Difficulties* (Grand Rapids: Zondervan, 1982), 425-27.

THE SECOND LETTER OF JOHN

When we come to 2 John, we come to the shortest letter minus one in the New Testament. If we allow thirty-six letters for the ancient line and count the letters of each, 2 John would have thirty-two lines, 3 John not quite thirty-one lines. It would have taken up one page of ordinary papyrus paper. In sum, it was not a long letter and in content, speaking comparatively, a rather insignificant letter.

Even though Eusebius (*Ecclesiastical History*, 3.25) lists both 2 John and 3 John among the *antilegomena*, the external evidence in their favor as apostolic letters, though scanty, is still weighty. Irenaeus (c. 140-203) in his *Against Heresies* (1.16.3; 3.16.8) twice quotes from 2 John. Clement of Alexandria (c. 155-c. 215) in his *Stromata* (2.15) speaks of "John's longer epistle," showing that he recognized that John had at least one other and that a shorter epistle. The Muratorian Canon (c. 170 A.D.), after referring to 1 John in connection with the fourth Gospel, speaks of "two epistles of the John who has been mentioned before," showing that 2 John and 3 John were highly regarded at Rome before the end of the second century. Cyprian, bishop of Carthage (c. 200-258), in his *Concerning the Baptism of Heretics* recounts that Aurelius, bishop of Chullabi, quoted 2 John 10-11 at the Council of Carthage (256 A.D.), and the Third Council of Carthage of 397 A.D. definitely recognized its canonicity. Alfred Plummer justifiably observes: ". . . precisely those witnesses who are nearest to S. John in time are favourable to the Apostolic authorship, and seem to know of no other view."[14]

THE THIRD EPISTLE OF JOHN

As we intimated above, 3 John is the shortest letter in the New Testament, a little less than thirty-one lines in length and taking up an ordinary-sized sheet of papyrus. Its brevity, the comparative unimportance of its content, as well as the fact that it was a private letter, caused it not to be widely read in churches. But in spite of these obstacles, the fact that this letter did become widely known and eventually attained formal canonical ranking testifies to the soundness of the tradition which had from earliest times assigned it to the apostle John.

Merrill C. Tenney, following Edgar J. Goodspeed, suggests that 2 John and 3 John "may have been written as 'cover letters' [for his Gospel and 1 John], one to the church, addressed under the figure of the 'elect lady,' and the other to Gaius, its pastor. They were intended to be private notes of counsel and greeting, where the main body of teaching was contained in the Gospel and in the First Epistle."[14]

---

14. A. Plummer, *The Epistles of St. John* (Cambridge: University Press, 1889), 53.
15. Merrill C. Tenney, *The New Testament, An Historical and Analytic Survey* (Grand Rapids, Mich.: Eerdmans, 1953), 375-76.

Goodspeed himself holds that all three epistles originally circulated as a corpus and that consequently the ancient authorities referred to them differently as either one, two, or three letters.[16]

THE REVELATION OF JOHN

Owing both to its enigmatic obscurity and to the dogmatic antichiliastic considerations expressed in some regions of the church, the Revelation of John came to be listed among the church's *antilegomena*, but Papias comments on Revelation 12; Justin Martyr (c. 100-165) in his *Dialogue with Trypho* (chapter 81) written around 155-60 A.D., states that John, the apostle of Christ, received this prophecy from Christ; Irenaeus (d. 202 A.D.) in his *Against Heresies* cited from virtually every chapter of the book, accepted it as Scripture, and attributed the book to "John, the Lord's disciple" (4.11; 5.26.1); Tertullian (c. 150-c. 225) frequently quoted from the book and accepted it as the work of John the apostle; Clement of Alexandria (155-215) and Origen (185-253) also accepted the Revelation as inspired Scripture written by the apostle John; and the Muratorian Canon (c. 170 A.D.) mentions it as a universally recognized book at Rome. Indeed, after A.D. 215 no serious question concerning its canonicity existed in the western church. And by the end of the fourth century the eastern church's resistance to it had abated.

From this overview one can see that there are historical data that can be cited in behalf of the "apostolic authority" of the so-called "disputed" books of the New Testament. Of course, in the final analysis, the Christian must and will rest confidently in the assumption that God led His church in those first four centuries to recognize what He had intended should be included in the New Testament canon, namely, just the twenty-seven commonly received books—books (1) that were inspired by Him, (2) that could and would bear truthful witness to the central redemptive events of the Christian faith, and (3) that He desired the church to preserve for its continuing spiritual soundness.

---

16. Edgar J. Goodspeed, *An Introduction to the New Testament* (Chicago: University of Chicago Press, 1937), 324.

APPENDIX C

The Historicity of Paul's Conversion

AFTER THE EVENTS of the Day of Pentecost, the risen Christ continued to display his divine power in the recorded events of Acts (see Luke's suggestive phrase in this regard, "all that Jesus *began* to do" in Acts 1:1). These authenticating events included the healing of the crippled man at the temple gate called Beautiful (Acts 3:6, 12–13, 16; 4:9–10), the many miracles performed through the apostles among the people (Acts 5:12), Christ's self–revelation to Stephen as "the Son of Man standing at the right hand of God" in the first martyr's moment of death (7:55–56), and the so–called Samaritan Pentecost (Acts 8:14–17). But it is arguable that no postascension act by the risen Christ has ever rivaled, in the significance of its effect on the on–going worldwide life of the church, his appearance to his arch–foe, Saul of Tarsus, on the road to Damascus, sometime between A.D. 32 and 35, the record of which is found in Acts 9:3–18; 22:6–16; and 26:12–18 (see also 1 Cor. 9:1; 15:8). Indeed, so significant is Saul's conversion to Christianity that it is not saying too much to declare that if he was *not* converted as the Acts accounts report, not only is Luke/Acts (as well as Luke's personal integrity as a careful historian) rendered immediately and directly a false witness to history, but the Pauline corpus is also rendered invalid as a trustworthy rule for faith and practice, because Paul claimed in all of his letters to be a legitimate apostle, meeting all of the requirements of one who would be an apostle, particularly the one Peter mentions in Acts 1:22: "a witness of his resurrection." Paul claimed to have "seen Jesus our Lord" (1 Cor. 9:1). He claimed that Jesus "last of all, . . . appeared to me also" (1 Cor. 15:8). He claimed that he had received his commission as an apostle "not from men nor by [any] man, but by Jesus Christ" (Gal. 1:1). And he claimed that he neither received his gospel from nor was he taught his gospel by any man, but to the contrary: "I received it by revelation from Jesus Christ" (ablative use of the genitive) (Gal. 1:12). So if Paul was *not* converted as Acts reports his conversion, then the Pauline corpus is no longer a trustworthy guide in anything it says with regard to matters of faith and practice, and also the church itself, honoring Paul as it has through the centuries as a true apostle of Jesus Christ and basing much of its theology on his writings, is a false witness to God. But no less certain is it that if Paul *was* converted as Acts reports, then this single event in a unique way establishes and validates not only the divine character of the Son of God but also the heavenly origination of Paul's teaching and the authenticity of the church's teachings.

It should surprise no one, then, to learn that a vast literature has grown up around the man Paul and the origin of his message. In fact, the literature on Paul's conversion along with its implications for his ministry is so absolutely enormous that I can do little more than recommend a few of the better treatments of the subject.[1] Moreover, I can do little more than mention the kinds of theories that have been advanced to explain on naturalistic grounds this extremely important event in the life of Saul of Tarsus and offer a few remarks by way of rebuttal.

RATIONALIZING EXPLANATIONS

Three extreme rationalizations of the event are that Saul suffered an epileptic seizure of some kind, or suffered a sun stroke, or saw a flash of lightning that blinded him and startled his horse (Acts nowhere mentions that Paul was on a horse) so that it threw him to the ground, and in the daze that followed he imagined that he had seen the Lord. But these explanations have not commended themselves generally even to the critical mind.

More popular is the view that, under the stress of his fanatical persecution of the church, Saul suffered a mental breakdown on the road to Damascus, and in this broken mental state imagined that the Lord of the very ones he was persecuting had called upon him to desist in his persecution and instead to serve him. Probably the most popular naturalistic explanation is that Saul was subconsciously being conditioned by the logic of the Christian position, plus the dynamic quality of

---

1. I would recommend George Lyttleton, *Observations on the Conversion and Apostleship of St. Paul* (1774), James Stalker, *The Life of St. Paul* (Edinburgh: T. & T. Clark, 1889), J. Gresham Machen, *The Origin of Paul's Religion* (1925; reprint, Grand Rapids, Mich.: Eerdmans, 1965), H. N. Ridderbos, *Paul and Jesus* (Philadelphia: Presbyterian and Reformed, 1957), Richard Longenecker, *Paul, Apostle of Liberty* (New York: Harper & Row, 1964) and *The Ministry and Message of Paul* (Grand Rapids, Mich.: Zondervan, 1971), F. F. Bruce, *Paul and Jesus* (Grand Rapids, Mich.: Baker, 1974) and *Paul: Apostle of the Free Spirit* (Exeter, U.K.: Paternoster, 1977), and S. Kim, *The Origin of Paul's Gospel* (Grand Rapids, Mich.: Eerdmans, 1981). Those readers interested in further reading are advised to consult the extensive bibliographies provided in these works.

THE HISTORICITY OF PAUL'S CONVERSION

Christians' lives and their fortitude under oppression. Then, it is said, when he underwent that "mood-changing" crisis experience on the road to Damascus, the precise nature of which we are now unable to recover (so there is an agnostic aspect to this suggestion), he became convinced because of this prior subconscious preconditioning of mind that he should become a follower of Christ rather than his persecutor.

Such psychologico/psychoanalytic solutions leave too many questions unanswered. In addition to the impossibility of psychoanalyzing a person who lived almost two thousand years ago, what real evidence is there that Saul suffered a mental breakdown? He certainly was not laboring under a deep guilt complex springing from his prosecutorial activities, for he was acting under the auspices of the chief priests (Acts 9:2; 22:5; 26:10, 12) and believed that he was doing God service. And what was the nature of the crisis experience that triggered it? Such questions as these, and many more besides, must be answered satisfactorily before any credence can be given to these theories.

Then there is Rudolf Bultmann, who believed that all such depictions of "biblical supernaturalism" are actually reflections of either Gnostic mythology or Jewish Apocalyptic. But his own explanation of Saul's conversion is wholly unsatisfactory in that it fails to come to terms to any degree with the historical character of the Acts narrative itself: "Not having been a personal disciple of Jesus, *he was won to the Christian faith by the kerygma of the Hellenistic church.*"[2] Neither is James D. G. Dunn's view much better: he concludes that it is impossible to know for sure whether Jesus was "'out there,' alive and making himself known to Paul." All that one can say with any certainty, Dunn continues, is that "Paul himself was convinced that what he saw was external to him" but it may have been "after all, all 'in the mind.'"[3]

THE BIBLICAL EVIDENCE

Such conclusions frankly fail to come to terms with Luke's historical narrative regarding Paul's conversion (recounted in the third person) in Acts 9 or with Paul's later accounts (told in the first person) in Acts 22 and 26, accounts which he gave on the solemn occasions of defending his office and actions under the auspices of the Roman commander and before high government dignitaries. There are pertinent

---

2. Rudolf Bultmann, *Theology of the New Testament,* trans. Kendrick Grobel (London: SCM, 1971), 1:187; emphasis original. Bultman wants the church to believe that Saul—convinced Pharisee that he was—simply came to believe the gospel and walked away from his entire Judaistic convictions, training, and friends with little or no fanfare, an incredible position.
3. James D. G. Dunn, *Jesus and the Spirit* (Philadelphia: Westminster, 1975), 107–8.

data which indicate that his conversion was neither merely mentally induced nor simply the result of evangelism. We are expressly informed that, while Saul alone saw Jesus, the men who were traveling with him both heard a voice (Acts 9:7), though they did not understand the words (22:9), and saw the brilliant light (22:9; 26:13–14). And while it is true that Paul would later call the event a "vision from heaven" (26:19), which description itself imputes an *ab extra* character to it ("*from heaven*"), the accounts make it clear that his conversion was not subjectively self-induced in the subconscious but, rather, that it resulted from an initiating action external to him (9:3–4; 22:6–7; 26:13–14). Indeed, the ascended Christ represents *himself* as the Initiator in 26:16: "I have appeared to you" (ὤφθην σοι, *ōphthēn soi*). And Ananias will say later that God had chosen Saul "to see the Righteous One and to hear words from his mouth" (22:14).

When all the facts in Acts 9, 22, 26, and 1 Corinthians 15 are taken into account, Richard Longenecker's judgment seems clearly justified:

> Only the Damascus encounter with Christ was powerful enough to cause the young Jewish rabbi to reconsider the death of Jesus; only his meeting with the risen Christ was sufficient to demonstrate that God had vindicated the claims and work of the One he was opposing. Humanly speaking, Paul was immune to the Gospel. Although he was ready to follow evidence to its conclusion, he was sure that no evidence could overturn the verdict of the cross; that is, that Christ died the death of a criminal. But . . . the eternal God "was pleased," as Paul says by way of reminiscence, "to reveal his Son to me" (Gal 1:16). Thus Paul was arrested by Christ, and made His own (Phil 3:12).[4]

---

4. Longenecker, *Ministry and Message of Paul*, 34–35. I must add to Longenecker's suggested reason for Saul's immunity to the gospel the additional reason that faith in Christ's obedience for salvation was surely for him incompatible with his Judaistic inclination to rely upon his own obedience to the law for salvation (see Jacques Dupont, "The Conversion of Paul, and Its Influence on His Understanding of Salvation by Faith," in *Apostolic History and the Gospel*, ed. W. Ward Gasque and Ralph Martin [Exeter: Paternoster, 1970], 178–94). E. Sanders has argued in his *Paul and Palestinian Judaism* (Philadelphia: Fortress Press, 1977) that Palestinian Judaism was not a religion of legalistic works-righteousness wherein right standing before God was earned by good works in a system of strict justice. It is true, of course, as Sanders points out, that one can indeed find references in the literature of the period to God's election of Israel and to his grace and mercy toward the nation. But Sanders makes too much of these facts, since Palestinian Judaism also taught that the elect man was obligated, even though he would do so imperfectly, to obey the law in order to remain in the covenant. Thus the legalistic principle was still present and ultimately governed the soteric status of the individual. But Paul rightly saw that *any* obligation to accomplish a "works-righteousness" on the sinner's part would negate the principle of *sola gratia* altogether (Rom. 11:6). For a detailed critical analysis of Sanders's thesis, see Karl T. Cooper, "Paul and Rabbinic Soteriology," *Westminster Theological Journal* 44 (1982): 123–39.

THE HISTORICITY OF PAUL'S CONVERSION

Paul's Own Argument

In support of his apostleship and the "revealedness" of the gospel he proclaimed, I can produce no better argument than the one which Paul himself adduced in Galatians 1:13–2:10 when he was defending his apostolic authority and message. The issue we are facing is: What was the ultimate origin of Paul's gospel and his apostolic commission? It is evident that he could have obtained his gospel and the authority to preach it from only one of three possible sources.

JUDAISTIC TRAINING

Did Paul obtain his gospel from his previous life in Judaism? To ask the question is to answer it. Certainly not! Paul himself describes that experience in Judaism for us four different times:

> For you have heard of my previous way of life in Judaism, how intensely I persecuted the church of God and tried to destroy it. I was advancing in Judaism beyond many Jews of my own age and was extremely zealous for the tradition of my fathers. (Gal. 1:13–14)

> I am a Jew, born in Tarsus of Cilicia, brought up in this city at the feet of Gamaliel, thoroughly trained in the law of our fathers, being zealous for God. (Acts 22:3)

> The Jews all know the way I have lived ever since I was a child, from the beginning of my life in my own country, and also in Jerusalem. They have known me for a long time and can testify, if they are willing, that according to the strictest sect of our religion, I lived as a Pharisee. (Acts 26:4–5)

> If anyone else thinks he has reasons to put confidence in the flesh, I have more: circumcised on the eighth day, of the people of Israel, of the tribe of Benjamin, a Hebrew of the Hebrews; in regard to the law, a Pharisee; as for zeal, persecuting the church; as for legalistic righteousness, faultless. (Phil. 3:4–6)

It is evident from these autobiographical descriptions that Paul was not proclaiming as the Christian apostle what he had learned from his life in Judaism. On the contrary, as the Christian apostle he directed men's trust away from the personal law–keeping in which his own trust had resided as a Pharisee, and toward Jesus Christ.

APOSTOLIC TRAINING AND AUTHORIZATION

Did Paul then obtain the gospel he was preaching after his conversion, if not at the feet of Gamaliel, at the feet of the apostles? He writes:

when God ... was pleased to reveal his Son to me ..., I did not consult any man nor did I go up to Jerusalem to see those who were apostles before I was, but I went immediately into Arabia and later returned to Damascus. (Gal. 1:15–17)

In this connection, there is separate evidence, if Paul intended by this reference to Arabia to refer to the Nabataean kingdom, that Paul did not simply devote himself to a life of quiet contemplation in Arabia after his conversion but in fact immediately began to missionarize the populace there. He informs us in 2 Corinthians 11:32–33 that "the governor under King Aretas guarded the city of Damascus in order to seize me." But one does not stir up the kind of trouble he alludes to in this passage merely by meditation. This would suggest that long before he made any contact with the Jerusalem apostles Paul had already been engaging himself in Gentile evangelism.

Then Paul informs us under a self-imposed oath (see Gal. 1:20: "I assure you before God that what I am writing to you is no lie.") that three years passed after his conversion before he finally met any of the apostles, and then it was only Peter and James he met, and even then it was for only the space of fifteen days (Gal. 1:18–19). This was doubtless the visit Luke records in Acts 9:26–28, and while it is likely that it was at this time that he "received" the precise details about Jesus' postresurrection appearances, particularly those to Peter and James, that he later "delivered" to the Corinthians in 1 Corinthians 15:5–7, it is evident that, since they had no opportunity, the apostles conferred no authority on him at that time. Furthermore, Paul assures his reader, "I was personally unknown to the churches of Judea" (Gal. 1:22). Then Paul declares that another eleven years passed (I am assuming the correctness of the South Galatia theory with respect to Paul's first missionary trip) before he saw the apostles again, this time on the occasion of his famine-relief visit to Jerusalem recorded in Acts 11:27–30. On this second visit to Jerusalem, Paul informs us, "I set before [the apostles] the gospel that I preach among the Gentiles" (Gal. 2:2). The outcome of this presentation, which surely would have included his view of Christ himself, was that the apostles "added nothing to my message" (2:6), but to the contrary, saw "that I had been entrusted with the gospel" (2:7), that "God who was at work in Peter as an apostle to the circumcision was also at work in me [as an apostle] to the Gentiles" (2:8), and "gave me the right hand of fellowship" (2:10). In other words, they again conferred no authority on him but rather only acknowledged or "confirmed" (Heb. 2:3) the authority which was already his and by virtue of which he had been engaged in his apostolic ministry among the Gentiles for many years. We conclude, then, that throughout this entire fourteen-year period (Gal. 2:1)—during the three-year period preceding his first visit to Jerusalem and during the eleven-year period preceding his second visit to Jerusalem—and beginning immediately after his conversion (Acts 9:20) Paul was "proclaiming Jesus, that this One is the Son of God" (Acts 9:20), "proving that this

One is the Messiah" (9:22), and "preaching the faith that he once tried to destroy" (Gal. 1:23)—a ministry that was only much later to be personally and directly acknowledged or confirmed as authentic by the other apostles.

Divine Authorization

Now if Paul was not preaching what he had learned during his life in Judaism, and if he was not preaching what he had learned from the original apostles either, the only remaining alternative is that he was proclaiming a gospel which he received, as he says, in and from his conversion experience itself—"by revelation from Jesus Christ" (Gal. 1:12)!

This does not mean, of course, that Saul had known nothing before his conversion about Jesus Christ or about the church's doctrinal teaching concerning him. He knew some things well enough, and he had violently opposed them often enough. What it does mean is that Jesus' postascension appearance to Saul on the Damascus road forced upon him an entirely new "hermeneutical paradigm" into which he had to place not only his understanding of Jesus' person and work but also his previous Judaistic instruction concerning law and grace.[5]

Nor does it mean that Paul did not grow in his understanding of Christ during those fourteen years, for indeed, he continued to grow in his knowledge of Christ to the very end of his life (Phil. 3:10–14). What it does mean is that in all his "growing up" he never "grew away" from that first clear "vision from heaven," as James Stalker so poignantly suggests when he writes: "His whole theology is nothing but the explication of his own conversion."[6]

---

5. See Machen, *Origin of Paul's Religion*, 144ff.
6. Stalker, *Life of St. Paul*, 40. See also Margaret E. Thrall, "The Origin of Pauline Christology," in *Apostolic History and the Gospel*, ed. W. Ward Gasque and Ralph Martin (Exeter, U.K.: Paternoster, 1970), 304–16.

APPENDIX D

Anselm's Satisfaction View of the Atonement

IN A.D. 1098 ANSELM (1033–1109), Archbishop of Canterbury, completed the greatest of his works, *Cur Deus Homo—Why [did] God [become] man?*—not a volume *per se* on the two natures of Christ in which one would expect to find the evidence being set forth for the full unabridged deity and the full unabridged humanity of Christ. Rather, it is a treatise on the Atonement in which he rejected the ancient (and also medieval) theory that the death of Christ was a ransom paid to the devil, and interpreted Christ's death rather, in light of the justice and mercy of God, as a vicarious *satisfaction* (*satis*, "enough"; *facio*, "to do") offered to God the Father as the legal representative of the Trinity for the sins of the world. In a word, Anselm argued that God owed the devil and his minions nothing. It was God's offended honor which required redress. He clearly saw that it was the exigencies arising from man's sin, namely, his natural depravity, his real guilt before God, and his inability to render satisfaction for himself that made the Incarnation and Christ's cross work necessary.

Anselm argued that man's sin, as failure to render to God that conformity to his will which the rational creature owes him, insults the honor of God and makes the offender liable to satisfaction. Since dishonoring the infinite God is worse than destroying countless worlds, even the smallest sin has infinite disvalue for which no created good can compensate by way of satisfaction. Though God's nature forbade that his purposes should be or would be thwarted by created resistance, his justice required that he not overlook such a great offence against him. So, Anselm reasoned, (1) because only God can do that which is immeasurably deserving, (2) because humans (unlike the fallen angels) come in biological families, and (3) because justice permits an offense by one family member to be compensated by another standing in his stead—if, given these circumstances, God then became a human family member, he could discharge man's debt for him. Hence, for Anselm the necessity of the Incarnation.

To elaborate, the terrible sin of man has offended the honor of the infinitely holy God, and the righteous requirements of his offended justice demand satisfaction. But this satisfaction cannot be made for human beings by an angel but must be achieved by a human being inasmuch as it is the sins of human beings which must be removed from the sight of God. The author of Hebrews, under inspiration, states this fact this way:

> Since the children have flesh and blood, he too shared in their humanity.... For surely it is not angels he helps, but Abraham's descendants. For this reason he had [ὤφειλεν, *opheilen*] to be made like his brothers in every way, in order that he might become a merciful and faithful high priest in service to God, and that he might make atonement for the sins of the people. (Heb. 2:14–17)

But since every sin, as we have said, carries within its bosom *infinite disvalue* since it is an assault against the *infinitely* holy God and deserves God's *infinite* wrath and curse,[1] full satisfaction requires recompense which may be met only by a payment of *infinite worth*. Such a payment, however, cannot be made for any single human being by either another sinful human being or even by the entire human race but only by a Being accredited with infinite worth before God, namely, by God himself! The One who makes such satisfaction must, therefore, be not only human but also God. Hence the necessity of the Godman, even Christ Jesus, our Lord. And because his divine nature, in accordance with the eternal decree,[2] communes with, and therefore concurs with, the suffering of his human nature in the one person of

---

1. Thomas Aquinas, *Summa theologica*, 1a2ac. 87, 4, rightly states: "... the magnitude of the punishment matches the magnitude of the sin.... Now a sin that is against God is infinite, the higher the person against whom it is committed, the graver the sin—it is more criminal to strike a head of state than a private citizen—and God is of infinite greatness. Therefore an infinite punishment is deserved for a sin committed against him."
2. John Calvin, *Institutes of the Christian Religion*, II.xvii.1, writes: "In discussing Christ's merit, we do not consider the beginning of merit to be in him, but we go back to God's ordinance, the first cause. For God solely of his own good pleasure appointed him Mediator to obtain salvation for us. Hence it is absurd to set Christ's merit against God's mercy. For it is a common rule that a thing subordinate to another is not in conflict with it. For this reason nothing hinders us from asserting that Christ's merit, subordinate to God's mercy, also intervenes on our behalf. Both God's free favor and Christ's obedience, each in its degree, are fitly opposed to our works. Apart from God's good pleasure Christ could not merit anything; but did so because he had been appointed to appease God's wrath with his sacrifice, and to blot out our transgressions with his obedience."

Christ in his work of redemption, the merit of his cross work is of infinite and eternal worth.[3] The author of Hebrews declares:

> Now there have been many [high] priests, since death prevented them from continuing in office; but because Jesus lives forever, he has a permanent priesthood. Therefore *he is able to save completely those who come to God through him, because he always lives to intercede for them. Such a high priest meets* [ἔπρεπεν, *eprepen*] *our needs—one who is holy, blameless, pure, set apart from sinners, exalted above the heavens.* (Heb. 7:23–26)

> How much more, then, will the blood of Christ, who *through the eternal Spirit offered himself unblemished to God,* cleanse our consciences from acts that lead to death, so that we may serve the living God. . . . In fact, the law requires that nearly everything be cleansed with blood, and without the shedding of blood there is no forgiveness. *It was necessary* ['Ανάγκη, *Anankē*], then, for the copies of the heavenly things to be purified with these sacrifices, but [*it was necessary for*] *the heavenly things themselves* [*to be purified*] *with better sacrifices than these.* For Christ did not enter a man-made sanctuary that was only a copy of the true one, he entered heaven itself, now to appear for us *in the presence of God.* (Heb. 9:14, 22–24)

It is *this* state of affairs—man originally created good but now fallen, totally corrupt through willful disobedience and unable to render satisfaction for himself—which Anselm contended lies behind and makes necessary the Incarnation and the cross work of Jesus Christ.

---

3. It should be noted here that Christ's cross work, while of infinite worth and thus *sufficient* to save countless worlds such as our own, was particularistic in its design and thus is salvifically *efficient* only for the elect.

APPENDIX E

The Five Points of Calvinism

THE ACRONYM TULIP represents the so-called five points of Calvinism, which are, in brief, as follows:

1. Total depravity. Both because of original sin and their own acts of sin, all mankind, excepting Christ, in their natural state are thoroughly corrupt and completely evil, though they are restrained from living out their corruptness in its fullness by the instrumentalities of God's common grace. Accordingly they are completely incapable of saving themselves.

2. Unconditional election. Before the creation of the world, out of his mere free grace and love, God elected many undeserving sinners to complete and final salvation without any foresight of faith or good works or any other thing in them as conditions or causes which moved him to choose them. That is to say, the ground of their election is not in them but in him.

3. Limited atonement. Christ died efficaciously, that is, truly savingly, only for the elect, although the infinite sufficiency of his atonement and the divine summons to all to repent and trust in Christ provide the warrant for the universal proclamation of the gospel to all men. I personally prefer the terms "definite atonement," "particular atonement," or "efficacious atonement" over "limited atonement," both because of possible misunderstanding of the word "limited" and because every evangelical "limits" the atonement either in its design (the Calvinist) or in its power to accomplish its purpose (the Arminian).

4. Irresistible grace. This doctrine does not mean that the nonelect will find God's grace irresistible; indeed, God's saving grace is not even extended to them. Nor does it mean that the elect will find God's saving grace irresistible the very first time it is extended to them, for even the elect may resist his overtures toward them for a time. What it does mean is that the elect are incapable of resisting forever

God's gracious overtures toward them. At his appointed time, God draws the elect, one by one, to himself by removing their hostility and opposition to him and his Christ, making them willing to embrace his Son.

5. *Perseverance of the saints.* The elect are eternally secure in Christ, who preserves his own and enables them to persevere in him unto the end. Those professing Christians who have apostasized from the faith (1 Tim. 4:1), as John states, "went out from us, but they did not really belong to us. For if they had belonged to us, they would have remained with us; but their going showed that none of them belonged to us" (1 John 2:19).

APPENDIX F

Whom Does the Man in Romans 7:14–25 Represent?

MANY OF THE ablest expositors, standing in the tradition of Augustine and the Western church at large, believe that Paul intended Romans 7:14–25 as a description of the Christian in his struggle against the power of indwelling sin (e.g., John Calvin, J. Fraser, F. A. Philippi, C. Hodge, J. Murray, C. E. B. Cranfield, John MacArthur). In my opinion (shared by J. A Bengel, H. A. W. Meyer, F. Godet, M. Stuart, W. Sanday and A. C. Headlam, J. Denney, J. Oliver Buswell Jr., A. Hoekema, M. Lloyd-Jones), however, the Romans passage is *not* a description of the regenerate person's struggle against indwelling sin. Rather, drawing upon his own experience as Saul, the most zealous law-keeping Pharisee of his day (Acts 22:3; 26:5; Gal. 1:14; Phil. 3:4–6) who had become aware through the law, as applied by the Spirit, of his own innate sinfulness, in this passage Paul, with words provided him from the enlightened vantage point which was now his as a Christian, sets forth both the impotence of the *unregenerate* ego to do good against the power of indwelling sin and the "inability" (ἀδύνατον, *adynaton* 8:3) and "weakness" (ἠσθένει, *esthenei* 8:3) of the law due to human depravity to deliver the unregenerate ego from sin's slavery.

Herman Ridderbos in his *Paul: An Outline of His Theology*,[1] concurs that this passage does not refer to the Christian struggle against sin. However, he rejects the view that "this ego of 7:7–25 . . . is to be taken in a biographical sense as a description of Paul's personal experience before or at his conversion" (129), preferring rather to interpret the passage by "redemptive-historical contrasts and categories"

---
1. Herman Ridderbos, *Paul: An Outline of His Theology*, trans. John R. DeWitt (Grand Rapids, Mich.: Eerdmans, 1975), 126–30.

(129), that is to say, the "I" in the passage represents Old Testament Israel and its experience with the law. I contend, however, that this is precisely what Paul intended—to employ his experience as the *unconverted* Saul of Tarsus, aroused from his spiritual torpor, convicted by the reality of his sinfulness, and struggling even more than before to please God through his efforts at law-keeping, as an illustration of the impotence of the law to sanctify the unregenerate heart and the frustration unto death that any and every unregenerate person will experience who would sincerely seek to achieve a righteousness before God on the basis of his own law-keeping. I say this for the following reasons:

1. Romans 7:7–13 is clearly autobiographical,[2] highlighting the facts that sin dwelling within Saul of Tarsus had always been his problem and that the law, while not the source of sin, for it is "holy, just, good, and spiritual" (7:12, 14), is impotent relative to the production of good in the sinful heart. The shift of verb tense from the past to the present at 7:14 in no way affects the autobiographical character of 7:14–25. Nor must the present tenses in 7:14–25 necessarily indicate Paul's experience at the time he is writing Romans as the mature Christian apostle and missionary. The "historical [or "dramatic"] present" is a well-known use of the present tense in Greek when the writer wished to make a past event or experience more vivid to his reader.[3]

2. The man describes himself as "carnal" (σάρκινός, *sarkinos*; 7:14), which according to 8:6 is descriptive of the state of spiritual death.

3. The man says of himself that he has been "*sold as a slave* [πεπραμένος, *pepramenos*] to sin" (7:14), that is, he is a slave of sin, which is descriptive only of the unregenerate man. Regenerate persons "*used to be* [ἦτε, *ēte*] slaves of sin" (6:17, 20) but now "have been set free from sin" and have now become "slaves to righteousness" (6:18, 22). They, "*were* controlled by the sinful nature" (7:5), but now (νυνί, *nyni*; 6:22) "are controlled not by the sinful nature but by the Spirit" (8:9), "having died to what once bound them" (7:6). They *did* "live according to the sinful nature" (8:4), but now *they are living* (περιπατοῦσιν, *peripatousin*) "according to the Spirit" (8:4b). and the law's requirements are being "fully met" in them (8:4a).

4. The man says of himself that his members are being mastered by "indwelling sin" (ἡ οἰκοῦσα ἐν ἐμοὶ ἁμαρτία, *he oikousa en emoi hamartia*; 7:17, 20). This is not true of the Christian for he is governed by the "indwelling Spirit"; if he is not so governed, he is not a Christian at all (8:9, 11)!

5. The man says of himself that "in me...dwells no good thing" (7:18), which is not true of the Christian for the Spirit of God dwells within him (8:9,11).

---

2. Murray, *The Epistle to the Romans* (Grand Rapids: Mich.: Eerdmans, 1959), 1: 248, 254.
3. E. Blass and A. Debrunner, *A Greek Grammar of the New Testament*, trans. Robert W. Funk (Chicago: Chicago University Press, 1961), 167, para. 321.

6. The man says of himself that a "law [of sin]" within him is "waging war against [ἀντιστρατευόμενον, *antistrateuomenon*] the law of his mind [that is, his desire to do good] and making him a prisoner [αἰχμαλωτίζοντά, *aichmalōtizonta*] of the law of sin at work within his members" (7:23). Here again he stresses his slavery to sin which is not true of the Christian (6:14), for the gospel has "liberated [him] from the law of sin and death" (8:2).

7. The man says of himself throughout the passage that he does not do the good that he wants to do; rather, he continually does, indeed, actually practices, what he does not want to do (Epictetus, *Enchiridion*, 1. ii. c. 26, says something almost identical with that of the apostle here). In sum, the man in this passage is enslaved by indwelling sin and sees his state as "wretched" and his body as the sphere in which sin is operative unto death (7:24). This is not true of the Christian nor can this be descriptive of the Christian.

8. The advocate of the Augustinian view contends that the unregenerate person could not and will not "delight in God's law after the inward man" as the man in the passage says he is doing (7:22); only Christians, they urge, can do that. But I beg to differ. Saul of Tarsus, as a Pharisee, did just that. It may legitimately be said that throughout his life as a self-righteous Pharisee he "delighted in the law of God with his mind"— observance of the law was his very reason for being. He was a "son of the law," was committed to it, and wanted to obey it. But when the tenth commandment truly "came home" to him at some point with condemning power (had he coveted Stephen's knowledge of Scripture and his exegetical power?) and made him aware of his indwelling sinfulness, the sin which had always dwelt within him "came to life" and he "died" (7:9). Paul also declared that the Jewish nation was "pursuing" a righteousness of its own through law-keeping (Rom. 9:31–32). Apparently, then, unregenerate people can sincerely desire to be obedient to the law. Their problem, as the passage teaches, is their impotence to do what they want to do or know to be right.

9. Some advocates of the Augustinian view contend that Romans 7:25b, as the conclusion of the argument, describes a condition only true of the Christian: he "is a slave to God's law with his mind but a slave to the law of sin with his members." But this radical dichotomy between what he wants to do (the good, obedience to God's law) and what he in fact *continually practices* (see πράσσω, *prassō*, 7:19) (evil, transgression of the law) is not true of the Christian. Romans 7:25b is either

> a. a conclusion descriptive of the unconverted but deeply convicted Pharisee, Saul of Tarsus, struggling to obey the law in his own power, with the preceding "Thanks be to God" phrase (7:25a) being the regenerate Paul simply interjecting into the flow of his argument as he occasionally does an anacoluthonic praise statement from his vantage point as a Christian (e.g., Eph 2:5), highlighting where he found the solution to his struggle,

or it is

b. following Theodor Zahn,[4] a rhetorical question (taking the ἄρα οὖν, *ara oun*, "Now therefore," of 7:25 as ἄρα οὖν, *ara oun*, "Shall I then?" which expects the negative response "Of course not!"), with the preceding "Thanks be to God" phrase then to be construed as an essential part of Paul's statement marking the point in the flow of his argument when he was converted and thus the point at which his *nonvictorious* struggle with sin's power ceased.

10. The man in Romans 7:14–25 is struggling against sin's power and he desires to obey God's law. But he is utterly defeated by the power of indwelling sin. This is not true of the Christian who, while he too experiences a struggle against sin (Gal. 5:16–18), is described as victorious in his struggle against sin's power because of his new master, the indwelling Spirit of Christ. Ridderbos writes:

> Undoubtedly it is said of the new man . . . that he continues to be engaged in conflict with the flesh. Thus, for example, in Galatians 5:17 where it is said: "the flesh lusts against [NIV— "desires what is contrary to"] the Spirit [to prevent you from doing the good that the Spirit wants you to do], and the Spirit against ["desires what is contrary to"] the flesh . . . to prevent you from doing [the evil that the flesh wants you to do]." And similarly it is said to believers in Romans 6:12 that sin may not (continue to) reign in their mortal bodies, etc. All this points to enduring battle, struggle, resistance of the flesh against the Spirit. But the absolute distinction between these and similar pronouncements and the portrayal of Romans 7 is that the former are spoken within the possibility and certainty of victory (see Rom. 6:14: "for sin shall not have dominion over you; for you are not under law, but under grace"; Gal. 5:24: "but they that are of Christ have crucified the flesh with its passions and lusts"), while in Romans 7 everything is directed toward throwing light on man's situation of death, his having been sold under sin, his having been taken captive by the superior power of sin. . . . The elements placed over against each other in Romans 7 are . . . not (as in Gal. 5) the Spirit and the flesh, or (as in Rom. 6) grace and the law, but the human ego, the "I-myself" (v. 25 !) and the flesh, the law of God and the law of sin. In the struggle between those parties the victory is to the flesh and sin, and the ego finds itself, despite all that it would will and desire, in absolute bondage and the situation of death. Other powers must enter the field, another than the "I-myself" must join the battle, if deliverance is to come. So far is it from any suggestion that since there is mention here of a *dis*-cord, this were able to furnish the proof that the struggle between the old and the new man is described [in Romans 7] in the manner of Galatians 5:17.[5]

---

4. Theodor Zahn, *Der Briefe des Paulus an die Romer* (Leipzig: A. Deichert, 1910), 370ff.
5. Ridderbos, *Paul: An Outline of His Theology,* 127.

WHOM DOES THE MAN IN ROMANS 7:14–25 REPRESENT?

Some Christians have employed the Augustinian view of the passage to undergird the antinomian's "carnal Christian" theology. I remember reading an antinomian tract once that actually argued, because Paul says of his evil practice here, "it is no more I that do it, but sin that dwells in me" (which means something on the order of, "my evil deeds show that I am impotent against sin in my own strength, that is, I am not my own master [the "it is not I that do it" phrase], but am rather a slave to indwelling sin which governs and controls me") (7: 17, 20), that the Christian need not worry about his carnal practice since, after all, it is not he who is sinning but simply his sin nature within him that is doing so! The antinomian has also used the Augustinian interpretation of the passage as his excuse for the sin in his life when confronted by his pastor: "Well, I've been taught that the man in Romans 7 is the apostle Paul, the most mature Christian of his day, who could never do what he wanted to do but rather continually sinned against his will. While I wish I didn't sin, and I hate it when I do, I guess, like Paul, I'm just the carnal man in Romans 7!" To use this passage in these ways is a travesty! Nothing Paul ever wrote did he intend the Christian to use as an excuse for the toleration of sin in his life, and no biblical passage should ever be used to justify a "carnal" Christian existence. The Bible denounces carnality *wherever* it is found. And it expects the Christian to denounce his carnality (which he will have) as a legitimate experience of Christian existence, and to repudiate and overcome the carnal thoughts and activities in his life (which, not without struggle, he will do).

It is better, I would urge, to hold that Paul is describing his state prior to his conversion on the Damascus Road but, due to his conscience having been awakened to his sinfulness but still "kicking against the goads" of Christ's gracious overtures (Acts 26:14), a state in which he is hopelessly struggling in his own power to be obedient to the law and thus to please God.

Why does Paul take his Christian reader back to his struggle against sin as a convicted Pharisee? How, in short, does this autobiographical piece fit into the context and the argument of the epistle? Paul, in his argument for justification by faith alone, knows he has said some things about the law which, if left unexplained, might lead his reader to the conclusion that the law of God is a bad and sinful thing. For example, he had said: "through the law we become conscious of sin" (3:20); "The law was added so that the trespass might increase" (5:20); and "the sinful passions aroused by the law were at work in our bodies" (7:5). Therefore, he pauses in the development of his argument at 7:7 to ask the question: "Is the law sin [that is, a sinful thing]?" Using his own experience as a Pharisee as his prime example, he answers this question with a resounding "Certainly not!," developing then the fact that it was not the law that made him covet; rather, it was his sinful human nature, seizing upon the opportunity provided it by the "holy, just, good, and spiritual" commandment, "Do not covet," that produced in him all manner of evil coveting. Not only this, says Paul, but his sinful human nature, seizing the opportunity provided by the commandment's unrelenting demand of obedience, also "killed" him (7:11). He asks then the question: "Did that which is good [the law], then, become death to me?" (7:13) In other words, was the law the "killing thing"? He answers, "By no means!" and declares again that it was his sinful human nature, through the "good" commandment that forbade coveting, that both produced death in him and showed, in its willingness to use the holy law for such a purpose, its "utter sinfulness" (7:13). It is both this last point—the "utter sinfulness" of his sinful nature—and the impotency of the law in the struggle against sin—that Paul develops in 7:14–25, arguing that even when as the convicted Pharisee he wanted to do the good and obey God, his sinful nature would not let him and the law did not help him; to the contrary, the sinful nature "waged war against the law of his mind [his desire to do good] and made him a prisoner of the law of sin at work within his members." His conclusion: his unregenerate state had been a "wretched" existence, so wretched, in fact, that he cried for deliverance from it! Not knowing where to turn (for he still did not believe that Jesus was the Messiah or that Jesus could help him), however, he continued in his impotency to struggle against sin's potency until his Damascus Road conversion finally brought him deliverance from his slavery to sin (8:1–4)!

Thus Paul restricts the source and locus of sin to man, the second cause, and while vindicating the "holy, just, good, and spiritual" law, showing that it is only the instrumental dynamic that the sinful nature, aroused by the law's prohibitions, uses in its hostility to God to lash out against God by enslaving his moral creature in sin and disobedience, highlights in doing so the law's "inability" and "weakness" to deliver from sin's enthrallment.

APPENDIX G

Selected General Theological Bibliography (Briefly Annotated)

Aquinas, Thomas. *Summa theologica.* 2 vols. *Great Books of the Western World,* vols. 19–20. Translated by Fathers of the English Dominican Province; revised by Daniel J. Sullivan. Chicago: Encyclopaedia Brittanica, 1952.
  Aquinas (1225–1274), the Schoolmen's purest and maturest representative of medieval Latin theology and of Rome's sacerdotal system, and the "Angelic Doctor" of Roman Catholicism, writes his theology from the "nature-grace" perspective.

Augustine. *The City of God Against the Pagans.* 7 vols. in the Loeb Classical Library. Cambridge: Harvard University Press, 1969–1988.
  ———. *Confessions.* Translated by E. B. Pusey. New York: John B. Alden, 1889.
  ———. *On the Trinity.* Translated by A. W. Haddan. Edinburgh: T. & T. Clark, 1873.
  Augustine (354–430), bishop of Hippo, the father of orthodox theology, wrote many books, chief among them being the above. Both Rome and Protestantism claim him as their own, but for different reasons: the former for his ecclesiology and sacerdotal tendencies, the latter for his doctrines of election, sin, and grace.

Bannerman, James. *Inspiration: the Infallible Truth and Divine Authority of the Holy Bible.* Edinburgh: T. & T. Clark, 1865.
  ———. *The Church of Christ: A Treatise on the Nature, Powers, Ordinances, Discipline, and Government of the Christian Church.* 1869. Reprint, London: Banner of Truth, 1960.
  Bannerman (1807–1868), professor of apologetics and pastoral theology at New College, Edinburgh (1849–1868), writes from a distinctly Reformed and Presbyterian perspective.

SYSTEMATIC THEOLOGY

Barth, Karl. *Church Dogmatics.* 12 vols. Translated by Geoffrey W. Bromiley. Edinburgh: T. & T. Clark. This work, in spite of its weak view of the inerrancy of Scripture and its misrepresentation of the Reformed faith, constitutes the weightiest contribution to Protestant theology since Schleiermacher.

Barth (1886–1968), the most significant theologian of the twentieth century and leader in the neo-orthodox movement, makes Christology the centerpiece of his entire theology.

Bavinck, Herman. *The Doctrine of God.* Translated by William Hendriksen. 1951. Reprint, Carlisle, Pa.: Banner of Truth, 1977. This is volume two of Bavinck's four-volume systematic theology, *Gereformeerde Dogmatiek*.

———. *Our Reasonable Faith.* Translated by Henry Zylstra. 1956. Reprint, Grand Rapids: Baker, 1977.

Bavinck (1854–1921), professor of systematic theology at Kampen (1882–1902) and the Free University of Amsterdam (1902–1920), writes from a Dutch Calvinist perspective.

Berkhof, Louis. *Introduction to Systematic Theology.* 1932. Reprint, Grand Rapids: Baker, 1979.

———. *Systematic Theology.* 4th ed. Grand Rapids: Eerdmans, 1939.

Berkhof (1873–1957), professor of systematic theology at Calvin Theological Seminary (1906–1944), writes from a Reformed perspective. His *Systematic Theology* has been the standard textbook in English-speaking Reformed seminaries for many years.

Berkouwer, Gerrit C. *Studies in Dogmatics.* 14 vols. English translations published in Grand Rapids: Eerdmans, 1952–1976. English titles are *The Church, Divine Election, Faith and Justification, Faith and Perseverance, Faith and Sanctification, General Revelation, Man: The Image of God, Holy Scripture, The Person of Christ, The Providence of God, The Return of Christ, The Sacraments, Sin,* and *The Work of Christ.*

Berkouwer (1952–1976), professor of systematic theology at the Free University of Amsterdam (1945–1976), writes from a somewhat critical Reformed perspective and is constantly interacting with other Dutch theologians, with Roman Catholic theology, and with Arminianism. His volumes on general revelation, the work of Christ, justification and sanctification are very good; his volumes on Scripture and election, in my opinion, do not espouse the classic Reformed position on these matters.

Boettner, Lorraine. *Immortality.* Philadelphia: Presbyterian and Reformed, 1962.

———. *The Millennium.* Philadelphia: Presbyterian and Reformed, 1958.

———. *The Reformed Doctrine of Predestination.* 1932. Grand Rapids: Eerdmans, 1951.

———. *Roman Catholicism.* Philadelphia: Presbyterian and Reformed, 1962.

———. *Studies in Theology.* Grand Rapids: Eerdmans, 1951.

Boettner (1901–1990) writes from a distinctly Reformed and postmillennial perspective. The seminarian, pastor, and intelligent layman will find all of Boettner's works very readable and trustworthy.

Boice, James Montgomery. *Foundations of the Christian Faith.* Revised one-volume edition. Downers Grove, Ill.: InterVarsity Press, 1986. Previously published in 4 volumes: *The Sovereign God* (1978), *God the Redeemer* (1978), *Awakening to God* (1979), and *God and History* (1981).

Boice, pastor of Tenth Presbyterian Church, Philadelphia, writes popularly from a Reformed and Presbyterian perspective. The laity will find Boice's volumes very helpful.

Boyce, James Pettigru. *Abstract of Systematic Theology.* 1887. Reprint, Christian Gospel Foundation, n.d.

Boyce (1827–1888), professor of systematic and polemic theology at the Southern Baptist Seminary in Louisville, Kentucky (1859–1888), writes from a Reformed and Baptist perspective.

Brunner, Emil. *Dogmatics.* 3 vols. Translated by Olive Wyon, David Cairns, and T. H. L. Parker. London: Lutterworth, 1949, 1954, 1962.

Brunner (1889–1966), professor of systematic and practical theology at the University of Zurich (1924–55), along with Karl Barth, was a leader of the neoorthodox movement, whose dialectical theology was influenced by Kierkegaard.

Buchanan, James. *The Doctrine of Justification.* 1867. Reprint, Grand Rapids: Baker, 1977.

Buchanan (1804–1870), writing from a distinctly Protestant perspective, provides us with the best classical treatment on the biblical doctrine of justification.

Buswell, James Oliver, Jr. *A Systematic Theology of the Christian Religion.* 2 vols. Grand Rapids: Zondervan, 1962–1963.

Buswell (1895–1977), professor of systematic theology at Covenant Theological Seminary (1956–1970), writes from a Reformed and Presbyterian perspective and provides interesting and original interpretations of many biblical texts. His *Systematics* is very readable.

Calvin, John. *Institutes of the Christian Religion.* 2 vols. Edited by John T. McNeill. Translated and indexed by Ford Lewis Battles. *The Library of Christian Classics,* vols. 20–21. Philadelphia: Westminster, 1960.

Calvin (1509–1564), Genevan Reformer and the greatest systematic theologian of the Reformation, writes from a Reformed perspective. His *Institutes* are the most influential Protestant systematic theology ever written.

Chafer, Lewis Sperry. *Systematic Theology.* 7 vols. plus an index volume. Dallas: Dallas Seminary Press, 1947–48.

Chafer (1871–1952), first president and professor of systematic theology at Dallas Theological Seminary (1924–1952), writes from a qualified Calvinistic and dispensational perspective.

Charnock, Stephen. *The Complete Works of Stephen Charnock.* 5 vols. Edinburgh: James Nichol, 1864–1866.

———. *The Existence and Attributes of God.* 1797. Reprint, Grand Rapids: Sovereign Grace, 1971.

Charnock (1628–1680) writes from a Calvinistic Puritan and Nonconformist perspective. These works are primarily his sermons, providing an excellent representation of Puritan preaching.

Chemnitz, Martin. *Examination of the Council of Trent.* Translated by Fred Kramer. St. Louis, Missouri: Concordia, 1971.

———. *Justification: The Chief Article of Christian Doctrine.* Translated by J. A. O. Preus. St. Louis, Missouri: Concordia, 1986.

———. *The Two Natures of Christ.* Translated by J. A. O. Preus. St. Louis, Missouri: Concordia, 1971.

Chemnitz (1522–1586), known also as Lutheranism's "second Martin," defined by his writings and labors for second-generation Lutherans the heart and substance of Lutheran theology.

Clowney, Edmund P. *The Church.* Downers Grove, Ill.: InterVarsity Press, 1995.

Clowney (1917–), professor of practical theology at Westminster Theological Seminary (1952–1984), writes from a Reformed and Presbyterian perspective.

Cunningham, William. *Historical Theology: A Review of the Principal Doctrinal Discussions in the Christian Church Since the Apostolic Age.* 2 vols. 1870. Reprint, London: Banner of Truth, 1960.

Cunningham (1805–1861), professor of theology (1844) and church history (1845) at the Free Church College, Edinburgh, writes from a Reformed perspective. This learned work, his *magnum opus*, is virtually a systematic theology.

Dabney, Robert Lewis. *Lectures in Systematic Theology.* 1878. Reprint, Grand Rapids: Zondervan, 1972.

Dabney (1820–1898), professor of systematic theology at Union Theological Seminary, Richmond (1853–1883), writes from a distinctly Reformed and Presbyterian perspective.

Denney, James. *Studies in Theology.* 1895. Reprint, Grand Rapids: Baker, 1976.

Denney (1856–1917), professor of systematic and pastoral theology (1897–1900) and professor of New Testament language and literature (1900–1915) at Glasgow College, writes from an orthodox perspective against Protestant liberalism but is willing to concede that the Bible might contain minor errors.

Dick, John. *Lectures on Theology.* 4 vols. Edinburgh: Oliphant, 1834.

Dick (1764–1833), professor of theology in the United Secession Church, Scotland (1820–1833), writes from a distinctly Reformed and Presbyterian perspective.

Edwards, Jonathan. *The Works of Jonathan Edwards.* 2 vols. Revised and corrected by Edward Hickman. 1834. Reprint, Edinburgh: Banner of Truth, 1974.

Edwards (1703–1758), perhaps America's greatest philosophical theologian, writes from a distinctly Reformed and Puritan perspective. He was a Congregationalist.

Erickson, Millard. *Christian Theology.* Grand Rapids: Baker, 1985.

Erickson, professor of systematic theology at Bethel Theological Seminary, St. Paul, Minnesota (1969–1991), writes from a moderate Reformed and Baptist perspective. His Christology is kenotic in some regards.

Finney, Charles G. *Finney's Lectures on Systematic Theology.* Edited by J. H. Fairchild. 1878. Reprint, Grand Rapids: Eerdmans, 1953.

Finney (1792–1875), professor of theology at Oberlin College (1836–1866), writes from a strong Arminian and perfectionist perspective.

Frame, John M. *Apologetics to the Glory of God: An Introduction.* Phillipsburg, N.J.: Presbyterian and Reformed, 1994.

———. *The Doctrine of the Knowledge of God.* Phillipsburg, N.J.: Presbyterian and Reformed, 1987.

———. *Cornelius Van Til: An Analysis of His Thought.* Phillipsburg, N.J.: Presbyterian and Reformed, 1995.

Frame, professor of apologetics and systematic theology at Westminster Theological Seminary, Escondido, California, writes from a Reformed perspective. Frame advocates a multiperspectival approach in interpreting the Holy Scripture.

Garrett, James Leo. *Systematic Theology: Biblical, Historical and Evangelical.* 2 vols. Grand Rapids: Eerdmans, 1990, 1995.

Garrett, professor of theology at Southwestern Baptist Theological Seminary, Fort Worth, writes from an evangelical Baptist perspective.

Geisler, Norman L., ed. *Inerrancy.* ("The Chicago Statement on Biblical Inerrancy" [1978] appears on 493–502). Grand Rapids: Zondervan, 1980.

Gill, John. *The Cause of God and Truth.* 1735–1738. Reprint, Grand Rapids: Baker, 1981.

Gill (1697–1771), a Baptist puritan pastor, writes a thorough defense of Calvinistic theology.

Grenz, Stanley J. *Theology for the Community of God.* Nashville, Tenn.: Broadman & Holman, 1994.

Grenz, professor of Baptist heritage, theology and ethics at Carey Theological College and professor of theology and ethics at Regent College, Vancouver, writes from an evangelical Baptist perspective.

Grudem, Wayne. *Systematic Theology: An Introduction to Biblical Doctrine.* Grand Rapids: Zondervan, 1994.

Grudem, professor of biblical and systematic theology at Trinity Evangelical Divinity School, writes from a Reformed and Baptist perspective. His *Systematic Theology* is very readable and informative.

Henry, Carl F. H. *God, Revelation, and Authority.* 6 vols. Waco, Texas: Word, 1976–1983.

Henry (1913–), professor of theology at Fuller Theological Seminary (1947–1955) and editor of *Christianity Today* (1956–1968) writes from a Reformed perspective as he interacts with many leading scholarly deviations from the faith in our time.

Heppe, Heinrich. *Reformed Dogmatics: Set Out and Illustrated from the Sources.* Revised and edited by Ernst Bizer. Translated by G. T. Thompson. 1861. Reprint, Grand Rapids: Baker, 1978.

Heppe (1820–1879) provides an extensive collection of citations from earlier Reformed writers topically arranged according to the subjects of systematic theology.

Hodge, Archibald Alexander. *The Atonement.* 1907. Reprint, Grand Rapids: Baker, 1974.

———. *Outlines of Theology.* 1878. Reprint, Grand Rapids: Eerdmans, 1949.

Hodge (1823–1886), professor of systematic theology at Princeton Theological Seminary (1877–1886), writes classically from a Reformed and Presbyterian perspective.

Hodge, Charles. *Systematic Theology.* 3 vols. 1871–1873. Reprint, Grand Rapids: Eerdmans, 1970.

Hodge (1797–1878), professor of systematic theology at Princeton Theological Seminary (1822–1878), writes from a Reformed and Presbyterian perspective. His *Systematic Theology* has been used extensively by pastors and theologians from the time it was published to the present.

Hoeksema, Herman. *Reformed Dogmatics.* Grand Rapids: Reformed Free Publishing Association, 1966.

Hoeksema (d. 1965), professor of dogmatics at the Theological School of the Protestant Reformed Churches, writes from a supralapsarian Reformed perspective and denies there is such a thing as common grace to the nonelect.

Kuiper, R. B. *The Glorious Body of Christ: A Scriptural Appreciation of the One Holy Church.* Grand Rapids: Eerdmans, 1958.

Kuiper (1886–1966), professor of practical theology at Westminster Theological Seminary, writes from a Reformed and Presbyterian perspective.

Kuyper, Abraham. *Principles of Sacred Theology.* Translated by J. Hendrik De Vries. 1894. Reprint, Grand Rapids: Eerdmans, 1954. This is volume 1, pp. 1–53, and volume 2 in its entirety of Kuyper's three-volume introduction to theology, *Encyclopaedie der Heilige Godgeleerdheid.*

Kuyper (1837–1920), founder (1880) and professor of systematic theology at the Free University of Amsterdam, writes from a distinctly Reformed (and presuppositional) perspective.

Ladd, George Eldon. *The Presence of the Future.* Grand Rapids: Eerdmans, 1974.

———. *Theology of the New Testament.* Grand Rapids: Eerdmans, 1974.

Ladd (1911–1982) writes from the historic or classical nondispensational premillennial perspective.

Lewis, Gordon R., and Bruce Demarest. *Integrative Theology.* 3 vols. Grand Rapids: Zondervan, 1987–94.

Lewis and Demarest, professors of systematic theology at Denver Seminary, write from a moderately Calvinistic and Baptist perspective.

Luther, Martin. *The Bondage of the Will.* Translated by Henry Cole. Grand Rapids, Baker, 1976.

Luther (1483–1546), the great German leader of the sixteenth-century Reformation, responds to the *Diatribe on Free Will* (1524) by Desidarius Erasmus, the leading humanist of the period, by urging the Augustinian theology of the "unfree will."

McGrath, Alister E. *Iustitia Dei: A History of the Christian Doctrine of Justification.* 2 vols. Cambridge: Cambridge University Press, 1986.

———. *Luther's Theology of the Cross.* Oxford: Blackwell, 1995.

McGrath, lecturer in Christian doctrine and ethics at Wycliffe Hall, Oxford, writes from a distinctly Protestant and Anglican perspective.

Melanchthon, Philip. *Loci Communes.* Translated by C. L. Hill. Boston: Meador, 1944.

Melanchthon (1497–1560), German reformer, Luther's coworker, and systematizer of Lutheran theology, writes from a first-generation Protestant perspective. In his own writings he departed from Luther's strong advocacy of the bondage of the will and (many interpreters think) from Luther's doctrine of consubstantiation.

Miley, John. *Systematic Theology.* 2 vols. Library of Biblical and Theological Literature, vols. 5–6. 1892, 1894. Reprint, Peabody, Mass.: Hendriksen, 1989.

Miley (1813–1895), professor of systematic theology at Drew Theological Seminary, authored the most scholarly Arminian systematic theology ever written.

Murray, John. *Christian Baptism.* Philadelphia: Presbyterian and Reformed, 1962.

———. *Collected Writings of John Murray.* 4 vols. Carlisle, Pa.: Banner of Truth, 1976–82.

———. *The Imputation of Adam's Sin.* 1957. Reprint, Nutley, N.J.: Presbyterian and Reformed, 1977.

———. *Redemption—Accomplished and Applied.* Grand Rapids: Eerdmans, 1955.

Murray (1898–1975), professor of systematic theology at Westminster Theological Seminary (1930–1966), writes from a distinctly biblical, Reformed and Presbyterian perspective. Students of theology will find all that Murray writes to be very informative and trustworthy.

Oden, Thomas C. *Systematic Theology* in three volumes: *The Living God; The Word of Life; Life in the Spirit.* San Francisco: HarperCollins, 1987–1992.

Oden, professor of theology at Drew University, once a "flaming liberal," writes now from what he himself describes as an Ancient Ecumenical-Vincentian-Anglican-Wesleyan perspective.

Ott, Ludwig. *Fundamentals of Catholic Dogma.* Edited by James Canon Bastible. Translated by Patrick Lynch. St. Louis: Herder, 1955. First published in German in 1952.

Ott writes from the traditional Roman Catholic perspective.

Owen, John. *The Death of Death in the Death of Christ.* 1858. Reprint, London: Banner of Truth, 1959. First published in 1647.

Owen (1616–1683), a Puritan congregationalist, writes here a defense of particular redemption from a distinctly Calvinistic perspective. No Arminian has ever answered his argument.

Packer, J. I. *Concise Theology: A Guide to Historic Christian Beliefs.* Wheaton, Ill.: Tyndale House, 1993.

———. *Evangelism and the Sovereignty of God.* Chicago: InterVarsity Press, 1976.

———. *"Fundamentalism" and the Word of God: Some Evangelical Principles.* Grand Rapids: Eerdmans, 1958.

———. *Knowing God.* Downers Grove, Ill.: InterVarsity Press, 1973.

Packer, professor of historical and systematic theology at Regent College, Vancouver (1979–), writes from a decidely evangelical and Reformed perspective. His writings are readable, enlightening, and informative.

Pannenberg, Wolfhart. *Systematic Theology.* 2 vols. Translated by Geoffrey W. Bromiley. Grand Rapids, Mich.: Eerdmans, 1991, 1994.

Pannenberg (1928–), professor of systematic theology, Protestant Theological Faculty, University of Munich, stressing the critical/historical approach to theology and particularly to Christology, presents a "Christology from below" which attempts to move from the historical man Jesus to the recognition of his deity.

Pieper, Francis. *Christian Dogmatics.* 4 vols. Translated by Theodore Engelder et al. St. Louis: Concordia, 1950–57. First published in German in 1917–1924.

Pieper (1852–1931), president and professor of theology at Concordia Seminary, St. Louis (1878–1831), writes from a distinctly Missouri Synod Lutheran perspective.

Radmacher, Earl D., and Robert D. Preus, eds. *Hermeneutics, Inerrancy, & the Bible.* ("The Chicago Statement on Biblical Hermeneutics" [1982] appears on pp. 881–904). Grand Rapids: Zondervan, 1984.

Reymond, Robert L. *Jesus, Divine Messiah: The Old Testament Witness.* Fearn, Ross–shire: Christian Focus, 1990.

———. *Jesus, Divine Messiah: The New Testament Witness.* Phillipsburg, N.J.: Presbyterian and Reformed, 1990.

SELECTED GENERAL THEOLOGICAL BIBLIOGRAPHY

———. *The Justification of Knowledge.* Phillipsburg, N.J.: Presbyterian and Reformed, 1976.

Ryrie, Charles C. *Basic Theology.* Wheaton, Ill.: Victor, 1986.

Ryrie, professor of systematic theology at Dallas Theological Seminary (1953–1958, 1962–1983), writes his introduction to systematic theology from a moderate Calvinistic and dispensational perspective.

Schaeffer, Francis A. *The Complete Works of Francis A. Schaeffer.* 5 vols. Westchester, Ill.: Crossway, 1982.

Schaeffer (1912–1984), founder of and primary teacher at L'Abri in Switzerland, is noted for his trilogy, *The God Who is There, Escape from Reason,* and *He Is There and He Is Not Silent.* He writes from a Reformed evangelical perspective. His analysis of twentieth-century culture is perceptive and informative.

Shedd, William G. T. *Dogmatic Theology.* 3 vols. in 4. 1889. Reprint, Minneapolis: Klock and Klock, 1979.

Shedd (1820–1894), professor of Bible and theology at Union Seminary, New York (1863–1893), writes from a Reformed and Presbyterian perspective.

Sproul, R. C. *Essential Truths of the Christian Faith.* Wheaton, Ill.: Tyndale House, 1992.

———. *Faith Alone: The Evangelical Doctrine of Justification by Faith.* Grand Rapids: Baker, 1995.

Sproul, founder and teacher of Ligonier Ministries, writes from a Reformed and Presbyterian perspective.

Strong, Augustus H. *Systematic Theology.* Valley Forge, Pa.: Judson Press, 1907.

Strong (1836–1921), professor of theology at Rochester Theological Seminary (1872–1912), writes from a moderate Calvinistic and Baptist perspective.

Thiessen, Henry Clarence. *Introductory Lectures in Systematic Theology.* 1949. Revised by Vernon D. Doerksen. Grand Rapids: Eerdmans, 1977.

Thiessen (1883–1947), professor and chairman of the faculty at the Wheaton College Graduate School, writes from a dispensational and Baptist perspective.

Thornwell, James Henley. *The Collected Writings of James Henley Thornwell.* 4 vols. Edited by John B. Adger. 1871–73. Reprint, Edinburgh and Carlisle, Pa.: Banner of Truth, 1974.

Thornwell (1812–1862), professor of didactic and polemic theology at the Presbyterian Theological Seminary, Columbia, South Carolina (1855–1862), writes from a Reformed and Presbyterian perspective.

Turretin, Francis. *Institutes of Elenctic Theology.* 3 vols. Translated by George Musgrave Giger. Edited by James T. Dennison Jr. Phillipsburg, N.J.: Presbyterian and Reformed, 1992–. Two volumes published to date.

Turretin (1623–1687), professor of theology at the Academy in Geneva (1653–1687), writing from a Calvinistic perspective, provided by his *Institutes* American Presbyterian ministers their textbook in systematic theology throughout the nineteenth century.

Vos, Geerhardus. *Biblical Theology: Old and New Testament.* Edited by Johannes G. Vos. Grand Rapids: Eerdmans, 1948.

———. *The Pauline Eschatology.* 1930. Reprint, Grand Rapids: Eerdmans, 1952.

———. *The Self-Disclosure of Jesus: The Modern Debate about the Messianic Consciousness.* 1926; corrected version republished in Grand Rapids: Eerdmans, 1954, and in Nutley, N. J.: Presbyterian and Reformed, 1976.

———. *The Teaching of Jesus Concerning the Kingdom of God and the Church.* 1903. Reprint, Grand Rapids: Eerdmans, 1951, 1958; Nutley, N.J.: Presbyterian and Reformed, 1972.

Vos (1862–1949), professor of biblical theology at Princeton Theological Seminary (1893–1932) and the "father" of evangelical biblical theology, writes from a Reformed biblical/theological perspective.

Warfield, Benjamin Breckenridge. *Biblical and Theological Studies.* Philadelphia: Presbyterian and Reformed, 1976.

———. *The Inspiration and Authority of the Bible.* Edited by Samuel G. Craig. Philadelphia: Presbyterian and Reformed, 1967.

———. *The Lord of Glory.* New York: American Tract Society, 1907.

———. *The Person and Work of Christ.* Philadelphia: Presbyterian and Reformed, 1950.

———. *The Plan of Salvation.* Revised edition. Grand Rapids: Eerdmans, 1942.

———. *Selected Shorter Writings of B. B. Warfield.* 2 vols. Edited by John E. Meeter; Nutley: Presbyterian and Reformed, 1970–1973.

Warfield (1851–1921), professor of didactic and polemic theology at Princeton Theological Seminary (1887–1921) and one of America's greatest theologians, writes from a Reformed and Presbyterian perspective.

Watson, Richard. *Theological Institutes.* 2 vols. New York: G. Lane and P. Sandford, 1843. First published in 1823.

Watson (1781–1833) writes from an Arminian and Methodist perspective.

Webb, Robert Alexander. *Christian Salvation: Its Doctrine and Experience.* 1921. Reprint, Harrisonburg, Va.: Sprinkle, 1985.

———. *The Reformed Doctrine of Adoption.* Grand Rapids: Eerdmans, 1947.

———. *The Theology of Infant Baptism.* 1907. Reprint, Harrisonburg, Va.: Sprinkle, 1981. Reprint of the 1907 edition.

Webb (1856–1919), professor of apologetics and systematic theology at the Presbyterian Theological Seminary of Kentucky at Louisville (1908–1919), writes from a Reformed and Presbyterian perspective.

Wiley, H. Orton. *Christian Theology.* 3 vols. Kansas City, Mo.: Nazarene Publishing House, 1940–43.

Wiley, a Church of the Nazarene theologian, writes from an Arminian perspective.

INDEX OF BIBLICAL REFERENCES

Old Testament

Genesis		1:26–27	257, 416 (2), 429, 770, 900 fn. 10	3:6	444, 445
1	117, 392, 393 (2), 393 fn. 11, 394, 417 (4), 1053			3:7	447, 534
		1:26–28	416	3:8	6, 448
		1:27	118, 414, 427, 428	3:10	447, 534
1–2	384 (2), 417	1:28	428, 507 fn. 9	3:12	355, 448 (2)
1–11	5, 117 (3), 118 (2), 383, 384 (2)	1:31	393	3:14	441
		2	117, 417 (2), 430, 432	3:15	406 (2), 449, 512, 534 (2), 535, 805, 806, 988
1–12	348	2–3	405 fn. 23		
1:1	299, 386, 387, 389 (5), 390 (2), 391 (4), 549 fn. 8	2:1	158		
		2:1–3	394 fn. 11	3:16	938 fn. 50
		2:2	398, 424, 487	3:17	445, 448
1:1–2	389	2:4	48, 117, 118, 388	3:17–18	448, 487
1:1–3	385, 387 (2), 388, 391, 414, 428	2:4a	388 (2)	3:19	448, 449 (2)
		2:4b	388, 389 (2)	3:21	407, 534, 536
1:2	76, 208, 313, 314, 386 (2), 387, 388, 389, 391, 392	2:4b–25	388 (3)	3:22	167, 207, 447
		2:5–25	416, 417	3:23	449
		2:7	36, 388, 417, 422 (2), 424	4:1	153, 466
1:3	208, 386 (2), 389 (3), 416			4:3–4	534
		2:15	449	4:4	512
1:5	393	2:16–17	5	4:4–5	872
1:6	416	2:19–20	416	4:6–12	6
1:8	393	2:21	424	4:7	447, 449
1:9	416	2:24	45, 398, 487	4:23–24	117
1:13	393	2:25	447	4:25	153
1:14	416	3	439, 440 (3), 441 (2), 445, 513, 1096	4:26	970
1:16–18	393			5	118, 394, 395 (3), 396
1:19	393	3:1	441, 442 (2)	5:1	117, 427
1:20	416	3:1–5	660	5:22–23	512
1:23	393	3:1–6	446	5:3	427
1:24	416	3:1–7	512	5:29	153
1:26	109, 167, 207, 257, 416, 425, 427 (3), 429	3:5	262 fn. 75	6–8	512
		3:5–6	1082	6:2	938 fn. 50

[1143]

6:5	356	14:19	155	20:6	6
6:5–6	450	14:22	155, 1090	21:4	938
6:5–7	180	15:1	6	21:9	366, 1025
6:8	358, 407	15:2	155, 156	21:12–13	358
6:8–9	512	15:6	xxx, 528, 729, 745 (2),	21:33	172, 970
6:9	117		746, 748, 749 (2)	22:1–2	208
6:13–21	6	15:8–18	177	22:9–10	749
6:18	406, 418, 512,	15:12	6 (2)	22:11–18	208
	618 fn. 17	15:16	999 fn. 32	22:12	351 fn. 5 (2), 749
6:21–22	400	15:18	406, 513 fn. 19	22:15–18	406
7:11	396	15:18–21	513	22:16–18	513
7:12–13	943 fn. 56	16:3	938 fn. 50	22:18	540, 988
7:21	417	16:7–13	6, 208	23:17–20	514 fn. 19
7:21–22	417	17:1–8	156	24:7	208
7:22	417	17:1–16	513, 937	24:12–17	358
8:21	450	17:5	153	24:40	208
9:1	6	17:7	513	25:8	395
9:6	427	17:7–8	517	25:12	117
9:8	6	17:7–9	881	25:19	117
9:8–17	406	17:7–14	406	25:22–23	368, 464
9:26	156	17:8	513, 536	25:23	358
9:26–27	512, 540	17:10	922	26:3–4	514, 939
10	512	17:12	927	26:4	540
10:1	117	17:14	939	26:6–7	938 fn. 50
10:25	153, 395	17:15	153	26:24	6
11	118, 394, 395 (5), 396	17:19	514	28:3	156
11:1–11	512	17:19–21	358	28:10–17	208
11:4	512	17:23–25	938	28:12	6
11:5	170	17:24	xxx	28:13	6
11:7	167, 207	18:14	191	28:13–14	939
11:10	117	18:16–18	949	28:13–15	514
11:27	117	18:19	466	28:14	540
12	349, 513 (2)	18:22–33	183	31:1	165
12–50	6, 117, 118	18:23–33	403	31:10	6
12:1	510 fn. 12 (2)	18:25	196, 1081	31:11	6
12:1–3	48, 358, 406, 513	19:16	1070	31:11–13	6, 208, 212
12:3	513, 517 (2),	19:24	1070	31:42	154
	540, 1031 (2)	19:26	1082	32:9–12	208
12:7	6	19:27	1070	32:20	637
12:8	970	19:28	1070	32:22–32	6
12:11–20	938 fn. 50	19:29	183	32:24–30	208
13:14–16	513	20:2–18	938 fn. 50	35:11	156
13:15	513 fn. 19, 536	20:3	6	35:12	514

[1144]

INDEX OF BIBLICAL REFERENCES

36:1	117	4:12	26	9:12	359, 359 fn. 19
36:9	117	4:13	8, 390	9:13	520
37:2	117	4:16	26	9:16	48, 360, 378
37:5	6	4:17	520	9:25–26	519
37:6	6	4:21	359, 359 fn. 19, 482 fn. 37	9:34	359 fn. 18
37:10	6			9:35	359, 359 fn. 18
38	401	4:22	759	10:1	359, 359 fn. 19
39:5	403	4:22–23	519	10:1–2	520
40:5–15	6	4:23	520	10:3	520
41:1	6	4:24–26	939	10:11	520
41:15	6	4:29	897	10:20	359 fn. 19
43:14	156	5:1	520	10:22–23	519
45:7	358	6:3	155, 156, 158	10:24	520
45:7–8	358	6:6	157 fn. 7, 518, 808 fn. 8	10:27	359 fn.19
45:13	165			11:7	519
46:2	5	6:7	157 fn. 7	11:9	359, 520
48:3	156	6:13	937 fn. 50	11:10	359 fn. 19
48:15–16	6, 208	6:20	394	12:5	634
49:1–27	58 fn. 7, 408	6:28	390	12:6	807
49:10	180, 987, 988	6:30	937 fn. 50	12:11–14	964
49:25	156	7:1	26	12:12	519
49:27	12, 358	7:3	359, 359 fn. 19, 482 fn. 37	12:12–13	520
				12:13	533
Exodus		7:1–4	25, 26	12:15	393
2:1	12, 180	7:3	520	12:21–23	520
2:1–10	358	7:4	26	12:24–27	520, 964
2:11–15	520	7:6–13	359	12:27	520
2:24	515	7:13	359, 359, fn. 18	12:37	520
2:25	466	7:14	359 fn. 18	12:46	964
3–14	359	7:16	520	13:8–10	964
3:2–6	208	7:22	359 fn. 18	13:20	520
3:4	58 fn. 7, 408	8:1	520	13:21	208
3:5	129	8:15	359, 359 fn. 18	13:21–22	520
3:11	8, 30	8:19	359, 359 fn. 18	14:4	359 fn. 19
3:14	157, 157 fn. 10, 167	8:20	520	14:8	359 fn. 19
3:14–15	157	8:22–23	519	14:13	518, 808 fn. 8
3:16	897	8:25	520	14:17	359 fn. 19
3:18	520, 897	8:28	520	14:19	208
3:19–20	519	8:32	359 fn. 18	14:21–23	520
4:5	515	9:1	520	14:30	808 fn. 8
4:10	8, 30	9:4	519	14:31	729
4:10–16	25, 26	9:7	359 fn. 18	15	520 (2)
4:11	21, 147, 358	9:8	933 fn. 41	15:2	157

[1145]

15:11	194	28:30	6	14:8–9	923
15:13	518, 808 fn. 8	29:20–21	933 fn. 41	14:46	390
15:18	986	31:3	386	15	923, 931
16:4	520	31:15–17	394	16:14	932 fn. 40
16:13–15	520	31:17	118	16:21–22	532, 634
17:1–6	520	32:9–10	180	16:33	807
17:5–6	897	32:10	637	18:5	439
17:8–16	520	32:12–14	515	19:2	195, 768, 770
17:14	6, 30	32:13	183	19:18	773, 776
18:8–12	1090	32:30	637	19:23	937 fn. 50
18:13	393	32:30–32	183	19:26	6
18:13–27	897	32:34	208, 212	20:27	6
19:5	406, 510 fn. 12 (2)	33:1	515	23	809
19:5–6	519, 806, 833	33:14	208	24:11	159, 226
19:6	767	33:19	158, 166, 199	24:16	228
19:7	897	34:24	360	25:8–54	1004 fn. 38
20:1–2	521	34:25	520	26:11–12	313
20:1–17	770	34:27	6 (2), 30	26:14–39	1083
20:3	142, 143	36:8	448	26:41	937 fn. 50
20:5	999 fn. 32	36:35	448	26:42	515
20:5–6	750	37:7–9	448		
20:6	881			**Numbers**	
20:7	159	**Leviticus**		1	832
20:11	118, 394 (2)	1:4	532, 634	3:17–19	395
21	774	1:5	933 fn. 41	3:27–28	395
23:7	196, 742 fn. 46, 744	1:11	933 fn. 41	4:35–36	395
23:14–17	809	3:2	532, 634, 933 fn. 41	6:1–21	924 fn. 26
23:20–23	208	3:8	532, 634, 933 fn. 41	6:24	208
23:23	212	3:13	532, 634, 933 fn. 41	6:24–27	925 fn. 28
24:1	897	4:4	532, 634	7:89	448
24:4	6, 30	4:6	932 fn. 40	8:12	532, 634
24:6	933 fn. 41	4:15	532, 634, 897	11:14–25	897
24:6–8	406	4:24	532, 634	12:1–11	411
24:7	6, 30	4:29	532, 634	12:6–8	6, 27 (2)
24:9–11	897	4:33	532, 634	14:5	807
24:16	393	6:27	932 fn. 40	15:32–36	1082
25:9	532	8:5–6	923	16–17	872
25:18–22	448	8:11	932 fn. 40	16:36–40	871
25:40	532	9:1–2	897	16:41–50	637
26:1	448	10:1–2	871, 872, 1082	17:1–8	411
26:30	532	11:44–45	195, 767, 770	19:18	932 fn. 40
26:31	448	12:3	393	20:6	806
27:21	393	14:7a	932 fn. 40	20:10	806

20:11	1082	9:4–6	361, 808 fn. 8	26:15		970
21:5–9	411	9:5	515	27:1		897
21:9	729	9:6–7	519	28:15–68		1083
22:20	6	9:10	806, 807 fn. 6,	28:58		226
22:28–30	441		808 fn. 9 (2)	29:1		406
23:19	177, 192, 201	9:26	518, 653, 808 fn. 8	29:9–13		939
23:21	986	9:27	515	29:12–13		515
24:17–19	987	10:4	806, 808 fn. 9 (2)	29:23		1071 fn. 10
25:11–13	637	10:15	361, 515	29:29		100, 101
27:21	6	10:16	937 fn. 50	30:6		937 fn. 51
33:2	6, 30	10:17	196, 310, 311	31:9		6, 30
34:6	241	12:29–32	871	31:9–13		6
		12:32–13:8	58 fn. 7	31:10–13		940
Deuteronomy		13:1ff.	43	31:24		6, 30
1:8	515	13:1–3	28, 60, 846	31:26		6
2:30	359 fn. 19, 360	13:3	351 fn. 5 (2)	31:30		806
2:34	1071	14:1	519	32:4		196
3:3	1071	15:11	892	32:5		700
3:6	1071	16:1–8	964	32:6		700
4:2	58	17:3	158	32:11		386
4:10	808	17:9–13	183	32:15		154
4:15	390	17:18	6	32:17		154
4:15–16	167	18:14	6, 28	32:31		1030
4:19	158	18:14–19	60	32:43		48
4:24	1040	18:14–21	27, 28	33:2		832
4:31	515	18:15	521, 564, 623, 988	33:4		832
4:32	118	18:16	806, 808 fn. 9 (2)	33:5		986
4:37	361, 515	18:18	6			
5:6–21	770	18:20–22	846	**Joshua**		
5:22	806	18:21–22	60	1:1		6
5:23	897	21:23	565	1:5		6
5:29	692 fn. 25	22:15–17	897	1:5–17		411
6:4–9	949	23	806	1:7–8		6
6:5	420, 776	23:1–3	807	2:10–11		412
6:6–7	881	24:1–4	938 fn. 50	3:16		430
6:13	45	24:2	386	4:23		412
6:16	45	24:14–15	892	5:2–9		939
7:6	519	25:1	743, 744	5:13–15		208
7:6–8	361, 519	25:4	35	7:6		897
7:8	515, 518, 652,	26:5–15	970	7:11		1082
	808 fn. 8	26:7	519	7:25		1082
8:3	45	26:10	970	8:30–35		6, 10, 808
9:3	1040	26:13–14	970	8:33		897

8:35	806, 940	2:25	361	8:27	169		
9:24	412	3	6	8:32	744		
11:19–20	361	4:4	159, 448	8:46	450		
11:20	359 fn. 19	5:9	390	8:55	807		
13:27	241	10:5–11	6	8:65	807		
15:12	241	10:10	386	9:2	7		
18:20	241	10:25	6	11:29–39	7		
21:44	516	12:7	198	12:15	362		
23:4	241	12:20–22	343	12:22–24	7		
24:3–4	516	14:41	6	13:2	7		
24:5	175	15:11	180	14:6–16	7		
24:14	519	15:29	166, 177, 192	17:1	7		
24:26	6	16:7	184	17:17–24	412		
		17:45	159	18:36–39	412		
Judges		17:47	806	19:18	806 fn. 2		
3:10	313	18:10–11	362	22:17–28	7		
4–5	900 fn. 10	19:9–10	362				
5:11	198	23:2–4	6	**2 Kings**			
6:11–24	208	23:9–13	373	1:10	412		
6:12	6	25:15	390	1:12	412		
7:13–15	6	25:25	153	2–13	7		
7:22	362	28:6	6	2:11	931		
8:18	258			5:15–18	1090		
9:23	362	**2 Samuel**		13:23	516		
13:3–22	208	6:2	159, 448	16:13	933 fn. 41		
13:5	924 fn. 26	6:6–7	1082	16:15	933 fn. 41		
13:7	924 fn. 26	7	430	19:15	986		
14:4	361	7:4–17	7	19:15–19	970		
20:2	806	7:11–16	406	20:8–11	412		
20:16	447	7:12–13	988	22:14–20	900 fn. 10		
21:5	806	12:1–14	7	23:10	1073		
21:8	806	12:21–23	946				
21:16	897	17:14	361	**1 Chronicles**			
		22:11	448	1	118		
Ruth		23:2	7 fn. 14	16:8–36	970		
4:18–20	118	24:16	208, 212	16:15–17	516		
				17:3	7		
1 Samuel		**1 Kings**		17:10–14	406		
1:9–11	970	3:5	7	17:16–27	970		
1:11	924 fn. 26	8:1–3	897	17:13	218		
2:1–10	970	8:14	806	21:1	660		
2:2	194	8:22	806	21:16	897		
2:3	184	8:22–61	970	28:2	809		

INDEX OF BIBLICAL REFERENCES

28:8	809	2:2–8	970	40:8	146		
29:10	809 (2)	5:13	809	42:2	358		
29:10–13	970	7:65	6	42:5–6	279, 723		
29:11–14	357	8:1–18	10				
29:12	8, 30	9:6	399	**Psalms**			
29:19	8, 30	9:6–7	358	1:6	466		
29:29	7, fn. 13	9:7	154	2	7 fn. 14, 213		
		9:7–8	516	2:1	48		
2 Chronicles		9:9–38	970	2:1–2	543		
5:12	825	9:20	313	2:2	531		
6:12	809			2:6	623, 624		
6:23	744	**Job**		2:7	158, 212 (2), 213 fn. 16,		
7:8	809	1–2	659, 660		218, 325 fn. 10		
7:12	7	1:4–5	183	2:8	222, 277		
9:29	7 fn. 13	1:12	659	2:8–9	861		
12:15	7 fn. 13	1:21	1090	2:8–12	987		
13:22	7 fn. 13	2:6	659	2:9	624, 1058 fn. 125		
18:20–22	362	2:7	660	5:4–6	195		
20:6	357	3:4	154	7:9	198		
20:13	940	4:13	6	7:11	197		
20:14	809	4:16	258	7:18	155		
20:34	7 fn. 13	11:7	101	8:1–3	166		
21:12–19	7	11:7–8	100, 101	8:2	233 (2)		
23:3	809, 825	12:10–23	358	8:3–8	416		
24:20	386	19:9	165	8:4	417		
24:20–22	1000 fn. 33	19:25–27	988	8:6	686 (2), 861		
25:20	362	20:8	6	9:7–8	197		
26:16–19	871, 872	21:26	1074	10:16	861		
26:22	7 fn. 13	24:20	1074	11:5–7	195		
28:3	1073	25:5	448	14:1–3	450, 714		
30:25	809	26:5–14	193	14:2–3	456		
30:26	809	26:13	392	16	51, 1044 (2)		
31:18	940	26:13a	314	16:3	390		
32:32	7 fn. 13	31:33	118, 440 fn. 29	16:8–11	286		
33:19	7 fn. 13	32:2	744	16:9:11	531		
		32:8	417	16:10	48, 531		
Ezra		33:4	36, 313, 417	16:11	1044		
1:1–2	362	33:15	6	17:1	198		
2:63	6	36:32	358	18:2	102		
7:27	362	37:16	184	18:10	448		
		38–41	358	18:20	198		
Nehemiah		38:4–7	177	18:21	198		
1:1–11	970	40:1	146	18:25–27	181		

[1149]

18:32	154	45:6–7	207, 212, 213,	76:2	159
19	7		213 fn. 16, 273	77:11–15	808 fn. 8
19:1	5, 56, 143, 153, 396	45:7	48	78:2	538, 995, 1012
19:1–4	396	45:7–8	273	78:56	155
19:3	5	45:16–17	165	80:3	724
19:7–9	71	47:2	861, 986	80:7	724
19:9	43, 166	47:3	155	80:19	724
22:1	46	47:7	861, 986	81:6	390
22:9	881	48:14	172	82:3–4	892
22:9–10	950, 954	50:4–6	988	82:6	230
22:16	531	50:22	154	83:5–6	366
22:28	861	51:1–2	924	84:3	986
22:31	198	51:4	1082	87	540, 832
24:7–10	861	51:5	450, 551 (2)	89:5–8	159
25:4	5	51:7–10	924	89:9	282 fn. 113
25:10	202	51:11	313, 793	89:14	198
29:10	172, 861, 986	51:12	793	89:19–37	430
31:1	198	51:15	198 (2)	90	6, 893
31:15	362	57:3	154	90:2	118, 131, 172, 174
32:1–2	528	58:3	71, 356, 451	90:4	172
32:4	793	58:9	390	90:17	xxxv
33:5	198	60:10	159	94:9	147
33:6	36, 118, 208	62:12	750	94:9–10	184
33:9	193	65:4	362, 380	95:3	861
33:13	184	65:5	198	95:7	48
34:8	289	67	540	95:7–11	158, 313, 394 fn. 11
34:15	198	68	832	96:5	201
34:22	198	68:8	832	96:10	986
35:10	892	68:16	832	96:10–13	197
35:23	198, 298	68:17	832	97:1	986
35:28	198	68:26	832	97:7	201
36:9	xxxi, 186	69:24	198	97:11	198
37:23–24	782	69:27	198	97:12	198
38:2	793	69:28	198	98:2	5
38:15	298	71:6	881	99:1–4	986
38:21	298	72:8–11	540	102	275
39:5	362	72:17	540	102:25–27	172, 213, 213 fn. 16, 273, 274, 276, 311
40:7	629	72:12–14	198		
40:10	198	73:1	199	102:26	48, 177
44:9	159	73:1–2	782	103	199
45:4	274	73:2	698	103:6	198 (2)
45:6	172, 273, 274, 623, 987	73:23	782	103:17	198
		73:23–24	698, 988	103:17–18	881

INDEX OF BIBLICAL REFERENCES

103:19	131, 356	119:40	198	147:19–20	676
103:19–21	159	119:86	71	148:2–5	118
104	199	119:105	87	149:2	209, 873
104:4	48	119:138	71		
104:10–30	401	119:142	71	**Proverbs**	
104:24	184	119:144	71	1:2–6	7 fn. 15
104:24–31	166	119:151	71	1:7	142, 143, 145
104:24	13	119:160	43, 71	3:12	310
104:30	313, 314, 392	127:3	937	8:22	598, 599
105:8–10	516	128:3–4	927	8:22–23	185
105:25	359 fn. 19, 482 fn. 37	130:3	451, 680	8:22–31	299 fn. 128,
105:42–43	516	130:4	756 fn. 66		325 fn. 10, 362
106:1	200	132:15	892	8:27–30	185
106:7–8	343	135:6	356, 362	13:13	750
106:9	282 fn. 113	136:5–9	118	15:3	169, 185
106:12	729	136:25	399	15:8	751
106:44–46	200	139:1–4	184	16:1	362
107	200	139:7–10	168, 313	16:4	362, 370
107:20	208	139:15–16	184	16:9	362
107:23–30	282	139:16	362	16:14	637
107:32	897	139:19	154	16:33	362
108:11	159	140:12	198	17:5	892
110	286 (2), 1044	141:12	892	17:15	744
110:1	155, 158, 208, 212,	143:1	198	17:23	744
	213, 213 fn. 16, 243,	143:2	451, 744	18:10	311
	273, 286, 987	143:11	198	19:7	892
110:1–2	623	143:15	200	19:21	362
110:1–7	861	144:3	466	20:12	147
110:4	623, 988	145:3	100, 101 (2)	20:24	362
110:5–6	987	145	399	20:27	5, 418, 447
111:9	808	145:4	101	21:1	362, 482
112:4	198	145:6	868	21:4	751
113:7	892	145:7	198	21:30	362
114:7	154	145:7–9	200	22:6	354
115:3	131, 191, 356, 362	145:9	5 fn. 7, 399	25:21–22	750
115:4–8	201	145:11	986	26:4	148
116:5	198	145:11–13	986	26:5	149
116:10	729	145:13	200, 399, 861, 986	29:7	892
116:11	71	145:15–17	399	29:14	892
118:1	200	145:16	200	30:1–4	216 fn. 23
118:22	289	145:17	131	30:5	154
118:29	200	147:4	186	31:8–9	892
119:15–19	198	147:15–16	208	31:20	892

[1151]

Ecclesiastes		10:22	530, 806	35:15	987		
7:20	451	11:1–9	987	37:16	159		
9:3	451	11:1–16	987	38:11	157		
12:1	209	11:2	313 (4), 314 (5)	40:2	196 fn. 65		
12:7	422, 424	11:3–5	198	40:3	311		
12:14	750, 988, 1071	11:6	514 fn. 19	40:12–31	131		
		11:6–9	988	40:13–14	185, 313		
Isaiah		11:9	987, 1014	40:15	363		
1:1	5, 30	11:10	540	40:17	363		
1:2	759	11:11	988	40:22	363		
1:2–3	519	13	988	40:23	363		
1:9	403, 1071 fn. 10	13:1	5	40:25–26	118		
1:10	1071 fn. 10	13:10	1003 fn. 37	40:27	102		
1:30	102	14:11	1074	40:27–28	185		
2:1	5	14:12	659	40:28	100, 101, 172		
5:7	221	14:24	363	41:22–23	186		
5:13	165	14:27	363	41:25–27	186		
5:16	197	19:1	8	42:1	208, 629		
5:23	742 fn. 46, 744	19:2	8	42:1–3	314		
6:1	30, 158, 195, 304	20:2–3	530	42:1–4	988		
6:1–3	194, 310	24:23	159	42:1–8	263		
6:2–3	159	25:1	179	42:5	118		
6:3	166, 304	26:19	988	42:6	530		
6:5	159, 279, 986	27:13	1004 fn. 38	42:8–9	186, 351 fn. 5		
6:8	167 (2), 207	28:16	289, 729	42:10	1013		
6:9–10	313, 365	29:1	390	43:1	808		
6:9–13	360 fn. 20	29:10–11	5	43:6	519		
6:10	304	29:16	369, 486	43:6–7	131		
7:14	213, 213 fn. 16, 225, 531, 547, 547 fn. 6, 552	30:8	8	43:6b-7	925 fn. 28		
		30:27	226	43:7	343		
8:1	8	30:33	1073	43:9–12	208		
8:11	8	31:33	198	43:10	281, 311		
8:12–13	289, 311	31:34	198	43:10–11	231		
8:13	194	32:15	987, 988	43:11–12	187		
8:14	311	32:39	198	43:15	986		
8:14b	289	32:40	198	43:19	1013		
9:2–7	987	33:8	198	43:21	343, 868		
9:4–5	987	33:22	208	43:25	198		
9:6	213, 213 fn. 16, 218, 531, 623	34:4–5	1003 fn. 37	43:27	118		
		35:2	987	44:3	881		
9:6–7	624	35:5–6	236	44:6	310, 311		
10:1–2	892	35:7	987, 988	44:7–8	187		
10:6–7	362	35:10	652	44:8	154, 351 fn. 5		

[1152]

INDEX OF BIBLICAL REFERENCES

44:9–10	201	53:10	634, 635	1:5	43, 174, 466		
44:13	258	53:10–12	529	1:6	8, 30		
44:20	201	53:11	629, 634	3:4	519		
44:24	118	53:12	46, 255, 264,	4:4	937 fn. 50		
44:24–28	187		634, 671, 673	6:3	30		
45:7	363	54:1–3	540	6:10	937 fn. 50		
45:9	369, 486	54:5	209	8:2	158		
45:12	118	54:9	118	8:6	723		
45:18–21	187	54:13	881	9:24	198		
45:21	198, 351	55:1	713	9:25–26	937 fn. 50		
45:22	221 (2), 311, 713, 735	55:3	48	10:2–16	201		
45:23	237, 263, 264, 312	55:5	624	10:7	986		
45:24	198 (2)	55:6–7	101	10:10	130, 201, 861		
45:24–25	746	55:7	101, 722	10:12	118		
45:25	199	55:8	101	12:15	175		
46:9–10	351 fn. 5	55:8–9	100, 101	13:1–11	530		
46:10	185, 390	55:11	208	13:11	343		
46:10–11	188, 363	57:13	776	13:23	453		
46:13	199	57:15	195, 304, 884	16:18	196 fn. 65		
48:3–7	188	57:16	424	17:9	356, 451, 456		
48:4–6	351 fn. 5	59:19	226	17:18c	197 fn. 65		
48:8–11	343	59:21	881	18:6	369, 486		
48:12	310	60:1–3	540	18:7–10	181 (2)		
48:16	208 (2)	61:1	208, 313, 892,	19:5	871, 872		
49:1	43		1004 fn. 38	19:13	158		
49:5	43	61:1–2	46, 314, 992	23:3	988		
49:5–7	988	61:10	746	23:5	198		
49:6	530, 540	63:9–10	209	23:14	1071 fn. 10		
49:24	102	63:10	208, 313, 314	23:23–24	169		
51:13	118	63:11	313	23:25	8		
52:13	629	63:16	519	23:28	8		
52:13–53:12	988	64:1–2	170	23:32	8		
52:15	932, 932 fn. 40 (3), 934	64:6	380, 451	25:13	8		
		64:8	369, 486, 519	26:1	30		
53	521, 530 (2), 654	65:17	798, 987, 988, 1013, 1016	26:3	351 fn. 5 (2)		
53:1	729			26:18	8		
53:4	634	65:17–25	987	27:1	30		
53:5	634	66:22	798, 987, 988, 1016	27:9	8		
53:5–10	805	66:22–24	1071 (2)	28:7ff.	43		
53:6	451, 634	66:24	1072	29:8	8		
53:7	529, 634			29:10	8		
53:7–8	932	**Jeremiah**		30:1–2	8, 30		
53:8	255, 263, 634	1:4–10	29 (2)	31:9	510		

[1153]

31:18	724	14:14	8	2:34–35	538, 995, 1006
31:31	525, 673	14:20	8	2:44	523, 544, 986, 987
31:31–34	406, 525, 988	16:49	892	2:44–45	538, 544 (2), 988, 995, 1006
32:17	192	18:23	692 fn. 25		
32:26–27	192	18:32	692 fn. 25	3:19	257, 258
32:35	351 fn. 5	20:9	8, 343	4:5	8
32:38–39	881	20:14	343	4:17	131, 363
33:1	30	20:22	343	4:25	131
36	30 (2)	20:44	343	4:27	892
36:2	8, 30	22:29	892	4:31–32	357, 363
36:4	30	22:30	183	4:34–35	363, 986
36:6	30	23:8	519	4:35	131, 482 fn. 37
36:27–28	8, 30	23:19	519	6:7	118
40:28	101	23:21	519	7	215, 216, 311, 1053
46:18	159, 986	24:1	8	7:1	8
48:15	159	24:2	8	7:2–14	998
49:14–22	8	24:15–24	530	7:9	310
49:18	1071 fn. 10	28:13	449	7:13	215, 1006 (2)
51:57	159	32:7–8	1003 fn. 37	7:13–14	216, 216 fn. 23, 225, 987, 988, 1006
		33:11	182, 183, 200, 692 fn. 25, 722	7:14	213, 213 fn. 16, 544, 861
Lamentations					
2:14	5	34	898		
4:6	1071 fn. 10	35:5	367	7:18	544
5:21	724	36:24–27	314	7:22	1006
		36:24–28	988	7:27	544
Ezekiel		36:25	198, 932, 933, 933 fn. 41	9:2	8 (2)
1:3	5, 8			9:4–19	970
1:4	5	36:25–26	924, 926	9:14	197
1:5–28	448	37:1	8	9:19	208
2:2	208	37:1–14	36, 314	9:2	523
3:16	30	37:12–14	314	9:24	84 fn. 51
3:22	8	37:25	881	9:24–27	523
4:4–8	530	43:11	8	9:27	45
5:1–12	530	43:18	933 fn. 41	10	311
8:1	30, 897	44:9	525 (2)	10:11–11:1	660
8:3	208			10:16	279
8:12	169	**Daniel**		11:31	45
11:19	198	2	412, 538, 995 (2), 1053	12:2	565, 988, 1072
11:24	386	2:1	8	12:4	8
12:3	351 fn. 5 (3)	2:3	8	12:11	45
12:8	30 (2)	2:19	8		
12:9	30	2:26	8	**Hosea**	
13:3	5	2:34	544	1:2	390

INDEX OF BIBLICAL REFERENCES

1:9	514 fn. 19	**Obadiah**		**Haggai**	
1:10	540	4	169	2:5–6	208
2:18	198	15–16	988	2:7	527
4:1–6	8	17	8	2:9	514
6:1–4	8				
6:7	405 fn. 23, 418,	**Jonah**		**Zechariah**	
	430, 430 fn. 16,	1:4–17	683	1:9	30
	440 fn. 29, 457, 512	2:9	201, 380	2:5	251, 271
11:1	519, 759	2:10	346	2:10–11	208
11:9	195	3:3–5	180	3:1	659, 660
12:3–4	6	3:10	180, 351 fn. 5 (2)	4:4–5	30
12:4	208			4:10	310
12:13	6	**Micah**		7:2	637
13:5	466	1:1	5	7:12	8, 208
		1:3–6	8	8:22	637
Joel		3:8	313, 314	9:4–6	8
1:15	988	3:12	8	9:9	198 (2), 988
2:1–7	988	5:2	325, 683	9:9–10	987
2:10	1003 fn. 37	5:4–5a	987	10:2	8
2:12–13	722	6:5	198	12:1	118, 424
2:15–16	940, 941 fn. 53	7:18	200	12:8	8, 208
2:16	809	7:20	516	12:9	8
2:28	198, 314, 686 (3)			12:10	312, 313, 530,
2:28–32	84, 285, 941,	**Nahum**			543, 1004
	988, 1011	1:3	213	13:7	530
2:31	1003 fn. 37				
2:32	8, 288, 311	**Habakkuk**		**Malachi**	
3:15	1003 fn. 37	1:1	5	1:2	367
3:16	8	1:5–6	363	1:3	367
		1:5–11	1083	1:6	519
Amos		1:13	182, 195	1:9	637
1:1	5	2	29 (2)	1:11	540
1:2	8	2:1	5	2:5–7	6
2:4	201	2:2	8, 30	2:10	519
3:2	466, 676, 806	2:2–3	28 (2)	3:1	45, 208, 213, 213 fn.16,
3:6	363	2:14	1014		564, 988, 989 fn. 17
3:7	5, 14	3:3	154	3:2–3	987
4:11	1071 fn. 10			3:2–5	988
4:13	118	**Zephaniah**		3:6	177
5:18–20	988	1:5	158	4:1–5	987
9:2–4	169	1:7	988, 1003 fn. 37	4:1–6	1083
9:11–12	524, 525, 527,	1:14–16	988, 1003 fn. 37	4:4	8, 58
	540, 828	2:9	1071 fn. 10	4:4–6	10

[1155]

SYSTEMATIC THEOLOGY

4:5	564, 988, 989 fn. 17 (2)	3:11–12	924 fn. 26	5:48	200, 271 fn. 87, 770
4:5–6	988	3:12	990, 1072	6:1	750
		3:15	629	6:1–2	1092
		3:16	313 (2), 930, 932	6:2	235, 750
		3:17	218, 293	6:4	750

New Testament

		4	262	6:5	235
		4:1–11	661	6:5–13	971, 973
Matthew		4:3	263, 293, 659	6:10	236, 993
1:1	394, 517	4:4	45, 663, 1104	6:11	271 fn. 87
1:1–17	546	4:6	263, 293	6:12	753
1:3	401	4:7	45, 508, 663, 1104	6:13	659, 973
1:8	394	4:8	263	6:14ff.	271 fn. 87
1:16	547	4:10	45, 663, 1104	6:16	235, 750
1:17	1000 fn. 34	4:11	660	6:18	750
1:18	547	4:13	242	6:19	271 fn. 87
1:18–20	314	4:17	538, 624, 723, 995	6:20	750
1:18–25	293	4:21	1106	6:22	271 fn. 87
1:20	10, 547	4:23–24	553	6:24	271 fn. 87
1:21	673	5–7	624	6:25–34	402
1:22–23	548, 552	5:3	271 fn. 87	6:26	364
1:23	213, 225	5:7	271 fn. 87	6:28	364
1:25	548	5:9	271 fn. 87	6:33	236
2:2	1090	5:10–12	271 fn. 87	6:34	271 fn. 87
2:10–12	1090	5:11	215	7:1	271 fn. 87
2:12	10	5:12	750	7:7–8	271 fn. 87
2:13	10	5:13	810 fn. 13	7:7–11	974
2:15	293	5:14	810 fn. 13	7:7	271 fn. 87
2:16	242	5:16	868	7:8	354
2:19	10	5:17	45, 46	7:11	271 fn. 87
2:22	10	5:17–18	45, 1104	7:12	45, 773
3:1–12	924 fn. 26	5:19	44	7:13	1074, 1078
3:2	10, 723, 924 fn. 26, 990	5:22	235, 271 fn. 87, 1074	7:14	1074
		5:24	648	7:16	271 fn. 87
3:3	294, 311	5:28	235	7:18	453
3:4	924 fn. 26	5:29	1074, 1078	7:21–23	271 fn. 87 (2), 993
3:6	924	5:30	1074	7:22	1005, 1083 fn. 24
3:7	637	5:32	235	7:22–23	466, 679
3:8	723, 924 fn. 26	5:34	235	7:23	692, 1083 fn. 24
3:9	1031	5:34–37	271 fn. 87	7:24	271 fn. 87
3:10	990	5:37	659	7:24–25	811 fn. 15
3:10–12	529, 990	5:39	235	7:26	271 fn. 87
3:11	285, 717, 723, 924, 926, 932 fn. 39, 934	5:44	5 fn. 7, 235	7:29	862
		5:45	200, 401	8:1–4	553

[1156]

INDEX OF BIBLICAL REFERENCES

8:4	45	10:23	215, 982, 1007 (2)	12:5	45
8:5–13	553	10:24–25	1008	12:8	217, 293
8:10	547	10:26–39	1008	12:9–13	553
8:11	517	10:28	422, 699, 1074	12:22–32	554
8:11–12	993	10:29	357	12:24	659, 659
8:12	1074	10:29–30	131, 186, 364	12:22–24	661
8:14	815	10:30	357	12:25–28	661
8:14–17	553	10:32	215	12:28	236, 314, 557, 992, 992 fn. 22
8:16	553	10:33	215		
8:17	263	10:40	844	12:29	236, 659, 661, 662, 1063 fn. 131
8:20	217	10:41	750, 1021		
8:23–27	554	11:2	294	12:31	223
8:27	282, 546	11:2–6	232, 236	12:31–32	314
8:28–34	553	11:4–5	554, 558	12:32	217, 997, 1008 fn. 43, 1064
8:29	662, 729, 1076	11:5	223		
8:34	242	11:7–14	924	12:36	271 fn. 87, 1005
9:1–8	553, 558	11:9–14	529	12:37	271 fn. 87, 744
9:2	11, 232	11:10	45 (2), 311, 1004	12:39	1000 fn. 34
9:4	619	11:12	992	12:40	45, 293 (2), 566 fn. 33
9:6	217, 232, 293	11:13	45, 924		
9:8	862	11:13–14	213	12:41	723, 1000 fn. 34, 1083 fn. 24
9:13	715	11:14	989, 989 fn. 17		
9:15	528, 559 fn. 19	11:16	1000 fn. 34	12:42	1083 fn. 24
9:18–19	553	11:18	924 fn. 26	12:45	1000 fn. 34
9:20–22	553	11:19	219	13	537, 538, 542, 810 fn. 13, 994, 996, 1012, 1013
9:23–26	553	11:20–21	723		
9:27	547	11:20–23	538, 995		
9:27–31	279, 553	11:20–24	219, 554	13:3–8	539, 996
9:29	663	11:22	1005, 1074	13:3–9	1012
9:34	659	11:23–24	45	13:11	508, 537 (2), 538, 994, 995
9:35	553	11:24	1005, 1074		
9:36	547, 897	11:25	220 (2), 676	13:13–15	539
10	982	11:25–26	283, 364	13:17	508, 537 (2), 995, 1012
10:1	862	11:25–27	218, 283		
10:2	813, 1106	11:25–28	1099	13:18–23	1012
10:3	1106, 1108	11:26	676	13:19	659
10:7	236	11:27	11, 100, 101, 218, 219, 220 (2), 223 (2), 223 fn. 37, 234, 235, 293 (3), 322, 579, 676, 713, 861	13:20–21	789
10:8	554			13:24–30	236, 539, 996, 1012
10:15	45, 1071, fn. 10, 1074 (2)			13:25	659, 660
				13:28	659
10:16–22	1008			13:28–29	403
10:20	313	11:28	221, 311, 736	13:31–32	539, 996, 1012
10:22	685	12:3	45	13:33	539, 996

[1157]

13:34–35	537, 538, 995, 1012	16:19	821, 821 fn. 36 (4), 862, 890	19:4–6	398, 487
13:36–43	236, 539, 996, 1012			19:5	48
13:37	539, 996	16:21	215, 559, 566 fn. 33	19:7–9	938 fn. 50
13:38	659	16:22–23	559, 815	19:8	938 fn. 50
13:39	659	16:23	660	19:12	236
13:40–43	1083 fn. 24	16:24–27	559	19:13–15	941
13:41	217, 223	16:27	217, 293, 750	19:14	538, 995
13:42	1075	16:28	560, 1007	19:23–24	538, 995
13:44–45	1012	17:1	1106	19:27	813
13:44–46	539, 996	17:2	561, 563 (2)	19:28	215, 236, 293, 993, 1012
13:47–50	539, 997, 1012	17:2–6	288		
13:49	223	17:4–5	815	19:29	750
13:50	1075	17:5	293	20:17–19	559
13:54	538, 996	17:5–6	564	20:18–19	216, 293
13:55	548, 1106	17:9	216, 293, 561, 562, 566 fn. 33	20:19	293, 566, 566 fn. 33
13:58	538, 996			20:20–28	816
14:15–21	554	17:10	564, 989 fn. 17	20:22	559
14:22–27	54	17:11–13	989	20:25–28	866, 886
14:28–29	813	17:12	293	20:28	216, 217, 293 (3), 557, 559, 629, 630, 634, 653, 657, 673, 680
14:33	282, 282 fn. 113, 293	17:14–21	553		
		17:17	1000 fn. 34		
14:35–36	553	17:19	566		
15:2	931	17:20	663	20:29–34	279, 553
15:3–6	45	17:22–23	216, 293, 559	21:13	45 (2)
15:9	872	17:23	293, 566	21:16	45, 233
15:13	364	17:24–25	813	21:18–22	554
15:15	813	17:24–27	554	21:21	969
15:21–28	553	18	820 fn. 35	21:22	969
15:22	242	18:1	816	21:25	728
15:30–31	553	18:6	729, 1075	21:32	728
15:32–39	554	18:7	365	21:33–39	221
15:39	242	18:8	1075	21:33–40	89
16	817, 818, 820 fn. 35 (2)	18:9	1075	21:37	581
		18:15–18	890	21:37–38	218, 293
16:4	1000 fn. 34	18:17	526, 811, 820, 824, 853	22:39	559
16:13	215, 583			21:42	45
16:16	281 (2), 282, 283, 293, 559	18:17–18	624	21:43	992, 1026
		18:18	821 fn. 36 (3), 822, 862	21:45	221
16:17	220, 283 (2)			22:1–14	810 fn. 13
16:17–19	282	18:20	234, 616, 1099	22:2	293
16:18	283 (2), 526, 811 (2), 813, 818 fn. 26, 819 fn. 31, 824, 829	19:1	242	22:13	1074
		19:4	45 (2), 48	22:14	365, 713
		19:4–5	45, 118 (2)	22:29	45

INDEX OF BIBLICAL REFERENCES

22:29–32	988	24:30b	1004	26:29	965, 994
22:31	45	24:30	215, 217, 234,	26:31	45, 46,
22:37–40	776		267, 293		521, 530
22:40	45	24:31	223, 293, 1004	26:36–44	970
22:41–45	208	24:32–33	1004	26:36–45	815
22:41–46	583	24:34	1004, 1005, 1007	26:36–46	630
22:42	1095	24:36	218, 293, 612,	26:37	547
23:8	147 fn. 34		1005 (2), 1006, 1007	26:38	547
23:13	236, 992	24:37	45, 993 fn. 25	26:39	612, 677
23:13–32	999	24:38	1028 fn. 76 (2)	26:41	969
23:32	999	24:37–39	118 (2)	26:42	612
23:33	1075	24:39	293, 993 fn. 25,	26:43	612
23:34	304		1006	26:45	215, 293
23:35	45, 118	24:42	1005, 1006 (2)	26:51–52	867
23:35–36	999	24:43–44	1005	26:51–54	815
23:36	1004, 1005	24:44	293, 1005, 1006	26:53–56	46
23:37	692 fn. 25	24:45–51	1005, 1007	26:54	521
23:37a	221	24:50	1005, 1006	26:56	521
24–25	624, 999	24:51	1083 fn. 24	26:63–64	293
24:2	1000, 1005	25:1–13	1005, 1022	26:64	267, 293 (2),
24:2–3	827	25:5	1007		576, 1004
24:3	993 fn. 25, 1000	25:13	1005, 1006	26:65–66	229
24:4–8	1001	25:14–30	1006	26:72	546
24:4–33	1005	25:19	1007	26:74	546
24:9–14	1001	25:31	217, 223 (2)	27:3	724
24:10	789	25:31–46	236, 293, 539,	27:4	629
24:11	845		687, 750, 994,	27:19–23	629
24:12	789		996, 1006, 1012	27:42	729
24:13	785	25:34	236	27:46	46, 982
24:14	1001, 1002	25:35	118	27:54	293
24:15	45	25:37–40	887	27:56	1106
24:15–21	1002	25:41	1075	27:61	566
24:19	1005	25:41–46	1083 fn. 24	27:62–66	566, 567
24:21	1000 fn. 34	25:46	679, 692, 1005, 1075	27:63	566 fn. 33
24:22	1005	26:2	293, 559	28:6	566
24:23–27	1003 (2)	26:11–12	559	28:8–9	569 fn. 35, 813
24:24	845	26:23–24	215	28:8–10	569
24:27	215, 293, 544,	26:24	45, 46, 293 (2),	28:12–15	566
	993 fn. 25		365, 521, 559, 1075	28:13	567
24:28	1003	26:26	956	28:16–20	570
24:29	1003 (2), 1005	26:27–28	922	28:18	11, 240, 579, 861
24:29–31	1003, 1005	26:28	559, 634, 654,	28:18–19	862, 878
24:30a	1004		658, 673, 956	28:18–20	*xxviii*, 880

[1159]

28:19	209, 218, 223, 225, 293 (2), 308, 313 (2), 810 fn. 13, 844, 922, 924, 927, 945, 956	3:10	554	8:1–10	554
		3:11	292	8:12	223
		3:14	61	8:14–21	223
		3:14–15	862	8:27	215
28:19–20a	225, 624 (2)	3:16	811, 813	8:29	281, 559
28:19–20	837	3:18	1106	8:30–32	282
28:20	234, 617, 825, 826, 889, 922	3:20–30	554	8:31	215, 292, 293, 559, 566 fn. 33
		3:21	223		
		3:22	659	8:33	660
Mark		3:27	236	8:34–37	559
1:2	1004	4:11	538, 995	8:38	217, 293
1:2–3	311, 924 fn. 26	4:11–12	360 fn. 20, 365, 1011, 1015	9:1	242, 560, 1007, 1008
1:3	294			9:2	561
1:4	723	4:26–29	236, 994, 997, 1012	9:3	563
1:4–5	924	4:29	544	9:4	561
1:8	285, 717, 926, 934	4:35–41	554	9:5	564
1:9	930, 932	4:39	617	9:6	563
1:10	930, 932	4:39–41	862	9:7	221, 292
1:9–11	20	5:1–20	553	9:9	216, 293, 561, 566 fn. 33
1:11	218, 221, 292	5:7	292		
1:15	723, 986, 992, 1012, 1013	5:17	242	9:11	564, 989 fn. 17
		5:22–24	553	9:31	216, 292, 293, 559, 566 fn. 33
1:22	862	5:25–34	553		
1:23–27	553	5:29	1078	9:32	559
1:24	281	5:30	1078	9:32–33	559
1:27	862 (2)	5:35–43	553	9:42	729
1:29–31	553	6:3	548, 1106	9:43	992 fn. 23, 1073, 1078
1:31	970	6:5	223	9:44	1078
1:32–34	554	6:6	547	9:46	1078
1:39	554	6:12	723	9:47	992 fn. 23
1:40–45	553	6:13	554	9:47–48	1073
1:41	547	6:34–44	554	9:48	1072, 1078
2:1–12	553, 558	6:45–52	554	10:1	242
2:5	232, 1099	6:56	554	10:6–8	118
2:7	218	7:3–4	931 (2)	10:13–16	941
2:8	1099	7:4	931 (2)	10:14	538, 547, 995
2:10	217, 218, 232, 292, 617	7:6–13	872	10:15	236
		7:7–8	871	10:17	223
2:17	715	7:24	242	10:18	200
2:20	528, 559 fn. 19	7:24–30	553	10:21	547
2:28	217, 218, 292	7:26	823 fn. 39	10:30	997
3:1–5	553	7:31	242	11:31	728
3:5	547 (2)	7:31–37	553	10:32–34	559

INDEX OF BIBLICAL REFERENCES

10:33–34	216, 292	14:25	965	1:37	192
10:34	293, 566 fn. 33	14:27	530	1:41	954 fn. 84
10:35	1106	14:32–42	630	1:47	551
10:35–37	559	14:34	547	1:54–55	516, 623, 989
10:38	559	14:38	973	1:68–73	516, 623
10:45	216, 217, 292, 542,	14:41	292	1:68–75	989
	557, 559, 629, 630,	14:49	46	1:76	989
	634, 652, 653, 657,	14:56	44	2:1–7	683
	671, 673, 680, 687	14:58	566 fn. 33	2:19	548
10:46–52	553	14:59	44	2:26	314
10:47–48	547	14:61	292	2:29–32	530, 990
11:12–14	554	14:61–62	229	2:34–35	530, 990
11:20–21	554	14:62	216, 267, 292,	2:38	990
12:1–11	221		576, 1006 (2)	2:41–51	546
12:6	218, 292, 581	14:71	546	2:51–52	629
12:8	559	15:34	223	2:51b	548
12:9	1083 fn. 24	15:39	292, 546	2:52	546, 630
12:14	629	15:40	1106	3	118
12:28	998	15:47	566	3:1–2	546
12:29–31	776	16	569 fn. 35	3:2–9	924 fn. 26
12:30	420	16:5–6	566	3:3	723, 924
12:31	773	16:5–7	569	3:4	311
12:33	420	16:7	793	3:7	637
13	999	16:9	569 fn. 35	3:8	723, 924 fn. 26 (2)
13:1	1000	16:9–20	951	3:10–14	924 fn. 26
13:3	1000, 1106	16:16	950 (2)	3:12–13	824
13:4	1000 fn. 35	16:19–20	575 fn. 43	3:16	285, 717, 926, 934
13:11	314	16:20	410	3:21	970
13:13	785			3:22	218, 294
13:22	292, 845	**Luke**		3:23	548
13:25	217	1:13–20	10	3:23–37	546
13:26	561	1:15	924 fn. 26, 954 fn. 84	3:36	395
13:26–27	293	1:16–17	311, 989	4:1–18	314
13:30	1007, 1008	1:19	213, 287	4:3	294
13:32	222, 223 (2), 224 (2),	1:20	728	4:6	660
	618, 619, 1007	1:27	548	4:9	294
14:7	892	1:28–37	10	4:16	629
14:8	559	1:32	294	4:16–18	208
14:9	965 fn. 106, 1007	1:32–33	989	4:16–21	xxvii–xxviii
14:12	632	1:33	624	4:17–21	1004 fn. 38
14:21	292 (2), 365, 559	1:34	192, 548	4:18	892
14:22	956	1:35	243, 294, 314,	4:18–21	623
14:24	559, 634, 956		548, 551	4:21	992

[1161]

4:22	548	7:37–38	279	10:7	11 (2), 35, 548
4:32	862	7:41–43	749 fn. 56	10:9	236, 554
4:33–37	553	7:44	931	10:12	1074
4:34	281	7:47–48	749 fn. 56	10:12–13	554
4:36	862	7:48	232	10:13	538, 723, 996
4:38–40	553	8:10	538, 995	10:14	1074
4:40	554	8:22–25	554	10:16	845
4:41	294	8:24	727	11:15	659 (2)
5	280	8:26–39	553	10:17	554, 663
5:1–11	554	8:28	294	10:19	554, 862
5:8	243, 278, 281	8:41–42	553	10:21–22	218, 294, 1099
5:12–16	553	8:42	326	10:22	100, 101, 218, 294
5:16	970	8:43–48	553	10:27	420, 421
5:17–26	553, 558	8:49–56	553	10:29	744
5:20	232	9:1	862	10:39	294
5:24	217, 232	9:1–6	11	10:41	294
5:32	715, 723	9:11	554	11:1–13	971
5:35	528, 559 fn. 19, 578	9:12–17	554	11:4	753, 973
6:5	217	9:18	215, 970	11:13	313, 356, 451
6:6–10	553	9:20	281, 559	11:14–23	554
6:7	862	9:22	215, 216, 294 (2), 559, 566 fn. 33	11:20	992, 992 fn. 22, 1012, 1013
6:12	970				
6:13	11	9:23–26	559	11:21	661
6:14	813	9:26	215, 294 (2)	11:21–22	661, 662
6:15	1106	9:27	560, 564, 989 fn. 17, 1007	11:22	661 (3)
6:16	1106, 1108			11:32	723
6:17–19	554	9:29	563 (2), 564	11:38	931
6:22	215	9:31	561, 563	11:39	294
6:35–36	5 fn. 7, 200	9:32	561, 562, 563 (2), 564	11:42	727
6:36	770	9:35	294	11:49	304
6:37–38	750	9:36	561	11:51	118
7:1–10	553	9:37	563	11:52	820 fn. 35, 992
7:9	547	9:37–43	553	12:5	1074, 1075 (2), 1078
7:11–16	553	9:38	326	12:6	186
7:12	326	9:43	563	12:8	215, 294
7:13	294	9:44	294	12:12	314
7:19	294	9:46	559	12:31	663
7:22	554, 558	9:48	38	12:41–48	1007
7:24	1004	9:52	1004	12:42	294
7:27	1004	9:54	1106	12:47	375
7:29	744	9:54–56	867	13:3	723
7:33	924 fn. 26	9:58	217	13:5	723
7:36–50	749 fn. 56	10:1	294, 554	13:10–17	553

INDEX OF BIBLICAL REFERENCES

13:11	660	18:15	941	22:20	406, 430, 634, 673, 957
13:15	294	18:15–17	941		
13:16	660	18:17	236, 538, 995	22:22	294, 360 fn. 20, 365, 465, 525
13:25–30	1083 fn. 24	18:23	724		
13:27	1075	18:29	236	22:24	816
13:28	1075	18:30	997 (2)	22:24–26	866
13:33	623	18:31	46, 294, 521	22:25–27	886
14:1–6	553	18:31–32	294	22:29	992
14:11	727	18:31–33	216	22:31	660
14:26	992 fn. 23	18:33	294, 566 fn. 33	22:31–32	677, 793, 813
15:1–2	232	18:34	559	22:32	813
15:7	183, 723	18:35–43	553	22:37	46, 263, 654
15:10	183, 723	19:2–8	824	22:39–44	630
16:8	997	19:8	294	22:48	215
16:15	744	19:9	796	22:49–51	553
16:16	9, 992	19:10	216, 294, 542	22:52	660
16:17	45	19:11	1007	22:53	660
16:19–28	1083 fn. 24	19:37	538, 996	22:54–61	793
16:23	1075, 1076	19:41–44	624	22:61	294
16:24	1075, 1076	19:43–44	1002	22:66	897
16:26	675, 680	20:5	728	22:69	294, 576
16:27	727	20:9–15	221	22:70	294
16:28	1075, 1076	20:13	218, 294	22:70–71	229
16:29	9	20:31	727	23:1–2	542
16:30	727	20:34	997	23:4	546, 629
16:31	45	20:35	997	23:6	546
17:1	365	21:3–36	999	23:14–15	629
17:2	1075	21:5	1000	23:28–31	1002
17:5	294	21:7	1000 fn. 35	23:43	423
17:6	294	21:9	785	23:47	546
17:11–19	553	21:20	45, 1002 (2)	23:55	566
17:13	547	21:23	637	24:3	294, 566
17:20–21	992, 1012	21:27	217, 294	24:3–7	569
17:22–27	999	21:28	656	24:6	566
17:25	1000 fn. 34	21:31	1004	24:6–7	566 fn. 33
17:26–27	118	21:32	1007	24:7	216, 294
17:29	1071, fn. 10	21:33	11	24:10	1106
17:32	45	21:36	294, 1083 fn. 24	24:12	569
18:1–8	971	22:7	632	24:13–15	570
18:6	294	22:16	965	24:22–24	566
18:13	279	22:18	965 (2)	24:25	729
18:13–14	455	22:19	634, 956 (2)	24:25–27	521, 537
18:14	920	22:19–20	654	24:27	*xxviii*, 10

24:31	577	1:14–18	617	2:22	726, 728		
24:34	288, 570	1:15	213, 214, 251	2:23	729		
24:36	577	1:17	10, 301, 307,	2:25	617, 619		
24:36–43	147, 167, 570		510 fn. 13, 1047	3:1–15	719		
24:39	167	1:18	100, 101, 159, 212,	3:2	1099		
24:44	9, 46 (2), 61		238, 300, 301 (2), 302,	3:3	453, 709, 719 (2)		
24:44–52	570		302 fn. 131, 303 (2),	3:5	453, 709, 719 (2), 926		
24:44–47	570		305, 306, 307, 312,	3:5–6	314		
24:45–47	46, 537		325, 336, 1098, 1099	3:6	549 fn. 8, 720		
24:46–47	723, 1088	1:23	311, 1046	3:7	719, 720		
24:46–48	863	1:23–27	924 fn. 26	3:8	107, 313,		
24:47	878, 880, 951,	1:25	932 fn. 40		314 (2), 720 (2)		
	952, 1104	1:29	309, 508, 529,	3:13	217, 227, 230,		
24:49	285 (2), 826		632, 924 fn. 26 (2),		303, 1046		
24:51	575		990, 1102	3:14	528, 543,		
		1:29–35	924 fn. 26		559 fn. 19, 1102		
John		1:30	213, 214, 224,	3:14–15	729		
1	591		251, 546	3:15	729		
1:1	10, 159, 212, 298,	1:31	266	3:16	22, 201, 238, 302,		
	299 (2), 300, 305,	1:32–33	314		304 (2), 325,		
	307, 312, 390,	1:33	285, 717, 926, 934		326 fn. 11, 477, 641,		
	625, 1097, 1099	1:34	213, 303, 314		666 (2), 685, 696 (4),		
1:1b	300 (2)	1:35	924 fn. 26 (2)		729, 1080		
1:1–2	391	1:35–37	924 fn. 26	3:16–21	304 (2)		
1:1–3	208	1:36	309, 632, 1102	3:17	304		
1:2	301	1:41	283	3:18	238, 302, 304 (2),		
1:2–3	118	1:42	811		684 fn. 16, 729,		
1:3	147, 299, 301, 336	1:45	546, 1102		1080, 1086 fn. 30		
1:4	307	1:47	617, 619	3:19	265, 304, 1088		
1:6	300	1:48	234	3:19–20	1088		
1:9	56, 147, 153,	1:49	227, 283, 303	3:23	930, 931		
	265, 307, 452	1:51	227	3:27–30	924 fn. 26		
1:12	300, 729 (2), 759, 761	2:1	548	3:28	529		
1:12–13	707, 719, 720	2:1–11	1099 fn. 10	3:31	304, 548, 708 fn. 7		
1:13	300, 369, 708,	2:4	1047, 1102	3:31a	304		
	719, 1031	2:11	260, 558 fn. 18,	3:31b	304		
1:14	10, 238, 241, 253,		729, 1099	3:31–36	304 (2)		
	260, 266, 271, 302,	2:13–4:3	528	3:32	304		
	307, 312, 325, 548,	2:17	1046	3:34	304 (2)		
	552, 558 fn. 18,	2:19	245, 543, 1102	3:35	304		
	625, 1097, 1098 (2),	2:19–21	566 fn. 33, 578	3:36	304, 637, 638, 729,		
	1098 fn. 9, 1099	2:19–22	528, 559 fn. 19		921, 1047, 1080		
	1100, 1101	2:21	1102	4	546, 1102		

INDEX OF BIBLICAL REFERENCES

4:1	305	5:39	46, 521, 537, 557, 1047	6:53			217, 280,
4:14	729	5:40	729				963 fn. 102, 964
4:21	728, 920	5:42	451	6:53–58			964
4:22–24	871, 872	5:46	xxviii, 537, 557,	6:54		280 (2), 963 fn. 102,
4:22	1030		728, 1031				964, 997
4:23	920, 1047	5:46–47	6, 46, 533, 726	6:56			964
4:24	162, 166	5:47	728	6:57		280, 307 (2), 548, 964
4:29	546, 617, 619, 1102	6	963 (3), 964	6:58			231, 280, 964
4:39	729	6:5–14	554	6:59			963
4:42	697	6:15	542	6:62			217, 227, 231, 280,
4:46–54	553	6:16–21	554				303, 576, 1046
4:50	726, 728	6:20	231, 232	6:63			964
5:1–15	553	6:22	280	6:63–64			966
5:12	546, 1102	6:23	305	6:65			280, 354, 365,
5:17	227	6:27	962				678, 720, 729
5:17–18	218	6:29	729, 921	6:66			963
5:18	260	6:30	728	6:68–69			280, 813
5:17–26	303	6:32	307	6:69		243, 279, 283, 303
5:17–29	218, 227	6:33	231, 280 (2), 962	6:70–71			280, 687
5:18	44, 228, 336	6:35	231, 729, 964 (4)	7:5			729
5:19	228	6:37–39	698	7:23			44
5:19a	227	6:37–40	782	7:27			546, 1102
5:19b	227	6:38	228, 231, 280,	7:30			1102
5:20	227, 234		548, 677	7:31			729
5:21b	227	6:39	280, 997	7:33			578
5:22	234, 861	6:40	218, 227 (2), 280 (2),	7:33–34			576
5:22–23	326		729, 964, 997	7:35			823 fn. 39
5:22–27	227	6:41	963	7:37–38			729
5:22–30	1083 fn. 24	6:42	546, 1102	7:37–39			973
5:23	228	6:44	280, 354, 453, 482,	7:38			314, 729
5:24	728, 921		678, 719, 729, 997	7:46			546, 1102
5:24–25	227, 1033, 1063	6:44–45	280, 364	7:48			729
5:25	230, 1047	6:45	101, 283, 354, 453,	8:12			231
5:26	307, 325, 326 (2), 612		678, 719, 1046	8:14			80 fn. 44
5:27	214, 218, 227, 234,	6:46	100, 101, 231	8:20			1047, 1102
	326 (2), 612, 861	6:47	964	8:21			576
5:28–29	227, 234, 687, 1076	6:48	231	8:23			231, 548, 1046
5:29	750	6:50	231, 280	8:24			231, 232, 303
5:30	228, 629	6:50–58	729, 966	8:26			23, 43
5:33–35	557	6:51	231, 241, 280 (2),	8:26–28			624
5:36	232, 412, 548, 557 (2)		634, 964	8:28			43, 231
5:37	557	6:51–59	962	8:28–29			629
5:38	728	6:52	963	8:30			729

[1165]

8:31	728, 785, 852	10:25	218, 232	11:52	759, 1047
8:33–58	1047	10:26	783	12:1–3	279
8:38	231	10:26–27	674	12:8	578
8:40	23, 546, 1101	10:27	624, 783, 783	12:10–12	1099
8:41	548	10:28	229	12:11	729
8:42	231	10:28–29	783	12:13–15	1046
8:43	354	10:28–30	698	12:20	823 fn. 39
8:44	659, 660 (2)	10:29	218, 229	12:20–23	687
8:45	728	10:30	167, 218, 229, 303	12:23	510 fn. 14, 577, 1047, 1102
8:46	629, 728	10:30–36	325
8:47	674 fn. 6, 852	10:32–33	218	12:24	628, 1102
8:56	517, 533	10:33	229 (2), 546, 1102	12:25	1047
8:58	231 (3), 251, 303, 616, 1099	10:33–36	336	12:26	886
		10:34	9	12:27	546, 547, 612, 1102
8:58–59	229	10:35	10, 44, 1104	12:31	659, 662, 663, 1047, 1063 fn. 131
8:59	232	10:36	218, 230 (2), 303, 548
9:1–7	553	10:37	218, 728	12:32	477, 685 (2), 687 (2), 1070
9:4	555	10:37–38	558
9:5	231	10:38	218, 232, 314, 324, 412, 728	12:36	729
9:6	546, 1102			12:37	729
9:11	546, 1102	10:42	729	12:37–40	365
9:16	546, 1099, 1102	11:1–54	553	12:37–41	1099
9:24	546, 1102	11:2	305	12:38	726, 728
9:29	548	11:3	547, 619	12:38–40	360 fn. 20, 1046
9:35	227, 729	11:4	218	12:40	304
9:35–37	216	11:5	547	12:40–41	194, 311, 1099
9:36	729	11:6	619	12:41	158
9:39	231, 360 fn. 20	11:11	620 (2)	12:42	729
10:7	231	11:11–14	617	12:44	729
10:9	231	11:14	620	12:44–50	10
10:11	231, 634, 654, 673, 674, 897, 1102	11:16	298	12:45	229
		11:24	997	12:46	231, 265, 729
10:14	231, 897	11:25	231, 307, 729	12:47	1083 fn. 24
10:14–16	839	11:26	729	12:48	997, 1083 fn. 24
10:15	634, 654, 673, 674, 1102	11:27	227, 265, 303	12:49	629
		11:33	546	12:49–50	624
10:16	624, 810 fn. 13, 1047	11:35	546, 1102	13–17	963
10:17	612	11:36	547	13:1	1102
10:18	234, 245, 612, 629, 631, 642	11:38	546	13:2	660
		11:45	729	13:3	576
10:22–29	229	11:45–48	1099	13:4–5	1034
10:24–25	558	11:47	546, 1102	13:8	1046
10:24–39	218	11:48	729	13:8–9	815

13:15	778, 920 fn. 19	15:24	557	17:21–23	738
13:18	521	15:26	209, 237, 313 (3),	17:24	175, 230, 678
13:19	231, 232		314 (2), 332 (2),	18:5–8	231, 232
13:20	845		332 fn. 22, 333 (3),	18:9	46
13:21	577		335 (3), 336, 717	18:17	546, 1102
13:27	660	16:5	1047	18:28	965
13:33	576, 578	16:5–15	209, 237	18:29	546, 1102
14:1	233, 729	16:7	313 (2), 314, 326,	18:32	46
14:2	576		332 fn. 22, 336	18:33–38	542
14:5	298	16:7–10	576	18:36–37	624, 867
14:6	72, 220, 231, 307,	16:8–11	314, 1083 fn. 24	18:37	231, 265
	581, 668, 872, 1088	16:9	729	18:38	629
14:9	229, 558	16:10	578	19:2	547, 1102
14:10	324	16:11	659, 662	19:3	547, 1102
14:10–11	558	16:12–14	47	19:4–6	629
14:11	232, 324, 558, 728	16:12–15	10, 11, 61, 89, 624	19:5	546, 1102
14:12	413 fn.. 29, 729	16:13	43, 313, 314	19:7	218, 229
14:13	218, 232, 629	16:13–14	314 (3)	19:11	307, 365, 708 fn. 7
14:13–14	974	16:13–15	332 fn. 22, 863	19:23	708 fn. 7
14:14	233	16:23–26	974	19:24	521, 1046
14:15	777	16:27	333, 548	19:25	548
14:16	313 (2), 314	16:28	231, 265, 335 (2), 548	19:28	521
14:16–26	209, 237	16:30	288, 303, 619	19:31–33	568
14:17	313, 453	17	364, 971	19:34	547, 1102
14:18	313	17:1	218, 230, 612, 1102	19:36	965
14:20	324	17:2	364, 400, 403, 579,	19:36–37	521, 1046
14:23	167, 229, 738, 852		678, 684, 862	19:37	312, 530, 548
14:25–26	11, 89	17:3	201, 306, 307	20:1–18	569 fn. 35, 813
14:26	47, 61, 313 (2), 314 (3),	17:3–4	306	20:1–29	578
	332 (2), 336, 863	17:3–8	10	20:3–9	569
14:28	228 (2), 576, 598	17:4	10, 344, 612	20:5–7	569
14:30	578, 659	17:5	230, 1047	20:5–8	566
15:1	231, 307	17:6	10, 344, 364, 678	20:6–7	567
15:1–8	738	17:6–24	624	20:9	521
15:4	737	17:8	10, 333	20:17	576, 619
15:4–5	453	17:9	364, 677, 678, 696	20:19	567, 577
15:5	146, 231, 810 fn. 13	17:12	364, 687	20:19ff.	575
15:6	785, 1076, 1083 fn. 24	17:13	547, 1047	20:20	305, 547, 1102
15:7	974	17:15–19	842	20:20–28	570
15:13	673	17:17	71, 768, 778, 780	20:21	863
15:14	777	17:20	11, 729, 845	20:22	332, 332 fn. 22, 336,
15:16	365, 974	17:20–23	839		821 fn. 36, 826
15:22–25	1083 fn. 24	17:21	324 (2)	20:22–23	822

20:23	821 fn. 36 (3), 863, 890	1:16	7 fn. 14	2:38–39		881
		1:22	846, 1113	2:39		941
20:25	1099	1:24	233	2:41		921
20:26	563 fn. 31, 577	2	284, 764, 765, 813, 951	2:42	780, 826, 845, 956
20:26–29	570	2:1–4	941	2:44–45		826
20:27	147, 547, 1099, 1102	2:2	821 fn. 36	2:46		780
20:28	159, 288, 297, 303, 305, 307, 312, 625, 1099 (2)	2:4	821 fn. 36	2:46–47		826
		2:5	1001, 1091	2:47	825 (2), 826
20:29	1099	2:5–6	525	3		826
20:30	85	2:11	1001	3:6		1113
20:20–31	11	2:12	285	3:12–13		1113
20:31	214, 227, 298, 303	2:14	525	3:16		1113
21	562	2:16	285	3:17–18		522
21:1–14	279, 554	2:16–21	285, 1003 fn. 37	3:19	723, 951 (2), 1091
21:1–22	570 578	2:17	288, 314, 332, 686 (2), 934, 997	3:20–21		1045
21:9–14	547, 1102			3:21	576, 1043 fn. 101
21:12	305	2:17–18	932 fn. 39	3:22		623
21:15–19	793	2:17–21	522, 1011	3:22–24		522
21:16	813	2:21	288	3:24		6, 537
21:18–19	1109	2:22	232, 412, 525, 546, 558 fn. 18, 1099	3:25–26		517
21:21–22	815			4:4		826
21:25	61, 85	2:22–36	1011	4:9–10		150, 1113
		2:23	131, 179, 190, 357, 360, 365, 465	4:12	311, 581, 668, 1086 fn. 31, 1088
Acts					
1	813	2:24	286	4:16		1099
1–12	825 (2)	2:24–25	1044	4:23		826
1:1	1113	2:24–31	51	4:24		48
1:2	575	2:25–28	522	4:24–26	7 fn. 14
1:3	575	2:25–31	531	4:24–28		465
1:4–9	570	2:27	579	4:24–30		971
1:5	285 (2), 821 fn. 36, 825, 926, 932 fn. 39, 934	2:29–31	286	4:25		48
		2:31	568	4:25–28	531, 543
		2:33	286, 287, 288, 313, 717, 821 fn. 36, 926, 932 fn. 39, 934 (2), 1044	4:27–28	131, 360
1:8b	863			4:28		365
1:8	285, 287, 311, 525, 821 fn. 36, 825, 826, 827, 880, 934			4:29		314
		2:33–35	576	4:31		969
		2:33–36	579	4:32–37		826
1:9	267, 575	2:34	286, 522	4:36	1108 fn. 4
1:11	267, 575	2:36	286 (2), 525, 579 (2), 826, 1044	5:1–10	826, 1082
1:13	813, 1106 (3), 1108			5:3	314, 660
1:13–15	826	2:37–41	926	5:3–4		313
1:14	549 fn. 8, 1109	2:38	288, 706, 723, 926, 950, 951 (3)	5:11	825 (2)
1:15	825			5:11–14		826

INDEX OF BIBLICAL REFERENCES

5:12	11, 1113	9:7	1116	11:14	942, 1091, 1092		
5:31	679, 1043 fn. 101	9:9	1009	11:15	314, 934		
6:1	826	9:10–17	233	11:17–18	287		
6:1–6	826, 892, 901 fn. 10	9:11	933	11:18	380, 679, 724 (2),		
6:1–7	899	9:15	863		827, 1091		
6:4	887	9:18	926	11:21	365		
7	827	9:20	1118 (2)	11:22	825 (2)		
7:8	937 fn. 50	9:20–22	xxix	11:26	825 (2), 829		
7:9	827	9:22	1095, 1119	11:27–30	1118		
7:23–29	520	9:23	829 fn. 44	11:30	837, 897		
7:25	513 fn. 19	9:26–28	572, 1118	12:1	825 (2)		
7:27–28	827	9:31	314, 825 (3), 829	12:2	1106		
7:31	314, 576, 724	9:42	729	12:5	825 (2)		
7:35	519, 808 fn. 8, 827	10	525, 764, 765,	12:17	624, 827		
7:38	10, 807 fn. 6,		813, 951	12:26	810 fn. 13		
	808 fn. 8, 825	10:1–11:18	827	13–28	828		
7:39–43	827	10:2	1090, 1092	13:1	825 (2), 829		
7:44	532	10:4	965 fn. 106	13:1–2	84		
7:53	832	10:10–16	815	13:1–3	829, 901		
7:55–56	1113	10:13–15	843	13:2	314 (4)		
7:56	576, 1009	10:15	1090	13:10	660		
7:59	233	10:19–20	314	13:24	723		
8	764, 765, 828, 951	10:25	933	13:27–30	523, 537		
8:1	825 (2)	10:25–26	279	13:30–31	572		
8:3	825	10:28–29	1091	13:30–41	1011		
8:12	236, 728	10:34–35	1090, 1092	13:31	578		
8:12–17	926	10:36	579	13:34	48		
8:14	287, 816, 901	10:38	314, 660	13:34–37	51		
8:14–17	287, 1113	10:38–39	559 fn. 18	13:35	48		
8:15–17	314	10:41	61	13:35–37	531		
8:16	926	10:42	581	13:38–39	755, 1091		
8:22	723	10:43	522, 537, 729, 742,	13:39	729, 746		
8:32	309		742 fn. 47, 1091	13:46–48	731		
8:32–35	263, 521	10:44	934	13:48	365, 380, 679		
8:33	255, 263	10:44–45	314	13:50	242		
8:35–38	926	10:44–46	287	14:3	62, 410, 412		
8:36–39	930, 932	10:44–48	926	14:11–15	279		
9	1115, 1116	10:45	827	14:16	5 fn. 7, 676,		
9:1–9	1108	10:47	937 fn. 50		1091 fn. 40		
9:2	810 fn. 13, 1115	10:48	927	14:17	56, 150, 200, 401		
9:3–4	1116	11:1	827	14:23	729, 825 (2),		
9:3–6	1009	11:1–18	816		829 (2), 837,		
9:3–18	1113	11:12	314		897, 907		

[1169]

14:27	365, 825 (2), 829, 901	17:22–34	150	20:32	710, 756, 780
15	524, 813, 816, 817, 828, 837, 901, 903, 1106	17:23	1091 fn. 40	20:35	61, 892
		17:25	131, 399, 414, 401	21:4	57
		17:25–28		21:10–11	57
15:1–16:5	xxx	17:26	357, 360	21:11	314
15:2	897, 907	17:27–28	169	22	1115, 1116
15:3	825 (2), 829 (2)	17:28	1109 fn. 6	22:3	1117, 1127
15:4	825 (2), 829	17:30	676, 684, 723, 735, 1091 fn. 40	22:4	810 fn. 13, 1028 fn. 76 (2)
15:13–17	1009				
15:13–18	540	17:30–31	713	22:5	897, 1115
15:13–21	1106	17:31	546, 578, 581, 1083 fn. 24	22:6–7	1116
15:15	524			22:6–11	1009
15:16	810 fn. 13	18:8	728, 926, 927	22:6–16	1113
15:16–17	527	18:9–10	624	22:8	250
15:18	351 fn. 5	18:10	365	22:9	1116 (2)
15:22	825 (3)	18:22	825 (2), 827	22:10	863
15:22–31	830	18:27	365, 380, 679, 732	22:14	1116
15:23	901	18:28	xxix, 150, 1095	22:15	863
15:28	314	19	764, 765, 951	22:16	922, 926, 950, 952 (2)
15:41	825 (2), 829	19:1–7	926	22:19	729
16:4	830, 901	19:4	529, 723, 729, 924 fn. 26, 990	23:6–8	565
16:5	825 (2), 829			24:14	726, 728, 810 fn. 13
16:6–7	314	19:5	927	24:15	1019 (2), 1034 fn. 84
16:6–8	676	19:6	934	24:22	810 fn. 13
16:7	313	19:8	xxix, 236	24:23	826
16:13–15	926	19:9	810 fn. 13	24:25	1083 fn. 24
16:14	365, 380, 679, 721, 731, 921	19:23	810 fn. 13	26	1115, 1116
		19:27	563	26:4	686
16:14–15	881	20:7	776	26:4–5	1117
16:15	921, 942 (2)	20:17	825 (2), 829, 837, 897 (2), 907 (2)	26:5	1127
16:30	921			26:6–7	523
16:30–34	926	20:18	837	26:10	1115
16:31	703, 706, 707, 729, 881, 921, 942	20:24	501	26:12	1115
		20:20–21	xxix	26:12–18	1113
16:31–34	942	20:21	706, 723	26:13–14	1116 (2)
16:32	933, 942	20:24	863	26:14	1131
16:33	921, 933, 942	20:27	917	26:16	1116
16:34	728, 942	20:28	159, 312, 626, 656, 657, 673, 825 (3), 830, 831, 889, 897, 898, 898 fn. 6, 1099	26:16–18	863
16:35	933			26:18	660, 710 (2), 756, 757
17:2	150			26:19	1116
17:2–3	xxix, 523, 1095			26:20	723
17:11	917	20:28–30	891	26:22–23	524, 537
17:17	xxix	20:28–31a	853	26:23	578

INDEX OF BIBLICAL REFERENCES

27	787, 788	1:18–32	379	2:15	5, 452, 772
27:15	39	1:18–2:16	57 fn. 3	2:16	638
27:22	787	1:18–3:20	638	2:17–24	1031
27:24	787	1:19–20	143, 1088	2:17–29	1031
27:25	728	1:19–21	397 fn.13	2:21	776
27:31	787	1:20	5, 56, 57, 132 fn. 4,	2:22	776 (2)
27:34	787		137 fn. 13, 143, 153, 192,	2:25–29	937 fn. 50, 1031
27:44	787		397, 401, 487, 490	2:26–29	951
28:15	1022	1:20–21	143, 150, 452	2:28–29	1025
28:23	236	1:20–22	166	3–8	366
28:25–27	313	1:21	56, 57 fn. 3, 132 fn. 4,	3:1–2	676
28:20	524		143 fn. 26, 1088	3:2	10, 59 fn 8, 62
28:23	524	1:21–23	645	3:4	71, 146, 201, 754
28:30	814	1:21–30	776	3:5	xxx, 637, 638
28:31	236	1:21–32	143 fn. 26, 545	3:5–6	197
		1:23	153, 1088	3:8	748
Romans		1:24	638	3:9	xxx
1	397	1:25	131, 153, 247, 1088	3:9–10	1088
1:1	755	1:26	638, 772	3:9–18	456
1:1–4	31	1:27	772	3:9–20	1089
1:2	10	1:28	153, 638	3:9–23	451
1:2–3	523	1:29	776 (2)	3:10–18	356, 379, 380
1:3	239 (2), 240, 241,	1:29–31	772	3:19	689, 696, 772, 1088
	244, 245, 268, 612	1:29–32	451	3:19–20	744
1:3–4	xxx, 237, 238 (2),	1:30	776	3:20	733, 1131
	243, 245 (2), 267 (2),	1:32	56, 57 fn. 3, 132 fn. 4,	3:20–22	733
	269, 878		143, 452, 638, 772 (2),	3:21	199, 755
1:4	245, 578, 1009, 1099		1083 fn. 24, 1088	3:21–22	746, 755
1:5	431	2:2	1083 fn. 24	3:21–31	638
1:7	237, 713	2:3	1083 fn. 24	3:22	707, 745
1:8	696, 1001	2:4	291, 1046	3:22a	688
1:9	31, 755	2:5	637, 638, 1083 fn. 24	3:22b-23	688
1:11–13	816	2:5–6	197	3:22–24	685 (2), 687
1:16	192, 755	2:5–10	750	3:23	166, 356, 380, 685,
1:16–17	31, 755	2:6	1021		687, 688 (4), 1087
1:17	199, 707, 740,	2:7	785, 1020, 1037	3:23ff.	755
	745, 746, 755	2:8	637, 638	3:24	199, 688 (9)
1:18	57 fn. 3, 132 fn. 4,	2:8–9	1019, 1078	3:24ff.	755
	143, 153, 397 fn. 13,	2:10	1020	3:24–25	746
	637, 638 (2)	2:12	1078, 1089	3:24–27	655
1:18–23	401	2:14–15	56, 57 fn. 3, 132 fn. 4,	3:25	626, 635, 637, 638,
1:18–25	868		143, 153, 1088		641 (2), 657, 680,
1:18–28	451	2:14ff.	772		687, 688, 745

[1171]

3:25–26	199, 688, 742	5:5	934	5:21	434, 436
3:26	624, 688, 707	5:6	628, 634	6	1130
3:27	688, 689, 754	5:6–8	680	6–7	748, 769
3:27–28	755	5:8	628, 634, 641, 646, 666	6:1	xxx, 1038
3:28	707, 733, 745, 754			6:1–10	658
3:29–30	755	5:8b-10	783	6:1–14	739, 748, 757, 771
3:30	707, 745 (2)	5:9	626, 631, 637, 647, 746, 755, 797, 1011	6:2	756
3:31	772, 1038			6:2–4	678
4:1	xxx	5:9–10	698, 699	6:2–6	934
4:1ff.	755	5:10	627, 646, 646 fn. 38, 647 (3), 738, 797, 1037	6:2–11	716
4:2	733			6:3	780, 927, 928
4:1–3	528			6:3–4	922, 923, 927, 927 fn. 31, 1015, 1016
4:3	728, 745	5:10–11	643, 646, 680		
4:5	729, 733, 742, 742 fn. 45, 742 fn. 46, 745, 754	5:11	651	6:3–6	925, 930
		5:12	265, 424, 434 (6), 435 (2), 437, 688, 1028	6:4	166, 245, 434, 578, 1015
4:6–7	528, 742, 742 fn. 47	5:12–14	439	6:5	578, 737
4:3–8	523	5:12–19	118, 262, 263, 375, 377, 379, 428, 430, 434 (2), 440 fn. 29, 500, 550, 738, 1082	6:5–11	678
4:5–8	755			6:6	520, 737, 756
4:6–8	752			6:9	578
4:9	745			6:10–14	739
4:9–10	921	5:13–14	434, 435	6:11	739, 780
4:11	806, 922 fn. 24, 937 fn. 50, 952	5:13–17	434	6:12	1130
		5:14	434, 436, 437	6:13	759
4:11–12	517	5:15	434, 435, 436	6:14	678, 759, 1020, 1129, 1130
4:13	513 fn. 19, 514 fn.	5:15–17	434		
4:14	259, 733	5:16	435, 436, 437, 744, 1083 fn. 24	6:15	xxx, 771, 1038
4:15	637			6:16	291
4:16	735 (2), 745, 810 fn. 13	5:16ff.	755	6:17	xxx, 50, 380, 878, 1013, 1128
4:17	719	5:17	435, 1033		
4:17–23	536	5:17–19	746, 755	6:17–22	520, 527, 678
4:22	745	5:18	434 (4), 435 (2), 435 fn. 24 (2), 436, 437, 477, 629, 685 (2), 1083 fn. 24	6:18	756, 810 fn. 13, 1013, 1128
4:23	745			6:19	380, 759
4:23ff.	755			6:20	380, 1128
4:23–24	52			6:21	1078
4:24	245, 729, 742	5:18a	685, 689	6:21–22	658
4:25	578, 1011	5:18b	689	6:22	810 fn. 13, 1013, 1128 (2)
5	437, 438 (2), 439, 449	5:18–19	439, 440		
5:1	650, 707, 742, 742 fn. 48, 745, 746, 755, 1011	5:19	434, 435 (2), 435 fn. 24, 436, 629, 689, 742, 742 fn. 48	6:23	1078, 1087
				7	1130 (4), 1131 (2)
5:1–2	646	5:19b	1088	7:1–6	755
5:2	745, 778	5:20	1131	7:4	578, 625

INDEX OF BIBLICAL REFERENCES

7:4–5	739	8:7–9	147	8:32	238 (2), 239 (2), 402, 477, 634, 635, 679, 680, 685 (2), 689 (3)
7:4–6	520, 658 (2), 756	8:9	313 (2), 336, 1128 (2)		
7:5	1128, 1131	8:9–10	313, 717		
7:6	1128	8:9–11	314	8:32–34	612, 673, 677
7:7	xxx, 773, 1131	8:10	1038	8:33	678, 689, 745, 810 fn. 13
7:7–8	776	8:10ff.	1017		
7:7–13	1128	8:11	245, 313, 314 (2), 578, 1038, 1128	8:33–34	744, 746
7:7–25	1127			8:34	576, 578, 579, 581, 689, 971
7:9	1129	8:13	769		
7:11	1132	8:13–14	779	8:35–36	784
7:12	772, 1128	8:14	810 fn. 13	8:35–39	624, 689, 780
7:13	773, 1132 (2)	8:15	313, 359, 759	8:37	784
7:14	772, 1128 (4)	8:15–16	314, 760, 791–92	8:38	791
7:14–25	380, 781 fn. 86, 1127 (2), 1128 (2), 1130, 1132	8:16	759	8:38–39	698, 699
		8:16–17	763	9	359, 365, 367, 501
		8:17	738, 762, 799, 832	9–11	367 fn. 22
7:16	772	8:18	377, 799	9:1–5	840 fn. 6
7:17	1128, 1131	8:19	359	9:3	755 fn. 64
7:19	1129	8:19–23	398, 487, 490, 492, 500, 513 fn. 19, 1019, 1036	9:4	519, 676, 759
7:20	1128, 1131			9:4–5	676, 806, 848 fn. 14
7:22	1129			9:5	109, 159, 237, 239, 241 (2), 243 (3), 245, 246, 248 (2), 248 fn. 64, 249 (2), 250, 268, 291 (2), 312, 580, 625, 1030, 1099
7:23	1129	8:20–22	448		
7:23–25	520	8:21	759		
7:24	651, 1129	8:23	655, 759, 760, 760 fn. 71, 798 (2), 800, 1019		
7:25a	1129				
7:25b	1129 (2)				
7:25	1130 (2)	8:26–27	314, 974		
8:1	657, 746	8:28	109, 200, 357, 403, 464, 624, 705 (2), 784, 791	9:5a	247
8:1–4	1132			9:5b	247
8:1–11	209	8:28–29	377, 713, 780, 912	9:6	366, 824
8:2	1129	8:28–30	678, 692	9:6–8	806
8:2–4	520	8:28–39	365, 370	9:6–9	1025
8:3	237, 238, 238, 239 (2), 241, 428, 634, 680, 1107	8:29	175, 251 (2), 357, 377, 414, 428, 466, 466 fn. 7, 641, 705 (4), 711, 714 (2), 762, 778, 798, 799 (2), 800	9:7–9	366
				9:8	759
				9:10–24	360 fn. 20
8:4a	1128			9:11	371, 483 fn. 38
8:4b	1128			9:11–12	371
8:4	771, 1128	8:29–30	465, 704 (2), 710	9:11–13	367, 368, 369, 370 (2), 464, 466, 486 (2)
8:4–13	773	8:30	689, 698, 699, 706, 714, 784		
8:6	1128				
8:7	354, 375, 380, 456, 679, 714, 773, 1088	8:30–39	784	9:11–16	690
		8:31	xxx	9:11–23	131, 678, 692
8:7–8	453	8:31–39	784	9:12	359, 368, 465

[1173]

9:13	367	10:13–15	1089	11:28b	1024 fn. 68
9:14	xxx, 369, 370	10:14	729	11:29	698, 699, 713,
9:14–18	485	10:14–17	147		714, 792
9:15	369, 485	10:16	728	11:30	434
9:15–18	369 (2), 485	10:17	727	11:30–31	691, 1028
9:16	190, 369, 380	10:17–18	1001	11:31	1027, 1029 fn. 77, 1030
9:17	10, 48, 369, 378,	11	1025, 1027 fn. 74	11:32	365, 477, 685 (2),
	485, 520, 520	11:1	xxx		690 (2), 691, 1029
9:17–18	359	11:2a	1025	11:32–36	377, 379
9:18	359 fn. 19, 369, 486	11:4–10	690	11:33	100, 101
9:18–24	365	11:5	xxx, 368, 465,	11:33–34	129
9:19	369		1025 fn. 69	11:33–36	185
9:19–24	485	11:5–6	754	11:36	146, 247, 357,
9:20	146	11:5–7	810 fn. 13		371, 1107
9:20–23	369 (2)	11:5–10	360, 371	12	773, 775
9:20–24	486, 701 fn. 36	11:6	735, 1116 fn. 4	12:1	868
9:21	359	11:6–7	678, 679, 692	12:1–2	755, 773
9:22	367 fn. 22 (2), 369,	11:7	xxx, 530	12:1–3	779
	485, 637, 1078	11:8	1025	12:2	769, 997, 1010, 1014
9:22–23	291, 495 fn. 54, 798	11:11	1030, 1032	12:3	50
9:23	369, 378, 485	11:12	696, 1025, 1026 (2),	12:4–5	830
9:24–25	540		1027 (3), 1029,	12:6	50
9:25–32	541		1030, 1032	12:6–7	887
9:27	530, 806, 810 fn. 13	11:13–24	810 fn. 13	12:9–21	779
9:27–29	1025 fn. 69	11:14	1030	12:19	637
9:29	1071 fn. 10	11:15	1025, 1026, 1027 (3),	13:1–5	452
9:32–33	311		1029, 1032	13:1–7	865
9:30	xxx, 483 fn. 38, 745	11:16–24	526, 824	13:7–14	779
9:30–31	679	11:17–24	1028	13:8–10	775
9:31–32	1025, 1129	11:18	1032	13:8–19	776
9:33	729	11:22–23	291	13:9	773, 776 (5)
10:3	746, 1010 fn. 44, 1025	11:23	1025	13:9–10	773
10:4	658, 733, 754, 1010 fn. 44	11:23–24	1033	13:10	773
10:5	439	11:24	1025	13:11	797, 1015
10:6	745	11:25	1025 fn. 69, 1027 (2),	14	698
10:8ff.	755		1028 (2), 1030	14:4	699
10:9	xxx, 727, 878	11:25–26	1025, 1028	14:7–9	1038
10:9–13	237, 288	11:26	527, 651, 1025, 1026,	14:8	699
10:11	729		1028, 1029 (2), 1030	14:9	581
10:12	579	11:26–32	1026	14:10	312, 1020,
10:12–13	268	11:28	527, 646 fn. 38, 678,		1083 fn. 24
10:13	311, 973, 1099		692, 737 fn. 41,	14:10–12	1078
10:13–14	102		806, 1025, 1032	14:11	624

INDEX OF BIBLICAL REFERENCES

14:12	376, 1020	1:13	925	3:1–9	840		
14:13	700	1:13–17	927 (2)	3:5–7	884		
14:15	680, 787	1:14	926	3:8–9	1021		
14:15a	699	1:15	925	3:9	810 fn. 13 (2)		
14:15b	685, 698 (2), 699	1:16	926, 942	3:11	820		
14:17	539, 997, 1033, 1037	1:17	259, 927 fn. 31, 951	3:11–15	1021		
15:4	34 fn. 10, 52, 518	1:18	625, 652, 699, 796	3:12–15	1020		
15:5–6	840, 868	1:18–25	656	3:13	750		
15:8	1107	1:19–21	545	3:15	698, 699, 785, 795 fn. 98, 797		
15:8–9	517, 623	1:20	32, 1010				
15:13	314	1:20–21	57 fn 4	3:16	810 fn. 13		
15:14	762, 889	1:21	57, 101, 149, 625, 916	3:16–17	842		
15:16	314, 887, 897 fn. 2			3:17	1078		
15:18–19	413	1:23	625	3:21–23	662		
15:19	313	1:23–28	371	3:22	797		
15:20	816	1:24	625 (2)	4:1	918 fn. 11 (2)		
15:24	829	1:26–30	713	4:5	750, 1021		
15:30	314	1:26–31	883	4:7	414, 679		
15:30–31	1107	1:30	371, 656, 658, 884	4:8	1017		
16:1	830, 900 fn. 9	1:31	380	4:9	1107		
16:4	830	2:1–5	884	4:17	830		
16:5	830	2:2	625	5:1–5	837, 853, 890		
16:16	830, 831	2:4–5	150	5:4–5	624		
16:17	44, 890, 891	2:6–8	1010	5:7	520, 527, 533, 625, 632, 679, 922, 964		
16:17–18a	853	2:6–13	32				
16:17–18	837	2:6–16	147 fn. 35 (2)	5:9	66 (2)		
16:20	440 fn. 29, 662	2:7	32, 377	5:13	853, 1083 fn. 24		
16:23	830	2:7–8	1012	6:2	1022		
16:25–26	1012	2:8	224, 580, 625	6:6	732		
16:26	10, 431 fn. 19	2:9	32	6:8	732		
16:27	185	2:10–11	313, 314	6:9	776 (2)		
		2:10a	32	6:9–10	236, 775		
1 Corinthians		2:11	153, 322	6:10	776 (2)		
1	927	2:11b	32	6:14	1038		
1:2	237, 710, 713, 756, 829, 830, 831	2:12	32 (2)	6:11	314, 710, 746, 756, 926, 1013		
		2:12b	32s				
1:2a	831	2:12–14	10	6:15	962		
1:2d	831	2:13	10, 21, 32 (2), 47	6:19–20	656		
1:5	737	2:14	32, 57, 147, 147 fn. 35, 354, 379, 380, 454, 679	6:20	657, 700		
1:8–9	698, 699, 713, 785			7	34		
1:9	706, 707, 713, 714			7:14	881, 942		
1:10	890	2:14–15	81, 148 fn. 35	7:15	713		
1:10–13	840	2:15	148 fn. 35	7:17	830 (2)		

[1175]

7:19	774 (2)	11:16	831	15:2	796
7:22	714	11:18	728, 890	15:3	628, 634, 680
7:23	652, 656, 657, 700	11:18–19	841 fn. 7	15:3–4	*xxx*, 523, 878
7:40	34	11:19	841 fn. 7, 891	15:3–5	269, 571
8	698	11:20	805 fn. 1, 956	15:3b–5	572
8:3	466	11:22	830, 831	15:3–7	572 fn. 36
8:6	357	11:23–24	959 fn. 89	15:4	565, 568, 578
8:9	699, 700	11:23–25	922	15:5	288, 570 (2), 572,
8:11	634, 680, 685,	11:23–30	853		813, 1033, 1034
	698 (2), 699, 787	11:23–32	921	15:5–7	1118
8:12	699	11:24	634, 956 (3), 965	15:6	284, 825, 1034
8:13	700	11:24–25	780	15:7	272, 570 (2), 572,
9:1	1113 (2)	11:25	957 (3)		1033, 1034, 1106
9:5	815	11:26	922, 964, 965 (2),	15:5–8	576
9:8–12	775		1028 fn. 76 (2)	15:8	1113 (2)
9:9–10	52	11:27	958	15:9	831
9:15	259	11:28	958	15:11	43, 846, 1036
9:16	501	11:29	958	15:12–20	578
9:20–21	775	11:30	34	15:17	566 fn. 33
9:21	1020	12:1–11	314	15:20–26	1033
9:27	785	12:3	*xxx*, 314, 354, 454, 878	15:21–23	1011
10:1–2	943	12:3–6	209	15:22	430, 685, 689,
10:1–11	518	12:4–6	313		738, 738
10:2	925, 927 (3)	12:11	314	15:23	993 fn. 25, 1022,
10:2–4	520	12:12–13	840		1033 (2), 1034
10:4	820, 822	12:12–27	830	15:23–25	1011
10:6	52	12:13	765, 925, 926,	15:24	1033 (2), 1034 (3),
10:11	52, 997		927, 928, 934		1035 (2), 1036
10:12	786	12:25	890	15:24–26	1035
10:14–17	852	12:27	810 fn. 13	15:24–28	581, 662
10:16	956 (2), 966	12:28	624, 830	15:25	624, 1028 fn. 76 (2),
10:16–17	923, 956	13:13	38		1033, 1034
10:17	961	14:12	888	15:25–26	1011
10:20	660	14:26	888	15:25–27	861, 1019
10:21	852, 956	14:29	57	15:26	236, 1035
10:22	1038	14:33	830 (2), 831, 854, 888	15:27	686 (2)
10:31	142, 144, 868	14:33b–36	900 fn. 10	15:28	228, 357, 414,
10:32	830, 831	14:34	775		580 fn. 51, 1019,
11:2	47	14:37	35		1070, 1083
11:8	424, 775	14:37–38	47	15:29	927, 928, 928 fn. 32
11:9	775	14:40	854, 888	15:33	1109 fn. 6
11:10	832 fn. 46	15	1116	15:42ff.	1037
11:14	772	15:1–2	785	15:42–43	1023

[1176]

INDEX OF BIBLICAL REFERENCES

15:44	421	3:11	1107	6:2	1013
15:45	243, 439, 506 fn.	3:18	428, 769, 778, 779	6:6	313
15:45–49	262, 428, 414	4:3	699	6:14–17	841 fn. 7
15:47	506 fn.	4:4	250, 258, 271, 427,	6:14–18	891
15:47–49	224		428, 659, 1010, 1015	6:14–7:1	842
15:48–49	738	4:6	211, 251, 1015	6:15	659
15:50	236, 1015	4:7	893	6:16	810 fn. 13
15:50ff.	236	4:11	1038	6:18	759
15:51–54	797, 1019	4:14	1038, 1039	7:1	768, 779
15:51–55	1034	4:16–18	1017	7:10	724 (2)
15:52	997	4:17	377, 799, 1037	8:1	830
15:54	1035	5:1	1018 (2)	8:1–4	830
15:55	1035	5:1ff.	1038	8:9	237, 552, 580, 634
15:55–56	662	5:1–10	423, 1017	8:18	830
15:56–58	1023	5:2	1018	9	892
16:1	830	5:2–4	1018 (2)	9:3	259
16:1–2	892	5:3	1018, 1018 fn. 61	10:3–4	867
16:1–3	830	5:4	1015	10:5	1014
16:2	776	5:4–5	1019	10:8	11, 863, 890
16:15	927	5:5	762, 763, 764, 1011	10:10	34
16:16	53	5:6	1018 (2)	10:16	816
16:19	830 (2)	5:7	69	11:3	118, 440 fn. 29
16:22	269, 728 fn. 30,	5:8	797, 1018 (4)	11:4	846
	755 fn. 64,	5:10	750, 1019, 1020,	11:8	830
	1077, 1078		1021, 1079,	11:9	893
			1083 fn. 24	11:14	660
2 Corinthians		5:14–15	477, 658, 678,	11:23–33	377
1:1	829, 830, 831, 1107		680, 685 (2), 691 (3),	11:28	830
1:3	247 (2)		748, 757	11:31	247, 248
1:3–4	201	5:15	520, 628, 634,	11:32–33	829 fn. 44, 1118
1:18	43		678, 680, 648	12:4	1038
1:20	192	5:17	520, 719, 810 fn. 13,	12:7	660
1:21–22	763		1013, 1015, 1016	12:7–10	377
1:22	314, 764, 1011	5:17–21	643, 647	12:8	233
2:4	66	5:18	647 (2), 698, 887	12:8–9	237, 975
2:5–10	837	5:18–20	680 (2)	12:9	739
2:14	663	5:18–21	810 fn. 13	12:9–10	624
2:15	796	5:19	477, 647 (4), 651,	12:12	11, 62, 413, 846
2:15–16	150, 360 fn. 20		685, 696, 698 (3)	12:13	830
2:16	823 (2), 1015	5:20	647, 648, 878	12:13–13:13	846
3:2–3	810 fn. 13	5:21	629, 634, 647, 680,	13:5	781, 792, 950, 958
3:3	313		698, 742, 746,	13:10	11, 864, 890
3:6	406, 525		753, 753 fn. 61	13:14	209, 313

[1177]

Galatians

1	1108	2:11	33	4:4	237, 238, 239, 240,
1:1	578, 1113	2:11–14	815, 854		545, 548, 629, 1013
1:2	829	2:11–21	755	4:4–5	656, 657
1:3	237	2:12	827	4:4–6	209, 314, 760
1:4	634, 680, 996, 997,	2:13	680	4:5	759
	1010, 1011, 1014 (3)	2:15ff.	755	4:6	313, 332 fn. 22, 792
1:5	247	2:16	707, 729, 733,	4:6–7	759
1:6	716		745 (2), 754,	4:7	832
1:6–9	755, 845		1011, 1031	4:21–31	366
1:8–9	31, 754,	2:17	746	4:21–5:1	1031
	755 fn. 64, 846, 852	2:20	634, 642, 673, 680	4:25	1025 (2), 1107
1:9	1077	2:20–21	733	4:26	1107
1:11–12	31, 863	2:21	754	4:27	540
1:11–2:21	31	3:1–5	748	4:29	366, 1025
1:12	31, 1108, 1113, 1119	3:1–14	755	5	1130
1:13	831	3:6	728, 745	5:1	658
1:13–14	31, 1117	3:8	48, 517, 540, 740, 745	5:1–4	755
1:13–2:10	1117	3:8–9	623	5:2	754
1:14	1127	3:9	517	5:2–4	1031
1:15	31, 714	3:10	1031	5:3	754
1:15–16	43	3:10–11	754	5:3–4	1031
1:15–17	1118	3:11	733, 745	5:4	733, 735, 754
1:16	829, 1116	3:12	439	5:6	749, 773, 774
1:16–2:10	31	3:13	634, 656,	5:13	713, 773
1:17	828, 829 fn. 44 (2)		657 (2), 680 (2)	5:13–16	779
1:18–19	572, 1118	3:13–14	517, 623, 679	5:16–18	314, 1130
1:19	288, 827, 1106	3:16	517, 536	5:17	781, 1130 (2)
1:20	1118	3:16–17	517	5:19–20	841 fn. 7
1:21	828, 830	3:19	832, 1107	5:19–21	356
1:22	830, 1118	3:21	666	5:20	891
1:23	50, 1119	3:22	451	5:22	766
2	1108 (2)	3:23	50, 658	5:22–23	314
2:1	1118	3:24	707, 745, 771	5:24	1130
2:1–9	288	3:24–25	771	5:26	776
2:2	269, 1118	3:25	50	6:1	854, 890 (2)
2:6	816	3:26	658, 754, 759	6:7	1083 fn. 24
2:6–9	269	3:26–27	927	6:7–9	750
2:7–8	815	3:27	780, 927 (2), 935	6:8	1015
2:8	1118	3:27–28	925	6:10	50, 892
2:9	271, 284, 813,	3:28	658, 840, 844	6:12–16	526, 755
	816, 827,	3:29	810 fn. 13	6:14	625
	1106 (2)	4:1–2	760	6:15	719, 1031
		4:2–5	658	6:15–16	810 fn. 13

INDEX OF BIBLICAL REFERENCES

6:16	824	1:22	830, 831 (2)	2:22	314
		1:22a	579	3:1–4	11
Ephesians		1:22–23	579	3:2–6	540, (2), 541
1	501	1:23	810 fn. 13, 831, 962	3:2–9	540
1:1	757, 810 fn. 13, 943	2:1	380, 714	3:3–5	1013
1:2	760	2:1–3	356, 379, 451, 456	3:3–6	491
1:3	247 (2), 679, 716, 736, 760, 911	2:1–4	709	3:3–12	508
		2:1–7	658	3:5	10, 43
1:3–4	379, 716, 731	2:2	445, 997	3:5–6	541
1:3–14	131, 209, 371, 495, 641	2:3	637, 684 fn. 16, 737, 1088	3:6	764
1:4	175, 177, 466, 736, 800			3:8	501
1:4–5	466, 678, 692, 705, 705 fn. 3, 760	2:4	201	3:9	118, 491 (2), 540 (2), 541, 918
		2:4–6	1063		
1:4–11	360 fn. 20	2:5	716, 719, 1015, 1129	3:9–10	343, 398, 414, 464, 487 (2), 490
1:5	759, 761, 800	2:6	576, 737, 1015, 1016, 1033		
1:6	166 (2), 344, 346, 377, 414, 490 fn. 51, 778, 868			3:9–11	490
		2:7	377, 490 fn. 51, 997 (2)	3:10	465, 491, 831
		2:8	796	3:11	345, 357, 379, 462, 463, 464, 641, 683
1:6–7	737	2:8–9	380, 466 fn. 8, 679, 732, 732 fn. 35	3:13	43
1:7	626, 655, 656, 658, 680, 716	2:10	716, 719, 737, 1020, 1020 fn. 63	3:14	760
				3:14–15	761
1:8–9	407	2:11	526, 937 fn. 50	3:16	314
1:9	463, 467, 918	2:11–13	526	3:20	974
1:9–10	414, 540, 1012	2:12	676, 737	3:21	247, 831
1:10	377, 1019, 1070, 1083	2:12–13	626, 824	4:1	713
1:11	190, 356, 374, 379, 464, 467, 678, 692	2:14	241, 649	4:3–6	841
		2:14–16	824, 841	4:4	713, 830, 831
1:12	166 (2), 344, 346, 377, 414, 490 fn. 51, 778, 868	2:14–17	643, 648	4:4–6	209, 313, 764
		2:15	649 (3), 1013	4:4–5	927 fn. 31
1:13	313, 737, 762, 763	2:16	627, 645, 648, 649, 680, 831	4:5	50, 927, 929
1:13–14	314, 763			4:6	760
1:14	166 (2), 344, 346, 377, 414, 490 fn. 51, 655, 764, 778, 868, 1011	2:17	524	4:7–8	579
		2:17–18	649	4:8	265, 864
		2:18	209, 313, 760, 911	4:8–9	237
1:17	313, 760, 911	2:18–19	761	4:8–10	576, 675
1:17–18	714	2:19	526, 761, 810 fn. 13 (2), 1107	4:10	579 (2)
1:19	192			4:10–11	864
1:19–20	192, 245	2:19–22	738	4:10–12	865
1:20	578	2:20	61, 84, 284, 821 fn. 35, 822, 845	4:11	579, 846 fn. 11, 880
1:20–22	576			4:11–12	624
1:20–23	865	2:20–21	823	4:11–13	624
1:21	267, 579	2:21–22	810 fn. 13	4:11–16	769

[1179]

4:12	831	6:2	775	2:10	237, 312
4:13	50	6:2–3	774, 776	2:10–11a	579
4:14	1038	6:4	881	2:10–11	240, 262,
4:15–16	738, 888, 962	6:11	660		1019, 1070, 1083
4:16	831	6:11–18a	867	2:11	414, 800
4:17–18	147, 148, 379,	6:12	659, 660 (2)	2:12	779, 993 fn. 25
4:17–19	356, 452, 456	6:12–13	660	2:12–13	752
4:17–32	779	6:13–20	969	2:13	190, 466 fn. 8, 779
4:18	1088	6:16	659	2:15	759
4:21	524	6:17	314, 663	2:20–21	815
4:21–24	429	6:18	969	3:3	526, 937 fn. 50
4:24	770, 843	6:19–20	1107	3:3–11	810 fn. 13
4:25	775, 776	6:23	760	3:4–6	1117, 1127
4:28	775, 776, 892			3:8–9	754, 755
4:30	183, 314 (2), 656,	**Philippians**		3:9	707, 733, 745 (2),
	762, 763, 1011	1:1	757, 837, 897		746 (2), 1079
4:32	656, 770	1:6	698, 785	3:10–14	1119
5:1	759, 760	1:9	769	3:10–17	779
5:1–2	762	1:11	778	3:12	1116
5:2	632, 634, 642, 656, 1107	1:19	313	3:13–14	711, 769
5:3	775, 776	1:21	800	3:14	713
5:5	775, 776 (2)	1:21–23	797 (2), 1017	3:20	578, 1016
5:6	637, 854	1:21–24	423	3:20–21	1022
5:8	760	1:22ff.	1038	3:21	761, 798, 1019
5:8–11	762	1:23	800, 1017	4:3	584
5:11	854	1:26	993 fn. 25	4:5	1039
5:18–21	765	1:28	732, 884	4:6	780, 969
5:19–21	766	1:29	380, 679, 729, 732	4:4–9	779
5:20	760	2:2	43, 841	4:20	2
5:22–23	738	2:5	253, 262, 778		
5:22–31	810 fn. 13	2:6	239, 258 (2), 259, 262	**Colossians**	
5:22–32	831	2:6–7	237, 264, 268, 616	1:1	1107
5:23–25	831	2:6–8	253, 612	1:2	757
5:23–26	673	2:6–11	237, 253, 269,	1:6	429, 696, 1002
5:25	642, 674		278, 377, 577	1:9	429
5:25–27	830, 843	2:7	261 fn. 73,	1:9–10	770
5:26	710, 756		268, 616, 629	1:12	250
5:27	831	2:7b	428	1:13	238, 250, 652, 660,
5:30	831, 962	2:8	629		823, 1011 (2), 1014,
5:30–32	398, 487	2:9	262, 264, 579, 1107		1015, 1016, 1033
5:31–32	830	2:9b	579	1:14	626, 652, 655,
5:32	831, 918	2:9–11	240, 253, 261,		658, 680
6:1	943		267, 268, 576, 579	1:15	250, 258 (2), 268,

[1180]

INDEX OF BIBLICAL REFERENCES

	325, 427, 428,	2:20–23	871, 872	2:16	637
	598, 799	3:1	576, 578, 579	2:19	993 fn. 25
1:15–16	237, 238	3:1–4	658	3:2	1107
1:15–17	268	3:1–25	779	3:5	659
1:15–20	237, 250, 251,	3:2	578	3:11	233
	253 (2), 269	3:3	769, 1016	3:12–13	770
1:16	118, 251, 391	3:4	993 fn. 25	3:13	993 fn. 25
1:16–17	400	3:5	769, 775, 776 (2)	3:14	864
1:17	146, 251	3:6	637	4:3	768, 776
1:18	251, 578, 624,	3:9	775, 776	4:5	57
	799, 810 fn. 13,	3:9–14	935	4:6	1083 fn. 24
	830, 831 (2)	3:10	427, 429, 770,	4:7	713, 768
1:19	239, 252 (2)		810 fn. 13	4:9	35, 846 fn. 11
1:19–22	644, 650	3:11	844	4:13	1023
1:20	251, 626, 627, 630,	3:12–14	841	4:13ff.	1023
	650, 1070, 1083	3:13	770	4:13–18	1017, 1019,
1:20–21	650, 680	3:15	713, 831		1022 (2),
1:21–22	627	3:15–17	765, 766		1023 (2), 1038
1:22	241, 625, 650	3:16	766, 889	4:13–5:11	1024
1:22–23	785	3:20	776	4:14	578, 727, 738
1:23	1002	3:23–24	750	4:15	993 fn. 25, 1023, 1039
1:24	540, 830, 831 (2)	4:3	969	4:15–17	1024
1:25–26	1013	4:4	969	4:16	738
1:25–27	540 (3)	4:11	236	4:16–17	981 fn. 3
1:27	252, 265, 739, 918	4:15	830	4:17	1037
1:27–28	429	4:16	11 (2), 66 (2),	4:18	1023
1:29	242		829, 830, 864	5:1–10	1039, 1083 fn. 24
2:2	252, 659 (2)			5:1–11	1023 (2)
2:2–3	265, 429	**1 Thessalonians**		5:2	1024
2:3	145, 146, 252	1:1	829, 830	5:3	1077
2:9	237, 239, 247, 252 (4),	1:3	749	5:6	1039
	253, 266, 268, 1099	1:5	242	5:8–22	779
2:10	253	1:9	706	5:9	637
2:11–12	527, 925, 926, 929,	1:10	578, 637, 638,	5:10	628, 1024, 1038, 1039
	930, 934, 937 fn. 50		651, 1023, 1077	5:11	889, 1024
2:12	578, 927	2:7	890	5:11ff.	1040
2:13	719	2:8	660	5:18	797
2:13c-15	663	2:12	713, 778	5:20	84
2:14f.	1015, 1016	2:13	*xxix*, 10, 11, 31 (2), 47	5:23	412, 758, 768,
2:14–15	627, 680	2:14	830, 831		779, 993 fn. 25
2:15	267, 660, 1103	2:14–16	1004	5:23–24	713, 714, 843
2:17	253, 513 fn. 19, 1107	2:15	85	5:25	1107
2:19	831	2:15–16	1025	5:27	11 (2), 864

[1181]

2 Thessalonians		1 Timothy		3:8–12	899
1:1	829, 830	1:3	907	3:8–13	901 fn. 10
1:4	831	1:3–4	880	3:9	50, 900
1:5	236	1:7	880	3:10	900, 1033
1:5–7	197	1:8–11	774	3:11	899, 900 fn. 9
1:5–10	1022, 1083 fn. 24	1:9	776	3:12	899 fn. 8, 900 (2),
1:6–10	1029	1:9–10	774, 776		900 fn. 9, 901 fn. 10
1:7	993 fn. 25, 1022,	1:10	776 (3)	3:15	810 fn. 13, 831 (3), 878
	1024, 1024 fn. 67	1:10–11	774	3:16	xxx, 237, 241, 253,
1:7–10	494	1:15	xxx, 237, 262 fn. 74,		265, 266 fn. 79, 268,
1:8	57, 624,		265 (2), 269 (2),		269, 576, 579, 878,
	1024, 1029		542, 668, 878		918, 993 fn. 25
1:8–10	1019	1:16	729	4:1	38, 50, 314 (2),
1:9	1077	1:17	167, 172, 247, 861		789, 891, 1126
1:9–10	344	1:19	789	4:4	34
1:10	993 fn. 25	1:20	854, 890	4:5	969
1:11	242	2:3–4	692	4:6	50
2	1063	2:1	693, 969	4:7–9	xxx
2:1	993 fn. 25, 1024	2:2a	693	4:8–9	878
2:1–11	1032	2:4	668, 672 fn. 3,	4:10	685, 693
2:3	891, 981 fn. 3		685 (2)	4:13	11, 84, 878
2:3–12	1083 fn. 24	2:5	581, 672 fn. 3, 1088	4:14	838
2:4	810 fn. 13	2:5–6	477, 685, 692,693	5:1	837
2:5	47	2:6	634, 655, 657, 685	5:8	50
2:6–7	1032 fn. 80	2:7	50	5:10	920
2:7	1032	2:8	578	5:15	659
2:8	993 fn. 25,	2:12	900 fn. 10	5:16	892
	1023, 1032	2:13	118, 1033	5:17	837, 907
2:10	727	2:13–14	440 fn. 29	5:17–18	775
2:11	372, 728	2:14	118, 445	5:18	11 (2), 35, 548
2:11–12	727	3	83, 897	5:19	837
2:12	728	3:1	xxx, 837, 878, 997	5:20	854
2:13	372, 467, 678, 692	3:1–7	527	5:21	481, 675
2:13–14	209, 714	3:1–13	624	6:7	265
2:14	713, 799	3:2	837, 899 (4),	6:8	402
2:15	xxx, 11, 62,		899 fn. 8, 906	6:10	50, 687 (2), 693
	85, 852, 878	3:2–7	899, 900 fn. 10	6:12	50, 713
2:16	233	3:3	899	6:13	402
3:2	679	3:4	899	6:14	993 fn. 25
3:5	659	3:5	831, 889, 899	6:15	861
3:6	11, 47, 837	3:6	899	6:16	100, 101, 167
3:14	11, 47	3:7	899	6:17	402, 683, 997
3:14–15	854, 890	3:8	900 (3), 906	6:20	xxx, 878

INDEX OF BIBLICAL REFERENCES

6:21	50	4:10	789, 997, 1010	3:4–6	209
		4:11	815	3:4–8	xxx
2 Timothy		4:16	815	3:5	314, 380, 719 (2),
1:6	838	4:18	247, 292, 581		733, 796, 926
1:7	314	4:21	814	3:8	728
1:9	372, 380, 464, 465,	**Titus**		3:10	624, 854, 890, 891 (2)
	466, 641, 678, 692,	1	897	3:10–11	837
	713 (2), 714, 716, 796	1:1	50		
1:9b-10	1013	1:2	110, 192, 201	**Philemon**	
1:10	993 fn. 25, 1015,	1:2–3	1013	1	1107
	1016 (2), 1037	1:5	837, 897 (2), 907 (2)	2	829, 830
1:12	698, 728, 791	1:5–9	527, 624		
1:13–14	880	1:6	899 (3), 899 fn. 8	**Hebrews**	
2:2	878	1:6–9	899, 900 fn. 10	1:1	581
2:8	244	1:7	837, 889, 897,	1:1–2	4, 10, 20 fn. 41,
2:10	1037		899 (2), 906, 907		118, 222, 273, 845
2:11–13	xxx, 878	1:8	899	1:2	222, 273 (2), 275,
2:12–13	1038	1:9	xxviii, 44, 889,		276, 277 (2),
2:13	177, 192		891, 899 (2)		392, 997, 1040
2:15	878, 917	1:9–11	880	1:2–3	273
2:19	466	1:10–11	854	1:3	131, 192, 251 (2), 271,
2:26	659, 660	1:12	1109 fn. 6		275 (2), 276, 325, 399,
2:25	679, 724 (2),	2:1	878		400, 576, 579, 580,
	727, 880	2:2	694		594, 612, 617, 1040
3:8	50	2:3	694	1:4	273, 276, 277 (2),
3:15	10, 83 fn., 528,	2:4	694		287, 1107
	881, 950	2:6	694	1:4–14	223, 267
3:15–17	119, 384	2:7–8	878	1:5	273
3:16	xxix, 8 (2), 33 (2), 71	2:9	694	1:5–6	212
3:16–17	37, 52, 55,	2:11	477, 685 (2), 693 (2), 694	1:5–13	21
	84, 408, 775	2:11–12	913	1:6	48, 273, 275, 799
3:16–4:2	864	2:12	997	1:7	274
3:16–4:4	852	2:13	159, 202, 237,	1:8	159, 172, 207, 213,
4:1	993 fn. 25,		246, 248, 249 (3),		273 (3), 274 (4),
	1083 fn. 24		250, 268, 289,		291, 312, 624,
4:1–5	883		291, 312, 580,		625, 1040, 1099
4:2	878		625, 797, 993 fn. 25,	1:8–9	273 fn. 91,
4:3	693 fn. 25		1022, 1039, 1099		274 (2), 300
4:5	880	2:14	634, 655, 657, 658,	1:9	276
4:6	1038		673, 680, 694	1:10	272 fn. 90, 275
4:7	50, 1021		1088	1:10–12	172, 213, 274,
4:7–8	750	3:3	720		311, 1099
4:8	993 fn. 25	3:3–7	878	1:11–12	275, 276, 1040
		3:3–8			

[1183]

1:13	213, 274, 276, 287, 576, 1040	3:7–4:13	776 fn. 82, 831	6:17–18	177, 192, 953
		3:11	637	6:18	110, 201
1:14	165, 273	3:14	786	6:20	576, 623
2:1–3	21 fn. 41, 845	4:3	637	7:3	273
2:2	832, 1107	4:3–6	394 fn. 11	7:9–10	424
2:2–3	1040	4:4–11	487	7:11	1040
2:3	272 fn. 90, 1108 (2), 1118	4:9	1040	7:18	1107
		4:11	1040	7:21	274
2:3–4	413	4:12	36, 421, 1028 fn. 76 (2), 1083 fn. 24	7:23–26	1123
2:4	11, 410, 660			7:24	632, 971
2:5	1040			7:24–25	581
2:9	276, 277 (2), 477, 576, 579 (2), 634, 680, 685 (2), 694 (2), 1040	4:12–13	34	7:25	698, 785, 971
		4:13	185, 186, 1083 fn. 24	7:26	579, 623, 629, 665
				7:26–27	632 (2)
		4:14	272 fn. 90, 273, 314, 576	7:27	625, 631, 633, 642, 1042, 1107
2:9–10	627				
2:10	276, 630 (2), 665, 694, 759, 1107	4:14–15	623	7:28	273, 276
		4:15	272, 629	8:1	576, 623, 1040
2:10–18	629	5:1–6	276	8:2	532
2:11	695 (2)	5:4	958	8:3–12	21
2:11–13	21	5:5	273, 274	8:5	532, 1041
2:12	695, 833	5:5ff	21	8:8–13	406, 525
2:12ff	276	5:5–6	623	8:13	1107
2:13	695, 1024	5:7	241, 272	9:8	21
2:13–14	759	5:7–9	612	9:10	933, 933 fn. 41
2:14	272, 428, 546, 552, 627	5:8	272, 273, 276, 277, 629, 630 (2)	9:11–14	527, 532, 632
				9:12	626, 654, 657, 1041, 1042
2:14–15	663, 680, 1063 fn. 131, 1103	5:8–10	629		
		5:9	630	9:13	933, 1040
2:14–17	1122	5:10	276	9:14	313 (2), 624, 626, 631, 633, 642, 1040, 1123
2:16	276, 481, 675, 695	5:11–14	791		
2:17	224, 272, 428, 546, 552, 624, 626, 635, 638, 642, 665, 680, 695, 831	6	791		
		6:1	723, 832	9:15	406, 430, 525, 628, 654, 657, 658, 673
		6:2	1079		
		6:4	1105		
2:18	272	6:4–6	789	9:19	933
3:1	623, 713, 1107	6:4–8	1083 fn. 24	9:21	933
3:2ff	276	6:5	997, 1011, 1040 (2)	9:22	509
3:5–6	273	6:5–6	790	9:22–24	581, 1123
3:6	273, 786, 831	6:6	273	9:23	632, 665, 679, 1041, 1042
3:7	48, 92, 314	6:9	791		
3:7–9	158, 313	6:13	80, 80 fn. 44	9:24	576, 624, 665, 1041
3:7–11	21	6:13–18	519	9:24–26	971
				9:26	266, 625, 632,

INDEX OF BIBLICAL REFERENCES

	679, 993 fn. 25,	11:9	513 fn. 19, 831	13:21	276 (2)
	997, 1040, 1043	11:9–10	533	13:23	1107
9:27	675, 680, 1040, 1079	11:10	513 fn. 19,		
9:28	624, 625, 631,		514 fn. 19, 988	**James**	
	633, 997, 1040	11:12	533	1:1	271 (2), 828
10:1	1107	11:13	810 fn. 13, 831	1:2	271 fn. 87
10:4	543	11:13–16	534, 988	1:4	271 fn. 87
10:5–9	21	11:19	988	1:5	271 fn. 87
10:7	629, 677	11:26	750	1:5–8	974
10:10	625 (2), 633,	11:26–27	533	1:7	272
	1040, 1042	11:33	1107	1:13	372, 441
10:12	576 577, 625,	11:35	242	1:17	178, 271 fn. 87, 892
	632, 633, 634	11:39	514	1:17–18	365
10:12–13	1040	12:1	831	1:18	715, 719,
10:14	625, 633, 1040	12:2	576		916 fn. 8, 1009
10:15	92, 314	12:5–8	759	1:19–27	779
10:15–17	21	12:6–8	762, 793	1:20	271 fn. 87
10:17	92	12:9	424	1:20–27	271 fn. 87
10:20	241	12:14	768	1:22–24	271 fn. 87
10:22	933	12:14–16	779	1:23	271 fn. 87
10:22–23	832	12:18–21	831	2:1	251, 271 (2)
10:24	679	12:22	810 fn. 13,	2:2	828
10:24–25	780, 887		1029, 1107	2:5	271 fn. 87, 365,
10:25	832, 833, 1040	12:22–24	831		828, 1009 (2)
10:26–27	1079	12:23	797	2:7	776
10:26–31	1083 fn. 24	12:24	933	2:8	1009
10:27	1040	12:26	21	2:10–11	776
10:28–31	1079	12:26–28	1040	2:11	776 (2)
10:29	273, 313	12:28–29	873	2:12–13	1009
10:30	21	12:29	162, 1040, 1079	2:13	271 fn. 87 (2),
10:31	1040	13:1–3	887		1083 fn. 24
10:33	1107	13:1–9	779	2:14	271 fn. 87
10:36	786	13:5	21, 776	2:14–17	749
10:37	1040	13:7	833	2:14–26	748, 779
10:37ff.	21	13:8	172, 275, 276	2:15–16	271 fn. 87
10:39	786, 1079	13:12	272, 1040	2:18	749
11	408	13:14	831	2:19	729, 776
11:1–40	508	13:15–16	527, 888	2:21	749
11:3	118, 392, 397, 414	13:17	528, 833, 889	2:22	749 (2)
11:4	118, 512, 534	13:18	1107	2:23	728, 745
11:5	512	13:18–24	1107	2:24	733, 734 fn. 38,
11:6	727	13:20	272, 465, 578 (2)		748, 749
11:7	118, 745	13:20–21	292	2:25	1004

[1185]

3:1	828	1:7	289, 795, 993 fn. 25	2:17	810 fn. 13, 833
3:2	271 fn. 87	1:8	578, 729	2:18	833
3:6	1079	1:10–11	30, 531, 624	2:21	289, 634, 713, 778
3:8	354, 454	1:10–12	37, 508, 522,	2:21–25	263
3:9	427		537, 834, 988	2:22	289, 522, 834
3:10–13	271 fn. 87	1:11	289 (5), 304, 313, 314 (2)	2:23	289, 1083 fn. 24
3:13–18	779	1:13	289, 993 fn. 25, 1045	2:24	289, 625, 630, 756
3:17–18	271 fn. 87	1:13–25	779	2:25	289, 834, 1043
4:2	780, 973	1:15–16	195, 770, 843	3:1–6	834
4:3	271 fn. 87, 973 fn. 118	1:16	834	3:7	834, 900 fn. 10
		1:17	750, 833	3:9	713
4:4	271 fn. 87	1:18	1043	3:10–12	834
4:5	314	1:18–19	626, 654, 657, 658	3:12	1083 fn. 24
4:7	663	1:19	289, 309, 632, 634	3:14–15	289, 311, 834, 1099
4:8	271 fn. 87	1:20a	289	3:15	880
4:11–12	271 fn. 87	1:20b	289	3:18	241, 289 (2), 634 (2), 680
4:12	272, 1083 fn. 24	1:20	131, 179, 266, 993 fn. 25, 997, 1043, 1045	3:19	675
4:13–14	271 fn. 87			3:20	118
4:15	272			3:20–21	943
5:2–3	271 fn. 87	1:21	289 (3)	3:21	289, 834
5:3	997	1:23	36, 715, 719, 916 fn. 8, 1043	3:22	267, 289, 579, 1043
5:7	993 fn. 25				
5:7–8	272 (2)	1:23–25	36, 834		
5:7–9	1009	2:2	770	4:1	241, 289
5:9	272, 1009	2:3	289	4:1–2	756
5:10–11	272	2:4–5	738	4:5	1045
5:12	271 fn. 87	2:5	289, 833	4:7	1045
5:13–14	272	2:6	289 (2), 729, 834	4:10–11	887
5:14	828, 837, 897, 907	2:6–8	522, 833	4:11	289, 292, 917
5:14–15	272	2:7	289, 834, 1083 fn. 24	4:13	289, 993 fn. 25, 1045
5:15	969	2:8	289, 834, 1083 fn. 24	4:14	289, 313
		2:8–9	372	4:17	1083 fn. 24
1 Peter		2:9	519, 521, 713, 810 fn. 13 (3), 833, 843, 850, 868, 1043	4:18	834, 1083 fn. 24
1	289			5:1	289 (2), 816, 834 (2), 837, 907, 1045
1:1	810 fn. 13, 815, 816, 834 (2)				
		2:9–10	810 fn. 13	5:1–2	834, 897
1:1–2	833	2:10	833, 1043	5:1–3	867
1:2	209, 289 (2), 313, 580, 626, 934	2:11	810 fn. 13, 833, 868	5:2	833, 889
		2:11–12	521	5:2–3	898
1:3	289 (3), 290	2:11–17	779	5:2b-3	934
1:4	762	2:12	1045	5:4	289 (2), 993 fn. 25
1:5	698, 762, 782, 785, 797, 997, 1045	2:13–14	833	5:5	834 (2), 1045
		2:16	833 (2)	5:8	659 (2), 833

[1186]

5:9	663, 810 fn. 13	2:9	289, 791, 1045	1:1–3	147, 697, 1098, 1102
5:10	289, 713, 714, 778, 1045	2:10	791	1:1–4	11
		2:10–19	791	1:2	266, 300, 305, 307
5:11	292	2:12	701	1:3	305, 697
5:13	814	2:13	700 (2)	1:4	697
5:14	289	2:19	291 (2)	1:5	162, 195, 372
5:15–16	969	2:20	289, 290, 292, 1043	1:5–7	697
		2:20–22	789, 790	1:7	305, 612, 626
2 Peter		3	1045, 1046	1:8	452, 757
1:1	159, 289 (2), 290 (3), 291 (4), 312, 580, 625, 1109	3:1	1109	1:9	198
		3:2	289, 291	1:10	452
		3:2a	834	2:1	638, 971
1:1–2	833	3:2b	834	2:2	477, 626, 634, 635, 638 (2), 672, 680, 685, 696, 697 (2)
1:2	291, 292, 792	3:3	997		
1:3	291, 714, 792, 1043	3:3–4	1043, 1045		
1:4	291, 1043	3:4	290, 993 fn. 25	2:3	777, 791, 792
1:5–6	792	3:5	118	2:3–11	779
1:5–10	779, 1045	3:5–6	1045	2:5–6	737
1:8	292, 792	3:6	118, 396	2:8	307, 1047
1:10	793	3:7	1045 (2), 1083 fn. 24	2:13–14	659
1:11	289, 290, 291, 544, 624, 1045 (2)	3:8	172, 289, 695	2:15	696 (2)
		3:9	289, 685 (2), 692 fn. 25, 695 (2), 1046	2:17	1047
1:12	1043			2:18	997, 1047
1:14	1109	3:10a	1045	2:18–19	891
1:16	38, 291 (2), 563, 564 (3), 993 fn. 25, 1045	3:10	289, 291, 1045	2:19	698, 790, 835, 1126
		3:10–12	291	2:20	835
		3:11	1013	2:22	305, 306
1:16–18	75, 147, 1109	3:11–12	1023	2:22–23	305
1:17	292, 564	3:12	291, 1045	2:23	1088
1:19	834	3:13	798, 1045	2:24	305
1:19b	38	3:14	1045	2:27	835, 846 fn. 11
1:20–21	8 (2), 21, 37, 38, 71, 119, 314, 384	3:14–18	779	2:28	993 fn. 25 (2), 1047 (3)
		3:15	289, 291 (2), 1046	2:29	314, 719
2	791, 833	3:15–16a	1046	3:1	666, 714, 759, 762
2:1	291, 295, 656 fn. 49, 685, 698, 700 (3), 701, 891, 1099	3:15–16	xxxi, 10, 33 (2), 39, 62, 288, 1109	3:1a	651
				3:2	578, 993 fn. 25, 1047
		3:16	11 (2), 22, 43, 291	3:2–3	1009, 1023
2:1–3	891	3:18	289, 290, 291, 292 (2), 711, 770, 792	3:3	1047
2:3	38, 791			3:5	266, 305, 993 fn. 25
2:3–10	1083 fn. 24			3:7	1083 fn. 24
2:4	481, 675, 1079	**1 John**		3:8	266, 305 (2), 661, 680, 993 fn. 25, 1083 fn. 24
2:5	118	1:1	300		
2:6–9	1071 fn. 10	1:1–2	305	3:9	314, 709, 719 (2)

[1187]

3:9a	709	5:13	305, 729, 792	20–21	209
3:9b	709	5:14	780	21	295 (4), 296, 534, 834, 1046
3:10	759	5:14–15	975		
3:12	118, 659	5:16	693, 969	22–23	795
3:14	147, 792, 1047	5:18	314, 709 (2), 719 (2)	23	834, 1046
3:15	776	5:18b	325, 326	24	1046 (2)
3:16	634, 835	5:18–19	659	24–25	292
3:17–18	892	5:19	452	25	295 (2), 296, 534
3:17–24	779	5:20	159, 201, 212, 305 (4), 306, 307 (3), 312, 1099		
3:20	185, 322			**Revelation**	
3:21–22	975			1–11	1058
3:23	305, 728	**2 John**		1:1	308, 309, 1048, 1049, 1054, 1056
4:1	241, 728, 835	1	810 fn. 13, 835		
4:1–3	846, 852	3	3–8	1:1–3	1058
4:2	305, 546 fn. 2, 1102	7	241, 305, 306	1:1–8	1058
4:2–3	305, 891	9–11	837, 852	1:3	11, 835, 864, 1048, 1054, 1056 (2)
4:3b	1047	10–11	835, 891, 1111		
4:6	11			1:4	209, 313, 1047, 1049, 1060
4:7	314, 719 (2)	**3 John**			
4:8	162, 200, 651	6	834	1:4–5a	1058
4:9	238, 302, 305 (2), 325	7	308	1:5	309 (2), 626, 642, 799, 821, 1059
4:9–10	641, 651	7–9	835		
4:10	305, 626, 634, 635, 638 (2), 666, 680	9	834	1:5b-6	292
				1:5b-8	1058
4:13	792	**Jude**		1:6	308, 309 (2), 310, 835, 850
4:14	305 (2), 697	1	295 (3), 834, 1109		
4:15	305, 308	2	834	1:7	530, 1054, 1058, 1059
4:16	162	3	xxxii, 834 (2), 878, 879	1:8	310, 311
4:17	1047	4	295 (4), 296, 534, 701, 834	1:9	308, 1049 (2), 1051, 1056 (1)
4:20–21	762				
5:1	305, 314, 709 (4), 719 (3), 727	4–6	1083 fn. 24	1:9–3:22	1058
		5	296 (2), 534	1:10	308, 776, 805 fn. 1, 835
5:1–20	762	6	481, 675, 1046	1:11	1047
5:2	759	7	1071 fn. 10, 1080	1:12–17	279
5:3	777	9	660	1:12–20	1058
5:4	663, 719, 727	11	118	1:13	308
5:5	305	12	834	1:13–18	310
5:6	305, 546 fn. 2	13	1083 fn. 24	1:14	310
5:8	43	14	296 (2), 534, 1046	1:16	333, 835
5:9	305	15	1046, 1083 fn. 24	1:17	310
5:10	150, 728, 729	17	295 (2), 296, 534, 834	1:18	310 (3)
5:11	305, 307	18	997, 1046	1:19	1048, 1054
5:12	305, 1088	20	834	1:20	918

INDEX OF BIBLICAL REFERENCES

2	835, 906	4	836	8:3–5	1057, 1059
2–3	1047, 1051, 1059	4–5	309	8:5	1057, 1058
2:1	835	4:1–5:5	1059	8:6–13	1060
2:1–7	907	4:1–8:5	1059	8:6–11:19	1060
2:2	845, 891	4:5	313, 1047	9:1–10:14	1060
2:6	1056	4:6–8	194	9:11	659 (2)
2:7	439, 1057, 1059	4:9	310	10:1–11	1060
2:8	310, 312	4:10	310	10:6–7	118
2:9	660, 835, 1055, 1056	4:10–11	752	10:7	1057, 1060, 1061
2:10	660	4:11	118, 131	10:11	1060
2:11	1057, 1059	5	836	11:1–2	1035, 1053, 1060
2:13	1051, 1056	5–6	309	11:2	1053
2:14	1056	5:5	309	11:3–14	1060
2:14–15	891	5:6	309 (2), 310, 313, 1059	11:8	1071 fn. 10
2:14–16a	854	5:6–14	310, 1059	11:11	313
2:15	1056	5:8	309	11:15	309, 310, 1057, 1060 (2)
2:16	1054	5:8–9	632	11:17–18	1060
2:17	1057, 1059	5:8–14	267	11:18	637, 1060
2:18	308, 309	5:9	309, 654, 657, 700, 1013	11:18–19	1057, 1060
2:20	854, 891			11:19	1058, 1060
2:23	310 (2)	5:9–10	627, 844, 850	11:19b	1057
2:25–27	1057	5:10	835	12	1112
2:27	308, 309 (2), 862, 1058 fn. 125	5:12	309 (2)	12–22	1060
		5:13	309, 310 (2)	12:1–17	1061
2:29	1059	6:1	309	12:1–14:20	1061
3	835, 906	6:1–17	1059	12:5	309, 1061 (2)
3:1	313	6:9	1051, 1056	12:9	659, 660
3:2	309	6:10	307, 836, 1051, 1056	12:10	309, 659
3:3	1057	6:11	1056	12:11	309 (2), 663
3:5	308, 309, 1057	6:12–17	1055 fn. 120, 1057, 1059	12:12	659
3:6	1059			12:13	309
3:7	307 (2), 310	6:16	309, 637	12:17	660
3:8	835	6:17	637, 1057	13:1–8	1061
3:9	660, 1055, 1056	7	835, 1048	13:3	1061
3:10	1054	7:1–8	1035, 1059, 1060	13:7	1061
3:10–12	1057	7:5–8	1060 fn. 129	13:8	309 (3)
3:11	1054	7:9	309, 799, 844	13:12	1061, 1062
3:12	309	7:9ff	309	13:14	1061, 1062
3:13	1059	7:9–17	1059	13:16–17	1062
3:14	307, 1057	7:10	309, 310	13:18	1035, 1052
3:19	310	7:14	309 (2)	14	835
3:21	308, 310, 1057	7:17	309	14:1	308, 309 (2)
3:22	1059	8:1–5	1059	14:1–5	1061

[1189]

Reference	Pages	Reference	Pages	Reference	Pages
14:3	454, 654, 657, 700, 1013	17:17	372	20:9–11	1055
14:4	309, 654, 657, 700	17:18	1052	20:9–15	1058
14:6–13	1061	18:1–3	1062	20:10	1075, 1080
14:7	1083 fn. 24	18:4	1062	20:11–15	1063, 1083 fn. 24
14:9–11	1068, 1083 fn. 24	18:6b-c	197 fn. 65	20:12–15	1080
14:10	309	18:9–19	1062	20:15	1068
14:10–19	637	19	836	21:1	1013, 1063
14:13	797, 1056, 1061	19:1–3	1083 fn. 24	21:1–17	1063
14:14	308	19:1–4	378	21:1–22:5	1068
14:14–16	310	19:1–5	1084	21:2	810 fn. 13
14:14–20	1057, 1061 (2)	19:1–8	494	21:3	271
14:15	1057	19:1–10	1062	21:4	798
14:16	1058	19:6	192	21:7	759, 776
14:17–20	1083 fn. 24	19:6–10	1084	21:8	776 (3)
14:19	1058	19:7	309 (2), 810 fn. 13	21:9	309, 810 fn. 13, 835
14:20	1061	19:7–8	835	21:9–27	494, 513 fn. 19
15:1	637, 1058, 1083 fn. 24	19:9	309, 713, 965, 1056, 1062	21:9–22:5	836
15:1–8	1062			21:14	284, 309, 822, 845
15:1–16:21	1062	19:9–10	279	21:22	309 (2)
15:3	309	19:10	310	21:23	309
15:7	637	19:11–21	310, 1058, 1062, 1083 fn. 24	21:27	309
16	1083 fn. 24			22:1	309 (2), 310 (2)
16:1	637	19:13	308, 309, 1062	22:1–5	494, 1064
16:1–12	1062	19:15	637, 1058	22:3	309, 310
16:11	1083	19:16	308, 309, 311, 579, 624, 861	22:3f	311
16:15	1056, 1062			22:4	1056
16:15–21	1058	19:18	1063	22:6	1054, 1064
16:17	1058	19:20	1062, 1068, 1080	22:6–21	1064
16:17–21	1055 fn. 120	19:21	1063	22:7	1048, 1055, 1056, 1064
16:18–21	1058, 1062	20	1033, 1034, 1035	22:8	308, 1049, 1064
16:19	637	20–21	1057	22:10	1048, 1055
16:20	1062	20:1–7	980	22:12	1055, 1064
16:21	1062, 1083	20:1–10	1055 fn. 120, 1063	22:12–13	312
16:30	1062	20:1–22:5	1063	22:13	310 (2), 311
17	1062	20:2–3	659	22:14	1056, 1064
17:1–19:21	1062	20:3	660	22:15	1083 fn. 24
17:7	918	20:4a	1033, 1063	22:16	309, 1049, 1064
17:8	1061	20:4b	1033	22:17	314, 713 (2), 736, 1009, 1064, 1085
17:9	1052	20:5	1063		
17:10	1035, 1051, 1052	20:6	310 (2), 1056, 1063	22:18	1064
17:11	1053, 1061, 1062	20:7	660	22:18–19	1048
17:14	308, 309 (3), 310, 311	20:7–9	1036	22:20	308, 969, 1055, 1064 (2)
		20:8	1036	22:21	308, 1064

INDEX OF PERSONS

(This index does not include biblical persons.)

Adams, Jay 931
Adamson, J. 270
Adler Mortimer, J. 347
Aland, Kurt 90
Aland, Barbara 90
Albright, W. F. 1100
Alexander 598, 599, 600
Alford, Henry 242
Allis, O. T. 187, 542, 985
Ambrose 331, 426, 1110
Ames, William xxxv, 948
Amyraldus, Moise 475
Anselm 132, 133, 657, 1121, 1122, 1123
Antipas 1051
Apollinaris 602
Aquinas, Thomas xxxv, 96, 135, 136, 186, 392, 470, 664, 746, 920, 1082, 1122, 1133
Aratus of Cilicia 1109
Archer, Gleason L., Jr. 59, 71, 1110
Archimedes 111
Arius 596, 598, 599, 600
Arminius, James 482
Athanasius 307, 330, 426, 596, 598, 599, 600, 601, 602, 1110
Athenagoras 587
Augustine xxxv, 74, 92, 173, 191, 331, 392, 392, 426, 468, 590, 607, 656, 664, 795, 818, 838, 918, 944, 972, 1107, 1110, 1127, 1133
Augustus, Caesar 1052
Aurelius of Chullabi 1111
Aus, Roger D. 1032
Ayers, A. J. 18

Bahnsen, Greg L. 91, 866
Ball, John 504
Bannerman, James 1133
Barkley, John M. 877
Barnabas of Alexandria 584, 585
Barr, James 13, 14, 16
Barth, Karl 43, 136, 347, 428, 470, 628, 684, 729, 844, 1134
Basil of Caesarea 601, 656
Basil the Great 1110
Basilides 589
Basinger, David 106, 190, 346
Bavinck, Herman xxxv, 162, 192, 197, 198, 357, 839, 1134
Baxter, Richard 882, 898
Beale, G. K. 359
Beasley-Murray, G. R. 270, 308, 310, 311, 992
Beckett, Samuel 18

Beckwith, Isbon T. 309, 310
Beckwith, Roger 60, 957
Bede 307
Behe, Michael J. 122
Bengel, J. A. 307, 1127
Benton, W. Wilson, Jr. 405
Berkhof, Hendrikus 984, 985
Berkhof, Louis xx, xxxii, xxxiii, xxxv, 8, 81, 82, 131, 159, 164, 167, 172, 173, 179, 191, 195, 199, 210, 211, 322, 324, 325, 332, 422, 438, 452, 468, 481, 484, 485, 584, 585, 587, 588, 592, 664, 665, 704, 708, 715, 716, 720, 726, 745, 769, 787, 807, 838, 855, 879, 892, 893, 902, 903, 907, 912, 915, 921, 944, 980, 1027, 1134
Berkouwer, G. C. xx, xxxv, 360, 367, 370, 418, 419, 424, 488, 568, 577, 600, 602, 608, 621, 684, 730, 787, 840, 850, 851, 918, 922, 940, 965, 1027, 1063, 1134
Bernard, J. H. 333, 656
Beyer, H. W. 886
Beza, Theodore 488, 946
Bigg, Charles 290, 1110

Bird, Herbert S. 935
Blaising, Craig A. 511
Blake, Thomas 504
Blocher, Henri 43, 44, 50, 51, 52, 932
Bloesch, Donald 741
Blomberg, Craig L. 556
Blum, Edwin A. 30
Bock, Darrell L. 510, 511
Bockmuehl, Klaus xxvi, xxxiii
Boettner, Loraine 335, 340, 347, 1134
Boice, James M. 1135
Bonar, Horatius 747
Bonhoeffer, Dietrich 882
Boniface VIII 846, 847
Boobyer, G. H. 561
Bornkamm, Günther 17, 572, 573, 574, 575, 807
Boston, Thomas 353
Boyce, James P. 1135
Bray, Gerald 327, 584, 590, 593, 594, 595, 604, 606, 608, 609
Bromiley, Geoffrey W. 584, 585, 588, 589, 921, 935, 943
Broadus, John 999, 1005
Brooke, A. E. 306
Brown, Raymond E. 274, 297, 298, 307, 326, 334, 1100, 1101
Bruce, A. B. 615
Bruce, F. F. 50, 65, 68, 276, 277, 278, 287, 307, 334, 1010, 1098, 1101, 1114
Brunner, Emil 43, 549, 729, 1135
Bucer, Martin 960
Buchanan, James 1021, 1135
Büchsel, Friedrich 637, 652
Bull, George 340

Bullinger, Johann Heinrich 503, 504, 505
Bultmann, Rudolf 17, 279, 282, 307, 556, 561, 572, 573, 574, 575, 984, 985, 1097, 1098, 1099, 1100, 1101, 1115
Bunyan, John 882
Buri, Fritz 1006
Burkett, Delbert 216
Burn-Murdock, H. 817
Burrows, Millar 924
Buswell, J. Oliver, Jr. xxii, xxxv, 133, 136, 141, 176, 183, 191, 192, 335, 336, 340, 427, 441, 551, 619, 664, 665, 841, 917, 980, 1127, 1135

Cadbury, Henry J. 821
Calvin, John xxi, xxxiv, xxxv, 56, 80, 148, 149, 163, 171, 191, 307, 319, 328, 329, 332, 335, 351, 352, 367, 372, 393, 409, 410, 426, 476, 482, 483, 503, 504, 551, 580, 629, 664, 668, 669, 672, 691, 693, 734, 755, 817, 819, 842, 856, 866, 870, 876, 946, 957, 959, 960, 961, 962, 963, 966, 972, 973, 1122, 1127, 1135
Cameron, John 476
Cameron, Nigel M. de S. 505
Campbell, J. Y. 807
Carey, William 882
Carnell, Edward John 78, 97
Carson, Alexander 930
Carson, D. A. 214, 231, 232, 233, 334, 811

Cartwright, Thomas 504
Casey, R. 1100
Celsus 586, 587
Cerinthus 835, 1101
Chafer, Lewis Sperry 771, 985, 1135
Chaney, James M. 935
Charnock, Stephen 1136
Chase, S. H. 1050
Chemnitz, Martin 1136
Chilton, David 1055
Chrysostom 63, 64, 818
Ciocchi, David M. 190
Clark, Gordon H. xxvii, 97, 98, 99, 100, 103, 141, 152, 173, 185, 321, 322, 323, 352, 353, 354, 374, 489, 491, 499, 576, 728
Clark, Kenneth W. 992
Clarke, W. Norris 178
Claudius, Caesar 1052
Clement of Alexandria 426, 593, 656, 1107, 1111, 1112
Clement of Rome 584
Clowney, Edmund P. 57, 810, 822, 851, 900, 925, 941, 959, 969, 970, 1136
Cocceius, Johannes 502, 504
Colani, T. 1006
Coleman, Thomas 908
Colwell, E. C. 214, 300
Constantine 597, 598, 599
Constantine IV 614
Conzelmann, H. 17
Cooper, Karl T. 1116
Craig, Clarence T. 992
Craig, William Lane 189
Cranfield, C. E. B. 50, 239, 241, 560, 561, 562, 900, 1127
Cross, Frank L. 587

[1192]

INDEX OF PERSONS

Cullmann, Oscar 68, 274, 275, 812, 984, 1006, 1017
Cunningham, William 503, 504, 818, 866, 902, 961, 962, 1136
Cupitt, Don 1095
Cyprian 818, 838, 944, 1111
Cyril of Alexandria 170, 307, 603, 604, 605, 606, 607, 617, 656
Cyril of Jerusalem 1110

Dabney, Robert Lewis *xxxv*, 131, 162, 174, 243, 307, 393, 470, 664, 665, 866, 947, 954, 961, 962, 1136
Dale, James W. 930, 931
Dale, Robert W. 906
Dana, H. E. 952
Dawkins, Richard 121
Deissmann, G. Adolf 38
Delitzsch, Franz 101, 102, 1072
Demar, Gary 866
Demarest, Bruce 1041, 1139
Denney, James 55, 642, 1127, 1136
Dennison, James T. 726
Denzinger, H. 297, 848, 1085
Descartes, Rene 319
DeWitt, John R. 935
Dick, John 1136
Diocletian 597
Dioscurus 607
Dixon, Larry 1085
Dodd, C. H. 10, 279, 281, 299, 306, 560, 561, 562, 636, 641, 983, 984, 991, 1044, 1045, 1100
Domitian 1049, 1050, 1051, 1056

Dunn, James D. G. 276, 277, 278, 1115
Dupont, Jacques 1116

Eddington, Arthur 123
Edgar, William *xxiv*
Edward VI 866
Edwards, David L. 1068, 1069, 1073, 1076
Edwards, Jonathan *xxxvii*, 134, 138, 139, 145, 149, 191, 353, 882, 1137
Eichrodt, Walther 347
Elizabeth I 866
Elliott, Charles 86
Elwell, Walter A. 511
Epictetus 1129
Epimanides of Crete 1109
Epiphanius 1110
Erastus, Thomas 907
Erickson, Millard J. 615, 616, 1069, 1086, 1087, 1103, 1137
Eusebius 599, 814, 1050, 1107, 1109, 1110, 1111
Eutyches 606, 607
Eward, Heinrich 387

Faber, Frederick W. 202
Fackre, Gabriel *xix, xxxiii*
Fairbairn, A. M. 270
Fee, Gordon D. 52
Ferdinand V 865
Finney, Charles G. 1137
Flavian 606, 607
Flew, Anthony 347
Forsyth, P. T. 640
Frame, John M. *xxii*, 12, 20, 57, 78, 86, 102, 103, 105, 112, 113, 114, 135, 138, 140, 141, 142, 143, 144, 146, 148, 149, 189, 201, 1137

France, R. T. 1006
Franzmann, Martin H. 62, 63, 68, 69, 1042, 1051, 1056
Fraser, J. 1127
Fuller, Daniel 431, 432
Fuller, R. H. 17, 282

Gaffin, Richard B. Jr. 57, 66, 69, 147, 411, 776
Gaius, Caesar (Caligula) 1052
Galba 1052, 1053
Garrett, James Leo 1137
Gasque, W. Ward 572
Gaunilo 133
Geisler, Norman L. 556, 1137
Gentry, Kenneth L. 1050, 1051, 1052, 1053, 1055
George, Timothy 347, 753
Georgius of Sicily 482
Gerstner, John *xxxv*, 4, 77, 78, 134, 140, 141, 347, 482, 679, 692, 746
Gesenius, Wilhelm 397
Gifford, E. H. 246
Gill, John 693, 1137
Glasson, T. F. 1006
Godet, F. 242, 615, 1127
Godfrey, W. Robert 431, 964
Gogarten, Fredrich 729
Gomarus, Franciscus 480, 488
Goodspeed, Edgar J. 1111, 1112
Gore, Charles 615, 905
Goulder, Michael 573, 574, 1095
Green, E. M. B. 1110
Green, James Benjamin 160, 624, 879

[1193]

Greeven, H. 969
Gregory of Nazianzus 315, 601, 602, 656, 1110
Gregory of Nyssa 601, 656, 818
Gregory VII 846
Gregory, (I) the Great 795, 846
Grenz, Stanley J. 1137
Grider, J. Kenneth 346, 472, 474, 475, 681
Grotius, Hugo 474
Grudem, Wayne xxxv, 57, 411, 901, 906, 1137
Gruenler, Royce G. 215, 216, 560
Gründler, Otto 489
Guinness, Os 882, 883
Gundry, Stanley N. xxvi, 266
Guthrie, Donald 573, 575, 1041, 1067, 1068, 1069, 1074, 1108, 1110

Habermas, Gary R. 572
Haenchen, E. 284
Hahneman, G. M. 63
Hall, David W. 866, 879, 883
Hall, Joseph H. 608, 904
Halsey, Jim 102, 103
Hanina, ben Dosa 556
Hanson, A. T. 636
Harris, Murray J. 159, 273, 306
Harris, R. Laird xxii, 60, 65, 157, 795, 1108
Harrison, Everett F. 652, 653, 655, 1091, 1110
Harvey, A. E. 556
Hasker, William 190, 346
Hatch, Edwin 905
Headlam, A. C. 242, 753, 1127

Heber, Reginald 315
Hegel, G. W. F. 112, 115
Helm, Paul 190, 504, 672
Hendriksen, William 540, 1027, 1053, 1057, 1059
Hengel, Martin 278
Henry, Carl F. H. 115, 136, 998, 1138
Henry VIII 866
Heppe, Heinrich xxxv, 1138
Heraclitus 299
Hering, J. 1041
Hermas 584
Hermogenes 589
Herrmann, J. 969
Heshusius, Tilemann 672
Hetherington, William Maxwell 339, 908
Hick, John 1086, 1095
Hilary of Poitiers 331, 656, 818, 1110
Hippolytus 63, 64
Hodge, A. A. xx, xxxv, 87, 179, 191, 373, 664, 665, 943, 945, 1138
Hodge, Charles xxii, xxxvii, 32, 131, 161, 174, 191, 242, 243, 307, 322, 323, 326, 340, 393, 425, 429, 437, 438, 486, 490, 491, 497, 541, 606, 615, 645, 649, 664, 665, 786, 788, 795, 877, 912, 918, 961, 975, 1127, 1138
Hodges, Zane 722
Hoekema, Anthony A. 542, 762, 985, 986, 988, 994, 1027
Hoeksema, Herman 489, 1138
Holmström, F. 983

Honi the Circle-Drawer 556
Hort, F. J. A. 302, 1050
Houlden, Leslie 1095
Howie, Robert 504
Hughes, Philip E. 276, 277
Hume, David 555
Hunter, W. Bingham 976
Hus, John 849

Ignatius 546, 549, 584, 585, 591, 904, 1101
Innocent III 846
Innocent IV 865
Irenaeus 549, 584, 586, 590, 591, 656, 814, 835, 943, 1052, 1101, 1111, 1112
Isadore of Pelusium 818

Jeans, James 123
Jeremias, Joachim 556, 687, 935, 965, 984
Jerome 186, 307, 331, 656, 812, 1050, 1107, 1109
Jewett, Paul King 929
John of Antioch 605, 606
John of Damascus 426, 610, 656, 818
Johnson, Phillip E. 122
Johnson, Terry L. 872, 877
Jones, David C. xxii, 5, 71, 84, 885, 890, 927, 928, 929, 936, 941, 947, 949, 958, 973
Josephus 59, 60, 1002
Joyce, Donovan 568
Judson, Adoniram 882
Julius Caesar 1052
Justin, Martyr 549, 586, 587, 588, 596, 598, 943, 1112
Justinian I 614

INDEX OF PERSONS

Kafka, Franz 18
Kaiser, Walter C., Jr. 22, 51, 527, 535
Kant, Immanuel 12, 113, 114
Kantzer, Kenneth S. *xxvi*, 550
Karlberg, Mark W. 103
Käsemann, Ernst 17, 43, 50, 291, 1100, 1101, 1102, 1103
Kaufman, Gordon D. 347, 348, 349
Keller, W. Phillip 898
Kelly, Douglas F. 347
Kelly, J. N. D. *xxx*, 34, 584, 754, 817, 879
Kendall, R. T. 672, 677
Kenrick, Peter Richard 819
Kevan, Ernest F. 777
Kierkegaard, Søren *xxvi*, 115
Kim, S. 1114
Kingsbury, Jack Dean 822
Kistemaker, Simon J. 1108
Kline, Meredith G. 69, 197, 431, 432, 433, 534, 536, 1071
Knight, George W. III 5, 53, 58, 265, 772, 774, 901
Kolb, Edward 121
Kuiper, R. B. 95, 104, 673, 1138
Kümmel, Werner G. 1006
Kuyper, Abraham *xxxv*, 732, 980, 1138

Lachman, David 877
Ladd, George E. 33, 236, 299, 300, 539, 572, 574, 638, 753, 765, 775, 982, 986, 987, 991, 992, 996, 997, 1009, 1010, 1011, 1014, 1019, 1024, 1032, 1036, 1037, 1042, 1043, 1046, 1060, 1061, 1063, 1064, 1139
Lagrange, M. J. 1006
Lampe, G. W. H. 573
Landis, R. W. 436
Lane, William L. 293, 560
Latourette, Kenneth Scott 584, 596, 606
Leblanc, L. 489
Leith, John 607, 920
Lenski, R. C. H. 523
Leo I 331, 606, 607, 608, 656
Leontius of Byzantium 610, 621
Leontius of Jerusalem 610
Lessing, G. E. 1105
Lewis, C. S. 556
Lewis, Gordon R. 162, 191, 1139
Lewis, Jack 393
Liefeld, Walter L. 563
Lightfoot, J. B. 258, 905, 908
Lindsley, Arthur 4, 77, 78, 134, 140, 141
Litton, Edward Arthur 905
Lloyd-Jones, Martyn 1127
Lock, Walter 249
Locke, John 319
Lohmeyer, E. 293, 562
Loisy, A. 284
Lombard, Peter 918
Long, Gary D. 700, 701
Longenecker, Richard N. 563, 1114, 1116
Loof, Friedrich 611, 612
Lucian 586, 587
Luther, Martin 67, 68, 191, 307, 393, 469, 503, 656, 734, 755, 756, 819, 850, 866, 915, 961, 1139
Lyon, R. W. 652, 653
Lyttleton, George 1114

MacArthur, John 1127
MacDonald, H. D. 423, 424
Machen, J. Gresham *xxvi*, 547, 549, 556, 557, 682, 683, 692, 1114, 1119
MacIntyre, Alasdair 151
Mackie, J. L. 193
Mackintosh, H. R. 615
Macleod, Donald 129, 130, 161, 163, 505, 877
MacMillan, J. Douglas 898
Maillot, Alphonse 50
Mantey, J. R. 821, 952
Marcian (Emperor) 607
Marsh, John 1011
Marshall, I. Howard 13, 235, 277, 279, 294, 295, 301, 305, 307, 308
Marston, George W. 95, 104
Martin, Ralph 572
Mascall, E. L. 175
Mavrodes, George 192
Mawhinney, Al 511
Maxwell, William D. 877
Mayor, J. B. 271
McCheyne, Robert Murray 801
McGrath, Alistair *xx*, 133, 347, 469, 1139
McMullin, Ernan 392
McNeill, John T. 972
Meek, Theophile J. 387
Melanchthon, Philipp 960, 1139
Menander 1109
Metzger, Bruce M. 214, 216, 247, 248, 297, 534, 695, 951, 1018, 1029, 1035, 1052, 1059, 1098
Meyer, H. A. W. 242, 1127
Michaelis, Wilhelm 560
Michaels, J. Ramsey 90
Micklem, Nathaniel 877

[1195]

Miley, John 1139
Minear, Paul 810
Mitchell, Alex F. 339, 340
Moffat, James 387
Molina, L. 189
Montgomery, John Warwick 4
Morris, Leon 10, 44, 167, 214, 280, 281, 299, 303, 304, 334, 413, 529, 557, 635, 637, 638, 639, 641, 743, 963, 1039, 1051, 1059, 1081, 1101
Morris, Thomas 619
Motyer, J. A. 1070, 1072
Moule, C. F. D. 34, 214
Moulton, James H. 34, 249
Mozely, J. B. 556
Muller, Richard A. *xxv*, 489
Murray, John *xx*, *xxviii*, *xxxv*, 50, 71, 89, 90, 92, 160, 192, 238, 239, 243, 244, 245, 258, 307, 320, 330, 331, 338, 340, 360, 373, 379, 401, 402, 403, 405, 418, 428, 434, 437, 438, 448, 449, 456, 457, 462, 467, 470, 471, 472, 480, 483, 486, 487, 502, 518, 551, 611, 612, 613, 621, 623, 630, 633, 638, 642, 643, 645, 646, 653, 655, 657, 658, 659, 660, 661, 664, 665, 666, 668, 678, 688, 689, 692, 697, 701, 704, 705, 709, 715, 716, 717, 728, 736, 737, 738, 743, 745, 746, 748, 751, 757, 761, 771, 778, 779, 784, 790, 793, 799, 809, 896, 898, 901, 925, 934, 935, 937, 938, 940, 941, 942, 946, 947, 953, 1013, 1016, 1017, 1020, 1021, 1022, 1026, 1027, 1032, 1035, 1089, 1127, 1128, 1139

Narborough, F. D. V. 1041
Nash, Ronald H. 103, 175, 176, 190, 1086
Nero 597, 1051, 1052, 1053, 1061
Nestorius 170, 603, 604, 605, 606, 607, 609, 617
Neve, J. L. 754
Nicholas of Cusa 846
Nichols, James Hastings 877
Nicole, Roger R. *xxii*, 90, 472, 476, 496, 497, 498, 637, 672, 673, 685
Nineham, Dennis 1095
Noll, Mark A. 883
North, Gary 866

Obermann, Heiko 432
Oden, Thomas C. 1140
Old, Hughes Oliphant 877
Olevianus, Caspar 504
Olshausen, Herman 307
Olson, Roger 347
Origen *xxxv*, 337, 424, 426, 584, 587, 593, 594, 596, 598, 656, 795, 818, 944, 971, 1107, 1112
Orlinsky, Harry M. 385, 386
Osborne, Grant R. 572
Osterhaven, M. E. 590
Otho 1053
Ott, Ludwig 848, 913, 1140
Outler, Albert C. 607
Overbye Dennis 120, 121
Owen John 662, 677, 680, 689, 695, 696, 698, 1140

Packer, James I. 18, 20, 47, 49, 50, 73, 82, 83, 104, 151, 178, 179, 334, 397, 532, 681, 720, 742, 755, 870, 880, 882, 1084, 1140
Pannenberg, Wolfhart 549, 572, 1099, 1140
Papias 584, 1112
Parker, T. H. L. 399, 400, 401, 402
Paul of Samosata 597
Paulus, Heinrich 555
Payne, J. Barton 157, 159, 347, 440, 443, 449
Pearson, John 340
Pelagius 468
Pelikan, Jaroslav J. *xxvi*, *xxxiii*
Perkins, William 488
Perrin, N. 17
Peterson, Robert A. 1069, 1085
Philippi, F. A. 1127
Phillips, Timothy 1087
Philo of Alexandria 299, 593
Pieper, Francis *xxxv*, 1140
Piggin, F. S. 470
Pighius, Albertus 482
Pinnock, Clark H. 30, 190, 346, 347, 348, 349, 350, 351, 352, 354, 355, 372, 378, 379, 380, 435, 1068, 1069, 1086, 1090, 1092
Piper, John 872, 901, 1092
Piscator, Johannes 489
Plato 424
Plummer, Alfred 333, 1111
Plumtre, E. H. 1110
Polanus, Amandus 946, 948
Polycarp 584, 585, 835
Pope Innocent III 817
Pope Paul VI 795, 848
Pope Pius IX 848

[1196]

INDEX OF PERSONS

Pope Pius XII 812
Porphyry 587
Powell, Ralph E. 1075, 1085
Poythress, Vern S. 18, 1024
Preston, John 504
Preus, Robert 915, 1140

Quick, O. 615

Radmacher, Earl D. 1140
Rahner, Karl 347, 1085, 1086
Ramm, Bernard 556
Rashi 387
Rayburn, Robert G. *xxii*, 877, 935
Rayburn, Robert S. 807, 881, 958
Reaume, John D. 928
Reymond, Robert L. *xxvi*, 4, 6, 17, 44, 47, 57, 58, 79, 96, 103, 111, 131, 137, 150, 213, 217, 251, 413, 547, 746, 811, 819, 862, 987, 1008, 1140
Reynolds, H. R. 333
Rice, Richard 190, 346
Richardson, Cyril 323
Ridderbos, Herman N. 61, 63, 66, 580, 1010, 1015, 1027, 1037, 1077, 1098, 1100, 1101, 1105, 1114, 1127, 1130
Ritschl, Albrecht 652
Robertson, A. T. 35, 732
Robertson, O. Palmer 57, 431, 513, 1027
Robinson, John A. T. 276, 278, 1006, 1083, 1084
Rollock, Robert 504
Ross Hugh 392
Rufinus Tyrranius 656, 838
Ruse, Michael 122
Russell, Bertrand 415

Rutherford, Samuel 903
Ryrie, Charles C. 507, 510, 1141

Sabellius 597, 600
Sagan, Carl 121, 122, 123
Salmond, S. D. F. 1109
Sanday, W. 242, 753, 1127
Sanders, E. 1116
Sanders, John 190, 346, 1086, 1090
Saucy, Robert L. 411, 511
Schaeffer, Francis A. 58, 78, 79, 115, 125, 1141
Schaeffer, Edith 125
Schaff, Philip 331, 584
Schiewind, J. 561
Schleiermacher, Friedrich 555
Schlier, Heinrich 50
Schmidt, K. L. 825
Schmiedel, Paul Wilhelm 222, 223, 224
Schnackenburg, Rudolf 307, 1101
Schonfield, Hugh 568
Schönmetzer, A. 297, 848, 1085
Schuller, Robert H. 455, 636, 637
Schweitzer, Albert 567, 982, 983, 1006
Schweizer, E. 573
Scobie, Charles H. H. 924
Scofield, C. I. 509
Seeberg, Reinhold 46, 584, 586, 588, 590, 591, 596, 601, 603, 604, 607
Seller, R. V. 602
Shakespeare, William 116, 457
Shedd, William G. T. *xxxv*, 1141

Shults, F. LeRon 611
Sidebottom, E. M. 270
Sixtus III 606
Skeat, S. K. 693
Smedes, Lewis B. 419, 420
Smith, C. R. 1060
Smith, Frank J. 877
Smith, Henry B. 438
Smith, Morton H. 162, 331, 340, 556, 717
Smith, Walter Chalmers 202
Spanheim, Friedrich 948
Speiser, Ephraim A. 387, 442
Spencer, Aida Besancon 1087
Sproul, R. C. 4, 74, 77, 123, 124, 134, 140, 141, 735, 741, 959, 1141
Spurgeon, Charles 882
Stalker, James 1114, 1119
Steele, David N. 466, 527
Stein, Gertrude 18
Steinman, Jean 924
Stewart, James S. 36
Stibbs, Alan 626
Stob, Henry 374
Stonehouse, Ned B. 952
Stott, John R. W. 639, 641, 671, 1068, 1069, 1073, 1076, 1080, 1081, 1082, 1083, 1087
Strauss, David 556, 567
Strimple, Robert B. 347, 556
Strong, Augustus Hopkins *xxxv*, 906, 907, 1141
Strossmayer, Josef 819
Stuart, Douglas 90
Stuart, M. 1127
Swete, H. B. 310, 1055
Swineburne, Richard 168
Sylvester I 846

Tatian 587

Taylor, Vincent 274, 560, 615
Temple, William 21, 22
Tenney, Merrill C. 563, 1111
Tennyson, Alfred Lord 107
Tertullian 549, 590, 591, 592, 593, 594, 595, 598, 607, 795, 818, 943, 944, 1101, 1112
Theodoret 818
Theodosius I 601
Theodosius II 603, 607
Theophanes 818
Theophilus of Antioch 587
Theophylact 818
Thiele, Edwin R. 7
Thiessen, Henry Clarence 5, 1141
Thomas, Curtis C. 466, 527
Thomas, W. Griffith 819
Thomasius, Gottfried 615
Thompson, Francis 124
Thornwell, James Henley xxxv, 947, 1141
Thrall, Margaret E. 1119
Tiberius, Caesar 1052
Tienou, Tite 1087
Tisdale, Sallie 354
Titus 1002, 1053
Toplady, Augustus 457
Trajan 1050
Trench, Richard C. 555, 556
Tryon, Edward P. 121
Turner, Nigel 34, 214, 248, 274
Turretin, Francis xxxv, 131, 190, 191, 206, 325, 497, 664, 665, 673, 726, 1141
Twisse, William 488
Tyconius 1052

Unger, Merrill F. 34, 60, 387, 388

Urban, William Marshall 18
Ursinus, Zacharias 504
Ussher, James 504, 948

Valentinus 589
Valla, Lorenzo 846
Van der Loos, H. 556
Van Oosterom, James 1027
Van Til, Cornelius 97, 98, 99, 103, 104, 105, 108
Venn, Henry 882
Vermes, G. 556
Vermigli, Peter Martyr 946
Vespasian 1002, 1053, 1061
Vilekin, Alex 121
Vitellius 1053
Voetius, Gisbertus 480, 488, 948
von Dodschütz, E. 284
von Harnack, Adolf 981
Von Rad, Gerhard 390
Vos, Geerhardus 9, 26, 156, 157, 158, 195, 197, 201, 212, 213, 217, 218, 219, 221, 222, 230, 283, 294, 357, 368, 370, 371, 406, 407, 408, 441, 443, 447, 465, 488, 503, 505, 512, 528, 529, 535, 536, 538, 550, 634, 821, 945, 946, 987, 991, 996, 1015, 1016, 1034, 1071, 1078, 1142

Waltke Bruce K. 7
Warfield, Benjamin B. xx, xxxv, 4, 6, 25, 26, 27, 30, 35, 36, 39, 40, 44, 48, 55, 65, 70, 81, 113, 140, 144, 149, 150, 206, 207, 209, 210, 211, 212, 218, 219, 220, 223, 225, 226, 228, 229, 242, 243, 244, 245, 258, 268, 269, 270, 271, 272, 279, 307, 308, 309, 326, 329, 330, 334, 335, 339, 340, 355, 373, 393, 395, 411, 413, 430, 436, 462, 468, 469, 471, 472, 473, 478, 480, 499, 502, 547, 550, 554, 580, 597, 618, 620, 633, 652, 673, 682, 691, 697, 726, 731, 849, 901, 930, 935, 946, 947, 1102, 1103, 1110, 1142
Warren, M. A. C. 640
Watson, Richard 1142
Watts, Isaac 640
Weaver, Gilbert 103
Webb, Robert Alexander 1142
Webber, Robert E. 873
Weiss, Johannes 982
Wells, David F. 236, 258, 469, 584, 602, 603, 610, 849, 882, 909
Wenham, Gordon J. 351
Wenham, John W. 44, 45, 47
Werner, Martin 1006
Wesley, Charles 650
Westcott, B. F. 229, 306, 308, 332, 333, 575, 577, 652
Whitaker, William 488
White, Andrew Dickson 392
White, R. Fowler 57, 1055
Whitefield, George 882
Wickham, E. C. 275
Wiles, Maurice 1095
Wiley, H. Orton 478, 681, 1142
William of Occam 847
Williamson, G. I. 871, 872
Witsius, Herman 726, 948
Wittgenstein, Ludwig 18
Wolterstorff, Nicholas 175

[1198]

Wycliffe, John 849

Yamauchi, Edwin M. 1100
Young, Edward J. 82, 83, 390, 391, 932

Young, Frances 1095

Zahn, Theodore 1130
Zanchius, Jerome 489, 948, 975

Zeller, E. 284
Zwingli, Ulrich 503, 819, 921, 957, 960, 961

INDEX OF SUBJECTS

Abrahamic covenant: O. Palmer Robertson's interpretation of the land promises of, 513–15, fn. 19; salvific definitiveness of and relation of to covenant of grace, 512–18.

Accomplishment of the atonement: see "The Character of the Cross Work of Christ," 623–69.

Adam, fall of: nature of, 440–6; seven effects of, 446–49.

Adam, sin of: imputation of, 436–39 (agnostic view, 436; realist view, 436–37; immediate imputation view, 437–38; mediate imputation view, 438–39).

Adoption: 759–62; biblical data for, 759–60; legal action, 761; consequences and responsibilities of adopted status, 761–62; summary of the doctrine, 762.

Amillennialism: definition of, 980, fn. 3.

Amyraldianism (inconsistent Calvinism): 475–79; its representation of the eternal salvific plan, 476; Warfield's objections to its representation of order of the decrees, 477–78; objections to its idea of universal atonement, 478–79.

Analogy of being (*analogia entis*): xix, 96–7, 470, fn. 16.

Analogy of faith (*analogia fidei*), of Scripture (*analogia Scripturae*): 50–2, 60.

Anselm: ontological argument of, 132–33; satisfaction view of the atonement of, see Appendix D, 1121–23.

Antilegomena, New Testament: see Appendix B, 1105–12.

Application of Christ's cross work (see also *ordo salutis*), 703–801.

Apocrypha: 59–60; Gleason L. Archer Jr. on, 59, fn. 8; not inspired, 59–60; Westminster Assembly's four confessional negatives concerning, 59–60.

Apollinarianism and Council of Constantinople: 601–3.

Arianism and Council of Nicea: 597–601.

Arminianism: see Universalism, evangelical.

Ascension of Christ: biblical data for, 575–77; historicity of, 575–81; significance of, 578–81.

Assurance of salvation: 790–4.

Attributes of the church: apostolicity, 844–46; catholicity, 843–44; holiness, 842–43; oneness, 839–42; papal interpretation of, 846–49.

Attributes of Scripture: authority, 73–9; finality, 88–93; inspiration, 59; necessity, 56–9; perspicuity, 87–8; self-authentication, 79–82; sufficiency, 83–7.

Augustinianism: 468–69.

Authority of Scripture: 73–9.

Authority of church: may draw up constitutions and manuals of church order, 889; discipline unruly and reprobate, 890; enforce laws of Christ, 888–89; keep itself separate from error and unbelief, 890–1; nature of, 865–67; source of, 861–65.

Baptism of Holy Spirit (see also Filling of Holy Spirit, Sealing of Holy Spirit): 764–65.

[1201]

Baptism, sacrament of (see also Paedobaptism, Sacraments as means of grace): 923–55; expositions of Pauline references to, 927–30; efficacy of, 950–5; import of, 925–26; institution of, 924–25; its "seal" character, 953–54; its "sign" character, 953; mode of, 930–35; Old Testament background to, 923–24; paedobaptism, 935–50.

Bible (see also Attributes of Scripture, Holy Scripture, Word of God): God's Word from another world, 3, Holy Spirit the primary author of, 3–4; its authority, 73–9; its divine "indicia," 80; its finality, 88–93; its infallibility, 70–3; its inspiration, 59; man's ποῦ στῶ for knowledge and personal significance, 111–26; its message's "revealedness," 25–37; nature of its versions, 90–2; nature of its truth, 95–110; its necessity, 56–9; New Testament evidence for its "revealed" character, 30–37; Old Testament evidence for its "revealed" character, 25–30; one meaning of, 23; its perspicuity, 87–8; its self-authentication, 79–82; its sufficiency, 83–7.

Biblical truth: Gordon H. Clark on nature of, 99–100; nature of, 95–110; paradoxical?, 103–10; univocal character of, 96–102; Cornelius Van Til on nature of, 97–9.

Bibliography, selected general theological: Appendix G, 1133–42.

Body, man's: effect of death upon, 1017–18; effect of resurrection upon, 797–99.

Calvinism, five points of (see also TULIP): Appendix E, 1125–26.

Canon (-ization): criteria of, 65; formation and close of, 60–70; Richard Gaffin on, 65–66.

Christ (see also Christology, God the Son, Jesus, Messiah): ascension of, 575–81; blood of, 625–27; body of, 625; cross of, 627; cross work of, 623–69; death of, 627–28; for whom he died, 473–75, 478–79, 671–702; destructive work of (against kingdom of evil), 658–63; miracles of, 553–59; of the antignostic fathers, 589–93; of the apologists, 586–89; of the apostolic fathers, 584–85; of the early councils, 583–622; Lord of the natural creation and of the spiritual creation, 250; of Monarchianism, 596–97; of Origen, 593–96; obedience of, 629–31; offices of, 623–24; Old Testament prophets prophesied of death and resurrection of, 521–25; propitiatory work of, 635–43; reconciling work of, 643–51; redemptive work of, 651–58; resurrection of, 565–75; sacrifice of, 631–35; supernatural, 545–81; theological method of, xxvii–xxviii; transfiguration of, 559–65; virgin birth of, 547–52.

Christology (see also Christ, Jesus, God the Son, Messiah): analysis of Nicene Creed on, 317–30; "from above and from below," 1095–1104; of James, 270–72; of Hebrews, 272–78; of Jesus, 214–37; of John, 296–311; of Jude, 295–96; of Paul, 237–70; of Peter, 278–92; of the Synoptists, 292–95; two modern kinds of, Appendix A, 1095–1104.

Church ("assembly"): attributes and marks of, 837–60; authority and duties of, 861–93; government of, 895–910; in Acts 1–12 (during Peter's ministry), 825–27; in Acts 13–28 (during Paul's ministry), 828–30; in Hebrews, 831–33; in James, 827–28; in Jesus' teaching, 811–25; in John's letters, 834–35, and in his Apocalypse, 835–36; in Jude, 834; in Old Testament, 805–10; in Paul's teaching, 830–31; in Peter's teaching, 833–34; its mandate to disciple the nations, xxviii; means of grace of, 911–76; nature and foun-

INDEX OF SUBJECTS

dation of, 805–36; one institutional means of grace, 911–12.

Common grace: a term for God's ordinary works of providence, 402–3.

Communication of attributes (*communicatio idiomatum*): Lutheran view of, 171, fn. 30.

Conscience: created aspect of human nature, 418; one expression of common grace, 452.

Conversion: see Repentance unto life; Faith in Jesus Christ.

Covenant of grace: special act of divine providence, 405–7; unity of, 503–44; five arguments for unity of, 512–35.

Covenant of redemption: as the explanation of Son's subordination to Father in Scripture, 228–29, 337–38; its referent as a title, 502.

Covenant theology: history and origin of, 503–5; confessional expression of, 505–7.

Covenant of works: continuing normativeness of, 439–40; exegetical basis for in Genesis 2, 430; nature of, 431–33; representative feature of, 434–39; special act of divine providence, 404–5.

Cross work (of Christ): absolute necessity of, 664–67; application of benefits of, 703–801; design behind, 671–702; destructive character of, 658–63; obedient character of, 629–31; perfection of, 667–69; propitiating character of, 635–43; reconciling character of, 643–51; redemptive character of, 651–58; sacrificial character of, 631–35.

Creation: age of, 394–96; days of, 392–94; God's work of, 383–98; out of nothing?, 384–92; man's special place in, 416–18; purpose of, 396–98.

Decree, divine: see "Eternal decree."

Death: in all its forms result of disobedience to original covenant of works, 439–40, 449; Christian's: is gain, 1017; ushers him into better (intermediate) state, 1017–18; eternal, 1068–85; physical: 449; spiritual: 449.

Definition of Chalcedon (see also Eutychianism): analysis of, 608–14; *anhypostasia* of, 610–11; Christology of, 608–14; departures from, 615–21; four "great negative adverbs of," 620–1.

Depravity, total: meaning of, 450–53; a state of man as fallen, 450–53; objections against, 454–55.

Destruction, Christ's work of: 658–63.

Diaconate: qualifications of, 899–900.

Dichotomy, 422–24.

Dispensationalism: critique of scriptural rationale for, 537–44; description of, 507–11; five arguments against, 512–35; two tragic implications of, 542–44.

Divine messiah: Old Testament predictions of, 212–14.

Double indemnity verses (so-called): 196–97, fn. 65.

Downgrade trends in evangelical eschatology: 1067–93; denial of literal return of Christ, 1067–68; eternal punishment construed as annihilation, 1068–85; non-necessity of conscious faith in Christ for final salvation, 1085–93.

Duties of church: administer sacraments, 885; bear witness to divine truth, 878–80; evangelize and grow church, 880–5; govern its affairs, 888–91; minister to saints, 885–88; perform deeds of benevolence, 892–93; worship and serve God, 868–77.

Effectual calling: 712–18; character and intention of, 713; "effecting" force (regeneration) in, 714–18; relation to the external presentation of the gospel, 713–14; summary of doctrine, 718.

Elders, rule by: duties of,

[1203]

897–98; qualifications of, 899.
Election: see God, eternal decree of; Plan (eternal) of salvation.
Empirical arguments: for God's existence, 135–52; Jonathan Edwards on, 138–39, 144–45, 149; Thomas Aquinas's "five ways," 135–36; ten arguments against, 137–51.
Empiricism, epistemological theory of, 112–13.
Eschatology, biblical (see also Eschatological dualism): 979–1065; debate over, 981–86; downgrade trends in, 1067–93 (which see); Hebrews on, 1040–43; James on, 1009; Jesus' kingdom of heaven parables, 994–97; Jesus' Olivet Discourse, 999–1006; Jesus' programmatic teaching on, 991–94; John's Apocalpyse, 1047–64; John's epistolary eschatology, 1047; John's Gospel eschatology, 1046–47; John the Baptist's teaching on, 990–91; Jude on, 1046; New Testament eschatology, 988–1064; Old Testament eschatology, 986–88; Paul on, 1009–40; Peter on, 1043–46; resolution of every other locus of theology, 980; summary of Jesus teaching on, 1008.
Eschatological dualism:

meaning of, 994.
Eternal decree: 343–81; Clark H. Pinnock's view of, 346–49, and author's analysis of, 350–56, 378–80; equal ultimacy of election and reprobation, 360, fn. 20; New Testament illustrations of, 364–72; Old Testament illustrations of, 358–64.
Eutychianism and Council of Chalcedon (see also Definition of Chalcedon): 606–8.
Evangelicalism: universalistic (Arminian), 471–75; particularistic (Calvinistic), 479–501.
Exodus: four great salvific principles revealed by, 519–21; Old Testament type of redemption, 518.

Faith in Jesus Christ: 725–36; absolute necessity of for final salvation, 1085–93; alone comports with grace, 735; diametrical opposite of law-keeping, 732–34; distinction between *fides generalis* and *fides specialis*, 726; "gift" character of, 731–32; human psychic character of, 729–30; instrumental function of, 730–31; nature of, 726–29; summary of doctrine, 735–36.
Fall of man: nature of, 440–46; seven effects of, 446–49.
Filioque: meaning of, 331–32.
Filling of Holy Spirit (see

also Baptism of Holy Spirit, Sealing of Holy Spirit): 765–67.
Finality of Scripture: 88–93.
Freedom: of indifference, 188–89, 191, 373; of spontaneity ("soft determinism"), 191, 373–75.
Future state (see also Eschatology, biblical; Glorification): Apostasy and Man of sin, 1032–33; Paul on, 1019–38; ingathering of "all Israel" present or future?, 1024–30; judgment of believers in, 1020–22; "millennial kingdom," Paul on, 1033–36; new heavens and new earth, 1036–38; "triggering mechanism" of, 1022–23.

Genesis, early chapters of: historical integrity of, 117–19, 383–84.
Glorification (Christian's): 795–801; nature of, 797–98; meaning of his glorification for creation, 798; meaning of his glorification for Christian himself, 798–99; meaning of church's glorification for Christ, 799–800; summary of the doctrine, 800–1.
God: as rational (logical), 109–10, 201; as spirit, 166–68; attributes of, 160–203; classifications of attributes of, 163–64; creator of and provider for all his works, 130–31, 383–

[1204]

INDEX OF SUBJECTS

414; empirical arguments for the existence of, 135–52; eternal decree of, 343–46; eternality of, 172–77; eternal plan of salvation of, 461–502; eternal purpose of, 463–65; ethical holiness of, 195–96; glory of, 165–66; goodness (love, mercy, pity, compassion) of, 199–201; immutability of, 177–84; introduction to the doctrine of, 129–52; justice of, 196–99; language-using, 20–1; majestic holiness of, 194–95; meaning of the glory of, 165–66; names and titles of, 153–60; nature of, 160–205; not the author or chargeable cause of sin, 372–76; omnipotence of, 191–93; omnipresence of, 168–71; omniscience of, 184–91; only living and true God, 130; ontological argument for the existence of, 132–35; presuppositional argument for the existence of, 145–49; relation between God's nature and the attributes of, 161–63; self-sufficiency of, 130–31; transcendent holiness of, 194–95; triune character of, 108–9, 205–316; truthfulness of, 201–2; why I believe in, 131–32; wrath of, 639–42.

God the Father: adopts believers, 759–61; definitively sanctifies believers, 756–57; effectually calls believers, 712–18; foreknew and predestined elect to salvation, 464–66; glorifies believers, 797–99; justifies believers, 742–45; originator of the universe, 359.

God the Holy Spirit (see also Pneumatology): coagent (with Son) in creating universe, 391–92; deity and personal subsistence of, 312–16; divine works of, 314; "eternal procession" of from God the Father (and the Son), 331–38; filling of, 765–67; sealing of, 763–64; testimony of, 81–2; titles of, 312–13.

God the Son (see also Christ, Christology, Jesus, Messiah): Father's coagent (with Spirit) in creating universe, 391–92; deity of, 211–312; eternal preexistence of, 230–32; God the Father's "eternal generation" of, 324–30; Old Testament predictions of, 212–13; unity of with God the Father, 229–30; universe dependent upon him, 251.

Government of church (see also Presbyterianism): 895–910; four distinguishable forms of, 896; congregationalism, 906–7; episcopacy, 904–6; Erastianism, 907–8; presbyterianism, 896–904.

Governmental theory of the atonement: 474–75.

Guilt, real: a state of man as fallen, 456–57.

Hebrews: Christology of, 272–78.

Hell (see also "Downgrade Trends in Evangelical Eschatology"): annihilation or conscious eternal torment?, 1068–85.

Hermeneutics: "paradox" a legitimate category of?, 103–10; principles of as implicates of inspiration, 49–53; principle of deduction by "good and necessary consequence," 86.

Holy Scripture: see Scripture, holy.

Holy Spirit: see God the Holy Spirit.

Humanity of Jesus: see Jesus: humanity of.

Image of God: see Man, as imago Dei.

Imputation of sin: see Adam, fall of.

Inability, total: a natural state of man as fallen, 453–56; objections against, 454–55.

Inerrant autographs and errant apographs: Augustine on distinction between, 92; justification of the distinction between, 91–2.

Infallibility of Bible: 70–3.

Infant baptism: see Paedobaptism.

Infralapsarianism: its representation of eternal

salvific plan, 480; historical principle governing, 479–81; six supralapsarian objections to, 481–88.
Inspiration of Scripture: an attribute of Scripture, 59; definition of, 70; three hermeneutical implications of, 49–53.
Intermediate state (see also Eschatology, biblical): Paul on, 1017–18.

James: Christology of, 270–72.
Jesus (see also Christ, Christology, God the Son, Messiah): divine attributes of, 234–35; humanity of, 546–47; kingdom of heaven parables of, 537–39, 994–97; miracles of, 553–59; Old Testament Yahweh passages applied to, 311–12; reference by to two other persons in Godhead, 236–37; self-testimony of to his deity, 214–37; teaching of, 235–36; virginally conceived, 547–52; use of ἐκκλησία, 811–25; witness of his acts to his deity, 232–34.
John: Christology of, 296–311; of his Gospel, 296–305, of his epistles, 305–8, of his Revelation, 308–11.
Jude: Christology of, 295–96.
Justification: 739–56; its character as a legal judgment, 743–45; heart and core of gospel, 740; meaning of, 742–43; righteousness of, 745–47; Rome's six objections to Protestant view of, 748–54; Rome's tragically defective understanding of, 741, fn. 44; summary of, 755–56.

Kant, Immanuel: epistemology of, 12–13, 113–15.
"Keys of the kingdom": meaning of, 820, fn. 35.
Kingdom of evil: Christ's triumph over, at cross, 660–63; power aspects of, 660; Satan the ruler over, 659–63.
Kingdom of God (heaven): meaning of, 538, 990, fn. 18; Old Testament perception of, 986–88; kingdom "of God" and "of heaven" synonymous terms, 538.
Knowledge, human: its relation to God's knowledge, 96–102; justification of, 111–16.

Language philosophy: its objection to verbal revelation, 17–18; rebuttal of, 18–23.
Law of God (ethical norm of covenant way of life): 770–78; relation of Christian to ("third use of"), 770–77; "three uses" of, 771.
Light of nature: meaning of, 56–7; John Calvin on, 56.
Limbus infantum: see Purgatory.
Limited atonement (see also Particular redemption): 672, fn. 3; Appendix E, 1125–26.
Lord's Supper, sacrament of (see also Sacraments as means of grace): 955–67; institution of, 956–57; import of, 964–67; observance of, 957–59; relation of Christ's presence to elements of, 959–64; terminology, 956.
Luke: Christology of, 294–95.

Man: biblical view of, 415–58; conscience of, 418, as a manifestation of restraining grace, 452; constituent elements of his nature, 418–29; as covenant breaker, 440–57; as covenant creature, 416–40; creature of God, 416–18; as imago Dei, 425–29; occupies special place in creation, 416–18; spiritual understanding of, 417–18; state of man as fallen, 450–57.
Man in Romans 7:14–25, whom does he represent?: see Appendix F, 1127–32.
Mark: Christology of, 292–93.
Marks (Protestant) of church: confessional witness to, 855–60; faithful exercise of church discipline, 853–55; purpose of, 850–51; right administration of the sacraments, 852–53; true proclamation of the Word, 851–52.
Matthew: Christology of, 293–94.

[1206]

INDEX OF SUBJECTS

Means of grace (see Word of God, Baptism, sacrament of, Lord's supper, sacrament of, Prayer): 911–76; not of common but of special grace, 913; do not work *ex opere operato*, 913; do not possess intrinsic power to convert and sanctify, 913; sacraments not necessary for saving grace, 913.

Merit, condign and congruent: definition of, 432, fn. 20.

Middle knowledge, theory of: 189.

Millennium (see also Eschatology, biblical): Paul on, 1033–36; John on, 1046–64.

Ministry to saints: goal of, 888; nature of, 886; scope of, 886–88.

Miracles: authenticating character of, 409–13; cessation of "miracles of power," 413; of Jesus, 553–59; special acts of divine providence, 409–13.

Miracles of Jesus: biblical data for, 553–54; critical responses to, 554–56; evangelical responses to, 556–57; historicity of, 553–59; significance of, 557–59.

Mission of church: 868–93.
Monogenes: meaning of, 326.

Names and titles of God: 153–60.

Nature of God: 160–203.

Natural theology (methodological): definition of, 137, fn. 13; critique of, 137–52; Ligonier apologists' form of, 134–35; 140–42.

Necessity of Christ's cross work: 664–67.

Necessity of Scripture: 56–9.

Neoorthodoxy: its objection to verbal revelation, 12–13; rebuttal of, 13–17.

Nestorianism and Council of Ephesus: 603–6.

New birth: see Regeneration.

New Testament church: theological activity of, *xxxii–xxxiii*.

New Testament prophets: relation of to the apostles, 27, fn. 3.

Nicene Creed: major affirmations on Christology and Trinity, 317–18; critique of, 317–30.

Niceno-Constantinopolitan Creed: its pneumatology, 331–32; critique of, 332–38.

Obedience of Christ: 629–31; biblical material for, 629–30; character of, 630–31, purpose of, 631; preceptive and penal, 631.

Offices of Christ: 623–24.

Ontological argument: 132–35.

Order of the decrees: principle governing, 479–501.

Ordo salutis (order of application): scriptural warrant for and aspects of, 704–11.

Original sin, Roman Catholic teaching concerning: 426, fn. 11.

Paedobaptism, sacrament of (see also Baptism, sacrament of, Sacraments as means of grace): 935–50; New Testament testimony favoring, 940–43; Old Testament testimony (via circumcision as type of) favoring, 937–40; relation of covenant children to church, 946–50; three undeniable truths concerning, 944–45.

Papacy, Roman Catholic teaching on: 812–13; Protestant response to, 813–19; true meaning of Matthew 16:18, 819–22.

Paradox: critique of, 105–10; R. B. Kuiper's definition of, 103–4; J. I. Packer's definition of, 104; Cornelius Van Til on, 104.

Particular redemption: meaning of, 672–73; exposition of passages used to rebut, 683–702; ten lines of evidence for, 673–83.

Paul, Christology of, 237–70; conversion of, see Appendix C, 1113–19.

Pelagianism, 468–70.

Perfection of Christ's cross work: 667–69.

Perichoresis: meaning of, 324.

Perseverance of saints (see also Assurance of salvation): 781–94; biblical data

[1207]

for, 782–85; meaning of, 782; response to Arminian objections to, 785–90; summary of doctrine, 794.

Person: meaning of, 319–20.

Personal significance: justification of, 116–26; Francis Schaeffer on, 125–26.

Perspicuity of Scripture: 87–8.

Peter: Christology of, 278–92.

Plan (eternal) of salvation, 461–502: Christ's cross work in, 465; election of men in, 466–67; the fact and central elements of, 462–67; God's foreknowledge and predestination of elect in, 465–66; nature of, 467–502; reflection of God's eternal purpose, 463–65.

Pneumatology (see also God the Holy Spirit): analysis of Niceno-Constantinopolitan Creed on, 331–37.

Postmillennialism: definition of, 980, fn. 3.

Postmodern theologians: xx, fn. 2.

Prayer as a means of grace (see also Means of grace): 967–76; biblical vocabulary, 968–69; significant discourses on in church history, 971–73; efficacy of, 973–76; in the Bible, 969–71.

Premillennialism: definition of, 980, fn. 3.

Presbyterianism (see also Elders, rule by): connectionalism, 900–4; history of, 897; meaning of, 896–97; significance of, 908–10.

Presuppositionalism, definition of: 145–49.

Pretribulationism: definition of, 980, fn. 3; Paul on, 1023–24.

Prophecy: nature of, 28–9; divine origin of, 37–9.

Prophet: definition of, 25–6; not merely a "robot," 39–43.

Propitiation, Christ's work of: 635–43; C. H. Dodd on, 636; Godward reference of, 639–40; Leon Morris and Roger Nicole on, 637–38.

Providence: God's works of, 398–413 (ordinary, 399–403; special, 404–13).

Purgatory, Roman Catholic teaching on: 795, fn. 98.

Ransom view of the atonement: 656–57; see also Anselm's view of the atonement, Appendix D, 1121–23.

Rationalism, epistemological theory of: 112.

Reconciliation, Christ's work: 643–51; biblical data for, 643–44; Godward reference of, 644–51.

Redemption, Christ's work of: Arminian interpretation of, 652–53; biblical data for, 653–56; Godward reference of, 656–57; manward reference of, 657–58.

Regeneration: 718–21; biblical data for, 718–19; divine monergism behind, 719–20; effects of, 719; summary of doctrine, 720–21.

Regulative principle in worship: see Worship, regulative principle in.

Repentance unto life: 721–25; aspect of evangelical preaching, 721–22; biblical data for, 722–23; distinction from "worldly sorrow, 724–25; gift character of, 723–24; summary of doctrine, 725.

Responsibility: meaning of, 375–76.

Resurrection of Christ: critical views concerning, 571–75; historicity of, 565–75; two great strands of evidence for, 566–71.

Revelation, general: definition of, 5, fn. 7.

Revelation, special: cessation of, 11–12, 56–59, 407–9; definition of, 4, fn. 3; nature of, 96–100.

Revelational process: came, not steadily, but in "spurts," 11–12, 56–59, 407–9; cessation of objective revelation, 11–12, 58, fn. 7, 84, 407–9, 413; fact of, 3–23; James Barr on, 13–16; language philosophy's objection to, 17–23; neoorthodoxy's objection to, 12–17; New Testament evidence for, 10–11; Old and New Testament terms for, 4–5;

INDEX OF SUBJECTS

Old Testament evidence for, 5–10; relation of to redemptive process (*Heilsgeschichte*), 407–8; special act of divine providence, 407–9.

Sacerdotalism: meaning of, 470; Warfield's three objections to, 471.

Sacraments (in general) as means of grace: 917–23: do not work *ex opere operato*, 919–20; meaning of word, 918–19; means of grace as "signs" and "seals," 922; not mere visible "representations" of certain truths, 921–22; not necessary for salvation, 920–21; only two, not seven, as Rome teaches, 919–20; require explanation of Word, 921; Roman Catholic view of, 919–21; three aspects to both sacraments, 922.

Sacrifice of Christ: as high priest, 632; as lamb of God, 632; as sacrificial offering, 632; significance of, 633–35.

Salvation: God's eternal plan of, 461–502; requisite condition for the same in Old and New Testaments, 528–34; tenses of, 796–97.

Sanctification, definitive: 756–59; biblical data for, 756–57; ground of Christian's breach with sin, 757–58; meaning of, 757; summary of doctrine, 758–59.

Santification, progressive (see also "Sanctified life"): 767–81; biblical data for, 767–68; summary of doctrine, 780–81.

Sanctified life: agents and instruments effecting, 778–80; goal of, 778; nature of, 768–80; threefold pattern (God's ethical holiness, law of God, Christ's life) of, 770–78.

Satan: activities of, 659–60; Christ's triumphant activity over, 660–63; final destruction of, 1063–64; names and titles of, 659; power aspects of the kingdom of, 660.

Satisfaction view of the atonement: see Anselm's view of the atonement.

Scripture, holy (see also Attributes of Scripture, Bible, Word of God): attributes of, 55–93; Christ's authentication of, 44–7; inspiration and authority of, xxxi; inspired nature of, 25–53; New Testament writers' identification of with God's Word, 47–9; "theopneustic" character of, 35–6.

Sealing of Holy Spirit (see also Baptism of Holy Spirit; Filling of Holy Spirit): 762–67; biblical data for, 763; to be distinguished from baptism of Holy Spirit, 764–65; to be distinguished from filling of Holy Spirit, 765–67; nature of, 763–64; summary of doctrine, 767.

Self-authentication of Scripture: 79–82.

Semi-Pelagianism, 469.

Semi-semi-Pelagianism, 469.

Sin: effects of, 446–57; deserves divine wrath, 456–57; God not the author or chargeable cause of, 372–76; imputation of Adam's, 434–39; nature of, 445–46; noetic effects of, 452–53.

"Son (of God)" title, meaning of, 218–29.

"Son of Man" title: meaning of, 214–18.

Soul: effect of physical death upon, 1017–18; origin of, 424–25 (creationist view, 424; traducianist view, 424–25).

Spiritual gifts: Wayne Grudem on, 57, fn. 5.

Sufficiency of Scripture: 83–7.

Supralapsarianism: its representations of the eternal salvific plan, 488–89; purposing principle governing, 488–89, 492–96; two exegetical objections against, 490–92; four theological objections against, 496–501.

Synoptists: Christology of, 292–95.

Systematic theology: definition of, xxv–xxvi;

specific task of, *xxxiii;* specific Reformed aspects of, *xxxiv–xxxv.*

Theodicy (biblical), 376–78.
Theology: apostolic model of, *xxviii–xxx;* classic *loci* of, *xxxvi;* definition of, *xxv;* departments of, *xxv;* general task of, *xxxii–xxxiii;* is Bible's "theology of the cross" incompatible with its "theology of glory"?, 1100, 1102–3; justification of as an intellectual discipline, *xxvi–xxxi;* specific illustration of the theological task, Appendix A, 1095–1104; specific Reformed aspects of, *xxxiv–xxxv.*
Θεός as a Christological title: in Hebrews 1:8, 273–75; in John 1:1, 298–301; in John 1:18, 301–3; in John 20:28, 297–98; in 1 John 5:20, 305–7; in 2 Peter 1:1, 289–91; in Romans 9:5, 245–48; in Titus 2:13, 248–50; summary of, 312.
This "systematic theology": not a slavish reproduction of orthodox or Reformed thought, *xxi–xxii;* reasons for, *xx–xxi.*
Tradition: Roman Catholic view of, 85–6.
Traditional arguments for God's existence: critique of, 131–52.
Traducianism, 424–25.
Transfiguration of Jesus: background of, 559–61; disciples' question concerning Elijah, 564–65; historicity of, 561–62; metamorphosis of Jesus in, 563–64; accompanying voice from the cloud, 564.
Trichotomy, 420–22.
Trinity, holy: analysis of Nicene Creed on, 317–30; analysis of Niceno-Constantinopolitan Creed on, 331–38; evidence for in deity of Christ, 211–312, and in personal subsistence of Holy Spirit, 312–15; God as, 205–316; historical nature of the revelation of, 207–11; in the creeds, 317–41; Old Testament adumbrations of, 207–9; relation of the "three" to the "one," 320–24; revelational ground of doctrine of, 206; three essential propositions of, 205–6; West-minster Assembly's view of, Nicene or Reformed?, 338–40.
TULIP, Calvinistic (see also Calvinism, five points of): L of, 672, fn. 3; explication of, Appendix E, 1125–26.

Union with Christ: 736–39: biblical data for, 736–38; reality of, 738–39; summary of doctrine, 739.
Universalism, evangelical (Arminianism): 471–75.

Versions, nature of: 90–92.

Virgin birth: biblical data for, 547–48; church testimony for, 548–49; historicity of, 547–52; purpose of, 550–52; reasons for believing in, 549, fn. 8.

Word of God as means of grace (see also Attributes of Scripture, Bible, Holy Scripture): 913–17; efficacy of, 915–16; ministry of, 916–17.
Works, good (criteria of): 751.
Worship, regulative principle in: 868–77.
Wrath of God: meaning of, 639–40; C. H. Dodd on, 641–42.